Lifespan Development

Kelvin L. Seifert

THE UNIVERSITY OF MANITOBA

Robert J. Hoffnung

UNIVERSITY OF NEW HAVEN

Michele Hoffnung

QUINNIPIAC COLLEGE

HOUGHTON MIFFLIN COMPANY   BOSTON   NEW YORK

To our children

Elizabeth Katherine and Michael David Seifert   K.L.S.

Aaron Hoffnung and David, Graham, and Heather Burbank   R.J.H.

Josh and Jesse Hoffnung Garskof and Sarah Grimké Faragher   M.H.

Sponsoring editor   David Lee
Basic book editor   Karla Paschkis
Senior project editor   Rosemary Winfield
Senior production/design coordinator   Jill Haber
Senior manufacturing coordinator   Florence Cadran
Marketing manager   David Lenehan

Cover design: Harold Burch, Harold Burch Design, New York City; cover photographs: Top—Minori Kawana-Photonica; bottom—Jake Wyman-Photonica

Anatomical and biological illustrations by Nancy Kaplan: Figures 3.14, 3.15, 8.4

Illustrations by Patrice Rossi: Figures 2.2, 9.1

Illustrations by Elizabeth Seifert: Figure 6.3

All other credits appear on page A-1, which constitutes an extension of the copyright page.

Library of Congress Catalog Card Number: 96-76960

ISBN: 0-395-69178-8

123456789-VH-99 98 97 96

Brief Contents

Contents

Early Childhood   181

Middle Childhood   257

PART FOUR

Adolescence   331

PART FIVE

Middle Adulthood   495

PART SEVEN

Chapter 14   Middle Adulthood: Physical and Cognitive Development   496

Late Adulthood   579

Death, Loss, and Bereavement   667

PART NINE

Chapter 18   Death, Dying, and Bereavement   668

Special Features

Perspectives

Preface

Students, we know, come to a lifespan course from many departments and are headed for a wide range of occupational and family roles that require an understanding of human development. They will be educators, health professionals such as occupational and physical therapists and nurses, social workers, parents, and family members. We have written our book with this in mind. We believe that lifespan psychology is relevant to current career and social issues that all adults face. It is especially relevant to those who will work or live with children, adolescents, or the elderly. We see personal involvement as positive and include a wide range of examples that will enable most readers to find themselves, and people they know, in the story of lifespan development.

stance, we trace the changes in cognitive competence, taking special care not to measure adult changes by adolescent standards. Because it focuses on context and experience, not only on age, our review of adult development of practical intelligence, expertise, and wisdom provides an optimistic view of adult cognition even in late life. Our discussion of Alzheimer's disease and other dementias makes clear that these are frequent but nonnormative late-life developments. Likewise, our discussion of moral development begins in middle childhood with a focus on age-related changes and is revisited in adolescence where we look at age and gender. When we look at this issue again in early adulthood, we broaden the focus to look at age, gender, experience, and the content or situation of the moral problem, which are important adult considerations.

A Focus on Growth

Human development is a lifelong process, yet most textbooks give precedence to childhood and adolescence as the growth portions of life and consider adulthood, particularly middle and late adulthood, from a decline perspective. Our goal in writing this book is to present development at every stage of lifespan from a growth perspective. While we do not overlook the losses and challenges associated with life experiences such as illness, primary aging, and death of loved ones that become more frequent with age, we view them within a framework that looks for growth potential in all aspects of the human condition. Chronic illness, for example, often requires permanent changes in physical, vocational, and social activities, and acceptance of the role of patient (Chapter 16). But chronic illness leads to positive outcomes as well. People offset the negative impact of their chronic conditions by rearranging their priorities and learning to appreciate each day, value their relationships more, and be more sensitive to others (Chapter 17).

Our growth orientation permeates the text. Growth engenders changing perspectives on our evolving roles and awareness of the continuities present even as we change. In the domain of cognitive development, for in-

Continuities

One of the ways in which we emphasize growth and change throughout the lifespan is by stressing the continuities from stage to stage—childhood to adolescence to early adulthood to middle adulthood to late adulthood. Each part closes with Looking Back/Looking Forward, a section that highlights the continuities between life stages. Every chapter examines how experiences at the stage under consideration have been shaped by earlier stages and shape the options and outcomes of stages yet to come.

The concept of attachment can serve as an example. First introduced in our overview of developmental theories (Chapter 2) and the discussion of psychosocial development during infancy (Chapter 5), we emphasize its lifelong importance by revisiting and refining the concept in discussions of psychosocial development in adulthood. Seeing how attachment to parents and siblings takes new behavioral forms during adolescence and adulthood helps students to understand their own relationships to their parents and children better and to develop a broader vision of what social support and connections mean.

Our coverage of physical development emphasizes the lifelong impact of health behaviors and health-compromising behaviors. For instance, we discuss the effects of prenatal nutrition in Chapter 3 and our coverage of physical development at every stage revisits the continuing importance of diet and weight. We link physical changes at each subsequent period to ones that occurred before and emphasize variability based on genetics, gender, race or ethnicity, and socioeconomic status.

Changing Perspectives

Our focus on growth also means that we view the family through different lenses at different stages of the life cycle. Parenthood takes new shapes as the ages of the children change; likewise, being a child takes different forms as we move from childhood to adolescence to adulthood. We look at parenthood from the perspective of expectant and new parents early in the book and examine the evolving nature of the parent-child relationship as the child grows. We explore the parenting of adolescents from the adolescent's perspective in Chapter 11 and from the middle-aged parent's perspective in Chapter 15. We look at grandparenting in middle and late adulthood and from the perspective of both the grandparent and the grandchild.

We consider death and dying to be a pertinent issue throughout the lifespan. Although we devote the final chapter of the book to issues of death, dying, and bereavement, we also address the normative developmental issues of facing one's own death or the deaths of loved ones in earlier chapters. In Chapter 4, our discussion of physical development during infancy includes consideration of sudden infant death syndrome. In Chapter 9, we extensively explore the problem of helping children with bereavement. Our Chapter 10 discussion of physical development during adolescence includes consideration of accidents, homicide, and suicide. Our discussion of physical development during early adulthood includes consideration of AIDS (Chapter 12). Our discussion of psychosocial development during middle adulthood considers bereavement related to the loss of one's parents (Chapter 15) and during late adulthood the loss of one's spouse (Chapter 17). Chapter 18 then focuses on issues of death and loss, which are more frequent during late adulthood. It also considers cultural similarities and differences in burial rituals and bereavement practices.

Emphasis on Diversity

Within each of the topics we cover we emphasize diversity. While human experience is in some ways universal, it is largely shaped by the particulars of an individual's culture, gender, and socioeconomic status (SES). Consideration of similarities and differences in developmen-

tal patterns due to these factors is an integral part of this book. We are careful not to overemphasize difference because males and females and people of different races, ethnicities, and sexual orientations are in many ways more similar than different. But we consider lifespan issues with an appreciation of the multicultural world in which we live. To present just a few examples, we consider

- Psychosocial and contextual theories that highlight developmental importance of cultural and historical change (Chapter 2);

- Ethnic and cultural differences in risk of genetic disorder and in perceptions of pain related to childbirth (Chapter 3);

- Cultural differences in infant temperament and in nonparental care giving (Chapter 5);

- Developmental influences of SES on health (Chapters 6 and 14), childrearing (Chapter 7), and parenting style (Chapter 11);

- Developmental influences of gender, SES, and culture on peer relations (Chapter 9) and on friendship and love (Chapter 13);

- Developmental influences of SES and culture on school dropouts (Chapter 11);

- Influences of gender and sexual orientation on cohabitation (Chapter 13);

- Gender and SES as factors in the midlife crisis (Chapter 15); and

- Influence of SES, race or ethnicity, and gender on leisure activities (Chapter 15).

In addition, each chapter includes "A Multicultural View" box that expands on a topic selected to broaden understanding of diversity.

Text Organization

The book's opening chapters discuss the field of human development, key theories, and genetics, prenatal development, and birth. The book is then organized chronologically: the first two years, early childhood, middle childhood, adolescence, early adulthood, middle adulthood, and late adulthood. Within each age period, we focus in one chapter on physical and cognitive development and in another chapter on psychosocial development. Although we frequently point out the interrelatedness of these three domains, we give each separate attention as well. By following the same organization throughout the book, we have made it easy for those who prefer to organize their courses topically rather than chronologically to use the book in their own way. Or one could teach the child and adolescent portions chronologically and the adult portion topically by first assigning the physical development portions of Chapters 12, 14, and 16, then the cognitive portions, and finally the psychosocial chapters 13, 15, and 17. In addition, we have integrated the coverage of death and dying at each stage of life so that although the final chapter adds perspective, a professor could responsibly save course time by skipping it.

Special Features

"Working with . . ." Interviews   Each chapter includes an interview with a person in a helping profession about the practical application of developmental issues featured in that chapter. For example, to enhance our discussion of pregnancy and preparation for childbirth, Robert Hoffnung interviewed an ob-gyn nurse practitioner (Chapter 3). Kelvin Seifert's interview with a preschool teacher about teaching sign language to hearing-impaired preschoolers enriches our discussion of cognitive development during early childhood (Chapter 6). When we consider death, we include Michele Hoffnung's interview with a social worker at a hospice (Chapter 18). Interviews enable students to see the relationship between the theoretical and the practical. Thought questions that follow the interviews stress the connections with the text. The interviews also provide occupational examples for students who are considering possibilities for their futures. For a complete list of featured careers and topics, see page xviii.

A Multicultural View   A boxed insert in each chapter highlights an issue of development from a cross- or multicultural perspective. While this perspective is a consistent aspect of the text, we use the boxes to focus on issues of particular interest. Topics include the cultural context of abuse and neglect (Chapter 7), culturally based attitudes about dieting and physical attractiveness (Chapter 8), and Japanese and North American views of menopause (Chapter 14). A complete list of these inserts appears on page xviii.

Perspectives   A boxed insert in each chapter expands the discussion in the text by highlighting a significant and timely issue. Topics include technological alternatives to normal conception (Chapter 3), the impact of SES on children's health (Chapter 6), anorexia nervosa and bulimia (Chapter 10), how stress relates to women's employment

(Chapter 12), and the double standard of sexuality in late adulthood (Chapter 17). See page xix for a full list.

Tools to Enhance Learning

For a textbook to be effective, it must be read. With this in mind, we held ourselves to high standards for clear, good writing. This text is approachable—filled with real-life examples that engage students in the issues of human development.

A Critical Approach to Research   We base our presentation on a firm understanding of current research in the field, balancing the inclusion of classic and recent studies. When discussing sexual attitudes and behaviors during early adulthood, for example, we present findings from the 1992 National Health and Social Life Survey (NHSLS) and consider them in light of the Kinsey sexual survey of 1948. Yet the book is not so data-driven as to be too technical for students new to the issues. Hypothetical and real-life examples balance our research-based discussions.

Since research findings do not always agree with each other, this book also focuses on how we know what we know, as well as what we know. We want students to understand how the data were generated and to be able to raise questions about the validity, reliability, and generalizability of research findings. We introduce methodological concerns in Chapter 1. In addition, we present critiques of studies as we discuss them (such as limitations of the Grant study in Chapter 16), as well as periodic sections on method where they will have the most meaning (such as "Studying Cognition and Memory in Infants" in Chapter 4's discussion of cognitive development during the first two years and the comparison of "Cross-sectional Versus Longitudinal Studies" in Chapter 14's discussion, "Does Intelligence Decline with Age?").

What Do You Think?   Questions designed to stimulate reflection and discussion about the issues and concepts of development are located periodically throughout every chapter. While addressed directly to the student, instructors also can use these questions as a basis for class activities and discussion. Many encourage collaboration among classmates and can be used as group assignments.

Rich Illustration Program   Numerous graphs, figures, and tables reinforce the text discussions by providing a visual guide to key concepts. Captions to line art and photos emphasize critical points and provide additional pedagogical support. We carefully selected photographs to reinforce our emphasis on diversity in culture, race or ethnicity, gender, and SES.

Special Learning Aids Opening chapter outlines, focusing questions, chapter summaries, and key terms lists serve as pedagogical supports by reinforcing the important themes, ideas, and concepts in each chapter. In addition to assisting in the mastery of content, these aids indirectly free students to develop their personal perspectives about lifespan psychology and its practical applications.

Ancillaries

Lifespan Development is accompanied by an extensive package of teaching and learning aids. Heading the list are a test bank, an instructor's resource manual, and a study guide that are unified by a shared set of learning objectives.

Test Bank The Test Bank, prepared by Robert Rycek of the University of Nebraska, Kearney, includes 100 multiple-choice and three essay questions per chapter. Each multiple-choice question is keyed to a text page number and a learning objective, and each is identified as requiring factual, applied, or conceptual knowledge. The emphasis has been placed on providing a wealth of applied and conceptual questions. The essay questions include sample response guides.

Instructor's Resource Manual The Instructor's Resource Manual, conceived and written by Gregory Cutler of Bay de Noc Community College, offers numerous resources to facilitate course preparation and student assessment. Each chapter begins with a chapter map that keys all activities and test questions to specific points in each text chapter. Also included are a chapter overview and an outline, learning objectives, notes on students' anticipated trouble spots and examples for use in class, lecture topics, news stories of relevance to developmental psychology, journal writing topics, in-class activities, out-of-class projects, and recommendations for Internet sites, videos, transparencies, and further readings.

Study Guide For each chapter, the Study Guide, prepared by Robert Rycek and Gregory Cutler, contains learning objectives, a chapter overview and an outline, a fill-in review of key terms and concepts, and two sets of multiple-choice practice questions, one that tests factual knowledge and one that tests applied knowledge. The

special multiple-choice answer key explains why each option is correct *or incorrect,* a feature particularly appreciated by students.

Computerized Test Bank The test items are available on disk, providing maximum flexibility for instructors who wish to generate tests electronically, as well as edit test items or add their own.

Videos A wide range of video programs on child development is available to qualified adopters. Your Houghton Mifflin representative has details.

Video Rental Policy Qualified adopters can also borrow films or videos free of charge through a consortium of university film libraries.

Transparencies The accompanying set of overhead transparencies contains images from both within and outside the text.

Acknowledgments

Our text benefits from the constructive suggestions and thoughtful reactions of many reviewers to the manuscript at various stages of its development, and we are very appreciative of their help. In particular, we would like to thank

Daniel R. Bellack, Trident Technical College
Marvin W. Berkowitz, Marquette University
Kathleen Bey, Palm Beach Community College
Joyce Bishop, Golden West College
Robert Bohlander, Wilkes University
Winfield Brown, Florence-Darlington Technical College
Paula Clarke, St. Mary's College of California
Stephen Coccia, Orange County Community College
Rita M. Curl, Minot State University
Lorraine DeJong, Furman University
Eric De Vos, Saginaw Valley State University
Bettye S. Elmore, Humboldt State University
Sam Joseph, Luzerne County Community College
Manolya Kayabasi, Harford Community College
Sally Kline, Henderson Community College
Joseph L. Miele, East Stroudsburg University
Walter D. Murphy, Lenoir-Rhyne College
Sarah C. O'Dowd, Community College of Rhode Island
Stuart I. Offenbach, Purdue University
Linda J. Palm, Coastal Carolina University
Robert H. Poresky, Kansas State University
Thomas M. Randall, Rhode Island College

Janice L. Rank, Victor Valley College
Robert F. Rycek, University of Nebraska at Kearney
Harriet Shaklee, Seattle University
Paul S. Silverman, University of Montana
Joan A. Sloman, Wheelock College
R. Bruce Tallon, Niagara College
Laura R. Thompson, Midlands Technical College
Tami Van Cleve, Fresno City College
Jerina Wainwright, Anne Arundel Community College

We wish to thank the individuals who participated in the "Working with . . ." interviews. We also thank the people at Houghton Mifflin who worked with us: Jane Knetzger, Ann Schroeder, and Rosemary Winfield. Our special thanks go to Karla Paschkis, who as basic book editor helped us write the text we had in mind. Working with her has been an unexpected pleasure of this project. We also thank Lisa Blyth and Marilyn Kline, who assisted us as we prepared the manuscript, and the Quinnipiac College Faculty Research Committee, which provided reduced teaching loads. We thank our families and friends for the support they provided as we worked on this book, as well as the many stories from their lives that serve as examples throughout the text. We especially thank John Mack Faragher and Barbara Fuller.

About the Authors

As developmental psychologists, college professors who teach adolescents and adults of many ages, and parents who have seen our children through many stages of development (some as far as early adulthood), the authors bring to this project a shared interest in human development as well as training and interests that complement each other. Kelvin's teaching has focused on early childhood and learning theory; his recent research is on children's cognition, although his earlier research looked at gender issues in early childhood teacher education. Robert has taught about childhood, adolescence, and lifespan development; he has also done clinical work with children, adolescents, adults, and families. Michele's teaching has been in the areas of research methods, psychology of women, and adult development; her recent research has focused on gender issues, motherhood, and balancing career and motherhood during adulthood.

We had a desire to work as a team, and we have been delighted with the result. Kelly and Rob had already successfully collaborated on a textbook. Rob and Michele, as siblings and close friends, had shared the creation and maintenance of a cooperative childcare center when their children were young and have been in a continuing dialogue about the problems, joys, and meanings of life's changes and challenges as they and their family members have been born, matured, and grown old. This text benefits both from former and new connections alike. Though we collaborated on the shape and focus of the text, Kelly and Rob shared the writing of the first eleven chapters; Michele wrote the adulthood chapters (12 through 18).

Kelvin Seifert is Professor of Educational Psychology at the University of Manitoba. He received his B.A. at Swarthmore College and his Ph.D. at the University of Michigan. He is author of *Educational Psychology* (1991) and has published research on gender issues in early childhood education as well as on teachers' and parents' beliefs about children and their development.

Robert Hoffnung is Professor of Psychology at the University of New Haven and Associate Clinical Professor of Psychiatry at the Yale University School of Medicine. He received his B.A. at Lafayette College, his M.A. at the University of Iowa, and his Ph.D. at the University of Cincinnati. He has published articles on educational, developmental, and mental health interventions with children, adolescents, and families.

Michele Hoffnung is Professor of Psychology and Director of Women's Studies at Quinnipiac College. She received her B.A. at Douglass College and her Ph.D. at the University of Michigan. She is Editor of *Roles Women Play: Readings Towards Women's Liberation* (1971) and author of *What's a Mother to Do? Conversations About Work and Family* (1992) and numerous articles and essays.

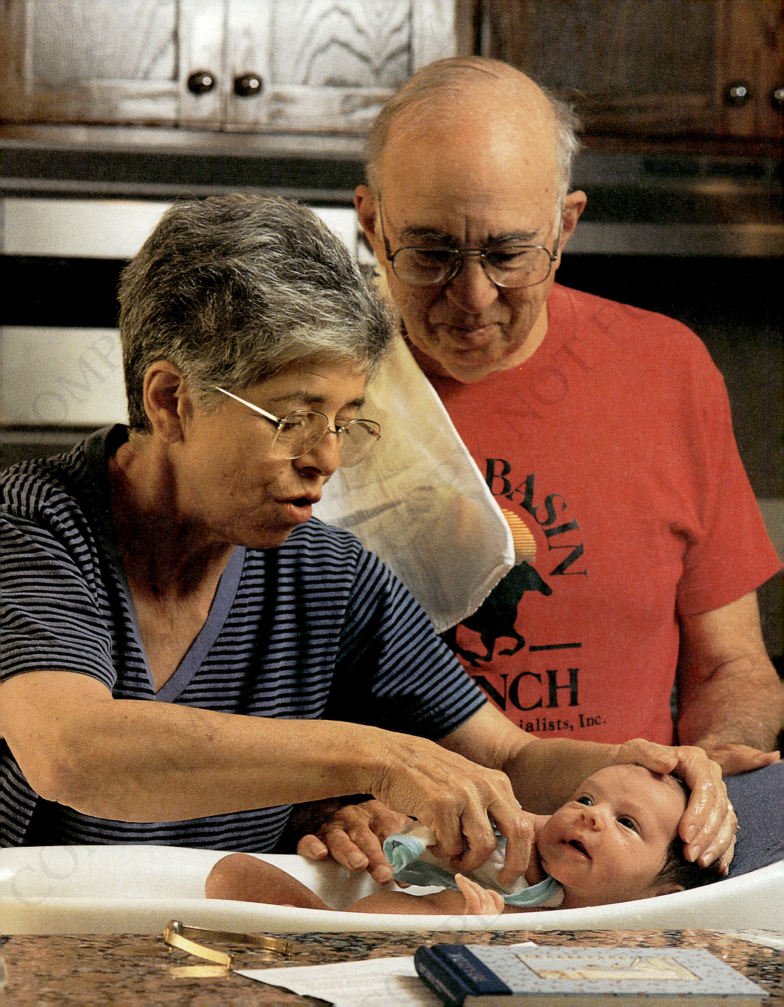

PART ONE

Beginnings

As infants grow into children, and children into adolescents and adults, a great many changes occur. Some of these changes are small and fleeting, while many others are relatively profound and long lasting. These developmental changes are the subject of this book and the field of study known as *lifespan developmental psychology*.

The study of lifespan development offers much insight into human nature—why we are what we are and how we became that way. Because describing development is a complex task, this book begins with three chapters which orient you to what lies ahead. The first two chapters explain just what development is and describe some of the most important tools of lifespan developmental psychology, namely the methods and theories that guide our understanding of the developmental changes that occur from conception through old age. The third chapter describes the genetic basis of human life, and the three major events that occur at the beginning of the lifespan: conception, prenatal development and birth. After completing these three chapters, you will be ready to begin exploring the main focus of lifespan development: people changing and growing throughout their lives.

1

INTRODUCTION

Studying Development

Focusing Questions

- What in general is human development?

- Why is it important to know about development?

- What general themes or issues are important in developmental psychology?

- How do developmental psychologists go about studying age-related change?

- What ethical considerations should guide the study of children?

- What special problems complicate the study of age-related change across the lifespan?

D o you remember your past? In important ways you were probably a different person as a child than you are now. When you were two, you probably could not tie a shoelace, button your coat, or turn a doorknob reliably. When you were six, you may have struggled to read even one line of print. When you were sixteen (or twenty, or thirty . . .) you may have wondered whether you would ever be truly liked and respected by your friends.

Changes such as these—and many others—mark every human life. Some are obvious, such as the transformation of a speechless infant into a talkative child or of an idealistic teenager into a thoughtful adult. Other changes are subtle and may go unnoticed, such as alterations in hormones circulating in the blood as children experience adolescence or as a midlife adult undergoes declines in fertility. But whether obvious or subtle, changes make us human and may alter our lives profoundly.

THE NATURE OF DEVELOPMENTAL CHANGE

This book is about change. In particular, it is about human **development**—changes in a person's long-term growth, feelings, and patterns of thinking. Some developmental changes are relatively specific, such as when an infant takes her first unassisted step. Others are more general, such as when an adult gradually becomes aware of mortality, of the finiteness of life itself. But on the whole, developmental changes tend to unfold gradually, even though once they appear they may seem quite unlike any behaviors a person showed previously. A ten-year-old boy, for example, may not believe that he will likely go on a date with a girl sometime during the next ten years; indeed, his own parents may find this hard to believe!

Not every change is truly developmental, however. Cold weather in the winter causes changes in behavior, such as putting on warmer clothing and selecting indoor activities more frequently. But when the weather warms up again, these behavioral changes tend to disappear. On the other hand, not every human development involves change in behavior or emotions. Some are characterized primarily by continuity; once a person's basic sense of self develops, it tends to remain constant for long periods of life.

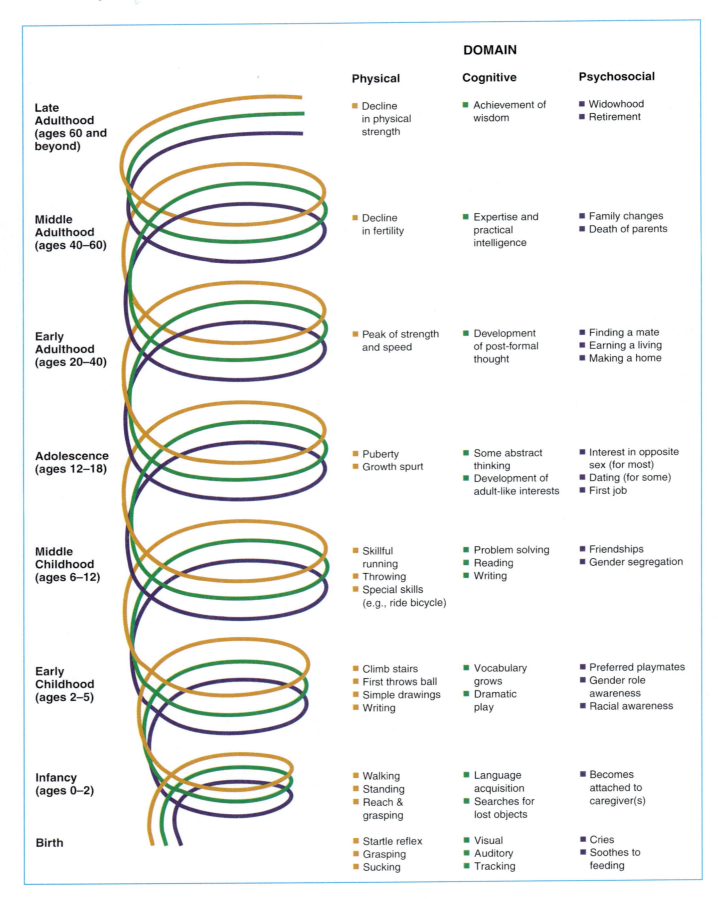

DOMAIN

	Physical	Cognitive	Psychosocial
Late Adulthood (ages 60 and beyond)	■ Decline in physical strength	■ Achievement of wisdom	■ Widowhood ■ Retirement
Middle Adulthood (ages 40–60)	■ Decline in fertility	■ Expertise and practical intelligence	■ Family changes ■ Death of parents
Early Adulthood (ages 20–40)	■ Peak of strength and speed	■ Development of post-formal thought	■ Finding a mate ■ Earning a living ■ Making a home
Adolescence (ages 12–18)	■ Puberty ■ Growth spurt	■ Some abstract thinking ■ Development of adult-like interests	■ Interest in opposite sex (for most) ■ Dating (for some) ■ First job
Middle Childhood (ages 6–12)	■ Skillful running ■ Throwing ■ Special skills (e.g., ride bicycle)	■ Problem solving ■ Reading ■ Writing	■ Friendships ■ Gender segregation
Early Childhood (ages 2–5)	■ Climb stairs ■ First throws ball ■ Simple drawings ■ Writing	■ Vocabulary grows ■ Dramatic play	■ Preferred playmates ■ Gender role awareness ■ Racial awareness
Infancy (ages 0–2)	■ Walking ■ Standing ■ Reach & grasping	■ Language acquisition ■ Searches for lost objects	■ Becomes attached to caregiver(s)
Birth	■ Startle reflex ■ Grasping ■ Sucking	■ Visual ■ Auditory ■ Tracking	■ Cries ■ Soothes to feeding

Changes happen in all domains at once—physical, cognitive, and psychosocial. As this baby refines her motor and thinking skills and develops a capacity for empathy and caring, she (hopefully) will grab the cat less and pet it more. Eventually she may display toward it the same degree of affection and loyalty shown by this woman for her cat.

Three Domains of Development

As these examples suggest, human development can take many forms. For convenience, this book distinguishes among three major types, or **domains,** of development: physical, cognitive, and psychosocial. The first domain deals with **physical development,** or biological growth. It includes changes in the body (in the brain, sense organs, muscles, bones, and so forth) and in the ways a person uses his or her body (motor skills and sexual development, for example). It also includes the effects of aging, such as changes in eyesight or in muscular strength. But it usually does not include physical changes that result from accidents, illnesses, or other special events. Like other forms of development, physical growth or maturation often spans very long periods.

Cognitive development involves gains, declines, and changes in reasoning and thinking, language acquisition, and the ways individuals gain, store, and remember or recall knowledge of their environments. It includes what we commonly call "learning," as well as the forgetting that nearly everyone experiences sometime during adulthood. Learning and forgetting refer to comparatively permanent changes in thinking, feeling, and behavior, but they tend to be limited to changes that result from relatively specific experiences or events. Often, too, the changes occur over a short time—sometimes just hours or even minutes—but, as later chapters show, both learning and forgetting can take much longer to occur.

Psychosocial development concerns changes in feelings or emotions as well as changes in how individuals relate to other people. It includes relationships with family, peers, and coworkers, as well as an individual's personal identity, or sense of self. Because identity and social relationships tend to evolve simultaneously, we discuss them together throughout this book. But both aspects of development also depend on other kinds of change. How a person looks physically can affect how she feels about herself and influence her relationships with her friends. Her powers of reasoning can influence her ability to understand the needs of others and, in this

FIGURE 1.1
Selected Landmarks of Development
Development is a continual unfolding and integration of changes in all domains, beginning at birth. Changes in one domain often affect those in another domain.

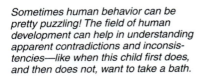

Sometimes human behavior can be pretty puzzling! The field of human development can help in understanding apparent contradictions and inconsistencies—like when this child first does, and then does not, want to take a bath.

way, affect the quality of her relationships with others. Each form of development appears to influence all of the others.

As Figure 1.1 shows, the three domains interconnect in many ways. For instance, physical growth makes the cognitive process of language acquisition possible, and language facilitates the development of social relationships. In turn, social relationships provide settings for cognitive learning and the nurturing of further physical growth. Later chapters point out connections such as these wherever appropriate.

An Example of Development: Jodi

You may have noticed that these opening comments are rather general; we seem to be speaking of changes that happen to *every* person. But what about changes that happen to just one individual? Can developmental psychology say anything about these? We believe it can, though it does so by framing specific experiences in relatively general terms. Specific changes—such as when a four-year-old "reads" his name or completes a somersault—can be understood both as examples and as creators of larger, more universal human changes. For this reason, among others, developmental psychology can be a very practical and useful field of study. To see what we mean, consider a child whom one of the authors knows personally: Jodi.

When Jodi was four, one of her brothers died. Roger had been 2½ years older, a friendly kid and a decent sibling. Jodi played with him more than with her sister and other brother, who were both older than Roger. He died suddenly one winter from complications of chicken pox. The doctors said he may have reacted to the aspirin he had taken for his fever. They said you weren't supposed to give aspirin to children, but Jodi didn't know that, and apparently her parents didn't know it either.

For a few years after that, they were a three-child family "with a hole in the middle," said Jodi to her best friend, where Roger was supposed to be. It was not ideal for Jodi, but it was tolerable: she didn't have the playmate she used to have, but she did have her family ("What's left of it!") and her friends from school. Life got back to normal—sort of.

When Jodi was nine, her parents adopted another child, a boy of twelve, about the same age Roger would have been had he lived. Frank had lived in numerous foster care homes, some of which had not been happy experiences for him. In two homes the discipline had been extremely strict, but it was hard for Jodi to know this, because Frank did not tell her as much as he told the social workers or his new adopted parents, and her parents did not say much about Frank's past. In fact, Frank said little to Jodi about anything; he seemed distinctly cool toward all three of his new siblings.

Except for his periodic visits to Jodi's room at night. The first time it happened, Jodi was startled out of her sleep: Frank was standing by her bed and demanded that she take off her nightgown. That was all for that time. But he came back every few weeks, each time asking for more than the time before and threatening to hurt her badly if she revealed "our secret."

So Jodi learned not to sleep deeply. She also learned to avoid being alone in the house with Frank. In high school and college, she learned to avoid talking to boys a lot, except in a joking way and in the presence of others. In class she learned to look interested in what the instructors said even though she often was "sleeping inside," as she put it. So Jodi learned a lot from Frank, though not things she wanted to learn and not things most of her classmates were learning.

Jodi's story shows several things about human development. It shows, for example, that the domains of development all unfold together. Jodi's thoughts and feelings about Frank occurred in the context of physical changes happening to herself. Being physically older or younger may not have protected her from abuse, but it probably would have altered the experience, either in impact or in quality.

Jodi's story also suggests the importance of unique, personal experiences when exploring developmental psychology in general. Some things about Jodi may always be unique because of her encounters with Frank; she may always be a bit mistrustful of boys and men, for example. But other things about Jodi can be understood as examples of human changes that are universal or nearly universal. In experiencing abuse, for example, Jodi responds to gender role differences that pervade nearly all societies; in most societies, women enjoy less power than men.

Urie Bronfenbrenner, a developmental psychologist, has originated a widely used framework for thinking about the multiple influences on individuals (Bronfenbrenner, 1989; Garbarino, 1992a). He describes the contexts of development as *ecological systems,* which are sets of people, settings, and recurring events that are related to one another, have stability, and influence the person over time. Figure 1.2 and Table 1.1 illustrate Bronfenbrenner's four ecological systems.

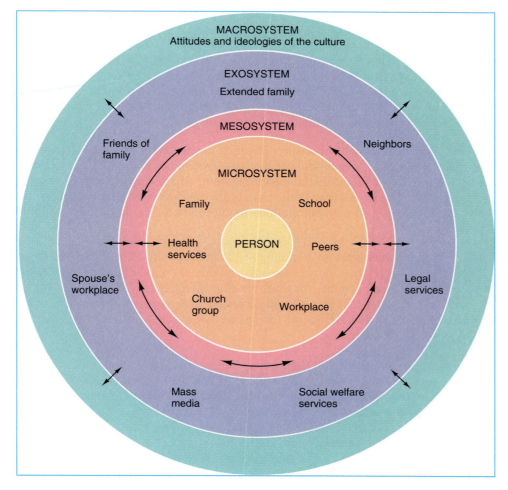

FIGURE 1.2
Bronfenbrenner's Four Ecological Settings for Developmental Change
As shown here, Bronfenbrenner describes human development as a set of overlapping ecological systems. All of these systems operate together to influence what a person becomes as he or she grows older. In this sense, development is not exclusively "in" the person but is also "in" the person's environment.
Source: Adapted from Garbarino (1982).

TABLE 1.1 **Ecological System Levels**

Ecological Level	Definition	Examples	Issues Affecting the Individual
Microsystem	Situations in which the person has face-to-face contact with influential others	Family, school, peer group, church, workplace	Is the person regarded positively? Is the person accepted? Is the person reinforced for competent behavior? Is the person exposed to enough diversity in roles and relationships? Is the person given an active role in reciprocal relationships?
Mesosystem	Relationships between micro systems; the connections between situations	Home–school, workplace–family, school–neighborhood	Do settings respect each other? Do settings present basic consistency in values?
Exosystem	Settings in which the person does not participate but in which significant decisions are made affecting the individuals who do interact directly with the person	Spouse's place of employment, local school board, local government	Are decisions made with the interests of the person in mind? How well do social supports for families balance stresses for parents?
Macrosystem	"Blueprints" for defining and organizing the institutional life of the society	Ideology, social policy, shared assumptions about human nature, the "social contract"	Are some groups valued at the expense of others (e.g., sexism, racism)? Is there an individualistic or a collectivistic orientation? Is violence a norm?

Source: Adapted from Garbarino (1982).

1. The *microsystem* refers to situations in which the person has face-to-face contact with influential others. For Jodi, the microsystem consists of her immediate family (though note that the membership of this family changed over time) as well as her teachers and peers at school.

2. The *mesosystem* refers to the connections and relationships that exist between two or more microsystems and influence the person because of their relationships. An example would be the contacts between Jodi's parents and the social workers responsible for Frank's adoption: their contacts led them (perhaps wrongly) to withhold information about Frank from Jodi.

3. The *exosystem* consists of settings in which the person does not participate but still experiences decisions and events that affect him or her indirectly. An example in Jodi's case might be the medical system, which either lacked the knowledge needed to save Roger at the time of his death or had been organized in a way that interfered with communicating needed medical knowledge to Jodi's parents.

4. The *macrosystem* is the overarching institutions, practices, and patterns of belief that characterize society as a whole and take the smaller micro-, meso-, and exosystems into account. An example that affected Jodi was gender role: a widespread belief that men should dominate women may have contributed to Frank's coercive actions against Jodi, as well as to Jodi's caution with boys and men as she got older.

In the pages ahead we will keep in mind these multiple systems, such as those implied by Jodi's story, as well as distinctions among the major domains of development. Only in this way will we be able to convince you that developmental psychology has something to say about the particulars of human change: about how you, I, or a specific friend change and grow and what those changes may signify. We therefore encourage you to return to Jodi from time to time to remind yourself that in real life, the particulars and universals both have meaning for human development.

WHY STUDY DEVELOPMENT?

Knowing about human development can help you in five major ways. First, it can give you realistic expectations for children, adolescents, and adults. Developmental psychology tells you, for example, when infants usually begin talking and when schoolchildren tend to begin reasoning abstractly. It also describes the issues faced by parents—and grandparents, for that matter. Admittedly, it often gives such information only as averages or generalities: when a "typical" person acquires a particular skill, behavior, or emotion. Nonetheless, the averages can help you know what to expect from specific individuals.

Second, knowledge of development can help you respond appropriately to a person's actual behavior. If a preschool boy tells his mother that he wants to marry her, should she ignore his remark or make a point of correcting his misconception? If a father is worried about his daughter's choice of friends, should he actively intervene in her social life or learn to have faith in her social judgments? Developmental psychology can help answer such questions by indicating the sources and significance of many patterns of human thought, feelings, and behavior.

Third, knowledge of development can help you recognize when departures from normal are truly significant. If a child talks very little by age two, should her parents and doctors be concerned? What if she still does not talk much by age four? If a fifty-year-old breadwinner reports feeling a lot less ambitious at work than he did when younger, are his feelings unusual or typical? We can answer these questions more easily if we know what *usually* happens to people as they develop through the lifespan. And knowing what usually happens—being aware of the universal trends—makes up a great deal of the content of developmental psychology.

Fourth, studying development can help you understand yourself. Developmental psychology makes explicit the processes of psychological growth, processes that each of us may overlook in our personal, everyday lives. Even more important, it can help you make sense out of your own experiences, such as whether it really mattered that you reached puberty earlier (or later) than your friends did.

Finally, studying development can make you a more professional advocate for the needs and rights of people of all ages, whether young, old, or in between. By knowing in detail the capacities of people of diverse ages and backgrounds, you will be in a good position to persuade others of their importance and value. All of us, including most readers of this book, have a common stake in making our society a more humane place to live. Yet, as the accompanying Perspectives box indicates, we as a society can do a better job of supporting human development than we in fact have done.

What Do You Think?

What do *you* hope to gain by studying developmental psychology (besides a college credit, of course!)? Take a minute to think about this question—maybe even jot down some notes about it. Then share your ideas with two or three classmates. How do they differ?

THE HISTORY OF DEVELOPMENTAL STUDY

Until just a few hundred years ago, children in Western society were not perceived as full-fledged members of society or even as genuine human beings (Ariès, 1962). During medieval times, infants tended to be regarded rather like talented pets: at best interesting and even able to talk, but not creatures worth caring about deeply. Children graduated to adult status early in life, around age seven or eight, by taking

Perspectives

Wanted: A Child and Family Policy

Parents generally do value their children, want the best for them, and make sacrifices on their behalf. In spite of this support, though, the lives of children are often difficult:

☐ In the early 1990s, more than 20 percent of all children in the United States under age six lived in families that were officially poor (Huston, 1994). This is more than twice the rate of poverty in Canada and about ten times the rate of poverty in Sweden.

☐ A similar proportion of children have failed to receive routine immunizations against polio, measles, and other childhood diseases. Here too the United States ranks much lower than many other developed countries.

☐ About a third of all children living today will eventually experience the divorce of their parents, with all of the stress it brings (Hetherington, 1995). One of the stresses will be poverty, because the parent who usually has major custody, the mother, tends to earn much less than the father.

☐ In the United States, on average, an infant is born into poverty every thirty-five seconds, a child is physically punished in school every four seconds, and a preschooler is murdered every fourteen hours (Children's Defense Fund, 1995).

A major reason these problems exist is that the United States lacks a comprehensive, integrated set of policies for caring for its children. Programs to remedy social problems have tended to focus on problems selectively rather than recognizing the impact of one problem on another. School programs to assist with learning difficulties, for example, tend to work with children individually, even though health, nutrition, illness, and family disrup-

tions contribute to learning difficulties in major ways. A more effective approach is to provide a set of related and coordinated services to support families: pediatric care, combined with special help at school and a supportive social worker or nurse to visit parents at home to provide encouragement and information. When Victoria Seitz and Nancy Apfel tried this approach with some low-SES families, they found improvements in cognitive abilities not only for the children originally at risk but also for their siblings who had not even been a focus of the intervention (Seitz & Apfel, 1994)!

Similar conclusions have followed from studies of the supports needed by low-SES single mothers who wish to attend college (Kates, 1995). The most effective form of support has not been restricted to the mothers as individuals. Career counseling and campus advocacy services, for example, are useful for low-SES single mothers. More useful is to combine these services with supports for the mother's family and friends, such as by providing child care as needed or help with finding housing. Best of all is to include, along with these services, programs to actively develop awareness of these students' needs among university faculty and administrators so that they in turn can help the students find what they need.

Such combined approaches to children's welfare may look expensive and difficult when organized as special demonstration projects, but experience in other developed countries suggests that costs decrease markedly when implemented universally and that organizational problems can in fact be solved (Chafel, 1993; U.S. General Accounting Office, 1993). The real challenge, it seems, may be political: enlisting the support of leaders in government and business to develop comprehensive policies for children, and thereby ensuring the future of society.

on major, adultlike tasks for the community. At that time, children who today would be attending second or third grade might have been caring for younger siblings, working in the fields, or apprenticed to a family to learn a trade.

Because children took on adult responsibilities so soon, the period we call *adolescence* was also unknown. Teenagers assumed adult roles. Although these roles often included marriage and childrearing, most people in their teens lived with their original families, helping with household work and with caring for other people's children until well into their twenties.

All this may seem harsh by modern, middle-class standards, but perhaps it was simply realistic. Relatively large numbers of children died early in life, especially in infancy. Some historians suggest that this made it unrealistic for parents to care too deeply about infants when they were first born. Others have argued that parents did care, but the economic circumstances of the community required early participation by children in community life (Hareven, 1986; Sommerville, 1990). There was little time left for play and fun, but children also enjoyed higher economic status than do most modern children.

The concept of childhood as a distinct period in a person's life is a relatively new invention, at least as judged by how children have been portrayed in paintings over the centuries. Until the nineteenth century, painters generally depicted children as miniature adults, with adultlike clothing, facial expressions, and bodily proportions. By the nineteenth century, though, childhood had come to be seen—and valued—as a unique time, one quite different from adulthood. Children were expected to wear special types of clothing and hairstyles and engage in their own kind of activities and pastimes.

Early Precursors to Developmental Study

Why did awareness of childhood eventually emerge? Society was becoming less rural and more industrialized. During the eighteenth century, factory towns began attracting large numbers of workers, who often brought their children with them. "Atrocity stories" became increasingly common: reports of young children in England becoming caught and disabled in factory machinery and of children being abandoned to the streets. Partly because of these changes, many people became more conscious of childhood and adolescence as unique periods of life, periods that influence later development. At the same time, they became concerned with arranging appropriate, helpful experiences for children.

The Emergence of Modern Developmental Study

During the nineteenth and twentieth centuries, the growing recognition of childhood led to new ways of studying children's behavior. One of these was the *baby biography,* a detailed diary of a particular child, usually the author's own. One of the most famous English biographies was written and published by Charles Darwin (1877) and contained lengthy accounts of his son Doddy's activities and accomplishments. The tradition of rich description continued in the twentieth century with Arnold Gesell, who observed children at precise ages doing specific things, such as building with blocks, jumping, and hopping (Gesell, 1926). After studying more than five hundred children, Gesell generalized standards of normal development, or **norms**—behaviors typical of children at certain ages. Although the norms applied primarily to white, middle-class children and to specific situations and abilities, they gave a wider-ranging picture of child development than was possible from baby biographies alone.

    The method of descriptive observation in developmental research has persisted into the present. An influential observer in this century has been Jean Piaget, who described many details of his own three children's behavior, as well as that of adolescents (Piaget, 1963). Others have provided sensitive commentary on adulthood, some (but not all) of it based on descriptive commentary; for example, Bernice

Neugarten (1967) has studied the lives of middle-aged adults from a number of perspectives. These works have begun to answer questions about the nature of human development. But they have created some new issues as well, issues that have become fundamental to current research and thinking in the field.

What Do You Think?

What are the merits and problems of descriptive study of human beings? One way to find out is for you and two or three classmates to make separate written observations of the "same" events. Visit a place with people in it (even your developmental psychology classroom), and separately write about what you see one particular person doing. Afterward, compare notes. How well do they agree, and when and how do they differ?

BASIC ISSUES IN DEVELOPMENTAL STUDY

As developmental psychology has evolved, four basic issues have emerged: nature and nurture, continuity and discontinuity, context and universality, and deficit and difference in development. These issues influence how developmental psychology is organized, and therefore also influence what you can expect when you study it. Table 1.2 summarizes these issues.

Nature and Nurture

How much are you the result of genetic, inborn qualities, and how much the result of learning and experience? The first alternative (genetics and inborn qualities) is your **nature,** and the second (learning and experience) is your **nurture**. It seems sensible to expect that each of us combines nature and nurture in a lot of ways. Your height depends on how tall your parents are (nature), but it also depends on the nutrition and exercise you get as you grow up (nurture).

Developmental psychologists have many questions about exactly how nature and nurture interact and whether one is sometimes more important than the other. Robert Plomin and his associates, for example, studied the temperaments (or emotional styles) of two groups of infants: one a group of identical twins, and therefore completely the same genetically, and the other fraternal twins, and therefore only as similar genetically as ordinary siblings (Plomin et al., 1993). The identical twins

TABLE 1.2   *Basic Issues In Developmental Psychology*

Issue	Crucial Question
Nature and nurture	How much are qualities, behaviors, and skills inborn, and how much are they acquired or lost through experience?
Continuity and discontinuity	How much does development simply continue earlier acquisitions, and how much does it lead to qualitatively new behaviors and skills?
Universal and context-specific development	How much can developmental psychology identify developmental changes that happen to everyone throughout the world, and how much should it take specific human and cultural contexts into account?
Deficit and difference	Are certain developmental changes and milestones inherently more desirable than others?

An important issue in developmental psychology has to do with the universality of human development. Are there principles of growth and maturation that hold true for all people, regardless of circumstances? What, for example, do the minds and feelings of these boys and girls have in common?

were somewhat more similar to each other in their emotional reactions than were the fraternal twins—they responded to strangers with similar degrees of shyness, for example—suggesting that genetics influenced their reactions and styles. But the tendency to be more similar was only modest, suggesting that experiences since birth also affected the babies' emotional temperaments.

Continuity and Discontinuity

Developmental psychologists also note, as perhaps you have too, that some long-term changes seem like obvious continuations of earlier qualities and skills, whereas others seem new and unprecedented. Take memory, for example: adults usually can recall and define more words than children can, as if this developmental change were simply a matter of accumulating more verbal memories. But is that all there is to it? In recalling and using terms, is an adult really just doing "more" of what a child does or doing something altogether different? Michelene Chi wondered about this question and, through some ingenious memory tests (Chi, 1985), concluded that later memory is not necessarily more of earlier memory but something altogether different in quality. She asked a first-grade girl to recall the names of as many of her classmates as possible. The girl performed this task quite well, but by using a strategy different than that used by most adults: instead of recalling classmates' names alphabetically, as adults probably would have done, the girl recalled them according to the children's seating arrangement in the classroom. When asked to recall a list of unfamiliar names in alphabetical order, on the other hand, she performed poorly compared to adults. It appeared, therefore, that her memory was limited, or "undeveloped," when she was expected to perform the task in an adult-like way. She did not lack knowledge of classmates' names; rather, she organized her knowledge differently.

Universal and Context-Specific Development

As a practical matter, most of us (including developmental psychologists) recognize that who we are and become depends in various ways on the settings and situations in which we grow up. If I grow up among English-speaking adults, I will learn to speak English, not some other language. If I grow up in a Hindu family in India, as described in the accompanying Multicultural View box, my entire personality will develop differently than if I grow up in a Christian family in the midwestern United States. What makes developmental psychologists curious is the extent

A Multicultural View

Growing Up in India

In many parts of the world today, childhood means something different than it does in the West, because most cultures emphasize interdependence among family members more than in the West (Greenfield, 1994). India is a good case in point. In the traditional Hindu sects of this society, infants and young children receive a good deal more protection and intimate nurturance than their counterparts in Western families do (Kakar, 1982; Kurtz, 1992). Typically, infants are breast-fed well into toddlerhood, far beyond what is usual in the West. During the first four or five years of life, children are rarely separated from their mothers; they come along on virtually all errands and visits, even when the excursions do not concern them. During this period, mothers take child nurturing very seriously and are expected to do so by Hindu society. Guidance, discipline, and spoiling—major concerns among Western parents—are not serious issues for traditional Hindu mothers, who see their primary task as helping children develop a deeply trustful attitude toward the world.

But eventually the protection and nurturance come to an end. For a boy, the end comes suddenly at about age five, when parents and other relatives expect him to begin conforming to adult standards of behavior, give up playing with younger children, and spend most of his time in the company of other boys and men. The boy must even give up eating meals with his mother and other females and take his meals exclusively with males.

For a girl, protection and nurturance persist a few years longer than for a boy. But she too faces a drastic change: sometime between ages eleven and thirteen she gets married, not to someone she chooses but to a young man selected by her parents and the man's parents. At this point, she is likely to leave home permanently to live with her husband's family. Many of her in-laws will be virtual strangers to her, sometimes including her new husband.

Because the changes occur so suddenly for each sex, they often create stress for young Hindus, as well as sadness and nostalgia for times past. Yet in most cases the changes are manageable, thanks to the emotional and practical supports provided by Hindu families. A major form of support is the extended family, which consists of adult relatives living together (usually brothers) who have brought their spouses to live with them after they marry. This arrangement helps reduce the loneliness children experience after they leave the intense early care of their mothers. A Hindu boy may miss his mother when he stops eating meals with her, but his new companions—his father and other males—have had similar experiences and respond to his feelings tactfully, albeit with reserve. A Hindu girl also may miss her mother when she marries, but she may become a mother herself by her late teens. In the context of an extended family, her pregnancy is not considered the burden that a teenage pregnancy is in the West. On the contrary, early pregnancy confers status on the mother-to-be, and in any case the girl's extended family is likely to contain other, more experienced women to assist her with child care.

and importance of such influences: when are they superficial and limited (such as wearing one color of clothing instead of another), and when are they profound, far-reaching, and part of our human essence?

Patricia Greenfield studied routine parent-teacher conferences between Anglo teachers and Hispanic mothers in terms of differences in personal and family values between the two groups (Greenfield, 1995). During the conferences, the Anglo teachers uniformly sought to highlight the individual achievements of the child ("Carmen is doing well with her spelling"). But many of the Hispanic mothers preferred to direct the conversation toward how the child fit into the family and into the classroom group ("Carmen is such a help to me, and so friendly"). The parents' remarks reflected differences in general cultural values—the Anglo parents valuing independence somewhat more, but the Hispanic parents (sometimes) valuing *inter*-dependence more. The result was frustration with the conference on the part of both teachers and parents and less effective support for the children in their efforts to succeed socially and academically.

Deficit and Difference

Given that individuals develop in different ways, are some people deficient compared to others, or are they merely different? Are certain developmental milestones

Compared to Western children, then, Hindu children experience longer and more intense nurturance from a larger number of relatives, but at the price of a relatively sudden transition away from intimacy with their mothers. Western children avoid such a sudden transition, but encounter more mixed responses about intimacy even from birth. Western parents admire and love their children, of course, but they are also likely to worry incessantly about fostering independence and self-reliance (Elkind, 1994b). These are reasonable concerns given the unique conditions of Western family life, where parents can count on much less help in raising children than in the majority of societies.

In the Hindu parts of India, mothers give their young children a good deal more physical care and emotional nurturance than commonly occurs in North America. Observing the effects of these differences can give insight into the impact and significance of parenting techniques in general.

inherently more desirable than others? To the extent that developmental psychologists (as well as the rest of the world) can agree on which changes are truly desirable, they (and other professionals) can actively work to encourage them and to discourage unwanted or undesirable directions of growth and change.

At some general level, some changes must surely be more desirable than others. Nearly everyone would agree, for example, that acquiring some sort of language is better than acquiring no language at all, because language provides a way to communicate with others. But as often as not, one developmental change is not clearly "better" than another. Although acquiring language in general may be good, it may not matter *which* particular language is acquired: Spanish, Chinese, American Sign Language, and all dialects (or "accents") of English are equally capable of expressing the full range of human thoughts and feelings. Speaking (or signing) these various languages makes people different, but does not make some people deficient compared to others.

The effort to identify general developmental trends sometimes makes developmental psychologists prone to equate differences in individuals with deficiencies. Recently a number of psychologists have explored an example of this tendency in studying how children and adults develop morality—a sense of ethics, or of right and wrong. Until the early 1980s, the psychological study of moral development focused on a person's general sense of justice or fairness (Colby et al., 1983). Is it always right, for example, to pay a person in proportion to his or her productivity? Is it always wrong to steal? More mature (and therefore "better") development seemed to be associated with the ability to reason abstractly about principles of fairness. An implication was that people who cannot or do not reason as abstractly as others do are not just different but deficient in their moral reasoning.

More recent research has suggested that this view of moral development is unfair to many people's ethical ideas. Carol Gilligan interviewed adolescent girls and young women who were considering having abortions and found that their sense of right and wrong focused much less on general principles of fairness ("Is abortion always/sometimes/never right?") and more on the welfare of the particular people affected (the baby, the father, the woman herself, her family). This approach, an "ethics of care" rather than of justice, becomes well developed in many women (and some men) and is used by them to resolve a variety of ethical dilemmas (Brown & Gilligan, 1992; Colby & Damon, 1992). Its existence suggests a new way of thinking about moral reasoning: perhaps people develop not toward a common endpoint but toward multiple possible endpoints. Some may develop moral reasoning oriented toward general principles of justice, whereas others develop an ethics of care. One orientation would be different from the other, but not necessarily deficient.

What Do You Think?

A psychologist once said that "every parent believes in nurture until they have their *second* child." What do you think she was getting at with this comment? If you happen to be a parent of at least two children, share your opinion of this comment with a classmate who is not a parent or with one who is a first-time parent. And vice versa: if you've raised no children, or only one, compare your opinions to those of a second- or third-time parent.

METHODS OF STUDYING DEVELOPMENTAL PSYCHOLOGY

Scientific Methods

All research studies of human development follow some form of **scientific method,** or systematic procedures to ensure objective observations and interpretations of observations. Even though it is not always possible to follow these methods perfectly, they form an ideal to which psychological research tends to aspire (Cherry, 1995; Levine & Parkinson, 1994). The procedures are as follows:

1. *Formulating research questions* Research begins with questions. Sometimes these questions refer to previous studies, such as when a developmental psychologist asks, "Are Professor Deepthought's studies of thinking consistent with studies of thinking from less developed countries?" Other times they refer to issues important to society, such as "Does preschool education make children more socially skilled later in childhood?"

2. *Stating questions as hypotheses* A **hypothesis** is a statement that expresses a research question precisely. In making a hypothesis out of the preschool education question above, a psychologist needs to be more specific about the terms *preschool education* and *socially skilled*. Does *preschool education* mean a part-time nursery or a full-time child care center? Does *socially skilled* refer to a child who initiates activities or only to a child who smiles frequently and cooperates?

3. *Testing the hypothesis* Having phrased a research question as a hypothesis, researchers can conduct an actual study about it. As the next section describes further, they can do this in a number of ways. The choice of method usually depends on convenience, ethics, and scientific appropriateness.

4. *Interpreting and publicizing the results* After conducting the study itself, psychologists have a responsibility to report their results to others by presenting them at conferences and publishing them in journal articles. Their reports should include reasonable interpretations or conclusions based on the results and enough details to allow other psychologists to replicate (or repeat) a study themselves to test the conclusions. In practice, the limits of time (at a conference presentation) or space (in a journal) sometimes compromise this ideal.

There is a wide range of ways to carry out these steps, each with its own strengths and limitations. Viewed broadly, studies can vary in time frame, the extent of intervention and control, and the sampling strategies used. These dimensions often get combined in various ways, depending on the questions the studies are investigating. Table 1.3 summarizes the various possible methods, and the following sections explain them more fully.

Variations in Time Frame

In general, developmental psychologists can either compare people of different ages at one point in time (called a *cross-sectional study*) or compare the same people at different times as they get older (called a *longitudinal study*). A method that combines elements of both time frames is the *sequential study*. Each method has its advantages and problems.

Cross-sectional Study   A **cross-sectional study** compares persons of different ages at a single point in time. One such study compared preschool children (age four) and early-school-age children (age six) on their ability to distinguish between real and apparent emotions (Joshi & MacLean, 1994). Half of the children lived in India, and the other half lived in Great Britain. All of the children listened to stories in which a character sometimes had to conceal his or her true feelings (such as when an uncle gives a child a toy that the child did not really want) and described both how the character really felt and how the character seemed to feel. The results shed light on how children distinguish sincerity from tactfulness. The older children were more sensitive to this distinction than the younger ones were, but the Indian children (especially girls) also were more sensitive to it than the British children were.

Longitudinal Study   A **longitudinal study** observes the same subjects periodically over a relatively long period, often years. A recent example is the twenty-

TABLE 1.3   *Methods of Studying Human Development*

Method	Purpose
Cross-sectional study	Observes persons of different ages at one point in time
Longitudinal study	Observes same group(s) of persons at different points in time
Naturalistic study	Observes persons in naturally occurring situations or circumstances
Experimental study	Observes persons where circumstances are carefully controlled
Correlational study	Observes tendency of two behaviors or qualities of a person to occur or vary together; measures this tendency statistically
Survey	Brief, structured interview or questionnaire about specific beliefs or behaviors of large numbers of persons
Interview	Face-to-face conversation used to gather complex information from individuals
Case study	Investigation of just one individual or a small number of individuals using a variety of sources of information

Communication Difficulties Across the Lifespan

Marsha Bennington works as a speech-language pathologist for a school district and in private practice. She thus sees individuals who range widely in age, from early childhood through adulthood. She talked, among other things, about how speech and language needs change across the course of development.

Kelvin: Speech-language pathologists used to be called "speech therapists," right? Why the name change?

Marsha: Our clientele has changed. We see people from a greater variety of language backgrounds now. Classrooms include more kids with disabilities, and more infants with medical problems at birth survive into adulthood, thanks to modern medicine. Our work is more diverse than it used to be, and the label "speech therapy" doesn't really describe it any more.

Kelvin: What do you mean?

Marsha: We address more than just speech problems. People may face an underlying inability to communicate and have a lot of difficulty with syntax or word choice. They might have trouble with reading, which really grows out of problems with focusing attention or with connecting printed and spoken language. We don't just deal with young children who mispronounce specific sounds—who say /t/ for /k/, for example.

Kelvin: Sounds like your job is as much about "cognition" as it is about speech.

Marsha: You're right, although even "cognition" may be narrowing it down too much. Motor skills can play a role, as can people's attitudes and feeling or their parents' attitudes and support. It depends on the individuals' particular needs and on their age.

Kelvin: Are the problems you see in young children different from those of older kids or adults you work with?

Marsha: You can't overgeneralize, but there do seem to be differences. A "typical" referral from a kindergarten or first-grade teacher tends to be specifically speech related. A child may articulate certain sounds incorrectly—*wun* instead of *run*—or a child may have some disfluency, that is, "stutter." I do see some young children with underlying language problems—constant syntax errors and trouble with finding words—but not many at this age.

Kelvin: Does this balance change among older students?

Marsha: It does change. By the upper elementary grades, students are most likely initially referred to me because they're having trouble with reading. By this age, reading can become a real effort because it depends so much on fluent speech. If your spoken sounds or your spoken syntax isn't "standard," it's hard to decipher written sounds or sentences!

Kelvin: What do you do in these cases?

Marsha: It depends! I might work on a child's oral language to build awareness of syntax or of phonological difficulties. But by the time a child is in fourth or fifth grade, strategies to compensate for reading difficulties may help more. I might encourage the child to listen carefully to the teacher's oral directions or to ask for them both orally and in writing.

Kelvin: Does that become more of a problem in high school and beyond?

Marsha: Well, adolescence can aggravate a person's self-consciousness, and any speech or language problems only add to it. The older kids I see definitely need reassurance to boost their motivation and confidence. They've started to learn to hide their problem from others, and that usually means they avoid reading and writing, avoid speaking in class, that sort of thing.

Kelvin: What happens after high school? The bigger world after graduation must pose challenges.

Marsha: It's fair to say that *every* transition poses a challenge: home to kindergarten, elementary to high school, high school and beyond. A teenager may have functioned all right in high school, thanks to some help from the speech-language pathologist, but find that her first job requires more language skills than she expected. So back she comes for more help . . . [pauses and frowns]

Kelvin: Except? . . .

Marsha: Except that help for adults, once they're not in school, can be hard to find and too expensive for many to afford.

What Do You Think?

1. Marsha described changes in the sorts of problems people of different ages bring to her. Do you think these should be called "developmental" changes, even though she is really talking about cross-sectional comparisons among age groups? Compare your opinion with that of a classmate.

2. Try retelling Marsha's comments from a more longitudinal (versus cross-sectional) perspective. Do they seem more or less true to life from this perspective? This question would make a good topic for an in-class debate if you and/or your instructor can organize one. In formulating your opinions, though, remember that you are talking about the development of a human *problem,* not about the normative course of development.

3. Given your ideas from questions 1 and 2, how helpful do you think the concept of "human development" is for a speech-language pathologist? Would it be more or less helpful for a regular classroom teacher?

three-year follow-up of the effects of a demonstration preschool program for low-income children that originally took place in 1967. The four-year-old "graduates" of the program were assessed (and continue to be assessed) every few years following the program; at the latest report, they were all twenty-seven years old (Schweinhart et al., 1993). Researchers gathered interviews, school achievement test results, and reports from teachers and (later) employers and compared them to results from an equivalent group of four-year-olds who had been identified at the time of the program but did not participate in it. The results are gratifying: the graduates have succeeded in school and employment better than the nongraduates and cost taxpayers less by needing less public aid and fewer medical and other services.

Cross-sectional and longitudinal studies both have advantages and limitations. Cross-sectional studies can be completed more quickly, but they do not guarantee to show actual change *within* individuals. In the study of children's knowledge of emotions, for example, the fact that older children were more knowledgeable does not ensure that each *individual* child becomes more knowledgeable. It shows only an average trend for the group; in certain individuals knowledge of emotions may improve little as they get older, or even decrease, whereas other individuals may experience a huge leap in knowledge! Why these differences in individual change occur remains a question—and an urgent one if you work with people as a teacher, a nurse, or a counselor. See, for example, the experiences described in the interview with Marsha Bennington, speech-language pathologist.

From the perspective of lifespan psychology, however, a more serious limitation of cross-sectional studies is their inability to distinguish among **cohorts,** or groups of people born at the same time and therefore having undergone similar developmental experiences. For example, a cohort of children born in 1930 shared experi-

Longitudinal studies are especially well suited to studying long-term constancy and change in particular individuals or groups. These brothers resemble each other and their father. But they also change from childhood to young adulthood: as children their faces are more round and their heads are larger relative to their bodies.

ences of less education and less comprehensive health care than a cohort born in 1960. As a result of this difference, comparing their abilities and health cross-sectionally in the 1990s may make the older cohort (the ones born in 1930) appear less intellectually able and less healthy. A cross-sectional study may leave the impression that differences in the cohorts reflect true developmental change instead of the effects of being born earlier in the century. Cross-sectional studies always contain this ambiguity, especially when they compare groups that differ widely in age, as is common in studies of adulthood.

Longitudinal studies do not eliminate the ambiguity created by historical changes in cohorts, but they at least reveal more truly "developmental" change because they show the steps by which particular individuals or groups actually change over time. But in doing so, they pose a practical problem: by definition, longitudinal studies take months or even years to complete. Over this much time, some of the original participants may move away; investigators may become hopelessly bogged down with other work and fail to complete the original study; or government funding to support the work may disappear prematurely. Given these problems, psychologists have organized cross-sectional studies much more often than longitudinal studies, despite the latter's special value.

Sequential Studies   The dilemmas and ambiguities posed by time frames can be partially solved by **sequential studies,** which combine elements of cross-sectional and longitudinal studies. In sequential research, at least two cohorts are observed longitudinally and comparisons are made both within each cohort across time and between the cohorts at particular points in time. This approach provides information about actual developmental changes within individuals, but also about historical differences among cohorts that might create the impression of truly developmental changes.

A good example of sequential research is the work by K. Warner Schaie (1994) studying changes in cognitive abilities of adults (see Chapter 14's discussion of cognitive development in middle adulthood for more details about this research). A variety of earlier, cross-sectional research suggested that adults' general reasoning ability *decreases* with age, for example, that older adults score lower than younger

Not all human differences are related to age; being older does not necessarily mean that a person knows more in all areas, or has more of all possible skills. Some human developments, like the computer skills referred to in this cartoon, result from historical changes, causing younger individuals to be more competent than older persons in selected areas. Another example (at least in the United States) is knowledge of the metric system, which, because of recent curriculum changes, children often understand better than their parents.

One of the joys of installing new software.

In naturalistic research, psychologists study human behavior as it normally occurs in everyday settings. What could be learned from observing this mother and father, or their infant children, relaxing at the park?

ones on tests of general academic intelligence. Schaie's sequential research, how-ever, modified this picture substantially. By testing several successive cohorts of young adults and then testing each cohort again at a later age, Schaie found that (1) many cognitive skills do not decline with age, particularly if they are used on a daily basis; (2) earlier cohorts generally achieved lower scores than later cohorts on tests of cognitive abilities; and (3) some individuals showed more decline with age than did others. None of these findings would have resulted from either a cross-sectional or a longitudinal study alone.

Variations in Control: Naturalistic and Experimental Studies

Developmental studies also vary in how much they attempt to control the circum-stances in which individuals are observed. When they are observed in naturally oc-curring settings, the studies are naturalistic; when circumstances are controlled tightly, the studies are experimental.

Naturalistic Studies   At one extreme, **naturalistic studies** purposely observe be-havior as it normally occurs in natural settings, such as at home, at school, or in the workplace. Reed Larson and Maryse Richards (1994) used this strategy to explore the daily emotional lives of parents in their forties and fifties and their adolescent children. For several weeks, each member of the family carried an electronic pager that beeped at random intervals to remind the person to report on his or her cur-rent moods and activities by telephoning a prearranged number. In every other respect, however, the family members engaged in their normal daily activities—school, job, homemaking, or whatever. The researchers discovered many interesting facts about individuals' responses to family life. Being at home *relieved* stress for midlife fathers ("Then I can relax"), for example, but often *created* it for midlife mothers ("Home is my 'second job'"). Figure 1.3 illustrates this trend. Teenage children felt far more hassled by small daily chores than their parents realized ("They don't notice it when they overdo the reminders about chores").

Experimental Studies   In contrast to naturalistic studies, **experimental studies** arrange circumstances so that just one or two factors or influences vary at a time. For example, Henry Wellman and Anne Hickling (1994) investigated how children understand the human mind: do they think of "the mind" as the center of a person, as adults do, or more as an impersonal switchboard, perhaps like a computer or the motor of a car? To study this question, the investigators designed an experiment in which children had to explain the meanings of metaphorical statements about the mind ("My mind wandered" or "His mind played tricks on him"). Many conditions of the experiment were held constant: all children were interviewed in the same room, by the same person, and asked exactly the same questions. Children were selected from specific ages between 2½ and 10 to allow investigators to infer when the children began believing in a personified view of the mind. The result? At 2½ children had only hazy notions of the mind as human or personified, but by age 8 most children did. Figure 1.4 depicts part of this trend.

Because this study was an experiment, Wellman and Hickling held constant all the factors that might influence children's responses to metaphorical notions *except* age, the one they were studying. This deliberately varied factor is often called the **independent variable**. The factor that varies as a result of the independent variable—in this case, the children's success at interpreting metaphorical statements about the mind—is often called the **dependent variable**.

The experimental method also requires making decisions about the population, or group, to which the study refers. When every member of the population has an equal chance of being chosen for the study, the people selected comprise a **random sample**. If not everyone in a population has an equal chance of being chosen, the sample is said to be *biased*. Investigators can never be completely sure they have avoided systematic bias in selecting individuals to study, but they can improve their chances by defining the population they are studying as carefully as possible and then selecting subjects only from that population. When Wellman and Hickling

FIGURE 1.3
Mothers' and Fathers' Self-Rated Emotions During Various Activities
The idea of "his" marriage and "her" job contains some truth. In this naturalistic study, in which family members reported their emotions at random intervals, mothers and fathers rated a number of activities (though not all) differently.
Source: Larson & Richards (1994).

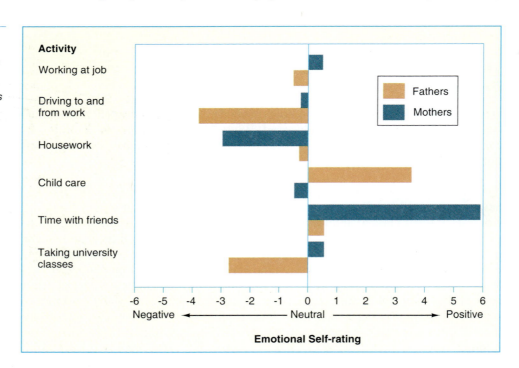

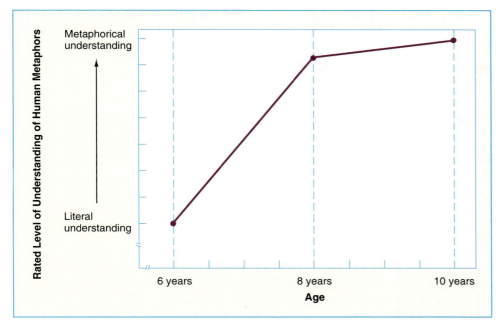

FIGURE 1.4
Children's Understanding of Human Metaphors of Mind
In this experimental study, children were asked to explain statements that contained metaphorical expressions for the human mind (e.g., "My mind fell asleep"). Results suggested that children begin understanding these expressions as metaphors sometime after their sixth birthday, but do not achieve full understanding until age ten.
Source: Adapted from Wellman & Hickling (1994).

studied children's beliefs about the human mind, for example, the population to which they limited their observations consisted only of children of a certain age range—2½ to 10 years—and they sampled children within this range at random. Interpretations of their results therefore apply only to this population of children. In later studies, they (or other investigators) could sample other populations, such as persons of other ages or specific ethnic backgrounds.

Experimental studies incorporate a number of precautions to ensure that their findings have **validity,** meaning they measure or observe what they intend to measure. One way to improve validity is to observe not one but two sample groups, one an experimental, or treatment, group and the other a control group. The **experimental group** receives the treatment, or intervention, related to the purposes of the experiment. The **control group** experiences conditions that are as similar as possible to the conditions of the experimental group, but without experiencing the crucial experimental treatment. Comparing the results for the two groups helps to explicitly establish the effects of the experimental treatment.

Comparisons of experimental and control groups are widespread in developmental research, but especially for problems involving interventions to improve the welfare of people at risk for difficulties. One team of investigators used the strategy to study the impact of a program to develop literacy skills in preschoolers from families of low *socioeconomic status* (*SES*), that is, families with low incomes and low levels of education (Whitehurst et al., 1994). The investigators used classrooms from Head Start, a nationwide early intervention program. They randomly assigned certain classrooms to an experimental group, which received the special literacy program. Other classrooms were randomly assigned to the control group, which received the usual Head Start program.

At the end of one year, they tested all classrooms in both groups for improvements in literacy skills. As you might expect, the experimental group improved more than the control group; children in the literacy program could identify more letters and their own names, for example. What is especially important is that the control group *also* improved somewhat, just by growing older, so the investigators were able to make allowances for this fact in evaluating the impact of the literacy program.

Because of its logical organization, the experimental method often gives clearer results than naturalistic studies do. But because people sometimes do not behave naturally in experimental situations, one criticism of the experimental method is that its results can be artificial. Naturalistic research does not face this particular problem, but it does run a greater risk of generating ambiguous results.

Correlations   Whether naturalistic or experimental, most research studies look for correlations among variables. A **correlation** is a systematic relationship, or association, between two behaviors, responses, or human characteristics. When the behaviors, responses, or characteristics tend to change in the same direction, the relationship is called a *positive correlation;* when they tend to change in opposite directions, it is called a *negative correlation.* The ages of married spouses are a positive correlation: older husbands tend to have older wives (though not strictly so). The age of a child and the frequency of bed wetting is a negative correlation: the older the child, the less frequent the bed wetting (though again, not strictly so).

When correlated factors can be expressed numerically, psychologists use a particular statistic, the *correlation coefficient* (abbreviated r), to indicate the degree of relationship between two behaviors or characteristics. The correlation coefficient is calculated in such a way that its value always falls between +1.00 and −1.00. The closer to +1.00 the value, the more positive the correlation; the closer to −1.00 the value, the more negative the correlation. Correlations near 0.00 indicate no systematic relationship between behaviors or characteristics, or an essentially random relationship. For various reasons, psychologists tend to consider correlations above +0.70 or below −0.70 as strong ones and those between +0.20 and −0.20 as weak ones.

When you read or talk about correlations, it is important to remember that correlations by themselves do not indicate whether one behavior or characteristic *causes* another; they indicate only that some sort of association exists between the two. The age of one spouse, for example, does not cause the age of the other spouse to be similar; the ages are associated only numerically. Additional information is needed to determine what causes the relationship to exist. In the case of spouses' ages, the correlation may be caused by society's beliefs about appropriate ages for spouses or by the way modern schools are age segregated and therefore facilitate the meeting of people of roughly your own age. A correlation only challenges us to consider these possible explanations; we would need further research to determine their truth or importance.

Sampling Strategies

In addition to all the variations described so far, developmental studies vary in how many people they observe or collect information about.

Surveys   At one extreme are large-scale **surveys,** specific, focused interviews of large numbers of people. Grace Kao (1995) used this method to examine patterns of school achievement among Asian American youth. She was particularly interested in a common stereotype of Asian youngsters as "model students," the belief that they always excel academically. Using interviews with about fifteen hundred Asian American students, parents, and teachers, as well as with about twenty-five thousand white counterparts, Kao compared family incomes, educational levels, and ethnic backgrounds with academic achievement. She found that the stereotype of the model student is rather misleading. Academic success varies substantially among particular Asian ethnic groups. It also depends more heavily on how much time and money particular parents invest in education for their particular children than on the educational, financial, or ethnic backgrounds of the family as such. In these ways, the Asian American students were no different from their white counterparts.

These conclusions seem especially persuasive because of the rather large sample of families on which they are based—an advantage of the survey method. But the method also has limitations. Survey questions tend to be "cut and dried" to ensure that responses can be compared among large numbers of respondents. They tend not to explore subtleties of thinking or the reasons people have for taking certain actions or holding certain beliefs. Did some of Kao's Asian American families invest more in education because their culture encourages them to do so or because they anticipated discrimination due to their ethnic background and regarded education as insurance against the negative effects of such discrimination? To answer questions such as these, researchers need methods that invite respondents to comment more fully, such as interviews and case studies.

Interviews   A research study that seeks complex or in-depth information may use **interviews,** or face-to-face directed conversations. Because they take time, interview studies usually focus on a smaller number of individuals than surveys do, perhaps several dozen or so. Regina Campos and her colleagues (1994) used interviews to assess how well low-SES youth in Brazil coped with daily life on the streets. Several dozen youngsters were interviewed both individually and in groups about their experiences, both stressful and satisfying. Some of them spent their days on the street either working at a low-paying job or begging, and came home only at night to sleep. Others were truly homeless and slept on the streets. As you might guess, the truly homeless individuals generally engaged in more illegal activities and experienced more stresses (such as illness). The interview format allowed insight into the reasons for the difference: even an impoverished home offered rest and refuge and provided adults who offered protection, occasional nurturance, and information useful for survival. By providing youngsters with social ties, furthermore, a home offered a reason to find work. Employment was therefore perceived as less burdensome to the home-based street youth than it was to the homeless ones.

Case Studies   When a study uses just one or a few individuals, it is called a **case study**. In general, a case study tries to pull together a wide variety of information and observations about the individual case and then present the information as a unified whole, emphasizing relationships among specific behaviors, thoughts, and attitudes in the individual. An example is a study by Robert Jimenez, Georgia Garcia, and David Pearson (1995) comparing the language skills and knowledge about reading of just three eleven-year-old children: one proficiently bilingual Hispanic student, one proficiently monolingual white student, and one modestly bilingual Hispanic student. Each child was interviewed at length about her perceptions of her own skills with each language. Each was also invited to "think aloud" while reading samples of text in each language (that is, the child told about her thoughts as she read along). Because of the time taken with each individual, the investigators were able to discover important subtleties about how each student read. The proficient bilingual reader, for example, thought of *each* language as an aid to understanding the other language, whereas the less fluent bilingual reader believed simply that her Spanish assisted her English.

By its nature a case study can explore an aspect of human development, looking for new or unexpected connections among behaviors, needs, or social relationships. This is the most common use of case studies. Second, it can confirm whether connections previously found in experimental studies actually occur in everyday, nonexperimental situations, even when conditions are not carefully controlled. The second use resembles the naturalistic studies described earlier in this section.

What Do You Think?

Are some methods of developmental study inherently more effective than others? Try answering this question by organizing a multisided debate. Pick a successful developmental study (you can use any of the ones described in this chapter, for example), and assign each of three or four debating teams to design and argue the merits of some *alternative* method of studying the same question. In a second round of the debate, each team can try to refute the arguments of any of the other teams. Remember: there will be more than two sides to this discussion!

ETHICAL CONSTRAINTS ON STUDYING DEVELOPMENT

Sometimes ethical concerns influence the methods researchers can use to study a particular question about development. Take the question of punishments administered by parents: what kinds of punishment are most effective, and for what reasons? For ethical reasons, we may be unable to experiment with certain aspects of this problem directly. Observing parents actually scolding and reprimanding their children would require delicacy at best. At worst, if the punishment became severe or physical, ethics might require our active intervention simply to protect the child from abuse.

For ethically sensitive questions, we may instead have to satisfy ourselves with less direct but more acceptable methods of study. We can interview a variety of parents about the methods of punishment they use, or we can ask experts who work directly with families what methods they think parents typically use. A few courageous families might allow us to observe their daily activities, with the understanding that we are interested in observing how they punish their children. But by being volunteers, these few families may not represent other families very well.

Generally, research about human beings faces at least three ethical issues: confidentiality, full disclosure of purposes, and respect for the individual's freedom to participate (American Psychological Association, 1992). In developmental psychology, all of these issues are complicated when the subjects are naturally vulnerable—when they are young, disabled, or elderly.

1. *Confidentiality* If researchers collect information that might damage individuals' reputations or self-esteem, they should take care to protect the identities of the participants. Observing parents' methods of managing their children might require this sort of confidentiality. Parents may not want just anyone to know how much and how often they experience conflicts with their children. Similar concerns might influence research on teachers' methods of classroom management or caregivers' styles of caring for elderly people. In such cases, investigators should not divulge the identities of participants in a study without their consent, either during the conduct of the study or afterward when the results are published.

2. *Full disclosure of purposes* Participants in a study are entitled to know the true purposes of any research study in which they participate. Most of the time, investigators understand and follow this principle carefully. But at times it can be tempting to mislead participants. In studying professionals' techniques for working with multiply handicapped adults, for example, researchers may suspect that stating this research purpose honestly will cause certain professionals, as well as the people under their care, to avoid participation. Investigators may

suspect that telling the truth about the study will make the subjects distort their behavior, hiding their less attractive behaviors and conflicts.

In this sort of study, therefore, it might seem that intentional deception would produce more complete observations and in this sense make the research more "scientific." But investigators would purchase this benefit at the cost of their long-run reputations with participants. Purposeful deception may sometimes be permissible, but only when no other method is possible and when participants are fully informed after the study of the deception and its reasons.

3. *Respect for individuals' freedom to participate* As much as possible, research studies should avoid pressuring individuals to participate. This may not be as simple as it first appears. Because psychologists have a relatively high status in society, some people may be reluctant to decline an invitation from them to participate in "scientific research." Investigators therefore may have to bend over backward to assure some individuals that participation is indeed voluntary. They cannot simply assume that every potential participant automatically feels free to decline if approached. After all, who wants to interfere with the progress of science?

When all three principles are closely followed, they allow for what psychologists call **informed consent:** the people or groups being studied understand the nature of the research, believe their rights are being protected, and feel free to either volunteer or refuse to participate. Informed consent therefore forms a standard, or ideal, for research to aim for and one that most studies do in fact approximate.

As the preceding discussion indicates, however, consent that is completely informed may prove difficult to achieve in some cases. This is especially so for research on vulnerable populations, such as children, people with certain disabilities, elderly individuals, or members of cultural groups who do not speak the native language. These people tend to depend on the goodwill and wisdom of others, including researchers themselves, to explain the purposes of a study and keep their best interests in mind. In studying an adult who speaks little English, for example, investigators may well wonder whether he fully understands the purposes of the study, even when those purposes are explained. Even if the person does understand, does he feel truly free to participate or to decline? Or does he, as an individual, simply assume he must cooperate with whatever investigators request?

In studying children in particular, the developmental levels of the participants should influence the way investigators resolve ethical issues (Thompson, 1990). As a rule, children understand the purposes of a research project less well than do adults, making it less crucial that children themselves be thoroughly informed but more important that the parents be informed. Children also are more vulnerable to stressful research procedures, such as experimentation with the effects of personal criticism. Older children and adults, on the other hand, are more prone to self-consciousness and are more likely to detect implied personal criticisms. Thus, investigators need to be more careful in studying problems that might shame a person publicly (such as by asking, "How often do you cry?" or "What problems have you had because your parents are divorced?").

Wherever possible, the right to decide about whether to participate in a research study rests with the individual, provided he or she understands the nature of the study and feels truly free to decline participation. When these conditions hold only partially, as with a child who speaks limited English, parents or other legal guardians share the ultimate right to decide whether the child should participate. When the conditions do not hold at all, such as with infants or adults with little oral language ability, parents and guardians essentially take over the right to decide about participation.

What Do You Think?

Why do you think ethics has become a bigger concern for developmental research in the past two decades? Brainstorm as many ideas about this as you can: have people changed, or research projects, or the conditions of modern life, or . . . ?

STRENGTHS AND LIMITATIONS OF DEVELOPMENTAL KNOWLEDGE

As this chapter has demonstrated, human development has to be studied in particular ways and with certain limitations in mind. Because time is a major dimension of development, its impact must be approached thoughtfully. Yet the very nature of time poses real problems for studying at least some major questions. Sometimes people "take too long" to develop within the time frame available to study them. Also, because developmental psychologists deal with people, they must treat their subjects with respect and abide by the usual standards of decency and consideration for human needs. Finally, because they sometimes deal with especially vulnerable people, developmental psychologists sometimes must take extra care to determine the true best interests of their subjects, even when those subjects do not know what they are being asked to do or do not feel free to refuse even when they do know.

Lest these limitations sound overly discouraging, be assured that in spite of them, developmental psychologists have accumulated considerable knowledge about people of all ages in recent decades and continue to do so. The remaining chapters of this book should make that point amply clear. Developmental psychology does not have definitive answers for some important questions about human nature, but it does have the answers for a good many others.

SUMMARY OF MAJOR IDEAS

The Nature of Developmental Change

1. Development concerns changes in a person's long-term growth, feelings, and patterns of thinking.

2. Development occurs in three major domains: physical, cognitive, and psychosocial.

3. The domains of development interact in many ways, and individuals always develop as whole persons rather than in separate parts.

Why Study Development?

4. Studying development can help give you appropriate expectations about human behavior and its changes throughout life.

5. A knowledge of development can help you respond appropriately to individuals' behavior.

6. A knowledge of development can help you recognize when unusual behaviors are cause for concern.

7. Studying development can give you self-knowledge and understanding of your past.

The History of Developmental Study

8. Until just a few hundred years ago, childhood and adolescence were not regarded as distinct periods of life.

9. Societal changes in the eighteenth century led to awareness of children's unique needs.

10. In the nineteenth and twentieth centuries, the first research studies of children consisted of baby biographies and structured observations of children at specific ages.

Basic Issues in Developmental Study

11. In general, developmental psychology focuses on four major issues: the impact of nature and nurture, the extent of continuity and discontinuity in development, the universality of development, and the problem of deficit and difference in development.

Methods of Studying Developmental Psychology

12. Research about developmental psychology tries to follow scientific methods: formulating research questions, stating them as hypotheses, testing the hypotheses, and interpreting and publicizing the results.

13. Studies vary in the time frame (cross-sectional or longitudinal), in control of the context (naturalistic or experimental), and in sampling strategies used (surveys, interviews, or case studies).

14. Cross-sectional studies compare individuals of different ages at one point in time.

15. Longitudinal studies observe human change directly by following the same individuals over relatively long periods of time.

16. Naturalistic methods observe individuals in natural contexts as much as possible.

17. Experimental methods try to control or hold constant extraneous conditions while varying only one or two specified variables.

18. Surveys, interviews, and case studies each sample different numbers of people, and each has unique advantages and problems.

Ethical Constraints on Studying Development

19. Ethical considerations guide how development can be studied and sometimes rule out certain studies altogether.

20. Generally, developmental studies should be guided by the principles of confidentiality, full disclosure of purposes, and respect for the individual's freedom to participate.

21. Research about children should strive for informed consent from children and their parents or guardians.

22. The specific ethical concerns in studying development depend on the age or developmental level of the individuals studied as well as on the content of the study itself.

KEY TERMS

development *(3)*

domain *(5)*

physical development *(5)*

cognitive development *(5)*

psychosocial development *(5)*

norms *(11)*

nature *(12)*

nurture *(12)*

scientific method *(16)*

hypothesis *(16)*

cross-sectional study *(17)*

longitudinal study *(17)*

cohort *(19)*

sequential study *(20)*

naturalistic study *(21)*

experimental study *(22)*

independent variable *(22)*

dependent variable *(22)*

random sample *(22)*

validity *(23)*

experimental group *(23)*

control group *(23)*

correlation *(24)*

survey *(24)*

interview *(25)*

case study *(25)*

informed consent *(27)*

2

Theories of Development

When Elizabeth, age three, began nursery school, she cried and screamed every day when her mother left her. "Home!" and "Mama!" were the only words she seemed able to produce between sobs, which continued for much of each morning. Her concerned teachers met to discuss what to do about Elizabeth.

"It's best to ignore the crying," said one teacher. "If you give her lots of special attention because of it, you will reinforce the crying, and she'll just keep going longer."

"But we can't just ignore a crying child," said another. "This is a new and strange situation, and her crying shows that she's feeling insecure and abandoned. Look at her! She needs comfort and emotional support so that she can feel safer and more secure. At least give her a hug!"

"I think she's unsure whether her mother really will come back for her," said a third teacher. "Maybe we can find ways to help her understand and remember our daily routine here."

The teachers decided to follow all of this advice. They agreed not to fuss too much over Elizabeth's tears and to give her lots of comfort and support when she was not crying. They also helped Elizabeth draw a picture chart of the daily schedule and tape it to her cubbyhole. Finally, they talked with her mother about what they had observed and the solutions they were trying.

How well did their approaches work? Elizabeth stopped crying—more quickly, in fact, than any of the teachers had expected. Although all three teachers agreed that Elizabeth clearly was happier and more at ease, no one was sure exactly how or why the change had come about.

Focusing Questions

- What are developmental theories? How are they useful?

- How have psychodynamic theories such as Freud's and Erikson's influenced thinking about development?

- How have developmental theories based on learning principles contributed to our understanding of developmental change?

- How does Piaget's theory of cognitive development help us understand changes in our capacity to think and solve problems throughout the lifespan?

- How have contextual approaches to development broadened our view of developmental change?

- How do adult developmental changes differ from child and adolescent changes, and what implications do these differences have for developmental theory?

THE NATURE OF DEVELOPMENTAL THEORIES

Each of Elizabeth's teachers' approaches reflects a different set of ideas and beliefs about children and their development. Whether they know it or not, most people—teachers, parents, grandparents, students, and even children themselves—are guided by "informal theories" of human development. And while the preceding example focuses on early childhood, informal theories of development are used to understand older children, adolescents, and adults as well, as we will see shortly.

What Is a Developmental Theory?

As we point out in Chapter 1, *development* refers to long-term changes that occur during a person's lifetime and the patterns of those changes. Theories are useful because they help us organize and make sense of large amounts of sometimes conflicting information about development. For example, how do we decide whether day care is good for children and, if so, what type of day care is developmentally best? What about day care for elderly adults? For that matter, how do we make developmental sense out of different approaches to parenting, family life, or education at various points in the lifespan? In contrast to informal theories, the more formal developmental theories we will discuss in this chapter attempt to provide clear, logical, and systematic frameworks for describing and understanding the events and experiences that make up developmental change and discovering the principles and mechanisms that underlie the process of change.

What qualities should a good theory ideally have? First, a theory should be *internally consistent,* meaning its different parts fit together in a logical way. Second, a theory should *provide meaningful explanations* of the actual developmental changes we are interested in, be they changes in children's thinking with age or the long-range effects of divorce on their social adjustment. Third, a theory should be *open to scientific evaluation* so that it can be revised or discarded if new or conflicting evidence appears or if a better theory is proposed. Fourth, a theory should *stimulate new thinking and research.* Finally, a theory should *provide guidance* to parents, professionals, and other interested individuals in their day-to-day work with children, adolescents, and adults.

Many motor skills, such as jumping rope or riding a bike, develop in predictable sequences or stages.

How Developmental Theories Differ:
Four Developmental Themes

Developmental theories differ in some important ways. In this chapter, we look at how each theory deals with the following four themes: (1) the *role of maturation* (nature) *versus experience* (nurture), (2) the *role of developmental stages* (continuity versus discontinuity), (3) *breadth of focus,* and (4) the *active versus passive role of the individual* in development.

Role of Maturation versus Experience   Theories differ in the importance they assign to nature and nurture as causes of developmental change. *Maturation* refers to developmental changes that seem to be determined largely by biology because they occur in all individuals relatively independently of their particular experiences. Examples of maturational changes include growth in height and weight and increases in the muscle coordination involved in sitting up, walking, and running. Examples of changes due to *nurture,* or experience, include increasing skill in playing baseball, basketball, or tennis, which clearly seems to be due mostly to formal and informal learning.

But for many developmental changes, the relative contributions of maturation and experience are less clear. Talking is a good example. To what degree do all children learn to talk regardless of their particular learning experiences? How much does their talking depend on their particular experiences in the family, community, and culture in which they grow up? (Hall & Lindzey, 1978; P. Miller, 1993).

The Role of Stages   Developmental theories also differ about whether developmental change is a *continuous* process, consisting of many small, incremental changes, or *discontinuous,* composed of a smaller number of distinct steps or *stages.* Theorists such as Erik Erikson and Jean Piaget assume developmental change occurs in distinct, discontinuous stages. All individuals follow the same sequence, or order. Each successive stage is qualitatively unique from all other stages, is increasingly complex, and integrates the developmental changes and accomplishments of earlier stages.

Erikson's theory, for example, assumes an infant must first master the crisis of *trust versus mistrust;* that is, she must come to trust her caregiver's ability to meet her needs. Only then can she move on to tackle the crisis that defines the next stage, *autonomy versus shame and doubt. Autonomy* refers to a person's capacity to be independent and self-directed in his or her activities. Similarly, mastery of the crisis of *intimacy versus isolation* during early adulthood prepares an individual for the crisis of *generativity versus stagnation* that occurs during middle adulthood. These and other stages of development proposed by Erikson are discussed later in the chapter.

Learning theories, on the other hand, see development as a relatively smooth and continuous process. The development of trust and autonomy or of more sophisticated thinking and problem-solving skills is thought to occur through the numerous small changes that unfold as a child interacts with his environment.

Still other theories, such as the cognitive approach of Robbie Case, take a more balanced view. They see developmental change as a sequence of more rounded, overlapping slopes rather than as one continuous incline or a series of sharply defined stages. Figure 2.1 illustrates these three views of the shape of developmental change.

Breadth of Focus   Developmental theories also differ in how broadly (or narrowly) they define the range of factors, circumstances, and contexts that may influence development, in how many areas of developmental change they seek to explain, and in the number of specific developmental processes and mechanisms they propose. For example, Uri Bronfenbrenner's *ecological systems theory* emphasizes the broad range of situations and contexts in which development occurs. These include the individual's direct and indirect experiences with family, school, work, and culture, all of which act together to create developmental change. However, these theories say little about the specific processes or mechanisms involved. On the other hand, *social learning theories* explain just a few specific issues, such as the development of gender roles and aggression, but describe several mechanisms—in this case, types of learning—that are involved.

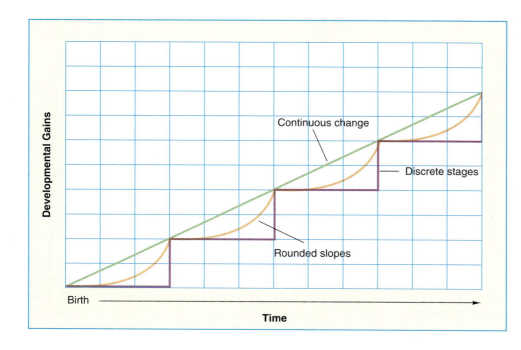

FIGURE 2.1
The Shape of Developmental Change
Developmental change may be viewed as a relatively continuous process consisting of many small changes or as a smaller number of distinct, step-like stages, or as a series of stages, each of which develops in a more gradual and continuous manner.

The Active Versus Passive Role of the Individual   Developmental theories also differ in their view of how actively individuals contribute to their own development. For instance, behavioral learning theorists believe developmental change is caused by events in the environment that stimulate individuals to respond, resulting in the learned changes in behavior that make up development. Theorists who are interested in how thinking and problem-solving abilities develop, such as Jean Piaget, propose that such changes depend on the person's active efforts to master new intellectual problems of increasing difficulty. Likewise, Erik Erikson's theory of identity development proposes that an individual's personality and sense of identity are strongly influenced by his or her active efforts to master the psychological and social conflicts of everyday life.

Table 2.8 on page 57 summarizes how developmental theories differ on the four developmental themes.

What Do You Think?

One of the four developmental themes concerns whether developmental change occurs in stages or is a continuous process. How might different answers to this question affect how parents raise their children? How might they affect how teachers educate their students?

PSYCHODYNAMIC DEVELOPMENTAL THEORIES

Psychodynamic theorists believe development is an active, dynamic process that is influenced by both a person's inborn, biological drives and his or her conscious and unconscious social and emotional experiences. According to Sigmund Freud, a child's development is thought to occur in a series of stages. At each stage, the child experiences unconscious conflicts that he must resolve to some degree before going on to the next stage. Other influential psychodynamic approaches, such as those of Erik Erikson and object relations theorists, place less emphasis on biological drives and unconscious conflict. These theorists focus more on the development of a sense of identity as a result of important social, emotional, and cultural experiences.

Sigmund Freud and his daughter Anna, who became a psychoanalyst herself and whose work with young children has been influential.

Freudian Theory

Sigmund Freud (1856–1939) was the originator of *psychoanalysis,* the approach to understanding and treating psychological problems on which psychodynamic theory is based. Much of Freud's formal theory is outdated. However, his ideas continue to influence our understanding of personality development, including such areas as early infant-caregiver attachment, diagnosis and treatment of childhood emotional disorders, adolescent identity formation, and the long-range consequences of divorce.

The Three-Part Structure of Personality   Freud described each individual's personality as consisting of three hypothetical mental structures: the id, the ego, and the superego.

The **id,** which is present at birth, is unconscious. It impulsively tries to satisfy a person's inborn biological needs and desires by motivating behaviors that maximize pleasure and avoid discomfort with no regard for the realities involved. In this view, the newborn infant is all id, crying for food and comfort but having no idea of how to get them because she cannot distinguish between wishful fantasy and reality.

The **ego** is the largely rational, conscious, problem-solving part of the personality. It is closely related to a person's sense of self. The ego functions according to the *reality principle,* a process by which the infant learns to delay his desire for instant satisfaction and redirect it into more realistic and appropriate ways to meet his needs. This involves a shift of psychological energy from fantasy to the real parents and other caregivers who can in fact meet the infant's needs. Thus, a hungry infant shifts from imagining that the wish for food will satisfy her hunger to a more realistic focus on anticipating the appearance of her parent or other caregiver, who will feed her. An infant's developing ego, or sense of self, is based on her internalized mental images of her relationships with these caregivers.

The **superego** is the moral and ethical component of the personality. It develops at the end of early childhood. The superego includes the child's emerging sense of *conscience,* or right and wrong, as well as the *ego-ideal,* an idealized sense of how he should behave. The superego acts as an internalized, all-knowing parent. It punishes the person for unacceptable sexual or aggressive thoughts, feelings, and actions with guilt and rewards him for fulfillment of parental standards with heightened self-esteem. The superego can sometimes be overly moralistic and unreasonable, but it provides the individual with standards by which to regulate his moral conduct and take pride in his accomplishments.

Stages of Psychosexual Development   Freud believed development occurs through a series of *psychosexual* stages. Each stage focuses on a different area of the body that is a source of excitation and pleasure. At each stage, developmental changes result from conflicts among the id, ego, and superego. These conflicts can threaten the person's ego, or sense of self. Pressures from the id push the person to act impulsively to achieve immediate pleasure; pressures from the ego encourage her to act more realistically by delaying satisfaction until it can be attained; and pressures from the superego push her to meet standards of moral behavior and achievement that may be overly strict or unrealistically high. Freud's psychosexual stages and the developmental processes that occur are summarized in Table 2.1.

The ego uses defense mechanisms to protect itself from such conflicts. *Defense mechanisms* are unconscious distortions of reality that keep conflicts from the ego's (self's) conscious awareness. One such defense mechanism is *repression,* in which unacceptable feelings and impulses are forced from memory and forgotten. Another is *projection,* in which a person's conflict-producing feelings, such as feelings of aggression, are mistakenly attributed to another person.

TABLE 2.1   *Freud's Psychosexual Stages and Developmental Processes*

Psychosexual Stage	Approximate Age	Description
Oral	Birth–1 year	The mouth is the focus of stimulation and interaction; feeding and weaning are central.
Anal	1–3 years	The anus is the focus of stimulation and interaction; elimination and toilet training are central.
Phallic	3–6 years	The genitals (penis, clitoris, and vagina) are the focus of stimulation; gender role and moral development are central.
Latency	6–12 years	A period of suspended sexual activity; energies shift to physical and intellectual activities.
Genital	12–adulthood	The genitals are the focus of stimulation with the onset of puberty; mature sexual relationships develop.

Developmental Processes

Development occurs through a series of psychosexual stages. In each stage the child focuses on a different area of her body, and how she invests her libido (sexual energy) in relationships with people and things reflects the concerns of the stage she is in. New areas of unconscious conflict among the id, ego, and superego, the three structures of personality, also occur. Conflicting pressures from the id to impulsively achieve pleasure, from the ego to act realistically by delaying gratification, and from the superego to fulfill moralistic obligations and to achieve idealistic standards all threaten the ego. The ego protects itself by means of unconscious defense mechanisms, which keep these conflicts from awareness by distorting reality.

Perspectives

Erik Erikson's Identity Crisis: An Autobiographical Perspective

How do theorists' own life experiences influence their theories of development? Here is what Erik Erikson has written about his own identity crises and how they influenced his developmental theory.

Erik Erikson was born in 1902 and died in 1994. He grew up in southern Germany with his mother, who was Danish, and her husband, a German pediatrician. Erikson recalls that "all through my earlier childhood, they kept secret from me the fact that my mother had been married previously; and that I was the son of a Dane who had abandoned her before my birth" (E. Erikson, 1975, p. 27).

As Erikson entered puberty and adolescence, identity conflicts intensified. "My stepfather was the only professional man in an intensely Jewish small bourgeois family, while I . . . was blond and blue-eyed, and grew flagrantly tall. Before long, then, I was referred to as a 'goy' [outsider] in my stepfather's temple, while to my schoolmates I was a 'Jew.' . . . Although during World War I, I tried desperately to be a good German chauvinist, [I] soon became a 'Dane' when Denmark remained neutral" (pp. 27, 28).

During this period, Erikson decided he would be an artist and a writer, rejecting his family's more middle-class values and expectations. He spent most of his time traveling, painting, writing, occasionally taking art classes, and teaching art. In looking back at these years,

Erikson said that he now considered them to be an important part of his training (pp. 25, 26).

In fact, it was not until Erikson was almost thirty and moved to Austria that his career as a psychoanalyst and developmental theorist really began. His training in psychoanalysis was conducted by Anna Freud, who accepted him as a student after observing his work with children as a teacher in a small private school. After studying and practicing psychoanalysis in Vienna, Erikson was forced to leave Austria by the rise of Hitler. He emigrated to the United States, where he lived and worked the rest of his life.

Erikson achieved his outstanding accomplishments as a teacher, scholar, and therapist without the benefit of even a college degree, much less any other professional credentials. In the 1930s, Erikson worked as a psychoanalyst with children and debated whether to return to school for a professional degree. Instead, he accepted a research appointment at Yale Medical School and the Yale Institute of Human Relations, where he worked with an interdisciplinary team of psychologists, psychiatrists, and anthropologists and conducted field studies of the Sioux Indians in South Dakota.

In the 1940s, Erikson moved to California to study the life histories of children living in Berkeley and then the lives of the Yurok Indians. He joined the faculty of the University of California at Berkeley in the early 1950s,

For these school-aged youngsters, learning new skills is part of mastering Erikson's developmental crisis of industry versus inferiority, while for their 90-year-old teacher, sharing her lifelong musical skills is one way of mastering the crisis of ego integrity versus despair.

but was soon fired because he refused to sign a "loyalty oath," part of the fanatical anticommunist crusade of Senator Joe McCarthy. Erikson was reinstated as politically dependable, but resigned in support of others who were not rehired. Erikson says of this experience, "As I think back on that controversy now, it was a test of our American identity; for when the papers told us foreign-born among the nonsigners to 'go back where we came from,' we suddenly felt quite certain that our apparent disloyalty to the soldiers in Korea was, in fact, quite in line with what they were said to be fighting for. The United States Supreme Court has since confirmed our point of view" (pp. 42–43).

Erikson continues, "It would seem almost self-evident now how the concepts of 'identity' and 'identity crisis' emerged from my personal, clinical, and anthropological observations in the thirties and forties. I do not remember when I started to use these terms; they seemed naturally grounded in the experience of emigration, immigration, and Americanization. . . . I will not describe the pathological side of my identity confusion, which included disturbances for which psychoanalysis seemed, indeed, the treatment of choice. . . . No doubt, my best friends will insist that I needed to name this crisis and to see it in everybody else in order to really come to terms with it in myself" (pp. 26, 43).

Using Freud's theory as a starting point, Erik Erikson expanded it to cover the lifespan and modified the stages to place more emphasis on social encounters.

According to Freud, unresolved id-ego and superego-ego conflicts can lead to a *fixation,* or a blockage in development. Fixation can also result from parenting that is not appropriately responsive to a child's needs. For example, overindulgence during the oral stage (see Table 2.1) may result in excessive dependence on others later in life. On the other hand, infants who experience severe deprivation and frustration of their needs may later feel they have to exploit or manipulate others to meet their needs. In this view, an individual's personality traits reflect the patterns typical of the stage at which a fixation occurred.

Erikson's Psychosocial Theory

Erik Erikson (1902–1994) grew up in Europe. He studied psychoanalysis with Freud's daughter, Anna, who strongly influenced his ideas about personality development. The accompanying Perspectives box describes the relationship between Erikson's life and his theory.

In Erikson's view, personality development is a *psychosocial* process, meaning internal psychological factors and external social factors are both very important. Developmental changes occur throughout a person's lifetime and are influenced by three interrelated forces: (1) the individual's biological and physical strengths and limitations; (2) the person's unique life circumstances and developmental history, including early family experiences and degree of success in resolving earlier developmental crises; and (3) the particular social, cultural, and historical forces at work during the individual's lifetime (for example, racial prejudice, poverty, rapid technological change, or war).

Psychosocial Stages of Development   Erikson proposed that development occurs in a series of eight stages, beginning with infancy and ending with old age. Each stage is named for the particular *psychosocial crisis,* or challenge, that every individual must resolve to be able to move on to the next stage. Successful mastery of the psychosocial crisis at a particular stage results in a personality strength, or *virtue,* that will help the individual meet future developmental challenges (Erikson, 1982; Miller, 1993). Table 2.2 summarizes Erikson's stages and developmental processes.

Stage 1: trust versus mistrust.   The earliest basic trust is indicated by the infant's capacity to sleep, eat, and excrete in a comfortable and relaxed way. Parents who reliably ensure daily routines and are responsive to their infant's needs provide the basis for a trusting view of the world. The proper ratio, or balance, between trust and mistrust leads to the development of hope. *Hope* is the enduring belief that one's wishes are attainable despite the many irrational impulses an infant experiences at birth. Failure to develop such trust may seriously interfere with a child's sense of security and compromise her ability to successfully master the challenges of the stages that follow.

Stage 2: autonomy versus shame and doubt.   This stage occurs during the toddler and preschool years. *Autonomy* refers to a child's capacity to be independent and self-directed in his activities and ability to balance his own demands for self-control with demands for control from his parents and others (Hall & Lindzey, 1978). *Shame* involves a loss of self-respect due to a failure to meet one's own standards (M. Lewis, 1992). During toilet training, for example, a child who is treated with firmness, reassurance, and respect for her failures as well as for her successes eventually will achieve autonomy (independence and self-direction) in this area. A child who is consistently shamed may have difficulty developing confidence in his ability to express himself freely and to self-regulate his thoughts, feelings, and behaviors. A successful outcome for this stage is the virtue of *will,* the capacity to freely make choices based on realistic knowledge of what is expected and what is possible.

TABLE 2.2   *Erikson's Psychosocial Stages and Developmental Processes*

Psychosocial Stage	Approximate Age	Description
Trust versus mistrust	Birth–1 year	Focus on oral-sensory activity; development of trusting relationships with caregivers and of self-trust (hope)
Autonomy versus shame and doubt	1–3 years	Focus on muscular-anal activity; development of control over bodily functions and activities (will)
Initiative versus guilt	3–6 years	Focus on locomotor-genital activity; testing limits of self-assertion and purposefulness (purpose)
Industry versus inferiority	6–12 years (latency period)	Focus on mastery, competence, and productivity (competence)
Identity versus role confusion	12–19 years (adolescence)	Focus on formation of identity and coherent self-concept (fidelity)
Intimacy versus isolation	19–25 years (early adulthood)	Focus on achievement of an intimate relationship and career direction (love)
Generativity versus stagnation	25–50 years (adulthood)	Focus on fulfillment through creative, productive activity that contributes to future generations (care)
Ego integrity versus despair	50 and older	Focus on belief in integrity of life, including successes and failures (wisdom)

Developmental Processes

Development of the ego, or sense of identity, occurs through a series of stages, each building on the preceding stages and focused on successfully resolving a new psychosocial crisis between two opposing ego qualities. No stage is fully resolved, and more favorable resolution at an earlier stage facilitates achievement of later stages.

Stage 3: initiative versus guilt. During this stage, which occurs during the preschool years, the child focuses on her genitals as a source of pleasure and on achieving greater mastery and responsibility. *Initiative* combines autonomy with the ability to explore new activities and ideas and to purposefully pursue and achieve tasks and goals. *Guilt* involves self-criticism due to failure to fulfill parental expectations. This crisis often involves situations in which the child takes on more than he can physically or emotionally handle, including the powerful sexual and aggressive feelings children often act out in their play.

If a child's conflicting feelings of love and hate and conflicting impulses to be independent and dependent are ignored, belittled, or ridiculed, destructive feelings of guilt can result. If a child is treated respectfully and helped to formulate and pursue her goals without feeling guilty, she will develop the virtue of *purpose* in her life.

Stage 4: industry versus inferiority. As a child leaves the protection of his family and enters the world of school, he must come to believe in his ability to learn the basic intellectual and social skills required to be a full and productive member of society and to start and complete tasks successfully. The virtue of *competence* is the result. A failure to feel competent can lead to a sense of inferiority. The child who consistently fails in school is in danger of feeling alienated from society or of thoughtlessly conforming to gain acceptance from others.

Stage 5: identity versus role confusion. This stage coincides with the physical changes of *puberty* and the psychosocial changes of adolescence. *Identity* involves a reliable, integrated sense of who one is based on the many different roles one plays. *Role confusion* refers to a failure to achieve this integration of roles. During this stage, teenagers undergo reevaluation of who they are in many areas of identity development, including the physical, sexual, intellectual, religious, and career areas. Frequently conflicts from earlier stages resurface. A successful resolution of this crisis is the development of the virtue of *fidelity*, the ability to sustain loyalties to certain values despite inevitable conflicts and inconsistencies. Failure to resolve this crisis may lead to a premature choice of identity, a prolonged identity and role confusion, or choosing a permanently "negative" identity that may be associated with delinquent and antisocial behavior. We take a closer look at identity development during adolescence in Chapter 11.

Erikson's final three stages focus on development during adulthood, a topic we discuss more fully at the end of the chapter.

Stage 6: intimacy versus isolation. Successful resolution of this stage results in the virtue of being able to experience *love*. The young adult, as we will see in Chapter 13, must develop the ability to establish close, committed relationships with others and cope with the fear of losing her own identity and separate sense of self that such intense intimacy raises.

Stage 7: generativity versus stagnation. This stage occurs during middle adulthood. Successful resolution brings the virtue of *care*, or concern for others. *Generativity* is the feeling that one's work, family life, and other activities are both personally satisfying and socially meaningful in ways that contribute to future generations. *Stagnation* results when life no longer seems purposeful. We look more closely at this crisis in Chapter 15.

Stage 8: ego integrity versus despair. This stage occurs during late adulthood, as we will see in Chapter 17. Successful resolution brings the virtue of *wisdom*. *Ego integrity* refers to the ability to look back on the strengths and weaknesses of one's life with a sense of dignity, optimism, and wisdom. It is in conflict with the despair resulting from health problems, economic difficulties, social isolation, and lack of meaningful work experienced by many elderly persons in our society.

According to Erikson, psychosocial conflicts are never fully resolved. Depending on his or her life experiences, each individual achieves a more or less favorable ratio of trust to mistrust, industry to inferiority, ego integrity to despair, and so on. Therefore, conflicts from earlier stages may continue to affect later development.

Other Psychodynamic Approaches

A number of psychodynamic theorists have sought to extend Freud's basic insights about the importance of a child's object relations. **Object relations** refer to the child's relationships with the important people (called *objects*) in his environment and the process by which their qualities become part of his personality and mental life. Object relations theorists such as Margaret Mahler, Heinz Kohut, and, more recently, Daniel Stern, have studied how personality development in children and adults is influenced by the mental representations they construct based on their experiences and attachment relationships with the significant people in their lives (Barlow & Durand, 1995; Eagle, 1984; Hamilton, 1989). (See Chapter 5 for a discussion of attachment.)

Margaret Mahler, for example, proposes that during the first three years of life, children go through four phases in developing a psychological sense of self. A newborn infant begins life in an *autistic phase,* meaning she is self-absorbed and has little psychological awareness of the world around her. Next, during the *symbiotic phase,* the infant experiences herself as being completely connected with and dependent on her primary caregiver rather than as a psychologically separate person. During the *separation-individuation phase,* she begins to develop a separate sense of self. Finally, during the *object constancy phase,* the infant achieves a more stable sense of self based on her increasing ability to form reliable mental representations of her primary caregivers (called *objects)* and their responses to her (Mahler et al., 1975). Table 2.3 summarizes Mahler's phases of development.

A second theorist, Heinz Kohut, suggests that a newborn infant's sense of self is at first fragmented and incomplete. Through a process called *empathic mirroring,* a caregiver responds to the infant in ways that accurately and sensitively reflect, or *mirror,* her awareness and appreciation of her baby's feelings, needs, and experiences. This empathic mirroring allows an infant to form a progressively more complete and well-organized set of mental representations of himself and his caregivers. From these mental portraits, the infant eventually constructs a reliable and independent sense of self (Eagle, 1984).

Daniel Stern offers an alternative description of the development of the psychological self based on detailed empirical studies of infant-parent interactions both in the laboratory and in naturalistic settings. According to Stern, from birth on, young infants display the capacity to coherently organize their experiences and to actively participate in their interpersonal world to a significantly greater degree than either Mahler or Kohut propose. Stern suggests that a *core self,* based on an infant's awareness of being physically separate from others, emerges between ages two and six months. A *subjective self,* based on an organized mental representation of relationships with others, appears between seven and nine months. Finally, a sense of *verbal self* emerges between fifteen and eighteen months with the development of language and symbolic thought (Cushman, 1991; Stern, 1985a, 1995). Table 2.4 summarizes Stern's stages of development.

TABLE 2.3   *Mahler's Phases of Development*

Phase	Approximate Age	Description
Autistic phase	Birth–2 months	Safe, sleeplike transition into the world
Symbiotic phase	2–6 months	Development of an emotionally charged mental image of the primary caregiver
Separation-individuation phase	6–24 months	Functions as a separate individual
Hatching subphase	6–10 months	Responds differently to primary caregivers versus others
Practicing subphase	10–16 months	Safe separation and disengagement
Rapprochement subphase	16–24 months	Experiments more fully with leaving and returning to the safe home base of the caregiver
Object constancy phase	24–36 + months	Maintains stable and reliable mental images of the primary caregivers

TABLE 2.4 *Stern's Stages of Development*

Stage	Approximate Age	Description
Emergent self	0–2 months	Active seeking of stimulation; more mature regulation of sleeping, eating, responsiveness, and emotional state
Core self	2–6 months	Development of sense of integrated self based on mental representations of past interactions that have been generalized (RIGs)
Subjective self	6–12 months	Organized perspective about relationships with others
Sense of verbal self	12 months +	Development of language and symbolic thinking skills

What Do You Think?

Erikson proposed that cultural and social forces play a major role in developmental change. With this in mind, how might growing up as a male versus a female of your own racial and ethnic background influence how an adolescent deals with the crisis of identity versus role confusion? Compare your conclusions with those of several classmates.

BEHAVIORAL LEARNING AND SOCIAL COGNITIVE LEARNING DEVELOPMENTAL THEORIES

Learning is generally defined as relatively permanent changes in the capacity to perform certain behaviors that result from experience. According to the learning theories, the learning experiences that occur over a person's lifetime are the source of developmental change. Thus, changes in existing learning opportunities or the creation of new ones can modify the course of an individual's development.

Behavioral Learning Theories

Pavlov: Classical Conditioning   Ivan Pavlov (1849–1936) was a Russian scientist who first developed his behavioral theory while studying digestion in dogs. In his well-known experiments, Pavlov rang a bell just before feeding a dog. Eventually the dog salivated whenever it heard the bell, even if it received no food. Pavlov called this process **classical conditioning**. He named the salivation itself the *conditioned response,* the food stimulus the *unconditioned stimulus,* and the dog's salivatory response the *unconditioned response*. The last was so named because the connection between the food stimulus and the dog's response was an inborn, *unconditioned reflex,* that is, an involuntary reaction similar to the eyeblink and knee-jerk reflexes.

Through the processes involved in classical conditioning, reflexes that are present at birth may help infants to learn about and participate in the world around them. For example, conditioning of the sucking reflex, which allows newborn infants to suck reflexively in response to a touch on the lips, has been reported using a tone as the conditioned stimulus (Lipsitt & Kaye, 1964). Other stimuli, such as the sight of the bottle and the mother's face, smile, and voice, may also become conditioned stimuli for sucking and may elicit sucking responses even before the bottle touches the baby's lips. Although even newborns' behavior may be classically conditioned, it cannot be reliably observed over a wide range of reflexes until about six months of age (Lipsitt, 1990). Figure 2.2 illustrates the process of classical conditioning.

B.F. Skinner developed one of the most well-known forms of behaviorism—operant conditioning. Its success may stem from its many practical applications to child and adolescent development.

Skinner: Operant Conditioning   B. F. Skinner (1904–1991) is best known for his learning theory, which is also known as **operant conditioning**. This theory is based on a simple concept called **reinforcement,** the process by which the likelihood that a particular response will occur again increases when that response is followed by a certain stimulus. *Positive reinforcement* occurs when, following a particular response (a baby saying "da-da"), a rewarding stimulus (his father smiling and saying "good boy!") is given that strengthens the response and increases the likelihood that it will recur under similar circumstances. *Negative reinforcement* also strengthens a response and increases the chance of its recurrence, but does so by removing an undesirable or unpleasant stimulus following the occurrence of that response. Consider Sarah, a four-year-old who has been crying and misbehaving at the dinner table. By quieting down once she gets her parents' attention, she may actually be negatively reinforcing (increasing) her parents' attention-giving responses by removing the unpleasant stimulus of crying and misbehaving.

FIGURE 2.2
Illustration of Classical Conditioning
In this example, the nipple in the baby's mouth is an unconditioned stimulus (US), which with no prior conditioning brings about, or elicits, the sucking reflex, an unconditioned response (UR). (A) The nipple in the mouth elicits a sucking reflex; (B) the sight of a bottle is a neutral stimulus (NS) and has no effect; (C) once the sight of the bottle (neutral stimulus) is repeatedly paired with the nipple in the mouth (UCS), the sight of the bottle becomes a conditioned (learned) stimulus (CS), which now elicits sucking, the conditioned response (CR).

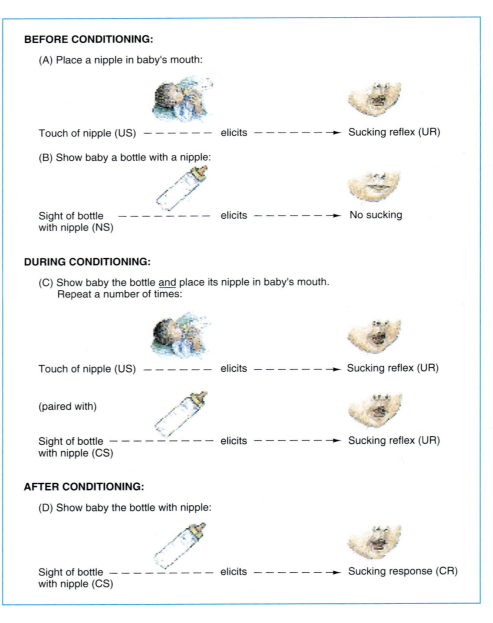

BEFORE CONDITIONING:

(A) Place a nipple in baby's mouth:

Touch of nipple (US) — — — — — elicits — — — — — → Sucking reflex (UR)

(B) Show baby a bottle with a nipple:

Sight of bottle — — — — — — elicits — — — — — → No sucking
with nipple (NS)

DURING CONDITIONING:

(C) Show baby the bottle and place its nipple in baby's mouth. Repeat a number of times:

Touch of nipple (US) — — — — — elicits — — — — — → Sucking reflex (UR)

(paired with)

Sight of bottle — — — — — — elicits — — — — — → Sucking reflex (UR)
with nipple (CS)

AFTER CONDITIONING:

(D) Show baby the bottle with nipple:

Sight of bottle — — — — — — elicits — — — — — → Sucking response (CR)
with nipple (CS)

Punishment weakens or suppresses a behavioral response by either adding an unpleasant stimulus or removing a pleasurable one following the response's occurrence. Taking away television privileges or adding an extra chore following a child's misbehavior are both forms of punishment. *Extinction* refers to the disappearance of a response when a reinforcer that was maintaining it is removed. Frequently the best way to extinguish an undesirable response is to ignore it and reinforce an alternative, more desirable response.

Shaping occurs when a child learns to perform new responses not already in his repertoire, or "collection." This is achieved by starting with an existing response and then modifying, or shaping, it by reinforcing small changes that bring it closer and closer to the desired behavior. Consider a dad who wishes to teach his seven-year-old daughter to hit a ball with a bat. Since she already can swing a bat, careful encouragement (a good reinforcer) for better and better swings and eventually for actually making contact with the ball (which is itself a good reinforcer) will transform, or shape, his daughter's bat-swinging behavior into ball-hitting behavior, a far more enjoyable and useful one.

Social Cognitive Learning Theory

Albert Bandura believes that developmental change occurs largely through **observational learning,** or learning by observing others. Learning is *reciprocally determined,* meaning it results from interactions between the child (including behaviors, cognitive processes, and physical capacities) and his physical and social environment.

Observational learning takes two forms: imitation and modeling. In *imitation,* a child is directly reinforced for repeating or copying the actions of others. In *modeling,* the child learns the behaviors and personality traits of a parent or other model through vicarious (indirect) reinforcement. A child learns to behave in ways similar to those of a parent or other model by merely observing the model receiving reinforcement for his or her actions. How influential the model will be depends on a variety of factors, including the model's relationship to the child, his or her personal characteristics, and how the child perceives them (Bandura, 1989; Miller, 1993).

It is likely that observational learning plays an important role as these girls learn to prepare bread dough.

According to Piaget, children think in qualitatively different ways as they develop. Very young children usually think about objects and experiences by looking and touching. Many adolescents, on the other hand, can plan and reason abstractly, as illustrated in the two photos.

Children's levels of cognitive development strongly influence their ability to observe, remember, and later perform in ways similar to the models they have watched.

The social cognitive learning approach has been useful in explaining gender development, the development of aggression, and the developmental impact of television and other media. It has also been useful to counselors and therapists who work with problems in the parent-child relationship and with children experiencing a variety of behavioral and adjustment difficulties in both outpatient and residential treatment settings. Refer to Table 2.8 on page 57 for a summary of how these theories deal with the four developmental themes.

What Do You Think?

Think of some examples of developmental changes in a young child's behavior that might be accurately explained using behavioral learning theories. Then think of an example of a developmental change that doesn't seem to fit the behavioral model.

COGNITIVE DEVELOPMENTAL THEORIES

In this section, we discuss three theoretical approaches to cognitive development: Piaget's cognitive theory, neo-Piagetian theories, and information-processing theory. All of these theories share a strong focus on how thinking and problem-solving skills develop and how such cognitive activities contribute to the overall process of development.

Piaget's Cognitive Theory

Jean Piaget (1896–1980) was one of the most influential figures in developmental psychology. Just as Freud's ideas radically changed thinking about human emotional development, Piaget's ideas have changed our understanding of the development of human thinking and problem solving, or *cognition*.

Key Principles of Piaget's Theory   Piaget believed that thinking develops in a series of increasingly complex stages, or periods, each of which incorporates and revises those that precede it. Table 2.5 summarizes Piaget's cognitive stages and developmental processes. We look at his theory in greater detail in the chapters on cognitive development.

TABLE 2.5 *Piaget's Cognitive Stages and Developmental Processes*

Cognitive Stage	Approximate Age	Description
Sensorimotor	Birth–2 years	Coordination of sensory and motor activity; achievement of object permanence
Preoperational	2–7 years	Use of language and symbolic representation; egocentric view of the world
Concrete operational	7–11 years	Solution of concrete problems through logical operations
Formal operational	11–adulthood	Systematic solution of actual and hypothetical problems using abstract symbols

Developmental Processes

The earliest and most primitive patterns, or schemes, of thinking, problem solving, and constructing reality are inborn. As a result of both maturation and experience, thinking develops through a series of increasingly sophisticated stages, each incorporating the achievements in preceding stages. These changes occur through the processes of assimilation, in which new problems are solved using existing schemes; accommodation, in which existing schemes are altered or adapted to meet new challenges. Together, these processes create a state of cognitive balance or *equilibrium,* in which the person's thinking becomes increasingly stable, general, and harmoniously adjusted to the environment.

What exactly makes a person develop from one stage of thinking and problem solving to the next? Piaget believed three processes are involved: (1) direct learning, (2) social transmission, and (3) maturation.

Direct learning results when a person actively responds to and interprets new problems and experiences based on patterns of thought and action he already knows. Piaget called these existing patterns *schemes*. A **scheme** is a systematic pattern of thoughts, actions, and problem-solving strategies that helps the individual deal with a particular intellectual challenge or situation.

According to Piaget, an infant's first understanding of the world is based on a limited number of *innate schemes* made up of simple patterns of unlearned reflexes that are inherited at birth, such as sucking, grasping, and looking. These schemes rapidly change as the infant encounters new experiences through the complementary processes of *assimilation* and *accommodation.*

Assimilation is the process by which an infant interprets and responds to a new experience or situation in terms of an existing scheme. For example, a two-month-old baby who is presented with a bottle for the first time understands what is needed to suck from the bottle based on her existing sucking scheme for her mother's breast. The infant has assimilated a new situation, sucking from a bottle, into her existing scheme for sucking. As children grow older, schemes involve increasingly complex mental processes. For example, a preschooler sees a truck but calls it a "car" because the concept of *car* is already well established in his thinking.

In **accommodation,** a child changes existing schemes, or ways of thinking, when faced with new ideas or situations in which the old schemes no longer work. Instead of calling a truck by the wrong name, the preschooler searches for a new name and begins to realize that some four-wheeled objects are not cars.

According to Piaget, development results from the interplay of assimilation and accommodation, a process called *adaptation*. **Adaptation** results when schemes are deepened or broadened by assimilation and stretched or modified by accommodation.

Social transmission, Piaget's second explanation for development, is the process through which one's thinking is influenced by learning from social contact with and observation of others rather than through direct experience. *Physical maturation,* Piaget's third explanation for developmental change, refers to the biologically determined changes in physical and neurological development that occur relatively independently of specific experiences. For example, a child must reach a certain minimal level of biological development to be able to name an object.

While research at least partially supports many of Piaget's ideas, it has found a number of shortcomings. One problem is how to explain why, in many instances, children master tasks that are logically equivalent at very different points in their development. It is also hard to explain why a child's cognitive performances on two logically similar tasks are often very different. A third problem is that Piaget's exclusive emphasis on the predetermined "logical" aspects of children's thinking often does not match the actual thought processes children appear to use and largely ignores the social, emotional, and cultural factors that influence the process (Case, 1992; Rogoff & Chavajay, 1995). Finally, Piaget's theory fails to recognize that cognitive development continues after adolescence, as we will see in Chapter 13. Some of these issues are discussed in the Multicultural View box on page 50.

Neo-Piagetian Approaches

Neo-Piagetian theories are new or revised models of Piaget's basic approach. Robbie Case, for example, proposes that cognitive development results from increases in the child's *mental space,* that is, the maximum number of schemes the child can apply simultaneously at any given time. During early childhood most cognitive structures are rather specific and concrete, such as drawing with a pencil, throwing a ball, or counting a set of objects. As the structures guiding these actions become coordinated with one another, they form new, more efficient, higher-level cognitive structures, which in turn begin to be coordinated with other, similar structures. Thus, a child's ability to use increasingly general cognitive structures enables him to think more abstractly. Different forms of the same logical problem may require different processing skills and capacities. As a result, a child's performance on two logically similar tasks may differ significantly, and mastery of each task may occur at very different points in her development (Case, 1991b, 1991c, 1991d).

Kurt Fischer, another neo-Piagetian theorist, accepts Piaget's basic idea of stages, but uses specific *skills* instead of *schemes* to describe the cognitive structures children use in particular problem-solving tasks or sets of tasks. The breadth of a skill is determined by both the level of maturation a child's central nervous system has reached and the range of specific learning environments to which the child has been exposed (Fischer, 1980; Fischer & Pipp, 1984a, 1984b). Thus, the type of support a child receives from parents, teachers, and others in the environment plays an important role in skill acquisition. Case's "breadth of skill" idea has much in common with Lev Vygotsky's "zone of proximal development," discussed later in this chapter.

The chess-playing abilities of these youngsters are closely tied to increases in their knowledge of chess and to their awareness and understanding of their own thought processes and problem-solving strategies.

Information-Processing Theory

Another alternative to Piaget's cognitive theory is **information-processing theory,** which focuses on the precise, detailed features or steps involved in mental activities (Klahr, 1989; Seifert, 1993). Like a computer, the mind is viewed as having distinct parts that make unique contributions to thinking in a specific order.

Key Principles of Information-Processing Theory   Figure 2.3 shows one information-processing model of human thinking. According to this model, when a person tries to solve a problem, she first takes in information from her environment through her senses. The information gained in this way is held briefly in the *sensory register,* the first memory store. The sensory register records information exactly as it originally receives it, but the information fades or disappears within a fraction of a second unless the person processes it further.

Information to which a person pays special attention is transferred to *short-term memory (STM),* the second memory store. The short-term memory corresponds roughly to "momentary awareness," or whatever the person is thinking about at a particular instant. The short-term memory can hold only limited amounts of information—in fact, only about seven pieces of it at any one time. After about twenty seconds, information in short-term memory is either forgotten or processed further. At this point, it moves into *long-term memory (LTM),* the third memory store.

Information can be saved permanently in long-term memory. But doing so requires various cognitive strategies, such as rehearsing information repeatedly or organizing it into familiar categories. Unlike short-term memory, long-term memory probably has unlimited capacity for storage of new information. The problem comes in retrieving information, which requires that we remember how it was stored in the first place.

Developmental Changes in Information Processing   As children grow older, they experience several cognitive changes that allow them to process information more efficiently and comprehensively. The most important developmental change in information processing is the acquisition of control processes. *Control processes* direct an individual's attention toward particular input from the sensory register and guide the response to new information once it enters short-term memory. Usually control processes organize information in short-term memory. Sometimes control processes also relate information in STM to previously learned knowledge from

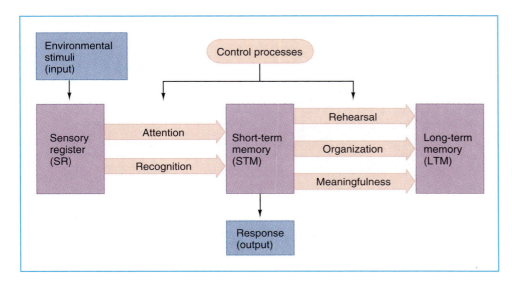

FIGURE 2.3
An Information-Processing Model of Learning
Information from the environment first enters the sensory register. With the aid of control processes, it is then transferred to short-term memory where it is either forgotten or processed further, and then to long-term memory where it is stored for future use.

LTM, such as when a teenager hears a song on the radio and notes its similarity to another song heard previously.

As children grow older they develop **metacognition,** an awareness and understanding of how thinking and learning work. Metacognition assists learning in a number of ways. First, it allows a person to assess how difficult a problem or learning task will be and to plan appropriate ways to approach it. More specifically, metacognition involves knowledge of self, knowledge of task variables, and knowledge of which information-processing strategies are effective in which situations (Forrest-Pressley et al., 1985).

In addition to metacognition, children acquire many other kinds of knowledge. Some children gradually become comparative experts in particular areas, such as math, sports, or getting along with peers. *Knowledge base* refers to children's current fund of knowledge and skills in various areas. A child's knowledge base in one area makes acquiring further knowledge and skills in the same area easier because the child can relate new information to prior information more meaningfully. Metacognition and an expanding knowledge base contribute to cognitive development throughout the lifespan.

According to many information-processing theorists, changes in the knowledge base are not general, stagelike transformations such as those proposed by Piaget (Chi et al., 1989). Instead, they are specialized developments of expertise based on the gradual accumulation of specific information and skills about a field, including information and skills about *how* knowledge in the field is organized and learned efficiently. A very good chess player is an expert in chess but is not necessarily advanced in other activities or areas of knowledge. Her skill probably reflects long hours spent in one major activity: playing chess games. Each hour of play enables her to build a larger knowledge base about chess: memories of board patterns, moves, and game strategies that worked in the past.

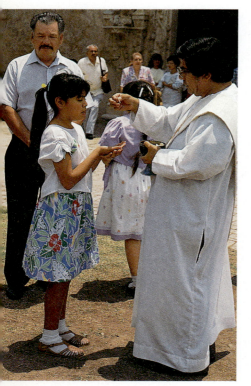

The particular cultural context in which communion and other important events occur can significantly influence a child's development.

What Do You Think?

How might the cognitive approach be useful to an elementary school math teacher who is preparing lesson plans? Would this theoretical approach be of any use in a health education class?

CONTEXTUAL DEVELOPMENTAL THEORIES

Contextual approaches view development as a process of reciprocal, patterned interactions between the developing child and his physical and social environment. A leading example of this approach is the ecological systems theory of Urie Bronfenbrenner. *Ecological systems theory* proposes that a person's development is influenced by four interactive and overlapping contextual levels: (1) the *microsystem*—the face-to-face physical and social situations that directly affect the person (family, classroom, workplace); (2) the *mesosystem*—connections and relationships among the person's microsystems; (3) the *exosystem*—the settings or situations that indirectly influence the person (spouse's place of employment, the local school board, the local government); and (4) the *macrosystem*—the values, beliefs, and policies of society and culture that provide frameworks, or "blueprints," for organizing our lives and indirectly influence the person through their effects on the exosystem, mesosystem, and microsystem. (See Chapter 1 for a discussion of Bronfenbrenner's theory.)

Another interesting example of contextual theory was developed by the Russian psychologist Lev Vygotsky (1896–1934). Vygotsky was interested in how changing historical and cultural contexts within which children's activities occur influence their cognitive development. According to Vygotsky, higher mental functions grow out of the social interactions and dialogues that take place between a child and parents, teachers, and other representatives of the culture. Through these interactions, children internalize increasingly mature and effective ways of thinking and problem solving. Some of these changes occur through discoveries that the child initiates on her own.

Many developmental tasks, however, occur in what Vygotsky called the *zone of proximal development*. The **zone of proximal development** refers to the range of tasks that a child cannot yet accomplish without active assistance from parents and others with greater knowledge, and the framework of support and assistance is called *scaffolding* (Blanck, 1990; Rogoff, 1990; Wertsch, 1989). See the accompanying Multicultural View box for a discussion of culture and cognitive development.

Ethological Theory

The ethological approach attempts to apply the principles of evolutionary biology and ethology to behavioral and psychological characteristics (Bowlby, 1979; Hinde, 1989; P. Miller, 1989). This approach has its roots in *ethology,* the study of various animal species in their natural environments. Ethology emphasizes the ways widely shared species behaviors evolved through the process of natural selection to ensure species survival. Developmental ethologists are interested in how certain behavioral and psychological traits or predispositions that appear to be widely shared among human beings may have developed to help ensure the evolutionary survival of the human species.

An underlying assumption is that just as human evolution has imposed certain constraints on our physical development, it may have influenced the range and nature of our behavioral development. Developmental ethologists also attempt to understand how individual differences in traits such as aggressiveness, shyness, competitiveness, and altruism reciprocally interact with the social environment to mutually influence development.

One area of ethological interest has been the study of infant emotions and *temperament,* relatively enduring individual differences in infant responsiveness and self-regulation that appear to be present at birth. (See Chapters 3 and 5 for a discussion of temperament.)

A second important application of the ethological approach is the study of infant-caregiver *attachment*—the mutually reinforcing system of physical, social, and emotional stimulation and support between infant and caregiver. This pattern of attachment behaviors has also been observed in other species, and ethologists presume it has survival value for humans as well (e.g., Bowlby, 1979) (See Chapter 5 for a discussion of attachment). Attachment has importance throughout the lifespan and is discussed again in Chapters 13, 15, and 17 on psychosocial development in adulthood.

What Do You Think?

To what degree does your informal theory of development include the different developmental contexts proposed by the theorists discussed in this section? Are there any you would add? Any you would delete?

A Multicultural View

Cultural Context and Cognitive Development

According to Lev Vygotsky's theory, cognitive development is largely "context specific," meaning it must be understood in terms of the particular social, cultural, and historical processes of people's everyday experiences (Vygotsky, 1978; Wertsch, 1985). Individuals growing up in different societies, cultures, and historical periods are likely to display differences in how they think and solve problems and in how cognitive development occurs. This view is very different from that of Jean Piaget, who believed cognitive development is largely "universal," meaning all individuals progress through the same developmental stages at approximately the same ages relatively independently of their particular situations and experiences.

Research based primarily on observations of children from Western industrialized societies, where formal schooling is heavily stressed, has generally supported Piaget's ideas. Studies of children growing up in other societies and cultures, however, have been more consistent with Vygotsky's views. Children growing up in cultures with little formal schooling have been found to take much longer to achieve the *concrete operational stage* of think-

ing and appear unable to achieve the *formal operational stage* of thinking, Piaget's final stage (Rogoff & Chavajay, 1995). Michael Cole, a pioneer in studying culture and cognitive development, concluded that the superior performance of children who had formal schooling was due to the common structure and activities of schooling and tests of cognitive development rather than to the effects of schooling on children's thinking (Cole, 1990).

Performance on tasks that require subjects to classify test items into categories is one good example. Whereas individuals from Western countries typically classify test items based on their type (for example, putting animals in one group, food items in another, and tools in a third), individuals in many other nations sort the same items based on their function (for example, putting a hoe with a potato because a hoe is used to dig up a potato) (Rogoff & Chavajay, 1995).

Logical tasks that require a person to draw conclusions based on abstract, hypothetical reasoning rather than on direct personal experience are another example. Nonliterate individuals who are able to make excellent

ADULTHOOD AND LIFESPAN DEVELOPMENTAL THEORIES

In this section we look at two theoretical approaches that focus on development during adulthood and across the entire lifespan: the *normative-crisis model* (also called the *stage-theory model*) and the *timing of events model*. As we will see, while these two models differ in important ways, they share the assumption that the process of individual developmental change does not end with adolescence but continues throughout a person's adulthood and old age, that is, throughout the life cycle.

Normative-Crisis Model of Development

The **normative-crisis model** of development assumes developmental change occurs in distinct stages that all individuals follow in the same sequence. Each successive stage is qualitatively unique from all other stages, is increasingly complex and more fully developed, and integrates the changes and accomplishments of earlier stages. This model generally presumes that developmental stages are at least in part influenced by biologically driven maturational changes.

Erik Erikson's psychosocial theory, discussed earlier in this chapter, is a good example. The crisis of *intimacy versus isolation,* which occurs during early adulthood, is discussed more fully in Chapter 13; the crisis of *generativity versus stagnation* during middle adulthood is covered in Chapter 15; and the crisis of *integrity versus despair* of late adulthood is discussed in Chapter 17. Here we will briefly look at two other normative-crisis views of adult development: George Vaillant's *adaptive mechanism* approach and Daniel Levinson's *seasons of adult lives* approach. We will look more closely at these and other theories of adult development in Chapters 13 and 15.

logical judgments when dealing with the immediate, practical problems of their everyday life experiences may, for cultural reasons, be unwilling to demonstrate similar reasoning abilities in situations that are not culturally familiar. The following example, taken from an interview with a nonliterate Central Asian peasant, illustrates this point:

Interviewer: In the Far North, where there is snow, all bears are white. Novaya Zemlya is in the Far North and there is always snow there. What color are the bears there?

Peasant: . . . We always speak of only what we see; we don't talk about what we haven't seen.

Interviewer: But what do my words imply?

Peasant: Well, it's like this: our tsar isn't like yours, and yours isn't like ours. Your words can be answered only by someone who was there, and if a person wasn't there he can't say anything on the basis of your words.

Interviewer: But on the basis of my words—in the North, where there is always snow, the bears are white—can you gather what kind of bears there are in Novaya Zemlya?

Peasant: If a man was sixty or eighty and had seen a white bear and had told me about it, he could be believed, but I've never seen one and hence I can't say. (Luria, 1976, pp. 108–109, quoted in Rogoff & Chavajay, 1995, p. 861)

Differences in performance of common cognitive tasks may also reflect cultural differences in how a problem is defined and how it should be solved (Goodnow, 1976). European Americans, for example, believe that intelligence involves technical rather than social skills. Kipsigis (Kenyan) parents include responsible participation in family and social life in their definition. For the Ifaluk of the western Pacific, intelligence means not only having knowledge of good social behavior but also performing it. Ugandan villagers associate intelligence with being slow, careful, and active, whereas westernized groups associate it with speed (Rogoff & Chavajay, 1995).

Future research will provide additional evidence regarding the social and cultural contexts of cognitive development.

George Vaillant: Styles of Adult Coping   Based on a long-term, longitudinal study of a sample of 268 men, Vaillant concluded that development is a lifelong process that is influenced mainly by relationships with others and by the adaptive mechanisms, or *coping styles,* that people used to deal with life events. Mature coping styles include sublimation, the redirecting of anxiety and unacceptable impulses toward acceptable goals, and altruism, the offering of help and support to others with no expectation of personal gain. According to Vaillant, the use of mature coping styles increases with age and is most likely to occur among individuals who have healthy brains and who have experienced long-term, loving relationships (Vaillant, 1977; Vaillant & Vaillant, 1990). Table 2.6 summarizes Vaillant's developmental periods.

Daniel Levinson: Seasons of Adult Lives   Based on his biographical study of the lives of forty men between ages thirty-five and forty-five from a variety of backgrounds, Levinson identified three eras, or "seasons," in male adult life: (1) *early*

TABLE 2.6   *George Vaillant's Phases of Adult Development*

Phase	Approximate Age	Description
Age of establishment	20–30	Increasing autonomy from parents; marriage, parenthood, and establishing more intimate friendships
Career consolidation	20–40	Consolidating and strengthening marriage and career; devotion to hard work and career advancement
Midlife transition	40–50	Painful reassessment and reordering of the experiences of adolescence and young adulthood; heightened self-awareness and exploration of forgotten "inner self," opens way for achieving greater generativity
Midlife	50 and older	Leave behind compulsive involvement with occupational apprenticeships; become increasingly self-reflective, nurturant, and expressive

adulthood, (2) *middle adulthood,* and (3) *late adulthood.* During each era, a new "life structure" is established that reflects the person's significant relationships with others and the desires, values, commitment, energy, and skills invested in them. The life structure evolves through a relatively orderly sequence during the adult years. Changes occur within each period, and each era brings transitions that provide an opportunity to reassess and improve on the preceding era (Levinson, 1986; Levinson et al., 1978).

Table 2.7 presents Levinson's three eras of adult development. In Chapters 13 and 15, we will take a more detailed look at his theory and its relevance for adult development among women.

Timing of Events Model

The **timing of events model** of development views *life events* as markers, or indicators, of developmental change. Life events may be normative or nonnormative. *Normative life events* are transitions that follow an age-appropriate social timetable; individuals create an internalized *social clock* that tells them whether they are "on time" in following that schedule (Neugarten, 1968). Normative life events include work, marriage, and parenthood during early adulthood, career advancement in middle adulthood, and physical decline, retirement, and widowhood during late adulthood.

Many life events, however, are nonnormative and less predictable. A *nonnormative life event* occurs at any point in time in a person's life and may include normative events that occur "off time," such as marrying "late," being widowed as a young adult, or returning to college in middle adulthood.

TABLE 2.7 *Daniel Levinson's Eras of Adult Development*

	Phase	Approximate Age	Description
Childhood and adolescence (Birth–17)			
Early Adult Era (17–45)	Early adult transition	17–22	Reassessing preadulthood and preparing for early adulthood
	Early life structure	22–28	Entering the adult world and building a first life structure. Novice phase: forming and living out the Dream of adult accomplishment; forming mentor relationships; developing an occupation; forming love relationships, marriage and family
	Age 30 transition	28–33	Reassessing and improving early life structure; transition may be smooth or painful
	Culminating life structure	33–40	Settling down: building a second adult life structure. Establishing occupational goals and plans for achieving them; becoming one's own person: achieving greater independence and self-sufficiency
	Midlife transition	40–45	Completing early adulthood and preparing for middle adulthood. Reappraising past progress toward achieving the Dream; revising the Dream and changing lifestyle around the themes of a new life structure. Midlife individuation through better resolving polarities of young/old, destruction/creation, masculine/feminine, attachment/separateness
Middle Adult Era (40–60)	Early life structure	45–50	Entering middle adulthood. Making and committing to new choices and building a life structure around them
	Age 50 transition	50–55	Modifying and improving the entry life structure
	Culminating life structure	55–60	Completion of middle adulthood
Late Adult Era (60 and older)	Late adult transition	60–65	Preparation for late adulthood

Marriage represents an important normative event in the lives of this couple and in the lives of their parents and grandparents as well.

The timing of events model reflects an awareness of two important ways in which the capabilities, life experiences, and developmental changes of adulthood tend to differ from those of childhood and adolescence. First, the changes during the adult years appear to be less closely tied to the substantial and predictable physical and cognitive maturational changes that characterize childhood and adolescence; rather, they seem to be more closely linked to the major social and psychological conditions, events, and experiences that adults encounter, many of which are considerably less predictable. Second, the physical, cognitive, and psychosocial competencies of adults allow them to play a much more active and self-conscious role in directing their own development through the decisions and choices they make. For example, individual decisions about whom (and when) to marry, whether or not to have children, where to live, what type of work to do, and what social, political, religious, and lifestyle commitments to pursue can all significantly affect development.

DEVELOPMENTAL THEORIES COMPARED: IMPLICATIONS FOR THE STUDENT

We have reached the end of our review of several of the most important theories in developmental psychology. What conclusions might we draw? In what ways are these theories useful as we investigate lifespan development in the remainder of this book?

Working with   John Daviau, RESIDENTIAL TREATMENT PROGRAM DIRECTOR

Understanding Multiproblem Adolescents

John Daviau was interviewed in a classroom at the University of New Haven, where he is currently enrolled as a part-time graduate student in the Community-Clinical Psychology Program. John has worked in residential treatment for the past ten years and was interested in discussing how developmental theory helps guide his day-to-day work.

Rob: Could you tell me a little about your work?

John: I'm a program director for an adolescent group home. Basically it's a long-term residential setting for abused, neglected, and emotionally disturbed adolescents.

Rob: How did you become involved in this type of work?

John: It's interesting. Years ago I was a landscape foreman and was looking for a career change, so I enrolled in a certificate program in counseling and human relations. When I finished the program, I got an entry-level position as a child care worker in a group home, where I eventually became director. After moving to Connecticut, I worked as a program director in a community criminal justice program for two years before beginning my present job.

Rob: Do you find that developmental theory influences how you work with these youngsters?

John: Actually, it influences me all the time. I think developmental theory is very important because disturbed adolescents can be very demanding, egocentric, frustrating people to work with. If you're not a parent and you haven't experienced adolescents as a parent or adult caregiver, it helps to know what to expect—what's normal or atypical behavior for a fourteen-year-old, for instance.

Rob: And theory can tell you this? Can you give some examples of how theory may be helpful?

John: Psychodynamic theories give us some useful guidelines for what is developmentally normal and age appropriate. They help us understand the adolescent's inappropriate behavior in terms of developmental delays and unresolved conflicts and crises. They also give us tools to better understand our own feelings as caregivers—and, hopefully, to see the difficulties that come up between these youngsters and staff as opportunities for positive change.

Rob: How might you apply developmental theory to your work?

John: Swearing is a good example. When teens get angry—and this population of adolescents is very angry—it often comes out as swearing. A lot

As we suggested at the beginning of this chapter, theories are useful because they help us systematically organize and make sense of large amounts of sometimes inconsistent information about lifespan development. Theories also stimulate new thinking and research and guide parents, professionals, and laypersons in their day-to-day involvements with children, adolescents, and adults.

Psychodynamic theories such as Erikson's help us anticipate and better understand the crises we encounter in our own development. For example, knowledge about the crisis of autonomy versus shame and doubt can help parents and day care teachers respond to toddlers with the right mixture of structure, control, and freedom. Similarly, knowledge of the crisis of identity versus role confusion can help us better understand normal and problematic identity development during adolescence and young adulthood (Glasser, 1967; Redl & Wineman, 1951; Selman, 1980). The accompanying interview with John Daviau discusses how developmental theories can provide insights into working with troubled adolescents. Finally, understanding the crisis of ego integrity versus despair can help us to respond more effectively to the needs of our aging parents and, eventually, to better adjust to our own later years.

Psychodynamic and object relations theories help us appreciate the considerable capabilities, needs, and vulnerabilities of infants, children, and adults. They have increased our awareness of the importance of the quality of parent-child relationships and have helped parents, teachers, pediatric nurses, and mental health professionals understand what constitutes quality parenting and caregiving both inside and outside the family and across the lifespan (e.g., Stern, 1995).

of times it will be directed at you to see what kind of reaction they can get from the authority figures. If you realize where they're coming from and what kind of anger and issues they have, you're going to react differently. You're better able to respond in a more constructive way that's respectful and empathic to their feelings, and not start yelling back at them.

Rob: Not always easy to accomplish.

John: No, it isn't.

Rob: What other ideas influence the work you do at the center?

John: Fritz Redl's ideas have been very useful. He established Pioneer House, a psychoanalytically oriented residential treatment program for antisocial adolescents in the 1940s. Redl believed that conscience and behavior controls break down in children who have been raised in disorganized and abusive environments. Since these environments have no adequate caregiving or role models, the children use hatred to defend themselves against the adults in their lives. This framework has certainly influenced how we structure our program and how we make individual treatment decisions.

Rob: Earlier you mentioned social cognitive learning approaches.

John: I was thinking of William Glasser's reality therapy approach, which helps children learn more effective problem-solving strategies and take responsibility for the consequences of their actions.

Rob: Can you give an example?

John: Yes. Sometimes it really helps to go through problem solving. It gets kids to realize consequences and to think about making changes. Simple things like "So when you get angry, what do you do?" "Well, I get angry and I punch the wall." "How does that make you feel?" "Well, I hurt my hand and I'm p---d off, and . . . " "Do you like that way of expressing anger? Does it help you? What does it do for you?" "Well, no, I guess I don't really like it, it doesn't really solve the problem." "Then maybe you could think about doing something differently."

What Do You Think?

1. How might unresolved crises related to Erikson's stages help explain the behaviors exhibited by these teenagers?

2. If you were a worker on John's staff, how might you respond to a teenager who swore at you?

3. What theoretical ideas would help you respond constructively?

Behavioral and social cognitive learning theories and the principles and techniques of classical and operant conditioning and social learning have helped parents and educators to concretely achieve some of the more abstract goals associated with good caregiving. For example, appropriate and respectful use of reinforcement and modeling have been helpful to nurse-midwives and school nurses working with sexually active or pregnant teens, probation officers and drug counselors working with troubled youths, and mental health professionals working with middle-aged adults facing the stresses of work, family life, and caring for their own aging parents.

Piaget's theory of cognitive development has helped parents and teachers to develop realistic expectations of children at different stages of thinking and to remember that readiness to solve certain types of intellectual problems depends not only on a suitable learning environment but also on a child's maturational readiness.

Concepts from contextual theories such as Lev Vygotsky's zone of proximal development have been useful in designing home, school, and work environments that provide the optimal amount of guidance and stimulation for children, adolescents, and adults. By focusing our attention on the multiple and overlapping situations in which development occurs, theories such as Urie Bronfenbrenner's ecological systems approach have helped us to more effectively respond to complex problems such as "at-risk" families, child maltreatment, school failure, drug use, juvenile delinquency, workplace alienation, and institutional care for elderly adults (for example, see Garbarino, 1992a, 1992b; Ramey et al., 1988).

Ethological theories help us understand how individual differences in temperament reciprocally interact with the social environment to influence development. The ethological approach has been particularly useful in the study of infant-caregiver attachment, the mutually reinforcing system of physical, social, and emotional stimulation and support between infant and caregiver that continues to be important in forming and maintaining intimate relationships during adolescence and adulthood.

Finally, lifespan theories of development help us understand that developmental change is truly a lifelong process and appreciate the similarities and differences in such changes across the life cycle. Normative-crisis theories of Erik Erikson, George Vaillant, and Dan Levinson provide useful frameworks for understanding the predictable challenges typically faced during the life course and guiding professionals and nonprofessionals in responding to these challenges. The timing of events approach highlights the degree to which a person's life course is influenced by nonnormative events and guided by individual choices.

Although each theory has significantly expanded knowledge in its particular area of focus, none should be thought to provide a complete explanation of development. Taken together, the theories are complementary and can be used in conjunction with one another to provide a fairly comprehensive view of lifespan development. Table 2.8 summarizes the main features, key concepts, and four developmental themes for each theoretical approach discussed.

Last, but not least, theories help us understand and actively participate in our own development. Theories can also broaden and deepen our understanding of ourselves, the factors influencing our development, and the choices we have. They can help us better understand how our family dynamics and relationships may have influenced our current personalities and our struggles with issues such as identity, intimacy, gender role, and sexuality.

However, uncritical reliance on theories poses several pitfalls. Because theories guide and direct our perceptions of and thinking about children, reliance on a given theory may lead us to focus on certain aspects of development, make certain assumptions, and draw conclusions about development that are consistent with the theory but not necessarily accurate. For example, overreliance on Piaget's cognitive approach may lead a teacher to underestimate the contributions of social and emotional factors to a child's academic difficulties. Similarly, parents who tend to interpret their child's irresponsible behavior in terms of psychological conflict may overlook the fact that the same behavior is frequently modeled and reinforced by the child's older sibling. Finally, the emphasis many developmental theories place on shared or even universal developmental trends may underestimate the role of individual differences in life conditions, events, and personal choices, not only during adulthood but during childhood and adolescence as well.

As you read the chapters that follow, notice that the theories are applied selectively based on the ages and developmental issues being discussed. We encourage you to refer back to this chapter whenever you have questions about the material and to make your own judgments about which theory (or theories) fits best. Finally, keep an eye on how your own theories of development change as you read the book and talk with your instructor and classmates. By the end of the course, if not sooner, you are likely to have a much clearer idea of your preferred theoretical orientation(s), as well as a much clearer perspective of what development is all about.

What Do You Think?

Remember three-year-old Elizabeth at the beginning of this chapter? Now that you have learned more about theories of development, which theory (or theories) do you think is most useful in understanding her situation and helping her adjust to her first days of nursery school? Why?

TABLE 2.8 *Developmental Theories Compared*

	Main Focus	Key Concepts	Four Developmental Themes				
			Role of maturation	Role of experience	Stages	Breadth of focus	Active role of individual
Psychodynamic							
Freud	Personality (social, emotional)	Id, ego, superego; psychosexual conflict; defense mechanisms	Moderate	Strong	Yes	Wide	Moderate
Erikson	Personality (social, emotional identity)	Lifespan development; psychosocial crises	Weak	Strong	Yes	Wide	Moderate
Mahler	Personality (social, emotional, self)	Birth of psychological self; separation-individuation	Strong	Moderate	Yes	Narrow	Moderate
Stern	Personality (interpersonal, cognitive, emotional, self)	Interpersonal sense of self; RIGs	Moderate	Strong	Yes	Moderate	Strong
Behavioral Learning							
Pavlov; Skinner	Learning specific observable responses	Classical and operant conditioning, extinction, reinforcement, punishment	Weak	Strong	No	Narrow	Weak
Social-Cognitive Learning							
Bandura	Learning behavior, cognitive response patterns, social roles	Imitation, social learning, modeling, cognitive learning, reciprocal determinism; skill capabilities	Weak	Strong	No	Moderate	Strong
Cognitive							
Piaget	Cognitive (thinking, problem solving)	Schemes, assimilation, accommodation, equilibrium; mental space, routinization of schemes	Strong	Moderate	Yes	Moderate	Moderate
Case; Fischer	Cognitive; problem-solving skills and capacities	Skill acquisition, optimal level of performance, higher-level skills	Moderate	Moderate	No	Moderate	Strong
Information Processing	Cognitive; steps and processes involved in problem solving and other mental activities	Sensory register, short-term memory (STM), long-term memory (LTM), meta-cognition, knowledge base, control processes	Strong	Moderate	No	Narrow	Strong

TABLE 2.8   Cont'd.

	Main Focus	Key Concepts	Four Developmental Themes				
			Role of maturation	Role of experience	Stages	Breadth of focus	Active role of individual
Contextual Approaches							
Bronfenbrenner	Contextual; interactive contextual influences	Ecological contexts; microsystem; ecosystem; mesosystem; macro-system	Weak	Strong	No	Wide	Strong
Vygotsky	Contextual; cultural/ historical influences	Dialogues; zone of proximal development	Weak	Strong	No	Moderate	Strong
Ethological	Contextual; biological and ethological influences	Behaviorial predispositions, ethological context	Moderate	Moderate	No	Moderate	Moderate
Vaillant	Personality (social, behavior, life structure)	Adult development; mature coping mechanisms	Weak	Strong	Yes	Moderate	Strong
Levinson	Personality (social, behavior, coping mechanisms)	Adult development; eras; transitions; life structures	Weak	Strong	Yes	Moderate	Strong
Timing of Events	Personality (social, behavior life structure)	Adult development; normative and non-normative events; social clock	Weak	Strong	No	Wide	Strong

SUMMARY OF MAJOR IDEAS

The Nature of Developmental Theories

1. Theories are useful in organizing and explaining the process of development and in stimulating and guiding developmental research, theory, and practice.

2. Developmental theories differ in the degree to which they emphasize maturation versus experience, continuous versus stagelike development, breadth of theoretical focus, and the individual's active versus passive participation.

Psychodynamic Developmental Theories

3. In the theories of Freud and Erikson, development is a dynamic process that occurs in a series of stages, each involving psychological conflicts that the developing person must resolve.

4. According to Freud, personality development is energized by three conflicting functions: the unconscious, irrational, pleasure-seeking id; the largely conscious, rational, realistic ego; and the superego, which is the voice of conscience and morality.

5. Erikson's psychosocial theory outlines eight developmental stages encompassing the lifespan, each defined by a unique psychological crisis that is never completely resolved.

6. During infancy, a basic sense of trust (versus mistrust) results in *hope*. During toddlerhood and the preschool years, a child achieves a sense of autonomy (versus shame and doubt) and initiative (versus guilt), resulting in *will* and *purpose*.

7. During the school years, a child must resolve the crisis of industry (versus inferiority) and during adolescence the crisis of identity (versus role confusion), resulting in *competence* and *fidelity*.

8. Erikson's final three stages occur after adolescence. They include young adulthood and the crisis of intimacy (versus isolation), middle adulthood and the crisis of generativity (versus stagnation), and old age and the crisis of ego integrity (versus despair). Successful resolution brings *love, care,* and *wisdom*.

9. Object relations approaches emphasize development as resulting from a child's mental representations of early social and emotional relationships with parents and important others.

10. According to Mahler, the infant goes through autistic, symbiotic, separation-individuation, and object constancy phases in developing a sense of psychological self. For Kohut, empathic mirroring by caregivers helps the infant to develop a cohesive and reliable set of mental representations out of which a sense of self emerges. For Stern, the process involves a core self, a subjective self, and a verbal self.

Behavioral Learning and Social Cognitive Learning Developmental Theories

11. Pavlov's theory emphasizes learning through classical conditioning as the main process by which developmental changes occur.

12. Skinner's operant conditioning theory emphasizes the influence of reinforcement, punishment, extinction, and shaping on developmental change.

13. Bandura's social cognitive theory emphasizes reciprocal and interactional processes involving direct, observational learning, modeling, and vicarious reinforcement.

Cognitive Developmental Theories

14. Piaget's theory explains the underlying structures and processes involved in the development of children's thinking and problem solving.

15. According to Piaget, thinking develops in a series of increasingly complex and sophisticated stages, or periods, each of which incorporates the achievements of those preceding it.

16. New ways of thinking and problem solving are achieved through the joint processes of assimilation (fitting a new scheme of thinking or action into an existing one) and accommodation (changing an existing scheme to meet the challenges of a new situation).

17. The neo-Piagetian theories of Robbie Case and Kurt Fisher emphasize the roles of mental space, skill acquisition, and information-processing capacity in cognitive development.

18. Information-processing theory focuses on the steps involved in thought processes. Information is first stored in the sensory register, then in short-term memory, and finally in long-term memory. As children grow older, they experience cognitive changes in control processes, metacognition, and their knowledge bases.

Contextual Developmental Theories

19. Bronfenbrenner's ecological systems theory proposes that the microsystem, mesosystem, exosystem, and macrosystem form interactive and overlapping contexts for development. Vygotsky emphasizes the contributions of history and culture to development that take place within a child's zone of proximal development.

20. Ethological theory focuses on the developmental roles of behavioral dispositions and traits, such as temperament and attachment, that are thought to have evolutionary survival value for the human species.

Adulthood and Lifespan Developmental Theories

21. Normative-crisis theories of adult and lifespan development focus on fairly predictable changes that occur over the lifespan, particularly during the adult years.

22. Timing of events theory emphasizes the role of both normative and nonnormative transitions in an individual's life course and how social expectations may be internalized in a "social clock" against which we judge our own development.

Developmental Theories Compared: Implications for the Student

23. Although developmental theories differ in both focus and explanatory concepts, together they provide a fairly comprehensive view of the process of developmental change.

24. By systematically organizing what we already know about development and proposing explanations that can be tested through formal and informal observations, developmental theories are so useful for experts and nonexperts alike that they are well worth the effort required to understand them.

KEY TERMS

id *(34)*
ego *(35)*
superego *(35)*
trust versus mistrust *(38)*
autonomy versus shame and doubt *(38)*
initiative versus guilt *(39)*
industry versus inferiority *(39)*
identity versus role confusion *(39)*
intimacy versus isolation *(39)*
generativity versus stagnation *(39)*
ego integrity versus despair *(39)*

object relations *(40)*
classical conditioning *(41)*
operant conditioning *(42)*
reinforcement *(42)*
punishment *(43)*
observational learning *(43)*
scheme *(45)*
assimilation *(45)*
accommodation *(45)*
adaptation *(45)*
information-processing theory *(47)*
metacognition *(48)*
zone of proximal development *(49)*
normative-crisis model *(50)*
timing-of-events model *(52)*

3

Genetics, Prenatal Development, and Birth

GENETICS

Inheritance affects a vast number of human qualities, from the color of our eyes and how tall we are to more complex characteristics such as athletic ability, intelligence, and temperament. We begin this section by describing the basic biological processes involved in human reproduction and how genetic information from two parents is combined and conveyed to their children. Next, we discuss genetic abnormalities. Then we address an issue that psychologists have found especially important: the relationship between heredity and environment. Finally, we describe ways to use knowledge of these relationships to benefit parents and children.

MECHANISMS OF GENETIC TRANSMISSION

The process by which genetic information is combined and transmitted begins with *gametes,* the reproductive cells of a child's parents. In the father the gametes are produced in the testicles, and each is called a **sperm** cell. In the mother they develop in the ovaries, and each is called an **ovum,** or *egg cell.* The sperm and egg cells contain genetic information in molecular structures called **genes,** which form threads called **chromosomes**. Thus, the chromosomes contain the genetic material the child will inherit from the parent. Each human sperm or egg cell contains twenty-three chromosomes. All other cells of the body contain forty-six chromosomes and approximately one hundred thousand genes. A single chromosome may contain as many as twenty thousand genes. Figure 3.1 shows pictures, or *karyotypes,* of the chromosomes for a normal human male. Figure 3.2 illustrates the genetic structures involved.

Focusing Questions

- How does inheritance work, and how are genetic differences usually transmitted from one generation to the next?

- What is our current state of knowledge about common genetic abnormalities and their causes?

- How can experts help parents diagnose and respond to potential genetic problems?

- What is required for normal conception to occur? What alternatives are available for couples who have problems conceiving a child?

- What important developmental changes occur during prenatal development? What risks do a mother and baby normally face during pregnancy, and how can they best be minimized?

- What methods are currently available to help parents prepare for the birth process?

- What happens during the birth process, what difficulties may occur, and how are they handled?

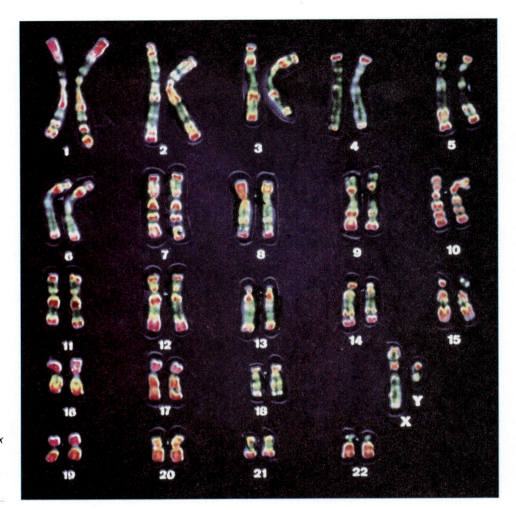

FIGURE 3.1
Chromosomes for the Normal Human Male
This karotype depicts the twenty-two pairs of chromosomes and the two sex chromosomes for the normal human male. In females, the twenty-third pair of chromosomes consists of an XX instead of an XY pair.

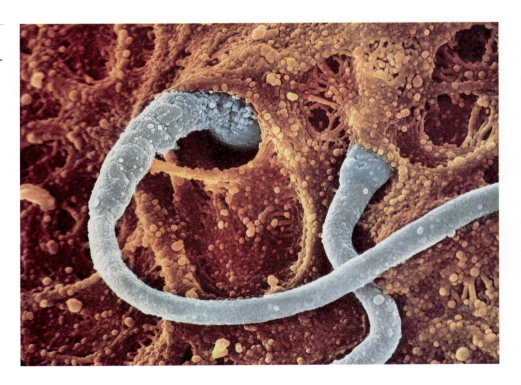

This color-enhanced photo shows a human sperm fertilizing an egg. Conception occurs when a sperm cell penetrates an egg cell, forming a zygote. Almost immediately, the wall of the new zygote changes so that no other sperm can enter.

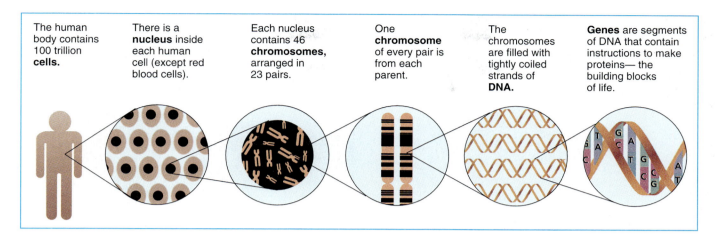

The human body contains 100 trillion **cells.**

There is a **nucleus** inside each human cell (except red blood cells).

Each nucleus contains 46 **chromosomes,** arranged in 23 pairs.

One **chromosome** of every pair is from each parent.

The chromosomes are filled with tightly coiled strands of **DNA.**

Genes are segments of DNA that contain instructions to make proteins— the building blocks of life.

FIGURE 3.2
Genetic Structures

The Role of DNA

The genes themselves are made of *DNA (deoxyribonucleic acid)*, the complex protein code of genetic information that directs the form and function of each body cell as it develops. DNA shares this information at conception, when a sperm from the father penetrates an egg from the mother, releasing their chromosomes, which join to form a new cell called a **zygote**. To accomplish this, reproductive cells, or gametes, divide by a process called *meiosis* and recombine into a zygote at conception. All of the other cells that make up a unique human being will develop from this original zygote through a simple division of their genes, chromosomes, and other cellular parts by means of a process called *mitosis*.

Meiosis and Mitosis

Meiosis involves the following steps. First, the twenty-three chromosomes of the egg (or sperm) cell duplicate themselves. Then they break up into smaller pieces and randomly exchange segments of genetic material with one another. Next, the new chromosome pairs divide to form two separate cells. Finally, the two new cells divide again. Each of the four new cells contains a unique set of genetic material in its twenty-three chromosomes, *one-half* the usual number of chromosomes carried by all other cells. This ensures that the new, single-cell zygote that forms during conception will contain the normal forty-six chromosomes: twenty-three chromosomes from the egg and twenty-three from the sperm. Figure 3.3 illustrates the process of meiosis for sperm cells.

Once the zygote forms, it and all of its descendants divide through the process of mitosis. *Mitosis* involves the following steps. First, the twenty-three pairs of chromosomes of a cell form a duplicate set. Next, the two sets of chromosomes move to opposite sides of the cell. Finally, a new wall forms between them, resulting in two new, identical cells, each containing the same unique set of chromosomes, genes, and DNA-based genetic code that will help guide the new organism's development. Figure 3.4 depicts the process of mitosis for sperm cells.

What Do You Think?

Sometimes a good way to check your understanding of rather complex material is to explain it to another person. Team up with a classmate and explain the roles of meiosis and mitosis to him or her in your own words. Then ask your classmate to explain it back to you. What unanswered questions do you still have?

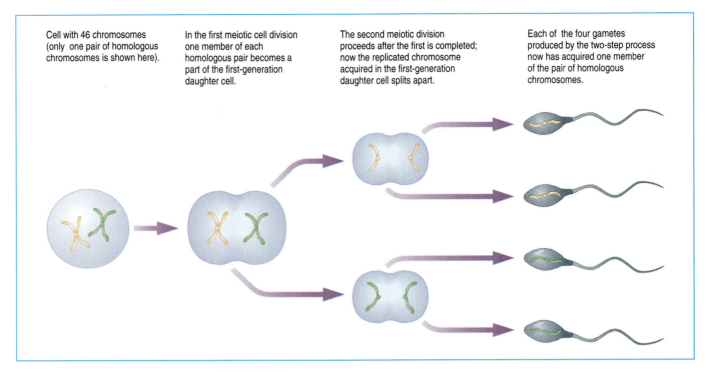

Cell with 46 chromosomes (only one pair of homologous chromosomes is shown here).

In the first meiotic cell division one member of each homologous pair becomes a part of the first-generation daughter cell.

The second meiotic division proceeds after the first is completed; now the replicated chromosome acquired in the first-generation daughter cell splits apart.

Each of the four gametes produced by the two-step process now has acquired one member of the pair of homologous chromosomes.

FIGURE 3.3
The Process of Meiosis for Sperm Cells
As meiosis begins, (a) DNA replicates. However, before the replicated arms split apart, one member of each pair of chromosomes moves to become part of each first-generation daughter cell (b). Once the first generation of daughter cells is established, the DNA copies itself, then splits as part of the second meiotic division (c). Thus, one copy of one member of the pair of chromosomes is contributed to each second-generation daughter cell (d). These two successive divisions produce four cells, each with twenty-three chromosomes.

FIGURE 3.4
The Process of Mitosis for Sperm Cells
Mitotic cell division produces nearly all the cells of the body except the gametes. During mitosis, each chromosome replicates to form two chromosomes with identical genetic blueprints. As the cell divides, one member of each identical pair becomes a member of each daughter cell. In this manner, complete genetic endowment is replicated in nearly every cell of the body.

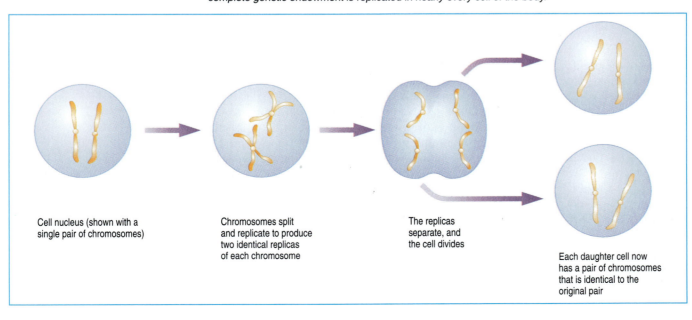

Cell nucleus (shown with a single pair of chromosomes)

Chromosomes split and replicate to produce two identical replicas of each chromosome

The replicas separate, and the cell divides

Each daughter cell now has a pair of chromosomes that is identical to the original pair

INDIVIDUAL GENETIC EXPRESSION

How does the genetic information contained in our cells influence the development of our unique physical, intellectual, social, and emotional characteristics? In the following section, we explore this question.

Genotype and Phenotype

Genotype refers to the specific genetic information a person inherits that has the potential to influence his or her observable physical or behavioral characteristics or traits such as eye color, height, intelligence, or shyness. **Phenotype** refers to the physical and behavioral traits an individual actually exhibits, such as blue eyes, a height of five feet, ten inches, a certain intelligence test score, or a certain level of shyness. A person's phenotype is always the product of the interactions of that person's genotype with the environmental influences that occur from the formation of the first cell at conception onward.

In some cases, there is a close match between a person's original genotype and the phenotype that results. For example, inheriting genes for blue eyes generally results in actually having blue eyes. In other cases, phenotype does not coincide so closely with genotype. Two newborn infants may have inherited the identical genotype for weight at the time of conception, but one may end up heavier (or lighter) than the other because of differences in prenatal nutrition and differences in diet and exercise during infancy and childhood. On the other hand, children with different genotypes for weight may end up the same weight (the same phenotype), one through dieting and the other simply by eating whatever she wanted.

Dominant and Recessive Genes

Genes are inherited in pairs, one from each parent. Some genes are dominant and others are recessive. A **dominant gene** will influence a child's phenotype even if it is paired with a recessive gene. A **recessive gene,** however, must be paired with another recessive gene to be able to influence the phenotype. If it is paired with a dominant gene, its influence will be controlled or blocked. More than one thousand human characteristics appear to follow the dominant-recessive pattern of inheritance (McKussick, 1988). Table 3.1 lists a number of common dominant and recessive traits.

Eye color is a good example. Suppose human eyes came in only two colors, blue and brown. Because blue eyes are a recessive trait and brown eyes are a dominant trait, a child's eyes will be blue only if he has received the appropriate blue-producing gene from both parents. If he has received it from only one parent or from neither, he will end up with brown eyes.

Transmission of Multiple Variations

The genes responsible for eye color—and, in fact, for many other traits—often take on two or more alternative forms called **alleles**. In addition to alleles for blue and brown, the gene responsible for eye color occasionally takes on a third allele, which often leads to hazel eyes. A person who inherits two identical alleles for a particular trait is said to be *homozygous* for that trait. A person who inherits two different alleles for the trait is said to be *heterozygous* for that trait. In the case of eye color, a heterozygous person (one brown and one blue/hazel allele) will therefore show the phenotype of the dominant allele and thus have brown eyes. Only a person who is homozygous will display the phenotype of one of the recessive alleles and have blue or hazel eyes. From a genetic standpoint, there are three times as many ways to have brown eyes as there are to have blue ones. Figure 3.5 illustrates this example.

TABLE 3.1   *Some Common Dominant and Recessive Traits*

Dominant Trait	Recessive Trait	Dominant Trait	Recessive Trait
Brown eyes	Gray, green, hazel, or blue eyes	Short fingers	Fingers of normal length
Hazel or green eyes	Blue eyes	Double-fingers	Normally jointed fingers
Normal vision	Nearsightedness	Double-jointedness	Normal joints
Farsightedness	Normal vision	Type A blood	Type O blood
Normal color vision	Red-green color blindness	Type B blood	Type O blood
Brown or black hair	Blond hair	Rh positive blood	Rh negative blood
Nonred hair	Red hair	Normal blood clotting	Hemophilia
Curly or wavy hair	Straight hair	Normal red blood cells	Sickle-cell disease
Full head of hair	Baldheadedness	Normal protein metabolism	Phenylketonuria (PKU)
Normal hearing	Some forms of congenital deafness	Normal physiology	Tay-Sachs disease
Normally pigmented skin	Albino (completely white) skin	Huntington disease	Normal central nervous system functioning in adulthood
Facial dimples	No dimples	Immunity to poison ivy	Susceptibility to poison ivy
Thick lips	Thin lips		

Note: Many common traits show dominant or recessive patterns. Sometimes too, a pattern may be dominant with respect to one trait but recessive with respect to another.

Keep in mind, however, that although all of the patterns of inheritance for dominant and recessive traits are possible, each genotype will not necessarily occur in each family, since genes are inherited randomly. In Figure 3.5 (example 1), for instance, although it is possible that the parents will have children with the eye color genotypes of BB, Bb, bB, or bb, all of their children may in reality be BB or bb. Thus, the increased probability of a particular genotype, such as Bb, does not mean that genotype will definitely be seen. In contrast, in the genetic transmission of a sex-linked trait such as hemophilia (discussed shortly), all daughters in a given family are carriers and all sons are affected (see Figure 3.7 on page 70).

FIGURE 3.5
Genetic Transmission of Eye Color
Example 1: Three out of four offspring will have brown eyes and one out of four will have blue eyes. Example 2: Two out of four offspring will have brown eyes and two out of four will have blue eyes.

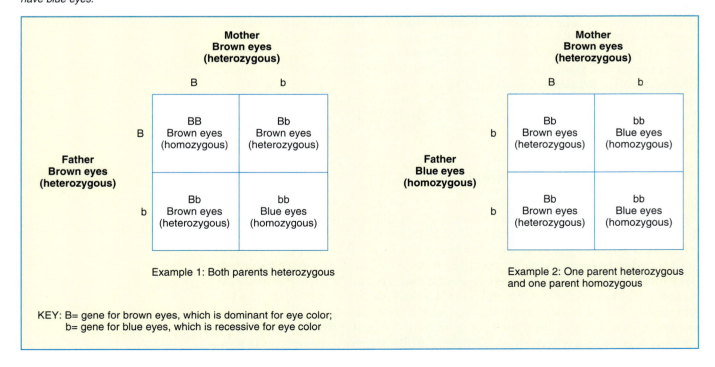

KEY: B= gene for brown eyes, which is dominant for eye color;
      b= gene for blue eyes, which is recessive for eye color

Many genes have more than two alleles. As a result, the traits they govern can vary in more complex ways. The four major human blood types, for example, are based on three alleles of the same gene. Two of these alleles, type A and type B, are dominant forms, and the O allele is recessive. Figure 3.6 illustrates how these three alleles for blood type can combine in six possible ways but produce only four blood types, A, B, O, and AB. The AB blood type is an example of *codominance,* a situation in which the characteristics of both alleles are independently expressed in a new phenotype rather than one or the other being dominant, or as a mixture of the two. Because each blood type has a unique chemistry that allows it to mix only with certain other blood types, determining the compatible blood genotype is very important for people who receive blood transfusions.

		Possible Alleles from Mother		
		A	B	o
Possible Alleles from Father	A	AA	AB	Ao
	B	AB	BB	Bo
	o	Ao	Bo	oo

FIGURE 3.6
Inheritance of Blood Type
In blood type inheritance, both A and B alleles are dominant and the O allele is recessive. Therefore, the following proportions of blood types are likely to occur in the general population:
Type A (AA or Ao): 3/9
Type B (BB or Bo): 3/9
Type AB: 2/9
Type O (oo): 1/9

Polygenic Transmission

Unlike eye color and blood type, which can vary only in a limited number of qualitatively distinct ways, the inheritance of most physical traits, including height, weight, and hair and skin color, and complex personality and behavioral traits, such as intelligence, shyness, alcoholism, and depression, do not fit the simple single-gene model just described. These traits are called *polygenic,* meaning they involve *many* genes, each with small effects, as well as environmental influences. In all of these cases, children show a marked tendency to have a phenotype that is intermediate between those of their parents, and for the most part the exact mechanisms of inheritance for such traits are still unknown (Plomin, 1989, 1990).

Because polygenic phenotypes vary by small degrees, environment can influence them in relatively important ways. An overweight person can become more slender through a change in diet, for example, and a shy person can learn to be more outgoing. Such experiences matter less for traits that are simply transmitted by a single gene; there is no way to change eye color, even though you can cover your irises with tinted contact lenses.

The Determination of Sex

Whether a person becomes male or female depends on events at conception. All ova, or egg cells, contain a single X chromosome, whereas a sperm cell may contain

Most physical traits result from the combined influences of gene pairs inherited from both parents. The degree of resemblance between a child and a given parent depends on the particular pattern of gene variations involved.

either an X or a Y. If a Y-bearing sperm happens to fertilize the egg, a male (XY) zygote develops; if the sperm is X-bearing, a female (XX) zygote develops.

During the first several weeks following conception, both male and female embryos possess a set of bisexual gonadal, or sex, tissues, meaning they can develop either male or female sex structures. However, between the fourth and eighth weeks, gonadal tissue develops into testes or ovaries depending on the presence or absence of a small section of the Y chromosome, referred to as *TDF* or *testis-determining factor*. For ova fertilized by a Y-bearing sperm, TDF is present, and male embryos result (Page et al., 1987).

More Y sperm than X sperm succeed in fertilizing the ovum, resulting in about 30 percent more male than female zygotes. By birth, however, boy babies outnumber girl babies by only about 6 percent on average, and by age thirty-five women begin to outnumber men, suggesting that males may be more genetically vulnerable than females. Much of this vulnerability is related to *sex-linked transmission*. Unlike women, who carry XX chromosomes, men carry XY chromosome pairs. Because the Y chromosome is much shorter than its matching X chromosome and therefore may lack many of the gene locations of that X chromosome, many genes from the mother may not be matched or counteracted with equivalent genetic material from the father. As a result, genetic abnormalities on the single complete X chromosome are more likely to result in phenotypic abnormalities in males than in females. Table 3.2 lists a number of **sex-linked recessive traits,** abnormalities that are transmitted on the single complete X chromosome.

One such trait is *hemophilia,* an inability of the blood to clot and therefore to stop itself from flowing. Since clotting is so slow, internal bleeding can at times be life threatening (American College of Obstetricians and Gynecologists [ACOG], 1990). Because the gene for hemophilia is located on the X chromosome, a female carrier is protected by having a normal gene on her second X chromosome. Each of her children will have a fifty-fifty chance of inheriting the abnormal gene. Daughters who get the gene will be carriers, like their mother, while sons will develop hemophilia because they lack a second X chromosome to counteract the gene's effects. Figure 3.7 illustrates this effect.

What Do You Think?

Now that you know how eye color and blood type are inherited, see if you can figure out how you inherited *your* eye color. How about your blood type?

FIGURE 3.7

Inheritance of Hemophilia, a Sex-Linked Disorder

In this example of the inheritance of hemophilia, the mother is a carrier of the disease. Each daughter has a 25 percent chance of inheriting a pair of normal chromosomes (XX) and a 25 percent chance of being a carrier (XX) like her mother. However, she herself will not be affected by the disorder because her second X chromosome protects her. Each son has a 25 percent chance of being normal (XY) and a 25 percent chance of inheriting the abnormal chromosome and being hemophilic. This is because as a male, his second chromosome is a Y, which does not protect him from the disorder.

		Carrier Mother	
		X	X
Normal Father	X	XX Normal Daughter (25%)	XX Carrier Daughter (25%)
	Y	XY Normal Son (25%)	XY Hemophilic Son (25%)

TABLE 3.2 *Sex-Linked Recessive Traits*

Condition	Description
Colorblindness	Inability to distinguish certain colors, usually reds and greens
Hemophilia	Deficiency in substances that allow the blood to clot; also known as *bleeder's disease*
Muscular dystrophy	Weakening and wasting away of muscles, beginning in childhood (Duchenne's form)
Diabetes (two forms)	Inability to metabolize sugars properly because the body does not produce enough insulin
Anhidrotic ectodermal dysplasia	Lack of sweat glands and teeth
Night blindness (certain forms)	Inability to see in dark or very dim conditions
Deafness (certain forms)	Impaired hearing or total hearing loss
Atrophy of optic nerve	Gradual deterioration of vision and eventual blindness

Note: All of the above traits are carried by the X chromosome, and all are recessive. As a result, they occur less often in females than in males.

GENETIC ABNORMALITIES

Once in awhile, genetic reproduction goes wrong. Sometimes too many or too few chromosomes transfer to a newly forming zygote. Sometimes the chromosomes transfer properly but carry particular defective genes that affect a child physically, mentally, or both. The changes almost always create significant disabilities for the child, if they do not prove fatal. Table 3.3 lists some common genetic abnormalities and the risk of their presence at birth.

Disorders Due to Abnormal Chromosomes

Most of the time, inheriting one too many or one too few chromosomes proves fatal. In a few cases, however, children with an extra or a missing chromosome survive past birth and even live fairly normal lives. One such example is Down syndrome.

Down Syndrome   People with **Down syndrome** have almond-shaped eyes, round heads, and stubby hands and feet. Many also have abnormalities of the heart and intestinal tract, and facial deformities. They also show greater than usual vulnerability to a number of serious diseases, such as leukemia. Most children with Down syndrome live until middle adulthood, but about 14 percent die by age one and 21 percent die by age ten.

Children with Down syndrome achieve many of the same developmental milestones normal children do, but at a much slower pace. Many children with Down syndrome learn to manage a good deal of their own lives and are able to hold routine jobs. Because their intellectual and psychosocial limitations prevent them from being fully independent, self-supporting adults, children with Down syndrome generally require extensive, ongoing support from their families and community service programs (Sloper et al., 1990; Stratford, 1994).

Children with Down syndrome, like this girl, learn academic material very slowly. But with special educational help and proper social support, they can lead satisfying lives.

TABLE 3.3   *Risk of Selected Genetic Disorders*

Disorder	Description	Risk of Having a Fetus with the Disorder	
		Overall	*With One Affected Child*
Chromosomal			
Down syndrome	Extra chromosome. Symptoms include almond-shaped eyes, round head, stubby hands and feet, abnormalities of the heart and intestinal tract, facial deformities, and vulnerability to disease. Most children with Down syndrome live until middle adulthood, but about 14 percent die by age one and 21 percent die by age ten.	1/800	1–2%
Klinefelter syndrome (XXY)	At least one extra chromosome, usually an X. Affected individual is phenotypically male, but has small testes and is sterile.	1/800 men	N/S[1]
Turner syndrome (XO)	Affects only females born with a single X in the sex chromosome. Grow to be very short as adults, "webbed" necks and ears set lower than usual; fail to develop secondary sexual characteristics; problems with spacial judgment, memory, and reasoning.	1/3,000 women	N/S[1]
Dominant Gene			
Polydactyly	Extra fingers or toes. Fairly common. Correctable by surgery.	1/300–1/100	50%
Achondroplasia	Rare disorder of the skeleton; afflicted person has shorter than normal arms and legs.	1/2,300	50%
Huntington disease	Usually first affects people in their 30s and 40s; gradual deterioration of the central nervous system, causing uncontrollable movements, mental deterioration, and death.	1/15,000–1/5,000	50%
Recessive Gene			
Cystic fibrosis	The most common genetic disease among white persons of Northern European descent. Abnormally thick mucus clogs the lungs, causing serious difficulties in breathing and digestion, delayed growth and sexual maturation, high vulnerability to infection, and shortened life expectancy.	1/2,500 white persons (risk of being a carrier is 1/25)	25%
Sickle-cell disease	Abnormal, sickle-shaped red blood cells clog blood vessels, reducing blood supply and causing pain. May cause increased bacterial infections and degeneration of brain, kidneys, liver, heart, spleen, and muscles. Shortened lifespan.	1/625 African Americans (risk of being a carrier is 1/10)	25%
Tay-Sachs disease	Found mostly in persons of Eastern European Jewish descent. Chemical imbalance of central nervous system. Symptoms first occur at six months of age, progressively causing severe mental retardation, blindness, seizures, and death by third year due to lowered resistance to disease.	1/3,600 Eastern European Jews (risk of being a carrier is 1/30–1/300)	25%
X Linked			
Hemophilia	Lack of substance needed for blood clotting. Risk of life-threatening internal bleeding; risk of AIDS from transfusions.	1/2,500 male babies	50% for boy, 0% for girl
Multifactorial			
Congenital heart disease	Structural and/or electrical abnormalities of the heart. May respond to medication or corrective surgery performed after birth.	1/125	2–4%
Neural tube defect	Tube enclosing the spine fails to close completely or normally. Brain may be absent or underdeveloped (anencephaly) or spinal cord and nerve bundles may be exposed. Death or severe retardation or other long-term problems for children who survive.	1–2/1,000	2–5%
Cleft lip/cleft palate	Gap or space in lip or hole in roof of mouth. May cause difficulties in breathing, speech, hearing, and eating. Corrective surgery at birth can repair most clefts.	1/1,000–1/5,000	2–4%

[1]No significant increase.

Sources: ACOG (1990); Blatt (1988); Diamond (1989); Selekman (1993); Stratford (1994)

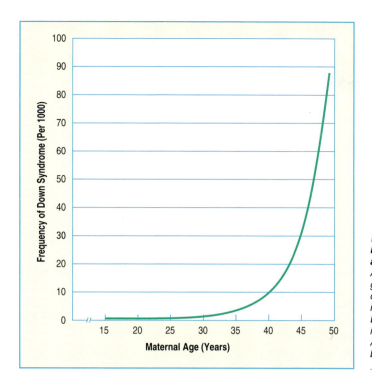

FIGURE 3.8
Relationship Between Maternal Age and Incidence of Down Syndrome
As women get older, their chances of giving birth to a baby with Down syndrome increase. At age twenty-one, 1 in every 1,500 babies is born with Down syndrome. At age thirty-nine, 1 in 150 babies is born with the disorder. At age forty-nine, 1 in 10 babies is born with Down.

Down syndrome is much more frequent in babies of mothers over age thirty-five and among older fathers. As women grow older, they experience longer exposure to environmental hazards, such as chemicals and radiation, that may affect their ovaries. In addition, since a woman's ova are formed before she is born, they are likely to undergo progressive deterioration with age (Baird & Sadovnick, 1987; Feinbloom & Forman, 1987). As we will see in Chapter 14's discussion of physical development in middle adulthood, older fathers are at risk because their sperm cells have divided so many times that there are many opportunities for errors (Angier, 1994). Figure 3.8 summarizes the risk of having a Down syndrome baby for women of different ages.

Abnormal Genes

Even when a zygote has the proper number of chromosomes, it may inherit specific genes that can create serious medical problems for the child after birth. In many cases, these problems prove lethal. In others, genetic diseases are at least manageable, if not fully curable.

As Table 3.3 shows, there are four main types of genetic disorders: dominant gene disorders, recessive gene disorders, X-linked disorders, and multifactorial gene disorders.

Dominant Gene Disorders   Dominant gene disorders require only one abnormal gene from either parent to affect a child. Figure 3.9 illustrates the inheritance of a dominant gene disorder.

Huntington Disease   Huntington disease is a dominant gene disorder that results in a gradual deterioration of the central nervous system, causing uncontrollable movements and mental deterioration. Typically it does not appear until affected people are in their thirties or forties, and it always proves fatal. Before that age, people usually have no way of knowing whether they will get the disease (ACOG, 1990).

FIGURE 3.9
Inheritance of a Dominant Gene Disorder
When one parent has a dominant gene disorder, each child has a 50 percent chance of inheriting the dominant abnormal gene for the disorder (D) and a 50 percent chance of inheriting a pair of recessive genes (rr) and being unaffected.

		Affected Parent (Has the Disorder)	
		D	r
Normal Parent	r	Dr Affected (25%)	rr Normal (25%)
	r	Dr Affected (25%)	rr Normal (25%)
		(50%)	(50%)

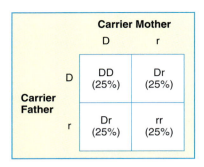

| | **Carrier Mother** | |
	D	r
Carrier Father D	DD (25%)	Dr (25%)
r	Dr (25%)	rr (25%)

FIGURE 3.10
Inheritance of a Recessive Gene Disorder
When both parents are carriers of a recessive gene disorder, each child faces the following possibilities: (1) a 25 percent chance of inheriting the pair of recessive genes (rr) required to have the disorder; (2) a 25 percent chance of inheriting a pair of dominant genes (DD) and being unaffected; or (3) a 50 percent chance of inheriting one dominant and one recessive gene (Dr) and being a carrier like both parents.

Researchers have recently identified specific sections of human genome that are exclusively linked to Huntington disease. The gene for the disorder appears to be located somewhere on chromosome four. Although it may now be possible to develop a genetic blood test for Huntington, an understanding of how the gene actually causes the disease and treatments are likely to be many years away (Horgan, 1993).

Recessive Gene Disorders   Recessive gene disorders can occur when the fetus inherits a pair of recessive genes, one from each parent. Figure 3.10 illustrates the inheritance of a recessive gene disorder.

Sickle-Cell Disease   About 1 in 635 African Americans are affected with sickle-cell disease, and about 1 in 10 are carriers of it. Sickle-cell disease is especially common in tropical climates such as Africa, the Mediterranean, India, and the Middle East. (ACOG, 1990).

In **sickle cell disease**, the oxygen-carrying protein in the red blood cells takes on an abnormal, rigid sickle shape inside the cells, which get caught in the blood vessels, cutting off circulation, reducing oxygen supply, and causing pain. Other symptoms include increased bacterial infections and degeneration of organs that need a great deal of oxygen, including the brain, kidneys, liver, heart, spleen, and muscles. Infants with sickle cell disease must be given daily doses of oral penicillin beginning at two months of age to reduce the chance of infection. Even with careful care, however, the majority of victims die before age twenty and few live past age forty (Diamond, 1989; Selekman, 1993).

Individuals who are *heterozygous,* meaning they carry just one abnormal sickle-cell allele along with one dominant, non-sickle-cell allele, show a few signs of sickle-cell disease but also a strong immunity to malaria. Most live normal lives, but when deprived of sufficient oxygen, such as during intense physical exercise or at high altitudes, the sickling of their red blood cells can be triggered, causing pain. Individuals avoid sickle-cell disease completely by having two dominant genes or suffer badly from it because they have two recessive genes. Although no cure exists yet for this disease, a new drug called *hydroxyurea* appears to reduce the production of sickle cells by switching on a gene that triggers the production of fetal hemoglobin, a type produced by babies before and shortly after birth that does not sickle (Leary, 1995).

Multifactorial Disorders   *Multifactorial disorders* result from a combination of genetic and environmental factors. The incidence of these disorders varies widely in different parts of the world, largely because of the great differences in existing environmental conditions. Table 3.3 describes a number of these disorders.

What Do You Think?

Woody Guthrie, the famous folk singer and father of Arlo Guthrie (also a famous folk singer), died of Huntington disease. Based on your new knowledge about this disorder, what questions might you ask Arlo about how his genetic inheritance has affected his life decisions, such as whether or not to have children?

GENETIC COUNSELING AND PRENATAL DIAGNOSIS

Some genetic problems can be reduced or avoided with the help of genetic counseling. Couples likely to benefit from counseling include those who may carry genetic disorders, know of relatives with genetic disorders, or belong to an ethnic group at risk for a particular disorder, such as African Americans, who are at risk for sickle-cell disease. More immediate signs of genetic risk include the birth of an infant with

TABLE 3.4　Who Should Seek Prenatal Counseling?

1. Couples who already have a child with some serious defect such as Down syndrome, spina bifida, congenital heart disease, limb malformation, or mental retardation
2. Couples with a family history of a genetic disease or mental retardation
3. Couples who are blood relatives (first or second cousins)
4. African Americans, Ashkenazi Jews, Italians, Greeks, and other high-risk ethnic groups
5. Women who have had a serious infection early in pregnancy (rubella or toxoplasmosis) or who have been infected with AIDS
6. Women who have taken potentially harmful medications early in pregnancy or who habitually use drugs or alcohol
7. Women who have had X rays taken early in pregnancy
8. Women with two or more of the following: stillbirth, death of newborn baby, miscarriage
9. Any woman thirty-five years or older

Source: Adapted from Feinbloom & Forman (1987) p. 129.

some genetic disorder or the spontaneous abortion of earlier pregnancies. Table 3.4 presents guidelines for determining who should seek prenatal genetic counseling.

Genetic counselors use potential parents' medical and genetic histories and tests to help couples estimate their chances of having a healthy baby and discuss alternatives from which a couple can choose. Two obvious alternatives are to avoid conception completely or take the chance of conceiving a healthy baby.

Modern medical techniques offer two additional options. Sometimes prenatal diagnosis can be used to detect genetic disorders after conception but before birth. Table 3.5 describes current diagnostic techniques to screen for genetic disorders. In addition, medical intervention early in infancy may help repair damage caused by a genetic disorder, depending on the severity.

Differences in cultural beliefs and expectations can affect who receives genetic counseling and the forms it takes. The accompanying Multicultural View box discusses this issue.

What Do You Think?

Do modern medical techniques unwittingly maintain several hereditary disorders by using heroic measures to keep alive severely impaired newborns who in the past might have died? If so, does this pose an ethical problem?

TABLE 3.5　Conditions That Prenatal Diagnosis Can Detect

Procedure	Timing	Conditions Detected
Ultrasound	Throughout pregnancy	Pregnancy; multiple pregnancies; fetal growth and abnormalities such as limb defects; tubal (ectopic) pregnancy; multiple pregnancies; atypical fetal position; fetal abnormalities (e.g., limb defects).
Amniocentesis	14–18 weeks	Chromosomal disorders such as Down syndrome; neurological disorders; gender of the baby
Chorionic villus sampling (CVS)	9–13 weeks	Tests for most of the same genetic disorders as amniocentesis, but is less sensitive to more subtle abnormalities
Fetoscopy	15–18 weeks	Used to confirm results from a prior prenatal test or to assess the severity of a disability already identified
Maternal serum alpha-fetoprotein (MSAFP)	15–18 weeks	Various problems, including neural tube defects and Down syndrome; positive first test is followed by additional testing, such as ultrasound and amniocentesis
Percutaneous umbilical blood sampling (PUBS)	18–36 weeks	Down syndrome, neural tube defects, Tay-Sachs disease, cystic fibrosis, sickle-cell disease; gender of the fetus; fetal infections such as rubella, toxoplasmosis, or AIDS

Sources: Feinbloom & Forman (1987); Blatt (1988); D'Alton & DeCherney (1993); ACOG (1990).

A Multicultural View

Cultural Difference and Genetic Counseling

The growing Asian American population in the United States tends to use genetic counseling infrequently. Reasons for this include lack of information and misperceptions about such services and cultural attitudes that strongly discourage seeking outside help for family problems.

In traditional Asian cultures, the family is the most important social unit. It is a source of material, social, and emotional support for its members and is responsible for maintaining the cultural and religious traditions that connect the present generation with past and future ones. The personal decisions and actions of an individual regarding pregnancy and genetic counseling reflect not only on herself but on her *nuclear family* (spouse and children), her *extended family* (parents, siblings, and other relatives), and *past and future generations* of her family (Chan, 1991; Wang & Marsh, 1992). John Roland, a psychologist who has studied personality development in India and Japan, believes that in addition to an *individual* and *spiritual* sense of self, individuals growing up in such traditional societies develop a powerful *familial* self. Within this sense of self, a person experiences himself as an inseparable part of the family unit and one whose actions will be largely determined by family needs and expectations (Roland, 1988).

Three other areas of cultural difference are important for genetic counselors to understand: (1) *collective versus* *personal autonomy,* (2) *shame and stigma,* and (3) *directive versus nondirective authority* (Wang & Marsh, 1992).

Collective Versus Personal Autonomy

A belief in *personal autonomy* is a cornerstone of Western genetic counseling, which views the patient as a self-determining individual who is largely free from the external control of family and other outside influences. The counselor's goal is to help the patient make an informed, autonomous decision about what is best by providing information in a nondirective and value-free way. This approach, however, frequently conflicts with cultural expectations of Asian patients, who hold a *collective* view of autonomy.

Collective autonomy presumes that a patient is an inseparable part of the traditional family unit and one whose actions will be largely determined by family interests. Family roles and responsibilities are rigidly and hierarchically defined based on generation, age, and gender, with the father occupying a position of unquestioned leadership and authority. This pattern serves to minimize family conflict by allowing little room for individuality and independence on the part of its members and to maintain family harmony and further the family's welfare and reputation (Wang & Marsh, 1992; Roland, 1988).

RELATIVE INFLUENCE OF HEREDITY AND ENVIRONMENT

Untangling the effects of heredity from those of environment has become the special focus of behavior genetics. *Behavior genetics* is the scientific study of how genetic inheritance (*genotype*) and environmental experience jointly influence physical and behavioral development (*phenotype*).

Key Concepts of Behavior Genetics

Every characteristic of an organism is the result of the unique interaction between the organism's genetic inheritance and the sequence of environments through which it has passed during its development. For some traits, variations in environment have minimal effect. Thus, once the genotype is known, the eventual form or phenotype of the organism is pretty well specified. For other traits, knowing the genetic makeup may be a poor predictor of the eventual phenotype. Only by specifying both the genotype and the environmental sequence can the character, or phenotype, of the organism be predicted.

Range of Reaction   **Range of reaction** refers to the range of possible phenotypes an individual with a particular genotype might exhibit in response to the specific sequence of environmental influences he or she experiences (Gottesman, 1963;

Shame and Stigma

In traditional Asian culture, which places tremendous importance on successfully marrying off a daughter, infertility is viewed as a handicapping stigma that will make a young woman unmarriageable and bring shame to herself and her family. Such problems are therefore managed within the family. To seek outside help from a genetic counselor would be a public admission of failure (Sue & Zane, 1987; Wang & Marsh, 1992).

Directive Versus Nondirective Authority

A *nondirective approach to authority* is a second cornerstone of genetic counseling that directly conflicts with the cultural expectations of Asian patients. This approach assumes the patient is responsible for making her own decisions and should not be influenced by the counselor's own views and values. In contrast, the *directive approach* assumes that as an expert authority, the counselor should provide the patient with clear and highly structured guidance about what he should do.

The directive approach is much more consistent with the authority relations and role expectations in Asian families. It therefore is more likely to relieve high levels of anxiety, shame, and doubt by providing practical and immediate solutions to problems (Wang & Marsh, 1992). Stanley Sue, who has written extensively about these issues, suggests that families from Asian and other traditional cultures will seek help from professionals who earn credibility and trust by responding to their need for directive, immediate assistance while also working with them to achieve more self-directed, long-term solutions (Sue & Zane, 1987).

As in the case of this multigenerational Asian American family, effective genetic counseling must be responsive to cultural differences.

Turkheimer & Gottesman, 1991). For example, if three infants start life with different genetic inheritances (genotypes) for intelligence—one low, one middle, and one high—the different levels of intelligence they actually develop (phenotypes), as measured by IQ tests, will depend on how well each child's intellectual development is nurtured by his or her experiences from conception onward, including the conditions created by the child's family, school, and community. Thus, in an enriched environment, the child with low genetic endowment may achieve an IQ that is actually equal to (or even higher than) that of the child with a middle-range endowment who grows up in a restricted or below-average environment. Nevertheless, the first child cannot be expected to achieve an IQ score equal to that of children with high genetic endowment, because this is beyond the upper limit of that child's range of reaction, that is, the highest level of intellectual functioning possible for that child. Figure 3.11 illustrates range of reaction for intelligence. Theorists such as Robert Sternberg (1988) and Howard Gardner (1990a), however, believe intelligence consists of several different factors or dimensions, and thus range of reaction may differ according to which aspect of intelligence is being measured. We will look more closely at these theories when we examine cognitive development in middle childhood in Chapter 8.

Adoption and Twin Studies

Adoption Studies   **Adoption studies** compare the degree of physical or behavioral similarity between adoptive children and members of their adoptive families (with

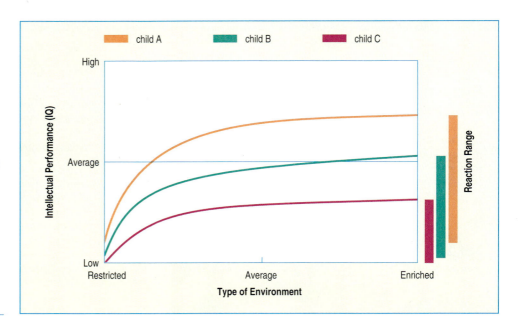

FIGURE 3.11

Range of Reaction for Intellectual Performance

Range of reaction *refers to the range of possible phenotypes as a result of different environments interacting with a specific genotype. As this figure shows, while intellectual performance will be retarded or facilitated for all children depending on whether the environment is restricted, average, or enriched, the range of potential intellectual performance in reaction to different environments will be limited by the child's genetic inheritance for intelligence.*
Source: Gottesman (1963); Turkheimer & Gottesman (1991).

whom they have little in common genetically) with the degree of physical or behavioral similarity between these same children and members of their biological families (with whom they share half of their genes). If adoptive children share similar environments (but not genes) with their adoptive family members, differences in trait similarity to their adoptive versus biological relatives should tell something about the influence of their genetic differences. For example, if the IQ scores of adopted children correlated more highly with the IQ scores of their biological families than with those of their adoptive families, we might conclude that heredity made a strong contribution to intelligence. However, if the IQ scores of these adoptive children were significantly higher (or lower) than those of their biological parents, this might also indicate the influence of family circumstances and other environmental factors.

Shared genes or shared experiences? Studies of genetically identical twins who are reared in different environments from birth attempt to evaluate the degree to which shared behavioral characteristics are determined by shared genes versus shared experiences.

Separated at birth, the Mallifert twins meet accidentally.

Twin Studies   **Twin studies** compare pairs of *identical twins* raised in the same family with pairs of *fraternal twins* (50 percent shared genes) raised in the same family. Since identical twins have the exact same genetic makeup, greater similarity between identical twins than between fraternal twins on a trait such as intelligence would probably reflect the influence of heredity.

Twin Adoption Studies   **Twin adoption studies** compare pairs of identical twins who are raised apart since birth in different environments. Twin adoption studies provide the most effective method for understanding the gene-environment relationship in humans. If we could study identical twins who inherit exactly the same genes but are raised in truly different family environments, we would be able to separate the relative contributions of heredity and environment. The catch is to find twins who are growing up in adoptive families. An additional problem is that adoptive families are most frequently chosen with the goal of offering twins similar socioeconomic, cultural, and religious conditions and experiences, raising the question of how different their adoptive family environments really are.

Linkage and Association Studies   Linkage and association studies allow researchers to identify *polymorphisms,* certain segments of human DNA that are inherited together in a predictable pattern—as genetic markers for the genes near which they are located. *Linkage studies* seek to discover polymorphisms that are coinherited, or "linked," with a particular trait in families unusually prone to that trait. This was the case in the discovery of a genetic marker for Huntington disease, which was described earlier in this chapter. *Association studies* compare the relative frequency of polymorphisms in two populations, one with the trait and one without it (Horgan, 1993).

Cautions and Conclusions about the Influence of Heredity and Environment

While substantial evidence exists that genetic inheritance plays at least a moderate role in differences in physical, intellectual, and personality traits, it is likely that such differences are due to *both* heredity and environmental experience. Currently, however, there is a growing trend toward minimizing environmental contributions in favor of *genetic determinism,* a belief that most, if not all, human characteristics, from intellectual functioning to gender roles and career choice, are determined primarily by genes. This tendency may in part be a reaction to *environmental determinism,* an equally simplistic view that sees experience as the central or sole cause of developmental change and dismisses the possibility that genes may also make a significant contribution. It may also reflect the explosive growth in biotechnology and the overly optimistic view it appears to have generated.

It is highly unlikely that either biogenetic or environmental determinism can ever lead to an adequate understanding of human characteristics. Rather, human development is always the product of multiple levels of influence of *both* genes and environment, be the influences molecular, biochemical, physical, social, or psychological.

What Do You Think?

Based on what you have just read, how do you view the relationship between genes and environment? To what degree do you believe most or all of human development will someday be explainable in terms of genetics? What unanswered questions do you have about these issues?

PRENATAL DEVELOPMENT AND BIRTH

From the moment of conception, a child becomes a biological entity. How do microscopic cells become people? In the following sections, we look at the events and processes that occur from conception through birth and how they may affect later development. We also look at how certain risks and problems of prenatal development and of birth and their long-term impact on the child.

STAGES OF PRENATAL DEVELOPMENT

Prenatal development begins with conception and continues through discrete periods, or stages. The first is the **germinal stage,** or *period of the ovum,* which occurs during the first two weeks of pregnancy; the second is the **embryonic stage,** which lasts from the third week to the eighth week; and the third is the **fetal stage,** which lasts from the eighth week until birth.

Conception

Conception occurs when, following intercourse, a sperm from the father successfully attaches itself to the surface of an ovum, or egg, from the mother. Once it becomes attached, the sperm gradually penetrates the egg. Within a few hours, the walls of the sperm cell and the *nucleus,* or center, of the egg cell both begin to disintegrate. In this process, as Figure 3.12 shows, the sperm and egg cells each release their chromosomes, which join to form a new cell called a zygote.

At this point, the zygote is still so small that hundreds of them could fit on the head of a pin. Yet it contains all of the necessary genetic information in its DNA molecules to develop into a unique human being.

The Germinal Stage (First Two Weeks)

The newly formed zygote now begins to divide and redivide to form a tiny sphere called a *blastocyst,* which looks something like a miniature mulberry. The blasto-

FIGURE 3.12
Gametes and Zygote
Each gamete, whether sperm or ovum, contains twenty-three single chromosomes. (Two chromosomes are shown in each gamete here.) At fertilization, sperm and ovum combine to form a zygote with forty-six chromosomes in twenty-three pairs. (Two pairs are shown here.) In each pair, one chromosome is from the mother and one is from the father.

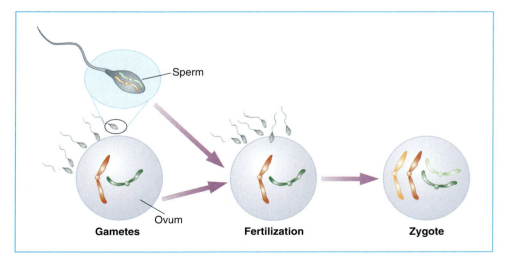

Sperm

Ovum

Gametes   **Fertilization**   **Zygote**

cyst differentiates into three layers. The *ectoderm* (upper layer) later develops into the epidermis, or outer layer of skin, nails, teeth, and hair, as well as the sensory organs and nervous system. The *endoderm* (lower layer) becomes the digestive system, liver, pancreas, salivary glands, and respiratory system. The *mesoderm* (middle layer) develops somewhat later and becomes the dermis (inner layer of skin), muscles, skeleton, and circulatory and excretory systems. In a short time the *placenta, umbilical cord,* and *amniotic sac* (to be discussed shortly) also will form from blastocyst cells.

After a few more days—about one week after conception—implantation occurs. During *implantation,* the blastocyst buries itself like a seed in the wall of the uterus. The fully implanted blastocyst is now referred to as the *embryo.* Figure 3.13 illustrates the changes that occur during the germinal stage of prenatal development.

The Embryonic Stage
(Third Through Eighth Weeks)

Growth during the embryonic stage (and the fetal stage that follows) occurs in two patterns: a *cephalocaudal* (head-to-tail) pattern and a *proximodistal* (near-to-far, from the center of the body outward) pattern. Thus, the head, blood vessels, and heart—the most vital body parts and organs—begin to develop earlier than the arms, legs, hands, and feet. Figure 3.14 (upper portion) on page 88 illustrates these changes.

At *three weeks,* the head, tail, brain, and circulatory system begin to develop and the heart has begun beating. At *four weeks,* the embryo is not much more than an inch long. The beginnings of a spinal cord, arms, and legs are evident, a small digestive system and a nervous system have developed, and the brain has become more differentiated (P. Harris, 1983). During *week five,* hands and lungs begin to form. During *week six,* the head grows larger, the brain becomes more fully developed, and hands, legs, and feet become more fully formed. During *week seven,* muscles form and the cerebral cortex begins to develop. By *week eight,* external genitals, fingers, and toes appear and facial features can be distinguished.

FIGURE 3.13
The Germinal Stage of Prenatal Development
The sperm and ovum join to form a single-celled zygote, *which then divides and redivides and becomes a multicelled* blastocyst. *The blastocyst buries, or* implants, *itself in the uterine wall. The fully implanted blastocyst is now called an* embryo.

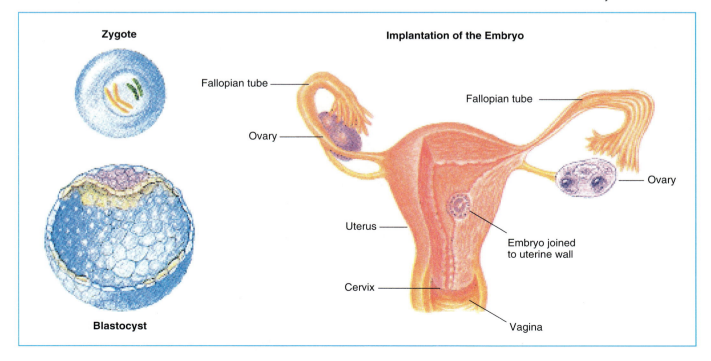

Zygote

Implantation of the Embryo

Fallopian tube

Fallopian tube

Ovary

Ovary

Uterus

Embryo joined to uterine wall

Cervix

Blastocyst

Vagina

While these developments are taking place, a placenta forms between the mother and the embryo. The **placenta** is an area on the uterine wall through which the mother supplies oxygen and nutrients to the embryo and the embryo returns waste products from her bloodstream. In the placenta, thousands of tiny blood vessels from the two circulatory systems intermingle. Although only minute quantities of blood can cross the separating membranes, nutrients pass easily from one bloodstream to the other through a process called *osmosis*. Although many toxic chemicals and drugs in the mother's system do not spread easily by osmosis, others do. As we discuss later, seemingly harmless chemicals sometimes prove devastating to the child.

The **umbilical cord** connects the embryo to the placenta. It consists of three large blood vessels, one to provide nutrients and two to carry waste products into the mother's body. The cord enters the embryo at a place that becomes the baby's belly button, or navel, after the cord is cut following birth.

By the end of the eighth week, an amniotic sac has developed. The **amniotic sac** is a tough, spongy bag filled with salty fluid that completely surrounds the embryo and serves to protect it from sudden jolts and maintain a fairly stable temperature. The embryo floats gently in this environment until birth, protected even if its mother goes jogging, sits down suddenly, or shovels heavy snow.

The Fetal Stage (Ninth Week to Birth)

At about *eight weeks* of gestation, the embryo develops its first bone cells, which marks the end of differentiation into the major structures. At this point the embryo acquires a new name, the *fetus,* and begins the long process of developing relatively small features, such as fingers and fingernails and eyelids and eyebrows. Their smallness, however, belies their importance. For example, the eyes undergo their greatest growth during this stage of development. The fetus's newly developing eyelids fuse shut at about ten weeks and do not reopen until the eyes themselves are essentially complete, at around twenty-six weeks.

Not only the eyes but most other physical features become more adult looking during this period and more truly human in proportion (P. Harris, 1983). The head becomes smaller relative to the rest of the body (even though it remains large by adult standards), partly because the fetus's long bones, the ones supporting its limbs, begin growing significantly. Thus, its arms and legs look increasingly substantial.

By *twelve weeks,* the fetus is about three inches long and able to respond reflexively to touch. By *sixteen weeks,* it has grown to about 4½ inches in length. If its palm is touched, it exhibits a grasp reflex by closing its fist; if the sole of its foot is touched, its toes spread (Babinski reflex); and if its lips are touched, it responds with a sucking reflex. In addition, the fetal heartbeat can now be heard through the wall of the uterus.

Between the *fourth* and *fifth months* (sixteen to twenty weeks), hands and feet become fully developed, eyes can open and close, hearing is present, lungs become capable of breathing in and out, and nails, hair, and sweat glands develop. Around the sixteenth week, most pregnant women feel *quickening,* the movement of the fetus inside the womb. Fetal movements appear to grow progressively stronger and more frequent from eighteen weeks on, reaching a maximum between twenty-eight and twenty-nine weeks, after which they diminish somewhat until delivery (Primeau, 1993).

By the beginning of the *seventh month,* the fetus is about sixteen inches long and weighs approximately three to five pounds. It is able to cry, breathe, swallow, digest, excrete, move about, and suck its thumb. The reflexes mentioned earlier are fully developed. Because of these capacities, the fetus is said to have attained *age of viability,* meaning it could survive if born at this point.

By the *eighth month,* the fetus weighs between five and seven pounds and has begun to develop a layer of body fat that will help it to regulate its body tempera-

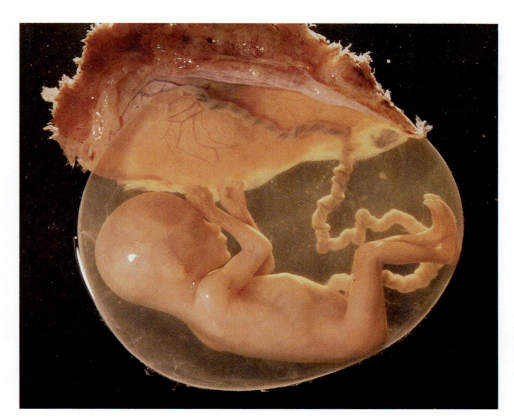

During the middle trimester of pregnancy, the fetus grows rapidly. By sixteen weeks, the fetus looks quite human, but it still cannot survive outside the womb.

ture after birth, and by *nine months* it has achieved its full birth weight. Toward the end of nine months, the average baby is about 7.5 pounds and almost 20 inches long. Growth in size stops, although fat continues to be stored, heart rate increases, and internal organ systems become more efficient in preparation for birth and independent life outside the womb.

The developing fetus is also responsive to stimuli in the external environment such as sound and vibration (Kisilevsky et al., 1992). For example, newborn infants have been found to show preferences for stories and rhymes read aloud to them during the final six weeks of pregnancy (DeCasper et al., 1994).

Infertility

Letisha and Alvin had always wanted children, but put off conceiving until both were in their early thirties and had established successful careers. After almost two frustrating years of unsuccessful attempts at conception, they finally decided to go to a fertility clinic to get help in finding out what might be causing the problem and what could be done about it.

Alvin and Letisha's situation is not uncommon. Approximately 15 percent of American couples experience *infertility,* meaning they are unable to conceive or carry a pregnancy to term after one year of unprotected intercourse. In about 80 to 90 percent of couples receiving medical treatment, it is possible to discover a clear medical reason for their infertility (ACOG, 1990; Greil, 1993a). We will look at the problem of infertility more closely when we discuss physical development in early adulthood in Chapter 12.

A growing number of new reproductive technologies are now available as alternatives to normal conception for couples who are infertile. These alternatives are discussed in the accompanying Perspectives box.

Perspectives

Technological Alternatives to Normal Conception

Earlier in this century, the only alternative for couples who were infertile was to adopt a child or to remain childless. But today's medical techniques offer a growing number of alternative options. These alternatives vary in practicality and popularity, but from a strictly medical standpoint they all work fairly reliably.

Artificial (donor) insemination (DI) is used in cases where infertility is caused by problems in sperm quality or production. In this procedure, fresh or previously frozen sperm from a donor are inserted into the woman's vagina and held in place for a few hours. While in most cases the donor is anonymous, he can also be a friend or a relative. Artificial insemination is safe and easy to carry out and induces pregnancy as effectively as does normal intercourse between fertile partners—a 20 percent success rate in any one month (Liebmann-Smith, 1993; Silber, 1991). A controversial application of artificial insemination is *surrogate mothering,* in which sperm from the future father are inserted into the womb of a woman who agrees (usually for a fee) to give up the baby once it is born.

In vitro fertilization (IVF) is used if both eggs and sperm are normal and infertility is caused by blocked fallopian tubes that cannot be surgically repaired. With IVF, ovulation is induced with medications that cause multiple eggs to be produced. With the aid of a laparoscope or ultrasound, one or more eggs are then removed through the woman's vagina under local anesthesia. They are mixed in a laboratory dish with sperm from the male and allowed to fertilize in an incubator. Two days later, the fertilized egg or embryo is transferred back into the woman's uterus through her vagina. Additional embryos can be frozen (cryopreserved) for future use. Although fertilization rates are high, getting the embryos to implant is much harder to achieve. Pregnancy rates with IVF are about 15 percent (Liebmann-Smith, 1993; Silber, 1991).

Gamete intrafallopian tube transfer (GIFT), a variation of IVF, solves the implantation problem and can be used by women with healthy fallopian tubes. The GIFT procedure is exactly the same as IVF, except that the sperm and eggs are both surgically placed directly into the woman's fallopian tube, where they are naturally

The Experience of Pregnancy

Sudah is nearing the end of her pregnancy—just eight weeks to go! She has been careful to eat a good, balanced diet and has gained about twenty-four pounds, which her doctor says is fine for her size and weight. Lately her belly feels like a basketball, and she sometimes worries whether Dan, her husband, still finds her attractive and whether she will ever get her normal figure back. During the first two months of pregnancy, Sudah felt nauseous a lot of the time and found it hard to keep food down. She found that eating small amounts of food (especially plain crackers) throughout the day helped, as did resting more frequently—which was hard to do, since she was still working full time.

Until recently, aside from getting tired more easily, Sudah has felt pretty good. During the last few weeks, however, she has had some swelling in her legs and some back pain, and has had to go to the bathroom much more frequently because of the pressure of the baby on her bladder. Although she and Dan can't wait for the baby to arrive, they are somewhat apprehensive about whether they are grown up enough to be parents and take on the responsibilities of parenthood.

Sudah's complaints are fairly typical of those associated with the hormonal and physiological changes of pregnancy. More than 50 percent of pregnant women experience some degree of nausea during the first trimester, but this usually disappears by the twelfth week. Strategies for relieving nausea include eating small amounts of food frequently, increasing protein intake, eating dry crackers or plain yogurt, and resting more often during the day. Frequent urination is another symptom of early pregnancy and is due to hormonally induced softening of the pelvic muscles, which allows the enlarged uterus to press on the bladder. Other symptoms include fatigue, headaches, dizziness and fainting, constipation, leg cramps, heartburn, shortness of breath, swelling of legs, hands, or face, varicose veins, and backache (Davis, 1993).

fertilized, and then moved to the uterus at the appropriate time. Pregnancy rates with GIFT are approximately three times higher than with IVF. With GIFT, it is also possible to use donor eggs when a woman no longer ovulates or has a genetic condition she wants to avoid passing on to her offspring (Silber, 1991).

Zygote intrafallopian transfer (ZIFT) is a modification of GIFT and IVF. After the egg and sperm are fertilized in the laboratory, the resulting embryo, or zygote, is placed in the fallopian tube rather than the uterus (with IVF, the "test-tube" embryo is placed in the uterus; with GIFT, the unfertilized sperm and eggs are placed in the fallopian tube). ZIFT is used when the sperm's ability to fertilize the woman's eggs is questionable. It also allows the surgeon to select and transfer only eggs that have been fertilized, thus increasing the chances of a pregnancy (Silber, 1991). GIFT and ZIFT produce identical pregnancy rates. However, whereas GIFT requires only a short (forty-five-minute) operation, ZIFT involves egg retrieval (aspiration) and in vitro fertilization, followed two days later by a procedure to transfer the embryo into the fallopian tube.

Finally, *micromanipulation (microfertilization)* is an experimental procedure in which a few sperm are microsurgically placed directly into the outside layer (zona) of the egg, making it possible for a man with very few viable sperm to fertilize his partner's egg.

What are the experiences of families with children conceived by the new reproductive technologies? In a recent British study that compared families with a child conceived by in vitro fertilization or donor insemination with families whose children were conceived naturally or adopted, Susan Golombok and her associates found no group differences in the quality of children's emotions, behavior, or overall relationships with their parents (Golombok et al., 1995). Mothers of IVF and DI children, in fact, showed greater warmth toward and deeper emotional involvement with their children, and both mother- and father-child interactions were more positive. At least for the families studied, genetic ties appeared to be less important for family functioning than a strong desire to become a parent.

In addition to the influence of hormonal changes, some of these symptoms are due to weight gain during pregnancy. Both a woman's weight before pregnancy and her weight gain during pregnancy influence the baby's birth weight. Current recommendations are that women of normal weight before pregnancy gain about thirty pounds, women who are overweight about twenty pounds, and women who are underweight about thirty-four pounds, with the exact amount reflecting the woman's height and prepregnancy weight.

Where does the weight gain go? The increased size of the uterus, breast tissue, blood volume, body fluid, and extra fat to prepare the woman to produce milk for breast feeding all contribute to the additional pounds (ACOG, 1990). Table 3.6 summarizes how the average weight gain during pregnancy is distributed.

Pregnancy is a powerful experience that can dramatically affect how both the mother and the father feel about themselves and each other. For most prospective parents, it raises the question "Am I ready to be emotionally and economically responsible for this baby?" Couples who are experiencing pregnancy together may

TABLE 3.6 *Average Weight Gain During Pregnancy*

Maternal stores (fat, protein, and other nutrients)	7.0 pounds
Increased fluid volume	4.0 pounds
Increased blood volume	4.0 pounds
Breast enlargement	2.0 pounds
Uterus	2.0 pounds
Baby	7.5 pounds
Amniotic fluid	2.0 pounds
Placenta	1.5 pounds
Total weight gain	30.0 pounds

Source: ACOG (1990).

Working with | Katie Glover, OB-GYN NURSE PRACTITIONER

Preparing for Childbirth

Katie Glover was interviewed in her office at the primary health care clinic where she works. Despite her hectic schedule, Katie has a relaxed and unhurried manner. She has a three-year-old son and is currently seven months pregnant. Our interview focused on preparation for childbirth.

Rob: What advice do you give pregnant women about their nutrition?

Katie: Pregnant women need three to four glasses of milk a day and should increase consumption of fruits and vegetables, which many people don't eat regularly. As a bottom line, we recommend a balanced diet plus a few extra calories and vitamin supplements. We also recommend a twenty-five-to-thirty-pound weight gain over the course of a pregnancy, depending on the woman's size, build, and weight.

Rob: Why do you recommend weight gain?

Katie: If you figure the average baby weighs roughly 6½ to 7½ pounds and the average placenta weighs maybe 3 to 5 pounds, and add the extra fluid a woman retains and extra subcutaneous fat her body stores as added protection, that's about twenty to twenty-five pounds right there.

Rob: How do weight gain and other changes of pregnancy affect women?

Katie: They certainly change their body image. How a woman feels about that directly relates to how she feels about being pregnant. Someone who's thrilled about pregnancy will be happy to see her belly getting bigger. Someone who resents the pregnancy is likely to have a harder time with her body's changes. It's not just that her breasts are getting larger or her stomach is getting bigger. She can't run up and down the stairs as easily, and she can't find a comfortable position to sleep in. Pregnancy gets in the

way of your life. You have to alter how you move and how you eat and how often you go to the bathroom—day and night. When all you really want is a good eight hours of sleep, you may start wondering if it's all worth it!

Rob: Pregnancy can be stressful, then.

Katie: Yes. In a way, pregnancy is a crisis. How a person copes with that crisis has a lot to do with her feelings about being pregnant as well as what her social and emotional support system is like. If her partner, parents, or friends provide good, solid support and appreciation for what she's experiencing, pregnancy is likely to be a more positive experience than if she doesn't have such support.

Rob: What preparation for childbirth do you offer your patients?

Katie: Most medical practices encourage some kind of childbirth classes.

---

wonder, "How will having a baby affect our relationship with each other?" We will take a closer look at these questions in Chapter 13's discussion of psychosocial development in early adulthood. See the interview with Katie Glover for a nurse-practitioner's observations regarding pregnancy and preparation for childbirth.

What Do You Think?

For those of you who have already experienced pregnancy, what was it like? For those of you who haven't, what do you imagine the experience might be like for you? How has what you have read so far in this chapter influenced your views about pregnancy?

PRENATAL INFLUENCES ON THE CHILD

Key Concepts

As we have noted, physical structures develop in a particular sequence and at fairly precise times. Psychologists and biologists sometimes call such regularity canalization. **Canalization** refers to the tendency of genes to narrowly direct or restrict growth and development of particular physical and behavioral characteristics to a single (or very few) phenotypic outcomes and to resist environmental factors that push development in other directions (McCall, 1981).

Classes typically cover the various stages of pregnancy, physiological and psychological changes a woman might experience, changes in the couple's relationship. We talk about labor and what the hospital will be like. We talk about the different kinds of pain medications that might be offered, their effects, and the risks and benefits. Most classes also teach basic relaxation and breathing techniques, which are very important. Knowing what to expect and how to deal with the anxiety and pain can really help make labor a more positive experience.

Rob: How do you feel about birth clinics and home deliveries?

Katie: For many people who don't want to give birth in a hospital, a birth center is ideal, whether it's freestanding or directly attached to a hospital. It offers a little more freedom of movement, a little more comfort, a different atmosphere, and reassurance that medical backup is available if needed, including quick transfer to a fully equipped hospital. Of course, parents who come to a birth center should be carefully screened beforehand for any potential medical complications.

Rob: What about home birth?

Katie: I think it's a good option for the very small percentage of people who are truly suited for it.

Rob: Why is that?

Katie: It takes a very high level of commitment to arrange a home birth. Real problems can arise if it's not something both partners agree on and believe in deeply. If both partners are always there for each other, if the home situation is a nice, clean, supportive place, and if a pediatrician and a well-trained, experienced obstetrician or midwife and good emergency medical backup are available, then go for it!

What Do You Think?

1. Katie suggests that pregnancy is a type of crisis and that how a woman copes with it will depend on her attitudes toward pregnancy and the social support she receives. How might this knowledge be used to design programs to help pregnant teenagers cope better with the "crisis" of pregnancy?

2. How might a woman's pregnancy affect the father and other family members?

3. Katie discusses alternatives to hospital birth. What additional information might you need to consider these alternatives for yourself?

Typically prenatal development is a highly reliable process, so prospective parents generally worry much more than they need to about whether their baby will be "all right." In fact, 97.5 percent of human infants are perfect at birth, and of the 2.5 percent who are not, half have only minor defects such as hammertoes, extra fingers or toes, or birthmarks (Guttmacher & Kaiser, 1984).

But certain conditions can interfere with even the highly canalized processes of fetal development. These conditions are sometimes called *risk factors*. Risk factors increase the chance that the future baby will have medical problems but do not guarantee that these problems will actually appear. Risk factors include the mother's biological characteristics, including age and physical condition, and exposure to diseases, drugs, chemicals, stress, and other environmental hazards during pregnancy.

As the complex sequence of prenatal growth proceeds, the timing of the development of each new organ or body part is especially important. **Critical period** refers to a time-limited period during which certain developmental changes are highly vulnerable to disruption. This "window of opportunity" is dictated by complex genetic codes in each cell *and* by the particular set of prenatal conditions that must be in place for each change to occur. If development is disturbed or blocked during a critical period, the changes that were scheduled to occur may be disrupted or prevented from occurring at all.

Especially during the early weeks of its life, development of the embryo is particularly vulnerable to disruption if it is exposed (through the mother) to certain harmful substances called *teratogens*. A **teratogen** is any substance or other environmental influence that can interfere with or permanently damage an embryo's growth. Named after an ancient Greek word meaning "monster-creating," teratogens can result in serious physical malformations and even the death of the embryo. Teratogens are most harmful if exposure occurs during the critical or sensitive period for the particular physical change to occur. Teratogens include many *medicinal and non-medicinal drugs; other chemicals; diseases* (viruses and bacteria); and certain *other harmful environmental influences,* such as radiation.

A teratogen's effects are influenced by several factors. The first is the *timing of exposure.* The nine months of pregnancy generally are divided into three *trimesters,* each lasting three months. Disruptions during the first trimester, when the critical periods for embryonic and fetal development occur, are most likely to result in spontaneous abortion or serious birth defects. During the third week, for example, teratogens can harm the basic structures of the heart and central nervous system that are just beginning to form. The effects of exposure in the second and third trimesters generally are less likely to be as severe. Figure 3.14 describes the effects of teratogens at different stages of prenatal development.

The impact of a teratogen is also influenced by the *intensity and duration of exposure.* For example, the higher the dose (intensity) and the longer the exposure to a harmful drug such as alcohol or cocaine, the greater the chances that the baby will be harmed and that the harm will be more severe than if dose and duration are less. The *number of other harmful influences* that are also present also makes a difference. The greater the number, the greater the risk. Finally, the *biogenetic vulnerability of the mother and the infant* will influence a teratogen's effects. Mothers and their infants will differ in the degree to which they will be affected by exposure to a particular type and level of teratogen. For example, whereas heavy and prolonged drinking is likely to affect almost all babies, very moderate drinking may cause considerable harm for one infant but no measurable harm for another.

FIGURE 3.14
Timing and Effects of Teratogens During Sensitive or Critical Periods
This figure illustrates the sensitive or critical periods in human development. The dark band indicates highly sensitive or critical periods; the light band indicates stages that are less sensitive to disruption caused by teratogens. Note that each structure has a critical period during which its development may be disrupted. Note also that development proceeds from head to tail (cephalocaudal) and from the center of the body outward (proximodistal).
Source: Reprinted from Before We Are Born: Basic Embryology and Birth Defects, 2nd ed., by K. L. Moore, p. 111, with permission of W. B. Saunders Company, ©1983.

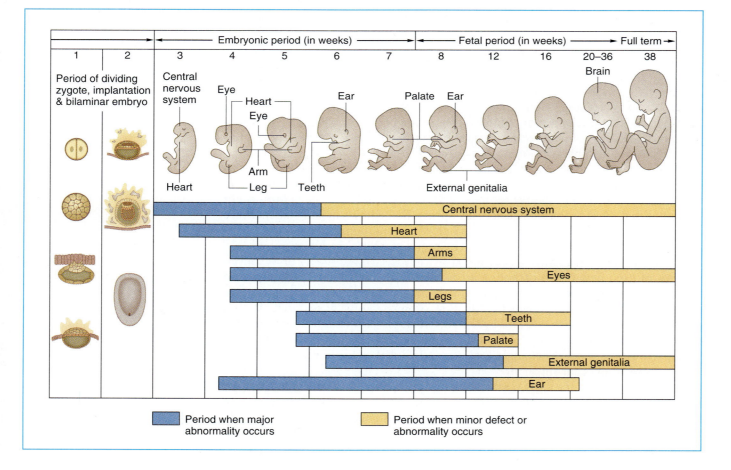

Maternal Age and Physical Characteristics

Healthy women over age thirty-five are not at significantly greater risk for any of these complications than younger women, although they are at greater risk for infertility and for having a child with Down syndrome (ACOG, 1990; Grimes & Gross, 1981; A. Stein, 1983). Very young mothers, especially those in their early teens, are at significantly greater risk of having low-birth-weight infants, stillbirths, or problems during delivery. This is partly because teenage mothers have not completed their own growth, so their bodies are unable to meet the extra nutritional demands of a developing fetus. Teenage mothers are more likely to be poor and less likely to get adequate prenatal care and have the maturity of judgment to adapt their lifestyles to the demands of pregnancy (Fraser et al., 1995; Furstenberg et al., 1989).

Maternal Diseases

Exposure of a pregnant woman to certain viral, bacteriological, and parasitic diseases can adversely affect her baby's development. Table 3.7 summarizes the teratogenic effects of exposure to selected diseases (and drugs) during pregnancy. In addition, some diseases can be directly transmitted from mother to fetus, often with devastating consequences; these include syphilis, gonorrhea, and AIDS.

Syphilis and Gonorrhea   A pregnant woman with untreated syphilis can transmit the disease to her fetus. In 25 percent of cases, death of the fetus results, usually during the second trimester. An additional 25 percent of infected fetuses die soon after birth. Of those who survive, about 25 percent show symptoms such as jaundice, anemia, pneumonia, skin rash, and bone inflammation (Blackman, 1990).

Fetuses that contract gonorrhea in the birth canal may later develop eye infections or become blind. It is now standard practice to put drops of silver nitrate or penicillin in newborns' eyes to protect them against these conditions, because gonorrhea may be present in the mother without obvious symptoms.

Pediatric AIDS   It is estimated that of the approximately 4 million babies born in the United States each year, between one thousand and two thousand will have HIV, the virus associated with the development of AIDS (Task Force on Pediatric AIDS, 1989; Lee, 1995). About three-fourths of AIDS cases in children involve perinatal (at the time of birth) transmission from an infected mother to her child, either through the placenta or through contact with HIV-contaminated blood at the time of delivery (American Academy of Pediatrics, 1991). In the majority of these cases, the mother's infection can be linked to her own intravenous (IV) drug use or that of her sexual partner. African American and Hispanic children from predominantly low-SES families make up three-quarters of all pediatric AIDS cases in the United States, although they account for only one-fourth of all American children. Because AIDS has an incubation period of up to five years in adults, pregnant women may be unaware that they have the virus or that it can be transmitted to their offspring. Although most children infected *perinatally* show symptoms before age one, some children who are infected may live for years without symptoms. Because newborns retain the protective antibodies they receive from their mothers for several months after birth, testing a newborn for HIV antibodies can give accurate information only about the mother (Lee, 1995; Richter, 1993).

Recent studies suggest that when the drug AZT is administered to AIDS-infected women during late pregnancy, administered intravenously during labor, and given intravenously to their newborns immediately after delivery, the risk of having an HIV-infected baby can be reduced by two-thirds (from 24 percent to about 8 percent) (Lee, 1995).

TABLE 3.7 *Teratogens and Their Effects*

Teratogen	Effects
Maternal Diseases	
Rubella	*First trimester:* blindness, deafness, heart defects, damage to central nervous system, mental retardation; *second trimester:* problems with hearing, vision, and language
Syphilis and gonorrhea	Fetal death, jaundice, anemia, pneumonia, skin rash, bone inflammation, dental deformities, hearing difficulties, blindness
Genital herpes	Disease of skin and mucous membranes, blindness, brain damage, seizures, and developmental delay
Cytomegalovirus	Jaundice, microcephaly (very small head), deafness, eye problems, increased risk for severe illness and infant death
AIDS	Abnormally small skull; facial deformities; immune system damage; enlarged lymph glands, liver, spleen; recurrent infections; poor growth; fever; brain disease; developmental delay; deteriorated motor skills
Toxoplasmosis	Spontaneous abortion, prematurity, low birth weight, enlarged liver and spleen, jaundice, anemia, congenital defects, mental retardation, seizures, cerebral palsy, retinal disease, blindness
Drugs	
Medicinal Drugs	
Thalidomide	Birth defects such as missing, shortened, or misshapen arms and legs, deafness; severe facial deformities; seizure disorders; dwarfism; brain damage; fetal/infant death
Diethylstilbestrol (DES)	*Grown daughters:* vaginal and cervical cancer; spontaneous abortions and stillbirth; autoimmune disorders such as pernicious anemia, myasthenia gravis (a nerve-muscle disorder), intestinal disorder, multiple sclerosis; *grown sons:* abnormalities in reproductive organs, testicular cancer
Nonmedicinal Drugs	
Heroin	Withdrawal symptoms, including vomiting, trembling, irritability, fever, disturbed sleep, an abnormally high-pitched cry; delayed social and motor development
Cocaine	Miscarriage or premature delivery, low birth weight, irritability, respiratory problems, genital and urinary tract deformities, heart defects, central nervous system problems
Alcohol	*Fetal alcohol effects (FAEs):* lower birth weight, lack of responsiveness and arousability, heart rate and respiratory abnormalities; delayed cognitive development; learning disabilities; *fetal alcohol syndrome (FAS):* central nervous system damage, heart defects, small head, distortions of joints, abnormal facial features; mental retardation; behavioral disorders such as hyperactivity and poor impulse control; impaired growth and/or failure to thrive
Tobacco	Spontaneous abortion, prematurity, fetal/infant death, reduced birth weight, poorer postnatal adjustment

Although children with AIDS appear to survive longer than AIDS-afflicted adults, the typical life expectancy of a child born with AIDS is not yet known. The medical aspects as well as the psychological consequences of AIDS/HIV are devastating. An AIDS-infected child faces not only physical deterioration, the social isolation and stigma associated with the disease, and early death but also the excruciating deterioration and loss of the mother (and frequently other family members and friends). As a result, an intensive, multidisciplinary team approach that simultaneously addresses the complex medical, psychological, social, and economic problems and stresses inflicted by AIDS has been found to be most effective in caring for afflicted infants and children (Task Force on Pediatric AIDS, 1989). Death, loss, and grieving during childhood are discussed in Chapter 9 and during adulthood in Chapters 13, 15, and 18.

Medicinal Drugs

Although a growing number of medications are being developed to help cure illness and relieve pain, many of these same medications may negatively affect fetal development if taken during pregnancy. A drug called *thalidomide* is a dramatic example of how such damage can occur. It also illustrates the political, economic, and social policy implications of new medical and scientific discoveries that affect human growth and development.

Thalidomide   *Thalidomide* is a seemingly harmless sedative that during the late 1950s and early 1960s was widely prescribed for calming the nerves, promoting sleep, and reducing morning sickness and other forms of nausea during the early weeks of pregnancy. Although it was advertised as being completely safe, between 1958 and 1962 thousands of babies were born with birth defects that included missing, shortened, or misshapen arms and legs, deafness, severe facial deformities, seizure disorders, dwarfism, and brain damage. Not until 1961 was the drug banned, in part because the effects of teratogens were less understood then and because the federal Food and Drug Administration (FDA) was under political pressure from the drug industry to keep thalidomide on the market.

It is estimated that there are currently about eight thousand thalidomide-affected adults and that twice that many babies were stillborn (dead at birth) or died shortly afterward because of defects caused by thalidomide (Stout, 1993). Teratogenic drugs pose an even greater developmental risk in developing countries in South America, Africa, and Asia, where drugs are less strictly regulated than in the United States. In Brazil, one of the world's largest producers of thalidomide, the drug is used to help treat the symptoms of leprosy, which afflicts almost 300,000 people in that country. This has led to a growing number of birth defects in babies born to mothers with leprosy who have taken the drug because they are not aware of its effects (Gorman, 1993).

Diethylstilbestrol (DES)   Unfortunately, the damage done by toxic drugs or chemicals does not always show itself as obviously or as soon as in the case of thalidomide. For about twenty-five years following World War II, another drug, *diethylstilbestrol (DES)*, was taken by 3 million to 6 million pregnant women with histories of spontaneous abortions to prevent miscarriages. The drug was especially useful during the early months, when miscarriages occur most often. At birth the babies of women who took DES seemed perfectly normal, and they remained so throughout childhood. As they became young adults, however, abnormal development of vaginal cells and structural abnormalities of the uterus were found in all female babies who had been exposed, and about one in one thousand eventually developed cancer of the vagina or of the cervix. The sons of DES mothers developed abnormalities in the structure of their reproductive organs and had a higher than usual rate of testicular cancer. Even the daughters who did not get cancer had significantly more problems than usual with their own pregnancies, including higher rates of spontaneous abortion and stillbirth as well as more minor problems, and they had them whether or not their families had histories of difficult births. As most of the individuals exposed to DES before birth are now reaching midlife, there is growing evidence of increased risk for autoimmune disorders such as pernicious anemia, myasthenia gravis (a nerve-muscle disorder), serious intestinal disorders, and multiple sclerosis as a result of DES damage to the immune system (Brody, 1993). DES support networks and social action groups for affected individuals and families have been formed in both Canada and the United States (Linn et al., 1988; Sato, 1993).

Nonmedicinal Drugs

Not surprisingly, drugs such as *heroin, cocaine, alcohol,* and *tobacco* also affect the fetus. Table 3.7 summarizes their effects.

Many babies born to mothers who consume alcohol during pregnancy display fetal alcohol effects (FAEs), and the most severely affected babies exhibit a cluster of defects known as *fetal alcohol syndrome* (*FAS*). *Fetal alcohol effects* refer to a set of symptoms that include lower birth weight, lack of responsiveness and arousability, and increased occurrences of heart and respiratory abnormalities in infants. These infants achieve lower mental development scores at eight months and at four years and have higher rates of learning disabilities (Barr et al., 1990; Streissguth et al., 1989).

Symptoms of **fetal alcohol syndrome (FAS)** include central nervous system damage and physical abnormalities of the heart, head, face, and joints; mental retardation and/or behavioral problems such as hyperactivity and poor impulse control; and impaired growth and/or failure to thrive. Babies of heavy drinkers, particularly in the last three months of pregnancy, are at much greater risk for these problems. It is estimated that 50 to 75 percent of infants born to chronically alcoholic women may be affected (Barr, et al., 1990; Blackman, 1990).

Even moderate daily drinking during pregnancy (two ounces of hard liquor, nine ounces of wine, or two beers) is associated with an increase in these disorders. The chance of fetal alcohol effects in the infant of a mother who consumes more than four drinks daily is estimated to be about 33 percent and about 10 percent for a woman who consumes between two and four drinks per day. However, no completely proven safe dosage of alcohol for a pregnant woman has yet been determined (Feinbloom & Forman, 1987).

Environmental Hazards

Currently the majority of women are employed outside the home, and most women who are employed when they become pregnant continue working throughout their pregnancies. Many of the environmental hazards to pregnant women and their babies are encountered in the workplace. These include (1) physical hazards such as noise, radiation, vibration, stressful physical activity, and materials handling; (2) biological hazards such as viruses, fungi, spores, and bacteria; (3) chemical hazards such as anesthetic gases, pesticides, lead, mercury, and organic solvents; and (4) radiation (Bernhardt, 1990). Risks to pregnancy also occur at home. In the next section we discuss one of the most disturbing of these risks: domestic violence.

Domestic Violence

Domestic violence presents another serious hazard to pregnant women and their babies. Studies of prenatal clinic patients report that between 7 and 8 percent of pregnant women are beaten by their partners and that women who are battered have twice as many miscarriages as women who are not. While 87.5 percent of pregnant women who are battered had been abused before, it is estimated that 1 percent of all pregnant women with no history of being battered will be abused during pregnancy (Helton et al., 1987). These rates probably are actually higher, since low-SES and teenage mothers, who are at greatest risk for abuse, are less likely to receive prenatal care or to be included in such studies. Abuse during pregnancy is correlated with unemployment, substance abuse, poverty, and family dysfunction, making it difficult to determine the relative contribution of each of these risks (Moran, 1993).

Teenage Pregnancy

The United States has the highest rate of teenage pregnancy of all industrialized countries (Lawson & Rhode, 1993). Pregnant teenagers are much less likely than pregnant adults to maintain nutritious diets and get adequate prenatal care during pregnancy and more likely to suffer complications and experience prolonged and difficult labor. Babies born to teenagers are more likely to be premature and suffer from low birth weight and its associated problems (see Chapter 4). They also have higher rates of neurological defects, have higher mortality rates during their first year, and are more likely to encounter developmental problems during the preschool and school years. We look more closely at the causes and consequences of teenage pregnancy in Chapter 11.

Diet and Nutrition

For mothers with poor diets, rates of prematurity and infant mortality are higher, birth weights are lower, and the risk of congenital malformations increases. Nutritionally deprived infants are less responsive to environmental stimulation and irritable when aroused. Malnourished infants are found to have a significantly reduced number of brain cells, especially when the malnutrition occurred during the last trimester or during the first three months following birth (Lozoff, 1989).

Recent research conducted by Larry Brown and Ernesto Pollitt (1996) in Guatemala found that when low-SES mothers and their infants regularly received a nutritious food supplement called *Atole* (a hot soup made from maize, a local grain), the rate of infant mortality decreased by 69 percent as compared to a similar group of mothers and infants receiving a less nutritious supplement called *Fresco*. As children, the Atole children displayed significantly greater gains in motor skills, physical growth, and social and emotional development than those who received the Fresco supplement. A long-term study of adolescents and adults who had been exposed to Atole or Fresco both prenatally and for at least two years after birth found that children who had received Atole early in life performed significantly better on academic achievement and general intelligence tests (Brown & Pollitt, 1996).

Prenatal Health Care

Adequate early prenatal care is critical to infant and maternal health, and mothers who begin prenatal care early in pregnancy have improved pregnancy and newborn outcomes, including decreased risk of low birth weight and preterm delivery. The quality of prenatal care is strongly influenced by the woman's life circumstances; race and SES, two factors that are closely linked in our society, play a major role. In 1988, for example, only 79 percent of white mothers and 61 percent of African American mothers began care in the first trimester. Five percent of white mothers and 11 percent of African American mothers delayed care until the last trimester or received no care at all. These mothers were most likely to be teenage, be unmarried, have less than twelve years of education, and already have three or more children (C. Lewis, 1993). Although the risk of problems increases the later prenatal care is begun, by far the worst outcomes occur for mothers receiving no care at all. Table 3.8 summarizes the relationship among timing of prenatal care, mother's education and race of baby, and the percentage of low-birth-weight deliveries.

How can the prenatal care of high-risk mothers be improved? The *Prenatal/Early Infancy Project* conducted by David Olds and his colleagues is one promising answer to this question (Olds, 1988). Beginning in the second trimester of pregnancy, program nurses made regular home visits during which they provided

TABLE 3.8 *Percentage of Full-Term Births of Low Birth Weight by Trimester of Pregnancy Prenatal Care Began, Educational Attainment of Mother, and Race of Child: 1988*
The percentage of low-birth-weight babies decreases the earlier prenatal care begins and the more years of education the mother has. Percentages of low-birth-weight infants are higher for African Americans (versus whites) among mothers who began prenatal care at the same time and had similar levels of education.

Educational Attainment and Race	Trimester of Pregnancy Prenatal Care Began			
	1st	2nd	3rd	No Care
White				
0–11	4.0%	4.3%	4.5%	8.7%
12	2.4	3.4	3.8	7.5
13–15	1.8	2.5	2.9	6.2
16+	1.5	1.8	2.1	*
African American				
0–11	6.6	7.1	7.5	14.6
12	5.3	5.9	6.3	12.8
13–15	4.3	5.6	5.5	14.5
16+	3.6	4.7	3.5	*

*Figure does not meet standard of reliability.
Source: C. Lewis (1993), p. 340.

education about diet and weight gain; the effects of cigarettes, alcohol, and drugs; signs of pregnancy complication; the importance of regular rest, exercise, and personal hygiene; preparation for labor and delivery and early care of the newborn; effective use of the health care system; planning for subsequent pregnancies; returning to school; and finding employment. Nurses also educated mothers about early infant temperament and how to promote infants' social, emotional, and cognitive development. Finally, nurses helped mothers expand their informal support network to include husbands, boyfriends, and other family and friends and to develop reliable, ongoing relationships with their pediatricians and other health and human service providers. Participation in the program lasted for two years, and a follow-up study was conducted when the children were four years old.

Pregnant women who participated in the program made more use of formal services, experienced greater informal social support, made more improvements in their diets, and reduced their smoking compared to similar women not in the program. Very young teenagers in the program showed a significant improvement in their babies' birth weights and a reduction in preterm deliveries. After delivery, these women displayed higher levels of infant and child care and made better use of health and social services. There was also a 75 percent reduction in verified cases of child abuse and neglect and a 42 percent decrease in subsequent pregnancies among low-SES unmarried women in the program (Olds, 1988).

Stress

Stress refers to chronic feelings of worry and anxiety. Women who experience severe and prolonged anxiety just before or during pregnancy are more likely to have medical complications and to give birth to infants with abnormalities than women who do not. Emotional stress has been associated with greater incidence of spontaneous abortion, difficult labor, premature birth and low birth weight, newborn respiratory difficulties, and physical deformities (Norbeck & Tilden, 1983; Omer & Everly, 1988). We will take a closer look at the role of stress when we discuss physical development in young adulthood in Chapter 12.

What Do You Think?

If good prenatal diet and health care are so closely related to healthy prenatal and postnatal development, why don't all expectant mothers follow nutritious diets and receive good health care? How can adequate health care be made available to all pregnant women?

BIRTH

After thirty-eight weeks in the womb, the fetus is considered to be "full term," or ready for birth. At this point it will weigh around 7½ pounds, but it can weigh as little as 5 or as much as 10 pounds and still be physically normal. The fetus measures about twenty inches or so at this stage, almost one-third of its final height as an adult.

During the final weeks, the womb becomes so crowded that the fetus assumes one position more or less permanently. This orientation is sometimes called *fetal presentation*. **Fetal presentation** (or *orientation*) refers to the body part of the fetus that is closest to the mother's cervix. The most common fetal presentation, and the most desirable one medically, is head pointing downward (called a *cephalic presentation*). Two other presentations also occur: feet and rump first (*breech presentation*) or shoulders first (*transverse presentation*). These two orientations used to jeopardize an infant's survival, but modern obstetric techniques have greatly reduced their risk.

Most fetuses develop normally for the usual thirty-eight to forty weeks and face their birth relatively well prepared. When the labor process begins, it too usually proceeds normally. The uterus contracts rhythmically and automatically to force the baby downward through the vaginal canal (see Figure 3.15). The contractions occur in a relatively predictable sequence of stages, and as long as the baby and mother are healthy and the mother's pelvis is large enough, the baby usually is out within a matter of hours.

Stages of Labor

It is common for the mother to experience "false labor," or *Braxton-Hicks contractions,* in the last weeks of pregnancy as the uterus "practices" contracting and relaxing in preparation for actual labor. These contractions do not open the cervix as real labor contractions do.

Labor consists of three stages. The *first stage of labor*, which lasts from the first true contraction until the cervix (the opening of the uterus) is completely open, or *dilated* to 10 centimeters (4.5 inches), is the longest stage. It usually begins with relatively mild and irregular contractions of the uterus. As contractions become stronger, more regular, and more frequent, *dilation,* or widening, of the cervix increases until there is enough room for the baby's head to fit through. As it stretches and dilates, the cervix also becomes thinner, a process referred to as *effacement*.

Toward the end of this first stage of labor, which may take from eight to twenty-four hours for a first-time mother, a *period of transition* begins. The cervix approaches full dilation, contractions become more rapid, and the baby's head begins to move into the birth canal. Although this period generally lasts for only a few minutes, it can be the most intense and challenging one because contractions become stronger and more deeply felt, lasting from forty-five to ninety seconds each. Managing each contraction involves a great deal of concentration and energy; women typically use the period between contractions to catch their breath and prepare for the next contraction. During transition, a woman often experiences a variety of physical changes, including trembling, shaking, leg cramps, nausea, back and hip pain, burping, and perspiring, and tends to be preoccupied with feelings of pain, pressure, and hoped-for relief (McKay, 1993).

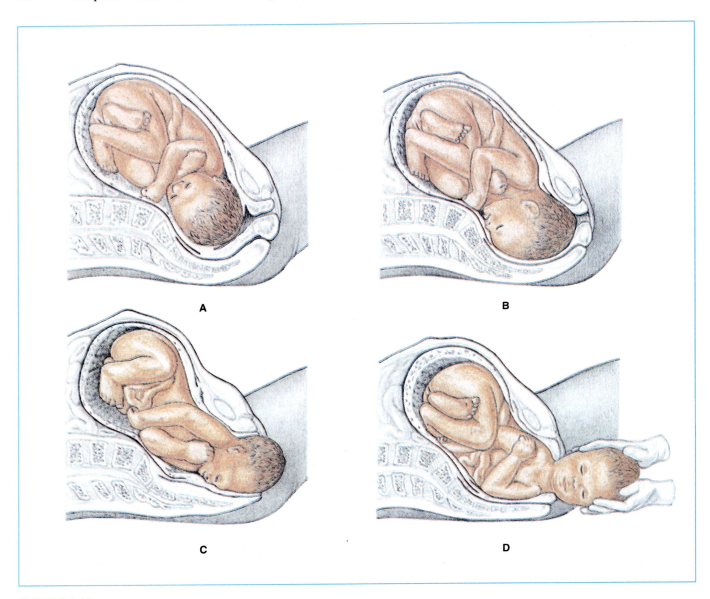

A

B

C

D

FIGURE 3.15
The Process of Delivery
(A) Before labor begins; (B) labor; (C) crowning; (D) emergence of the head

The *second stage of labor* ranges from complete dilation of the cervix to birth. Contractions continue, but may be somewhat shorter, lasting forty-five to sixty seconds. Although the baby now has only a few more inches to move down the vagina to be born, the process can be slow, usually lasting between one and two hours for a first baby and less than a half-hour for women who have previously given birth. Although dilation is complete, for most women the reflexive urge to push the baby out by bearing down full strength usually develops toward the end of this stage, and often becomes irresistible. When a woman first begins to push, she may be uncoordinated and need to learn to push "with" the contraction and rest in between. How hard she pushes will depend on the strength of the contractions, which varies throughout labor. If a woman doesn't feel the urge to push, guidance from a partner can help, particularly if she had an epidural block or other local anesthetic that interferes with her bearing-down reflex.

During the *third stage of labor*, which lasts between five and twenty minutes, the afterbirth, which consists of placenta and umbilical cord, is expelled. Contractions still occur but are much weaker, and the woman may have to push several times to deliver the placenta. The medication oxytocin is frequently given to help

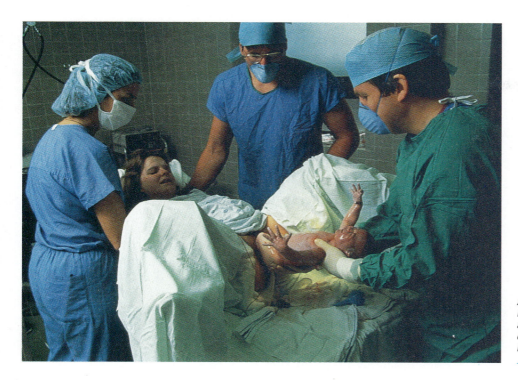

After all the hard work of labor, a baby! No matter how exhausted she may feel a mother is usually glad to see her new child, especially once reassured that it is healthy.

the placenta to detach from the side of the uterus. Putting the baby to the mother's breast also can help, because stimulation of the nipple naturally releases oxytocin (McKay, 1993).

Childbirth Settings and Methods

Until the 1800s, births in the United States generally took place in the woman's home. Usually it was attended by midwives, friends, neighbors, and family members and was viewed as a natural process rather than as a medical procedure. The *midwife* was a woman experienced in pregnancy and childbirth who traditionally served as the primary caregiver during pregnancy, childbirth, and the month or so following birth. During the 1800s, political and social factors and the emergence of medicine as a scientifically based and politically powerful profession led to the replacement of midwives by physicians as the chief birth attendants. In the 1900s, delivery moved to the hospital, where it was increasingly treated as a medical rather than a naturally occurring community event (Bogdon, 1993; Steiger, 1993).

These changes brought the benefits of modern medical technology to the birth process and resulted in decreased mortality rates for mothers and their babies, particularly in the case of high-risk pregnancies. However, they also shifted the birth process from being a natural event controlled by the pregnant woman, her family, her friends, and the community to a medical event controlled by physicians. As a result, all babies and their mothers were exposed to the risks associated with hospital-based medical practices, including overreliance on medication and on procedures such as episiotomies and caesarian sections (discussed a bit later).

Hospital Births   Currently more than 90 percent of all births in the United States occur in hospitals under the supervision of a physician. In recent years, the maternity wards of many hospitals have modified their environments to be more comfortable and supportive of pregnant women and their families. A growing number of hospitals now have *birthing rooms* with more comfortable furniture, muted colors and lighting, and soft music, and facilities for *rooming in* that allow mother and baby to stay together until both are ready to leave the hospital. Most hospitals now allow a partner to be present during the delivery, a practice that was rarely allowed just two decades ago (Steiger, 1993).

Nonhospital Settings   *Freestanding birth centers* (*FBCs*) are nonhospital facilities organized to provide family-centered maternity care for women who are judged to be at low risk for obstetrical complications (Rooks et al., 1989). Equipped and staffed to handle all but the most serious medical emergencies and designed like simple but comfortable hotels, birth centers encourage the active involvement of the mother, her family, and her friends in a birth process that minimizes technical intervention deemed to be medically unnecessary and physiologically and psychologically stressful in low-risk deliveries (Eakins, 1993).

Home birth is another alternative to hospital birth available for low-risk pregnancies. In a typical home birth, normal daily activities continue through the first stage of labor. When contractions increase, the nurse-midwife or physician is called to monitor the labor. Backup arrangements with a doctor or hospital are generally in place should they be needed, and women planning on home birth are carefully screened to minimize last-minute complications requiring hospital equipment or procedures. In addition to the widely held view that hospitals are the place of choice for birth, difficulty in obtaining malpractice insurance and resistance by the medical profession are major barriers to widespread acceptance of home birth.

Prepared Childbirth   The majority of hospitals and nonhospital birth settings now offer programs to help women and their partners prepare for the physical and psychological experience of birth. These include preparatory visits to the hospital or birth facility, where pregnant women and their partners can become familiar with the physical setting and procedures. Various methods of **prepared childbirth** have been devised to help parents rehearse, or simulate, the actual sensations of labor well before the projected delivery date. Although the these methods differ from one another in certain details, all generally emphasize educational, physical, and emotional preparation for the birth process and active involvement of the mother and father (or other partner). Typically, they encourage the mother to find a coach (often her spouse or a relative) to give her personal support during labor (Lamaze, 1970).

Pregnant women and their "birth coaches" attend a Lamaze birth class to help them prepare for the experience of childbirth.

One well-known preparation program, the Lamaze method, strongly advocates participation of *both* mother and father during the weeks preceding delivery and during the delivery itself. Women are taught techniques for managing the discomfort of labor that include relaxation techniques and breathing methods for each stage of labor. Labor either without drugs or with minimal drugs is encouraged, and the importance of birth as a shared emotional experience is stressed.

Women who have participated in Lamaze and similar childbirth approaches report more favorable attitudes toward labor and delivery, less discomfort and stress during the birth process, less reliance on medication, and more sensitive interaction with the newborn baby (Cogan, 1980; Lindell, 1988). A father's involvement in preparing for and participating in the delivery process has been found to positively influence his experience of birth, his behavior toward mother and baby during delivery, and his relationship to his new infant (M. Hoffnung, 1992; Markman & Kadushin, 1986).

Medicinal Methods During Delivery   Despite adequate psychological preparation, most mothers feel some pain during labor contractions. Under good conditions, many mothers can endure this pain until the baby is delivered. But if labor takes an unusually long time or a mother finds herself less prepared than she expected, pain-reducing drugs such as narcotics or other sedatives can make the experience bearable. But such medications must be used cautiously. Most pain relievers cross the placenta and therefore can seriously depress the fetus if they are given at the wrong time or in improper amounts.

During the final stages of delivery, two other forms of pain relief are available. Doctors may inject a sedative into the base of the woman's spine. The two most common of these procedures are called an *epidural* and a *spinal*. They allow the mother to remain awake and alert during the final stages of labor, but also prevent her from helping in the delivery process by regulating her own contractions. Nitrous oxide, which dentists commonly use, also has been used to take the edge off the pain of the peak contractions while allowing the mother to remain conscious.

Giving a mother either a general or a local anesthetic before delivery removes all pain, of course, but both mother and child may take a long time to recover from it. Mothers who receive general anesthetics for delivery stay in the hospital for more days after delivery, on the average, than do mothers who receive other kinds of medication. This is partly because it takes several days for them to recover from the medication (Hamilton, 1984). In addition, the bonding between mother and child may be delayed while both are recovering from the effect of anesthesia. Table 3.9 lists the major types of medications used during labor and delivery, their administration, and their effects (Feinbloom & Forman, 1987).

Problems During Labor and Delivery

Interference with labor and delivery can occur in three ways: through *faulty power* in the uterus, a *faulty passageway* (the birth canal), or a *faulty passenger* (the baby itself). These problems actually interconnect in various ways, but it is convenient to distinguish among them (Buckley & Kulb, 1983).

Faulty Power   Sometimes the uterus does not contract strongly enough to make labor progress to a delivery. The problem can occur at the beginning of labor or develop midway through a labor that began quite normally, especially if the mother becomes tired after hours of powerful contractions. In many cases, the doctor can strengthen the contractions by giving the mother an injection of the hormone oxytocin. Such *induced labor* must be monitored carefully so that the artificial contractions it stimulates do not harm both baby and mother by forcing the baby through the canal before the canal is ready.

TABLE 3.9   *Major Medications During Childbirth and Their Effects on the Baby*

Type	Administration	Positive Effects for Mother	Negative Effects for Baby
Analgesics	By injection (in controlled doses) during the first stage of labor to reduce pain	Reduces pain, causes some drowsiness and euphoria (sense of well-being and tranquility); women participate in labor and delivery	May cause drowsiness and decreased responsiveness for first few hours after birth or longer; naloxone hydrochloride (Narcon) can be used to reverse these effects
Local anesthesia			
Spinal	By injection into spinal canal in controlled doses when cervix is fully dilated (beginning of second stage of labor); numbs sensory and motor nerves so that mother's pelvic area and legs cannot move voluntarily	Mother can remain awake and aware during labor and delivery; can be used for either vaginal or caesarean birth; is highly effective in eliminating pain	No negative effects reported
Epidural	By injection during active phase of first stage of labor to numb sensory nerves after their exit from spinal canal	Pain and sensations are generally eliminated; mother is awake; some voluntary movement is preserved, although it is less effective because a woman's sense of position and tension are blocked by the medication	No negative effects reported
General anesthesia	A mixture of nitrous oxide and oxygen is inhaled; is less commonly used than blocking agents	Easily administered, rapid onset of effect; anesthetic of choice in emergencies in which time is critical and baby must be delivered quickly	Decreased alertness and responsiveness following birth

Source: Feinbloom & Forman (1987).

Faulty Passageway   Sometimes the placenta partially or completely covers the cervix and blocks the baby from moving down the birth canal during labor. This condition, called *placenta previa,* occurs in late pregnancy and causes bleeding when the cervix starts to open. If left untreated, it may leave the fetus somewhat undernourished, because it prevents sufficient blood from reaching it. Sometimes it blocks a normal delivery entirely so that the baby must be delivered by caesarean section (ACOG, 1990).

Faulty Passenger   Usually a baby enters the birth canal head first, but occasionally one turns in the wrong direction during contractions. A breech presentation—with the bottom leading—is risky for the baby, since its spine can be broken if a contraction presses it too hard against the mother's pelvis. Or the baby may not get enough oxygen because it cannot begin breathing on its own until after its nose comes out. In some cases a skilled midwife or a doctor can deliver a breech baby with no problem, but if the baby gets stuck partway out of the vagina, medical staff may use *forceps* to pull it the rest of the way out. In most cases, breech babies are either turned to the right position during delivery or delivered surgically by caesarean section.

A small but significant proportion of babies are simply too big to pass through the mother's pelvis and vaginal canal, a problem sometimes called *cephalopelvic disproportion (CPD)*—literally, a disproportion of the head and pelvis. If the mismatch is too severe and threatens the life of the mother or the child, the doctor may interrupt the labor and deliver the baby surgically.

Caesarean Section   *Caesarean section,* or *C-section,* is a procedure used in cases where the baby cannot be safely delivered through the vagina and therefore has to be removed surgically. Techniques for this surgery have improved substantially over the past decades. The operation now takes only about half an hour, most of which is devoted to sewing the mother up after getting the baby out. Partly because of these improvements, the number of C-sections for live births, which almost quadrupled between 1970 and 1988, currently appears to have leveled off at about one in four births. Many experts and parent advocates remain concerned that the rates are still too high and reflect medical practices that are not in the best interests of mothers and their babies (ACOG, 1990; Taffel, 1989, 1993).

Both supporters and critics of caesarean birth agree that there are a number of good reasons for selecting a caesarean birth as the safest way to deliver a baby. These include some of the problems of placenta previa and cephalopelvic disproportion (CPD) already noted, as well as prolapsed cord, where the umbilical cord cuts off the baby's oxygen; unusual positions of the baby that make delivery impossible; severe fetal distress that cannot be corrected; and active herpes, where the baby may be infected through vaginal birth.

Selection of a caesarean delivery purely for the convenience of the physician, a previous caesarean delivery (currently the most common reason for doing the procedure), inactive herpes, and suspected cephalopelvic disproportion not confirmed by a period of strong, frequent contractions are all no longer accepted as valid reasons for a caesarean delivery. Reasons for considering a vaginal birth after a previous C-section include less risk of surgical complications, shorter recovery time, and the opportunity for greater involvement of the mother in the delivery process (ACOG, 1990).

Fetal Monitoring   Most hospitals use *electronic fetal monitoring* to record uterine contractions and the fetal heart rate. Uterine contractions are externally measured by a pressure gauge strapped to the mother's abdomen that electronically represents changes in the shape of the uterus on graph paper. Fetal heart rate can be picked up by an *external* ultrasound monitor placed on the abdomen over the uterus or *internally* by a wire, leading through the vagina and screwed into the fetus's scalp, that records more subtle electrical changes in the fetus's heart.

Although internal fetal monitoring is extremely helpful in high-risk and emergency situations, experts have questioned its routine use for low-risk deliveries. Some have suggested that the procedure may itself contribute to fetal (and maternal) distress. In addition, the mother must lie in bed for as long as the wires are attached (Feinbloom & Forman, 1987). Experts have also noted that by shifting the center of focus from the experience of mother and baby to readouts from the equipment, "high-tech" births may reduce certain aspects of clinical awareness that are central to good obstetric care (Davis-Floyd, 1986).

Birth and the Family

The arrival of a new baby can be particularly difficult for parents who lack the economic resources, knowledge, and social and emotional support that are so important in adjusting to the complicated demands of caring for a new baby. Having a baby that is low birth weight or other problems can be even more traumatic. While it is unwise to generalize too broadly, adolescent parents, single parents, and parents who are educationally and economically disadvantaged are more likely to find parenthood difficult.

Nevertheless, the great majority of births in this country occur without significant problems and to families whose economic, social, and psychological resources enable them to become effective parents. For women (and their partners) who receive good preparation and training for the birth process and obtain adequate social and emotional support from family, friends, and culture, birth is likely to be a very positive and welcome event. For most families, the arrival of a new baby brings many changes that take some time to adjust to. For first-time parents, learning to

Birth is a family event. Involving children in the preparation for birth can play an important role in helping them adjust to the changes.

care for a new baby and rearranging family schedules to be able to provide the almost constant attention a newborn requires are very big challenges, to say the least. We will look at these and related issues in Chapter 13's coverage of psychosocial development in early adulthood.

For parents who already have children, a newcomer to the family also creates stresses. Children naturally worry that they will lose their special place in the family and the exclusive attention they enjoy once the newcomer arrives. Involving the child in the preparation for birth, for the period when the mother is in the hospital, and for the changes that will occur with the new arrival are all important ways to help a child adjust to the changes. Talking to the child about these things and listening carefully to his or her questions and concerns are particularly important. Especially with preschoolers, providing concrete information about birth, newborn babies and what they are like, and the specific changes that will occur in the family before and after the baby's birth can help allay their fears.

After the new baby arrives home, parents can do a number of things to assist the adjustment process. Giving the older child lots of verbal reassurance helps, but concrete actions often speak louder than words. One strategy is to give the child an important role in the event by providing special activities, asking friends and family members to bring a gift for the child as well as for the new baby, and including the child in daily activities with the new infant. High priority should also be placed on continuing routine activities with the older child and ensuring that each parent spends lots of special time just with him or her.

What Do You Think?

How might the process of birth vary depending on a family's circumstances such as age, marital status, income, race, and culture? To explore this question, have yourself and several classmates play the roles of expectant parents from different life circumstances. What did you discover?

LOOKING BACK/LOOKING FORWARD

The process of prenatal development presents a contradictory picture. On the one hand, it seems highly predictable and relatively insensitive to the influences that might change its course. Starting from a single cell, the process rapidly unfolds and develops in an increasingly complex sequence of interrelated patterns of change, all of which have become highly canalized over the thousands of years of human evolution. It is as though from the moment of conception, the emergence of the newborn baby nine months later was never in doubt. Although deviations from these normal developmental pathways occur, they are not genuine departures from normal prenatal development; rather, they seem to further emphasize the predictability of most embryos and fetuses.

On the other hand, although birth marks the end of prenatal development, it is only the beginning of the incredible range of developmental changes that follow—changes that are much less canalized or predictable. The fact that biology seems to lose its hold on the child once she or he emerges from the womb and the environment and experience take over may be overwhelming to a new parent. Nevertheless, as we discover in the chapters that follow, biology and experience remain too closely intertwined to be sharply distinguishable from each other. The path a child's development takes will be only partly determined by the child's experiences, including the efforts of the parents.

SUMMARY OF MAJOR IDEAS

GENETICS

Mechanisms of Genetic Transmission

1. Genetic information is contained in a complex molecule called *deoxyribonucleic acid (DNA)*.

2. Reproductive cells, or gametes, divide by a process called *meiosis* and recombine into a zygote at conception.

3. The process of meiosis gives each gamete one-half of its normal number of chromosomes; conception brings the number of chromosomes up to normal again and gives the new zygote equal numbers of chromosomes from each parent.

4. Other body cells produce new tissue by simple division of their genes, chromosomes, and other cellular parts by means of a process called *mitosis*.

Individual Genetic Expression

5. A person's genotype is the specific pattern of genetic information inherited in his or her chromosomes and genes at conception.

6. A person's phenotype refers to the physical and behavioral traits the person actually shows during his or her life. Phenotype is the product of the interactions of genotype with environment.

7. Although most genes exist in duplicate, some, called *dominant genes*, may actually influence the phenotype if only one member of the pair occurs.

8. Recessive genes do not influence the phenotype unless both members of the pair occur in a particular form.

9. Many traits are polygenic, meaning they are transmitted through the combined actions of several genes.

10. Sex is determined by one particular pair of chromosomes, called the *X* and *Y* chromosomes, and a testis-determining factor (TDF) located on a small section of the Y chromosome.

Genetic Abnormalities

11. Some genetic abnormalities, such as Down syndrome, occur when an individual inherits too many or too few chromosomes.

12. Other genetic abnormalities occur because particular genes are defective or abnormal even though their chromosomes are normal. Examples are Huntington disease and sickle-cell disease.

Genetic Counseling and Prenatal Diagnosis

13. Experts on genetics can provide parents with information about how genetics influences the development of children and about the risks of transmitting genetic abnormalities from one generation to the next.

14. Several methods now exist for diagnosing genetic problems before a baby is born, including ultrasound, fetoscopy, amniocentesis, chorionic villus sampling (CVS), and various blood tests.

15. Personal circumstances and cultural differences in beliefs and expectations must be considered in helping couples reach informed decisions about pregnancy.

Relative Influence of Heredity and Environment

16. According to behavioral geneticists, every characteristic of an organism is the result of the unique interaction between the genetic inheritance of that organism and the sequence of environments through which it has passed during its development.

17. Behavioral geneticists use the concept of range of reaction to describe the strength of genetic influence under different environmental conditions.

18. Studies of identical twins and of adopted children suggest that heredity and environment operate jointly to influence developmental change.

19. Linkage and association studies use repeated DNA segments called *polymorphisms* as genetic markers to locate abnormal genes.

20. Neither biogenetic nor environmental determinism is likely to give us an adequate understanding of human development, which is the product of *both* genes and environment.

PRENATAL DEVELOPMENT AND BIRTH

Stages of Prenatal Development

21. Prenatal development begins with conception, in which a zygote is created by the union of a sperm cell from the father and an egg cell, or ovum, from the mother.

22. Prenatal development consists of discrete periods, or stages.

23. The germinal stage occurs during the first two weeks following conception; the zygote forms a blastocyst, which differentiates into three distinct cell layers and then implants itself in the uterine wall to form the embryo.

24. During the embryonic stage, which lasts from the third through eighth weeks of pregnancy, the placenta and umbilical cord form and the basic organs and biological systems begin to develop.

25. During the fetal stage, which lasts from the ninth week until the end of pregnancy, all physical features complete their development.

26. Infertility is the inability to conceive or carry a pregnancy to term after one year of unprotected intercourse.

27. The experience of pregnancy includes dramatic changes in a woman's physical functioning and appearance, as well as significant psychological changes, as prospective mothers and fathers anticipate the birth of the baby.

Prenatal Influences on the Child

28. Although prenatal development is highly canalized, or directed, there are critical periods (particularly during the first trimester) when embryonic development is highly vulnerable or at risk for disruption from teratogens.

29. Teratogens are substances or other environmental influences that can permanently disrupt and damage an embryo's growth. Their effects depend on the timing, intensity, and duration of exposure, the presence of other risks, and the biological vulnerability of baby and mother.

30. Risk factors for prenatal development include the physical and biological characteristics of the mother; diseases such as syphilis, gonorrhea, and AIDS; certain medicinal drugs such as thalidomide and DES; and nonmedicinal drugs such as heroin, cocaine, alcohol, and tobacco.

31. Environmental hazards also pose risks for pregnant women. These include physical hazards such as noise and radiation, biological hazards such as viruses and bacteria, chemical hazards such as pesticides, and radiation.

32. Domestic violence and teenage pregnancy are two serious problems that increase risks to healthy prenatal and postnatal development as well as developmental risks to the mother.

33. Adequate prenatal nutrition and health care for the mother and her developing baby is associated with a successful pregnancy, a normal birth, and healthy neonatal development.

Birth

34. Labor occurs in three distinct but overlapping stages. During the first stage of labor, which may last from eight to twenty-four hours for a first-time mother, uterine contractions increase in strength and regularity, and the cervix dilates sufficiently to accommodate the baby's head. The second stage of labor lasts from the complete dilation of the cervix until birth and takes from sixty to ninety minutes. During the third stage of labor, which lasts only a few minutes, the afterbirth is expelled.

35. Nonhospital birth centers and home birth are two alternatives to hospital-based birth.

36. Prepared childbirth is now widely used in both hospital and nonhospital birth settings to help women actively and comfortably meet the challenges of giving birth.

37. Pain-reducing medications can make the experience of childbirth more comfortable, but in recent years they have been used more cautiously because of their potentially adverse effects on the recovery of both infant and mother.

38. Problems during labor and delivery include insufficient uterine contractions, or *faulty power*; a *faulty passageway* caused by blockage of the birth canal; and a *faulty passenger*, which may occur if the baby's physical position or large head size prevents completion of the journey through the birth canal.

39. Most hospitals use electronic fetal monitors to keep track of fetal heart rate and uterine contractions.
40. Low-birth-weight babies may experience significant complications after birth; however, the bigger and more mature they are at birth, the greater are their chances for survival and healthy development.
41. While learning to care for a new baby is a welcome challenge for most new parents, it may be especially difficult for adolescent parents, single parents, and parents who are educationally and economically disadvantaged.

KEY TERMS

sperm *(63)*
ovum *(63)*
gene *(63)*
chromosome *(63)*

zygote *(65)*
genotype *(67)*
phenotype *(67)*
dominant gene *(67)*
recessive gene *(67)*
alleles *(67)*
sex-linked recessive traits *(70)*
Down syndrome *(71)*
sickle-cell disease *(74)*
range of reaction *(76)*
adoption study *(77)*
twin study *(79)*
twin adoption study *(79)*

germinal stage *(80)*
embryonic stage *(80)*
fetal stage *(80)*
conception *(80)*
placenta *(82)*
umbilical cord *(82)*
amniotic sac *(82)*
canalization *(86)*
critical period *(87)*
teratogen *(87)*
fetal alcohol syndrome (FAS) *(92)*
fetal presentation *(95)*
prepared childbirth *(98)*

PART TWO

The First Two Years of Life

As parents and other proud relatives keep discovering, infants grow and change more rapidly than the rest of us. Every few weeks, or sometimes even in a matter of days, infants seem to do something new. In a matter of months they are able to smile, sit, and babble. In just a few more months, they begin acquiring language, show signs of make-believe play, and take their first tentative steps.

These miracles invariably impress caregivers—provided, of course, that the caregivers are receiving the support *they* need to nurture infants. In reality, the infant is not the only person who is learning and changing. Parents are changing, too, as a result of witnessing and supporting the baby's emerging talents. For example, as they watch their baby grow, they revisit their relationships with their own parents and begin seeing those relationships with new breadth and wisdom. We take a close look at these experiences in Part Six on early adulthood. For now, we look at infancy in terms of the child himself or herself.

4

THE FIRST TWO YEARS

Physical and Cognitive Development

A nne was looking at the journal she had kept about her daughter since Michelle was seven months old.

■ April 9: For two weeks she has been sleeping through the night! Maybe it helped to start nursing her just before bedtime—but it's so hard to tell. She is starting to enjoy bedtime stories, too; babbles at the book and points at the pictures.

■ June 10: Michelle has been crawling all over—mostly after the dog. Gets mad, cries when King walks away; struggles to crawl after him; but then forgets all about him.

■ August 10: Here's Michelle's latest words: "dada" (daddy), "tigg'n" (Tigger, the cat), "buh" (book). Maybe not polished English, but she's getting there. At this rate, I'm going to lose track of her full vocabulary soon.

As Anne can attest, during the first months of life a baby's behaviors evolve rapidly. In this chapter, we trace some of these changes through the first two years of life. We begin by discussing young infants' physical growth: what they look like, how they sleep, hear, and see, and what behaviors they can already perform at birth. We also look at variations in growth and in infants' nutritional needs in the first months of life. In the second part of the chapter we take a second look at infants' development, this time from a cognitive perspective. We explore infants' perceptions and representations of their surroundings and how they learn from their world even before they learn to speak. Finally, we consider one of the most universal yet remarkable of all human accomplishments: the acquisition of language.

Focusing Questions

- What do infants look like, and how do they act during the first two years of life?

- How do infants' sleep and wakefulness patterns change as they get older?

- How do infants' senses operate at birth?

- What are some motor skills that evolve during infancy?

- What are the risks of low birth weight on infant development?

- What do infants need nutritionally?

- Do infants see and hear in the same way adults do?

- How does thinking evolve or change during infancy?

- What phases do infants go through in acquiring language?

PHYSICAL DEVELOPMENT

APPEARANCE OF THE YOUNG INFANT

As we saw in the last chapter, birth continues rather than initiates physical development. Most organs have already been working for weeks, or even months, prior to this event. The baby's heart has been beating regularly, muscles have been contracting sporadically, and the liver has been making its major product, bile, which is necessary for normal digestion after birth. Even some behaviors, such as sucking and arm stretching, have already developed. Two physical functions, however, do begin at birth: breathing and ingestion (the taking in of foods).

The First Few Hours

When it first emerges from the birth canal, the newborn infant (also called a **neonate**) definitely does not resemble most people's stereotypes of a beautiful baby. No matter what its race, its skin often looks rather red. If born a bit early, it may also have a white, waxy substance called *vernix* on its skin, and its body may be covered with fine, downy hair called *lanugo*. If the baby was born vaginally rather then delivered surgically, its head may be somewhat elongated or have a noticeable point on it; the shape comes from the pressure of the birth canal, which squeezes the skull for several hours during labor. Within a few days or weeks, the head fills out again to a more rounded shape, leaving gaps in the bones. The gaps are sometimes called *fontanelles,* or "soft spots," although they are actually covered by a tough membrane that can withstand normal contact and pressure. The gaps eventually grow over, but not until the infant is about eighteen months old.

Is the Baby All Right? The Apgar Scale

The Apgar Scale (named after its originator, Dr. Virginia Apgar) helps doctors and nurses to decide quickly whether a newborn needs immediate medical attention. The scale consists of ratings that are simple enough for nonspecialists to make, even during the distractions surrounding the moment of delivery (Apgar, 1953). To use it, someone present at the delivery calculates the baby's heart rate, breathing effort, muscle tone, skin color, and reflex irritability and assigns a score of 0 to 2 to each of these five characteristics. Babies are rated one minute after they emerge from the womb and again at five minutes. For each rating they can earn a maximum score of 10, as Table 4.1 shows. Most babies earn nine or ten points, at least by five minutes after delivery. A baby who scores between four and seven points at one minute is given immediate special medical attention (Apgar & Beck, 1973), which usually includes examination by a pediatrician, and is then carefully observed during the next few hours and days for any problems that may develop.

TABLE 4.1   The Apgar Scale

Characteristic	Score		
	0	*1*	*2*
Heart rate	Absent	Less than 100 beats per minute	More than 100 beats per minute
Efforts to breathe	Absent	Slow, irregular	Good; baby is crying
Muscle tone	Flaccid, limp	Weak, inactive	Strong, active motion
Skin color	Body pale or blue	Body pink, extremities blue	Body and extremities pink
Reflex irritability	No response	Frown, grimace	Vigorous crying, coughing, sneezing

Source: Apgar (1953)

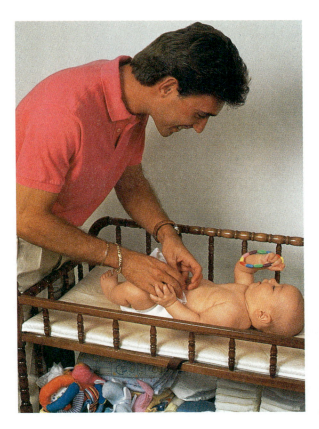

The normal facial features of infants—large forehead and eyes, high cheekbones, small mouth—may help stimulate attachment in adults. Similar facial proportions also exist in the young of many other animals; puppies, for example, have larger eyes and cheekbones than adult dogs.

Size and Bodily Proportions

A newborn baby weighs about 7½ pounds and measures about 20 inches lying down. Her length matches her adult size more closely than her weight does: her 20 inches represent more than one-quarter of her final height, whereas her 7½ pounds amount to only a small percentage of her adult weight.

Babies' proportions and general physical appearance may have psychological consequences by fostering *attachments*, or bonds, with the people who care for them. Such bonds promote feelings of security. The cuteness of infants' faces in particular seems to help. No matter what their racial or ethnic background, most babies have unusually large foreheads, features that are concentrated in the lower part of the face, eyes that are large and round, and cheeks that are high and prominent. A pattern of babyish features occurs so widely among animals, in fact, that biologists who study animal behavior suspect it has a universal and genetically based power to elicit parental or nurturing responses among adult animals (Lorenz, 1970). Mothers in some species of ducks, for example, take care of baby ducks even when the babies are not their own. Among human parents and children, attachments may start with this sort of inherent attraction of parents to infants, though, of course, it deepens as additional personal experiences accumulate across the lifespan. We discuss some of these experiences when we look at psychosocial development in early adulthood (Chapter 13) and middle adulthood (Chapter 15).

What Do You Think?

What do you think attracts parents to their newborn children? Explore this question with the parents of a physically handicapped infant. How did they feel about their child (and about themselves) when the child was first born?

DEVELOPMENT OF THE NERVOUS SYSTEM

The **central nervous system** consists of the brain and nerve cells of the spinal cord, which together coordinate and control the perception of stimuli as well as motor responses of all kinds. The more complex aspects of this work are accomplished by the brain, which develops rapidly from just before birth until well beyond a child's second birthday. At seven months past conception, the baby's brain weighs about 10 percent of its final adult weight, but by birth it has more than doubled to about 25 percent of final adult weight. By the child's second birthday, it has tripled to about 75 percent of its final adult weight (Parkins, 1990).

Most of this increase results not from increasing numbers of nerve cells, or **neurons,** but from the development of a denser, or more fully packed, brain. This happens in two ways. First, the neurons put out many new fibers that connect them with one another. Second, certain brain cells called *glia* put out fatty sheathing, or *myelin,* that gradually encases the neurons and their fibers.

States of Sleep and Wakefulness

One important function of the brain is to control infants' states of sleep and wakefulness. The brain regulates the amount of stimulation infants experience, both ex-

Infants spend more time sleeping than doing anything else. Unfortunately their sleep may not all occur at night, so chronic sleep deprivation can be a real problem for some parents, particularly primary caregivers. If it can be arranged, it sometimes helps to nap at the same time as the baby, as this mother is doing.

ternally and internally. Thus, periodic sleep helps infants to shut out external stimulation and thereby allows them to obtain general physical rest.

Sleep   In the days immediately after birth, newborns sleep an average of sixteen hours per day, although some sleep as little as eleven hours a day and others as much as twenty-one (Michelsson et al., 1990). By age six months babies average just thirteen or fourteen hours of sleep per day, and by twenty-four months only eleven or twelve. But these hours still represent considerably more sleeping time than is typical for adults.

As Figure 4.1 shows, newborns divide their sleeping time about equally between relatively active and quiet periods of sleep. The more active kind is named **REM sleep,** after the "*rapid eye movements*," or twitchings, that usually accompany it. In the quieter kind of sleep, **non-REM sleep,** infants breathe regularly and more slowly, and their muscles become much limper.

Unfortunately for parents, a baby's extra sleep time does not usually include long, uninterrupted rest periods, even at night. In the first few months, it is more common for the baby to waken frequently—often every two or three hours—but somewhat unpredictably. Studies of brain development suggest that much of the unpredictability may result from the physical immaturity of the baby's nervous system: his brain may have frequent, accidental "storms" of impulses because it is not yet fully formed (Sheldon et al., 1992). As the accompanying Perspectives box

FIGURE 4.1
Developmental Changes in Sleep Requirements
Sleep changes in nature as children grow from infancy to adulthood. Overall they sleep less (shown by the top line decreasing to the right), and the proportion of REM (rapid-eye-movement) sleep decreases sharply during infancy and childhood (shown by the space decreasing between the two lines).

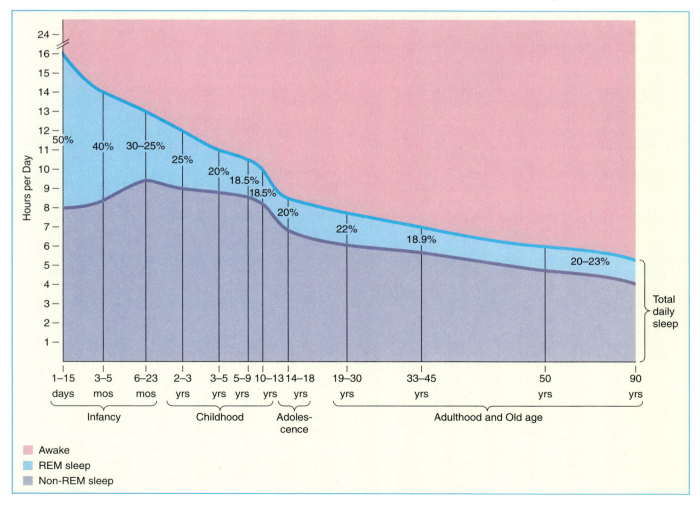

Perspectives

Sudden Infant Death Syndrome

Each year about two out of every one thousand young infants die in their sleep for no apparent reason. Doctors call this phenomenon **sudden infant death syndrome (SIDS),** or "crib death." The problem is most frequent among infants between ages two months and four months, although SIDS can affect babies as young as one month and as old as one year. It is the leading cause of death among infants who survive the first few weeks after delivery.

SIDS is disturbing because it is so mysterious. Typically parents put a seemingly healthy baby down to sleep as usual, but when they come in to get her up again, they discover she is dead. Sadly, because the baby had exhibited no health problems, the parents often blame themselves for the death, suspecting that somehow they neglected their child or hurt him in some way (Kaplan, 1995). Even more unfortunately, friends and relatives often concur in blaming the parents, simply because they can think of no other way to explain SIDS. Other obvious causes simply do not happen. The baby does not choke, vomit, or suffocate; she just stops breathing.

What causes SIDS? One theory is that SIDS is an exaggerated form of normal *sleep apnea,* temporary cessations of breathing during sleep (Hunt, 1992). Another theory suggests that SIDS occurs primarily at a special transition in development, just when inborn reflexive control of breathing begins to fade in importance but before infants have firmly established voluntary control of breathing. For most infants, this transition occurs at about two to four months of age, just when SIDS strikes most often. A third theory suggests that SIDS infants suffer from heart problems: their nervous systems may fail to prompt regular, strong heartbeats and in essence cause them to suffer a heart attack (Levy & Schwartz, 1994). Unfortunately, no clear evidence points to any of these alternative explanations.

If medical researchers could identify a basic cause, they would help future infants at risk for SIDS. Those babies could wear monitors that would indicate interruptions in breathing (if lungs are the problem) or heart rate (if that is it) and prompt parents or medical personnel to give the baby immediate, appropriate help. But so far the use of monitors has not been practical on a widespread scale because they can be cumbersome, cause a lot of unnecessary alarm, and occasionally fail to function properly.

Medical research has identified several factors that make a particular family or infant more likely to experience SIDS (Byard & Cohle, 1994). Very young mothers and fathers (less than twenty years) stand a greater chance of having a SIDS infant; so do mothers who smoke cigarettes or have serious illnesses during pregnancy. Mothers who are poorly nourished during pregnancy also carry more risk than mothers who keep reasonably well nourished. But certain babies also are at greater risk for SIDS independently of their parents' qualities or behaviors. Boys die of SIDS more often than girls, for example, and infants born small (less than seven pounds) die more often than bigger infants. These relationships do not mean, however, that being a boy or being small actually *causes* SIDS; they imply only that for reasons still not understood, SIDS seems to strike boys and small infants more frequently.

Even taken together, these factors do not predict SIDS very accurately. The vast majority of high-risk infants never die, whereas some infants with few risk factors die of SIDS anyway. This circumstance creates problems in translating the studies of risk factors into concrete recommendations for medical personnel and parents, because taking the risk indications too literally can arouse fears in parents unnecessarily. The most useful recommendations tend to be valid for all families, whether or not they are at risk for SIDS (U. S. Department of Health and Human Services, 1994b). For example, it is a good idea to recommend that parents not smoke and that an infant's room be humidified, if possible, whenever the baby catches a cold. Recent research also has found that SIDS is less likely to occur if infants sleep on their backs rather than on their stomachs. These are good pieces of advice for everyone, but unfortunately they do not guarantee complete protection from SIDS. For parents whose babies do die, many hospitals and communities have created support groups in which couples can share their grief and come to terms with it.

describes, irregularities in neural activity may be related to "crib death," or sudden infant death syndrome, in a very small percentage of infants.

The unpredictability of infants' sleep can create chronic sleep deprivation in some parents; obviously somebody has to wake up during the night to calm or feed a crying baby! Eventually the cure for fussiness depends on physical maturation, but parents can also influence their infant's sleep patterns by developing regular (though not rigid) times for and methods of waking, feeding, and sleeping that involve the infant. One study found, for example, that infants change toward more adultlike levels of wakefulness and sleep within six weeks after arriving home, provided routines are (relatively) regular (Bamford et al., 1990). Another found that regularity offers dividends later in childhood: comparisons of Dutch and American families found fewer sleep problems among the young children of Dutch families, whose culture encourages regularity of daily routines more strongly than North American society does (Harkness & Keefer, 1995).

The advice to strive for (relatively) regular routines is widely supported among parent advice experts, but note that it makes assumptions about families that are not always true. In some families, routines cannot be made regular because of competing pressures from other children, because of exhaustion from work or from earlier ill-timed wakings or feedings, or because the family has only one parent to begin with. Under these conditions, parents need additional support from friends, extended family, or social service workers. They cannot do it all themselves.

States of Arousal   As Table 4.2 shows, infants exhibit various states of arousal, from sleep to full wakefulness. As they get older, their patterns of arousal begin to resemble those of older children (Berg & Berg, 1987). The largest share of time, even among older infants, goes to the most completely relaxed and deepest form of sleep.

Obviously a fully alert state is a time when babies can learn from their surroundings, but it may not be the only time. During REM sleep, infants' heart rates speed up in reaction to sounds, suggesting that infants may process stimulation even while asleep. But the meaning of a faster heart rate is ambiguous: changes in it may also show neural *dis*organization or an inability to shut out the world. Babies who are born prematurely confirm this possibility, because they show more variablity in heart rate than normal babies when they hear sounds in their sleep (Spassov et al., 1994).

What Do You Think?

How do parents deal with differences in children's sleep patterns? Ask a classmate or friend who is a parent of more than one child, or ask your own parent(s), how he or she responded to sleep differences in the children as infants. Combine your information with several other classmates'. Do you see any trends?

TABLE 4.2   *States of Arousal in Infants*

State	Behavior of Infants
Non-REM sleep	Complete rest; muscles relaxed; eyes closed and still; breathing regular and relatively slow
REM sleep	Occasional twitches, jerks, facial grimaces; irregular and intermittent eye movements; breathing irregular and relatively rapid
Drowsiness	Occasional movements, but fewer than in REM sleep; eyes open and close; glazed look; breathing regular, but faster than in non-REM sleep
Alert inactivity	Eyes open and scanning; body relatively still; rate of breathing similar to drowsiness, but more irregular
Alert activity	Eyes open, but not attending or scanning; frequent, diffuse bodily movements; vocalizations; irregular breathing; skin flushed
Distress	Whimpering or crying; vigorous or agitated movements; facial grimaces pronounced; skin very flushed

Source: Wolff (1966).

VISUAL AND AUDITORY ACUITY

Infants can see at birth, but they lack the clarity of focus or *acuity* (keenness) characteristic of adults with good vision. When looking at stationary contours and objects, newborns see more clearly at short distances, especially at about eight to ten inches—about the distance, incidentally, between a mother's breast and her face. Their vision is better when tracking moving objects, but even so their overall vision is rather poor until about one month of age (Banks & Dannemiller, 1987).

Visual acuity improves a lot during infancy, but it does not reach adult levels until the end of the preschool years. An older infant (ages one to two) often has 20/30 or 20/40 vision, meaning he can see fine details at twenty feet that adults can see at thirty or forty feet. This quality of vision is quite satisfactory for everyday, familiar activities; in fact, many adults can see no better than this, without even realizing it. But this level of visual acuity does interfere with seeing distant objects.

Auditory acuity refers to sensitivity to sounds. Infants can hear at birth, but not as well as adults. Any sudden loud noise, such as that caused by dropping a large book on the floor, demonstrates they can hear. Such a sound produces a dramatic startle reaction, called a *Moro reflex*: the neonate withdraws her limbs suddenly, sometimes shakes all over, and may also cry. Not all noises produce this reaction; pure tones, such as the sound of a flute, cause relatively little response. Complex noises containing many different sounds usually produce a stronger reaction; a bag of nails spilling on the floor, for example, tends to startle infants reliably.

What Do You Think?

Do parenting books agree with our comments that young infants have the use of vision and hearing? Check the comments made in two or three books about the capabilities of newborn babies. Do they seem consistent, or at least not *in*consistent?

MOTOR DEVELOPMENT

Early Reflexes

Pediatricians have identified more than two dozen inborn **reflexes,** or automatic responses to specific stimuli. Table 4.3 summarizes the most important ones. A few reflexes, such as sucking, clearly help the baby to adapt to the new life outside the womb. Others look more like evolutionary vestiges of behaviors that may have helped earlier versions of *Homo sapiens* to cope, for example, by clinging to their mothers at the sound of danger. A few reflexes, such as blinking, breathing, and swallowing, persist throughout a person's life, but most reflexes disappear from the infant's repertoire during the first few months. Their disappearance, in fact, helps doctors to judge whether a baby is developing normally. Newborn reflexes that persist over many months may suggest damage to the nervous system or generally retarded development (Menkes, 1994).

The First Motor Skills

Motor skills are voluntary movements of the body or parts of the body. They can be grouped conveniently according to the size of the muscles and body parts involved. *Gross motor skills* involve the large muscles of the arms, legs, and torso. *Fine motor skills* involve the small muscles located throughout the body. Walking and jumping are examples of gross motor skills, and reaching and grasping are examples of fine motor skills.

TABLE 4.3 **Major Reflexes in Newborn Infants**

Reflex	Description	Development	Significance
Survival Reflexes			
Breathing reflex	Repetitive inhalation and expiration	Permanent, although becomes partly voluntary	Provides oxygen and expels carbon dioxide
Rooting reflex	Turning of cheek in direction of touch	Weakens and disappears by six months	Orients child to breast or bottle
Sucking reflex	Strong sucking motions with throat, mouth, and tongue	Gradually comes under voluntary control	Allows child to drink
Swallowing reflex	Swallowing motions in throat	Permanent, although becomes partly voluntary	Allows child to take in food and to avoid choking
Eyeblink reflex	Closing eyes for an instant ("blinking")	Permanent, although gradually becomes voluntary	Protects eyes from objects and bright light
Pupillary reflex	Changing size of pupils: smaller in bright light and bigger in dim light	Permanent	Protects against bright light and allows better vision in dim light
Primitive Reflexes			
Moro reflex	In response to a loud noise, child throws arms outward, arches back, then brings arms together as if to hold something	Arm movements and arching disappear by six months, but startle reaction persists for life	Indicates normal development of nervous system
Grasping reflex	Curling fingers around any small object put in the child's palm	Disappears by three months; voluntary grasping appears by about six months	Indicates normal development of nervous system
Tonic neck reflex	When laid on back, head turns to side, arm and leg extend to same side, limbs on opposite side flex	Disappears by two or three months	Indicates normal development of nervous system
Babinski reflex	When bottom of foot stroked, toes fan and then curl	Disappears eight to twelve months	Indicates normal development of nervous system
Stepping reflex	If held upright, infant lifts leg as if to step	Disappears by eight weeks, but later if practiced	Indicates normal development of nervous system
Swimming	If put in water, infant moves arms and legs and holds breath	Disappears by four to six months	Indicates normal development of nervous system

Viewed broadly, the sequence in which skills develop follows two general trends. The **cephalocaudal principle** ("head to tail") refers to the fact that upper parts of the body become usable and skillful before lower parts do. Babies learn to turn their heads before learning to move their feet intentionally, and they learn to move their arms before they learn to move their legs. The **proximodistal principle** ("near to far") refers to the fact that central parts of the body become skillful before peripheral, or outlying, parts do. Babies learn to wave their entire arms before learning to wiggle their wrists and fingers. The former movement occurs at the shoulder joint, near the center of the body, and the latter occurs at the periphery.

Gross Motor Development in the First Year Almost from birth, and before reflex behaviors disappear, babies begin doing some things on purpose. By age four weeks or so, most babies can lift their heads up when lying on their stomachs. At six or seven months, many babies have become quite adept at using their limbs; they can stick their feet up in the air and "bicycle" with them while a parent struggles valiantly to fit a diaper on the moving target. At ten months the average baby can stand erect, but only if an adult helps. By their first birthday, one-half of all babies can dispense with this assistance and stand by themselves without toppling over immediately (Savelsbergh, 1993). By age seven months, on the average, babies become able to locomote, or move around, on their own. At first, their methods are crude and slow; a baby might simply pivot on her stomach, for example, to get a better view of something interesting. Consistent movement in one direction develops soon after this time, although the movement does not always occur in the direction the baby intends!

Even before learning to walk, infants can reach for and handle small objects. With time and practice, they learn to modify their grasping to fit the physical requirements of a variety of objects and circumstances. As a result, babies already have useful grasping skills when locomotion finally begins, around their first birthday.

Reaching and Grasping   Even newborn infants will reach for and grasp objects they can see immediately in front of them. They often fail to grasp objects successfully; they may make contact with an object but fail to enclose it in their fingers. This early, crude reaching disappears fairly soon after birth, only to reappear at about four or five months of age as two separate skills, reaching and grasping (Pownall & Kingerlee, 1993). These skills soon serve infants in many ways. For example, by their second birthday most babies can turn the pages in large picture books one at a time, at least if the paper is relatively indestructible. But they can also point at the pages without grasping for them.

Walking   A reasonably predictable series of events leads to true walking in most children; Figure 4.2 describes some of these milestones. By about twelve to thirteen months, most children take their first independent steps. Well before two years, they often can walk not only forward but backward or even sideways. Some two-year-olds can even walk upstairs on two feet instead of on all fours. Usually they use the wall or a railing to do so. Usually, too, coming downstairs proves more difficult than going up; one solution is to creep down backward, using all four limbs.

Cultural and Sex Differences in Motor Development   Differences in motor development exist among cultures and between the sexes, though they are not always large or dramatic. Certain African cultures, for example, give their infants unusually frequent chances to sit upright and to practice their "walking" reflex when held at a standing position by adults and older children (Munroe et al., 1981). These opportunities seem to stimulate toddlers in these societies to learn to walk earlier and better than North American toddlers. Early walking, in turn, may prove especially valuable in these societies, which do not rely heavily on cars, bicycles, or other vehicles that make walking less important. Yet early walking may also be a genetic trait (at least partially) for these groups; without comparable training in reflex walking for North American infants, there is no way to be sure.

Yet differences in motor skills do not always appear where we might expect. Take the Navaho Indians, whose infants spend nearly all of their first year bound and swaddled tightly to a flat board, with their arms and legs extending straight down along their bodies (J. Whiting, 1981). Apparently as a result, Navaho toddlers

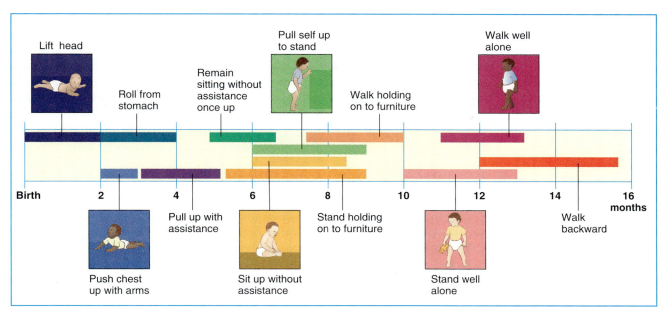

FIGURE 4.2
Milestones of Motor Development
Walking alone is one of the major physical achievements of the first year of life. Quite a few other physical skills usually develop prior to walking, as the figure shows. Note, though, that skills appear at different times for different individuals. As a result, some skills may even appear "out of sequence" in some children.

do tend to acquire walking a little later than Anglo-American children. But they do not show delays in other skills inhibited by swaddling, notably reaching and grasping, and the deficit in walking disappears by the end of the preschool years in most cases (Kagan, 1984).

Culture aside, do boys and girls differ, on average, in motor development? The answer depends on distinguishing what infants *can* do from what they typically *do* do. What they can do—their competence—has relatively little relationship to their sex. Girl and boy babies sit upright at about the same age, for example, and stand and walk at about the same time. Similar equality exists for all of the motor milestones of infancy.

Swaddling infants, as is done with this Navajo infant, is practiced in many cultures. Swaddling tends to slow motor development at first, but not permanently. It may also allow caregivers to carry infants with them during daily activities—a circumstance that could make the skill of vocalizing by infants less urgent to develop.

How infants use their time is another matter. Almost as soon as they can move, boys show more activity than girls do. The trend begins even before birth, when male fetuses move about in their mothers' wombs more than female fetuses do (Ames, 1983). After birth, the trend continues: girls spend more time using their emerging fine motor skills. Of course, the differences in use of time may stem partly from parents' encouragement (praise) for "gender-appropriate" behaviors. Given the young age of the children, though, and the fact that activity actually precedes birth, part of the difference must come from genetic endowment: an inborn tendency to be more (or less) active.

It is important to note that whatever their source, sex differences in infants' motor development are only averages and that they are in any case rather slight. As groups, boys and girls are more alike than different, and numerous individual boys are quieter motorically than numerous individual girls despite "average" behavior. As a practical matter, it is therefore more important for parents and teachers to respond to the qualities of the individual children for whom they are responsible than to any stereotypical "gender" average.

What Do You Think?

If motor skills develop partly through learning, why not just deliberately teach infants to walk? What do you think would be the result of doing so? Do similar considerations apply for certain other important developments in infancy?

IMPAIRMENTS IN INFANT GROWTH

Low-Birth-Weight Infants

A small percentage of newborns are considered **low-birth-weight** infants if they are born weighing less than 2,500 grams, or about 5½ pounds. The condition can result from several factors. One of the most common causes is malnourishment of the mother during pregnancy. But other harmful practices, such as smoking cigarettes, drinking alcohol, or taking drugs, also can depress birth weight. Mothers from certain segments of the population, such as teenagers and those from very low-SES backgrounds, are especially likely to give birth to low-birth-weight babies, most likely because of their own poor nourishment or their lack of access to good prenatal care. But even mothers who are well nourished and well cared for sometimes have infants who are smaller than is medically desirable. Multiple births (e.g., twins, triplets) usually result in small babies; so do some illnesses or mishaps, such as a serious traffic accident that causes damage to the placenta.

Consequences of Low Birth Weight   When birth weight is very low (less than 2,500 grams), infants' reflexes tend to be a bit sluggish, weak, and poorly organized (Brooten, 1992). Such infants do not startle as reliably or grasp as automatically and strongly at objects. Their muscles often seem flabby or overly relaxed. After delivery, the infants must cope with many tasks for which they are inadequately prepared physically, including breathing and digesting food. They also have trouble regulating their own sleep to keep it peaceful, sustained, and smooth.

Neurological limitations can often persist for the first two or three years of life, causing the baby to develop specific motor skills a bit later than other infants. A four-month-old baby who is small due to being born two months preterm, for example, in many ways resembles a two-month-old born at full term; both infants have lived eleven months from conception. Some of the delay may reflect stresses associated with early birth (such as parents' overprotectiveness) rather than the physical effects of early birth as such. Unless they are extremely small, though, most low-birth-weight infants eventually develop into relatively normal preschoolers (Goldson, 1992).

What Do You Think?

Imagine that you are writing a brief (two-paragraph) article for expectant mothers in the local newspaper about "What to do if your baby is born two months early." What would you say, and where would you find further information for your article? Sketch out your answers, but also consult with a few classmates about how to construct this article.

NUTRITION DURING THE FIRST TWO YEARS

Of course, the physical developments described in this chapter depend on good nutrition during the first two years. Like adults, babies need diets with appropriate amounts of protein, calories, and specific vitamins and minerals. For various reasons, however, infants do not always get all the nutrients they need. Often poverty accounts for malnutrition: parents with good intentions may be unable to afford the right foods. In other cases, conventional eating practices interfere: despite relatively expensive eating habits, such as going to fast-food restaurants, some families may fail to provide their children with a balanced diet.

Compared with older children, infants eat less in overall or absolute amounts. A well-nourished young baby in North America might drink somewhat less than one liter (about .95 quarts) of liquid nourishment per day. This amount definitely would not keep an older child or a young adult well nourished, although it might prevent starving. In proportion to their body weight, however, infants need to consume much more than older children or adults do. For example, every day a three-month-old baby ideally should take in more than two ounces of liquid per pound of body weight, whereas an eighteen-year-old needs only about one-third of this amount (Queen & Lang, 1993).

Breast Milk Versus Formula

Someone (usually parents) must provide for an infant's comparatively large appetite. Whenever breast feeding is possible, health experts generally recommend human milk as the sole source of nutrition for at least the first six months or so of most infants' lives and as a major source for at least the next six months. In some cases, of course, this recommendation proves difficult or impractical to follow. Babies who need intensive medical care immediately after birth cannot be breast fed without special arrangements. Also, for one reason or another, some women may choose not to breast feed, for example, if they are taking medications that might be passed on to the baby, or if job situations make breast feeding difficult to do. For these infants, formulas can be either safer or more convenient.

Why do pediatricians recommend breast feeding? First, human milk seems to give young infants more protection from diseases and other ailments. Second, human milk matches the nutritional needs of human infants more closely than formula preparations do; in particular, it contains more iron, an important nutrient for infants. Third, breast feeding better develops the infant's jaw and mouth muscles because it requires stronger sucking motions than bottle feeding does and because it tends to satisfy infants' intrinsic needs for sucking better than a bottle does. Fourth, breast feeding may encourage a healthy emotional relationship between

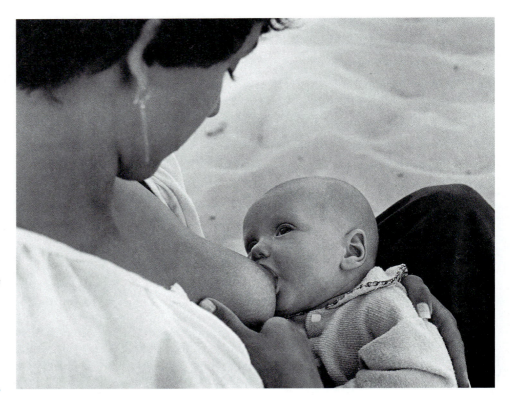

In recent decades, increasing numbers of mothers in our society have chosen to breast-feed their babies as recommended by most pediatricians. For a significant number of parents and infants, however, partial or complete bottle-feeding remains a better option—for example, if fathers wish to be involved in feedings.

mother and infant, simply because it involves a lot of close physical snuggling (La Leche League International, 1991).

Nutrition in Later Infancy

After about six months, infants can be introduced gradually to solid foods such as strained cereals and strained fruits. As babies become tolerant of these new foods, parents can introduce others that sometimes require a more mature digestive system, such as strained meats and cooked eggs. Overall, the shift to solid foods often takes many months to complete (see Table 4.4 for guidelines about how to do this). As it occurs, parents must begin paying more attention to their baby's overall nutritional needs, since many solid foods lack the broad range of nutrients that breast milk and formula provide.

Malnutrition in North America   Often North American diets fail to provide enough of three specific nutrients: vitamin A, vitamin C, and iron. Prolonged deficiencies of vitamins A and C seem to create deficits in motor ability (Pollitt et al., 1984), and deficiency of iron appears to lead to deficits in cognitive performance (Pollitt, 1987). For about 4 to 5 percent of infants, these nutritional deficiencies are serious and require immediate remedy. For another group about the same size, the nutritional deficiencies are less severe but are still a cause for concern.

Even when undernourished infants appear healthy and "bright," they may be at risk for later developmental problems because poorly nourished families often experience other serious deprivations, such as poor sanitation, inadequate health care, and lack of educational opportunities. Under these conditions, it may not take much to turn mild undernourishment into severe malnutrition and thus reduce cognitive and motor performance to below satisfactory levels.

Obesity and Overnutrition In calorie-loving societies such as our own, eating too much can pose a serious problem for some individuals. The most obvious result of eating too much is to become extremely overweight, or **obese**. The nature and extent of obesity depend partly on how much an infant overeats and when during development the overeating occurs.

In the short run, what infants eat affects how much they weigh. Big, heavy infants tend to have diets high in calories. They tend to drink more milk than usual and to be started early on solid foods, which often are relatively high in calories. They even breast feed more vigorously and in this way take in more calories per meal than other babies. Contrary to what some parents fear, however, weight in infancy correlates little with weight in childhood and even less with weight in adulthood (Williams & Kimm, 1993). Heavy babies stand only a slightly greater chance than lighter ones of becoming heavy children, and then only if they are very heavy indeed to begin with.

Failure to Thrive An infant or a preschool child who fails to grow at normal rates for no apparent medical reason suffers from a condition called **failure to thrive**. About 6 percent of North American children exhibit this condition at one time or another, although not necessarily continuously (Woolston, 1993). In some ways the condition resembles malnutrition, especially as it occurs in developing nations. Failure-to-thrive and malnourished children both develop motor and cognitive skills more slowly than usual; both experience higher rates of school failure and learning disabilities; and both are more likely to live in disadvantaged circumstances and to have parents who are enduring physical or emotional stress.

At one time, professionals tended to attribute failure to thrive to lack of nurturing and love between parent and child. A more complex picture may be closer to the truth: failure to thrive may have many sources, both physical and psychological, and depend on both the child and the environment. Consider this pattern. An infant has a genetically quiet, slow-to-respond temperament, making it more difficult for her mother to establish emotional contact. If the mother also is experiencing a number of other stresses (low income, illness, or disapproval of the new baby from others), the relationship between mother and infant is put at risk. A vicious cycle may develop of poorly timed feedings and ineffective efforts to nurture the infant, who persistently resists the mother's love and even her food. Parents in this situation often can benefit from professional help and support in learning new patterns of interacting with their babies.

TABLE 4.4 *Changing Nutritional Needs During Infancy*

Age in Months	Parents May Begin
Birth–4	Complete diet of breast milk or baby formula
4–6	Introduce puréed single-grain cereal, preferably iron-fortified. Begin with 1–2 teaspoons, work up to 1/2 cup, twice per day.
5	100% fruit juices, could be diluted, 1/2 cup serving per day.
6–8	Introduce puréed vegetables or fruit, one at a time. Begin with 1–2 teaspoons, work up to 1/4–1/2 cup per serving, twice per day. Introduce "finger" foods (e.g., chopped banana, bits of dry cereal).
10–12	Introduce puréed meats or poultry, beginning with 1–2 teaspoons, working up to 1/4–1/2 cup per serving, 3–4 times per day. Introduce soft but chopped foods (e.g., lumpy potatoes). Introduce whole milk, 1/2 cup per serving, 4–5 times per day.
24	Introduce low-fat milk, 1/2 cup per serving, 4–5 times per day.

Source: Adapted from International Food Information Council, 1993.

TABLE 4.5 *Infant Mortality in Selected Nations*

Nation	Infant Mortality (per 1,000 live births)
Finland	5.5
Japan	6.3
Sweden	6.7
Switzerland	6.9
Hong Kong	7.5
Canada	7.9
Denmark	7.9
Netherlands	7.9
France	8.0
United States, white	**8.5**
Norway	8.5
Germany	8.9
Ireland	8.9
Singapore	9.3
United Kingdom	9.3
Belgium	9.4
Australia	10.0
Spain	10.5
United States, average	**10.6**
New Zealand	10.8
Italy	10.9
Austria	11.0
Israel	12.3
Greece	14.0
Czechoslovakia	14.0
United States, nonwhite	**17.5**

Sources: UNICEF (1993); U.S. Bureau of the Census (1992b).

Infant Mortality

In the past several decades, health care systems in North America and around the world have substantially improved their ability to keep infants alive. The **infant mortality rate,** the proportion of babies who die during the first year of life, has declined steadily during this century. In 1950 in the United States, about twenty-nine out of every one thousand infants died; forty decades later, this number was fewer than ten out of every one thousand infants (U.S. National Center for Health Statistics, 1991). The averages conceal wide differences within society, some of which are listed in Table 4.5. Families with very low incomes are about twice as likely to lose an infant as are families with middle-level incomes (about eighteen to twenty babies per one thousand versus nine per one thousand). Likewise, African American families are twice as likely as white families to lose an infant, perhaps because of the historical correlation of race with income level and access to health care in American society (Pritchett, 1993). As a result, mortality rates in some nonwhite, low-SES areas of major cities rival the rates found in less developed countries around the world.

On average, infant mortality rates in the United States and Canada are two or three times lower than those in many less developed countries. Even so, infant mortality in the United States actually is *higher* than in nineteen other developed nations, including Canada, Japan, Sweden, France, and Great Britain (United Nations International Children's Emergency Fund, 1995). Cross-cultural investigations of infant mortality rates in European countries have given further clues about the reasons for the relatively high U.S. rate and have suggested ways to improve it. The research overwhelmingly indicates that parents need social supports as much as they need access to basic medical services and knowledge. Most European countries provide pregnant mothers with free prenatal care, for example, and also protect women's right to work during and after pregnancy. Pregnant women get special, generous sick leave, get at least four months of maternity leave with pay, and are protected from doing dangerous or exhausting work (such as night shifts). Policies such as these communicate support for pregnant mothers and their spouses in ways not currently available in the United States.

What Do You Think?

If you (or your spouse) were expecting a child, would you prefer that the baby be breast fed or bottle fed? Discuss this question with a classmate of the *same* sex; then compare your responses with a classmate of the *opposite* sex. Do your responses differ?

COGNITIVE DEVELOPMENT

While infants are growing physically, they are also thinking: noticing the world around them, organizing their impressions, and even remembering their experiences. Although these activities are often simply called "cognitive development" or "cognition," psychologists frequently classify them according to their mental complexity. **Perception** is the less complex process and refers to the brain's immediate or direct organization and interpretation of sensations. Perceptual processes occur when an infant notices that a toy car is the same car no matter which way she orients it. **Cognition** is the more complex process and refers to thinking and other mental activities. It includes reasoning, attention, memory, problem solving, and the ability to represent objects and experiences. Infants engage in both cognition and perception, even as newborns.

STUDYING COGNITION AND MEMORY IN INFANTS

How can we know whether an infant, who cannot talk about his or her experiences, is actually noticing sights and sounds, organizing information about them, and remembering them? Psychologists have developed two main strategies: studying changes in infants' heart rates and studying infants' tendency to *habituate,* or get used to, novel stimuli.

Arousal and Infants' Heart Rates

One way to understand an infant's cognition is to measure his heart rate (HR) with a small electronic stethoscope attached to his chest. The changes in HR are taken to signify variations in the baby's arousal, alertness, and general contentment.

Psychologists who study infants make this assumption because among adults, HR varies reliably with attention and arousal. Typically HR slows down, or decelerates, when adults notice or attend to something interesting but not overly exciting, such as reading the newspaper. If adults attend to something *very* stimulating, their HRs speed up, or accelerate. Watching a lab technician draw blood from your own arm, for example, often causes your HR to speed up. On the whole, novel or attractive stimuli produce curiosity and a slower HR, whereas potentially dangerous or aversive stimuli produce defensiveness, discomfort, and a faster HR, at least among adults.

Very young infants, from one day to a few months old, show similar changes, but we need to take several precautions when we study their HRs. For one thing, observations of infants' attention should be made when infants are awake and alert, and, as we already pointed out, newborn babies often spend a lot of time being drowsy or asleep. For another, newborn and very young infants are much more likely to respond to relatively gentle and persistent stimuli, such as a quiet, continuous sound or a soft light that moves slowly or blinks repeatedly (Slater & Morrison, 1991). Many stimuli that lead to deceleration in adults or older children lead to acceleration in infants. Many one-month-olds show a faster HR at familiar sights, such as their mothers, even though the infants may look like they are just staring calmly into space. Despite these problems, however, studies of HR have provided a useful way to measure infants' attention, perception, and memory.

Recognition, Memory, and Infant Habituation

Although infants cannot describe what they remember, they often indicate recognition of particular objects, people, and activities. Familiar people, such as mothers, bring forth a special response in one-year-olds, who may coo suddenly at the sight of them, stretch out their arms to them, and even crawl or walk to them if they know how. Less familiar people, such as neighbors or the family doctor, tend not to produce responses such as these and may even produce active distress, depending on the age of the infant.

Babies' responses to the familiar and the unfamiliar offer infant psychologists a second way to understand infant perception and conceptual thought. Psychologists study infants' tendency to get used to and therefore ignore stimuli as they experience them repeatedly; this tendency is called **habituation** (Bornstein, 1989). One habituation strategy repeatedly offers a baby a standard, or "study," stimulus—a simple picture to look at or a simple melody to hear. Like most adults, the baby attends to the study stimulus carefully at first, but on subsequent occasions gradually pays less attention to it. As this happens, the baby is said to be *habituating* to the stimulus. After the baby has become habituated, the investigators present the original study stimulus along with a few other stimuli. If the baby really recognizes the original, she probably will attend to the others *more* because they are comparatively novel. Her HR will slow down as well.

This method has shown that young babies recognize quite a lot of past experiences. One classic habituation study found that four-month-old girls recognized a familiar visual pattern among three others that differed from the original (McCall & Kagan, 1967). Another showed that HR slowed down when five-month-olds heard a familiar melody replayed in a different rhythmic pattern (Chang & Trehub, 1977b). Still another found habituation even in newborns: they "noticed" when a light brush on their cheeks changed location, as revealed by changes in their HRs (Kisilevsky & Muir, 1984). Sometimes, too, recognition persists for very long periods. Three-month-olds, it seems, can still recognize a picture or a toy two weeks after they first see it, as long as the objects are presented in a familiar context the second time—a performance that matches adults' recognition memory (Hayne et al., 1991).

What Do You Think?

Given the research described in this section, when is it fair to say that a young infant first begins to "recognize" his or her parents? Talk to a recent parent about when he or she felt sure of being recognized. Does the parent's experience confirm that infants have memory?

INFANT PERCEPTION

As mentioned earlier, *perception* refers to how the brain organizes and interprets sensations. Perception operates relatively automatically: when your best friend walks up to you, your brain almost instantly converts an oval-shaped pattern of colors and lines from an unorganized batch of sensations into an organized whole called your friend's face. The automatic quality of perception has made many psychologists suspect that it is either genetically programmed or learned very early in infancy. Either way, perception is a primary feature of infant cognition.

Children acquire a number of important perceptual skills during infancy. The most important ones correspond to the two dominant human senses, vision and hearing, and the relationships between these two senses.

Visual Perception

Given that children can see almost from birth, what do they perceive? Some of the earliest research on this question stirred up a lot of interest because it seemed to show that infants, even those just two days old, could discriminate between human faces and abstract patterns and that they looked at faces longer than at either patterned disks or plain, unpatterned disks (Fantz, 1963). The researchers presented infants with various combinations of these stimuli side by side and carefully observed which object the babies spent the most time looking at. At all ages studied (birth to six months), the infants showed a clear preference: they stared at a picture of a human face almost twice as long as at any other stimulus picture. Young infants, it seemed, were inherently interested in people.

More recent studies of visual preferences, however, have qualified this conclusion substantially (Yonas, 1988). It is not the humanness of faces that infants enjoy looking at but their interesting contours, complexity, and curvature. Newborns are particularly attracted to contours, or the edges of areas of light and dark. But such edges can be provided either by the hairline of a parent's head or by a properly constructed abstract drawing. When infants reach age two or three months, their perceptual interest shifts to complexity and curvature. At this age, infants look longer

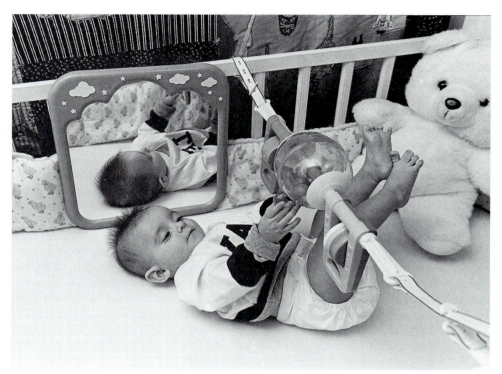

Young infants concentrate longer on certain shapes and contours, even when these are not part of a human face. Newborns are especially attracted to contours and to patches of light and dark. A few months later, they prefer complex patterns over simpler ones and curved lines over straight ones. Such changes are one reason (among many) why a baby's interest in crib toys waxes and wanes over time.

at a pattern of many small squares than at one containing just a few large squares. They also look longer at curved lines than at straight ones. These qualities too are conveniently provided by human faces, but not by faces alone.

Object Perception   *Object constancy* refers to the perception that an object remains the same in some way despite constant changes in the sensations it sends to the eye. A baby's favorite toy duck never casts exactly the same image on her retina from one second to the next. The image continually varies depending on its distance and its orientation, or angle of viewing. Somehow the baby must learn that this kaleidoscope of images really refers to only one constant duck—that the duck always *is* the same but keeps *looking* different. Several studies show that infants begin acquiring this knowledge very early indeed.

Consider the development of *size constancy,* the perception that an object stays the same size even when viewed from different distances. In a typical study, newborn babies are conditioned to suck on pacifiers at the sight of a cube of some specified size and placed at some precise distance. During conditioning training, sucking at the sight of cubes of other sizes or distances is deliberately *not* reinforced so that the sucking provides an indicator of the baby's recognition of an object of a particular size and at a given distance.

Later the conditioned infants are shown several cubes of different sizes and placed at different distances. The test cubes include one that casts an image exactly the size of the original but is in fact *larger* and *farther away,* as shown in Figure 4.3. Typically, the babies are not fooled by this apparent identity of retinal images. They prefer to look at the original cube regardless of its distance; that is, they suck on their pacifiers more vigorously while looking at the original cube than while looking at any substitute. Apparently they know when an object really is the same size and when it only looks the same size.

Depth perception refers to a sense of how far away objects are or appear to be. Infants begin acquiring this kind of perceptual skill about as soon as they can focus on objects at different distances, at around two or three months of age. This conclusion is suggested by research that has developed out of the now classic experiment with the visual cliff (Gibson & Walk, 1960). In its basic form, the **visual cliff** consists of a table covered with strong glass under which is a textured surface with colored squares, such as that shown in the photograph on the next page. Part of the textured surface contacts the glass directly, and another part is separated from it by several feet. Visually, then, the setup resembles the edge of a table, but the glass provides ample support for an infant, even in the dropped-off area. A baby who is placed onto it will seem to float in midair.

On this apparatus, even babies just two months old discriminate between the two sides of the visual cliff. They find the deep side more interesting, as suggested by the extra time they take to study it. Young babies show little fear of the deep side, judging either by their overt behavior or by their heart rates, which tend to decrease during their investigations of the cliff. This finding implies they are primarily curious about the cliff rather than fearful of it.

Babies old enough to crawl, however, show significant fear of the visual cliff. Their heart rates increase markedly, and they will not crawl onto the deep side despite coaxing from a parent and the solid support they feel from the glass. Why the change? Perhaps infants' crawling skills allow them to perceive distances more accurately than before, since the motion of crawling causes faraway objects (including the deep side of the cliff) to move less than nearby objects (such as the shallow side). Perhaps, too, infants old enough to crawl are also old enough to focus their eyes more accurately on each side of the cliff, a physical skill that provides further perceptual information about the difference in distance of the two sides (Kermoian & Campos, 1988).

Auditory Perception

Infants respond to sounds even as newborns. But what do they perceive from sounds? What sense do they make of the sounds they hear? These questions are important, because infants' ability to discriminate among sounds makes a crucial difference in their acquisition of language, as discussed later in this chapter.

Localization of Sounds   Infants just two months old can locate sounds, as suggested by the fact that they orient their heads toward certain noises, such as a rattle (Morrongiello, 1994). But they often take much longer to respond than do older children or adults. Instead of needing just a fraction of a second, as adults do, full-term infants require an average of two to three seconds before orienting toward ("looking at") a sound that occurs off to one side. Infants born one month preterm require even more time to respond. These delays may explain why pediatricians and others used to believe newborn infants cannot hear: the sounds they offered to the babies, such as a single hand clap, may not have lasted long enough for the infants to respond.

FIGURE 4.3

Size Constancy in Infancy
Even babies just a few weeks old show size constancy; that is, they distinguish between an object that is larger but farther away and one that is smaller but closer. In general, they prefer looking at objects that are relatively close in distance, whatever their size.

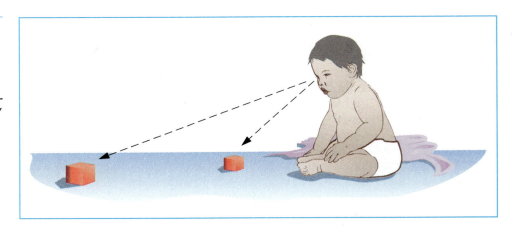

Infants' behavior on a visual cliff reflects both their knowledge and their feelings about depth. Even babies too young to crawl or creep find the deep side of the cliff more interesting than the shallow side. But only babies who have begun crawling or creeping show fear or wariness of the deep side.

Although infants can locate sounds, their skill at doing so is somewhat limited. They are better able to locate relatively high-pitched sounds, such as those made by a flute or a small bird, than low-pitched sounds, such as that made by a foghorn (Spetner & Olsho, 1990). This fact has sometimes led some experts to suggest that infants have a "natural" preference for female—that is, high-pitched—human voices. Studies of voice preferences, however, have not confirmed this possibility consistently, probably because newborns' range of special sensitivity lies well above the pitch of even female voices and because male and female voices usually are more similar in overall quality than gender stereotypes suggest. Instead, it is more accurate to say that infants prefer sounds in the middle range of pitches, which is the range most similar to human voices, male or female.

Coordination of Vision and Hearing   The localization of sounds suggests that even very young babies coordinate what they see with what they hear; they seem to use sound to direct their visual gaze. But is this what really happens? As reasonable as this interpretation seems, the evidence suggests a more complicated story (Morrongiello, 1994). In their first efforts to turn their heads, very young babies (one or two months old) act more as though head turning is a reflex than a search for something to see. The behavior does not habituate, meaning a young baby is just as likely to turn toward a sound after many presentations as he was after the first presentation. Also, the behavior occurs even in the dark, when there is no chance to actually see the source of a sound. Only by age five or six months do these reflexive qualities change: by that age, babies habituate quickly to repeated presentations and search only in the light, when there is something to see. In these ways, then, hearing and vision have become coordinated, but it has taken several months of learning for the change to occur.

Culture and Infant Perception   How, if at all, might culture influence the ways infants see and hear? Research on this problem is sketchy; most psychologists, even those with a special interest in culture, usually assume cultural influences require time after birth to develop and therefore begin to emerge only toward the end of infancy. Even among older children and adults, however, cultural influences on perception seem to be much smaller than on language, problem solving, styles of thinking, or social relationships. For example, adults from twenty different societies all perceive the same color of blue to be the "best," or truest, example of blue regardless of their culture of origin or the number of color terms in their particular language (Berlin & Kay, 1969). If the adults show such unanimity, presumably young infants from these cultures do so as well.

What Do You Think?

Might there be a way to help babies coordinate vision and hearing better and sooner? Think of one or two ways to accomplish this, and also consider any negative side effects of deliberately encouraging this development. Ask a classmate—or, better yet, a recent parent—for an opinion about whether your ideas would in fact succeed.

INFANT COGNITION

As perceptual skills develop, children begin to put them to cognitive uses. A one-month-old infant may notice the dark eyes painted on the face of a doll and stare a long time at them out of interest. But an eighteen-month-old can do more than that: he can talk to the doll in babbles that resemble language or cuddle the doll briefly as though it were a real person. All in all, the older infant combines perception with other skills he is developing. In doing so, he shows the first signs of cognition, or methods for thinking or gaining knowledge about the world.

At first, infant cognition has little to do with the symbolic forms that develop in most children and adults. Instead, it emphasizes active experimentation with and manipulation of materials. Only by the end of infancy does truly symbolic thought emerge. Even then it is still interspersed with large amounts of concrete doing, seeing, and hearing. Nevertheless, its mere existence marks a significant new development for the child. The interview with Gillian Luppiwiski describes firsthand how this happens for some children in an infant care center.

Piaget's Theory of Sensorimotor Intelligence

Piaget's theory of cognitive development, described in Chapter 2, provides one of the most complete outlines of infant intelligence available (Piaget, 1963). According to this viewpoint, infants think by way of *sensory* perceptions and *motor* actions, by doing things to and with the objects they see. Piaget called this activity **sensorimotor intelligence**. He identified six stages during infancy that mark significant developments in sensorimotor intelligence; Table 4.6 summarizes these stages.

In general, the stages of infant cognition show two trends. First, infants show a trend toward symbolic thinking. Instead of needing to handle a toy car to understand it, an infant becomes increasingly able to visualize, or think about, a car without actually touching or seeing one. This ability becomes very strong by the end of the first two years of life; to Piaget, it helps mark the end of infancy. Changes in infants' toys reflect this developmental trend, as indicated in Table 4.7.

Second, infants form cognitive structures that Piaget called *schemes*. In relation to infants, **schemes** are organized patterns of actions or concepts that help the baby to make sense out of and adapt to the environment. Schemes develop well before infants can represent objects or events through language or motor skills. A newborn baby's initial grasping motions constitute an early scheme, as do her earliest sucking motions. Eventually, as described shortly, internal, or mental, concepts and ideas develop out of such patterns of behavior. These too are sometimes called *schemes* (or sometimes *schemas* or *schemata*); but Piaget himself more often called cognitive structures and patterns that develop later by names such as *operations* or *systems,* depending on their exact nature (Miller, 1993).

As we discuss more fully in Chapter 2, Piaget argued that sensorimotor intelligence develops by means of two complementary processes, assimilation and accom-

Working with Gillian Luppiwiski, INFANT CARE PROVIDER

Fostering Infants' Thinking

Gillian Luppiwiski has worked as a caregiver in an infant day care center for ten years. She made numerous comments about her work: the changes she sees in the babies as they grow, the responses of mothers and fathers, the interest that even infants and toddlers show in one another. When I asked her to comment on infants' thinking abilities, she began talking about their language and problem-solving behaviors and about how she and other caregivers support it.

Kelvin: What do you notice most about these children when you're working here?

Gillian: They change so much! Like day and night. Last fall Jocelyn could hardly move; she got so frustrated watching the older children walk around! But now she's all over the place, into *everything*—and happy as a lark.

Kelvin: Can you figure out what she thinks about? Does it even make sense to ask about her "thoughts"?

Gillian: Oh, yes. Like when we get out the play doh, and she starts using it—poking it with her fingers, talking about it. She just started naming it, you know; she says "doh" and looks at you with a smile. And "wed" when it's red. That's her favorite color.

Kelvin: So her language is developing?

Gillian: Yes, and the play doh helps with that. It gives her something to talk about. We support her comments, saying things like "That's right! We've got red play doh today."

Kelvin: What about other times? Even when she's not talking, does it seem like Jocelyn's "thinking"?

Gillian: Definitely! Take the climber: she loves to climb up there and sit with Joel. That teaches her about space and depth, but she learns more by *doing* it than by talking about it. Shelley (another caregiver) might talk about it, comment on it verbally when she sees Jocelyn climbing. But Jocelyn mainly learns it by doing it.

Kelvin: Do you ever "teach" them anything directly?

Gillian: We don't so much teach them as make it possible for them to learn. That's how I'd put it. Shelley or I might put out a few puzzles one day, and talk with a child when she chooses to work on one—encourage her to persist in putting it together, maybe give a hint or two, but not do it for her.

Or the other day Danny started getting out *all* the trucks! He lined them all up with the big ones at one end and the smaller ones at the other end. Sorted them! It was great to see. He needed help, though, in finding enough room to do this without tripping over Jocelyn and the others. He commented on the lineup: "All the trucks!" And so did I, by challenging him gently: "Are you sure you have them *all*?"

Kelvin: So he was grouping? Classifying things?

Gillian: Yes. In his own way, his own two-year-old way. "Developmentally appropriate practice"—that's what educators are always talking about. That's what makes us a real *infant* center, and different from a preschool center. We try to provide developmentally appropriate things and support the children for using them.

What Do You Think?

1. Considering what Gillian said, how important is an infant care center for fostering a child's thinking ability? How does it compare to experiences that an infant or toddler might have at home?

2. Gillian says, "We don't so much teach them as make it possible for them to learn." How comfortable are you with this idea? Can it apply to working with older children (preschoolers, school-age, adolescents) or only to infants and toddlers? Consult with a few classmates about this question; what do they think about it?

3. At times Gillian seems to equate language development with cognitive development. Is there some way to distinguish these two processes in an infant center? Brainstorm an example or two of how you might do this if you were a caregiver.

---

modation. **Assimilation** consists of interpreting new experiences in terms of existing schemes. A baby who is used to sucking on a breast or bottle may use the same action on whatever new, unfamiliar objects he encounters, such as rubber balls or his own fist. **Accommodation** consists of modifying existing schemes to fit new experiences. After sucking on a number of new objects, an infant may modify this action to fit the nature of each new object; she may chew on some new objects (her sweater) but not on others (a plastic cup).

The interplay of assimilation and accommodation leads to new schemes and eventually to the infant's ability to symbolize objects and activities. Let's see how Piaget believed this transition occurs.

Stage 1: Early Reflexes—Using What You're Born With (Birth to One Month)
According to Piaget, cognitive development begins with reflexes, those simple,

TABLE 4.6 *Some Features of Infant Cognition According to Piaget*

Stage	Age in Months	Characteristics
1: Early reflexes	Birth–1	Reliance on inborn reflexes to "know" the environment; assimilation of all experiences to reflexes
2: Primary circular reactions	1–4	Accommodation (or modification) of reflexes to fit new objects and experiences; repeated actions focusing on infant's own body
3: Secondary circular reactions	4–8	Repeated actions focusing on objects; actions used as means toward ends, but haphazardly; early signs of object permanence
4: Combined secondary circular reactions	8–12	Deliberate combinations of previously acquired actions (or schemes); AnotB error; early signs of sense of time
5: Tertiary circular reactions	12–18	Systematic application of previously acquired actions (or schemes); well-organized investigation of novel objects, but always overt
6: The first symbols	18–24	First symbolic representations of objects; true object permanence; deferred imitation

Source: Piaget (1963).

inborn behaviors that all normal babies can produce at birth. As it happens, the majority of such reflexes remain just that—reflexes—for the individual's entire life; sneezing patterns and blinking responses, for example, look nearly the same in adults as they do in infants. But a few are notable for their flexibility, chiefly sucking, grasping, and looking. These behaviors resemble reflexes at birth, but they quickly begin to be modified in response to experiences such as sucking on the mother's breast, on toys, and on the child's own hand. They give infants a repertoire from which to develop more complex skills, and their susceptibility to influence makes them especially important to cognitive development during infancy.

Stage 2: Primary Circular Reactions—Modifying What You're Born With (One to Four Months)   Soon after the baby begins modifying his early reflexes, he begins to build and differentiate action schemes quite rapidly. In fact, within a month or so he sometimes repeats them endlessly for no apparent reason. Because of its repetitive quality, Piaget calls this behavior a **circular reaction**. The baby seems to be stimulated by the outcome of his own behavior, so he responds for the mere joy of feeling himself act. At this point the circular reactions are called *primary circular reactions,* because they still focus on the baby's own body and movements. Waving an arm repeatedly constitutes a primary circular reaction; so does kicking again and again.

During this period, the young infant practices her developing schemes widely, and the behaviors rapidly become less reflexive. The baby may shape her mouth dif-

TABLE 4.7 *Toys That Support Cognitive Development in Infancy*
As infants get older, their toys tend to involve more complex motor skills, as well as language and make-believe. Can you see how these trends are reflected in the lists below?

Birth–2 Months	6–12 Months	12–24 Months
Mobile in crib Rattle	Squeeze toys Nested plastic cups Boxes with lids Soft ball Stuffed animals Pots and pans Picture books (especially cloth or cardboard)	Dolls, especially large ones Toy telephone Puzzles (5–10 pieces) Vehicles (cars, boats, train) Sandbox, shovel, and pail Water toys (cups, funnel, etc.) Picture books with simple words

ferently for sucking her fist and for sucking her blanket. In this sense she begins to recognize the objects all around her, and implicitly she also begins to remember previous experiences with each type of object. But this memory has an automatic or object-focused quality, unlike the large variety of more conscious memories children have later in life.

Stage 3: Secondary Circular Reactions—Making Interesting Sights Last (Four to Eight Months)   As they practice their first schemes, young infants broaden their interests substantially. Before long, in fact, they shift their attention beyond their own bodily actions to include objects and events immediately around them. Shaking his arm, for example, no longer captivates a baby's attention for its own sake; he has become too skilled at arm shaking for it to do so. Now a behavior such as this becomes useful rather than interesting. A baby at this stage may accidentally discover that shaking his arm will make a mobile spin over his head in his crib, or create an interesting noise in a toy he happens to be holding, or make parents smile with joy. In all these cases, shaking an arm becomes a means to other ends. At best it is a primitive means, however, because the usefulness of the behavior originally develops by chance.

Once primitive means are discovered, a baby at this stage will repeat a useful procedure endlessly to sustain and study the interesting results. The repetition is a circular reaction like those in the previous stage, but with an important difference: now the circular reactions orient toward external objects and events rather than to the baby's own body and actions. Now results matter. If arm shaking fails to keep the mobile spinning, the baby will soon stop her effort. If she finally figures out the nature of the mobile, she will also stop. Either way, the repetition is not governed by her earlier motivation to simply move. To differentiate this new orientation from the earlier one, Piaget called such repetitions *secondary circular reactions:* repetitions motivated by external objects and events.

Secondary circular reactions create two parallel changes in the child's motor schemes. On the one hand, the infant uses existing schemes even more widely than before. He tries to suck on more and more of the toys that come his way. On the other hand, he begins to discover that schemes can be combined to produce interesting results. He may happen to reach toward an object (one scheme) and discover that doing so makes it possible to grasp the object (another scheme). At first, the combination occurs accidentally; but once it does occur, the baby at this stage can produce the new combination of schemes deliberately on future occasions.

Secondary circular reactions also implicitly show that the infant is now acquiring at least a hazy notion of **object permanence,** a belief that objects exist separately from her own actions and continue to exist even when she cannot see them. In the first two stages of infant cognition, objects often seem to disappear from the baby's mind as soon as she loses sight of them or no longer touches them. She may stare at or grasp a toy duck, but a parent or an older sibling can sometimes take it from her without causing distress; at most, the baby will simply keep staring blankly where the duck used to be and then turn to other activities. As Piaget might have claimed, out of sight is out of mind in early infancy.

This is not so, however, as babies enter the second half of their first year. By stage 3, they will look for an object briefly if they have been watching it carefully or manipulating it just beforehand. Naturally their first searching skills leave something to be desired, so it helps if the hidden object is actually partly visible and within easy reach: the toy duck's tail should stick out from under a blanket if that is where the toy is hidden. But the first signs of symbolic thought are there, because the infant must have some idea of the toy duck if she is going to bother searching for it.

Stage 4: Combined Secondary Circular Reactions—Deliberate Combinations of Means and Ends (Eight to Twelve Months)   At this stage, instead of just happening on connections among schemes by accident, the infant intentionally chooses to

Playing peek-a-boo becomes popular with babies as they approach their first birthday. Even though the father disappears for a moment, the baby seems to believe that he still exists behind the door, as shown by the baby's delight when he reappears.

use a scheme as a means toward an end. In stages 1 and 2, he may have developed separate schemes for opening his mouth and for chewing food. In stage 3, he may have accidentally discovered that the first scheme is a means toward the other: mouth opening is a means toward eating. Now, in stage 4, the baby starts using this means-end connection purposefully. Like a young bird in a nest, he opens his mouth to "produce" food to chew on. Of course, he may eventually discover that the connection does not always work: sitting with his mouth wide open may sometimes produce no food at all or occasionally produce bad-tasting medicine instead of good-tasting food.

At this stage, too, the infant still lacks alternatives to the single-purpose, fragmented schemes he has developed so far. As he encounters the limitations of these schemes, he gradually modifies and expands (or accommodates, as Piaget would say) his initial schemes that connected means with ends. He may learn to open his mouth at the sight of some foods but not others. He may also add other behaviors to the mouth-opening scheme, such as pointing to favorite foods, thereby turning the original scheme into a more general food-requesting scheme. As these accommodations occur, the infant moves into the next stage of cognition.

Stage 5: Tertiary Circular Reactions—Active Experimentation with Objects (Twelve to Eighteen Months)   At stage 5, the infant deliberately varies the schemes for producing interesting results, or ends. Previously, at stage 4, she could intentionally combine schemes, but only one pair at a time and only if an appropriate situation for using the combination happened to occur. Now, in dealing with a new object, the baby can run through a repertoire of schemes in a trial-and-error effort to learn about the object's properties. Piaget called the variations *tertiary circular reactions,* meaning third-level circular reactions, to distinguish them from the simpler forms of repetition that dominate the earlier stages.

These variations in behavior, however, are still organized largely by trial and error rather than by systematic plans. Given a rubber ball, for example, some babies may try dropping it from different heights and onto different objects. But no matter how delighted these infants are with the results of these variations, they will not think to vary the dropping conditions carefully or experimentally. Such actions require planning and consequently also require considerably more ability to represent objects and situations than the infant has yet developed.

Stage 6: The First Symbols—Representing Objects and Actions (Eighteen to Twenty-Four Months)   At this stage, the motor schemes the child previously explored and practiced overtly begin to occur symbolically. For the first time, the infant can begin to envision, or imagine, actions and their results without actually having to try them out beforehand.

Consider a stage 6 child who wants a favorite toy that is just barely out of reach on a high shelf. Near the shelf sits a small stool that she has played with numerous times. How to get the toy? Earlier in infancy, the baby might simply have stared and fussed and eventually either given up or cried. At this later stage, things are quite different. The baby surveys the situation, observes the stool, and pauses briefly. Then, with a purposeful air, she places the stool under the toy, climbs up, and retrieves the toy. What is important here is the lack of false starts or, conversely, the presence of only a single, correct attempt. The infant may succeed even though she never before used the stool to reach high-up objects. According to Piaget, trial and error is no longer the method of choice; now the infant tries out solutions mentally to envision their results.

Skill with mental representations makes true object permanence possible. A child at the end of infancy will search for a toy even after it has been fully hidden and even if it was hidden without his witnessing the act of hiding. If a ball disappears behind a bookcase, he will go around to the other side to look for it. He will search appropriately, even though he cannot know in advance exactly where behind the bookcase the ball will turn up. In the ball-and-blanket situation described earlier, the child can now play more complex games of hide-and-seek. She usually looks first under the blanket where the toy disappeared; if she fails to find it there, she will search under any and all other blankets and sometimes even under the table and in the experimenter's pockets. Relatively extensive search is made possible in part by the child's new conviction that toys and other objects have a permanent existence independent of her own activities with them. In other words, they do not just disappear.

Mental representations also make possible deferred imitation, a behavior that will figure prominently in play and learning later in childhood. In *deferred imitation,* the child copies, or duplicates, a behavior—or at least aspects of a behavior— at a significantly later time than when he first witnessed it, sometimes days or even weeks later. Having seen her father brush his teeth, the stage 6 child does so too, but she may also do so twelve hours later, when her father is not even around. Or, having heard his older sibling exclaim, "Yum! Good!" at one night's dinner menu, the child may do so as well. But he makes his exclamation at dinner two days later, even if none of the other family members feel quite so ecstatic about the food.

All of these behaviors depend on the child's ability to form and maintain representations (thoughts or memories) of the relevant experiences, which later become available for expression again. As we will see, representational skill proves crucial in early childhood. It contributes to children's play, because much play involves reenactment of previous experiences and roles. It makes possible much language development, because the child must learn to use words and expressions when they are appropriate and not just at the time she hears them uttered. And it makes possible the first real self-concept, because sooner or later the child realizes that he too has a (relatively) permanent existence akin to the permanence of all the things and people in his life, whether toys, pet dogs, or parents.

Assessment of Piaget's Theory of Infant Cognition

Piaget's theory has stimulated considerable study of infant cognition. A lot of this research has confirmed the main features of the theory, whereas other research has called attention to additional aspects of infancy that at least complicate Piaget's original presentation, if they do not contradict it outright. Following is a sampling of both the confirmations and the complications.

The Integration of Schemes   Do infants begin life with fundamentally separate sensorimotor schemes, as Piaget argued, and only gradually learn to combine, or integrate, them? Some such combining surely must occur, but there is also evidence for the opposite trend: some important schemes may begin as integrated wholes and only later become differentiated into parts (Lewkowicz & Lickliter, 1994). Newborn infants will reach for and grasp a small object placed in front of them at the proper distance, and will do so even if the object is only a projected image of one. Such behavior implies that young babies tend to regard sight and touch as connected rather than separate, or that, in Piagetian terms, they have a single early scheme for seeing and reaching rather than one scheme for seeing and another, separate scheme for reaching.

Vision and hearing also may have inborn integrated schemes. As pointed out earlier, infants just a few days old will turn, as though by reflex, to look at the source of a sound as long as the direction lies within their physical capacity to turn. In addition, they show signs of connecting their parents' faces and voices within two or three weeks: they will look longer at a photograph of their mothers, for example, if a recording of the mothers' voices is playing. And infants just a few months old prefer looking at sights that match a soundtrack to sights that do not match. Suppose a young infant looks at two films side by side, one with a kangaroo bouncing up and down and the other with a toy donkey doing the same thing but at a different speed. If a soundtrack of bouncing rhythms is made to coincide with one film but not the other, the infant will spend more time watching the soundtrack-coordinated picture.

Such evidence complicates Piaget's assertion that schemes begin primarily as separate, discrete reflexes and do not begin to be integrated until midway through infancy. At the same time, however, the evidence does not really contradict Piaget. Given the complexity of human beings, it is perfectly possible for both trends to occur at once. Some schemes may begin as integrated wholes and develop that way in at least certain situations, and others may begin as relatively specific reflexes and combine later.

Motor Versus Cognitive Limitations   Some infant psychologists question Piaget's six stages because they believe the descriptions of the stages confuse the child's motor abilities with his or her cognitive or thinking abilities (Meltzoff et al., 1991). Object permanence, for example, implicitly depends on a child's capacity to conduct a manual search: to walk around the room, lift and inspect objects, and the like. Perhaps younger infants "lack" classic object permanence, this argument goes, simply because they lack motor skills or at best use them only clumsily.

To test this possibility, psychologists have designed new tests of object permanence that require only visual search rather than motor coordination (Baillargeon, 1993). In one experiment, infants were habituated to (repeatedly shown) the sight of a toy car sliding down an inclined track from the left and then rolling off to the right, as shown in Figure 4.4. In the middle of this track was a small screen concealing the middle portion of the track and obstructing a view of the car for part of its trip along the track. During habituation, the babies watched the car slide down the ramp, behind the screen, and out the other side. Between car trips, the screen was lifted temporarily to show that there was nothing behind it that might affect the car's movements.

After the infants had gotten used to seeing this setup and watching the car disappear and reappear predictably, they were shown one of two test events. In the first event, the screen was lifted and a toy mouse was placed directly behind the tracks. Then the screen was lowered, and the car made its usual run down the ramp and out the right side of the screen. This was called the "possible test event." The second test event was the same, except that the toy mouse was placed directly *on* the tracks. Then the screen was lowered, the car was released, it disappeared behind the screen, and—surprise!—it reappeared out the right side of the screen anyway, even though the mouse had been placed on the tracks. This was called the "impossible test event." In reality, the experimenters secretly removed the toy mouse before the car could hit it, using a hole concealed in the back of the test apparatus.

Under these conditions, infants as young as 3½ months looked significantly longer at the *im*possible test event than at the possible test event. The most plausible interpretation is that the impossible event violated assumptions the infants made about the permanence of objects: they seemed to assume the toy mouse should cause a collision, presumably because they believed it continued to exist behind the screen even when they could not see it. They also seemed to assume objects retain their usual physical properties even when invisible—that the car could not simply pass through the mouse, for example, just because it was hidden.

This evidence of early object permanence, though, does not mean young infants are now ready to reason about hidden objects in the ways older children or adults might do. If a preschool child experienced the experiment just described, he or she would very likely suspect a trick of some sort and consciously puzzle over what the trick might be. The three- or four-month-old infant still has much developing to do before being able to do this kind of thinking. By requiring manual search skills, Piaget's tasks may have delayed children from displaying their preexisting object permanence until rudimentary reasoning skills had become established. Hence Piaget's assertion that full object permanence (the stage 6 described earlier) involves conscious problem solving: a deliberate search for the object.

The Effects of Memory   Considerable evidence suggests that memory does in fact affect infants' performance on many tasks. Imposing slight delays—just a few seconds—when an infant searches for an object lowers success rates much more for younger infants than for older ones (Baillargeon, 1993). Much of the change may

FIGURE 4.4
Evidence of Object Permanence in Infants
First, the infant becomes habituated to watching a car roll down a track, behind a screen, and out the other side. In one test condition, a toy mouse is placed behind the tracks but is hidden while the car rolls past. In the other test condition, the mouse is placed on the tracks but is secretly removed after the screen is in place so that the car seems to roll "through" the mouse. Infants stare longer at the second impossible event, suggesting that they already "believe in" object permanence.
Source: Baillargeon & DeVos (1991).

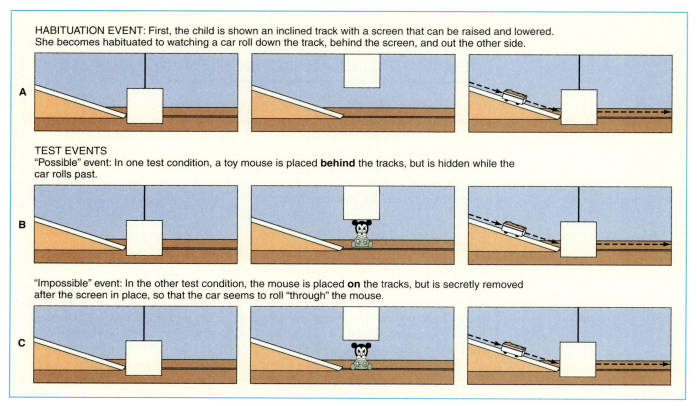

HABITUATION EVENT: First, the child is shown an inclined track with a screen that can be raised and lowered. She becomes habituated to watching a car roll down the track, behind the screen, and out the other side.

A

TEST EVENTS
"Possible" event: In one test condition, a toy mouse is placed **behind** the tracks, but is hidden while the car rolls past.

B

"Impossible" event: In the other test condition, the mouse is placed **on** the tracks, but is secretly removed after the screen in place, so that the car seems to roll "through" the mouse.

C

reflect younger infants' difficulties in attending to and retaining relevant cues about the object to be searched for. Younger babies seem to remember less of what they are looking for.

These trends imply that infants may have a notion of object permanence, but find it demanding to remember the relevant facts needed to search: where they last saw the object and when and whether the object was in fact moved. Perhaps infants use memory when they can but supplement it with Piagetian motor schemes whenever necessary (Case, 1992). If an infant cannot recall where a toy is hidden, at least she can reenact the means she used to find it in the past. This multiple strategy actually resembles the way adults sometimes search for a lost object: if you cannot recall where you left it, you may retrace your steps up to the time you remember seeing it last—in essence, using an action scheme.

Performance Versus Competence   These questions about motivation illustrate a more general problem with Piagetian theory as applied to both children and infants: by emphasizing the nature of competence, it tends to neglect the immediate causes of performance. An infant—or anyone, for that matter—may be *able* to do something but fail to perform the action for any of a number of reasons. Even if an infant shows his highest competence in one situation, he may fail, for various reasons, to do so in a situation that differs from the first one only slightly. As mentioned earlier, even a few seconds' delay can change some infants' success rates on a memory task, creating very different impressions about their underlying competence based on performance.

What Do You Think?

Between about eight and twelve months of age, many babies show distress at separations from their primary caregiver (usually the mother). Some psychologists suggest that the distress is a partial result of their budding belief in object permanence. Do you think this might be true? How you might explain your position to a new parent who is concerned about her baby's distress?

BEHAVIORAL LEARNING IN INFANCY

One framework for studying the specific performance of infants has come from **behaviorism,** or what psychologists sometimes also call *learning theory*. As described in Chapter 2, learning theory focuses on changes in particular behaviors (sometimes called *responses*) and on the specific, observable causes and consequences (reinforcements, or lack thereof, and punishments) of those behaviors. Typically learning theorists identify three kinds of behavioral learning: classical conditioning, operant conditioning, and imitation.

Operant Conditioning

In operant conditioning as most infants experience it, a child gets a reward, or positive reinforcement, if she performs some simple action or set of actions. By turning her head, for example, she may get to see an interesting toy or picture. In this case the reinforcement is viewing the interesting toy, and head turning becomes the learned, or conditioned, behavior. Such actions tend to be performed more often than actions that are not reinforced.

As the examples of research in this chapter show, infants are quite capable of learning through operant conditioning. Newborns will learn to suck on their hands longer if doing so yields a tiny amount of sugar water delivered through a tube in the corners of their mouths. Or they will learn to blink their eyes more often if doing so causes a pleasant voice to speak or a melody to play. One reason infants seem to learn to breast feed so easily is the strong reinforcement the behavior brings in the form of mother's milk and being touched and held closely.

Infants are predisposed to learn these particular behaviors. All examples of operant conditioning in infants rely on those few behaviors that young babies already exhibit, which are mainly their inborn reflexes. By nature, reflexes occur easily—in fact, almost *too* easily. As parents often discover, any slight provocation, such as a touch on the baby's cheek, can stimulate sucking movements in young babies. Such readiness to respond creates confusion about when infant responses really constitute learning rather than general excitement. For example, when do sucking movements show true operant learning: a specific behavior performed more often because a particular reinforcement results from it? And when do sucking movements simply amount to a reflex that is itching to occur, so to speak, and would occur in response to almost any stimulus?

The confusion between learning and excitement diminishes as babies grow older, because they acquire behaviors that are more truly voluntary. Even as babies get older, however, they acquire many behaviors, both desirable and regrettable, through what appears to be operant conditioning. A six- or nine-month-old will babble longer and more frequently if parents smile and express praise when he does so. A twelve-month-old will learn to wave good-bye sooner and more frequently if reinforced with praise or encouragement. And a two-year-old may learn to scream at her older sibling when she wants a toy the older child has because her screaming has been inadvertently reinforced: it causes the older child to simply abandon the toy, or it summons a parent who assumes (not always accurately) the older child somehow caused the screaming.

Of course, these effects refer primarily to immediate, short-term ones, which sometimes differ from long-term effects of reinforcement. An example often important to parents is crying: will picking up the baby to quiet his crying actually reinforce him for crying in the long term? Conditioning theory would predict that it would, but most research on the impact of crying has found that fast, sensitive response to crying actually leads to *less* crying (St. James-Roberts et al., 1993). The quieting, though, is not reliable in the short term, but may take many months to become a definite, obvious response to being picked up. This is a long enough delay to cause parents a lot of worry about whether they are "spoiling" their child by responding to her crying.

Imitation

As make-believe play demonstrates, children obviously learn to imitate at some point in development. But exactly how early, and by what processes? Early research on these questions generally suggested that infants can engage in different kinds of imitation at different points during infancy (Piaget, 1962). It found that infants imitated actions they could literally see themselves perform (for example, in a mirror) sooner than those they could observe only in a model. Much research over the past two decades confirms this hypothesis. Imitating a hand gesture such as waving, for example, proves easier than imitating an unusual face made by an adult (Meltzoff & Kuhl, 1994). Also, deferred imitation may not appear until close to a child's second birthday; by that time, the child can imitate a gesture an entire day after seeing a model perform it.

Despite their preference for visible actions, infants sometimes imitate actions that are relatively invisible to themselves. One-week-old babies tend to stick out their tongues in imitation of adults and wiggle their fingers after seeing adults model this behavior. Distinguishing voluntary imitation from general, automatic excitement, however, remains a problem, as it does with other studies of very young

Imitation provides a rich source of learning for most children, even during infancy. This toddler appears to be learning how to brush its teeth by copying its mother! To be effective, though, imitation requires both symbolic thought and the development of motor skills—and adults interested in providing models.

babies. One research study highlighted this ambiguity especially well. It showed babies pictures of human faces depicting various emotions (Kaitz et al., 1988). Although the babies responded with emotional facial expressions of their own, their expressions did not match those in the pictures. In fact, the emotions on the babies' faces were hard to classify at all; they just looked "wrought up" at the sight of expressive human faces. At present, therefore, we still have more to learn about the origins of imitation during the newborn period.

What Do You Think?

Shift your focus from infants to mothers for a moment. How do you suppose *mothers* might become conditioned to breast feeding, either positively or negatively? Think about "what's in it" for them, as well as what hassles breast feeding can create. If possible, talk to a breast-feeding mother about her experiences.

LANGUAGE ACQUISITION

When Michael, the son of one of the authors, was an infant, he went through several phases in using language. At twelve weeks, Michael made open-mouthed, cooing noises when he was feeling content. Sometimes these sounds were vaguely similar to ordinary vowel sounds, but they seemed to vary unpredictably. Michael cooed a lot in the morning when he first woke up, which pleased his father and mother.

By six months, Michael had added consonant sounds to his vocalizations to produce complicated babbling noises. His most productive time for this activity continued to be the morning, although he "said" quite a lot whenever he was feeling generally content. Certain sounds seemed to be favorites: *da* and *gn*. Sometimes Michael repeated these and other sounds—*da, da, da, da*. His father thought Michael repeated sounds when he was feeling especially happy.

At fifteen months Michael could produce about six words, but he did not pronounce them as adults would. The family cat was *dat;* his favorite food, yogurt, sounded like *yugun;* and airplanes were simply *der!* (as in "Look there!"). He seemed to understand dozens of words and sentences, although it was hard to be sure because he probably picked up clues about meaning from the behavior of his parents. When Michael was tired one day, he came immediately when his mother said, "Come sit here" in a sympathetic tone of voice. But when she said the same thing in a cross tone of voice the next day, he looked at her with an impish smile and went the other way.

One day close to his second birthday, Michael sat "reading" a children's book to himself. Occasionally real phrases could be heard ("bug ate leaf"), but mostly Michael sounded as though he were mumbling or talking in the next room. When he finished, he walked to the kitchen and phrased a three-word question: "What's for lunch?"

As these examples show, language is a fundamental feature of infant and child development. A great deal of language develops during infancy; indeed, language is one of the most clearly human of all developments of this age period and perhaps of the entire lifespan.

Language has several aspects, and infants must acquire them all to become verbally competent. When listed separately, the array is an impressive set of achievements for such young people!

- They must learn the sounds of the language (its *phonology)*.
- They must learn its words (its *lexicon)*.
- They must learn the meanings of words (*semantics)*.
- They must learn the purposes and ways in which words and sentences normally get used in conversation (*pragmatics)*.
- They must piece together the organization of words into sentences and connected discourse (*syntax)*.

Infants must acquire all of these aspects of language to be able to express their feelings, get what they want, and describe their activities to others. In this chapter we concentrate on phonology and semantics and leave the other aspects for later chapters.

Phonology

Every language uses a finite number of **phonemes,** or sounds that speakers of the language consider distinctive and that combine to make the words of the language. English has about forty-one phonemes; other languages have more or fewer than this number. In acquiring language, infants must be sensitive to phonemes and ignore any meaningless variations. Although the task may seem demanding, it actually proves surprisingly easy, even for a baby—so easy, in fact, that some language specialists suspect human beings are genetically and physiologically predisposed toward noticing phonemic differences (Archibald, 1995).

Babbling Although skill at producing phonemes takes longer to develop, it too seems to be biologically influenced. Sometime between four and eight months of age, infants begin babbling in increasingly complex ways. They apparently do so for the sole reward of hearing themselves vocalize, a form of play with sound and an example of a Piagetian primary circular reaction.

What suggests that babbling is motivated intrinsically? The most important evidence is the fact that all physically normal infants begin babbling at about the same age (about six months), regardless of the culture or language to which they are exposed. Furthermore, an observational study of deaf infants found the babies "babbling" with their hands. These infants could not babble orally, but they had been exposed to American Sign Language and were observed to make repetitive hand gestures analogous to the oral babbling of hearing infants (Pettito & Marentette, 1991).

Despite this finding, most research suggests a significant influence on babbling by parents and other members of an infant's language community. Although the study on deaf infants observed a type of babbling in these babies, the fact that the babbling was gestural rather than oral suggests that the infants' language environment influenced the form their babbling took. Other research on deaf infants has confirmed this conclusion. Contrary to a long-held belief, deaf infants do *not* babble orally in the same way hearing infants do; rather, they begin oral babbling some months later, and even then babble only if they hear sound that is amplified, such as through a hearing aid (Marschark, 1993).

Semantics and First Words

The **semantics** (or meanings) of a language, and of words in particular, are never mastered fully, even by adults. To test this idea on yourself, scan any page of a large, unabridged dictionary and see how far you go before you encounter an unfamiliar word. Most people, it seems, never learn even a majority of the words or terms in their native language. This is because words get much of their meanings from the real world rather than from other words. Most of us simply do not live long enough to encounter all of these relationships with the real world.

What words do children use first? On the whole, they prefer nominals—labels for objects, people, and events—much more than other kinds of words, such as verbs or modifiers (Hart, 1991). Among nominals, they are most likely to name things that are used frequently or that stand out in some way. The child's own mother or father therefore may be named early, but not always as early as the parents expect. *Dog* may appear as an early word more often than *sun* or *diaper* does, even though children probably experience the latter two objects more frequently than they do dogs.

Other research has found that children vary in how much they emphasize different language functions in their first utterances (Bloom, 1993). Most children have a *referential style,* meaning their first words refer to objects and objective events—*car, book,* and so on. Others have an *expressive style,* using words to express feelings and relationships—*hello* and *goody!* During the second year of life, infants with a referential style tend to make more rapid advances in vocabulary, though whether this advantage continues into the preschool years is unclear. Presumably these differences are encouraged partly by differing family environments. Some families may speak of objects more often than they do of feelings, or vice versa. But to some extent, word preferences may also represent a learning strategy adopted by the child; just as she may find a word easier if she already knows the phonemes in it, she may also find an utterance easier if she already has used similar ones on previous occasions.

Influencing Language Acquisition

Although many of these comments may make language acquisition seem beyond human influence, adults do in fact affect this process. The most important influence is parents, as you might expect. But other adult caregivers can also make a difference for infants and toddlers who have regular contact with them.

Parental Influences   Even when infants are very young, parents often talk to them as though they were full-fledged adult partners in a conversation (though not equally in all cultures; see the accompanying Multicultural View box). Consider this mother speaking to her three-month-old child:

Mother: How is Kristi today? *(pause)* How are you? *(pause)* Good, you say? *(pause)* Are you feeling good? *(pause)* I'm glad for that. *(pause)* Yes, I am. *(pause)* What would you like now? *(pause)* Your soother? *(pause)* Um? *(pause)* Is that what you want? *(pause)* Okay, here it is.

By asking questions in this "conversation," the mother implies that Kristi is capable of responding, even though her infant is much too young to do so. Furthermore, the mother leaves pauses for her baby's hypothetical responses. Observations of these kinds of pauses show that they last just about as long as in conversations between adults (Roth, 1987); it is as though the mother were giving her baby a turn to speak before taking another turn herself. When her child remains silent, the mother even replies on her behalf. In all these behaviors, the mother teaches something about turn taking in conversations, and she expresses her faith that the infant eventually will learn these conventions herself.

When infants finally begin speaking, parents continue this strategy. At the same time, however, they also simplify their language significantly. Sentences become shorter, although not as short as the child's, and vocabulary becomes simpler, although less restricted than the child's (Gallaway & Richards, 1994). These extra strategies help to teach a new lesson, namely that words and sentences do in fact communicate and that language is more than interesting noises and babbling. By keeping just ahead of the infant's own linguistic skills, parents can stimulate the further development of language.

This style is called **infant-directed speech,** or *caregiver speech,* meaning a dialect or a version of language characteristic of parents talking with young children. In addition to shorter sentences and simpler vocabulary, caregiver speech has several unique features. It tends to unfold more slowly than speech between adults and to use a higher and more variable, or singsong, pitch; it generally contains unusually strong emphasis on key words ("Give me your *cup*"). Parents speaking to infants also tend to repeat or paraphrase themselves more than usual ("Give me the cup. The cup. Find the cup, and give it.").

Research shows clearly that parents' conversations with babies are extremely important to the infants' development. The Harvard Preschool Project, a longitudinal study conducted at Harvard University, observed the contacts between parents

Siblings serve as important models of behavior and language for younger infants as they grow and develop. What do you suppose this girl is saying to her infant sister, and what do you suppose the infant will learn from it?

A Multicultural View

Cognitive Effects of Talking to Infants: A Cross-Cultural Perspective

Although the text implies strong support for mothers' talking with their infants, a different impression of this practice occurs if you view it in a cross-cultural context. Then the frequent one-way "conversations" and direct gazing between mother and baby seem a bit less natural or inevitable, and even a bit strange.

In North America, the practice is widely regarded as a positive experience: talking with and gazing at a nonverbal infant increases in frequency until the child begins producing her own language, around the first birthday, and cuddling and holding close decrease at the same time. Parents are even given professional assistance when these changes in interaction do not occur (Yoder & Warren, 1993)! Mothers themselves believe that talking with and gazing at infants stimulates infants' intellectual competence.

Research evidence seems to support the mothers' belief. Children who have verbally interactive mothers during infancy do show better language comprehension as four-year-olds and do show higher competence at solving simple problems involving both verbal and nonverbal reasoning (Bornstein & Tamis-Lemonda, 1989). But there is contrary evidence as well. In China, for example, mothers talk to infants relatively little but cuddle and hold them relatively a lot (Ho, 1994). Yet Chinese culture values educational success and Chinese children perform well in school.

The fact is that the effects of maternal talk on infants are not really clear. But it is probably not a matter of stimulating thinking and language development, as many mothers themselves might believe. Maternal talk probably is much too complex for a two- or three-month-old infant to learn by hearing it directly. Instead of providing a language model directly, therefore, early verbal interaction may serve other purposes in infants' development: maybe it simply reflects the mother's general interest in and responsiveness to her child. Parents who enjoy talking to their babies as newborns are likely to still enjoy talking to them several years later, when the babies have become capable of learning and using language more effectively. If so, the relationship between early talk and later competence is a good example of a *correlation* (an association) that is not also a *cause.* In that case, too, North American mothers could (in theory) talk with their

and their infants that occurred naturally in the families' own homes (B. White, 1993). At various intervals, the infants were assessed for both intelligence and social skills. When the assessments were correlated with the results of the home observations, one result stood out clearly: the most intellectually and socially competent infants had parents who directed large amounts of language at them. The most competent babies received about twice as much language as the least competent infants in this study did. But the most competent infants also stimulated interactions with their parents, primarily by procuring various simple kinds of help, such as in pouring a glass of juice or placing the final block on a tower. These "services" probably benefited the infants by offering many opportunities for parents to talk with them ("Shall I put the block on top?").

Influences of Professional Caregivers   Language acquisition can also be supported by other adults who interact with infants extensively, notably professional caregivers in family child care or infant care centers. Their forms of influence parallel those of parents (Koralek et al., 1993). *Contingent dialogue* (extending the child's verbal initiatives), for example, can easily take place at an infant care center: a toddler may name objects in the room ("Book!") or pictures displayed on the wall ("Cat!"), and the caregiver can extend those early initiatives into longer dialogues ("Yes, it's a pretty cat. Do you like cats?"). *Contextual dialogue* (familiar language routines or rituals) can also occur: a caregiver and child may engage in predictable exchanges in preparing to go home each day ("Have you found your coat?"; "Now zipper it up"). To succeed, these dialogues must be simplified; that is, they should rely on infant-directed or "caregiver" speech that takes the infant's early stage of language into account. Table 4.8 lists some additional ways caregivers can assist in language development.

But important differences also exist between caregiver influences and parent influences. One concerns intensity and frequency: caregivers usually do not see a par-

Constant close contact between caregiver and infant, as between this mother and her children, may encourage more nonverbal communication and result in infants who fuss relatively little. Crying and fussing, which we associate with infancy in our society, may actually be a precursor to verbal communication, which parents tend to encourage in North American society.

newborns a good deal less in the earliest months and still expect the babies to end up with good language skills eventually! This would be true, though, only if a mother were responsive and caring throughout the child's infancy, and only if the mother did begin interacting verbally as soon as the infant showed signs of actually understanding and using language. This developmental pattern in fact describes mother-infant relationships in China to a certain extent (though not perfectly).

These ideas remain speculation, though, because mothers' language practices cannot, and probably should not, be manipulated simply to explore their effects on children. In any society, parents need to interact with their babies in ways they consider natural. But comparing cultural beliefs can nonetheless give clues about the deeper, less obvious effects of particular cultural practices (Greenfield, 1994). Mother-infant "conversations" are a good example of a culture-bound practice: virtually all parent advice books urge parents to talk with their babies. Yet in doing so, the books join parents in assuming a particular cultural value: that skillful oral expression is desirable and should be encouraged as much as possible.

ticular infant or toddler for as many hours as a parent does, nor do they develop relationships as emotionally intense as parents'. Another difference concerns cultural expectations: it is common for caregivers (but rare for parents) to come from a cultural or language background that differs from the children's. The gap can create confusion and misunderstanding between caregiver and child or between caregiver and parent. If a caregiver and a child speak different primary languages, one may lack facility with some of the words and expressions needed to communicate with the other.

At a more subtle level, a language gap may contribute to differences in fundamental attitudes or values. In observing parent-teacher conferences for grade-school-age children, Patricia Greenfield found that teachers focused much more on a child's individual achievement, whereas parents focused on the child's social compatibility

TABLE 4.8   *Interactions That Support Language Development*

Interaction	Purpose
Sitting on the floor with infant and reading books, telling stories, or singing songs	Builds trust, models interesting activities using language
Holding infant close, looking into infant's face, smiling, and talking to infant	Builds trust, models dialogue or conversation
Responding to infant's first words and gestures using caregiver's own words and gestures	Encourages dialogue and conversation, shows respect for infant's language initiatives
Offering simple choices to infant verbally ("Do you want to paint or to play outside?")	Stimulates infant to attend to language; calls attention to relationship between language and actions
Encouraging infant (especially if a toddler) to express desires and resolve differences using words ("What do you want to do?")	Encourages child to practice language; demonstrates power of verbal expression

(Greenfield, 1995). The result was misunderstanding and dissatisfaction with the conference. Presumably a similar problem could occur between parents and care-givers of infants, though research has not yet tested this possibility specifically.

All things considered, parents, caregivers, and others constitute a much more positive than negative influence on language development. Given their importance to the process, it should not be surprising that nearly all children acquire high ver-bal competence in just a few years. Language acquisition is "overdetermined": soci-ety supports language learning in so many ways that if a child fails to experience that support in one way, she or he is likely to experience it in some other way. So most of us do learn to talk!

What Do You Think?

Find out, if you can, the words you produced first as an infant and the setting in which you produced them. Pool your results with a few classmates. Are there any features common to either the words or the settings?

THE END OF INFANCY

During the first two years of life, infants become much more like individuals than they are on the day they are born. By their second birthday they walk about, grasp at objects, and direct their attention toward particular people and activities. These physical skills facilitate certain cognitive activities, such as searching for objects that an infant "knows" exist even though he cannot see them.

The language skills that develop at the same time, in turn, contribute to the for-mation of social skills and relationships, as we will see in the next chapter. By age two a child knows, and can say, who her parents and siblings are. She can also be-gin expressing her feelings about these people verbally: whether she is happy or sad, angry or fearful, likes someone or not. In the next chapter we take a closer look at these social changes, which have a basis in the physical and cognitive developments of infancy.

SUMMARY OF MAJOR IDEAS

PHYSICAL DEVELOPMENT

Appearance of the Young Infant

1. The average newborn has rather red-looking skin, is often covered with a waxy substance, and has a skull somewhat compressed on the top.
2. The health of newborns born in hospitals is assessed quickly after delivery with the Apgar Scale.
3. The average newborn at full term weighs about 7½ pounds. Regardless of cultural background, the newborn's bodily proportions make the infant look appealing to adults and may foster the formation of attachments with adults.

Development of the Nervous System

4. Infants sleep almost twice as much as adults do, but the amount of sleep gradually decreases as they get older. They also experience distinct states of arousal from deep sleep to full alertness.

Visual and Auditory Acuity

5. At birth infants already can see and hear, but with less ac-curacy or acuity than adults do.

Motor Development

6. Infants are born with a number of innate reflexes.
7. Motor skills appear during the first year of infancy and in-clude reaching, grasping, and walking.
8. Motor skills develop differently depending on cultural background and sex.

Variations in Growth and Motor Development

9. One of the most important impairments to early growth is low birth weight.
10. Low-birth-weight infants often have difficulties with breathing, digestion, and sleep, and their reflexes may be poorly developed.

Nutrition During the First Two Years

11. Infants need more protein and calories per pound of body weight than older children do.

12. Compared to formula and bottle feeding, breast feeding has a number of advantages.

13. After weaning from breast or bottle, infants need a diet rich in protein and calories. Most North American families can provide these requirements, but many cannot.

14. A common problem in North American diets is overnutrition, which can make infants seriously overweight, or obese.

15. For a variety of reasons, infants sometimes fail to thrive normally.

16. Infant mortality has decreased in the recent past, but in the United States it is still higher than it should be.

COGNITIVE DEVELOPMENT

Studying Cognition and Memory in Infants

17. Infants' arousal and attention can be studied by noting changes in their heart rates.

18. Infants' recognition and memory of familiar things can be studied by observing their habituation to stimuli, or tendency to attend to novel stimuli and ignore familiar ones.

Infant Perception

19. Perception refers to the immediate organization and interpretation of sensation. Cognition refers to all the processes (including perception) by which humans acquire and process knowledge.

20. Studies of visual perception show that infants under six months of age perceive, or at least respond to, a variety of patterns, such as those usually found on a human face.

21. Young infants, including newborns, show size constancy in visual perception, meaning they respond to objects somewhat independently of the objects' distance and orientation.

22. Infants also show sensitivity to depth, as indicated in the visual-cliff experiments.

23. Infants can localize sounds to some extent at birth, but do not do so accurately until about six months of age.

24. Cultural background probably plays a small role in infant perception, at least during the first year of life.

Infant Cognition

25. Piaget has proposed six stages of infant cognitive development during which infants' schemes become less egocentric and increasingly symbolic and organized.

26. Research on Piaget's six stages generally confirms his original observations, but it also raises questions about the effects of motor skills, memory, and motivation on infants' cognitive performance.

Behavioral Learning in Infancy

27. Like older children and adults, infants can learn through behavioral conditioning and imitation.

28. Behavioral learning tends to be ambiguous in infants less than three months old because it is difficult to distinguish true learning from general, automatic excitement.

Language Acquisition

29. Babbling begins around six months of age and becomes increasingly complex until it disappears from use sometime before the infant's second birthday.

30. Infants show important individual differences in their selection of first words, but generally they use words for objects in their environment that are distinctive in some way.

31. Adults influence language acquisition mainly through modeling simplified utterances, recasting their infants' own utterances, and directing considerable language at the child as she or he grows.

32. Professional caregivers influence language acquisition in ways similar to parents, but they must also recognize the potential effects of a cultural gap between caregiver and child.

KEY TERMS

neonate *(110)*
Apgar Scale *(110)*
central nervous
   system *(112)*
neuron *(112)*
REM sleep *(113)*
non-REM sleep *(113)*
sudden infant death
   syndrome (SIDS) *(114)*
reflex *(116)*
motor skills *(116)*
cephalocaudal
   principle *(117)*
proximodistal
   principle *(117)*
low birth weight *(120)*
obese *(123)*
failure to thrive *(123)*

infant mortality rate *(124)*
perception *(124)*
cognition *(124)*
habituation *(125)*
visual cliff *(128)*
sensorimotor
   intelligence *(130)*
schemes *(130)*
assimilation *(131)*
accommodation *(131)*
circular reaction *(132)*
object permanence *(133)*
behaviorism *(138)*
phonemes *(141)*
semantics *(142)*
infant-directed
   speech *(143)*

5

Psychosocial Development

Focusing Questions

- In what ways is a newborn infant capable of participating in the social world? How does caregiver-infant synchrony expand an infant's social capabilities?

- What emotional capabilities does an infant have? How do differences in infants' temperaments affect their social development?

- What experiences enable infants to develop secure emotional attachments with their caregivers? What are the consequences if secure attachments fail to develop?

- How do an infant's interactions with father, siblings, and peers differ from those with his or her mother? What are the effects of day care and maternal employment on infant and toddler development?

- Why is autonomy so central to development during toddlerhood? What qualities of parenting contribute to its successful development?

E ven as a newborn, Alberto was an easy baby to feed and comfort. He was also very active and responsive to the sights and sounds in his environment. Even when tired or overstimulated by the people around him, he seemed able to calm himself with just a little help from his caregiver. When he was five weeks old, Alberto just loved attention. His smiles and excitement were irresistible, and he responded to anyone who paid attention to him—from his parents to his older brother and sisters to Luisa, the family dog. However, a special mutual responsiveness seemed to be present whenever Alberto interacted with his mother, Maria, or his father, José. With either of them, Alberto's smiles, sounds, and movements seemed so highly in tune with theirs that they appeared to be having a real conversation.

By the time Alberto was four months old, he began to show a preference for his mother and his oldest sister, Lydia, who helped Maria care for him. When he saw or heard either of them, he became especially happy, active, and noisy, which caused some jealousy among other family members.

Between ages nine and eleven months, Alberto's preferences for specific people became much stronger and more obvious. He clearly preferred his mother to any other adult and responded to his sister Lydia more than to any of the other children. Now able to crawl, he tried to follow his mother wherever she went, and he cried when she left the room. During this period, he also began to do something he had never done before: he sometimes became upset when unfamiliar people visited, even if they were friendly to him.

By the time he was almost two, Alberto was walking and talking well, had begun toilet training, and could do many things himself. He continued to be an active and happy child, but sometimes he became frustrated and upset if he did not succeed at a task. Fortunately, talking to him and giving him just the right amount of helpful guidance usually worked. Although he still demanded a good deal of attention from his mother and still preferred to play with Lydia, he rarely got upset when other family members cared for him. He also seemed quite happy to socialize with almost all friendly visitors, even those he had never met before.

These changes in Alberto are typical of some of the important psychosocial changes that occur during infancy. From the moment of birth, infants differ in their characteristic activity levels and stylistic patterns of responding to the people and events in their new environment. And although infants highly depend on their caregivers to meet their needs, they are anything but passive. Infants become active, sophisticated observers and participants in their own psychosocial development.

As an infant grows older, she comes to form close and enduring emotional attachments with the important people in her life and sometimes shows her concerns about them very dramatically. She wails when a strange nurse approaches her in the doctor's office, and she greets her mother or father warmly when one of them "rescues" her from the nurse. At other times, the baby may participate in relationships

149

Each member of a family has a unique style of interacting with a new friend.

in more subtle ways, such as attending closely to older brothers and sisters while they play—more closely than her siblings attend to her. At still other times, she may express her needs or feelings in ways that confound the people around her; for example, she may refuse particular foods when a parent offers them but take them happily from a baby sitter.

These behaviors convey two major themes of psychosocial development in infancy: *trust* and *autonomy*. Infants learn what to expect from the important people in their lives. They develop strong feelings about whom they do (and do not) like to be with and what foods they prefer. The conflicts of trust versus mistrust and autonomy versus shame and doubt, which we examined in Chapter 2, intertwine closely during their first two years, although many observers of children believe trust develops earlier than autonomy does (Erikson, 1963; Maccoby, 1980; Stern, 1985a).

In this chapter, we first discuss the importance of emotions and temperament in infancy. Next, we explore the essential role of early social interactions and attachments in the development of a sense of basic trust (versus mistrust) and in the achievement of autonomy (versus shame and doubt). We examine the ways in which attachments are formed. Finally, we look at the emergence of self-knowledge and self-awareness during later infancy and toddlerhood.

EMOTIONS AND TEMPERAMENT IN INFANCY

The healthy cries of a newborn infant make it clear that infants are capable of feeling and expressing their emotions even at birth. During the first three months, infants spend about two hours crying during a typical day. Healthy babies produce four types of cries—the basic hunger cry, the angry cry, the pain cry, and the fussy irregular cry—all of which provide their caregivers with useful information about their physiological states of discomfort (Bruner, 1983; St. James-Roberts & Halil, 1991). Over time, as infants gain better control over their crying, crying serves to convey a wider range of messages to their caregivers (Zeskind et al., 1985). In the following sections, we discuss the role of early emotions and *temperament*—the infant's characteristic way of feeling and responding.

Emotions in Infancy

While researchers have long recognized changes in infants' crying, smiling, frustrations, and fear of strangers and novel stimuli, there is now a growing appreciation of the range and complexity of infant emotions. For example, videotape studies reveal that an infant only a few weeks old is able to produce facial expressions corresponding to the range of adult emotional states, even though the infant's expressions of emotion, particularly negative emotions, do not always result from the same events that typically produce them in adults. Similarly, while physiological aspects of emotion, such as changes in heart rate, can be reliably measured, their relationships to specific emotions are not always clear (Camras et al., 1993; Oster et al., 1992). One reason for this lack of specificity is that babies' expectations and understandings appear to play an important role in their emotional reactions. For example, an incongruous stimulus, such as a mother's face covered with a mask, will produce a fear response in some situations but smiling and laughter in others.

While researchers still disagree about the earliest age at which particular emotions are present, they generally agree that most babies can reliably express basic joy and laughter by three or four months, fear by five to eight months, and more complex emotions such as shame, embarrassment, guilt, envy, and pride during toddlerhood (Izard, 1994; Izard & Malatesta, 1987; Lewis, 1992; Lewis et al., 1989; Weinberg & Tronick, 1994). Table 5.1 shows the approximate ages at which certain infant emotions appear.

Expressions of emotion play an important role in development by providing vital information to infants and their caregivers about ongoing experiences and interactions. Caregivers "read" these messages and use them to guide their actions in helping the infant to fulfill his needs (Gianino & Tronick, 1988; Tronick, 1989). Very young infants also appear to be sensitive to the positive and negative emotions of their caregivers; they are quite capable of responding to adult fears and anxieties. These responses are likely based on cues similar to those adults use, such as slight variations in voice quality, smell, and touch, as well as variations in facial expression and body language. As they get older, infants display these feelings with increasing frequency and predictability.

Another important change in an infant's emotional life during the first year is the baby's growing ability to regulate her own expressive behaviors and associated emotional states, especially negative ones. These *self-directed regulatory behaviors* include looking away, self-comforting, and self-stimulation. They allow the infant to control her negative feelings by shifting her attention away from a disturbing event or by substituting positive for negative stimuli. This helps the infant adjust her emotional state to a comfortable level at which she can successfully maintain interaction with her surroundings (Gianino & Tronick, 1988; Thompson, 1990; Tronick, 1989). During the second year, increases in the capacity for emotional self-regulation also reflect her growing ability to respond to the feelings and needs of others through helping, sharing, and providing comfort (Zahn-Waxler et al., 1992). Claire Kopp (1982) has proposed that the modulation, or self-regulation, of behavior develops over a series of five successive phases. Table 5.2 describes these phases. Emotional self-regulation in infancy from the view-point of developmental theorists was discussed in Chapter 2.

TABLE 5.1 *Development of Infant Emotions*

Approximate Age (in months)	Emotion
0–1	Social smile
3	Pleasure smile
3–4	Wariness
4–7	Joy, anger
4	Surprise
5–9	Fear
18	Shame

Sources: Izard (1982); Sroufe (1979).

TABLE 5.2   *Development of Behavioral Self-Regulation (modulation) During Infancy: Phases of Self-Regulation*

Phases	Approximate Ages	Features	Cognitive Requisites
Neurophysiological modulation	Birth to 2–3 months	Modulation of arousal, activation of organized patterns of behavior	
Sensorimotor modulation	3 months–9 months+	Change ongoing behavior in response to events and stimuli in environment	
Control	12 months–18 months+	Awareness of social demands of a situation and initiate, maintain, cease physical acts, communication, etc. accordingly; compliance, self-initiated monitoring	Intentionality, goal-directed behavior, conscious awareness of action, memory of existential self
Self-control	24 months+	As above; delay upon request; behave according to social expectations in the absence of external monitors	Representational thinking and recall memory, symbolic thinking, continuing sense of identity
Self-regulation	36 months+	As above; flexibility of control processes that meet changing situational demands	Strategy production, conscious introspection, etc.

Source: Kopp (1982), p. 202. Table 2.

During phase 1 (neurophysiological modulation), the infant becomes able to regulate its patterns and states of sleep, arousal, and waking activity. During phase 2 (sensorimotor modulation), the sensorimotor schemes described by Piaget are used to regulate behavior. During phase 3 (control), the infant intentionally controls and directs its behavior and is aware of the social demands of others. During phase 4 (self-control), language and representational thinking allow increased behavioral self-control. During phase 5 (self-regulation), self-control becomes more conscious, purposeful, and flexible in response to changing demands of the situation.

Temperament

Temperament refers to an individual's consistent pattern or style of reacting to a broad range of environmental events and situations. Most researchers agree that differences in primary reaction tendencies such as sensitivity to visual or verbal stimulation, emotional responsiveness, and sociability appear to be present at birth, prior to any significant interaction with the external environment. However, researchers disagree on how much such differences are due solely to genetic inheritance and how much they reflect prenatal influences and more subtle environmental experiences during and shortly after birth (Kagan & Snidman, 1991; Kagan et al., 1995; Rothbart, 1989). For example, although identical twins have been found to be significantly more alike than fraternal twins in smiling behavior and in the tendency to be anxious or curious in response to strangers, they may elicit more similar responses from their parents than fraternal twins do, making it hard to sort out the reasons for these early differences (Freedman, 1976; Plomin & Rowe, 1979).

Parents certainly report differences in their infants' temperaments even shortly after birth. The parents of baby Alberto and his sister Lydia, for example, clearly remember that unlike Lydia, who was a fussy and somewhat difficult baby to care for and comfort during her first few months, Alberto was a very easy baby who was no trouble at all.

In a now classic study of temperament, Alexander Thomas and Stella Chess used parents' reports of differences in their babies on the following nine dimensions: (1) activity level (2) rhythmicity (regularity of eating, sleeping, and elimination), (3) approach-withdrawal to or from novel stimuli and situations, (4) adaptability to new people and situations, (5) emotional reactivity, (6) responsiveness to stimulation, (7) quality of mood (positive or negative), (8) distractibility, and (9) attention span (Thomas & Chess, 1977, 1981). They found three general patterns of temperament.

Easy babies (40 percent of the sample) showed mostly positive moods, regular bodily functions, and good adaptation to new situations. *Difficult babies* (10 per-

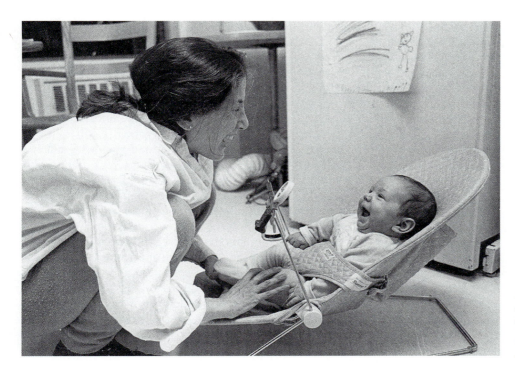

Infants vary in temperament. Some are easygoing like the baby in this photo, while others are more difficult. These variations may affect their long-term development.

cent) displayed negative moods, irregular bodily functions, and high stress in new situations. *Slow-to-warm-up babies* (15 percent) resembled the difficult ones but were less extreme; they were moody and relatively unadaptable, but did not react vigorously to new stimuli. Finally, *mixed-pattern babies* (35 percent) did not fall neatly into any of the first three groups.

Because the original classification of temperaments was based solely on parents' reports, which sometimes can be unreliable, more recent studies have used two additional measures of temperament: multiple behavior ratings (by pediatricians, nurses, teachers, and other individuals familiar with the child) and direct observation of the child. These studies have confirmed earlier findings of temperamental differences at birth (Plomin, 1989; Seifer et al., 1994).

Classifying babies by temperamental pattern has been helpful in predicting problems for the minority of children who are difficult or slow to warm up, but not for the majority of children whose temperaments are less extreme. For example, newborn infants whose biological rhythms are irregular, who experience discomfort during feeding and elimination, and who do not communicate their needs clearly often are difficult for their parents and are more likely to experience problems in developing close relationships with them. This is particularly true when mothers have little or no help and emotional support from relatives and friends in caring for their difficult babies, although parenting can improve when such emotional support is made available (Kerr et al., 1994; van den Boom & Hoeksma, 1994; Crockenberg & McCluskey, 1986).

How stable are early differences in temperament? Predictions of later temperament based on temperamental differences among newborns are not very reliable, although predictions based on differences observed toward the end of the first year are somewhat better (Carlson et al., 1995; Gunnar et al., 1995; Kagan & Snidman, 1991; Rothbart, 1989). This may in part reflect the influence of experience and context on temperament. In most cases, the degree to which an infant's early temperamental style contributes to personality development is likely to be influenced by how good a *fit* exists between the child's temperamental style and the attitudes, expectations, and responses of parents and other caregivers. For example, an infant who is very active and demanding is more likely to maintain that temperament if these qualities are consistent with his parents' expectations and responses than would be the case if his parents expected him to be more passive and less demanding (Rickman & Davidson, 1995).

The particular culture a child grows up in may also influence various temperamental characteristics by assigning them different meanings and by responding to them differently. Margot Prior and her colleagues (1987) compared parent ratings of temperament in four-to-eight-month-old infants from four cultural groups: American, Chinese, Australian, and Greek. Table 5.3 presents their results.

Prior suggests that the temperamental differences she found may be as much a product of the mother's behavior as the infant's. For Chinese and Greek infants who are low on rhythmicity, mothers may be more "child centered," placing greater emphasis on immediately fulfilling the infant's needs. For American and Australian infants (high rhythmicity), mothers are more likely to set meal and sleep times according to their own adult schedules. Similarly, the lower adaptability and distractibility scores of Greek and Chinese infants may reflect the fact that they have not learned to adapt to varying demands of the social environment as early as Australian and American infants have and may be more persistent and less easily distracted from their attempts at self-gratification. An alternative possibility is that the differences found reflect inherited group differences in temperament. This interpretation is consistent with recent reports by Jerome Kagan and his associates (1995) of temperamental differences among four-month-old infants in Boston; Dublin, Ireland; and Beijing, China.

What conclusions can we draw? Infant temperament is certainly an important influence on early social and emotional development. In most cases, however, its contribution is best understood as a product of the ongoing interactions among an infant's inherited temperamental predispositions, the responses of his or her parents and other caregivers, and the overall developmental environment.

What Do You Think?

What advice would you give to parents about how to respond to differences in their children's temperaments? What have you noticed about temperamental differences among members of your own family?

TABLE 5.3   *Parent's Ratings of Their Infants' Temperament in Four Cultural Groups*

	Cultural Group			
Dimension	*American*	*Australian*	*Greek*	*Chinese*
Activity level	H	H	L	L
Rhythmicity	H	H	L	L
Approach-withdrawal	H	H	L	L
Adaptability	H	H	L	L
Emotional reactivity	L	L	H	H
Responsiveness to stimulation	L	L	H	H
Quality of mood	H	H	L	L
Distractibility	H	H	L	L
Attention span	H	H	L	H

Note: H = high level of the temperamental quality; L = low level of the temperamental quality.

American and Australian infants were rated low on emotional reactivity and responsiveness to stimulation and high on all others. Greek infants were rated high on emotional reactivity and responsiveness to stimulation and low on all others. Chinese infants were rated high on emotional reactivity, responsiveness to stimulation, and attention span, and low on all others. Further research is needed to determine the degree to which these differences are due to child care practices and to differences that are present at birth.

Source: Prior et al. (1987).

EARLY SOCIAL RELATIONSHIPS

Infants seem to have a natural tendency to be social participants. Not only do newborns show preferences for their mothers' voices shortly after birth; some evidence also suggests that their perception of speech can be influenced by prenatal exposure to their mothers' speech (DeCasper & Spence, 1986; DeCasper et al., 1994). Immediately after birth, infants are capable of many social responses. For example, a newborn will turn his head toward the sound of a human voice and actively search for its source, attend to and show preference for a voice with a female pitch, and pause regularly in his sucking pattern for human voices but not for similar, nonhuman tones. He will even prefer the smell and taste of human milk over those of formula, water, or sugar water (Brazelton, 1976).

Transition to Parenthood

Parent-child relationships begin even before a child is born. Almost as soon as pregnancy is confirmed, parents form *images* of what their child will be like and of how they as parents will respond and cope with this new human presence (Galinsky, 1987). They often experience both excitement and fear, the precise mix depending on how much support they have for becoming parents as well as the history of support, or lack thereof, that they had for being children themselves years ago. Even after the baby is born, these images can influence the parents' internal experiences and expectations regarding a child, although this "mental portrait" is now subject to continual revision based on the parents' ongoing interactions and experiences with their baby (Ferholt, 1991; Stern, 1985a, 1985b; 1995).

As we will see in Chapter 13's discussion of psychosocial development in young adulthood, having a child, particularly if it is the first, represents a major life transition that is accompanied by personal, familial, social, and, for many people, professional changes. For most parents, having a child leads them to become less concerned about themselves and more concerned with the well-being of others and about the future as embodied in their child. This shift away from self-centeredness usually comes at some emotional cost, however. During the first two years of rearing an infant, many mothers find themselves removed from much of their normal contact with other adults to devote themselves to infant care and fathers report working harder at their jobs (Bronstein, 1988; C. Cowan et al., 1991).

To accommodate the additional family tasks involved in caring for a new infant, the division of roles between husband and wife tends to become more traditional, regardless of the wife's employment, educational level, preexisting arrangements, or beliefs about gender roles. Social and emotional patterns between parents also appear to change, as reflected in significant decreases in shared leisure and sexual activities, in fewer positive interactions with each other, and in decreased marital satisfaction and greater marital conflict (C. Cowan et al., 1991; Levy-Shiff, 1994).

To better understand these changes, Rachel Levy-Shiff (1994) studied marital adjustment in 102 couples from diverse sociocultural backgrounds from pregnancy through the first eight months following the birth of their first child. She found that higher levels of *paternal involvement* with the baby, especially in caregiving, was the most important factor in maintaining marital satisfaction for *both* spouses at a time when opportunities to spend time together in leisure and sexual activities are greatly reduced due to the demands of infant care. Levy-Schiff suggests that during the transition to parenthood, men and women must first solve the internal and interpersonal dilemmas of reorganizing their lives to adjust to the new demands and responsibilities of childrearing. In most families, the birth of a first child results in gender roles becoming more differentiated and traditional, with women assuming

Sharing children and household tasks plays a positive role in dealing with the transition to parenthood.

both the main responsibilities for child care and most of the housework. The physical and emotional drain new mothers experience may lead them to feel resentment toward their husbands because of "overload" and because of unfulfilled prenatal expectations that caring for the new baby would be more fully shared.

Fathers who are more involved in *coparenting* (sharing child care) and sharing housework demonstrate that they are not just husbands but also good friends who are committed to meeting their partners' needs in ways that are caring and fair. It is also likely that such shared involvement increases a husband's empathy and appreciation for his wife's experience. Self-respecting participation by men is also likely to reduce the guilt they would feel if they failed to take an active role in sharing these new responsibilities. Interestingly, by freeing up their wives' time and conveying a spirit of cooperativeness, husbands create opportunities for more high-quality time with their wives, the lack of which is a major cause of dissatisfaction for many new fathers (Belsky et al., 1995; Levy-Schiff, 1994). The transition to parenthood is the start of a lifelong process that will be discussed throughout the book.

Caregiver-Infant Synchrony

Frequently the social interactions between parent (or other caregiver) and infant involve a pattern of close coordination and teamwork in which each waits for the other to finish before beginning to respond. This pattern of closely coordinated interaction is called **caregiver-infant synchrony**. Recall the description of Alberto at the beginning of this chapter. Even infants only a few weeks old are able to maintain and break eye contact with their mothers at regular intervals and to take turns with them in making sounds and body movements. Furthermore, videotape studies

Parents and their toddlers often show a striking synchrony in their movements and gestures. In these exchanges, it is often hard to tell who is leading whom.

reveal that mother and baby have "conversations" that resemble adult dialogue in many ways, except for the child's lack of words (Fish et al., 1993; Stern, 1985b, 1992; Tronick, 1989).

Until an infant is several months old, responsibility for coordinating this activity rests with the caregiver. But after a few months, the baby becomes capable of initiating social interchanges and influencing the content and style of his caregiver's behavior. Not surprisingly, babies who are particularly sociable early in infancy are likely to have mothers who form especially strong emotional attachments, or connectedness, with them later in infancy (Tronick et al., 1982). Some of this continuity is created by the baby rather than the mother. The smiles, gazes, and vocalizing of a friendly infant prove hard for her mother to resist, and after several months of experience with such a baby, the mother becomes especially responsive to her infant's communications, further reinforcing the baby's sociable tendencies.

As we will see shortly, a good caregiver-infant temperament "fit" and a well-developed capacity for caregiver-infant synchrony both contribute in important ways to the establishment of the high-quality caregiver-infant relationships that serve as the basis for healthy development. Caregiver-infant relationships that lack the mutual awareness and responsiveness that make synchrony possible may reflect childrearing difficulties and can place an infant at risk for developmental problems. Studies of interactions between depressed mothers and their infants, for example, have found that mothers' negative moods influence their babies' moods and can affect their longer-term relationships and vulnerability to depression later in life (Field, 1987; Isabella & Belsky, 1991; Nolen-Hoeksema et al., 1995; Radke-Yarrow et al., 1993).

Social Interactions with Fathers and Siblings

Although infants may interact more with their mothers than with anyone else, they actually live in a network of daily social relationships in which a number of other people make at least minor—and sometimes major—contributions to their social lives (Hodapp & Mueller, 1982). Fathers often belong to this network, and so do siblings. How do a baby's contacts with these people compare to those with his or her mother?

Father-Infant Interactions   In recent years, fathers have become increasingly involved in the care of infants and young children, spending around two or three hours per day compared to nine hours for mothers. In a small but significant number of instances, fathers assume the role of primary caregiver, reversing the traditional expectations that fathers should set personal and professional goals over investing time and care in their children and the paternal role (Belsky et al., 1984b; Garbarino, 1993; Lamb et al., 1987). As with mothers, fathers' success at maintaining high levels of caregiver-infant synchrony is related to the goodness of fit between their stress levels, personality characteristics, attitudes and expectations, and the characteristics and needs of their babies (Noppe et al., 1991; Yogman et al., 1977).

Although mothers and fathers engage in similar forms of play with their infants, their styles differ. Play episodes with fathers tend to have sharper peaks and valleys: higher states of excitement and more sudden and complete withdrawals by the baby. Fathers tend to jostle more and talk less than mothers do, and they roughhouse more and play ritual games such as peek-a-boo less. Fathers also devote more time with their babies to play than mothers do—40 percent versus 25 percent (Kotelchuck, 1976). These differences in style also appear in middle childhood, and such playful interactions may help prepare infants for future play with peers of both genders (Parke et al., 1988).

How do we explain these differences? Past experience with infants, the amount of time routinely spent with young children, demanding work schedules, and fathers' expectations about the stresses and responsibilities of parenting may all play a role. When researchers compared fathers who served as primary, full-time caregivers with fathers who took the more traditional secondary-caregiver role, they found differences in how the two groups played with their infants. Primary-caregiver fathers acted very much like mothers, smiling more and imitating their babies' facial expressions and vocalizations more than secondary-caregiver fathers did. However, all of the fathers were quite physical when interacting with their infants (Field, 1987; Hwang, 1986; Noppe et al., 1991). These findings suggest that "cohort" effects may be at work here. (*Cohort effects* refer to developmental changes shared by individuals growing up in a particular place or under a specific set of historical circumstances.) As successive generations of fathers assume greater responsibility for the care of infants due to changing societal and cultural conditions and expectations, differences in how fathers and mothers interact with their babies will likely decrease.

Interactions with Siblings   Approximately 80 percent of children in the United States and Europe grow up with siblings. The time they spend together in their early years frequently is greater than the time spent with their mothers or fathers. In many cultures, children are cared for by siblings. From age one or two they are fed, comforted, disciplined, and played with by a sister or brother who may be only three or four years older (Dunn, 1985; Weisner & Gallimore, 1977). Firstborn children are likely to monitor the interactions of their mother and the new baby very closely and try to become directly involved themselves. Children as young as eighteen months attempt to help in the bathing, feeding, and dressing of their sibling. At times they also try to tip over the baby's bath, spill things, and turn the kitchen upside down when they feel jealous of their mother's attention to the new baby. Conflict between siblings is most likely to occur when parents are seen as giving preferential treatment to one child (Dunn, 1985, 1988; Stewart et al., 1987).

In talking to their younger siblings, children make many of the same adjustments their parents do, using much shorter sentences, repeating comments, and using lots of action-getting techniques (baby talk, or "parentese"). In turn, infants tend to respond to their siblings in much the same way they do to their parents. But they also quickly learn the ways siblings differ from parents, particularly young siblings. Because younger children lack their parents' maturity and experience, they are less able to focus consistently on meeting the baby's needs rather than their own. For example, a four-year-old who is playing with his eight-month-old sister may not notice that she is becoming overstimulated and tired and needs to stop. On another occasion, he may become jealous of the attention she is getting and "accidentally" fall on her while giving her a hug. If parents (and other caregivers) keep in mind the needs and capabilities of each of their children and provide appropriate supervision, interactions with siblings are likely to benefit the development of both their new infant and his or her brothers and sisters.

Interactions with Nonparental Caregivers

In recent years, caregiving has become increasingly important in the lives of preschool children because many more mothers have returned to working outside the home, even before their children have begun public school. By 1990, about 55 to 60 percent of all mothers with children less than six years of age worked outside the home, and experts predict the proportion will rise even higher by the end of the century (Children's Defense Fund, 1992; U.S. Bureau of the Census, 1991). (We will take a closer look at changes in the nature of families and family life when we discuss psychosocial development in early adulthood in Chapter 13.) All of these parents require suitable, high-quality care for their children for either all or part of the day. The arrangements they actually make depend on the age of the child, on their own preferences (usually familylike settings), and on the kinds of services available in the community. Among all parents who work at least part time or more, about 45 percent arrange for a relative to come into the home or take the child to the relative's home (U.S. Bureau of the Census, 1991). Another 40 percent arrange for a nonrelative to care for the child in the child's home or, more commonly, in the caregiver's home. That leaves only about 15 percent of infants, toddlers, and preschoolers to be cared for in licensed infant and toddler child care centers and in family day care homes. Figure 5.1 summarizes current child care arrangements for children under two years of age.

In addition to good physical facilities and developmentally appropriate programs, high-quality care for infants is best ensured by employing caregivers who are well trained and supervised and responsive to the physical, cognitive, social, and emotional needs of infants and their families (Bredkamp, 1987; Phillips, 1987).

For parents who are considering day care for their infant, knowing what to look for in a center is extremely important. Table 5.4 presents guidelines for choosing infant day care.

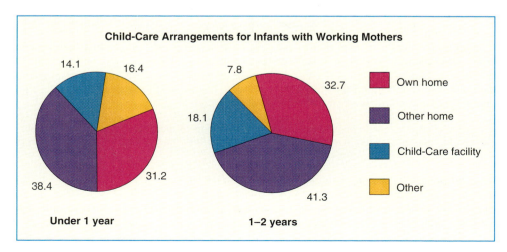

Child-Care Arrangements for Infants with Working Mothers

Under 1 year:
14.1, 16.4, 38.4, 31.2

1–2 years:
7.8, 32.7, 18.1, 41.3

Own home
Other home
Child-Care facility
Other

FIGURE 5.1
Current Child Care Arrangements for Working Mothers with Children under One Year and with Children Between One and Two Years
The majority of infants and toddlers whose mothers work are cared for in their own or another home. Somewhat more toddlers than infants go to child care facilities. Infants are more likely than toddlers to be cared for in "other" situations, such as accompanying their parents to work.

TABLE 5.4 *Guidelines for Choosing a Good Infant Daycare Program*

In choosing an infant day care program, parents should look for the following characteristics.

Interactions Among Caregivers and Children

Caregivers hold and carry infants frequently; engage in many one-to-one interactions; talk in a pleasant, soothing voice; and use simple language and frequent eye contact.

Caregivers are especially attentive to infants during routines such as changing diapers and feeding and respond quickly to infants' cries or calls of distress in a soothing and tender way.

Caregivers playfully interact with babies in ways that are sensitive to the infants' interests and level of tolerance for stimulation.

Caregivers frequently talk with, sing to, and read to infants, and play games such as peek-a-boo and "This Little Piggy."

Caregivers greet infants and their parents with warmth and enthusiasm, hold the baby upon arrival, and gradually help the child become part of the small group.

Caregivers consistently respond to infants' needs for food and comfort and adjust to infant's individual feeding and sleeping schedules, food preferences, and eating styles.

Caregivers praise infants for their accomplishments, respect infants' curiosity about one another, and support children in interacting with one another in a gentle and respectful way.

Environment

Diapering, sleeping, feeding, and play areas are separate to ensure sanitation and provide quiet, restful areas.

Children have their own cribs, bedding, clothing, comforting objects, etc.

Environment is cheerful, and attractively decorated, and designed for children, with child-oriented pictures and objects, soft and hard objects, mirrors, and contrasts in color and design for infant stimulation.

Healthy fresh air, light, and heat/humidity/cooling conditions are maintained; floors are covered with easy-to-clean carpet; space is arranged so children can enjoy quiet play by themselves, have space to roll over, and crawl toward interesting objects.

A variety of music is provided for enjoyment in listening/body movement/singing.

The area that is the focus of play changes periodically during the day from the floor, to strollers, to being carried, to rocking or swinging, and other variations to give infants different perspectives on people and places. Children are cared for both indoors and outdoors.

Equipment

Toys are safe, washable, and too large for infants to swallow; range from very simple to more complex.

Toys are responsive to the child's actions: bells, busy boards, balls, vinyl-covered pillows to climb on, large beads that snap together, nesting bowls, small blocks, shape sorters, music boxes, squeeze toys that squeak.

Toys are scaled to a size that enables infants to grasp, chew, and manipulate them (clutch balls, rattles, spoons, teethers, rubber dolls); mobiles are designed to be seen from the child's viewpoint.

Toys, books, and familiar objects are available on open shelves so children can make their own selections.

Low climbing structures and steps that are well padded and safe for exploration are provided.

Health, Safety, and Nutrition

Health and safety precautions are taken to limit the spread of infectious diseases.

Written records are maintained for each child, including immunizations, special health needs, and up-to-date emergency information.

Staff members are in good health and use good health care practices in working with children, including washing hands before and after diaper changing and before and after feeding each infant.

Staff members are aware of the symptoms of common illnesses, environmental hazards such as lead poisoning, and food and other allergies.

Children are always under adult supervision. Children are dressed appropriately for the weather and type of play they engage in.

Infants are held when fed, and children who can sit up eat in small groups with caregivers who provide assistance as needed. A variety of healthy foods are fed, and eating is a sociable and happy time.

Staff-Parent Interactions

Parents are viewed as the child's primary source of affection. Staff support parents and work with them to help them feel confident as parents.

Parents and staff talk daily to share pertinent information about the child. Staff help parents anticipate the child's next areas of development and prepare them to support the child.

Staff members welcome and encourage appropriate parent input and involvement in various day care center activities; parents feel welcomed and respected by day care staff and confident that the staff will be responsive to their needs and concerns.

Staff Qualifications

Staff members enjoy working with infants and toddlers and are warmly responsive to their needs.

Staff members have training specifically related to infant and toddler development and caregiving.

Staffing

The group size and ratio of adults to infants is limited to allow for one-to-one interaction, intimate knowledge of individual babies, and consistent caregiving. Babies need to relate to the same, very few people each day. A ratio of one adult to no more than three infants is best.

Low staff turnover ensures caregiver continuity.

Hours of Operation

Center has hours that accommodate the complicated schedules of working parents.

Center Philosophy

The child care, developmental, and educational values and goals of the center and its staff should be compatible with those held by families that are involved and respectful of cultural and lifestyle differences.

Adapted from Bredkamp (1987), pp. 34–38.

For many families, grandparents play an important role in raising young children.

Grandparents   For the majority of well-functioning families, and in most cultural groups in North America, grandparents become welcome companions for the new child (Werner, 1991), as well as secondary sources of practical advice and child care. This is especially true when the grandparents live geographically close to the parents, they are relatively young and in good health, and the family itself belongs to a cultural group (such as Mexican Americans) that values the participation of the extended family in raising children (Ramirez, 1989; Slomin, 1991). We will look at the importance of grandparenting and the variety of grandparenting styles in Chapter 15, where we examine psychosocial development in middle adulthood.

Interactions with Peers

Young babies show considerable interest in other infants and in much the same ways they show interest in their parents: by gazing, smiling, and cooing. Sociability of this kind develops with peers at the same time and at the same rate that it does with parents (Field & Roopnarine, 1982; Vandell, 1980). When given the choice, infants often prefer playing with their peers to playing with their mothers. In play situations, infants more frequently look at and follow their peers, and toddlers are more likely to talk with, imitate, and exchange toys with their peers than with their mothers (Rubenstein & Howes, 1976).

Toddlers in day care spend about 25 percent of their time interacting positively with other toddlers. They are more likely to express positive feelings and play competently with peers than with adults or when by themselves. Repeated contact with a peer in a familiar setting with a familiar caregiver and minimal adult interference appears to facilitate the development of peer friendship. Peers also support the autonomy of the toddler from the mother and offer the toddler an alternative source of stimulation and comfort (Hartup, 1989; Rubenstein & Howes, 1983).

In conclusion, although infants' social interactions with their parents generally are their most important early social experiences, interactions with siblings and peers also contribute to their social development. The quality and developmental

Infants show considerable interest in interacting with other infants and when given the opportunity may prefer playing with their peers than with their parents.

impact of experiences with siblings and peers will reflect, to some extent, the degree to which parental supervision of such contacts considers the needs of both the baby and the other children.

What Do You Think?

What advice would you give to prospective parents about maternal employment and child care arrangements for infants? How will (or do) your own child care arrangements differ from those of your parents?

ATTACHMENT FORMATION

Attachment refers to the strong and enduring emotional bond that develops between infant and caregiver during the infant's first year of life. This relationship is characterized by reciprocal affection and a shared desire to maintain physical closeness (Ainsworth, 1973; Bowlby, 1969).

The concept of attachment has been most strongly influenced by the ethological perspective (see Chapter 2) and, to a lesser extent, by the psychoanalytic approach. In the ethological view, the ties between infant and caregiver develop from the activation of a biologically based motivational system that is an inherited adaptation of human evolution. This system helped ensure survival by protecting infants from environmental dangers (Bowlby, 1969). Because the nature of the child-caregiver relationship is widely viewed as being central to successful child development, studies of attachment have come to play an important role in developmental theory. Another influence has been the work of theorists who emphasize the importance of "working models," or internalized perceptions, feelings, and expectations regarding social relationships with significant caretakers (Biringen, 1994).

Although attachment cannot be observed directly, it can be inferred from a number of commonly observed infant behaviors that help establish and maintain physical closeness with caregivers (Bowlby, 1969, 1973, 1980). Three of these behaviors—crying, cooing, and babbling—are *signaling behaviors;* four others—smiling, clinging, nonnutritional sucking, and following—are *approach behaviors.* While researchers do not agree as to whether these *specific* attachment behaviors are biologically inherited, many believe that the tendency to seek and maintain physical closeness with caregivers is biologically determined and essential to infant survival in much the same way food is.

One important source of support for attachment theory comes from a well-known series of studies of infant rhesus monkeys by Harry Harlow (Harlow, 1959; Harlow & Harlow, 1962). Infant monkeys who were taken away from their mothers at birth and raised with artificial wire and terrycloth substitute mothers displayed many of the attachment behaviors just mentioned. When forced to choose, they preferred physical *contact comfort* with a warm, soft, terrycloth substitute mother that did not provide food to contact with a cold, hard, wire mother that provided milk from a bottle but was not soft and huggable. Harlow also found that infant monkeys that were deprived of physical closeness but were otherwise well cared for exhibited extreme fear and withdrawal, an inability to establish social and sexual relations with peers, and much higher rates of illness and death.

Although we must be cautious in drawing conclusions about human infants from studies of monkeys, Harlow's findings suggest that contact comfort, a key attachment behavior, may be a primary need during infancy that is relatively independent of the need for food and the other sources of oral pleasure that psychodynamic theorists such as Freud thought to be the basis of emotional development. They also suggest that severe deprivation of physical closeness with a caregiver may have major negative consequences for subsequent development. The work of René Spitz (1945, 1946), who studied infants reared in institutional settings, suggests that consistency and reliability of caregiver responsiveness is also important. Spitz found that infants who experienced frequent changes in caregivers and who lacked at least one caregiver who was consistently responsive to their needs found it extremely difficult to establish social and emotional infant-caregiver connections.

Currently most developmental psychologists believe attachment relationships develop over time as a cumulative product of the infant's repeated experiences in interaction with her main caregivers during the first year (Isabella, 1993). They also believe attachment involves a highly mutual and interactive partnership between caregiver and child, both of whom have strong, although unequal, needs to achieve physical and emotional closeness with each other. This view is influenced by recent discoveries about the interactive nature of social relations between infants and their caregivers.

According to attachment theory, once attachment with the mother (or other primary caregiver) is established, the infant uses her as a *secure base* from which to explore the environment. As the infant gradually increases his distance from the mother, the *attachment behavioral system* and accompanying feelings of fear and anxiety are more likely to be activated, and the infant begins to seek proximity (closeness) to the caregiver once again. This pattern is also activated when the infant encounters dangers such as strangers, darkness, or animals approaching. The balance between activation of the attachment system and activation of exploratory behaviors varies with the particular context and developmental level of the child (Biringen, 1994).

Phases of Attachment Formation

John Bowlby (1969) believes that attachments develop in a series of phases determined partly by cognitive changes (described in the previous chapter) and partly by interactions that appear to develop quite naturally between infants and their caregivers. Table 5.5 presents these four phases. Note that *separation anxiety,* an infant's disturbance at being separated from her caregiver, and *stranger anxiety,* a

TABLE 5.5   *Four Stages of Attachment Formation*

Phase 1: Indiscriminate Sociability (birth–2 months)

Responds actively with cries, smiles, coos, and gazes to promote contact and affection from other people; uses limited attachment behaviors less selectively than when older.

Phase 2: Attachments in the Making (2–7 months)

Increasing preference for individuals most familiar and responsive to needs; preferences reinforce parents' affection; accepts certain forms of attention and care from comparative strangers; tolerates temporary separations from parents.

Phase 3: Specific, Clear-cut Attachments (7–24 months)

Preferences for specific people become much stronger due to ability to represent persons mentally (Piaget's fourth stage of sensorimotor development; see Chapter 6); ability to crawl and walk enables toddler to seek proximity to and use caregiver as a safe base for exploration; increasing verbal skills allow greater involvement with parents and others; both *separation anxiety*—an infant's disturbance at being separated from the caregiver—and *stranger anxiety*—a wariness and avoidance of strangers— appear near the beginning of this phase.

Phase 4: Goal-coordinated Partnerships (24 months onward)

By age two, increasing representational and memory skills for objects and events; growing ability to understand parental feelings and points of view and to adjust his or her own accordingly; growing capacity to tolerate short parental absences and delays and interruptions in parents' undivided attention makes possible cooperation with others to meet needs; changing abilities are related to secure attachment relationships grounded in a sense of basic trust.

Source: Bowlby (1969).

wariness and avoidance of strangers, appear near the beginning of phase 3. The achievement of object permanence (see Chapter 2) is thought to be an important basis for separation anxiety and attachment development.

Assessing Attachment: The "Strange Situation"

The most widely used method for evaluating the quality of attachment to a caregiver is called the **Strange Situation**. Originally developed by Mary Ainsworth for infants who are old enough to crawl or walk, the procedure consists of eight brief social episodes with different combinations of the infant, the mother, and an unfamiliar adult (Ainsworth et al., 1978). It presents the infant with a cumulative series of stressful experiences: being in an unfamiliar place, meeting a stranger, and being separated from the caregiver.

The first episode lasts for thirty seconds and the remaining seven for three minutes each: (1) parent and infant enter the room with the experimenter; (2) parent as a secure base: the baby plays with toys and explores the room while her mother is seated; (3) reaction to an unfamiliar adult: a stranger enters the room, sits down, and talks to the mother; (4) separation anxiety: the parent leaves the infant alone with the stranger, who responds to (and comforts) the infant if necessary; (5) reaction to reunion: the parent returns, greets (comforts) the baby, and the stranger leaves; (6) separation anxiety: the mother leaves and the baby is left alone in the room; (7) comforted by a stranger: the stranger again enters the room and offers comfort to the infant; (8) reunion: the parent again returns, the stranger leaves; the parent greets/comforts the baby and tries to interest her in playing with the toys.

Based on the infants' patterns of behavior in the Strange Situation, Ainsworth and her colleagues identified three main groups. Most of the infants studied (approximately 65 to 70 percent) displayed a **secure attachment** pattern. When first alone with their mothers, they typically played happily. When the stranger entered, they were somewhat wary but continued to play without becoming upset. But when they were left alone with the stranger, they typically stopped playing and searched for or crawled after their mothers; in some cases, they cried. When the mothers returned, the babies were clearly pleased to see them and actively sought contact and interaction, staying closer to them and cuddling more than before. When left alone with the stranger again, the infants were easily comforted; although they showed stronger signs of distress, they quickly recovered from the upset by actively seeking contact with their mothers on their return.

The second group of infants (about 10 percent) were classified as displaying an **anxious-resistant attachment** pattern. They showed some signs of anxiety and, even in the periods preceding separation, stuck close to their mothers and explored only minimally. They were intensely upset by separation. When reunited with their mothers, they actively sought close contact with them but at the same time angrily resisted the mothers' efforts to comfort them by hitting them and pushing them away. They refused to be comforted by the stranger as well.

The third group of infants (about 20 percent) displayed an **anxious-avoidant attachment** pattern. They initially showed little involvement with their mothers, treating them and the stranger in much the same way. They rarely cried when separated and, when reunited, showed a mixed response of low-level engagement with their mothers and a tendency to avoid them.

The three attachment patterns have been studied in many other countries. In all cases, around 60 to 65 percent of the children are reported to be securely attached, whereas rates of insecure attachment are much more variable (van Ijzendoorn & Kroonenberg, 1988). The accompanying Multicultural View box discusses cross-cultural variations in attachment.

Consequences of Different Attachment Patterns

Secure attachment early in infancy benefits babies in several ways during their second year of life. For one thing, securely attached toddlers tend to cooperate better with their parents than other babies do (Londerville & Main, 1981). They comply better with rules such as "Don't run in the living room!", and they are also more willing to learn new skills and try new activities their parents show them (such as when a parent says, "Sit with me for a minute and see how I do this"). When faced with problems that are too difficult for them to solve, toddlers who are securely attached are more likely than others to seek and accept help from their parents. At age five, these children tend to adapt better than other children to changes in preschool situations (Arend et al., 1979; Matas et al., 1978; Slade, 1987).

Less securely attached infants may not learn as well from their parents (Matas et al., 1978). Anxious-resistant infants often respond with anger and resistance to their parents' attempts to help or teach them. Such babies may at times invest so much time and energy in conflicts that they are unable to benefit from their parents' experience and to explore their environment. Given a roomful of toys and a mother who has recently returned from an absence, for example, a child may use up a lot of time alternating between being angry at and snuggling with his mother instead of getting on with his play. Anxious-avoidant infants do not have this particular problem, but because of their tendency to avoid interaction with their parents, they also miss out on parental efforts to teach or help them and ultimately may discourage parents from even trying to help.

Such differences in attachment appear to persist even into the preschool years. One study found that children rated as securely attached at age one seemed more likely to seek attention in positive ways in nursery school at age four (Sroufe et al., 1983). When they needed help because of sickness or a hurt, or just wanted to be friendly, they found it easy to secure attention by approaching their teachers fairly directly, and they seemed to enjoy the attention when they received it. Less securely attached infants, whether anxious avoidant or anxious resistant, tended to grow into relatively dependent preschool children. They sought more help more frequently but seemed less satisfied with what they got. However, methods of seeking attention differed between the two groups. Anxious-resistant children showed signs

A Multicultural View

Cross-cultural Variations in Attachment

Almost all infants become attached to their parents in some way. However, the patterns by which they do so vary around the world. Studies on the Strange Situation report that whereas 60 to 65 percent of children studied appear to be securely attached, rates of insecure attachment are much more variable (van Ijzendoorn & Kroonenberg, 1988). Among infants from northern Germany, for example, anxious-avoidant attachment patterns occur twice as often as they do among North American infants. Among infants from Japan, on the other hand, anxious-resistant responses occur approximately three times as often as they do in the United States, while anxious-resistant attachment is virtually nonexistent (Bretherton & Waters, 1985; Takahashi, 1990).

These variations result partly from differences in cultural values around the world and partly from the childrearing practices these values foster. In northern Germany, people value personal independence especially strongly (Grossmann et al., 1985) and believe children should obey parents more consistently than is usually expected in North America. As a result, infants need to learn not to make excessive demands on parents; they must minimize crying and fussing and do without extra bodily contact. During early infancy, mothers encourage these qualities by remaining relatively unresponsive to their infants' moment-by-moment behavior. Thus, in northern Germany, unresponsiveness may not signify personal rejection of the child as much as a desire to raise a good citizen. The results show up in the Strange Situation as anxious-avoidant attachment: a larger than usual number of young children seem indifferent when reunited with their mothers.

Childrearing practices probably also influence the attachment responses of Japanese children. Separations between Japanese infants and their mothers are quite rare by North American standards. Most Japanese infants have very little experience with strangers. Typically they are left alone or with another adult only two or three times per month on average, usually someone already intimate with the child, such as the father or a grandparent (Mikaye et al., 1985). Their extreme protests to the Strange Situation resemble the anxious-resistant pattern of crying, anger, fear, and clinging when the mother returns. As with the German infants, however, it is more likely that these

of chronic complaining or whining, whereas anxious-avoidant children tended to approach their teachers very indirectly, literally taking a zigzagging path to reach them. Having done so, they typically waited passively for the teachers to notice them.

Attachment is not limited to the periods of infancy and early childhood. As we will see when we discuss psychosocial development in adulthood in Chapters 13 and 15, attachment is a lifelong process.

Influences on Attachment Formation

So far we have emphasized the general aspects of attachment. In this section, we discuss some of the factors that appear to influence the quality of attachment between infants and their mothers, as well as other important caregivers.

The Role of the Mother   A major determinant of individual differences in attachment is the quality of the infant-mother relationship during the first year of life. A mother's capacity to respond sensitively and appropriately to her infant and to feel positively about her baby and the baby's strengths and limitations appears to be more important than the amount of contact or caregiving. Mothers of securely attached infants are more responsive to their babies' crying, more careful and tender in holding them, and more responsive to their particular needs and feelings during both feeding and nonfeeding interactions than are mothers of less securely attached infants (Ainsworth et al., 1978; Belsky et al., 1984b; Crockenberg & McCluskey, 1986).

Differences in infant temperament are likely to affect the mother-infant relationship and the quality of attachment. Infants with irritable temperaments tend to receive less maternal involvement, which in turn may negatively influence the quality of attachment. With the appropriate interventions, however, such negative cycles may be interrupted.

behaviors represent the fulfillment of typical cultural practices rather than failures in childrearing.

Some researchers have also noted that distribution of attachment types may vary within as well as across cultures. In a study of infants from southern Germany, the distribution of attachment types did not differ significantly from those reported for infants in the United States (Grossmann & Grossmann, 1990; van Ijzendoorn & Kroonenberg, 1988). Studies of attachment among Israeli infants raised in kibbutz communities provide further evidence of cultural differences in attachment within a particular society. Kibbutz children were raised in communal peer groups by *metapelot* (nurse/educators), spending regular time with their families during evenings, weekends, and holidays. Kibbutz infants successfully formed attachments to both their parents and their communal caregivers, but a larger proportion displayed insecure attachment patterns compared to Israeli infants raised in the city or infants raised in the United States (Aviezer et al., 1994; Sagi et al., 1994).

Cultural values and practices, however, cannot explain all the differences. Even in northern Germany, for exam-

ple, many babies become securely attached even though their mothers follow culturally approved practices of aloofness. In Japan, some infants become anxious-resistant even though their mothers follow essentially Western childrearing styles, which include considerable experience with baby sitters and other nonparental caregivers. Observations of these babies in their homes suggest that they were born with somewhat irritable or fussy temperaments, which may predispose them to becoming anxious-resistant despite their mothers' practices.

On balance, attachment seems to result from the combination of several influences, including cultural values, inborn temperament, and the childrearing practices of the particular family. The developmental meaning of attachment may vary too. What looks like an attachment failure for one child may be a success for another, depending on the circumstances.

In one recent study of the influence of temperament and mothering on attachment, Dymphna van den Boom (1994) helped mothers to respond to their temperamentally difficult six-month-old infants in more sensitive and developmentally appropriate ways by adjusting their behaviors to the infants' unique cues. Mothers gained practice in imitating their infants' behaviors and repeating their own verbal expressions. They also learned to notice when their infants were gazing at them and when they were not and to coordinate the pace and rhythm of their own behavior with those of their infants. Mothers who received such help were found to be significantly more responsive, stimulating, visually attentive, and controlling of their infants' behavior than a similar group of mothers who did not get assistance. Infants of these mothers had higher scores on sociability, self-soothing, and exploration, cried less often, and at twelve months of age were much more likely to be securely attached.

Being securely attached herself makes the mother more likely to have a child who is securely attached. The quality of the mother-child relationship is influenced by the mother's perceptions, expectations, and assumptions (sometimes called *working models*) about her infant, herself, and their relationship. Past mother-infant interactions, the mother's memories of her own childhood, and similar factors also may play a significant role in mother-child attachment relationships (Biringen, 1990; Stern, 1985b). A mother's capacity to establish and maintain a secure attachment relationship with her infant is also influenced by her socioeconomic status (SES), which affects her ability to focus on her infant rather than on finding housing, food, work, and other necessities.

The Role of the Father While children are most likely to form strong attachment relationships with their mothers, who most often are their primary caregivers, they may form equally strong attachments with their fathers. Studies of father-infant attachment in the United States and other countries suggest that the processes involved are similar and that fathers display the same range of attachment relation-

Attachment—the tendency of young infants and their caregivers to seek physical and emotional closeness—provides an important basis for achieving secure and trusting relationships during early childhood.

Good-quality day care can play an important role in the lives of working mothers and their children.

ships mothers do, and most studies have found no differences in most babies' preferred attachment figures during their first two years.

As we pointed out earlier in the chapter, however, fathers and mothers interact with their infants somewhat differently. Fathers generally are more vigorous and physical in their interactions, and mothers are quieter and more verbal (Belsky et al., 1984c; Lamb, 1977a, 1977b). Such differences in the quality of mother-infant versus father-infant attachment relationships are likely to reflect gender-related differences in caregiving opportunities, experiences, and expectations, as well as gender-related differences in the current division of child care and other household responsibilities within the family (Akande, 1994; Cox et al., 1992; Ferketich & Mercer, 1995; Rosen & Rothbaum, 1993; Volling & Belsky, 1992).

For example, Martha Cox and her colleagues (1992) found that the security of father-infant attachment at twelve months can be predicted from the qualities of their interactions at three months, the father's attitudes toward and reports about the infant and the paternal role, and the amount of time spent with the infant. In addition, research by Nathan Fox and his colleagues (1991) found that the security of attachment to one parent also appears to be closely related to the security of attachment to the other parent. Thus, an infant with a secure (or insecure) attachment to her mother is likely to have the same quality of attachment to her father.

The Effects of Maternal Employment   As we noted earlier, approximately 50 percent of mothers with infants one year old or under and around 60 percent of mothers with three-to-five-year-olds are in the work force. The number of working mothers with young children is expected to continue to increase (U.S. Bureau of the Census, 1990b). Family-leave policies in the United States and Europe are discussed in the accompanying Perspectives box.

Most infants of mothers who are employed either full or part time are securely attached, although full-time employed mothers are somewhat more likely than part-

Family-Leave Policies in the United States and Europe

In 1993, the United States enacted its first national family-leave policy, guaranteeing up to twelve weeks of unpaid leave per year to any worker who is employed for at least twenty-five hours per week at a company with more than fifty employees. Family leaves are allowed after the birth of a child or an adoption to care for a child, spouse, or parent with a serious health condition, as well as for a health condition that makes it impossible for the worker to perform a job. After the leave, the worker is assured of his or her old job or an equivalent position (*The New York Times*, 1993).

How does U.S. family-leave policy compare with that in other countries? Most industrialized countries have much more generous policies than those in the United States, providing not only more extended leaves of absence so that working parents can take care of their young children but also financial support for part or all of the leave period (Kamerman, 1991; Zigler & Frank, 1988). In Sweden, West Germany, and France, one parent can take a paid infant care leave supported by the employer or a social insurance fund. If both parents choose to continue to work, they are guaranteed access to high-quality day care for their child. In Sweden, either the mother or the father is entitled to a twelve-month paid leave to stay home with a new infant. The parent on leave is reim-

bursed 90 percent of her or his salary for the first nine months following the child's birth, receives $150 per month for the next three months, and then is allowed to continue with an unpaid leave and a job guarantee for six additional months until the child is eighteen months old. An interesting sidelight is that only a very small percentage of fathers actually take advantage of this opportunity, and when they do, the bulk of feeding and nurturance during nonwork hours still appears to be performed by the mother (Kamerman, 1991; Lamb et al., 1982).

In France, a working parent is entitled to 90 percent reimbursement for four months through the social security system and then up to two more years of unpaid leave with a job guarantee, provided she or he works for a company with more than two hundred employees. In West Germany, a parent taking a leave of absence from work is entitled to 100 percent reimbursement for three months and then $285 per month for four more months.

It seems evident that while the twelve weeks of unpaid leave provided by the recent U.S. family-leave policy is a step in the right direction, policies in Europe go much farther in helping parents to directly meet the needs of their babies without undue economic hardship and risk to their jobs.

time employed and nonemployed mothers to have insecurely attached infants (Belsky, 1988; Clarke-Stewart, 1989; L. Hoffman, 1989). However, these results must be viewed with caution, since the effects of maternal employment on the infant or young child are rarely direct. They are almost always based on a variety of family factors, including SES and cultural differences, the mother's "morale," the father's attitude toward his wife's employment, the type of work and number of hours it demands, the husband-wife relationship, the father's role in the family, the availability and quality of nonmaternal care, and the mother's own feelings about separation (L. Hoffman, 1989; Silverstein, 1991).

The work of Cynthia Stifter (1993) and her colleagues is a good example. They compared mother-child interactions and attachment patterns in families in which mothers returned to full- or part-time employment outside the home before their infants were five months old with those in families in which mothers remained home full time, and found that employment did not directly affect attachment. However, when employed mothers were experiencing high levels of separation anxiety as a result of the severe time constraints imposed by work schedules, they were more likely to have infants who developed anxious-avoidant attachments. Although they were equally sensitive and responsive to their infants as working mothers who were not anxious, highly anxious mothers were much more likely to be "out of synch" and overcontrolling when interacting with their infants.

The Effects of Day Care and Multiple Caregivers   The growing number of dual-wage and single-parent families and changing views about childrearing and family life have led to increased interest in nonmaternal child care to supplement the care

Working with   Rachelle Turner, INFANT DAY CARE COORDINATOR

Understanding Infant Social Development

Rachelle is the infant coordinator in a day care center, where she has taught for the past four years. She began working as a day care teacher during her college years and plans to eventually work as a therapist in a program serving young children and their families. Rachelle was interviewed in my office.

Rob: What do you like most about working with infants?

Rachelle: I find working with infants fascinating because so much is packed into the first year of life. It's amazing to see how rapid the changes are. Because you're with the children eight hours a day, five days a week, you can observe the very small changes in development that happen, even on a week-to-week basis.

Rob: What differences in early infant temperament do you find?

Rachelle: There are differences in napping patterns, for example. If, as an infant, a child needs you to rub his back or rock him gently to go to sleep, often he will want the same kind of thing as a three-year-old when he is going down for a nap on a cot. Or you might see him rocking himself to go to sleep. On the other hand, there's the child you can just put in his crib, and he'll just grab his blanket and go to sleep. When he's older, you can say, "OK, it's nap time," and he'll get on his cot and go to sleep. It often seems like children are their own person from day one.

Rob: Do you have another example?

Rachelle: Some infants aren't happy until they can crawl and go get what they want, while others seem perfectly content with just sitting up and having you plop toys in front of them. Infants can really differ in how active or passive they are in learning to crawl or walk and in their style of exploring their physical and social world. They also differ in their moods and in whether they are irritable or not.

Rob: What about their social relationships?

Rachelle: Their changing interactions with other children are interesting. A five-month-old infant will be attracted to another child, but will not, of course, play with the child. She'll pull the other infant's hair and touch its face and clothes. She'll want to explore it and see what it is, just like a doll. Toward the end of the first year, infants recognize their friends, and smile and laugh when they see them. They now want to go on the climber or play blocks together.

Rob: So their social skills change from exploring each other as objects to interacting with each other as unique individuals?

Rachelle: Yes.

Day care, even for infants and toddlers, has few negative effects on children, as long as the care is of high quality and parents feel satisfied with it.

Rob: What changes do you see during the second year?

Rachelle: Once they can actually say the child's name, they'll call him to come play. Games like hide-and seek, chasing each other, or knocking blocks over together. They interact because the child makes it fun. It's not the imagination that three-year-old friends have, but it's definitely play and excitement when they see each other. They'll run up to each other, and they'll hug and kiss and be affectionate, and they know the other child isn't a doll. And if one gets hurt, they'll say, "Oh, Anne has a boo-boo," because she's a person in their life.

Rob: What have you observed about infants' ability to form attachment relationships with nonparental adult caregivers?

Rachelle: If you are affectionate and responsive to an infant's unique habits

and needs around feeding, changing, and sleeping, and comforting and stimulation, she'll quickly come to know you and form an attachment to you. Particularly if a child is in day care full time, if an unfamiliar parent or delivery person comes into the center, or if a child is upset for some other reason, she will crawl or run to a caregiver or want to be held or to sit in your lap.

Rob: How does it feel from the caregiver's perspective?

Rachelle: Very strong feelings of attachment develop. Remember, unlike a typical household where laundry, cooking, and other tasks compete with child care, we spend almost all of our time observing and interacting with the children. I get very attached. When children leave, it's very hard to have children coming in and out of your life. You think about them constantly.

Rob: Are parents sometimes jealous of your relationship with their baby?

Rachelle: Yes. A parent might give the child excessive gifts, or become critical of the teacher, or make a point of telling the teacher something she didn't know about the child. I try to reassure parents by asking them for information about their child and by being interested in changes they have observed rather than just focusing on changes I have noticed.

What Do You Think?

1. What qualities do you think make a good day care teacher?

2. As a current or prospective parent, how comfortable would you feel putting your child in Rachelle's care? Why?

3. How closely do Rachelle's examples of temperamental differences and attachment fit your own understandings based on reading the chapter?

given within families. The effects of day care and other forms of nonmaternal care on attachment in infants and toddlers are difficult to evaluate for many of the same reasons cited in the discussion of maternal employment. The gender of the child, the child's temperament, the mother's (and father's) feelings about both day care and maternal employment, and the mother's reasons for working all play a role. Other factors include the type of child care arrangement (day care center, in-home day care, relative), the stability of the arrangement, the child's age of entry, the quality of day care, and the quality of the child-caregiver relationship (Belsky & Rovine, 1988; Scarr et al., 1989). See the interview with Rachelle Turner for a look at social interactions in an infant day care center.

While some infant care researchers have found evidence that one-year-olds who attend centers more than twenty hours per week tend to form less secure attachments to their parents (Belsky & Nezworski, 1988; Belsky & Rovine, 1988), others have reported that negative attachment outcomes tend to be associated with little or part-time rather than full-time infant care and that babies in infant care centers show *more* social confidence than do infants reared at home (Anderson, 1989; Roggman et al., 1994).

The majority of infants receiving full-time center care actually appear to be quite securely attached to one or both of their parents (Clarke-Stewart, 1989). For the minority who appear to have insecure attachments, it is not yet clear whether the infant center care per se makes them less secure or whether the variety of other factors just mentioned are responsible.

What about attachments to multiple caregivers? While expectations based on infant-mother attachment relationships may help guide an infant in forming new attachments, infants and nonmaternal caregivers are capable of establishing unique and independent relationships based more on their reciprocal exchanges and individual qualities than on a "model" developed from mother-child interactions (Zimmerman & McDonald, 1995). The attachments infants form with their center caregivers, for example, appear to be no less secure than their attachments to their parents, and the two sets of attachments are relatively independent of each other. Thus, even an infant who exhibited an insecure pattern of attachment relationships with his or her family might still form secure attachments with other caregivers (Goosens & van Ijzendoorn, 1990).

There is also evidence that in a variety of other contexts, including extended families and communal childrearing settings such as the Israeli kibbutz and the Efe people of Zaire, secure relationships with multiple professional and nonprofessional caregivers are not only possible but may even contribute to the child's well-being by either adding to a network of secure attachments or compensating for their absence (Aviezer et al., 1994; Tronick et al., 1992). On the Israeli kibbutz, infants and toddlers are raised in same-age peer groups by community child care providers. Among the Efe, infants and toddlers experience a pattern of multiple relationships—with mother, father, other adults, and children. In such cases, the extended family or community childrearing network may be more predictive of attachment relationships than the mother-child relationship alone.

Limitations of Attachment Theory

The Strange Situation has had mixed success at helping us understand the development of the parent-infant relationship. Atypical infants who differ from normal infants in their everyday parent-infant interactions often cannot be reliably distinguished based on attachment classifications. In addition, it frequently is not possible to reliably predict later attachment from early mother-infant attachment classifications. Tiffany Field (1987) suggests that the problem may lie in overreliance on the Strange Situation as the standard for measuring complex processes involved in the parent-infant and other caregiving relationships. The Strange Situation depends on a single occurrence of a limited number of rather specific mother-infant interactions that take place in a context that does not represent the broad range of situations within which attachment relationships naturally occur. Understanding and prediction of attachment may therefore require a more complex and ecologically meaningful model.

More valid assessments of attachment might be achieved by studying caregiver-infant interactions longitudinally over the entire first year, for longer periods of time, and in contexts that more closely represent those in which caregiver-infant relationships typically occur. It is also likely that the types of detailed and sophisticated methods that have helped us in studying caregiver-infant synchrony and infant emotional states will be needed to better understand both the complex parent-child interactions and the internal experiences, expectations, and working models that are central to the development of attachments and the overall parent-infant relationship.

What Do You Think?

What advice would you give new parents about the roles of fathers, maternal employment, and infant day care in supporting secure attachment and optimal social/emotional development for their infants? What recommendations would you give to your elected representatives regarding infant and toddler day care programs for families with working and nonworking mothers?

After their first birthday, infants begin to show increasing autonomy in their play and other activities, which sometimes leads them to unsafe situations. This autonomy is fostered by their improving motor skills and cognitive development.

TODDLERHOOD AND THE EMERGENCE OF AUTONOMY

By the second year of life, infants who have experienced adequate levels of caregiver-infant synchrony and achieved relatively secure attachment relationships with their parents and other caregivers have developed a sense of *basic trust* (versus *mistrust*) about the world. According to Erik Erikson (1963), an infant's trusting view of the world leads to the development of *hope,* the enduring belief that one's wishes are attainable.

Despite lingering anxieties about separations, the achievement of a basic sense of trust in their relationships with their caregivers enables toddlers to become increasingly interested in new people, places, and experiences. For example, an eighteen-month-old may no longer bother to smile at his mother while he plays near her, and he does not need to return to her for reassurance as often as he used to.

Parents may welcome these changes as a move toward greater independence and at the same time experience a loss of intimacy for which they may not be quite ready. This shift is both inevitable and developmentally important. For one thing, an older infant can move about rather easily and therefore find much to explore without help from others. The newfound abilities to crawl, climb, and walk make her more interesting as a playmate for other children and thus less dependent on her parents for her social life. For another, her rapidly developing thinking and communication skills contribute to her increasing autonomy.

These competencies create new challenges for both toddlers and their families as a new developmental crisis emerges: the psychosocial crisis of *autonomy versus shame and doubt.* **Autonomy** refers to a child's capacity to be independent and self-directed in his activities and his ability to balance his own demands for self-control with demands for control from his parents and others. *Shame* involves a loss of self-respect due to a failure to meet one's own standards. Toddlers must somehow practice making choices—an essential feature of autonomy—in ways that cause no serious harm to themselves or others.

Parents must learn to support their child's efforts to be autonomous, but must do so without overestimating or underestimating the child's capabilities or the external dangers and internal fears she faces. If they are unable to provide such support and instead show their disapproval of failures by shaming their child, a pattern of self-blame and doubt may develop. Shame appears to arise out of both the loss of approval by important people and the child's negative thoughts about herself for failing to live up to certain expectations or standards (Lewis, 1992). In such a case, the child is more likely to be either painfully shy and unsure of herself or overly demanding, self-critical, and relatively unable to undertake new activities and experiences freely.

Parents also must help their infant master this crisis of autonomy by continually devising situations in which their relatively mature baby can play independently and without undue fear of interference—by putting the pots and pans within reach but hiding the knives, for instance. Children also need social as well as physical safety. Chewing on a sister's drawing or dumping the dirt out of the flowerpots may not have dangerous physical consequences, but it can have negative social effects. Thus, parents must help their infant learn how to avoid social perils by being selective about the child's activities.

Sources of Autonomy

Why should infants and toddlers voluntarily begin to exert self-control over their own behavior? Developmental psychologists have suggested several possible answers to this question based on the various theories outlined in Chapter 2. Each has some plausibility, although none are complete in themselves.

Identification   According to psychoanalytic theory, *identification* is the process by which children wish to become like their parents and other important attachment figures in their lives. The intensity of a young child's emotional dependence on parents creates an intense desire to be like them to please them and guarantee their love. This dependence also creates anger because of the helplessness and fear of abandonment the infant inevitably experiences during even brief periods of separation. Because it is so upsetting to be angry at the very person you depend on for love and care, identification can also be motivated by the unconscious desire to protect oneself from the distress by being like the person who is the object of that anger. Both mechanisms, of course, may operate at once, and either may function without the child's knowledge.

Operant Conditioning   *Operant conditioning* stresses the importance of reinforcement for desirable behaviors. According to this view, adults will tend to reinforce a child for more grown-up behaviors, such as independent exploration ("What did you find?") and self-restraint ("I'm glad you didn't wet your pants"). Operant conditioning resembles identification in assuming parents can motivate children, but it also assumes their influence occurs in piecemeal ways; that is, the child acquires specific behaviors rather than whole personality patterns.

Observational Learning   According to the theory of *observational learning*, the key to acquiring autonomy and self-control lies in the child's inherent tendency to observe and imitate parents and other caregivers. If parents act gently with the child's baby sister, for example, the child will come to do so too (although his interpretation of *gently* may occasionally be influenced by feelings of sibling rivalry). Similarly, if a young child observes her mother taking pots and pans from the kitchen cabinet, it is a fair bet that she will attempt to do the same. In fact, much home "childproofing" is necessitated by a young child's skill at observational learning. The process of observational learning implies that autonomy and self-control are acquired in units, or behavioral chunks, that are bigger than those described by operant conditioning but smaller than those acquired in identification.

Social Referencing: A Common Denominator   All three explanations of developing autonomy have something in common: they involve **social referencing,** the child's sensitivity to the feelings of his parents and other adults and his ability to use these emotional cues to guide his own emotional responses and actions (Campos & Stenberg, 1981; Tronick, 1989). For example, infants and toddlers exhibit social referencing when they visit a strange place. Should they be afraid of the new objects and people or not? How safe is it to be friendly and to explore? In the absence of past experiences of their own, they evaluate such situations based on their parents' responses: if their parents are relaxed and happy, they are likely to feel that way too; if their parents are made tense or anxious by the situation, the children probably will feel that way also. Even very young infants use their caregivers and even strangers to guide their responses, for example, approaching and playing with unfamiliar toys if a nearby stranger is smiling and avoiding them if the person looks fearful (Klinnert et al., 1986).

Development of Self-knowledge and Self-awareness

The sense of self that develops late in infancy shows up in everyday situations as well as in situations involving self-control. One very interesting series of studies explored the development of self-knowledge in infants nine to twenty-four months old by testing their ability to recognize images of themselves in mirrors, on television,

This toddler's responses to her own reflection in the mirror are an important indicator of her developing self-knowledge and self-awareness.

and in still photographs (M. Lewis & Brooks-Gunn, 1979a; M. Lewis et al., 1985). Because most of the infants could not verbally indicate whether or not they recognized themselves, the researchers secretly marked each infant's nose with red rouge. When placed in front of a mirror, infants from fifteen to twenty-four months of age touched their bodies or faces more frequently than they did before they were marked. Infants around fifteen to eighteen months also began to imitate their marked images by making faces, sticking out their tongues, or watching themselves disappear and reappear at the side of a mirror. These self-recognition behaviors never occurred in infants younger than fifteen months and increased from 75 percent at eighteen months to 100 percent at twenty-four months. When presented with videotaped images of themselves in which a stranger sneaked up on them, infants as young as nine months displayed self-recognition based on *contingent cues,* that is, connections between their own movements and the movements of the image they were viewing. By approximately fifteen months, infants were increasingly able to distinguish themselves from other infants by using *noncontingent cues* such as facial and other physical features (M. Lewis & Brooks-Gunn, 1979a).

Aspects of Self-awareness   By the end of their second year, most children show an increasing appreciation of the standards and expectations of others regarding their behavior toward both people and things. For example, a broken toy can trouble a child even if she did not break it; she may show it to an adult and verbally express concern and a need for help ("Broken!" or "Daddy fix?"). A crack in the kitchen linoleum may now receive close scrutiny, even though several months earlier it went unnoticed and several months later it may go unnoticed again. Language that implies *knowledge of standards*—evaluative vocabulary such as *bad, good, dirty, nice*—appears as well (Bretherton et al., 1981). Such knowledge combines with other behaviors to suggest that the child is beginning to sense an identity for himself. There is also reason to believe that verbal and nonverbal reactions of toddlers to flawed objects are associated with the early development of a sense of morality. When faced with situations in which they believe they have been responsible for a "mishap" such as breaking a toy, toddlers' responses include acceptance of responsibility, apologies, a focus on reparations (repairing the wrong), and distress (Kochanska et al., 1995).

By age two, children show satisfaction in *initiating challenging activities* or behaviors for themselves, and they often smile at the results. A child builds a tower of blocks higher than usual and smiles broadly the moment she completes it. Another makes a strange noise—say, a cat meowing—and then smiles with pride. In each case, the child confronts a task that is somewhat difficult by her current standards, but attempts it anyway. Her behavior suggests an awareness of what competent performance amounts to and of her own ability to succeed. This knowledge reflects part of her sense of self and contributes to its further development.

Development of Competence and Self-esteem

From the beginning of infancy through the end of toddlerhood, children achieve a growing sense of basic trust, autonomy, competence, and ultimately self-esteem. In fact, these developments go hand in hand. Autonomy, as we discussed earlier, is made possible by a child's secure and basically trustworthy relationships with her primary caregivers. **Competence**—skill and capability—develops as a result of the child's natural curiosity and desire to explore the world and the pleasure she experiences in successfully mastering and controlling that world (B. White, 1975, 1993). Much like the infant's need for proximity and attachment to caregivers, her motivation to explore and master the world is thought to be relatively autonomous and independent of basic physiological needs for food, water, sleep, and freedom from pain.

Based on many years of observational study, Burton White (1993) suggests that a socially competent toddler is likely to display capabilities in the following areas:

1. Getting and holding the attention of adults in socially acceptable ways
2. Using adults as resources after first determining that a task is too difficult
3. Expressing affection and mild annoyance to adults
4. Leading and following peers
5. Expressing affection and mild annoyance to peers
6. Competing with peers
7. Showing pride in personal accomplishment
8. Engaging in role play or make-believe activities

What everyday rules for behavior guide parents' efforts to socialize their toddlers and preschool-age children? To answer this question, Heidi Gralinski and Claire Kopp (1993) observed and interviewed mothers and their children in these age groups. They found that for fifteen-month-old toddlers, mothers' rules and requests centered on ensuring the children's safety and, to a lesser extent, protecting the families' possessions from harm; respecting basic social niceties ("Don't bite"; "No kicking"); and learning to delay getting what they wanted (versus getting it immediately). As children's ages and cognitive sophistication increased, the numbers and kinds of prohibitions and requests expanded from the original focus on child protection and interpersonal issues to family routines, self-care, and other concerns regarding the child's independence. By the time children were three, a new quality of rule emerged: "Do not scream in a restaurant, run around naked in front of company, pretend to kill your sister, hang up the phone when someone is using it, fight with children in school, play with guns, or pick your nose."

Not surprisingly, a toddler's social competence is influenced by the nature of the parent-toddler relationship. Even though they do not spend more time interacting with their children than mothers of less competent children, mothers of highly competent children support and encourage their toddlers' curiosity and desire to explore the world around them by providing a rich variety of interesting toys and experiences that are both safe and appropriate to the children's level of competence. They also play with their toddlers in ways that are responsive to the children's interests and needs and use language their toddlers can clearly understand.

Observations of mothers and their two-year-olds found that toddlers' capacity for both compliance with parental directions and self-assertion was associated with *authoritative parenting* relationships (see Chapter 7) consisting of a combination of control and guidance and an appropriate sharing of power with warmth, sensitivity, responsiveness, and child-centered family management techniques. High levels of defiance and parent-toddler conflict were most likely to be associated with more authoritarian, power-assertive control strategies. In situations where the toddler had said "no" to the mother, maternal negative control was most likely to elicit defiance (B. White, 1975; Crockenberg & Litman, 1990).

Mothers of competent toddlers are also more likely to encourage their children to accomplish the tasks they had initiated themselves by actively guiding them and praising them for achievements rather than actually performing the tasks for them (B. White, 1975). As you might expect, this approach requires considerable patience, the ability to tolerate the child's frustration when things do not work out the first few times, and a firm belief in the child's need and potential to be an autonomous and competent person. Perhaps the most important quality of these mothers is their ability to interact sensitively and appropriately with their children and to experience pleasure and delight in these interactions (at least most of the time). The same quality appears to be most important in the development of secure attachment relationships and continues to be important throughout childhood.

Toddlers who grow up in supportive environments are likely to be better adjusted in their development than children whose environments are less supportive. A natural outcome of such parenting is the early emergence of a strong sense of **self-esteem**: a child's feeling that he is an important, competent, powerful, and worthwhile person whose efforts to be autonomous and take initiative are respected and valued by those around him (Erikson, 1963; Harter, 1983). The development of self-esteem during infancy and toddlerhood is closely tied to the achievement of a positive ratio of autonomy versus shame and doubt and initiative versus guilt during the developmental crises that, according to Erikson, occur during this period (Erikson, 1963). As we shall see, the childhood experiences that follow infancy continue to make major contributions to this important aspect of identity.

What Do You Think?

How do you think seeing your toddler develop competence and self-esteem would affect your feelings and self-evaluation as a parent and caregiver? How might these feelings affect your child in turn?

LOOKING BACK/LOOKING FORWARD

In a matter of just months, a baby may have tripled in weight and doubled in height. She has learned to move about freely and independently and has formed important relationships with particular people and places. The mature toddler is starting to know that she is a unique individual like everyone else. As we saw in Chapter 4, she has also made a good start in developing her capacities to think, listen, and talk. It generally becomes clear somewhere around her second birthday that she is definitely not a baby anymore!

But what, then, has the child become? As we will see in the next two chapters, although children in the early childhood years are too young to begin elementary school, a considerable number attend day care centers, family day care, or nursery school on a regular basis. Even at this early age, the preschool child definitely is ready—and eager—to learn more about the physical and social worlds outside his or her immediate family. If all has gone reasonably well up to now, the family can serve as a secure base from which the child can explore these larger worlds, which include the children next door, the local mall, and peers and teachers at a nursery school or day care setting.

Psychosocial development during the early childhood years will bring about increasingly sophisticated play activities and greatly expanded relationships with parents, siblings, and peers. The competencies achieved in infancy and toddlerhood will also help the preschool child to develop a capacity for empathy and prosocial behavior, managing conflict and aggression, forming and maintaining lasting friendships, and acquiring a sense of gender and the roles and behaviors it entails.

SUMMARY OF MAJOR IDEAS

Emotions and Temperament in Infancy

1. Infants appear to be capable of a complex range of emotional responses and are quite sensitive to the feelings of their caregivers. They probably use cues similar to those

adults use, such as variations in voice quality, smell, touch, facial expression, and body language.

2. Even at birth, infants exhibit differences in temperament, patterns of physical and emotional responsiveness, and ac-

tivity levels. These differences both influence and are influenced by the feelings and responses of their caregivers.

Early Social Relationships

3. Newborn infants have a natural tendency to actively participate in their social world.

4. *Caregiver-infant synchrony* refers to the closely orchestrated social and emotional interactions between an infant and his or her caregiver and provides an important basis for the development of attachment relationships.

5. The similarities in the type and quality of an infant's interactions with mother and father are much greater than the differences.

6. The effects of nonmaternal care and maternal employment on infant and toddler development depend on the specific circumstances, but in general do not appear to be negative.

7. When given the opportunity to do so, infants engage in active social interactions with their siblings and peers and often prefer them to their parents as playmates.

Attachment Formation

8. Attachment, the tendency of young infants and their caregivers to seek and maintain physical and emotional closeness with each other, is thought to provide an important basis for achieving secure and trusting relationships during early infancy.

9. Attachment develops in a series of phases from indiscriminate sociability at birth to goal-coordinated partnerships at two years.

10. The Strange Situation, in which the infant is confronted with the stress of being in an unfamiliar place, meeting a stranger, and being separated from his or her parent, has been used to study the development of attachment.

11. Secure attachment is most likely to develop when the caregiver responds sensitively and appropriately to the infant and the infant can use the caregiver as a safe base for exploration.

12. Insecurely attached infants tend to be less able than securely attached infants to get help from parents and teachers when they need it or to accept it when it is offered.

13. Infants are equally capable of forming secure attachments to their mothers and to their fathers, and to other caregivers as well, even though in the majority of families the mother is the primary caregiver.

14. The effects of both maternal employment and day care on attachment depend largely on how the mother feels about herself and her role as a parent and how the situation helps or hinders her ability to care for and enjoy her baby. The quality of her experience and the quality and consistency of the day care are also important.

Toddlerhood and the Emergence of Autonomy

15. Sources of the growing autonomy that characterizes the second year of infancy include identification, operant conditioning, observational learning, and social referencing.

16. Toddlerhood also brings significant increases in self-knowledge and self-awareness. These changes are reflected in the toddler's increasing awareness of adult standards, distress at behaviors modeled by unknown adults, and pride in her or his accomplishments.

17. Toddlers are strongly motivated to achieve greater competence through successfully mastering and controlling the physical and social worlds around them. Competence is fostered by parents who encourage their infant's curiosity by providing opportunities that are challenging, safe, and appropriate to the child's capabilities.

18. Increased self-esteem in the infant is the natural outcome of supportive parenting.

KEY TERMS

temperament *(152)*
caregiver-infant
  synchrony *(156)*
attachment *(162)*
Strange Situation *(164)*
secure attachment *(164)*
anxious-resistant
  attachment *(165)*
anxious-avoidant
  attachment *(165)*
autonomy *(174)*
social referencing *(175)*
competence *(176)*
self-esteem *(178)*

PART THREE

Early Childhood

 lthough most of us remember relatively little of our pre-school years, parents often believe those years are among the most gratifying for their children. Perhaps this is be-cause children become more equal participants in their fam-ilies during this time than during infancy; yet they have not begun the process of creating lives for themselves outside the family. Parents therefore have much to do during these years, and they may still believe they can shape or influence their children fully. Later it will become harder to hold to this idea.

Preschoolers become more social during this period, partly because of the more complex motor skills they acquire—skills such as riding a tricycle or climbing a jungle gym, which can im-press parents as well as friends. In addition, new cognitive skills allow preschool children to express themselves more precisely than they could as infants and even try out new social roles in play. Their world expands rapidly during these years, a process that is both exhausting and exhilarating for children as well as for their parents.

6

EARLY CHILDHOOD

Physical and Cognitive Development

itty run!" says Zöe, age three. She is pointing to the local cat. "Yes," replies her father. "She's chasing a bird."

Zöe nods and says, "Bird gone now. Bad kitty?" and looks to her father for confirmation.

"It's OK this time," says her father. "The bird flew away soon enough."

At this, Zöe walks off to find the cat, curious to learn what else it might do.

Two features of this incident are especially noteworthy: Zöe's language and her mobility. Little more than a year ago, neither could have occurred. As a preschooler, however, she is developing the ability to deal with her world in symbols, in this case through oral language. She is also developing new physical skills that serve her interests and abilities; for example, she can walk up to the cat simply to learn more about it.

In this chapter, we look in detail at physical and cognitive development during early childhood. Many of the examples will suggest relationships between the two domains, as well as their impact on the third domain of psychosocial development. Furthermore, as we will see in the chapters on development in adulthood, the physical and cognitive changes in preschoolers influence the development of the adults who care for them. The fact that preschoolers sleep less than they did as infants, for example, is the beginning of a lifelong trend that will affect both child and parent, creating new options for each. For the child, keeping awake longer facilitates attending school; for the parent, the child's attending school makes adult-focused activities such as a job or a hobby easier to arrange than before. Parents who are ready for the growth and changes in their preschoolers but do not feel pressured to hurry those changes will likely influence their children's development in many positive ways.

Focusing Questions

- What influences how rapidly preschool children grow?

- How is poverty connected to children's health?

- When and how do children achieve bladder and bowel control?

- What motor skills do children acquire during the preschool years?

- How does children's growth affect parents and other adults?

- What are the special strengths of preschoolers' thinking?

- How does the language of preschool children differ from that of older children, and what social and cultural factors influence its development?

- What constitutes good early childhood education?

PHYSICAL DEVELOPMENT

INFLUENCES ON NORMAL PHYSICAL DEVELOPMENT

Physical growth in the preschool years is relatively easy to measure and gives a clear idea of how children normally develop during this period. Table 6.1 and Figure 6.1 show the two most familiar measurements of growth, standing height and weight. At age two, an average child in North America measures about thirty-three or thirty-four inches tall, or about two feet and ten inches. Three years later, at age five, he measures approximately forty-four inches, or about one-third more than before. The typical child weighs about twenty-seven pounds on his second birthday but about forty-one pounds by his fifth. Meanwhile, other measurements change in less obvious ways. The child's head grows about one inch in circumference during these years, and his body fat decreases as a proportion of his total bodily tissue.

For any preschool child who is reasonably healthy and happy, physical growth is remarkably smooth and predictable, especially compared to many cognitive and social developments. All in all, physical growth contains no discrete stages, plateaus, or qualitative changes such as those Piaget described for cognitive development. At the same time, however, large differences develop among individual children and among groups of children. Sometimes these differences affect the psychological development of young children; at other times they simply create interesting physical variety among human beings.

TABLE 6.1 *Average Height and Weight During Early Childhood*

Age (Years)	Height (Inches)	Weight (Pounds)
2	34.5	27.0
3	37.8	31.5
4	40.9	36.0
5	43.6	40.5

Source: Engels (1993).

As a result of improvements in nutrition and health care, children in industrialized nations are more often taller than in earlier times. But there are important variations among societies—even among industrialized ones—that apparently are genetically influenced.

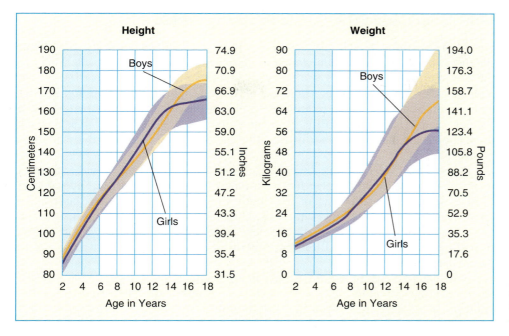

FIGURE 6.1
Growth and Height from Two to Eighteen Years

The overall smoothness of growth means that childhood height and weight can predict adult height and weight to a significant extent, although not perfectly. A four-year-old who is above average in height tends to end up above average as an adult. Nevertheless, correlation between childhood height and adult height is imperfect because of individual differences in nutrition and health and, most of all, in the timing of puberty. In particular, children who experience puberty later than average tend to grow taller than children who experience it early (Sanfilippo et al., 1994).

Genetic Background

Most dimensions of growth are influenced substantially by heredity. Tall parents tend to have tall children, and short parents usually have short children. Weight shows similar patterns, although it can be influenced strongly by habits of exercise and diet.

Races and ethnic groups around the world also differ in growth patterns (Eveleth & Tanner, 1990). Children from Asian groups, such as Chinese and Japanese, tend to be shorter than European and North American children. The latter, in turn, are usually shorter than children from African societies. Shape differs among these groups as well, although the differences do not always become obvious until adolescence. Asian children develop short legs and arms relative to their torsos, and relatively broad hips. African children do just the opposite: they develop relatively long limbs and narrow hips. Olympic athletes reflect these differences; records consistently show that Asians perform better in events requiring upper-body strength, such as wrestling, gymnastics, and weightlifting, whereas Africans tend to excel in events requiring a long stride, such as running (Falkner & Tanner, 1986).

Disease

Although serious illnesses interfere with growth, it often is hard to judge exactly how much. The trouble is that children with serious illnesses often have other conditions that retard growth; they may have been small for date or suffered from chronically poor nutrition during infancy. These conditions can lead not only to slow growth but also to various illnesses, which in turn may contribute to the hindered growth.

Nutritional Needs During the Preschool Years

For a time, a young preschooler (such as a three-year-old) may eat less than he or she did as a toddler and become much more selective about foods as well. Michael, the son of one of the authors, ate every meal voraciously as a two-year-old; a year later he rarely finished a meal, even though he was significantly taller and heavier by then. Elizabeth, his sister, followed a similar but more pronounced pattern. As a toddler she ate most foods except ice cream ("Too sweet," she said!), but as a young preschooler she sometimes hardly ate—though she did decide then that she liked ice cream.

Parents may worry about such changes, but in fact they are normal and result from the slowing down of growth after infancy. Preschool children simply do not need as many calories per unit of their body weight as they did immediately after birth. They do need variety in their foods, however, just as adults do, to ensure adequate overall nutrition. Given preschoolers' newfound selectiveness about eating, providing the variety needed for good nutrition can sometimes be a challenge to parents and other caregivers.

How can one ensure healthy variety in a preschool child's diet? Experts generally discourage coercion ("Eat your vegetables because I say so!"), since it teaches children to associate undesired foods with unpleasant social experiences (Endres & Rockwell, 1993). They also discourage using sweet foods as a reward for eating undesired foods ("If you eat your vegetables, then you can have your ice cream"), because it implicitly overvalues the sweets and undervalues the undesired food still further. The best strategy seems to be casual, repeated exposure to the food without insisting that the child eat it (Andrien, 1994). Observations of children's eating habits confirm what parents often suspect as well: children's food preferences are influenced by the adult models around them. In the long term, preschoolers tend to like the same foods their parents and other important adults like. More generally, as we will see in Chapter 12's discussion of physical development in early adulthood, they practice many of their parents' other health behaviors (such as exercise) as well.

Social Influences on Growth

Variations in growth can result from cultural and psychological factors. Sometimes much stress in a family can keep children from growing normally, a condition called **failure to thrive** (Money, 1992). Children with this condition seem apathetic and weak, and their relationships with parents tend to involve conflict and impaired rapport.

The condition is believed to result from situations that interfere with normal positive relationships between parent and child, especially during infancy or the early childhood period. For example, parents suffering from the stresses of unemployment, chronic conflicts, or other painful circumstances may make a scapegoat of a child who needs more attention than other children in the family do. The result is a difficult relationship that may lead the child to eat poorly or be plagued by constant anxiety. This nervousness can interfere with sleep or even the production of growth hormones. With help from a counselor or a social worker, however, failure to thrive can be reversed, as long as it has not persisted for too long.

What Do You Think?

How do you suppose parents evaluate their child's height and weight? Explore this problem by asking two or three parents how satisfied they are with their child's height and weight. Do you think parents' feelings have any relationship to the actual size of their child?

THE CONNECTION BETWEEN HEALTH AND POVERTY

In middle- and high-SES settings, preschool children are among the healthiest human beings alive: they experience comparatively few major illnesses as long as they get enough of the right things to eat and as long as their parents have reasonable access to modern medical care. As parents often note, preschoolers do experience frequent minor illnesses: various respiratory infections, ear infections, and stomach flus. These typically strike a young child several times per year, which is three or four times as often as for adults and about twice as often as for school-age children (Engels, 1993). For well-fed children whose families have access to medical care, however, these illnesses rarely prove serious or life threatening. For their parents, of course, colds and flu cause worry, as well as challenges in arranging child care if a parent works.

Poverty as a Health Problem

But this optimistic picture of preschoolers' health may be misleading. About 30 percent of all families in the United States and countless other countries worldwide have poor access to medical care, mainly because they live at or near the poverty

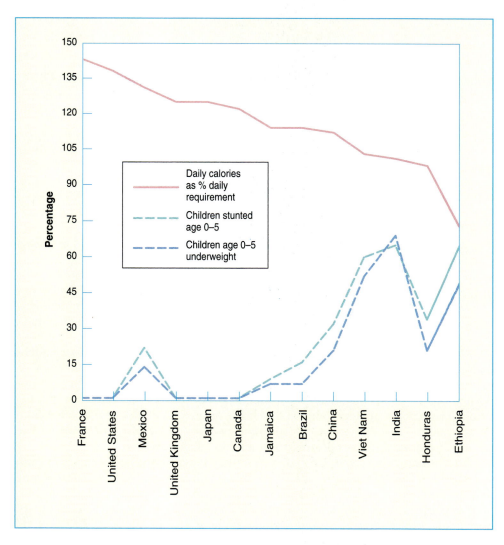

FIGURE 6.2
Physical Impact of Poverty on Growth
The percentage of children who are underweight and stunted (excessively short) tends to be smaller in countries where children receive more food calories, but the relationship is far from perfect.
Source: United Nations International Children's Emergency Fund (1995).

Perspectives

Reforming Children's Health Care

The health care system provides less help to poor families than it does to more well-off ones. The gap begins before birth: low-SES mothers are less likely to receive medical attention during pregnancy, causing health problems in themselves or their fetuses to be overlooked. The gap continues after birth: infants of low-income mothers are less likely to receive checkups from a doctor and less likely to be seen by a doctor if they get sick (United States Select Committee on Children, Youth, and Families, 1992).

Why does access to health care depend so heavily on personal income? In the United States, medical services for the poor are paid through Medicaid, a federally sponsored insurance program created in the 1960s. Medicaid pays for basic health services, but only up to a point; it will pay for taking a child with an earache to a general practitioner, for example, but it will reimburse the doctor only up to a certain point. Doctors who wish to charge more are free to do so, but in the process they price themselves out of the market for low-SES families. In effect, therefore, low-SES parents have significantly fewer doctors and clinics to choose from than higher-SES parents do, even though (as pointed out in this chapter) their children experience more illnesses than do children from middle- and upper-SES families (Fitzgerald et al., 1994).

For this and other reasons, low-SES parents are more likely than others to wait until a child's illness is serious, or even life threatening, before seeking medical help. Instead of getting antibiotics immediately when a preschooler shows signs of a bacterial ear infection, for example, parents may wait until the infection threatens the child with actual hearing loss or until the child has become chronically run down and therefore will require more time to regain strength.

To make matters worse, efforts to limit the soaring costs of medical services have led many states to make the standards for eligibility for Medicaid stricter than they originally were (United States Congressional Budget Office, 1993). In recent years, therefore, a person or a family has had to be "poorer" than before, in some states even living at only *one-half* the income level of the official federal poverty line. Some states have also set limits on services, such as the number of days a person can stay in a hospital or the number of visits permitted to a doctor per year. Still others have required preauthorization from state health authorities for services that exceed a certain cost (say, $500).

What can society and concerned individuals do to reduce these economically based inequalities in health

level. Young children from these families are substantially less healthy than those from middle- and high-SES families. Low-SES preschoolers contract 25 to 50 percent more minor illnesses than do preschoolers as a whole, and they are more often malnourished, meaning they chronically lack essential vitamins, iron, or protein (American Academy of Pediatrics, 1993; Wadsworth, 1986). Figure 6.2 illustrates the impact of child poverty on some aspects of health.

Whether in North America or around the world, minor illnesses and malnourishment put children's health at risk for additional illnesses, both minor and major. Malnourishment also seems to contribute to delays in social, language, and cognitive development, possibly because of a lack of energy. In one study based in Kenya (Africa), even a temporary food shortage (due to a few months of local drought) impaired children's health and school performance two years later (McDonald et al., 1994).

How can we counteract these problems? In general, strategies can focus either on individuals and their particular communities or on systematic reorganization of the health care system as a whole. Among individually oriented strategies, an important one is to educate children and families about health and nutrition. For example, pamphlets can be distributed in schools or medical clinics, and public health nurses can make presentations in classrooms, community clubs, or churches. The accompanying Perspectives box proposes additional alternatives.

Educational activities can be effective if they build on the knowledge of health and nutrition low-SES parents and their children already have and avoid assuming that the public is completely ignorant about these matters. Mexican American children as young as four years, for example, have good knowledge about the effects of cleanliness, but often need more information about nutrition (Olvera-Ezzell et al.,

care? Numerous reforms have been proposed, most of them centering on one of three ideas: community involvement, prevention, and reorganization of services. Reforms that focus on community involvement seek to reduce the distance, both psychological and geographical, between medical staff and the people they serve. Some hospitals and cities have established small community health clinics in areas of greatest need (the inner city). They hire medical staff who deliberately try to establish rapport with the parents and children who seek help, recruit local community members to serve on their governing and advisory boards, and charge low fees based on families' ability to pay.

Reforms that focus on prevention seek to keep disease from striking in the first place. By their nature these actions may not seem strictly related to "health," because they often deal with relatively healthy children (who have not gotten sick yet) and with the conditions that make illness likely rather than with illness itself. Lead poisoning is a good example: community health experts often cite this substance as the most hazardous health threat to preschool children in modern society (Tesman & Hills, 1994). Lead accumulates in the body and eventually causes damage to the nervous system, sickness, and even death. Children (and adults) pick it up accidentally from

many sources, but the most prominent culprit is the interior wall paint used in about 75 percent of all homes and apartments built before 1980. Since there is no real cure for lead poisoning, prevention strategies have dominated the response of the health care profession: educating parents to the dangers, pressing for legislation outlawing lead-based paints (and also lead-based gasoline, incidentally), and even removal of leaded paint in some homes.

Reforms that focus on reorganization generally involve more self-conscious planning of medical services. Basing immunization and health screening programs in schools, for example, often allows the programs to reach a higher percentage of children than basing the same programs in a community health clinic (Behrman, 1993). Also, making better use of "front-line" professionals often can improve access dramatically without compromising quality of care: the majority of childhood illnesses, for example, can be treated effectively by a nurse rather than a medical doctor, as long as the nurse knows when a particular illness deserves referral to the doctor.

1994). A similar pattern exists among their parents (Sanjur, 1995). In this sort of situation, it is helpful to organize intervention programs aimed at providing parents and children with the knowledge they need. However, such programs must respect the culture and economic situations of the families, which usually influence food preferences in major ways.

What Do You Think?

Suppose you are a teacher or caregiver at a child care center, and one of your children often seems hungry throughout the day. How could you tell whether the child is undernourished or simply has a big appetite? Compare your strategies for answering this question with those of a classmate.

BLADDER AND BOWEL CONTROL

Sometime during the preschool years, to parents' great relief, most children acquire control of their bladder and bowels. The process includes many false starts and accidents. Most commonly, daytime control comes before nighttime control, sometime before a child's third birthday, although individual children vary widely and somewhat unpredictably. Typically too daytime control of the bladder and bowels occurs at very nearly the same time. Some pediatricians believe this fact implies that children decide when they wish to begin exercising control, perhaps to begin feeling more grown up. In the early stages of toilet training, therefore, reminders and

In the long run, successful bladder control depends on both physical growth and the child's own motivation. Forcing a child prematurely to control herself or himself may produce results, but only in the immediate future.

parent-led visits to the toilet may make little difference to most toddlers. Nonetheless they may help in the long term as a form of behavioral conditioning: a child comes to associate seeing and sitting on the toilet with the relief of emptying a full bladder, as well as with the praise parents confer on the child for successes.

Nighttime bladder control often takes much longer to achieve than daytime control. About one-half of all three-year-olds still wet their beds at least some of the time, and as many as one in five six-year-olds do the same (American Psychiatric Association, 1994). The timing of nighttime control depends on several factors, such as how deeply children sleep and how large their bladders are. It also depends on anxiety level; worried children tend to wet their beds more often than relaxed children do. Unfortunately, parents sometimes contribute to young children's anxieties by becoming overly frustrated about changing wet sheets night after night.

Achieving control over bladder and bowels reflects the large advances children make during the preschool years in controlling their bodies in general. It also reflects parents' accumulated efforts to encourage physical self-control for their children. The combined result is that children of this age can begin focusing on what they actually want to do with their bodies.

What Do You Think?

Imagine how you would talk to a parent who was concerned about the child's bet wetting at night. What would you say? If you or your instructor can arrange it, try acting out a meeting to discuss bed wetting between a concerned parent and a child care center worker or director.

MOTOR SKILL DEVELOPMENT

As young children grow, they become more skilled at performing basic physical actions. Often a two-year-old can walk only with considerable effort; hence the term *toddler*. But a five-year-old can walk comfortably in a variety of ways: forward and backward, quickly and slowly, skipping and galloping. A five-year-old also can do other vigorous things that were impossible a few years earlier. He can run, jump, and climb, all with increasing smoothness and variety. He can carry out certain actions that require accuracy, such as balancing on one foot, catching a ball reliably, or drawing a picture.

In this section, we examine in more detail how children reach milestones such as these under naturally occurring conditions. Because natural conditions vary a great deal in real life, we must take a certain range of conditions for granted. In particular, we must assume children have no significant fears of being active—that they have a reasonably (but not excessively) daring attitude toward trying out new motor skills, they are in good health, and their physical growth has evolved more or less normally.

Fundamental Motor Skills

Preschool children obviously have moved well beyond the confines of reflex action, which constituted the first motor skills of infancy. From ages two to about five, they experiment with the simple voluntary actions that adults use extensively for their normal activities, such as walking, running, and jumping (Kalverboer et al., 1993). For older children, these actions usually are the means to other ends. For very young children, they lie very much in the foreground and frequently are goals in themselves. Table 6.2 summarizes some of these activities.

Walking and Running From a child's point of view, walking may seem absurd at first: it requires purposely losing balance, then regaining balance rapidly enough to

TABLE 6.2   Milestones in Preschool Motor Development

Approximate Age	Gross Motor Skill	Fine Motor Skill
2.5–3.5 years	Walks well; runs in straight line; jumps in air with both feet	Copies a circle; scribbles; can use eating utensils; stacks a few small blocks
3.5–4.5 years	Walking stride 80 percent of adult; runs at one-third adult speed; throws and catches large ball, but stiff-armed	Buttons with large buttons; copies simple shapes; makes simple representational drawings
4.5–5.5 years	Balances on one foot; runs far without falling; can "swim" in water for short distance	Uses scissors; draws people; copies simple letters and numbers; builds complex structures with blocks

Note: The ages given above are approximate, and skills vary with the life experiences available to individual children and with the situations in which the skills are displayed.
Source: Kalverboer et al. (1993).

keep from falling (Rose & Gamble, 1993). As older infants, children still must pay attention to these facts, even after a full year or so of practice. Each step is an effort in itself. Children watch each foot in turn as it launches (or lurches) forward; they may pause after each step before attempting the next. By their second or third birthday, however, their steps become more regular and their feet get closer together. Stride, the distance between feet in a typical step, remains considerably shorter than that of a typical adult. This makes short distances easy to walk but long distances hard to navigate for a few more years.

Jumping   At first, a jump is more like a fast stretch: the child reaches for the sky rapidly, but her feet fail to leave the ground. Sometime around her second birthday, one foot, or even both feet, may finally leave the ground. Such early successes may be delayed, however, because the child may thrust her arms backward to help herself take off, as though trying to push herself off the floor. Later, perhaps around age three, she shifts to a more efficient arm movement—reaching forward and upward as she jumps—which creates a useful upward momentum.

Success in these actions depends partly on the type of jump the child is attempting. Jumping down a step is easier than jumping across a flat distance, and a flat or broad jump is easier than a jump up a step. By age five or so, most children can broad-jump across a few feet, although variations among individuals are substantial.

Throwing and Catching   For infants and toddlers, first throws may consist of simply waving an object, releasing it suddenly, and watching it take off. Once intentional throwing begins, however, children actually adopt more stereotyped methods initially, using a general forward lurch, regardless of the ball's size or weight. As skill develops, children vary their movements according to the size of the ball. Catching proceeds through analogous phases, from stereotyped, passive extension of arms to flexible movement of hands in a last-minute response to the oncoming ball.

Fine Motor Coordination: The Case of Drawing Skills

Not all motor activities of young children involve the strength, agility, and balance of their whole bodies. Many require the coordination of small movements but not strength. Tying shoelaces calls for such **fine motor coordination;** so do washing hands, buttoning and zipping clothing, eating with a spoon, and turning a doorknob.

One especially widespread fine motor skill among young children is drawing. In North American culture, at least, virtually every young child tries using pens or pencils at some time and often tries other artistic media as well. The scribbles or

Skills that require fine motor coordination—like painting this butterfly—develop through identifiable steps or stages. At first children tend to make random marks or scribbles; later they coordinate these into patterns; still later they coordinate patterns into representations of objects that become increasingly recognizable by parents and teachers.

drawings that result probably serve a number of purposes. At times they may be used mainly for sensory exploration; a child may want to get the feel of paintbrushes or felt-tip pens. At other times, drawings may express thoughts or feelings; a child may suggest this possibility by commenting, "It's a horse, and it's angry." Children's drawings also probably reflect their knowledge of the world, even though they may not yet have the fine motor skills they need to convey their knowledge fully. In other words, children's drawings reveal not only fine motor coordination but also their self-concepts, emotional and social attitudes, and cognitive development.

Drawing shows two overlapping phases of development during early childhood. From about 2½ to 4 years, children focus on developing nonrepresentational skills, such as scribbling and purposeful drawing of simple shapes and designs. Sometime around age four, they begin attempting to represent objects (Coles, 1992). Yet, although representational drawings usually follow nonrepresentational ones, the two types stimulate each other simultaneously. Children often describe their early scribbles as though they referred to real things, and their practice at portraying real objects helps them to further develop their nonrepresentational skills.

Prerepresentational Drawing   Around the end of infancy, children begin to scribble. A two-year-old experiments with whatever pen or pencil is available to him, almost regardless of its color or type. In doing so, he behaves like an infant and like a child. As with an infant, his efforts focus primarily on the activity itself: on the motions and sensations of handling a pen or pencil. But like an older child, the two-year-old often cares about the outcome of these activities: "That's a Mommy," he says of his drawing, whether it looks much like one or not. Contrary to a popular view of children's art, even very young children are concerned not only with the process of drawing but with the product as well (Dyson, 1990).

A child's interest in the results of her drawing show up in the patterns she imposes on even her earliest scribbles. Sometimes she fills up particular parts of the page quite intentionally—the whole left side, say, or the complete middle third. And she often emphasizes particular categories of strokes: lots of straight diagonals or many counterclockwise loops (Raines, 1990). Different children select different types of motions for emphasis, so the motions are less like universal stages than like elements of a personal style.

Representational Drawing   While preschool children improve their scribbling skills, they also develop an interest in representing people, objects, and events in their drawings. This interest often far precedes their ability to do so. A three-year-old may assign meanings to scribbles or blobs in his drawing; one blob may be "Mama," and another may be "our house." Events may happen to these blobs, too: Mama may be "going to the store" or "looking for me." During the early childhood years, and for a long time thereafter, the child's visual representations are limited by his comparatively rudimentary fine motor skills. Apparently he knows more, visually speaking, than his hands can portray with pens or brushes. Figure 6.3 shows this tendency for one particular child. Only as the child reaches school age do her drawings of people become relatively realistic.

Gender Differences in Physical Development

As is true during infancy, preschool boys and girls develop at almost exactly the same average rates (Malina & Bouchard, 1991). This applies to practically any motor skill of which young children are capable, and it applies to both gross and fine motor skills.

On the average, boys and girls develop motor skills at almost the same rate during the preschool years. But marked differences emerge among individuals within each sex even at this age.

3 years, 2 months

3 years, 7 months

4 years, 0 months

4 years, 0 months

4 years, 2 months

4 years, 9 months

5 years, 1 month

FIGURE 6.3

Samples of a Preschooler's Drawings (Ages Three to Five)

Any nursery classroom therefore is likely to contain children of both sexes who can run very well and children of both sexes who can paint well or tie their shoelaces without help. This is especially true among younger preschool children (age three or four).

By the time children begin kindergarten (usually at age five), slight gender differences in physical development and motor skills appear, with boys tending to be (slightly) bigger, stronger, and faster. Yet these differences are noticeable only as averages and only by basing the averages on very large numbers of children (Tanner, 1990). Despite the slight differences, therefore, more than 95 percent of children are more skillful and bigger than some members of *both* sexes and less skillful and smaller than certain others of both sexes.

By the time children start school, a few children in any community are bigger, stronger, and faster than *any* other children, and most of them are boys. Furthermore, these few individuals may get much more than their share of attention because of their superior physical skills. This contributes to the (mistaken) impression that boys are larger and more skillful than girls *in general*. In this way (among many others), stereotypes are born.

The differences in motor skills might be more accurately called *gender* differences than *sex* differences, because they probably derive partly from the social roles boys and girls begin learning early in the preschool years. Part of the role differences includes how preschool children spend their time. Preschool boys do spend more time than girls in active and rough-and-tumble play, and girls spend more time doing quiet activities such as drawing or playing with stuffed animals. Children of both sexes, furthermore, reinforce or support one another more for engaging in gender-typed activities (Davies, 1991). These differences may give the impression that boys are incapable, or at least less capable, of fine motor skills and that girls are physically weaker.

What Do You Think?

Suppose you are a child care center worker, and one of your four-year-olds seems to be especially clumsy at throwing and catching a ball. Should you do something about this, and if so, what should you do? Consult with a classmate for a second opinion. Would you feel the same way if the child seemed clumsy or "uninspired" at drawing?

EFFECTS OF CHILDREN'S GROWTH ON ADULTS

Changes in Facial Features

From birth—and despite any biases from their own parents—children vary in how attractive their faces seem to adults and other children. As a rule, some individuals look younger than others of the same age. In general, having a young-looking face depends on having large features and a large forehead; that is, facial features should be wide-set and located relatively low on the front of the skull. Even slight changes in these proportions (just a fraction of an inch) can make an adult seem many years older or younger, an infant seem six months older or younger, or a preschooler seem one or two years older or younger.

In general, younger-looking children are also rated as more attractive than older-looking children by both adults and peers, and adults tend to expect more mature behaviors from older-looking children (Langlois et al., 1990). This coincidence of stereotypes—of youthfulness and attractiveness—may contribute to important differences in how parents and other adults respond to preschoolers as individuals. Parents and other caregivers need to be made aware of the impact of facial attractiveness (Langlois, 1992).

The new motor skills that preschoolers develop bring with them new risks and create new safety concerns for their parents and other caregivers. What hazards may be waiting for these three-year-olds? And how should parents or other adults deal with them?

Changes in Size and Motor Skill

Consider the changes in size that preschool children experience. A two-year-old often is still small enough to be handled. When necessary, parents can pick her up and move her from one place to another, physically remove her from danger, and carry her (at least partway) if a distance is too far for her to walk. By age five, a child often has outgrown these physical interactions, not only figuratively but literally. Parents or other adults may still lift and cuddle him sometimes in play or in an emergency, but they probably are beginning to avoid doing so on a regular basis. To a significant extent, the child may now simply be too bulky and tall. More and more rarely can parents save a child from danger by picking him up suddenly or speed him along a long hallway by carrying him piggyback. They must somehow get the child to do these things for himself.

Usually, of course, parents succeed at this task. By age five, a child can think and talk about her own actions much more than before, and these improvements help guide her own actions. The handling that used to be literal now becomes mostly figurative: now *handling* means negotiating and discussing with the child rather than lifting her up or carting her around.

Improvements in motor skills also change the agenda for a child's daily activities. A two-year-old may spend a good part of his day experimenting with fundamental skills: walking from one room to another, tearing toilet paper to shreds, or taking pots and pans out of a cupboard. These activities often are embedded in an active social and cognitive life: the child may smile (or frown) at his parents while he works and may "talk" about what he is doing as well. But the motor aspects of his activities absorb a significant part of his attention throughout the day. The child may return repeatedly to a staircase, for instance, as though compelled to get the hang of climbing it; no reward needs to lie at the top step except the satisfaction of a job well done.

A two-year-old's parents therefore must spend a lot of time ensuring that the child comes to no physical harm in her motor explorations. They must make sure the child does not fall down the stairs, tumble into the toilet bowl, or discover a sharp knife among the pots. Their role as safety experts can dominate their contacts with the child, particularly if the child is active. Table 6.3 lists common accidents, remedies, and preventions.

By the end of early childhood, minute-to-minute physical surveillance recedes in importance, even though, of course, a concern about safety remains. Rules about dangers make their appearance ("Don't climb on that fence; it's rickety"), along with the hope that a five-year-old can remember and follow the rules at least some of the time. The shift toward rules also results from increasing confidence in the child's motor skills. Now parents are apt to believe their child can go up and down stairs without stumbling very often—and they are usually right.

During the preschool period, many parents discover a special need for patience in their dealings with their children. Simple actions such as tying shoelaces or putting on socks may take longer than before simply because children now insist on doing many of these things themselves. For similar reasons, walking to the store may now take longer; a three- or four-year-old may prefer to push the stroller rather than ride in it, thus slowing everyone down. And preschoolers may have their own agenda on a walk, such as noticing little rocks on the sidewalk or airplanes in the sky, that differs from parents' goals. On good days these behaviors offer some of the joys of raising children, but on bad days they often irritate even the most patient of parents.

What Do You Think?

How might different work schedules, the number of children in a family, and family finances influence the amount of joy or irritation experienced by a well-meaning family? This question makes a great topic for exploration with others. If possible, discuss it with an actual parent or two.

TABLE 6.3 *Common Accidents, Remedies, and Preventions among Preschoolers*

Accidents	What to Do	How to Prevent
Drowning	Unless you are trained in water safety, extend a stick or other device. Use heart massage and mouth-to-mouth breathing when and as long as needed.	Teach children to swim as early in life as possible; supervise children's swim sessions closely; stay in shallow water.
Choking on small objects	If a child is still breathing, do not attempt to remove object; see a doctor instead. If breathing stops, firmly strike child twice on small of back. If this does not help, grab child from behind, put your fist just under his or her ribs, and pull upward sharply several times.	Do not allow children to put small objects in mouth; teach them to eat slowly, taking small bites; forbid vigorous play with objects or food in mouth.
Cuts with serious bleeding	Raise cut above level of heart; apply pressure with cloth or bandage; if necessary, apply pressure to main arteries of limbs.	Remove sharp objects from play areas; insist on shoes wherever ground or floor may contain sharp objects; supervise children's use of knives.
Fractures	Keep injured limb immobile; see a doctor.	Discourage climbing and exploring in dangerous places, such as trees and construction sites; allow bicycles only in safe areas.
Burns	Pour cold water over burned area; keep it clean; then cover with *sterile* bandage. See a doctor if burn is extensive.	Keep matches out of reach of children; keep children well away from fires and hot stoves.
Poisons	On skin or eye, flush with plenty of water; if in stomach, phone poison control center doctor for instructions; induce vomiting only for selected substances.	Keep dangerous substances out of reach of children; throw away poisons when no longer needed. Keep syrup of ipecac in home to induce vomiting, but use *only* if advised by doctor.
Animal bites	Clean and cover with bandage; see a doctor.	Train children when and how to approach family pets; teach them caution in approaching unfamiliar animals.
Insect bites	Remove stinger, if possible; cover with paste of bicarbonate of soda (for bees) or a few drops of vinegar (for wasps and hornets).	Encourage children to recognize and avoid insects that sting, as well as their nests; encourage children to keep calm in presence of stinging insects.
Poisonous plants (e.g., poison ivy)	Remove affected clothing; wash affected skin with strong alkali soap as soon as possible.	Teach children to recognize toxic plants; avoid areas where poisonous plants grow.

Sources: Adapted from Green (1994); Bain (1993).

COGNITIVE DEVELOPMENT

THINKING IN PRESCHOOLERS

In addition to their physical changes, preschool children develop new abilities to represent objects and experiences. They begin to notice, for example, that their particular way of viewing the objects across a room differs from the perspective of a family member already sitting on the other side. They begin to distinguish between appearances and reality; that is, when you cover a doll with a costume, it still is "really" the same doll. And they become able to communicate new understandings such as these to others. The changes are in thinking, or *cognition,* and are called *cognitive development.*

Much of the research on cognitive development owes its intellectual roots to the observations and theorizing of Jean Piaget. During the 1960s and 1970s, considerable effort went toward testing his ideas about cognitive development. On the whole, the research led first to modifications of and, in some cases, challenges to Piaget's major proposals, such as the existence of comprehensive cognitive stages that unfold in a predictable order (Case & Edelstein, 1993). To put these later findings in proper context, however, we must first keep in mind Piaget's key ideas about the changes young children experience during the preschool years.

Piaget's Preoperational Stage

At about age two, according to Piaget, children enter a new stage in their cognitive development (Piaget, 1963). Infancy has left them with several important accomplishments, such as the belief that objects have a permanent existence and the capacity to set and follow simple goals, such as removing all the clothes from every drawer in the house. Infancy has also left them with the knowledge that all of their senses register the same world; now a child knows that hearing his mother in the next room means he will probably see her soon and that seeing her probably also means he will hear from her.

The preoperational stage, roughly ages two through seven, extends and transforms these skills. During this stage, children become increasingly proficient at using *symbols,* words or actions that stand for other things. During this period, they also extend their belief in object permanence to include *identities,* or constancies, of many types: a candle remains the same even as it grows shorter from burning, and a flower growing out of the sidewalk remains the same flower even though its growth changes its appearance from day to day.

Preoperational children also sense many *functional relationships,* or variations in their environments that normally occur together. Preschool children usually know that the hungrier they are, the more they will want to eat; the bigger they are, the stronger they tend to be; and the faster they walk, the sooner they will arrive somewhere. Of course, they still do not know the precise functions or relationships in these examples—exactly how *much* faster they will arrive if they walk a particular distance more quickly—but they do know that a relationship exists.

Preschoolers' play often relies on their growing abilities to represent objects and events symbolically. A carpet becomes a zoo, and rows of blocks become fences enclosing zoo animals. New language skills are stimulated by this sort of activity as well.

These are all cognitive strengths of preschool children, and they mark cognitive advances over infancy. But as the *pre-* in the term *preoperational* implies, Piaget's original theorizing actually focused on the limitations of young children's thinking relative to that of school-age children. The term *operations* referred to mental actions that allow a child to reason about events he or she experiences. Piaget's observations suggested that from age two to seven, children often confuse their own points of view with those of other people, cannot classify objects and events logically, and often are misled by single features of their experiences. As later sections of this chapter point out, however, more recent research has substantially qualified this perspective; in essence, it has found that children often are more cognitively astute than Piaget realized. Their specific cognitive skills are all based on a key ability that Piaget *did* recognize: the ability to represent experiences symbolically.

Symbolic Thought

As we just noted, *symbols* are words, objects, or behaviors that stand for something else. They take this role not because of their intrinsic properties but because of the intentions of the people who use them. A drinking straw is just a hollow tube and does not become a symbol until a preschooler places it in the middle of a mound of sand and declares it to be a birthday candle. Likewise, the sound /bahks/ lacks symbolic meaning unless we all agree that it refers to a hollow object with corners: *box*.

Probably the most significant cognitive achievement of the preoperational period is the emergence and elaboration of **symbolic thought,** the ability to think by making one object or action stand for another. Throughout their day, two-year-olds use language symbolically, such as when they say "Milk!" to procure a white, drinkable substance from the refrigerator. They also use symbolic thought in make-believe play by pretending to be people or creatures other than themselves. By about age four, children's symbolic play often combines complex actions (getting down on all fours), objects (using a table napkin for a saddle), language (shouting "Neigh!"), and coordination with others (getting a friend to be a rider).

Symbolic thinking helps preschool children organize and process what they know. Objects and experiences can be recalled more easily if they have names and compared more easily if the child has concepts that can describe their features. Symbols also help children communicate what they know to others, even in situations quite different from the experience itself. Having gone to the store, they can convey this experience to others either in words ("I went shopping") or through pretend play ("Let's play store, and I'll be the clerk."). By its nature, communication fosters social relationships among children, but it also fosters cognitive development by allowing individual children to learn from the experiences of others. More precisely, communication allows individuals to learn from the symbolic representations of others' experiences.

Egocentrism in Preschool Children

Egocentrism refers to the tendency of a person to confuse his or her own point of view and that of another person. The term does not necessarily imply selfishness at the expense of others, but a centering on the self in thinking. Young children often show egocentrism in this sense, but not always. Piaget illustrated their egocentrism by showing children a table on which models of three mountains had been constructed and asking them how a doll would see the three mountains if it sat at various positions around the table. Three-year-olds (the ones in Piaget's preoperational stage) commonly believed the doll saw the layout no differently than they did (Piaget & Inhelder, 1967).

On the other hand, when the task concerns more familiar materials and settings, even preschool children adopt others' spatial perspectives (Steiner, 1987). For example, instead of using Piaget's three-mountain model, suppose we use a "police officer" doll that is searching for a "child" doll and place them among miniature barriers that sometimes obscure the dolls' "view" of each other and sometimes do not. In this experiment, four-year-olds have relatively little difficulty knowing when the two dolls can "see" each other and when the barriers truly are "in the way" (Cohen, 1983).

In oral communication, preschoolers also show distinct but incomplete egocentrism. A variety of studies have documented that preschoolers often explain tasks rather poorly to others, even though their language and understanding are otherwise skillful enough to explain them better (Flavell, et al., 1986; Foster, 1990). Copying a simple diagram according to instructions from a preschooler can prove next to impossible, no matter how sensitive the listener is. On the other hand, preschool children do show awareness of the needs of a listener. They explain a drawing more clearly, for example, to a listener who is blindfolded (Cohen, 1983), apparently because the blindfold emphasizes the listener's need for more complete information.

In these studies, young children show both similarity to and difference from the adults they will become. All of us, young or old, show egocentrism at times; indeed, our own thinking is often the only framework on which we can base our actions and conversations with others, at least initially. As we mature, though, we learn more about others' thoughts, views, and feelings, as well as more about how to express ourselves more precisely. In these ways, we (hopefully!) differ from four-year-olds.

Other Aspects of Children's Conceptual Development

Along with their symbolic skills, preschool children develop specific cognitive skills. They become able to classify objects, and by the end of the early childhood period some can even attend to changes in objects involving more than one feature at a time. They move beyond rote counting to a meaningful understanding of the concept of *number*. They also acquire an intuitive sense of the differences among fundamentally different types of concepts, such as the difference between a living dog and a toy robot made to act like a dog.

Classification Skills   **Classification** refers to the placement of objects in groups or categories according to some specific standards or criteria. Young preschool children, even those just three years old, can reliably classify objects that differ in just one dimension, or feature, especially if that dimension presents fairly obvious contrasts. Given a collection of pennies and nickels, a preschooler usually can sort them by color, which is their most obvious dimension of difference. Given a boxful of silverware, a young child might sort the items by type: knives, forks, and spoons. Or she might group dishes by how they are used in real life, putting each cup with one saucer rather than separating all the cups from all the saucers. These simple groupings represent cognitive advances over infancy.

Reversibility and Conservation   Some classification problems require **reversibility** in thinking, or the ability to undo a problem mentally and go back to its beginning. If you accidentally drop a pile of papers on the floor, you may be annoyed, but you know that in principle the papers are all there: you believe (correctly) that the papers that have scattered can be "unscattered" if you pick them up and sort them into their correct order again. Reversibility, it turns out, contributes to a major cognitive achievement of middle childhood: **conservation,** or the ability to perceive that certain properties of an object remain the same or constant despite changes in the object's appearance. On average, children do not achieve conservation until about age six.

To understand reversibility and conservation, consider the task shown in Figure 6.4. First, you show a preschool child two tall glasses with exactly the same amount of water in each. Then the child watches you pour the water from one of the glasses into a third, wide glass. Naturally, the water line in the wide glass will be lower than it was in the tall one. Finally, you ask the child, "Is there more water in the wide glass than in the [remaining] tall glass, or less, or just as much?"

Children less than five years old typically say that the tall glass has either less or more water than the wide glass, but not that the two glasses are the same. According to Piaget, this happens because the child forgets the identity of the water levels that she saw only a moment earlier; in this sense, she is a nonreversible thinker and cannot imagine pouring the water back again to prove the glasses' equality. Instead she is limited to current appearances. More often than not, a big difference in appearance leads her to say that the amount of water changes as a result of its being poured. In Piagetian terms, she fails to conserve, or believe in the constancy of the amount of liquid despite its visible changes (Inhelder & Piaget, 1958). Not until the early school years do conservation and reversibility become firmly established.

In the meantime, tasks that require conservation are affected significantly by how they are presented or described to the child. When given a series of conservation tasks, for example, a child tends to alternate conserving with nonconserving responses (Elbers et al., 1991). Why? Perhaps repeating the question makes some children believe the experimenter wants them to change their response; after all, why else would he repeat himself? Because most children begin the conservation task by agreeing that the glasses hold equal amounts of water, obliging children may feel compelled to give nonconserving responses against their own better judgment. It seems, therefore, that children may take Piagetian tasks as social events as well as cognitive ones.

The Concept of Number   Like many parents, Piaget correctly noted that children do not fully grasp how the conventional number system works during the first few years of life (Piaget, 1952). Preschoolers may, of course, count, such as when a three-year-old says, "One, two, three, blast off!" before tossing a ball high into the air. But such counting, Piaget argued, lacks understanding; it essentially is a rote activity. To fully understand number, a child must comprehend three ideas. The first is that a one-to-one correspondence exists between items in a set and number names; the second is *cardinality,* the idea that the total number of a set corresponds to the last number named when the items are counted; and the third is *ordinality,* the concept that numbers always occur in a particular order (the second item to be counted is always called the "second," for example).

Research stimulated by these ideas about number generally has concluded that Piaget underestimated preschoolers' knowledge of number. Many four-year-olds,

FIGURE 6.4
Conservation of Liquid Quantity
Does a child believe liquid quantity remains constant (is "conserved") despite changes in its shape? The method illustrated here, or some variation of it, is often used to answer this question.

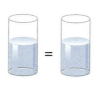
First, you show a preschool child two tall glasses with exactly the same amount of water in each.

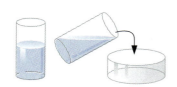
Then the child watches you pour the water from one of the glasses into a third, wide glass.

Finally, you ask the child, "Is there more water in the wide glass than in the (remaining) tall glass, or less, or just as much?"

A child who lacks reversibility (is non-conserving) in thinking about liquids says either, "The tall glass has more," or "The wide glass has more." She is fooled by its appearance.

and even some three-year-olds, can reliably say the numbers in sequence, at least up to some modest limit such as *five* or *six*. They also know that different sets of items should be counted with the same sequence of numbers, that each item should be counted only once, and that any set can be counted in more than one order. For this and other reasons, some psychologists have argued that children may have an innate conception of number (Gelman & Greeno, 1988), though of course they must also learn the conventional number names from experience.

How Cognitive Development Occurs

Variations in cognitive performance occur in part because preschool children depend on the social context or circumstances to develop new cognitive skills. Children do not simply learn fundamental thinking skills alone, merely interacting with and thinking about objects and experiences. Instead, either directly or indirectly, they learn from adults or older, more experienced peers (Rogoff et al., 1993). The older children provide models for how to solve problems, and they offer hints and information about how to approach or think about a problem. The help sometimes is deliberate (such as in school) or accidental (such as at home in many cases), but either way it allows a child to handle problems that are just a bit beyond those she or he can deal with alone.

The gap in difficulty between independent thinking and socially supported thinking is called the **zone of proximal development (ZPD),** the area in which problems are too difficult to solve alone but not too hard to solve with support from adults or more competent peers. The concept originated with the Russian psychologist Lev Vygotsky (Newman & Holzman, 1993) and has created a lot of interest among developmental psychologists because it suggests how stages and skills may emerge and evolve. In learning about number, for example, everyday conversations between parent and child play a significant role:

PARENT: Here are four books for you and the same for your brother.

CHILD: The same? *(He investigates his brother's pile of books.)* No, he has more *(spoken with annoyance)*.

A lot of cognitive change occurs because of the mutual development of meaning that happens in the "zone of proximal development," where two people focus on a common activity. In this case the father stimulates the son to learn adult ideas about recycling, and the son stimulates the father to learn about the son's growing knowledge and abilities.

PARENT: No, really, they're the same. Take another look.

CHILD: He does have more.

PARENT: Try laying his out in a row. Then lay yours out, too. Then compare.

CHILD *(does as suggested, then counts each row)*: One, two, three, four. One, two, three, four. The same! *(He looks satisfied.)*

In this example, the parent provides a framework that the child cannot provide for himself and that allows the child to solve the problem for himself. First, the parent states the problem in a helpful way ("They're the same"); then she gives hints about how to solve it. But the final solution remains with the child. The help occurs in the child's personal zone of proximal development. Without it, the child might not have solved the problem, at least at this point in his cognitive development.

As you might suppose, the nature of the ZPDs that any particular child experiences depends on the child's cultural and economic circumstances. Parents with a "bookish" and school-oriented background will more often provide ZPDs that encourage bookish and school-oriented skills. Those with special skills and concerns for interpersonal sensitivity may more often provide ZPDs that promote interpersonal sensitivity. Those with few resources, either economic or social, may have difficulty providing any sort of assistance to the child's cognitive development.

Neostructuralist Theories of Cognitive Development

As the studies described so far suggest, preschoolers show considerable new strengths in using symbolic thought. They can take others' perspectives to some extent, develop a usable theory of how the human mind works, and distinguish between appearances and reality at least some of the time. Many of Piaget's classic observations on Swiss children have proven true: preschool children have trouble focusing on two dimensions of an object at once and therefore have difficulty with conservation tasks throughout most of the preschool period. Other Piagetian observations have underestimated children's ability and stimulated research that has led to new ways of thinking about children's capacities. For example, unlike Piaget's claims, preschool children do have a partial understanding of number.

Research has complicated our picture of children's cognitive development. Many psychologists have sought to keep Piaget's commitment to stagelike progressions in development and at the same time revise the content or details of those progressions (Case & Edelstein, 1993). Instead of proposing comprehensive, "grand" stages of thinking, as Piaget did, they argue that stages may be much more focused in content. Research based on this premise has in fact identified stages of spatial representation, of mathematical ability, and of interpersonal awareness, among others (Case, 1992). Each of these skills seems to develop through predictable stages, but do so independently of the other domains. As individuals, children therefore show unique patterns and timing of development across many areas of thinking and skills (Wozniak & Fischer, 1993).

This newer view of cognitive stages is sometimes called **neostructuralist** or *neo-Piagetian theory* because of its roots in the ideas of Piaget. As a result of focusing attention on more specific cognitive achievements, it has also paid more attention to *how,* or by what processes, children acquire new cognitive skills. One neostructuralist line of research explored the process of learning to draw by noting how it consists of the successive coordination of simpler skills (Dennis, 1992). An infant begins her second year of life able to visually track objects as well as reach for objects. With practice, by the time she reaches age three, the child has learned to coordinate these two schemes into a single cognitive skill that enables scribbling. As the child continues to practice with this newly consolidated scheme, she begins coordinating it with other, more advanced schemes, such as *comparing* scribbles with the orientation and edges of the paper. When tracking edges of a paper and tracking scribbles eventually become coordinated, the child can finally begin controlling lines and curves. Now the stage is set for her first representational drawings, such as stick-figure people.

From the neostructuralist perspective, then, cognitive development during early childhood is not all of one piece when it unfolds but has many components—many forms of thinking, as well as perceptual and language developments. As a result, it is important to understand each piece separately from the others and to combine them to get a well-rounded picture of young children. Therefore, in the next section we look at another major piece of the puzzle of children's thinking: language acquisition.

What Do You Think?

What do you think parents of young children believe about preschoolers' cognitive abilities? What if you asked parents (1) how much their *children* know when *parents* are happy or upset and (2) would their children think that a clay ball was the same "amount" if it were squashed into a pancake shape? Would parents' expectations about these questions coincide with the research described in this section? If possible, interview a real-life parent or two to test your prediction.

LANGUAGE ACQUISITION IN THE PRESCHOOL YEARS

For most children, language expands rapidly after infancy. Dramatic development occurs in *syntax,* or the way the child organizes utterances. But significant changes also occur in semantics and in pragmatics. As we mentioned in Chapter 4, *semantics* refers to what the child means by his utterances. *Pragmatics* is how the child adjusts his utterances to the needs and expectations of different situations and speakers; it might also be called "communicative competence."

The Nature of Syntax

The **syntax** of a language is a group of rules for ordering and relating its elements. Linguists call the elements of language *morphemes. Morphemes* are the smallest meaningful units of language; they include words as well as a number of prefixes and suffixes that carry meaning (the /s/ in *houses* or the /re/ in *redo*) and verb-tense modifiers (the /ing/ in *going*).

Syntactic rules operate on morphemes in several ways. Sometimes they mark important relationships between large classes or groups of words. Consider these two pairs of sentences:

1a. John kissed Barbara. *and* 2a. Frank kisses Joan.
1b. Barbara kissed John.   2b. Frank kissed Joan.

These sentences differ in meaning because of syntactic rules. In the first pair, a rule about the order, or sequence, of words tells us who is giving the kiss and who is receiving it: the name preceding the verb is the agent (the kisser), and the name following the verb is the recipient (the "kissee"). In the second pair, the morphemes /es/ and /ed/ tell something about when the event occurred; adding /es/ to the end of the word signifies that it is happening now, but adding /ed/ means it happened in the past. These rules, and many similar ones, are understood and used by all competent speakers of the language. Unlike textbook authors, however, the speakers may never state them and may be only barely aware of them.

Unfortunately for a child learning to talk, some syntactic rules have only a small range of application, and still others have irregular exceptions. Most words, for example, signal pluralization (the existence of more than one) by having an /s/ or /es/ added at the end; *book* means one volume, and *books* means more than one. But a few words use other methods to signal the plural. *Foot* means one, and *feet,* not *foots,* means more than one; *child* means one and *children* more than one; and *deer* can mean either one animal or several.

Thus, in acquiring syntax, a young child confronts a mixed system of rules. Some apply widely and regularly, and others apply narrowly and exceptionally. Added to these complexities is the fact that the child often hears utterances that are grammatically incomplete or even incorrect. Somehow he or she must sort these out from the grammatically acceptable utterances while at the same time trying to sort out the various syntactic rules and the contexts for using them.

Beyond First Words: Semantic and Syntactic Relations

Before age two, children begin linking words when they speak. Initially the words seem to be connected by their *semantic relations,* or the meanings intended for them, rather than by *syntactic relations,* the relations among grammatical classes of words such as nouns, verbs, and adjectives. This is particularly true when the child is still speaking primarily in two-word utterances (sometimes called *duos*). As the mean length of a child's utterances increases to three words and more, syntactic relations become much more noticeable.

Duos and Telegraphic Speech   These ideas were documented in a classic set of three case studies of early language acquisition by Roger Brown (1973). When the children Brown observed were still speaking primarily in two-word utterances, their utterances were organized around eight possible semantic relationships; these are listed in Table 6.4, along with examples. The meanings of the utterances were determined by the intended relationships among the words, and the intentions of the preschool speakers often were discernible only by observing the context in which the utterances were made. "Mommy sandwich" could mean "the type of sandwich Mommy usually eats," or "Mommy is eating the sandwich," or "Mommy, give me a sandwich," all depending on the conversational context.

TABLE 6.4 *Semantic Relations in Two-Word Utterances*

Relationship	Example
Agent + action	Baby cry
Action + object	Eat cookie
Agent + object	Bobby cookie
Action + locative (location)	Jump stair
Object + locative	Teddy bed
Possessor + possessed	Mommy sandwich
Attribute + object	Big dog
Demonstrative + object	There Daddy

A child's earliest utterances are organized not according to adultlike grammar but according to particular semantic or meaning-oriented relationships such as those listed in this table. Often the intended, underlying relationships are ambiguous and can be discerned only by an attentive, observant adult at the time of the utterance.

The reason for the ambiguity is that two-word utterances leave out indicators of syntactic relationships. One syntactic indicator is word order: due to word order, "the boy chased the girl" means something different than "the girl chased the boy." Children who still speak in duos do not use word order randomly, but they do tend to be less predictable about it than more linguistically mature children, whose utterances can be several words long. Another indicator of syntactic relationships is inflections, prepositions, and conjunctions. An older child will add 's to indicate possession (as in "Mommy's sandwich") and use words such as *in* and *on* to indicate location (as in "jump on the stair"). Leaving these indicators out makes the speech sound stilted and ambiguous; therefore, it is also called **telegraphic speech,** presumably because it sounds like a telegram. Telegraphic speech is characteristic of children's first efforts to combine words (around eighteen months to two years), but it can persist well after children begin using longer, more syntactic utterances some of the time.

Regularities and Overgeneralizations   After highly individual beginnings, certain aspects of syntax develop in universal and predictable patterns. The present progressive form *-ing* occurs quite early in most children's language, the regular plural morphemes *-s* and *-es* somewhat later, and articles such as *the* and *a* still later (Marcus et al., 1992).

At a slightly older age, most children begin using auxiliary verbs to form questions, but they do so without inverting word order, as adults normally do. At first, a child will say, "Why you are cooking?" and only later "Why are you cooking?" This suggests that language acquisition involves more than just copying adult language; after all, adults rarely model incorrect forms. To a certain extent, children's language seems to compromise between the new forms children hear and the old forms they already can produce easily.

Sometimes, in fact, early syntax becomes *too* regular, and children make **overgeneralizations**. Around age three, preschool children often make errors such as those in Figure 6.5. In each case, the child uses the wrong but more regular form as opposed to the correct but irregular forms of an earlier age. Usually by early school age he shifts back again, although not necessarily because anyone teaches him or forces him to do so. Apparently his overgeneralizations represent efforts to try out new rules of syntax that he has finally noticed.

The Predisposition to Infer Grammar   As these examples suggest, young children seem to infer grammatical relationships rather than simply copy others' speech. A classic study of early syntax showed the importance of the child's own inferences

Preschoolers are skilled at acquiring syntactic rules, even though much syntax must be learned by rote.

"I runned to the store"

"Unpour the water, please"

"All the childs came!"

about grammatical rules. Instead of asking children about real words, the experimenter showed them pictures of imaginary creatures and actions that had nonsense words as names (Berko, 1958). With one picture, a child was told, "Here is a wug." Then he was shown two pictures and told, "Here are two of them. Here are two _____." Most children, even those as young as 2½, completed the sentences with the grammatically correct word, *wugs*. Because they could not possibly have heard the term before, they must have applied a general rule for forming plurals, one that did not depend on copying any language experiences specifically but came from inferring the underlying structure of many experiences taken together. The rule most likely operated unconsciously, because these children were very young indeed.

The Limits of Learning Rules   Preschoolers' skill at acquiring syntactic rules, however, obscures a seemingly contradictory fact about the acquisition of syntax: much syntax must be learned by rote. As we have pointed out, most children use irregular forms (such as *foot/feet*) correctly before they shift to incorrect but more regular forms. The most reasonable explanation for the change is that they pick up the very first sentence forms simply by copying, word for word, the sentences they hear spoken. Presumably they copy many regular forms by rote, too, but the very regularity of these forms hides the haphazard, unthinking way in which children acquire them.

Although children eventually rely on rule-governed syntax, they probably still learn a lot of language by rote. Many expressions in a language are *idiomatic*, meaning they bear no logical relation to normal meanings or syntax. The sentence "How do you do?", for example, usually is not a literal inquiry as to how a person performs a certain action; and the sentence "How goes it?", meaning "How is it going?", does not even follow the usual rules of grammar. Because words and phrases such as these violate the rules of syntax and meaning, children must learn them one at a time.

Mechanisms of Language Acquisition

Exactly how do children learn to speak? For most children, several factors may operate at once. In general, current evidence can best be summarized as follows: language seems to grow through the interaction of an active, thinking child with certain key people and linguistic experiences. The preceding sections describe in part this active, thinking child; the following sections describe some possible key interaction experiences.

Reinforcement   A commonsense view, one shared by behaviorally oriented psychologists, is that children learn to speak through reinforcement. According to this idea, a child's caregiver reinforces vocal noises whenever they approximate a genuine word or utterance, and this reinforcement causes the child to vocalize in increasingly correct (or at least adultlike) ways (Skinner, 1957). In the course of babbling, an infant may happen to say "Ma-ma-ma-ma," to which his proud parent smiles and replies cheerfully, "How nice! You said 'Mama'!" The praise reinforces the behavior, so the infant says "Ma-ma-ma-ma" more often after that. After many such experiences, his parents begin to reinforce only closer approximations to *mama,* leading finally to a true version of this word.

Among preschool children, the same process could occur if parents reinforced correct grammatical forms and ignored or criticized errors or relatively immature utterances. Parents might respond more positively to the sentence "I have three feet" than to the sentence "I have two foots." According to the principles of reinforcement (see Chapter 2), the child would tend not only to use the correct version more often but also to generalize the correct elements of this sentence to other, similar utterances.

Analysis of conversations between parents and children confirms this possibility, at least in indirect form and for the early stages of language acquisition. One study compared parents' responses to simple but grammatical sentences made by

Imitation accounts for a very large part of human learning. This grandmother is reading to her granddaughter before the girl can actually read. Without explicitly realizing it, the grandmother is helping the girl to be more ready when reading is taught in school. The girl's earliest reading skills are being "caught," not taught.

their two- and three-year-old children to their responses to ungrammatical utterances (Penner, 1987). Parents did not correct their children's grammar directly, but they were more likely to elaborate on the child's topic if the utterance was a grammatical one.

Imitation and Practice   In some sense, children obviously must imitate their native language to acquire it. This is an idea borrowed from the social learning variety of behaviorism. In daily life, though, the process of imitation is subtle and often indirect. Children do not imitate everything they hear, but most copy certain selected utterances, often immediately after hearing them. Sometimes the utterances chosen for imitation involve familiar sentence forms that contain new, untried terms, and sometimes they contain familiar terms cast into new, untried forms. The imitated terms and forms return later in the child's spontaneous speech. At first these utterances resemble the rote learning mentioned earlier, and they seem to help the child by emphasizing or calling attention to new morphemes and syntax.

Imitation may also help children acquire language by initiating playful practice with new expressions. The child in essence plays around with the new forms she learns and in doing so consolidates her recently acquired knowledge (see Chapter 7's discussion of play). Because quite a bit of language play remains unobserved by adults, its extent is hard to judge, but a lot obviously does go on even in children as young as two years (Messer, 1994).

Innate Predisposition to Acquire Language: LAD

The ease and speed children show in acquiring language have caused some linguists and psychologists to conclude that children have an innate predisposition, or built-in tendency, to learn language (Chomsky, 1994). For convenience, the innate tendency is sometimes called the *language acquisition device,* or *LAD*. According to this viewpoint, LAD functions as a kind of inborn road map to language. It guides the child to choose appropriate syntactic categories as he tries to figure out the comparatively confusing examples of real speech that he ordinarily hears. It helps him find his way through the mazelike structure of language with relatively few major errors instead of having to explore and construct his own language map, as the Piagetian viewpoint implies.

The most persuasive reason for postulating the LAD is the *poverty of content* in the speech to which most infants and preschoolers are exposed. According to this argument, the language children encounter is too incomplete and full of everyday grammatical errors (too "impoverished") to serve as a satisfactory guide in learning the grammatical structure of the language (Baker, 1995). Parents sometimes speak in incomplete sentences, sometimes make grammatical errors, and sometimes do not speak at all when speaking might prove helpful to a child learning the language.

Despite the poverty of content, however, children seem remarkably resilient in acquiring language. Children isolated from language through parental neglect, for example, have learned some language later in life, but their language usually is limited in amount and complexity. In a less tragic example, identical twins often create a private language that they speak only with each other. In many cases their private language seems to delay normal language development, though the delay rarely causes serious lasting damage to their development (Mogford, 1993).

A final piece of evidence that a LAD exists is that preschool children do not simply copy their parents' language directly, yet they seem to figure out and use many of its basic syntactic relationships remarkably well. The classic "wug" experiment discussed earlier illustrates this ability dramatically. In forming plurals they have never heard spoken before, children seem to demonstrate a grammatical skill that is more innate than learned.

The Limits of LAD   Although this evidence suggests that children have a built-in ability to acquire language, it does not show that experience plays no role at all. The evidence from twins and neglected children emphasizes just the opposite: that certain experiences with language may be crucial, especially early in life. Ordinarily practically every preschooler encounters these experiences. They may consist of hearing others talk and of being invited to respond to others verbally. But the fact that they happen to everyone does not mean children do not learn from them; it means only that what children learn is universal.

Furthermore, experiences affect the version of language children acquire, even when they supposedly grow up in the same language community. As pointed out earlier, children vary in the vocabulary they learn and in the grammar they use; even by age three or four, children often do not define grammatical categories as abstractly as adults do or necessarily in the same way other children do. Most preschoolers eventually revise their grammatical categories to coincide with conventional adult grammar, thus obscuring their individuality. But as we will see in Chapter 8, large differences persist in older children's styles of communicating, even after they have mastered the basic structure of language.

All things considered, the fairest conclusion we can draw is a moderate one: that children are both predisposed to acquire language and in need of particular experiences with it. Skill with language is neither given at birth nor divorced entirely from other cognitive development. A special talent for language may be given to all normal children, however, and many crucial experiences for developing that talent may happen to occur rather frequently among infants as they grow up.

Parent-Child Interactions

Certain kinds of verbal interactions apparently help children acquire language sooner and better. Parents can help by speaking in relatively short sentences to their preschoolers and using more concrete nouns than pronouns, though this also depends on whether the task or topic at hand calls for concrete or abstract ideas (Sorsby & Martlew, 1991). In the following pair of comments, the first helps a child learn language more than the second does:

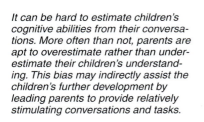

It can be hard to estimate children's cognitive abilities from their conversations. More often than not, parents are apt to overestimate rather than underestimate their children's understanding. This bias may indirectly assist the children's further development by leading parents to provide relatively stimulating conversations and tasks.

PARENT 1: Take your shoes off. Then put your shoes in the closet. Then come kiss Mama goodnight.

PARENT 2: After you take off your shoes and put them in the closet, come kiss me goodnight.

As we noted in Chapter 4, the simplified style of the first set of comments is one aspect of a version of language called **infant-directed speech,** or sometimes "motherese." Another aspect of this version is the use of a high-pitched voice. Infant-directed speech is used intuitively by adults with young children and even by older children with younger children (Messer, 1994).

One of the most helpful kinds of verbal interactions is *recasting* a child's utterances: repeating or reflecting back what the child says, but in slightly altered form. For instance:

CHILD: More milk.

PARENT: You want more milk, do you?

Recasting helps because it highlights slight differences among ways of expressing an idea. In doing so, it may make the child more aware of how she expresses her idea—its form or organization—as well as call attention to the idea itself.

Most of the techniques for stimulating language development provide young preschoolers with a framework of language that simultaneously invites them to try new, unfamiliar language forms and simplifies and clarifies other aspects of language. Some psychologists call this framework *scaffolding* (Bruner, 1983): like real scaffolds used in building construction, parents' language scaffolds provide a temporary structure within which young children can build their own language structures. As such, it functions much like Vygotsky's zone of proximal development mentioned earlier: helpful scaffolding changes and grows in response to the child's continuing development, always building a bit beyond the child's current independent abilities but never very far beyond.

These and similar findings have been translated into curricula for education of young children and even of infants (Spodek & Saracho, 1993). Fortunately, the most useful methods of interaction often are those that parents and teachers use intuitively anyway; training for them therefore really consists of emphasizing and refining their use.

What Do You Think?

Suppose you were asked to speak to a parent group, and a parent complained of her four-year-old's use of poor grammar. What advice could you give to this parent? Rehearse your comments with a classmate to determine how appropriate they are.

LANGUAGE VARIATIONS

Not surprisingly, parents vary in how they talk to their children, and these differences may influence the version of language children acquire as they grow up. It is unclear, however, how language variations affect other aspects of children's development, such as thinking ability. Later, in Chapter 8, we discuss variations related to cultural differences—for example, the "Black English" that some African Americans speak in certain situations. First, though, let's consider three other sources of language variation: gender, socioeconomic status, and hearing ability.

Gender Differences in Language

Within any one community, girls learn nearly the same syntax boys do, but they acquire very different pragmatics, or discourse patterns. On the whole, the differences reflect society's gender stereotypes. For example, girls phrase requests indirectly more often than boys do; girls more often say, "Could you give that to me?" instead of "Give me that." Also, they more frequently expand on comments made by others rather than initiating their own. These differences appear especially in mixed-gender groups and are noticeable not only in adults but in children as soon as they are old enough to engage in conversation (Coates, 1993).

The sexes reinforce their language differences with certain nonverbal gestures and mannerisms. Girls and women tend to maintain more eye contact than boys and men do; they blink their eyelids at more irregular intervals and tend to nod their heads as they listen (Arliss, 1991). Boys and men use eye contact a good deal less in ordinary conversation, blink at regular intervals, and rarely nod their heads when listening.

Gender differences in discourse patterns may contribute to gender segregation: members of each sex may feel that members of the other sex do not really understand them, that they do not "speak the same language." Boys and girls therefore begin drifting apart during the preschool years almost as soon as they begin using language (Ramsey, 1995) and as a partial result of acquiring language. The emerging segregation, in turn, reinforces gender differences in language patterns (Fagot, 1994). Boys reinforce one another for their assertive discourse style, and girls and their (mostly female) teachers reinforce one another for their "considerate" style. In the end, then, cognitive development supports social development, and social development supports cognitive development.

Socioeconomic Differences in Language

Most research has found low-SES children to be less verbal than middle- or high-SES children (Heath et al., 1991). In practice, this means low-SES children perform less well in verbal test situations, but outside of those situations their language differences are less clear-cut. These facts have created controversy about the importance of socioeconomic differences in language development.

What is the significance of socioeconomic differences in tests of language development? Some psychologists point out that most tests of language skills favor middle-SES versions of English in both vocabulary and style of *discourse,* or conversational patterns. This bias is due to the content selected for individual test questions and to the ways tests are normally conducted. A question on one of these tests might ask children to describe a dishwasher, but few low-SES families own this appliance. Other questions might draw on experiences that only middle-SES children usually enjoy, such as trips on airplanes or visits to museums.

Sign language has the qualities of oral language, including grammar, subtlety, and expressiveness. This mother and child are communicating about the child's day at nursery school. Unfortunately in hearing communities (such as classrooms), it can be hard to appreciate the capacities of sign language.

Perhaps most important, middle-SES families use styles of discourse that include many "test" questions or questions to which parents already know the answers. At the dinner table, parents may ask their preschooler, "What letter does your name begin with?" even though they already know the answer and their child knows that they know. Exchanges such as these probably prepare young children for similar exchanges on genuine tests by making testing situations seem more natural and homelike.

In contrast, low-SES children more often lack prior experience with "test" question exchanges. They can give relatively elaborate answers to true questions such as "What did you do yesterday morning?" when the adult really does not know the answer. But they tend to fall silent when they suspect the adult already can answer the question (for example, "What are the names of the days of the week?"). Their silence is unfortunate, because rhetorical, or "test," questions become especially common when preschoolers enter school and because active participation in questioning and answering helps preschoolers' learning substantially.

Language of Deaf and Hearing-Impaired Children

Children with hearing impairments often do not develop oral language skills as fully as other children do, but they are quite capable of acquiring a language of gestures called **American Sign Language (ASL)**. In fact, language development in ASL children provides much of the reason for considering ASL a true language, one as useful for communication as any verbal language, such as English.

How can this be so? Signing consists of subtle gestures of the fingers and hands made near the face. In general, each gesture functions like a morpheme. For example, holding the fingers together gently (which signers call a "tapered *O*") can mean either *home* or *flower,* depending on whether it is placed near the cheek or under the nose. Other sign-morphemes affect the syntax of expressions: gestural equiva-

Carolyn Eaton, PRESCHOOL TEACHER

Introducing Sign Language to Young Children

Carolyn Eaton teaches in a nursery school that serves only children who are deaf or who have moderate or severe hearing impairment. Everyone in the school communicates in American Sign Language (ASL): teachers, the children themselves, and (as much as possible) the parents. When they start the program, the children and parents often know very little ASL. How do they acquire this new language? Carolyn talked about some of the ways.

Carolyn: In a lot of ways the program really looks like any other nursery program, though maybe one with a lot of language emphasis. We always have a theme for the week. That's how we organize the vocabulary, the signs.

Kelvin: Can you give an example of a theme?

Carolyn: Last week's theme was "The Three Little Pigs." I told the story in ASL and read a picture book—one of the children had to hold it because I needed two hands to sign with. I emphasized key signs, like the ones for *pig* and *three* and the signs for *brick,* and *straw,* and *house.* I invited the children to make those signs with me when I came to them in the story.

Kelvin: Do you do other things related to the week's theme?

Carolyn: We'd have other conversations—in ASL, of course—about pigs and animals. And about trusting strangers, for that matter—that's in that story too! We might act out the story at some point, with signs instead of words. It depends partly on the vocabulary and fluency of the children.

Kelvin: Is it harder to understand preschoolers' signing than adults'?

Carolyn: It varies with the child, just like oral language. Most three- and four-year-olds tend to use less complex sign vocabulary and simpler expressions than adults. I found it hard at first to simplify my signing appropriately, the way you simplify oral language for young hearing children. There's a signing equivalent of "motherese" that you have to learn, or you won't be understood.

Kelvin: I noticed a parent today in the class signing to the kids. Does that happen a lot?

Carolyn: We have a parent volunteer just about every day. Since not all parents can volunteer, we have the kids take home a page each day that describes what's going on in the class and shows drawings of the signs we're currently emphasizing. We encourage the parents to learn them and use them at home. We also run two signing classes for the families of the preschoolers to help them communicate with their signing child.

Kelvin: Is it hard for them to learn?

Carolyn: Like everything else, people vary a lot. Some start learning immediately as soon as they learn that their child will always be deaf, and they're fluent by the time the child is a toddler. Others still haven't learned by the time the child is in grade school.

Personally, I think it has a lot to do with how accepting the parents are of the child's hearing impairment. If they're still grieving over the child's loss, they make less progress at ASL.

Kelvin: Your program does seem language oriented—ASL oriented that is.

Carolyn: It really is, though we also deal with all the other stuff that happens to children—friendships among peers, for example. Did you see that argument between two kids that was going on just as you were arriving today?

Kelvin: It looked fierce, judging by the children's faces. What was it about?

Carolyn: Well, Billy wrecked a roadway that two other kids had made in the sand table. They were upset, signed Billy to get lost, and that got Billy upset. That's when I stepped in.

Kelvin: I noticed how intently you were looking at Billy when you gave him a "talking to."

Carolyn: I sure was—but in all ASL conversations, not just scoldings, you have to look to see the signs. You get good at reading people's moods that way too, especially if you learn signing as early as these children did.

What Do You Think?

1. Judging by Carolyn's comments, how does the acquisition of ASL resemble the acquisition of oral language? How does it differ?

2. Among speech-language pathologists and deaf people generally, there has been heated debate about whether to emphasize ASL experiences, even if they sometimes segregate children from the hearing community, or to emphasize oral language experiences, even if hearing-impaired children have trouble acquiring them. How might you decide between these alternatives? Compare your thoughts on this issue with one or two classmates' thoughts.

lents of *-ing* and *-ed.* Individual signs are linked according to syntactic rules, just as in English. After some practice, signers can "speak" (or gesture) as quickly and effortlessly as people who use English can.

What happens to infants and young children with hearing impairments who grow up learning ASL from their parents as their first language? Studies show they experience the same steps in signing development that speaking children do in language development. At about the age when infants babble, signing children begin "babbling" with their hands, making gestures that strongly resemble genuine ASL signs but that signers recognize as gestural "nonsense" (Marschark, 1993). As with verbal babbling, signing infants apparently engage in gestural babbles playfully when waking up in the morning or going to sleep at night.

When signing infants reach ages two and three, they experience a phase of one-word signing similar to the holophrases often observed among speaking children. They also experience two-word, telegraphic signing. As with speech, their signs at this point often omit important syntactic gestures and do not follow the usual conventions of word order (or, in this case, signing order) (Bellugi et al., 1993). Signing vocabulary increases rapidly during the early preschool period, in amounts comparable to the increases speaking children experience. Even the kinds of words acquired parallel those speaking children acquire; signing preschoolers tend to learn signs for dynamic, moving objects first, as is true for speaking children. The interview with preschool teacher Carolyn Eaton describes some of these developments.

Still another reason to consider ASL a true language comes from observations of hearing preschoolers whose parents purposely used both English and ASL during the period when the children normally acquired language (Prinz & Prinz, 1979). During their preschool years, these children became thoroughly bilingual, using ASL and English interchangeably. Especially significant, however, were their patterns of language development, which essentially paralleled those shown by conventionally bilingual children. A clear example concerned vocabulary. Like verbal bilinguals, these children first acquired a single vocabulary that intermingled elements from both ASL and English but included few direct translations. If a child understood and used the sign for "tree," she or he would be unlikely to understand and use the spoken word *tree*. The children eventually acquired translations and thus finally possessed duplicate vocabularies. But acquiring duplicate terms took several years, just as it does with verbally bilingual children.

What Do You Think?

How do you think early childhood teachers should respond to language variety in preschoolers? Should they encourage it, discourage it, or simply accept it? This is an important issue in education and would make for a lively debate in class!

EARLY CHILDHOOD EDUCATION

Developing cognitive skills influence an important experience for many preschool children: early childhood education. Programs for three- and four-year-olds take many forms. Look at these experiences:

- Juan goes to *family day care* for three full days each week. His care occurs in his caregiver's home, with only four other children.

- Denzel goes to a *child care center* full time, five days a week. The center consists of two rooms modified from a church basement. About twenty children attend the center and are cared for by four adults.

- Cary goes to a part-time *nursery school* four mornings per week. There are twelve children and two adults.

Early Education and Cognitive Theories of Development

Despite the diversity these examples imply, high-quality early education programs are usually based on some sort of developmental perspective. Some programs draw heavily on Piaget's ideas about cognitive development (Demetriou & Shayer, 1992). They provide sensorimotor activities, such as sand and water play, as a basis for fostering preoperational activities such as make-believe play. Other programs organize cognitive activities around structured materials, which teachers guide children to use in particular ways. Nurseries and centers inspired by Maria Montessori (Montessori, 1964; Cuffaro, 1991) give children sets of cylinders graded by size and designed to fit snugly into a set of size-graded holes in a board. A child experiments with the cylinders and holes to discover the best way to fit them.

Still other early education programs borrow from Vygotsky's views of cognition as originating in social and cultural activities. These programs emphasize cooperative problem-solving activities and *emergent literacy*, a way of introducing reading and writing by situating it in everyday, valued experiences (Morrow, 1993). For example, instead of teaching children to recognize letters or familiar words at a special time each day, the early childhood teacher might simply provide a classroom rich in print materials and encourage children to come to him with words or letters that they themselves want to learn.

Effectiveness of Early Childhood Education

Evaluations of early childhood programs suggest that a wide range of approaches, including those just mentioned, are about equally effective in promoting overall cognitive growth, although the choice of curriculum does seem to influence the *pattern* of skills children acquire (Schweinhart et al., 1993).

Three factors seem to underlie successful early childhood programs, whatever their format and curriculum. First, the staff of successful programs regard themselves as competent observers of children's educational needs and as being capable of making important decisions in tailoring a curriculum to particular children (Hills, 1992). Second, the vast majority of successful programs and teachers view an early childhood curriculum as an integrated whole rather than consisting of independent subject areas or skills (Bredekamp & Rosegrant, 1992). Singing a song, for example, is not just "music"; it also fosters language development, motor skills (if the children dance along), arithmetic (through counting and rhythm), and social studies (if the words are about people and life in the community).

Third, successful early childhood programs involve parents, either directly as volunteers in the classroom or indirectly as advisers on governing boards, in certain school activities, or in additional services that support families. The federally sponsored program of early education called *Head Start,* for example, owes much of its effectiveness to parent involvement (U.S. Department of Health and Human Services, 1994). To get federal funding, local centers are required to create parent advisory boards to guide policy and practice at the centers. They are also encouraged to provide other family support services, such as parent support groups and dental screening for children.

Cultural Diversity and Best Practice in Early Education

A careful look at successful programs for young children raises an important question: are there "best" ways to support children's learning despite the cultural and individual diversity among children? A major professional association for early childhood education, the National Association for the Education of Young Children (NAEYC), argues that there are and has described its recommendations in detail in an influential book called *Developmentally Appropriate Practice: Birth to Age Eight* (Bredekamp, 1987; Kostelnik, 1992). **Developmentally appropriate practices** are ways of assisting children's learning that are consistent with children's developmental needs and abilities. Table 6.5 lists a few of the practices recommended by the NAEYC as they relate to the preschool years.

The NAEYC recommendations seem reasonable in many ways. Who can object, for example, to providing children with choices for their preschool play or to supporting their dialogues and initiatives with comments from the teacher or caregiver? Yet cross-cultural comparisons of early childhood programs complicate the picture

TABLE 6.5 *Developmentally Appropriate Practices with Preschoolers*

Principle	Examples
Caregivers provide ample space for active play	Program has access to outdoor space or gymnasium with climbing apparatus, tricycles, etc.
Caregivers allow children choices in activities	Classroom has several learning centers: dramatic play (dress-up), block building, books and reading area, art area, etc.
Caregivers provide long periods of uninterrupted time	Group transitions (e.g., from indoor to outdoor activities) are kept to a minimum; activities tend to begin and end individually
Activities and materials are relevant to children's experiences	Books are gender fair and culture fair; relevant cultural holidays are noted and celebrated through appropriate activities in class
Caregivers ensure that the environment is safe and free of hazards	Climbing apparatus has soft mats underneath (if indoors) or soft sand (if outdoors); furniture is sturdy; sharp objects (knives, scissors) are supervised carefully when used

Source: Adapted from Bredekamp (1987).

somewhat by revealing that some practices in early education in North America are really culture bound rather than universally beneficial to children.

In Japan, for example, early childhood programs are more likely to value large-group activities (such as singing or putting on a skit) in the belief that such activities develop commitment to the child's community—in this case, the community of the classroom (Kotloff, 1993). The time given to large-group activities, however, would probably seem excessive to some preschool educators in North America, where the development of individual initiative is more highly valued.

In Italy, early childhood programs emphasize involvement of parents much more heavily than do most North American programs. They also place children in permanent groups from their entrance at age three until they leave the program for public school at age six. Unlike in North America, little effort is needed to maintain and justify these practices, because Italian culture already supports them: women

Early childhood programs often serve children from differing cultural backgrounds. The diversity can be enriching if caregivers encourage cooperative activities, like the game these two children are playing, and if caregivers include stories, activities, and information that recognize and respect children's cultural differences.

(but not men) are expected to avoid paid employment and form extended social networks of support with other relatives, with one another, and (in this case) with their children's teachers (Edwards et al., 1993).

These comparisons suggest that the best practices in early education may need to take account of cultural differences and values regarding children's development (Mallory & New, 1994). For programs in ethnically diverse societies such as the United States, this means more than including songs and brief mentions of the holidays of various cultural groups. The central values and attitudes of cultural groups served by a particular center or nursery school must find their way into the daily activities of the program. Particular centers will therefore experience cultural diversity in different ways:

- A program serving a rural community of Amish or Hutterite children will need to take seriously the value of learning outdoors from the natural environment, sometimes even in the winter (Wardle, 1995).

- A program serving urban Appalachian children in northern schools will have to recognize and honor the importance of religion in the lives of many Appalachian families, even if these families now live in a much more secular, urban environment (Klein, 1995).

- A program serving Native American children in the Northwest will need to recognize the importance of cooperation to many of these children and their families and their aversion to individual striving to "better" oneself (Soldier, 1993).

As the accompanying Multicultural View box shows, in these culturally diverse programs cognition, or thinking, itself can take on diverse meanings. Educators who work with young children therefore need to do more than understand preschool cognition: they also need to explore how it might be understood and used by particular children and communities with specific social relationships and values. The next chapter turns to these important topics.

What Do You Think?

Is early childhood education a "social" or a "cognitive" activity? Decide what you think about this question. Then, if you can, talk about it with one or two experienced teachers of young children. How does your opinion compare to theirs?

FROM PRESCHOOLER TO CHILD

The physical and cognitive changes of early childhood create new relationships with parents and other caregivers. Due to preschoolers' physical developments, adults can begin encouraging new skills in the young child more actively and with more focus than before. Adults may find such teaching and learning easier because they no longer have to monitor the child's every fundamental physical action. A few years before, one false step might have made a young child fall. But now this term has a metaphorical meaning; false steps for a five-year-old now may mean mistakes rather than actual physical mishaps.

Because of preschoolers' cognitive development, adults can now sense even more personality in the child than previously. In the preschool years conversations become possible; moods can be expressed verbally rather than only through bodily gestures and facial expressions; a child's preferences and activities become increasingly clear. These changes set the stage for the psychosocial developments described in the next chapter. And, as we will see when we look at psychosocial development in young adulthood in Chapter 13, they simultaneously trigger parents' reexaminations of their own values, emotions, and identities.

A Multicultural View

Parents' Beliefs about Intelligence: A Cross-cultural Perspective

In our society, parents mean particular things when they refer to children's *intelligence:* they are usually talking about a child's verbal skills and reasoning abilities, especially as they occur in school or school-like tasks. This view of intelligence is so deeply grounded in our culture that an entire psychological field has developed to measure it, complete with standardized "intelligence" tests and experts to help teachers and parents interpret the tests.

But not all societies think of intelligence in this way. The Kipsigis in East Africa frame the idea of intelligence rather differently, placing it more explicitly in its social context (Harkness & Super, 1992). They speak of a child being *ng'om,* meaning not only verbally skilled and sociable but also responsible to others. A child who is *ng'om* is quick to learn household tasks, for example, but also reliable about doing them without being reminded. The Kipsigis recognize, in principle, that a child can have verbal skill in the abstract. In practice, however, they regard such an isolated or abstract skill as a unique ability that requires a special term to describe it: *ng'om en sukul,* or "smart in school." Furthermore, *ng'om* is a quality shown

only by preschoolers; neither an infant nor an adult can be *ng'om,* since she or he is not expected to be responsible to others in the same way preschoolers are.

Such a socially embedded notion of intelligence differs radically from the usual North American idea. In our society, parents are likely to distinguish clearly between a child's sense of responsibility to others and his or her intelligence (Goodnow, 1996). They may consider the former desirable but not an intrinsic part of intelligence as such. When interviewed about the qualities shown by preschoolers, parents of preschoolers tend to name relatively "cognitive" features: an intelligent child is inquisitive, curious, imaginative, self-reliant, and able to play independently (Harkness & Super, 1992). These features of intelligence take individual autonomy for granted rather than social harmony: being intelligent is something you do by or on behalf of yourself, not with or on behalf of others.

These cultural differences begin to make sense if we consider the settings in which Kipsigis and North American parents and preschoolers live. A Kipsigis preschooler

SUMMARY OF MAJOR IDEAS

PHYSICAL DEVELOPMENT

Influences on Normal Physical Development

1. Between ages two and five, growth slows down and children take on more adultlike bodily proportions.

2. Usually growth is rather smooth during the preschool period, though genetic, social, and nutritional differences can affect growth to some extent.

3. Children's appetites are often smaller in the preschool years than in infancy, and children become more selective about their food preferences.

The Connection Between Health and Poverty

4. Although high-SES preschoolers tend to be very healthy, a substantial percentage of preschoolers live in poverty and consequently lack adequate health care.

Bladder and Bowel Control

5. Children tend to achieve daytime bladder and bowel control early in the preschool period and nighttime bladder control late in this period.

Motor Skill Development

6. Preschoolers acquire and refine many fundamental motor skills, including walking, jumping, throwing, and catching.

7. Fine motor skills such as drawing also emerge during the preschool years, progressing from prerepresentational to representational drawings.

Effects of Children's Growth on Adults

8. Preschoolers' facial features and changing size and motor skills influence parents' responses and methods of child-rearing to some extent.

COGNITIVE DEVELOPMENT

Thinking in Preschoolers

9. The preoperational stage of thinking, defined by Piaget, is characterized by increased symbolic thinking and new knowledge of identities and functional relationships.

10. Children's new reliance on symbolic thought helps them recall experiences, solve problems more effectively, and communicate with others about their experiences.

11. Preschool children can classify objects accurately as long as the system or criteria for classifying are relatively simple.

12. At age three preschoolers have some knowledge of how the number system works, but they do not achieve full understanding until about age four or five.

13. Preschoolers often cannot solve problems that require reversible thinking, such as the classic Piagetian tasks of conservation.

14. Neostructuralist theories of cognitive development use Piaget's belief in stages but focus on relatively specific cognitive skills of the child.

typically is part of an extended family. There are likely to be children of all ages close at hand, related to one another in largely complex ways; older children typically care for younger children from an early age; and children's chores are likely to take on "real" economic importance as children get older. Such a setting seems sure to reward children for showing responsibility to others.

In our own society, a preschooler is likely to live with a small family; relatively few or even no immediate relatives may be close at hand; parents expect that school will figure prominently in the preschooler's future; and parents themselves (including mothers) are likely to be working for a living. This sort of setting favors children who can "teach themselves" to a certain extent, that is, play with and learn from materials on their own. It also favors children who orient themselves toward school-like activities—toward number and memory games, for example, and books and letters. An "intelligent" child is one who can do these things, which have much less to do with responsibility to others than is the case for a Kipsigis child (Harkness et al., 1992). Cultural differences such as these can pose problems for many preschoolers in our

own society when they finally enter school. Historically, modern schooling has encouraged the culturally conventional definitions of intelligence as individual activity and those of cognitive activity as separate from the daily needs of the community. Students generally "do their own work" and focus on tasks (such as a set of math problems) that are created specially for school settings.

When these assumptions do not fit the cultural expectations of particular children or their families, however, teachers are challenged to modify them. Teachers must then find other ways for children to "be intelligent"—ways that involve greater responsibility to others, for example, and greater concern for the real needs of the child's community. Though it takes effort, there are ways to accomplish these changes in teaching philosophy; some of these changes are discussed in Chapter 8.

Language Acquisition in the Preschool Years

15. During the preschool years, children make major strides in acquiring the syntax, or grammar, of their native language.

16. Young children's first word combinations are related by semantics and omit syntactic relationships.

17. One important syntactic error of preschool children is overgeneralization.

18. Although preschoolers learn a great deal of language through the process of inference, they also learn some language by rote.

19. Infants and preschoolers are reinforced, though only indirectly, for using correct syntax in their earliest utterances.

20. Children probably acquire some syntax through imitation and practice of language models.

21. The ease of language acquisition and the poverty of the content of speech that infants hear may mean children possess an innate language acquisition device, or LAD.

22. Parents probably assist children's language acquisition by recasting the children's own utterances, providing scaffolding that supports children's language efforts, and using a special style of talk called *infant-directed speech*.

Language Variations

23. Language varies between girls and boys in ways that support gender stereotypes.

24. Language varies according to socioeconomic class in ways that prepare middle-SES children better than low-SES children for school settings.

25. Children who are deaf or hearing impaired often learn American Sign Language, which has all of the properties of an oral language.

Early Childhood Education

26. Early childhood education programs come in a variety of forms, many of which have been influenced by theories of cognitive development.

27. Three factors characterize successful programs in early education: a staff oriented to observing the children, an integrated view of the curriculum, and significant involvement of parents in the program.

28. Cultural diversity challenges early childhood educators to identify teaching practices that are not only developmentally appropriate but also culturally appropriate.

KEY TERMS

failure to thrive *(186)*
fine motor
   coordination *(191)*
symbolic thought *(198)*
egocentrism *(198*
classification *(200)*
reversibility *(200)*
conservation *(200)*
zone of proximal
   development (ZPD) *(202)*

neostructuralist
   theory *(203)*
syntax *(204)*
telegraphic speech *(206)*
overgeneralization *(206)*
infant-directed speech *(210)*
American Sign Language
   (ASL) *(212)*
developmentally appropriate
   practices *(215)*

7

EARLY CHILDHOOD

Psychosocial Development

When Melissa was two, she would crouch down on the floor with her rear end sticking out in imitation of the prominent haunches of Tigger, the family cat. From time to time, she made a noise sort of like a cat's meow. Keeping her head low, she looked around carefully for acknowledgment from her parents. Occasionally she walked like a cat, although her walk looked more like a rabbit's hopping. Tigger himself was not impressed by all of this.

Melissa's skills as a performer and her active awareness of her audience illustrate an important milestone during the early childhood years: the development of psychological and social skills. During early childhood, many activities and events that occupy a child's waking hours involve social interaction with other people. These others include parents and siblings, as well as friends and acquaintances in the neighborhood and community. The social skills and unique personality a preschool child develops are largely a result of social interactions within and outside his or her family.

In this chapter, we first look at three areas of psychosocial development: play, relationships with others, and gender roles. We conclude by examining the tragic problem of child abuse and neglect.

Focusing Questions

• What important developmental achievements occur during early childhood?

• What distinguishes play from other activities, and why is play so important in preschoolers' development?

• What types of play occur among preschoolers? What changes are observed as they approach school age?

• How do different styles of parenting influence preschoolers' relationships with their peers?

• How do preschoolers handle conflicts with their peers?

• How does a young child's understanding of gender change during the preschool years? What are some of the important factors that influence a child's flexibility about gender role stereotypes?

• What appear to be the main factors that contribute to child abuse and neglect? What are the consequences of maltreatment?

PLAY IN EARLY CHILDHOOD

In our society and many others, play dominates the preschool years. Every child plays, it seems, and virtually all observers of young children see lots of examples of play. What are the play activities of a preschooler like, and what important contributions does play make to a child's development? Before we tackle these questions, we must first agree on what we mean by *play*.

The Nature of Play

One useful approach to defining *play* focuses on the attitudes and dispositions of children themselves (Rubin et al., 1983). First, play is *intrinsically* (rather than *extrinsically*) motivated. Children engage in play mainly because it is enjoyable and reinforcing for its own sake rather than because it is useful in achieving external goals.

Second, play is *process* oriented rather than *product* oriented. At the local playground, for instance, children may care very little about the goal of using the slide, to get from top to bottom, but likely care a lot about their style of sliding—whether they go head first or feet first, or how fast they go.

221

In early childhood, the process of doing things often matters more than the outcome. Even taking a bath can seem like play.

Third, play is *creative* and *nonliteral*. Although it resembles real-life activities, it differs from them in that it is not bound by reality. For example, a child who is "play fighting" looks different than one who really is fighting, and a child playing Mommy typically acts differently than one who is actually caring for a baby brother or sister. The features that reveal an activity as play rather than the real thing vary with the particular type of play and the situation; a play fight may include smiles and laughter, and a make-believe mother may be overly bossy. Whatever the signs, they communicate the message that "this behavior is *not* what it first may appear to be." Even so, it is common for a preschooler to become so caught up in a round of dramatic play that he forgets for a moment that it is not real and becomes truly frightened when his make-believe mother tells him he has been bad and must sit in the corner.

Fourth, play tends to be governed by *implicit rules,* that is, rules that can be discovered by observing the activity rather than rules that are formally stated and exist independently of the activity. For example, although no rule book exists for playing house, children implicitly understand that there can be only one mother and one father and that these actors must live up to certain expectations. If one player deviates too widely from the expected role, the other children are likely to correct her for it ("Hey, mommies don't suck on baby bottles; only babies do!").

Fifth, play is *spontaneous* and *self-initiated,* meaning it is engaged in only under a child's own free will and is not evoked or controlled by others.

Finally, play is *free from major emotional distress*. Play does not normally occur when a child is in a state of fear, uncertainty, or other kind of significant stress.

Theories of Play

There are three main theoretical approaches to play: psychoanalytic, learning, and cognitive. Although each theory emphasizes a somewhat different aspect of play, all hold that play activities make a major contribution to the development of important social and emotional skills and understandings during the preschool years.

Psychoanalytic Theory   Psychoanalytic theories emphasize the social and emotional importance of play in early childhood. Play gives a child an opportunity to *gain mastery* over problems by rearranging objects and social situations in ways that allow her to imagine she is in control. Following an especially painful and up-setting experience such as being suddenly separated from a parent who is hospitalized for a serious illness, a child may display *repetition compulsion,* repeating the experience over and over in her symbolic play with dolls or other toys to gain greater control, or resolution, of her distress.

Play also allows a child to use fantasy to *gain satisfaction for wishes and desires* that are not possible to fulfill in reality due to limitations in the child's abilities and life situation. Play also provides an opportunity for *catharsis,* the release of upsetting feelings that cannot be expressed otherwise. Finally, play allows a child to *gain increased power* over the environment by rearranging it to suit his own needs and abilities (J. Lewis, 1993).

Learning Theory   Learning theorists view play as a major means by which children progressively learn adult skills and social roles. A child learns in three ways: through his own experience of being praised or encouraged for his own actions (direct reinforcement), through observations of adults and other children being reinforced for their activities (vicarious reinforcement), and through the experience of setting a goal and achieving it (cognitive or self-reinforcement).

For example, what might a three-year-old who is playing with wooden blocks be learning about the adult world? For one thing, building with blocks gives the child an opportunity to learn about the nature and design of physical structures and space. The child also learns about how hard blocks are, how high they can be piled, and how many small ones equal a larger one. He might also learn about his own capabilities and limitations as a builder: how high he can reach, how many blocks he can carry at once, and so forth.

Playing with blocks also exposes the child to adult expectations and practices, such as when and where blocks can be used, picked up, and stored and how to share blocks, take turns, and cooperate with others.

Cognitive Theory   Cognitive theorists, discussed in Chapter 2, have identified four major kinds of play that they believe develop sequentially in parallel with the major stages of cognitive development (Piaget, 1962; Smilansky, 1968). Table 7.1 describes the different types of cognitive play.

Cognitive Levels of Play: Developmental Trends

Functional Play   **Functional play,** which involves simple, repeated movements such as splashing water or digging in a sandbox, is most common during the sensorimotor period. Because it requires no symbolic activity, functional play makes up more than one-half of the play activity of older infants and toddlers. By the time a child reaches kindergarten or first grade, however, functional play has decreased to

TABLE 7.1 *Types of Cognitive Play*

Type	Description and Examples
Functional play	Simple, repetitive movements, sometimes with objects or own body. Example: shoveling sand; pushing a toy
Constructive play	Manipulation of physical objects to build or construct something. Example: building with blocks
Pretend play	Substitutes make-believe, imaginary, and dramatic situations for real ones. Example: playing house or Superman
Games with rules (age 5 or 6)	Play is more formal and governed by fixed rules. Example: jumping rope; hide-and-seek

Constructive play, such as block building, is probably the most common form of play in early childhood.

less than one-quarter of her total play time. This shift occurs partly because some of the physical activities typical of functional play become incorporated into more symbolic forms of play (Hetherington et al., 1979; Sponseller & Jaworski, 1979).

Constructive Play   **Constructive play** involves manipulation of physical objects, such as using blocks to build or construct something. This form of play is evident in older infants and preschoolers, although it is not always clear where functional play ends and constructive play begins. For example, a child who at first appears to be building a mountain out of sand may forget about her goal and end up just shoveling the sand for the fun of it. As the child grows older, however, the constructive elements of play become quite clear. Not only does she build a mountain; she builds it in a certain shape and adds a road leading to it and perhaps a car or two to make the trip.

Pretend Play   **Pretend play** (also called *fantasy* or *dramatic play*) substitutes imaginary situations for real ones, such as in playing house or Superman, and dominates the preoperational period. Pretend play occurs even among toddlers and probably begins as soon as a child can symbolize, or mentally represent, objects. Family roles (including mother, father, brother, sister, baby, and even family pet) and *character roles* based on fictionalized heros such as Batman, Ninja Turtles, and Power Rangers are most likely to be dramatized by preschool children. Pretend play grows in frequency and complexity during the preschool years and eventually decreases again later in childhood, when social pressures to act more "grown up" reduce it in public settings {Dunn, 1985; Howes & Matheson, 1992; Lytinen, 1991; Rubin & Krasnor, 1980). The complexity, flexibility, and elaborateness of preschoolers' fan-

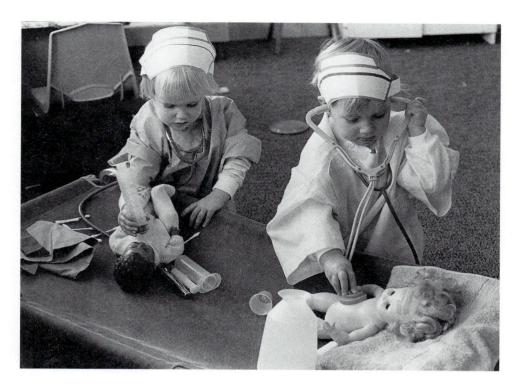

In dramatic play, children take on pretend roles, like the two "nurses" here. Realistic props, such as the uniforms, stethoscopes, and bottles in this photograph, encourage dramatic play, but they are not always necessary.

tasy play also appear to be positively related to both the support and the nurturance preschoolers receive from their parents, as well as to the specific reinforcement parents give them for such play (Ladd & Hart, 1992).

Pretend play is a good example of how new forms of experience are assimilated into existing schemes of cognitive understanding. In addition to allowing the child to practice and expand schemes already acquired, such play contributes to the consolidation and expansion of cognitive skills during the early childhood years (Piaget, 1962; Vygotsky, 1967).

Games with Rules   Games with rules, such as Simon Says and hide-and-seek, first appear during the concrete operational period, when children are five or six years old, and peak in frequency toward the end of elementary school (Eifermann, 1971; Rubin & Krasnor, 1980). Piaget (1964), in fact, did his original studies of moral development by interviewing and observing children playing rule-based games. The rules for many such games apparently develop out of the more flexible, "made-up" rules of pretend play. Instead of continuing to negotiate roles and behaviors as they go along, young children gradually learn to agree on them beforehand and to stand by their agreements throughout a play episode. Due to their greater formality, games with rules can become traditions handed down from one sibling to another, from older to younger playmates, and from generation to generation. Hopscotch, for example, has been around in some form for many generations (Opie & Opie, 1969).

Social Levels of Play

Play also varies according to how social it is, that is, how much and in what ways children involve others in their play activities. Several decades ago, Mildred Parten studied social participation among children ages two to five and proposed that children's play develops in six stages, or levels, of sociability (Parten, 1932). Although subsequent researchers have questioned whether Parten's categories actually form a developmental sequence, her distinctions continue to be useful to people who study young children. Table 7.2 describes the six types of play Parten identified.

TABLE 7.2   *Parten's Social Levels of Play*

Type	Description and Examples
Unoccupied play	The child wanders about, watching whatever is of momentary interest, but does not become involved in any activity
Solitary play	The child plays alone with different toys or other objects and with no direct or indirect awareness of or involvement with other children, even if nearby
Onlooker play	The child watches others play without actually entering into the activities; is clearly involved with what is happening and usually is within speaking distance of the participants
Parallel play	Involves two or more children playing with the same toys in a similar way, in close proximity and with an awareness of each other's presence; do not share toys, talk, or interact except in very minimal ways
Associative play	Children engage in a common activity and talk about it with each other, but do not assign tasks or roles to particular individuals and are not very clear about their goals
Cooperative play	Children consciously form into groups to make something, attain a goal, or dramatize a situation; one or two members organize and direct the activity, with children assuming different roles and responsibilities

Source: Parten (1932).

Changes with Age   As we saw in Chapter 5's discussion of psychosocial development during infancy, even very young infants actively interact with the objects and people in their environment, and by twelve months their play interactions with peers become more frequent, particularly those that involve toys. Access to peers through play groups or day care and parental support tend to increase the likelihood of peer play.

Mildred Parten (1932) found that parallel play accounted for almost half of early childhood play activity, whereas solitary play occupied about one-fourth, associative play one-fifth, and cooperative and unoccupied play less than one-tenth of the total. Parallel and solitary play appeared to decline throughout the preschool years, whereas associative play and cooperative play, which involve greater social participation, increased with age.

These children are involved in parallel play. They are probably aware of each other's presence, but they are using separate toys and are preoccupied primarily with their own activities.

Working with Javier Hernandez, PRESCHOOL PROGRAM COORDINATOR

Play and Friendships Among Preschoolers

Javier Hernandez coordinates a privately run preschool program that serves a middle- and working-class community. A parent himself, he has a degree in early childhood education and has worked in preschool and day care programs for almost six years. Javier was interviewed during nap time in the day care center office and talked about ways in which children's playing styles evolve over time.

Rob: Your program serves a pretty wide age range. Do you see the kids' play change as they grow older?

Javier: Yes, I do. Most of the two-year-olds' play involves sharing toys and turn taking—"it's my turn, it's your turn." They might share building blocks or share crayons when they draw. They can follow simple directions, like for circle time at the beginning and end of the day and for various other activities.

Rob: How do three-year-olds play differently?

Javier: Between 3 and 3½, you see an amazing increase in dramatic and fantasy play. The games become more complex and are rarely what they appear to be. The two-year-olds see the climber as just a climber, but the three-year-olds see it as a car, a spaceship, a house, or anything else they decide. The kids all make up different names and are deeply into imaginative role playing. They're always trying to involve you in their fantasy play.

Rob: What about rules?

Javier: They're very interested in rules—setting them and following them. They'll tell each other, "Oh, we can't do that now" or "We can't go that way" or "That's not the way we do it," or "You have to sit down." They're really into structure and delight in pointing out the right and wrong way

to do things. There's a lot of tattling; I'll frequently overhear "You're going to get in trouble if you do that" or "You can't walk up the slide."

Rob: This is quite different behavior than the two-year-olds.

Javier: Yes. The two-year-olds are more apt to hit or push another kid, who will cry until the teacher comes over. With three-year-olds, the one who gets hit or pushed cries, but goes and then tells the teacher, "He hit me" and watches to see what you're going to do about it.

Rob: So this also reflects the superior verbal and cognitive abilities of three-year-olds?

Javier: Yes. The two-year-olds do a lot of copycatting. What one wants, the other one wants, and they want everything to be the same. Their attention spans are much shorter, and they change their minds quickly. They often forget what they want, and you can never be sure just what they're after.

Rob: And the three-year-olds?

Javier: They have much longer attention spans. They'll get so involved in a story that they won't move a muscle. And you have to point out and explain every detail of every picture in the book.

Rob: You have to satisfy their desire to fully understand exactly what is going on?

Javier: Exactly. Two-year-olds will keep on saying *why* just for the sake of it. Three- and four-year-olds really want a solid answer and are generally satisfied once they hear one they like. They're really listening to what you're saying, whereas the two-year-olds are mainly practicing their verbal skills.

Rob: What about friendships and prosocial behavior among preschoolers?

Javier: If one two-year-old is aggressive toward another and you say, "That wasn't very nice, you hurt his feelings and I think you need to say you are sorry," she may go over to the child and say, "sorry," but five minutes later might do the same thing again. Three- and four-year-olds tend to be more aware of other children's feelings and of their own. They base their friendships on who is nice to them and are better able to appreciate how it feels to be hurt. If you say, "Well, would you like it if she did that to you?" they are likely to say, "No, I wouldn't like it."

Rob: Are they better able to take care of each other?

Javier: Yes. We have two children who started in the infant room and went all the way up to kindergarten together. By the last few months they were here, if Larry said anything to Jenelle that she was sensitive about, she would just fall apart because "He's my best friend." She would get very sad and look to us to help them make up and mend their friendship. Then Larry would apologize, and they would hug. Older preschoolers seem to know a lot about each other's personalities. They know what to expect of each other and are very aware of what other children are doing.

What Do You Think?

1. In what ways do Javier's examples of preschool play and peer interactions demonstrate the interplay of cognitive and social development?

2. In what ways do Javier's descriptions of preschool friendships parallel the discussion of preschool friendship and its management in the chapter?

As preschoolers get older, play involving coordinated interactions increases. These interactions include imitation; complementary exchanges in which playmates take different roles, such as driver or passenger in pretend play; and more complex combinations of imitation and complementary exchanges (Eckerman et al., 1989). Preschool children's highest level of peer social play also increases with age, progressing through a sequence of parallel play, simple social play, complementary and reciprocal play, cooperative social pretend play, and finally complex social pretend play. Children who spend more of their play time in complex forms of play appear to have greater overall social competence with their peers (Howes & Matheson, 1992). See the accompanying interview with Javier Hernandez for a discussion of play during the early childhood years.

Other Influences on Play

Setting   The composition of a particular child's play is also likely to be influenced by the range of play opportunities caregivers provide and the types of play they encourage. For example, a parent or caregiver who insists that the child always be learning something or trying something new may make play a stressful rather than a rewarding experience for the child. Outside the home, children who attend child care centers with qualified staffs, developmentally appropriate programs, and safe, well-designed, and well-equipped play areas have been found to develop more complex forms of pretend play at earlier ages, engage in much less unoccupied and solitary play, and interact more positively with adults than children in less adequate centers (Howes & Matheson, 1992; Susa & Benedict, 1994).

Having adequate time for play is also important. Large amounts of television viewing can reduce the amount of time available for play, and watching programs with high levels of violence has been associated with decreased levels of fantasy play (van-der-Voort & Valkenburg, 1994). We will take a closer look at the developmental effects of television later in this chapter.

Although play is a universal activity and occurs in all cultures, its frequency, forms, and functions also vary with cultural and socioeconomic contexts (Roopnarine et al., 1994). For example, in countries such as Kenya, India, Ecuador, and Brazil, where many children spend a large part of the day doing household chores and assisting their families in getting food or money, time and opportunity for play are far more limited than for children in Mexico, the Philippines, or the United States (Campos et al., 1994; A. Hoffnung, 1992; Whiting & Whiting, 1975).

Even when free time, space, and toys are limited, however, most children find a way to play. They use common household objects such as pots, pans, and furniture, as well as outdoor items such as trees, sticks, rocks, sand, empty cans, and discarded equipment, as props for their make-believe and sociodramatic play. However, the range and developmental appropriateness of play activities under such circumstances are likely to be more restricted than in the case of children who play in more supportive settings.

Table 7.3 summarizes age-appropriate recommendations for preschool play materials for children growing up in the United States. Readers may wish to compare these recommendations with those made for infants and toddlers in Chapter 5 (Table 5.4).

What Do You Think?

Many political leaders (and a significant number of parents who have voted for them) have criticized spending money on preschool programs in which children spend their time "playing" rather than learning important preschool skills. How would you respond to such critics regarding the importance of play for preschool children?

RELATIONSHIPS WITH OTHERS

As our discussion of play shows, young children spend a good deal of time relating to others. In this section we discuss children's relationships with parents, siblings,

TABLE 7.3 *General Characteristics and Appropriate Play Materials for the Preschool Child*

Age	General Characteristics	Appropriate Play Materials
2	Uses language effectively. Large-muscle skills developing, but limited in the use of small muscle skills. Energetic, vigorous, and enthusiastic, with a strong need to demonstrate independence and self-control.	Large-muscle play materials: Swing sets, outdoor blocks, toys to ride on, pull toys, push toys. Sensory play materials: Clay, fingerpaints, materials for water play, blocks, books, dolls and stuffed animals.
3	Expanded fantasy life, with unrealistic fears. Fascination with adult roles. Still stubborn, negative, but better able to adapt to peers than at age two. Early signs of product orientation in play.	Props for imaginative play (e.g., old clothes). Miniature life toys. Puzzles, simple board games, art materials that allow for a sense of accomplishment (e.g., paintbrushes, easels, marker pens, crayons).
4	Secure, self-confident. Need for adult attention and approval—showing off, clowning around, taking risks. More planful than threes, but products often accidental. Sophisticated small-muscle control allows for cutting, pasting, sewing, imaginative block building with smaller blocks.	Vehicles (e.g., tricycles, Big Wheels). Materials for painting, coloring, drawing, woodworking, sewing, stringing beads. Books with themes that extend well beyond the child's real world.
5	Early signs of logical thinking. Stable, predictable, reliable. Less self-centered than at four. Relaxed, friendly, willing to share and cooperate with peers. Realistic, practical, responsible.	Cut-and-paste and artistic activities with models to work from. Simple card games (e.g., Old Maid), table games (e.g., Bingo), and board games (e.g., Lotto), in which there are few rules and the outcomes are based more on chance than on strategy. Elaborate props for dramatic play.

Source: Fergus Hughes (1991), p. 70.

and friends. Then we examine the prosocial behavior and aggression interactions that typically occur during the early childhood years. Finally, we look at the effects of television on preschoolers and their relationships with others.

Relationships with Parents

During the preschool years, the attachment relationships between children and their parents and other caregivers discussed in Chapter 5 continue to play a central role in children's social and emotional development. However, young children's

All parents discipline their children sometimes. Their methods make a difference; calling attention to the consequences of misbehaving is generally more effective than spanking, at least in the long run.

expanding ability to initiate verbal and physical activity and their exploding powers of imagination can at times be a challenge to their parents. These changes require parents to support their preschoolers' efforts to take on the world while also appreciating young children's limitations and need for restraints that ensure their physical and emotional safety and protect their self-esteem. Preschoolers often test the limits their parents impose and are frequently inconsistent in their ability to understand and conform to parental wishes. At times they express their strong desire to control their environment by refusing to eat certain foods or wear certain clothing, or by insisting on playing the same game or having the same story read to them over and over again.

Understanding the need for family rules poses a challenge to preschoolers, but making them also creates a challenge for parents, at least those living in the individualistic culture of mainstream North America. In this society, unlike most others, parents are expected to devise their own standards for rearing children, largely independently of other families' standards or expectations—a kind of "private enterprise" system of childrearing. For instance, it is up to parents as individuals to decide how much anger their child should be allowed to express, how early and well she should learn manners, or how much candy she can eat. Parents' independence in deciding on these standards increases their power to shape their child's behavior in the short run. But it also increases their dilemma over which standards to choose, since they observe that other parents often make choices different than their own. These factors may help explain why community members are often reluctant to say something to someone else's child who misbehaves or to offer advice or assistance to a parent who might find it useful. And, as we will see in Chapter 12, the lack of clear standards for good parenting is precisely the kind of ambiguous role that creates stress during early adulthood.

Enforcing family rules may be less of a problem in cultures and societies that encourage less individualism and stronger, more prolonged interdependence among kin, community, or both. In Chinese American and Japanese American families, for example, grandparents and other relatives retain considerable prestige and influence in childrearing matters even after a couple has married and given birth to children (Chao, 1994; Huang & Ying, 1989; Nagata, 1989). Even as preschoolers, children are taught ways to show respect for their elders, such as caution in asking questions and readiness to obey orders. In such a situation, parents lose some decision-making authority to grandparents, in-laws, or "the community." But parents also gain family and community backing for their position: it is not just an adult or two, Mom and (sometimes) Dad, who decide whether talking in a loud voice is rude but an extended array of relatives and friends (Skolnick & Skolnick, 1989). See the accompanying Perspectives box for a discussion of extended family members' participation in childrearing.

Patterns of Parental Authority   One of the most important aspects of a parent-child relationship is the parent's style of authority. Observations of North American families of preschoolers suggest that childrearing styles can be classified into four groups: *authoritative, authoritarian, permissive-indulgent,* and *permissive-indifferent* (Baumrind, 1971, 1973; Darling & Steinberg, 1993; Maccoby & Martin, 1983). In most families, however, none of these styles exist in a "pure" form and parenting styles can change as children grow older and as other family changes occur. Table 7.4 summarizes the main patterns of parental authority.

Authoritative Parenting   **Authoritative** parents exert a high degree of control over their children and demand a lot of them, but they are also responsive, child centered, and respectful of their children's thoughts, feelings, and participation in decision making. For example, although it may be easier for a parent to respond to her child's request for help in building something or getting dressed by doing it for

Perspectives

Extended Family Supports for Childrearing

In American society in particular, parents are held, and hold themselves, responsible for the physical care of their children. Whether parents are rich or poor, Caucasian or African American, divorced or married, society expects them to provide food for their children as well as clothing and a place to sleep. In reality many families share these responsibilities with relatives, friends, and professionals of various kinds. In a typical week, a child may spend significant time not only with his biological parents but also with a grandparent, a neighbor, and (depending on the child's age) a teacher or day care center worker. The mixture of responsibility depends partly on the local circumstances of the particular family. It also reflects cultural and economic differences. Mexican American families, for example, value the participation of grandparents and other relatives in childrearing. Many nonwhite families report the participation in family life of *fictive kin,* neighbors or friends who develop a relationship with the family that closely resembles that of a blood relative (Ramirez, 1989). Though fictive kin are more common among ethnic and racial minorities, they are also an important part of the white experience, as we will see in Chapter 17.

These additional adults supplement what parents provide, often literally by providing alternative persons to cook meals and arrange other daily routines and by bolstering the psychological goals and emotional supports provided by the biological parents. A study of African American families confirmed this conclusion by investigating the emotional climate in two- and three-generational families (Tolson & Wilson, 1990). Interviews with all members of the families, including the children, found that three-generational families (those with a resi-

dent grandparent) saw themselves as organized more informally and spontaneously than two-generational (two-parent) families, which in turn saw themselves as organized more informally and spontaneously than one-parent families. In other words, the greater the number of parents (including a grandparent), the *fewer* the rules for children to follow and the *more* flexible the daily scheduling of activities, even though larger families had to coordinate the activities of more individuals. While this trend may seem contradictory, the family members themselves suggested the reason when interviewed: more adults in the house meant individual parents had more back-up support in carrying out their functions as parents and therefore needed to rely on preset procedures less heavily.

The benefits of back-up support are psychological as well as physical. The interviews just described also found that African American families with more than one parent placed significantly greater emphasis on moral and ethical issues and on determining how best to deal with both individual members and people outside the family (Tolson & Wilson, 1990). To achieve this benefit, however, it did not matter whether the second "parent" was a father; it occurred just as frequently when a mother and a grandmother were the resident parents. Other research, in fact, suggests that it may not even matter whether the additional parents live at home, as long as they participate actively in the life of the family. In another interview study, successful minority single parents reported developing and depending on networks of family and personal relationships (Lindblad-Goldberg, 1989). What mattered was not the form or pattern of the networks but their existence and importance in helping the parent carry out the roles of childrearing.

TABLE 7.4   Patterns of Parental Authority

Pattern	Control	Clarity of Communication	Maturity Demands	Nurturance
Authoritative	High	High	High	High
Authoritarian	High	Low	High	Low
Permissive-indulgent	Low	Mixed	Low	High
Permissive-indifferent	Low	Low	Low	Low

Authoritative parents display high levels of control, clarity of communication, demands for mature behavior, and nurturance. Authoritarian parents also show high levels of control and maturity demands but are low on clarity of communication and nurturance. Permissive-indulgent parents are low on control and maturity demands, high on nurturance, and inconsistent in how clearly they communicate with their children. Permissive-indifferent parents display low levels of all four dimensions.

him, an authoritative parent is likely to provide only the amount of help that will enable him to successfully accomplish the task himself. Such parents tend to be democratic and rational in their decision making and to respond to their children with warmth and empathy. When their children misbehave, these parents attempt to understand why and to explain the reasons for the restrictions or punishments that follow.

Preschoolers of authoritative parents tend to be self-reliant, self-controlled, and able to get along well with their adults and peers (C. Hart et al., 1992; Kuczynski & Kochanska, 1995; Pettit et al., 1988). For example, Leon Kuczynski and Grazyna Kochanska (1995) found that children who experienced authoritative childrearing as toddlers were more responsive to parental guidance and had fewer behavior problems at age five. In particular, the demands of these authoritative mothers emphasized competence, prosocial behavior, and positive actions ("Ask him to share"; "Pour the milk carefully"; "Put away your toys") rather than demands to inhibit behavior ("Don't hit"; "Don't spill the milk; "Don't leave a mess").

Authoritative parenting is also associated with high self-esteem, internalized moral standards, psychosocial maturity, autonomy, and academic success. In addition, it appears to foster relationships with peers and family that display the same qualities of warmth and respect for others during middle childhood, adolescence, and beyond (Baumrind, 1991a, 1991b; Darling & Steinberg, 1993; Franz et al., 1991). We will look at the relationship between authoritative parenting and prosocial behavior later in this chapter.

Authoritarian Parenting   **Authoritarian** parents also are demanding of their children and exert high control over them. However, they tend to be less warm and responsive than authoritative parents. They also tend to be arbitrary and undemocratic in decision making, imposing their rules or views on their children based on their own greater power and authority, with little sensitivity to their children's thoughts and feelings. Parent-child relationships that depend on arbitrary, "power-assertive" control and ignore children's feelings and need for independence often have a negative effect on children. Children of authoritarian parents tend to be relatively distrustful of others and unhappy with themselves and to have poorer peer relations, poorer school adjustment, and lower school achievement than do children with authoritative parents (C. Hart et al., 1990; Putallaz, 1987). We discuss the impact of authoritarian parenting on older children in Chapters 9 (middle childhood) and 11 (adolescence).

In the extreme, the combination of rigid and arbitrary power assertion and insensitivity to a child's thoughts and feelings can increase the likelihood of child maltreatment. By modeling disrespectful and insensitive behavior, such parenting can elicit and reinforce similar behavior in children and lead to escalating cycles of negative reinforcement and coercion (Patterson, 1982).

Authoritarian parenting is more frequent in large families and in working-class families (Greenberger et al., 1994), and fathers are more likely to be authoritarian than mothers. Authoritarian parenting is also more common in cultures in which family relations are hierarchically structured based on age, family role, and gender. Ruth Chao (1994) has questioned the validity of Western European concepts of authoritative and authoritarian parenting for Chinese families. Chinese childrearing is based on Confucian principles that require children to show loyalty to and respect for their elders and require elders to responsibly train, discipline, and otherwise "govern" young children. High degrees of parental authority and control are viewed as positive and essential aspects of the *chiao shun,* or "training," needed to set a standard of acceptable family and community conduct. Chao suggests that cultural differences such as these may explain why authoritarian parenting, which is associated with poor school achievement among European American children, is linked to high levels of school achievement among Chinese children. Central to such cultural differences are differences in values and assumptions about what kind of people parents want their children to be and what kinds of parenting and other developmental influences will best help them get there.

Permissive Parenting   *Permissive parents* appear to show two patterns. **Permissive-indulgent** parents are warm, sensitive, caring, and generally responsive to their children's thoughts and feelings. However, they exert low levels of control and make relatively few demands, permitting their children to make almost all of their own decisions. Also, while they clearly communicate their warmth, love, and caring, their communication tends to be less clear in situations requiring them to set limits on their children's behavior. **Permissive-indifferent** parents are detached and emotionally uninvolved. They are inconsistent in setting and maintaining age-appropriate standards and expectations for their children and in fulfilling their parental responsibilities (Maccoby & Martin, 1983).

Children with permissive-indulgent parents tend to lack self-reliance and self-control and to have lower self-esteem as they enter their adolescent years. This is also true of children with permissive-indifferent parents, who seem to be emotionally detached and not to care what their children do (Loeb et al., 1980). Children with permissive-indifferent parents may turn to peers or others for help in setting limits and learning morality. These children tend to have various degrees of developmental difficulties, including a low ability to tolerate frustration and control their impulsive and aggressive behavior. They also tend to have difficulty in making life choices and setting long-term goals. At the extreme, permissive-indifferent parents may neglect their children's physical and emotional needs in ways that place them at risk for serious developmental and emotional problems. Child neglect and abuse are discussed later in this chapter.

While most parents are fairly consistent in their parenting styles, under certain circumstances they may exhibit other styles. For example, a parent with an authoritative style may, on occasion, respond to an overtired child in an impatient and authoritarian manner after explaining to her for the tenth time why it is time to go to bed.

Changes over Time   Patterns of childrearing tend to change over time. Authoritarian parents, for instance, often ease up and shift to a more permissive or authoritative style as their children grow older. Changes in the family situation, such as the birth of another child, also can make a difference. The experience gained from rearing their first child frequently enables parents to be more comfortable and flexible in rearing the children who follow. Help from older children in caring for younger children can also reduce the stresses of parenting. On the other hand, additional children increase the family's overall child care and economic burdens, so more relaxed parenting is not always the outcome. As we will see when we look at psychosocial development in adulthood in Chapters 13 and 15, other changes within a family, such as separation, divorce, and remarriage, as well as changes in employment, standard of living, and health, also may influence childrearing. Families that are under stress tend to be more rigid, arbitrary, and authoritarian in rearing their children than families that are not.

Relationships with Siblings

Brothers and sisters are major participants in the social activities of many preschoolers. Studies have shown that most young children are very interested in babies and speak to their baby brothers and sisters in ways very similar to those of adult caregivers. Preschoolers also listen carefully to conversations between their parents and older brothers and sisters, as reflected in their efforts to join in family conversations; and their awareness of caregiving interactions between their parents and younger siblings helps them to respond to their younger siblings' distress with appropriate caregiving behaviors (Dunn & Shatz, 1989; Garner et al., 1994).

Older siblings show similar behavior when they simplify their language while explaining a task to a younger sibling (Hoff-Ginsberg & Krueger, 1991). They also provide important role models for their preschool brothers and sisters, helping them learn social skills and parental expectations. Both the friendly and the aggressive interactions of siblings contribute to the development of preschoolers' understandings of the feelings, intentions, and needs of people other than themselves (J. Brown & Dunn, 1992; J. Dunn, 1985).

Given the social opportunities siblings offer, one might expect children growing up with brothers and sisters to develop social skills earlier and more rapidly, and perhaps end up with better skills, than children who lack siblings. But having siblings can have its down side as well. For instance, caring for a younger sibling is likely to enhance the younger child's social competence, but being burdened with her care may also limit the older child's opportunities to spend time with his peers. How siblings will affect a particular child's social development is likely to depend on the degree to which parents recognize and respond appropriately to the social needs of all of their children. Siblings continue to play an important role in childhood and adolescence, and, as we will see, while they become less important in early adulthood (see Chapter 13), they regain importance in middle adulthood (Chapter 15) and late adulthood (Chapter 17).

Friendships in Early Childhood

Preschool children are simultaneously pulled in two directions. On the one hand, they seek the security and intimacy that come from playing continually with a familiar friend; on the other, they want to participate in the variety of activities that many different children make possible.

The Evolution of Friendship   John Gottman and Jennifer Parkhurst (1980) made extensive home observations of preschoolers between ages three and six as the chil-

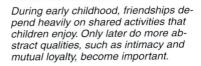

During early childhood, friendships depend heavily on shared activities that children enjoy. Only later do more abstract qualities, such as intimacy and mutual loyalty, become important.

dren played with friends and new acquaintances. They found that play between younger children and their friends included frequent and extensive fantasy role playing, whereas older children's friendships focused more on the actual activities they were doing than on make-believe roles. Younger children communicated more clearly with their friends than did older children and were more responsive to their friends' requests for information or explanation. They also worked harder to create a "climate of agreement" by avoiding disagreements. They did this by immediately discussing the reasons for a disagreement or explaining them away and by using positive social comparisons with their friends to create a sense of common ground and solidarity. Older children were better able to tolerate differences and disagreements and had less need to use positive social comparisons to manage conflict in their friendships.

Due to the "management" problems just noted and the emphasis on overt, concrete, shared activities—such as whether to build a sand castle, how to draw a dog, how to cook a pretend dinner—early friendships tend to be somewhat unstable and may change on a weekly or even daily basis. A preschool child will drop a friend relatively easily and later make up to her just as easily. Sometimes she will even exchange goods for friendship: "If you give me a piece of candy, I'll be your best friend!"

Preschoolers are also capable of sustaining relationships with playmates that last for a year or more (Howes, 1988). These preferences are an important step toward forming more lasting friendships later in childhood, as well as a basis for learning to get along with others. By age three to four, friendships become more involved and durable. Certain pairs of children develop a liking for each other and purposely try to spend time together. In fact, approximately 80 percent of three-to-four-year-olds spend a substantial amount of time with at least one special "associate," or playmate. Children in nursery school spend at least 30 percent of their time with one other peer. Typically the pairings develop in situations that encourage physical proximity, such as the children's neighborhood play group, day care center, or preschool classroom (Hinde et al., 1985). Pairs of preschool friends exhibit greater reciprocity and interdependence with each other in their parallel play, requesting, and following/imitating activities than they do with mere acquaintances (Goldstein et al., 1989). The "Working With" interview on page 227 discusses friendships among preschoolers.

By the end of the preschool period, stable friendships do emerge. However, generally they are not as reciprocal or intimate as friendships become in middle childhood, adolescence, and early adulthood.

Conceptions of Friendship   In the minds of younger preschoolers, a friend is someone who does certain things with you; she is someone (anyone, in fact) whom you like to play with, share toys with, or talk with a lot. "A friend," as one preschooler put it, "lets you hold his doll or truck or something."

As children near school age, more permanent, personal qualities enter into their conceptions (Furman, 1982). Now the crucial features of a friend are more often dispositional, that is, related to how the friend is likely to behave in the future. A friend is still very much "someone you like," but she is also someone whom you trust, whom you can depend on, and who likes and admires you. To be friends in this sense, two children must know each other's likes and preferences better than before, and they must also be increasingly aware of thoughts and feelings that the friend may keep hidden. Nevertheless, each child is still likely to focus primarily on his own needs to the exclusion of his friend's. As one child said, "A friend is someone who does what you want"; and as another said, "A friend doesn't get you in trouble." Neither of these children understands that sometimes he or she should return these favors; later, during the school years, they will likely think of this.

These two toddlers are concerned about the unhappy baby. Important gains in children's capacity for empathy and emotional support develop during the preschool years.

Empathy and Prosocial Behavior

Empathy is the ability to vicariously experience the emotions of another person and is thought to play an important role in the successful development of friendships and other close emotional relationships (Eisenberg et al., 1989). *Prosocial behavior* refers to positive social actions that benefit others, such as sharing, helping, and cooperating. Some prosocial behaviors are *altruistic,* meaning they are voluntarily aimed at helping others with no expectation of rewards for oneself. The development of both empathy and prosocial behavior is related to sound parent-child relationships and secure attachment during infancy and toddlerhood, which we discussed in Chapter 5.

Preschool children will respond helpfully to another person's distress in a variety of situations. For example, mothers' observational reports of the prosocial behavior of their four- and seven-year-olds at home indicate that spontaneous helping occurred in both age groups more frequently than did sharing and giving, affection and praise, or reassuring and protecting (Grusec, 1991). Young children are able to empathize in other settings as well. One study of children at a day care center playground found that more than 90 percent of the time, a crying child generated concerned and mostly helpful responses from the other children (Sawin, 1979). About half of the children who were near the distressed child looked as though they would cry themselves. Almost 20 percent of the nearby children tried to console the child directly (and their actions did, in fact, help reduce the crying); other children sought out an adult on the playground; still others threatened revenge on the child who caused the upset. Carolee Howes and her colleagues have also found that young children in day care settings respond to crying with empathic, prosocial behavior, although at lower rates (Howes & Farver, 1987; Phinney et al., 1986).

Developmental Trends   Prosocial behavior, or helpfulness, is well established by the time a child reaches the preschool years. An early, classic study found that all of the following helping behaviors occurred with significant frequency among four-year-olds (Murphy, 1937): assisting another child, comforting another child, protecting another child, warning another child of danger, giving things to another child, and inquiring of a child in trouble. Fifty years later, these and similar helping behaviors are still quite evident, not only among preschool children but even among children younger than two (Eisenberg & Mussen, 1989; Radke-Yarrow & Zahn-Waxler, 1987).

Between ages two and six, children give increasingly complex reasons for helping and are more strongly influenced by nonaltruistic as well as altruistic motives and concerns (Eisenberg et al., 1989; Yarrow & Waxler, 1978). An older child may justify her helpfulness in terms of gaining approval from peers in general rather than in terms of her concern for the well-being of the child in distress. Or she may justify withholding help because of fear of disapproval from adults, for example, if she has been instructed to let the day care or nursery school teachers handle children in trouble. In fairness to older preschoolers, however, younger children also may have reasons such as these but are not yet able to verbalize them clearly (Fabes et al., 1988).

Sources of Prosocial Behavior   Potential sources of individual differences in prosocial responses include age, gender, temperament, child care experience, social competence with peers, and friendship status (Farver & Branstetter, 1994). Prosocial behaviors increase with age due to gains in cognitive functioning, social skills, and moral reasoning and to more socialization experiences that enhance prosocial responsiveness (Eisenberg & Mussen, 1989). No consistent gender differences in prosocial responses have been found, although some studies have found girls to be more prosocial than boys.

There is some evidence that differences in temperament affect children's prosocial behavior. Young children who display high levels of prosocial behavior tend to be active, outgoing, and emotionally expressive. This pattern is similar to the temperamentally *easy child,* whose high levels of adaptiveness, positive mood, and approachfulness (tendency to approach) may help him initiate and sustain more peer interaction than *difficult* or *slow-to-warm-up children,* who are more likely to avoid peer contact (Buss & Plomin, 1984; Farver & Branstetter, 1994).

Early exposure to prosocial experiences with peers, parents, and other important individuals may be the best predictor of later prosocial behavior. Jo Ann Farver and Wendy Branstetter (1994) studied prosocial behavior among preschoolers ages 3 to 4½ in three child care programs. They found that the type and quality of peer contact children experienced more than the length of time children spent in their prior or current preschool programs influenced their prosocial tendencies. Early peer relationships are most likely to foster prosocial responsiveness when teachers, parents, and other adults create an environment that supports it and provides models for children to observe and imitate.

Prosocial competence among preschoolers may also depend on how often parents initiate informal play activities. Gary Ladd and Craig Hart (1992) found that children whose parents frequently arranged for them to play with peers and actively involved them in arranging play activities displayed higher levels of prosocial behavior. Children who more frequently initiated informal peer contacts were better liked by their classmates.

Overall differences in parenting styles also appear to influence preschoolers' prosocial behavior. Children whose parents are authoritative in their disciplinary styles engage in more prosocial, empathic, and compassionate behavior and less

Hostile aggression among preschoolers is frequently associated with frustrations at being unable to solve a conflict over toys and with angry and jealous feelings that may result when excluded from a desired activity with peers.

antisocial behavior in day care, playground, and other play settings than do children whose parents have authoritarian discipline styles (Hart et al., 1992; Main & George, 1985; Zahn-Waxler et al., 1979).

Cross-cultural studies have provided some additional insights into the significance of parental support and encouragement. In mainly rural societies where mothers worked in the fields and children assumed major child care and household responsibilities, children had more opportunities to experience prosocial roles and to behave prosocially. Firstborn children, who had the most helping experience, tended to be more prosocial than lastborn or only children. Children raised in close-knit, communal Israeli kibbutz communities, which place high value on cooperation and prosocial behavior, exhibited higher levels of cooperation and prosocial behavior than did children from rural or big-city areas (Eisenberg et al., 1990; Whiting & Edwards, 1988).

What practical steps can parents and teachers take to increase altruism and prosocial behavior in the children they care for? Two techniques that have proven successful in increasing such behavior among preschoolers are (1) verbal approval and encouragement for being empathic, respectful, and helpful to others and (2) arranging regular play opportunities that support and encourage sharing, cooperation, and helping.

Conflict and Aggression

So far our discussion of social relationships has focused on the ability of preschoolers to get along reasonably well with one another. However, preschoolers also get very angry and express their feelings in aggressive ways: grabbing one another's toys, pushing, hitting, scratching, and calling names. What types of interpersonal conflicts make preschoolers angry, and how do they cope with their angry feelings? Richard Fabes and Nancy Eisenberg (1992) observed the causes of anger and reactions to provocations among preschool children between ages 3 and 6½ while they were at play. Conflict over possessions was the most common cause of anger, and physical assault was the second most frequent cause. In most types of anger conflicts, the majority of children responded by expressing angry feelings (particularly boys) or by actively attempting to defend themselves in nonaggressive ways (particularly girls). Active resistance was most likely in conflicts over material things such as toys and least likely in conflicts involving compliance with teachers and other adults. In contrast, venting of angry feelings was least likely in material conflicts and most likely in compliance conflicts with adults, suggesting that the particular coping strategy chosen depends in part on how controllable the child sees the situation to be. Children's use of aggressive revenge (hitting or threatening) and tattling was most frequent when their anger was caused by physical assault.

The Nature of Aggression   **Aggression** refers to actions that are intended to harm another person or an object. Aggressive actions frequently are divided into two types. **Instrumental aggression** involves actions in which one person hurts another as a means to achieving a nonaggressive end. Instrumental aggression frequently involves conflicts over objects, territory, and perceived rights or privileges. **Hostile aggression** refers to actions in which hurting another person is the major goal, such as when a child who is teased or taunted by another child retaliates by pushing or hitting. Quite frequently aggressive behavior is associated with a child's frustration at being unable to solve a conflict; for example, one child hits another because her attempts to get a turn with a favorite toy have all failed. Generally, judgments about whether a child's aggressiveness is instrumental or hostile are based on the child's motivations, his level of knowledge about the effects of his actions, previous patterns of response in similar situations, and whether or not destructive consequences have resulted.

Changes in Aggression During Early Childhood   During the preschool years, the frequency of instrumental aggression declines as children become better able to understand the reasons for their frustration and anger, whereas the frequency of hostile aggression increases (Shantz, 1987). Young preschoolers show aggression in more physical ways than older preschoolers do. As children get older, verbal aggression such as making insulting remarks increases, whereas physical aggression such as pushing, hitting, and grabbing declines (McCabe & Lipscomb, 1988).

Influences on the Development of Aggression   When expressed in acceptable ways, aggression may be not only tolerable but even desirable. Assertive or instrumental-aggressive actions allow a child to communicate and fulfill legitimate needs, such as when he takes back a toy that is rightfully his or stands up for his integrity against unfair insults. Often, however, hostile motivations complicate matters and create additional distress. The anger and rage children sometimes experience can be quite upsetting to them as well as to their parents and others. For example, a mother who observes her four-year-old attack a playmate, perhaps biting her or pulling her hair, is likely to be upset for multiple reasons, including her own child's unhappiness, the pain and distress of the other child, her belief that biting is "dirty fighting," and concerns about how all of this reflects on her as a parent.

Temperamental Differences   Temperamental differences that are present at birth may make aggressive behavior and parent-child conflict more likely during early childhood. For example, babies who are low in their ability to regulate their physical and emotional states and high in emotional intensity may be especially prone to overt expressions of anger, frustration, and aggressive behavior, whereas babies with a high ability to regulate these states are more likely to cope more constructively with their anger and frustration.

Consistent with this view, Nancy Eisenberg and her colleagues found that babies with especially "difficult" temperaments at six months of age experienced significantly more conflict with their mothers at age three than did babies with less difficult temperaments (Eisenberg & Fabes, 1992; Eisenberg et al., 1994). As three-year-olds, these children were more likely to be uncooperative, ignore their parents' disciplinary efforts, and respond in insulting and unpleasant ways. Their frustrated parents used a wide variety of methods to attempt to control them, including forbidding certain activities, threatening punishment, and using physical restraint. Thus, the ongoing interactions between these difficult children and their parents seemed likely to be escalating a cycle of aggression (Eisenberg et al., 1994). Of course, many active or difficult babies do not become aggressive three-year-olds, perhaps because the expression of temperament is largely a product of child-caregiver interactions.

Gender   Throughout the preschool years, boys exhibit more overall aggressive behavior than girls do (Maccoby & Jacklin, 1980). This difference holds true across a broad range of social classes, ethnic groups, and cultures and across a wide spectrum of aggressive behaviors. Contrary to common belief, however, girls do not "specialize" in verbal aggression (such as name calling) or boys in physical aggression (such as pushing and hitting). Although girls and boys do not appear to differ significantly in the types of anger conflicts they experience, boys are more likely than girls to vent their feelings when angered, whereas girls are more likely to actively resist by verbally defending themselves (Fabes & Eisenberg, 1992).

One reason for these differences may be that girls and boys have different goals when they respond to anger provocations. Boys may be more likely to use coping strategies designed to meet their own needs, whereas girls may select strategies to maximize interpersonal harmony. The childrearing and educational philosophies and practices of parents and teachers may contribute to such differences. For example, parents tend to play more roughly with boys and be more tolerant of their physically assertive and aggressive actions and to be less tolerant of similar behavior in girls, encouraging them instead to use verbal accommodation in such situations (Mills & Rubin, 1990; Ross et al., 1990).

Childrearing Styles   As in the case of prosocial behavior discussed earlier, styles of childrearing and the overall quality of the parent-child relationship are likely to significantly influence children's use of aggression in coping with interpersonal anger. There is some evidence that both permissive-indifferent and extremely authoritarian parenting styles are likely to be associated with higher levels of aggression and lower levels of prosocial behavior. In one study conducted by Grazyna Kochanska (1992), children who were abrasive and aggressive in interacting with their mothers and whose mothers used control tactics that were negative and unclear were more likely to be aggressive, low in prosocial behavior, and unsuccessful with their peers compared to mothers whose guidance was more respectful. Children whose parents depend on arbitrary, "power-assertive" control and ignore their thoughts, feelings, and need for independence have also been found to display greater distrustfulness of others and unhappiness with themselves, poorer peer relations, and poorer school adjustment and academic achievement than other children (Hart et al., 1990; Putallaz, 1987).

All of the following childrearing characteristics have been found to contribute to aggressiveness in preschoolers, especially when they are part of an ongoing pattern (Baumrind, 1971; Hart et al., 1990; B. Martin, 1975; Putallaz, 1987):

1. Lack of acceptance of the child, dislike of the child, and criticism of the child for being the sort of person she or he currently is or is becoming

2. Excessive permissiveness, particularly if it includes indifference to the child's true needs for reasonable but consistent limits and emotional support

3. Discipline that does not respect the child's ability and need to understand the reasons for the punishment and its meaning to the parent

4. Inconsistent discipline, which fails to provide the child with a reasonable and predictable basis for learning to regulate his or her behavior

5. A "spare the rod and spoil the child" attitude, which often results in impulsive and overly harsh use of discipline

6. Unclear rules and expectations for the child, particularly those regarding interactions with other family members

Children whose parents are able to accept their hostile-aggressive impulses and actions and respectfully guide their efforts to discover nonhostile methods for resolving conflicts and asserting their needs are most likely to learn to manage their aggression. The childrearing orientation of such parents closely corresponds to the authoritative parenting style, which is strongly associated with the development of prosocial behavior.

Peer Influences   Peers can also contribute to aggression by acting in ways that provoke aggressive retaliation. A child surrounded by provocative peers is likely to acquire a similar style herself, and, in doing so, stimulate further aggressive behavior in her peers.

Some preschool children are continually involved in conflicts. They constantly either lose battles and arguments or lose potential friends by depending too much on hostile, aggressive actions to get what they need. Kenneth Dodge and his colleagues (Dodge et al., 1986; Dodge & Coie, 1987) believe that a combination of low peer status and lack of social competence in the preschool period may contribute to a child's tendency to behave aggressively. When entering a new group, for example, aggressive children have difficulty in accurately processing and evaluating information about what is expected and generating appropriate responses when faced with threats or provocation. Such children may have a social-cognitive bias that leads them to overestimate the harmful intentions of their peers and to respond aggressively in situations that do not warrant it. The aggressive, hostile behavior of an unpopular preschooler may also be his way of externalizing anger and distress he is experiencing due to similar problems at home.

Media Influences   As many concerned parents realize, television, films, and other media exert a strong influence on children, and much of that influence centers on physical violence. Researchers estimate that three-to-four-year-olds watch two or more hours of television each day and that viewing TV violence increases children's aggressive behavior, at least in the short run. Numerous studies indicate that watching violence *disinhibits,* or releases, violent behavior in children who are already prone to anger and aggression (Huston et al., 1989). Longitudinal studies have found that the amount of TV violence viewed at age eight may be predictive of the seriousness of boys' aggressiveness at age nineteen and of the average severity of criminal behavior at age thirty for both males and females (Eron, 1987; Huesmann et al., 1984). In addition to violent TV programs, violent video games are a growing concern for parents of young children.

Preschoolers have a special problem in coping with violence in the media: their lack of skill in figuring out the motives of characters portrayed and the subtleties of plots. A heinous murder on television may look the same to a preschooler as one committed in self-defense or to protect innocent people (Collins et al., 1981). Also, some of the most violent TV programs are those produced for children; Saturday morning cartoons average more than twenty violent acts per hour (Gerbner et al., 1986). Programs such as "Spider Man," "Mighty Morphin Rangers," "Masked Rider," and "X-Men" and many videotapes that young children view also contain substantial amounts of violent content (Fabrikant, 1996). Adult supervision and help in understanding television programs therefore are especially important for very young children. Unfortunately, one of television's main attractions for some parents is that it makes adult supervision unnecessary by keeping children passively occupied.

Recent widespread concern about childrens' exposure to television violence has led to a new U.S. communications law stipulating that all new TV sets be equipped with a "violence chip," or V-chip. The V-chip "reads" TV programming and allows parents to tune out shows that they consider too violent for their children based on a rating system that is currently under development (Andrews, 1996). Several unanswered questions remain, however. Will the V-chip really give parents control over their children's exposure to TV violence? What criteria should be used for deciding which programs are too violent for preschoolers? Are the same criteria appropriate for older children and adolescents? We will look at the broader developmental role of television in the lives of preschool-age children later in this chapter.

Responding to Aggressive Behavior   Children who have difficulty controlling their aggression experience considerable problems. Often they become aggressive at inappropriate times and in self-defeating ways, getting into fights with children and adults who are stronger than they are. Peers and parents alike find it difficult not to attribute malicious motives to children who seem out of control and appear unresponsive to generally agreed-upon standards of behavior (Kutner, 1989). Children who are overly aggressive can stimulate strong feelings of inadequacy, guilt, anger, and loss of control in their parents, leading to an increased risk that parents will respond in angry, punitive ways.

Spanking and Other Forms of Punishment   In general, preschoolers conform to parental expectations, especially if those expectations are communicated in a clear, understandable way that conveys warmth and respect for the child. Even when preschoolers resist, patient explanation and responsiveness to the child's feelings and perceptions generally resolve the problem. In instances when a preschooler "loses it" and throws a tantrum or refuses to comply with a parent's reasonable and necessary demands, firm but respectful physical restraint and guidance may also be needed until the child has regained self-control. In dangerous situations requiring immediate action, such as when a child runs into the street or is about to touch something hot, parents may use strong reprimands or spanking to stop the risky behavior and prevent it from happening again.

Some parents, however, rely on spanking and punishment as a regular part of their childrearing discipline. James Comer and Alvin Poussaint (1992), two prominent child psychiatrists, point out that children who were spanked by thoughtful, loving parents rarely have problems as a result of the spanking. They also note that while many well-behaved and well-adjusted adults were never or rarely spanked as children, many others were spanked fairly often. Nevertheless, Comer and Poussaint caution that punishment is not the best way to provide discipline, especially in cases where parents are having difficulty with their preschoolers.

What problems are associated with spanking and punishment in general? While verbal or physical punishment can suppress misbehavior in the short run, it is not an effective or desirable long-run strategy, particularly if it is harsh or frequent. One obvious problem is that preschoolers are very likely to imitate the behavior of the adult models who punish them (Bandura, 1991; Emery, 1989). Using aggressive behavior such as verbal threats or spanking to reduce a child's unacceptable behavior is likely to increase the very behavior it seeks to control. A child who is hit by an angry parent learns to act on her own anger in similar ways, which is surely not the lesson her parents intend. Even moderate use of spanking appears to contribute to child aggression. One large-scale study conducted by Robert Larzelere (1986) using a nationally representative sample of parents with at least one child age three to seventeen living at home found that the use of physical punishment was positively associated with child aggression. In situations where spanking was frequent and reasons were rarely provided, the association between spanking and child aggression dramatically increased. Excessive reliance on spanking and other forms of punishment is strongly linked to child maltreatment, a topic we discuss later in this chapter.

A second problem with spanking and other forms of punishment is that a child quickly learns to fear and avoid the punishing adult, thus reducing opportunities for adult supervision and constructive adult-child interactions. Third, because punishment quickly suppresses the child's undesirable behavior in the short run, it serves to reinforce adult reliance on punishment and reduce the likelihood of exploring other ways to respond to the child's unacceptable behavior. Fourth, to the extent that punishment reduces the guilt a child feels for misbehaving, it reinforces the child's reliance on external (parental) control rather than internal, self-control of his behavior (Comer & Poussaint, 1992).

Helping Aggressive Children and Their Parents   Several principles have emerged from work with aggressive children and their families. The most successful approaches frequently involve working with the entire family. The first step is to carefully observe the child's interactions with peers and adults to discover consistent patterns in what triggers the aggression and how each family member may unintentionally reinforce the patterns of problem behavior (Kutner, 1989; Patterson, 1982; Patterson et al., 1989).

Structure, predictability, and consistency of routine are important for all preschoolers, especially for children who have difficulty controlling their aggressive behavior. For such children, aggressive outbursts are most likely to occur in unstructured and ambiguous situations. Such circumstances aggravate their tendency to distort information about potential harm and to perceive themselves as being at risk. Thus, neutral behavior, such as the approach of another child, is misinterpreted as an aggressive act (Dodge, 1986).

Once the patterns of aggression are discovered, parents can learn to recognize the early signs and intervene by either changing the situation or removing their preschooler before things escalate. The most successful methods involve reinforcement of positive behaviors through warmth, affection, and parental approval; assertiveness training to help the child meet her needs for attention in less self-destructive ways; and increasing predictability and consistency in the child's everyday life (Kutner, 1989; Patterson, 1982).

Another successful approach to modifying destructive family processes and problems with childhood aggression uses social learning theory methods such as coaching, modeling, and reinforcing alternative patterns of parent-child interaction. After carefully observing the parent-child interaction, the therapist describes and then demonstrates alternative ways to deal with the child's hostile, aggressive, or disobedient behaviors. As parents gain more confidence in their competence, they become more effective parents; as children learn to resolve conflicts in more appropriate ways, their problematic behavior decreases (Patterson, 1982, 1985).

The Effects of Television on Preschoolers' Development

Ninety-eight percent of American homes have at least one television set, and a TV set is on for a total of 7.1 hours per day in a typical household (Huston et al., 1989). Most children are exposed to television from the time they are born, and American children spend more time, on average, watching TV than in any other waking activity, including play (Liebert & Sprafkin, 1988).

As Figure 7.1 shows, a typical two-year-old is in front of a TV set almost 1.5 hours per day. Viewing time increases during the preschool years and peaks at about 2.5 hours per day; it then decreases slightly with the beginning of school, but at about age eight it increases steadily, reaching an average of about four hours per day during adolescence. Boys and girls appear to watch equal amounts of television. The same basic developmental pattern has been found in a number of European countries, Canada, and Australia, although the amount of viewing time varies with program availability and the number of broadcast hours (Liebert & Sprafkin, 1988).

Not surprisingly, the types of programs children prefer to watch also change with age. Until they are three or four, children prefer programs such as "Sesame Street" and "Mister Rogers' Neighborhood," which are designed for children and feature language, characters, and events at a level children can readily understand. Children ages three to five tend to watch more cartoons, and children ages five to seven increasingly watch comedies, action shows, and special-interest programs that are more cognitively demanding and aimed at general audiences (Huston et al., 1990).

Television viewing has been found to influence children's social development in a number of areas, including aggression, prosocial behavior, consumer behavior, and gender stereotypes. The relationships between viewing aggression on TV and children's aggressive behavior were already discussed.

Television programs designed for children (and for adults) often convey a highly stereotyped and distorted social world that values being male, youthful, beautiful, and white over being female, old, handicapped, dark-skinned, or foreign born (Greenberg, 1986; Huston et al., 1989; Liebert & Sprafkin, 1988). Despite efforts to broaden the portrayals of gender roles, women continue to be cast in strongly sex-typed roles such as teacher, secretary, nurse, or (most commonly) homemaker. On television, women solve problems less frequently, need help more often, listen better, and talk less than men do and behave in other gender-stereotypical ways (Huston & Alvarez, 1990). These patterns also prevail for children's television despite widespread concern about the ways gender stereotypes limit girls' expectations. One reason for this may be that boys, who are reinforced largely by their peers, show much greater interest in shows with action heroes than in programs that present less stereotypic male activities. The significance of these patterns is not lost on advertisers, who are interested in buying time on programs that most effectively sell their products (Huston & Alvarez, 1990).

However, television is also a very useful educational tool for supporting children's intellectual and social development. Studies have found, for example, that programs that model cooperative, prosocial behavior are likely to increase children's prosocial behavior and that children who are exposed to non-gender- and

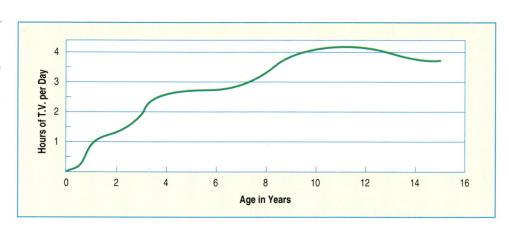

FIGURE 7.1
Changes in the Amount of TV Viewing with Age
Daily TV viewing time increases during the preschool and school years, with children viewing 1.5 hours daily at age two, 2.5 hours at age four, 3.5 hours at age eight, and a peak of 4.0 hours at age eleven.
Adapted from Liebert & Sprafkin (1988), p. 5.

non–racially stereotyped programs are more likely than other children to behave in less stereotypic ways (Liebert & Sprafkin, 1988).

Differences in family circumstances significantly affect young children's TV viewing. Children from lower SES levels watch more television than those from families that are better off (Greenberg, 1986). Having a mother who works outside the home and attending day care or preschool, however, may decrease the amount of TV viewing. And while having an older brother or sister to play with may decrease TV watching, having younger siblings may increase it (Pinon et al., 1989).

Both the types of programs TV networks provide and the choices parents make about what their children view strongly affect young children's viewing patterns (Huston et al., 1990). Families vary considerably in their attitudes toward television and the amount and type of guidance they provide for their children. While nearly 40 percent of parents of preschoolers sometimes use TV to keep their children occupied, almost 40 percent regularly limit the number of hours their children can watch, and close to 50 percent have consistent rules regarding which types or which specific programs their children are allowed to view (Comstock, 1991).

Michelle St. Peters and her associates conducted a two-year longitudinal study of how families with five-year-olds regulate their children's TV viewing (St. Peters et al., 1991). Whereas the majority of children's programs were viewed without parents, most adult programs were watched with parents, although watching programs together declined with age. Based on the degree to which parents regulated their children's TV viewing (high versus low regulation) and on how much they encouraged TV watching (high versus low), St. Peters and her colleagues classified families into four types. *Laissez-faire* parents provided low levels of regulation or encouragement; *restrictive* parents provided high regulation and low encouragement; *promotive* parents had few regulations and high levels of encouragement; and *selective* parents highly regulated their children's TV watching and encouraged specific types of viewing.

As Table 7.5 indicates, the number of hours of TV children viewed per week was highest for the promotive style (21.2) and lowest for the restrictive style (11.9), with selective (19.2) and laissez-faire (17.6) supervisory styles falling in between. The same pattern was found for the types of programs children watched. For example, children whose parents encouraged TV viewing watched more educational programs, such as "Sesame Street" and "Mister Rogers' Neighborhood," and more adult programs, including comedy, game shows, and action-adventure shows, than children who were not encouraged. Children whose TV viewing was regulated watched similar amounts of educational programs but significantly fewer

TABLE 7.5 *Styles of Parental Regulation and Number of Hours of Television Their Children Watch Each Week*

Style of Supervision	Degree of Regulation	Degree of Encouragement	Hours of TV Viewed per Week
Laissez-faire	Low	Low	17.6
Restrictive	High	Low	11.9
Promotive	Low	High	21.2
Selective	High	High	19.2

Source: Adapted from St. Peters et al. (1991), p. 1419.

Children whose parents do not encourage TV viewing (laissez-faire and restrictive) watch the fewest hours of TV; children whose parents encourage viewing (promotive and selective) watch the most hours.

adult programs. These findings suggest that parents can substantially influence their children's TV viewing by providing appropriate supervision and guidance.

Many older preschoolers, especially those with school-age brothers and sisters, also spend a lot of time watching prerecorded videos and playing video and computer games. In a recent survey of households with at least one child in the two-to-twelve-year age range, 33 percent reported that the child watched videotapes, 33 percent that the child had used a personal computer, and 14 percent that the child had played video games "some or a lot" during the previous day. Since 1984, industry studies have found a 1 percent decrease in the average number of hours of TV viewing among children ages two to eleven, due largely to their increased viewing of video-tapes and use of computer games (Fabrikant, 1996). Here, too, parental supervision is needed to ensure that such activities are appropriate in content and do not inter-fere with their children's involvement in other important play and related activities.

What Do You Think?

What style of parental authority best describes what you experienced as a child? How did it change during middle childhood and adolescence? If you now have children or expect to in the future, which pattern of parenting do (will) you use? Why?

GENDER DEVELOPMENT

Gender influences important aspects of social development in early childhood. As used here, the term **gender** refers to learned or socially constructed categories (feminine and masculine) in contrast to *sex,* which refers to biological categories (male and female). Most children go through at least three steps in gender devel-opment (Shepherd-Look, 1982). First, they develop beliefs about *gender identity,* that is, which sex *they* are. Second, they develop *gender preferences,* attitudes about which sex they wish to be; gender preference does not always coincide with gender identity. Third, they acquire *gender constancy,* a belief that the sex of a per-son is biologically determined, permanent, and unchanging no matter what else about the person changes. All three aspects of gender contribute to a child's gen-eral knowledge of **gender role stereotypes** (also called *sex roles*), the very power-ful (but not necessarily welcome or accurate) culturally sanctioned messages regarding which gender-related behaviors are and are not acceptable. Different cultures have different stereotypes and therefore send different messages to par-ents and children.

Developmental Trends During Early Childhood

From age two onward, preschoolers use gender role stereotypes to guide their be-haviors. Children's gender preferences and knowledge of stereotypes regarding toys and activities increase significantly with age: whereas twenty-four-month-old infants typically do not show consistent gender preferences in toys and activities, thirty-month-olds consistently prefer "same-gender" over "opposite-gender" ob-jects and activities. Gender role stereotypes about personal qualities develop more slowly. Only by age five or so do children begin to know which gender is "sup-posed" to be aggressive, loud, and strong and which is "supposed" to be gentle, quiet, and weak. Knowledge of gender stereotypes regarding personal qualities continues to develop throughout childhood and adolescence (Huston, 1983; S. Thompson, 1975).

Most children acquire *gender identity,* the ability to label themselves correctly as boys or girls, between ages two and three and are able to correctly label other children and adults as well (Huston, 1983). Some children develop gender identity early, before age twenty-eight months, and others not until later. Early identifiers exhibit significantly more gender-stereotyped play, such as car play for boys and doll play for girls, than later identifiers do (Fagot & Leinbach, 1989; Fagot et al., 1992).

Gender constancy, the understanding that one's sex is permanent and will never change, first appears by age four or five. A young preschool child may say she can switch gender just by wanting to or say that even though she is a girl now, she was a boy as an infant or may grow up to become a man as an adult. And a two-year-old may have only a hazy notion of what defines gender, believing perhaps that certain hairstyles, clothing, and toys make the crucial difference. Most children, however, achieve a reliable sense of gender constancy between ages seven and nine (Emmerich & Sheppard, 1982).

Gender Schema Theory   A *gender schema* is a pattern of beliefs and stereotypes about gender that children use to organize information about gender-related characteristics, experiences, and expectations. A child's *gender schema* is thought to develop through a series of stages. First, a child learns through social experiences what kinds of things are directly associated with each sex, such as "boys play with cars" and "girls play with dolls." Next, around age four to six, the child moves to the second stage and begins to develop more indirect and complex associations for information relevant to his own sex but not for the opposite sex. For example, a child who knows that boys like trucks and boys like cars should now be able to infer that someone who likes trucks will also like cars. Finally, by age eight or so, the child moves to the third stage, where he has also learned the associations relevant to the opposite sex and has mastered the gender concepts of masculinity and femininity that link information within and among various content areas. Thus, a child will know the pattern of interests that are stereotypically associated with being masculine (cars, action toys, football) or feminine (dolls, "dress-up", dancing) (Bem, 1983; Martin et al., 1990; Ruble, 1988).

Influences on Gender Development

Parents   Many theorists hold parents responsible for the development of gender differences, either blaming or congratulating them depending on the theorist's point of view. When asked about their childrearing philosophies, parents tend to express belief in gender equality, but their actions often differ from their statements (Fagot, 1982). Observations of parents playing with their preschool children reveal that parents support their children for gender-stereotyped activities more than for cross-gender activities. Boys get praised more for playing with blocks than for playing with dolls, and parents generally support physical activity in boys more than in girls. As children approach school age, parents begin assigning household chores according to gender: girls more often fold the laundry, and boys more often take out the trash. Parents are also more likely to reward sons for being assertive, independent, active, and emotionally unexpressive and to reward daughters for being accommodating, dependent, more passive, and emotionally expressive (Fagot & Hagan, 1991; Lytton & Romney, 1991).

Nancy Chodorow (1978) has proposed that the gender differences between girls and boys are related to differences in their experiences of identity formation during their early years, when women are usually their exclusive caregivers. In this view, girls' identities and personality development are based on similarity and attachment to their mothers, who provide models for nurturing, caregiving, and closeness. Boys' identities and personality development are based on difference, separateness, and independence from these qualities, for to be a male in our society means possessing qualities that are incompatible with those traditionally associated with being a woman. Thus, Chodorow believes, women's capacity to nurture, raise children, and develop close relationships and men's capacity to separate themselves from their feelings and participate in the isolating and alienating world of work are rooted in these early experiences.

According to this view, the task of identity formation for a boy may be more difficult in that it requires a certain degree of rejection of essential qualities of his primary female caregiver. At the same time, the higher degree of similarity and continuity of experience between daughter and mother may make it more difficult for a girl to separate from her mother and establish an independent identity. After discussing the influence of peers and the media on gender differences, we will return to the question of how we define gender difference and what its consequences are.

Peers   In some ways, peers may shape gender differences more strongly than parents do. Early in the preschool years, even before age three, children respond differently to partners of the opposite sex than to those of the same sex (Maccoby, 1990). In play situations, girls tend to withdraw from a boy partner more often than from a girl partner, and boys heed prohibitions made by another boy more often than they do those that come from a girl. Even when preschoolers are not playing actively, they watch peers of the same sex more often than they do peers of the opposite sex.

Children of this age also respond to a reinforcement more reliably if it comes from a child of their own sex. If a boy compliments another boy's block building, the second boy is much more likely to continue building than he is if a girl compliments it. Conversely, if a boy criticizes the building, the other boy is more likely to stop than if a girl criticizes it. Parallel patterns occur for girls, who tend to persist in whatever other girls compliment or praise and stop whatever they criticize or ignore. For both sexes, teachers' reinforcements have less influence than peers' in determining children's persistence at activities (Fagot, 1982). What makes these patterns important is that children tend to reinforce play activities that are considered appropriate for their own sex. Children who deviate from expected gender-stereotyped activities, such as boys playing with dolls, often find themselves largely ignored, even after they return to expected activities (Lamb & Roopnarine, 1979). Thus, peer pressures to practice conventional gender roles are both strong and continuous, and they occur even if teachers and other adults try to minimize gender-typed play.

Androgyny

Androgyny refers to a situation in which gender roles are flexible, allowing all individuals, male and female, to behave in ways that freely integrate behaviors traditionally thought to belong exclusively to one or the other sex (Kaplan & Bean, 1976). In this view, both girls and boys can be assertive *and* yielding, independent *and* dependent, instrumental (task oriented) *and* expressive (feelings oriented). Sandra Bem (1974, 1976) and others (e.g., Lamke, 1982a, 1982b) have found that adolescent and young adult males and females use both masculine and feminine characteristics to describe their own personalities. Bem believes androgynous individuals are less concerned about which activities are appropriate or inappropriate and therefore are more flexible in their responses to various situations (Bem, 1981).

How we choose to define *gender* also can affect our understanding of what it means to be male or female. On the one hand, definitions that tend to exaggerate

The ease with which this preschool girl included in her play both the traditional male role of bus driver and the traditional female role of her mother vividly illustrates the flexible qualities associated with androgyny.

positive gender differences run the risk of perpetuating gender role stereotyping and inequality; on the other hand, definitions that minimize real differences may be used to deny boys and girls the physical, cognitive, and social developmental opportunities appropriate to their different gender-related needs. One positive consequence of focusing on differences associated with gender is that doing so increases our awareness and appreciation of feminine (and masculine) qualities. A positive consequence of efforts to minimize gender differences is to help equalize treatment under the law and access to equal opportunity for males and females (Hare-Mustin & Marecek, 1988).

What are the implications of androgyny? Because the notion of androgyny challenges certain fundamental beliefs that individuals have about gender, it holds the potential to reduce gender role stereotyping and its detrimental developmental effects in early childhood and beyond. The idea of androgyny also contributes to our understanding of sexual orientations that are not traditionally heterosexual, a topic we address in Chapter 11, where we discuss psychosocial development in adolescence.

What Do You Think?

A hockey coach's five-year-old son enjoys playing with dolls with his female peers. Because of this, his dad has encouraged him to play with GI Joe dolls and play football more often, since he is worried that his son may become homosexual. What gender influence is this hockey coach having on his son's gender development? What advice would you give this parent based on your reading of this chapter?

A Multicultural View

The Cultural Context of Child Abuse and Neglect

Can the ideas one culture holds about child abuse and neglect be validly applied to others? According to Jill Korbin, who has extensively studied child abuse and neglect in many different cultural and societal contexts, culturally appropriate definitions of child abuse and neglect require an awareness of both the viewpoint of an "insider" to a particular culture, termed the *emic* perspective, and the viewpoint of an "outsider" to that culture, or the *etic* perspective (Korbin, 1991, 1987, 1981). Such definitions must include three dimensions: (1) cultural differences in childrearing practices, (2) treatment of children that deviates from cultural norms, and (3) societal abuse and neglect.

Cultural differences in childrearing include practices considered acceptable in the culture in which they occur but abusive or neglectful by outsiders. For example, most middle-class American parents believe it is developmentally important for young children to sleep separately from their parents, but traditional Japanese and Hawaiian-Polynesian cultures, which highly value interdependence among family members, view isolating chil-

dren at night as potentially dangerous to healthy child development. Another example concerns a woman in London who cut the faces of her two young sons with a razor blade and rubbed charcoal into the cuts. She was arrested for child abuse, but officials soon learned that she and her children belonged to an East African tribal group that traditionally practiced facial scarification. When viewed from within her culture, her actions were an attempt to protect her children's cultural identity, for without such markings they would be unable to participate as adults in the culture of their birth (Korbin, 1987).

Many cultures have practiced such initiation rights as a normal part of childrearing before and during adolescence. Where, for example, is the line drawn between circumcision during adolescence and circumcision at birth? How would a European or an American convince traditional people in highland New Guinea that circumcision is more painful for an adolescent than for an infant? How would traditional highland New Guinea people convince Europeans or Americans that (1) circumcision has no meaning for an infant, who cannot understand its

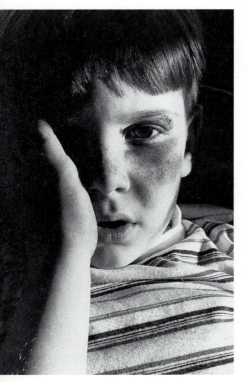

Preschoolers are particularly vulnerable to child abuse because of their immaturity and dependence. The destructive impact of abuse is often serious and long term.

CHILD MALTREATMENT

Child maltreatment by parents and other caregivers is a serious social problem, with more than 1 million new cases reported each year. A significant number of these cases involve infants, toddlers, and preschool-age children, who are particularly vulnerable because of their immaturity and dependence. Maltreatment may consist of physical, sexual, or emotional *abuse* or of physical or emotional *neglect* (Finkelhor, 1995; Krugman & Davidson, 1990; Rosenberg, 1989).

Causes

The causes of physical child abuse and neglect are best understood within the developmental-ecological contexts within which they occur. These include parent and child characteristics, parenting and parent-child interactions, and the broader context of family, community, and culture (Belsky, 1993).

Parent and Child Characteristics   One explanation for maltreatment is that the aggressive and antisocial behavior involved in abuse was previously learned by the parent during her or his own childhood, through modeling and direct reinforcement. The risk of maltreatment is much higher when parenting is extremely authoritarian (overly harsh and lacking in empathy) or when it is permissive-indifferent and neglectful of a child's needs. This explanation, however, fails to explain why two-thirds of parents who were abused themselves do not abuse their own children.

A second, more promising explanation of the causes of abuse is based on the idea of *internal working models*, the mental representations that organize and

deep cultural significance, and (2) infancy is a time when the child should be spared all discomfort? How is the line drawn between facial scarification and orthodontia (braces), both of which cause pain and discomfort but are intended to enhance the child's attractiveness?

Idiosyncratic child abuse and neglect involves treatment of children that deviates from established standards of acceptable treatment within a particular culture. Although they may differ, all societies have such standards. For example, in one Polynesian culture known for its indulgence of children, a child can be pinched lightly on the mouth for misbehavior, but more severe punishments are prohibited. When one man left a scratch on the lip of his grandchild, he was severely criticized by his cultural group. By their *emic* standards his behavior was abusive, although from the *etic* perspective of American parents it is unlikely that such behavior would be of great concern.

Societal abuse and neglect refers to harm caused to children by societal conditions such as poverty and inadequate housing, health care, and nutrition, all of which either contribute significantly to abuse or neglect or are considered abusive or neglectful in themselves. For example, the widespread famine in Ethiopia and Somalia and the inadequate nutrition in India and Chile have had devastating effects on the physical, cognitive, and socioemotional development of millions of children. In many countries physical, sexual, and emotional exploitation and abuse of children are very common. Even in affluent countries such as our own, social policy regarding aid to parents with dependent children, early childhood health care and nutrition, child care, and employment can significantly harm (or help) the development of young children. Where does responsibility lie, and what should be done about this?

It seems likely that neither a single, universal standard nor a completely relativistic, "anything goes" standard for determining abuse and neglect is acceptable. The challenge, then, is to develop an approach that incorporates developmental values and standards for "good enough" care and treatment of children that should be universal and values standards that afford more room for cultural and societal diversity.

guide a parent's experiences, relationship, and interactions with the child (Bowlby, 1988; Farrangy et al., 1991; Stern, 1985b). The internal working models of an abusive parent are based on past experiences with the child, the parent's own childhood experiences, and the beliefs and expectations held by his or her own abusive parents. These models are often characterized by a distorted, unbalanced view of the child (overly negative or overly positive) and are associated with pervasive failures in parental empathy, parent-infant synchrony, and attachment (Belsky, 1993; Ferholt, 1991; Main & Goldwyn, 1989; A. Miller, 1990; van Ijzendoorn, 1992).

Mothers who were abused as children are much less likely to abuse their own children if they experienced one nonabusive, supportive, and close relationship while growing up. They are also likely to display greater self-awareness regarding their own abuse, be involved in a more satisfying social relationship, and have more extensive social supports than mothers who do abuse (Belsky, 1993; Caliso & Milner, 1992).

Personality characteristics that significantly compromise a parent's ability to provide good parenting may also increase the risk of abuse, particularly if they interfere with getting social and emotional support from others. Difficulty with impulse control, emotional instability, high levels of depression, anxiety, or hostility, and abuse of alcohol or drugs can all impair a parent's capacity to respond to a child in empathic and responsible ways.

Finally, although a young child is never to blame for his or her own abuse, in some circumstances certain characteristics of a child, such as a difficult temperament, prematurity, a physical disability, hyperactivity, or other developmental problems, may contribute to an increased risk of abuse (Belsky, 1980).

Parenting and Parent-Child Interactions   Parenting and parent-child interactions also play a role. Abusive parents are more likely than nonabusive parents to rely on physical punishment and negative control strategies such as hitting, grabbing, and pushing, or threats and disapproval, rather than on reasoning to guide or discipline their children. They are also less likely to appropriately adjust their disciplinary techniques to different kinds of misbehavior (Belsky, 1993). During an abusive episode, the instrumentally aggressive behavior (physical punishment) on which an abusive parent relies is transformed into an act of interpersonal violence. A parent with a strong predisposition toward anxiety, depression, and hostility may become so irritated with the child that she or he loses control and physical or verbal punishment escalates into abuse.

Family, Community, and Cultural Factors   Poverty, unemployment, marital conflict, social isolation, and family pathology can increase the risk of abuse; so can shorter-term stressors such as emotional distress, economic or legal problems, or the birth of a new baby (Belsky, 1988b; Cicchetti & Olson, 1990; Garbarino, 1992b). Economic conditions, child and family social welfare policies, and cultural values and expectations regarding the care and protection of children can indirectly contribute to the risk of abuse and neglect. For example, societies that condone the use of violence against women (who are the primary caregivers of children) are likely to have higher rates of child abuse than societies that treat women with respect. Chapter 13's Multicultural View box (see page 476) looks at the problem of wife abuse. The role of differing cultural values and expectations regarding child maltreatment is discussed in the accompanying Multicultural View box.

Consequences

Neglected infants, toddlers, and preschoolers often are deprived of sufficient food, clothing, shelter, sanitation, and medical care, which may interfere with their physical, intellectual, social, and emotional development and place them at risk for serious illness or even death (Egeland, 1988). Abused or neglected preschoolers often develop emotional problems that include insecure attachment relationships, lack of empathy, and emotional detachment. They are also more likely to exhibit behavioral problems, such as aggressiveness and withdrawal, toward peers than other children are (Cicchetti & Olson, 1990; Dodge et al., 1990; Klimes-Dougan & Kistner, 1990; Pianta et al., 1989). Physical abuse in early childhood is linked to aggressive and violent behaviors in adolescents and adults, including violence toward nonfamily members, children, dating partners, and spouses (Kendall-Tackett et al., 1993; Malinosky-Rummell & Hansen, 1993).

The most common symptoms reported for preschoolers who have been sexually abused include nightmares, general posttraumatic stress disorder (see Chapter 12's discussion of physical development in early adulthood), depression and emotional withdrawal, regressive and immature behavior, anxiety disorders, and problems with aggression and inappropriate sexual behavior (Kendall-Tackett et al., 1993). The developmental stage at which sexual abuse occurs is particularly significant in determining longer-term outcomes. For example, incest (sexual abuse by a parent or other family member) disrupts the development of social functioning and self-esteem and increases risk for borderline and multiple personality, eating disorders, and substance abuse in adolescence and early adulthood (Finkelhor, 1995; Spaccarelli, 1994), as we will see in Chapters 10 and 12.

Treatment and Prevention

Dealing with child maltreatment involves working directly with the abused infant, toddler, or preschooler, the parents, and the family after abuse (or the threat of abuse) has been discovered. One goal is to protect the child from further mistreatment and help her recover from the physical and psychological consequences. Another is to assist the abusing parent(s) in establishing a parent-child relationship and family environment that adequately ensures the preschooler's safety and supports his developmental needs.

Intensive professional help, including family counseling and psychotherapy, often are used to help parents and child understand the causes, consequences, and personal meanings of their destructive feelings and behaviors so they will be able to live together in less destructive ways. A key aspect of treatment is to help parents improve their parenting skills. Self-help groups such as Parents Anonymous, parent aides who assist abusive and neglectful families in their homes, crisis nurseries, foster care for the abused child, and short-term residential treatment for family members or the entire family unit are among the treatment alternatives that have met with some success (Helfer & Kempe, 1987; Willis et al., 1992).

Early intervention programs that target "high-risk" families, including those headed by low-SES teenage mothers and minorities, have focused on helping parents improve their parenting skills, the family climate, and their ability to better cope with the stressful life events and conditions. Such programs include early and extended contact between parents and their newborn infants to improve the early parent-child relationship, parent education about child development and everyday child care problems, and home visitors and parent aides who assist parents with young children. They also offer training and support in home safety, money management, job finding, health maintenance and nutrition, leisure time counseling, and help in developing stronger social support networks (Rosenberg & Reppucci, 1985; Willis et al., 1992).

Other prevention efforts attempt to reduce or eliminate the causes of abuse by changing more general conditions that affect *all* children and families. These *social policy* efforts include education for parenthood programs, elimination of corporal punishment, the development of a bill of rights for children, and various social policy supports for parents and their children, including more and better jobs, funding for preschools and day care centers, affordable health care, and so forth.

What Do You Think?

If you were a preschool teacher, what behaviors in a child might lead you to suspect child maltreatment? What help is available to parents who may be at risk for abusing or neglecting their children?

LOOKING BACK/LOOKING FORWARD

Although the preschool period, considered as a whole, may not bring about physical changes as dramatic as those of infancy, the cognitive, social, and emotional changes that occur may be even more striking. By age five or six, a child has both worked and played with symbolic skills quite a lot, and sometimes is beginning to do so according to prearranged rules. He can form friendships that last at least a bit beyond the here and now and that both foster and draw on genuine understanding of others. His increasing social sophistication may also allow him to use less aggressive means of asserting his needs and dealing with conflict. All of these new skills, both positive and negative, are strongly guided by the child's gender role, a concept to which the child himself makes important contributions during the preschool years.

But human development is far from over at this point. The child's social world broadens widely in the years ahead, most obviously through her entry into school and the development of important social relationships outside her family. Major changes also occur in the child's cognitive abilities, physical growth, and motor skill development. The following chapters explore these and other important features of the child's development as she progresses through middle childhood.

SUMMARY OF MAJOR IDEAS

1. Even the physical and cognitive activities of preschool children are highly social.

Play in Early Childhood

2. Play is the major waking activity of preschoolers.

3. Play involves intrinsic motivation, process rather than product, pretense, and implicit and flexible rules.

4. Psychoanalytic theory emphasizes the mastery and wish fulfillment functions of play, whereas learning theory stresses the acquisition of social skills through imitation and observation.

5. Cognitive theory emphasizes that play develops in a sequence that generally parallels the major stages of cognitive development.

6. Functional play involves simple, repeated movements or manipulation of the body or inanimate objects. In constructive play, a child manipulates objects to build or construct something. Pretend, or make-believe, play allows the child to practice motor skills and rehearse social roles. Play involving games with rules focuses more heavily on the rules themselves.

7. Parten has identified six social levels of play: unoccupied, solitary, onlooker, parallel, associative, and cooperative play.

8. The type of setting is important to the development of social play.

Relationships with Others

9. Authoritative parents show a high level of control, strong demand for maturity, and high sensitivity and responsiveness to their children's needs and feelings. Their children tend to show greater self-reliance, self-control, and achievement.

10. Authoritarian parents exhibit a high degree of control and strong demand for maturity but low sensitivity and responsiveness to their children's thoughts and feelings. Their children tend to be more distrustful, be unhappy with themselves, and show lower school achievement than other children.

11. Permissive-indulgent parents are warm, caring, and responsive to their children's feelings, but exert little control and make few maturity demands. Their children tend to lack self-reliance and self-control.

12. Permissive-indifferent parents are detached, uninvolved, and inconsistent in their parenting. Their children tend to lack self-reliance and self-control and may be at risk for more severe social and emotional problems.

13. Parents often use mixtures of parenting styles and may change their preferred style as their children grow older.

14. Both siblings and friends contribute to social development during the preschool years. Ultimately, however, it is the parent's responsibility to establish the sort of parent-child interactions that foster positive social relationships.

15. Whereas early friendships are unstable and depend on specific shared activities, friendships among older preschoolers involve expectations about future behavior and popularity considerations.

16. Preschoolers' friendships become more durable and involve a greater degree of shared activity with age. As they near school age, the more permanent and personal qualities of friendship become increasingly important.

17. As children grow older, the support and judgments of parents and other adults contribute increasingly to children's feelings of empathy and prosocial activities.

18. Preschoolers commonly exhibit both hostile aggression and instrumental (nonhostile) aggression to assert their needs and resolve conflicts. As they grow older, verbal methods replace physical ones and overall aggression declines.

19. Temperamental differences, gender, family childrearing practices, peers, and the media all influence the form and frequency of aggressive behavior.

20. Children who cannot control their aggression can be helped to do so with methods such as assertiveness training and social learning theory strategies. Parents can learn to spot the triggers of their children's aggression and respond effectively.

21. Television viewing significantly influences preschoolers' social development in such areas as aggression, prosocial behavior, and gender stereotyping.

Gender Development

22. During early childhood, children acquire an understanding of gender-typed behaviors and gender identity. A sense of gender constancy, the belief that being male or female is biologically determined and permanent, typically is not achieved until ages seven to nine.

23. Because the development of stereotypes about personal qualities appears to depend on the ability to think abstractly, children do not gain a clear and stable concept of gender until the school years.

24. Influences on gender development include differential expectations and treatment of boys and girls by parents, peers, and the media.

25. A more flexible approach to gender roles enables children to adopt more androgynous behaviors and attitudes.

Child Maltreatment

26. More than 1 million cases of child maltreatment are reported annually. Types of abuse include physical, psychological, and sexual abuse. Neglect can be physical or emotional.

27. Causes of maltreatment occur at the levels of the individual parent, the family, the community, and the culture.

28. Consequences of child maltreatment include a range of developmental, adjustment, and emotional problems.

29. Responses to child maltreatment frequently focus on treating the victims and their families. Prevention efforts include early intervention programs targeting "high-risk" families and attempts to change more general conditions that affect all children and families.

KEY TERMS

functional play *(223)*
constructive play *(224)*
pretend play *(224)*
games with rules *(225)*
authoritative
    parenting *(230)*
authoritarian
    parenting *(232)*
permissive-indulgent
    parenting *(233)*
permissive-indifferent
    parenting *(233)*

empathy *(236)*
aggression *(239)*
instrumental
    aggression *(239)*
hostile aggression *(239)*
gender *(246)*
gender role
    stereotypes *(246)*
androgyny *(248)*

PART FOUR

Middle Childhood

Because growth slows after the preschool years, children in middle childhood have more time and energy to develop skills of all sorts, from riding a skateboard to making friends. An accumulation of language practice and symbolic, make-believe play pay off: school-age children can think more logically than ever before, at least if they choose to and usually only when thinking relates to concrete matters. These new competencies, combined with children's experience of attending school, make peers more important than ever before.

Adults often remember middle childhood as the best years of their youth, though it is not clear that children themselves would agree with this assessment. For high-SES families, the world now likely seems secure, children's health is excellent, and children's skills and abilities improve steadily and visibly year by year. Unfortunately, not all families enjoy high SES; for them, the middle childhood years can be just as challenging as the periods before and after.

8

MIDDLE CHILDHOOD

Physical and Cognitive Development

PHYSICAL DEVELOPMENT

Trends and Variations in Height and Weight

Motor Development and Athletics in Middle Childhood

Health and Illness in Middle Childhood

Social Influences on Illness
Attention Deficit Hyperactivity Disorder

COGNITIVE DEVELOPMENT

Piaget's Theory: Concrete Operational Skills

Conservation in Middle Childhood
Conservation Training
Other Concrete Operational Skills
Piaget's Influence on Education

Information-Processing Skills

Memory Capacity
Difficulties with Information Processing: Learning Disabilities

Language Development in Middle Childhood

Understanding Metaphor
Bilingualism and Its Effects
Black English

Defining and Measuring Intelligence

Psychometric Approaches to Intelligence
Information-Processing Approaches to Intelligence
Sociocultural Approaches to Intelligence

The Changing Child: Physical, Cognitive, and Social

C armen and Mercedes were sisters. When Carmen was six and Mercedes nine, they both decided they wanted to buy skates. The problem was to find the money. They sold lemonade at the curbside: "DRINX, 25 SENTS" said a sign made by Carmen. In three days they had sold ten drinks. "That's $2.50," noted Mercedes. "Not nearly enough." Carmen puzzled over how long it would take them to earn enough; she thought maybe about a year, but she was not sure.

After a few more days—and increasing discouragement—their mother brought home one pair of used skates. "It's to share," she said, "because it's all I can afford. And besides, the two of you are nearly the same size!" This arrangement was not ideal, but the girls did attempt to take turns with the skates. And that is where the real trouble began: Carmen soon proved more skillful at using the skates than her older sister. After a few months, Mercedes gave up taking her turns with them, despite her mother's encouragement.

These events suggest the close relationship that can exist between physical and cognitive development in middle childhood. Physical growth follows individual paths, with some children growing tall (or short) for their age and children of different ages ending up relatively similar for periods of time. Cognitive skills emerge more strongly than in the preschool years and are often "recruited" into the service of goals related to physical and motor skill growth, such as skating.

In this chapter, we look at physical and cognitive development in the middle childhood years. Although we discuss each domain of development separately, as in earlier chapters, Carmen and Mercedes' experience emphasize that both domains evolve together.

Focusing Questions

- What trends in height and weight occur among school-age children?

- What improvements in motor skills do children usually experience during the school years, and how do they affect children's involvement in athletic activity?

- What kinds of illnesses occur among schoolchildren? How does children's socioeconomic status affect their health?

- What new cognitive skills do children acquire during the school years? What are the psychological and practical effects of these new skills?

- How does memory change during middle childhood? How do these changes affect thinking and learning?

- What new changes in language emerge during middle childhood?

- What is general intelligence, and how can it be measured?

- How does acquiring two languages affect a child's cognitive development?

PHYSICAL DEVELOPMENT

In general, children's physical growth slows during middle childhood (ages six to twelve) even more than it does during early childhood. Specific physical skills are easier to teach than they used to be because children now find them easier to learn. For a school-age child, instruction and practice in baseball make a more obvious difference in skill development than they did when she was still a preschooler. This means the child can now acquire physical and athletic skills that may give her a lifetime of satisfaction. But children *can* get hurt during physical activity, and athletic games can emphasize competition that is unrealistic or unpleasant.

Children are relatively healthy during the school years, but they do sometimes have accidents or get sick. A few children also develop problems that have ambiguous physical causes, and such children may show excessive motor activity even in quiet situations or difficulties in learning specific academic skills. Such problems may originate from subtle differences in how the nervous system operates in these children, although this is far from certain.

In the sections that follow, we review these ideas in more detail. We begin by looking at normal trends and variations in overall growth during middle childhood. Then we examine specific motor skill and athletic development and their psychological effects on children. Finally, we discuss health in the school years, with special reference to children who are overly active.

TRENDS AND VARIATIONS IN HEIGHT AND WEIGHT

As Figure 8.1 shows, children grow steadily during the middle childhood years, from about forty-six inches and forty-five pounds at age six to almost sixty inches and eighty pounds at age twelve (Engels, 1993). At the same time, variations among children are often significant. Figure 8.2 shows, for example, that the average height of eight-year-old girls varies from forty-five inches in South Korea to almost fifty-one inches in Russia. And at any one age within any one society, individual variations are even more dramatic. The shortest and tallest six-year-olds in North America differ by only two or three inches, but the shortest and tallest twelve-year-olds differ by more than one foot. The changes are a source of both pride and dismay to individual children.

Toward the end of elementary school, girls tend to become significantly taller than boys of the same age. The difference results partly from girls' earlier puberty and partly from the timing of the growth spurt associated with puberty for each sex. For boys, a spurt in height tends to follow the other physical changes of adolescence, such as the growth of pubic hair and the deepening of the voice. For girls, a

Late in childhood, girls often grow taller and faster than boys of the same age. The disparity can create awkward moments for members of both sexes, though many children do not seem to be concerned about it at all. When these children become older adolescents or young adults, they may not even remember that a disparity occurred.

FIGURE 8.1
Growth in Height and Weight from Two to Eighteen Years
During the early school years, children continue to grow at a smooth rate, though more slowly than in early childhood and infancy. By the middle and later parts of this period, however, weight and height begin to accelerate as children move into puberty. The growth spurts usually begin sooner for weight than for height and sooner for girls than for boys.

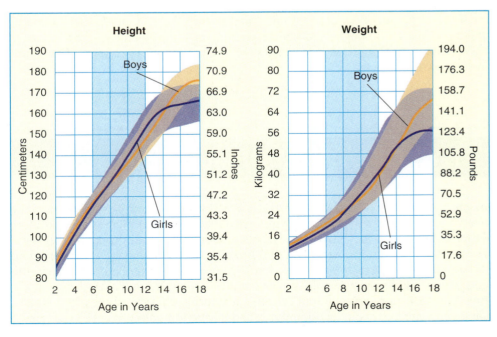

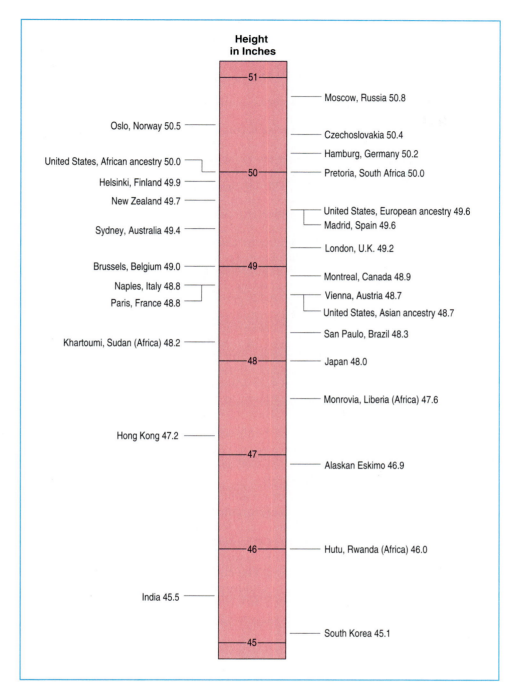

Height in Inches

Moscow, Russia 50.8

Oslo, Norway 50.5

Czechoslovakia 50.4

Hamburg, Germany 50.2

United States, African ancestry 50.0

Pretoria, South Africa 50.0

Helsinki, Finland 49.9

New Zealand 49.7

United States, European ancestry 49.6
Madrid, Spain 49.6

Sydney, Australia 49.4

London, U.K. 49.2

Brussels, Belgium 49.0

Montreal, Canada 48.9

Naples, Italy 48.8
Paris, France 48.8

Vienna, Austria 48.7

United States, Asian ancestry 48.7

Khartoumi, Sudan (Africa) 48.2

San Paulo, Brazil 48.3

Japan 48.0

Monrovia, Liberia (Africa) 47.6

Hong Kong 47.2

Alaskan Eskimo 46.9

Hutu, Rwanda (Africa) 46.0

India 45.5

South Korea 45.1

FIGURE 8.2
Ethnic and Cultural Differences in Growth
Differences in height are associated strongly with cultural and ethnic background. This chart summarizes the heights of eight-year-old girls from a number of nations and regions of the world. Girls from eastern and northern Europe are nearly six inches taller than girls of the same age from India and South Korea. Similar trends occur for boys.
Source: Adapted from Meredith (1978).

spurt in height usually occurs before the growth of breasts and pubic hair. We look again at these and other physical changes of puberty in Chapter 10.

At least one American child in ten suffers from **obesity,** meaning the child weighs more than 130 percent of the normal weight for his or her height and bone size (Cassell, 1994). This means that a child who is fifty-four inches tall weighs more than eighty-five pounds instead of a normal weight of about sixty-five pounds. Psychologically, the condition can be particularly difficult for girls, since cultural norms emphasize physical thinness more heavily in females than in males. (But note: in some other cultures, physical size is not important to individuals' social success; see the accompanying Multicultural View box.) Throughout life, obesity causes physical problems as well. As pointed out in Chapter 12's discussion of physical development

A Multicultural View

Dieting in Cross-Cultural Perspective

In our society, self-administered dieting and exercise has become a major industry. Countless books have been published to help individuals lose weight and gain muscle, and many of them are intended for children (see, for example, Schwarzenegger & Gaines, 1994). Attaining a culturally valued bodily "look" can become a major personal project, one that for many children begins in late childhood and continues well into adulthood.

At the heart of North Americans' preoccupation with body image is not only a concern with nutrition and health but also a commitment to crucial cultural values. One of these values is *individualism,* a belief that people are fundamentally autonomous and responsible for themselves. From this notion comes the belief that your body indeed belongs to you and that you personally are responsible for how it looks. How it compares to social ideals of physical beauty therefore indicates your success as a member of society as well as your ongoing commitment to participation in society. A lean, thin body (supposedly) shows self-discipline and restraint, two socially admired qualities, because it implies that you have been eating and exercising responsibly. To achieve these

things, numerous individuals embark on exercise and diet programs for varying periods of time. Girls and women are especially likely to do so, since they are almost certain to be judged by their physical appearance repeatedly, even during childhood (Bordo, 1993).

Yet a preoccupation with diet and exercise is not universal. The Fiji islanders in the South Pacific, for example, seem generally indifferent to the size or weight (Becker, 1994). At the same time, they have definite ideals about physical appearance: a person should have sturdy calf muscles, for example, and generally look "well fed" (a bit plump by our standards). Furthermore, despite their indifference to size and weight, the Fijians comment on one another's physical looks constantly and directly. Everyday greetings often include teasing about whether a person looks fatter (or thinner) than in the past. Daily conversations about persons not present ("gossip") also refer frequently to a person's size, particularly if his or her size seems to have changed.

The paradox of personal indifference combined with public frankness is accounted for by the Fijians' fundamental orientation to their *community* rather than to

in early adulthood, people who were obese as children and continue to be obese as adults risk a variety of minor illnesses, as well as a few major ones such as heart disease and diabetes (Rotatori & Fox, 1989).

Unfortunately, for either a child or an adult, losing weight permanently is difficult to do. For a child, dieting or exercise must have the full support of parents and siblings, because these people have such substantial influence on meal preparation and on a child's daily activities (Pittman & Kaufman, 1994). Yet family members may find support is difficult to sustain over the long periods of time most weight control programs require. The collective will power may simply be lacking, especially because overweight children tend to have siblings and parents who are overweight themselves. Table 8.1 lists some additional guidelines for treating a childhood weight problem successfully.

TABLE 8.1   *Guidelines for Responding to a Child's Weight Problem*

1. *Make sure the child really needs to lose weight.* Weighing only a little (10 percent) more than average poses no medical risk and may cause a child few social problems in the long term. If a child is teased for his or her weight, learning ways to cope with the teasing may be more effective than trying to lose weight.

2. *Consult with a doctor or a trained nutritionist before starting the child on a diet program.* A diet should aim at stabilizing weight or causing a loss of only about one pound per week at most. It should be balanced nutritionally and include snacks. Crash diets or food fads should be avoided at all costs; they are not effective and can seriously jeopardize a child's health.

3. *Develop a program of exercise appropriate for the child.* Start slowly and build up gradually. Try to incorporate activities that the child enjoys and that can fit into his or her daily routines conveniently.

4. *Seek support from the child's whole family, as well as from teachers or others whom the child sees regularly.* These people must show respect for the child's efforts, offer encouragement, and avoid tempting the child to break a diet or give up on exercise. Most of all, participate *with* the child in programs of activity or programs to control eating.

themselves as individuals. What is important to an individual Fijian is not personal achievement or standing out from the average but showing a nurturing and caring attitude toward friends, family, and children. A primary vehicle for attaining these goals is food: serving food is a major way to show interest and attention to others' needs, both physical and emotional. According to custom, Fijians open their windows and doors during mealtimes so that the event becomes more truly public, and anyone passing by is cordially (and sincerely) invited in to share the food. Extra food is routinely prepared for each meal to allow for this possibility, because it is considered a social disgrace to be unable to share food generously with whoever happens to come by.

The Fiji islanders, therefore, consider dieting to be self-centered and irresponsible because it prevents a person from either giving or receiving nurturance from the community. In a sense, a person's body "belongs" to the community rather than to the individual. Secret eating is a serious social mistake, as is secret noneating (dieting). Parents observe their children carefully for changes in appetite, as well as for changes in weight (either up or down) that may imply fluctuations in appetite. They do so not because they want their children to achieve a certain size but because they want them to participate fully in both the giving and receiving of community care, and an important way of participating is through food.

In Fiji, it is not the cultivation of a certain body image that confers prestige, as in North American society. Instead, it is the cultivation of social relationships, particularly those that make nurturance possible. Is this orientation preferable to our own? The focus on caregiving spares most Fijian children from worries about their physical appearance, as well as from discouragement caused by unsuccessful dieting or exercise programs to improve physical looks (Sault, 1994). But a negative effect also is possible: the focus on community can create problems for children who *must* limit their eating for health reasons, such as diabetes or intestinal flu. In a strongly communal society, these situations can prove especially worrisome to both child and family, since they require deliberately limiting participation in a central social practice: the daily abundant sharing of food.

What Do You Think?

Is concern about height and weight really a gender issue? Why or why not? Check your perceptions by polling ten male and ten female acquaintances (it's easier if you collaborate in doing this task) about whether they weigh more than, less than, or close to the ideal. Then ask them how they think members of the opposite sex would answer the same question, on average.

MOTOR DEVELOPMENT AND ATHLETICS IN MIDDLE CHILDHOOD

Fundamental motor skills continue to improve during the school years and gradually become specialized in response to each child's particular interests, physical aptitudes, life experiences, and the expectations of others. Unlike a preschooler, an older child no longer is content simply to run, jump, and throw things; now she puts these skills to use in complex, active play. Sometimes this consists of informal, child-organized games, such as hide-and-seek, in which the child uses her motor skills. At other times, active play involves formal sports such as gymnastics, swimming, or hockey.

During the school years, children develop the ability to play games with rules. Some of these games are informal, such as after-school hopscotch, and some are formal and adult sponsored, such as Little League softball. In any case, traditional team sports now begin to have meaning for children because they can understand and abide by a game's rules. At the same time, children's improvements in coordination and timing enhance their performance in all kinds of sports, whether individual or group.

School-age children continue to refine fundamental motor skills, such as running, walking, or throwing. They show the biggest improvements in activities—like this game involving jumping and leaping—that require both coordination and timing simultaneously.

What lasting physical and psychological effects do early athletics have on children? This question has not been studied as thoroughly for children as it has for adolescents and adults, but a few tentative answers are possible. On balance, athletic activity probably helps children much more than it hurts them, though it does carry some risks. Table 8.2 lists examples of the physical effects, and Table 8.3 lists some psychological effects.

In North America, girls are especially likely to drop out of athletic activity late in middle childhood. On the whole, they do so for cultural rather than physiologi-

In addition to obvious physical benefits, early athletics can also encourage achievement motivation, discipline, and a sense of self-esteem. Critics worry, though, that some sport activities may also cause injuries and destructive competition.

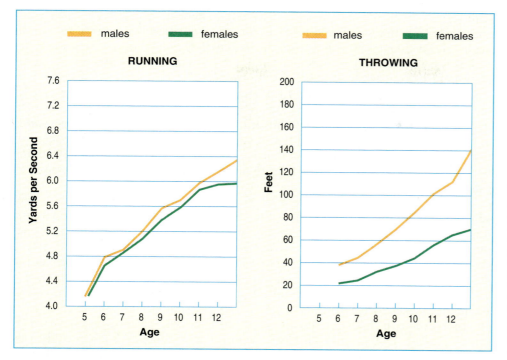

FIGURE 8.3
Running Speed and Throwing Distance for Boys and Girls at Different Ages
As the data indicate, despite changing gender roles in society, boys still tend to run faster and throw farther than girls during middle childhood. The data summarize a number of studies carried out since 1960. The gender gap increases as children enter adolescence.
Source: Gallahue (1989), adapted from Haubenstricker & Seefeldt (1986).

cal reasons (Scraton, 1992). Throughout childhood girls compare favorably with boys in strength, endurance, and motor skill, and late in childhood girls also tend to be physically more mature than boys. But beginning at about age twelve, they begin to perform less well than boys on tests of physical skills: they run slower, jump less far, and lift less weight (see Figure 8.3). (This particular gender difference continues well into middle age, as we will see when we discuss psychosocial development in middle adulthood in Chapter 15.) Because physical training can eliminate these differences (Hunter-Griffin, 1990), girls' relatively poor performance most likely results from social expectations about gender. At the time of puberty, some girls begin to emphasize nonathletic pursuits such as listening to rock music or reading or talking with friends. (Some boys, of course, do the same.) Fortunately, gender role standards may be shifting, and athletic activity may be getting more attractive for both sexes, as well as more accessible for girls than in the past (Ontario Ministry of Culture, Tourism, and Recreation, 1994).

What Do You Think?

Do childhood athletics by nature foster a competitive spirit among players? Or does competitiveness develop from stimulation by coaches and parents? This issue can spark a lively in-class discussion, especially if you can include a person who has been successful at competitive athletics as well as someone who has not!

HEALTH AND ILLNESS IN MIDDLE CHILDHOOD

Whether they are physically active or not, children usually are relatively healthy in the middle childhood years in the sense that they experience illnesses or accidents

TABLE 8.2 *Physical Effects of Childhood Athletics*

Postive

Better physical fitness
Improved motor coordination

Negative

Sports-related injuries: knee injuries (football), back problems (gymnastics), shoulder pain (baseball), among others

TABLE 8.3 *Psychological Effects of Childhood Athletics*

Postive

Training in achievement motivation (e.g., bettering previous running times) support for team work (e.g., basketball)

Negative

Competition (e.g., more concern with winning than with performance as such)

Excessive pressure from adults to practice, perform well, and win

with serious medical consequences only rarely. School-age children also have colds and minor viral illnesses less often than preschool children and infants do. But illnesses and accidents can still disrupt the lives individual children, which partly accounts for why medical professionals and parents may disagree about whether or not schoolchildren are "really" healthy in general.

One sign of good health is very low **mortality,** or the proportion of persons dying at a given age. In recent years, only about three or four children in every ten thousand die between ages six and thirteen, compared to twice this number among preschoolers and four times this figure among adolescents (U.S. Department of Commerce, 1995). The low rate of mortality is part of a historical trend extending back over the past century in which death rates have declined for all age groups, but especially for children.

On the average, schoolchildren get sick only about one-half as often as preschoolers do, though still about twice as often as do their parents. From parents' point of view, therefore, illnesses probably still seem rather frequent; nearly one-quarter of the parents in one survey reported that during the preceding two weeks their children were "too sick to carry on as normal" (Coiro, 1994), meaning the children stayed home from school for at least one day. As parents often point out, a sick child has a substantial impact on the work and leisure schedules of the rest of the family, especially parents.

Most common childhood diseases are **acute illnesses,** meaning they have a definite beginning, middle, and end. Most childhood acute illnesses, such as colds, gastrointestinal flu, chicken pox, and measles, develop from *viruses,* complex protein molecules that come alive only when they infect a host tissue (such as a child's nose). Despite popular belief, no drugs can combat viral infections. (This is not the case with bacteria that invade the body; they can be effectively fought off with antibiotic drugs.) Instead, viral illnesses must run their course, and the child's natural immunities must work the real cure.

By the school years, about 5 to 10 percent of children develop **chronic illnesses,** or conditions that persist for many months without significant improvement. In the United States and other developed countries, the most common chronic conditions occur in the lungs and affect breathing (United Nations International Children's Emergency Fund, 1995). Some children develop *asthma,* or persistent congestion in the lungs; others develop chronic coughs or allergies. Other chronic complaints concern specific sensory organs. About one child in one hundred, for example, experiences problems in hearing or seeing. These and other chronic health problems become more frequent with age; among elderly people they become commonplace, as we will see in Chapter 16's discussion of physical development in late adulthood.

Social Influences on Illness

The seriousness of illnesses varies according to children's social and socioeconomic status, but not the frequency. In general, parents in higher-SES families report that their school-age children get sick just about as often as those from lower-SES families, but higher-SES parents report keeping their children at home for shorter periods of time (Fitzgerald et al., 1994). What accounts for the difference? Low-SES families probably lack money for doctors' visits, access to special child care when a child is sick, and permission to take time off from work to tend to a sick child. Therefore, to merit staying home from school or visiting a doctor, a child must have a relatively major illness, such as a seriously high fever or severe diarrhea. The result of these circumstances shows up in the longer average stay at home when illness finally receives special attention.

Race and sex appear to matter too. African American families report *fewer* illnesses per child than do white families of similar SES, and all families of both races report *more* illnesses for girls than for boys of the same age (Johnson, 1995). In fact, school-age girls appear to get sick almost as often as preschool children of both sexes do; boys, however, get sick less frequently as they get older. Each of these differences probably reflects cultural influences. Medical care and an "on-call," stay-at-home parent may be less available to African American children than to white children, for example, necessitating that they continue to attend school even with minor illnesses. Furthermore, gender expectations may encourage girls to seek care for minor ailments and encourage boys to ignore such ailments, trends that continue into adulthood.

Attention Deficit Hyperactivity Disorder

A small number of school-age children, especially boys, seem to be extremely active and have considerable trouble concentrating on any one activity for long (American Psychiatric Association, 1994). Their problem is called **hyperactivity,** or **attention deficit hyperactivity disorder (ADHD)**. A second-grade teacher described one student with ADHD like this:

> Joey was friendly when you greeted him; "Hi!" he would say brightly, and smile. But he would never settle down. First he dumped the class's main supply of pencils out on a table; he sort of lunged at one of the pencils, but before he began writing, he left the table, looking for something new. During a reading lesson, I asked Joey to read silently until I finished helping another child; but Joey found this hard to do. He glanced in my direction; tapped a neighboring child on the shoulder; giggled; and kept scanning the room for "more." A child happened to drop a book; Joey laughed at this harder than the others, and jumped up quickly to pick the book up. He was probably trying to help, but in doing so he knocked his own papers all over the floor. Instead of picking up the papers, he only picked up his pencil, and headed off to sharpen it. And the morning was still only half over!

Note that *most* children show excessive activity—behavior such as Joey's—*some* of the time. Only a few children really exhibit extremely high activity levels consistently enough to warrant professional attention. Experts suggest five criteria for deciding when activity poses a truly serious problem (Ingersoll & Goldstein, 1993):

1. The overactivity occurs even when it is clearly inappropriate, such as when the child is riding in a car or sitting at a meal.
2. Seriously overactive children consistently fail to respond to pressures to inhibit their activity.
3. Seriously overactive children seem to always respond at the same rapid pace, even when they are trying to respond more slowly, such as when drawing a picture.
4. Seriously overactive children show other, related problems, such as high distractibility and difficulties in making friends.
5. Seriously overactive children exhibit poor academic achievement without evidence of sensory, physical, or cognitive disability.

Only children who meet all or most of these criteria warrant the often misused label *hyperactive;* all others probably should be considered simply *very active* or *overactive.*

Causes of ADHD   Most psychologists and medical researchers agree that ADHD has biological roots, but they do not know for sure what those roots are (Rutter,

1995). It seems likely that ADHD in individual children has different causes: one child may have suffered oxygen deprivation during birth, for example, whereas another child may have been exposed to toxic substances such as lead (found in the paint in many older houses). Head injuries are more common among children with ADHD than among other children, but it is not clear whether the injuries caused high activity or whether hyperactivity made children prone to the injuries (by bumping into things at high speed, for example).

In addition to biological explanations, it is tempting to believe that a child's parents or social environment may accidentally precipitate hyperactivity in some way, such as by setting rules for behavior that are too precise or rigid. Yet it is unclear whether strict childrearing is a cause of ADHD or an effect; having a very active child naturally drives parents to impose more rules and restrictions on her or his activities! In one study, ADHD children were given medication to reduce their activity levels; subsequent observations revealed that the parents became less strict than they were before the medication was given (Barkley, 1985). It is also true that many parents are strict without their children becoming hyperactive. The most reasonable conclusion, then, is that parents or teachers probably do not cause hyperactivity directly, but they may inadvertently aggravate it in some cases by responding to very active children inappropriately. What adults need are not new personalities but specific techniques and advice for dealing with such children.

Helping Children with ADHD and Their Families   Because no one is sure what makes some children overactive, and because ADHD usually persists throughout an individual's childhood and beyond, no single strategy for treating or dealing with the condition exists. However, a group of strategies have proven helpful for the majority of children with this problem.

To reduce immediate symptoms, the most effective treatment is a stimulant medication. One common and effective stimulant has been *Ritalin* (also called *methylphenidate*), which, paradoxically, quiets the child's behavior by "waking up" the central nervous system, that is, making it more alert. When used properly, Ritalin has no short-term, negative side effects; contrary to popular belief, it does not make the child lethargic, depressed, drowsy, or lacking in spontaneity (Johnston, 1991). Instead, it makes the child less bossy, argumentative, and noisy and better able to focus on tasks.

In addition to medication, behavior modification often helps to alter some of the most undesirable or counterproductive behaviors of an ADHD child. As the term implies, **behavior modification** is a psychotherapeutic technique that identifies specific behaviors that need changing, as well as straightforward techniques for eliminating or reducing them (Kazdin, 1994). In classrooms, one behavior modification technique consists of using high-status peers to model or demonstrate appropriate behaviors. The active child simply watches a classmate complete an assignment slowly instead of at lightning speed; then the child tries to copy the same slow style in doing the assignment himself. The teacher, of course, reinforces (usually with praise) the modulated behavior when it occurs.

One key quality of behavior modification is its consistency and predictability, and parents and teachers can help significantly by striving to provide these qualities in the child's everyday environment. At home this means meals, play times, and bedtimes should come at about the same times every day and follow roughly the same pattern. At school, lessons should have a regular, predictable format. In either setting, rules of acceptable and unacceptable behavior should be clear, simple, and relatively consistent. All of these strategies help the ADHD child by temporarily reducing the demands on her attention-directing capacities and allowing these abilities to develop at her own pace.

When these strategies are followed, about half of all ADHD children eventually outgrow the problem, although they often report continuing to feel restless and distractible as adults (Weiss & Hechtman, 1993). The remaining ADHD children show some greater risk as adults for minor antisocial behaviors, such as failure to pay parking tickets or carrying (but not using) a weapon. Psychiatric experts generally believe, however, that such behaviors may result not so much from ADHD itself as from the extensive interpersonal conflicts these individuals experience in growing up: many ADHD children live in chronic conflict with teachers and parents for years and, in this sense, are "driven to distraction" (Hallowell & Ratey, 1994).

What Do You Think?

Some experts argue that children with ADHD are not so much "disturbed" as "disturbing." What do you suppose they mean by this comment? Speculate about ways that home and school could be made less "disturbing" for a hyperactive child. Offer your ideas to a teacher or some other person who has experience with children's behavior problems. What does this person think?

COGNITIVE DEVELOPMENT

While school-age children are coping with the challenges of physical growth, they are also developing a wide range of cognitive skills and abilities. Viewed from the perspective of Piaget's theory, they are developing concrete operational thinking, a concept we will look at more closely in the next section. Viewed from the newer perspective of *information-processing theory,* children are acquiring new memory and learning strategies (though not necessarily using them effectively yet).

School-age children are also making new strides in language. Later in the chapter, we will see how children differ in their styles of speaking and how these variations can affect children's educational and social success. We will also discuss how and why psychologists consider these variations to be part of a very general human quality, *intelligence.* First, though, let's look at Piaget's ideas about cognition in middle childhood.

PIAGET'S THEORY: CONCRETE OPERATIONAL SKILLS

As we discussed in Chapter 2, Jean Piaget developed a comprehensive theory of cognitive development from birth through adolescence. During middle childhood, according to this theory, children become skilled at **concrete operations,** mental activities focused on real, tangible objects and events. Concrete operations have three interrelated qualities, none of which is reliably present among preschool children: decentration, sensitivity to transformations, and reversibility (Piaget, 1965). *Decentration* means attending to more than one feature of a problem at a time. For example, in estimating the number of pennies spread out on a table, a

In one of the most widely known Piagetian tasks, children evaluate whether the amount of liquid stays the same when poured into a beaker of a different shape. Most children over the age of six believe that the amount does stay the same, a dramatic change from the preschool years.

school-age child probably will take into account not only how large the array is but also how far apart individual pennies seem to be. *Sensitivity to transformations* means having different perceptions of the same object and combining them in logical ways. For example, when judging whether the amount of liquid in a glass stays the same after being poured into a new container, a school-age child concentrates on the actual process of change in appearance—the transformation—rather than on how the liquid looks either before or after pouring. *Reversibility* of thought means understanding that certain logical operations (for example, addition) can be reversed by others (subtraction). All in all, the concrete operational child constructs a view of the world that emphasizes quantitative relationships for the first time. Now many facts seem logically necessary that earlier appeared arbitrary or even incomprehensible. In judging whether the amount of liquid stays the same when transferred to a new container, the child now reasons that the amount *must* be the same if nothing was added or taken away when the liquid was poured.

Concrete operations cause important transformations in the cognitive skills children develop in the preoperational period. In classifying objects, children can group things in more than one way at a time by about age seven. They know that a person can be *both* a parent and a teacher at the same time, for example, rather than just one or the other. They also understand that some classifications are inclusive of others, for example, that a particular animal can be both a dog and a pet. As a result, they usually can answer correctly a question such as "Are there more boys in your class or more children?" Preschool children, in contrast, often fail to answer such a question correctly unless it is further simplified or clarified.

Conservation in Middle Childhood

Some cognitive skills make their first real appearance during middle childhood. Probably the best known of these skills is **conservation,** a realization that certain properties of an object necessarily remain constant despite changes in the object's appearance. An example of conservation of quantity is the one described in Chapter 6 in which two tall, narrow glasses contain exactly the same amount of water. If you empty one glass into a wide, low tray, you create a substantial perceptual change in the water; it looks quite different than before and quite different than the water in the remaining tall glass, as Figure 8.4 shows. Will a child know that the wide tray has the same amount of water the tall glass does? If he does, he conserves, meaning he shows a belief in the water's underlying constancy despite a perceptual change.

Piaget (1965) found that after about age seven, most children did indeed conserve quantity in the water glass experiment. In fact, he found that by a year or two later, children conserved on a lot of other tasks as well, including the ones illustrated in Figure 8.4. Each of the tasks depicted requires believing in some form of invariance despite perceptual change. The clay balls, like the water glasses, require believing that mass remains constant; the bent wires and the pencils, that distance or length remains constant; and the coins, that number remains constant.

Conservation Training

Specialists agree that children do not begin life conserving but instead acquire this skill somehow. How do they do it? Piaget argued that biological maturation and countless experiences with physical objects that show conservation properties enable children to mentally construct conservation. These experiences are numerous

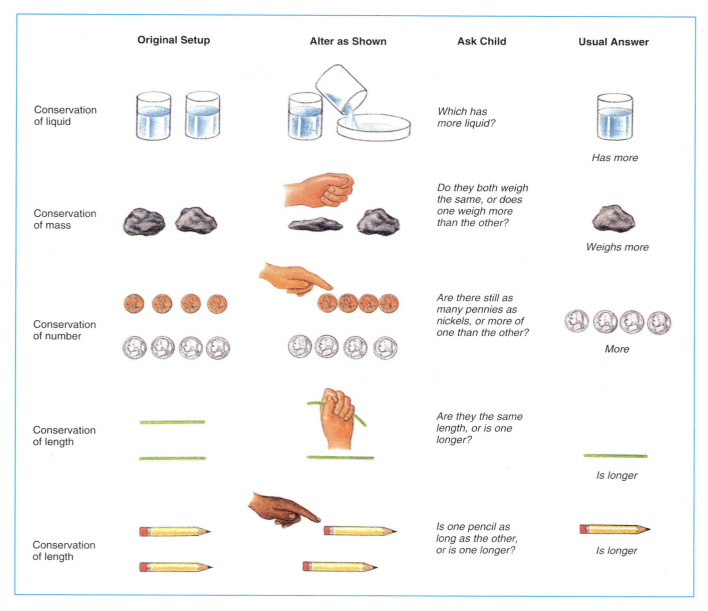

Original Setup	Alter as Shown	Ask Child	Usual Answer

Conservation of liquid — *Which has more liquid?* — *Has more*

Conservation of mass — *Do they both weigh the same, or does one weigh more than the other?* — *Weighs more*

Conservation of number — *Are there still as many pennies as nickels, or more of one than the other?* — *More*

Conservation of length — *Are they the same length, or is one longer?* — *Is longer*

Conservation of length — *Is one pencil as long as the other, or is one longer?* — *Is longer*

FIGURE 8.4

Conservation Experiments
As Piaget demonstrated, conservation (or the perception of invariance) emerges on a wide scale in middle childhood. In some cases, the child realizes that amounts of liquid or of solid mass remains constant; in other cases, he or she realizes that length or number remains constant. Early in middle childhood, however, the child often holds one of these beliefs without necessarily holding another, or holds one belief only on some occasions and not on others.

and diverse, and although they can be taught explicitly, Piaget believed they have a fuller, more general influence on development if allowed to emerge naturally.

But many psychologists have tried to teach conservation anyway. In recent studies, investigators tried to prevent children from being distracted by coaching them to talk about what was happening ("Nothing is being added or taken away") or to compare the important dimensions closely ("Watch the height *and* the width"). Such efforts do produce greater conserving in a large number of children, though not in all (Bijstra et al., 1991; Field, 1987). Conservation has even been taught successfully to children with mental retardation (Hendler & Weisberg, 1992).

However, trained children often do not maintain conservation concepts the same way "natural" conservers tend to do; they are more likely to give up their belief when even slightly challenged. "Natural" conservers are more steadfast in their commitment to conservation (although even they can be led to give it up if an experimenter shows strong skepticism about it). All in all, it seems that conservation may not develop during childhood as inevitably as Piaget first believed.

School-age children can use their spatial relations skills to make accurate maps of familiar places, such as their own neighborhoods. But like some adults, they often have trouble using a map as a guide to an unfamiliar place.

Other Concrete Operational Skills

Piaget described many other forms of knowledge that emerge during middle childhood (Piaget, 1983). For one thing, children become able to *seriate,* or arrange objects in sequence according to some dimension such as length or size. For another, they understand *temporal relations,* or the nature of time, better than they did as preschoolers; an eight-year-old knows that time unfolds in a single, constant flow marked by calendars, clocks, and landmark events. Children at this age can also represent the *spatial relations* of their surroundings. They can make maps and models of familiar places, such as their homes, their classrooms, or the local shopping mall.

Piaget's Influence on Education

Although Piaget commented on educational issues (Piaget, 1970), he never intended his research to serve as a theory of education. At no time, in particular, did he offer advice about problems that normally concern teachers, such as how to teach reading or other conventional school subjects, how to motivate students, or how to evaluate students' learning. Nonetheless, his ideas and approach have significantly influenced educators, particularly those in early childhood education (Elkind, 1994a). At the heart of this influence is Piaget's *constructivist philosophy:* the assumption that children develop their own concepts through active engagement with the environment. Also at the heart is Piaget's emphasis on universal stages of cognition. These ideas have lent support to curricula that encourage students' choice of activities and self-discovery of new concepts, particularly during the early parts of an educational program or unit of study.

What Do You Think?

Given Piaget's ideas about how thinking develops in middle childhood, what would be a good way to evaluate a student's work in elementary school? Devise a way to evaluate a favorite elementary school activity. Then see how your plan compares to one devised by a classmate or (if possible) to one composed by an experienced teacher.

INFORMATION-PROCESSING SKILLS

Another way to understand the cognitive changes of middle childhood is in terms of how children begin organizing and remembering information. This perspective utilizes the information-processing theory described in Chapter 2. By school age, children's short-term memories already are well developed. Their skills at processing information for long-term memory, however, show significant limitations compared to those of adults, but the limitations diminish during this age period.

Memory Capacity

According to popular wisdom, children remember better as they get older. But how true is this idea really? In everyday life, children obviously do not perform as well as adults do on some tasks, such as remembering to put away their clothes at the end of the day. But in other ways they seem to perform equally well; for example, they will remember their grandparents when they see them again after months or even years of absence.

Short-Term Memory   Some of these differences in memory may depend on which parts of the information-processing model the children happen to be using. Some tasks rely primarily on *short-term memory (STM)*, a feature of thinking that holds information only for a short period, perhaps up to twenty seconds (see Chapter 2). On tasks that emphasize short-term recognition memory, school-age children perform less well than adults do. Experimenters have demonstrated this tendency by showing subjects a set of digits briefly and then immediately asking them whether the set included a particular digit (Cowan, 1995; Dempster, 1981). Under these conditions, recognition of a test digit improved steadily, with eight-year-olds remembering only about three digits and adults remembering about seven. Not surprisingly, too, the time it took a subject to recognize a test digit *did* depend on how many digits were shown in the original set, regardless of the person's age. Showing six digits made the task take longer than showing just three, no doubt because the subject evaluated the test digit against a larger number of alternatives.

This study assessed a variation of **recognition memory,** in which a person merely compares an external stimulus or cue with preexisting experiences or knowledge. Recognition memory is involved when children look at snapshots of a holiday celebration months in the past: their faces light up, and they may describe aspects of the celebration they had apparently forgotten. **Recall memory,** in contrast, involves remembering information in the absence of external cues, such as when trying to remember a friend's telephone number without looking it up. Recall generally is more difficult than recognition, but it shows the same developmental trend recognition does: school-age children can recall better than preschoolers, but not as well as adults. Figure 8.5 illustrates this trend.

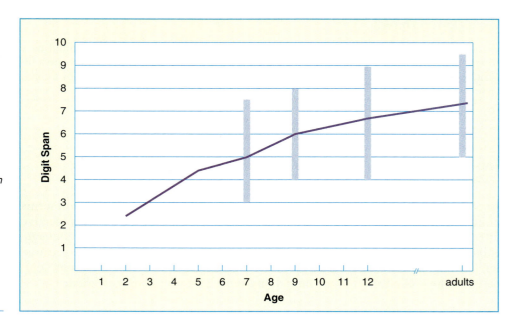

FIGURE 8.5
**Developmental Changes in
Recall Memory**
*In the study represented here, children
were asked to recall a series of digits
shortly after hearing them. The points
on the graph represent the average
number of digits subjects were able
to recall, and the bars represent the
ranges of typical performance at each
age. Recall of digits improves during
middle childhood and almost reaches
adult levels by age twelve, though not
quite.*

Long-Term Memory   *Long-term memory (LTM)* is the feature of thinking that holds information for very long periods, perhaps even indefinitely. It is not clear how much long-term memory changes during childhood, or even whether it changes at all, because LTM relies increasingly on complex strategies of information storage and retrieval. Younger children may remember less because they have experienced fewer memorable events or because they use fewer methods of deliberately remembering information and experiences.

To understand how LTM changes during childhood, consider how children and adults recall short stories they have heard (Wolf, 1993). By age six, children already understand the basic narrative structure of stories—that such stories contain characters, situations, and plots with a beginning, a middle, and an end. Not surprisingly, therefore, children show many similarities to adults in recalling stories. Like adults, they recall important features of a story ("Goldilocks was not supposed to enter the bears' house") and ignore or forget trivial details ("Goldilocks was wearing brown shoes"). They also recall the essences of sentences rather than their exact wording.

But compared to adults, the recollections of school-age children include fewer inferences based on the sentences they actually hear (McNamara et al., 1991). As children get older, they begin to "read between the lines" more frequently, at least when recalling stories. This tendency lends color and detail to their retellings as they get older, although they sometimes risk misstating the facts of a story.

Implications for Elementary Education   The structure, or "architecture," of memory may affect how children can learn during the school years. A younger student who can remember only three bits of information needs to have information organized in smaller chunks than an older student who can remember six bits at a time. The younger child may have trouble remembering a phone number long enough to dial it, for example, unless the teacher can offer some learning strategies for doing this task (see the next section for some suggested strategies). More significant for learning, research shows that elementary school students' ability to solve arithmetic problems is correlated with the extent of their short-term memories; in one study, "larger" short-term memory meant greater accuracy in solving problems (Swanson et al., 1993). The majority (80 percent) of these children are boys. Children's limitations in terms of long-term memory, on the other hand, pose a different challenge: school-age children *can* remember ideas and facts for long periods, but their teachers may need to help them see connections among the stories, ideas, and other material they learn in school.

Difficulties with Information Processing: Learning Disabilities

During middle childhood, about 5 percent of children develop **learning disabilities,** disorders in basic information processing that interfere with understanding or using language, either written or spoken (Lerner, 1993). Usually a learning disability causes poor academic achievement, although low achievement is not in and of itself evidence of a learning disability. Learning disabilities have no obvious physical cause, as blindness or hearing impairment do, and do not result from a general slowness of thinking, as mental retardation does.

Learning disabilities take many forms. One of the more common forms is called *dyslexia,* literally an inability to read. The diversity of symptoms among children with dyslexia reflects the diversity among learning disabilities in general. For some children, dyslexia consists of "word blindness": they can read letters singly (such as *c, a,* or *t*) but not in combinations that make words, such as *cat.* In other forms of dyslexia, children can read words but fail to comprehend them. They can copy words accurately or transcribe them from oral dictation, but they cannot explain what they have written afterward, no matter how simple the vocabulary. Some children with dyslexia can read combinations of digits that make large numbers; for example, they can read *123* as "one hundred and twenty-three" but not as "one, two, three," even when they try. Most children with dyslexia have these problems in combination. Yet they seem normal in every other respect; their everyday conversations seem perfectly intelligent and their motor skills just as developed as other children's.

Causes of Learning Disabilities   What causes some children to have a learning disability such as dyslexia? The symptoms sometimes resemble what happens to individuals who suffer injuries to their brains (Rourke & Del Dotto, 1994). For this reason, some professionals have suggested that many learning disabilities, including dyslexia, may reflect undetected minimal brain damage that occurred during the birth process or even before birth. This hypothesis is extremely hard to prove, however. It also discourages some parents and professionals from helping children with learning disabilities on the grounds (probably mistaken) that organically based problems are beyond control.

A more helpful explanation for learning disabilities focuses on cognitive functions rather than on brain anatomy. In this view, disabilities may result from subtle differences in how the mind of a child normally organizes and processes information. To see what this idea means, consider what children must do to read an ordinary page of print. First, they must perceive the letters and words as visual patterns. Then they must combine those patterns into larger strings that constitute phrases and sentences. Finally, they must connect those strings with meanings to form ideas. While all of these steps are going on, they must also scan ahead to recognize the upcoming visual patterns on the page. If any of these steps fails to occur or occurs in the wrong sequence or at the wrong speed, a child may appear to be dyslexic.

Such problems in processing information may lie at the heart of many learning disabilities. Some children with dyslexia may, for example, find visual recognition especially difficult or time consuming. Several researchers have reached this

Working with **Terry Wharton, SPECIAL EDUCATION TEACHER**

Giving Children a Second Chance to Learn

Terry Wharton has a wide range of experience in classroom teaching and special education. He currently teaches a class of 2nd to 4th graders who have shown significant behavioral and emotional problems in regular classrooms. There are only eight students in his class, all of them boys, and two teacher assistants—definitely not the typical teacher-to-student ratio. Terry spoke about the philosophy guiding his program and about how he and his assistants reconcile it with conventional academic expectations for the primary grades.

Terry: We emphasize making the class nonpunitive and nonaversive. For these kids, school has been a disaster socially—lots of fights with classmates, conflicts with teachers and other adults. We have to provide successes and confidence to counteract the downward spiral of their self-esteem.

Kelvin: How do you do that without leading to further fights and conflicts? Eight of these kids in one room could be explosive!

Terry: Well, we do have to plan activities carefully and guide their choices more than usual. At the start of the year, the children only come for half a day, and I plan a series of activities they are sure to enjoy and to be able to do, like setting up a personal datebook or calendar to use later in the year. By the end of that first day, they really feel successful.

Kelvin: Given your students, how much is it like ordinary school?

Terry: Oh lots, actually! Academics is a priority. We have a "news" time where everyone relates some interesting personal experience. Then I read to them for a few minutes. Then they write in journals, either about the story or about something else that concerns them.

Kelvin: Do the kids like the journals?

Terry: I must admit, at first they resisted. They seemed very self-conscious about their writing skills and about revealing their thoughts and feelings. But lately it's been amazing; you should read them! Their growth with the journals is impressive. They talk about the story, or about their fears and hopes for their family.

Kelvin: What about math?

Terry: They don't seem as uncomfortable about math as they do about writing and reading; I'm not sure why. We work on basic arithmetic skills using some of the latest manipulatives.

Kelvin: Manipulatives?

conclusion after studying a phenomenon called *perceptual masking,* in which some letters are hard to read because of the presence of other letters nearby. To understand this problem, consider the following arrangement of letters:

$$w\,e\,k$$
$$q\,w\,e\,k\,l$$
$$a\,q\,w\,e\,k\,l\,m$$
$$s\,a\,q\,w\,e\,k\,l\,m\,n$$
$$d\,s\,a\,q\,w\,e\,k\,l\,m\,n\,p$$
$$g\,f\,d\,s\,a\,q\,w\,e\,k\,l\,m\,n\,p\,y\,b$$
$$c\,v\,g\,f\,d\,s\,a\,q\,w\,e\,k\,l\,m\,n\,p\,y\,b\,h\,t$$

If you look at the *e* in the top line, you probably will still be able to see the letters *w* and *k* clearly using your peripheral vision (the corner of your eye). If you look at the *e* in a line farther down, you can still see the end letters relatively clearly, but the middle letters become almost impossible to pick out clearly. Trying to notice the middle letters does help you to perceive them, but when you make this effort, the end letters become hard to discern. Perceiving one set of features in this display masks others; hence the term *perceptual masking.* Without a lot of practice, few people, adults or children, can see very many letters at once.

Some (though not all) children with dyslexia show especially strong perceptual masking (Vellutino, 1991). Compared to normal readers, they must stare at words for rather long periods, consciously shifting attention from one subset of letters to another in a way similar to the staring required to "see" the letters displayed on this page. Once they figure out the letters in a word, however, they can connect mean-

Terry: Like sets of unit blocks that you can combine to illustrate addition problems. They seem to like that. But you know what surprised me the most? Workbooks! When I taught a regular primary-grade class, I tried to avoid those because I felt they were too structured, but these students love them; they even ask to do them! I think it gives them a feeling of clear progress and a sense of control over their own efforts. They can *see* clearly that they are getting work done.

Kelvin: So your program is indeed academic? You do work on cognitive skills?

Terry: Absolutely. The cognitive skills develop only because we're also supporting these students socially, though. The two go hand in hand. I think that's true for all children, but working with these kids with behav-

ior problems has really brought that idea home to me.

Kelvin: Where else do you see academic and social connections?

Terry: With the parents, certainly. We make a big effort to involve the parents in our program. Several times a year we have "family celebrations," lunches where the child's whole family is invited. The parents have responded enthusiastically. Some parents work as volunteers in the school. They've been a real help, and even if they are not in the same classroom, it's reassuring to be in the same building as their child.

Kelvin: These sound like good ideas for *all* classrooms and parents. Do you agree?

Terry: Yes, I do. But they're especially valuable for these particular parents because they've had so many bad experiences with schools, either because

of their child's problems or when they were students themselves. It builds their confidence as parents.

What Do You Think?

1. Do you think that Terry would define the word *cognitive* the same way this chapter does?

2. Terry did not comment on the fact that his class is all boys. Do you think gender is important to consider in teaching a class like this? Why or why not?

3. Terry mentions that his students enjoy workbooks for mathematics, even though he personally did not consider them a good idea initially. How do you feel about this issue? What do you suppose Piaget or an information-processing theorist would say about using workbooks?

ings with them fairly quickly and accurately. For these children, verbal association may occur much sooner than visual perception does.

The gap in speed between perceiving and associating may account for many errors made by children with dyslexia. A ten-year-old may look at the word *conceal* and say something like "concol," or look at *alternate* and say "alfoonite." In making these mistakes, children may literally be reading what they see and guessing about the rest. Unfortunately, they may see fewer letters than normal readers usually discern. To put it differently, trying to see all letters clearly may simply take too much time and effort, and overall reading comprehension breaks down as a result.

Helping Children with Learning Disabilities   Because learning disabilities become a problem primarily in school settings, school professionals have taken increasing responsibility in recent years for helping children who develop these problems. Most commonly, help consists of careful diagnosis of which steps of thinking cause difficulty for a child, followed by individual instructional plans to strengthen those particular steps (Lyon, 1993). Children with problems in perceptual masking can be given exercises in which they purposely work to improve this skill. Often such special work can be done in a regular class during a normal school day, but at least some of it requires individual tutoring so that the professional can monitor and give precise assistance to the child's thinking as it actually occurs. Depending on the child's needs and the school's circumstances, regular classroom teachers, parents, or trained special educators can act as tutors as well as additional sources of encouragement and support for the child. The interview with Terry Wharton discusses issues of special education in more detail.

There are numerous ways of helping children with learning disabilities, but no single way is guaranteed to be effective. This teacher, for example, is helping two boys with their reading by using a computer that deliberately slows down the presentation of words, "reads" the text out loud if the boys request it, and offers hints if the boys do not answer its reading-related questions correctly.

Note that children with learning disabilities usually are old enough to have feelings and opinions about their problems. Eventually, in fact, the major problem in some learning disabilities may become *self-consciousness* about failing to learn, in addition to any cognitive or perceptual problems as such. A child who cannot read well usually becomes painfully aware of this fact sooner or later and worries about what teachers, parents, and peers may think of her as a result. Adults can help with this problem by being optimistic about the child's eventual capacity to learn academic skills and encouraging tolerance of differences among classmates and other peers.

What Do You Think?

Think about the methods you yourself have used to remember new information. What are they, and how are they consistent with the discussion in this chapter about how memory develops during middle childhood? Compare your own memory strategies with those of classmates. How are they similar? How are they different?

LANGUAGE DEVELOPMENT IN MIDDLE CHILDHOOD

Language continues to develop during middle childhood. Vocabulary keeps growing, of course, and the ways children use words and sentences become more subtle and complex and more like adults' (Anglin, 1993). Contrary to the impressions young school-age children sometimes give, they have not necessarily mastered syntax. They often are confused by a number of common sentence forms until well into the elementary school years. To six-year-olds, for example, the sentence *The baby is not easy to see* means "The baby cannot see very well"; the sentence *I don't think it will rain tomorrow* is likely to mean "I know for a fact that it won't rain."

Understanding Metaphor

One of the most interesting language developments in middle childhood concerns understanding metaphor. A **metaphor** is a figure of speech in which a word or an expression ordinarily used for one thing is used for another ("the perfume is bright sunshine"). Children can understand a variety of metaphors even in the preschool years, comparing color and personality ("He is blue") and objects and personality ("It was a friendly house"), among other things (Broderick, 1991). At first, however, they often assume a metaphor refers to a physical similarity rather than to an underlying conceptual relationship. The sentence *My brother is a rock,* for example, is taken to mean "My brother sits very still, like a rock" or "My brother is very hard when you touch or punch him, like a rock." Even the types of physical similarities are restricted at this age. In one study comparing preschoolers and school-age children, youngsters listened to tones of various pitches, some very low and some very high, and were asked which pitch was brighter or dimmer and bigger or smaller (Marks et al., 1987). Four-year-olds readily described the low pitches as "dim" and the high pitches as "bright." But not until age eleven did children also reliably describe low pitches as "big" and high ones as "small," as adults tend to do.

Children do not reliably interpret a metaphor in conceptual or relational terms until about age ten (Winner, 1988). By that age, the sentence *My brother is a rock* is taken psychologically rather than physically: now the term *rock* is assumed to refer to a personality trait, so the sentence might mean "My brother is unfeeling or reserved." The sentence *Your words are music to my ears* no longer means literally that you are singing, as some preschoolers assume, but that "Your ideas produce a pleasurable feeling in me, like the feeling I get listening to music."

Bilingualism and Its Effects

Although most monolinguals may not realize it, a majority of children around the world are able to speak two languages and therefore are bilingual (Paulston, 1988). Bilingualism is common in the United States even though the nation is officially monolingual; somewhere between 30 million and 35 million individuals

Fully bilingual children have cognitive advantages over monolinguals, but only as long as both languages and their related cultures are treated with respect by teachers and society. These Vietnamese children are well on their way to becoming bilingual; what attitudes will they encounter about their language and heritage?

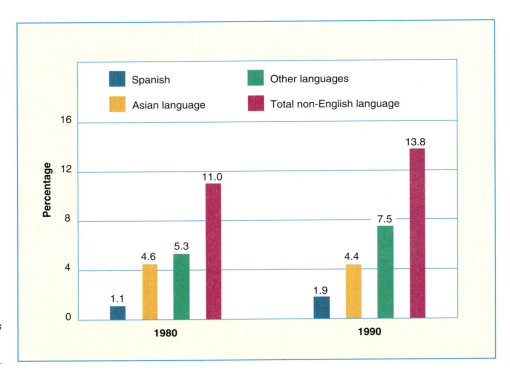

FIGURE 8.6

Children Five Years and Older from Homes Where a Language Other Than English Is Spoken, 1980 and 1990
The percentage of homes in which a non-English language is spoken has been growing. The single most common non-English language is Spanish. In some cities and regions, the proportion of non-English speakers is far higher than shown in this graph.
Source: U.S. Bureau of the Census, 1993.

regularly use another language in addition to English (U.S. Bureau of the Census, 1993) (see Figure 8.6). This represents about 10 to 15 percent of children overall, but the proportion is actually much higher in some cities and regions.

Does bilingualism benefit children's cognitive development? Research suggests that it does, but primarily when children acquire both languages equally well and when both languages are treated with respect by teachers and other representatives of the community (Bialystok & Hakuta, 1994). Language specialists call such children **balanced bilinguals**.

Cognitive Effects of Bilingualism   For one thing, balanced bilingual children show greater cognitive flexibility—skill at detecting multiple meanings of words and alternative orientations of objects—than monolingual children do. Bilingual children can substitute arbitrary words for normally occurring words relatively easily without changing any other features of the sentence. If asked to substitute *spaghetti* for *I* in the sentence "I am cold," bilingual children more often produce the exact substitution "Spaghetti am cold" and resist the temptation to correct the grammar ("Spaghetti is cold"), as monolinguals more often do. Such flexibility shows **metalinguistic awareness,** the knowledge that language can be an object of thought. Metalinguistic awareness develops because bilingual experiences often challenge children to think consciously about what to say and how to say it (Jimenez et al., 1995). A question such as "What if a dog were called a cat?" therefore poses fewer conceptual problems for bilinguals. So do follow-up questions such as "Would this 'cat' meow?" or "Would it purr?"

However, all of these cognitive advantages apply primarily to balanced bilingual children, those with equal skill in both languages. What about the unbalanced bilinguals, those with more skill in one language than in the other? Does knowledge of a second language help, even if it is limited? Evidence is scarce, but what there is suggests that unbalanced bilingualism has mixed effects on children's thinking skills, largely because of the interplay of social attitudes surrounding language differences in society (Pease-Alvarez, 1993).

Social Effects of Bilingualism   When children acquire two languages, one language usually has more prestige than the other. In the United States, the "best," or most important, language almost always is English. Its prestige results not only from its widespread use but also from its association with success and power: all the important people in American society, it seems, speak English fluently. These circumstances create negative attitudes or stereotypes about people who speak other languages and challenge educators to overcome social prejudices at the same time they facilitate learning new grammar, vocabulary, and usage.

The influence of language on attitudes has been well documented through experiments using the *matched guise technique* (Giles & Coupland, 1991). In this type of experiment, perfectly balanced and fluent bilinguals tape record standard messages in each of their two languages, and the messages are interspersed among other tape-recorded messages to disguise the identities of the bilingual speakers. Then listeners evaluate the competence and social attractiveness of each speaker. Time after time, two consistent trends occur in studies of this type. First, speakers of English are rated more highly than speakers of other languages. Second, listeners from non-English-speaking cultural groups rate the English speakers more highly than they do speakers of their own language. The prestige of English, in other words, comes from sources in addition to English speakers themselves.

Negative attitudes toward non-English languages reduce children's school performance by making them less willing to use their primary, or first, language in public and reducing their self-confidence about linguistic skills in general. Fortunately, however, educational programs exist that can counteract these effects by treating children's first language as an educational resource rather than a liability. Overall, research favors *additive bilingual education,* programs that develop language skills in *both* of a child's languages rather than attempting to replace a first language with English (Perez & Torres-Guzman, 1992). As a practical matter, such programs usually are conducted partly in each language, depending on children's current language skills, but they do not confine either language to isolated "lessons" lasting only short periods each day. The challenge is a double one: to foster new language skills while promoting respect for a child's original language and culture. In countries where language is less strongly associated with economic or social status (for example, Canada, where about 25 percent of the population speaks French as a first language), bilingual education often does not include this double agenda. Therefore, successful bilingual programs more often emphasize simple immersion in a second language and tend to ignore a child's first language without negative educational effects (Lambert et al., 1993).

Black English

In the United States, some African Americans use a dialect, or version of English, called **Black English,** that differs from the middle-class dialect that linguists call *Standard English.* The two versions differ in three ways (Sutcliffe, 1992). First, certain sounds occur differently: for example, the sound /th/ becomes /d/, making the word *this* sound like *dis.* Second, certain grammatical forms differ. The verb *to be* is used to indicate a continuing situation or condition. The sentence "The coffee be cold" means approximately "Every day the coffee is always cold"; but the sentence "The coffee cold" is closer to meaning "The coffee is cold this time." Third, Black English contains many words and expressions that have meanings very different than those in Standard English. The word *bad* can mean something undesirable ("I have a bad cold") but also something highly desirable ("She look bad" usually means "She looks very good").

Studies of Black English have found it to be as complex as any other language, including Standard English, and equally capable of expressing the full range of human thought and emotion (Smitherman-Donaldson, 1994). Unfortunately, society's attitudes toward it remain rather negative, which has created dilemmas for teachers of students who use Black English. Should students be allowed to speak this dialect in class, or even be encouraged to do so, because they know it best? Or should they always be expected to use Standard English to prepare them to function better in mainstream (white) society? Educators typically recommend a compromise: teachers should respect Black English, appreciate its richness, and allow students to use it in class some of the time. But they should also show students how Black English has influenced and enriched Standard English (Holloway & Vass, 1993)—where, for example, did the term *cool,* meaning "terrific," come from? Teachers should also encourage students to practice Standard English because it probably will help them in situations where they must communicate more formally.

What Do You Think?

Think about a language you wish you could speak fluently. Why would you like to be able to use this language? In forming your opinion, what assumptions are you making about the culture or people who use this language?

DEFINING AND MEASURING INTELLIGENCE

All of the cognitive changes discussed so far—concrete operational thinking, memory development, and language—constitute aspects of **intelligence,** a term that refers to adaptability, or a general ability to learn from experience. Often intelligence also refers to the ability to reason abstractly, especially by using language, as well as an ability to integrate old and new knowledge. In recent years, some psychologists have broadened the term *intelligence* to refer to social skills, talents of various kinds (such as a talent for music), or bodily skills. The traditional orientation toward reasoning and problem solving, however, still dominates discussions of intelligence, and partly as a result many standardized tests have been developed to measure these forms of intelligence.

The multitude of definitions of intelligence can create confusion for parents and professionals who have responsibility for helping children to develop their fullest potentials. Some of the complexity can be sorted out by noting that views of intelligence can be organized around three major theoretical approaches. The oldest and therefore best developed view is the **psychometric approach,** which is based on standardized, quantitative measurement of abilities and achievement. More recently, researchers oriented toward *information processing* and toward

As Calvin's scribbling implies, there are obviously many forms of intelligence, but not all are recognized in academic settings! Often in everyday thinking, intelligence is equated with the school-related abilities of reading and mathematics, which is one reason why students may worry if they think that they lack it.

sociocultural issues also have developed theories of intelligence, although these approaches have not been tied to standardized testing to any significant extent.

Psychometric Approaches to Intelligence

Psychometric definitions of intelligence have developed out of *standardized tests,* all of which share three important features. First, they always contain clearly stated questions that have relatively specific answers. The questions usually draw on logical reasoning and verbal skills, which schools typically require. Second, standardized tests always include clear, standard procedures for administration and scoring. Often they provide a script for the person giving the test, as well as specific printed guidelines about when and how to credit particular answers. Third, such tests present information about how large groups of comparable individuals perform to allow evaluation of the performances of particular groups or individuals (Scarr, 1991).

Kinds of Standardized Tests   Standardized tests serve many purposes, but for convenience we can classify them into two major groups: achievement tests and aptitude, or ability, tests. **Achievement tests** measure individuals' existing skills or knowledge; they try to assess current attainment in a particular realm of human behavior. Children often encounter such tests in the form of scholastic achievement tests, such as tests of reading achievement or of arithmetic achievement. By nature, such tests usually draw heavily on the typical curriculum content of the subject area being tested.

Aptitude tests measure ability or try to estimate future performance in some realm of behavior. A test of scholastic aptitude, for instance, tries to estimate a child's potential for success in school. Because of their goal, aptitude tests contain a broader range of questions than achievement tests do. A scholastic aptitude test probably would include questions from several major school subjects and draw on basic academic skills such as reading and mathematical reasoning.

In practice, aptitude and achievement tests are less distinct than these definitions make them sound. Often achievement tests are very effective predictors of future performance; children's current skills in arithmetic, for instance, predict their future mathematical performance about as well as any aptitude test can do. Also, aptitude tests can successfully predict future progress only by sampling skills and knowledge children have already attained. Nonetheless, the distinction remains useful for those who develop and use tests. In general, measuring aptitude means looking to the future, whereas measuring achievement means assessing the past.

Once norms have been calculated, standardized tests, and especially achievement tests, can serve two purposes. On the one hand, they can help educators know how well particular schools or classrooms are functioning in general. For example, all classrooms using a particular curriculum can be compared with classrooms using another curriculum, or all classrooms in one school can be compared with all classrooms in the city or even with a national cross-section.

On the other hand, standardized tests sometimes can aid individual children. The most common approach involves screening students who need special educational help. If teachers find that a certain student is learning the curriculum very slowly, they may ask a school psychologist to test the child's general scholastic ability in the hope of diagnosing or clarifying his or her learning problems. Although the results of such a test cannot stand alone, they often contribute to the complex process of assessing the learning needs of a particular child. Standardized tests can also help to identify students with superior abilities in specific areas; the accompanying Perspectives box looks at educational issues pertaining to these gifted students.

Gifted Students: Victims or Elite?

For years certain educators have expressed concern about *gifted students,* those capable of high performance in some or all academic areas, in social leadership, or in the performing arts (see Table 8.4 for a summary of their characteristics). Because of their talent, some educators feared that these students are especially likely to become bored with the normal curriculum, become isolated from their peers socially, and, in some cases, become permanently unproductive in school and career as a result (Ross, 1993). Even though their "problem" was too much talent, some educators believed gifted students were potential victims of conventional schooling in much the same way students with learning disabilities or physical challenges are.

In response to these concerns, some schools have created programs of gifted education. Typically these include a "pull-out" program: for an hour or two each week, students designated as gifted work in a separate classroom on activities designed to meet their needs. Often students work independently on projects of their own choosing, such as learning all about local butterflies, designing their own computer program, or creating a portfolio of paintings. Sometimes they are also linked with experts from the community (called *mentors*) to assist them in developing these interests. Their regular classroom teachers are encouraged to recognize the gifted students' interests and abilities by allowing extra time to pursue the projects and periodically grouping the more gifted children together for tasks related to the regular curriculum (Gallagher & Gallagher, 1994).

This portrait of gifted education is attractive, but it has proven highly controversial. A number of educators, parents, and political leaders argue that gifted education creates an elite, overprivileged group of students (Margolin, 1994). Particularly in the pull-out part of gifted programs, students receive much more time and attention from a teacher than in a typical classroom, and they enjoy much more freedom in using their time. Ironically, it is argued, the curriculum for gifted students is much *less* rigorous than that for regular students; even though they are capable of it, gifted children do not necessarily read more books, write more essays, or learn more mathematics than others do. Furthermore, the gifted programs tend to treat students as if they were broadly talented in all areas, even though research and professional teachers' experiences suggest that almost all students have selected talents—math but not English, for example, or music but not athletics (Gardner, 1993b). This circumstance makes gifted programs more compatible with the preexisting strengths of high-SES families and of white, English-speaking families, which may constitute a subtle form of racism.

How has gifted education responded to these criticisms? One strategy has been to make entrance into gifted programs more flexible: rely less on standardized test scores and more on students' own interest in volunteering for the program. Another is to arrange more activities for gifted students in the regular classroom and fewer in pull-out situations (Maker, 1993). A third is to redefine gifted education as *enrichment:* activities that tie

As you may suspect, standardized tests do not serve either of these purposes perfectly. Factors other than ability, such as a child's health or motivation to succeed, affect performance. So do physical disabilities, such as visual impairment. More indirectly, cultural and language differences among children affect performance on standardized tests. These additional influences deserve special discussion because they affect all children throughout society.

Biases of Intelligence and General Ability Tests   Although they attempt to measure general qualities, tests of ability and intelligence contain various biases. For example, many intelligence tests rely heavily on language in all of its forms—listening, speaking, and reading. Many also emphasize problems that have specific answers and that play down divergent or creative thinking. Also, although they do not focus on speed, intelligence tests tend to favor children who answer fairly rapidly and take little time to mull over their solutions.

Because schools also emphasize all of these features, intelligence tests measure academic ability better than they do any other skill. Some psychologists, in fact, have suggested calling them measures of *academic intelligence,* or school ability, to make this limitation clear (Anastasi, 1989).

conventional curriculum goals (reading, arithmetic, and the like) to students' own prior interests and talents. When pull-out activities are offered, therefore, all students may be invited, and the activities focus only on particular areas of the normal curriculum.

Integrating gifted and regular education in these ways is more equitable, but it does not eliminate the basic educational controversy underlying gifted education: the tension between fostering excellence and fostering equality of education. Some researchers argue, for example, that having highly talented students work with less talented ones may actually accentuate elitism rather than reduce it. Differences between higher and lower performers become obvious to all students, day in and day out, and may create tensions within the classroom (Gallagher, 1993). Students may still prefer classmates with similar levels of academic motivation, both to work with and to be friends with; so informal social segregation may develop even in a room that is officially integrated. In addition, enrichment activities are harder to schedule if they invite volunteers and focus on specific school subjects; they cannot overlap with regular class times since some students, although ahead and motivated in the enrichment subject, may need extra help in the "regular" subject that they happen to be missing. That leaves lunch periods and before and after school for enrichment periods, times that teachers may already need for class preparations and for "refueling." Given these problems, it is to their credit that many excellent enrichment programs exist in the schools and that they have succeeded reasonably well in creating flexible yet challenging learning opportunities.

TABLE 8.4 *Some Characteristics of Gifted Students*

Characteristic	Examples
Well-above-average ability	Can think abstractly; skilled at verbal and numerical reasoning; adapts well to novel situations; rapid and accurate memory
Task commitment	Shows high level of interest, enthusiasm, perseverance, and self-confidence; sets high standards for success
Creativity	Shows original thoughts; open to new experiences and information; curious, speculative, sensitive to detail and to aesthetic characteristics of ideas and things

Source: Renzulli (1986).

The biggest problem with intelligence tests, however, comes from their cultural assumptions, which have originated entirely from white, middle-SES experiences in Western Europe and North America. The tests show their assumptions or biases in at least two ways. First, individual questions often demand knowledge that children can gain only by thorough immersion in white, middle-SES society. One question might ask children to describe the purpose of a garden hose, thereby assuming previous contact with a garden in their backyards. Another question might ask children to define the word *drama* or *concerto,* thereby assuming the sort of education that provides this information.

Even when tests avoid this type of bias, they suffer from other, more subtle cultural assumptions. Some ethnic groups and cultures do not value conversations that emphasize abstract or general propositions, as is common in classrooms or intellectual discussions; using this style may seem rude or at least boring (Heath, 1993). Children from these groups therefore cannot be expected to take tests that rely heavily on this form of dialogue. Also, in some cultural groups contact with strange adults is extremely rare, so children from such groups may find sitting alone in a room with an unfamiliar test administrator rather perplexing or even frightening. For such children, any questions the administrator asks may seem much less important than figuring out this adult's real motives.

Information-Processing Approaches to Intelligence

Some psychologists have responded to the limitations of psychometric views by developing other definitions and theories of intelligence. One way or another, all of the newer approaches broaden the nature and sources of intelligence. From these perspectives, more children seem to qualify as "intelligent" than is the case when children are assessed psychometrically.

The Triarchic Theory of Intelligence   An approach that draws explicitly on principles of information-processing theory is the **triarchic theory of intelligence** proposed by Robert Sternberg (Sternberg, 1994). This theory broadens the psychometric approach by incorporating recent ideas from research on *how* thinking occurs. To do this, Sternberg proposed three realms of cognition or, in his words, "subtheories" (hence the name *triarchic*), each of which contributes to general intelligence.

The first realm of intelligence concerns the *components* of thinking. These resemble the basic elements of the information-processing model described in Chapter 2. Components include skills at coding, representing, and combining information, as well as higher-order skills such as planning and evaluating one's own success in solving a problem or performing a cognitive task.

The second realm of intelligence concerns how individuals cope with their *experiences*. How effectively do they respond to novelty in solving new problems? For example, a person may follow a dinner recipe accurately when it is written in imperial measurements (ounces, teaspoons) but fail miserably when the same recipe is presented in metric units (milliliters, grams). How quickly can that person adjust to the new form of the task and solve it as automatically as was possible with the old form?

The third realm of intelligence concerns the *context* of thinking. People show this form of intelligence to the extent to which they can adapt to, alter, or select environments relevant to and supportive their abilities (Sternberg & Wagner, 1994). In taking a university course, for example, a student may try diligently to complete the course assignments as given, in essence adapting himself to the environment of the course. If this strategy does not work satisfactorily, the student may complain about the assignments to the professor in an effort to alter them. If the altered assignments do not work for him, the student may drop the course and select another. All of these behaviors show contextual intelligence (though not necessarily of a kind that may please professors!).

Table 8.5 summarizes the three realms of thinking, or cognition. These realms describe the processes of intelligence in more detail than classic psychometric approaches to intelligence have done. They also suggest an explanation for why individuals sometimes seem intelligent in different ways: perhaps one person has an advantage at internal processing of information, another adjusts to new experiences

TABLE 8.5   *The Triarchic Theory of Intelligence*

Realm of Intelligence	Examples
Componential	Coding and representing information; planning and executing solutions to problems
Experiential	Skill with novel problems and familiar problems in novel settings; skill at solving problems automatically as they become familiar
Contextual	Deliberate adaptation, alteration, and selection of learning environments to facilitate problem solving

The triarchic theory of intelligence, developed by Robert Sternberg, identifies three different realms of thinking: componential, experiential, and contextual. Philosophically, the theory is rooted in information-processing theory.

Musical intelligence is not well assessed on most classical tests of general ability, even though some psychologists (for example, Howard Gardner) believe that it constitutes a unique form of talent or intelligence. Children who play an instrument may—or may not—be particularly studious at school.

especially well, and a third has a knack for adapting, altering, or selecting appropriate environments in which to work. Given these possibilities, it would not be surprising if psychometric tests favored certain children and cultural groups more than others, since the environments of some families and cultures foster the learning of testlike behaviors more than others do.

Gardner's Theory of Multiple Intelligences   Like Sternberg, Howard Gardner (1993a) has proposed that general ability consists of several elements or factors. However, Gardner has defined these factors in ways that reflect the influence of culture and society even more explicitly than the triarchic theory does. He argues that not one but **multiple intelligences** exist and take the following forms:

1. *Language skill* A child with this talent speaks comfortably and fluently and learns new words and expressions easily. She also memorizes verbal materials, such as poems, much more easily than other children do.

2. *Musical skill* This child not only plays one or more musical instruments but also sings and discerns subtle musical effects. Usually musical talent also includes a good sense of timing, or rhythm.

3. *Logical skill* A child with this skill organizes objects and concepts well. Using a microcomputer, for example, comes easily, as does mathematics.

4. *Spatial skill* This child literally can find his way around. He knows the streets of the neighborhood better than most children his age do; if he lives in the country, he can find his way across large stretches of terrain without getting lost.

5. *Kinesthetic, or body balance, skill* This child is sensitive to the internal sensations created by body movement. As a result, she finds dancing, gymnastics, and other activities requiring balance easy to learn.

Even though repairing a fishnet may be too difficult for this boy to do alone, he is able to make repairs successfully when assisted by a more experienced adult. Changes in performance because of such assistance is part of what Vygotsky meant by the zone of proximal development.

6. *Interpersonal and intrapersonal skills* A child with interpersonal skill shows excellent understanding of others' feelings, thoughts, and motives. A child with intrapersonal skill has a good understanding of his own. For children with either or both of these skills, handling social encounters comes relatively easily. (Interpersonal and intrapersonal skills may really amount to two distinct forms of intelligence, but the research evidence has made Gardner unsure about this.)

Gardner argues that the six intelligences are distinct, for several reasons. First, some of them can be physically located within the brain. Certain language functions occur within particular, identifiable parts of the brain, as do kinesthetic or balance functions. Second, the intelligences sometimes occur in pure form; some individuals with mental retardation play a musical instrument extremely well, even though their language ability may be limited and they cannot reason abstractly. Third, each intelligence involves particular, core skills that clearly set it off from the others. Being musical requires a good sense of pitch, but this skill contributes little to the other intelligences.

Like Sternberg's ideas, the theory of multiple intelligences implies criticisms of psychometric definitions of intelligence and of the standardized intelligence testing associated with psychometric definitions. Strictly speaking, however, the notion of multiple intelligences may really criticize the *use* of conventional tests beyond their intended purposes.

Sociocultural Approaches to Intelligence

Sociocultural definitions of intelligence give even more importance than information-processing theories do to the social setting. In the **sociocultural perspective,** intelligence is not actually "in" individual persons but instead resides in the interactions and activities that occur *among* individuals (Wertsch et al., 1995). In this view, it is not the individual who adapts to, learns, and modifies knowledge but the person and his or her environment in combination. For example, a child may make many mistakes on a test of arithmetic computation but be able to locate the most economical items at the local candy store almost infallibly, even if the items come in odd sizes (1⅛ versus 2¼ ounces) or odd prices (34 cents versus 49 cents) (Chaiklin & Lave, 1993). That is because the knowledge needed for comparison shopping is contained not only in the shopper's mind but also in the overall structure of shopping in the candy store's environment. With practice, a child learns how to sort out pricing clues that depend very little on the computational procedures learned in grade school. Some of the clues involve rough estimations, such as when the prices of two items differ widely but their sizes differ only a little. Others involve nonarithmetic knowledge, such as recommendations from other shoppers or memories of where the store kept the bargains on previous visits. The intelligence needed for comparison shopping thus is only partly "in" the child; the rest is more accurately said to be distributed among the store shelves, the conversations with other shoppers, and the history of events at the store.

A key concept in understanding the sociocultural view of intelligence is the *zone of proximal development (ZPD),* originated by the Russian psychologist Lev Vygotsky and discussed in Chapter 6 (Vygotsky, 1978; Wertsch, 1985). The ZPD refers to the level of problem solving at which a child cannot solve a problem alone but can do so when assisted by an adult or a more competent peer. For example, a six-year-old may find the telephone directory too difficult to use alone but may be quite able to look up a phone number when given a bit of help from a parent. Implicit in the ZPD is the idea of shared knowledge, or shared cognition. Knowledge of how to use the phone directory exists at first in the interaction or relationship between two people—parent and child—and only gradually becomes located fully within the developing child. Likewise, knowledge of academic skills such as reading and mathematics also begins in the interactions between adults and children and only later becomes internalized by individual children. In fact, as the internalization progresses, children tend to perform better on tests of reasoning and language and therefore seem more "intelligent" in the psychometric sense.

Note that in emphasizing the social context of intellectual development, the sociocultural approach turns the issue of cultural bias on psychometric tests into an outcome to be expected and explored rather than a problem to be overcome or minimized. From the sociocultural perspective, cultural influences are the source, or foundation, of thinking rather than a mere backdrop or secondary factor that modifies individuals' cognitive performances. What becomes puzzling instead is why individual families and cultures vary so much in the social settings and interactions—the zones of proximal development—that they arrange for their children (Goodnow et al., 1995). Why does one culture promote skills in verbal dialogue more heavily than another culture does? And why do some families in a particular culture nonetheless adopt their culture's priorities more completely than others do?

What Do You Think?

Should standardized tests of ability be used in schools? If so, when and with whom, and for what purpose? Consult with several classmates about this issue. Then, if possible, compare the opinions of several professionals, such as a special education teacher and an occupational therapist. How do you think their work affects their opinions?

THE CHANGING CHILD: PHYSICAL, COGNITIVE, AND SOCIAL

Among the examples of development discussed in this chapter, one quality occurs repeatedly: neither physical nor cognitive development occurs in isolation from a child's social experiences. Even a child's height and weight influence acceptance by peers and personal self-esteem. Thinking skills such as conservation or long-term memory are influenced not only by a child's own efforts to make sense of her world but also by learning experiences often provided by others. And language turns out to be more than an automatic acquisition of grammatical rules; it also involves learning *how* a child's community prefers to communicate. Evidently a child's social surroundings—the people around him, both young and old—make quite a difference in development during these years. In the next chapter, we look at these surroundings in more detail.

SUMMARY OF MAJOR IDEAS

PHYSICAL DEVELOPMENT

Trends and Variations in Height and Weight

1. Although growth slows during middle childhood, children of any single age still show significant differences in height and weight.

2. Toward the end of the elementary school years, girls tend to grow taller than boys, and this difference can create embarrassment for some children.

3. A few children weigh significantly more than average, and they sometimes experience social rejection and risk medical problems if their condition persists.

Motor Development and Athletics in Middle Childhood

4. Improvements are especially marked for skills that emphasize coordination and timing rather than strength and size.

5. Gender differences in athletic skills develop during middle childhood, probably because of social expectations.

Health and Illness in Middle Childhood

6. Overall, schoolchildren are among the healthiest people in society, as shown by their low mortality.

7. Compared to preschoolers, school-age children catch fewer minor acute illnesses, but a small percentage do suffer from significant chronic medical problems.

8. Family SES and parents' beliefs about illness affect how much children actually stay at home as a result of getting sick.

9. Attention deficit hyperactivity disorder (ADHD) affects a small percentage of school-age children and may result from a combination of genetic, physical, and social causes.

10. Treatment of ADHD sometimes includes medications and behavior modification techniques.

COGNITIVE DEVELOPMENT

Piaget's Theory: Concrete Operational Skills

11. School-age children develop concrete operational thinking, or reasoning that focuses on real, tangible objects.

12. A very important new skill is conservation, the belief that certain properties, such as size and length, remain constant despite perceptual changes in the object.

13. Efforts to train children in conservation have had moderate success, although when applied in a variety of circumstances training does not persist as strongly as naturally developed conservation does.

14. Concrete operational children also acquire new skills in seriation, temporal relations, and spatial relations.

15. Considered as a whole, Piagetian ideas about cognitive development have influenced educators' styles of teaching and the content of curricula.

Information-Processing Skills

16. Information-processing models divide thinking into several components, including short-term memory, long-term memory, recognition memory, and recall memory.

17. Both short-term and long-term memory improve with age, partly as a result of other cognitive developments such as growing skills in using learning strategies.

18. Improvements in logical reasoning sometimes assist the development of long-term memory, as does increasing richness or familiarity of knowledge as schoolchildren grow older.

19. Learning disabilities can be understood in part as the result of problems in information processing.

20. Providing learning assistance that focuses on specific aspects of information processing can sometimes benefit students.

Language Development in Middle Childhood

21. Although school-age children already are quite skillful with language, they continue to have difficulties with certain subtle features of syntax.

22. During middle childhood, children become much better able to understand metaphorical uses of language.

23. Bilingual children develop certain cognitive advantages over monolingual children, at least if their bilingualism is relatively balanced; these advantages include cognitive flexibility and metalinguistic awareness.

24. Often, however, bilinguals must cope with prejudices against one of their languages and against the culture that language represents.

25. Black English is an example of an important dialect of English spoken by some African Americans in some situations (but not by all or in all circumstances).

Defining and Measuring Intelligence

26. Intelligence is a general ability to learn from or adapt to experience.

27. Traditionally intelligence has been studied from the perspective of psychometric testing, but newer perspectives based on information-processing theory and on sociocultural principles have challenged this perspective.

28. A view of intelligence based on information-processing theory is the triarchic theory of Robert Sternberg, which divides intelligence into components, experiences, and the context of thinking.

29. Howard Gardner's theory of multiple intelligences identifies six distinct cognitive capacities: language skill, musical skill, logical skill, spatial skill, kinesthetic skill, and interpersonal and intrapersonal skills.

30. The sociocultural view of intelligence regards thinking as being distributed among individuals who interact and communicate, and it locates cognitive development in the zone of proximal development.

KEY TERMS

obesity *(261)*
mortality *(266)*
acute illness *(266)*
chronic illness *(266)*
hyperactivity *(267)*
attention deficit
    hyperactivity disorder
    (ADHD) *(267)*
behavior modification *(268)*
concrete operations *(269)*
conservation *(270)*
recognition memory *(273)*
recall memory *(273)*
learning disability *(275)*
metaphor *(279)*

balanced bilingual *(280)*
metalinguistic
    awareness *(280)*
Black English *(281)*
intelligence *(282)*
psychometric approach
    to intelligence *(282)*
achievement test *(283)*
aptitude test *(283)*
triarchic theory of
    intelligence *(286)*
multiple intelligences *(287)*
sociocultural
    perspective *(288)*

9

MIDDLE CHILDHOOD

Psychosocial Development

Nickie is nine years old and in second grade. Between practicing soccer, baseball, and basketball and playing with his friends, playing video games or watching TV with his older brother Alex, doing his homework, walking the dog, and carving a model race car for his Cub Scout den with his father, he is always on the go. Until recently, if asked about his popularity or how he was doing at school or sports, Nickie would answer with a noncommittal "OK" or "I don't know." Lately, however, he has begun to talk more about himself: who he is and how well he is (or is not) doing as a ballplayer, a friend, a student, a brother, and a son.

Middle childhood is a time when the developmental changes of early childhood are rapidly consolidated and children ready themselves for adolescence and the movement to full adulthood. By the time they start school, most children have learned something about human nature and are beginning to pick up various practical skills. During middle childhood, society fosters these developments further by requiring children to attend school to learn socially valued skills such as reading and writing.

School also provides children with more contacts with **peers,** other children of similar age and maturity. Peers offer certain benefits, such as freedom from the watchful eyes of parents and teachers. But they also demand loyalty and conformity. "Be nice to everyone except Rachel" may be a rule in one circle of friends; "Do the assignment, but don't work too hard on it" may be a rule in another. School-age children must learn to coordinate these expectations with those of parents, who sometimes disagree with peers.

To meet all of these demands simultaneously, children must learn to regulate their behavior from within. Somehow they must find ways to control their expressions of aggression, impatience, grief, and other strong impulses and emotions. Doing so becomes easier as they develop concepts of themselves as individuals, knowledge of their own needs and values, and a sense of how these needs and values compare with those of other people. In this chapter, we discuss these developments as they occur from approximately age six to about age twelve.

Focusing Questions

• What major developmental challenges do children face during middle childhood?

• What important changes occur in a child's sense of self during middle childhood?

• What is meant by *achievement motivation,* and what forms does it take?

• How do peers contribute to development during middle childhood?

• How have changes in the nature of the family, such as increases in the proportion of single-parent and dual-wage-earner families, affected children's development?

• In what important ways do schools influence development during middle childhood?

293

PSYCHOSOCIAL CHALLENGES OF MIDDLE CHILDHOOD

During the school years, children's psychosocial development includes five major challenges: the challenge of knowing who you are, the challenge to achieve, the challenge of peers, the challenge of family relationships, and the challenge of school. We will first summarize the nature of those challenges and then discuss them in greater detail in the sections that follow.

The Challenge of Knowing Who You Are   Throughout middle childhood, children develop a deeper understanding of the kinds of people they are and what makes them unique. They also acquire a more fully developed sense of self as a framework for organizing and understanding their experiences. These notions do not yet constitute a final, stable identity, such as that developed during adolescence and adulthood, but they do lay the groundwork for later development. During middle childhood, a child at least can ask, "Am I a popular sort of person?" or "Am I a good athlete?" The answers may still be rather simplistic, but they are beginning to take on meaning nonetheless.

The Challenge to Achieve   Some psychologists consider the major crisis of this age period to be the development of competence, self-confidence, and willingness to achieve to the best of one's ability. Of course, children care about their competence even in infancy. But during middle childhood, this motive is complicated by children's growing awareness of others' opinions about their efforts.

The Challenge of Peers   The third major challenge of middle childhood is relationships with other children, or peers. As we point out later in this chapter, peers serve even more important purposes for schoolchildren than they do for preschoolers, and most school-age children choose to spend a great deal of their time in peer-related activities.

The Challenge of Family Relationships   Despite the strong influence of peers, family relationships have far from disappeared from the lives of schoolchildren. Later in this chapter we discuss several important aspects of family life, including recent changes in family roles and family membership due to changing employment patterns and divorce rates. These changes in the traditional family structure have raised the questions of who is responsible for doing what within a family and what constitutes a family in the first place. Furthermore, all too often school-age children must share the challenge of holding the family together.

The Challenge of School   During middle childhood, school is second only to the family in influence on children's social and emotional development. Observing and interacting with a large number of diverse children and adults other than their parents give children an opportunity to learn new social skills, values, and beliefs and to develop a fuller sense of identity. In this chapter we explore how school culture and curriculum, teacher influences, and the student's own experiences contribute to development during middle childhood.

THE SENSE OF SELF

Throughout infancy, childhood, and adolescence, children actively construct a **sense of self,** a structured way of thinking about themselves that helps them organize and understand who they are based on the views of others, on their own experiences,

During the middle years, children develop preliminary notions of their personal qualities and psychological identity. What do you suppose this girl's sense of herself might be?

and on cultural categories such as gender and race. This structure rapidly evolves during middle childhood and becomes increasingly organized and complex. In fact, although a sense of self often is called a *self-concept,* it functions more as a theory that organizes a pattern of related ideas than as a single concept. A child actively constructs and continually revises his or her sense of self based on increasing age and experience (Wylie, 1974/1979).

For example, at age six, Mina loved playing with dolls and also loved holding and caring for babies. She noticed that her parents and others commented on this preference, so nurturance became part of Mina's idea of herself: "I'm someone who likes babies," she sometimes thought. But later experiences modified this idea. Toward the end of elementary school, Mina discovered that she often preferred playing softball to playing house. Somehow, at age ten or eleven, she had to incorporate this reality into her sense of self: "I'm a good ballplayer," she realized. By the start of adolescence, she still was not sure how to reconcile these two concepts of herself: her interest in child care and her interest in sports. Someday she may succeed in doing so, but not at age twelve.

To a large extent, a child's notion of self grows out of social experiences with other selves or, put more plainly, out of contacts with other children and adults. Learning what it means to be female in their cultural context, for example, occurs as girls meet other individuals who also are female. Learning what it means to be happy occurs as children see other people express happiness. As personal and individual as a sense of self is, then, it reflects generalizations about others, and it cannot develop without considerable social contact (Lewis & Brooks-Gunn, 1979b).

The Development of Self in Childhood

How do children acquire a sense of self? The first step involves basic social labels or categories. By the end of the second year of life, most children can correctly label their gender ("I'm a boy" or "I'm a girl"), their age ("I'm two"), and their species

("I'm a person"). Labels such as these pave the way for later, more complete knowledge of self.

Self-constancy   At first, however, most such labels lack permanence. At age two or three, a boy may claim he can become a girl under certain circumstances—"when I grow up" or "if I grow my hair long" (Marcus & Overton, 1978). Or a very young child may say she can become a different individual "if I change my name" (Guardo & Bohan, 1971). **Self-constancy,** a belief that identity remains permanently fixed, does not become firm until the early school years, sometime after age six. At this time, a child becomes convinced he will stay the same person indefinitely into the future, will remain human in all circumstances, and will keep his gender forever. Beliefs such as these are what a sense of self means.

The First Beliefs in Psychological Traits   Younger children, up to age five or six, tend to define themselves in terms of observable features and behaviors such as hairstyles or how fast they can run (Rosenberg, 1979). Around age eight, some children form a more stable sense of self by including psychological traits in their self-descriptions. At first, the traits are feelings and qualities that have no apparent reference to other human beings; "I am brave," says the child, or "I am cheerful." By implication these traits describe her as an entire personality and in all possible situations, with little recognition of people's usual variations in moods. At first, too, the child describes the traits in bold, global terms that ignore the possibility that opposing feelings or qualities sometimes exist within the same person. The child may vacillate in describing her own qualities without realizing it. Sometimes she will say, "I am dumb," meaning *completely* dumb, and other times she will say, "I am smart," meaning *completely* smart (Harter, 1977). Neither statement suggests the child recognizes that both descriptions contain an element of truth.

By the end of middle childhood, fuller integration of contradictory traits occurs. Around age ten or twelve, children begin to recognize that they can feel more than one way about any particular situation or person; they can both like and hate their teachers or enjoy and dislike school more or less at the same time (Selman, 1980). As they do so, they also begin using trait labels in less global ways and more often to express qualities in particular situations. When an older child says, "I am smart," he no longer means "I am always smart in every possible way and in every activity." Now he more likely means "I am smart in a number of significant situations, but not in all." During middle childhood, children become increasingly able to interrelate the different categories of traits and develop more patterned and integrated self-descriptions (Damon & Hart, 1988; Fischer et al., 1990).

These changes contribute to the development of a more flexible sense of self, in which the same individual can be characterized in a variety of ways depending on the circumstances. The situation-bound qualities school-age children express usually describe them more accurately than the global traits and observable features younger children rely on. But a school-age child's consciousness of inner traits still lacks the subtlety and flexibility found in adolescents and adults, who recognize that the stability of self involves multiple dimensions and ongoing change.

However, significant cultural differences exist in how the concept of self is constructed, and the idea of self is probably not a discrete psychological entity in all cultures (Hoare, 1994). In Asian countries such as India, Japan, and Nepal, for example, three distinct senses of self appear to exist simultaneously even in adulthood: a familial self, in which one's sense of self is defined almost exclusively in relationship to one's family; a spiritual self, which is defined and organized in terms of religious beliefs; and an individualized self, which is closer to the European-American sense of self just described (Roland, 1988).

Processes in Constructing a Self

To a large degree, the process of developing an identity and a sense of self during middle childhood reflects a growing awareness of relationships with other people (Damon & Hart, 1988). Children construct their identities by distinguishing their thoughts and feelings from those expressed by others. When children of various ages are asked how they would feel if their parents expressed certain emotions, such as sadness, anger, or happiness, preschoolers are likely to say they would feel the same emotions: they would be angry if their parents were angry, sad if they were sad, and so on. Older children, however, are more likely to name complementary rather than identical emotions; if their parents felt angry, for example, they would feel fearful (Harter & Barnes, 1983).

Additional evidence comes from studies of how children gradually acquire a fuller understanding of shame and pride. By the early school years (age six or seven), children begin explicitly mentioning an external audience in defining these two terms (Seidner et al., 1988). For example, one seven-year-old's definition was "My teacher was proud when I earned 100 percent on the test"; another's was "My mother was ashamed when I lost my temper at the neighbor." Such attention to others implies awareness that others sometimes observe the child's self. More important, it suggests that school-age children distinguish between their own emotions and those of others—something they must do to develop a mature sense of self.

A child's emerging sense of self during middle childhood is part of a broader process of personality development. In the following section, we briefly discuss how two major developmental theorists, Sigmund Freud and Erik Erikson, view this process.

What Do You Think?

What do you remember about changes in your sense of self during your school years? What conflicting traits do you recall, and how did those traits get integrated?

THE AGE OF INDUSTRY AND ACHIEVEMENT

When viewed as part of the overall lifespan, the years from six to twelve seem especially important to the achievement of competence. Children spend countless hours in school acquiring skills in reading, writing, and mathematics. Many of these hours also contribute to learning the unofficial curriculum of school: how to get along with teachers and with other children. Outside of school, children often devote themselves to the long, slow mastery of particular skills. One child may spend years learning to play baseball; another may devote the same amount of time to learning how to care for a zoo of pet hamsters, dogs, and birds.

Latency and the Crisis of Industry

Psychodynamic theories such as those proposed by Freud and Erikson explain such behavior in terms of the emotional relationships that precede it in early childhood. As we describe in Chapter 7, preschool children feel envy, awe, and competitiveness with respect to their parents. At first, these feelings have a magical quality: children simply want to be like their parents. Inevitably they are disappointed to learn that merely wanting such things does not make them come true.

School-aged children often devote themselves to the long, slow mastery of complicated skills, such as learning to hit a ball.

In this regard, Freud emphasized the emotional hardship of preschoolers' disappointment and their consequent repression of their magical wishes regarding their parents (Freud, 1983). A five-year-old, he argued, cannot continue indefinitely to wish for intimacy with his opposite-sex parent and for success in competition with his same-sex parent. These feelings (which Freud termed the *Oedipus* and *Electra conflicts*) disrupt life if they persist too long. Thus, the child eventually represses the feelings, meaning he pushes them completely out of awareness. As it happens, this repression occurs at about the time most children begin school—around age six or seven—and continues until adolescence. Freud called this the **latency** period, meaning a child's earlier unresolved feelings have gone underground and are waiting to resurface in the future (at the beginning of adolescence). During this period, the schoolchild focuses on building competencies and skills as a defense—an unconscious, self-protective behavior—against her earlier romantic feelings toward her parent. Developing talents, whether in sports, art, academics, or whatever, also helps to keep the child's mind off her earlier disappointment, which lingers on unconsciously.

Erikson agreed with Freud's account up to this point, but he went beyond it to stress not only the defensive, negative functions of skill building but its positive functions as well (Erikson, 1963, 1968). According to Erikson, children respond to their romantic feelings toward their parents not only by repressing them but also by trying consciously to become more like their parents and more like adults in general. Becoming competent helps children reach this goal in two ways. First, it helps them through *identification,* a process by which they experience themselves as being like their parents and thus capable of becoming genuine adults; second, it helps them to gain similar recognition from others.

Erikson called this process the crisis of **industry versus inferiority,** meaning children of this age concern themselves with their capacity for *industry,* or the ability to do good work. Children who convince themselves and others of this capacity develop relatively confident, positive concepts of themselves. Those who do not tend to suffer from feelings of poor self-esteem and *inferiority,* a sense of inadequacy or general lack of competence. According to Erikson, most children end up with a mixture of self-confidence and fear of inferiority, but self-confidence predominates in most cases (we hope).

In addition, the crisis of industry versus inferiority gives healthy school-age children a more or less permanent motivation to achieve particular, definable standards of excellence. A child's continuing sense that she can achieve and that her industry will pay off is shaped by her earlier successes and failures in school. No longer is she happy just to draw pictures, for example; now she must draw *well.* With persistence and support, children often do reach higher standards of excellence in many activities than they did as preschoolers, and most of the time they are happy about doing so.

Partly because of the connection between industry and increasing competence, psychologists have devoted a lot of attention to the development of achievement motivation in school-age children. In the next section, we look at some of this work.

Achievement Motivation

Achievement motivation is the tendency to show initiative and persistence in attaining certain goals and increasing competence by successfully meeting standards of excellence (Atkinson & Feather, 1966; Beck, 1978). What matters most is the approach to a task rather than the importance of the task itself. An individual can reveal achievement motivation as either a student or a college professor, for example, and as either an amateur checkers player or a world-class chess grand master. As long as the individual strives toward a standard of excellence that is reasonable for him, he possesses achievement motivation. Usually too his motivation leads to increased competence compared to his previous level.

Differences in Achievement Motivation   There appear to be two distinct kinds of achievement motivation. The first, called **learning orientation,** relies on *intrinsic motivation,* that is, motivation that comes from within the learner and relates directly to the task and its accomplishment. A learning orientation leads children to concentrate on learning as an end in itself; they will practice jumping rope just to see whether they can do it. The second type of motivation, called **performance orientation,** involves *extrinsic motivation,* meaning motivation comes not from the learner but from other individuals who see and evaluate her. In this instance, the person the child is trying to please or satisfy is not herself but others (Chapman & Skinner, 1989; Dweck & Leggett, 1988; Ginsburg & Bronstein, 1993).

Motivational orientations play an important role in children's development. For example, higher levels of intrinsic motivation have been associated with an internal sense of control, feelings of enjoyment, and various mastery-related characteristics such as curiosity, creativity, exploration, and persistence in completing tasks and a preference for taking on challenges. They are also linked to higher academic performance and learning, feelings of academic competence, and perceptions of what contributes to academic success or failure (Ginsburg & Bronstein, 1993).

Achievement Motivation in Middle Childhood   During middle childhood, children become more performance oriented than they were at earlier ages. At the beginning of this period, children express considerable optimism about their abilities. Kindergartners tend to rank themselves at the top of their class in scholastic ability, even though they rank other children relatively accurately (Stipek & Hoffman, 1980). This implies a learning orientation; for young children, achievement is something they do without either the involvement or the evaluations of others (Frieze et al., 1981).

During the next several years, however, children begin to believe that having an ability depends partly on whether other people give them credit for having it. This belief lies at the core of the performance orientation. It does not replace a learning orientation; rather, it takes a place alongside it. Now being "smart" means partly that a child's teachers, parents, and friends *say* she is smart and partly that she possesses certain skills in reading, mathematics, and the like regardless of what others say (Feld et al., 1979).

Successful achievement becomes more complicated in middle childhood. Consider swimming. Late in infancy and during the preschool years, a child may be motivated to learn to swim simply by being given chances to experiment in the water. During the school years, however, he may ask himself what other people, especially parents and friends, will think about his learning to swim. Most people will value swimming to some extent, of course. But even very respectable progress in swimming may not look like much of an achievement if the child's family and friends hold very high athletic standards or place little value on athletics in the first place.

As we saw in Chapter 8, academic achievement is one of the principal types of achievement children focus on during middle childhood. Also, since schools tend to group children homogeneously by age and ability, children of similar age and ability form the principal peer group for many developing children. The main exception to this pattern is siblings, who often are an important peer system influence as well. We will take a closer look at both sibling and school influences later in this chapter.

Environmental factors also can influence motivational orientation. Environments that provide optimal challenge, offer feedback that promotes competence, and support children's autonomous and independent behaviors are likely to facilitate the development of intrinsic motivation, whereas environments that strongly emphasize extrinsic rewards, deadlines, and adult control tend to undermine intrinsic motivation and foster an extrinsic motivational orientation (Deci & Ryan, 1987).

Family factors are also important. Golda Ginsburg and Phyllis Bronstein (1993) examined how parental monitoring of homework, parental reactions to grades, and general family style influenced achievement motivation orientation among fifth-grade children. When parents heavily supervised homework (by helping, checking, reminding, or insisting), reacted to grades with punishment, criticism, uninvolvement, or extrinsic rewards, and displayed overcontrolling (authoritarian) or undercontrolling (permissive) styles of parenting, children were more likely to have extrinsic (performance) motivational orientations and lower academic performance. On the other hand, children whose parents responded to grades with encouragement and were supportive of their children's autonomy (authoritative parenting style) were more likely to have intrinsic motivational orientation and higher academic performance. We explore the contributions of SES to differences in parenting style in Chapter 11.

Differences in cultural backgrounds also can influence children's achievement orientations. For example, Chinese and Japanese mothers believe more strongly than American mothers do that academic success depends on one's own efforts rather than on factors beyond one's control, such as inborn ability or external conditions. This intrinsically motivated, achievement-oriented view is likely shared by their children and may help account for the higher academic achievement of Asian students over American students (Stevenson & Lee, 1990). The accompanying Multicultural View box discusses ethnic differences in parental expectations for academic achievement.

As children grow older, they shift toward a performance orientation and become more similar to adults in their achievement motivation. This in part reflects the increasing importance of peers and children's changing perceptions of social comparisons (Pomerantz et al., 1995). At this stage, children take others' opinions more and more seriously and often seek out those opinions on a variety of matters. Achievement motivation, it turns out, is just one peer-related concern among many.

What Do You Think?

Survey several classmates about their current learning orientations and the extent to which those orientations grew out of middle childhood experiences. What advantages and disadvantages do you see in each of these orientations?

PEER RELATIONSHIPS

Throughout childhood, some of children's most important relationships involve peers. The peer group is second only to the family as a context within which developmental changes occur (Hartup, 1989). As early as age two, children enjoy playing with or next to one another, and by age three or four they often prefer the company of peers, even when adults are available. Time spent with peers increases steadily during middle childhood. By the late elementary school years, about one-half of children's social interactions are with peers (Ellis et al., 1981). Peer relationships acquire a special intensity during late childhood and the transition to adolescence that typically occurs between fifth and seventh grades. During this period, children have increased unsupervised contact with peers and begin to place greater importance on peers' approval, views, and advice. At the same time, they spend less time with their parents and display greater emotional distance and psychological independence from them (B. Brown, 1990; Larson & Richards, 1991).

What Theorists Say About Peer Relationships

Piaget   According to Jean Piaget, one important function of peers is to help school-age children overcome their *egocentrism,* or their tendency to assume everyone views the world in the same way they do (Piaget, 1963). In the course of playing together, children inevitably run into conflicts over toys and priorities, arguing over who should use a new set of felt pens or over what and where they should draw. In settling such disagreements, children gradually come to understand and value different points of view, a capacity that is central to living successfully in a pluralistic, democratic society.

Sullivan   The most comprehensive theory about peers was proposed by Harry Stack Sullivan. Like Piaget, Sullivan argued that relationships with peers have fundamentally different qualities than those with adults (Sullivan, 1953; Youniss, 1980). In particular, peers foster skills in compromise, cooperation, and competition. But unlike Piaget, Sullivan emphasized the value of peers in promoting emotional health. Peers create a life for children outside their families, and in doing so they help correct the emotional biases families inevitably give their children, biases that Sullivan called emotional *warps.* For instance, an eight-year-old with shy, reserved parents may learn from peers that not all people are shy and reserved. Or a ten-year-old whose parents care little about competitive athletics may discover from peers that athletic competition matters quite a lot to some people.
　　According to Sullivan, this form of learning occurs during the **juvenile period,** which begins around age five and continues until nine or ten. In this period, children

A Multicultural View

Parental Expectations and Academic Achievement

Differences in academic achievement among African American, white, and Hispanic children appear early during the elementary school years and continue throughout elementary, junior, and senior high school. One study found that at second grade, about 5 percent of white children and more than 15 percent of African American and Hispanic children were performing below grade level in mathematics, and by sixth grade 20 percent of white children, more than 40 percent of Hispanic children, and 50 percent of African American children were performing below grade level (Norman, 1988).

One popular explanation is that lower achievement of minority children is due to low levels of achievement motivation resulting from poverty, family disruption, inadequate academic support, and low parental expectations for children's academic success. This view has been challenged by a large-scale study of African American, Hispanic, and white urban elementary school children and their mothers (Stevenson et al., 1990). In that study, Harold Stevenson and his colleagues examined the role parents played in their children's education and parents' and children's beliefs about children's current school performance and their educational future. Mothers and teachers were also asked how the children's performances might be improved.

What did the researchers find? First, when only families from similar economic and educational backgrounds were compared, the achievement levels of the African American and Hispanic children were *not* substantially lower than those of the white children. Second, beliefs about the children's educational achievement held by both the Hispanic and African American children and their mothers were very similar to those typically associated with higher rather than lower levels of achievement.

When the entire sample was looked at, the following findings emerged. All mothers agreed that parents should work closely with their children on schoolwork. African American mothers expressed the greatest interest in helping their children, followed by Hispanic and then white mothers. Hispanic mothers were less confident about their knowledge of English and of the American school system, but were still eager to help their children with schoolwork, stressed the importance of school, and had high regard for their children's intellectual abilities and academic achievement. They also shared with the African American mothers (and their children's teachers) a strong belief in the importance of homework, the necessity of competency examinations, and the potential value of a longer school day. They held high expectations for their children's futures, though not as high as those of the African American and white mothers.

Most of the African American mothers were familiar with what teachers expected of their children. They reported spending more time teaching their children academic skills than the other parents and evaluated their children's skills, abilities, and academic achievement in reading and math very highly. Their children rated their own performances very highly as well and believed they were working hard. Surprisingly, though, African American students' evaluations of their school performances were unrelated to their actual levels of achievement in reading and math, which suggests they had not received or internalized realistic feedback about their academic performances from either their parents, their teachers, or both (Alexander & Entwisle, 1988; Bock & Moore, 1986).

These findings challenge the view that the low performances of African American and Hispanic elementary

show increasing interest in playmates of similar age and status. As they near the end of the elementary school years, they supposedly focus this interest on just a few select friends of the same sex, whom Sullivan called *chums*. These relationships provide children with models for later intimate relationships.

The Functions of Peers

Peer activities appear to serve several important functions. First, they provide a context for sociability, enhancement of relationships, and a sense of belonging. Second, they promote concern for achievements and a reliable and integrated sense of who one is. Finally, they provide opportunities for instruction and learning (Zarbatany et al., 1990). The accompanying Perspectives Box discusses the nature and function of peer activities.

Children's reliance on peers versus parents for help appears to increase with age. According to fourth-graders, friends provide support less frequently than do

As discussed in the multicultural view, active encouragement and support from parents plays an important role in fostering academic achievement during the middle years.

school children are due to low levels of achievement motivation, parental expectations, or parental support. What, then, accounts for the decreasing academic achievement of minority elementary school children and increasing rates of academic failure and dropping out in junior and senior high school? One possibility is that teachers and staff may have lower academic expectations for minorities, who are overrepresented in the low academic tracks compared with other student groups, leaving these students with both inadequate preparation and unrealistic expectations about the academic demands of junior and senior high school (Reed, 1988). As these children approach adolescence, the schools they attend and the families in which they live fail to adequately meet their emerging needs for intellectual challenge and academic support, for adult supervision and independence, and for relationships with teachers and parents that enable them to believe a relationship exists between their academic efforts and the rewards available to them in American society (Eccles, 1993; Stevenson et al., 1990).

mothers and fathers, the most frequent providers. Seventh-graders, however, believe same-sex friends and parents are equally supportive, whereas tenth-graders view same-sex friends as the most frequent source of support (Furman & Buhrmester, 1992). Although the functions of children's peer relationships show considerable similarity to those with adults, several features are unique to peer relationships. Attachments with parents and other adults or older children are "vertical and complementary," meaning they involve individuals who have greater knowledge, competence, and social power. Peer relationships, in contrast, are "horizontal and symmetrical" in that they involve individuals of approximately equal knowledge, competence, and social power (Hartup, 1989). They are by nature voluntary and reciprocal relationships among comparative equals. This means that a child must act in a way that explicitly supports the relationship—be friendly, that is—if he expects the relationship to survive. Children apparently understand these differences intuitively, because they typically attribute an obedience orientation to relationships between adults and children but attribute play and recreation orientations to relationships among children (Berndt, 1988; Youniss, 1980).

Perspectives

The Psychological Functions of Preadolescent Peer Activities

Peer activity is a central feature of middle childhood. It plays an important role in acquiring skills and knowledge and developing the personal and interpersonal goals that guide and give meaning to children's behavior and values. To learn more about the psychological functions of preadolescent peer activities, Lynne Zarbatany, Donald Hartmann, and Bruce Rankin asked fifth- and sixth graders from middle-class neighborhoods in Canada to keep weeklong diaries of important types of peer activities (Zarbatany et al., 1990). Children also kept track of the specific behaviors their peers exhibited during each activity and which behaviors they liked and disliked. A second group of fifth- and sixth-grade children then rated the frequency of each activity, its importance, and which positive and negative behaviors they would most (or least) like to occur during the ten most frequently reported activities.

Table 9.1 lists the twenty most common activities reported and how girls and boys ranked the importance of each. It reveals substantial similarities as well as some differences, a theme that holds true for many aspects of gender across the lifespan. Despite some variations in order, eight of the ten activities judged "most important" by both girls and boys were the same. As expected, some gender differences were also found. Boys preferred contact and noncontact sports more and played more contact sports than girls did, whereas girls tended to rate talking about hairstyles, clothing, shopping, attending church, and baby sitting higher than boys did and spent more time in these activities.

Such peer activities appear to serve three major functions. First, they provide a context for sociability, enhancement of relationships, and a sense of belonging. Second, they promote concern for achievement and self-worth. Third, they provide opportunities for instruction and learning. Peers also provide validation

TABLE 9.1   Peer Activities of Fifth- and Sixth-Graders

Activity	Importance		
	All	Boys	Girls
*Noncontact sports	1	1	4
*TV/music	2	2	1
*Conversing	3	4	2.5
*Telephone	4	6.5	2.5
*Physical games	5	3.5	5.5
Parties	6	3.5	7
Hanging out	7	6.5	8.5
Acting silly	8	8	10
*Shopping	9	13.5	5.5
Cards/board games	10	7	15.5
*Contact sports	11	5	22
Baby sitting	12	15	8.5
Secrets	13	13.5	11
Clubs (e.g., scouts)	14	10	13
Play with pets	15	9	17
*Academic	16	13	15.5
Arts and crafts	17	15	14
*Travel/school	18	10.5	17.5
Walking to school	19	13.5	18
*Eating	20	12	21.5

* = ten most frequently reported activities.
Source: Adapted from Zarbatany et al. (1990).

Listed above are the twenty most important peer activities reported, ranked in order of importance for fifth- and sixth-grade boys and girls combined and separately. With the exception of shopping and contact sports, two highly gender-stereotyped activities, boys and girls are quite similar on which of the ten most frequently reported activities are most important.

Influences on Peer Group Membership

Most of children's peer interactions occur in groups. In defining a peer group, elementary school children emphasize the importance of shared activities such as walking to school, talking on the telephone, listening to music, playing games, and just hanging out; however, sharing attitudes becomes most important as children approach adolescence (O'Brien & Bierman, 1988; Zarbatany et al., 1990). Living in the same neighborhood, attending the same school, and participating in the same community organizations all contribute to the likelihood that peer groups will form.

Children's peer groups are not simply random assortments of individuals but are influenced by many factors. Three of the most important factors are age, gender, and race or ethnic background.

from others of emerging aspects of the self, such as attitudes, interests, and worthiness, and serve as a comparison group against which children can gauge their skills and abilities. Acceptance and inclusion by peers and opportunities for assessing the unique capabilities of self are important functions served by preadolescent peer activities.

Different peer activities appeared to support different psychosocial achievements. For instance, noncompetitive activities such as TV watching and "hanging out" provide opportunities for socializing and enhancing relationships but less opportunity to identify unique aspects of the self. In contrast, competitive activities such as noncontact sports are less relationship oriented but enable youngsters to evaluate their own unique skills and abilities.

These researchers see several implications in their findings. First, children may require exposure to a variety of activities to benefit from the full range of psychosocial experiences. For example, cultural norms that limit a girl's exposure to team sports may deprive her of opportunities to learn skills important to the world of work, such as negotiation and conflict resolution. Likewise, a boy's strong investment in team sports and lower interest in relationship-oriented activities such as baby sitting or talking on the telephone may inhibit the development of skills for establishing intimacy.

The results also suggest that peer behavior is best understood in the context in which it occurs. For example, while supportive peer behaviors that occur while watching TV or listening to music may serve to promote better interpersonal relationships, these same behaviors are more likely to promote skill achievement or a greater sense of self-worth if they occur during noncontact sports activities. In addition, the desirablility and effectiveness of a particular behavior appeared to vary with the nature of the activity in which it occurred. The use of humor is a good example. While humor tended to be a highly desirable behavior in many situations, indiscriminate use of humor was not particularly valued if it occurred while playing competitive team sports, where it could easily be misinterpreted as criticism. Likewise, "ragging" and other forms of criticism were not much of a problem if they occurred while traveling to and from school with friends, but could create serious problems if they occurred while in the school cafeteria, where chances for public embarassment were much greater.

Age Children play mostly with others of approximately the same age and, when asked, say they prefer to be friends with their agemates. But contrary to a common impression, schoolchildren may spend anywhere from one-quarter to one-half of their time with companions who are more than two years older or younger and say they prefer to seek help and comfort from older children (Ellis et al., 1981; French, 1984). School imposes an upper limit on these cross-age contacts, however, because classrooms usually group children according to age.

Groups with mixed ages have certain special qualities. Older children show more nurturant behavior, such as tying the shoelaces of a younger child or buttoning the child's sweater. Younger children show greater dependence by asking for help with schoolwork or agreeing to older peers' preferences for play activities. However, mixed-age groups also tend to be less "sociable" than same-age groups; they chat or have friendly conversations less often, for example. Same-age groups encourage the opposites of all of these qualities: children give and receive less practical help, show more friendliness to one another, and get into conflicts more often (Brody et al., 1983; Furman & Buhrmester, 1992).

Gender   Although mixed-gender play occurs during the elementary school years, first-graders generally name children of their own gender as best friends. Observations of younger schoolchildren during free play show that during cooperative play periods, they interact about four times as often with children of their own gender as they do with those of the opposite gender (Maccoby & Jacklin, 1987). This ratio actually increases as children approach adolescence; by third grade most peer groups contain only one gender, and by fifth grade virtually all do. As children move into middle school and adolescence, however, the trend reverses (Shrum et al., 1988).

How do we interpret this tendency toward gender-based separation during middle childhood? Eleanor Maccoby argues that gender differences emerge primarily in social situations and vary with the gender composition of the dyads (two-person relationships) and groups involved (Maccoby, 1990). She suggests that children spontaneously choose same-gender playmates even in situations where they are not under pressure from adults to do so because they find same-gender play partners more compatible.

During the later preschool years, two factors seem to be important. First, the rough-and-tumble style and emphasis on competition and dominance that is characteristic of boys appear to be unappealing to most girls, who in general prefer play that is more cooperative and less aggressive. Second, girls discover that their growing reliance on polite suggestion to influence others is increasingly ineffective with boys and therefore avoid choosing boys as playmates (Maccoby, 1990).

Further support for the idea that playmate selection may be more heavily influenced by sharing gender-based play activities than by merely being of the same gender comes from a recent laboratory study of playmate choice among six-to-eight-year-olds conducted by Gerianne Alexander and Melissa Hines. When given the choice of selecting a playmate based on gender versus preferred style of play, style of play appeared to be more important for both boys and girls. Boys chose female playmates who had masculine play styles (including toys, rough-and-tumble play, and activity level), whereas girls chose male playmates with more feminine play styles (Alexander & Hines, 1994).

Girls' long-term friendships more often tend toward exclusive intimacy than boys' do. For example, in one study that asked children to name their best friends, girls more often made mutually exclusive choices (dyads, or two-person relationships). Triads, in which a third girl's choice was not reciprocated, also occurred more often. Boys more often formed patterns in which no choice was reciprocated, picking one another as friends, even though no one was picked in return. Judging by these choices, boys' friendships tend to be more extensive and spread more widely, whereas girls' tend to more intensive and focused on just a few individuals. (Eder & Hallinan, 1978; Hallinan, 1981). Figure 9.1 illustrates these differences in friendship patterns between girls and boys.

Over time, children find same-gender play partners more compatible and segregate themselves into same-gender groups. As children enter adolescence, childhood patterns carry over into cross-gender interactions in which girls' styles may put them at a disadvantage. While patterns of mutual influence may be more symmetrical in intimate, young adult male-female couples, these gender-related differences in style are still present and subsequently manifest themselves in the roles and relationships of parenthood (Maccoby, 1990). We will look at the impact of these differences on parenthood in Chapter 13's coverage of psychosocial development in early adulthood.

Adult norms and expectations regarding gender stereotyping can also have an impact. For example, children growing up in families that downplay gender typing in their childrearing values and practices are less stereotyped in their activities, interests, and gender-typed beliefs. However, gender flexibility in children's play behavior or

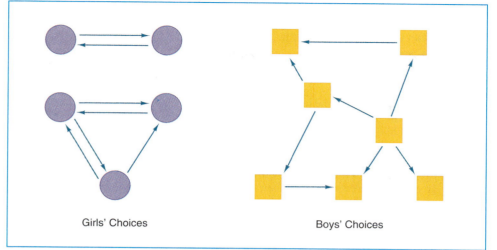

Girls' Choices   Boys' Choices

FIGURE 9.1
Typical Patterns of Peer Friend-
ships among Girls and Boys
Girls' friendships tend to involve recip-
rocal, two-person relationships and
three-person relationships in which a
third girl's choice is not reciprocated.
Boys more often form patterns in
which no choice is reciprocated.

friendship preferences is more likely to be evident in situations where it is supported, or at least not actively discouraged, by parents, teachers, and other adults (Hoffman, 1989; Maccoby, 1990; Moorehouse, 1991; Weisner & Wilson-Mitchell, 1990).

Even when parents work hard to encourage friendships that are not gender stereotyped, peers often exert considerable pressure toward conformity with same-gender friendship patterns. On his ninth birthday, Alex solved this problem by having an all-boy "public" birthday party and later having a special "private" one with his lifelong best friend, Katie. For interesting firsthand observations of the role of gender in peer group play, see the interview with Lisa Truong.

Race and Ethnic Background   Patterns of segregation and preferences based on racial and ethnic differences are a fact of life in much of our society (Asher et al., 1982; Shrum et al., 1988). Racial and ethnic awareness are especially important

A school setting that is ethnically
diverse may foster peer interactions
and friendships among schoolchildren
from different ethnic groups.

Working with Lisa Truong, FOURTH-GRADE TEACHER

Reducing Gender Role Stereotyping in Play

Lisa Truong is a fourth-grade teacher at a "follow-through" elementary school that serves students from citywide head-start preschool and kindergarten programs as well as children from the local neighborhood. Her classroom is a well-organized, friendly, cheerful place filled with children's drawings and other projects. Lisa provides richly detailed observations of gender differences in peer group and play activities among fourth-graders.

Rob: How would you describe peer relations among fourth-graders?

Lisa: Often children's academic ability sets the tone and pace for their friendships. Children who do well academically tend to be friends with other kids who are bright.

Rob: Why do you think this is so?

Lisa: In part because of parent pressure. Parents are interested in their children having good friends. Another reason

may be that much of the teaching here occurs in small skill groups. These group children with the same academic needs together. They also focus on group dynamics, teaching the children to work with other people. When we go outside for recess, the children do tend to stay in those same groups.

Rob: What other factors seem to influence peer groups?

Lisa: Boy-girl differences are very important. As much as I've tried to encourage girls to play football or soccer and boys to do things like four-square and jump-rope, it really does break down by gender as to how they play outside. Girls tend to play jump-rope, and boys tend to play soccer on the field—it's almost automatic. Girls also tend to go to the swings and slide much more than the boys.

Rob: Why do you think this happens?

Lisa: At this age, girls are getting more

social and interactive. Often I see girls walking slowly and talking. Even their jump-rope is more consistently interactive and coordinated— with turn taking and things like that—than the boys' play. You should see the girls play four-square! It involves a lot of verbal interaction and social coordination.

Rob: How so?

Lisa: Four people stand in a 10-foot-by-10-foot square drawn in chalk and divided into four smaller squares. The person in the fourth square is in control of whatever the category will be. So, for example, that person will say "Colors" and then bounce the ball into any of the other players' squares. They will have to name a color and catch the ball, or they're out.

Rob: There's a rhythm to it?

Lisa: You have to keep the rhythm, and you can't name the same color

during middle childhood, because children of this age are in the process of committing themselves to society and to the values and standards of the majority culture. They are also developing their own self-concepts.

Racial segregation and racial preference often reflect certain types of prejudice. *Prejudice* is a positive or negative attitude toward an individual based solely on the person's membership in a particular group. Prejudices are frequently based on *stereotypes,* patterns of rigid, overly simplified, and generally inaccurate ideas about the characteristics of another group of people. Stereotypes often involve negative ideas associated with race, ethnic or cultural background, religion, SES, age, gender, and sexual orientation. While prejudices based on stereotypes do not necessarily determine a person's overt behavior, they often do. Frequently prejudice is associated with *discrimination*—actions toward members of the targeted group, such as exclusion or mistreatment, that reflect prejudicial attitudes toward that group.

Studies that asked children to name their friends have found that children are more likely to name peers of their own race, particularly if that race is the majority one. This trend begins in the preschool years and increases throughout middle childhood until children reach junior high school (Asher et al., 1982; Shrum et al., 1988; Singleton & Asher, 1979). The degree to which family, neighborhood, and school settings are supportive (or unsupportive) of cross-race friendships is also likely to influence a child's peer preferences. For example, cross-race friendships are more likely to develop in integrated schools but are difficult to maintain outside of school unless the children live in interracial neighborhoods or participate in team sports or other integrated activities (DuBois & Hirsch, 1990; Howes & Wu, 1990).

Can racial and ethnic prejudice be reduced? Elementary school programs that emphasize multicultural competence and awareness by integrating multicultural

twice—or animal, country, movie star, or whatever the category is. The categories get more complex as the year goes on. The kids almost always start the year with colors, and by the end of the year it will be something much more specific, like Madonna's songs or names of rock stars. This group of girls also made up a great hand-clapping game about music groups; the way they thought it through and the rules they made up were fascinating.

Rob: What are the boys doing?

Lisa: They're playing soccer and kick-ball, building forts, or skateboards, if they can. Or they'll collect things and investigate the environment. At the beginning of the year, we studied insects and their natural habitats in science. Once the boys got outside, they tried to find every single little bug they could, and they would come in and show it.

Rob: It seems fourth-grade boys are less interested in make-up games than girls.

Lisa: Yes, that's true. Boys tend to play games that emphasize physical rather than social interaction and where they follow rules that are already made up for them.

Rob: How permanent are these peer group patterns?

Lisa: They seem long-lasting. The group I described was made up of five girls who are very, very close. They're all good students, and all happen to be white. I've been trying to encourage them to be less of a clique and interact with other people more.

Rob: How else might teachers encourage greater interaction?

Lisa: Our school is committed to helping children interact in a way that doesn't break down along sex role or racial lines. I talk to them about it

very up-front, and I say I think there should be more interaction between boys and girls and blacks and whites. When we have social studies activities, the rule is that groups will be mixed. The children understand this and help make it work.

What Do You Think?

1. Lisa's observations of her students illustrate how closely play and social development are interrelated. What examples in the interview demonstrate this?

2. How has Lisa attempted to reduce gender role stereotyping in her fourth-graders' peer group and play activities? Based on this chapter, what additional things might she consider trying?

3. Discuss how Lisa's observations demonstrate the interaction of physical, cognitive, and social domains in her fourth-graders' development. How are the three domains reflected in gender differences in peer groups and play activities?

activities in both academic and extracurricular activities and actively involve children's families and other community members in school activities can successfully foster friendship and peer acceptance among students from different racial, ethnic, and cultural backgrounds (Bojko, 1995). *Magnet schools* that use specialized programs in science, language, or the arts to attract students from school districts representing a variety of ethnic and cultural backgrounds have also successfully increased diversity on a long-term basis (Rossell, 1988).

Cooperative learning experiences that allow mixed groups of children to work as a team to achieve common academic goals also have had some success in fostering cross-race acceptance and enhancing children's self-esteem (Johnson et al., 1984; Katz & Zalk, 1978; Slavin, 1986). In one program based on this "jigsaw" technique, children from different racial and ethnic backgrounds were assigned to different parts of a single project. They quickly learned to work together to complete the task and developed more positive feelings about both themselves and one another (Aronson & Bridgeman, 1979).

Popularity, Social Acceptance, and Rejection

When peers are asked to evaluate one another's popularity, or likability, by "nominating" whom they like most or would choose to play with, children generally are classified as "popular" or as occupying one of three unpopular statuses: "rejected," "controversial," or "neglected." Popular children receive many positive and very few negative votes from their peers; rejected children receive many negative and few positive peer nominations; controversial children receive many positive and negative peer nominations; and neglected children receive few positive or negative nominations (Coie et al., 1982).

The Popular Child   Easily noticed characteristics, such as having the "right" hair-style, the "right" body build, or an attractive-sounding name, are quite important to acceptance and popularity in the early grades. As children get older, they increasingly choose their friends on the basis of personal qualities such as honesty, kindness, humor, and creativity (Furman & Bierman, 1983; Reaves & Roberts, 1983).

Popular children are well liked, are able to easily initiate and maintain social interactions, and understand social situations. They possess a high degree of interpersonal skills and tend to behave in ways that are prosocial, cooperative, and in tune with group norms (Asher et al., 1982). Popular children are viewed by their peers as being confident, good-natured, kind, outgoing, and energetic. Highly visible abilities and achievements help, especially in athletics, but also in academics or social activities. Stylish clothing and special material possessions, such as an expensive fashion watch, also influence status with peers (Dodge, 1986; Hartup, 1983). Recently there has been a trend among some schools to adopt strict "dress codes" or school uniforms to reduce differences in dress and their perceived negative effects. No systematic research has yet been reported on how this trend affects the popularity hierarchy, although a number of school boards have been challenged by students (and sometimes parents) on the grounds that such codes infringe on children's right to freedom of expression.

Some of the assets just noted, such as peer competence and athletic ability, remain valuable to children as they move into adolescence, and others (such as the fashion watch) may not. But during childhood, such advantages create prestige for individual children within particular peer groups and also make membership in the "best," or highest-status, groups possible. Because of the importance of peer relationships during the school years, the interpersonal competencies associated with peer acceptance and popularity are likely to have a positive impact not only on a child's current adjustment but also on her or his longer-term psychological well-being.

The Unpopular Child   Peers describe unpopular children, particularly those classified as "rejected," as unpleasant, disruptive, selfish, and having few positive characteristics. Such children are likely to exhibit socially inappropriate aggression, overactivity, inattention or immaturity, and, not surprisingly, behavioral and academic problems in school (Bierman et al., 1993). Because they lack the social skills needed to successfully join and participate in peer groups, they are blamed by peers for their own deviance and are often actively disliked and excluded from activities (Coie et al., 1991; Dodge et al., 1990; Juvonen, 1991; Pope et al., 1991).

Aggression   Among both boys and girls, the highest levels of aggression are displayed by children who are classified as unpopular-rejected. However, girls and boys appear to differ in the form their aggressive behavior most typically takes. Boys are more likely to attack peers through *overt aggression* (such as hitting, pushing, or verbally threatening to hurt others), whereas girls are more likely to display *relational aggression* involving harming others through purposeful manipulation and damage of their peer relationships (Crick & Grotpeter, 1995).

The likelihood of aggressive behavior toward rejected peers is also influenced by social context. For example, one study of seven-to-nine-year-old African American boys found that aggressive behavior between two children was more likely in group situations characterized by a tense, negative atmosphere; high levels of aversive verbal and nonverbal behavior, such as criticizing, teasing, grabbing, and pushing; high levels of competitiveness; and low levels of cooperation and group cohesion (DeRosier et al., 1994).

Family and neighborhood contexts also are important. In a large-scale study of second-through-fifth-graders, Janis Kupersmidt and her colleagues found that living in middle-SES neighborhoods had a strong protective effect on aggressive behavior and peer rejection, particularly among African American children from low-SES, single-parent families who lived in such neighborhoods (Kupersmidt, et al., 1995).

For children living in war zones or in other dangerous environments such as communities where gang and drug activity and the wounding and killing of friends and relatives are everyday occurrences, the developmental toll on children and their parents is immense. Youngsters who are exposed to ongoing violence suffer from chronic emotional distress, learning problems, sleep disturbances, and preoccupation with their own safety and the safety of those they depend on and care about. They are also more likely to have problems with aggression, impulse control, and conflict resolution in both school and nonschool settings. Children may cope with chronic danger by adopting a world view that may be dysfunctional in any "normal" situations in which they are expected to participate. For example, although being hyperaggressive may help ensure survival in a dangerous neighborhood, it is likely to be dysfunctional and stimulate peer and teacher rejection if used to cope with disappointments and disputes in most school situations (DeAngelis, 1991; Garbarino, 1992; Garbarino & Kostelny, 1996; Garbarino et al., 1991; Kozol, 1995).

In addition, some adaptations to chronic danger, such as emotional withdrawal, may cause problems for the next generation when those individuals themselves become parents. Finally, the same links between danger and trauma observed in children may operate directly among parents. Parental adaptations to dangerous environments may produce childrearing strategies that interfere with normal development. For example, a parent who forbids her child to play on the floor to keep him away from the poison put there to kill rats that infest the apartment may deprive her child of opportunities for exploratory play. Likewise, a parent who forbids his child to play outside for fear of shooting incidents may limit the child's opportunities for athletic and social interaction with other children and adults outside the immediate family (Garbarino et al., 1991).

How successfully such children cope with their circumstances also depends on the support and guidance they get from family members and school personnel, social services, and the community at large. Considerable success in reducing aggression and fostering prosocial behavior has been reported for school-based intervention programs designed to teach older elementary and junior high school children assertiveness and interpersonal cognitive problem-solving skills (Hudley & Graham, 1993; O'Donnell et al., 1995; Shure & Spivak, 1988). Despite such efforts, however, it is unlikely that these problems will be resolved without social and economic changes that significantly reduce or eliminate the dangerous conditions under which many children and their families currently live.

Friends   During the early school years, friendships provide an arena for "activity and opportunity"; children base friendships on shared interests and activities, exchanges of possessions, and concrete supportive behaviors. By second or third grade, children become better able to live with differing perspectives within their friendships and feel less pressure to choose between one or the other (Rawlins, 1992; Selman, 1981).

As children move into later childhood and preadolescence, *equality* and *reciprocity* become key elements of friendship interactions. Exchanging favors and sharing activities continue to matter as children get older, but by the time they enter fifth and sixth grades they place greater emphasis on psychological qualities such as intimacy, trust, mutual support, and loyalty. Friendship begins to involve a concept of a relationship based on a reciprocity between equals, each with distinct but compatible personalities. Sharing between friends shifts from an unreflective, *symmetrical reciprocity* based on "tit-for-tat" to a *cooperative reciprocity* based on mutual and deliberate sharing of assistance and resources that are intended to serve as tokens of friendship. Actually doing the same things or sharing the same objects becomes correspondingly less important. (Keller & Wood, 1989; Rawlins, 1992).

By fifth or sixth grade, children can even adopt an independent, or third-party, perspective, comparing their own points of view with those of their friends (Berndt,

1988; Furman & Bierman, 1984; Selman, 1980). As one eleven-year-old put it about a good friend, "He thinks that I don't study enough, and that he studies just about the right amount for schoolwork. But you know what *I* think? I think that I'm just trying to keep schoolwork from bothering me too much, and that *he* works too hard. I wonder what the teachers think." Judging by statements such as this, friendship at this stage appears to be an intimate collaboration between two people who are mutually committed to building the relationship, which has acquired an importance beyond the particular needs of either friend.

In a recent study of the current literature on friendships and their developmental significance, Willard Hartup (1996) argues that the developmental implications of friendships cannot be specified without distinguishing among *having friends,* the *identity of one's friends,* and *friendship quality*. He concludes that friends provide one another with cognitive and social *scaffolding* that differs from what nonfriends provide and that having friends supports favorable developmental outcomes across *normative transitions,* predictable changes that almost all children experience, such as entering school, starting middle school, and puberty. However, predicting developmental outcomes also requires knowledge of the attitudes and behavioral characteristics of children's friends as well as the qualitative features of those relationships. Cognitive and social scaffolding are similar to Vygotsky's zone of proximal development, and normative transitions are similar the *normative crisis model* of adult development, both of which we discussed in Chapter 2.

Conformity to Peers

Because peer groups involve social equals, they give children unique opportunities to develop their own beliefs without having parents or older siblings dominate or dismiss them. But in doing so, peer groups also present challenges. Acceptance and support by groups matter intensely to children, who are still learning what kind of people they are and acquiring the skills they need to interact with others. As a result, peer groups often influence their members very strongly indeed: they demand conformity to group expectations in return for continued acceptance and prestige.

Pressures to conform sometimes lead children to violate personal values or needs or those of parents and other adult authorities. One child might feel pressured into paying dues she cannot afford, joining fights she does not want to participate in, or shunning children who do not belong to her own group. Another might feel pressured to wear clothes that his parents consider outrageous or to perform poorly at school. In return for these behaviors and attitudes, the children remain in good standing with their peers. Despite these differences, however, there tends to be high agreement between peer group and parents on important issues such as moral and ethical standards, standards of appropriate behavior, schooling, and future goals (Damon, 1988; Fine, 1982).

Peer groups can exert positive pressures as well. For example, they can encourage athletic and academic achievement and create commitments to fairness and reciprocity, at least within an immediate circle of peers: "When someone buys a candy bar at the drugstore, she shares it with the rest of us. Then we do the same thing the next time if *we* get something nice." Peer conformity can also support "good" behavior such as avoiding smoking, drinking, or other drugs or abstaining from risky sexual activity. Whether the pressures are positive or negative, however, peer groups offer a key setting for acquiring social skills, evaluating and managing personal relationships, and handling competition and cooperation.

A study of the natural, self-selected peer groups of fourth- and fifth-graders conducted by Thomas Kindermann (1993) found that children tend to associate with peers who share similar norms regarding involvement in school. Children who were academically oriented and highly engaged in school tended to affiliate with classmates who had similar motivational orientations; the same was true for children who were disengaged from school and lacked academic motivation. Although their memberships changed somewhat during the year, peer groups remained quite stable in terms of their norms regarding academic orientation.

What Do You Think?

Children's growing exposure to peer group influences during middle childhood is a source of concern for both parents and teachers. What advice might you give to parents and teachers regarding the best ways to deal with this challenge?

FAMILY RELATIONSHIPS

Despite the growing importance of peers, families continue to influence children's development strongly during middle childhood. However, parental influence differs from that of peers due both to parents' greater experience and psychological maturity and to the greater material resources and power they possess. In this section, we discuss how the particular circumstances and characteristics of families affect family relationships and psychosocial development during middle childhood.

The Quality of Parent-Child Relationships in Middle Childhood

During middle childhood, as children gradually learn more about their parents' attitudes and motivations and the reasons for family rules, they become better able to control their own behavior. This change has a major impact on the quality of rela-

During the course of middle childhood, the degree of closeness a child experiences with each parent varies with the particular individuals and often changes over time.

"During the next stage of my development, Dad, I'll be drawing closer to my mother—I'll get back to you in my teens."

tions between school-age children and their parents (Galinsky, 1987). Parents find themselves monitoring the moment-to-moment behavior of their children less closely than in earlier years. They need not always watch carefully as their child pours a glass of milk, and they do not always have to remind him to use the toilet before getting in the car.

Nevertheless, parents do continue to monitor children's efforts to take care of themselves, but in more indirect ways (Maccoby, 1984). Instead of simply arranging for a child's friend to visit, parents increasingly use comments such as "If you want to have Lin sleep over next week, you'd better call by tomorrow." Instead of helping their child put on each item of clothing in the morning, they will more likely confine themselves to some simple reminder ("It's time to get dressed") on the assumption that the child can take care of the details of dressing.

These changes contribute to one stereotype of parenting during middle childhood: the notion that parenting consists only of fixing meals, providing taxi service, and enforcing a few rules. In reality, this stereotype does not take into account the activities parents and children often still do together, from shopping to watching television to holiday celebrations. It also fails to consider the emotional ties that underlie these activities. If children have become securely attached during the preschool years, they and their parents often enjoy each other's company more than ever during middle childhood.

The Changing Nature of Modern Families

The stereotype of a typical family—a father who works, a mother who cares for the family full time—shows little similarity to families of today. In 1955, 60 percent of families in North America fit this popular stereotype. By the early 1990s, only 7 percent of North American families conformed to this model (Children's Defense Fund, 1993; Hodgkinson, 1985).

Today an increasing number of mothers work outside the home. Sixty-nine percent of married women and 60 percent of single women with children under eighteen are employed. This is more than double the rates in 1960 and a trend that is expected to increase through the year 2000 (U.S. Bureau of Labor Statistics, 1995). Figure 9.2 summarizes this trend.

Divorce also has become much more common, as Figure 9.3 shows. Between 1960 and 1993, the U.S. divorce rate tripled, with more than half of all marriages in the United States ending in divorce. Approximately 25 percent of children

FIGURE 9.2
Percentage of Working Mothers, 1940–1994
The long-term trend for working mothers with children is expected to increase through the year 2000.
Source: U.S. Bureau of the Census (1995c).

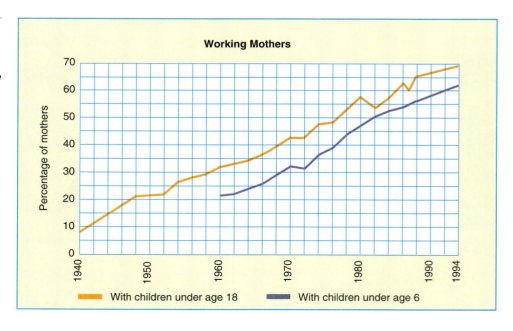

FIGURE 9.3
Percentage of U.S. Marriages Ending in Divorce, 1900–1993
Since the mid-1980s, approximately half of all marriages in the United States have ended in divorce.
Source: U.S. Bureau of the Census (1995a).

younger than eighteen live in single-parent households, 88 percent with their mothers and 12 percent with their fathers. It is estimated that children of divorce spend an average of six of their first eighteen years in a single-parent home (Children's Defense Fund, 1993; U.S. Bureau of the Census, 1995a). Because approximately two-thirds of divorced parents remarry, most children of divorce will live in a *reconstituted family* consisting of parent, stepparent, siblings, and stepsiblings. And in almost half of these cases, the second marriage will end in divorce as well (Glick & Lin, 1987; Hetherington et al., 1989).

Divorce and Its Effects on Children

Most parents who divorce must make major adjustments in their lives, and these adjustments often affect their children deeply. First, many divorcing parents face sudden economic pressures. Some find themselves financially responsible for two households, that of their former spouse and children and that of the new spouse and children. Many divorced mothers must take on new or additional employment to meet their household responsibilities, and even so their standard of living frequently declines (Hetherington et al., 1989). For many of these women, a reduction of economic resources often is accompanied by dependence on welfare; poorer-quality housing, neighborhoods, schools, and child care; and the need to move to a neighborhood they can afford, which often leads to loss of social support for the child from familiar friends, neighbors, and teachers. In contrast, both noncustodial and custodial fathers are more likely to maintain or improve their standard of living following divorce.

Divorce involves many psychological pressures as well. The parent who takes primary custody of the children must learn to manage a household alone, which is a major physical and psychological burden. Some parents may feel deeply isolated from relatives or friends to whom they used to feel close. If relatives do live nearby, divorcing parents often must rely on them for the first time, simply to procure help with child care and household work. Even before actual separation and divorce, many such families go through long periods of distress, tension, and discord. For most, these pressures continue to create stress for two or three years following separation (Hetherington et al., 1982; Hetherington et al., 1989).

Divorce is especially hard for children during the school years. Having outgrown the self-centeredness of the preschool years, school-age children increasingly identify with and rely on their parents as role models to help them establish their own sense of who they are and how they should behave. At a time when children are just learning to be independent from home life, divorce threatens the safe base they have come to rely on to help make increasing independence possible. The loyalty conflicts

For children of divorce, Mother's Day and other family holidays serve as painful reminders of the changes and losses that have occurred. Children often respond to such challenges in creative ways.

frequently created by parents who are competing for their children's allegiance can make children fearful that they will lose one of their parents in the process.

Judith Wallerstein (1987, 1989) conducted a long-term follow-up study of middle-SES children who were between six and eight years old at the time of their parents' divorce. She found that even ten years later, these children were burdened by fear of disappointment in love relationships, lowered expectations, and a sense of powerlessness. When compared to children who were older or younger at the time of the breakup, school-age children fared far worse in their emotional adjustment and overall competence, including school and social relationships. The profound unhappiness with current relationships and concerns regarding future ones that these children experienced often were masked by their overall conformity to social expectations. Table 9.2 summarizes the psychological tasks of children of divorce.

Some critics have questioned the degree to which Wallerstein's findings, which were based on naturalistic, case study techniques with a middle-SES sample, represent the entire population of parents and children of divorce. Further research using more quantitative approaches and families from a broader range of backgrounds will help determine the validity of her findings (Hetherington & Furstenberg, 1989; R. Weiss, 1989).

Differing Effects on Boys and Girls   On the whole, girls and boys tend to respond differently to divorce. Boys often express their distress in *externalizing* ways, becoming more aggressive, willful, and disobedient during the period surrounding separation and divorce. They often lose access to the parent with whom they identify most strongly—their father—because the majority of divorced children live with their mothers and are more frequently victims of parental power struggles and inconsistencies in matters of discipline (Santrock & Warshak, 1979). In a study of children six years after divorce, Mavris Hetherington (1988, 1991) found that

TABLE 9.2   *The Psychological Tasks of Children of Divorce*

Task 1: Understanding the divorce	Children must first learn to accurately perceive the immediate changes that divorce brings. Later they learn to distinguish between fantasized fears of being abandoned or losing their parents and reality so that they can evaluate their parents' actions and draw useful lessons for their own lives.
Task 2: Strategic withdrawal	Children and adolescents need to get on with their own lives as quickly as possible and get back, physically and emotionally, to the normal tasks of growing up. This poses a dual challenge to children, who must actively remove themselves emotionally from parental distress and conflict to safeguard their individual identities and separate life course.
Task 3: Dealing with loss	Children must overcome two profound losses: the loss of the intact family, together with the symbolic and real protection it provided, and the loss of the presence of one parent, usually the father, from their lives. They must overcome the powerful sense of rejection, humiliation, unlovableness, and power-lessness they feel and feelings of self-blame for causing the divorce.
Task 4: Dealing with anger	The major task for children is to resolve their anger at being hurt by the very people they depend on for protection and love. They must recognize their parents as human beings capable of making mistakes and respect them for their efforts and courage.
Task 5: Working out guilt	Young children often feel responsible for divorce, thinking their misbehavior may have caused one parent to leave. They need to separate from guilty "ties that bind" them too closely to a troubled parent and go on with their lives.
Task 6: Accepting the permanence of the divorce	At first, children's strong need to deny the divorce can help them cope with the powerful realities they face. Over time, they must accept the divorce as a permanent state of affairs.
Task 7: Taking a chance on love	Achieving realistic hope regarding relationships may be the most important task for both the child and society. Children must create and sustain a realistic vision of their own capacity to love and be loved, knowing that separation and divorce are always possible. Mastering this last task—which depends on successfully negotiating all of the others—leads to psychological freedom from the past and to a second chance.

Source: Adapted from Wallerstein & Blakeslee (1989).

whereas mothers and daughters had reestablished close and positive relationships, problems between mothers and sons persisted. Whereas the most common parenting style for divorced mothers with daughters was authoritative, the most common style with sons was authoritarian and the next most common was permissive, suggesting that mothers either tried to control their sons' behavior with power assertiveness or gave up trying.

Girls appear to become less aggressive as a result of divorce, tend to worry more about schoolwork, and often take on more household responsibilities. This suggests they are *internalizing*, or holding inside, their distress by trying to act more helpful and responsible than usual (Block et al., 1981). Daughters of divorced parents may also become overly preoccupied with their relationships with males. They are more likely to become involved in dating and sexual activities at an early age, sometimes before the end of elementary school, and more likely to get pregnant and have conflict-ridden relationships with males during their teen years. Girls also may encounter increased risk of sexual abuse from stepparents and parents' dating partners in the period following divorce (Spaccarelli, 1994; Wallerstein, 1987; Wallerstein & Blakeslee, 1989).

Perhaps the most important factor in reducing the negative effects of divorce during the school years are parents' efforts to reduce their own conflicts and cooperate in providing the best parenting possible for their children (Kline et al., 1989). Also important is the appropriate use of professional help to successfully work out postdivorce arrangements, resolve emotional conflicts more effectively, and develop the skills needed to sustain strong and supportive parent-child relationships (Stolberg & Walsh, 1988). Table 9.3 presents suggestions for parenting during or following divorce.

Custody Arrangements   Relationships between parents and children frequently deteriorate during and immediately after a divorce. The parent with physical custody of the children (usually the mother) finds herself dealing not only with her children but also with major new responsibilities for earning a living and making peace—at least in her mind—with the reality of divorce.

TABLE 9.3   *Suggestions for Divorcing Parents with School-Age Children*

1. Don't pretend that the divorce is "good," and don't expect your child to appreciate your reasons for the divorce.
2. Avoid assigning blame for the divorce or criticizing the other party in your child's presence.
3. Reassure your child that she or he did not cause the divorce and will continue to be loved and cared for by both parents.
4. Don't put your child on the spot by involving him or her in divorce-related decisions.
5. Keep your child informed about divorce-related events and decisions in a timely and frank manner.
6. Avoid making changes in your child's normal routines as much as possible.
7. Allow your child full freedom to express his or her feelings both to you and to other trusted adults.

Here are some suggestions for helping children handle parental dating and remarriage:

1. Wait until you know your new romantic interest fairly well before arranging for your friend and your child to spend time together.
2. Allow your child to get used to this person gradually, at the child's own pace.
3. Keep your child informed about your relationship, but don't force your child to make decisions about it.
4. Involve your child in plans regarding living arrangements, marriage, and other important changes in an appropriate manner.
5. Seek agreement with your new partner or spouse on childrearing philosophy and practices.

Source: Adapted from Philadelphia Child Guidance Center (1994), pp. 85–90.

Parents without physical custody of the children (usually fathers) do not face these daily hassles, but they do report feeling rootless, dissatisfied, and unjustly cut off from their children. Seeing his children every other week or on school vacations may prevent a father from knowing them intimately and being part of their everyday lives, and lead him to become increasingly reliant on special events (such as going to Disney World) when contacts do occur. Noncustodial parents may also believe their financial and emotional support for their children go unappreciated. Perhaps for these reasons, although fathers often increase the amount of time they spend with their children immediately after divorce, many soon decrease such time well below what it was before the divorce (Furstenberg et al., 1982; Hetherington et al., 1989).

Sometimes parents are able to establish *joint custody,* a legal arrangement in which parental rights and responsibilities continue to be shared in a relatively equal manner. The mechanics of the arrangement vary with the child's age and the family's circumstances. The children may live with each parent during alternate weeks, parts of weeks, or even parts of the year. Or, when the children are older, one or more children may live with one parent and the rest with the other parent. Joint custody tends to promote greater contact with both parents after divorce, facilitate fathers' involvement, and make mothers' parenting responsibilities less burdensome. Its success, however, depends on parents' willingness and ability to rearrange their lives and maintain the levels of mutual respect and cooperation required to make this arrangement work (Arditti, 1992).

Remarriage and Blended Families   Most divorced parents remarry within a few years, creating **blended families** consisting of the remarried parents and their children. The most common type of blended family occurs when a mother marries a man who does not have custody of his children by a previous marriage, but families with stepmothers occur as well. In both situations, the stepparent and stepchildren must somehow acknowledge the previous attachments they bring to the new family. Children must recognize and accept the fact that their new stepparent has other children, about whom he or she cares a great deal, living somewhere else. Also, the new stepparent must accept the fact that the stepchildren have another, "real" father or mother somewhere and strong attachments to that parent.

Younger children appear able to eventually form an attachment with a competent stepparent and to accept the stepparent in a parenting role. Older children and young adolescents are more vulnerable and less able to adapt to the transition of remarriage due to the developmental tasks they face. Stepfathers who establish parent-child relationships based on warmth, friendly involvement, and mutual respect rather than on assertion of parental authority are more likely to be accepted by both boys and girls, although daughters, especially those approaching adolescence, appear to have a more intense and sustained negative reaction to their mothers' remarriage and more difficulty accepting and interacting with their new stepfathers (Giles-Sims & Crosbie-Burnett, 1989; Vuchinich et al., 1991).

Stepmothers generally are more emotionally involved and take a more active role in discipline than stepfathers do, but gaining acceptance from the stepchildren is not easy for them either (Ganong & Coleman, 1987; Hetherington et al., 1989). In one study of parent-child relationships in stepmother families, John Santrock and Karen Sitterle (1987) found that despite their active involvement in parental and childrearing activities and ongoing efforts to establish good relationships with their stepchildren, stepmothers tended to be viewed as somewhat detached, unsupportive, and uninvolved, a feeling the stepmothers themselves shared. One explanation for these negative views is that the stepmother may be a target for her stepchildren's displaced anger, hurt, and disappointment toward their noncustodial mother. It is also possible that since families in which mothers have custody are still the norm, stepmother families are stigmatized, thereby keeping alive the myth of the "wicked stepmother."

Because divorce is a social reality that affects development throughout the lifespan, we will return to this issue when we discuss psychosocial development in adolescence (Chapter 11) and in early adulthood (Chapter 13). In the next section, we look at the developmental effects of death and dying during the school years.

Death, Loss, and Grieving During the School Years

While for obvious reasons interest in death and dying has been greatest for those interested in the adult years (see Chapters 15, 17, and 18), experiences with death have a developmental impact throughout the lifespan. For example, approximately 1.5 million children in the United States live in single-parent families because the other parent is dead (U.S. Bureau of the Census, 1995b). One study of death, loss, and grieving among middle school children found that 41 percent had been personally involved with death within the previous year; death of a grandparent or great-grandparent was most frequently mentioned (Glass, 1991). However, deaths of parents, siblings, other relatives, family friends, other children, and pets were also noted. While the loss of a parent may be the most difficult for children, the death of a sibling due to an illness such as sudden infant death syndrome (SIDS), AIDS (see Chapter 3), cystic fibrosis, or cancer, or to accidents or suicide, also can have a profound effect on children at various ages (Birenbaum et al., 1991; Davies, 1995; Fangos & Nickerson, 1991; Powell, 1991).

Children's Understanding of Death   Between ages five and seven, when the transition from preoperational to concrete operational modes of thinking occurs (see Chapter 8), most children come to understand that death is an irreversible, nonfunctional, and universal state: that once a living thing dies, it cannot be made alive again; that all life-defining functions cease at death; and that all living things eventually die. Under at least some circumstances, younger children think death is reversible, attribute various life-defining functions to dead things, and think that certain individuals (often including themselves) will not die (Speece & Brent, 1984).

The Process of Grieving for a Childhood Loss   *Loss* refers to being separated from someone to whom one was emotionally attached; *grieving* refers to the complex emotional, cognitive, and perceptual reactions and experiences that accompany

Approximately 1.5 million children in the United States live in single-parent families because the other parent has died, and experiences with death have developmental impact throughout the lifespan.

the loss (Mullan et al., 1995). John Baker and his colleagues propose that for bereaved children the grieving process includes three phases, each involving certain psychological tasks (Baker et al., 1992).

Early-phase tasks include understanding the fact that someone has died, the implications of the death, and protecting oneself and one's family from both physical harm and the full emotional impact of the loss. Children need information at an age-appropriate level about death in general and about the nature of the particular death. Euphemistic explanations (e.g., "Mother has gone to sleep") should be avoided because they tend to interfere with children's need to understand what really happened. Bereaved children listen intently and watch others' reactions, ask questions, and reenact elements of the events in their play; if there are gaps in their understanding, they tend to fill in the missing pieces with fantasy. Children also need to feel they are safe and in a secure environment. Because of fears that they too will die or that their families will disintegrate, children and their families may engage in a variety of self-protective mechanisms such as denial, distortion, emotional numbing, and even physical isolation from people.

Middle-phase tasks of grieving include accepting and emotionally acknowledging the reality of the loss, exploring and reevaluating one's relationship to the person who died, and bearing the intense psychological pain involved. *Late-phase tasks* require that the child consolidate a new sense of personal identity that includes both the experience of the loss and identifications with the deceased person; safely develop new emotional relationships without excessive fear of loss or guilt; construct his or her own inner representation of the deceased, based on past and current experiences, thoughts, and feelings, that enable the child to maintain an ongoing emotional connection (attachment) with the deceased; wholeheartedly resume the age-appropriate developmental tasks and activities that were interrupted by the loss; and successfully cope with the painful memories associated with the loss that are likely to resurface at points of developmental transition or on specific anniversaries, such as the date of the person's death.

Just as the adopted child faces the question "How could they give me up?" and the child of divorce the question "Why did my father (or mother) leave me?", the child who has lost a parent must deal with how and why the parent died and what the parent's presence may have been like had it continued over time. Children's efforts to remain connected to the deceased parent include locating the deceased (for example, "in heaven"), experiencing the deceased (such as believing the parent is watching them), reaching out to the deceased (visiting the cemetery and "speaking" to the person), having waking memories of the deceased, and cherishing physical objects linked to the deceased (Silverman et al., 1992).

Developmental Impact   The developmental impact of death experienced during childhood depends on a number of factors, including the significance of the person to the child, the nature of the death and the conditions surrounding it, the child's strengths and vulnerabilities at the time of the loss, the amount of support available to the child to successfully grieve the loss, the amount of material and psychological disruption in the child's family as a result of the loss, and the quality of the child's relationships with the survivors of the deceased. Studies of college students and older adults who experienced the death of a parent during childhood have found that being able to talk freely with the surviving parent about the circumstances of the death, express sorrow about the death, or ask questions about the deceased parent helped to protect them from the onslaught of depression in adulthood. Greater involvement in activities such as attending funeral-related events, keeping mementos of the dead parent, openly expressing anger to someone else about the death, hearing stories about the deceased parent, seeing pictures in the home of the dead parent, and visiting the grave decreased the risk of subsequent depression (Saler & Skolnick, 1992).

Helping Children with Bereavement   The work of Kelly Lohnes and Neil Kalter (1994) is an excellent example of preventive intervention with groups of parentally bereaved elementary school–age children. Groups of five to seven children met for twelve weeks of one-hour sessions designed to achieve the following: (1) normalize children's reactions to and experiences of the death of a parent, (2) clarify confusing and frightening death-related issues, (3) provide a safe place for children to experience and rework emotionally painful aspects of the death and the stresses of living in a single-parent household, (4) help children develop coping strategies for particularly troubling feelings and family and peer dynamics, (5) help children maintain an emotional connection (attachment) to the deceased parent, and (6) share the children's concerns about parental death and its aftermath with surviving parents (and stepparents) through newsletters.

Group activities included bereavement stories, drawings, role playing, and discussion to help children express and understand their feelings and experiences related to loss and bereavement. Some of the thoughts, feelings, and experiences of these children, which in other contexts might have raised concerns about severe disturbance, were in fact common for parentally bereaved children who were otherwise developmentally normal. For example, children typically reported hallucinations of their dead parent, believed the parent would return, and wished to be "dead" in order to be reunited with their parent. If ignored or misunderstood by adults, such fantasies, distortions, and symptoms may contribute to psychological disorder. Knowledge that such behaviors are normal for such children, however, can enable mental health professionals, surviving parents, school personnel, pediatricians, and other concerned individuals to more effectively help these children mourn their loss and minimize negative developmental effects such as health problems, decline in school performance, and emotional problems (Lohnes & Kalter, 1994).

The Effects of Work on Families

Work affects family life profoundly, although not always in simple or straightforward ways. Jobs determine daily schedules, of course, which in turn affect how much time parents have for their children. Job schedules also influence which parent or child does particular household chores. At a more subtle level, work affects parents' self-esteem and thus their happiness as human beings and as parents. Jobs also contribute to SES and therefore affect many aspects of family life (Greenberger

In families where mothers work, other family members often share household responsibilities. Sometimes this results in less stereotypic role models of male and female behavior.

et al., 1994; Kohn et al., 1986). All of these effects are magnified by the fact that an increasing number of families are headed by two working parents or by a single parent who works.

Effects of Maternal Employment   Despite the once popular view that mothers should stay at home to care for their children, research suggests that maternal employment as such usually does children no developmental harm (Hoffman, 1984a, 1984b). What does matter is whether a woman chooses to work or not to work. Mothers who can make this choice and who live in relatively supportive families apparently suffer no setbacks in their relations with their children. Mothers who feel forced either to work or not to work are less fortunate; they report more stressful relations with their children.

However, maternal employment often does influence children's development in some ways. Most of these influences are positive, or at least not negative. For example, families with working mothers divide housework and child care more evenly than do families without employed mothers (Hoffman, 1983). In dual-worker families, fathers do some household chores relatively more often and spend more time alone with their children (although mothers still do the majority of housework and child care). In families with working mothers, children often are expected to help with household chores and caring for younger brothers and sisters.

The blend of housework and breadwinning seems to create less stereotyped attitudes in the children of working mothers regarding the "proper" roles of mothers and fathers. Both sons and daughters witness nurturant behavior in their fathers and occupational competence in their mothers. Especially as they approach adolescence, children are likely to support women's employment in general (Hoffman, 1989; Scarr, 1984), and daughters usually expect to work outside the home when they get older. Studies of school-age children of employed women indicate they are as well or better adjusted and hold less rigid views of gender roles than do children of women who do not work outside the home (Hoffman, 1980, 1984a, 1984b; Moorehouse, 1991).

Many working mothers compensate for possible negative effects of their employment through more frequent shared activities or "quality time" with their children. A high level of shared mother-child activities serves as a buffer against the long hours and other disruptive demands of full-time jobs. Also, children are likely to match or exceed their peers in school achievement and adjustment when shared mother-child activities are more frequent (Moorehouse, 1991).

Effects of Paternal Unemployment   Involuntary paternal unemployment can create significant economic, social, and psychological disruption for children and their families. Loss of income can require parents and their children to make major sacrifices in their lifestyles. In many cases, the search for a new job or for affordable housing may cause a family to uproot itself, forcing children and parents to leave their friends and social support network behind. Leaving their existing school and neighborhood peers and gaining acceptance in a new neighborhood and school is particularly difficult during middle childhood (Liem & Liem, 1988; McLoyd, 1989; R. H. Price, 1992).

Children who experience family economic hardship are vulnerable to a broad range of difficulties, including problems with peer relations, academic performance, and psychological adjustment. However, the impact of such hardships is significantly influenced by how severe they are, how long they last, and how well parents can mobilize their material and psychological resources to deal with adversity while continuing to provide good parenting for their children (Bolger et al., 1995).

After-School Care   One common challenge working parents face is finding after-school supervision for their children. In cases where after-school programs do not exist and siblings, friends, and other relatives are not available, older (and sometimes younger) elementary school–age children are left at home by themselves. Many parents in this situation carefully work out after-school procedures, including strict limits on what a child may do and a checkup phone call from work to ensure that everything is okay; others leave their children to their own resources.

Jill Posner and Deborah Vandell (1994) recently compared the effects of formal after-school programs with three other arrangements (mother care, informal adult supervision, and self-care) for a sample of low-SES third-graders from nine urban schools. They found that attending after-school programs was associated with better grades and conduct in school as well as with better peer relations and emotional adjustment. Children who attended such programs were exposed to more learning opportunities, spent more time in enrichment lessons (such as music and dance), and spent less time watching TV and in unstructured neighborhood activities than children in other forms of care.

Formal after-school programs may be less important for children who live in communities that provide safe and constructive after-school opportunities. Nevertheless, even for these children, close parental monitoring of their after-school plans and activities and authoritative parenting (respectful acceptance and firm control) tend to promote academic performance and social adjustment as well as keep them out of trouble. Lower levels of such parental involvement and stressful, unsupportive family circumstances are associated with poorer academic and social adjustment and more problem behaviors (Galambos & Maggs, 1991; Steinberg, 1986; Vandell & Ramanan, 1991).

Other Sources of Social Support

So far we have emphasized two major sources of social experiences for children: peers and parents. Most school-age children establish other sources of social support as well. One study conducted by Brenda Bryant (1985) documented this fact by interviewing schoolchildren about people, places, and activities that they found satisfying and helpful in conducting their lives. To stimulate the children's thinking, the interviewers took them on long walks around their neighborhoods. From time to time, the interviewers asked questions about what they saw ("Do you know who lives there?"; "Is this where you go to relax?"). This approach revealed a large number of social supports for school-age children, which are summarized in Table 9.4.

Sibling Support   Perhaps most noteworthy is the high frequency with which siblings (as well as peers) were named as sources of support. During middle childhood, brothers and sisters provide one another with companionship, friendship, social support, and mentoring. They help one another master the psychosocial challenges of knowing who they are, achievement, peers, family relationships, and school that we looked at earlier in this chapter. Because of their greater maturity, older children frequently serve as role models and mentors to younger siblings, helping to transmit customs and family expectations and providing challenges that (hopefully) lead the younger children to new learning (Azmitia & Hesser, 1993; Ervin- Tripp, 1989; Weiser, 1989). As we will see in later chapters, siblings continue to serve as an important source of social support through adolescence and adulthood as well.

In a study comparing the impact of siblings and peers on learning to construct toy models, Margarita Azmitia and Joanne Hesser (1993) found that young school-age children conferred a unique role on their older siblings by prompting them to use effective teaching strategies such as explaining and transferring responsibility. Compared to interactions with their older peers, these strategies enabled children to better "corregulate" their interactions with their younger siblings. In unstructured learning situations, they were more likely to observe, imitate, and consult their older siblings, who in turn were more likely to spontaneously provide them with guidance than were older peers. In more structured

During the school years, grandparents and other adults and other children within and outside the immediate and extended family provide invaluable sources of social support for children.

TABLE 9.4 *Sources of Support Reported by School-Age Children*

Support	Average Number Mentioned in Interviews
Homes and informal meeting places where child feels free to visit	5.5
Peers and siblings named among ten most important individuals	4.5
Formally sponsored activities (public library, community pool, church or temple)	4.5
Adults (including parents) named among ten most important individuals	3.0
Hobbies that child attributes to self	2.3
Special places to go to be alone	2.1
Pets (including neighbors') considered as a special friend	1.7
Make-believe friends and make-believe identities	1.6
Grandparents and others of grandparents' generation named among ten most important individuals	1.3

Source: Bryant (1985).

"teaching" situations, older siblings provided more explanations and positive feedback and gave learners more control over the task than did older peers; young children more often prompted their older siblings' explanations, pressured them into giving them more control over tasks, and performed at higher levels than when taught by their peers.

It is not surprising that older brothers and sisters tend to develop relationships with younger siblings that combine dominance and nurturance, the two major elements of mentoring relationships. However, a survey conducted by Duane Buhrmeister and Wyndol Furman (1990) with third-, sixth-, ninth-, and twelfth-graders found that as children moved toward the end of middle childhood, relationships between siblings became less domineering and more egalitarian and that reported levels of intensity and conflict also decreased.

Siblings also tend to be less domineering and more nurturant in families in which children feel secure and parents get along well together (Brody et al., 1987; Brody et al., 1992; Dunn & Plomin, 1990; Dunn et al., 1994). For example, Gene Brody and his colleagues (1992) found that school-age siblings whose fathers treat them with equality and impartiality during problem-solving discussions, whose families are generally harmonious even when discussing problems, and whose parents perceive family relationships to be close are less to likely experience sibling conflict than children in families that are functioning less effectively.

Other Sources of Support   Many of the children studied by Brenda Bryant (1985) also reported seeking out adults other than their parents, especially grandparents, to talk with and confide in. Family pets and sometimes even neighbors' pets also served as confidants (Bryant, 1990). Children also reported using hobbies to unwind and feel better about themselves (although some of the hobbies, such as collecting stamps or playing a musical instrument, were relatively nonsocial). Other children reported having special hideaways where they went to be alone for awhile. Many children sought out peers for activities when they needed an emotional lift or felt confused; but this was not the case on every occasion, and not all of the children did so.

In general, Bryant (1985) found that as children moved through middle childhood, their sources of support increasingly broadened. This made them better able to manage particular stresses, whether inside or outside their families. At all ages during the elementary school years, children seemed happiest when they reported the widest range of social supports and when that range emphasized informal rather than formal supports.

What Do You Think?

What are your views about the impact of maternal employment on child development? In what ways do your views reflect your own experiences as a child?

SCHOOL INFLUENCES

Next to the family, school probably is the single most important developmental influence during middle childhood. Each year children spend more than eleven hundred hours at school and often many additional hours in school-related activities. According to Erik Erikson (1963), school is one of the main arenas in which children resolve the crisis of industry versus inferiority. Interactions with teachers and peers give children important opportunities to develop cognitive and social skills, gain knowledge about the world, and cultivate peer relationships (see the discussion of peers earlier in this chapter) that are central to the development of self-concept during middle childhood.

School Culture

Each school has its own culture, which includes the values, beliefs, traditions, and customary ways of thinking and behaving that make it unique and distinguish it from other schools and institutions. One school may especially value its innovative academic programs and the high achievement levels of its students, another the degree of student involvement in school-sponsored activities, and a third the active involvement of parents in providing special resources. The closer the fit between the school culture and the values and expectations of the children (and families) it serves, the more likely will the school's developmental impact be positive. Students both learn and feel better in classrooms in which the instructional approach, pattern and rhythm of verbal interaction and student participation, and strategies for motivating students are in tune with their family and cultural expectations (Minuchin & Shapiro, 1983; Tharp, 1989).

The Informal Curriculum

Schools influence children through two curricula. The **formal curriculum** helps children acquire the academic knowledge and skills thought to be necessary for successful participation in society. The **informal curriculum**—the implicit norms, expectations, and rewards for certain ways of thinking and acting that are conveyed by a school's social and authority relationships—teaches students the social roles and behaviors society expects. The left side of the report card, which evaluates a child's academic performance, reflects the formal, more explicit curriculum; the right side, which includes such areas as attendance, work habits, social skills, cooperation, competition, friendship, gender roles, sexuality, and relationships to other racial and ethnic groups, reflects the informal, or "hidden," curriculum (Ruble, 1983; Thorne, 1986).

Teacher Influences

With the exception of their parents, most elementary school children spend more time with their teachers than with any other adults. Teachers therefore play a very significant role in the lives of school-age children. Observational studies of daily classroom life reveal that the elementary school teacher engages in as many as one thousand interpersonal exchanges with pupils each day (Cazden, 1988). Many of these interactions involve communicating academic material, regulating students' verbal and nonverbal activity, evaluating student participation and providing feedback, dispensing supplies, and keeping track of time so that things go as scheduled.

Teachers' styles of classroom management vary considerably. However, all effective teachers establish learning environments that are calm, predictable, and engaging and provide smooth transitions from one activity to the next. Effective teachers also stay on top of the classroom situation by keeping in tune with their students, in both their communication of academic content and their responses to the constantly changing social and emotional needs of thirty or more children (Linney & Seidman, 1989).

Teachers' beliefs and expectations regarding their students' potential also can affect students' performance and overall school adjustment by changing students' behavior in the anticipated direction and thereby serving to create a *self-fulfilling prophecy*. Early research by Robert Rosenthal and Lenore Jacobson found that when elementary school teachers were given information that falsely identified randomly selected students as potential academic "bloomers," those gains actually did occur for first- and second-graders but not for students in grades three through six (Rosenthal & Jacobson, 1968). Although they were generally unaware of doing so, the teachers treated students for whom they had high expectations differently, giving them more challenging materials and demanding (and more frequently rewarding) better performance (Brophy, 1983; M. Harris & Rosenthal, 1985).

Teachers may also unintentionally communicate negative expectations of students who do not conform to their own. In one classic, four-year observational study of an urban elementary school classroom, Ray Rist (1973) found that by the eighth day of kindergarten, the teacher had assigned students to permanent "slow-learner," "average," and "fast-learner" groups. Because she had no knowledge of the children's academic ability or cognitive development, her evaluation was based primarily on students' SES. Children who were assigned to the slow-learner table turned out to be those who were poorly dressed and whose families were on welfare; students who were middle class in their dress and behavior were seated together in the average or fast-learner groups. A similar pattern of classroom organization was repeated by their first- and second-grade teachers, the only difference being that these teachers based their decisions on children's test scores and readiness material from the prior year rather than on their subjective judgments. The result of this "objective" placement was to reinforce the social class divisions initiated by the kindergarten teacher.

Rist and other investigators have found that these different groups within the same classroom receive different treatment. The fast-learner group is much more likely to receive academic assignments and the slow learners busywork. In most grades, the teacher directs two to five times as much control-oriented and somewhat less supportive behavior toward the slow-learner group than toward the fast-learner group. Controlling behavior includes verbal and nonverbal reprimands, time-out, and physical restraint; supportive behavior includes verbal praise, smiles, and hugs (Dusek, 1985).

The Student's Experience

What do students experience in the classroom? According to Philip Jackson, particularly in traditional, teacher-centered classrooms, students spend a great deal of time waiting for the teacher or other students, delaying fulfillment of their needs until given permission to do so by the teacher, and contending with distractions and social disruptions. Students must wait to ask a question, wait to get permission to leave their seats, wait to have a question answered, wait for the next assignment, or wait for their chance to use the stapler (Jackson, 1968, 1986).

Although these observations are cause for concern, many classrooms are conscientiously organized to minimize such difficulties and provide a learning environment that is academically stimulating and supportive of children's developmental

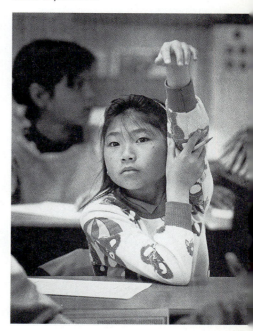

Waiting to be called on in class can sometimes seem to take forever. Unfortunately, in many classrooms, waiting to get the teacher's attention constitutes a major aspect of a student's experience.

needs (Lightfoot, 1983). While the teaching styles may vary, the experiences of the great majority of students in well-run classrooms are largely positive. Students in such classrooms feel like respected members of their classroom and school communities. They are eager to learn and are active participants in classroom activities, both academic and nonacademic.

Various factors may contribute to creating positive classroom and school experiences for children. For example, small class size and teachers' aides can enhance the quality of classroom life for both students and teachers (Finn & Achilles, 1990). The *open classroom* approach, which encourages children to take an active role in the learning process, and *cooperative learning* techniques, which support children of varying abilities in working together to achieve both individual and shared learning goals, also have proven to enhance the quality of classroom life and students' psychological and academic performances (Horwitz, 1979; Slavin, 1990a, 1990b).

Effective schools provide an environment with clear rules and expectations, effective controls, open communication, high nurturance, and respectful relationships that encourage students to participate as fully as possible in school and classroom life. Not surprisingly, effective teacher-student relationships tend to be authoritative in that their qualities parallel those of the authoritative parenting style discussed in Chapter 7.

Finally, effective school environments provide children with opportunities to freely interact with and form developmentally beneficial relationships with children of different ages, developmental levels, and backgrounds. Many of the peer-related developments discussed earlier in this chapter occur in school-related settings. We take a closer look at schooling when we discuss psychosocial development in adolescence in Chapter 11.

What Do You Think?

How did teacher expectations regarding gender, race, and SES influence your own elementary school performance? Did you note any differences between those described in the text and your own experiences?

LOOKING BACK/LOOKING FORWARD

In a variety of ways, middle childhood is the time when a child becomes a person in a more adult sense than ever before. This happens partly because the child has begun accumulating considerable experience with other people of roughly the same age and maturity and partly because of cognitive developments. Children begin setting goals and working toward them in more adult ways by taking into account others' opinions about their achievements as well as their own interest in learning.

As we point out several times in this chapter, the developments of middle childhood do not always result in happy feelings and experiences. With their newly developed maturity, children are able to hurt and snub some of their peers as well as make new friends, and they are now able to worry about peer evaluations as well as be commendably open-minded. Life has not gotten happier just because the child has gotten older, but it is not necessarily unhappier either.

Taken together, these experiences create a new, more mature sense of self within children of this age, one that has more inward or psychological properties than that of early childhood. In the years ahead, during adolescence, this psychological self becomes still more elaborate. As we will soon see, contrary to widespread belief, for the majority of children the adolescent years do not necessarily prove any more or less difficult than the school years or early childhood do.

SUMMARY OF MAJOR IDEAS

Psychosocial Challenges of Middle Childhood

1. During middle childhood, children face challenges concerning the development of an identity or a sense of self, achievement, peer relationships, family relationships, and school.

The Sense of Self

2. During middle childhood, children develop a sense of self, acquire a belief in self-constancy and in relatively permanent psychological traits, and learn to distinguish their thoughts and feelings from those of others.

The Age of Industry and Achievement

3. According to some psychodynamic theorists, schoolchildren repress their earlier romantic attachments to their parents and focus instead on developing a sense of industry and achievement.

4. During middle childhood, children shift their achievement orientation from an exclusive focus on learning, or a task orientation, to a performance orientation that includes others' responses to their achievements.

Peer Relationships

5. Piaget believes that peers help children overcome their egocentrism by challenging them to deal with perspectives other than their own.

6. According to Sullivan, peers help children develop democratic ways of interacting and also offer the first opportunities to form close or intimate relationships with others.

7. In general, peers seem to serve unique functions by creating voluntary relationships of equality among children.

8. Groups of peers vary in membership and behavior in terms of age, gender, and race or ethnic group. Peer groups tend to segregate themselves by gender, race, and SES.

9. Popular children possess a number of socially desirable qualities, including well-developed social skills and confidence in themselves. Unpopular children exhibit less desirable qualities, such as aggression, selfishness, and bossiness.

10. Early in the school years, a friend is someone with whom a child shares activities and toys, but later in this period a friend becomes someone whom the child can count on and with whom she or he can share intimacies.

11. Peers exert pressure to conform on individual children, and this pressure can have either positive or negative effects.

Family Relationships

12. In recent years, divorce has become more common in North American families and usually creates stress for all members of the family, although girls and boys react differently to divorce.

13. Blended families, which result from remarriage, pose considerable challenges; however, younger children form attachments with stepparents more easily than adolescents do.

14. Between ages five and seven, most children come to understand that death is an irreversible, nonfunctional, and universal state: that once a living thing dies it cannot be made alive again; that all life-defining functions cease at death; and that all living things eventually die.

15. Prevention groups help parentally bereaved children normalize their reactions to and experiences of death, clarify confusing and frightening death-related issues, safely deal with emotionally painful aspects of the death and the stresses of living in a single-parent household, cope with troubling feelings and family and peer dynamics, maintain an emotional attachment to the deceased, and help the survivors understand the children's concerns.

16. Many mothers now work at least part time, and their employment generally does not seem to have any negative effects on their children. Nevertheless, maternal employment influences the division of household labor and children's attitudes about gender roles.

17. When fathers are unemployed, both they and their families experience significant stress.

18. Providing good after-school supervision is a challenge for working parents. Formal after-school programs offer considerable benefits, especially for children in unsupportive environments.

19. Schoolchildren often find emotional support from adults other than parents, as well as from friends, pets, and hobbies.

School Influences

20. Children are influenced by their school's culture. This influence is more likely to be positive if the school's culture and the child's familial culture are compatible.

21. The informal, or hidden, curriculum—the school's implicit values, norms, and expectations—has a subtle but powerful effect on children.

22. The environment a teacher creates and his or her expectations of students shape children's school experiences.

23. From the students' perspective, school is often a place where they may encounter denial of needs, interruptions, delays, and social distractions. Cooperative learning and open classrooms, however, can contribute to greater student involvement and learning.

KEY TERMS

peers *(293)*
sense of self *(294)*
self-constancy *(296)*
latency *(298)*
industry versus
    inferiority *(298)*
achievement
    motivation *(299)*
learning orientation *(299)*
performance
    orientation *(299)*
juvenile period *(301)*
blended family *(318)*
formal curriculum *(326)*
informal curriculum *(326)*

PART FIVE

Adolescence

The adolescent years present new and unique challenges for everyone. We must come to terms with our bodies as they suddenly grow taller and sexually mature. We must seek more equal relationships with parents. And we must begin thinking about leaving home someday, even if not immediately. Achieving independence becomes an issue, though one that will take years to resolve.

How stressful these challenges turn out to be depends on a variety of circumstances. For some teens, the timing of puberty can make adolescence especially hard—or easy. For others, newly forming abilities to think about life's larger issues can make life seem suddenly confusing, though at the same time full of exciting future possibilities. For many young people dating or even just talking to the opposite sex becomes both intriguing and frustrating as they overcome childhood habits of relating only to members of their own sex. All in all it is a challenging time, but on average neither more nor less so than other periods of life, either in childhood or in adulthood.

10

ADOLESCENCE

Physical and Cognitive Development

THE CONCEPT OF ADOLESCENCE

Adolescence is the stage of development that leads a person from childhood to adulthood. Marked by the major physical changes of puberty and important cognitive and social developments, it is generally considered to begin around age ten and end sometime around age twenty-two. *Early adolescence* lasts roughly from ages ten to fourteen, including the middle school (or junior high school) years. *Middle adolescence,* ages fifteen through seventeen, includes the high school years. *Late adolescence* occurs between ages eighteen and twenty-two.

Every society uses ceremonies and rituals such as confirmation, bar mitzvah, graduation, and marriage to signify important changes in a person's life stage status, and the transition to adulthood is one of the most important and widely recognized changes that all people experience. In societies that still have relatively simple, agricultural economies and traditional cultural and social practices, this transition is fairly smooth and predictable and grows out of a long period of preparation. For example, when a teenage Australian aborigine goes on his year-long walkabout through the desert with only a few simple weapons to protect him, his chances of returning safely are high because he has spent much of his childhood learning skills to help him meet this challenge. Similarly, in many tribal cultures, a girl's initiation into womanhood is preceded by years of instruction in and imitation of the adult roles and activities she is now expected to perform.

In modern industrial societies such as ours, however, the roles and responsibilities a person is expected to assume when reaching sexual maturity are much less predictable, largely because our technology and values are changing so rapidly. Our rites of passage tend to be more symbolic than real, and the transition from childhood to adulthood can be rather difficult and prolonged. For example, a girl in a hunting-and-gathering society such as the Innuit of Alaska or the Bushman of Africa has a good idea of what her adult work will be: bearing and caring for children, gathering and preparing food, and the like. But a girl in computer-age North

Focusing Questions

- What is meant by *adolescence,* and what changes in society contributed to its gaining recognition as a developmental stage?

- What changes in height, weight, and appearance can be expected during adolescence, and how do they differ for girls and boys?

- What are the social and emotional effects of early, "on-time," and late pubertal development, and how do they differ for girls and boys?

- What major health problems do adolescents face, and in what ways are adolescents more at risk than other age groups?

- To what extent and in what situations are adolescents capable of abstract reasoning?

- How do adolescents show their improved information-processing skills in everyday activities?

- How can one support or foster skillful and critical thinking in adolescents?

- How does cognitive development affect adolescents' knowledge and beliefs about their identities and about morality?

America has little idea of what kind of work she will do, what kind of family she will have, or even where she will live.

Adolescence: From Idea to Social Fact

Most of us take the idea of adolescence for granted, but in fact it is a relatively modern concept. Its discovery, or recognition, in technological societies was largely a response to the social changes that accompanied industrial development in the nineteenth century in Europe and the United States (see Chapter 1 for a discussion of this development).

In fact, some researchers have proposed that adolescence was defined as a separate stage of development that occurred primarily to prolong the years of childhood so that the aims of the new urban-industrial society that rapidly developed after the Civil War could be fulfilled (Bakan, 1975). According to this view, the spread of railroads and the telegraph, accompanied by a general shift in population from the country to the industrial cities and the addition of a huge number of immigrants, threatened the American way of life. Because so much was changing so fast, people felt a growing fear that society would get out of control—that the country would be overrun by foreigners and the crowded, dirty cities would breed crime and immorality. There were three major legal responses to this national "identity crisis": compulsory education, requiring children to attend school; child labor laws, regulating the age and hours children and adolescents could work; and special legal status and procedures for juveniles, including those who were "delinquent." Together these developments played a major role in making adolescence a social reality (Bakan, 1975).

Theoretical Views of Adolescence

Since the "discovery" of adolescence in the United States, two somewhat conflicting views about its basic nature have emerged. One view sees adolescence as a time of "storm and stress," a period when major physical, intellectual, and emotional changes create tremendous distress and crisis within the individual and conflict between the person and society. As you may recall, Sigmund Freud believed develop-

Compared to children, teenagers think more often about possibilities and about the future; they also daydream and fantasize more. What do you suppose these boys are talking and thinking about?

ment is full of conflict, especially in adolescence. Erik Erikson and others have suggested that a lack of stable and predictable role expectations due to rapid changes in society may make the transition from childhood to adulthood more difficult (Erikson, 1963, 1968; Elkind, 1984).

Current research, however, suggests that adolescence is not intrinsically a time of severe "storm and stress" in personality development or in relationships with parents. Most adolescents in the United States adapt to the changes in themselves quite well and adjust to the changing demands and expectations of parents and society in a relatively smooth and peaceful way. The same appears to be generally true in a number of other cultures, including Australia, Bangladesh, Hungary, Israel, Turkey, and Germany, where approximately 75 percent of teenagers have been found to have positive self-images and good emotional adjustment (Offer et al., 1988).

While adolescence is not an unusually problematic period for most youngsters, in the United States and Great Britain the onset of adolescence is associated with more frequent negative feelings among many adolescents and increased rates of behavioral and psychological problems for some (Brooks-Gunn & Warren, 1989; Hamburg, 1994; Larson & Ham, 1993). In certain ethnic groups, for example, between 15 and 20 percent of adolescents in the United States drop out of school before completing high school; adolescents have the highest arrest rate of any age group; and a growing number of adolescents use alcohol and drugs on a regular basis (Eccles et al., 1993). How negative or positive the changes associated with adolescence are likely to be will depend on the degree of fit between adolescents' developing needs and the opportunities offered them by their social environments, school and home being two of the most important. Furthermore, the increased stress some adolescents experience may be due not simply to the external environment but also to developmental changes in adolescents' subjective construction of their environments (Larson & Ham, 1993).

We discuss these and other social aspects of adolescence in greater detail in this chapter and the next. First, let's look more closely at the physical changes of adolescence and their effects on development.

What Do You Think?

In what ways has the "discovery" of adolescence as a developmental stage been helpful for teenagers and their families? In what ways has it been a problem? What has your personal experience with adolescence been?

PHYSICAL DEVELOPMENT

GROWTH IN HEIGHT AND WEIGHT

Compared to childhood, the years of adolescence include less overall growth in height and weight but significantly greater irregularity and unevenness in the pattern and pace of growth. As Figure 10.1 shows, the average height for both boys and girls at twelve years is about fifty-nine or sixty inches. By age eighteen, the average height for boys is sixty-nine inches, whereas the average for girls is only sixty-four inches.

Much of this rapid change in height and weight is due to a dramatic **growth spurt,** which is preceded and followed by years of comparatively little increase. The change in height is particularly striking, as Figure 10.2 shows. The maximum rate of growth occurs around age eleven or twelve for girls and about two years later for

Adolescence is a time of rapid growth, which makes teenagers need more calories than either earlier in childhood or later in adulthood. In spite of the increased overall need, though, it is important for them to eat a balanced and sensible diet.

boys. In those years, many girls grow three inches in a single year and many boys grow more than four inches (Marshall, 1978).

The reason for males' greater average height is that boys start their growth spurt two years later than girls do and thus undergo two additional years of childhood growing. The average girl is around fifty-four or fifty-five inches tall when she begins her growth spurt, whereas the average boy is fifty-nine or sixty inches tall when he begins his. Because both boys and girls add around nine or ten inches during adolescence and grow relatively little afterward, women end up being shorter than men on average (Tanner, 1981; Thissen et al., 1976).

Interestingly, growth patterns and height during childhood are better predictors of adult height than growth patterns and height during adolescence are. That is, a tall ten-year-old is more likely to become a tall adult than is a tall thirteen-year-old who was short as a ten-year-old (Faust, 1977). Although weight also increases during adolescence (see Figure 10.1), it is more easily influenced than height by diet, exercise, and general lifestyle, and therefore changes in weight are less predictable. Girls begin puberty with slightly more total body fat than boys do. During puberty, total body fat declines for boys from an average of 18 or 19 percent to 11 percent of body weight, whereas for girls it increases from about 21 percent to around 26 or 27 percent (D. Sinclair, 1990). The average weight gain during the growth spurt is about thirty-eight pounds for girls and forty-two pounds for boys, although how it is distributed varies considerably among individuals.

In the long term, of course, not everyone ends up with the height, weight, and other physical characteristics that match society's ideals or, for that matter, the indi-

FIGURE 10.1
Growth in Height and Weight from Two to Eighteen Years
During adolescence, young people reach their final adult size. On average, young men end up significantly taller and heavier than young women, though of course many exceptions to this trend exist.

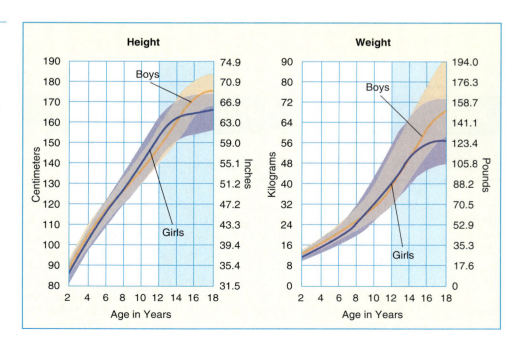

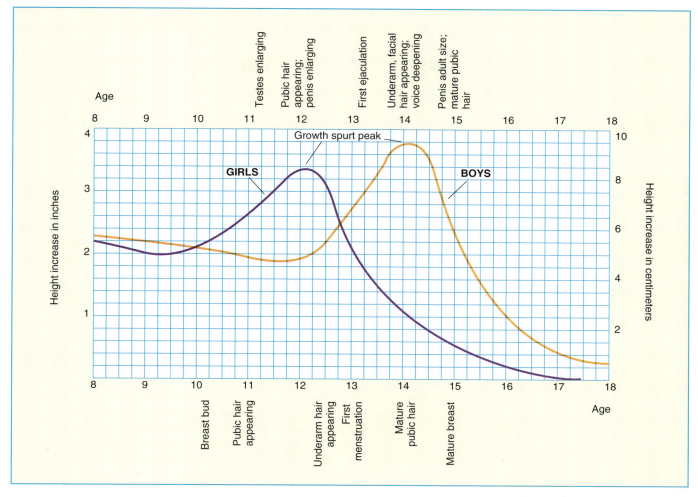

FIGURE 10.2
Physical Development During Adolescence
Puberty involves a number of specific changes in both boys and girls, as this graph shows. One of the most obvious changes, the "growth spurt" or rate of increase in height, occurs significantly sooner in girls than in boys. But as with trends in final adult size, many individual exceptions exist.

vidual's own. Later in this chapter, we discuss how the increase in body fat in adolescent girls and rigid cultural norms regarding body shape and size may contribute to fairly widespread problems with diet and nutrition and, in some cases, to eating disorders such as anorexia and bulimia.

What Do You Think?

What pattern (timing, rate) did changes in your own height and weight follow during adolescence? What do you remember thinking and feeling about those changes?

PUBERTY

Rapid increases in height and weight are only one part of a large pattern of changes, called **puberty,** that lead to the completion of sexual development, or *reproductive maturity*. For females, the completion of reproductive maturity is signaled by the beginning of *menstruation;* for males, it is heralded by the *ejaculation of mobile sperm*. Puberty is marked by striking changes in both primary and secondary sex characteristics. **Primary sex characteristics** make sexual reproduction possible. For girls, these include complex changes in the vagina, uterus, fallopian tubes, and ovaries; the most obvious sign of these changes is the beginning of menstrual periods. For boys, changes in primary sex characteristics include development of the penis, scrotum, testes, prostate gland, and seminal vesicles, which lead to the production of enough sperm to enable successful reproduction. Changes in **secondary sex characteristics** include enlargement of the breasts, growth of body hair, and deepening of the voice. Associated with these developments are important changes in the levels of hormones present in the blood stream. These powerful chemicals play a major part in initiating and regulating all of the changes associated with puberty.

Primary Sexual Maturation

For boys, the most significant sign of sexual maturation is rapid growth of the penis and scrotum (the sack of skin underneath the penis that contains the testicles), which begins at around age twelve and continues for about five years for the penis and seven years for the scrotum (Meredith, 1967). The penis typically doubles or triples in length, so locker room comparisons are almost inevitable as boys become increasingly aware of obvious changes in themselves and their friends. Although penis size has almost nothing to do with eventual success at overall sexual functioning, for adolescent boys it sometimes seems to be an all-important sign of their new status as men (Malina, 1990; Marshall & Tanner, 1974).

During adolescence, enough live sperm are produced in the testes to make reproduction a real possibility for the first time. Sometime around age twelve, boys are likely to experience their first ejaculation of *semen,* a sticky fluid produced by the prostate gland, which is located near the penis just inside the body cavity. Semen carries the sperm to the penis and provides it with a medium in which to live after ejaculation. Most boys have their first ejaculation during masturbation; as *nocturnal emissions,* or "wet dreams," during sleep; or, less frequently, as emissions that occur spontaneously upon waking. Most males report experiencing nocturnal emissions about one or two years before puberty; the accompanying dreams are frequently but not always erotic in nature. The sexual changes just discussed and the unexpected erections and uncomfortable sexual fantasies and sensations that boys sometimes experience are common sources of embarrassment. Less frequently, they are a source of more serious discomfort and conflict.

For girls, the appearance of the first menstrual period, called **menarche,** signals sexual maturity. In most societies, menarche also symbolizes the shift from girlhood to womanhood (Logan, 1980). Nevertheless, menarche occurs rather late in a girl's sexual maturation and is preceded by a number of other changes, including enlargement of the breasts, the appearance of pubic hair, and broadening of the hips and shoulders. Next, as the growth spurt peaks, the uterus, vagina, labia, and clitoris develop, as do the ovaries.

Maturation of Secondary Sex Characteristics

Breasts   Girls first develop breast "buds," or slightly raised nipples, at the beginning of puberty. During the following several years, the nipples grow darker, the areolas (the pigmented areas surrounding the nipples) increase in size, and the breasts continue to grow until they reach their full size.

Given the attention our culture devotes to breasts, it is not surprising that breast development is a potential source of concern for many adolescent girls. Breasts that are "too big," "too small," or the "wrong" shape may cause embarrassment, and in many cases girls experience outright harassment due to these physical developments.

Boys too undergo a small amount of breast development, and their areolas become larger and darker much as they do in girls. A few boys experience enough tissue growth to cause them some embarrassment, but these "breasts" usually return to typical male size in a year or two.

Hair   When their genital development is relatively advanced, both boys and girls acquire more body hair, although boys generally grow more of it than girls do. The first growth is simply a fine fuzz around the genitals called **pubic hair,** which then darkens and becomes coarser. At the same time, underarm or **axillary hair** begins to appear; this eventually becomes dark and coarse as well.

Voice   In both sexes, the voice deepens near the end of puberty and becomes richer in overtones so that it sounds less like a flute or whistle and more like a violin or clarinet. These changes make the adolescent's voice sound more truly adult, but the fluctuations in voice qualities that some adolescents experience can be a cause of considerable (although usually temporary) embarrassment.

Hormonal Changes and Their Physical Consequences

For both boys and girls, the onset of puberty brings increases in the levels of all sex hormones in the blood, but the pattern by which it does so differs for each sex. **Testosterone** (also called *male sex hormone*), a particular type of androgen, and **estrogen** (or *female sex hormone*) are two of the most important sex hormones. Although both hormones are present in males and females, the high concentration of testosterone in boys stimulates the growth of the penis and related male reproductive organs, and the high concentration of estrogen in girls stimulates the growth of the ovaries and vagina. Androgens are thought to influence the strength of the sex drive in both sexes.

Hormones affect more than just sexual characteristics. For example, they are responsible for the typical differences between girls' and boys' overall body builds. In general, the sex that has shorter bones and more rounded curves (female) also has higher estrogen levels, and the sex that has longer bones and larger muscles (male) also has higher levels of testosterone (Cheek, 1974; Tanner, 1990).

Testosterone stimulates muscle and bone growth in both sexes. Throughout childhood, boys and girls are about equally muscular. They have roughly the same number and sizes of muscle fibers, and they can exert about the same amount of strength with their muscles. Although individual children vary around the averages, as groups the two sexes differ very little (Malina, 1990).

Puberty significantly changes this equality. During puberty, boys typically become more muscular looking than girls, even though girls too become more muscular as they grow. Boys experience close to a fourteenfold increase in the size of the largest muscle fibers between early childhood and adolescence, with most of the increase occurring during adolescence. Girls, in contrast, experience only a tenfold increase (Brasel & Gruen, 1978; Malina, 1990).

Some of this difference may result from life experiences more specific to boys than to girls. For example, teenage boys receive greater encouragement and opportunity to participate in sports and more responsibilities that involve physical work and other heavy muscular activity (Frisch, 1983). Differences in hormone levels may also be influenced by differences in behavior and life experiences. Sustained exercise, for example, tends to increase a person's level of testosterone (Rogers & Walsh, 1982).

Estrogen stimulates increased deposits of subcutaneous fat (fat under the skin). It also stimulates the final maturation of bones, a process in which the growing areas within individual bones finally become hard and fixed in size. Throughout childhood, boys and girls tend to possess almost identical amounts of fat (or adipose) tissue (F. Johnston et al., 1974).

During adolescence, however, the two sexes begin to differ noticeably in their proportions of fat tissue. Boys tend to keep most of their fat deposits, which are simply stretched over their increasingly larger bodies. Because boys' muscles and bones tend to grow particularly rapidly during puberty, boys' fat tissue decreases as a proportion of their total body weight. The overall result is a relatively muscular, bony-looking person, at least compared to a typical girl (Chumlea et al., 1983). Girls, on the other hand, develop significant new deposits of subcutaneous fat during adolescence while maintaining those produced during childhood. The new fat develops in all the locations that make girls look typically female: in their breasts, hips, buttocks, thighs, and upper arms. The new fat tissues combine with girls' smaller muscles and bones to make young females significantly more rounded than young males. By the end of adolescence, fat accounts for more than one-fourth of their body weight compared to about one-eighth in males, a trend that continues throughout adulthood.

What Do You Think?

Do you think puberty is easier or more difficult for the opposite sex? In what ways? Compare your opinion on this question with the opinion of someone of the opposite sex.

PSYCHOLOGICAL EFFECTS OF PHYSICAL GROWTH IN ADOLESCENCE

Given how rapid the physical changes of puberty are, it is not surprising that adolescents often are preoccupied and dissatisfied with the way they look. Although dissatisfaction is most noticeable during the early adolescent years, it is also very common during the later teen years (Harter, 1990a; Heilbrun & Friedberg, 1990). Part of teenagers' concerns about appearance results from the timing of puberty, particularly if it happens very early or very late. The positive and negative effects of early, on-time, and late maturation, however, depend partly on the individual's sex and partly on whether the effects are considered in the short term or in the long term.

Early-maturing boys seem to experience certain initial advantages. Their more muscular appearance appears to gain them favorable responses from peers, teachers, and other important people sooner and for longer than their agemates. Early-maturing boys seem to respond to these changes and the favorable attitudes they elicit in very positive ways: they appear to be more self-confident and generally strike others as being more mature and competent than their peers, and are more likely to be chosen as leaders in high school (Livson & Péskin, 1981a, 1981b; Tobin-Richards et al., 1983). There are also some disadvantages, however. Early-maturing boys are found to be more somber, less spontaneous and creative, more submissive, and less flexible than their peers. They tend to be less open to new experiences and more conforming to adult values and expectations, perhaps due to pressures they feel to live up to the expectations that accompany their adult, masculine body image (Brooks-Gunn, 1987).

What about the long-term effects? Adult males who were early maturers have been found to be relatively responsible, sociable, and self-controlled, but they also continue to be more rigid, moralistic, and conforming than their peers. This may be partly because although their muscular physiques enabled them to excel early in athletics and to physically resemble culturally desirable stereotypes, they became overdependent on these early advantages and experienced a loss of self-esteem when their on-time and later-developing peers eventually caught up.

Late-maturing boys still resemble children, at least physically, as late as age sixteen. Teachers, parents, and other observers tend to judge them unfavorably, viewing them as impulsive, immature, and lacking in self-confidence. In school, late-maturing boys tend to be regarded as socially inferior to earlier-maturing peers and often regard themselves this way as well. Boys who are late developers may be perceived as childish and socially immature, in part because their self-consciousness about their delayed physical development limits their opportunities to become involved in sports and social activities. On the other hand, their physical immaturity may, to some degree, protect them from the increasing pressures to become sexually and socially active—which their on-time and early-developing peers find hard to resist—and allow them greater freedom to develop their own unique identities.

Early-maturing girls often feel less attractive and more concerned about their physical appearance, are more awkward and ill at ease in social situations, experience less support from their peers, and have poorer self-concepts (Peskin, 1973; Tobin-Richards et al., 1983). Unlike with early-maturing boys, who frequently experience athletic achievement and expectations for leadership and success, early maturation often puts a girl out of step with common standards for female beauty. Because of the hormonal changes of puberty, she becomes relatively tall, muscular, and sometimes heavyset for her age, whereas her later-developing agemates remain relatively slender and short. And because she also becomes more shapely and sexually mature, she may find herself in dating and sexual encounters for which she is not psychologically ready. Although a girl who has achieved puberty may have mature physical characteristics, there is no reason to assume she is emotionally ready to make decisions about birth control or sexual relationships. Nor should she be assumed to be developmentally ready to take on greater responsibility for adult work in or outside the home.

Studies in the United States, Sweden, and Finland found that early-maturing girls have more problem behaviors, including truancy, academic problems, and drug and alcohol use (Aro & Taipale, 1987; Peterson, 1987; Simmons et al., 1987; Statton & Magnusson, 1990). However, once early-maturing girls successfully navigate the next several years, they are likely to enjoy increased status and popularity and be better able than their peers to cope with the challenges of adolescence. This may partly be a result of the skills they learned in dealing with earlier problems or because life may have become easier for these early maturers as their later-blooming peers caught up.

Late-maturing girls exhibit a less clear-cut pattern. In contrast to their early-maturing peers, they appear to experience social advantages throughout adolescence. In one study, teachers and other observers rated late-maturing girls as more attractive and as better leaders, and these girls did in fact become school leaders relatively often (Livson & Peskin, 1981b). As with boys, the long-term effects of maturation differed from the immediate or short-term effects. At age thirty, women who were early maturers were found to be more poised and self-directed than late maturers, especially those who had encountered difficult circumstances in adulthood, such as divorce or serious illness.

What about adolescents who mature "on time"? *On-time- maturing boys* tend to feel less attractive than do early-maturing boys but more attractive than do later maturers. This suggests that their perceptions of attractiveness are related to how close they are to physical adulthood. *On-time-maturing girls* typically have more positive body images and greater feelings of social attractiveness than do early- or late-maturing girls (Tobin-Richards et al., 1983).

Table 10.1 summarizes the reactions to puberty of early-, on-time-, and late-maturing adolescents.

What Do You Think?

Talk with one or two classmates about how the timing of maturation affected their experience of adolescence. How closely did their experiences fit the patterns discussed in the text? What might teachers and parents do to help early- and late-maturing adolescents deal with the awkwardness sometimes associated with the physical changes of puberty?

TABLE 10.1   *Adolescents' Reactions to the Onset of Puberty*

Time of Onset	Reaction	Male	Female
Early	Initial	Positive	Negative
	Later	Negative	Positive
On time	Initial	Positive	Positive
	Later	Positive	Positive
Late	Initial	Negative	Positive
	Later	Positive	Mixed

For adolescents who begin puberty on time, initial and later reactions are positive for both males and females. For early-maturing males, initial reactions are positive and later reactions are negative, while the reverse is true for early-maturing females. Late-maturing males first react negatively and later react positively. Late-maturing females first react positively, and later reactions are mixed.

HEALTH IN ADOLESCENCE

In some ways, adolescents are among the healthiest of all people. They tend to have fewer colds and ear infections than young children or adults do (Fry, 1974). Compared to adults, they suffer fewer of the illnesses and physical damage associated with prolonged exposure to physical and emotional stress and with aging.

Nevertheless, adolescents actually experience *greater* health risks than either younger children or adults do. Compared to either age group, they are much more likely to be injured in motor vehicle accidents, misuse alcohol and other substances, experience unwanted pregnancy, and have inadequate diet and health and mental health care (Dougherty, 1993; Jessor, 1993; Takanishi, 1993).

Continuity with Health in Childhood

The health and health care patterns of most children show considerable consistency and continuity from early childhood through adolescence. This is true of common, recurring illnesses, patterns of use of medical services, and children's overall levels of health as judged by doctors and other health care professionals. Children who visit the doctor frequently when young continue to do so as adolescents, whereas those who visit less frequently early in life tend to maintain this pattern (Starfield & Pless, 1980). As we we will see when we discuss physical development in early adulthood in Chapter 12, continuity in patterns of health also continues beyond adolescence.

Factors such as SES and the quality and accessibility of services play a major role in adolescent patterns of use (and underuse) of health and mental health services and health-related behaviors (Hamburg, 1994; Taylor et al., 1991; Terre et al., 1992). Because health care and health insurance are extremely expensive, many families cannot afford to pay for care that adequately meets their needs. If such families receive inferior medical care and are treated in belittling ways (as is often the case), their children are more likely to develop negative attitudes toward doctors and hospitals. In contrast, children and adolescents from families whose financial resources allow them more regular and positive contacts with the health care system are likely to have more favorable attitudes and better health habits.

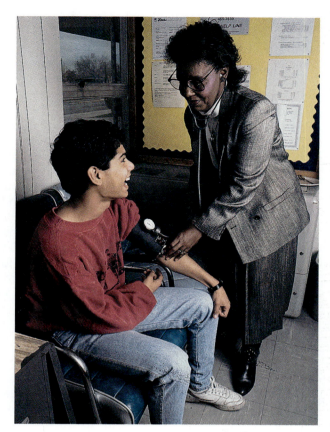

School-based health care programs that are responsive to the special needs and vulnerabilities of adolescents can make an important contribution to helping teenagers to take responsibility for their own health care. As teenagers get older, it may be less and less realistic to rely on parents to ensure that young persons get the medical attention that they need.

Inadequate understanding of the relationship between their behavior and their health may also affect how much responsibility adolescents assume for their own health. As we saw in Chapter 8's discussion of physical development in middle childhood, not until adolescence are children able to understand health in terms of multiple causes and cures and to realize that interrelationships among thoughts, feelings, and changes in physical health are important (Hergenrather & Rabinowitz, 1991; Millstein, 1989; Sigelman et al., 1993). But although adolescents may be similar to their parents in their estimates of risks to their health and in their cognitive decision-making processes regarding health care, they (and their parents) still frequently display significant gaps in their knowledge about what does and does not cause illness and how to safeguard their health (Quadrel et al., 1993).

For many teenagers, health care that is affordable, accessible, and responsive to their particular developmental needs and level of understanding appears to be the most important factor in determining whether they receive adequate care. Consider Genelle, a teenager from a low-SES family who recently discovered she was pregnant. It is very likely that her family's lack of health insurance and a regular doctor, along with the difficult psychological issues involved, will substantially reduce her chances of seeking or receiving adequate prenatal care. There is growing evidence, however, that under the right circumstances, adolescents (and even younger children) from a broad range of backgrounds can become very competent managers of their own health. Programs to encourage self-care have had significant success, especially when they are based in junior and senior high schools and offer comprehensive health care and family planning to teenagers. The success of such programs is due not only to the quality and appropriateness of the health services provided but also to their accessibility, assurances of confidentiality, and the reduction or elimination of financial barriers (Hamburg, 1994; Millstein, 1989).

Causes of Death Among Adolescents

Although adolescents are less affected by the health problems that lead to death in younger children and adults, the death rate during adolescence is one of the highest for all age groups. Both the risky environments in which many teenagers live and the risk-taking behavior associated with adolescence undoubtedly contribute to this statistic (Eccles et al., 1993).

Because of their riskier lifestyles, males are significantly more at risk than females are. Middle-SES males are likely to believe that risk taking and experimentation with cars and motorcycles, alcohol, and drugs are signs of masculinity. Males from low-SES families and those from minority groups are at still greater risk for accidental death and homicide, because the dangerous inner-city environments in which many of them live and the lifestyles they often lead are likely to involve the use and sale of drugs, participation in gangs, and exposure to various forms of physical violence, including the use of lethal weapons (Takanishi, 1993). Leading causes of adolescent deaths are motor vehicle accidents (more than fifteen thousand per year), homocide and other forms of intentional violence (more than six thousand per year), and self-inflicted harm or suicide (more than five thousand yearly) (Garland & Zigler, 1993; Hammond & Yung, 1993; Millstein, 1989; Spivak et al., 1988).

Adolescent Health Problems

Although adolescents are not prone to the infectious diseases of childhood, they often adopt habits that are damaging to their health. Poor diet, lack of sleep, use of alcohol or drugs, and unsafe sexual practices can all lead to a number of serious diseases. As Table 10.2 shows, infectious mononucleosis, hepatitis, and a variety of *sexually transmitted diseases* (*STDs*) constitute major health risks during adolescence.

Sexually Transmitted Diseases   Teenagers and young adults under twenty-five account for more than 50 percent of the 20 million STD cases reported annually. It is estimated that 25 percent of adolescents will become infected with an STD before graduating from high school (Shafer & Moscicki, 1991). With the exception of prostitutes and homosexual men, adolescent females have the highest rates of gonorrhea, cytomegalovirus, chlamydia, and pelvic inflammatory disease of any age group (Cates & Rauh, 1985). STDs can cause pelvic inflammatory disease, which places young women at risk for subsequent development of ectopic pregnancy and infertility (Shafer & Moscicki, 1991).

Risk factors for STDs include the increased acceptability of early sexual activity throughout our culture and inadequate use of contraceptives. Use of the birth control pill has replaced condoms as the favored method for birth control among teenagers. But condoms provide significant protection against venereal diseases, whereas the pill provides none. Inadequate health and sex education at home and in the schools must also be held accountable (Brooks-Gunn & Furstenberg, 1989; U.S. Bureau of the Census, 1992). As we discuss next, sexual experimentation and unprotected sex, particularly in the case of low-SES and minority adolescents who participate in the sex-for-drugs exchanges common in the drug subculture, place adolescents at great risk for all STDs, including AIDS.

First diagnosed in the United States in the early 1980s, *AIDS* (*acquired immunodeficiency syndrome*) is perhaps the best-known and most feared sexually transmitted disease in the 1990s. AIDS destroys the body's ability to maintain its normal immunity to diseases; death often results from pneumonia or related complications. The disease is transmitted through introduction of the *human immunodeficiency virus* (*HIV*) through body fluids from an infected person. The most common methods of transmission are sexual intercourse with an infected person, contact with the

TABLE 10.2   *Common Infectious Diseases During Adolescence*

Disease	Cause	Symptoms	Incidence	Treatment
Non–Sexually Transmitted Diseases				
Infectious mononucleosis	Virus	Sore throat, fever, swollen glands, extreme fatigue, enlarged spleen		Rest and good nutrition
Hepatitis	Virus transmitted through blood transfusions, injections, or sexual activity; also, inadequate sanitation	Acute infection of liver		Antiviral drugs
Sexually Transmitted Diseases				
Syphilis	Bacteria; transmitted by direct sexual contact with infected individual	Sores and lesions on genitals and mucous membranes; if untreated, CNS damage	134,000 new cases per year	Antibiotics
Gonorrhea	Bacteria; transmitted by direct sexual contact with infected individual	Infection of mucous membrane of urethra and genital areas; pain in urinating, vaginal discharge; if untreated, may cause pelvic inflammatory disease and sterility in women	1.9 million new cases per year	Antibiotics
Genital warts	Virus; transmitted by direct sexual contact	Small, painless growths on penis, urethra, rectal areas in males, genitals and anus in females; if untreated, increased risk of cervical cancer	1 million new cases per year	Removal
Genital herpes	Virus; transmitted by direct sexual contact with infected individual	Chronic, painful inflammation and lesions on genitals and other areas of sexual contact	200,000 to 500,000 new cases per year	Antiviral drugs; no cure as yet
Chlamydia	Bacteria; transmitted by direct sexual contact	Pain in urination, discharge from penis; vaginal discharge, abdominal discomfort; if untreated, may cause pelvic inflammatory disease, sterility	4 million new cases per year; most common STD	Antiviral drugs
Acquired immunodeficiency syndrome (AIDS)	Virus transmitted by body fluids from infected person		As of 1992, 671 males and 275 females age thirteen to nineteen, and 7,820 males and 1,762 females ages twenty to twenty-four	New antiviral drugs such as AZT may slow replication of the virus. No effected treatment has been developed so far.

Sources: Centers for Disease Control (1993a, 1993b); Shafer & Moscicki (1991); Amschler (1991).

blood of an infected person (through sharing of needles or through a blood transfusion), and contact of a child with an infected mother during pregnancy, birth, and (possibly) breast feeding (Shafer & Moscicki, 1991). Because the virus cannot survive in air, water, or things people touch, it does not spread through casual, day-to-day contact. AIDS has *never* been transmitted by sharing food; shaking hands; hugging; using the same dishes and utensils; being spit, drooled, or cried on; or having any form of casual contact.

A growing number of teenagers now receive formal instruction about AIDS in school. Most know that sexual intercourse and sharing needles are the main routes to getting AIDS and that condoms reduce the risk of transmission. Perhaps most important is to know how to practice safe sex, including massage, petting, masturbation, and kissing (provided there is no chance of direct contact between the body fluids of the partners). Kissing on the lips also is safe. No cases of AIDS have been traced to deep-tongue, "French" kissing, but because small amounts of HIV have been found in saliva, people who have open sores in their mouths or wear braces on their teeth are better off avoiding this practice. There is no such thing as "100 percent safe" sexual intercourse, but some sexual practices and behaviors are *safer* than others in that they very significantly reduce (but do not eliminate) the risk of contracting AIDS (Hein & DiGeronimo, 1989).

Drug and Alcohol Abuse   High rates of experimentation with drugs and of drug abuse are typical of adolescence. In our society, as in many others, drinking alcoholic beverages represents a rite of passage associated with the adolescent's transition to adulthood. Although drugs differ in many ways, experimentation with psychedelics and other "mind-altering" drugs, such as LSD, psilocybin, and mescaline in the 1960s and traditional use of peyote among Native American cultures in the southwestern United States, can also be thought of as serving a rite of passage function. Choices of drugs and patterns of use may, of course, change over time. More important, drug use has great potential for harm, particularly for adolescents.

Use of alcohol and drugs is associated with motor vehicle accidents, homicides, and suicides, the leading causes of death and injury among teenagers. Close to half of all deaths from motor vehicle crashes in this age group involve alcohol use. As Figure 10.3 shows, as of 1991 88 percent of high school seniors had used alcohol, 36.7 percent had tried marijuana, and 7.8 percent had used cocaine at least once. These figures indicate a decline in the use of marijuana, stimulants, and sedatives by high school students over the five-year period shown (L. Johnston et al., 1992). As we point out in Chapter 12, similar trends occur among young adults.

Developmental Effects of Drug Abuse   For several reasons, the effects of drug abuse on development are extremely destructive, particularly if the use is prolonged or chronic. First, even short-term use of illegal drugs such as heroin, cocaine, and crack exposes the user to considerable physical risk of injury or death due to overdose, contamination of the drug, or both. Second, even moderate use of certain drugs may have destructive physical and psychological effects; they may disrupt

Drinking and cigarette-smoking make some teenagers feel more grown-up and more sociable and accepted by their friends. As a result, alcohol and cigarettes are used by more teenagers than any other drug.

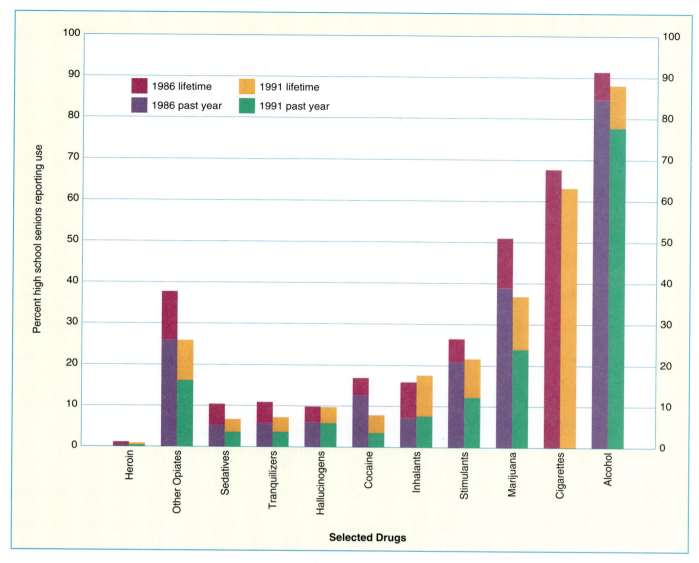

Percent high school seniors reporting use

Legend:
- 1986 lifetime
- 1986 past year
- 1991 lifetime
- 1991 past year

Selected Drugs

Heroin, Other Opiates, Sedatives, Tranquilizers, Hallucinogens, Cocaine, Inhalants, Stimulants, Marijuana, Cigarettes, Alcohol

normal patterns of eating, sleeping, and physical activity and mask psychological problems that require attention. Third, a number of these drugs cause physical addiction and psychological dependence. Physical addiction involves a biological dependence on the drug; withdrawal can be painful and sometimes life threatening. In most cases, tolerance to the drug increases with prolonged use, requiring higher doses to maintain the same level of effect and thus increasing the user's exposure to the drug's negative effects.

Finally, even if a proper medicinal dose of the drug itself is not physically dangerous, as is true with heroin, the physical, social, and psychological risks involved in supporting a habit are enormous. Teenagers addicted to heroin are, with few exceptions, forced to sell drugs and steal to support their habit. They are at great risk for using unreliable and contaminated drugs and for contracting hepatitis or even AIDS from dirty and infected needles. They are exposed to situations that are both physically and psychologically violent. And the time and energy needed to support a habit often force them to abandon normal social, emotional, and intellectual endeavors and threaten to halt their identity development prematurely. Teenagers living in poverty-stricken, crime-ridden areas and homeless teens are vulnerable to involvement in the drug trade, which to them may appear to be the only route to success or even survival (R. Price, 1992; Rotheram-Borus et al., 1991).

FIGURE 10.3
Use of Selected Drugs among High School Seniors, 1986 and 1991
Between 1986 and 1991, the percentage of high school seniors who reported using the drugs listed in the figure declined for all drugs except hallucinogens and inhalants. The largest decreases occurred for marijuana, cocaine, and other opiates. Source: L. Johnston et al. (1992).

Alcohol and Tobacco   Chronic alcohol abuse can lead to severe health problems, including destruction of the liver and damage to the central nervous system. It also seriously disrupts the drinker's ability to function effectively in school, at work, at home, and in other settings. Because alcohol is heavily advertised and socially valued as a sign of adulthood and independence, is readily available at low cost, and is a potent short-term reducer of anxiety, it continues to be very popular among adolescents. For the same reasons, it continues to be popular among young adults as well. We will discuss problems of substance abuse among adults in detail when we look at physical development in early adulthood in Chapter 12.

The use of tobacco products also has been widely advertised as a sign of adulthood. Early adolescents are particularly susceptible to this "ready-made" symbol of maturity. Although most adolescents are aware that smoking causes cancer and heart disease, more than one-third (36.0 percent) of all students in grades nine through twelve report using tobacco (Centers for Disease Control, 1991a). While overall smoking rates for teenagers have decreased over the last fifteen years, smoking among females and minorities has risen, at least in part because advertisers have targeted them as a highly lucrative market (L. Johnston et al., 1992).

Patterns of both drinking and smoking are strongly influenced by the lifestyles of family members and peers and by the environments in which they live. Among family members, minimal, moderate, and heavy levels of drinking, smoking, and drug use, including legally prescribed medications, are strongly associated with very similar patterns of use among adolescents. Peer pressure is also thought to significantly influence which drugs a teenager uses, in what circumstances, and how much and how often, although some findings indicate that its contribution may be overestimated (Bauman & Ennett, 1994).

Because most initial experiences with cigarettes, alcohol, and illicit drugs occur during the early teenage years, prevention efforts are now being directed at this age group. These efforts have focused on reducing exposure to drugs, altering the social environment, and changing the attitudes and behaviors of the drug user (or potential user). In general, however, drug prevention programs have not proven very effective. Those that show promise are peer programs and school-based prevention efforts involving life skills training designed to increase knowledge and build confidence and overall social competence in areas such as risk assessment, decision making, self-directed behavior change, capacity to cope with anxiety, and conflict resolution (Botvin & Tortu, 1988; Hamburg, 1994; Newcomb & Bentler, 1989).

Nutritional Problems   Adolescents have the highest "unsatisfactory" nutritional status of any age group. The average teenage girl requires approximately 2,200 calories per day, and the average adolescent boy needs about 2,800. Boys' nutrient intakes come closer to recommended daily allowance levels than girls' do, because boys eat relatively larger amounts of food for their body weight; also, girls diet more frequently on a long-term basis (as do young women, as we will see in Chapter 12).

The food habits of adolescents, which include an increased tendency to skip meals (especially breakfast and lunch), snacking (particularly on "junk" foods), consumption of fast foods, and dieting, place them at dietary risk. Surprisingly, iron-deficiency anemia, one of the most common nutritional disorders in this age group, is found more frequently in boys than in girls (American Academy of Pediatrics, 1985). Inadequate nutrition can interfere with a teenager's ability to concentrate at school and work and to actively engage in activities with peers. Poor nutritional habits established during adolescence can have more serious health consequences if continued on a long-term basis.

Like dependence on drugs, food dependence and the obesity that frequently results are problems that affect a significant portion of the teenage population. Currently it is estimated that 15 percent of today's teenagers are significantly over-

Whereas most teenagers suffer no shortage of calories, their diets often lack balance. These adolescents' meal consists entirely of refined sugar (in the drinks) and of fat and starch (in the French fries). Achieving a more balanced diet is a matter partly of knowledge of good nutrition, partly of coping with peer pressure to eat "junk" food, and partly of getting food sellers to provide more nutritious alternatives.

weight. Major causes of obesity include a biologically inherited tendency to be over-weight, childhood diet and family attitudes and habits regarding food, and lack of exercise (Epstein & Wing, 1987; Maloney & Klykylo, 1983). Adolescents and young adults who are oveweight suffer increased health risks, including hyperten-sion, respiratory disease, orthopedic disorders, and diabetes.

Obesity is particularly difficult for adolescents who already are struggling to de-velop a comfortable and realistic view of their changing bodies. It can significantly impair teenagers' sense of themselves as physically attractive people and their over-all identity development. In some cases, obesity can severely limit social oppor-tunities due to both exclusion by peers and self-isolation. Because overweight adolescents do not conform to the social ideal of thinness, they also suffer from dis-crimination that limits their access to education, employment, marriage, housing, and health care (DeJong, 1993; Gortmaker et al., 1993).

Excessive thinness is also a problem. Despite a growing appreciation of physi-cal strength and fitness in women, a lean body is still the dominant cultural stan-dard for feminine beauty. Many adolescent girls try to lose weight to achieve a degree of slenderness that may not be possible for them. Inadequate knowledge about dietary requirements and poor judgment lead to inadequate nutrition for many teenage girls.

An extreme form of this quest for thinness is **anorexia nervosa,** a physical and psychological disturbance in which the afflicted teenager starves herself, exercises compulsively, and develops an increasingly unrealistic view of her body. Ninety-five percent of anorexics are females. Many anorexics also suffer from **bulimia,** a disor-der that compels them to eat huge amounts of food and then make themselves vomit to avoid gaining weight. The accompanying Perspectives box looks at the causes, symptoms, and treatment of these disorders.

What Do You Think?

Why do you think adolescents are at such high risk for injury, death, and health problems? What recommendations for preventing such serious outcomes might you make to a group of high school students and their parents?

Two Serious Eating Disorders: Anorexia Nervosa and Bulimia

Anorexia nervosa and bulimia are two emotional disorders characterized by severely abnormal eating patterns, an obsession with food and weight, and the "relentless pursuit of excessive thinness" (Bruch, 1979). *Anorexia nervosa* affects approximately 0.2 percent, or one in five hundred, adolescent girls and young women, and bulimia affects between 1.0 and 2.8 percent. Also, it is estimated that approximately 20 percent of adolescent girls (2.5 million) exhibit less extreme bulimic behaviors and an additional 20 percent engage in less extreme but still unhealthy dieting behaviors (Graber et al., 1994).

The major symptom of anorexia is extreme weight loss (approximately 20 to 25 percent of body weight) through self-starvation that is tied to an obsessive fear of becoming fat. Anorexic youngsters experience severe disturbances in three areas of psychological functioning. First is a *disturbance in body image.* A girl (we'll call her Jill) is five feet, six inches tall and weighs eighty-seven pounds. Jill looks like a walking skeleton, but when she views herself in the mirror, she sees someone who is too fat and needs to continue dieting. The second disturbance is *misinterpretation of internal and external stimuli:* although she is literally starving to death, Jill enjoys the feeling of hunger and her flat, empty stomach, both of which make her feel thinner. The third disturbance is a *pervasive sense of ineffectiveness and helplessness* about her ability to direct her life (Attie & Brooks-Gunn, 1989; Bruch, 1979, 1988). Other symptoms of anorexia include excessive, compulsive exercise; amenorrhea (the cessation of menstruation); hyperactivity; social isolation; and feelings of insecurity, loneliness, inadequacy, shame, and guilt (Attie et al., 1990; Frank, 1991; Solnit et al., 1986).

Bulimia is a related eating disorder that frequently involves a recurrent "binge-purge" syndrome in which as many as 4,800 calories are eaten at a time, mostly in the form of sweets and other "forbidden" and fattening foods, and then immediately "purged" by forced vomiting, laxatives, and other cathartics. Approximately half of all anorectics also have bulimic eating patterns (Attie et al., 1990; Leon & Dinklage, 1989; Solnit et al., 1986).

Causes

Women at greatest risk for bulimia likely are those who have accepted and internalized most deeply the social and cultural norms that equate fat with bad, thinness with beauty, and beauty with good (Streigel-Moore et al., 1986). Most anorectics are girls from financially and socially successful upper-middle-class and upper-class families. Many feel burdened by their parents' success and an overwhelming obligation to be at least as special and successful as their parents were. Their eating behaviors serve as a means of forestalling and/or avoiding the physical, sexual, and psychosocial changes and challenges of puberty and adolescence, which they do not feel ready to face. The behaviors also give them a means of asserting control over their own bodies and daily activities and of resisting the intense pressure to conform to the parental expectations they experienced throughout their childhood (Bruch, 1979; Leon & Dinklage, 1989; Romeo, 1984).

Anorexia and bulimia are frequently associated with a serious family disturbance, and in particular with a mother-daughter relationship that is overprotective, rigid, and rejecting or hostile and with mothers who themselves are preoccupied with thinness and have dis-

COGNITIVE DEVELOPMENT

Teenagers' growing cognitive competencies broaden the horizons of their world substantially. For example, the question "What if a nuclear war broke out?" is more meaningful to an adolescent than to a child, even though both are equally inexperienced with actual nuclear war. So is the question "What if I had been born really poor or fabulously rich?" Adolescents can imagine what these situations might be like even though they have not experienced them in a concrete way. In general, thinking about the possible creates a new skill for speculating about important events and guessing about daily experiences (Kahlbaugh & Haviland, 1991). It also stimulates adolescents to daydream or fantasize about their actions and feelings. And it helps them make more astute inferences about human motivations ("Perhaps she did that because . . .").

Psychologists have explained and interpreted these new talents from two major points of view. The first is the *cognitive developmental viewpoint,* often associated

turbed eating patterns (Attie et al., 1990). There is also evidence that sexual abuse may be involved in some cases (Shapiro & Rosenfeld, 1987).

Treatment

Successful treatment generally requires a multiple focus. First, it must deal with the starvation problem in a way that addresses both the anorectic's need for control and the distortions in her thinking. This typically requires a highly restricted hospital environment that allows careful observation and the use of behavior modification to strictly reduce or eliminate rewards for behaviors leading to weight loss and reinforce more appropriate eating behaviors. Antidepressant medications have also proven helpful in reducing the depression and risk of suicide that are present in many cases (McDaniel, 1986). Second, the treatment must address the underlying family problems and abnormal interactions among family members that are invariably related to anorexia. Finally, individual therapy with the anorectic adolescent must focus on helping her to uncover her own abilities and resources for independent thinking, judging, and feeling. It must help her to achieve autonomy and self-directed identity by helping her to become aware of, express, and act on her own impulses, feelings, and needs (Bruch, 1979, 1980; Leon & Dinklage, 1989; Shapiro & Rosenfeld, 1987).

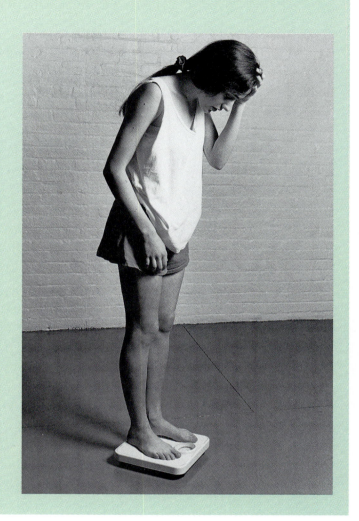

Individuals with anorexia, like this teenage girl, suffer from serious confusion about their body image. Their compulsive dieting and exercise are attempts to attain culturally imposed standards of female beauty and gain control over their lives. No matter how thin they become, they are likely to view themselves as "too fat."

with the work of Piaget. The second is the more recent approach of *information-processing theory,* which analyzes human thinking as a complex storage, retrieval, and organizing system for information, much like a computer. Both theories have been discussed elsewhere in this book (see especially Chapter 2); here we focus on how they relate to adolescence in particular.

THE COGNITIVE DEVELOPMENTAL VIEWPOINT: FORMAL THOUGHT

The cognitive developmental viewpoint (the one discussed in Chapter 2) interprets adolescents' cognitive changes as a stage of cognitive development, one in which a person acquires **formal operational thought**. This sort of thinking differs from *concrete operational thought* (discussed in Chapters 6 and 8) in three important ways: emphasizing the possible versus the real, using scientific reasoning, and skillfully combining ideas (Keating, 1991).

Possibilities Versus Realities

Formal thought involves attention to possibilities rather than merely to actual realities. A parent discovered this feature when he tried to get his two children to make suggestions about how to improve the humdrum weekly chicken dinner. "Fried is fine," said his nine-year-old. "I like it the way we always have it." But the fourteen-year-old insisted on a more complicated response: "Let me think about that," she said. Later she remarked, "Can we make some brand-new sauce for it? Maybe one of the cookbooks has some ideas." Even though the older child had never eaten chicken cooked this way, she thought about trying it.

Scientific Reasoning

Formal thought also involves scientific reasoning, the same kind psychologists use in designing many of their studies of human development. This quality reveals itself when adolescent students must solve some problem systematically. For example, how do youngsters in an art class figure out methods for mixing basic colors of paint to produce various intermediate shades and other colors? Those capable of formal operations in effect design an experiment to test all the available combinations of colors. They form hypotheses, or hunches, about how certain colors affect each other when mixed. Then they try out their hypotheses by mixing each basic color with every other basic color, being careful to try every possibility. By carefully observing the results of this procedure, they can draw logical conclusions about how to mix colors. This procedure in effect uses the scientific method.

In contrast, concrete operational children rarely act so systematically. Like the formal operational thinkers, they probably would mix colors, but they would do so hap-

Many teenagers become able to solve problems scientifically. But like these students in a biology laboratory class, and like most adults, they still need ample concrete experiences to support their abstract thinking. Commonly, too, they may have trouble using scientific thought outside a structured school situation.

hazardly and might not take careful note of the results of their experiments. As a result, they may not learn to mix colors as rapidly as older, formal operational thinkers do. When confronted with this problem, of course, some younger children might draw on previous experience with art materials to solve it; but then their performance would reflect memory about how to mix colors rather than true scientific reasoning.

Logical Combination of Ideas

The third feature of formal operational thought involves combining ideas logically. Unlike less cognitively mature children, formal thinkers can hold several ideas in mind at once and combine or integrate them in logical ways. When asked to explain why some students perform better in school than others do, concrete operational thinkers are likely to latch on to one reason or another: "Some kids are smarter" or "Some kids work harder." In contrast, formal operational thinkers often give combinations of reasons, as this first-year university student did:

> Well, I think it depends. Sometimes it pays just to be smart. But it also helps to work hard—except when the teacher doesn't notice. Some kids do better too because they have taken courses before in the same area. Your first class in literature is likely to be harder than your fifth class in that subject.

As this example shows, the ability to combine ideas sometimes makes formal operational thinkers qualify their opinions more than pre–formal operational thinkers do.

Cognitive Development Beyond Formal Thought

Piaget and other psychologists have identified formal, or abstract, thought as a major achievement of the adolescent years. But for most human beings, it may not be the final or highest cognitive achievement. One clue to this possibility comes from adolescents themselves: some teenagers overuse logical thinking when they first achieve facility with it (Leadbetter, 1991). They may believe all problems, including ambiguous ones such as achieving world peace, can be solved by the proper application of rational principles and careful reasoning. Teenagers may fail to notice that some problems by nature resist the application of general logic and may inherently have multiple, partial solutions.

Consider Ana, a twelfth-grader who recently has begun sleeping with her boyfriend. Ana gets along well with her parents, and she knows they will worry and feel hurt if they learn of her sexual involvement. She also believes that in general, friends and family should have no secrets. By continuing her sexual activities, she seems to be violating this principle. On the other hand, she and her boyfriend regard their intimacy as a private matter, and she worries that telling her parents would violate this privacy, which she also considers her right. Telling her parents might also create a lot of bad feelings among Ana, her boyfriend, and her parents. In this case, her principles do not seem to point her toward a good solution: Ana believes that no matter what she does, somebody will get hurt, some ethical principle will be violated, or both.

Ana's situation suggests the importance of nonrational choices or judgments in solving real-life problems. Like Ana, many people may wish to be reasonable; that is, they may wish to rely on formal logic and may even believe they use it a lot. But in practice, most people use formal logic consistently only when solving academic problems posed by teachers, especially when the problems are deliberately scientific in nature (Bartsch, 1993). Less systematic reasoning serves as well or better for solving daily problems.

For older adolescents, the cognitive challenge consists of converting formal reasoning from a goal in itself to a *tool* used for broader purposes and tailored to the problems at hand (Myers, 1993). Ana cannot reach a sound decision about informing her parents of her sexual activities if she focuses on formal principles about truthfulness and privacy to the exclusion of more personal facts, which in this case include her knowledge of her boyfriend's and her own parents' probable responses and feelings. Taking these circumstances into account leads to the "best," or most mature, solution, but it may not lead to a solution that is fully logical in Piaget's sense. As adolescents grow into young adults, this sort of postformal thought becomes more common, as we will see in Chapter 12 when we discuss cognitive development in early adulthood.

Implications of the Cognitive Developmental Viewpoint

According to Piaget, formal operations begin developing early in adolescence and are fully formed by the end of the high school years. All teenagers supposedly develop wide-ranging thinking abilities that have a formal, abstract nature and apply to many specific experiences and daily problems. In reality, however, the actual cognitive performances of adolescents fail to conform to this picture in several ways. First, a majority of adolescents (and even adults) use formal thinking inconsistently or even fail to use it at all (Lakoff, 1994). In explaining why a car is not working properly, for example, many adolescents and adults merely describe the car's symptoms: "The brakes are making a weird noise" or "It won't shift into third gear."

It seems, then, that formal operational thought does describe adolescents' thinking, but only partially or intermittently. Formal thought helps teenagers to argue with their parents more skillfully than they could as children, thereby contributing to the stereotype of teenagers as being relatively "rebellious." Formal thought also makes teenagers more skillful at cultivating friendships, potential dates, and social contacts; now they can imagine and anticipate the consequences of various friendly (and unfriendly) strategies. And formal thought means teenagers are more ready than children are to grapple with philosophical and abstract topics at school: literary analysis can now begin to make sense, for example, and so can at least some theoretical concepts in science.

What Do You Think?

Outside of school- or job-related tasks, most people actually use formal operational thinking rather little in their everyday lives. How much do *you* actually use it? Think of a situation other than school (shopping, visiting a friend, cooking) in which you need to use abstract thinking to function effectively. What does your answer imply about the place of formal thought in adolescents' overall development?

INFORMATION-PROCESSING FEATURES OF ADOLESCENT THOUGHT

As we saw in Chapter 2, information-processing theory sees human cognition as a complex storage and retrieval system, governed largely by an "executive" control system that transfers information between short- and long-term memory and organizes information for more efficient and meaningful handling and retrieval. When cognition is viewed this way, development consists largely of overcoming the bottlenecks in processing information, especially those caused by the limited capacities of the executive and short-term memory. As children mature into adolescents, they develop strategies for taking in, organizing, and remembering larger amounts of information more quickly and with less effort. The most important of these strategies are included in Figure 10.4 and explained more fully next.

Improved Capacity to Process Information

Typically an adolescent can deal with, or process, more information than a child can. A first-grader may remember three or four random digits (3 9 5 1), but a teenager usually can remember six or seven. And when a first-grader asks an adult how to spell a word, he can hold only two or three letters in his mind at a time; the adult has to dole them out singly or in very small groups (*LO . . . CO . . . MO . . . TI . . . VE*). A teenager, however, can more often encounter much longer groupings of letters and still reconstruct the word accurately.

Expertise in Specific Domains of Knowledge

By adolescence, many individuals have become comparative experts in specific domains of knowledge or skill. These domains may or may not have much to do with school learning. One teenager excels in knowledge of mathematics, whereas another excels in knowledge of baseball and still another excels in getting along with people.

Much of such expertise may depend not on generalized development of cognitive structures, as Piagetian theorists would claim, but on the long, slow acquisition of large amounts of specific knowledge, along with better organization of that knowledge. Studies of experts and novices among adults suggest this possibility. Experts in physics know many more concepts about physics than beginners do, but they do not necessarily know more about geography, English grammar, or other areas of knowledge (Gregg & Leinhardt, 1995). Experts also know more about problem solving in their particular field of expertise. A mathematician remembers countless formulas, equations, and solution methods, thanks to years of experience in memorizing them. Her memories naturally help her to solve new problems as they come up; she may realize that a new equation is similar to one she has worked with before and simply recall how she responded to the earlier formula.

Implications of the Information-Processing Viewpoint

By focusing on the detailed features of problem solving, the information-processing viewpoint provides a valuable complement to the broader approach of cognitive developmental theory. By focusing on the fine details of thinking, information-processing theory offers more insights into why individuals vary in their thinking

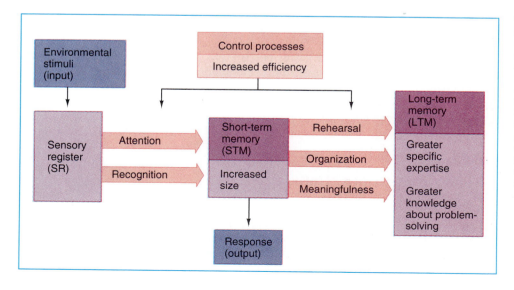

FIGURE 10.4
Developmental Changes in Information Processing
Although the basic nature of information processing remains constant from childhood to adolescence, important changes occur in several features, as the figure indicates. Short-term memory may increase in capacity, control processes become more efficient, and long-term memory contains more specific knowledge as well as knowledge about problem solving, or "how to think."

Compared to younger girls who like to make pottery, these teenagers are more planful and more able to carry out complicated projects. These changes in their pottery skills probably happen both because they are able to hold more ideas and plans in mind at one time, and because they can coordinate their activities—and even their hand movements—more skillfully than before.

performances from one occasion to the next. Some psychologists have also tried to identify developmental trends in information processing (Case & Edelstein, 1993). Their research has emphasized specific sequences within particular domains of thinking rather than the more global stages of the cognitive developmental approach. In this way, the information-processing viewpoint resembles research on adolescents' cognition about interpersonal and social knowledge.

What Do You Think?

Think of an activity or area of knowledge in which you consider yourself a relative expert. How much of your expertise has resulted from knowing a lot of specific facts about the area? How much has resulted from organizing your knowledge better than other people do? Compare your opinions with those of a classmate or friend who is an expert in an area other than yours.

SUPPORTING ADOLESCENTS' COGNITIVE DEVELOPMENT

Adolescents' cognitive changes result partly from informal everyday experiences, such as discussions with friends or family members about ideas and points of view that are new or with which the teenager does not agree. But they can also be influenced deliberately, as sometimes happens in school curricula or other educational programs intended to stimulate young people to think in new ways and adopt new perspectives. What do such interventions involve?

The Nature of Critical Thinking

Programs to encourage adolescents' thinking vary somewhat and go by a variety of names, including *problem solving, reflective thinking,* or *creativity.* For our purposes here, we will use the term **critical thinking,** meaning reflection or thought about complex issues, usually to make decisions or take actions. Despite its name, critical thinking refers not to thinking that is negative or complaint ridden but to thinking that is thoughtful, yields new insights, and provides a basis for intelligent choice. Critical thinking is a broad, practical skill: it can help a person figure out why an unfamiliar appliance broke down, compose a term paper, resolve a conflict with a friend, or decide what kind of career to pursue.

What does critical thinking involve? Educators and psychologists have analyzed it in various ways, but usually point out the following elements (King & Kitchener, 1994):

1. *Basic operations of reasoning* To think critically, a person must be able to classify, generalize, deduce conclusions, and perform other logical steps mentally.

2. *Domain-specific knowledge* To deal with a problem, a person must know something about its topic or content. To evaluate a proposal for a new, fairer tax system, a person must know something about the existing tax system. To resolve a personal conflict, a person has to know something about the person with whom he is having the conflict.

3. *Metacognitive knowledge* (knowledge about how human thinking works, including one's own) Effective critical thinking requires a person to monitor when she really understands an idea, know when she needs new information, and predict how easily she can gather and learn that information.

4. *Values, beliefs, and dispositions* Thinking critically means valuing fairness and objectivity. It means having confidence that thinking does in fact lead to solutions. It also means having a persistent and reflective disposition when thinking.

Interestingly, research has found that students themselves understand these elements of critical thinking (Nichols et al., 1995). Furthermore, as Figure 10.5

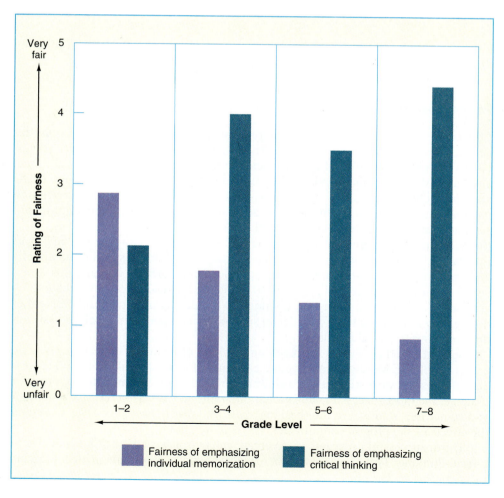

FIGURE 10.5
Students' Ratings of Fairness of Critical Thinking as a Goal of School
As students get older, they perceive critical thinking to be a fairer or more appropriate goal of schooling. In other parts of this particular study, students also increasingly rated critical thinking as more likely to get students excited about learning and to get them to help one another more.
Source: Adapted from Nichols et al. (1995).

A Multicultural View

Cross-cultural Misunderstandings in the Classroom

Consider these classroom situations and their impact:

☐ Student 1 is quiet when his teacher speaks to him, but he generally looks down at the floor or away from her when she speaks. Even when the teacher encourages him to express his own ideas, the Student pauses and looks away for what feels like an eternity to the teacher.

☐ Student 2 writes an essay for a social studies class entitled "Jobs in the Coming Global Economy." To the teacher, the essay seems to meander all over the place and does not state its theme until the final paragraph. "It's as if you were telling me what you were thinking," the teacher wrote on the essay afterward, "instead of stating and then justifying a position."

☐ Student 3 rarely answers questions completely when the teacher calls on her in class; she just mumbles an answer or remains silent. But when collaborating with a small group on a project or an activity, she is lively, talkative, and focused on the task.

There are many possible reasons for these situations. One common explanation is *cross-cultural miscommuni-*

cation, culturally based differences in how individuals interpret comments and behaviors. Observations of conversations show that cultures vary in communication styles and that children acquire the styles in the course of learning their native language (Scollon & Scollon, 1994).

Cultural communication styles can vary in the following ways, among others:

1. *Timing:* speakers expect different lengths of pauses between conversational turns, from many seconds to only a fraction of a second or even to a "negative" pause (overlapping comments).
2. *Deductiveness/inductiveness:* in some cultures, speakers are expected to state their point immediately (use a "topic sentence") and then justify their position; in others, speakers more often lead up to the main point indirectly, describing their thought processes along the way.
3. *Politeness indicators:* in some cultures, it is especially important to indicate respect for those in authority, chiefly by listening quietly and allowing an authority to determine the topic and length of a conversation.

indicates, compared to grade-school children, adolescents regard critical thinking as a fairer and more appropriate purpose of schooling.

Programs to Foster Critical Thinking

Educators have devised a number of programs intended to foster the qualities needed for critical thinking (French & Rhodes, 1992), many of which serve adolescents. The programs differ in their particulars: they last for various lengths of time, emphasize different thinking skills, and draw on content from different areas of the standard school curriculum. Some programs are integrated into the curriculum, meaning they replace a traditional course in some subject area; others are taught separately and draw content from several areas at once.

But experts do agree on several general principles that enhance the quality of programs that teach critical thinking. First, teaching thinking is best done directly and explicitly. Critical thinking does not develop on its own by unconscious osmosis, so to speak (Keefe & Walberg, 1992). Watching the teacher or a classmate think critically does not guarantee that a student will become a better thinker. Neither does giving a student a lot of practice in simple mental operations, such as basic addition or simple logical puzzles.

Second, good programs for teaching thinking offer lots of practice at solving actual problems. Merely describing the elements of critical thinking (as this text is doing) does not turn students into skillful thinkers. To accommodate the need for practice, the most successful educational programs last as least a full academic year and sometimes also weave the thinking skills into other, related courses to extend the effects of the program still further.

Third, successful programs try to create an environment explicitly conducive to critical thinking. Typically they expect teachers to model important critical thinking

These cultural differences can pose problems whenever members of more than one culture come together to interact. For children and adolescents, therefore, cultural mismatch is especially likely in classrooms, particularly in contacts between teachers and students. If the teacher "speaks the culture" of white, mainstream English, she or he will tend to use and expect relatively short pauses between conversational turns in classroom discussions. The teacher will also tend to use and expect a deductive style of turn taking, with the topic stated immediately by whoever initiates a conversational exchange. And although the teacher may expect moderate indications of respect for his or her right to initiate topics of conversation, she or he may also expect students to initiate ideas and concerns of their own.

When a student's culture supports other communication styles, the teacher can easily get the impression that the student is either unintelligent, lacking in confidence, or deliberately resistant to learning (Lustig & Koester, 1993). Yet these sorts of mismatches are precisely what occur, and always to the disadvantage of the student. What the teacher sees and hears are pauses that are too long, eye contact that is poor, comments that stray from the topic, and silence in response to invitations to speak. What the student experiences, though, may be quite different: he or she may see and hear a teacher who is too talkative, stares at individuals too much, and seems insincere in issuing invitations to ask questions.

But such misunderstandings can be overcome. Training in intercultural communication exists and is effective when focused on the key cultural misunderstandings of particular conversational partners. In the teaching profession, some of the most elaborate training occurs for teachers of English as a Second Language (Paulston, 1992), but programs are also developing in many business communities (Brislin & Yoshida, 1994; O'Hara-Devereaux & Johansen, 1994), where economic activity increasingly spans more than one country, language, and cultural community. The programs vary in detail, of course, but share a common assumption: that awkwardness between culturally different speakers is likely the result of legitimate differences in communication styles rather than of inferiority of one style or the other.

skills themselves, such as thinking out loud while they explain a solution to a problem. The programs also expect teachers to convey confidence in students' ability to think while providing constructive, explicit criticism of ideas, whether their own or the students'. For example, one technique is to invite individual students to temporarily act as teacher or constructive critic (Slavin, 1995). To make time for these activities, most critical thinking programs tend to minimize individual seatwork, a time-consuming activity that is found in much traditional classroom instruction but gives students little on-the-spot feedback about the quality of their thinking processes.

Whatever their differences, programs that teach critical thinking draw on the spirit, if not the literal research findings, of several strands of cognitive theory concerning the adolescent years. One strand is Piagetian, with its concern for how logic and reasoning gradually develop. Another is information-processing theory, with its focus on specific ways of organizing ideas and coordinating new ideas with pre-existing ones. A third strand is the concern with the social and cultural context of cognitive development in adolescence: how people and settings affect a young person's thinking. As the accompanying Multicultural View box indicates, cultural differences and misunderstandings can complicate teachers' efforts to encourage critical thinking skills in the classroom. Social influences are so important, in fact, that we discuss them more fully in the next section.

What Do You Think?

Some educators argue that you cannot teach thinking skills in *general,* since a person always thinks about something in *particular*. Why do you think they take this position? This issue makes for a useful debate in class, especially if you adopt the position contrary to the one you truly embrace!

THE DEVELOPMENT OF SOCIAL COGNITION

No matter which approach they take, most developmental psychologists agree that the new cognitive skills of adolescents have important effects on their **social cognition,** or their knowledge and beliefs about interpersonal and social matters. In this section, we look at the most important forms of social cognition. We begin with a description of the special form of self-centeredness, or **adolescent egocentrism,** that affects teenagers' reactions to others and their beliefs about themselves. We consider what causes this form of egocentrism and how those causes affect three other important kinds of social cognition: moral beliefs, political attitudes, and religious orientation. Another perspective on the impact of social cognition appears in the interview with Carole Castleton, a psychiatric group worker.

Egocentrism During Adolescence

When adolescents first begin to reason abstractly, they often become overly impressed with this skill; it seems to them that anything can be solved "if only people would be reasonable" (that is, logical). This attitude can make teenagers idealistic and keep them from appreciating the practical limits of logic (Bowers, 1995). They may wonder why no one has ever "realized" that world war might be abolished simply by explaining to all the world powers the obvious dangers of war. Or they may wonder why their parents have not noticed the many "errors" they have made in raising children.

Teenage egocentrism is often expressed as a preoccupation with how others respond and as a belief in personal invulnerability. This girl may be spending a lot of time choosing clothes because she is concerned about what others will think of how she looks. The boy may be willing to risk a broken limb in skateboarding because he does not really believe that he can be injured.

Cognitive Strategies for Social Problems

Carole Castleton has worked for seven years as a group therapist at an adolescent psychiatric treatment center. Most of the teenagers who come to the center have emotional difficulties; often they are depressed, withdrawn, or even suicidal. When I began the interview, I expected Carole to describe numerous social problems among the teens at the center. What I learned, though, is that it's more accurate to think of their problems as social and cognitive simultaneously.

Kelvin: What exactly do you do at the treatment center?

Carole: I'm a group therapist. I coordinate several dozen groups, both for outpatients and inpatients. We try to find out what sort of group will best help each teenager on arrival.

Kelvin: So the groups differ, not just the teens?

Carole: For sure. We create groups in all sorts of modalities—psychoeducational, expressive, supportive, insight oriented. Each kid thinks and feels in a unique way, so each needs a unique style of group.

Kelvin: I'm not familiar with many of the terms you just used—for instance, what's a psychoeducational group like?

Carole: Well, that group would have some structure and a theme or goal—"communication," for instance. All group activities would focus on how kids talk and listen, on nonverbal "messages," on differences between assertive and aggressive, and so on. If I needed to talk about managing personal stress with these kids, I would do it in a way that also dealt with issues of communication.

Kelvin: Wouldn't you do this sort of thing with *all* of the groups?

Carole: Not in the same way. An expressive group, for instance, would revolve around art work, art explorations—clay, free drawing, that sort of thing. Sometimes the leader might suggest a task, like "try drawing your family," but the emphasis is always on the artistic activity itself: the kids communicate through their art, not with words.

Kelvin: How do you decide which group might be the "best fit" for a particular teen?

Carole: That's the big challenge of my job! When teenagers first arrive, I meet with them to learn something about their background and why they came to the center. Even that initial meeting reveals something about their communication styles— do they use words, do they like to work with their hands? Do they like—even *need*—to move around a lot? We also have whole-staff meetings to assess each youngster's strengths and to figure out what sort of experiences she's likely to respond to positively. Very few actually seem suited to insight therapy— explicit talking about their problems. They do seem to function well in other ways.

Kelvin: So the *way* a teenager thinks makes quite a difference for treatment! It's not just "pure emotion" that's the challenge?

Carole: It's everything—emotion, social life, thinking. You can really see it when you look at their school experiences. Usually these have been wrecked by terrible home experiences—by abuse, by a nasty divorce between the parents, by family "secrets" that make it hard for a kid to think straight.

Kelvin: An example?

Carole: This boy who came last spring, just thirteen or fourteen years old, "young" compared to most others here. He had been hyperactive when he was in elementary school, on Ritalin [a drug to control hyperactivity]. His parents were divorced. When he came, his stepdad kept say-

ing, "The boy doesn't listen, he's not disciplined"—as if it were the boy's choice, the boy's fault. He wasn't reading or writing in school, got in fights with teachers.

Well, our observations confirmed some of this—he *was* restless, he *would* fidget during groups and seem like he wasn't listening, he *did* get really mad sometimes. But we also found that he *could* read, though at a pretty basic level.

One day he came to group late. We were building Lego models, copying from photos. The other kids had been taking a long time, but he got his done much faster than everybody else!

Kelvin: What did that tell you about him?

Carole: That he was visual and tactile— sight and touch oriented. He was not verbally oriented, yet his stepdad and his teachers had been "talking at" him for years, trying to get through to him and to make him function verbally. It just didn't work. He didn't think that way. His strengths had been missed, and all sorts of emotional conflict had been the result.

What Do You Think?

1. The different groups Carole describes seem consistent with Gardner's notion of "multiple intelligences" (see page 287). How, then, do you account for her comment that "very few [teens] actually seem suited for insight therapy"? What might prevent these teenagers from fully developing this sort of thinking?

2. How could the center prepare a teen who prefers to communicate nonverbally (e.g., via art work) to return to school, where most academic activities depend on verbal give-and-take?

3. Suppose most of the teenagers at the treatment center had criminal records instead of histories of depression and withdrawal. How might that change the center's treatment priorities? Would that influence the emphases of the groups?

The development of formal thought also leads to a new kind of confusion between an adolescent's own thoughts and those of others. This confusion of viewpoints amounts to a form of egocentrism. Unlike the egocentrism of preschoolers, which is based on concrete problems, adolescent egocentrism concerns more abstract thoughts and problems.

The Imaginary Audience   Adolescent egocentrism sometimes shows itself in teenagers' preoccupation with the reactions of others. Thirteen-year-olds often fail to differentiate between how they feel about themselves and how others feel about them. Instead, they act as though they are performing for an **imaginary audience,** one that is as concerned with their appearance and behavior as they themselves are (Elkind, 1985).

Teenagers also reveal concern with an imaginary audience through *strategic interactions* with their peers, encounters that aim to either reveal or conceal personal information indirectly. Telephoning often serves as a strategic interaction, especially for younger teenagers. Frequent phone calls help sustain a belief in personal popularity with an imaginary audience, so a teenager may subtly encourage others to phone by casually promising to share special gossip or secrets "if you call me tonight." An adolescent can also create the appearance of popularity by talking on the phone for very long periods of time so that potential callers get a "busy" signal, implying that the youngster is too popular to reach easily by telephone. This message can also be conveyed to the person on the line with an offhand comment such as "Gotta go; I'm expecting some other calls."

The Personal Fable   As a result of their egocentrism, teenagers often believe in a **personal fable,** the notion that their own lives embody a special story that is heroic and completely unique. For example, one high school student may be convinced that no love affair has ever reached the romantic heights of his involvement with a classmate. Another may believe she is destined for great fame and fortune by virtue of (what she considers to be) her unparalleled combination of charm and academic talent.

In experiencing these feelings and ideas, adolescents fail to realize how other individuals feel about them as well. Early in adolescence, they still have only limited empathy, or the ability to understand reliably the abstract thoughts and feelings of others and compare those thoughts and feelings with their own. In fact, much of adolescence consists of developing these social skills. So does most of adulthood, for that matter; we never really finish learning how to understand others or comparing our own experiences with those of others. But adolescence is the time when most people begin learning to consider other viewpoints in relation to their own and developing complex ideas about moral, political, and religious questions, among others, in response.

However, not all teenagers seem equally egocentric, and even those who do show this quality only when compared to adults, not to younger children. Investigations of adolescents' belief in an imaginary audience show that teenagers are just as likely to develop greater empathy or interpersonal sensitivity during this developmental period as they are to develop greater self-centeredness (Lapsley, 1991). Accurate awareness of others' opinions about oneself apparently develops alongside, and sometimes even instead of, self-conscious preoccupation with others' opinions. The relative balance between these two developments depends, among other things, on the quality of relationships between parents and the adolescent: closer and more supportive relationships lead to greater realism and less self-consciousness.

What Do You Think?

1. Think back to your early adolescence. Who were the people or groups whose opinions concerned you the most? Did they amount to an "imaginary audience" in the sense described in the text?

2. Have you ever felt that you are telling the "story of your life" in a way you have rehearsed before? If so, does that story constitute a personal fable such as that described in the text?

3. Do some young people seem relatively unconcerned about what others think? If so, might they be caught up in an imaginary audience and a personal fable, contrary to the assertions made in the text?

MORAL DEVELOPMENT: BELIEFS ABOUT JUSTICE AND CARE

As adolescents gradually overcome egocentrism in their personal relationships, they develop a personal **morality,** or sensitivity to and knowledge of what is right and wrong. Moral thinking develops in two ways: in the form of increasingly logical and abstract principles related to fairness and justice and in the form of increasingly sophisticated ways of caring about the welfare of friends, family, and self (Noam & Wren, 1993). Each of these trends is somewhat related to gender: boys tend to emphasize ethical thinking about justice rather abstractly, and girls typically emphasize an ethics of care. But the gender difference is not large; most individuals develop both kinds of ethical thinking to a significant extent. A major theory of the development of justice was originated by Lawrence Kohlberg, and a major theory of the development of care was conceived by Carol Gilligan. Both are stage theories in the cognitive developmental tradition, reminiscent of Piaget's approach to cognitive development.

Kohlberg's Six Stages of Moral Judgment

Lawrence Kohlberg proposed six stages of moral judgment that develop slowly, well into middle adulthood (Schrader, 1990). The stages were derived from interviews conducted in much the same style as Piaget's classic interviews about cognitive

"Ben is in his first year of high school, and he's questioning all the right things."

A youth's level of moral judgment depends on the reasoning that leads to the judgments, not on the judgments as such. In this cartoon, Ben may express judgments that seem principled, but if they were adopted simply to conform, as his mother implies, then his level of moral thinking is closer to Kohlberg's middling conventional level.

development: children and adults of various ages responded individually to hypothetical stories that contained moral dilemmas. The original interviewees were all
males, but in later studies Kohlberg and his associates extended the research to include females.

Table 10.3 summarizes the six proposed stages. The stages form a progression
in two ways. First, earlier stages represent more egocentric thinking than later
stages do. Second, earlier stages by their nature require more specific or concrete
thinking than later stages do. For instance, in stage 1 (called *heteronomous morality*), a child makes no distinction between what he believes is right and what the
world tells him is right; he simply accepts the perspectives of the authorities as his
own. By stage 4 (social system orientation), when the child is an adolescent, he realizes that individuals vary in their points of view, but he still takes for granted the
existing overall conventions of society as a whole. He cannot yet imagine a society
in which those conventions might be purposely modified, for example, by passing
laws or agreeing on new rules. Only by stages 5 and 6 (ethics) can he do so fully.

In the school years, children most commonly show ethical reasoning at stage 2,
but some may begin showing stage 3 or 4 reasoning toward the end of this period
(Colby & Kohlberg, 1987). For the majority of youth and adults, stage 3 (interpersonal orientation) and stage 4 (social system orientation) characterize their most
advanced moral thinking. In stage 3, a person's chief concern is with the opinions
of her peers: an action is morally right if her immediate circle of friends says it is
right. Often this way of thinking leads to helpful actions, such as taking turns and
sharing possessions. But often it does not, such as when a group of friends decide
to let the air out of the tires of someone's car. In stage 4, the person shifts from concern with peers to concern with the opinions of community or society in the abstract: now something is right if the institutions approve. This broader source of
moral judgment spares stage 4 children from the occasional tyranny of friends'
opinions; now they will no longer steal hubcaps just because their friends urge them
to do so. This change makes teenagers less *opportunistic* than children are, less inclined to judge based on immediate rewards or punishments they experience personally. Instead they evaluate actions on the basis of principles of some sort. For the
time being, the principles are rather conventional; they are borrowed either from
ideas expressed by immediate peers and relatives or from socially accepted rules
and principles, whatever they may be. If friends agree that premarital sex is permissible, many teenagers are likely to adopt this idea as their own, at least as a general

TABLE 10.3   *Kohlberg's Stages of Moral Judgment*

Stage	Nature of Stage
Preconventional Level (*emphasis on avoiding punishments and getting awards*)	
Stage 1 Heteronomous morality; ethics of punishment and obedience	Good is what follows externally imposed rules and rewards and is whatever avoids punishment
Stage 2 Instrumental purpose; ethics of market exchange	Good is whatever is agreeable to the individual and to anyone who gives or receives favors; no long-term loyalty
Conventional Level (*emphasis on social rules*)	
Stage 3 Interpersonal conformity; ethics of peer opinion	Good is whatever brings approval from friends as a peer group
Stage 4 Social system orientation: conformity to social system; ethics of law and order	Good is whatever conforms to existing laws, customs, and authorities
Postconventional Level (*emphasis on moral principles*)	
Stage 5 Social contract orientation; ethics of social contract and individual rights	Good is whatever conforms to existing procedures for settling disagreements in society; the actual outcome is neither good nor bad
Stage 6 Ethics of self-chosen universal principles	Good is whatever is consistent with personal, general moral principles

principle. But if friends or family believe premarital sex is morally wrong, teenagers may adopt this alternative belief as a principle. (Note, however, that whether a teenager actually acts according to these principles is another matter. Moral action does not always follow from moral belief.)

A few older teenagers develop **postconventional moral judgment,** meaning that for the first time ethical reasoning goes beyond the judgments society convention- ally makes about right and wrong (Colby & Kohlberg, 1987). Adolescents' growing ability to use abstract formal thought makes this possible; unlike schoolchildren, they can evaluate ethical ideas that *might* be right or wrong given certain circum- stances that can only be imagined.

Enduring Issues About the Development of Moral Judgment

As Figure 10.6 indicates, Kohlberg's six stages of moral judgment have held up well when tested on a wide variety of children, adolescents, and adults. The stages of moral thinking shown in Table 10.3 do seem to describe how moral judgment de- velops, at least when individuals focus on hypothetical dilemmas posed in stories. When presented with stories about risky but fictional sexual behaviors, adolescents of both sexes evaluated the actions of the stories' characters in line with Kohlberg's stages (Jadack et al., 1995).

Even so, Kohlberg's theory of moral judgment leaves a number of important questions unanswered. One is whether the theory really recognizes the impact of prior knowledge on beliefs; another is whether the theory distinguishes clearly enough between conventions and morality. One especially important question has to do with gender differences: does Kohlberg's theory really describe the moral de- velopment of girls as well as that of boys?

Issue 1: Form Versus Content of Moral Beliefs Despite the theory's plausibility, a number of developmental psychologists have questioned important aspects of it. Can the form of ethical thinking really be separated from content to the degree

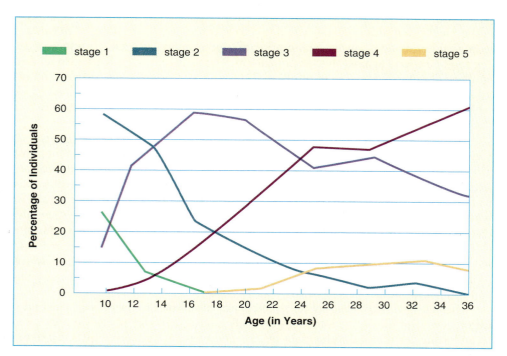

FIGURE 10.6
Longitudinal Development of Moral Reasoning
In a longitudinal follow-up study of Kohlberg's original sample, Colby and her colleagues confirmed that subjects showed consistent upward advances in moral reasoning with age. The graph shows the extent to which subjects gave responses characteristic of each of Kohlberg's six stages from age ten through adulthood. With development, responses associated with the precon- ventional level (stages 1 and 2) de- clined, whereas responses associated with the conventional level (stages 3 and 4) increased. Few young adults moved to the postconventional level of moral reasoning.
Source: Adapted from Colby et al. (1983).

Kohlberg proposes? Perhaps not. Some studies have found that when people reason about familiar situations, they tend to have more mature (that is, higher-stage) ethical responses (Lickona, 1991). For instance, children have a better sense of fairness about playing four-square on the playground than about whether to steal a drug for a spouse who is dying (one of Kohlberg's fictional dilemmas). In addition, young women think in more mature (more "developed") ways about ethical problems of special concern and familiarity to women, such as whether to engage in premarital sex or whether to have an abortion (Bollerud et al., 1990). To some extent, therefore, what someone thinks about affects the ethics she or he applies.

Issue 2: Conventions Versus Morality   According to some psychologists, some inconsistencies in moral beliefs may arise because the theory does not fully distinguish between social conventions and morality (Nucci & Turiel, 1993). **Social conventions** refer to the arbitrary customs and agreements about behavior that members of society use, such as table manners and forms of greeting and dressing. *Morality,* as we already pointed out, refers to the weightier matters of justice and right and wrong. By nature, social conventions inevitably generate widespread agreement throughout society, whereas morality does not necessarily do so. Yet Kohlberg's six-stage theory glosses over these differences by defining some of its stages in terms of social conventions and others in terms of morality. Stage 4 (social system orientation), for example, seems to refer to social conventions as well as to moral matters, but stage 5 (social contract orientation) refers only to moral judgment.

Issue 3: Gender Differences in Morality?   One especially important criticism of Kohlberg's theory of moral justice has to do with possible gender bias. Do Kohlberg's stages describe both sexes equally well? And does his theory undervalue ethical attitudes that may develop more fully in girls and women than in boys and men? The best-known investigations of these questions have been pursued by Carol Gilligan and her associates, described next.

Gilligan's Ethics of Care

According to Gilligan, boys and girls tend to view moral problems differently (Gilligan, 1982, 1990). As they grow up, boys learn to think more often in terms of general ethical principles that they can apply to specific moral situations. They might learn that deceiving is always bad in principle and evaluate a specific instance of deception of a friend against this generalization. The principles boys learn also tend to emphasize independence, autonomy, and the rights of others. This orientation biases boys to ignore or minimize others' possible needs: if a friend is at home sick with a cold, it may seem better to leave the friend alone until he gets better rather than check on how well he is recovering.

Girls tend to develop a different sort of morality as they grow up. Instead of seeing moral judgment as a set of abstract principles to apply to specific situations, girls tend to develop an ethics of care, a view that integrates principles with the contexts in which judgments must be made. A girl therefore may think deception is usually bad but also believe deception is ethical in certain circumstances, such as when a friend needs reassurance about the quality of a term paper that is actually mediocre but took a lot of time and effort. Viewing ethics in context grows out of a general concern for the needs of others more than for one's independence. A friend who is depressed therefore deserves a visit or a phone call; leaving her alone seems more like neglect than like respect for her autonomy. Table 10.4 summarizes Gilligan's stages of moral development.

These differences are only tendencies, not dramatic or sharply drawn gender differences. But they are enough, argues Gilligan, to make Kohlberg's theory seem to underrate the moral development of girls and women. Concern with context and

TABLE 10.4   *Gilligan's Stages of Moral Development*

Stage	Features
Stage 1 *Survival orientation*	Egocentric concern for self, lack of awareness of others' needs; "right" action is what promotes emotional or physical survival
Stage 2 *Conventional care*	Lack of distinction between what others want and what is right; "right" action is whatever pleases others best
Stage 3 *Integrated care*	Coordination or integration of needs of self and of others; "right" action takes account of self as well as others

Source: Gilligan (1982).

with others' needs causes girls to score closer to the middling, conventional levels of moral judgment, where peers' opinions matter most. Asked if a child should inform authorities about a friend who often shoplifts small items from a local department store, a girl is likely to give priority to one part of the problem in particular: that of balancing each person's views and needs in the particular situation. Doing so means wondering, among other things, whether informing will alienate peers not only from the shoplifter but also from the informer. On the other hand, it also means wondering whether keeping silent will make her risk losing the trust and respect of important adults, such as parents and teachers. It also means considering the amount of emotional pain that will befall the shoplifting friend at the hands of either angry parents or the police. Taking all of these considerations into account can make the final decision seem hesitant, tentative, and apparently lacking in principle, whichever way the decision goes.

Reviews of moral judgment have qualified Gilligan's ideas somewhat but have also lent them support. When faced with hypothetical dilemmas, females show as much capacity as males to reason in terms of abstract ethical principles (Gilligan & Wiggins, 1987). When faced with real-life dilemmas, however, girls make different choices (Bollerud et al., 1990; J. Brown, 1990). For example, adolescent girls who personally confront the decision of whether to engage in premarital intercourse often show more concern than do boys for the context in which they make their decisions and for the impact of their decisions on the emotional needs of others. As with Kohlberg's justice-oriented stages, however, a needs-oriented ethics of care takes time—years, in fact—to develop.

The Ethics of Care During Adolescence

As with the morality of justice, young people develop an ethics of care during adolescence, but like ethical justice, it remains somewhat conventional during the teenage years. During the school years, children develop significant concern about others' needs and welfare and begin viewing actions as good if the actions take others' needs and welfare into account (Larrabee, 1993). However, egocentrism persists in that teenagers often fail to distinguish between actions that merely *please* others and actions that are "right" in a deeper, ethical sense. For example, if parents will be pleased if their adolescent enrolls in complex science and mathematics courses in high school, doing so may seem "right" to the youngster, even if he has little interest or aptitude in those areas.

As with the ethics of justice, a few individuals move beyond conventional pleasing of others toward *integrated care,* in which the young person realizes that pleasing everyone is not always possible but it is important to balance everyone's needs, including her own (Larrabee, 1993). Deciding whether or not to take a part-time job, for example, now becomes a matter of reconciling the impact of the job on family, friends, and self. Some individuals may gain (the teenager herself may earn more money and make new friends), but others may lose (parents and

Moral development involves more than learning to reason about moral principles. It also involves learning to care about others and to reconcile their needs for care with your own. This girl seems to be on her way to care by providing companionship for the elderly in a retirement home.

friends may see less of her). The gains and losses must be balanced rather than viewed completely as gains.

Overall, then, the moralities of justice and care begin taking into account a broader array of both interpersonal circumstances and general principles than was true during the school years. Teenagers more often refer to principles in evaluating actions, although they still do not always act on their principles. Often they also regard pleasing others as ethically good or right, even though they are learning to deal with the impossibility of pleasing everyone perfectly. Like many other cognitive developments, these changes result from adolescents' growing capacities to reason abstractly.

What Do You Think?

Suppose you are starting your first job in a helping profession, such as nursing or teaching. How much would you want your work to be guided by an ethics of justice and how much by an ethics of care? Exchange your feelings about this question with a classmate or a friend.

SUMMARY OF MAJOR IDEAS

The Concept of Adolescence

1. Adolescence, which begins around age ten and lasts until about age twenty-two, is a developmental period of transition between childhood and adulthood.

2. Adolescence was "discovered" in the early part of this century as a way of prolonging childhood in a period of rapid social and economic change.

3. Some theories of adolescence emphasize the "storm and stress" of this period, whereas others find it no more conflict ridden than earlier periods of development. For most youngsters, adolescence is mixed.

PHYSICAL DEVELOPMENT

Growth in Height and Weight

4. Adolescents make significant increases in height and weight, but variations in the "growth spurt" among teenagers are even more striking.

Puberty

5. In addition to increases in height and weight, a larger pattern of changes occur that lead to full physical and sexual maturity, or puberty.

6. Primary sexual maturation among boys includes rapid growth of the penis and scrotum and the production of fertile semen.

7. Menarche, or the beginning of menstrual cycles, is a complex biological process that signals the beginning of sexual maturity for girls.

8. Maturation of secondary sex characteristics includes enlargement and development of the breasts, growth of body hair, deepening of the voice, and increased production of sex-related hormones.

9. Although girls and boys are equally muscular prior to adolescence, during puberty boys experience significantly greater increases in muscle tissue than girls do. Girls experience a somewhat greater increase in body fat than boys do.

10. Differences in how muscle and body fat are distributed rather than in their absolute amounts account for many of the differences in the physical appearances of male and female adolescents.

Psychological Effects of Physical Growth in Adolescence

11. Most adolescents are preoccupied with their physical appearance; a teenager's body image is influenced by conventional standards of attractiveness, as well as by evaluations by peers and parents.

12. For boys, the effects of early maturation are positive in the short run but somewhat negative in the long run. Late maturation appears to have the reverse effects.

13. For girls, early maturation is more stressful in the short term but positive in the long run. Late maturers tend to experience benefits during adolescence and no serious long-run negative effects.

Health in Adolescence

14. There is considerable continuity between childhood and adolescent patterns of illness and health care. Both are influenced by individual and family attitudes and resources.

15. Adolescents are a high-risk group for injury and death due to risky lifestyles and their myth of invulnerability.

16. Major health problems during adolescence include sexually transmitted diseases; alcohol, tobacco, and drug abuse; and inadequate diet.

COGNITIVE DEVELOPMENT

The Cognitive Developmental Viewpoint: Formal Thought

17. During adolescence, teenagers develop formal operational thought, or the ability to reason about ideas regardless of their content.

18. Formal thought is characterized by an ability to think about possibilities, by scientific reasoning, and by an ability to combine ideas logically.

19. In daily life, however, adolescents (and adults) often do not use formal thinking, even when it would be appropriate to do so.

20. Some research suggests that formal operations are not the final point of cognitive development.

Information-Processing Features of Adolescent Thought

21. During adolescence, information-processing skills continue to improve.

22. Teenagers acquire greater expertise in particular areas of knowledge or skill, and they come to allocate their attention to tasks more efficiently.

Supporting Adolescents' Cognitive Development

23. Teachers and other adults can intervene to encourage critical thinking, or reflection about complex issues to make decisions or take actions.

24. Programs to foster critical thinking usually do so explicitly and directly, offer lots of practice in solving problems, and create an environment conducive to critical thinking.

The Development of Social Cognition

25. Despite their improved cognitive skills, adolescents still sometimes show egocentrism by believing in an "imaginary audience" and in a "personal fable," or a biography of their lives.

Moral Development: Beliefs About Justice and Care

26. Adolescents develop two forms of morality at the same time, one oriented toward justice and one oriented toward caring.

27. Kohlberg proposes six stages in the development of moral judgments oriented toward justice.

28. A number of issues have not been resolved about Kohlberg's theory, including the role of form versus content of moral beliefs, the difference between conventions and morality, and the possibility of gender differences in morality.

29. Carol Gilligan proposes a theory of moral development oriented toward interpersonal caring; on average, it may be slightly more characteristic of females than males, though many exceptions exist.

KEY TERMS

adolescence (333)
growth spurt (335)
puberty (337)
primary sex characteristics (337)
secondary sex characteristics (338)
menarche (338)
pubic hair (339)
axillary hair (339)
testosterone (339)
estrogen (339)
anorexia nervosa (349)
bulimia (349)

formal operational thought (351)
critical thinking (356)
social cognition (360)
adolescent egocentrism (360)
imaginary audience (362)
personal fable (362)
morality (363)
Postconventional moral judgment (365)
social conventions (366)

11

ADOLESCENCE

Psychosocial Development

A s we have discovered, a number of dramatic physical and cognitive changes occur during puberty and adolescence. Although the rate at which these changes occur varies greatly, by the end of this period most adolescents look like adults and are physically and intellectually capable of most adult activities. But as important as these physical changes are, the changes that occur in the psychosocial domain may be even more significant. Perhaps the most important change is the progress adolescents make in achieving a full-fledged and integrated psychological identity that is mature, adult, unique, and separate from those of parents, friends, and other important childhood figures. An identity gives teenagers a more integrated and more permanent sense of who they really are, what they really need, what they believe in, and what they are and are not capable of doing. Barbara, who has just begun her senior year of high school, put it this way:

> It's not just that I'm all grown up now—physically, I mean. It's that I have grown up inside, too. I feel different, more like a grownup than a child. Although there are still many things I'm unsure of, I finally have a much clearer sense of who I am and what is important to me and what I believe in. And this may sound strange, but the sense of independence and separateness that I now feel means I can often be close to my parents and friends without losing a sense of who I am and my confidence in my ability to succeed at achieving the things I really want. In a way, it feels like I'm at the end of a long journey and ready to start off on a new one.

As Barbara's thoughts suggest, an enhanced capacity for psychological autonomy, intimacy, and relatedness to parents, family, and friends and significant strides in achievement and self-esteem are also important accomplishments of adolescence (Allen et al., 1994).

In this chapter, we look at the process of adolescent identity development as well as the related processes by which adolescents develop a healthy sense of autonomy, industry and achievement, intimacy, and sexuality. We explore several important aspects of the teenager's social world, including relationships with parents and peers, the development of friendships, and the impact of school and work. We also look at adolescent sexuality and how it is influenced by current social trends and personal beliefs. Finally, we explore the special problems adolescents face today and some strategies for preventing them.

Focusing Questions

- What conflicts do adolescents typically experience in their search for identity? What factors support or hinder successful identity development?

- What special challenges does adolescence pose for parents? How do differences in parenting style affect parent-teenager relationships?

- In what ways do adolescent friendships and peer groups play a constructive role, and how are concerns about their negative influence justified?

- What changes in sexual activities and attitudes occur among teenagers? How are they related to other aspects of adolescent development?

- Why are adolescents at risk for problems such as pregnancy, depression, and delinquency?

THEORIES OF IDENTITY DEVELOPMENT

Ruthellen Josselson: Individuation and Identity Development

Individuation is the process by which an adolescent develops a unique personal identity or sense of self, one distinct and separate from all others. Borrowing from Mahler's views on individuation in early childhood that we discussed in Chapter 2,

For each of these adolescents, it is likely that their willingness to engage in activities that diverge from cultural expectations reflects a strong sense of individual identity and self-direction.

"Soon you will be entering a phase, son, in which you will no longer pay attention to anything I have to say. Please let me know when that changeover occurs."

While the transition to adolescence is not without its stresses, parental fears of losing their influence are sometimes greatly exaggerated.

Ruthellen Josselson (1980) has proposed that the individuation process consists of four separate but overlapping subphases: differentiation, practice and experimentation, rapprochement, and consolidation of self.

During the *differentiation* subphase, which occurs early in adolescence, the teenager recognizes that she is psychologically different from her parents. The discovery that parents are not as wise, powerful, and all-knowing as she thought earlier sometimes leads her to question and reject her parents' values and advice, even if they are reasonable.

In the *practice and experimentation* subphase, the fourteen- or fifteen-year-old may believe he knows it all and can do no wrong. He may deny any need for caution or advice and actively challenge his parents at every opportunity. He also increases his commitment to friends, who provide the support and approval he previously sought from adults. In a discussion of plans to go to a heavy-metal rock concert, for example, Alonzo will completely dismiss his parents' concerns about the dangers in attending, insisting that his friends, who went to last year's concert, have assured him that it was perfectly safe.

During the *rapprochement* subphase, which occurs toward the middle of adolescence, a teenager has achieved a fair degree of separateness from her parents and is able to *conditionally* reaccept their authority. Often she alternates between experimentation and rapprochement, at times challenging her parents and at other times being conciliatory and cooperative. Although Maria, who has just turned fifteen, goes to great lengths to accept responsibility around the house, she often becomes highly indignant when her parents still insist on a curfew and on knowing where she is going when she leaves the house in the evening.

During the final, *consolidation-of-self* subphase, which lasts through adolescence and into early adulthood, youngsters develop a sense of personal identity, which provides the basis for understanding self and others and for maintaining a sense of autonomy, independence, and individuality. Parents often are surprised at how much careful thought an eighteen- or nineteen-year-old has given to who he is and how strong his sense of personal direction can be. For example, in a two-hour discussion with his mother that occurred quite by chance, Jorge, a high school senior, revealed that first and foremost he thought of himself as an artist and worked very hard to develop a special way of seeing and translating what he saw into creative works. He also considered himself a person who was good at helping others. He said he planned to first attend art school and become an artist, but thought he would eventually earn his living as a social worker or some other type of mental health professional.

The process of individuation continues throughout the teenage years and often into early adulthood. As we will see shortly, it dovetails with Erikson's theory, which holds that the major task of adolescence is to resolve the crisis of identity successfully.

Erik Erikson: The Crisis of Identity Versus Role Confusion

According to Erik Erikson (see Chapter 2), the key developmental challenge of adolescence is to resolve the crisis of **identity versus role confusion** (Erikson, 1963). In forming an identity, an adolescent selectively accepts or rejects the many different aspects of herself that she acquired as a child and forms a more coherent and integrated sense of unique identity (Damon & Hart, 1988; Harter, 1989; Harter & Monsour, 1992). During middle childhood, she may have simply formed disconnected, relatively separate impressions about herself: her athletic ability, popularity, capabilities as a student, and the like. In adolescence, however, she mulls over the significance of all of these impressions taken together: Do they mean that I am generally athletic? That I am popular? Intelligent? Or that I am merely a conformist, just devoting myself to whatever others value? An adolescent's increasing capacity for abstract thought and self-understanding (see Chapter 10) plays a central role in this process.

Psychosocial Moratorium   According to Erikson, adolescence provides a **psychosocial moratorium,** a period during which the youth is free to suspend or delay taking on adult commitments and to explore new social roles. The goal of role experimentation is to find a place, or niche, that is clearly defined and yet seems uniquely made for him. He may devote this time to academics, to trying out different jobs, to travel, to social causes, or even to delinquency, depending on prevailing social, cultural, and economic conditions as well as on his individual capacities and needs.

The type of psychosocial moratorium an adolescent encounters (or whether she encounters one at all) will largely depend on the opportunities for exploring a variety of roles provided by her family, culture, society, and the particular historical period in which she lives. For example, children growing up under conditions of poverty and deprivation or during periods of war and social upheaval are likely to experience more limited and less supportive moratorium opportunities than children living under more optimal circumstances.

Identity Diffusion   **Identity diffusion,** or the failure to achieve a relatively coherent, integrated, and stable identity, may take a number of forms. The first is *avoidance of closeness* with others. A second form, *diffusion of time perspective,* involves the belief that one is out of step with others, that important opportunities may be lost forever. It is sometimes accompanied by feelings of depression and despair over whether the pain and confusion surrounding identity will ever end and a comfortable sense of identity will finally be achieved. The third form, *diffusion of industry,* may involve an inability to concentrate on school- or work-related tasks or an excessive preoccupation with a single activity, such as reading or dating, that interferes with accomplishing other things. A final form of identity diffusion is the choice of a negative identity. A **negative identity** involves the disparagement and rejection of the roles and opportunities that are valued and made available by one's family and community and an acceptance of socially undesirable roles, such as that of a juvenile delinquent, a problematic identity that we discuss later in the chapter.

The Relationship Between Identity and Intimacy   Successful resolution of the crisis of identity versus role confusion prepares the adolescent for the crisis of intimacy versus isolation, which occurs in early adulthood. A clear and coherent sense of identity provides a basis for achieving intimacy in friendships and love relationships and for tolerating the fear of losing one's sense of self when intimacy becomes very intense and of experiencing loneliness and isolation if a relationship ends. However, as we will see in Chapter 13's discussion of psychosocial development in early adulthood, the establishment of an intimate relationship with a partner frequently occurs prior to the resolution of identity issues. The tendency for adolescent and young adult couples to break up suddenly and then unexpectedly reconcile may in part reflect a level of identity resolution that is not yet up to the task of sustaining intimacy. It is much more difficult to work out conflicting needs and expectations with someone who lacks a clear picture of who she is and what she needs.

Identity Status   Guided by Erikson's ideas, researchers such as James Marcia have empirically studied identity development during adolescence. Marcia interviewed students ages eighteen to twenty-two about their occupational choices and religious and political beliefs and values, all central aspects of identity (Marcia, 1967, 1980). He classified students into four categories of **identity status** based on (1) whether or not they had gone through an "identity crisis" as described by Erikson and (2) the degree to which they were now committed to an occupational choice and to a set of religious and political values and beliefs. Table 11.1 describes these categories.
    Marcia's findings were as follows:

1. *Identity-achieved* individuals had experienced and successfully resolved a period of crisis concerning their values and life choices and were now able to feel commitment to an occupation and to a religious and political ideology. Their occupational choices and their religious and political beliefs were based on serious consideration of alternatives and were relatively independent of those of their parents.

2. *Identity-diffused* individuals may or may not have experienced a crisis, but showed little concern or sustained commitment regarding occupational choice and religious and political beliefs.

TABLE 11.1 *Crisis and Commitment in Marcia's Theory of Identity Status*

Identity Status	Crisis	Commitment
Achieved	Present	Present
Diffused	Present/absent	Absent
Moratorium	In process	In process
Foreclosed	Absent	Present

Source: Marcia, (1980).

According to James Marcia, students can be classified into four categories of identity status based on the presence or absence of an identity crisis and whether or not they are committed to an occupational choice and a set of religious values and beliefs.

3. *Moratorium* individuals were presently *in* crisis, actively struggling to make commitments and preoccupied with achieving successful compromises among their parents' wishes, the demands of society, and their own capabilities.

4. *Foreclosed* individuals had "prematurely" committed themselves to important aspects of identity without having experienced any significant conflict or crisis. Consequently, it was difficult for them to distinguish their own goals from those of their parents. Their college experiences served mainly to confirm the childhood beliefs to which they rigidly held rather than provide challenging alternatives.

Most adolescents seem to progress toward a status of identity achieved. For both males and females, identity achievement is rarest among early adolescents and most frequent among older high school students, college students, and young adults. During junior and senior high school, identity diffusion and identity foreclosure are the most common identity statuses. Although diffused and foreclosed statuses significantly decrease during the later high school and college years, only about one-third of college juniors and seniors and one-quarter of adults studied have been found to be identity achieved (Archer & Waterman, 1988; Meilman, 1979).

The proportion of individuals at each identity status appears to vary with the specific identity area involved. Identity achievement was the most frequent status in the area of *religious beliefs;* identity achievement and moratorium were the most frequent statuses where *vocational choice* was concerned; identity foreclosure was the most common status in the area of *sex role preferences;* and identity diffusion was the most frequent status in the area of *political philosophies* (Archer, 1982; Meilman, 1979; S. Pomerantz, 1979; Waterman, 1982, 1985).

Few differences between males and females have been found on measures of identity. Both genders are equally represented among the four identity statuses and seem to develop in similar ways. Although early studies suggested that the identity statuses may have different psychological meanings and consequences for males and females, more recent research indicates that the meanings and implications appear to be quite similar for both sexes (Archer & Waterman, 1988; Gilligan, 1987).

What Do You Think?

To what degree have you experienced the developmental crisis of identity versus role confusion proposed by Erikson? Which of Marcia's four identity statuses best describes your own at the present time?

SOCIAL RELATIONSHIPS DURING ADOLESCENCE

The search for identity and the achievement of a mature psychological sense of autonomy and relatedness affect all of an adolescent's relationships. Ties with parents must make room for an increasing interest in peers and a new commitment to the life among comparative equals that peers provide. A young teenager's efforts to become more physically and emotionally separate from his parents and closer to his friends may be stressful, but more often than not the problems and conflicts of this period are relatively minor. Full-blown upheavals and more serious problems of adolescence are most likely to occur in families and communities in which a poor fit exists between the developmental needs of adolescents and the opportunities and supports that are available (Eccles et al., 1993; Offer & Schonert-Reichl, 1992).

Before we discuss social relationships during adolescence, let's take a brief look at how adolescents spend their time and whom they spend it with. Mihaly

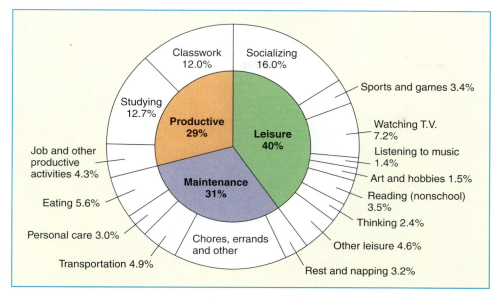

FIGURE 11.1
How Adolescents Spend Their Time
Source: Csikszentmihalyi & Larson (1984).

Csikszentmihalyi and Reed Larson (1984) asked seventy-five ninth-through-twelfth-grade girls and boys from different ethnic and SES backgrounds to carry electronic pagers for a week. Each teenager was "beeped" eight times during waking hours each day and, after each beep, completed a self-report form describing the activity, where it occurred, and who else was involved at the time. Figures 11.1 and 11.2 show the results of the study. The teenagers spent 41 percent of their waking hours at home, 32 percent at school, and 27 percent in public places, including work, friends' homes, yard or garage, cars, and stores or restaurants. Almost three-quarters of their reported activities occurred at home or in school, settings that generally have a great deal of adult supervision.

As Figure 11.1 indicates, 29 percent of adolescents' activities (about 4.6 hours per day) involved classwork, studying, or other "productive" activities; 31 percent (5.0 hours per day) involved maintenance; and 40 percent (6.4 hours per day) consisted of leisure pursuits, socializing being the most frequent. Figure 11.2 shows that

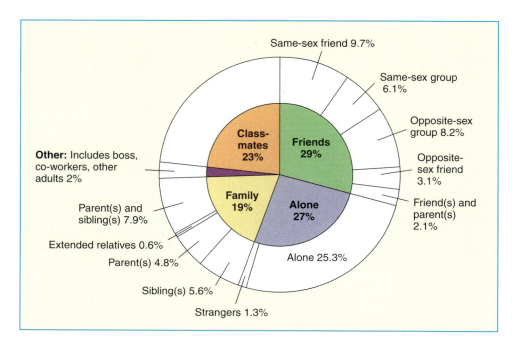

FIGURE 11.2
With Whom Adolescents Spend Their Time
Source: Csikszentmihalyi & Larson (1984).

Although leaving home is often accompanied by mixed feelings, the overall quality of adolescent-parent relationships often improves after teenagers have left.

about one-fifth (19 percent) of their waking hours were spent alone and more than half were spent with peers, 27 percent in class and 29 percent outside the classroom.

Relationships with Parents

Even though the majority of teens get along well with their parents on a daily basis, parent-teenager relationships are likely to feel slightly unstable or "out of joint" some of the time (Csikszentmihalyi & Larson, 1984). In part, this is because teenagers are likely to perceive discrepancies between themselves and their parents in how their families function—whether individuals really get along with one another, for example, and who really makes decisions around the house (C. Carlson et al., 1991). Parents may think they listen to their teenager's opinions about what household chores she should do, but she herself may regard the "listening" as shallow or meaningless, since parents evidently decide who does what chores anyway. When discrepancies such as these come into the open, conflicts usually arise ("You always say X, but you really mean Y!"). That is the bad news. The good news is that the conflicts frequently serve as catalysts for further growth in teenagers' social maturity and to reconcile gaps between parents and their nearly grown children (Holmbeck & O'Donnell, 1991). An important task of adolescence is to achieve adequate psychological separation, or independence, from one's parents.

Achieving psychological separation entails four important accomplishments: *functional independence,* the ability to manage one's own personal and practical affairs with minimal help from one's parents; *attitudinal independence,* a view of oneself as unique and separate from one's parents and having a personal set of values and beliefs; *emotional independence,* freedom from being overly dependent on parents for approval, intimacy, and emotional support; and *conflictual independence,* freedom from excessive anxiety, guilt, resentment, anger, or responsibility toward one's parents (Moore, 1984, 1987; Sullivan & Sullivan, 1980). From the perspectives of adolescents themselves, the most significant indicators of successful separation from parents are gaining economic independence, living on their own, graduating from school, and being free to make their own life choices without being overly concerned about what their parents may think (Moore, 1987).

In our culture, leaving home is a powerful metaphor for achieving psychological separation, and differences in how parents and adolescents understand and react to this experience are fairly common. For example, parents generally expect their children to leave home at an older age and for a specific purpose, such as marriage. Their adolescent children, on the other hand, often expect to live on their own before they get married (Goldscheider & Goldscheider, 1987, 1989). Many of the everyday conflicts between adolescents and their parents over chores, curfews, school, and social activities reflect different perspectives about the approaching separation. Adolescents' tendency to view themselves as increasingly emancipated from their parents' conventional perspectives and control may create conflict between a parent's need to maintain the usual family norms while allowing the child increasing independence (Smetana, 1988).

The changes and conflicts teenagers experience often stimulate similar unresolved feelings in their parents. As one parent put it, "Sometimes I'm not sure which is more upsetting to me, my teenage daughter's pain and confusion about who she is or similar feelings that are stirred up from my own difficult adolescence." Higher levels of parent-adolescent conflict are more likely to occur in families experiencing divorce, economic hardship, or other serious stressors (Flanagan, 1990; Smetana et al., 1991). Keep in mind, too, that high overall levels of adolescent-parent conflict are frequently a continuation of a pattern that existed during middle childhood.

The overall quality of adolescent-parent relationships often improves for adolescents who have successfully left home and are living on their own, as we will discuss in Chapter 13. In one study, students who no longer lived at home during their first year of college showed greater affection toward their parents, improved communication, and a greater sense of independence than students who remained living at home (Sullivan & Sullivan, 1980). Reasons for leaving home are, of course, quite important. Separating is often much more difficult for adolescents who leave home because of stressful family relationships. They are more likely to experience feelings of emotional detachment, broken ties, irregular communication, and visits home that are uncomfortable and infrequent (Moore, 1984).

Despite the many changes taking place, however, the majority of adolescents and parents continue to get along rather well together. They also tend to share similar attitudes and values about important issues and decisions such as ideas of right and wrong, what makes a marriage good, or the long-run value of education. (Collins, 1991; Csikszentmihalyi & Larson, 1984; Larson & Richards, 1994; Youniss & Smollar, 1985).

Where adolescents and parents do differ is in the emphasis, or strength, of those attitudes and values. Most disagreements between teens and parents are about matters affecting the teenager's current social life and behavior, such as styles of dress, hair length, choices of friends, dating, curfews, telephone use, participation in household chores and family activities, and choice of music. For preferences such as these, teenagers agree more with their peers than with their parents. Yet when it comes to the basic attitudes and values that guide long-term life choices, adolescents have consistently rated their parents' advice more highly than their friends' (C. Carlson et al., 1991).

Parenting Styles   During adolescence, a fine line exists between sensitive, respectful parental involvement and intrusive overinvolvement that fails to adequately appreciate adolescents' need for separateness and independence. As in the early and middle childhood years, a parent-adolescent relationship that establishes a secure emotional base is most likely to result in a mutually satisfactory exploration of autonomy and relatedness (Allen et al., 1994). Adolescents whose families display an *authoritative parenting style* (high levels of acceptance, supervision, and respect for children's autonomy) and a high degree of parental involvement in schooling have been found to experience better relationships at home and better performance and social adjustment at school (Smetana, 1995; Steinberg et al., 1992).

Of course, not all families provide this type of relationship. While warm, caring, and supportive parenting appears to be associated with constructive and effective solutions to family problems and positive overall adjustment, parent-child relationships that are hostile and uncooperative frequently result in conflict and failure (Fuhrman & Holmbeck, 1995; Rueter & Conger, 1995).

Parenting style and the quality of the parent-child relationship can exert influence far beyond the boundaries of the family. This is important, since during adolescence youngsters spend increasing amounts of time outside the home. Contact among parents in a community and between adolescents and nonfamilial adults can benefit (or harm) children by creating and supporting shared community expectations regarding adolescent behavior (Coleman, 1988). Anne Fletcher and her colleagues surveyed approximately forty-five hundred fourteen-to-eighteen-year-olds concerning their families' parenting practices and their own academic achievement, psychosocial competence, behavior problems, and internalized distress. Adolescents whose friends described their parents as authoritative earned higher grades in school, spent more time on homework, felt more academically competent, and reported lower levels of delinquency and substance abuse (Fletcher et al., 1995).

How children perceive their relationships with their parents may also influence their relationships with peers, particularly during early adolescence (Fuligni & Eccles, 1993). Early adolescents strongly desire relationships with parents that are less restrictive and provide increased opportunities to participate in decisions that affect their own lives. Children who fail to perceive these opportunities may lose hope that their parents will ever acknowledge that they are maturing and deserve to be treated more like adults. These teenagers may sacrifice developmentally important experiences with adults for the sake of peer relationships that appear to offer greater opportunity for respect and support. They are less likely to seek advice from their parents and more likely to consult with friends about important issues. In some cases, they may orient toward peers so strongly that they are willing to forgo their parents' rules, their schoolwork, and even their own talents to ensure peer acceptance (Fuligni & Eccles, 1993).

Although parent-adolescent alienation and excessive peer orientation can have serious negative long-term implications, this is the exception rather than the rule. More commonly, the parent-child relationship undergoes positive changes during middle and later adolescence and is frequently aided by constructive relationships that teenagers develop with other adults, including relatives, teachers, coaches, camp counselors, and other community members.

In summary, parents and adolescents get along best when decision making is consistent and collaborative, decisions are perceived as being fair and reasonable rather than arbitrary, and the developmental needs and sensitivities of all family members, both parents and children, are respected. Self-reliance and self-control and the successful academic and social achievement associated with authoritative parenting during childhood are also fostered by these qualities during the adolescent years (Baumrind, 1989, 1991a; Hart et al., 1990).

SES Differences   As noted earlier, adolescents are significantly influenced by the type of family in which they grow up. One useful way to describe families is by **SES** (*socioeconomic status,* or *social class*), which is determined by parents' levels of education, incomes, and type of work, as well as by their lifestyles and cultural values. Studies of families in the United States, Great Britain, and Italy have found that differences between the values, childrearing practices, and expectations of middle-class parents and those of working- and lower-class parents closely parallel differences in the amount of autonomy, independence, and satisfaction enjoyed in their day-to-day work experiences (Greenberger et al., 1994; Kohn, 1969; Kohn et al., 1986).

These studies found that adolescents in middle-class families were encouraged to be independent and to regulate or control their own behavior rather than rely on the rewards or punishments of others to determine how they would act. The parents' childrearing styles tended to be democratic or authoritative rather than authoritarian. Working-class parents were much more authoritarian than middle-class parents in their childrearing patterns and were less likely to support their children's attempts to be independent and participate in family decision making until their children were ready to leave home (Kohn, 1969; Kohn et al., 1986).

Recent research supports these findings (Greenberger et al, 1994; Steinberg et al., 1991). For example, Laurence Steinberg and his colleagues found similar relationships among parenting styles and SES in a sample of ten thousand ninth-through-twelfth-grade students from different ethnic backgrounds and family structures (biological parents or other parenting arrangement). Authoritative parenting (based on student reports of high levels of parental acceptance, control, and autonomy) was generally more common in middle-class than in working-class families, although ethnic differences and differences in family structure were also important. Table 11.2 presents the percentages of authoritative families for each level of SES and ethnic group. In addition, for all ethnic groups and family types, adolescents from authoritative families had better school grades, were more self-reliant, and exhibited less delinquent behavior than those from nonauthoritative families (Steinberg et al., 1991).

Divorce, Remarriage, and Single Parenthood

The impact of separation and divorce on adolescent development depends on a variety of factors. These include when the divorce occurs, the nature and duration of family conflict before and after the divorce, the quality of the child's relationship with each parent, and the family's economic circumstances following the divorce. Separation from the father early in life seems to have a greater effect on both girls and boys than later separation does (Frost & Pakiz, 1990; Hetherington & Clingempeel, 1992; Wallerstein & Corbin, 1989). (See Chapter 9 for additional discussion.)

TABLE 11.2: *Percentages of Families with Authoritative Parenting Styles in Different SES Levels, Ethnic Groups, and Parenting Situations*

Ethnic Group	Working-Class Family Structure		Middle-Class Family Structure	
	Biological Parents	Other*	Biological Parents	Other
White	17.2	11.5	15.0	17.6
African American	13.4	12.2	14.0	16.0
Hispanic	10.7	9.8	15.8	12.9
Asian	7.5	6.1	15.6	10.8

Adapted from Steinberg et al. (1991), Table 1, p. 25.

*Includes single-parent households, stepfamilies, and other family arrangements.

SES differences: *Middle-class parents were more likely to be authoritative than working-class parents in all ethnic groups, with the exception of white biological parents.*

Ethnic differences: *The highest percentage of authoritative parenting occurred for whites, followed by African Americans, Hispanics, and Asians.*

Differences in family structure: *In both working-class and middle-class Hispanic and Asian families and for working-class white and African American families, authoritative parenting occurred more frequently with biological parents than with other parenting arrangements. For both middle-class white and African American families, however, authoritative parenting was less frequent with biological parents than with other parenting arrangements.*

Adolescents who experience multiple changes in parenting are most severely affected. They are much more likely to experience unhealthy family climates, display more disruptive behavior, and have poorer school achievement than children whose parenting has been more stable (Kurdek et al., 1995). Divorce and its aftermath are particularly hard for teenagers, who tend to be sensitive about being "normal" and insecure about their identities. Even ten years after the divorce, many adolescent children continue to have feelings of anger and self-blame and difficulty accepting the permanence of the divorce (Wallerstein & Blakeslee, 1989; Wallerstein & Corbin, 1989). Similar long-term consequences of divorce for adolescents and young adults have been reported for Switzerland, England, and Finland (Aro & Palosaari, 1992; Binder et al., 1981; Wadsworth et al., 1990).

Judith Wallerstein (1983) found that divorce often makes it more difficult for teenagers to achieve realistic hopes about their own love relationships. Jay, who is fourteen, said, "Dad left because Mom bored him. I do that all the time." Pamela, also fourteen, said, "I'm afraid to use the word *love*. I tell my boyfriend that I love him, but I can't really think about it without fear" (Wallerstein, 1983, p. 241). Nevertheless, most adolescents of divorce do make their way, although it usually isn't easy. Sarah, a seventeen-year-old whose parents separated when she was ten, reported the following: "My mom and I are real close now. I stopped being angry at her when I was fifteen, when I suddenly realized that all of the kids who lived in tract houses with picket fences were not any happier than I was. It took me a long, long time to stop blaming her for not being in one of those houses" (Wallerstein, 1983, p. 239).

As in middle childhood (see Chapter 9), adjustment to divorce during adolescence is strongly influenced by parents' ability to resolve their own angry feelings and allow their child to do the same. The quality of relationships with divorced parents and with current family members also appears to play a key role in how successfully these youngsters negotiate the tasks of later adolescence and early adulthood (Portes et al., 1992; Wallerstein, 1987; Wallerstein & Blakeslee, 1989).

Although a single-parent family is the most likely outcome of divorce, several other possibilities exist. The single parent may remarry and bring a stepparent into the family or may not remarry but bring a new partner into the family who serves as a "stepparent." In some cases, divorced parents continue to share parenting with or without sharing legal custody. Living with a stepparent can be particularly hard for an adolescent because of the lack of commonly accepted roles for stepparents and stepchildren and the teenager's intense need to be independent of adult control and authority. Both teenagers and their parents may also find it difficult to switch to a new set of rules and expectations (Hetherington, 1989a; Lutz, 1983). For additional discussion of living with and being a stepparent, see Chapters 9 and 13.

Although relationships with parents are very important in shaping an adolescent's development, another set of social influences are extremely important as well. In the following sections, we discuss the roles of friendship and peer relationships in adolescent development.

Friendship

Friends matter a lot during adolescence. Unlike most adults, who often try to "improve" many of a teenager's behaviors and skills, friends offer easier and more immediate acceptance and thus ease the uncertainty and insecurity of the adolescent years. They also offer reassurance, understanding and advice, and emotional and social support in stressful situations. The opportunity to share inner feelings of disappointment as well as happiness with close friends enables the adolescent to better deal with her emotional ups and downs. Furthermore, a capacity to form close, intimate friendships during adolescence is related to overall social and emotional adjustment and competence (Buhrmester, 1990; Reid et al., 1989).

Sharing interests with friends is important to teenagers, as it is to children. At the same time, though, less tangible qualities such as loyalty, mutual respect, and intimacy become increasingly important in friends, especially among older adolescents.

Especially during early and middle adolescence, friendships help teens to become more independent of parents and other authority figures and to resist the seemingly arbitrary demands of family living. Friends provide one another with cognitive and social scaffolding that differs from what nonfriends provide. Having good friends supports positive developmental outcomes during periods of developmental change (Hartup, 1996). Friends also promote independence simply by providing knowledge of a world beyond the family. Teenagers learn that not every young person is required to be home by the same hour every night, that some parents expect their children to do more household chores than other parents do, and that other families hold different religious or political views. The processes of sharing feelings and beliefs and exploring new ideas and opinions with friends play an important role in helping adolescents define their sense of self (Rawlins, 1992).

Qualities of Adolescent Friendships   Friends strongly influence an adolescent's development by virtue of their positive and negative characteristics, attitudes, values, and behaviors and through the quality of the friendship. A friendship based on mutual respect and trust, intimacy, and prosocial behavior is likely to help the adolescent cope with stressful situations in the family and in school. Friendships that lack these qualities are likely to be less helpful or even destructive (Dusek, 1991; Hartup, 1996).

During the teenage years, the basis of what makes a close friendship changes. When asked to define close friendships and how they are initiated, maintained, and ended, adolescents report that *mutual understanding* and *intimacy* are most important, whereas school-age children emphasize shared activities. Unlike cooperation between younger children, adolescent mutuality depends on the understanding that other people share some of one's own abilities, interests, and inner experiences and on an appreciation of each person's uniqueness. In fact, early adolescents share a fascination with the particular interests, life histories, and personalities of their friends; young teenagers want to understand friends as unique individuals and be understood by them in the same way. The ability of adolescents to recognize the advantages of complementary relationships—relationships in which two people with different strengths and abilities cooperate for mutual benefit—makes possible friendships that involve greater commitment, permanence, and loyalty. Intimacy in adolescent friendships includes self-revelation, confidence (in keeping secrets), and a sense of exclusivity (Damon, 1983; Youniss, 1980).

Gender Differences   Friendships formed by boys generally involve lower levels of intimacy than those of girls, who are better able to express feelings and more comfortable with giving emotional support to one another. During the junior high and early high school years, girls appear to develop greater intimacy with the opposite sex than boys do. They also tend to have one or two close friends, whereas adolescent boys often have many friends with whom they are less intimate. Adolescent boys may be more likely to equate intense intimacy exclusively with heterosexual friendships, whereas girls at this age can be comfortably close with both male and female friends. Toward the end of the eleventh grade, however, differences between same-sex and opposite-sex friends decrease (Buhrmester & Furman, 1987; Furman & Buhrmester, 1992; Sharabany et al., 1981). We take a closer look at these and related issues later in this chapter.

Interethnic Friendships   Friendships between adolescents from different ethnic groups tend to be the exceptions. One national study of students enrolled in more than one thousand public and private high schools in the United States found that fewer than 3.5 percent of the eighteen thousand friendships identified by students involved African American and white friends (Hallinan & Williams, 1989). As we saw in Chapter 9's discussion of psychosocial development in middle childhood, the social contexts in which potential friendship interactions occur seem to make an important difference. In a recent study of school and neighborhood friendship patterns among African American and white students attending integrated junior high schools, most students reported having a close other-race school friend, but only about one-quarter saw such a friend frequently outside school. Interracial school friendships that extended to nonschool settings were significantly more common among youngsters who lived in integrated rather than segregated neighborhoods (DuBois & Hirsch, 1990; Giordano et al., 1993).

Peer Groups

Peer groups play an even greater role in the everyday lives of adolescents than they do for younger children. They also tend to be more structured and organized, frequently include individuals from a relatively wide age range, and are much less likely to be all male or all female (Dusek, 1991; Furman, 1989). Peer groups are an important component of an adolescent's *social convoy,* the network of social relationships that follow a person over his or her lifetime, changing in structure but providing continuity in the exchange of support, as we will see in Chapter 17 on psychosocial development in late adulthood. Who is included in this social convoy of support is determined by the adolescent's emotional attachment to the person and by the person's role in the adolescent's life (Levitt et al., 1993). Peers provide a teenager with critical information about who he is, how he should act, what he is like, and so forth. They offer him an environment for making social comparisons between his own actions, attitudes, and feelings and those of others. These are important ingredients in an adolescent's development of self-concept and identity

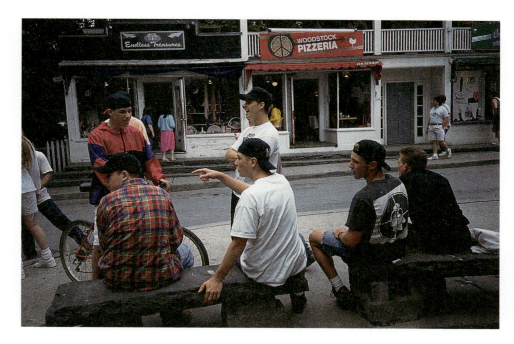

It is probably no coincidence that all these teenagers wear similar clothing. Adolescent peer groups do encourage conformity, although they also allow for a certain amount of diversity and role distinctions among their members.

(Connolly et al., 1987). Most important, peer groups provide a support base outside of the family from which the teenager can more freely try on the different identity roles that ultimately will contribute to her adult personality: popular, brain, normal, druggie, outcast, partyer, punk, grind, clown, banger, nerd, lover, and so forth (B. Brown et al., 1993; Durbin et al., 1993; Gavin & Furman, 1989). Peer groups can also exert powerful pressures to conform. Especially when the family fails to serve as a constructive corrective force, such pressures may contribute to a prolonged period of identity diffusion or to premature identity foreclosure, for example, as a teenage parent, drug addict, or gang member (Dishion et al., 1988; Patterson & Dishion, 1985).

Peer Group Structure   Adolescent peer groups generally are of two types, the clique and the crowd. The **clique** is a small, closely knit group of two or more members (with an average of six members) who are intimately involved in a number of shared purposes and activities and exclude those who are not. The **crowd** is a larger, less cohesive group of between fifteen and thirty members (with an average of twenty members) and generally consists of from two to four cliques (Dunphy, 1963).

Clique membership allows a teenager to have a few select friends whom she or he knows well and who share important interests and activities, whereas membership in a crowd provides contact with a much broader group of peers on a more casual basis. The small size and intimacy of a clique make it like a family in which the adolescent can feel comfortable and secure. The major clique activity seems to be talking, and cliques generally meet during the school week. Advantages of clique membership include security, a feeling of importance, and acquisition of socially acceptable behaviors (such as academic, social, or athletic competence) that are part of conforming to the clique's norms. However, conformity can also suppress individuality and may promote "in-group" snobbishness, intolerance, and other negative values and behaviors. Involvement with a clique of antisocial peers is associated with various adolescent adjustment problems, including substance abuse, dropping out of school, delinquency, and gang membership, although which is cause and which is effect is uncertain (Dishion et al., 1988; Patterson & Dishion, 1985).

Can Parents Influence Their Adolescent's Choice of Peer Group?

It has been a long accepted view that parental influence sharply declines during adolescence due to the increasing counterinfluence of peer groups over which parents have little control. However, recent large-scale studies of high school students have challenged this view.

Bradford Brown and his colleagues studied parenting practices and peer affiliation in a sample of more than thirty-seven hundred high school students ages drawn from a variety of socioeconomic brackets, ethnic backgrounds, family structures (e.g., first-time two-parent, divorced, remarried), and types of communities (urban, suburban, and rural) (B. Brown et al., 1993). To determine peer group affiliation, they asked school administrators to identify a set of boys and girls in each grade, within each ethnic group in multiethnic schools, who represented a good cross-section of the student body. They then interviewed these students in small groups composed of individuals of the same sex, grade level, and ethnic background. Each group then developed a list of the school's major crowds and identified two boys and two girls in the same grade who were the leaders or most prominent members of each crowd.

A sample of the identified leaders, each accompanied by a friend of her or his own choosing, were then individually interviewed and asked to place each student in the same grade level in one of the crowds that had been named. In addition, the entire sample of students were surveyed about family characteristics, parenting practices, and adolescent behaviors related to academics, drug use, and self-reliance.

Brown and his colleagues found that differences in levels of authoritative parenting as reflected by parental monitoring, encouragement of achievement, and support for joint decision making were significantly associated with teenagers' levels of academic achievement, drug use, and self-reliance. These factors, in turn, were closely related to the type of crowd an adolescent belonged to (popular, jock, brain, normal, druggie, and outcast). Figure 11.3 diagrams the relationships among parenting practices, adolescent behaviors, and peer group membership.

The authors concluded that parents have the capacity to indirectly influence the behaviors by which teenagers become associated with a particular crowd and that peer group norms serve to reinforce behaviors and predispositions to which parents have already contributed through their parenting strategies and/or family background characteristics. Although parenting practices and family background cannot *determine* a teenager's crowd affiliation, their influence should be taken seriously.

How might this parental influence work? In a survey of approximately forty-five hundred fourteen-to-eighteen-year-olds from the same schools we have just described, Anne Fletcher and her colleagues attempted to answer this question (Fletcher et al., 1995). They asked students about parenting practices in their families and about their academic achievement, psychosocial competence, behavior problems, and personal distress. The researchers also asked each student's friends to independently evaluate the degree to which authoritative parenting was present in the peer network, as indicated by parental acceptance and involvement, behavioral supervision and strictness, and granting of psychological autonomy.

What did they find? Adolescents whose friends described their parents as authoritative earned higher grades in school, spent more time on homework, had more positive perceptions of their academic competence, and reported lower levels of delinquency and substance abuse. Fletcher and her colleagues suggest that authoritative parenting is associated with adolescent competence; that competent, well-adjusted adolescents with authoritative parents select (and are selected by) peers who are similar in competence and background;

Crowds usually gather at parties and other organized social functions, which typically take place on weekends. They tend to include both males and females, thereby providing opportunities for mixed-gender interactions and promoting transition from same-gender to mixed-gender cliques. Crowd membership also provides opportunities to interact with individuals from a broad range of backgrounds and experiences, but can also promote snobbishness and can pose real or imagined threats to parental and teacher authority.

Parental Influence   Parents of adolescents are frequently concerned that their children will be excessively influenced by peer pressure and that peer influence will replace their own guidance. Laurence Steinberg and Anne Levine (1990) suggest that parents can help their adolescents with their friendships and relationships with peers in a number of ways. Table 11.3 lists these guidelines. The accompanying Perspectives box discusses recent research findings on parental influence.

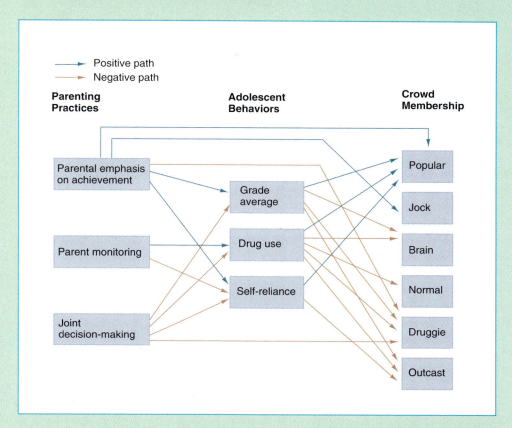

FIGURE 11.3

Parenting Practices, Adolescent Behaviors, and Crowd Membership
Parenting practices such as emphasis on achievement, monitoring of teenagers' behaviors, and joint decision making positively influence adolescents' grade averages, drug use, and self-reliance. These adolescent behaviors, in turn, are associated with the type(s) of crowd(s) a teen belongs to, as indicated by the arrows.
Source: B. Brown et al. (1993), Figure 3, p. 476.

and that experiences within their peer group maintain and strengthen their higher level of adjustment. Less competent adolescents with nonauthoritative parents are more likely to select peers who are similar to themselves, thus maintaining and amplifying their limitations. The presence of authoritativeness among one's friends' parents may decrease the likelihood that an adolescent will engage in delinquent activities due to the higher level of shared social control provided by a network of authoritative parents.

The Influence of School and Work

In the United States and other modern, industrialized countries, school plays a central role in adolescents' development. American teenagers spend most of their days attending school, engaging in extracurricular activities, and doing homework. Laws that require them to attend school until age sixteen, social expectations, parental pressures, and vocational requirements help keep most adolescents in high school through graduation and, increasingly, in post–high school education of some kind, as we will see in Chapter 12's discussion of cognitive development in early adulthood.

Schools serve two primary functions: they provide students with an opportunity to grow socially and emotionally, and they offer them the skills and knowledge they need to become economically independent and productive members of society (Dusek, 1991). As we saw in Chapter 9, schools influence identity development

TABLE 11.3   *Guidelines for Parents Concerning Their Adolescents' Friends*

Helping Adolescents to Deal with Peer Pressure

- Build self-esteem by helping your adolescent discover her or his strengths and special talents.
- Encourage independence and decision making within the family.
- Talk about situations in which people have to choose among competing pressures and demands.
- Encourage your adolescent to anticipate difficult situations and plan ahead.
- Encourage your adolescent to form alliances with peers who share his or her values and your family's values.
- Know your adolescent's friends.
- Don't jump to hasty conclusions based on peers' appearance, dress, language, or interests.
- Allow time for peer activities.
- Remain close to your adolescent.

When to Be Concerned

- If your adolescent has no friends at all.
- If your adolescent is secretive about her or his social life.
- If your adolescent suddenly loses all interest in friends.
- If all of your adolescent's friends are much older than him or her.

Source: Adapted from Steinberg & Levine (1990), pp. 183–187.

through the academic demands of the *formal curriculum,* which includes basic knowledge and skills in such areas as reading, writing, mathematics, and science, and through an *informal curriculum,* which exposes students to teachers (and peers) who serve as role models for academic achievement, motivation to learn, skill mastery, self-improvement, assumption of responsibility and leadership, and respect for authority.

For early adolescents, the transition to middle school or junior high school may be a period of increased social and emotional stress. Compared to students who remain in elementary school through eighth grade, students entering junior high school appear to have less positive attitudes toward school, poorer academic achievement, less adequate leadership skills, and lower levels of participation in ex-

For many high school students, working a moderate number of hours provides an opportunity outside of the home for gaining experience and the material rewards needed to have an independent life with peers.

tracurricular activities following school entry. Girls display a drop in self-esteem, and boys are more likely to be bullied than boys who remain in elementary school for seventh and eighth grades (Eccles et al., 1993; Simmons & Blyth, 1987).

School transition is particularly difficult for low-SES urban youth. In one study, the negative effects of transition to junior high included decline in self-esteem, inadequate preparation for class, and lower grades. Daily hassles with the school increased while social support and extracurricular involvement decreased, and peer values were perceived as more antisocial. These changes were common across races/ethnic groups and for both sexes (Seidman et al., 1994).

Critics have questioned whether the structure, curriculum, and overall climate of the middle school fits the developmental needs of early adolescents. They suggest that young adolescents still require a protective school environment that provides levels of supervision and support from teachers, administrators, and parents that will allow them to safely develop autonomy and independence. In these critics' view, middle or junior high school settings should be more like elementary schools, and transitions between settings should be more gradual (Eccles et al., 1993; Eccles & Harold, 1993; Simmons, 1987).

School Failure and Dropping Out   Approximately 25 percent of all students drop out of high school, and dropout rates approach 60 and 70 percent in some urban high schools. Michele Fine, who has extensively studied this problem, reports that 22 percent of the poorest students drop out; dropout rates are 22.7 percent for Native Americans, 18.7 percent for Hispanics, 16.8 percent for African Americans, 12.2 percent for whites, and 4.8 percent for Asian Americans (Fine, 1991). Interviews that Fine conducted with high school students who dropped out or were forced to leave before graduating revealed a number of different reasons for leaving. Some students left because they did not believe a high school diploma is worth working for, since people they knew who did finish school remained unemployed due to an unavailability of jobs. A second group left school to provide economic and other support for their families. A third group left because their impoverished life circumstances made it too difficult for them to fit in either academically or socially. A final group dropped out because they had difficulty adjusting to the demands of teachers and school administrators and felt too alienated to continue (Fine, 1986).

Adolescents who have recently immigrated, particularly those from impoverished or war-torn countries, are also at risk for dropping out. Not only must they adjust to the economic and social stresses of a new country, language, and culture; frequently they must also deal with a profound sense of cultural exclusion and lack of social acceptance in schools whose standards for academic performance and social behavior fall far below those of their own culture. Many of these students report that the disillusionment and sense of *cultural vertigo* they experienced, rather than the other challenges they faced, caused them to lose their sense of purpose for going to school and therefore to drop out (Salett & Koslow, 1994). It is unlikely that a single set of educational standards and strategies can effectively serve the diverse needs of the many ethnic groups that attend our schools. (The accompanying Multicultural View box discusses adaptive strategies used by families of ethnic minority youth.)

How can schools for adolescents be improved? The Carnegie Council on Adolescent Development established a Task Force on Education of Young Adolescents to help answer this question for middle schools (Carnegie Council on Adolescent Development, 1989; Hamburg, 1992). The task force commissioned papers, interviewed experts, and met with teachers and principals, health professionals, and leaders of youth-serving organizations. Their main recommendations, called "Turning Points," are summarized in Table 11.4.

Many of these same recommendations apply to high schools. Ted Sizer (1992) has suggested that good schools do the following: (1) allow students and teachers to

A Multicultural View

Adaptive Strategies of Families of Minority Youth

Nearly one-third of all adolescents in the United States are from non–European American family backgrounds (see Figure 11.4), and by the year 2000 the majority of children in our school systems will belong to ethnic minority groups from diverse cultural backgrounds (Carnegie Council on Adolescent Development, 1992). Ethnic minority families face many challenges. These include mastering a new language and set of cultural norms; coping with the economic, social, and emotional stresses of relocation; and dealing with the negative stereotypes, ethnic and racial prejudice, and economic and social discrimination they frequently encounter. *Adaptive strategies* are the unique cultural patterns ethnic minorities use to promote the survival and well-being of the community, families, and individual members of the group. Adaptive strategies help them gain access to educational, medical, political, and legal services, employment, housing, and other important resources and services. These strategies are reflected in the childrearing goals and practices found in these groups (Harrison et al., 1990). Three of the most important adaptive strategies are (1) the extended family, (2) biculturalism, and (3) ancestral world views.

The *extended family* includes parents, children, and other relatives such as aunts, uncles, grandparents, and cousins, as well as some individuals not biologically related. In African American extended families, for example, the high degree of interdependence among three or more generations of kin (child, parent, grandparent), as well as nonbiological family members, helps to provide the material aid such as food, shelter, clothing, money, child care, household maintenance, and social and emotional support that are critical for effective family functioning (Harrison et al., 1990; Stack, 1981). Hispanic American families also show high degrees of connectedness, loyalty, and solidarity with parents and other relatives and of interdependence and mutual support (McGoldrick et al., 1982).

Biculturalism involves the ability to function optimally in more than one cultural context and to flexibly switch patterns of thinking and behaving in ways that are appropriate and adaptive to what the particular situation demands. Benefits of bicultural (and multicultural) competence include greater cognitive flexibility and the ability to appreciate differing cultural values and perspectives (Harrison et al., 1990).

Ancestral world views refer to the basic beliefs and assumptions held by a given culture regarding human beings and the world in which they live. For example, the dominant European American world view emphasizes an *individual self* that places motivations, rights, and responsibilities primarily within the individual. In Asian cultures, two additional senses of self also are present: a "familial self," based on a person's relationships, roles, responsibilities, and expectations as an inseparable part of the extended family, and a "spiritual self," which reflects one's relationship to religious beliefs, practices, and philosophical orientations (Roland, 1988). In many Native American tribal cultures, for example, adolescents commonly undertake a quest for a guardian spirit. Once attained, the person's relationship with that spirit plays a major role in guiding future life choices and development (Harrison et al., 1990). Ancestral world views emphasize *collectivism,* or loyalty to the family and group, and a more fluid, flexible, and multidimensional sense of self than is the case in the majority European American culture, both of which may help ethnic minorities deal with the challenges they face.

Adaptive strategies appear to be related to two important aspects of childrearing among ethnic minority families. The first is a *positive orientation toward ethnic groups* (their own and others), which helps to promote biculturalism and acceptance of ancestral world views by teaching children to view their role within the family and society in terms of relationships and obligations to the

work and learn in their own appropriate ways, (2) insist that students clearly exhibit mastery of their schoolwork, (3) provide appropriate and effective incentives for students and teachers, (4) focus students' work on using their minds, and (5) keep the structure simple and therefore flexible. Ernest Boyer (1983), who conducted a nationwide study of secondary (high school) education in the United States, found that successful, high-quality high schools emphasized high academic standards; a common, core curriculum; flexible electives; and a humanistic approach to education that considered the developmental needs of the students and communities they served.

Despite the shortcomings just discussed, the majority of high schools still do a fairly good job. Studies of a variety of successful traditional and *alternative high schools,* both private and public, indicate that high school education that is responsive to the educational and developmental needs of adolescents from the broadest range of backgrounds and life situations is possible, provided the motivation and resources are available (Lightfoot, 1983; Trickett, 1991).

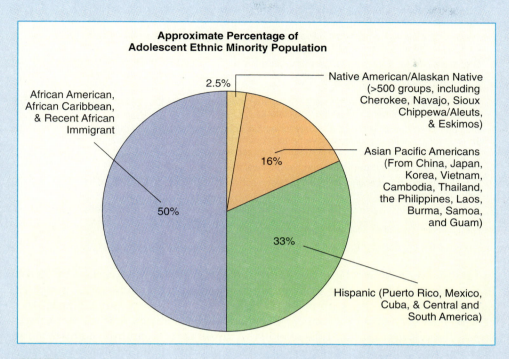

Approximate Percentage of Adolescent Ethnic Minority Population

African American, African Caribbean, & Recent African Immigrant — 50%

2.5%

Native American/Alaskan Native (>500 groups, including Cherokee, Navajo, Sioux Chippewa/Aleuts, & Eskimos)

16%

Asian Pacific Americans (From China, Japan, Korea, Vietnam, Cambodia, Thailand, the Philippines, Laos, Burma, Samoa, and Guam)

33%

Hispanic (Puerto Rico, Mexico, Cuba, & Central and South America)

FIGURE 11.4

Ethnic Minority Youth in the United States
Adolescents with African origins make up the largest percentage of ethnic minority youth in the United States, followed by adolescents from Hispanic, Asian Pacific, and Native American/Alaskan Native backgrounds.
Source: Adapted from Harrison et al. (1990), p. 350.

family and to maintain solidarity with their ethnic group. The second, a stress on *socialization for interdependence,* is a logical extension of an emphasis on interdependence within extended families and of the ancestral world view of collectivism. Given the formidable barriers to achieve-ment confronting ethnic minorities in American society, the pathway frequently has been through collective actions that create opportunities for individual achievement (Harrison et al., 1990).

Employment The majority of teenagers report participating in "formal" paid work outside the home, and many others engage in "informal" paid work such as babysit-ting and yardwork within their own homes (Fine et al., 1990; Mortimer et al., 1992a). Informal work is likely to be a first paid job. Because it is fairly continuous with the chores and responsibilities of childhood, it provides a more gradual transi-tion to the demands of adult work. Formal adult work typically takes place in com-mercial or other organizational settings. It represents a greater departure from childhood work and involves more impersonal relationships with adults, closer su-pervision, and more systematic monitoring of job performance (Mortimer et al., 1992b). The types of jobs frequently reported by teenagers include supermarket, restaurant, or retail store worker; bus driver; office worker; and semiskilled worker (Green, 1990).

Work during adolescence serves three important functions. First, it facilitates the transition from school to work. Second, it provides structure for involvement

TABLE 11.4:   *Turning Points: Recommendations for Transforming Middle School Education*

1. Create communities for learning by dividing large middle-grade schools into smaller ones.
2. Teach a core curriculum of substantive knowledge to all students in ways that foster curiosity, problem solving, and critical thinking.
3. Organize schools in ways that maximize opportunities for success for *all* students through cooperative learning, flexible scheduling, and expanded opportunities for learning within and outside of the school.
4. Provide teacher training that specifically prepares teachers to meet the unique academic and developmental needs of young adolescents.
5. Shift primary responsibility and authority for middle schools to teachers and principals, and establish community-school governance committees composed of teachers, parents, administrators, support staff, and community representatives.
6. Create school environments that promote physical and mental health.
7. Establish respectful, working alliances between school staff and parents of middle school students.
8. Establish cooperative partnerships between the school and community organizations.

Sources: Carnegie Council on Adolescent Development (1989); Hamburg (1992).

in family- and school-related activities. Finally, it provides an arena outside of home and school for gaining social experience and the material rewards needed to have an independent life with peers (Green, 1990). How work influences adolescent mental health and adjustment depends on the type and level of workplace stress, the relevance of job-related skills to future careers, and the compatibility between the demands and experiences of work and school (Mortimer et al., 1992a).

The intensity of formal work as measured by the number of hours worked per month is also important. Students who work more than ten hours per week do more poorly academically, report more psychological problems (depression, anxiety, fatigue, sleeping difficulty), and physical problems (headaches, stomachaches, colds) than other students. They are also more likely to use drugs, smoke cigarettes, and engage in delinquent activities, regardless of ethnicity, SES, or age. In contrast, working fewer than ten hours per week generally appears to have no negative effects. (Mortimer et al., 1992a, 1992b; Steinberg et al., 1993; Steinberg & Dornbusch, 1991). Additional research is needed to rule out the possibility that students with intensive work involvements had more problems to begin with.

For most high school students, working more than a moderate number of hours per week may be developmentally unwise, because it interferes with academic activities, exposes them to negative environments and role models, and limits the amount of monitoring and supervision they receive from parents, teachers, and other positive role models. Many students, particularly those receiving appropriate levels of adult monitoring and support, make sensible decisions about the role of work in their lives, adjusting their choice of work and number of hours to meet their other important academic and social needs (Green, 1990). We will continue our discussion of the developmental impact of work in the adulthood chapters that follow.

What Do You Think?

Think about your own separation and individuation with regard to your parents. How similar were your concerns to those described in the chapter?

In what ways are your own experiences similar to the text's description of the development of friendship and peer groups? In what ways do they differ?

SEXUALITY DURING ADOLESCENCE

The popular idea that adolescence is a highly sexual period of life is correct. However, people tend to focus on sexual intercourse and the risks of pregnancy rather than the broader pattern of interrelated changes involved. During adolescence, the expression of sexual urges interacts closely with the need to establish a secure sexual identity that is reasonably free from anxiety and the need for intimate relationships with others.

Sexual Fantasies and Masturbation

Sexual fantasies about real or imaginary situations often accompany masturbation, although adolescents of all ages report having sexual fantasies throughout their waking hours. Both sexes have reported that they most commonly fantasize about "petting or having intercourse with someone [they] are fond of or in love with" (P. Miller & Simon, 1980). Regarding the second most common fantasy, however, males reported imagining anonymous sex ("petting or having intercourse with someone you don't know"), whereas females reported imagining intimate but not explicitly sexual activity ("doing nonsexual things with someone you are fond of or in love with").

Approximately 70 percent of boys and 45 percent of girls surveyed have reported having masturbated by age fifteen, and about 65 percent of boys and 50 percent of girls ages sixteen to nineteen have reported masturbating once a week or more. Sexually experienced adolescents tended to masturbate more than those who were less experienced, but boys tended to give up masturbation when they were involved in an ongoing sexual relationship, whereas girls tended to masturbate more often (Coles & Stokes, 1985; Dreyer, 1982). Feelings of discomfort and guilt resulting from cultural and religious beliefs about masturbation have decreased in recent years. However, many teenagers still find the subject embarrassing; fewer than a third of teenagers questioned in one study reported that they felt no guilt at all (Coles & Stokes, 1985). It is likely that current efforts to encourage safe sexual practices in the face of the threat of AIDS will lead to increased acceptance of and decreased guilt about masturbation.

Heterosexuality

Sexual Experience   During the last thirty years, sexual activity among college-age adolescents has significantly increased, particularly among females. As Figure 11.5 shows, in the mid-1960s only 29 percent of college-age females and 65 percent of males reported having had premarital intercourse; in 1980, roughly 63 percent of college females and 77 percent of college males reported having had premarital intercourse at least once; and by 1988, 74 percent of college females and 82 percent of college males reported having had premarital intercourse (Murstein et al., 1989; Robinson & Jedlicka, 1982). The percentage of college-age men and women who report having had sex with only one person and believing in having sex only with someone they are deeply involved with emotionally has also increased (Abler & Sedlacek, 1989).

The timing of first sexual intercourse is related to several factors. First intercourse at an early age is more likely with early puberty, a personality style that is risk taking and impulsive, a history of substance abuse, fewer years of education, a single-parent family, low SES, and nonwhite ethnicity. First intercourse at a later age is more likely with late timing of puberty, a personality style that includes a religious

For these teenage couples, the junior/senior prom is an opportunity to experiment with intimacy, sexuality, commitment, as well as other complex activities and roles associated with adulthood.

orientation and traditional values, absence of substance use, higher levels of education, a two-parent family, high SES, and white or Hispanic ethnicity (B. Miller & Moore, 1990; Sonenstein et al., 1991).

Sexual Attitudes   Although types of sexual activity may now be fairly similar for boys and girls, differences in attitudes and expectations persist. On the whole, girls still tend to be more conservative than boys in their sexual attitudes, values, and actions, whereas boys tend to be more sexually active and to have more sexual encounters. Girls are more likely to emphasize intimacy and love as a necessary part of sexual activity and less likely to engage in sex merely as a physically pleasurable activity (Leigh, 1989; S. White & DeBlassie, 1992). One study of thirty-six hundred Canadian high school students found that although there was fairly high agreement between males and females about holding hands and kissing on the first date and a fair degree of agreement regarding necking, males were much more likely to think it was all right to pet on the first date and to have intercourse either on the first date or after a few dates (Bibby & Posterski, 1985).

When asked to recall their reasons for first intercourse and how they felt about the experience, female and male college students differ. While both frequently report that "we both wanted to," were curious, and loved or cared deeply about their partners, many more women cite partner pressure and many more men report sexual arousal and a desire to "score" as reasons (Koch, 1988).

Women and men also differ in their emotional reactions to their first experience with intercourse. Both are equally likely to say it was "okay," "fine," or "all right"; however, men more frequently report that it was "pleasant," "pleasurable," "terrific," or "fantastic," whereas women are more likely to say it was neither positive nor negative or that it was a disappointment or a disaster (Koch, 1988). Women also are more likely than men to have been in a committed relationship and to have had intercourse again with their first partner (Darling et al., 1992).

Dating   Since the beginning of this century, dating has tended to begin earlier, thus increasing the time span over which teenage dating takes place. Currently many adolescent girls begin dating at age twelve and boys at age thirteen, with almost one-half of boys and more than one-half of girls reporting dating at least once a

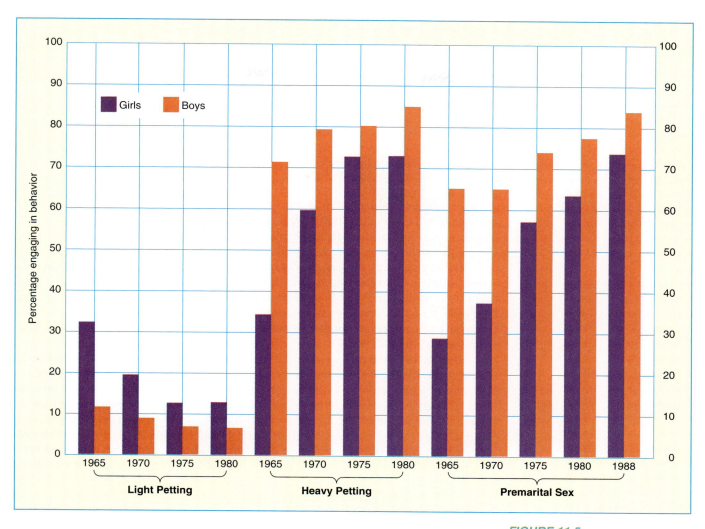

FIGURE 11.5

Sexual Activity among Older Adolescents, 1965–1988
Sources: Murstein et al. (1989); Robinson & Jedlicka (1982).

week and approximately one-third dating two or three times per week. Only 10 percent of male and female seniors report never having dated (Savin-Williams & Berndt, 1990).

Dating is a major avenue for exploring sexual activity. In recent years, there has been a growing awareness that dating situations may lead to sexual activity that is coerced. It is estimated that as many as 25 percent of sixteen-to-nineteen-year-old females are victims of *date rape*, a situation in which a person, usually a female, is forced to have sex with a person she is dating (Sorenson & Bowie, 1994). In one large-scale study of college men and women, more than three-quarters of the women reported having been treated in a sexually aggressive way (being forced to engage in sexual acts ranging from kissing to petting to sexual intercourse) and more than one-half of the men reported acting in a sexually aggressive manner on a date, either in high school or in college (Muehlenhard & Linton, 1987).

Date rape and other forms of sexual aggression were most likely to occur between two partners who knew each other fairly well, often for almost a year prior to the incident. It was also more likely when a man initiated the date, provided transportation, and paid for the date, and was also more likely if both people got drunk and ended up in the man's dorm room or apartment (Muehlenhard & Linton, 1987). The cultural expectation that the boy initiate sexual activity and the girl limit how far to go and the persistent tendency in our culture to blame the victim continue to contribute to this problem (Blumberg & Lester, 1991).

Nonheterosexual Orientations

Due largely to the political and educational efforts of the "equal rights" and "gay rights" movements, public acceptance of gay, lesbian, and bisexual orientations has increased significantly during the past several decades. This acceptance acknowledges the right of individuals to freely practice their own sexual orientations and lifestyles and to receive protection from discrimination. In one interview study, approximately two-thirds of the adolescent respondents said that in principle they approved of same-sex petting and kissing in its various forms (Dreyer, 1982). However, other researchers have found that **homophobia** (dislike and fear of homosexuals) remains strong among adolescents. One study found that 75 percent of females and 84 percent of males expressed disgust for homosexual acts; however, females seemed to be more tolerant of homosexuality and less fearful about being identified as homosexual than males were (Stokes, 1985). Another found that most heterosexual college students, both male and female, would not want to marry someone who had had even a single homosexual experience (Williams & Jacoby, 1989).

Reliable statistics on sexual orientation are difficult to obtain. In one large-scale study of thirty-eight thousand adolescents in grades seven through twelve, 88.2 percent described themselves as predominantly heterosexual (exclusively interested in the other sex), 1.1 percent as predominantly homosexual or bisexual (interested in members of both sexes), and 10.7 percent as uncertain about their sexual orientation (Remafedi et al., 1992).

Because of persisting widespread homophobia, gay, lesbian, and bisexual adolescents are likely to experience feelings of attraction for members of the same sex for several years before *coming out,* or publicly acknowledging their sexual orientation (C. Patterson, 1995). A study by Ritch Savin-Williams (1995) found that for gay males initiation of sexual behavior with same-sex partners was closely associated with biological changes of puberty (early maturers initiated same-sex encounters earlier than did late maturers), whereas sexual behavior with opposite-sex partners began according to a youngster's age and level of social and emotional development.

As yet no agreement exists on the specific pattern of factors that lead to the development of nonheterosexual orientations. Experiences within the family have long been considered an important contributor. Cross-gender behavior in childhood appears to be strongly associated with nonheterosexual orientations in adolescence and adulthood for both males and females, but a substantial proportion of gay and lesbian adults report no or few cross-gender behaviors in childhood (Bailey & Zucker, 1995; Golombok & Tasker, 1996; R. Green, 1987). In a unique longitudinal study, Susan Golombok and Fiona Tasker (1996) compared the sexual orientations of twenty-five adults who had been raised as children by lesbian mothers with a group of twenty-one adults who had been raised by heterosexual single mothers. Although children from lesbian families were more likely to explore same-sex relationships, all but two children raised by lesbian mothers (and all children raised by heterosexual mothers) identified themselves as heterosexual in adulthood, a difference that was not statistically significant.

A number of researchers are also exploring the contributions of biological and genetic predispositions to the development of nonheterosexual orientations (Byne, 1994; LeVay & Hamer, 1994; Patterson, 1995). One approach has sought to discover physical differences between the brains of male and female animals and humans; the second has explored the role of genes by using family and twin adoption studies to analyze the frequencies with which homosexuality occurs in families and by directly examining DNA. To date, there is little reliable evidence of differences in brain structure that correlate with differences in sexual orientation and no reason to think that the discovery of such differences would explain the cause of sexual orientation. The search for genetic causes of homosexuality suffers from the same methodological and conceptual problems discussed in Chapter 3.

The challenging task of achieving a secure sexual identity is considerably more difficult for nonheterosexual adolescents, who have the added burdens of grappling with their difference and the anxieties and dangers involved. Homosexual and bisexual teenagers frequently experience rejection by their families, peer groups, schools, places of worship, and other community institutions—the very groups adolescents depend on for support. The verbal abuse, the AIDS-related stigmatization, the threat of physical attack, and other forms of victimization they encounter put them at greater risk for mental health problems. However, strong support from family, friends, school and community, and antidiscrimination legislation and education about nonheterosexuality can all serve as buffers against these negative outcomes by creating an environment that allows these adolescents to successfully master the challenges of identity formation (Hershberger & D'Augelli, 1995).

Sex and Everyday Life

Although sexuality plays an important role in adolescents' feelings, fantasies, and social relationships, it does not necessarily dominate their lives. Sexual experience involving intercourse is the exception for most junior high school students. Sexual activity increases during high school, but most adolescents have intercourse on a rather sporadic, unpredictable basis, if at all. Masturbation and various forms of petting appear to be the mainstay of many adolescents' sexual activity (Rodgers & Rowe, 1993). Keep in mind, however, that the nature and role of sexual activity in the lives of adolescents vary considerably depending on culture, SES, and overall life circumstances (Seidman & Rieder, 1994).

As we noted earlier, changes in sexuality during adolescence involve not only physical maturation and the development of new social skills; they also play a major role in the development of intimacy and personal identity. Sometimes identity development is complicated by sexual issues. It can also be affected by social problems specific to teenagers, as we will see in the next section.

What Do You Think?

When you were an adolescent, what were your attitudes toward premarital sex, dating, and nonheterosexual orientations? In what ways, if any, have your attitudes changed since then?

SPECIAL PROBLEMS OF ADOLESCENCE

In Chapter 10, we looked at the special physical and health risks adolescents face as a group. Their lack of experience, their need to experiment with new and sometimes risky social roles, and the lack of educational and economic opportunities and social support they frequently encounter can place adolescents at high risk for developing certain psychosocial problems. In this section, we discuss three special problems of adolescence: teenage pregnancy and parenthood, adolescent depression and suicide, and juvenile delinquency.

Adolescent Pregnancy and Parenthood

Each year more than 1.1 million American teenagers ages fifteen through nineteen become pregnant; most of those pregnancies were not intended (U.S. Department

Working with | Janet Whallen, NURSE PRACTITIONER

Helping Pregnant Teenagers

Janet Whallen was interviewed in her office, which is located in a neighborhood health care center serving disadvantaged Hispanic and African American individuals and families. Janet's warm, low-key style made it easy to see why teenagers would find her easy to talk with. Our interview focused on the experiences of pregnant teens.

Rob: What special problems do pregnant teenagers face?

Janet: Most of the sexual relationships these teenagers are involved in are fairly short-lived. A young woman or man might have three or four partners in a year. When a young woman becomes pregnant, the chances that she'll still be with the same boyfriend when she delivers nine months later are fairly slim.

Rob: Nine months would be a long relationship?

Janet: For someone who is only fourteen or fifteen, it is. Very few of these girls have the baby's father with them in any way, shape, or form at the time of delivery.

Rob: Why is this so?

Janet: Sometimes the guy gets scared or loses interest because the girl is starting to get fat. Or the girl or guy was already losing interest even before the pregnancy occurred. Whatever the reason, I think shorter relationships are fairly typical of early adolescent behavior.

Rob: In what other ways are the experiences of pregnant teenagers typical of adolescents in general?

Janet: They have very little sense of the implications of the decisions they make. They make most choices based on short-term consequences, and those choices are tightly connected to peer approval. There are also lots of rebellion issues against important adults, whether parents or teachers.

Rob: How does this rebelliousness affect pregnancy?

Janet: Teenagers are very sensitive about many things, from small issues to big ones: being told to eat certain things or to wear certain clothes—you know, "you're going to look fat if you wear that"—about smoking or not smoking, getting home on time after school or staying out late on Friday night, about how their parent will feel about their being sexually active or getting pregnant. I have to be very careful to give advice in a way that they don't find threatening.

Rob: Sounds like typical adolescent behavior.

Janet: I have kids who will come in for an appointment with four or five giggling teenage friends, who'll sit outside the office and heckle and laugh. They'll all be talking about who is going out with whom, who passed notes to whom in class, who cut class for what reasons, where they bought their clothes. You would never know you were in the middle of an inner-city clinic for pregnant teenagers.

of Health and Human Services, 1990a). It is estimated that 19 percent of white females and 41 percent of African American females become pregnant by age eighteen and that close to 66 percent of all white and 97 percent of all African American teenage first-time mothers were unmarried when they became pregnant (Earle, 1990; Furstenberg et al., 1989). Janet Whallen, a nurse practitioner, discusses her work with pregnant teenagers in the accompanying interview.

Unsound Contraceptive Practices   The great majority of teenage pregnancies are the result of inadequate or no contraception. Many teenagers are startlingly uninformed about the basics of reproduction, believing they are "immune" to pregnancy or at least at very low risk. Approximately one-half of all teenagers do not use contraceptives the first time they have sex, and many, particularly younger adolescents, delay using contraception for a year or more after the first intercourse (Hofferth & Hayes, 1987; U.S. Bureau of the Census, 1992b).

Although birth control pills are popular, they are not reliable during the first month of use. Only foam and condoms or a diaphragm and contraceptive jelly are really effective for first intercourse. But adolescents do not like to use these contraceptives because they imply a preparedness for sex, are expensive or unavailable when needed, can be messy, reduce pleasure, and increase anxiety due to inexperience in their use. Irregular use of contraception is associated with lack of knowledge about contraceptives, low SES, poor communication with parents, having

Rob: Are these pregnant teenagers in danger of losing connection with their peer culture?

Janet: Not as much as you might think. Unlike in middle-class communities, where teenagers are expected to complete high school and go to college, there is relatively little stigma attached to becoming pregnant during high school—although there may be a little bit more if pregnancy occurs in junior high.

Rob: Why do teenagers become pregnant in the first place?

Janet: I wish I knew the answer to that one! Failure to use effective birth control is, of course, the immediate factor. And some teenagers want to have a little baby to care for and be close to and to feel important and needed, or they see pregnancy as a way to gain adult status. Another reason is that sex is a big deal and getting pregnant isn't.

Rob: What do you mean?

Janet: Many of these kids become sexually active at age twelve or thirteen, and some even before they start having their periods. Most of them have little extra money, so they don't go shopping, or buy CDs, or collect this or that. A lot of them are involved in Pentecostal or Baptist churches, so they don't do drugs and they don't drink. But they do sex.

Rob: It's an enjoyable activity, and it's inexpensive.

Janet: Well . . . intimacy is involved too, but for many young teens, sex is mainly a way to have immediate fun. Getting pregnant simply happens, with little thought about its deeper social, emotional, or philosophical significance.

Rob: What social supports are available to these youngsters?

Janet: Family or extended family members often will babysit and share other child care responsibilities. Sometimes the boyfriend's family will also be-

come involved, even when he's out of the picture. Many teen moms are back to being teenagers fairly soon after having their babies. Some graduate from high school and get a job, and a few go on to college. A significant number do not finish school. Unfortunately, we are finding that an increasing number get pregnant again soon after the first baby.

What Do You Think?

1. If Janet Whallen were working with pregnant teens in the community in which you spent your adolescence, in what ways might her observations be different? In what ways might they be the same? Why?

2. What are your views about the causes of teenage pregnancy?

3. What strategies might you recommend for preventing teen pregnancy among low-SES, inner-city youth?

---

teenage friends who became parents, low educational achievement and aspirations, high levels of anxiety, low self-esteem, and feelings of fatalism, powerlessness, and alienation (Brooks-Gunn & Furstenberg, 1989).

Choosing Between Abortion and Parenthood   Although most teenage mothers report that they did not plan to become pregnant and would not choose to do so if they had a choice, the more than 50 percent who decide to have their babies become increasingly committed to motherhood during the course of the pregnancy. A teenager's reactions to unplanned pregnancy are influenced by a variety of factors, including her feelings about school, her relationship with the baby's father, her relationship with her parents, perceived family support for keeping the child, how many of her peers have become parents, and her sense of self-esteem (Furstenberg et al., 1989; Faber, 1991).

Approximately 44 percent of all teenage pregnancies end in abortion, which is roughly 25 percent of all abortions performed in the United States (U.S. Bureau of the Census, 1992; Hayes, 1987). The experience of an abortion may be psychologically stressful for teenagers. How an abortion will affect a particular teenager depends on her feelings and attitudes about pregnancy and abortion; the attitudes and support available from parents, other adults, peers, and her sexual partner; and her overall personal adjustment and life circumstances (Franz & Reardon, 1992; Hardy, 1991).

Teenage pregnancy is no joke. Young teenagers face increased risks of complications during pregnancy and childbirth and of delivering premature and low birth weight babies who continue to experience developmental problems. Young teenage mothers encounter difficulties in becoming competent parents while they are still in need of parenting themselves.

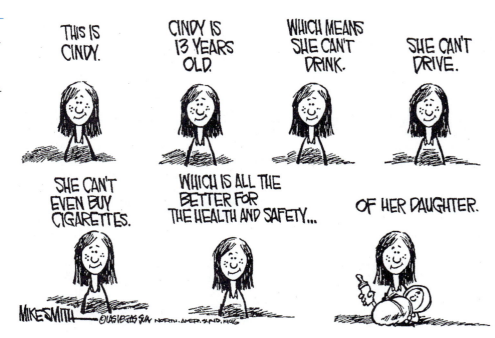

Consequences of Teenage Parenthood   Many teenage mothers may see having a baby as a way to prematurely crystallize their identities, because motherhood and marriage promise to establish them in a secure adult role and help them escape role confusion (Furstenberg et al., 1989). Such fantasies are generally not realized, however. Teenage mothers are less likely to finish high school, find a stable paying job, enter secure marriages, or achieve equal job status or income in their lifetimes. Teenage fathers are less negatively affected, largely because they generally do not assume responsibility for raising their children (Furstenberg et al., 1989).

Teenage mothers are more likely than older women to experience complications such as anemia and toxemia during pregnancy, as well as prolonged labor. Their babies are more likely to be premature, have low birth weight, and have neurological defects, and are also more likely to die during their first year. The children of teen mothers are more likely to suffer developmentally, displaying poorer cognitive and social functioning in preschool and elementary school and a higher rate of learning and social adjustment problems as adolescents, than are children born to older mothers. They are also more likely to become teenage parents themselves. Because they are still children themselves and focused on their own developmental needs, teenage mothers may be less emotionally equipped to be competent parents (Furstenberg et al., 1989). As we will see in Chapter 13, the transition to parenthood is also difficult for young adults.

Prevention and Support Programs   Prevention of teenage pregnancy requires a delay of early sexual activity as well as improved use of contraceptives among sexually active teenagers. Prevention programs have taken four approaches: (1) educating teens about sexuality and contraception, (2) changing their attitudes about early sexual involvement, (3) providing contraceptive and family-planning services, and (4) increasing girls' self-esteem to give them higher aspirations for education and career. Currently contraception and family-planning services appear to have the highest chance of success, in part due to the increased awareness of the need for contraception to help protect against AIDS.

Most services aimed at providing medical, educational, financial, and parental support have had only moderate success. Prenatal care programs have been the most successful, because teens who obtain adequate prenatal care are more likely to have healthy babies than those who do not (see Chapter 3 for a discussion of such programs). School-based medical clinics that provide easy access to contraceptives and support for teenagers and their problems also have been very effective. Different prevention approaches may be needed for different types of at-risk teenagers. Teens who are at risk for pregnancy because they are problem prone in general may need different help than teens who are depressed or teens whose alternative lifestyles place them at risk for pregnancy (Lancaster & Hamburg, 1986; McCullough & Scherman, 1991).

Teenage Depression and Suicide

Between 20 and 25 percent of adolescents report having experienced depressed moods during the last six months. A *depressed mood* involves periods of sadness, unhappiness, or blue feelings for an unspecified period of time and is usually experienced with other negative emotions, such as fear, guilt, or anger, and with other problems, such as anxiety and social withdrawal (Petersen et al., 1993). Approximately 5 percent of all adolescents display a *depressive syndrome,* a pattern of depressive symptoms that include feeling lonely, unloved, mistreated, worthless, nervous, fearful, guilty, self-conscious, suspicious, sad, or worried (Petersen et al., 1993).

Finally, at any given point in time, approximately 7 percent of adolescents suffer from a **clinical depression,** meaning their depression is severe enough to be diagnosed as an emotional disorder that requires treatment by a mental health professional. The symptoms of clinical depression include (1) a depressed or irritable mood for most of the day,(2) decreased interest in pleasurable activities, (3) abnormal weight gain or loss, (4) sleep problems, (5) psychomotor agitation or retardation (being physically tense and overactive or slowed and underactive), (6) fatigue or loss of energy, (7) feelings of worthlessness and excessive guilt, (8) impaired concentration and decision-making ability, and (9) repeated thoughts about suicide, plans of suicide, or actual suicide attempts (Petersen et al., 1993).

Suicide is the third leading cause of death among children ages fifteen to nineteen. Between 6 and 13 percent of adolescents have reported attempting suicide at least once in their lives, and the ratio of attempted to successful suicides is estimated to be as high as fifty to one (Garland & Zigler, 1993; Meehan et al., 1992). Suicide attempts are estimated to be three to nine times more common among girls, but boys succeed three times as often, in part because they use more effective methods such as knives and guns (Holden, 1986).

The majority of teenagers who attempt suicide have experienced serious family difficulties, including parent-child conflict, parental divorce, neglect, and abuse. Depression often is a factor. Suicide attempts almost always represent cries for help with the personal turmoil and feelings of intense loneliness, isolation, and hopelessness that such youngsters experience (Rubenstein et al., 1989; Spirito et al., 1989; Trautman & Shaffer, 1989). Although most teenagers who are not depressed still experience moments of unhappiness, and most who are depressed do not attempt suicide, signs of unhappiness and depression should not be dismissed, particularly if they persist. Also, because a large percentage of those who attempt suicide have threatened or attempted it before, such threats should be taken very seriously. Adolescent egocentrism, the exaggerated feeling that one's uniqueness makes it impossible for anyone else to truly understand one's problems, may intensify a teenager's feelings of loneliness and isolation and contribute to a tendency not to seek help and to reject help that is available.

Attempts to prevent suicide include early detection and intervention in family and personal crises, school-based education about depression and suicide risk factors, training in problem solving and coping skills, crisis counseling, and emergency hot lines. Treatment for teens who attempt suicide generally involves therapy with both the adolescent and his or her family (Garland & Zigler, 1993; Rubenstein et al., 1989). The film *Ordinary People* provides an excellent portrayal of a teenager's suicide attempt, the events and family circumstances involved, and the treatment received.

Juvenile Delinquency

Juvenile delinquency refers to a pattern of destructive or antisocial activities and lawbreaking offenses committed by adolescents. In 1990, more than 1.75 million juveniles were arrested for less serious *status offenses* such as vandalism, joy-riding, drug abuse, or running away and almost 650,000 for more serious crimes such as larceny or theft, robbery, or forcible rape (Federal Bureau of Investigation, 1991; Patterson et al., 1989). Arrests and imprisonment for status offenses may serve as an introduction to the criminal world for some adolescents, especially those who already feel very weak ties to the rest of the majority society.

There is some evidence that the route to chronic delinquency follows a predictable developmental sequence of experiences. The first step involves ineffective parenting and problematic family interaction processes, both of which frequently contribute to childhood conduct disorders. In the second step, the conduct-disordered behaviors lead to academic failure and peer rejection. During later childhood and early adolescence, continuing failure at school and peer rejection lead to a third step: increased risk for depressed mood and involvement in a deviant peer group. Children who follow this developmental sequence are assumed to be at high risk for engaging in chronic delinquent behavior (Patterson et al., 1989).

Factors associated with delinquency include a caregiver-child relationship characterized by hostility, lack of affection, underinvolvement, and lack of supervision; overly harsh and authoritarian methods of discipline; a high degree of family conflict and disorganization; a parent with a personality disturbance and a delinquent history of her or his own; impoverished living conditions; lack of attachment to any prosocial institution such as school, job, or church; lack of positive adult role models; and exposure to neighborhood environments in which violence, crime, and delinquent behavior are prevalent (Dishion et al., 1995; Romig et al., 1989; Sarafino & Armstrong, 1986).

Gangs   Many delinquent youngsters belong to gangs. A *gang* is a relatively permanent group of individuals with a clearly identified leadership and organizational structure and clear role expectations for its members. Gangs identify with or claim control over "territory" in the community and engage in violence and other forms of illegal activities such as fighting, vandalism, theft, and dealing drugs, on an individual or group basis (W. Miller, 1990). A gang is likely to have a group name, an initiation rite, nicknames for members, and gang symbols such as colors, tattoos, hand signs, or jewelry (Winfree et al., 1994).

The rising incidence of gang-related homicides, drive-by shootings, home invasions, and related violent and illegal activities in schools and communities is a growing national concern (Pryor & McGarell, 1993; Takata & Zevitz, 1990). Typically gangs are formed by individuals from low-SES and racial or ethnic minority and immigrant backgrounds. Traditionally gang members have mainly been adolescent males, but the growth of gangs in prisons and increased gang involvement in the drug trade have expanded the age range to include children as young as nine as well as adults, and also increased female involvement to some degree (Goldstein & Soriano, 1994; Lasley, 1992).

Gangs are thought to provide alternative economic opportunities and social supports for disadvantaged and alienated youths who face high levels of uncertainty, instability, and danger in their families and neighborhoods. For such adolescents, gang membership offers a surrogate "family," a sense of identity and belonging, and status, power, and protection, as well as the material benefits of criminal activity (Curry & Spergel, 1988; Knox, 1991).

A gang typically reinforces its members for associating exclusively with other members, conforming to pro-gang attitudes and behaviors, and rejecting the values of parents, teachers, and mainstream peers (Winfree et al., 1994). Many of the individual, family, and social factors associated with gang membership, gang activity, and its prevention are similar to those linked to juvenile delinquency.

Reducing and Preventing Delinquency   Most adolescents, of course, do not become delinquents or join gangs. Adolescents who are at risk for delinquency can sometimes be helped by programs that make available the support and opportunities that will allow successful experimentation with other roles and identities. These include community houses, YMCAs, police athletic leagues, summer camps, crisis drop-in centers, and telephone hot lines, as well as outpatient and residential treatment programs to assist more disturbed teenagers and their families. Unfortunately, such interventions have been found to produce mostly short-term effects and lose their impact unless continued on a long-term basis (Patterson et al., 1989).

Intensive early childhood intervention programs for at-risk preschool children and their families have achieved significant success in reducing delinquency and related problems later in life (Zigler et al., 1992). The High/Scope Perry Preschool Program, for example, provided a high-quality preschool, weekly home visits by teachers, and extensive parent involvement for three- and four-year-olds from low-SES families. Long-term longitudinal follow-up studies of these children at age nineteen and again at age twenty-seven found significantly lower rates of school dropout, illiteracy, unemployment, welfare dependence, and arrests for delinquent or criminal behavior than for a comparable group of children who did not participate in the program. They reveal how early childhood intervention can help generate and support ongoing family processes that are supportive of positive development into the adulthood years (Hamburg, 1992; Luster & McAdoo, 1996; Schweinhart & Weikart, 1992).

What Do You Think?

What advice might you give to concerned parents regarding how they can protect their children from teenage pregnancy and delinquency? What advice might you give to the governor of your state regarding programs to prevent these problems?

LOOKING BACK/LOOKING FORWARD

We have reached the end of our discussion of adolescence. We saw how relationships with parents, friendships, and activities with groups of peers contribute to the development of identity during this stage. We also discussed the important contribution of sexuality and sexual experiences to identity formation and explored several special problems that can interfere with identity achievement. Just as the growth spurt and physical changes of puberty and the development of formal cognitive thinking at the beginning of adolescence culminate the long series of maturational and cognitive changes that begin with conception and birth, the achievement of identity culminates the psychosocial developments that precede it.

The social changes of adolescence show vividly one of the major themes of this book: individuals change dramatically as they grow up. As we have seen, in a matter of months an infant who smiles at everyone becomes devoted to particular adults and siblings, and in just a few years more people well outside the family compete seriously with these attachments. The other domains of development show equally dramatic changes. In just a few years, a child grows physically from diapers to climbing trees and riding a bicycle; in just a few years more, she or he starts looking (almost) like an adult. Cognitive changes are equally sweeping: individuals change from infants who think by looking and touching to children who can reason out concrete problems to teenagers who can imagine possibilities they have never personally experienced.

Although adolescence marks the end of childhood, it by no means marks the end of development. As we note at the beginning of this section of the text, adolescence is a period of transition to adulthood. In the chapters that follow, we will explore the many important and exciting developmental changes of adulthood that are yet to come.

Summary of Major Ideas

Theories of Identity Development

1. The process of individuation, or becoming a separate and independent person, appears to follow a fairly predictable pattern: differentiation, practice and experimentation, rapprochement, and consolidation of self.

2. A key task of adolescence is successful resolution of the psychosocial crisis of identity versus role confusion.

3. Identity formation involves selectively keeping and integrating certain aspects of one's earlier childhood identity and discarding others.

4. Successful resolution of the identity conflicts typical of adolescence depends in part on having adequate opportunities to experiment with different identities and roles.

5. Erikson calls the period of experimentation and uncertainty that precedes the achievement of a stable adult identity the *psychosocial moratorium.*

6. Marcia has identified four identity statuses among older adolescents: identity achievement, identity diffusion, moratorium, and foreclosure.

Social Relationships During Adolescence

7. While they are not conflict free, relationships between adolescents and their parents are for the most part mutually rewarding.

8. Teenagers appear to feel most positive about authoritative parenting styles and more negative about parents who are authoritarian.

9. Although adolescents and their parents may differ about some of the details of everyday life, they generally agree on the more important questions involving basic values.

10. SES differences influence the educational and career expectations parents have for their adolescent children and adolescents have for themselves.

11. In recent years, an increasing number of adolescents have encountered the stresses of growing up in a family that has experienced divorce, remarriage, or single parenthood.

12. During adolescence, friendships become increasingly stable, intimate, and mutual.

13. Both small, cohesive cliques and larger, less intimate crowds appear to be important aspects of peer group participation.

14. Teenagers participate in peer groups to please parents and teachers, gain peer acceptance and popularity, and conform.

15. The difficulties many young adolescents experience during the transition to junior high school have raised questions about redesigning schools to better meet young teenagers' developmental needs.

16. The quality of a school's curriculum and the social relationships offered within and outside the classroom affect students' academic performance, personal development, and the likelihood of dropping out.

17. Work can be a constructive experience for adolescents if it is kept to moderate levels and is appropriate to their educational and other developmental needs.

Sexuality During Adolescence

18. Adolescents' sexual needs are closely tied to their need to establish a secure identity and to achieve both intimacy and independence.

19. Masturbation and sexual fantasies play a significant role in adolescents' sexual development.

20. Girls and boys differ in their reasons for their first experience of sexual intercourse and in their attitudes toward sexual activities.

21. In the United States, dating is the major pathway to adolescents' sexual activity. Unfortunately, sexual aggression and date rape continue to be a serious problems.

22. Although acceptance of youngsters with nonheterosexual orientations has increased, the prejudice and discrimination that still exist make identity development more difficult for these adolescents.

Special Problems of Adolescence

23. Although a great deal is known about the causes, pregnancy and parenthood continue to be a major problem faced by a growing number of adolescents.

24. Two other problems common during adolescence are depression and juvenile delinquency.

KEY TERMS

individuation *(372)*
identity versus role confusion *(374)*
psychosocial moratorium *(374)*
identity diffusion *(374)*
negative identity *(375)*
identity status *(375)*
SES *(380)*
clique *(385)*
crowd *(385)*
homophobia *(396)*
clinical depression *(401)*
juvenile delinquency *(402)*

PART SIX

Early Adulthood

While we are children, and especially as adolescents, we often look forward to adulthood as a time when we will be "all grown up" and have fewer problems to cope with. Certainly we expect to be in charge of our own lives; no longer will parents and teachers tell us what we can and cannot do. Therefore, as young adults, it comes as a shock to many of us that although we are fully grown in size and reproductive capacity, we do not feel as grown up as we expected to.

Development continues during early adulthood, roughly from twenty to forty years of age, as physical and cognitive skills expand and psychosocial concerns change to include independent households, self-supporting work, intimate partnerships, and parenthood. These are complex roles and responsibilities that call on all we have learned thus far, as well as push us to new learning.

In Part Six, we explore the issues of early adulthood. Just as in childhood and adolescence, in adulthood physical, cognitive, and psychosocial aspects of development are intertwined. The psychosocial choice to become a parent, for example, raises concerns about fertility, involves the physical and psychological demands of pregnancy, postpartum, and childrearing, and causes changes in work, marriage, and other family relationships. Likewise, experience at earlier stages of development influence choices and problems during early adulthood, which in turn affect middle and late adulthood. Although we focus separately on the physical, cognitive, and psychosocial domains in early adulthood, keep in mind that our lives are continuous and the domains are inseparable.

12

EARLY ADULTHOOD

Physical and Cognitive Development

A t age thirty-five, Lilly is the mother of two-month-old Billy. When she and Marc married, she was thirty-three and he was twenty-nine, and both wanted a baby soon. Once they bought a little house and got settled, they stopped using contraception. Much to their dismay, it took almost a year for Lilly to get pregnant, and a couple of months later she miscarried. Her doctor advised her to wait two months before trying to conceive again. A few months later, Lilly got pregnant again. During this pregnancy, Lilly was more health conscious than usual. She exercised daily and tried to follow a nutritious diet. Her job as a bartender, however, exposed her to considerable secondhand smoke. Because of that she stopped working six weeks before the baby was due, even though she felt fine.

Now that Billy is two months old, Lilly has returned to work three days a week. She has arranged her hours so that on two of those days, Marc cares for Billy; on the third day, she drops Billy off at her mother's. The combination of infant care, employment, and postpartum adjustment are physically and emotionally demanding. Trying to do all she would like as a mother, wife, daughter, and employee creates stress and leaves her little time or energy for herself. She might choose not to work for awhile longer, but her family needs her income and she does not want to lose her job.

Early adulthood, generally the years between twenty and forty, is a period of assuming adult roles, earning a living, and taking on the responsibilities of a household. These changes usually occur sometime in the twenties, but there is considerable variability. The main tasks of early adulthood are establishing oneself in work and forming intimate connections with another person, usually leading to marriage and family. While in their twenties, Lilly and Marc each still lived in their parents' homes; they worked, but were not fully independent. Like many of their peers, as postadolescents they entered *youth* as a stage of life before proceeding to early adulthood. Youth is a distinctive period of growth devoted to figuring out who you are and who you want to be (Miller & Winston, 1990). Young people who find jobs and start families right after high school enter the conventional adult world sooner than those who take time to explore alternative paths before settling down. Being adult, then, depends on behaving in adult ways rather than on reaching eighteen, or twenty-one, or any other "magic" age.

Focusing Questions

- What does it mean to be a young adult?

- Why is early adulthood typically a time of physical well-being?

- How do adopting health behaviors and avoiding health-compromising behaviors contribute to the quality and longevity of adult life?

- What is the relationship between stress and illness?

- In what ways are women and men similar in their sexual responses? In what ways do they differ?

- In what ways does adult thought differ from adolescent thought?

- How does attending college contribute to cognitive development?

- What kinds of cognitive skills do adults need to deal with real-world problems?

In this chapter, we focus on physical and cognitive aspects of the early adult years. First we look at physical functioning and issues of health, stress, sexuality, and infertility. Later in the chapter we look at cognitive aspects of early adulthood, including the contributions of college and work to cognitive development. In the next chapter, we focus on psychosocial development during the early adult years.

PHYSICAL DEVELOPMENT

PHYSICAL FUNCTIONING

Young adults are at the peak of their physical abilities. The heart, lungs, and other body organs have reached maturity and are at their strongest by the mid-twenties. In fact, researchers use early adulthood as the baseline against which to measure declines in functioning during middle and late adulthood. Although signs of normal aging do appear between ages twenty and forty, any decline in physical functioning is likely to be so gradual that it goes unnoticed. In this section, we consider three aspects of physical functioning: growth in height and weight, strength, and age-related changes in body systems during early adulthood. We will look at how genetic make-up, diet, exercise, and stress affect these changes.

Growth in Height and Weight

Recent generations of adults have been getting taller and heavier, as well as maturing earlier, than previous ones. We see this in our own families when we grow taller than our aunts, uncles, parents, and grandparents. These generational changes in height, weight, and maturation constitute a secular trend. As we saw in Chapter 6's discussion of physical development in early childhood, a variety of factors have contributed to this trend, including better nutrition, healthier environmental conditions, and interbreeding of genetically dissimilar individuals, which produces hybrid vigor.

While many people reach their full height during adolescence, virtually all reach it by their mid-twenties. Skeletal development is completed in the twenties as the process of ossification changes the cartilage to bone. While women tend to reach their maximum height and go through the ossification process earlier than men do, considerable variability in cessation of growth occurs for both women and men (Spirduso, 1995). Both sexes achieve maximum bone mass by age thirty. The combination of exercise and good nutrition while bone mass is developing produces a reservoir of bone and calcium that can alleviate the bone loss associated with aging in later stages of adulthood (Recker et al., 1992).

Both women and men experience weight increases during early adulthood as their bodies continue to fill out. Women's breasts and hips and men's shoulders and upper arms generally increase in size. For most people, the high activity level of adolescence gives way to a more sedentary routine; if they do not adjust their diets, they gain weight. As we saw in our discussion of adolescence, normal body changes during puberty result in a higher proportion of body fat in females than in males. During the early twenties, the average body fat percentage is 15 percent for men and 27 percent for women. This increases to an average of 21 percent body fat for men and 39 percent for women at age seventy (Spirduso, 1995). Most researchers believe the larger amounts of fat in women of normal weight are related to sex-specific reproductive functions.

Both women and men experience weight increases during early adulthood as their bodies continue to fill out and high activity levels of adolescence give way to more sedentary routines. Because contemporary American society emphasizes being slim as an essential element of female attractiveness, women are particularly attuned to weight and weight control.

While physiological differences account for the different proportions of body fat in women and men, social factors also contribute to adult patterns of weight gain. Contemporary American society puts heavy emphasis on physical attractiveness, and being slim is an essential element of this, particularly for females. Models and movie stars are thinner than ever, at a time in human history when women's bodies are larger than ever before. As a result, females are very attuned to weight and weight control, long before they reach adulthood (Striegel-Moore et al., 1986). Twelve- to twenty-five-year-old females suffer from the eating disorders anorexia nervosa and bulimia ten times more often than males do. See Perspectives in Chapter 10. During early adulthood, women continue to be more concerned about their weight than men are.

Strength

Strength continues to increase after full height is reached. The muscular system gains in strength throughout the twenties and peaks in the early thirties. The middle and late twenties are the prime time for doing hard physical labor or playing strenuous sports. Lilly's husband Marc, for example, typically runs four miles after his eight-hour shift of heavy factory work and still faces the evening full of energy. After the peak comes a slow but steady decline in strength—so slow that it has little impact on most people until age forty or fifty.

Professional dancers, athletes, and others who depend on their physical skills for their livelihood are likely to feel these changes more acutely. They are likely to feel older sooner than people who count more on their intellectual or social skills for their self-esteem (Striegel-Moore et al., 1986). Individuals who are strong are likely to remain strong compared to their cohort, but younger adults will have the

The muscular system gains in strength throughout the twenties and peaks in the early thirties. This makes the middle and late twenties prime time for doing strenuous activities such as quarry rock climbing, as this woman is doing in Quincy, Massachusetts.

edge in activities that rely on strength after the peak in the thirties. Most young adults will notice a change only under unusual circumstances, such as chopping wood on a camping trip or moving heavy boxes, because under ordinary circumstances we do not use our full capacity. The declines of aging primarily affect our **organ reserve**, the extra capacity each body organ has for responding to particularly intense or prolonged effort or unusually stressful events, such as running for a bus (Fries & Crapo, 1981).

Age-Related Changes

Appearance changes relatively little during early adulthood, although by the late twenties some people may get a few creases in the face or a few gray hairs, the first visible signs of aging. These signs of aging reflect changes in skin elasticity and a reduction in the number of pigment-producing cells (Warren et al., 1991).

Age-related changes occur in all body systems: cardiovascular, respiratory, nervous, and sensory. In our twenties our body systems are at peak performance, after which gradual decline begins, proceeding at different rates for different systems.

Cardiovascular Changes   The cardiovascular system undergoes a steady decline in functioning throughout the adult years. The function of this system is to pump blood through the body in an efficient and continuous manner to provide the cells with nutrients and oxygen and rid them of waste products, both when the body is at rest and during exertion. In healthy individuals free of cardiac disease, the major age-related cardiovascular change is a gradual decrease in maximum heart rate; resting and submaximal heart rate are relatively unchanged (Spirduso, 1995). The maximum rate at which the heart can beat during heavy exertion decreases about five to ten beats each decade following peak capacity in the twenties (Shephard, 1987).

Respiratory Changes   The respiratory system enriches the blood with oxygen and rids it of carbon dioxide by exchanging air from outside the body with air inside. Because pollutants are so pervasive, it is hard for researchers to distinguish between normal aging of the lungs and respiratory system and aging due to damage caused by environmental factors such as smoking and air pollution. Sam, who smokes a pack of cigarettes a day, often finds himself out of breath while playing basketball with his friends, even though he is in his twenties and they are in their thirties. Gradual decreases in respiratory efficiency start at about age twenty-five and noticeable decreases by age forty.

Sensory System Changes   Peak central nervous system functioning characterizes early adulthood. Although age-related changes in the central nervous system begin during this period, they are very gradual. As Figure 12.1 shows, nerve conduction speed decreases less during early adulthood than other physiological functions do, although most decreases are small.

The senses vary in the degree of age-related changes during early adulthood. Visual acuity increases until the twenties or thirties and remains relatively constant to age forty or fifty (Pitts, 1982). From about age thirty, the eyes become progressively more farsighted as the lenses thicken and flatten, but most people usually do not notice changes in vision until middle adulthood, when they may need reading glasses for the first time (Whitbourne, 1985). Hearing peaks at age twenty, followed by a gradual loss, usually too small to be noticed by young adults. Taste and smell sensitivity remain constant during early adulthood, whereas sensitivity to touch continues to increase until age forty-five.

What do these physiological changes mean for most young adults? Typically, not much. This is the period of life when physical functioning is most stable; growth is

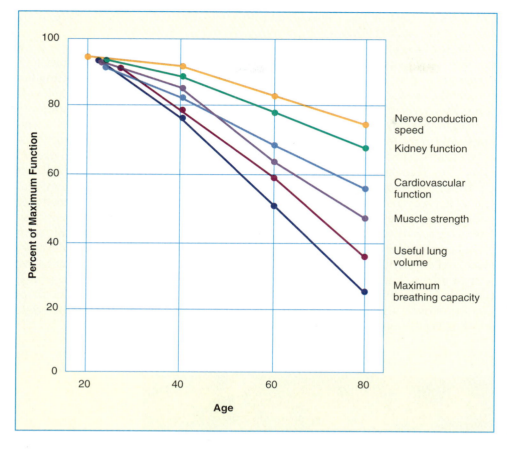

FIGURE 12.1
Average Declines in Major Biological Systems
Age-related changes occur in all bodily systems. The rate of decline differs for each system, with nerve conduction speed showing the slowest decline and maximum breathing capacity the fastest decline. Decline in all systems is minimal during early adulthood.
Source: Rybash et al. (1995).

virtually complete, and decline is only beginning and is largely unseen. While in the early adult years, people feel young and strong; the slight physical changes usually do not concern them. As we will see next, however, these feelings of strength may make young adults less sensitive to their health habits than they should be.

What Do You Think?

Are concerns about weight common among your friends? Are they more frequent among your female friends than your male friends? How can you explain any differences?

HEALTH IN EARLY ADULTHOOD

Young adults are generally healthy. Even if disease is present, the person is likely to feel fine because the disease is likely to be in the early stages, unsymptomatic, and undiagnosed. For example, adolescents and young adults have sex with more different partners than do people in any other age group, which puts them at higher risk for contracting the human immunodeficiency virus (HIV). The period between contracting the virus and developing full-blown AIDS may be as long as eight or nine years, however, so infected young adults often feel fine. Similarly, young adults with poor health habits such as smoking are not yet likely to suffer from the negative effects, although the damage is already going on in their bodies. A body system, such as the respiratory system in the case of a smoker, need not be working at its best for the person to still feel fine. Because of this, most young adults feel healthy and vigorous, regardless of genetic make-up, environmental factors, socioeconomic factors, and health behaviors.

Many of the losses in functioning people suffer as they age may result not from the normal aging process but from **pathological aging** caused by illness, abnormality, genetic factors, or exposure to unhealthy environments. **Health-compromising behaviors** that lead to illness, such as smoking, can also lead to pathological aging. It is hard for researchers to separate the effects of normal aging on the respiratory system, for example, from the effects of smoking, air pollution, radiation, and respiratory infections that people are subject to during their lifetimes. Because socioeconomic status (SES) determines the environment where one lives, works, and goes to school, it affects biological functions that in turn influence health status (Adler et al., 1994). Different neighborhoods present different levels of exposure to environmental hazards such as toxic waste or other pollutants. High-SES neighborhoods are rarely near factories that emit various kinds of wastes. SES-linked environments also impose different levels of exposure to interpersonal aggression or violence; different socialization experiences that influence attitudes, moods, and cognitive development; and different health behaviors. Certainly some neighborhoods are safer to live in than others, but the benefits of such neighborhoods may be very far reaching. Concern for healthy aging, therefore, has turned to encouraging people to adopt lifestyle choices and health behaviors that set the stage for long-term health while avoiding health-compromising behaviors.

While the primary benefit of regular aerobic exercise is to the cardiovascular system, its positive impact on health and well-being are far reaching. This man incorporates jogging into his routine by taking his baby along.

Health Behaviors

In this section, we focus on three health behaviors that people engage in to maintain or improve their health—consuming a healthy diet, exercise, and weight control—and three health-compromising behaviors—smoking, alcohol and drug abuse, and unsafe sex. While subsequent chapters point out that adopting health behaviors and avoiding health-compromising behaviors promotes better health in any stage of adulthood, young adults are in the best situation to prevent illness from developing.

Diet   What we eat affects our health. Diet plays a major role in the development of cardiovascular disease and is increasingly being recognized as a significant contributor to the development of cancer. About 35 percent of cancers are believed to be diet related (Alexander & LaRosa, 1994); for instance, high fat and low fiber intake is associated with the development of colon and rectal cancers. In addition, high calorie intake is associated with obesity, high salt intake with hypertension and cardiovascular disease, and high fat and cholesterol intake with atherosclerosis (hardening and narrowing of the larger arteries due to the formation of plaques that reduce the flow of blood) and coronary heart disease (Taylor, 1995). All of these negative health effects are under the control of the person making food choices.

A healthy diet is low in cholesterol, fats, calories, and additives and high in fiber, fruits, and vegetables. Fats should contribute fewer than 30 percent of one's daily calorie intake, protein no more than 12 percent, complex carbohydrates about 60 percent, and refined sugar around 10 percent (Russell, 1992). As Figure 12.2 shows, the U.S. Department of Agriculture (USDA) recommends that fruits, vegetables, and grains make up the bulk of what we eat. The National Cancer Institute recommends five servings (each roughly one-half cup) of fruits and vegetables a day as a cancer prevention measure. Unfortunately, this is not the typical American fast-food diet. Many adults learned poor eating habits when they were children and adolescents and need to modify their diets to make them healthy. Lifelong dietary change is hard to induce, even when an individual is at high risk for coronary heart disease (Taylor, 1995). Attitudes have an important effect on diet; people who feel

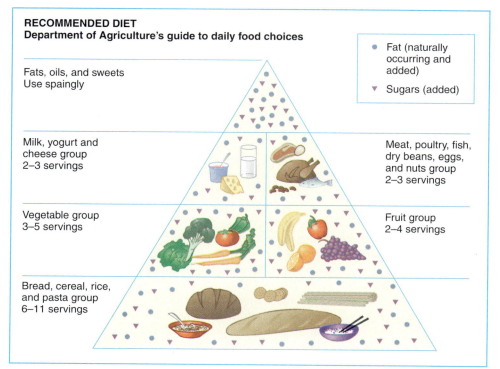

RECOMMENDED DIET
Department of Agriculture's guide to daily food choices

Fats, oils, and sweets
Use spaingly

• Fat (naturally occurring and added)
▼ Sugars (added)

Milk, yogurt and cheese group
2–3 servings

Meat, poultry, fish, dry beans, eggs, and nuts group
2–3 servings

Vegetable group
3–5 servings

Fruit group
2–4 servings

Bread, cereal, rice, and pasta group
6–11 servings

FIGURE 12.2
Recommended Daily Diet
The USDA food pyramid shows that fruits, vegetables, and grains should make up the bulk of what we eat, while fats, oils, and sweets should be eaten sparingly.
Source: U.S. Department of Agriculture (1992).

able to change, have a high level of health consciousness, have an interest in exploring new foods, and are highly aware of the link between eating habits and illness are better able to establish good dietary habits (Hollis et al., 1986). As we will see next, people can amplify the positive effects of a good diet by exercising.

Exercise   Physical activity is associated with staying healthy (Bouchard et al., 1990; Spirduso, 1995). The positive effects of regular aerobic exercise are well documented and far reaching. Aerobic exercise such as jogging, bicycling, and swimming is high-intensity, long-duration, and high-endurance activity. It is recommended that a healthy individual exercise at 70 to 85 percent of maximum heart rate nonstop for at least twenty to thirty minutes three times a week. Moderate exercise will increase fitness and decrease the risk of early death for less fit individuals (Alexander & LaRosa, 1994).

The primary benefit of exercise is to the cardiovascular system. Regular aerobic exercise counteracts the age-related decreases in cardiovascular functioning we discussed earlier. People who exercise maintain higher levels of cardiac functioning and blood flow than those who do not. The heart can more efficiently supply blood to the other tissues of the body, and the respiratory, muscular, and nervous systems all benefit as well. The benefits do not stop there, however; exercise improves endurance, helps to optimize body weight, builds or maintains muscle tone and strength, and increases flexibility. It reduces or controls hypertension and improves cholesterol levels. Exercise also seems to improve mood and self-esteem and reduce stress (Plante & Rodin, 1990). People who exercise tend to engage in fewer health-compromising behaviors, including smoking, alcohol consumption, and poor diet (Leon, 1983; Leon & Fox, 1981). Weight gain is one of the key age-related changes that people try to counteract with exercise.

Weight Control   Obesity, the excessive accumulation of energy in the form of body fat, is a major health problem. When people weigh in the range of 20 percent above their ideal body weight, they are considered overweight; if they weigh more than 20 percent, they are considered obese. Obesity is associated with heart disease, atherosclerosis, hypertension, diabetes, some forms of cancer, gall bladder disease, and arthritis. Because of its connection with these chronic diseases, obesity is associated with early *mortality* (death). As we saw in Chapter 10's discussion of physical development in adolescence, it is also associated with a poor self-image. Beverly Mendelson and Donna White (1995) found that children and adolescents who had positive feelings about their appearance and high opinions about others' evaluations of their looks tended to have high self-esteem. Obese boys and girls reported worrying significantly more about their weight and bodies than did their nonobese peers (Wadden et al., 1991). Although obesity was a poor predictor of self-esteem among African American inner-city youngsters (Kaplan & Wadden, 1986), in a three-year longitudinal study, Robert O'Brien and his coworkers (1990) found that obese inner-city African American children ages nine to twelve with high self-esteem were more likely than those with low self-esteem to lose weight. Because being overweight is viewed negatively in American society, children as young as six years old exhibit prejudice against overweight people (Wadden & Stunkard, 1985).

Many Americans are overweight or obese. As Table 12.1 shows, in 1991 more than one-third of the adult population fell into one of these categories. Despite changes toward healthier diets, the percentage of overweight adults has been growing over the last twenty years, particularly among economically disadvantaged groups (Taylor, 1995).

Several factors are known to increase the risk of obesity. First, overweight parents are more likely to have overweight children. This is because both the tendency toward obesity and eating patterns may be genetic. Children who became obese were found to have had distinctively vigorous feeding styles very early in life (Agras

TABLE 12-1 *Overweight Adults in America*
Weight control is an important health behavior. National weight surveys of people twenty to seventy-four years old indicate that increasing percentages are 20 percent or more over ideal weights. Before 1980, Hispanic people were not treated as a separate category, so percentages are unavailable.

	1962	1974	1980	1991	Increase from 1980 to 1991
Both sexes	24.4%	24.9%	25.4%	33.3%	31.1%
Men	22.9	23.6	24.0	31.6	31.7
Women	25.6	25.9	26.5	35.0	32.1
White men	23.1	23.8	24.2	32.0	32.2
White women	23.5	24.0	24.4	33.5	37.3
African American men	22.2	24.3	25.7	31.5	22.6
African American women	41.7	42.9	44.3	49.6	12.0
White, non-Hispanic men			24.1	32.1	33.2
White, non-Hispanic women			23.9	32.4	35.6
Black, non-Hispanic men			25.6	31.5	23.1
Black, non-Hispanic women			44.1	49.5	12.2
Mexican American men			31.0	39.5	27.4
Mexican American women			41.4	47.9	15.7

By Age Group (Years)	20–34	35–44	45–54	55–64	65–74	75 and Over
Men	22.2%	35.3%	35.6%	40.1%	42.9%	26.4%
Women	25.1	36.9	41.6	48.5	39.8	30.9

All figures for women exclude pregnant women.
Source: *The New York Times,* July 7, 1994, p.18.

et al., 1987). When feeding, they sucked more rapidly, more intensely, and longer and took shorter breaks between sucking than other children did, meaning they consumed more calories and gained more weight. Childhood patterns of eating and exercise contribute to obesity in childhood and adulthood. Children who were encouraged to overeat and those with low daytime activity are more likely to become obese (Berkowitz et al., 1985). About 80 percent of people who were overweight as children are overweight as adults (Taylor, 1995). SES is another significant factor in the incidence of obesity. Lower SES is associated with more obesity and less exercise. These relationships appear to be stronger for men than for women (Adler et al., 1994).

The best strategies for weight loss include an increase in exercise and a switch to a healthy diet such as the one discussed earlier. Exercise burns calories by increasing one's basal metabolic rate, which controls the automatic activities of the body, such as breathing and heartbeat, and regulates body temperature. Long-term changes like these, rather than fasting, following a fad diet, or taking diet pills, will promote gradual weight loss without leaving the dieter hungry. It is also important to be realistic about one's body type and not strive to be unrealistically thin.

Health-Compromising Behaviors

While many young adults incorporate a good diet, exercise, and weight control into their daily lives, they still engage in behaviors that put them at increased health risk. Smoking, alcohol and drug abuse, and unsafe sex—all prevalent among adolescents, as we saw in Chapter 10—persist among young adults as lingering adolescent egocentrism enables them to maintain the personal fable of invincibility.

Smoking and heavy drinking are promoted by certain social settings young adults frequent, such as this California fern bar. The illnesses related to these health-compromising behaviors take years to develop, enabling young and healthy people to deny or ignore the threat to their health.

Smoking   The media bombard young adults with images that link smoking to being grown up and popular. Since the early 1980s, cigarette consumption in the United States has been declining due to heightened health awareness, and cigarette advertising expenditures have been steadily rising (Cooper, 1994). Tobacco companies have developed advertising techniques that target young people, African Americans, and women. Cigarette ads depict glamorous, elongated female models and proclaim words such as "slims," "thins," and "lights" to capitalize on women's concern with being thin.

Smoking is responsible for more preventable illnesses and deaths than any other single health-compromising behavior. Of the 2,148,000 Americans who died in 1990, 400,000 of the deaths were related to tobacco use (McGinnis & Foege, 1993). Smoking is associated with cancer of the lung, larynx, oral cavity, and esophagus; it is also a major risk factor for other cancers throughout the body. Smoking is also related to cardiovascular *morbidity* (illness) and mortality. It accounts for 21 percent of all deaths from coronary heart disease (U.S. Department of Health and Human Services, 1990). Smoking increases the risk of emphysema, chronic bronchitis, peptic ulcers, cirrhosis of the liver, and respiratory disorders and aggravates the symptoms of allergies, diabetes, and hypertension. In women, smoking increases the risk of osteoporosis and lowers the age of menopause (Taylor, 1995).

Smoking does not only pose health risks to smokers. *Passive smoking*, or the breathing in of secondhand smoke from other people's cigarettes, increases the health risks to nonsmokers who are subjected to air contaminated by smokers. Children and spouses of smokers are at particular risk (Greenberg et al., 1984; Hirayama, 1981). John Reif and his colleagues (1992) found that even dogs owned by smokers had a 50 percent greater risk for lung cancer than dogs owned by nonsmokers.

Although the negative health consequences of smoking are clear, smoking-related illnesses take years to develop, which enables young, healthy people to deny or ignore the threat to their health. As we saw in Chapter 10, adolescents are more likely to smoke if their parents, older siblings, best friends or peers smoke. There is some evidence of a genetic component within families, as well as evidence of imitation. Smoking is inversely related to SES; the lower the SES, the higher the rate of smoking (Adler et al., 1994). As just mentioned, the cultural emphasis on being slim puts women at risk for smoking. Phyllis Pirie, David Murray, and Russell Luepker (1991) found that 58 percent of women smokers were concerned about gaining weight if they quit smoking, compared to 26 percent of men smokers.

Jacqueline Royce and her associates (1993) analyzed racial/ethnic differences in smoking patterns and attitudes. They interviewed about twelve hundred smokers and twelve hundred nonsmokers, 22.5 percent of whom were African Americans. African Americans started smoking significantly later than white respondents at all levels of education. African Americans of both genders on average smoked fewer cigarettes than whites, yet there were some indicators that they were more nicotine dependent. First, they more often smoked menthol cigarettes (which are higher in tars and nicotine). Second, they were more likely to be "wake-up" smokers (which is a measure of nicotine dependence). Third, they had more difficulty quitting. Royce and her colleagues also found that significantly more African Americans had made at least one serious attempt to quit in the preceding year; of the total sample interviewed, African American women made up the highest proportion of those who had tried to quit and white men the lowest. More than 65 percent of the sample wanted to quit smoking; more African American than white smokers wanted to quit "a lot." Royce and her associates point out the many life factors, such as stress and tobacco company focused advertising campaigns, that may contribute to the difficulty African Americans have in quitting even with their higher motivation to quit.

People who suffer from multiple addictions report that smoking is harder to stop than taking drugs or drinking alcohol (Kozlowski et al., 1989). Media campaigns have been effective in providing knowledge about the health risks caused by smoking, establishing an antismoking attitude in the general public, encouraging adults to remain nonsmokers, and encouraging smokers to want to quit. They have been less effective in getting smokers to quit and not return to smoking. Many programs have been developed to help people quit smoking, but none have been especially effective.

Public health campaigns aim to help adolescents resist smoking. Smoking prevention is particularly important because nicotine appears to serve as an entry-level drug that makes one more likely to use other drugs in the future (Fleming et al., 1989). In addition, laws restrict where people can smoke. For example, smoking is no longer permitted on domestic flights or in many public buildings. Such restrictions not only reduce the amount a smoker can smoke; they also protect all of us from passive smoke.

Alcohol and Drug Abuse   Adolescents and young adults between ages twelve and twenty-five are particularly vulnerable to becoming chemically dependent (Dupont, 1988). In Chapter 10 we focus on the destructive effects of drugs; here we concentrate on the effects of heavy drinking.

Moderate alcohol consumption, defined as up to two drinks a day for men and one drink a day for women, can affect health in many ways. Alcohol consumption increases the risk of some cancers and cirrhosis of the liver, and the calories in alcoholic beverages can contribute to obesity. Yet light to moderate alcohol consumption, especially of red wine, may improve longevity by decreasing coronary heart disease, which is the leading cause of death for both women and men (Kushi et al., 1995). Alcohol abuse, however, sharply reduces longevity (Criqui & Ringel, 1994). Among people with higher SES, consumption of alcohol is more frequent, and so is better health (Adler et al., 1994). Alcohol abuse, not alcohol use, is a health-compromising behavior.

Even one or two drinks a day may be too much for many people, however. As discussed in Chapter 3, Genetics, Prenatal Development, and Birth, women who are trying to get pregnant, are pregnant, or are breast feeding should not consume any alcohol because there are no "safe" levels for the fetus and the infant. Heavier drinking greatly increases the risk of fetal alcohol syndrome in the infant. Even for nonpregnant women, the physiological costs of heavy drinking (more than two drinks a day) may be more severe than for men. Research indicates that women get more intoxicated than men do from the same amount of alcohol (Frezza et al, 1990). This is because they have more fatty tissue, which retains alcohol, and less body water, which dilutes it, than men do and a less active stomach enzyme to break down the alcohol before it reaches the bloodstream.

Alcohol abuse can damage nearly every organ and function of the body. It is responsible for or associated with more than one hundred thousand deaths per year. Alcohol-related accidents are the leading cause of death in young adult men (McGinnis et al., 1992). For men ages 25 to 44 years old HIV infection is a close second; while for women in this age group cancer is the leading cause of death, followed by accidents, heart disease, then HIV (U.S. Bureau of the Census, 1994). Alcohol abuse increases risks for liver, larynx, esophagus, stomach, colon, breast, and skin cancers and for cirrhosis of the liver, and is also associated with hypertension and high blood pressure. Drinking also causes temporary and permanent cognitive impairments. A drunk driver, for example, may have blurred vision, poor perception of speed, and slowed reaction times.

Problem drinking and alcoholism are two behavior patterns that can result from heavy drinking. Alcoholism is characterized by the inability to control one's drinking, a high tolerance for alcohol, and withdrawal symptoms when drinking is stopped. Problem drinking does not produce those symptoms, but like alcoholism it creates social and medical problems. Problem drinkers and alcoholics are likely to consume large amounts of alcohol at times, often resulting in a loss of memory and violent outbursts. They often have family- and job-related problems. Sometimes, however, alcoholism and problem drinking are hard to recognize because many afflicted individuals drink privately and quietly.

Several factors have been found to increase the risk of problem drinking. Drinking and heavy drinking are more common among younger adults than older adults (Barnes et al., 1992; Hilton, 1988) (see Figure 12.3). About 84 percent of college students are drinkers, about 44 percent are binge drinkers (consumption of five drinks in a row for a man and four drinks in a row for a woman), and about 19 percent are frequent binge drinkers (Wechsler et al., 1994). Young adult males have the highest rate of alcohol misuse of any age group (Barnes et al., 1992). Gerardo Gonzalez (1989) found that people who began drinking during adolescence were at greater risk for both heavier drinking and alcohol-related problems. Grace Barnes and her colleagues (1992) found that beginning to drink at an early age and growing up with a father who was a heavy drinker were strong predictors of both later heavier drinking and alcohol-related problems, especially for males. They also found that living in a college dorm contributed to alcohol misuse.

Unsafe Sex In addition to posing direct health risks, drug and alcohol use facilitates the health-compromising behavior of unsafe sex. People who ordinarily would not engage in risky sexual activities may be less inhibited about doing so when under the influence of these substances (Desiderato & Crawford, 1995; Leigh & Stall, 1993).

Sex without a barrier to protect against potentially infected blood, semen, or vaginal fluids constitutes unsafe sex and creates risk for STDs and HIV infection.

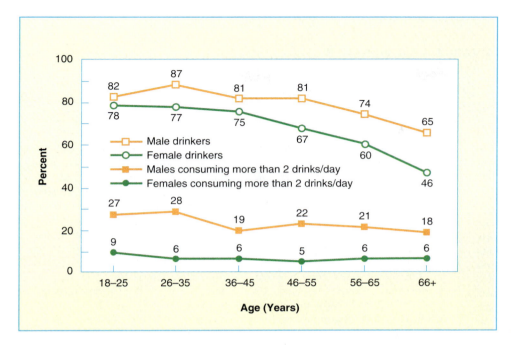

FIGURE 12.3
Percentage of Drinkers and Heavy Drinkers by Age and Sex
Heavy drinking can lead to alcohol-related problems. Drinking and heavy drinking (more than an average of two drinks a day) are more common among young adults than older adults. Findings are from a general population study of 6,364 adults in New York state.
Source: Barnes et al. (1992).

As we saw in Chapter 10, adolescents and young adults are at greater risk than other age groups because they have more sexual partners. As a result of HIV infection in their teens and twenties, more young adults ages thirty to thirty-nine died of AIDS in 1992 than any other age group—45 percent of AIDS deaths (U.S. Bureau of the Census, 1994). For sexually active people condoms provide the best protection from infection, although vaginal spermicides also reduce the risk of catching STDs. The best way to deal with STDs is to avoid getting them in the first place. Many women and some men have no symptoms, so they do not know to seek treatment. Furthermore, some diseases, such as HIV and genital herpes, have no cures at this time.

AIDS is the most feared sexually transmitted disease because it is fatal, but other STDs—such as pelvic inflammatory disease—also present serious complications and may cause infertility, discussed later in this chapter. Young adults often do not consider the consequences of unsafe sex, forget about them when under the influence of alcohol or drugs, or protect themselves from AIDS but not other STDs. Andrew and Kathy provide an example of this last behavior. When they first became intimate, they always used a condom because Andrew was open about his many previous sexual partners. After each tested negative for HIV twice over a six-month period, they stopped using condoms. Since genital herpes is not always active, they did not worry about the fact that Kathy had it. Now Andrew is also infected with herpes.

Risk for AIDS has been greatest for homosexual men, intravenous drug users, and minority populations, but the number of women affected is growing (Ickovics & Rodin, 1992). David Longram, an AIDS case worker, talks about these issues in the Working With interview on page 422. African American and Hispanic women make up 73 percent of female AIDS cases, even though they are only 19 percent of the female population (Centers for Disease Control, 1991). Socioeconomic factors influence the progression from HIV+ to AIDS, as well as how quickly the individual dies after AIDS is diagnosed. Low-income African Americans and Hispanics develop AIDS twice as fast as whites, possibly because of less healthy lifestyles, poorer general health, and less available health care (Taylor, 1995).

Table 12.2 summarizes the factors that promote and compromise health.

Working with Daniel Longram, CASE MANAGER

Helping Families Cope with AIDS

Daniel Longram is a case manager at AIDS Project New Haven (APNH), a nonprofit community organization that works to improve the quality of life of area residents who are affected by HIV-associated illnesses.

Michele: What is APNH?

Daniel: APNH was started ten years ago by six gay men in their living room. It's modeled after a program in New York City called Gay Men's Health Crisis. As the spread of AIDS has changed, APNH has evolved to include a multicultural approach in helping HIV+ people and their families.

Michele: What do you do?

Daniel: I'm a full-time case manager. Overall I would describe myself as a broker of services, but I do all sorts of jobs. I run errands, I coordinate volunteer services, I console overwhelmed caregivers. My caseload includes Hispanic, African American, and heterosexual people as well as gay men. To work in this field, you need to be bilingual.

Michele: So do you mainly counsel individuals?

Daniel: No, most of my caseload is made up of families. Sometimes the husband is HIV+ and I provide him with physical support while the wife gets emotional support from support groups at APNH. Other times the husband, wife, and/or some of the children are HIV+ and the whole family needs a combination of physical and emotional support through APNH.

Of the people I see, women seem to suffer the most, especially heterosexual women. They die a third quicker than men and have more problems associated with the disease. Women are at greater risk than men of contracting HIV through heterosexual sex. I'm seeing many more married heterosexual women infected by AIDS. I think it's because more married men are engaging in unprotected sex with male and female prostitutes.

Michele: What aspects of your job do you find difficult?

Daniel: In this line of work, it's important to be nonjudgmental and to go with the flow, and that can be tough. I had one case where my client was an Hispanic woman who was HIV+. She was a mother of four children and had her mother living with her. Over a nine-month period I helped her make hospital visits, provided groceries, and did the majority of her communicating for her because she couldn't speak. Her mother was giving her traditional Puerto Rican folk medicines during that time, which worried me. I felt uneasy about those herbal remedies. But I'm glad I kept my mind open, because nine months after I started visiting her, she started to speak.

Michele: What other services does APNH provide?

Daniel: We have the Caring Cuisine program, community outreach, support groups, a hot line, and the buddy program. The Caring Cuisine program provides isolated home-bound clients with daily meals that meet their specific nutritional needs. The buddy system is also set up to reach isolated clients who need a supportive friendship. The support groups and the hot line are targeted to reach not only the AIDS community but also the general public that are affected by AIDS. The community outreach program is targeted to educate the general public, both young and old. This is done in a variety of ways, ranging from high school and college talks to discussing risky behavior with people who are prostitutes.

What Do You Think?

1. How are changes in the populations at risk for AIDS reflected in Daniel's caseload and in the concerns of APNH?

2. The discussion of STDs in the chapter emphasizes prevention. How does Daniel's description of the work of APNH reflect a concern for this issue?

Fear of STDs causes stress for sexually active adults of all ages, but particularly for young adults who are delaying marriage and consequently are likely to have multiple partners. Other life changes make early adulthood a stressful period as well, as we will see next.

What Do You Think?

Discuss with your classmates your levels of health consciousness. Which health behaviors and which health-compromising behaviors do you regularly engage in? What changes could you make to reduce your long-term health risks?

TABLE 12.2 *Behaviors That Affect Lifelong Health*
Individuals can promote good health by adopting health behaviors and avoiding health-compromising behaviors.

Health Behaviors	Health-Compromising Behaviors
Low-fat, high-fiber diet	Smoking
Regular aerobic exercise	Drug abuse
Weight near realistic ideal level	Alcohol abuse
	Unsafe sex

STRESS

Stress, the arousal of the mind and body in response to demands made on them by unsettling conditions or experiences (stressors), is not unique to the early adult period. However, early adulthood is a time of life when the demands of establishing a career and starting a family are likely to bring new levels of stress. Unfortunately, many young adults ignore or deny stress as they do other health-related issues and rely on health-compromising behaviors to make them feel better. Tobacco, alcohol, and drugs are used to reduce tension and anxiety and to improve mood; yet they are not very effective ways to cope with stress. Learning to identify and cope with stress at this stage of life can provide lifelong benefits.

Stress can be *eustress* (positive stress), such as when you are chosen to give a speech, or *distress* (negative stress), such as when your car will not start and you need to get to an exam or a job interview. What serves as a stressor for one person may not be a stressor for another person or for the same person at another time. Important to the definition of stress is the person's appraisal of whether his or her personal resources are sufficient to meet the demands of the situation. Studies have consistently found that the level of stress is associated with a wide range of health problems.

Stress affects all the systems of the body. Hans Selye (1985) identified a pattern of physical response to stress that he called the **general adaptation syndrome**. This pattern has three stages: alarm, resistance, and exhaustion. Confrontation with a stressor sets the stress response in motion. During the alarm stage, the body becomes mobilized to meet the threat. The sympathetic nervous system (which helps to control the heart) and the adrenal glands increase the production of hormones that bring on typical stress responses; rapid heart rate, dilated pupils, shallow and quick breathing, and higher blood pressure all result from increased blood supply to heart, brain, liver, and peripheral muscles. During the resistance stage, the body mobilizes to cope with the stressor. The adrenal glands produce hormones that attempt to keep the stressor as localized as possible while still being able to overcome it. If the energy of the system is depleted before the body has overcome the stressor, the exhaustion stage is reached and illness results. The syndrome appears to be irreversible and accumulates to constitute the signs of aging. Wear and tear on the system brought about by repeated or prolonged stressors depletes the body's resources and lays the groundwork for disease.

Stress and Health

There is ample evidence that stress causes illness, but how? The answer is not simple. Stress can have a direct effect by increasing wear and tear on the physiological system and producing physiological changes that lead to illness. Tight shoulders,

Young adults face stress on the job as they leave school and begin their careers. Occupational stress often results from high job demands combined with lack of clarity of expectations.

trembling hands, and fatigue are all signs of stress that, if untreated, can lead to conditions such as headaches, psoriasis, ulcers, skin rashes, colitis, gastritis, chronic lower back pain, heart attack, vertigo (dizzy spells), and high blood pressure (Schafer, 1987). Some people have personalities or health conditions that predispose them to stress. Stress, for example, may create chronic hypertension only in individuals with already elevated blood pressure. People with negative affectivity (depression, anger, hostility, or anxiety) may be disease prone. Stephen Almada and his associates (1991) studied more than eighteen hundred men age forty or older to assess their degree of cynicism toward life. They found that cynicism scores were significantly related to coronary death and total mortality. Stress can also cause illness by influencing health behaviors. Smoking, eating poorly, or drinking more due to stress can lead to illness.

The Experience of Stress

Psychological factors significantly contribute to a person's experience of stress; the meaning a person attaches to an event determines the degree of stress. Richard Lazarus (1993) identified a two-step process, which he calls *primary* and *secondary appraisal,* that people go through when faced with a stressor. During *primary appraisal,* the person determines if the stressor is positive, neutral, or negative. If it is a negative stressor, the individual assesses its potential for harm, threat, or challenge. *Harm* refers to the present damage. If a police officer pulls you over and gives you a ticket for speeding, the harm might include the cost of the fine, the embarrassment in telling your parents or spouse, and the distress of being late for work. *Threat* refers to future damage, in this case the increase in automobile insurance premiums, the difficulties that might arise from the additional points on your license, and the history of being late for work. *Challenge* involves the potential to overcome and benefit from the event. In this case, the challenge lies in learning not to speed or getting up earlier so there is less need to speed. *Secondary appraisal* refers to the person's assessment of whether he or she has sufficient coping resources to meet the harm, threat, and challenge of the negative stressor. The experience of stress involves the balance between primary and secondary appraisal. High stress arises when harm and threat are high and coping ability is low.

People tend to perceive negative, uncontrollable, ambiguous, or overwhelming events as more stressful than positive, controllable, clear-cut, or manageable ones. Planning a wedding requires time and energy that often taxes the resources of a busy family, but it is a positive event and unlikely to be reported as stressful. Planning a funeral, on the other hand, is typically less work but is experienced as far more stressful. When faced with a negative event, feeling that it can be predicted, changed, or stopped reduces the person's experience of stress. Being able to predict and control allows the individual to adjust to the stressful event and reduces the physiological reactions to stress (Bandura et al., 1988).

Ambiguous events increase stress because the person does not know how to react to them. Unlike with a clear-cut stressor, an individual must devote resources to figuring out the ambiguous stressor rather than being able to confront it directly and effectively. For Lilly and Marc, the couple described at the beginning of this chapter, new parenthood is an ambiguous event. Although Billy's arrival was long desired and a positive event, his needs appear uncontrollable, ambiguous, and overwhelming to young adults who have never before been responsible for a child. Similarly, occupational stress often results from role ambiguity, or not knowing what the expectations are for job performance. Young adults face this kind of stress as they leave school and begin their careers. Longitudinal data from the Framingham Heart Study indicate that high job demands in combination with lack of clarity of expectations and feedback from supervisors lead to an increased risk of coronary heart disease (LaCroix & Haynes, 1987). People who are "overloaded"—who have more responsibilities than they can meet in the available time—are subject to more stress. On the other hand, having too few or no roles is also associated with poor health, as discussed in the accompanying Perspectives box.

Societal stress is also related to illness. War and natural disasters, as well as geographical mobility that disrupts social ties, produce psychological distress. The term **posttraumatic stress disorder (PTSD)** describes the physical and psychological symptoms of a person who has been the victim of a highly stressful event, such as war, rape, or earthquake, that last long after the event is over (Herman, 1992; Leor et al., 1996; Steinglass & Gerrity, 1990). Typical PTSD reactions include feelings of numbness, reliving aspects of the trauma, sleeping problems, difficulty in concentrating, and strong reactions to other stressful events. Lower SES exposes individuals to more stress and associated health problems (Adler et al., 1994). Individuals with lower SES are more likely to encounter negative events that create stress, such as loss of a job. Also, individuals with lower SES have fewer resources to cope with stressful events, such as savings to live on until they find a new job or friends who can hire them, and thus experience even greater stress.

Decisions about sexual intimacy may create interpersonal stress for young adults. As our discussion of STDs and HIV indicated, sexual activity can pose high risks for those who are in the process of establishing intimacy and not yet in steady relationships. Sexual functioning is the one area of physical development of which most young adults are very aware. We turn to this subject next.

What Do You Think?

What stressors can you identify in your life? What mechanisms do you use to cope with them? Which of these mechanisms are good ways of coping with stress? Which are not?

SEXUALITY

Early adulthood is a time of sexual and reproductive maturity. Although many of today's adolescents are sexually active (as discussed in Chapter 11), adult status brings a greater demand for sexual intimacy. Sexuality is one of the most important aspects of adult relationships. In this section we look at the physiology of the human sexual response, a survey of contemporary sexual behavior, and common sexual problems.

The Sexual Response Cycle

William Masters and Virginia Johnson (1966) watched and measured women's and men's physiological responses in more than ten thousand episodes of sexual activity

Perspectives

How Does Stress Relate to Women's Employment?

Without considering the positive role employment can have and the fact that men have always been expected to be workers as well as husbands and fathers, the mental health field predicted serious negative health effects in the 1940s when women began their rapid influx into the labor force. Psychologists and sociologists predicted that working women would suffer "role strain" from the multiple roles of worker, wife, and mother.

This prediction was based on two faulty assumptions concerning stress. First, the assumption that employment simply adds one more complex and demanding role to a woman's life ignores the reality that homemaking is work and homemakers' lives often already include many different and demanding roles. The role of daughter, for example, can be a complicated one that creates role strain in a homemaker's life. Also, people are likely to make more demands of a full-time homemaker, assuming that if you are at home anyway, you can be asked to baby-sit, shop, plan a shower, or give a ride to the doctor's office.

The second faulty assumption is that people have a limited amount of energy, so the more activities one has, the less energy one has available for any one of them. This ignores the fact that a different role can call on different resources and give different satisfactions and therefore can create more energy than it depletes. Going for a run after work, for example, often refreshes rather

than depletes energy. Likewise, the workplace can feel refreshing after a weekend of doing laundry, cleaning house, and entertaining guests. Role strain is a function not only of how many roles but of what roles and in what combinations.

Nonetheless, for years multiple roles were viewed as a negative experience for women. Only as researchers have examined the lives of women have we been able to ascertain the actual effects of multiple roles. Phyllis Moen, Donna Dempster-McClain, and Robin Williams (1989) interviewed mothers in the 1950s and recontacted them thirty years later. They found that multiple roles predicted a longer, not a shorter, life. In an early review of the literature, Lois Verbrugge (1982) investigated how multiple roles affect women's health status. She found that having several key roles was associated with good health for women; having too many roles may tax health, but having few or no roles may impair it.

Employment, marriage, and parenthood are all related to good health for women (Verbrugge, 1989b). Two of these roles combined are better than one, and all three are better than any two. Multiple roles provide more privileges, more resources, more social support, and more avenues for attaining self-esteem and social involvement. Women without multiple key roles were found to be more subject to boredom, social isolation,

and made several important discoveries. First, they found that while sexual excitement can come from many different sources, such as touch, smell, or fantasy, healthy individuals go through the same physiological process. Second, male and female sexual responses are much more similar than different. Masters and Johnson describe four physiological stages in the human sexual response cycle: excitement, plateau, orgasm, and resolution. Other researchers have suggested the desire stage as an initial stage that precedes the other four (Kaplan, 1979; Zilbergeld & Ellison, 1980).

Feelings or thoughts that awaken sexual interest and desire begin the sexual cycle. In the *desire stage,* both physiology and emotion contribute to sexual arousal. Desire, which is mainly an emotional state, leads to excitement. In the *excitement stage,* both women and men experience the first signs of physiological arousal called *vasocongestion,* when increased blood flow to the surface of the skin causes swelling of the pelvic region, a more rapid heartbeat, and erection. The excitement phase can be rapid or it can be slow. Whether ardent and passionate or slow and gentle, the physiological process of building arousal remains the same. When the changes of the excitement stage reach a high state of arousal and then level off, the *plateau stage* has been reached.

Young men often reach plateau very quickly, but as they approach forty they may find that sexual responsiveness is slower. They need more time and more direct stimulation to get fully erect. Women too vary in the time needed for arousal; variations occur among women and at different times for the same woman. Although with age women sometimes reach the plateau stage more slowly, this is not as common as it is with men. Since orgasm is the shortest part of the sexual response cycle, the slowing with age has the benefit of lengthening the pleasure and providing women with more opportunity for orgasm (Brecher, 1984).

and stress. Employment is the single most important factor. Employed women had the best health; full-time homemakers had the worst health.

Grace Baruch, Rosalind Barnett, and Caryl Rivers (1983) assessed the ways major areas of life contribute to a woman's sense of well-being. Based on a survey of three hundred women, they found two major components of well-being: *mastery*, which includes self-esteem, sense of control, and low levels of depression and anxiety, and *pleasure*, which includes satisfaction, happiness, and optimism. The women who scored highest on all the indices of well-being were married women with both children and high-prestige jobs. This is the group role strain theorists would have predicted to be the most harried and overloaded, but in fact they were the happiest and healthiest and scored highest in mastery and pleasure.

The women who scored lowest on mastery were those with the fewest roles: married, childless, full-time homemakers. Their self-esteem was very closely tied to their husbands' lives; if anything went wrong, they had no individual resources. They were underloaded in terms of roles but, more important, they felt they had little control over their lives.

Mothers who are married and employed clearly have strains in their lives. Dona Alpert and Amy Culbertson (1987) used questionnaires to assess the levels of stress experienced by working and nonworking mothers who lived with men who worked full time. They found that although the working mothers reported more "little" hassles than the nonworking ones, the intensity of their hassles was no greater than that of the nonworking mothers, and they were no more stressed. Married, employed mothers have the rewards and resources associated with each of their roles. If something goes wrong at the office, the successes of home—a dinner with the family and talk about everyone's day—can renew the spirit and give perspective to the office problem. If something goes wrong at home, such as a fight with a husband or teenager, a day at the office can provide self-esteem and civility and perhaps give perspective on the problems of home. In fact, evidence suggests that employment serves as a buffer for women, protecting them from the worst effects of difficulties experienced in other parts of their lives. In a Detroit health study, Verbrugge (1987) found that both women and men who had multiple roles were happier and healthier than those with few. Employed, married parents had the best health profile. In a survey of all the available studies, Faye Crosby (1991) argues convincingly that maternal employment benefits not only the mothers but the fathers and children as well.

Orgasm, the involuntary, rhythmic contractions in the muscles of the pelvis, releases the buildup of muscular tension and vasocongestion. Most women describe the feeling of orgasm as a burst of pleasure in the clitoris (Masters et al., 1994). Men describe the contractions that ejaculate the semen as the most pleasurable part of orgasm. A man typically has only one orgasm, whereas a woman may have no orgasm, only one orgasm, or multiple orgasms. Whether single or multiple, orgasms typically result from direct clitoral stimulation, either oral or manual, rather than from the indirect stimulation provided by sexual intercourse alone.

After orgasm, the body returns to its nonaroused state. During this *resolution stage,* men have a refractory period during which orgasm is impossible. The refractory period varies from thirty minutes to several hours. It is shorter for younger men and longer for older men.

Sexual Attitudes and Behaviors

Sex involves psychosocial and cognitive aspects in addition to physical ones. While Masters and Johnson studied the physiology of the sexual response, other investigators have focused on sexual attitudes and behaviors.

In 1992 Robert Michael, John Gagnon, and Edward Laumann conducted the National Health and Social Life Survey (NHSLS), interviewing 3,432 U.S. residents ages eighteen to fifty-nine, about their sex lives, histories, and attitudes (Gagnon et al., 1994; Michael et al., 1994). They found that respondents' attitudes about sex fell into one of three broad categories—traditional, relational, or recreational—and that "people's beliefs about sexual morality are part of a much

Feelings or thoughts that awaken sexual interest constitute the desire stage that begins the sexual response cycle. Desire can be awakened in nonromantic settings, such as while riding bikes.

broader social and religious outlook that helps define who they are" (Michael et al., 1994, p. 240). Traditional people said that "their religious beliefs always guide their sexual behavior." Relational people said that "sex should be part of a loving relationship, but that it need not always be reserved for marriage." Recreational people said that "sex need not have anything to do with love." Older married people were found to hold more traditional views of sex, whereas younger unmarried people held more recreational views. These differences may have been due to cohort differences (the age groups learned different attitudes about sex when they were young) age differences (attitudes about sex changed as individuals grew older), or a combination of both.

The NHSLS data also show clear differences in behaviors among attitudinal groups, as shown in Table 12.3. Whereas only 30 percent of traditional men and 14 percent of traditional women who were not living with a partner had two or more sex partners in the past year, about 60 percent of recreational men and 49 percent of recreational women had two or more partners. Even among married respondents, recreationalists of both genders were more likely to have had two or more partners than either traditionalists or relationalists and to engage in oral sex with their primary partners. Evidently, sexual attitudes influence how much sexual variety people choose.

Despite attitudinal differences, the NHSLS data uncovered some large similarities in adults' sexual lives: (1) once married, people tend to have only one sexual partner; (2) before marriage, people tend to be in one intimate relationship at a time; and (3) because people have become sexually active at younger ages while delaying marriage, younger adults are more likely to have more life partners than older adults. The data also revealed that "Americans of the same age and marital status are remarkably alike in the frequency with which they have sex" (Michael et al., 1994, p. 115). Younger people have more frequent sex than older people; married and cohabiting people have more sex than noncohabiting people do; and race, religion, and attitudinal groupings seemed to make little difference in this regard.

One surprising finding was the percentage of NHSLS respondents who considered themselves homosexual. Based upon Alfred Kinsey and his colleagues' survey of sexual behavior of American men, 10 percent has been the accepted estimate of homosexuals in the male population (Kinsey et al., 1948). Yet only about

TABLE 12.3   ***Selected Sexual Behaviors within Attitudinal Groups***
The National Health and Social Life Survey of eighteen- to fifty-nine-year-olds indicates that beliefs about sex fall into three attitudinal groups and are reflected in differences in sexual behaviors reported.

MEN   **WOMEN**

Sexual Behaviors	Attitudinal Group			Sexual Behaviors	Attitudinal Group		
	Traditional	Relational	Recreational		Traditional	Relational	Recreational
Partners last year: noncohabiting				Partners last year: noncohabiting			
None	40.6%	22.4%	12.8%	None	46.7	25.2	14.6
One	30.2	41.0	27.9	One	39.1	52.6	36.6
Two or more	29.2	36.6	59.4	Two or more	14.1	22.2	48.8
Partners last year: married				Partners last year: married			
Zero or one	97.0	96.0	84.9	Zero or one	98.0	98.5	92.5
Two or more	3.0	4.0	15.1	Two or more	2.0	1.5	7.5
Last-year sex frequency				Last-year sex frequency			
None	12.5	8.8	8.4	None	18.5	10.8	8.0
Three times a month or less	31.4	34.2	35.9	Three times a month or less	31.5	34.0	39.6
Once a week or more	56.1	57.1	55.7	Once a week or more	50.0	55.1	52.4
Had oral sex (active or passive) with primary partner in last year				Had oral sex (active or passive) with primary partner in last year			
Yes	56.4	78.2	80.7	Yes	55.9	73.9	83.6
Ever had same-gender partner since age 18				Ever had same-gender partner since age 18			
Yes	2.6	4.5	7.8	Yes	0.8	3.0	8.6

Note: Percentages in columns total 100 percent within the categories; the "no" percentages are omitted in the last three.
Source: Adapted from Michael et al. (1994).

3 percent of the NHSLS men identified themselves as gay or bisexual. About 2 percent said they had had sex with a man in the past year, and about 5 percent reported they had had sex with a male partner at least once since turning eighteen. Kinsey did not publish comparable figures for women, but of the NHSLS women, 1.4 percent identified themselves as lesbian or bisexual, fewer than 2 percent said they had had sex with a woman in the last year, and 4 percent said they had had sex with a woman at least once since turning eighteen. The discrepancy between the Kinsey and NHSLS figures may be due to several causes, including different sampling methods that either overrepresented gay men in Kinsey's sample or underrepresented them in the NHSLS sample; different interviewing circumstances and styles that enabled more gay men to be honest in the Kinsey study; or different criteria for being considered gay. These data highlight the difficulty of relying on self-report because people can present themselves in whatever light they choose. They also call attention to the difficulty of defining homosexuality, which we discuss further in the next chapter.

Common Sexual Dysfunctions

Sexuality, as we have seen, includes physical, psychosocial, and cognitive aspects. It depends on healthy body functioning, on feelings and attitudes conducive to arousal, and on thinking ahead about protection from disease and unwanted pregnancy. As with any behavior that depends on integration of all of these domains, problems with sexual performance are not uncommon. A **sexual dysfunction** is an inability to function adequately in or enjoy sexual activities. Most couples have some sexual problems at some time in their relationship, but these are usually of a temporary nature. In one study of married couples, 77 percent of the wives and 50 percent of the husbands reported some sexual dysfunction (Frank et al., 1978).

Low Sexual Desire   Low sexual desire is a common complaint of both women and men. It can stem from a variety of physical causes. Androgen (the sex hormone associated with sex drive) deficiencies, either those caused naturally or those caused by medications for nonsexual ailments, can lower sex drive in both sexes, as can a wide range of medical conditions. Although biological causes are important to consider, the majority of cases of low sexual desire are due to psychological factors. Preoccupation with problems of work or children, fear of sexual intimacy, anger or hostility toward one's partner, low self-esteem, or negative attitudes about sex are all examples of psychological causes of low sexual desire.

Female Orgasmic Problems   If a woman has never experienced an orgasm, she is considered to have *primary orgasmic dysfunction.* Although the causes of this problem are little known, they are usually psychological rather than physiological. Learning from an early age that one's body is "dirty" or that masturbation and sex are "bad" can contribute to guilt about sexual feelings and sometimes lead to dysfunction of the orgasmic response. A religious upbringing that is extremely negative about sex can have a negative impact on a woman's orgasmic functioning (Kelly et al., 1990). Sexual responsiveness requires shedding inhibitions, which is relatively difficult if the inhibitions are strong and deeply ingrained. Part of successful treatment for primary orgasmic dysfunction entails therapy designed to defuse negative attitudes about sex.

More frequently women are orgasmic, but they fail to have orgasms without direct clitoral stimulation. Manual or oral stimulation is more likely than intercourse alone to lead to orgasm. Inability to experience orgasm during intercourse is not considered a sexual dysfunction, but it does make many women (and their partners) unhappy and therefore is sometimes seen as a problem.

Male Ejaculatory and Erectile Problems   The most common male sexual dysfunction, *premature ejaculation,* exists when a man reaches orgasm with minimal sexual stimulation before, during, or right after insertion of the penis into the vagina. The causes are typically psychological rather than physiological. Using a condom can sometimes help, because it reduces penile sensitivity. Fortunately, counseling helps many men learn to delay ejaculation.

Most men are unable to get or keep an erection at some point due to illness, fatigue, stress, or heavy alcohol consumption. This condition is considered an *erectile dysfunction* when a man is generally unable to get or keep a firm enough erection to have intercourse. Erectile dysfunctions affect an estimated 10 percent of men and frequently cause feelings of shame, helplessness, anxiety, and depression (Masters et al., 1994). Physical causes such as alcohol and drug abuse, diabetes, vascular disease, side effects from medications for medical problems (notably high blood pressure), or severe chronic illnesses play a role in about half the cases; psychosocial factors contribute to the other half. Depression is a common psychological cause. Upsetting life events, such as losing a job or failing in a business venture, may threaten a man's self-confidence and lead to erectile difficulties. As we saw with female primary orgasmic dysfunction, an upbringing that stresses strong negative attitudes about sex may cause erectile dysfunction in men. Current difficulties in a relationship may set off the problem. Treatments vary as widely as causes do. Physically based erectile dysfunctions sometimes respond to medication or surgery. In many cases, couples are treated together in sex therapy.

So far we have discussed sexuality for the pleasures it can bring on its own terms, but, as we all know, sex is very much connected to developing intimacy. Establishment of intimacy during early adulthood frequently leads to the decision to start a family. A significant minority of couples, such as Lilly and Marc at the beginning of this chapter, have trouble conceiving a child. For this reason, we now turn to a discussion of infertility.

What Do You Think?

Attitudes about sex seem to play an important part in sexual functioning. Where did you acquire your attitudes about sex? Would you want to pass on these attitudes to your children? Why or why not?

INFERTILITY

Many couples who look forward to having children experience difficulty when they try to conceive. **Infertility** refers to a couple's inability to conceive a pregnancy after one year of sexual relations without contraception. Between 10 and 15 percent of married couples in the United States are estimated to be infertile (Davajan & Israel, 1991). Many couples who face infertility eventually do conceive, but according to one study, it took 20 to 35 percent of couples over a year to conceive at some time in their reproductive lives (Page, 1989).

In the United States, infertility has become a more frequent problem in the last twenty-five years (Mosher & Pratt, 1991). The number of couples with primary infertility (never having had a biological child) doubled from 1965 to 1988 (Stanton & Dunkel-Schetter, 1991). The number of young women ages twenty to twenty-four with infertility problems increased dramatically from 3.6 percent in 1965 to 19.6 percent in 1982. This rise in infertility among young women is attributed to changing patterns of sexual behavior and the increase in sexually transmitted diseases in this age group (U.S. Congress, Office of Technology Assessment, 1988). African American women are at greater risk for infertility than white women because of higher rates of pelvic inflammatory disease and sexually transmitted diseases, greater use of intrauterine devices, greater exposure to environmental hazards, and less access to medical care (Stanton & Dunkel-Schetter, 1991). Other factors contributing to the overall increase in infertility include greater exposure to environmental pollution and toxic substances. On a larger scale, delayed childbearing has meant that couples are trying to conceive when they are more likely to be infertile (Mosher & Pratt, 1991).

Although women are likely to seek treatment for infertility before men do, the problem can be due to the woman, the man, the combined infertility of the couple, or to undetermined causes. Often multiple causes contribute to infertility. About 40 percent of infertility cases have been found to have female causes and about 40 percent to have male causes (Speroff et al., 1983). The remaining 20 percent are due to immunity or incompatibility between the man's sperm and the woman's egg or to unknown causes.

Female Infertility

The two major causes of female infertility are failure to ovulate and blockage of the fallopian tubes. Ovulatory problems may be treated with drugs that induce ovulation. However, these drugs pose the risks of multiple pregnancies and forming ovarian cysts (Davajan & Israel, 1991). Blocked fallopian tubes may be due to scarring after a pelvic infection associated with an STD such as gonorrhea or chlamydia or by endometriosis (a condition where the tissue lining the uterine cavity grows outside of the uterus into other pelvic or abdominal organs). Treatment for blocked fallopian tubes usually entails corrective surgery. The pregnancy rate after surgery varies greatly, depending on the location of the blockage (Davajan & Israel, 1991).

Male Infertility

Male infertility may be due to a low sperm count, low sperm mobility, poor semen quality (a high percentage of abnormal or immature sperm), or blockage of the ducts of the reproductive tract. Less attention has been paid to developing treatments for male infertility than for female infertility, and the treatments have been studied less thoroughly; thus, their usefulness is less well documented. Hormonal treatments can improve testicular functioning, while reproductive tract infections often respond to antibiotics. Surgery can repair varicose veins in the scrotum and correct blockage of ducts of the reproductive tract. Most male infertility cases are managed with artificial insemination.

Psychological Reactions to Infertility

Infertility becomes apparent only over a period of time. When a couple has been trying to conceive month after month and nothing happens, what are the psychological reactions? Christine Dunkel-Schetter and Marci Lobel (1991) describe five common emotional responses to infertility. Most frequently, people respond with grief and depression. Feelings of sadness, mourning, and disappointment at being unable to have a child predominate. Anger, another very common response to infertility, may be directed inward, but may also be directed at the spouse or others who have children. Guilt, the next most common emotional response, may be linked to prior sexual behavior, delaying childbearing, or any other previous "transgression."

When people receive an infertility diagnosis, they respond initially with shock or denial. Anxiety often accompanies treatment for infertility, in part because the treatment is stressful and in part because the outcome is uncertain. These emotional effects have an impact on the person's general functioning. A feeling of loss of control may result because the person's life goal of having a child cannot be met and also because treatment for infertility directs a couple's sexual relationship and invades their privacy. Self-esteem may be threatened. Some people develop negative body images, others believe their potency is threatened, and still others question their gender identity. All of these psychological effects have an impact on the marriage and other relationships.

Reproductive Technologies

Given that infertility is so common and its effects on couples who experience it are so emotionally trying, it is not surprising that many treatments for infertility have been developed. As we saw in Chapter 3, couples may try artificial insemination, in which doctors inject the male partner's (or a donor's) sperm at the mouth of the cervix; in vitro fertilization, in which doctors combine egg and sperm outside the body and reintroduce fertilized eggs into the uterus; or intrafallopian tube transfers, in which gametes or zygotes are placed in the fallopian tube rather than the uterus. These treatments are not without drawbacks; they tend to be expensive and are not always successful. For couples who do conceive with these treatments,

Treatments for infertility tend to be expensive and stressful and are not always successful. When they do succeed, however, the joys of parenthood are the same as for those who do not need help from reproductive technologies.

though, any drawbacks quickly fade. For others, adoption can provide the joys of parenthood.

What Do You Think?

How could one convince adolescents (who think they are never going to die) to give up risky sexual behavior? Do you think that explaining the connection to infertility would be likely to have an impact?

ADULT CHOICES

Early adulthood is a time of major life decisions. Although we vary greatly in how rapidly and in what order we assume the tasks that will make us independent from our parents and connect us in intimate relations with peers, we typically face these challenges in our twenties and thirties. When Lilly and Marc were still living at home at about age thirty, their mothers worried that their children would never marry and move out. Three years later, Lilly and Marc delighted their parents with their new marriage, new home, and new baby. The early adult years, which extend through our thirties, provide time for trying different paths and finding ones that suit us. They also set some limits for the years to come. We establish attitudes and habits that will affect our physical well-being for the rest of our lives. We also make decisions about sexuality and childbearing. These choices have major implications for our cognitive and psychosocial development, for what we will think about and what roles we will play, for which struggles we will face and what regrets may later haunt us.

We now turn our attention to cognitive development in early adulthood. In addition to being of theoretical interest, adult cognition has implications for many aspects of people's lives. We begin by considering the development of postformal thought after adolescence, of contextual thinking, and of adult moral reasoning. Then we look at the effects of college on intellectual functioning. Finally, we consider issues of work, occupation, and career during early adulthood.

COGNITIVE DEVELOPMENT

Cognition concerns how and why people know rather than what and how much they know. While there is little doubt that adults continue to accumulate new information throughout their lives, disagreement abounds about when cognitive functions are fully developed and if and when cognitive loss begins. Jean Piaget's strong influence on cognitive developmental theory has led to the belief that cognitive development reaches its final stage during adolescence with the emergence of formal operations. Some cognitive theorists accept his idea that the structures of mature thinking are in place by the time we reach adulthood; others believe this view is too limited. This is the first issue we will explore as we focus on cognitive development in young adults.

POSTFORMAL THOUGHT

Formal operational thought is the final Piagetian stage of cognitive development. A person progresses through the *sensorimotor stage,* based on direct experience, as an infant; through the *preoperational stage,* based on language and symbols; through *concrete operations,* based on concrete problem solving; to *formal operations.* According to Piaget, as we saw in Chapter 10's discussion of cognitive development in adolescence, formal operational thought emerges between ages eleven and sixteen. It enables the adolescent to think abstractly in addition to thinking about the properties of concrete objects. Formal thought involves the ability to generate possibilities, use scientific reasoning, combine ideas logically, and think critically. A high school senior, for example, uses formal operational thought when she systematically compares the advantages and disadvantages of the three colleges that have accepted her. For Piaget, formal thought does not involve specific behavior; rather, it represents a generalized orientation toward problem solving (Blackburn & Papalia, 1992). Formal operations emphasize logical-mathematical thought structures, the solving of problems by using rational principles, logic, and careful reasoning.

Because formal operational thought is Piaget's final stage, it has been taken to represent his conceptualization of mature cognition and has occupied a central place in the study of adult cognition. Researchers using Piagetian methods and assumptions have focused on the development and use of formal operational thought in late adolescence and adulthood. Chapter 10 points out limits of the applicability of Piagetian theory to the study of adolescent cognitive development. Not all adolescents achieve formal thought, and those who do achieve it do not use it in all situations. In addition, emotions influence thought. Our college senior may generate a logical conclusion that she should attend the local university (it is the cheapest, has the best reputation, and offers the program that interests her), yet feel it is the wrong choice for her.

Critiques of Formal Operations

John Rybash, William Hoyer, and Paul Roodin (1986) have criticized the theory of formal operations. They acknowledge that emergence of formal thought is a significant achievement, but see it as an unsatisfactory description of adult thought. This is because formal operational thinking emphasizes finding the one right answer to a problem regardless of the specific nature of the problem, overemphasizes abstraction, and underemphasizes the ambiguities of real life. When you consider the complex, open-ended problems that mature adults encounter every day, the inapplicability of formal operations to adult thought becomes clearer. Whereas choosing the best car to buy in your price range may be possible using formal operational comparisons and contrasts, deciding whether or not to have a child, as Lilly did, is not. Lilly's decision depended on the circumstances of her life (Did she have emotional support? Could she afford a child? Was she healthy? Would there be someone to care for the baby when she works? Would waiting increase the chances of infertility?) and not on abstract possibilities. As Robert Sternberg (1992, p. 393) points out, "Solving a problem is less important than solving an important problem," and important problems often do not fit the laboratory model.

These limitations to Piaget's conception of formal operational thought have led cognitive psychologists to construct other formulations for mature thought. Dierdre Kramer (1989) found three basic characteristics these models of **postformal thought** have in common. First, postformal thinkers understand that knowledge is *relative and nonabsolute*. They realize that knowledge always has a subjective component that necessarily makes it incomplete (Sinnott, 1989). Second, postformal thinkers *accept contradiction* as a basic aspect of reality. For example, physicists must recognize that light can be both a wave and a particle. Similarly, an intense personal relationship can call forth the contradictory emotions of both love and hate. Third, postformal thinkers can *synthesize contradictions* into coherent wholes. Instead of choosing among alternatives, they construct a framework that integrates the contradictions. When planning a dinner for guests who include both vegetarians and meat-and-potato lovers, for example, a choice of Mexican or Indian fare can include a coherent array of meat and nonmeat dishes that suits all. As we examine some of the formulations of postformal thought, these features will be apparent.

Is There a Fifth Stage?

Patricia Arlin (1989) proposes *problem finding* as a postformal mode of thinking. In contrast to the problem-solving nature of formal operational thought, **problem finding** entails generating new questions about oneself, one's work, or one's surroundings. Arlin used interviews to assess problem finding in high school students involved in science or in art. When asked "Why do you do science?", an example of a problem-finding response was "Because many of the questions in nature and space intrigue me—I am looking for answers to them" (p. 203). When asked "Why do you paint?", a problem-finding response was "Because it is fun to create new ideas and discover myself" (p. 203). Arlin measured problem solving (formal thought) and problem-finding (postformal thought) and found that while not all of the formal thinkers were postformal thinkers, only a rare nonformal thinker exhibited postformal thought. She attributes these few exceptions to the imperfect measures of assessing levels of thought. Her findings confirm the notion of problem finding as a fifth stage.

As Table 12.4 shows, other researchers have made various proposals for a **fifth stage of cognitive development** that follows formal operations, the last of Piaget's four stages. Klaus Riegel (1973, 1976) sees *understanding and seeking out contradictions* as the important achievement of adult cognitive development. Adult thinkers accept conflict and change rather than always trying to resolve contradictions. They realize that both problems and solutions have inherent ambiguities. Whereas Piaget's theory emphasizes stability and equilibrium, Riegel's emphasizes change and disequilibrium.

Michael Basseches (1984), following the work of Riegel, proposes dialectic thinking as the postformal cognitive stage. *Dialectical thinking* is the art or practice of aiming at the truth by using conversation involving question and answer. Basseches' dialectical stage is a synthesis of Piaget's and Riegel's approaches. Individuals master formal thought, in which they analyze relationships within a

TABLE 12.4 *Theories of Adult Cognition*
Because many adults move beyond the absolute nature of formal operational thought as they face the ambiguities of real life, several theorists have proposed a fifth stage of adult postformal thought. These fifth-stage formulations emphasize the prag- matic, relative, and changing nature of adult knowledge. All four theorists propose postformal thought as a fifth stage; Labouvie-Vief proposes a fifth and sixth stage.

Piaget's Stages of Cognitive Development in Childhood	Proposed Fifth Stages of Adult Cognitive Development			
	Arlin	Basseches	Commons & Richards	Labouvie-Vief
Sensorimotor—direct experience	Problem finding—generating new questions about oneself, one's work, or one's surroundings	Dialectical postformal thought—search for truth through analyzing relations among systems	Metasystematic operations—movement from analysis of elements within a problem to relationships among sets of relationships	Intrasystemic thought (formal operational thought)—abstract, distanced, and objective thought
Preoperational—language and symbols				Intersystemic thought (fifth stage)—truth from multiple intellectual perspectives
Concrete operations—problem solving				Autonomous thought (sixth stage)—truth from perspective of personal values
Formal operations—generate possibilities, combine ideas logically, think critically				

problem or system, and then move to *dialectical postformal thought,* in which they analyze competing systems.

Michael Commons and Francis Richards (1984a, 1984b) propose *metasystem- atic operations* as a fifth stage. In this stage, people move beyond the analysis of single elements in a problem and begin to look at the relationships among sets of relationships. Instead of focusing on how to match the paint to the counter in the kitchen, for example, the person becomes interested in how matching paint is similar to or different from other problems of logic. Thoughts about operations of elements of a system are formal, whereas thoughts about the operations of diverse systems and their relationships are metasystematic. Commons and Richards (1984b), using stories that could be interpreted in a concrete, formal, or postfor- mal manner, found that whereas most graduate students displayed metasystematic thinking, few undergraduates did. As their stage theory predicted, not all the stu- dents capable of formal thought were capable of metasystematic thought, whereas all but one of the metasystematic thinkers displayed formal thought.

While the proposals for a fifth stage considered so far focus on the more ab- stract quality of postformal thought, Gisela Labouvie-Vief (1985) sees the clash be- tween logic and reality as the impetus for development of a more pragmatic type of adult cognition. Labouvie-Vief and Julie Hakim-Larson (1989) propose two modes of thought, one abstract and one emotional. The *formal mode* is distanced and ob- jective; the *internalized mode* is intuitive, subjective, and imaginative. Formal oper- ations represent the development of the first mode, but mature thought requires the balanced use of both ways of knowing. Labouvie-Vief (1992) stresses that the mature thinker must reconnect reason with emotional and social reality, making decisions within the context of commitments to careers, relationships, and children. A less mature thinker, for example, would take an individualistic approach to a work problem, do it singlehandedly at the cost of work overload and some blun- ders, with hope for career advancement. A more mature thinker would admit his or her limitations and rely on a team of experts and advisers. In Labouvie-Vief's theory *intrasystemic thought*, which is the last phase of formal operations, is the precursor to mature cognition, which she calls *intersystemic thought.* Intersystemic thought enables thinkers to understand multiple intellectual perspectives and to see the truth as part of a changing reality. Her final stage is *autonomous thought.* Autonomous thinkers see the role of their perspectives and values in the construction of their personal truths.

Taken in combination, these many different ideas reflect the emergence of a new view of adult thought and are shown together in Table 12.4. The multiplicity of postformal models indicates recognition that Piaget "failed to represent adequately the thought and emotions of mature people" (Blackburn & Papalia, 1992, p. 141). While the theoretical formulations we have discussed vary, most emphasize the increasingly pragmatic, relative, and changing nature of adult knowledge. Current thinking emphasizes that adult intellectual performance cannot be separated from its social and cultural context.

What Do You Think?

Have you noticed ways in which your thinking has changed since you have been in college? Does it fit the description of postformal thought?

DEVELOPMENT OF CONTEXTUAL THINKING

While the researchers discussed so far have used experiments to try to discover the stages of adult thinking, other psychologists have used other approaches. K. Warner Schaie (1994) measured intellectual development in the same individuals over many years (see Chapter 14). Based on twenty years of longitudinal research, Schaie (1977/1978) proposes three or four stages of adult thought that represent different goals of knowledge corresponding to changing adult patterns of commitment.

Schaie's Stages of Adult Thinking

Schaie's stage theory of lifespan intellectual development builds on Piaget's stages. Schaie believes cognitive abilities develop as Piaget described, but become more

College interactions with professors and other students foster the development of contextual relativism, a postformal mode of thinking that enables the person to embrace abstract ideals and to develop an ethical point of view.

goal directed during adulthood. His stages highlight a clear relationship between psychosocial and cognitive development; external context, such as the demands of work and family, rather than internal organizing structure define each stage. Thus, whereas Piaget's stages describe how an individual acquires new information, Schaie's stages go another step, considering how adults use knowledge differently throughout adulthood.

Childhood and adolescence, according to Schaie, constitute the **period of acquisition** and encompasses all four of Piaget's stages, as shown in Figure 12.4. During the period of acquisition, the person builds basic skills and abilities, from walking and talking to abstract reasoning about future possibilities.

Young adults are in the **achieving stage**. They direct their intelligence toward specific goals rather than following every inclination as might an adolescent who has not yet formulated clear personal choices. Young adults must consider both the contexts and the consequences of their decisions when solving real problems associated with planning careers and establishing families. The decision about whether to take a job, for example, must balance consideration of short-term factors, such as salary and commuting distance, with longer-term factors, such as retirement benefits and promotion opportunities. The decision about when to have a baby must balance the desire for parenthood, the ability to support a child, and the willingness to rearrange other commitments to care for an infant.

In middle adulthood, people enter the **responsible stage**. While in the achieving stage, people strive to meet personal goals. In the responsible stage, people also consider their responsibilities to others—mates, children, aging parents, and community—when making decisions. A middle-aged lawyer, for example, cannot just leave a well-paying job that he dislikes to begin a private practice that will take time to develop when his family depends on the steady income. A promotion may have to be rejected if it requires the family to relocate.

Some middle-aged people have powerful positions that bring broader and more complex responsibilities. For them, middle adulthood also brings the **executive stage**. This calls for a new type of cognition—applying postformal thinking about systems to practical problems—as they work to understand and meet the needs of competing groups in a large organization, such as a business or community organization, that affects many people beyond themselves and their families. A college president, for example, must make decisions about community relations that concern not only members of the college but local residents and perhaps an entire city

FIGURE 12.4
Schaie's Stages of Adult Thinking
Schaie focused on how adults use their knowledge at different periods of adulthood, in contrast to Piaget, who focused on how children and adolescents acquire knowledge. Young adults are typically in Schaie's achieving stage; they direct their intelligence toward specific personal goals.
Source: Adapted from Schaie (1977/1978).

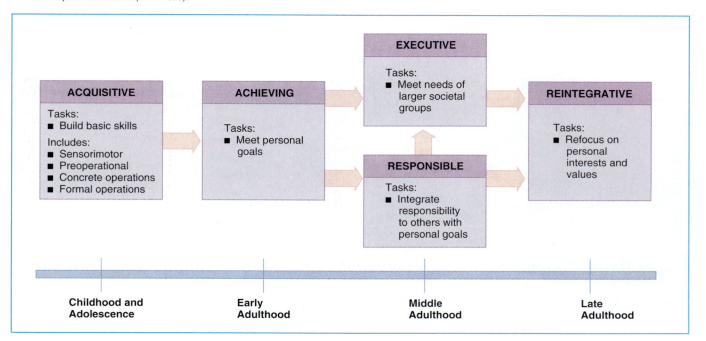

economy and social structure as well. Not all middle-aged individuals have an opportunity to use their cognitive skills to meet this kind of challenge, which is why Schaie talks of three or four adult stages.

Late adulthood is the **reintegrative stage**, when people have fewer long-range plans to make and fewer responsibilities to job and family. This enables them to focus again on their personal interests and values. Older adults are more likely to focus selectively on the issues that have meaning for their own personal lives rather than on abstract questions or the needs of others. It is a time during which they use their intellectual skills to make sense of their own lives, as we discuss in Chapter 17.

Contextual Relativism

William Perry (1970) was the first to examine how adult critical thinking develops over time. He interviewed students at Harvard University about their educational and personal experiences, starting when the students were freshmen and reinterviewing them as they progressed through their college years. Freshmen had a perspective toward intellectual and ethical problems that Perry called **basic dualism**. They saw things in terms of right or wrong, good or bad, we or they. They expected the professor to teach them how to distinguish the one right answer. Students who are dualistic thinkers are often frustrated when the professor presents competing theoretical approaches to a topic and does not say which one is right. Perry's participants gradually became aware of the diversity of opinions, and dualism gave way to *multiplicity*. In this case, students understand that authorities can differ, that many questions have no single right answer. During this stage, students come to see opinions as subjective and to consider their opinions as good as any other. But not all answers are equally good. Perry found that as professors challenged students' personal opinions by demanding evidence to support them, students moved into **contextual relativism**. In this stage, students begin to see that truth is relative, that the meaning of an event depends on its context and on the framework of the knower who is trying to understand the event. Abortion, for example, has different meaning from a "pro-choice" perspective than from a "pro-life" one. Understanding the importance of perspective pushes students to make a commitment to a particular intellectual and/or ethical point of view. As they make a personal commitment to a world view, they transcend subjectivity and the limits of formal operations.

Limitations of Perry's Work Perry's (1970) sample of Harvard University students, however, did not represent all adults or even all college students. Although a few female students participated, Perry used only the male students' responses to establish his scheme of intellectual and ethical development. In addition, Harvard University represents only the most prestigious of colleges, and the students Perry interviewed were all of traditional college age.

Broadening Perry's Approach Nevertheless, Perry's work has had a great deal of influence on subsequent researchers, who have tried to broaden the picture to include women, less prestigious institutions, and a broader range of adult ages.

In one such study, Mary Belenky, Blythe Clinchy, Nancy Goldberger, and Jill Tarule (1986) interviewed 135 women from six academic institutions ranging from an inner-city high school to a prestigious women's college, as well as several family agencies, or "invisible colleges," that assist clients with questions about parenting. They believed that relationships to authority matter in how we know. Given the diversity of participants, they found some women (none of whom were in college) who experienced *silent knowing*. These women felt "passive, reactive, and dependent, they see authorities as being all-powerful, if not overpowering" (p. 27). Among college freshmen, they found women who were concrete and dualistic in their thinking, as Perry's dualistic thinkers were. Belenky and her associates call this *received knowing,* because the women were receiving the truth from others. Whereas the dualistic Harvard men in Perry's study identified with the authority, the women in Belenky et al.'s study saw the authority as "other."

The next development among the women was *subjective knowing.* Subjective knowing is like Perry's multiplicity in many ways, but subjectivist women seem to be less concerned than men with persuading others. They also distrust logic, analysis, abstraction, and language, as well as authorities such as teachers, doctors, scientists, and men in general. Women at this stage feel in flux because they are lacking a secure, integrated, and enduring self-concept. Their predominant learning mode is one of inward listening and watching. Some women move from subjective knowing to *procedural knowing,* which is based on abstract reasoning (formal operations) and represents a shift from subjective opinions to reasoned arguments. Making this transition requires interacting with authorities who teach how to reason; the women who reached this stage were attending college or had graduated from college.

When women integrate subjective and objective knowing, they move to *constructed knowing.* This stage corresponds to Perry's contextual relativism. Women at this stage see that all knowledge is constructed, that truth is a matter of context, that frame of reference matters, and that they are responsible for developing the systems they will use to construct knowledge. At the most advanced ways of knowing, problem finding and other ways of critical thinking that are beyond formal thought become prominent.

You may have noticed that while the men in Perry's study all seemed to develop contextual relativism, only some of the women in Belenky et al.'s study reached procedural or constructed knowing. Why? Belenky and her associates interviewed women from a wide spectrum of institutions, whereas Perry interviewed only Harvard men. The differences in findings may be due to gender, or to one group being homogeneous and privileged and the other being diverse, or to a combination of both factors. In this regard, it is significant that the women who did progress to higher levels of thinking were those with college experience. A more recent three-year study of Harvard undergraduate men and women found that despite levels of educational achievement, success, or satisfaction, women bring more self-doubt to education than do their male counterparts (Light, 1990). Because men have historically been the "fact makers," women, especially minority women, feel more alienated in academic settings (Gallos, 1993; Maher & Tetreault, 1994). Thus, differences due to educational level, SES, race/ethnicity, and gender are probably at work.

Whether called *contextual relativism* or *constructed knowing,* the development of a postformal mode of thinking enables the person to embrace abstract ideals and develop an ethical point of view. As we will see, these developments allow young adults to transcend conventional levels of moral reasoning.

What Do You Think?

With your classmates, consider ways in which your college may be less hospitable to female than male students. How might this discrepancy affect male and female students' ways of knowing?

ADULT MORAL REASONING

As we saw in Chapter 10's discussion of cognitive development in adolescence, moral development depends on cognitive structures. Lawrence Kohlberg, building on Piaget's cognitive stages, developed stages of moral judgment. At the *preconventional level,* punishment and reward guide individual morality; at the *conventional level,* social rules guide it; and at the *postconventional level,* moral principles guide it. Just as Piaget's stages focus exclusively on logical skills and ignore social or emotional context, Kohlberg's stages focus on the abstract ethic of justice (or rules) and ignore the social or emotional context of moral decision making. Carol Gilligan and her associates have criticized Kohlberg's one-sided view of morality. Empathy, they argue, is a primary motivator for moral judgment and ethical behavior. They provide their own three-stage model of moral development. At the *survival orientation* stage, the person focuses on caring for the self to ensure survival. At the *conventional care* stage, she or he focuses on responsibility to others. At the *integrated care* stage, she or he coordinates the needs of self and of others.

How do the justice and care perspectives compare when directed toward the same issue? The public abortion debate serves as an example (Gilligan & Attanucci, 1988). When approached from the perspective of justice, the claims of the fetus and the pregnant woman are placed in opposition. Is the fetus a person? Should its claims take precedence over the pregnant woman's? From the perspective of care, on the other hand, the connection between the fetus and the pregnant woman is central and the moral question becomes whether it is responsible or irresponsible to extend or end this connection. Which is caring and which is careless? We saw in Chapter 10 that adolescents develop more ethical beliefs about both care and justice, though few develop postconventional moral judgment or integrated care.

Context and Moral Orientation

Research investigating adult moral development has assessed orientation (justice or care) and level of moral reasoning as a function of gender, age, experience, and the content or situation of the moral problem. Much of the work has been done with college students. Mary Rothbart, Dean Hanley, and Marc Albert (1986) found that the content of the dilemma, or situational factors, had a strong influence on moral orientation. They interviewed undergraduate men and women about three different moral dilemmas: Kohlberg's classic Heinz dilemma (Should Heinz steal medicine from a druggist who is charging an outrageous price, in order to save his wife's life?), a dilemma concerning physical intimacy, and a dilemma from their own lives. Responses were coded according to their justice or care orientation. The investigators found that all respondents used both care and justice orientations in the course of the interview, and only 4 percent used one orientation on any one dilemma exclusively. Whereas the Heinz dilemma more often called forth a justice orientation and the physical intimacy dilemma a care orientation, the "own life" dilemma was equally divided for both genders. Nancy Yacker and Sharon Weinberg (1990) studied male and female law and social work students and found social work students were more likely to use care and law students justice, regardless of gender. Nancy Clopton and Gwendolyn Sorell (1993) studied the moral reasoning orientations of men and women presented with parenting dilemmas and found no gender differences. These studies support the conclusion that differences in moral reasoning result from different types of dilemmas women and men encounter rather than from gender characteristics.

Gender and Moral Voice

Kathleen Galotti (1989) asked male and female undergraduates to write responses to the question "When faced with a moral dilemma, what issues or concerns influence your decision?" The responses were coded according to one or more of thirteen themes. "Feminine" themes included *what others would think and/or feel, effects on others, situation specifics, effect on self, gut feeling/intuition,* and *personal guilt.* "Masculine" themes included *greater societal good, legal issues, general principles, reasoning systematically, religious teachings, personal code of*

A Multicultural View

Moral Orientation in the United States and China

A basic criticism of Lawrence Kohlberg's stage theory of moral development is that it is based on data gathered from a culturally homogeneous and all-male sample. The problem of gender has received a lot of attention thanks to the work of Carol Gilligan and her colleagues. Studies looking at social class (e.g., Bardige et al., 1988; Ward, 1988) have shown that low SES status does not hinder moral development; urban youth use both justice and care orientations and can sustain both orientations simultaneously when discussing real-life events. To understand their moral perspective, however, we need to expand the analytical framework to include categories of justice and of care and combined categories.

What about moral orientations in different cultures and subcultures? John Snarey (1985) has criticized Kohlberg's theory for being too bound to Western culture, especially at the postconventional level of reasoning. While Kohlberg's guidelines for scoring include examples of reasoning from a broad range of viewpoints at lower levels of reasoning, the guidelines and examples for scoring the fifth and sixth stages of moral reasoning are particularly culture bound. An answer to the Heinz dilemma that places the right to life over the right to property, for example, earns a stage 5 designation. However, a response such as "Everyone has the obligation to relieve human misery and suffering, if possible . . . I do think you have certain obligations to your wife and your friends or relatives that are just deeper" earns only a stage 4 designation because of the contextual consideration. This makes it difficult for people of other cultures to be con-

sidered to have reached the postconventional level of moral development or for someone in this culture who has developed a *contextual relativism* in Perry's sense (Murphy & Gilligan, 1980). Rosemary Mennuti and Don Creamer (1991) call for a sensitivity to the variations in moral perspectives in other cultures and within a culture.

The Chinese culture, for example, has been oriented toward collectivism and conciliation rather than justice and autonomy. Because of this, Valerie Stander and Larry Jensen (1993) expected that, compared to Americans, Chinese people might exhibit more of an orientation toward care than toward justice. They studied men and women undergraduates in the United States and China using two groups of Americans—Mormons and non-Mormons attending Brigham Young University—and one group of Chinese students from Beijing Normal University. The Chinese students all reported no religion. The non-Mormon Americans were predominantly Christians of various faiths.

To assess moral orientation, the investigators asked each participant to fill out the World View Questionnaire. Each of the forty items consisted of a pair of adjectives, one representing each orientation, from which the participant was to choose. Sample items appear in Table 12.6. The Chinese students' form was printed in Chinese, the Americans' in English.

Stander and Jensen found differences in scores on the questionnaires based on culture. Unlike their prediction, the Chinese students chose the smallest number of caring adjectives, the Mormons chose the most caring adjectives,

ethics, and *rights of others*. The people who coded the responses did not know whether men or women had written them. Galotti found that the essays of men and those of women were not distinguishable. There was no difference in the proportion of women and men who gave postconventional responses. Likewise, no differences were found in theme usage for twelve of the thirteen themes (men were more likely to use the theme *reasoning systematically*). Overall, usage of themes identified as feminine was double or triple the usage of themes identified as masculine.

Studies of adult moral development therefore show that the "different voice" Carol Gilligan (1982) identified is not just a "female voice." Most adults use more than one moral orientation. Many studies show no gender differences in moral orientation, whereas some show that women exhibit more diversity in their moral reasoning than men do (Stiller & Forrest, 1990). Women sometimes respond to dilemmas with further questions: "What does Heinz wish?" "What is the condition of Mrs. Heinz's life?" "Why is the druggist behaving so?" "Does Heinz have children dependent upon him for care?" "Who would care for the children if Heinz went to jail?" (Belenky et al., 1986). These questions reflect the importance of context.

Critics of Gilligan believe her assertion that women tend to resolve dilemmas using the care approach whereas men tend to use the justice approach exaggerates

and the non-Mormon Americans fell in between. The two American groups were more like each other than either was to the Chinese group. This clearly indicated cultural differences based on both nationality and religion.

Why did the cultural differences not confirm the prediction that the Chinese students would be more caring?

It may be that the Chinese viewpoint of collectivism represents a different form of caring than that measured by the World View Questionnaire. Appropriate cross-cultural measurement may require more than just a language translation of a questionnaire. It may also be that Chinese culture is changing or is misunderstood.

TABLE 12.6   *Selected Items from World View Questionnaire*
The World View Questionnaire was designed by Jensen et al. (1991) to differentiate between caring and justice orientations; one adjective in each pair represents each orientation. Stander and Jensen (1993) gave the World View Questionnaire to American Mormons, American non-Mormons, and Chinese subjects reporting no religion. The Chinese respondents chose the fewest caring adjectives and the Mormons the most, indicating cultural differences in moral orientation based on both nationality and religion.

Circle the contrasting adjective you think is more important to you personally.

1. Logic	Intuition
2. Compromise	Power
3. Consistency	Forgiveness
4. Organized	Creative
5. Those we love	Self
6. Justice	Mercy
7. Principles	People
8. Getting along with others	Achievement
9. Sense of right	Sensitivity to others
10. Educating the mind	Educating the heart
11. Competitive ability	Cooperative ability
12. Loyalty	Leadership

Source: Adapted from Stander & Jensen (1993).

gender difference. Rachel Hare-Mustin and Jeanne Marecek (1990) point out that care orientation may reflect a lack of power in the current situation more than it reflects enduring gender differences. Those in dominant positions tend to promote rules, as in the justice orientation, whereas those in subordinate positions tend to appeal to understanding, as in the care orientation. Men more often use the justice approach because they more often hold powerful positions, not because of their gender. Carol Stack (1993) looked at moral reasoning of African Americans living in conditions of economic deprivation and found a convergence between men's and women's modes of thinking that she attributes to conditions of poverty. See the accompanying Multicultural View box for a multicultural perspective. Differences in moral reasoning should be expected when women's and men's daily lives differ and similarities when their daily lives are similar.

What Do You Think?

Think of a moral dilemma that you expect would call forth similar orientations from male and female students. Think of one that would not. Try your choices out on some friends or classmates. What aspects of each dilemma seem to be important?

Informal discussions in the dorms, such as these students are having, are one reason why living on campus provides an intellectual advantage. But the largest advantage is that young adults who attend college grow in intellectual skills as compared to those who do not attend college.

COLLEGE

The work of Perry (1970) and Belenky et al. (1986) clearly demonstrates that the college experience cultivates intellectual development, that college not only teaches large amounts of information but also fosters a progression in ways of thinking. Darrin Lehman and Richard Nisbett (1990) studied 165 undergraduates majoring in the natural sciences, humanities, and social sciences and found they showed improvements in reasoning from the first through fourth years in college. Ernest Pascarella and Patrick Terenzini (1991) found that traditional- and nontraditional-age seniors performed better than freshmen in abstract reasoning and critical thinking; they were also more intellectually flexible and better able to develop abstract frameworks. It appears that all measures of adult cognition increase with level of education, as does maintenance of cognitive performance as people age (Labouvie-Vief, 1985; Reese & Rodeheaver, 1985). Susan Heidrich and Nancy Denney (1994) examined the effects of age, gender, education, and intellectual abilities on problem-solving performances of eighteen- to eighty-one-year-olds. They found that level of problem solving was positively related to higher levels of education and not to age.

Compared to other large industrialized countries, the United States has the most educated population, as Figure 12.5 shows. In 1991 only young Japanese men (ages twenty-five to thirty-four) were more likely than young American men to complete college. Young American women were much more likely to have completed college than women of any other country and than men of any country but Japan (U.S. Department of Education, 1993).

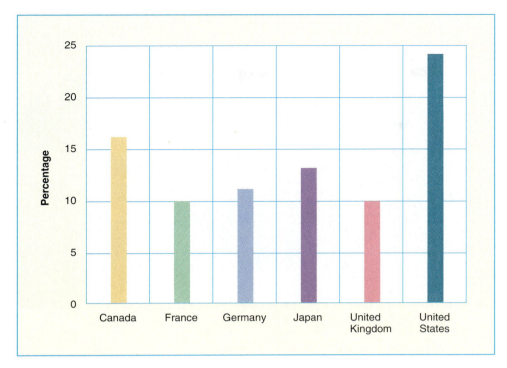

FIGURE 12.5

College Graduates in Large Industrialized Countries, 1991

In 1991, a larger percentage of twenty-five- to sixty-four-year-olds in the United States had completed four or more years of college than in any other large, industrialized country.
Source: U.S. Department of Education (1993).

FIGURE 12.6

Probability of Attaining a B.A.
In tracking the progress of 1980 high school graduates, Lee, Mackie-Lewis, and Marks (1993) found that whether students went directly to a four-year college or went to a community college and then transferred to a four-year college did not change the likelihood of their graduating from college by 1986. The groups also did not differ in whether or not they went on to enroll in graduate school.

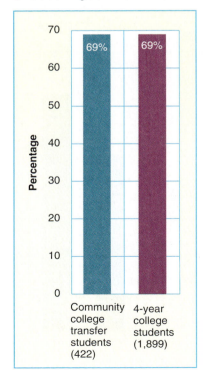

Public and private colleges and universities offer two- and four-year programs that address a diverse range of student needs. Junior and community colleges offer vocational training or the first two years of coursework at the college level. Colleges offer four-year programs leading to a bachelor's degree, as well as professional and graduate programs. Family income and mother's highest level of education are two aspects of family background that are strongly associated with the type of institution a student attends (U.S. Department of Education, 1993). Students from low-income families are more likely to attend public two-year colleges than any other type; students from high-income families are more likely to enroll in four-year, Ph.D.-granting universities. Children of less educated mothers are more likely to attend two-year colleges; whereas children of well-educated mothers are more likely to attend Ph.D.-granting colleges and universities. Attendance at four-year colleges without Ph.D.-granting programs is not associated with mother's educational level.

Does the kind of school you attend matter? Most studies have shown that the benefits of college can be realized at any type of school. Pascarella and Terenzini (1991) found that while there were differences in cognitive growth as a function of the kind of education, the largest difference was the fact that those who attended college grew in intellectual skills compared to young adults who did not attend college. Living on campus does seem to provide an intellectual advantage. Ernest Pascarella and his associates (1993) found that resident students made significantly larger freshman-year gains in critical thinking than commuting students. Another factor that leads to cognitive growth is the amount of contact between students and faculty, especially informal interaction (Lamport, 1993; Pascarella & Terenzini, 1991). As Figure 12.6 indicates, attending a community college is as likely to lead to a B.A. as attending a four-year college directly.

The college student body became more diverse in age and race/ethnicity the last two decades.

FIGURE 12.7
Changes in Percentage of High School Graduates Enrolling in College, 1973 and 1991
The percentage of high school graduates enrolling in college has increased substantially since 1973. The number of older students enrolling in college increased even more rapidly during the 1980s.
Source: U.S. Department of Education (1993).

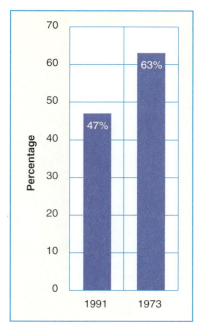

Who Attends College?

While most high school graduates go directly to college, colleges enroll adults of all ages in addition to adolescent students. As Figure 12.7 shows, the rate of college enrollment for younger students has grown substantially, but the number of older students has been growing even more rapidly. Between 1980 and 1990, enrollment of students under age twenty-five increased by 2 percent, while enrollment of students twenty-five and older rose by 32 percent (U.S. Department of Education, 1992).

Students go to college for a variety of reasons. Younger students may attend because their parents and teachers expect them to, because they wish to obtain a liberal arts education or attain specific career goals, or simply because they do not know what else to do. Some gifted young adolescents forgo the high school experience in favor of the intellectual challenge of early entrance to college (Noble & Drummond, 1992). Middle-aged adults are more likely to be preparing for careers or career changes, and older adults are more likely to be learning for the sake of learning (O'Connor, 1987).

Women and Racial/Ethnic Minorities

Women are more likely than men to attend college. In 1991, 67 percent of female high school graduates were in college, compared to only 58 percent of male graduates. Women are also more likely than men to complete college within four years of starting (U.S. Department of Education, 1993).

Is the college experience different for women and men? Marcia Magolda (1989) investigated gender differences in cognitive development and the relationship between ways of viewing knowledge and approaches to learning. Men and women viewed the acquisition of knowledge differently, but no differences were found in the bases of cognitive structures or learning styles. In a review of the literature on gender differences in the experience of higher education, John Richardson and Estelle King (1991) found little consistent or valid evidence for gender differences in the amount learned and some evidence for parallel but distinct development of ways of knowing similar to the findings of Perry and Belerky et al. we discussed earlier in this chapter.

The college student body became more racially and ethnically diverse in the last two decades, from 15 percent minority students in 1976 to 21 percent in 1991 (U.S. Department of Education, 1993). Figure 12.8 shows the likelihood of going to college by race/ethnicity.

What about the college experience for minority students? Erica Gosman and her colleagues (1983) found significant differences between African American and white students in terms of attrition rates, overall progression rates (defined as length of time to graduation), and tendency to follow the prescribed progression pattern (sophomore in the second year, junior in the third year, senior in the fourth year, and graduate after the fourth year). Racial differences disappeared when the effects of other student and institutional characteristics were statistically controlled.

According to Joseph Ponterotto (1990), higher dropout rates among African Americans, Hispanics, and Native Americans result from an inhospitable climate on most predominantly white college campuses. Marvalene Hughes (1987) distributed questionnaires to eighty-nine African American undergraduates attending predominantly white and predominantly African American college campuses. Students reported greater satisfaction at predominantly African American campuses because the social support systems assisted students in their social, cultural, emotional, intellectual, and spiritual development. Fewer incidents of misunderstanding or hostility enabled students to adjust better on these campuses. Researchers point out that colleges and universities must help minority students to develop academically, socially, and personally, or they will become increasingly segregated (Cheatham & Berg-Cross, 1992; Gosman et al., 1983; Ponterotto, 1990; Wright, 1987). One way they suggest for improving campus climate is to provide education on cultural diversity in such areas as the meanings underlying the interpretations of nonverbal behavior, individual achievement, and competition.

College is one of the major events of early adulthood. For many people, it is the first step in the transition from adolescence to independence. The next step is establishing a career; for those who do not go to college, work is often the path to independence.

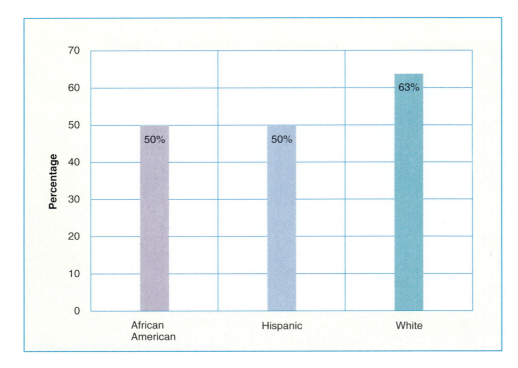

FIGURE 12.8
Percentage Attending College by Race/Ethnicity, 1990
Over the last two decades the college population has become more racially and ethnically diverse. African Americans and Hispanic Americans are equally likely to attend college, but less likely than white Americans.
Source: U.S. Department of Education (1993).

What Do You Think?

Imagine that your younger brother tells you he plans to be a carpenter and does not want to go to college. Use the research on college and cognition to try to convince him to attend.

WORK

Work is a major social role of adult life; it forms a critical part of one's identity. One of the first questions we ask when we meet someone new is "What do you do?" Except for the few who are very rich, adults need to work to support themselves and their families. Most would choose to work even without financial necessity (Opinion Roundup, 1980).

Experience with work generally starts long before an individual reaches adulthood. Many children set up lemonade stands or do chores for relatives or neighbors to earn spending money. Teenagers often baby-sit, mow lawns, walk dogs, or get part-time jobs. Work starts early in life and develops and changes throughout the life cycle. During early adulthood, individuals typically establish an occupation or a career. *Occupation* refers to all forms of work, whereas *career* usually refers to professional occupations such as doctor, lawyer, or engineer. In addition to providing economic rewards, one's occupation helps to define one's self, gives structure to one's life, establishes a context for relating to other people, organizes one's time, and gives meaning to one's life.

Career Stages

Jeffrey Greenhaus (1988) has proposed the five-stage ladder of career development shown in Table 12.5. Each stage has an approximate age range and a set of major tasks. The first three stages—preparation for work, organizational entry, and early career—usually take place prior to and during early adulthood, but they may occur at any time. For example, a midlife woman who has finished raising her family may

In addition to gaining competence on the job, during the early career stage these men must learn about other work options and develop a balance between work and nonwork involvements.

TABLE 12.5   Characteristics of Different Career Stages
Each of Jeffrey Greenhaus's five stages of career development has a typical age range and a set of major tasks. The first three stages typically take place during early adulthood, when establishing an occupation is a major developmental task, but these may occur or reoccur in middle adulthood as men and women reassess their earlier occupational choices.

1. Preparation for Work
   Typical Age Range: 0–25
   Major Tasks: Develop occupational self-image; assess alternative occupations; develop initial occupational choice; pursue necessary education

2. Organizational Entry
   Typical Age Range: 18–25
   Major Tasks: Obtain job offer(s) from desired organization(s), select appropriate job based on accurate information

3. Early Career
   Typical Age Range: 25–40
   Major Tasks: Learn job and organizational rules and norms: fit into chosen occupation and organization; increase competence, pursue Dream

4. Mid-career
   Typical Age Range: 40–55
   Major Tasks: Reappraise early career and early adulthood; reaffirm or modify Dream; make choices appropriate to middle adult years; remain productive at work

5. Late Career
   Typical Age Range: 55–Retirement
   Major Tasks: Remain productive in work; maintain self-esteem; prepare for effective retirement

Source: Adapted from Greenhaus (1987, Table 5.4, p. 87).

begin preparing for work by entering college at the same time her children do, or a midlife man may prepare to enter a different occupation once his family is no longer dependent on him. Nonetheless, young adults are usually concerned with these three stages of career development. The stages of mid-career and late career are typical of middle adulthood.

Preparation for work includes self-exploration to discover one's interests, talents, and preferences. It includes training, such as college or vocational school, apprenticeship, or on-the-job skill development. It should also include learning about the actual work one does on the job. Many academic programs now include internships to give students the opportunity to learn about jobs that interest them, as well as to learn skills necessary for the jobs. This on-the-job experience can help reduce *reality shock,* the disappointment felt when the actual experience of being on a new job fails to meet the unrealistic, often idealistic expectations. Reality shock is common (Reilly et al., 1981). It occurs when a new teacher realizes that being a teacher includes lunchroom duty, parent conferences, and many other practical tasks that do not involve planning curriculum and working with students, or when a new reporter discovers that not all stories she will cover are exciting or even interesting.

Organizational entry involves finding a job. This means knowing what work one wants to do, but it also means responding to the demands of the job market. Among twenty-five- to twenty-nine-year-olds who have not completed high school, employment rates are substantially lower than among those who have. For males ages thirty to sixty-four, employment rates have increased among those with a bachelor's degree compared to those with only some college work. For females of both age groups, employment rates have increased substantially with each higher level of education (U.S. Department of Education, 1993).

The early career stage involves gaining competence on the job as well as developing a balance between fitting into the organization and learning about other options and directions for one's career. John Keller (1985) points out that because of the increasing incidence of career changes, career and occupational counselors need to encourage people just beginning their first jobs to think about career change options. The early career stage also involves developing a balance between work and nonwork commitments. Given the challenges of establishing this balance, it is not surprising that older people tend to be more satisfied with their jobs than younger people are. As we will see in Chapter 14, there are many reasons for this difference.

Other factors play a role in career development as well. Sometimes a person cannot achieve personal goals because of an inhospitable or discriminatory work environment, as we will see next.

Gender, Race, and Socioeconomic Status

If we look around us, it is easy to see that women and minorities are not equally represented in all occupations. Gender, race, and socioeconomic status (SES) affect which jobs people attain. Sociologists define **discrimination** as the valuation in the labor market of personal characteristics of a worker that are not related to productivity. Discrimination can be based on differences in prework experiences, such as educational background, health, and marital status, or on prejudice on the part of employers, coworkers, or customers (Thornborrow & Sheldon, 1995). An employer that requires a high school diploma even though one is not necessary for doing the job is practicing discrimination, as is a patient who will see only a male doctor. Women, racial/ethnic minorities, and individuals from lower socioeconomic backgrounds experience differential treatment and opportunities before they enter the labor force and face differential treatment once they are in it. These factors account for their overall lower incomes and status in the labor market.

How do women fare in the world of work? In 1992, women made up 45 percent of the labor force and 58 percent of all women were in the labor force. The median annual earnings of women working full time were 69 percent of men's (Thornborrow & Sheldon, 1995). All of these statistics represent significant gains for women over the twentieth century. But women still face serious discrimination in hiring and evaluation and are less likely than men to be promoted to upper-level managerial positions (Good for Business, 1995).

Occupational Segregation   The major limiting factor is the fact that most jobs today are held by either men or women; few are truly integrated. This situation is called **occupational segregation**. In 1990, for example, 82 percent of architects were male and 95 percent of typists were female (Amott, 1995). Whereas over the past three decades women have been entering traditionally male occupations, men have not been entering traditionally female occupations. Women have been able to make much greater inroads into male-dominated professions than into male-dominated blue-collar jobs. In 1990, for example, fewer than 2 percent of carpenters were women. Occupations that depend on education have been more receptive to women than have occupations that require physical strength and skill (Lips, 1993). As we saw in the last section, women today are more likely to attend college than men are. Having a degree gives them proof of their qualifications for professions, but does not help them enter jobs that require on-the-job training. In a study of more than fifteen hundred individuals, Patricia Gurin (1981) found that white and African American women had tried job training or job changes less often and had acquired additional schooling more often than white or African American men. The largest gains for women have been in the higher-paying executive, administrative, and managerial positions, which explains why the wage gap between women and men has been narrowing (Thornborrow & Sheldon, 1995). However, women are not a homogeneous group in the work force.

In a study of African American and white low-income youth, William Kenkel and Bruce Gage (1983) found that anticipation of working, achievement motivation, perceived barriers to achieving one's desired occupation, encouragement from parents, work experience, and the rewards sought in an occupation all contributed to most females' aspiring to "gender-appropriate" occupations. A large proportion of females stated preferences for one of five specific jobs: teacher, nurse, secretary, beautician, and social worker.

Differences Between Jobs   Economists divide jobs into two categories, which they call the primary and secondary sectors. The *primary sector* includes high-wage jobs that provide good benefits, job security, and advancement opportunities. It includes professional jobs that require training and certification as well as manufacturing jobs that offer relatively high wages and job security. The *secondary sector* includes low-wage jobs with few fringe benefits and little advancement opportunity. The white-collar jobs in this sector include sales and clerical; the blue-collar jobs include private household, laborer, and most service jobs. It is very hard to move between sectors, since no career ladders connect the two types of jobs. Pat, for example, started as a departmental secretary and worked her way up to become the dean's secretary. When a new dean was hired, she did the work of an administrative assistant, since she knew the system better than he did. When it was time to hire an assistant dean, however, Pat was not considered because she was a secretary, not a managerial employee. Pat left the secretarial position and returned to college, which will enable her to get a job in the primary sector.

How do ethnic and racial minorities fare in terms of the job sectors? Amott (1995) reports, "For decades, the majority of women of all racial-ethnic groups, along with most men of color, were found in the secondary sector" (p. 209). This means they tend to have less desirable jobs and less job security than white men do. In 1993 the unemployment rate for whites was 6.0 percent, whereas for African Americans it was 12.9 percent and for Hispanics 10.6 percent (U.S. Department of Labor, 1994). Minority men earned less than white men, and women in each category earned less than the men in that category. Various factors contribute to the income differentials, including prejudice against minority workers, different access to education, and internalized negative self-images as an effect of racial/ethnic discrimination.

Phillip Bowman (1990) found indicators revealing more gender similarities than differences among male and female African American youth (nineteen to twenty-eight years old) in the school-to-work transition. The young men and women faced similar stress as they searched for jobs. Because tests used to measure vocational interests have not been validated with racial/ethnic group members, vocational counselors are less able to help racial/ethnic minorities. Robert Carter and Jane Swanson (1990) reviewed the literature and found that scales used to measure vocational interest, such as the widely used Strong Interest Inventory, have not been properly tested with African Americans. They report that studies have found African Americans and whites exhibit different patterns of interests, but this does not tell us whether these differences reflect within-group cultural characteristics, an understanding of the occupational opportunity structure, or both.

What Do You Think?

Has occupational segregation had any influence on the jobs you have had so far and/or the occupation you would like to enter? If so, how has it influenced your life? Has it affected what you think you can do?

GROWTH AND CHANGE

As we have seen, early adulthood is a time of cognitive growth in response to higher education and the increasingly complex responsibilities that typically accompany this period. Young adults change as they meet the challenges of finding an occupation, establishing new friendships and families, and maintaining relationships with the families that raised them. As our discussions of physical and cognitive development indicate, the social context has a major impact on all aspects of development. In the next chapter, we direct our attention to psychosocial development in the early adult years.

SUMMARY OF MAJOR IDEAS

1. Early adulthood, roughly the period from ages twenty to forty, entails assuming responsibility for the adult tasks of earning a living and establishing a household.

PHYSICAL DEVELOPMENT

Physical Functioning

2. Young adults are at the peak of their physical functioning. They reach their full height, their body systems are fully mature, and they are unlikely to have many noticeable signs of aging.

3. Age-related changes begin in many body systems during early adulthood, but the declines are gradual. The cardiovascular and respiratory systems show the most noticeable changes by age forty.

Health in Early Adulthood

4. Young adults generally feel healthy. Although disease may be present, it is likely to be in early stages, undiagnosed, and unsymptomatic.

5. Many of the losses in functioning suffered by aging adults are due to pathological aging resulting from unhealthy environmental conditions and health-compromising behaviors rather than to normal aging.

6. Young adults can set the stage for healthy aging by eating a nutritious diet, doing regular aerobic exercise, controlling their weight, and avoiding smoking, alcohol and drug abuse, and unsafe sex.

Stress

7. Stress is arousal of the mind and body in response to demands made on them by stressors. The general adaptation syndrome, a pattern of physical response to stress, accumulates to lay the groundwork for disease.

8. Stress has psychological dimensions as well. Negative, uncontrollable, ambiguous, or overwhelming events are perceived as more stressful than positive, controllable, clear-cut, or manageable events.

9. Stress contributes to illness in multiple ways. It can have a direct physical effect that wears down the physiological system. It can affect people with personalities that predispose them to stress. It can also contribute to illness by negatively influencing health behaviors.

Sexuality

10. The sexual response cycle has five stages—desire, excitement, plateau, orgasm, and resolution—that are very similar for men and women.

11. People's beliefs about sexual morality are part of a broader social and religious outlook and affect sexual practices in some ways but not others.

12. Sexual dysfunctions are not uncommon. Both sexes often complain of low sexual desire. For women, orgasmic problems are a frequent complaint. For men, ejaculatory problems and erectile dysfunctions are common problems.

Infertility

13. Infertility affects a substantial minority of couples at some time in their reproductive lives and often leads to psychological reactions of grief, anger, and guilt.

COGNITIVE DEVELOPMENT

Postformal Thought

14. Cognitive theorists have proposed a fifth postformal stage of adult thought characterized as relative and nonabsolute, accepting contradiction, and synthesizing contradiction.

Development of Contextual Thinking

15. Schaie's stage theory of intellectual development includes three or four stages that go beyond Piaget's formal operations and reflect the goal-directed and contextual nature of adult thinking.

16. Examination of the development of critical thinking has led to an understanding that mature thought depends on the context of the event and the framework of the knower.

Adult Moral Reasoning

17. Studies of adult moral reasoning indicate that the content or situation of the problem may be more important than gender in influencing whether a justice or a care orientation is used.

College

18. The college experience fosters intellectual development. Although different types of schools provide different benefits, the biggest difference in cognitive growth occurs between adults who attend college and those who do not.

19. Today's college student body is diverse in terms of age, gender, and race/ethnicity. Older students often go to college for different reasons than younger students. More women go to college than men. Racial/ethnic minorities face an inhospitable climate on predominantly white college campuses and need more social support services than are currently provided.

Work

20. Work is a critical part of adult life that helps define the self, give structure to life, and provide means of support. Work starts early and continues throughout life, but with different emphases or stages.

21. Gender, race, and SES affect which jobs people are likely to attain. Discrimination and occupational segregation channel white men into the primary sector of the economy and African American men, as well as all women, into the secondary sector.

KEY TERMS

organ reserve *(412)*

pathological aging *(414)*

health-compromising
    behaviors *(414)*

general adaptation
    syndrome *(423)*

posttraumatic stress
    disorder (PTSD) *(425)*

sexual dysfunction *(429)*

infertility *(431)*

postformal thought *(435)*

problem finding *(435)*

fifth stage of cognitive
    development *(435)*

period of acquisition *(438)*

achieving stage *(438)*

responsible stage *(438)*

executive stage *(438)*

reintegrative stage *(439)*

basic dualism *(439)*

contextual relativism *(439)*

discrimination *(450)*

occupational
    segregation *(451)*

13

EARLY ADULTHOOD

Psychosocial Development

Focusing Questions

- How does development in adulthood differ from development in childhood and adolescence?

- What are the various forms intimacy can take in early adulthood?

- In what ways has marriage changed in the last few decades?

- What are the lifestyle choices for young adults who choose not to marry?

- What is the impact of parenthood on couples, on single parents, and on remarried parents?

B ill is twenty-six. He has been living with his girlfriend, Karen, who is twenty-five, for six months. They met in college. Bill had been working for a year as a part-time tutor at the Writing Resource Center when, at the beginning of their junior year, Karen joined the staff. Each was already involved in a romantic relationship, but Karen and Bill became friends. They found they had a lot in common: both came from the same area of Connecticut, and they knew a few of the same people. They would chat at the Writing Resource Center and sometimes go out for coffee.

During their senior year, the nature of their relationship changed. Both had ended their romantic relationships over the summer, and they began to spend more and more time together. By second semester, Bill and Karen were lovers as well as friends; they had become a couple. That was four years ago.

After graduation, Bill got a job as a reporter for a newspaper in Connecticut; Karen entered law school in Massachusetts. Bill worked four long days, Monday through Thursday. After work on Thursday he would drive to Boston and stay with Karen until Monday morning, then drive back to work. Karen studied much of the time Bill was with her, but they liked being together and he used some of the time to look for a job in the Boston area. Before Karen completed her first year of law school, Bill found a job in the area and moved to a town outside of Boston. Although he would have liked to live with Karen, she had a lease and a commitment to roommates, and he felt he needed experience living on his own. They liked being closer, but each was very busy, so they still saw each other mostly on weekends and one night during the week. By the time Karen graduated from law school, Bill had a new job as assistant editor for a magazine, and they were ready and eager to look for a place to live together.

As you can see, Bill and Karen have faced the developmental tasks that are paramount in early adulthood. They have simultaneously begun the key tasks of establishing an intimate relationship, embarking on careers, and establishing independence from their parents. Much more still lies ahead. Karen has yet to find a full-time position as an attorney. Bill is balancing the benefits of on-the-job advancement and getting a graduate degree. Both will have to decide about marriage in the next few years, and both say they want children while they are still young. These challenges are easy to anticipate, but they will face many others.

THEORIES OF ADULT DEVELOPMENT

Contrary to what many believe, reaching early adulthood is not the end of development, but it does mark a significant change. Physical maturation plays a key role in child and adolescent development and paves the way for new challenges at similar ages. As we saw in Chapter 12, physical changes in early adulthood have little effect on behavior. This continues to be true in middle adulthood for most individuals and in late adulthood for many. Biology has much less to do with adult development than do cultural, social, and personal factors, which serve as the impetus for change and growth. As adults face new challenges, they develop new behaviors, cognitive skills, and ways of interacting. They take on new roles, which set the stage for new demands.

While there are similarities in the challenges of adulthood, individuals can follow many different paths. Adult development is marked by much greater diversity than child or adolescent development, and this diversity increases with age. People may marry early, late, or never. They may become parents early, late, or never. These are just two examples of variability, and each represents a very different set of social roles and responsibilities adults will face at similar ages. Whether or not adults marry, they will still have similar needs to establish intimacy with other people. Whether or not they become parents, they will still have similar needs to pass on what they know and care about to the next generation.

Given the diversity of developmental paths during adulthood, theorists have had a difficult time developing a neat stage model of adult development. Theories of adult development focus on common elements in diverse experiences, paying particular attention to the two basic psychosocial needs of mentally healthy adulthood first articulated by Freud: to love and to work. These theories suggest the various changes most people can expect more than they describe a specific developmental pattern. The theories fall into two broad categories: timing of events theories and normative crisis theories. *Timing of events theories* focus on the importance of the developmental context to adult psychosocial development. They would predict that Bill will marry Karen in the next few years because he has internalized his family's expectations about when to marry and because his friends are marrying. In contrast, *normative crisis theories* focus on the importance of stirrings within the individual, or inner crises. Because they highlight impulses within the individual, crisis theories are also considered to be psychodynamic theories, as Erikson's theory is (see Chapter 2). Crisis theories would predict that Bill will marry Karen in the next few years because of his inner needs for intimacy and emotional support now that he has separated from his parents. For Bill and Karen to marry, of course, Karen will have to feel similar social expectations or inner needs, depending on the theory.

Despite the differing premises underlying these theories, most tend to overlook differences due to gender, race/ethnicity, or socioeconomic status (SES) and to be based on white, middle-class, male experiences. They tend to focus on one developmental domain rather than trying to map all of adult functioning. Most theorists look at adulthood in its entirety, or at the entire lifespan, rather than focusing only on early, middle, or late adulthood. Thus, we will revisit many of the theories presented here in subsequent chapters.

Timing of Events: Social Clocks

Marty entered law school when he was thirty-two years old, married, and the father of two young children. Twelve years later, he feels he is behind in his career as an attorney because of his "off-time" schooling. What is the origin of his sense of what is appropriate at a given time? For one thing, comparisons with others in his

The social clock tells if we are "on time" in following the age-appropriate timetable of our social group. These two "on time" mothers provide social support for each other in their transitions to parenthood. Social support from friends makes adjustment to significant life events easier.

social group. His agemates are already established in their legal careers and have entered what Schaie calls the *responsible stage*, as we saw in Chapter 12. In contrast, Marty's former classmates are in Schaie's *achieving stage*. Marty finds himself alone; his level of career development places him in the achieving stage, while his family's maturity places him in the responsible stage. As a result, Marty feels "off time."

One way to understand the consistencies among disparate lives is to recognize that social expectations create an internalized **social clock** that tells us whether we are "on time" in following the age-appropriate social timetable (Neugarten, 1968). Cultural groups tend to develop a shared sense of when men and women "should" marry, have children, or attend school, for example. These social norms dictate when certain life transitions should occur, and people strive to time their major life events to match societal expectations. People who follow the expected pattern experience fewer difficulties than people who deviate from it (Kogan, 1990). Social support from friends who are "on time" in going through a significant life event, such as parenthood, makes that experience easier for individuals within the group. The social life of the new parents changes in ways similar to their friends. As a group, they can share resources and advice. As the Perspectives box on page 486 indicates, being "off time" does not necessarily have negative outcomes, but it often creates discomfort. In Chapter 15, Psychosocial Development in Middle Adulthood, we will see how family life cycle, another timing of events theory, emphasizes similarities within family stages that depend on the children's ages.

Since the 1960s, American society has become less rigid in its expectations of when significant life events should occur (Neugarten & Neugarten, 1987). Although the social clock still ticks, the range of acceptable ages for graduating from school, marrying, or starting a family is wider. Taking time off before completing college or graduate school has become common. Many people delay marriage and parenthood until their thirties, particularly college-educated individuals. Returning to school is acceptable at any age. Nonetheless, in everyday conversation people often refer to themselves as having been "early to marry" or "late to start a family," which indicates that although there may be more latitude, people still know when "on time" is. Age-graded roles have lessened in importance, but they have not disappeared. They have also changed. Jen's mother had Jen, her fourth child, at the exact age Jen is now; Jen and her husband have just begun thinking about having children. Both Jen and her mother are "on time" for their cohort, since expectations for women have changed considerably in a generation.

While all developmental theories strive to describe and explain consistencies in development, timing of events theories are better able than normative crisis theories to explain dissimilarities among groups, or cohorts. Differences in marriage or retirement patterns in other times or within other cultures result from different shared expectations. Crisis theories, on the other hand, emphasize the internal normative crises adults experience and tend to underrepresent diversity.

Crisis Theory: George Vaillant and the Grant Study

Life abounds with events that require a constant series of adaptations. How men adapt determines their levels of physical health, mental health, and life satisfaction. These are the basic premises of George Vaillant's many years of work on the Grant Study (Vaillant,1977; Vaillant & Vaillant, 1990). In 1937, when Vaillant was four years old, William T. Grant funded a longitudinal study of college men to follow the course of their development and see what led them to function effectively in work, play, and love. Vaillant, a psychiatrist, joined the project in 1967. The Grant Study participants were a homogeneous sample of 204 white men who were attending Harvard and were selected because they seemed healthy. Vaillant notes that "the absence of women in the Grant Study was an unforgivable omission, an omission that will require another study to correct" (Vaillant, 1977, p. 13). Participants went through twenty hours of tests, physical examinations, and interviews while in college and completed detailed questionnaires and had physical examinations at regular intervals after graduation. Tests included rating scales of adult adjustment, childhood environment, marital happiness, maturity of adaptive mechanisms, and outcome of children. As of 1990, 173 of the men were still alive and active members of the study (Vaillant & Vaillant, 1990). Six left the study when they dropped out of college, twenty-three died before age sixty, and only two had data too incomplete to include. We will address the problem of *attrition* (who drops out) in longitudinal studies in the next chapter.

The Grant Study led Vaillant to three basic conclusions about adult development (Vaillant, 1977). First, growth and development are a lifelong process. The men in the study clearly showed evidence of intellectual and moral development after age twenty and at least up to age fifty. Second, isolated events, unexpected or traumatic as they might be, rarely mold individual lives; rather, sustained relationships with other people are what shape lives. Vaillant found that the loss of a parent, for example, was less devastating in the long run than the continued relationship with a disturbed parent. Third, the **adaptive mechanisms,** or coping styles, that people use to adapt to life events determine their level of mental health. Vaillant categorized four types of adaptive mechanisms. *Mature mechanisms* include sublimation, the redirecting of anxiety and unacceptable impulses toward acceptable goals, and altruism. *Immature mechanisms* include *hypochondriasis,* or the development of ailments without physical bases, and fantasy. *Psychotic mechanisms* include distortions of reality, such as hearing voices. *Neurotic mechanisms* include irrational fears and repression (Vaillant, 1977).

Development of Adaptive Mechanisms   Vaillant found that adolescents (ages twelve to nineteen) were twice as likely to use immature mechanisms as mature ones, young men (twenty to thirty-five) were twice as likely to use mature mechanisms as immature ones, and midlife men (thirty-six to fifty) were four times as likely to use mature mechanisms as immature ones (Vaillant, 1977). For instance, when faced with disappointment, an adolescent might slam his fist through the wall or throw a tantrum, whereas a young adult or midlife man might go for a run or do some work. Not every man made the maturational shifts in adaptive styles. Some, whom Vaillant labels *Perpetual Boys*, failed to show any significant shift, whereas those he labels *Generative Men* shifted so completely that in midlife they showed almost no use of immature mechanisms.

What factors contribute to the development of mature adaptive mechanisms? Among the Grant study's rather privileged group (white, male, American, well educated), it was not happy childhoods or good genes that were important: "The evolution of mature defenses seemed surprisingly independent of social and genetic good fortune" (Vaillant, 1977, p. 335). According to Vaillant, ego development (the problem-solving aspect of the personality) grows in adversity as well as in prosperity. Two elements contribute to the development of mature adaptive mechanisms. The first is a healthy brain. Injuries and alcoholism lead to regression to immature or psychotic defenses, such as fighting or domestic violence. The second is sustained and loving relationships. Adaptive mechanisms are not so much taught as absorbed. During childhood, close, loving relationships provide models for coping with life events, even if the life events are unhappy. Seeing loved and trusted adults cope with adversity sets the stage for the child's ego development. During adulthood, the critical people for Vaillant's subjects were friends, wives, and psychotherapists. "No single variable . . . predicted mental health as clearly as a man's capacity to remain happily married over time" (Vaillant, 1977, p. 320). We will look at marriage in more detail shortly.

Love and Work in the Grant Study   Like Schaie and Greenhaus (see Chapter 12), Vaillant (1977) sees work as the focus of development between the twenties and forties, a period he calls **career consolidation.** During career consolidation the men tended to work hard, devote themselves to career advancement, and sacrifice play. As Table 13.1 shows, Vaillant sees the Grant Study as confirming Erikson's adult life

TABLE 13.1   *Adolescent and Adult Stages of Normative Crisis Theories Compared*
Normative crisis theorists take a psychodynamic view of development. They see each developmental period as focused around an internally motivated crisis, such as the need for intimacy to overcome isolation in early adulthood, when adults turn to their parents less frequently. Normative crisis theories were developed in studies of middle-class males and tend to underrepresent the diversity of adult experience.

	Grant/Vaillant	**Levinson**	**Erikson**
Adolescence	Forging identity Separating from parents (12–19)	Era of preadulthood	Identity versus role confusion
		Early adult transition (17–22) establishing independence	
Early adulthood	Development of intimacy (20s)	Era of early adulthood	Intimacy versus isolation
	Career consolidation (30s)		
Middle adulthood	Generativity (40s and 50s)	Era of middle adulthood	Generativity versus stagnation
Late adulthood		Era of late adulthood	Ego integrity versus despair

According to Daniel Levinson's theory, having a mentor plays an important role in helping a young man achieve his Dream. This older executive can teach, sponsor, host, guide, and serve as a model for the young man beginning his career.

patterns. Recall from Chapter 2 that Erikson saw the normative crisis of early adulthood to be intimacy versus isolation and that of middle adulthood to be generativity versus stagnation. Vaillant describes a similar progression of development: career consolidation fits between Erikson's stages of intimacy and of generativity. Adolescence is the stage of forging identity by separating from parents. The twenties is a period for developing intimacy. Young adult men replace adolescent friendships with mature ones and seek out wives. The thirties is a period for career consolidation. The forties and fifties are a period of generativity, which Vaillant (1977) describes as a "second adolescence." "At age forty—give or take as much as a decade—men . . . once more become explorers of the world within" (p. 220). We will discuss his findings on his male participants' middle years in Chapter 15.

Crisis Theory: Daniel Levinson's Seasons of Adult Lives

In contrast to Vaillant, who at age thirty-four devoted himself to the study of developing young men, Daniel Levinson, at age forty-six, wanted to study the transition into middle age so he could better understand his own experience. His formulation of developmental stages in early and middle adulthood also comes from the study of men. Levinson (1978) studied forty men between ages thirty-five and forty-five, a smaller and older group of participants than in the Grant Study. To ensure some variety in levels of education, SES, and race/ethnicity, Levinson selected his sample to include four occupational subgroups: hourly workers in industry, business executives, university biologists, and novelists. In contrast to the Grant Study's longitudinal method, Levinson (1986) used what he calls the *biographical method* to learn about these men's lives. The **biographical method** entails reconstructing the life course by interviewing the person and using a variety of other sources, such as visiting the person's home and place of work and, in the case of Levinson's novelists, reading the novels and reviews. Each man was interviewed for ten to twenty hours over a span of two or three months and given a series of tests, such as personality scales. There was also a follow-up interview two years later.

Based on the "biographies" of the forty participants, Levinson (1978) identified three eras, or "seasons," in the male adult life, as shown in Figure 13.1: the era of early adulthood, the era of middle adulthood, and the era of late adulthood. During each of these eras a man builds a life structure, which is the underlying pattern for his life at a given time. Significant relationships form primary components of the man's life structure, usually work and marriage/family. Bill's life, for example, includes significant relationships with his career and with Karen. As a man outgrows these structures, he moves into a transition during which he builds a new life structure for the new era. For instance, Marty has moved into a transition as he reappraises his current position in the law firm and readies himself to strike out on his own. Change goes on within each era, and then a transition is needed for the shift from one to the next. Although the content of life structures varies greatly from individual to individual, "the life structure develops through a relatively orderly sequence of age-linked periods during the adult years" (Levinson, 1986, p. 7).

The Novice Phase   The first three periods of early adulthood are its novice phase. The *novice phase* begins with the early adult transition from about ages seventeen to twenty-two. As Figure 13.1 shows, the transition applies to both the earlier era of preadulthood and the coming era of early adulthood, but is not fully a part of either. This is similar to the stage of youth we discussed in Chapter 12. During the early life structure for early adulthood, ages twenty-two to twenty-eight, the young man explores the possibilities for adult life, tests some initial choices, and creates a provisional entry life structure. The age thirty transition is an opportunity to reassess and improve the first adult life structure. Most of the men in Levinson's study felt too committed or too rootless and experienced a stressful transition.

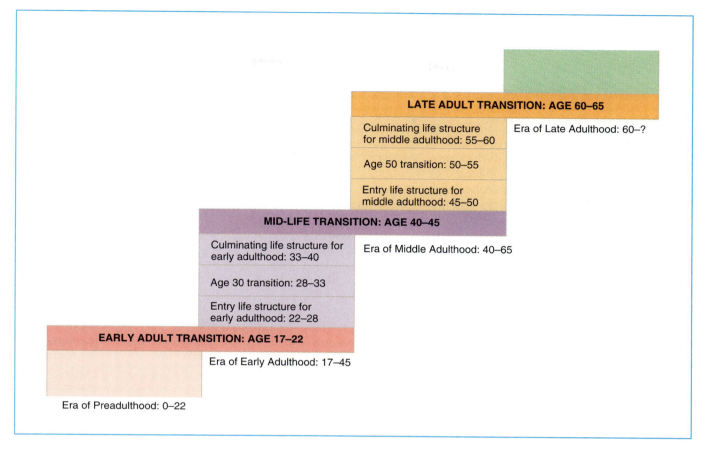

LATE ADULT TRANSITION: AGE 60–65

Culminating life structure
for middle adulthood: 55–60

Era of Late Adulthood: 60–?

Age 50 transition: 50–55

Entry life structure for
middle adulthood: 45–50

MID-LIFE TRANSITION: AGE 40–45

Culminating life structure for
early adulthood: 33–40

Era of Middle Adulthood: 40–65

Age 30 transition: 28–33

Entry life structure for
early adulthood: 22–28

EARLY ADULT TRANSITION: AGE 17–22

Era of Early Adulthood: 17–45

Era of Preadulthood: 0–22

FIGURE 13.1
Levinson's Developmental Periods in the Eras of Early and Middle Adulthood
Daniel Levinson devised his developmental periods by using the biographical method to analyze the lives of forty men. Each era is preceded by a transition that applies to both the earlier era and the coming era. Each era has three parts: the entry life structure, the transition, and the culminating life structure.
Source: Levinson (1986).

The novice phase includes four major tasks. The first is forming a *Dream* of adult accomplishment and giving it a place in the life structure. Bill's Dream might be to write a successful novel, be a successful sports reporter, or edit a successful weekly magazine. The second task is forming mentor relationships. The third is developing an occupation. The fourth is establishing intimate relationships and finding the *special woman,* one who is "lover, friend and helper in search of the Dream" (p. 332).

The Dream can take various forms; it may be down to earth, unrealistic, or even grandiose. In any case, it is important. Without a Dream, the young man has no vision. A vision inspires activity that helps him move toward a satisfactory life structure. The Dream represents a sense of self in the adult world; it helps the young man define himself and decide on a path. Important in achieving the Dream is the *mentor,* who is usually a somewhat older person with experience in the world the novice is entering. Mentors teach, sponsor, host, guide, and serve as models. Mentoring relationships do not last indefinitely. As the novice becomes more competent, he may feel limited or overly criticized by the mentor. The relationship is likely to break off, sometimes with rancor, or become a friendship after a period of separation. The "special woman" also facilitates the realization of the Dream by believing in it and encouraging her man.

The Culminating Phase   The two final periods of early adulthood constitute the *culminating phase.* They bring to fruition the efforts of the era. The culminating life structure, ages thirty-three to forty, benefits from the experiences of the novice phase and is better integrated than the entry life structure was. During this period, the young man establishes his occupational goals and makes plans for advancing them. His need for more stability creates great pressure to marry or to form some other formal lifestyle choice, if he has not done so already. This is a time of building a life around initial choices, of settling down. By the end of this period, the man is more independent and self-sufficient. He has accomplished some of his goals, is at the peak of early adulthood, and begins to feel the stirrings of what will come next. At around forty he enters the midlife transition, which bridges the final period of early adulthood and the initial period of middle adulthood, yet is not completely in one period or the other. We will discuss the era of middle adulthood in Chapter 15, but keep in mind that it follows a similar pattern, although the content differs.

Do Women Have the Same "Seasons"?   Levinson (1978) excluded women from his initial study because he believed they might well have a different course of development. Priscilla Roberts and Peter Newton (1987) reviewed four unpublished doctoral dissertations that interviewed a total of thirty-one white and eight African American women, ages twenty-eight to fifty-three, using Levinson's methodology. In response to criticism for his male-only theory, between 1980 and 1982 Levinson (1996) interviewed forty-five women: fifteen homemakers, fifteen businesswomen, and fifteen academics. Based on this limited research with women, Levinson (1986) reported that his formulations fit women as well as men. If we look at the tasks he considered most important for novice men, however, that conclusion is far from clear. In contrast to the men in the earlier study, most of the women lacked well-defined goals (Levinson, 1996).

Roberts and Newton found that while women do have Dreams, their Dreams differ from those of men. Men's Dreams focus on career achievement and are unified, whereas most women's Dreams are split between achievement and relationships. Roberts and Newton (1987) reported that only about 18 percent focused on achievement alone and only about 15 percent focused on relationships alone. Even those women who had career as part of their Dream were likely to moderate it, to be "special women" and place it within the context of their husbands' goals. Women were unlikely to have had mentors; only four of the thirty-nine women in

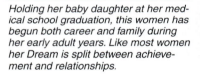

Holding her baby daughter at her medical school graduation, this women has begun both career and family during her early adult years. Like most women her Dream is split between achievement and relationships.

the older studies were able to find a mentor. Levinson (1978) pointed out the problem of fewer women being available to serve as mentors and the complications of male mentors for women because of the likelihood of stereotyping and sexual involvement. Similarly, developing an occupation followed different time lines for women and men.

Integrating career and family was difficult for the women in the studies Roberts and Newton analyzed. Many women who fixed on a career in the twenties had not established it until age forty or later because of the demands of family relationships. Others followed a male career pattern until the age thirty transition and then shifted their focus to personal relationships. The age thirty transition was stressful for both women and men, but for different reasons. Men faced the stress of reevaluating their careers, whereas women were resetting their priorities regarding occupational and family goals and experienced the stress of balancing the two or building a new life structure. Finally, the women did not have a "special man" to help them pursue their Dream. These women were expected by their husbands to be "special women" and encourage their men's Dream rather than seek encouragement for their own, especially if theirs might threaten the importance of their men's. With women now in the work force, Dreams of achievement have been added to Dreams of marriage and motherhood for women, but men's Dreams continue to center around achievement. This leaves women at a double disadvantage. As we will see when we discuss marriage, men are not committed to relationships in ways that provide women with career encouragement, and women are left with family responsibilities.

Crisis Theory: Erik Erikson's Intimacy Versus Isolation

As we saw in Chapter 2, **intimacy versus isolation,** the crisis of early adulthood, follows and builds on Erikson's earlier stages of ego development. Trust versus mistrust, autonomy versus shame and doubt, initiative versus guilt, and industry versus inferiority precede the adolescent crisis of identity versus role confusion, in which the task is to develop a unique and integrated sense of self. During the intimacy versus isolation crisis, the young adult must develop the ability to establish close, committed relationships with peers and the ability to tolerate the threat of fusion and loss of identity that intense intimacy raises. As Bill and Karen have become closer, for example, Bill has begun to use the term *we* when he talks of plans and desires. This sharply contrasts with the strong *I* perspective he had as an adolescent. For Erikson, the development of identity is the necessary basis for establishing intimacy because true intimacy necessitates sacrifice and compromise, which require that you know who you are and what you want.

The avoidance of intimacy, or the distancing of oneself from closeness, leads to isolation and self-absorption. An isolated young adult would, for example, continue to have adolescent sexual encounters in which his concerns remained conquest and his own gratification rather than reciprocally satisfying sex. Intimacy often includes sexuality, but not always. We can have intimate relationships with friends as well as lovers, and we can have sex with people with whom we are not emotionally close.

Critics of Erikson have suggested that good interpersonal relationships can form the basis for identity, in the same way identity forms the basis for intimacy. For women, according to Jean Baker Miller and her colleagues at the Stone Center, relationships are primary and continuous (Jordan et al., 1991). In contrast to Erikson's theory, in which identity forms first and then intimacy, in the Stone Center's theory identity and intimacy develop simultaneously. Autonomy, creativity, and assertion can all grow within the context of relationships. Agnes is a good example of this. She had been out of college two years and lacked career direction. A biology major, she had tried several related jobs and disliked them all. At age twenty-four, she took a position teaching science and fell in love with John, also a science teacher. John had just graduated from college and was taking a year off before applying to graduate school in biology. In her year of intimacy with John, Agnes first attached herself to his occupational plan; then she came into conflict with John and developed her own "similar but different" vision. Two years later she is no longer in a relationship with John, but she is in graduate school on a clear career direction she developed within an intimate relationship.

In Erikson's theory, one stage builds on another and at the same time issues from earlier periods can reemerge and be resolved in new ways at later stages (Erikson & Erikson, 1981). Identity formation remains an issue in early adulthood, even as intimacy becomes a focus. As young adults face new life events and engage in new relationships, they redefine their sense of identity and alter their relationships.

What Do You Think?

Think of a life decision you are considering or have recently made. Construct a timing of events explanation and a normative crisis explanation. Which one better fits your vision?

INTIMATE RELATIONSHIPS

The need for intimacy, or attachment, begins at birth and continues throughout life. The first attachment, as you may remember from Chapter 5's discussion of psychosocial development in the first two years, is between the infant and the caregiver and changes as the child develops. Although attachment is a lifespan developmental process, developmental stages influence the nature of social relationships (Antonucci, 1990). We saw in Chapter 11 that during adolescence, friendships become important sources of loyalty and intimacy as relationships with parents became more strained. Nonetheless, adolescents continue to depend on parents for security when the going gets rough.

During early adulthood, attachment to friends and lovers increases while attachment to family decreases. Establishing independence requires gaining emotional independence from parents as well as setting up a separate residence. The safe-base function parents continue to provide for adolescents shifts during early adulthood to a significant other, a spouse, or a friend (Hazen & Shaver, 1990). When Bill had a problem with his taxes, Karen was the first to hear about it and provide advice and emotional support. Only when he had calmed down and wanted additional expertise did Bill consult his mother who is knowledgeable about tax matters. He does not share many of his personal issues with his parents these days and discusses others with them only in retrospect.

While parents and siblings continue to be important in young adults' lives, they are not as important as they were during the earlier life stages. We will see in Chapters 15 and 17 how secure attachment in early years results in continuing relationships with parents and siblings that contribute to health and happiness during middle and late adulthood. The developmental tasks of establishing an occupation, an independent household, and an intimate relationship push young adults to relinquish the primacy of their attachment to their parents and turn to peers for security.

Friendship

Friendship is one form of personal relationship that, while important throughout adult life, is particularly significant during early adulthood. As young adults relinquish dependence on their families, they rely increasingly on friends for intimacy and support. Joan Pulakos (1989) found that young adults felt closer to their friends than to

During early adulthood, attachment to friends increases while attachment to family decreases. These friends are going to do something together, which is typical of male friends. All close friendships include some shared activities and some sharing of confidences.

their siblings. They discussed most topics more frequently and engaged in most joint activities more often with friends. Mary Levitt, Ruth Weber, and Nathalie Guacci (1993) found that compared to their mothers or grandmothers, young adult women included fewer family members and more friends in their social networks and received more support from friends. When young adults do not have established friendships, telephone hot lines may "fill in" for friendship roles by providing emotional supports, as Marilyn Kline discusses in the Working With interview on page 466).

Characteristics of Friendship   Friendship takes many different forms, which makes it hard to define. Pat O'Connor (1992) suggests that the essential elements are its voluntary nature and its ability to provide at least some of the following: enjoyment, ego support, validation, stimulation, intimacy, trust, acceptance, and companionship. High levels of practical support are not necessary characteristics of friendship (LaGaipa, 1990). This Western cultural perspective locates friendship in the private arena. Barry Wellman (1990) points out that in the First World (the West), people rely on friendship mainly to meet sociable and emotional needs or minor practical domestic needs. In contrast, friendship in the Second World (the former communist bloc) short-circuits bureaucracy—for instance, a well-placed friend might arrange for a job—and in the Third World (the developing nations), people need friends for basic survival, such as sharing food and shelter. Friendship also plays a survival function within poor African American communities (Stack, 1974).

Benefits of Friendship   Research consistently shows a positive relationship between friendship and individual well-being, especially for mental health (O'Connor, 1992). Friends bolster positive feelings by sharing activities, feelings, and ideas. They also serve as buffers against stress by providing intimacy and comfort during hard times such as the breakup of a romantic relationship, the failure to get a job, the death of a loved one, or a health crisis. Karen, for example, relies on Bill's encouragement as she sends out résumés and waits for interviews. His belief in her abilities, stories about his job searches, and computer assistance provide emotional and practical support.

Working with   Marilyn Kline, SUICIDE HOT LINE WORKER

Helping Individuals Through Crises

Marilyn Kline is a twenty-six-year-old college senior majoring in human services. With more life experience than the traditional-age college student, she is very sensitive to the problems young adults face. When we spoke, she was a paid worker at Helpline, a telephone counseling service that helps young adults who don't have friends to turn to for emotional support.

Michele: What is Helpline's purpose?

Marilyn: I think is serves several purposes. Mainly we give callers emotional support, pass on information about available services, and give referrals. Just today I got a call from a person who was really drunk; he felt awful and wanted to know where to go for help. After talking to him for awhile, I referred him to an AA meeting.

Michele: How do you know what to do in a situation like that?

Marilyn: You need to be able to listen responsibly, to be genuine and non-judgmental. You can be trained to listen, but I think it helps to be a good listener to begin with.

Michele: What was the listening training like?

Marilyn: It was pretty extensive—five hours a week for eight weeks. We focused on active listening skills. We worked in small groups and did a lot of role plays. It felt like group therapy! The role playing helps you understand who you are and what issues you're dealing with, and that helps you help callers.

Michele: Who goes through the training?

Marilyn: Everyone who takes calls does. Most workers are volunteers who commit to working at least four hours a week for a year, but most people stay longer.

Michele: Who tends to call hot lines like yours?

Marilyn: Even though we're listed as a suicide prevention service, we get most calls from people who are having trouble handling their feelings.

Maybe they're in an abusive situation, spousal or child, and don't know where else to turn. People who have recurring suicide thoughts and attempt to follow through will call. They're in crisis, and you help them get through it—to make a safety contact.

Michele: Do your callers tend to be younger or older?

Marilyn: Well, there's a range: I talk mostly to people between ages twenty and fifty. I know that two of my callers are college students.

Michele: Does that wide range match what you learned about suicide in your training?

Marilyn: Not really. Older white men have the highest suicide rates. Adolescent boys and young adult white males have the next highest rate. Then come elderly women and, last, adolescent girls.

Michele: You say that older adults have the highest suicide rates but most of your callers are young adults. Can you explain that?

Marilyn: Young adults are more willing to ask for help outside the family than this generation of elders. Also, most callers at Helpline are young adults because they have problems with their families and have not established friendships they can turn to.

Michele: What's a typical call like?

Marilyn: A twenty-six-year-old woman is upset at her mother. She has two children, both under four, and is on welfare. Her husband is in jail. Her brother stays with her to help, but he drinks heavily and often abuses her. She's angry at her mother for her not being there when she was growing up and for not helping her now. She needs help.

Michele: What would you do for her?

Marilyn: Validate her feelings and offer emotional support. For callers like this, we're their support system, we're their friends, we're their family. We hear from them repeatedly.

Michele: How may calls would you expect on a typical shift?

Marilyn: Weekends are really busy. On my Saturday nights, I usually get about fifty calls. Of those, forty calls are for emotional support. One or two might be crisis calls, someone who's taken pills or has a loaded gun. We call a mobile crisis team at the associated clinic if the crisis warrants it. The rest of the callers need information and referrals.

Michele: Why do you think people need Helpline?

Marilyn: I think they need the communication we offer. Many of our regular callers just want to chat. They say hello and tell you what they did during the day. They don't have skills to talk about things with their friends. They have people around them, but they just don't feel comfortable talking about these issues with them. I think they appreciate that we're unconditional. They know there's a nice person on the other end of the phone who is willing to listen.

Michele: Do you find your work rewarding?

Marilyn: I really like to help people, and being on a hot line is the epitome of that. I don't honestly know why I love it so much, but I sure do. I love going there. I love being there for people. Sometimes the crisis team will call back to say that they got there and took the caller to the hospital. You know that what you did saved them.

What Do You Think?

1. Many Helpline callers are looking for emotional support and companionship. To whom do young adults more typically turn? Why is this a stage of life when people may not have secure personal relationships?

2. In what ways do the things Marilyn learned during training resemble skills that we all need to be good friends and lovers?

Social relationships with friends have also been shown to encourage health-promoting behaviors such as healthy patterns of eating, exercising, and avoiding abuse of alcohol (House et al., 1988; Rakowski et al., 1988; Umberson, 1987). A running buddy helps to keep you running, while a friend from a twelve-step program such as Alcoholics Anonymous (AA) helps you to stay on the wagon. Friends encourage each other to seek medical attention when symptoms occur and encourage behaviors that reduce acute conditions, such as following special diets (Anson, 1989; Antonucci et al., 1989).

Gender Differences in Friendship   Although friendships answer basic human needs for intimacy and support, men and women tend to have different styles of friendships. When Bill and his male friends get together, they typically watch basketball or football on TV, play basketball, or talk "shop" or sports. When Karen sees her female friends, they talk about the issues in their lives: Karen discusses her job search, her relationship with Bill, a fight she had with her sister, what to wear to an interview. In same-sex friendships, men tend to define intimacy in terms of proximity and shared activities and interest, whereas women tend to define it in terms of emotional sharing of confidences. William Rawlins (1992) found that even when men and women talked with their friends about the same topics, women tended to do so in deeper and more self-revealing ways. The only areas of personal experience in which women appear to confide less than men do is their strengths, victories, and achievements (Cancian, 1986).

Several investigators have related these gender differences in friendship style to the issues of power and control. Masculine friendships protect men from situations of emotional vulnerability and potential loss of control (Helgeson et al., 1987). Men do not reveal their weaknesses and failures, and therefore they appear strong and successful. Feminine friendships, which involve admitting dependency, sharing problems, and being emotionally vulnerable, are incompatible with control (Cancian, 1986). Emotional sharing means acknowledging vulnerability and relinquishing control.

More typically, psychologists have focused on the advantages of the feminine style and highlighted it as the epitome of friendship (O'Connor, 1992). It provides emotional support for concerns and problems and helps to prevent loneliness. Almost all studies show that women have more close friends than men do and, at all stages of life, are more likely to have a confidant, someone in whom they confide. Recent research shows, however, that while intimacy of this kind has great benefits, it is not without costs. For instance, Kathryn Ratcliff and Janet Bogdan (1988) found that intimate friendships frequently were not helpful when a married woman lost her job because her friends believed she should not be working in the first place. The feminine style of friendship also imposes considerable costs in time and energy, since it requires that a woman be available for friends in need.

As you read this section, you may well be thinking that your friendship style does not follow the gender stereotypes described. As with all behavior, individual differences exist in friendship styles. Many women have friends at the gym or at work with whom they share activities, in addition to intimate friends in whom they confide. Likewise, many men have emotionally sharing conversations with one or more of their male friends, at least some of the time. Paul Wright (1988) cautions against "dichotomous thinking" because "Virtually all close friendships involve shared interests and activities, various kinds of intimacy including self-disclosures and the sharing of confidences, emotional support, small talk, shop-talk and exchanges of tangible favors. . . . Rather we should think in terms of what qualities or characteristics are more typical on average of the friendships of women than of men and vice-versa" (p. 370). Both women and men find friendship deeply significant (Rawlins, 1992).

Single adults have more cross-gender friendships than any other group. Contact at work and school provides opportunities for men and women to become friends. Although cross-gender friendships are not considered inappropriate, especially for unmarried people, others often perceive them as unconscious or deceptive precursors to romantic involvement (Rawlins, 1992). Women have similar types of relationships with women and men friends that differ from their relationships with their partners. In contrast, men experience more self-disclosure, intimacy, and emotional involvement with women than with men and distinguish less closely between women friends and partners. As a result, men are more likely than women to consider cross-gender friends as potential romantic partners.

Love

Intimacy is also an important ingredient of love. While friendship is important, most young adults expect to find love in the form of a mate who will be a lover and a friend and with whom life will be shared. Contemporary young adults are marrying later than did their earlier cohorts, so they typically have more experience with love relationships and more sexual partners before they marry (Michael et al., 1994). Nonetheless, each relationship is likely to be monogamous, resulting in a pattern of **serial monogamy**, or a series of committed, intimate relationships. Love differs from friendship, differs from person to person, and even differs within the same person. Like the person, love develops and changes over time.

The Triangle of Love   Robert Sternberg (1987) developed a triangular theory of love to explain the similarities and differences among love relationships. According to Sternberg, love has three essential components: intimacy, passion, and decision/commitment. *Intimacy* refers to feelings in a relationship that promote closeness, bondedness, and connectedness. Sternberg's definition of intimacy includes self-disclosing communication with the loved one, desiring to promote the welfare of the loved one, experiencing happiness with the loved one, holding the loved one in high regard, being able to count on the loved one in times of need, having mutual understanding with the loved one, sharing oneself and one's possessions with the loved one, receiving emotional support from the loved one, giving emotional support to the loved one, and valuing the loved one. His research indicates that not all of these elements are necessary at any one time to experience intimacy; the number varies for different situations and different people, as we will see in the upcoming discussion of gender differences in love. *Passion* refers to the expression of desires and needs for self-esteem, nurturance, affiliation, dominance, submission, and sexual fulfillment. Once again, the relative strengths of these needs vary among situations, individuals, and types of loving relationship. *Decision/commitment* includes both short-term and long-term commitment. *Short-term* refers to a commitment to love and *long-term* to a commitment to maintain that love. Marriage, according to Sternberg, represents the legalization of the commitment to maintain the relationship.

The three components of love have different properties and vary in different kinds of love relationships. Intimacy and commitment are relatively stable in close relationships, whereas passion is unstable and likely to fluctuate. In short-term romantic involvements, passion tends to play a large part, intimacy may play only a moderate part, and commitment plays no part at all. In long-term close relationships, intimacy and commitment play large parts while passion typically plays a moderate part. Passion tends to be most intense at early stages of a relationship and to be intermittent after that.

Different combinations of these three components characterize different types of love (see Figure 13.2). Sternberg describes seven possibilities (although liking is not actually a form of love):

1. *Liking:* Intimacy without passion or commitment. This describes many friendships. A relationship can be frustrating if one of the friends feels passion as well

as intimacy and the other does not. Friendship can have some of the other elements as well as intimacy, but in that case it is more than liking.

2. *Infatuation:* Passion without intimacy or commitment. "Love at first sight" falls into this category, as does an infatuation with an unrealistic partner. Infatuation can be long-lasting but only if it is unrequited.

3. *Empty love:* Commitment without intimacy or passion. This is a long-term relationship that has lost the intimacy and passion it once had. The people stay married because of their commitment to love each other rather than because of their feelings of love. Sternberg also points out that an arranged marriage may start out as empty love, but intimacy and/or passion may develop.

4. *Romantic love:* Intimacy and passion without commitment. This is the addition of physical attraction to liking.

5. *Companionate love:* Intimacy and commitment without passion. It is a long-term relationship in which the physical attraction has waned.

6. *Fatuous love:* Passion and commitment without intimacy. This is a "whirlwind" romance, often associated with Hollywood or with quick commitment on the rebound. Such a relationship is not likely to last.

7. *Consummate love*: Intimacy, passion, and commitment. This is what most of us are searching for: a balance of all the essential components in equal measure. It is hard to attain and, once you have it, takes work to maintain.

Sternberg's triangular theory of relationships is dynamic. Intimacy, passion, and commitment each change over time, and as a result the nature of relationships changes over time. Romantic love is difficult to maintain for a long period because passion is likely to fade. This helps to explain why young adults who are not ready for long-term commitment often find themselves in a series of intimate relationships. Relationships take work, and work takes commitment. As Sternberg puts it,

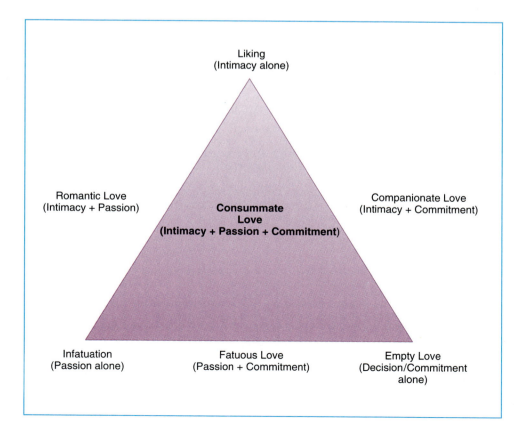

FIGURE 13.2
The Kinds of Loving as Different Combinations of Sternberg's Three Components of Love
The three components of love, intimacy, passion, and commitment have different properties and vary in different love relationships. Consummate love consists of all three components in equal measure.
Source: Sternberg (1988).

"Relationships are constructions that decay over time if they are not maintained and even improved. A relationship cannot take care of itself, any more than a building can. Rather, we must take responsibility for making our relationships the best they can be, and constantly work to understand, build, and rebuild them" (1987, p. 83).

Gender Differences in Love   Enduring love is a combination of instrumental qualities such as shared activities and expressive qualities such as shared feelings. We care for and assist our loved ones, and we express physical and emotional closeness to our loved ones. Women report significantly higher confidence in expressing liking, love, and affection to men than men do for women (Blier & Blier-Wilson, 1989). Consistent with the gender differences we saw in friendship, men and women seem to place different values on the instrumental and expressive aspects of love. Men consider practical help, shared physical activities, spending time together, and sex more important. Women place more emphasis on expressive qualities such as emotional involvement and verbal self-disclosure (Cancian, 1986). Most of us would probably choose a relationship that integrates both the masculine and feminine styles of loving, but women are much more likely to complain that their male partners lack verbal expressiveness, whereas men often do not understand this complaint because they express their feelings by doing so many things for the women they love (Tannen, 1990).

Although men and women value different aspects of love, they still think about it in similar ways, as Donna Castañeda (1993) found when she asked eighty-three Mexican American college students, "What qualities and characteristics are important in a love relationship to you personally?" As Table 13.2 shows, the top ten categories among women and men largely overlapped. Although the order differs, eight categories appear on both lists: trust, mutual respect, communication/sharing, honesty, friendship, shared values/attitudes, understanding, and compassion. The fact that men and women look for very similar qualities in a love relationship helps to explain why most succeed in finding partners.

Mate Selection

Early adulthood is a time when people look for partners, or mates. How do they find them? Many cultural myths lead us to believe that "opposites attract" or that we "will meet a stranger across a crowded room." These myths do not hold up

TABLE 13.2   Top Ten Categories among Women and Men to the Question "What Qualities and Characteristics Are Important in a Love Relationship to You Personally?"
When asked what qualities and characteristics are important in a love relationship, men and women mentioned similar things. Although the order is different, the top ten categories for each gender largely overlap.

Women		Men	
Category	**Number**	**Category**	**Number**
Trust	25	Shared values/attitudes	16
Mutual respect	21	Trust	13
Communication/sharing	20	Communication/sharing	13
Honesty	11	Honesty	9
Friendship	10	Freedom	8
Shared values/attitudes	9	Mutual respect	8
Understanding	8	Understanding	7
Affection	8	Friendship	6
Compassion	7	Compassion	6
Humor	7	Mutual support	4

Source: Castañeda (1993).

to the scrutiny of scientific study. Similarities are what bring people together into romantic or sexual relationships (Murstein, 1988). Bill and Karen are a good example. They met on the same job on the same university campus and found they came from the same area and knew some of the same people. In the National Health and Social Life Survey (NHSLS), Robert Michael and his associates (1994) found that people's sexual partners were overwhelmingly like them in race/ethnicity, age, and educational level. They varied only in religion, and the couples that married were likely to have the same religion as well.

Most people meet their partners in very conventional ways. They are introduced by people they know well, or they introduce themselves in familiar places where people come together because of their similarities. Although people do sometimes meet in outside settings, such as on a vacation or at a bar, very few go outside of their network to establish sexual relationships and, when they do, the relationships are likely to be short term (Michael et al., 1994). Sixty-three percent of the NHSLS participants who were married had been introduced by family and friends, coworkers, classmates, and neighbors, as were 60 percent of couples living together and 55 percent of couples not living together and in a relationship lasting more than one month. The most common places people met were school, work, a private party, or a religious institution, all places where they were likely to find others similar to themselves. The NHSLS study found that when people in the same social network introduced each other or met each other in a preselected place, each person's friends and family were more likely to approve of the relationship, which helped the partnership last (Michael et al., 1994).

You may be wondering why, since we meet a lot of people similar to ourselves in familiar places, some relationships "click" while others do not. It appears that we are more vulnerable to falling in love when our lives are turbulent (Hatfield, 1988). If we have experienced the loss of another relationship or are unsettled by life events, we are more likely to be open to romantic love (Bergmann, 1988). Potential partners may be in sight, but we do not notice them unless we are in need of them.

How does sex affect the development of romantic relationships? Getting to know someone as a friend before having sex is more likely to lead to a long-term relationship than responding to passion first and then trying to build intimacy. The more permanent the relationships of the NHSLS participants, the longer the partners had known each other before they had sex (Michael et al., 1994). In 90 percent of the married couples the spouses knew each other more than a month before they had sex, and in about 50 percent they knew each other more than a year. This does not necessarily mean they were dating for a long time before they had sex; rather, like Bill and Karen, they probably knew each other and were friends for awhile before dating. Most people were unlikely to have had sex immediately after meeting, and when they did the relationship was likely to have lasted a month or less. It seems that people proceed differently if they are interested in a casual sexual relationship than if they seek a long-term partnership.

What Do You Think?

How have your intimate relationships changed from when you were an adolescent? In what ways, if any, have they become more important to you than family relationships?

MARRIAGE

During early adulthood, almost everybody finds a marriage partner. Although contemporary men and women are marrying later than previous cohorts, 90 percent of Americans have married by age thirty (Michael et al., 1994). As we will discuss later in the chapter, marriage is not the only lifestyle choice of young adults, but it is the most frequent choice. Marriage is the socially sanctioned union of a man and a woman that, to some extent, symbolizes being an adult. It represents the establishment of a new household and the beginning of a new family, even though households and families do not necessarily begin with marriage. It is also the institution to which we look for love, companionship, emotional gratification, and the context for ego development (Melville, 1988). With expectations for marriage being so multifaceted in a changing society that includes many different types of people, not all marriages are the same.

Marriage Types

In a 1989 Gallup poll that asked 1,234 randomly selected adults about marriage, 57 percent said the ideal marriage is one in which both husband and wife have jobs and share the responsibilities of child and home care (DeStefano & Colasanto, 1990). Another 37 percent said the ideal arrangement is the traditional division of roles, with man as provider and woman as homemaker. These two responses represent very different views of marriage.

Equal Partnerships   The majority of respondents in the poll were describing an *equal-partner relationship.* Based on a study of sexual relationships, John Scanzoni and his associates (1989) characterize the **equal-partner relationship** as one in which negotiating about shared concerns and responsibilities is the norm. Everything (who works, who cooks, who pays the bills) is open for renegotiation except the principle that everything is negotiable. Instead of a preset assignment of roles and responsibilities, both partners expect change as they and their relationship grow and develop. This enables each partner to cultivate his or her capacity to function effectively both at home and at work. Equal partners would, for example, rene-

In an equal-partnership marriage, husband and wife share responsibility for work and family. Here Dad folds the laundry and cares for the children. In a junior-partnership marriage, Dad (typically the senior partner) would help with family responsibilities but Mom (typically the junior partner) would have primary responsibility.

gotiate household tasks if one of them faced a new job opportunity that required a longer commute. This form reflects the contemporary belief that each partner should be able to count on the loved one in times of need and to promote the welfare of the loved, as we saw in Sternberg's theory of love.

Conventional Marriages   In contrast, the substantial minority in the poll described what Scanzoni and associates call a **conventional relationship,** in which the man is the head of the household and the sole economic provider and the woman is the mother and the homemaker, responsible for all domestic tasks. If a personally meaningful opportunity came along that would interfere with the assigned division of labor, the conventional husband or wife would be expected to turn it down. This agreement between conventional-style marriage partners sometimes leads to conflict when the wife decides she wants to return to school or take a job. A frequent outcome is that she can take the job, but only if it does not interfere with her responsibilities at home. The conventional relationship used to be the dominant model for marriage, but not any longer.

Junior Partnerships   A third type of relationship, the **junior-partner relationship,** has elements of both equal partnership and conventional relationships. The junior partner, typically the wife, brings in some of the income and takes on some decision-making responsibilities. The senior partner, usually the husband, often *helps* the wife at home, but he does not *share* family responsibilities such as cooking and child care. Thus, a husband may speak of "baby sitting" for his own child. This, we will see, is the most common form of marriage today. Scanzoni and associates (1989) point out that it is very difficult to move from junior partner to equal partner because doing so leads to a series of conflicts that call for renegotiation of the relationship. Usually it falls on the wife to raise the issues that create the conflict, because she feels the inequity more keenly. Husbands are more satisfied with their relationships when they have a voice equal to or greater than their wives' and least satisfied when their wives have more say than they do. In these cases, husbands would want to renegotiate. Wives are more satisfied when decision making is equal and less satisfied when there is an imbalance in either direction. This is the more typical situation (Steil, 1995).

Marital Equality

Endorsing equal partnership as the ideal is not the same thing as having an equal-partnership marriage. Although most wives today are employed outside the home, Janice Steil (1995) estimates that employed wives still do 60 to 64 percent of the household labor and husbands do about 20 percent. Employed wives fill in the gap by paying for baby sitting, house cleaning, and carry-out foods. Only 14 to 20 percent have regular paid housekeeping help (about the same as for nonemployed wives). Employed wives also reduce their standards so that meals become simpler and cleaning gets done less often. We see here a pattern of women having what Arlie Hochschild (1989) has labeled the *second shift*: they work the first shift at their jobs and the second shift in the family. If sharing roles is the measure of equal partnership, very few marriages reach the ideal. While more women now share the conventional male role of earning money, men still have a larger share of financial responsibility. And while husbands of employed wives now help more at home, few men share the conventional female role of caring for home and family.

Decision-making power in relationships is another measure of equality researchers have examined. Family size, social class, ethnicity, husband's income, and wife's employment are associated with the degree of the husband's dominance in the marriage. In a summary of available studies, Janice Steil (1989) found that white husbands in the United States have more power than African American husbands and Asian American husbands may have more power than white ones.

More women now share the conventional male role of earning money and more husbands of employed wives now help at home, but few men share the conventional female role of caring for home and family. As a result many women do a "second shift" when they get home from work.

"Thank goodness you're here. His dish is empty."

Working-class husbands have less power than middle-class husbands. Steil reports, "White middle-class housewives who do not work outside the home may well have less power in their marital relationships than any other group" (p. 141). The more women earn, the greater their influence in decision making at home (Blumstein & Schwartz, 1983; Steil, 1995). This exemplifies one of the benefits of multiple roles discussed in Chapter 12's Perspectives box (see page 426).

Marital Satisfaction

Do different types of marriages lead to different levels of satisfaction with marriage? Indeed, that seems to be the case. In comparisons of couples with different types of marriages, both spouses in equal partnerships express the highest levels of marital satisfaction and psychological well-being. Inequitable relationships cause distress in the form of a diminished sense of self-worth and negative judgments about the relationship (Keith & Schafer, 1991). Wives have fewer depressive symptoms when husbands help than when they do not (Steil, 1995). Couples that are satisfied with their division of household labor report greater marital happiness and lower marital conflict and aggression (Suitor, 1991). While not all dissatisfaction leads to physical violence, wife abuse is the most frequent form of family violence, as discussed in the accompanying Multicultural View box. After reviewing many studies using many different measures, Steil (1995) concludes that "across these diverse measures the general pattern of findings seem to support equality as a desirable basis for marriage" (p. 154).

What about comparisons between married and unmarried people? Married people generally fare better than unmarried people in terms of mortality, morbidity, men-

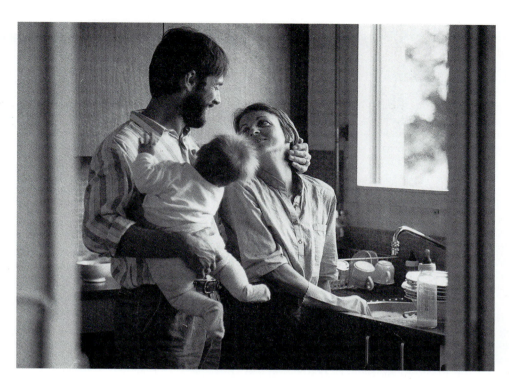

Wives and husbands in equal partner-ships express the highest levels of marital satisfaction and psychological well-being.

tal health, and more general measures of psychological well-being (Friedman et al., 1995; Lee et al., 1991). While it is true that happier and healthier people are more likely to be selected as marriage partners, researchers agree that being married provides strong and important benefits (Gove et al., 1990). Formerly married people (divorced and widowed) have the lowest levels of well-being of all types, never-married people have intermediate levels, and married people the highest levels. Men seem to benefit more than women do (Ross et al., 1990). Married people are financially better off, which probably contributes to their health and happiness. They also care for each other and provide comfort and support. Perhaps men derive the greater advantage from marriage because wives typically provide more care, comfort, and emotional support than they receive. The evidence is clear, however, that having a partner has advantages, even if the partnership has some problems.

Both marriage and employment status have positive effects on mental health. Peter Guarnaccia, Ronald Angel, and Jacqueline Worobey (1991) were interested in the interactive effects of marital status and economic resources on mental health. They looked at young adult (ages twenty to forty-five) Mexican Americans, Cuban Americans, and Puerto Ricans in the United States to assess the relative effects of marital status, employment status, and culture on mental health status. They found large differences among the three nationality groups. Cuban Americans had the highest educational and employment levels and the highest incomes; Puerto Ricans and Mexican Americans had similar levels of educational attainment; and Puerto Ricans had the lowest incomes. The researchers also found significant differences in SES between married and unmarried adults. The unmarried individuals were less likely to be employed and, especially women, had lower income levels. Respondents who were both unemployed and unmarried had substantially poorer mental health than those who were employed and married in all of the nationality groups. Both women and men were less depressed if they were both married and employed, further evidence that partnership relationships are healthier for husband and wives.

While married people are still happier and healthier than never-married people, differences in personal happiness between the two groups have decreased in recent years. Gary Lee and his associates (1991) found that among young adults ages

A Multicultural View

Cross-Cultural Similarities in Wife Abuse

Young adults seek love and support from intimate partners. Yet high levels of physical aggression against one's marriage or cohabiting partner, or wife abuse, are evident in almost all societies (Hoffman et al., 1994). In a cross-cultural study of small-scale and peasant societies, David Levinson (1989) found that wife beating was the most common form of domestic violence, occurring in about 85 percent of the societies studied. Other researchers have found high rates of physical wife abuse in European, industrialized societies (Gelles & Cornell, 1983). In the United States, the reported rate of wife abuse is between 11 and 22 percent (Straus & Gelles, 1990). Particularly high rates of wife abuse have been found among Hispanic families in the United States and among African American families (Cazenave & Straus, 1990; Straus & Smith, 1990). Although female-against-male violence also occurs in families, male violence against women is of greater concern because it causes the most damage (Cantos et al., 1994). What factors contribute to violence within the very relationships we turn to meet our most intimate needs?

Researchers who have studied wife abusers have found that certain demographic and structural characteristics of married men seem to influence their levels of domestic violence. Factors that cause economic frustration, stress, and strain, which might include occupation, educational level, and income, increase the likelihood of wife

abuse. All measures of SES—educational level, occupational level, and income—are negatively related to domestic violence (Straus et al., 1980). Individuals who have witnessed or have been the object of aggression are more likely to be aggressive themselves (Lackey & Williams, 1995). Alcohol usage is positively related to spouse abuse; about one out of four instances of wife abuse in the United States involves alcohol (Julian & McKenry, 1993; Kantor & Straus, 1990).

Two types of theories have been used to explain why, although wife abuse occurs at all levels of SES, it appears to be more common and more severe among those with lower SES. The first theoretical approach focuses on structural factors associated with having fewer resources. Violence, like money or status, is perceived to be a resource. When husbands lack other resources to control their wives, according to this theory, violence becomes the "ultimate" resource (Yllo & Bogard, 1988). Those with fewer resources generally experience higher levels of frustration and stress because they have fewer financial, emotional, and social supports to help them cope. Husbands resort to violence when stress is high and resources are low.

The second theoretical approach focuses on cultural factors. According to this theory, people who grow up in cultural environments that expose them to more physical aggression and approve of it more learn to be violent

twenty-five to thirty-nine, the never-married ones have become happier, the married ones have become less happy, and as a result the gap between the two has lessened. Both never-married young men and women were happier in the 1980s than they were in the 1970s. In addition, young married women were less happy in the 1980s than they were in earlier years. The authors suggest that young women are entering marriage with expectations for equal partnerships, but their expectations are not being met. The difficulties in finding partners who share their views about marriage are one of several reasons many young adults delay marriage and choose alternative lifestyles, to which we turn next.

What Do You Think?

What type of marriage did your parents have when you were growing up? If you are (or were) married, what type of marriage do (did) you have? What type of marriage would you like to have?

ALTERNATIVE LIFESTYLES

Although the majority of Americans spend most of their adult lives in marriages, many spend significant portions as singles and some never marry. Singlehood can be the result of delaying marriage, a lack of opportunity to marry, divorce, widowhood,

(Stets, 1990). Adults who as children were physically punished engage in wife and child abuse significantly more than those who had not been physically punished (Straus & Smith, 1990). The culture of violence is very much affected by the socioeconomic forces that create high population density and high rates of unemployment, poverty, and crime in the inner cities (Zinn, 1989). Murray Straus and Christine Smith (1990) found, for example, that physical punishment was more closely related to spouse abuse in lower-SES Hispanic families than in higher-SES ones. In a dangerous environment, children and adults witness violence with some frequency and are more likely to see it as a necessary means of protection for themselves and their families. Parents see the risks of their children's misbehavior as potentially life threatening and so are perhaps more likely to use physical punishment in this situation. Exposure to physical punishment adds to the experience of violence in the children's lives. The long-term effects of violence in daily life seem to be increased use of aggression within the family, since spouse abuse and child abuse are often linked (McKay, 1994).

Karen Hoffman, David Demo, and John Edwards (1994) studied a sample of married individuals in Bangkok, Thailand, to see the relative impact of structure and culture on physical wife abuse. Women in Thailand have high status compared to women in other developing countries; more than half of Thai wives are employed. Yet the culture emphasizes conventional division of labor within the family and "macho" characteristics in males. Buddhism, the dominant religion in Thailand, prescribes principles of compassion, responsibility, and caring for others and emphasizes mutual caring and respect between spouses. Given these various economic and cultural forces in Bangkok, what is the incidence of wife abuse?

Hoffman and associates interviewed 619 husbands in intact marriages with at least one child and wives who were no more than forty-five years old. About 20 percent of these urban Thai husbands reported having hit, slapped, or kicked their wives at one time or another. The researchers found evidence that structural factors were highly significant; a higher level of resources decreased the likelihood of physical wife abuse. Cultural factors were at work as well. Cultural norms prescribing male dominance and power within a conventional marriage encouraged wife abuse in Thailand. Thus, both structural and cultural forces appear to contribute to wife abuse in Bangkok. Clifton Marsh (1993) found that a similar interplay of forces was correlated with African American domestic violence.

or a choice to remain single. Although parents, religious leaders, and politicians still exhort marriage as the ideal state against which other lifestyles are judged, today's unmarried people have a variety of lifestyle choices that carry less stigma than in earlier times (Ganong et al., 1990). Unmarried adults are no longer expected to continue to live with their parents, as they were before the 1960s. They can live without a partner, in a heterosexual partnership, or in a homosexual partnership.

Singlehood

Many contemporary Americans spend early adulthood single. Peter, for example, always expected to marry. During his early adult years he lived with and planned to marry a series of three women, but each relationship failed for a different reason. At age forty, he had all but given up. He bought a house for himself and prepared to be happily single. Three years later his wife and infant daughter live with him in that house, but Peter represents a large proportion of his cohort who spent many adult years single. Of his two brothers, Jimmy has never married; after many years as a single, he now lives with his gay partner. Barry, the remaining brother, married at age twenty-four, divorced at age thirty, and spent six years as a single before he remarried. Their cousin Sandy will be forty-three on her next birthday and remains single. She has devoted herself to her acting career, a career she does not consider to be compatible with family life. As these examples show, singles are not a homogeneous group.

In a survey of three thousand singles in thirty-six states, Jacqueline Simenauer and David Carroll (1982) found that one-third of the men and one-fifth of the women reported they were single by choice. Some were in religious orders that required chastity. Some considered marriage to be incompatible with their careers. A small minority were gay or lesbian. The rest saw being single as a waiting period, a special, limited time to do things that they had never done or a time to look for a new partner. The best part of being single, they reported, was the freedom; the worst was the loneliness.

These two extremes capture the advantages and disadvantages of the single life. When Sandra Dalton (1992) interviewed never-married women, they talked about the trade-offs between opportunities for freedom, independence, and personal growth and the loneliness resulting from the absence of a mate and children. They described self-reliance, openness, and self-acceptance as positive aspects of singleness. They also described it as a burden and as a form of rootlessness. Never-married women and men seem to see similar benefits and drawbacks in marriage, although women report being more motivated to marry (Inglis & Greenglass, 1989). Single women also report being happier than single men and are better adjusted socially and psychologically than either single men or married women (Johnston & Eklund, 1984). This reflects the decreasing gap between never-married and married individuals. Being single as a young adult appears to be getting better. In a comparison by year from 1972 to 1989, never-married young adults of both genders ages twenty-five to thirty-nine showed steady increases in personal happiness (Lee et al., 1991). Never-married young adults may have become happier because their single status is now more widely accepted.

Heterosexual Cohabitation

As Figure 13.3 shows, contemporary young adults are marrying later than earlier cohorts did. However, they are forming sexual partnerships at about the same rate and same age at which older cohorts married. As in the case of Bill and Karen, the first union is now more likely to be **cohabitation,** or living together. Of the women in the NHSLS sample born between 1963 and 1974, only half were married by age twenty-five but almost 90 percent were in partnerships (Michael et al., 1994). The trend toward cohabitation replacing early marriage is most pronounced for the least educated segment of the population, those who have not completed high school (Bumpass et al., 1991).

Koray Tanfer (1987) examined the patterns of heterosexual cohabitation among more than 8 million twenty to twenty-nine year-old, never-married American women. She found that African American women were no more likely to be cohabiting or to have cohabited than white women. While heterosexual cohabitation was a common occurrence for single women in their twenties, they saw it not as a permanent replacement for marriage but as part of the courtship process. A similar pattern appears to exist in Australia, where cohabitation is also prevalent (Khoo, 1987). The younger, never-married participants view living together as a temporary arrangement prior to marriage. They live together when they have just finished their education or just started working and do not feel financially or emotionally prepared to take the more serious step of marriage. In one survey, half of the cohabiting adults indicated that they saw living together as a good way to test for compatibility before marriage (Bumpass et al., 1991).

Heterosexual cohabitation typically does not last long. Within a few years, most relationships have either broken up or the couple has married. There are many social pressures to marry, and most adults do want to marry eventually. And, as we discussed earlier in this chapter, for those who remain not ready for marriage, the changes in intimacy and passion that are to be expected in a relationship over time mitigate against the romance continuing. Despite all the social pressures to marry, Larry Bumpass and associates (1991) report that 20 percent of cohabiting adults

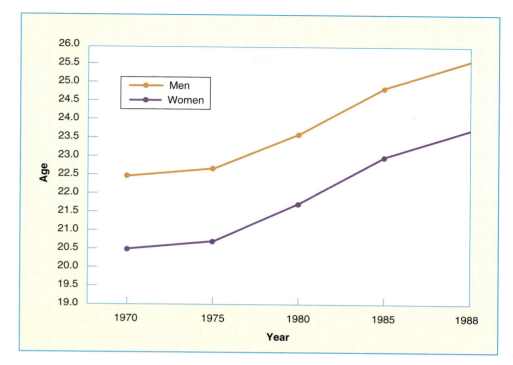

FIGURE 13.3
Median Age at First Marriage, 1970 to 1989
Since 1970, young adults have been marrying later than earlier cohorts. They are forming sexual partnerships at about the same age earlier cohorts did, but these unions are more likely to be cohabitation.
Source: U.S. Bureau of the Census (1995).

do not expect to ever marry. They point out that "the picture that is emerging is that cohabitation is very much a family status, but one in which levels of certainty about the relationship are lower than marriage" (p. 926).

Does living together first improve the quality of a marriage? The evidence is inconclusive. One study found that for recently married white couples, premarital cohabitation seemed to make no difference in level of satisfaction with marriage, but for African American couples it seemed to have a negative impact (Crohan & Verhoff, 1989). Perhaps the difficulties for African American couples are so much greater to begin with that the transition from cohabitation to marriage is more stressful; or perhaps cohabiting before marriage has different meanings for African Americans and whites. Other studies show that couples who had cohabited before marriage report more problems, are at higher risk for divorce, and have less commitment to the institution of marriage than couples who had not lived together first (Booth & Johnson, 1988; Thomson & Colella, 1992). One way to understand these contradictory results is to look at who chooses cohabitation.

People who have chosen cohabitation tend to have personal and demographic characteristics that put them at higher risk for divorce. Female cohabitors tend to be white, less educated, and less likely to be employed than noncohabitors, according to Tanfer's (1987) large survey. They also are likely to live in large metropolitan areas and are one-third more likely to have grown up in a single-parent family. They are more likely to be unconventional, to describe themselves as free of traditional gender role characteristics, and to think of themselves as assertive and independent. Alfred DeMaris and Vaninadha Rao (1992) report that cohabiting couples tend to be less conventional, less religious, and lower in SES. Because these qualities are associated with higher divorce rates, as we will discuss shortly, the differences in the quality of marriages between couples that first lived together and those that did not are likely due to the differences in the kinds of people selecting those routes rather than to the cohabitation experience itself. Some confirmation of this possibility comes from evidence that the differences in marital quality have become smaller as cohabitation has become more conventional (DeMaris & Rao, 1992; Schoen, 1992). Alfred De-Maris and William MacDonald (1993) found that only serial cohabitation was associated with marital instability. While cohabitation is seen as a choice, the lesbian or gay lifestyle is often perceived as more than a conscious choice, as we will see next.

Lesbian/Gay Sexual Preference

Several factors make it difficult to know how many gay persons there are. First, sexual preference is not set early in life and is not unchanging. While some women and men remember knowing, since some time between ages six and twelve, that they were different from their heterosexual friends, others perceive themselves to have made a conscious choice to be gay or lesbian (Golden, 1994). Claudia Card (1995) stresses the importance of choice in determining sexual orientation. Second, as we discussed in Chapter 12, it is hard to know how to define *homosexuality.* Does a single homosexual experience define you as gay? Does desire for a same-sex person, in the absence of homosexual behavior, define you as gay? Or does self-identification as a homosexual define you as gay? Third, gay people are hard to count since, except in the privacy of their sexual relationships, they look and act just like everybody else. Fourth, **homophobia,** which refers to fear, dread, hostility, or prejudice directed toward gay people and the resulting mistreatment and discrimination, discourages many gay men and lesbians from making their sexual identity public.

Ethnic minority gay men and lesbians face the multiple stresses of coping with the gay and lesbian community's racism, the dominant culture's homophobia, and the homophobia of their own ethnic group (Greene, 1994). Since the ethnic community provides a protective buffer against racism, "coming out" may have greater costs for ethnic minorities.

The NHSLS provides two estimates of the percentages of homosexuals in the United States (Michael et al., 1994). Among men, 2.8 percent identified themselves as gay or bisexual, while 10.1 percent reported some behavior or desire, or self-identification as gay. Among women, 1.4 percent identified themselves as lesbian or bisexual, while 8.6 reported some behavior or desire, or self-identification as lesbian. Using either set of figures, the percentages of gay men and lesbian are small, considerably smaller than Kinsey's estimate (see Chapter 12), but they still represent a great many individuals.

Most gay men and lesbians live in larger cities and the surrounding suburbs. Concentrating in these areas makes it easier to establish the social networks that facilitate making friends and finding sexual partners. Within these networks, gay men and lesbians are a varied group. They work in all occupational fields, participate in all religious traditions, come from all ethnic and racial groups, and have the full range of political outlooks (Bell & Weinberg, 1978; Bell et al., 1981). Depending on the study, between 40 and 60 percent of gay men and between 45 and 80 percent of lesbians are involved in close, steady same-sex relationships (Peplau & Cochran, 1990); some are in heterosexual marriages, others are single and have casual encounters, and still others are abstinent. Some pass as heterosexual, some are "out," and many are "out" with some of their friends but not at work or in all social settings.

Lesbian/Gay Cohabitation

It is estimated that one-half of gay male couples and three-quarters of lesbian couples live together (Peplau & Cochran, 1990). Cohabiting gay couples face the same pressures cohabiting and married hetrosexual couples face, plus the additional problems that result from negative attitudes toward and treatment of homosexuals. While some cohabiting gay couples establish conventional roles and division of labor, most form equal partnerships and share household tasks and decision making (Peplau & Cochran, 1990). Many see gay relationships as "an opportunity for breaking away from heterosexual stereotypes . . . trying to establish and maintain a truly equal partnership, with both . . . taking responsibility for matters emotional and practical" (National Lesbian and Gay Survey, 1992, p. 109). In a review of studies of gay couples, Letitia Peplau and Susan Cochran concluded that "most gay men and lesbians perceive their close relationships as satisfying and that levels of love and satisfaction are similar for homosexual and heterosexual couples who are

matched in age and other relevant characteristics" (p. 333). Lawrence Kurdek (1994) found that gay male couples do not differ from heterosexual men in their levels of relationship satisfaction (although gay men are more expressive than husbands) and that lesbians do not differ from wives in their levels of relationship satisfaction. Lesbians and gay men report high levels of sexual satisfaction with their partners (Peplau & Cochran, 1990). William Masters, Virginia Johnson, and Robert Kolodny (1992) report that homosexual couples share more information about their sexuality and have better communication than heterosexual couples do.

Cohabiting gay and lesbian couples have levels of satisfaction similar to those of heterosexual couples who are matched in age and other relevant characteristics. They face the same pressures that cohabiting and married couples face, plus the additional ones that result from the negative attitudes and treatment of homosexuals.

Perhaps because legal marriage does not exist as an expectation or a possibility for them, gay and lesbian cohabiting partnerships often last a long time. When Philip Blumstein and Pepper Schwartz (1983) set out to study couples, they had difficulty finding heterosexual cohabitors who had been together for more than ten years, but they had no trouble finding gay and lesbian partnerships of that duration. In their comparisons of lesbian, gay male, and cohabiting heterosexual couples, they found that all were about equal in their personal expectations of staying together, that breakups were rare in couples who had been together for more than ten years, and that among shorter-term relationships lesbians' breakup rate was 20 percent, gay male couples' was 16 percent, and heterosexual cohabitors' was 14 percent. Compared to married couples, gay couples are more likely to break up in the first ten years, but after that the rates of breakup are about the same.

These findings suggest that lasting intimate partnerships do not depend on marriage. Forming an intimate relationship helps the young adult establish independence from parents. It also raises the issue of starting a family of one's own.

What Do You Think?

With a few classmates, compare your experiences as singles with those of your same-sex parents. Which generation spent more time being single? Which cohabited? To what factors do you attribute any differences? Is your case consistent with the trends discussed in the chapter?

CHANGING FAMILIES

Not so long ago, the word *family* brought to mind a breadwinner husband and a homemaker wife with at least two children. We have already seen that this image no longer reflects the typical marriage; today most wives and mothers are employed. We have also seen that many people now live together before or in place of marriage and that some people remain single. When we add high rates of divorce and remarriage to this picture, it becomes even clearer that American families are taking new forms.

Divorce

Marriage is expected to meet such a wide array of social, emotional, personal, and sexual needs that it is little wonder many people find their actual marriages disappointing. About 50 percent of first marriages and 40 percent of all marriages end in divorce (Ruth, 1995). Most divorces occur during early adulthood, although, as Figure 13.4 shows, the age at which people divorce has been rising since the mid-1970s. In an analysis of more than fifteen hundred responses to surveys conducted from 1973 to 1988, Norval Glenn (1991) found that the percentage of people in intact marriages who reported that their marriages were "very happy" declined a little each year of the survey for both men and women, and overall the declines were statistically significant. His findings, combined with the increase in the divorce rate, led Glenn to conclude that the probability of marital success has dropped between 1970 and 1990. He points out that if the rate of marital success had stayed the same but more unhappily married couples ultimately divorced, partners in intact marriages should have been happier because only the more successful marriages would remain. This is not the case.

Glenn (1991) identified two social changes that have contributed to the rising divorce rates. First are the increased expectations of marriage, the breakdown of consensus about marital and gender roles, and the issues of equality within marriage that we discussed earlier. With both marriage partners typically working, the conventional image of marriage has not kept pace with the reality, a reality that causes conflict and disappointment for many married women and men. Consider Charles and Kathy: When they met, he was a musician and a part-time chef and she was a teacher. They fell in love, moved in together, and married within a year's time. A month later, Kathy was pregnant. She was eager to be a mother. When the baby was born, Charles was dismayed to find that Kathy no longer intended to work. He had looked forward to being a caregiving parent and musician and expected her to

FIGURE 13.4
Median Age at Divorce, 1970 to 1990
The age at which people divorce has been rising steadily since the mid-1970s, but most divorces still occur during early adulthood.
Source: U.S. Bureau of the Census (1995).

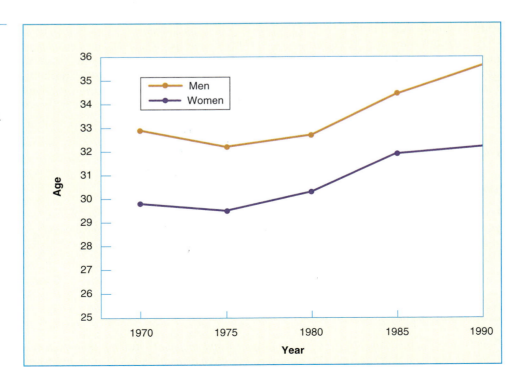

be a caregiving parent and teacher. They held different unspoken ideals of what marriage should be like. Charles had an equal-partner model; Kathy's model was conventional. Charles found himself working longer and longer hours and having little time with his baby. Kathy felt cooped up alone in the house with the baby, but believed that was where she belonged. They tried their best to work out their conflict, but their views were irreconcilable and they eventually separated.

The second social change is the decline in the belief that marriage really means "until death do us part." Many young adults are children of divorce, and as adults they tend to hold more negative views of marriage (Tasker & Richards, 1994). These young adults have witnessed their mothers becoming **displaced homemakers,** women who committed themselves to the conventional roles of wife and mother, lost those roles due to separation, divorce, or widowhood, and were unprepared for employment and single parenthood. An estimated 3 to 5 million women age thirty-five and older were displaced homemakers in the 1980s (Greenwood-Audant, 1989). Children of divorce have seen their fathers suffer the anguish of no longer living with their children or have not seen their fathers at all. Children of divorce thus fear becoming fully committed to marriage. According to Glenn (1991, p. 269), "when the probability of marital success is as low as it is in the United States today, to make a strong, unqualified commitment to a marriage—and to make the investments of time, energy, and forgone opportunities that entails—is so hazardous that no totally rational person would do it." But as we saw in our discussion of love, if a person withholds commitment and is constantly comparing his or her marriage with alternatives to it, that marriage will not get the effort any relationship requires to stay healthy.

Remarriage

The end of a particular marriage does not generally mean the end of a desire for a good marriage. Americans remarry at almost the same rate at which they marry; divorced people are more likely to remarry than never-married people are (Ruth, 1995). Based on data from 1982, Larry Bumpass, James Sweet, and Teresa Martin (1990) estimate that overall, 72 percent of divorced people will remarry, with divorced young adults remarrying at the highest rates. About half of these remarriages will end in divorce, and many of these divorcees will remarry again. The pattern in marriage, as in cohabitation, is to move from one exclusive relationship to another, that is, engage in serial monogamy.

People who have divorced and remarried several times report less happiness and more frequent depression than people who have divorced once; the latter, in turn, report more frequent depression than those who have never divorced (Kurdek, 1991). Remarried people report as much satisfaction with their marriages as do people in first marriages and find their second marriages more sexually satisfying than their first ones (Call et al., 1995).

Joshua Gold, Donald Bubenzer, and John West (1993) found that the types of relationships marriage partners had with ex-spouses were related to the quality of their current marriages. Questionnaires were completed by sixty-nine male (ages twenty-five to sixty-four) and fifty-eight female (age twenty-two to sixty-two) spouses. The questionnaires measured the degree of emotional attachment and interpersonal conflict between ex-spouses as well as the level of current marital intimacy. Respondents came from stepmother, stepfather, or blended families. Among both men and women, the more attached they were to the ex-spouse, the less intimate they were with the current spouse. There was also a significant negative relationship between conflict with the ex-spouse and marital intimacy for men and women. Relationships with ex-spouses that were low in conflict and low in emotional attachment had the best outcome for the new marriage.

Some people choose not to remarry. In a study of women in their mid-thirties to mid-fifties who had redefined their sexuality from heterosexual to lesbian, Claudette Charbonneau and Patricia Lander (1991) found that half of the respondents had been

Americans remarry at almost the rate at with they marry, with divorced young adults remarrying at the highest rates. Remarriage contributes to the changing nature of families. Since this bride and groom each have a daughter, their marriage forms a blended family.

divorced for several or more years before their lesbian "awakening." Many mentioned as a turning point leaving the marriage and reevaluating expectations of relationships with men. Whether people remarry, remain single, or form gay or lesbian partnerships, the families that result are different. As we saw in Chapter 9's discussion of psychosocial development in middle childhood, the changing nature of families has had a direct impact on the experience of parenthood, the subject of the next section.

What Do You Think?

What evidence can you think of in your own life that the image of marriage does not fit with the reality? How has this affected your views of marriage?

PARENTHOOD

People have many different reasons for wanting children. Some really like children and want an opportunity to be involved with their care. Some women strongly desire the experience of pregnancy and childbirth. Many young adults see parenthood as a way to demonstrate their adult status, since parenting is an acknowledged adult role in our society. For people who come from happy families, it is a means of recreating their earlier families. For those from unhappy families, it can be a means of doing better than their parents did. Many people never consider their own reasons for having children but do so to conform to social expectations; social pressure from family, religious institutions, and the media pushes people, especially women, to have children. Because society places so much emphasis on the fulfillment motherhood is supposed to bring, some women who are unsure of what they want to do with their lives use having a child as a way to create an identity.

Whatever reasons one has for becoming pregnant, pregnancy and childbirth are major life experiences for women and are the initial stages in the transition to parenthood for women and men. As we discussed in Chapter 3, Genetics, Prenatal Development, and Birth, couples who want to have children but have difficulty conceiving can turn to an array of reproductive technologies for help, or they can adopt. Pregnancy is both a biological and a psychological event in a woman's life. A successful pregnancy leads to the birth of a healthy child. It also contributes to the development of a healthy mother and a new family unit. Whether a couple is having its first child together or a woman is having a first child on her own, one of the biggest adjustments is developing a family in which the young adults put some of their own needs and concerns on the back burner and take on the responsibilities of caring for the next generation. This is an enormous change in the lives of the new parents (and, as you will remember from Chapter 11's discussion of problems of adolescence, an important reason teenage parenthood has such negative effects).

Transition to Parenthood

People prepare less for the parenting role than for the other important new roles of early adulthood, employment and marriage (Rossi, 1982). Young adults train for employment in school, in volunteer positions, in internships, or on the job. The experiences of dating, courtship, engagement, and cohabitation all help the young adult prepare for marriage and other forms of intimate relationships. But many young adults have no experience with children before they become parents. They frequently find themselves expecting a child as a result of recreational sex rather than active reproductive choice. Furthermore, schools and other social institutions do not teach the skills necessary for adequate parenting, such as empathy, interpersonal competence, and caring for a child. Unlike the young adult's other new roles, parenthood cannot be undone. You can quit a job that does not suit you, change professions, break an engagement, or get a divorce, but you cannot "give back" a child. You do not even get time off. Parenthood hits full force with the birth of the baby. No other transition is so abrupt and complete. This is

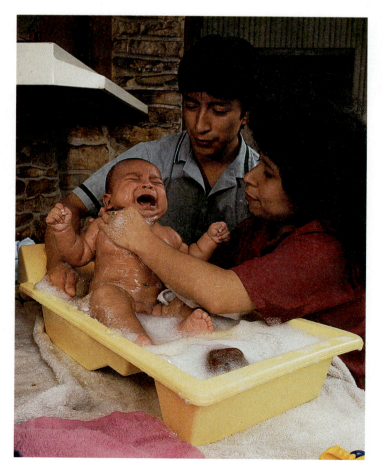

Many young adults have no experience with children before they become parents and find themselves unprepared for the abrupt and demanding transition to parenthood. Although they experience some difficulty adjusting, most find parenting rewarding.

How Does the Timing of Parenthood Influence the Parenting Experience?

With safe and effective contraception readily available, couples can now decide not only whether they will have children but when they will have children. How does the decision about timing affect the quality of the parenting experience? To investigate this question, Pamela Daniels and Kathy Weingarten (1982) interviewed eighty-six couples who represented parents of "early," "late," and "very late" firstborn children. The early-timing parents (thirty-six couples) had their first child in their late teens or early twenties. The late-timing parents (thirty-six couples) had their first child in their late twenties or early thirties. The very-late or midlife parents (fourteen couples) had their first child in their late thirties or early forties. These couples reflected the diversity of occupations, incomes, ethnicities, and religions of white Americans. They also represented a time when couples were expected to have their first child in their mid-twenties. More recently, a sample of about two hundred adults reported that the most appropriate time to have the first child is when the parents are twenty-seven years old (Rook et al., 1989). While the age-related expectations have changed, there is little evidence that the experience of being "off time" has.

Daniels and Weingarten found that couples had four different images, or *family-timing scenarios,* about when a child should enter their lives. The *natural ideal* refers to letting nature take its course. The *brief wait* refers to deferring parenthood for two or three years after marriage. *Pragmatic postponement* means waiting until other personal or occupational goals have been met. The *mixed script* reflects that some couples do not agree about ideal timing. Finally, some couples have no thoughts or expectations about timing and thus have an *unformed scenario.* The natural ideal was most common among women who did not go to college. College-educated women were equally divided between the brief wait and pragmatic postponement.

Only 60 percent of the couples had their first child according to the family-timing scenario they would have chosen. Of those who did not, about half became parents earlier because they did not use contraception consistently or contraception was faulty. The other half became

one reason late timing of parenthood can be advantageous (see the accompanying Perspectives box).

New fathers feel the strain as well as mothers, but mothers feel it more fully because they are expected to take primary responsibility for infant care and encouraged to believe they will feel fulfilled by motherhood. Fulfillment, however, comes not from the experience of a biological event but from development of and dedication to values, interests, and competencies over time (M. Hoffnung, 1995). The gap between many a new mother's expectations of fulfillment and the realities of exhaustion and distraction is often enormous. Whereas almost everybody gets excited about pregnancy and birth, no one gets excited about colicky babies and dirty diapers. After being the center of attention during labor and delivery, a new mother soon finds herself very much alone at home. This aloneness may be heightened by the fact that the new father needs to increase his work hours to meet the new financial responsibilities of the family. The birth of a first child is, therefore, the event that is most likely to cause the greatest psychological disruption in American middle-class women, especially if the birth is not followed by full-time involvement outside the home (M. Hoffnung, 1992).

Adapting to New Roles In a longitudinal study of the adult-to-parent transition at the birth of the first child, Nicolina Fedele and her colleagues (1988) followed thirty working- to upper-middle-class couples in conventional marriages from early pregnancy to five years after the birth. They found that expecting the birth of the first child aroused anxieties in men about their capacity to provide. Women tended to become completely immersed in the world of mother and infant and greatly reduce their involvement with their husbands and the rest of the world. Fedele and associates measured *affiliation* (need for relatedness) and *autonomy* (need for separateness) in the parents-to-be early in the pregnancy and found these needs were related to parental adaptation in the postpartum period. Women who expressed high need for affiliation experienced less postpartum depression two months after the baby's birth,

parents later because of infertility. When asked if they were pleased with the timing of their first child, 54 percent of the parents said they were. Many more of the late-timing (67 percent) than early-timing (42 percent) parents were satisfied with how the timing worked out for them. More than half of the early-timing parents (56 percent) would have had their first child later than they did. Only 24 percent of the late-timing parents would have had their first child earlier, and 7 percent would have waited even longer.

How does family timing affect the couple? Late timing seems to be beneficial in this area. Early-timing parents are less mature, less ready to nurture each other and the baby, and more likely to be in conventional marriages in which they do not share child and home care, which leads to lower marital satisfaction (Cowan & Cowan, 1988). They are still adjusting to marriage when they begin adjusting to parenthood. Late-timing parents typically have worked out their identities, have separated from their parents, have developed nurturing marriages, and are able to share the work of caring for a child.

How does family timing affect mothers' work outside the home? Since mothers' employment has historically been affected more than fathers', this is an important question, especially today when most young women want careers as well as families (M. Hoffnung, 1992). For a woman with an occupational dream, the twenties are an essential period for giving it form. A career is hard to develop at the same time one is a new parent. Postponement of children frees the twenties for career development; late timing seems to offer the best solution. Combining parenthood and an established career is more workable than starting both at the same time. This has contributed to "on-time" parenting moving to one's late twenties or early thirties. On the other hand, infertility is less likely with early timing. And when two young adult parents share childrearing responsibilities, both can start their careers with plans to develop them more vigorously when their children enter school.

but their sense of well-being declined by the time the child reached the first birthday. Women with higher autonomy scores felt a greater sense of well-being at two months and at one year after the baby's birth. Men's affiliation scores during pregnancy had no relation to their well-being in the postpartum period, but the more autonomous their wives were, the greater was the men's well-being at one-year postpartum.

The researchers found that fathers in families in which the mother was more autonomous were more skillful parents. They conclude that "in families, things are often not what they seem. A mother who is completely devoted to her firstborn infant, who is always warm and empathetic, who never seems to miss a cue from the baby is satisfying to observe but is probably a mixed blessing for her family. It is probably mixed for her infant because, on the one hand, it provides the empathetic bond that allows the baby to thrive, but on the other hand, it may cement that bond in a way that will make it much harder for the baby to develop an early important attachment to his or her father" (p. 108). This means the father has little room for involvement with the child, thus depriving the father of the growth-producing experience of active parenting, depriving the child of early attachment to the father, and depriving the mother of an empathetic partner.

The combination of the new mother's complete devotion to her firstborn and the father's increased time at work creates particular problems for the development of the family, but problems also arise when mothers continue employment. Employment has multiple benefits for mothers, but it is not without costs (see Chapter 12's Perspectives box on page 426). The most pressing problem for working mothers is lack of time: there are more tasks to be done than hours in the day. Although many people think that fathers today are more involved with their children than fathers in the past, contemporary evidence indicates that women still carry more than 90 percent of the responsibility for children (LaRossa, 1992). This leaves working mothers with the heavy demands of doing two jobs. Despite the practical problems, however, continuing maternal employment is strongly associated with paternal skillfulness at parenting and with maternal adjustment to motherhood.

Marital Satisfaction in New Families   Almost all studies that measure martial satisfaction before and after the birth of the first child have found that marital satisfaction declines (Cowan & Cowan, 1988). Jay Belsky and Michael Rovine (1990) found that couples who were least satisfied with their marriages before the birth were most likely to report decline in satisfaction after, since problems that existed before were likely to have been magnified by the additional stresses brought on by the birth. Babies do not appear to create severe marital distress where none existed before; nor do they bring couples with distressed marriages closer together. Rather, the early postpartum months bring on a period of disorganization and change. The leading conflict in these first months of parenthood is division of labor in the family. Couples may regain their sense of equilibrium in marriage by successfully negotiating how they will divide the new family responsibilities. Husbands' participation in child and home care seems to be positively related to marital satisfaction after the birth. One longitudinal study found that the more the men shared in doing family tasks, the more satisfied were the wives at six and eighteen months postpartum and the husbands at eighteen months postpartum (Cowan & Cowan, 1988).

While many couples experience a difficult transition to parenthood, they also find it rewarding. Children affect parents in ways that lead to personal growth, enable reworking of childhood conflicts, build flexibility and empathy, and provide intimate, loving human connections. They also give a lot of pleasure. In follow-up interviews of new parents when their children were eighteen months old, Philip Cowan and Carolyn Cowan (1988) found that almost every man and woman spoke of the delight they felt from knowing their child and watching the child develop. They reported feeling pride for and closeness to their spouses, more adult with their own parents, and a renewed sense of purpose at work.

As you read about the young, married adult's transition to parenthood, you may have wondered how single parents cope with this critical change. As you can imagine, single parents face very different issues than their married counterparts.

Single Parenthood

One important change in family life has been the dramatic increase in single-parent families. The rise in the number of single parents is due to increasing numbers of divorces and delayed marriages and the shifting social values we have been considering. In 1990, 46 percent of all single-parent households resulted from divorce, 26 percent from out-of-wedlock births, 21 percent from marital separation, and 7 percent from the death of a spouse ("Single Parents," 1992). Single-parent households are characteristically low-income families; 45 percent of all female breadwinners with children and 19 percent of male breadwinners with children live in poverty. Because poverty is so frequent among single-mother families, and because 85 percent of single parents are mothers, it is hard to separate the effects of single parenting from the effects of poverty (Edmondson et al., 1993). Women generally face discrimination in employment, as we discussed in Chapter 12, and single mothers often face increased discrimination because employers fear they may be unreliable due to their sole responsibility for their children. These factors contribute to female heads of household earning less than their male counterparts. For women who were full-time homemakers, the transition to becoming both provider and parent is a difficult one that typically includes a dramatic decrease in income. In addition to facing financial pressure, single parents often feel socially isolated, as we discussed in Chapter 9. The demands of work and parenting may leave little time for their social and sexual needs.

The problems of single parenting are particularly acute for African American families. More than 50 percent of African American families with children under eighteen are now headed by single mothers. This is due to changes in the status of African American males, such as high unemployment, mortality, and incarceration rates, that make them less marriageable ("It's Not Working," 1986). The proportion of African American teenagers who have had babies and not gotten married has increased dramatically, from 42 percent in 1960 and 63 percent in 1970 to 89 percent in 1983 (Zinn, 1989). Pregnant teenagers are more likely to marry their boyfriends if the boyfriends have jobs. As Maxine Zinn (1989) points out, out-of-wedlock births are sometimes preferred by the pregnant teens' parents when marrying the father would mean adding another unemployed person to the burden of the extended family. "The mother-only family structure is thus the consequence, not the cause, of poverty" (Zinn, 1989, p. 868).

Extended families provide many single parents with support systems. Roland Wagner (1993) found that Mexican American mothers, despite being younger, less educated, and having more children, encountered fewer problems than white single mothers during their first year of single parenthood. Because members of the young mother's extended family tended to live close together, they offered a better family support network. In contrast, white single mothers, who often did not live near their extended families, were more likely to be upset or depressed. However, many single parents build wider support networks composed of non–family members to help combat their isolation (Donati, 1995). Most single mothers say they turn to their partners, boyfriends, friends, or relatives for help on a regular basis (Parish et al., 1991). Financial security and social support, basic needs of any family, are harder for single-parent families to attain.

Although research shows that single parents and their families suffer from more externally imposed stress than other parents—financial pressure, for example— many successfully raise happy and healthy children (Vosler & Proctor, 1991). Myrna Olson and Judith Haynes (1993) interviewed twenty-six single parents who were considered successful by qualified professionals. What contributed to their success? Olson and Haynes identified seven factors these parents had in common. First, they recognized and accepted the responsibilities and challenges of single parenthood. Second, they gave priority to the parental role; effective parenting requires time and energy. Third, they used consistent, nonpunitive discipline. Fourth, they emphasized open communication with their children. Fifth, they fostered individuality within a supportive family unit. Sixth, they recognized their need for self-nurturance. Last, they established and followed rituals and traditions, which contributes to the feeling of being a family.

As family structures have become more diverse, so has the group known as single parents. Most are women, but some are men. Some have partners, some have family support networks, some have friendship networks, and some are isolated. The stereotypes that portray single mothers as the cause of poverty, alcohol and drug abuse, and other social problems are belied by the wide variety of causes, attitudes, and activities of single parents. A more constructive approach would be to develop community services, such as sick-child care, to ease the stress with which single parents must cope.

Stepparent/Blended Families

Remarriage frequently reconstitutes a single-parent family into a stepparent or a blended family, as we discussed in Chapter 9. Comparisons among single-parent, remarriage, and conventional families indicate that remarriage families show the highest number of within-family problems (Vosler & Proctor, 1991). Consider the complexity of the relationships in these families. The remarriage brings together not only two adults but children and ex-spouses as well. Stepparents need to establish good relationships with the stepchildren as well as respect the bonds the children have with their biological parents. Stepparents have to accommodate their partners' ex-spouses, who need to be in communication about visitation, disciplinary or school problems, and other important matters concerning their children. If the remarriage involves stepsiblings, differences in treatment of biological siblings and stepsiblings by the newly married parents usually arise. Family relationships are likely to be awkward for a time until the inconsistencies are ironed out.

Lawrence Ganong and Marilyn Coleman (1993b) studied the relationships among members of stepfamilies. They measured stepsibling, stepparent-child, and stepfamily relations in 105 stepfamilies consisting of adults and their seven- to twenty-year-old children. Children's interactions with half-siblings and siblings were slightly more positive than those with stepsiblings (especially among cross-sex stepsibling pairs), although all relationships were relatively positive. Parental relationships with the children depended on whether the household was a stepfamily (one marriage partner with children from a previous relationship) or a blended family (both marriage partners with children from previous relationships). Parents in blended families felt closer to their biological children than did parents without stepchildren. They also believed that stepchildren negatively affected their relationship with their biological children. In blended families, parents more often disciplined only their biological children. In stepfamilies, the stepparent was more likely to be perceived as playing a parental role, which included disciplining the stepchildren. In general, adults in stepfamilies had more difficulty than children did in coping with stepsibling relationships.

Being a stepparent is an ambiguous role; one is neither a parent nor a nonparent. The problems are easier to resolve with younger children, who are likely to form special attachments to their stepparents. They are also easier with same-sex stepchildren. Men generally have an easier time being stepfathers than women do being stepmothers. This may be due to the fact that stepparenting relationships work best when the relationship is friendly but not intense, and men have less difficulty maintaining friendly distance than women do. When family roles are ambiguous, however, some men step over the line and become sexual abusers (Clark, 1993). Stepmothers tend to be more involved with their stepchildren than are stepfathers, but neither is as involved as the biological parent.

Many researchers have been interested in what factors affect the development of children in stepfamilies. (Chapter 9 discusses these issues in more detail.) Stepfamilies vary on a great many dimensions, including age of parents and children when the families are formed; gender of stepchildren and stepparents; degree of similarity in values, attitudes, and practices of prior families; and SES and amount of social support. These and many other factors determine the outcome for any given stepfamily. In a review of twenty-four studies comparing self-esteem and behavior problems of stepchildren and children in nuclear and single-parent households, Ganong and Coleman (1993a) concluded that stepchildren do not differ greatly from children in other family structures.

Child Free

Only about 5 percent of married couples choose not to have children (M. Hoffnung, 1995). This figure underrepresents the number of voluntarily childless people, since some women and men who intend not to have children choose not to marry. In a study of college undergraduates' attitudes toward parenting, neither gender saw child-free-by-choice as a positive option. Women, however, thought having children would make both parents more satisfied with their lives, whereas men thought having children would make both less satisfied (Ross & Kahan, 1983). This may be because although family and friends pressure both women and men to want children, women are encouraged to believe that children will provide them with fulfillment, whereas men are not.

People who choose not to have children pay a social price. Marsha Somers (1993) found that voluntarily child-free men and women perceived themselves as being viewed more negatively by relatives and friends because of their parenting choice than did parents. Examples of the negative stereotypes include "selfish," "abnormal," and "immature." Relatives were perceived as being more negative than friends, and women perceived themselves as being evaluated more strongly than men by both relatives and friends.

A majority of child-free couples say they like children but are committed to being child free so they can pursue their marriage relationships, their work, and the other opportunities that life affords—such as taking cruises.

In couples who choose to forgo parenthood, the woman almost always makes the initial decision and remains more committed to the decision than the man (Seccombe, 1991). The choice to be child free is more frequent among women who are college educated and career oriented. For example, Susan, now in her late forties, always knew she did not want children. She has two master's degrees and holds a vice-presidential position at a university. In addition to her demanding job, she leads several important civic organizations. She and Tom have been in a stable marriage since early adulthood. Tom says he would like to have been a parent, but he did not feel as strongly about the issue as Susan did.

Susan is an example of what Jean Veevers (1980) calls an **early articulator,** someone who knew from childhood that she or he did not want children. In her longitudinal study of fifty-two voluntarily childless marriages, Veevers found two types of child-free couples: early articulators and postponers. In about a third of Veevers' couples one partner, usually the woman, was an early articulator. Some early articulators knew they disliked children and were committed to a child-free lifestyle. The majority liked children but were committed to being child free so they could pursue their marriage relationship, their work, and the other opportunities life affords. **Postponers** were likely to be less definite about whether they would have children. First they delayed childbearing for a definite time, then for an indefinite time, then finally weighed the pros and cons and decided to remain child free. Veevers found the postponers were likely to see their decision as specific to the particular relationship they were in. If they had married someone else, their decision might have been different.

Women who complete their education, postpone marriage, and hold jobs outside their homes tend to have higher childlessness rates, which includes those who are child free by choice and those by chance (Ambry, 1992). Early articulators leave the path clear to develop their careers. Those who feel ambivalent usually decide not to become a parent bacause of the stress and worry associated with motherhood (Seccombe, 1991). In a comparison between childless adults in their twenties and those in their thirties, Mary-Joan Gerson, Linda Berman, and Ann Morris (1991) found that the younger respondents expressed a greater desire to become parents than the older ones. Though both groups saw the benefits of parenting, the older group was more attuned to the costs.

Kathleen Gerson (1985) found that because of the structural contradictions between career and motherhood, women on the career path felt ambivalent about childbearing. Respondents who chose to be child free saw their choice as the only responsible one given their level of commitment to work. Among college-educated, high-SES couples, African Americans were found to delay marriage longer and have higher rates of voluntary childlessness than white couples (Boyd, 1989). This may be because they perceive the obstacles to getting ahead as even greater than whites do and consequently believe the costs of parenthood are greater. Similarly, in China many urban couples are deciding not to have any children because they believe a child would be a liability and curb their freedom. Urban couples believe they can remain much happier without a child, since they can pursue their individual interests without any hindrance. In contrast, rural couples in which wives do not work outside the home see childrearing as their primary goal and are more likely to resist the one-child social policy and have larger families (Bian, 1994).

Since children introduce a great deal of stress into a marriage, as we saw in our discussion of the transition to parenthood, we might expect child-free couples to be happier. Somers (1993) compared voluntarily child-free adults with parents. Both groups gave very similar reports of their marriages. There were no differences in the expression of affection or overall agreement between the two groups, but minimal differences existed in terms of satisfaction in life. The couples with no children showed a slightly higher degree of overall satisfaction and closeness.

What Do You Think?

Do you have children or plan to have children? What would the advantages and disadvantages to you of being a parent versus being child free?

Looking Back/Looking Forward

In this chapter we examined intimacy, marriage, alternative lifestyles, and parenthood from the perspective of the young adult. While young adults typically view these issues in more mature ways, many of these issues are first faced by adolescents. But adults in their middle years also confront these issues. The need for intimacy, the decisions about whom to love and live with, whether to divorce or remarry, and even whether to be a parent or remain child free may occur for the first time or be revisited in middle adulthood. When Sylvia turned forty, she had just remarried after living with Aaron and their respective children for seven years. As the mother of a teenage daughter and stepmother of two teenage sons, she was facing middle adulthood in a maturing family. Peter, as you might remember from our discussion of singles, was past forty when he married and started a family. He and his forty-year-old wife are confronting the tasks of forming a family in their middle years. As we have seen, adult life follows many different patterns. When we discuss stages of adulthood, the boundaries are very unclear.

Summary of Major Ideas

Theories of Adult Development

1. Physical maturation plays a key role in child and adolescent development, but in adult development cultural, social, and personal factors serve as the impetus for growth and change.

2. Social clocks are internalized age expectations that govern when people marry, become parents, and retire. Age grading has become less rigid in the past few decades, but it has not disappeared.

3. The Grant Study indicates that development is a lifelong process, that sustained relationships have more of an effect on the shape life takes than isolated events do, and that the maturity of adaptive mechanisms determines level of mental health.

4. Daniel Levinson considers early adulthood as one era in adult life. During the novice phase men have a Dream, form mentor relationships, develop an occupation, and establish intimate relationships.

5. Both the Grant Study and the research on which Daniel Levinson built his theory excluded women. While Levinson has tried to place women within his theory, other researchers have found that women's experiences do not neatly fit.

6. During Erik Erikson's stage of intimacy versus isolation, young adults who have established their identities develop close, committed relationships with peers. Critics suggest that good interpersonal relationships can form the basis for identity as well as identity forming the basis for intimacy.

Intimate Relationships

7. Friendship is a particularly important form of intimacy when young adults are establishing independence from parents. It is voluntary in nature, meets social and emotional needs, and contributes to individual well-being.

8. Another form of intimacy most young adults expect to find is love. Contemporary young adults are delaying marriage and typically experiencing more love relationships and more sexual partners than earlier cohorts did.

9. Robert Sternberg's triangular theory of love highlights three essential components of love: intimacy, passion, and decision/commitment. These components have different properties and vary in different kinds of love relationships.

10. Most people meet their mates in familiar places or are introduced by friends or family. This preselection leads to similarity in race/ethnicity, age, and educational level.

Marriage

11. While most people say the ideal marriage is an equal-partnership relationship, most contemporary marriages are junior-partner relationships and some are conventional relationships. Marital equality, as measured by role sharing and decision-making power, leads to greater marital happiness and lower marital conflict.

12. Marriage is associated with psychological well-being, although differences in health and happiness between married and never-married people have decreased in recent years. Women and men both benefit from marriage, but men benefit more.

Alternative Lifestyles

13. Singlehood has become frequent among young adults who are delaying marriage while they go to school and establish their occupations.

14. Heterosexual cohabitation is common among young adults who typically see it as a step in the courtship process and a way to test for compatibility before marriage.

15. Most gay men and lesbians are involved in close, steady same-sex relationships. Gay and heterosexual couples have similar levels of love and satisfaction.

Changing Families

16. High divorce rates are due to increased expectations from marriage and to decreased expectations for marital permanence.

17. Divorce often leads to remarriage; more than 70 percent of divorced people remarry, and half of those who do divorce again. The result is a pattern of marriage called serial monogamy.

Parenthood

18. Most people want to have children, although their reasons for wanting children vary. The birth of the first child creates an enormous change in the lives of new parents as they are forced to put some of their own needs on the back burner and take on the responsibilities of caring for the next generation.

19. While fathers and mothers both feel the strain of the transition to parenthood, mothers feel it more fully because the primary responsibility for infant care usually falls on them. Employment of mothers is beneficial to the family, but it often leaves mothers doing two jobs.

20. Single parenthood has increased due to high divorce rates and out-of-wedlock births. Because single-parent households are characteristically low-income families, it is hard to separate the effects of single parenting from poverty. Despite the financial and social pressures they face, many single parents successfully raise happy families.

21. Remarriage often leads to the creation of stepparent or blended families. These families have more within-family problems than other families because of the inherent complexity of the relationships.

22. Couples who choose to be child-free are likely to be college educated and career oriented. They seem to differ only minimally in life satisfaction from those who choose to be parents.

KEY TERMS

social clock (457)
adaptive mechanisms (458)
career consolidation (459)
biographical method (460)
intimacy versus isolation (463)
serial monogamy (468)
equal-partner relationship (472)

conventional relationship (473)
junior-partner relationship (472)
cohabitation (478)
homophobia (480)
displaced homemaker (483)
early articulator (491)
postponer (491)

Middle Adulthood

Because the human lifespan has lengthened over the course of this century, middle adulthood begins later and lasts longer than it used to. Middle adulthood, considered roughly the years from ages forty to sixty, is continuous with early adulthood at its beginning and with late adulthood at its close; no abrupt change occurs at either end. As we will see in Part Seven, middle-aged adults resemble in many ways both younger and older adults, depending on the person and the life circumstances.

Middle adulthood is a stage characterized by change—gradual physical decline, occupational peaks, and new family relationships. The changes in physical functioning that began in early adulthood continue, leading to physical decline so gradual that it rarely impairs normal functioning. Society makes its maximum demands on middle-aged adults for social and civic responsibility; this is the time when men and women reach the peak of their influence on society. It is also the stage of life when individuals reconsider their priorities, their occupations, and their perspectives on mortality. And, as children grow up and parents die, family relationships change as well. In Part Seven we examine physical, cognitive, and social development during middle adulthood.

14

MIDDLE ADULTHOOD

Physical and Cognitive Development

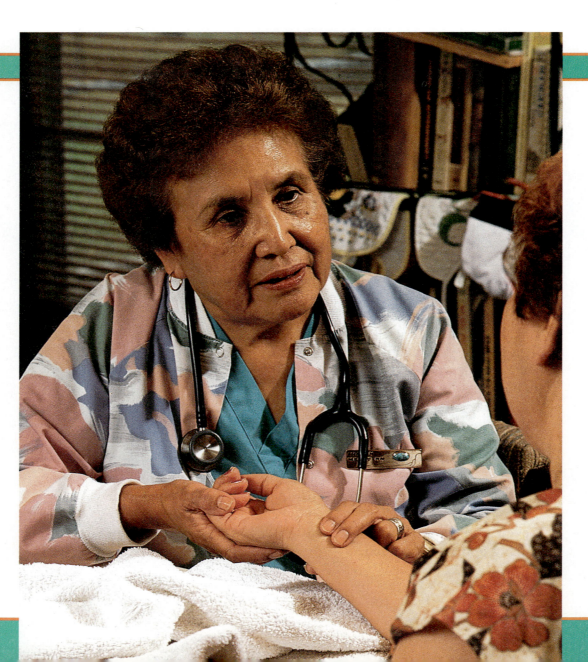

PHYSICAL DEVELOPMENT

THE BIOLOGY OF AGING

Middle adulthood, a period characterized by changes in appearance and functioning of the body, spans roughly ages forty to sixty. There is enormous variability, however, in when and how these changes show up. Despite being over fifty and a grandfather, Mick Jagger continues to prance around the stage more actively than most young adults could. At age forty-five, George Foreman defeated a twenty-six-year-old's bid for the heavyweight boxing championship. Chronological age, the measure of life in the years since birth, is not a good indicator of level of functioning because individual differences are so great. In determining physical or psychological functioning, it is more useful to measure the distance from death than the distance from birth. This has been done in some longitudinal studies but is not practical in everyday life, where we usually know date of birth but rarely know when death will occur. By age fifty, almost all adults show enough bodily changes to mark them clearly as being physically in middle adulthood.

The timing of middle adulthood depends on life expectancy. **Life expectancy** refers to a statistical estimate of the probable number of years remaining in the life of an individual based on the likelihood that members of a particular birth cohort will die at various ages. Life expectancy changes for each cohort from year to year as some people die and some survive. As Table 14.1 shows, life expectancy increased dramatically from 1900 to 1990. As life expectancy has increased, so have the number of years in each stage of adulthood. In 1900, for example, when a white female was expected to live 48.7 years, early adulthood ended much earlier than it does today; old age began earlier as well, and the middle years were the decade of the thirties. In 1990, life expectancy for a white female was 73.6 years, old age began at 60 years old and the middle years were the decades of the forties and fifties.

TABLE 14.1 *Life Expectancies by Sex and Race, 1900–1990.*
Life expectancies have increased dramatically since 1900, changing the timing and duration of adult life stages. Middle adulthood, the thirties early in the century, is now ages forty to sixty.

| | 1900 | | 1950 | | 1960 | | 1970 | | 1980 | | 1990 | |
Age	White	African American	White	African American	White	African American	White	African American	White	African American	White	African American
Male												
At birth	46.6	32.5	66.5	58.9	67.4	60.7	68.0	60.0	70.7	63.8	72.7	64.5
65	11.5	10.4	12.8	12.9	12.9	12.7	13.1	12.5	14.2	13.0	15.2	13.2
Female												
At birth	48.7	33.5	72.2	62.7	74.1	65.9	75.6	68.3	78.1	72.5	79.4	73.6
65	12.2	11.4	15.1	14.9	15.9	15.1	17.1	15.7	18.4	16.8	19.1	17.2

Source: National Center for Health Statistics (1993).

To understand why the variability in aging is so great, it helps to distinguish between primary aging and secondary aging. **Primary aging** refers to normal age-related changes that everyone experiences, such as menopause in women and similar hormonal changes in men. While differences exist in when primary aging occurs, the experience is universal and falls within a normal age range. **Secondary aging** refers to pathological aging, or the effects of illness or disease on the body due to environmental exposure or health-compromising behaviors. Because of vast differences in genetic make-up, health behaviors, and life circumstances, secondary aging shows much more variability. Some individuals experience secondary aging in their twenties or thirties, whereas others do not until their seventies or eighties.

By the middle years, birthdays take on new meaning and are often greeted with mixed feelings. Each additional candle reminds us that we are likely closer to the end of our lives than to the beginning. Contemporary birthday cards dwell on the theme that after age thirty (just thirty!), one is "over the hill." However, the normal aging process has little impact on the day-to-day experience of middle age. Gradual changes take place and become noticeable in this period, but most middle-aged adults are healthy and function much as they did as young adults. In this chapter, we look at primary aging and its effects on physical functioning and cognitive competence. We save our discussion of the common health problems and cognitive losses of secondary aging for Chapter 16, because these experiences more frequently occur in late adulthood.

PHYSICAL FUNCTIONING IN MIDDLE ADULTHOOD

Physical functioning reaches its peak during early adulthood, plateaus for a period of time that depends on the particular bodily system, then gradually declines after that. Most adults do not feel the impact of the decline before age fifty, and some do so much later than that. Most people enjoy good health and active lives for most, if not all, of their middle years. They continue to do the activities they have been doing, as well as try new activities.

Strength

Strength slowly but steadily declines after its peak in early adulthood, so slowly that few people notice the change until age forty or fifty. After that, until sixty or sev-

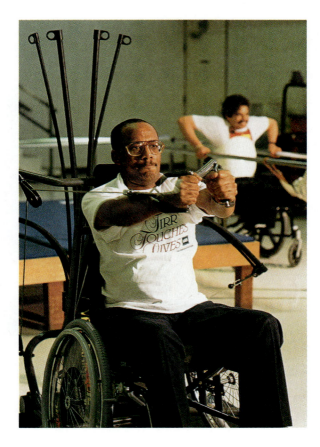

After its peak in early adulthood, strength slowly but steady declines. By working out regularly at his gym, this man retards muscle atrophy and may actually gain in muscle strength.

enty, the loss seems to be minimal, on the order of 10 to 20 percent of the peak in early adulthood (Spirduso, 1995). People differ greatly in the amount of strength lost. During a ten-year study, Douglas Kallman, Chris Plato, and Jordan Tobin (1990) found that 29 percent of the middle-aged subjects and 15 percent of the older subjects lost no strength. Through experience people develop greater skill and learn to use their strength more wisely, expending maximum effort only at the exact moment it is required. Strategies such as this conserve energy and make the decline in strength barely noticeable to most people.

Atrophy of the muscle fibers, which results in the loss of muscle mass, leads to the loss of muscular strength that is part of the aging process. As muscles atrophy from disuse, they are replaced with fat. How much muscle mass a person loses depends on the level of exercise he or she has maintained as a lifelong pattern. Efficient exercise can retard atrophy and may actually facilitate gain in muscle strength (Spirduso, 1995). Although exercise is best started early in life, even sedentary individuals can make improvements in strength during their middle years by participating in an exercise training program. Muscle fibers do not regenerate, but those that have not atrophied become more efficient.

Bone mass also begins to decrease once growth stops in early adulthood. This is due to the loss of mineral content that occurs throughout adulthood. The loss multiplies for women after menopause. Robert Cumming (1990) found that women who took no supplemental calcium lost about 2 percent of bone density each year in early menopause, whereas those who took calcium supplements lost only about 0.8 percent. Because they start out with denser bones and do not experience the hormonal changes of menopause, men lose bone mass more slowly and at a later age. Women can slow the process of bone loss by ingesting sufficient levels of calcium, engaging in weight-bearing exercise such as weightlifting, jogging, or walking, and taking replacement estrogen after reaching menopause (Spirduso, 1995). As in other areas of physical functioning, starting good nutrition and exercise habits in early adulthood can reduce the potential problems in middle and late adulthood.

In the middle years the outward signs of aging become apparent. The changes we can see in this woman's face from when she was in her early twenties to when she was about fifty result from the combination of primary aging of muscle, fibrous tissue, and skin and secondary aging from years of exposure to sun and wind.

Age-Related Changes in Appearance

In the middle years, the outward signs of aging become apparent. The skin becomes less elastic with age, so when it is stretched during movement or facial expressions, it is less likely to return to its original shape. As the skin stretches out, it wrinkles, sags, and loses its firmness. Loss of fat and muscle underneath the skin contribute to the sagging and wrinkling, as does the decrease in activity of the sweat glands and sebaceous glands that lubricate the skin. Exposure to sun and wind accelerates these changes, so the face and other exposed areas of the body suffer the most damage. Sun and wind exposure at young ages is particularly damaging, although the damage does not show up until the middle years. In a comparison of young (twenty-five to thirty-one years) and middle-aged (forty-five to fifty-one years) women who had low sun exposure (less than two hours per week) and high sun exposure (more than twelve hours a week) over the prior year, high exposure did not significantly affect the appearance of the young women's skin, but the middle-aged group had significantly more wrinkles and lower skin elasticity (Warren et al., 1991). Judges perceived the high-exposure middle-aged women to be older than the low-exposure ones. During middle age bags under the eyes, jowls, and double chins may develop as the underlying muscle and fibrous tissues weaken.

Age-related changes in hair color and distribution of hair growth also affect appearance. Although hair tends to darken with age, this process is reversed when graying begins due to loss of pigment, which may occur as early as the thirties. Half of men and women over age fifty have at least 50 percent gray scalp hair (Ashburn, 1992). In both men and women, the hair on the head becomes thinner and loses its youthful texture. It also grows more slowly. Body hair also becomes thinner and grayer. Women in their fifties begin to develop hairs on their chins, and men begin to have more hair growing out of their ears and nostrils and longer eyebrow hairs.

Aging also changes body build. People tend to gain weight through the mid- to late fifties as fatty tissue and muscle are redistributed throughout the body. When individuals begin to lose muscle, fat will replace muscle if they do not increase their exercise or decrease their calorie consumption. After the muscle is replaced by fat, fat will accumulate outside the muscle and under the skin. Middle-aged adults tend to store fat in the thighs, abdomen, waist, back, and upper arms. As we saw in Chapter 12's discussion of physical development in early adulthood, women tend to add more body fat than men do. So-called "middle-age spread" is not inevitable, however; regular exercise and proper diet can prevent or correct the addition of excess fat. Jane Fonda, though well into her fifties, shows no sign of middle-age spread. Adults who stay active in sports or run marathons lose little muscle and gain little weight (Kavanaugh & Shephard, 1990; Pollock et al., 1987). Even sedentary adults in their middle and later years can strengthen muscles and lose body fat by engaging in regular endurance-type exercise such as walking, biking, or jogging (Spirduso, 1995).

Cardiovascular System Changes

The cardiovascular system loses efficiency during middle adulthood. Both cross-sectional and longitudinal research shows decreases in maximum oxygen consumption and the heart rate attained during maximum levels of exertion starting in early adulthood and proceeding by about 10 percent per decade throughout the adult years (Bouchard & Shephard, 1993). Age-related changes in the bodily system cause these losses in cardiovascular functioning. First, the left ventricle of the heart gradually loses its capacity to contract completely, which reduces its ability to pump out a large volume of blood when it empties. As a result, the amount of blood pumped at each beat decreases and, because less blood is flowing, the amount of oxygen that can be extracted is reduced (Spirduso, 1995). Second, arterial walls become more rigid with age; thus, blood cannot pass through them as easily, especially during exercise, when more blood is needed.

Continuous and regular exercise helps to counteract these changes. Ample evidence indicates that athletes who continue their sports into their middle and later years experience considerably smaller reductions in cardiovascular functioning, though they still see some age-related reductions (Pollock et al., 1987). In a thirteen-year longitudinal study of 954 healthy adult males matched by age, Ronald Grossarth-Maticek and his associates (1990) found that the lowest mortality overall and from heart disease (12 percent) occurred among men who were actively engaged in sports and the highest mortality overall and from heart disease (25 percent) occurred among those who had given up sports. Nonathletes can also reduce, but not reverse, the loss of aerobic power and prolong their lives by maintaining physical fitness. In a study of more than four thousand men ages thirty to sixty-nine, Lars-Goran Ekelund and colleagues (1988), found that lower levels of physical fitness were associated with higher risk of death from diseases of the heart.

Respiratory System Changes

The changes in the respiratory system that began in early adulthood continue and progress with age. Primary aging includes changes in the breathing apparatus and tissues of the lungs that are not due to pathological aging (Christiansen & Grzybowski, 1993). The amount of oxygen in the blood after it has passed through the lungs decreases with age across adulthood. This is due to loss of elasticity in the lung tissue, structural changes in the alveoli (the sacs in the lungs where the exchange of oxygen and carbon dioxide takes place), and resistance to expansion of the chest wall during breathing.

Getting regular exercise and avoiding environmental pollutants and tobacco smoke beginning in early adulthood can prevent some, but not all, of the age-related respiratory system changes. The loss of elasticity in the lungs cannot be modified, but exercise can strengthen the chest wall and thereby increase the amount of air moving in and out of the lungs. Lifelong endurance training increases **vital capacity**, the total volume of air that moves in and out of the lungs during maximal exertion. Short-term training does not affect vital capacity, but it does increase breathing rate. As with the cardiovascular system, regular aerobic activity can slow age effects in the respiratory system (Bouchard & Shephard, 1993).

Sensory System Changes

The middle adulthood years are when people start complaining that their arms have become too short to hold a paper far enough away from their eyes to read it. By age fifty, most people require reading glasses or bifocals if they already wear glasses because they were nearsighted. The lens of the eye continually grows new fibers without shedding the old ones, so the lens continues to thicken and gradually loses its capacity to accommodate. *Accommodation* is the process of changing the shape of the lens to focus on things that are close by.

Hearing loss begins gradually in early adulthood and progresses until the eighties. The loss comes sooner and is greatest in the high-frequency range and is due to several changes in the inner ear, including loss of receptor cells, atrophy of the nerve fibers, changes in the conducting fluid, and deficiency in the vibrating motion of the basilar membrane, which helps transform sound vibrations into electrical signals. Men have poorer hearing in the high frequencies than women do, perhaps because they have been exposed to more environmental noise at their jobs. During the middle years the accumulation of noise exposure takes its toll, whether the noise is from occupational sources, listening to loud music, or living near an airfield. Despite the measurable losses, however, most adults in the stage are able to function normally. They may turn up the volume on the television set or ask someone to speak up, but only a small percentage have a loss that qualifies as a hearing impairment.

Although some losses occur due to primary aging, regular body maintenance starting in early adulthood can keep bodily systems in optimal shape so that aging does not take a serious toll on physical functioning during the middle years. While some adjustments are necessary, such as wearing glasses or getting better seats at a concert, quality of life is not negatively affected. Nevertheless, secondary aging can accelerate overall aging by adding pathological changes to age-related ones. These changes make health an important concern in the middle years, as we will see next.

What Do You Think?

Try to imagine the kinds of physical changes you will experience at midlife, or consider the changes you have already experienced. How will (do) these changes affect the kinds of activities you currently engage in? How might (do) you compensate for these changes?

HEALTH IN MIDDLE ADULTHOOD

Middle-aged adults become more aware of health issues than they were when they were younger as they continue to enjoy active healthy lives. Bernice Neugarten (1968) found that men paid increased attention to their health as they felt their bodies become less efficient and learned of male friends and colleagues their own age having heart attacks, whereas women were more concerned with their husbands' health than their own and worried about becoming widows. This change in "body monitoring," or continual, low-key concern about health and well-being, reflects the realities that some chronic diseases do become apparent in the forties and fifties as the effects of lifelong behaviors take their toll and that they are likely to affect men sooner than women. Men are much more often victims of premature death, as the accompanying Perspectives box indicates. Both morbidity and mortality rates increase in the middle years. **Morbidity** refers to the number of cases of a disease; **mortality** refers to the number of deaths. Poor diet, lack of exercise, smoking, obesity, and alcohol abuse influence the cardiovascular and respiratory symptoms, as do environmental elements. The cumulative effects of stress on the body may produce signs of wear and tear by the middle years because, as we discussed in Chapter 12, physiological responses to psychosocial stress can lead to fatigue, hypertension, ulceration, impotence, decreased growth and repair, and decreased immune system response.

The lines between early, middle, and late adulthood are blurring as increasing numbers of Americans continue to be healthy and vigorous well into their later years. Most middle-aged adults are not much different in physical health than young adults, whereas some already suffer the chronic diseases that are more common in late adulthood. Even among older adults, fewer than ever are reporting limitation in activities due to health (Neugarten & Neugarten, 1986). For this reason, although cardiovascular disease, hypertension, cancer, and arthritis are chronic diseases that do show up with some frequency in middle adulthood, we save our discussion of them for Chapter 16 because they are more representative of health in late adulthood.

Health and Health-Compromising Behaviors

Many of the factors that contribute to secondary aging are related to the health behaviors and health-compromising behaviors we considered in our discussion of early adulthood in Chapter 12. Because life is continuous, behaviors at younger ages lay the groundwork for health and well-being in the years to come and for the next generation as well. One study found that a year after teaching parents (ages thirty to forty-five) how to improve their diets, both parents and children (ages four to twenty-one) had less fat in their diets and better eating habits (Kashani et al., 1991). Smoking has a negative health impact on the smoker and on his or her immediate family, especially young children.

Health-promoting behaviors positively affect health in multiple ways. For example, in addition to benefiting the cardiovascular and respiratory systems and

Smoking, like all health-compromising behaviors, contributes to secondary aging. Not only smokers are harmed. The passive smoke from these men's cigarettes has a negative health impact on other workers in the company cafeteria.

Perspectives

The Gender Gap in Life Expectancy

Women have a longer life expectancy than men do. Although the gender gap narrows with increasing age, it never disappears. This reflects the fact that women are afflicted less often by the leading causes of death at all ages. The two leading causes, heart disease and cancer, are excellent examples.

Diseases of the heart, the number one cause of death, afflict men earlier and more often than they afflict women. Figure 14.1 shows 1991 death rates for heart disease by age and sex. Among the age group forty-five to fifty-four years, the rate for men was three times the rate

for women; among individuals eighty-five years and over, the rate for men was 1.14 that for women.

The second leading killer is cancer. As Figure 14.2 shows, men and women have essentially the same death rate from cancer in the forty-five to fifty-four-year group. In this case, the gap widens rather than narrows with age.

Although no one knows why the gender gap exists, biological and psychosocial factors are clearly involved. Female sex hormones seem to provide biological protection from some diseases (Markides, 1990). This is especially clear for diseases of the heart, where rates for women in-

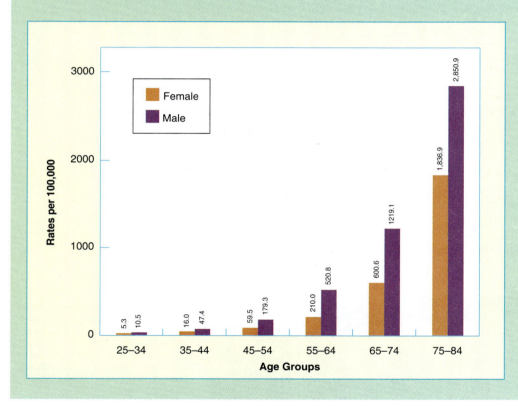

FIGURE 14.1

Death Rates from Heart Disease by Sex and Age, 1991

Although the gender gap gets smaller with age, it never disappears. Both biological and psychosocial factors contribute to women's lower death rates from heart disease.
Source: U.S. Bureau of the Census (1994).

helping to control weight, exercise enhances the ability to cope with psychosocial stressors (King et al., 1993). Compared to nonexercisers, regular aerobic exercisers have lower levels of chronic stress, react less strongly to stressors, and recover more efficiently from stressors (Spirduso, 1995). Coming from a family that exercises regularly, having a positive attitude toward physical activity, and believing people should be responsible for their health increase the likelihood that a person will get involved in an exercise program (Taylor, 1995). Practical barriers and social attitudes that discourage exercise among middle-aged and older women, however, make it especially unlikely that they will get exercise (Lee, 1992).

Health-compromising behaviors often are linked; individuals who smoke heavily are also likely to drink heavily, for example. Gary Friedman and his associates (1991) explored the relationship between alcohol drinking and cigarette smoking

crease dramatically after menopause and can be positively affected by postmenopausal estrogen replacement. Psychosocial factors include men's greater tendency to engage in smoking and other health-compromising behaviors, their greater risk taking, and their greater exposure to occupational toxins and hazards. There is reason to believe that psychosocial factors have more to do with the gender gap in cancer deaths. The gender gap in life expectancy has narrowed since 1980, a fact that has been attributed to the increase in smoking rates among women since World War II (Verbrugge, 1989a).

Although women have longer life expectancies, they suffer more from illnesses that are serious but not life threatening, such as arthritis. Lois Verbrugge (1989b) reanalyzed several large-scale health studies and found that morbidity was influenced by social factors such as less employment, more deeply felt stress and unhappiness, stronger feelings of vulnerability to illness, fewer formal time constraints, and less physically strenuous leisure activities. While women have a biological advantage that protects them from mortality, they have a social disadvantage that puts them at risk for morbidity.

FIGURE 14.2
Death Rates from Cancer by Sex and Age, 1991
In the case of cancer, the gender gap increases with age. There is reason to believe that psychosocial factors contribute more to the gender gap in cancer deaths since the gap has narrowed as more women have become smokers.
Source: U.S. Bureau of the Census (1994).

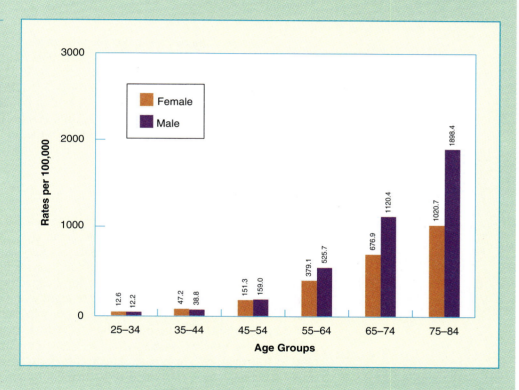

among middle-aged white and African American men and women. They found a strong association between drinking and smoking; the percentage of cigarette smokers increased as the amount of alcohol consumption increased, as Table 14.2 shows. The number of cigarettes smoked per day was the best predictor of how much alcohol was consumed. The investigators also found that alcoholic beverage preference was related to smoking: liquor drinkers smoked the most, followed by beer drinkers, then those with no preference, and finally wine drinkers. Arthur Klatsky and his colleagues (1990) looked at traits of people who choose wine, beer, or liquor. They found that people who preferred wine were likely to be women, temperate drinkers, young or middle-aged, nonsmokers, better educated, and free of symptoms or risk of illness. People who preferred liquor were likely to be men, heavier drinkers, middle-aged or older, less educated, and afflicted with symptoms

TABLE 14.2 *Percentage of Subjects Reporting Current Cigarette Smoking by Race, Sex, and Alcohol Consumption*
The percentage of cigarette smokers increased as the amount of alcohol consumption increased. This example illustrates the link between health-compromising behaviors.

Drinking Category	Percentage Reporting Current Cigarette Smoking			
	Black		White	
	Women	Men	Women	Men
Never, occasional	26%	24%	23%	23%
<1 drink/day	43	43	26	22
1–2 drinks/day	58	55	32	27
3–5 drinks/day	65	58	50	38
6–8 drinks/day	60	66	50	46
9+ drinks/day	92	63	80	54

Source: Friedman et al. (1991).

or risk factors for major illness. People who preferred beer were likely to be young men who were intermediate between wine and liquor preferrers on most traits. Ronald Grossarth-Maticek and Hans Eysenck (1991) found that stress and drinking combined to form a risk factor for disease. In their thirteen-year follow-up of men, drinking to "drown sorrows" was more of a risk factor for cancer and coronary heart disease than "pleasure" drinking. Health-compromising behaviors are also linked to cancers that become frequent in the middle years, such as breast and prostate cancer.

Breast Cancer

Breast cancer is frightening to women, young and old, because it is so prevalent in the United States. Breast cancer rates in Japan are less than half the rates in North America, which points to lifestyle factors as likely causes (Lock, 1993). Although more women in the United States die of lung cancer than of breast cancer annually, more new cases of breast cancer than lung cancer are diagnosed each year. The widely published statistic that one out of eight women will develop this disease in her lifetime is both scary and misleading—scary because it indicates that breast cancer is bound to hit close to home and misleading because this figure is for women who live to be ninety-five years old. For women under age seventy, the incidence is one in fourteen. While breast cancer can occur at any age, incidence increases rapidly between ages thirty and fifty, then continues to rise but more slowly after fifty (Harris et al., 1992).

Death rates from breast cancer used to be higher for white women than for African American women. As Figure 14.3 shows, while death rates from breast cancer among white women have remained stable over the past four decades, they have been rising among African American women. In 1980 African American death rates were higher for the first time, and they have continued to increase, The rate of breast cancer for young African American women has doubled and is now higher than the rate for young white women (Harris et al., 1992).

Still the overall incidence of breast cancer is higher for white women than for African American women, yet the death rate is greater for African Americans (Neale, 1994). Socioeconomic, genetic, and cultural factors each contribute to this inequity. Early detection of breast cancer predicts a higher survival rate, and African American women are less likely to be diagnosed at an early stage of the disease. Furthermore, minority women have less access to cancer prevention services, such as mammography, and use them less. This is probably related to socioeconomic fac-

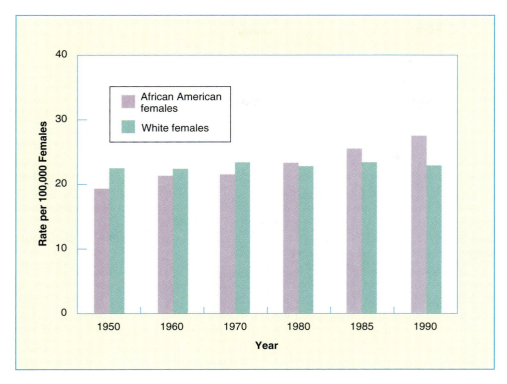

FIGURE 14.3
Death Rates from Breast Cancer, White and African American Women, 1950–1990
Over the past four decades, death rates from breast cancer have been rising among African American women while remaining stable among white women. Socioeconomic, genetic, and cultural factors all contribute to this inequity.
Source: National Center for Health Statistics (1993).

tors, since higher-income and better-educated women also use mammography more than do lower-SES women. With higher SES comes the greater likelihood of medical insurance and regular checkups rather than reliance on emergency medical care. Yet when Beth Jones and associates (1995) studied 145 African American and 177 white women newly diagnosed with breast cancer, they found that mammography was better able to protect white women than African American women from late-stage diagnosis. Genetic factors may affect how the cancer progresses (Shiao et al., 1995).

Cultural factors can also contribute to differences in medical care by affecting attitudes toward seeking or following medical advice about breast cancer screening. Cultural values also lead to differences in dietary patterns and alcohol use, which have been related to the development of breast cancer. Racism contributes as well. In a survey of African Americans and Hispanics, 43 percent complained of lack of respect from medical providers (Haynes, 1991). Treatment that leads to these feelings is unlikely to convince minority women to accept the medical advice that might help early detection.

We see differences, then, in breast cancer rates between U.S. women and Japanese women and among ethnic/racial groups within the U.S. Diet, obesity, and alcohol abuse all appear to contribute to these differences. Similar factors play a role in prostate cancer.

Prostate Cancer

Prostate cancer is the most common cancer in men; for men over fifty, it is the second leading cause of cancer deaths in the United States. Since 1968 incidence has risen in England, Italy, Japan, Sweden, and the United States, although increased detection rates account for part of this rise (Whittemore, 1994). Causes of prostate cancer are unknown. Risk increases with age and with family history of the disease (Whittemore et al., 1995). Marked differences in ethnic and racial trends have been observed both in the United States and internationally. Rates for African American men are higher than those for white men, which in turn are higher than those for Asian American men, although the reasons are not understood (Harlan et al., 1995). An analysis of incidence of prostate cancer among non-Hispanic whites, Hispanics, Native Americans, and African Americans in New Mexico for the period 1969 to 1991 indicated that Native Americans have the lowest incident rates of all groups (Gillialand et al., 1994). Incidence rates of early-stage cancers increased over that time period among non-Hispanic whites and Hispanics and were stable for Native Americans and African Americans, but incidence of later-stage cancers increased among Hispanics and mortality rates from prostate cancer decreased among all groups except Hispanics. As Figure 14.4 shows, African American men have both higher incidence and higher mortality rates from prostate cancer than do white men in the United States. This is most evident between ages fifty to seventy (Powell, 1994). As we saw with breast cancer, African Americans are diagnosed with prostate cancer at a more advanced stage, which partially accounts for their higher mortality rate. Socioeconomic, environmental, dietary, and genetic factors may be involved as well (Morton, 1994).

Prostate cancer is slow growing and unlikely to produce symptoms. It is usually discovered during surgery to relieve urinary problems, by a routine digital exam, or by a blood test called *PSA*. PSA measures blood levels of the prostate-specific antigen, a protein that may be elevated when cancer is present. Since "normal" PSA levels vary from man to man and can be elevated by other diseases, the blood test sometimes fails to detect cancer and sometimes falsely indicates prostate cancer. Even when detected, there is no standard recommended treatment. Treatment recommendations vary from waiting until evidence of cancer progression appears to treating with radiation or radical prostatectomy (removal of the prostate) soon after detection. Treatment varies widely by geographic regions and by ethnicity of patient (Harlan et al., 1995). No clear evidence exists that more aggressive treatment reduces mortality (Lu-Yao & Greenberg, 1994).

By the middle years health concerns are more prevalent than in early adulthood, but behaviors in early adulthood and the early middle years can lead to healthy later years. Not all aspects of aging are under the control of the individual, however. Genetic factors, for example, can be taken into consideration but not controlled. As we will see in the next section, some physical changes are not linked to illness. Changes in the reproductive system are normative and age related. Although menopause is perhaps more familiar, both men and women experience reproductive changes.

FIGURE 14.4

Age-Adjusted Prostate Cancer Incidence and Death Rates by Race, 1980–1988

African American men have both higher incidence and higher mortality rates from prostate cancer than white men in the United States. Socioeconomic, genetic, and cultural factors all contribute to this difference. Source: "Trends in Prostate Cancer— United States" (1992).

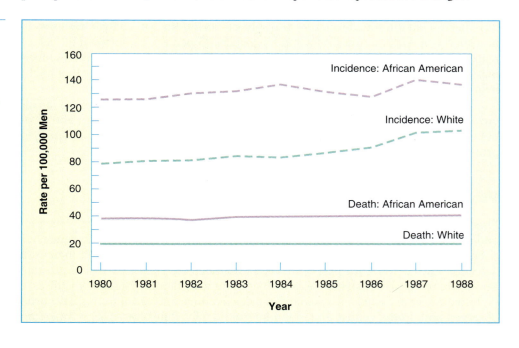

What Do You Think?

What health behaviors could you adopt that would reduce your risk for secondary aging?

REPRODUCTIVE CHANGES

Primary aging in the middle years includes a reduction in sex hormone production. This process, which happens gradually over the course of five to twenty years, is known as the **climacteric**. It begins when the production of testosterone, estrogen, and progesterone declines significantly and ends when the ability to reproduce stops. During the process, fertility decreases. The climacteric is more noticeable in women because it leads to menopause, the end of menstruation, but men also experience changes in their reproductive systems that significantly decrease, but do not end, fertility. What changes occur within the body? How do they affect how middle adults function and feel?

Menopause

When a previously menstruating woman has gone an entire year without a menstrual period, she has reached **menopause**. The term *climacteric* more properly refers to the entire process that ends with menopause, but most people think and talk about the process as menopause—that is, if they talk of it at all. Until recently, menopause has been a little discussed and poorly understood topic. Attitudes toward menopause and menopausal women have been generally negative, especially within the largely

During middle adulthood, decreased ovarian functioning gives rise to the physiological changes of menopause. Despite the negative stereotypes of menopause that abound in the United States, most postmenopausal women enjoy good health and active lives during their middle years.

male medical profession. Doctors in the United States have considered menopause as an illness to be treated with hormones, tranquilizers, and surgery rather than as a natural process in women's bodies (Cowan et al., 1985). Not all cultures share this view of menopause; Japanese doctors, for example, prescribe surgery and hormones infrequently (Lock, 1993). Scientific research has failed to show that depression in midlife women is associated with menopause (Gitlin & Pasnau, 1989; Matthews et al., 1990; McKinlay et al., 1987; Strickland, 1988a). Despite the evidence the myths live on, and menopause is still stereotyped in the United States as causing extreme moodiness, irritability, depression, and despair. As we will see in the next chapter, middle adulthood can be a difficult time for women, but more because of social factors than biological ones (Notman, 1990).

Physical Changes   Decreased ovarian functioning causes menopause. Because of age-related changes, the ovarian follicles, or egg-forming cells, are no longer able to react to the follicle-stimulating hormone (FSH), and estrogen production gradually decreases. When ovulation does not occur, progesterone, which is secreted after the egg ruptures from the follicle, is not produced. The reduced levels of estrogen and progesterone give rise to the physiological changes of menopause.

Menopause is a gradual process and occurs in three stages. During *pre-menopause*, the first stage, the ovaries gradually decrease hormone production. This decrease begins around age forty and continues until menstruation stops. A premenopausal woman may notice a change in her menstrual cycle, with periods becoming more closely spaced, more widely spaced, or irregular. Her menstrual flow may change, becoming lighter or heavier. Decreased progesterone causes lighter flow, whereas an unusually high level of estrogen causes heavier flow. Some women experience no menstrual changes and simply stop menstruating. Inconsistent hormone production may cause erratic flow. As her body tries to adjust to the inconsistency, a woman may have more severe premenstrual symptoms, such as water retention and breast tenderness. Women tend to gain weight during premenopause, but this can be reduced by restricting salt intake and exercising regularly.

Menopause itself is actually the second stage of the female climacteric. Hormone production declines further, the ovaries cease to produce eggs, and menstruation ceases. Because a woman may still ovulate sporadically after regular periods have stopped, she is said to have reached menopause when she has had no period for a year; at that point the woman is sterile, and pregnancy is no longer possible. The average age for menopause in the United States is 51.4 years (Ashburn, 1992), a shift from an average of forty years in the last century (Mishell & Brenner, 1986). Age of menopause seems to be genetically determined; daughters and mothers tend to have similar timing. It is not related to number of pregnancies, breast-feeding experience, race, education, SES, age of onset of menstruation, or height or weight. It is related to health status; women who are malnourished or who smoke tend to have an earlier menopause (Mishell & Brenner, 1986).

During *postmenopause*, the third stage, hormonal levels stabilize and menopausal signs subside. A woman is not totally without estrogen during post-menopause because the ovaries continue to produce small amounts and the adrenal glands produce the precursors of estrogen, which are converted to estrogen by stored body fat. The estrogen level is far lower, however, than when the ovaries were producing large amounts.

Physical Signs.   The most common sign of menopause in the United States is the *hot flash,* a sensation of internally generated heat beginning in the chest and moving to the face and the rest of the body. Hot flashes are often accompanied by heavy perspiration and may be preceded or followed by a chill. They result from blood rushing to the surface of the skin when decreased estrogen causes vasomotor instability. Fifty to 75 percent of women experience hot flashes, which most frequently occur at night (McKinlay et al., 1991). Night sweats, as nighttime hot flashes are called, disrupt sleep and may bring on the insomnia that menopausal women some-times experience. Some women have no or only occasional hot flashes, many have them once a day, and some have them more than once a day (Mishell & Brenner, 1986). Obese women have fewer hot flashes because they have more estrogen con-verted from stored fat. While a majority of American women experience hot flashes and/or night sweats, only 10 percent experience severe symptoms (Gannon, 1985). Hot flashes are not common in all cultures, as the accompanying Multicultural View box indicates. When they do occur, hot flashes typically last about two or three years. They are sometimes referred to as *power surges* because they come at a time when women are relieved of their reproductive functions and, as we will see in the next chapter, likely to be gaining power at home and at work.

Vaginal changes are another common physical sign of menopause. *Atrophy of the vagina* is the label given to the thinning of the vaginal lining, loss of elasticity, and foreshortening or narrowing of the vagina that frequently follow menopause. This may be accompanied by decreased lubrication. These changes can lead to vagi-nal dryness, itching, painful intercourse, and greater susceptibility to infection. Some vaginal changes can occur as early as premenopause, but more often they occur during postmenopause and sometimes not until late adulthood.

Other less frequently reported signs include palpitations (rapid heartbeat), ner-vousness, dizziness, short-temperedness, mood swings, weight increase, and mem-ory changes. These signs usually last only while the hormonal balance is unstable and are at least partly due to the disruption of sleep that night sweats cause and changes in lifestyle that often accompany midlife.

Surgical Menopause   Thus far we have been discussing natural menopause. Surgi-cal menopause is the sudden onset of menopause due to removal of the ovaries or, in some cases, removal of the uterus. Surgical removal of the uterus, called **hys-terectomy**, is performed so frequently in the United States that it has aroused a good deal of controversy. At present rates, 37 percent of all women will have had a hysterectomy by the time they reach age sixty (Bachmann, 1990). In a cross-cultural comparison, Margaret Lock (1993) found that only 8.7 percent of Japanese women ages forty-five to fifty-five had had hysterectomies, in contrast to 28.1 percent of U.S. women. Hysterectomy is a risky procedure that is called for under certain cir-cumstances, such as in the treatment of advanced cancers, but is performed for many more questionable reasons, such as menstrual irregularities.

Whereas hysterectomy sometimes triggers menopause, **oophorectomy**, surgical removal of the ovaries, always does. Oophorectomy suddenly and drastically re-duces estrogen production, bringing on surgical menopause. Lock (1993) found that only 3.4 percent of the Japanese women in her study had had bilateral (both sides) oophorectomy, in contrast to 16.2 percent of the U.S. women. The symptoms of surgical menopause are more numerous and severe than those of natural menopause because the body does not have a chance to adjust gradually to the changing hormonal levels. For this reason, studies of menopausal symptoms that have included women experiencing surgical menopause give an artificially negative picture of the natural process.

Hormone Replacement Therapy   Since the natural decrease in hormones brings on menopausal symptoms, one way to alleviate them is to replace the hormones. Replacement can be made by **estrogen replacement therapy (ERT)**, the taking of replacement estrogen, or by **hormone replacement therapy (HRT)**, the taking of a combination of estrogen and progestin (artificial progesterone). ERT is usually rec-ommended to reduce the symptoms of surgical menopause. For women who have not had a hysterectomy, ERT has been shown to increase the risk of endometrial cancer (cancer of the lining of the uterus) by 500 to 800 percent (Kaufert & Mc-Kinlay, 1985). HRT does not increase the risk of endometrial cancer. There is evi-dence that the incidence of other kinds of cancer, particularly breast cancer,

A Multicultural View

Japanese and North American Attitudes Toward Menopause

Although the cessation of menstruation is a natural and universal aspect of primary aging for women in their middle years, its meaning and experience depend on cultural ideas and expectations. Margaret Lock (1993) set out to study middle age in Japan and the experience of *konenki*, which is what Japanese people call the change of life. Because Japanese women had suffered due to war, poverty, and oppressive social conditions, she assumed they would have a difficult time with *konenki* and would report many symptoms. Her findings surprised her and differed so widely from the North American experience that she went on to do a comparison of 1,316 Japanese women, 1,226 Manitoba (Canadian) women, and 2,565 Massachusetts (U.S.) women between ages forty-five and fifty-five. None of the women had surgical menopause or medical treatment that would interfere with natural menopause.

The surveys listed fifty-seven possible symptoms and asked participants to place check marks next to any they had experienced in the last two weeks. The Japanese women reported very few symptoms, especially in contrast to both North American groups. Only thirteen symptoms were reported by more than 100 Japanese women (8% of the sample). As Table 14.3 shows, hot flashes were reported by approximately 12 percent of Japanese women, 30 percent of Canadian women, and 35 percent of U.S. women; insomnia was reported by around 12 percent, 30 percent, and 31 percent, respectively; and feeling blue or depressed was reported by about 10 percent, 23 percent, and 36 percent, respectively.

Japanese women reported a very low incidence of hot flashes, the most frequent menopausal symptom among North American women. In fact, the Japanese language does not include a term equivalent to *hot flash*. Overall

This family's typical Japanese meal includes many soy products such as tofu and miso, which are rich in phytoestrogens. This natural estrogen rich diet contributes to the low incidence of hot flashes among Japanese women during menopause.

incidence was lower than 25 percent in contrast to ? percent for the two North American groups combined. an interview study Lock conducted with 105 Japane women in the same age group about their experience beliefs, and concerns about *konenki*, not one complain of major sleep disturbance or night sweats. Amo Japanese women surveyed, the most frequent sympton reported were shoulder stiffness (52 percent) a headaches (28 percent). While about a third of Nor American women reported headaches (see Table 14.? these groups reported shoulder stiffness so infrequen that it was not considered a core symptom in the study.

What can account for these differences in menopau symptoms? First, there may be some biological diffe

increases with the replacement of estrogen, whether through ERT or HRT (Colditz et al., 1995). Although cancer can be treated if detected early, it is a serious risk factor associated with ERT and HRT.

Nevertheless, ERT and HRT have benefits beyond alleviating menopausal signs. In combination with exercise and diet they can help prevent **osteoporosis**, the degeneration of the bone that affects an estimated one in three postmenopausal women (Doren & Schneider, 1989). They also reduce LDL ("bad") cholesterol and increase HDL ("good") cholesterol, thereby reducing the risks of coronary heart disease and strokes (Mishell & Brenner, 1986). However, studies measuring the impact of taking hormones have been done by following women who undergo ERT or HRT and those who do not, but the women are not randomly assigned to taking or not taking the hormones. This means that women who take hormones are generally more affluent and healthier than those who do not and would have lower rates of disease anyway (Payer, 1992).

A woman's decision about hormone replacement requires weighing the risks and the benefits in conjunction with her family history and personal risk factors.

ences based on genetics, nutrition, or a combination of the two. The typical Japanese diet, for example, includes many soy products, such as tofu and miso, that are rich in phytoestrogens. This natural, estrogen-rich diet may contribute to the significant difference in the incidence of hot flashes (Adlercreutz et al., 1992). It may also contribute to a different cultural expectation as to whether *konenki* typically includes hot flashes. Culture is a second possible explanation for the difference in incidence of hot flashes. Cultural expectations encourage members of the culture to experience biological changes in culturally appropriate ways. Japanese culture encourages concern about problems such as shoulder stiffness, headaches, and backaches, whereas North American culture emphasizes hormonal changes, hot flashes, and mood swings.

The possibility that the method used to conduct the study caused underreporting of symptoms by the Japan-ese subjects must also be considered. Because no Japanese equivalent of the term *hot flash* exists, perhaps the Japanese women did not understand the meaning of that term as it was translated, or maybe they were embarrassed to report hot flashes. Lock argues against both possibilities. First, since people in Japan are highly sensitive to their bodies and their language offers many ways to express bodily changes, she reasons that a word for *hot flashes* would exist if that symptom were common. In addition, some Japanese women did report hot flashes and so must have understood the term. Second, the Japanese speak very frankly and openly with others of the same gender about physical changes, sometimes to the embarrassment of outsiders. Third, other studies confirm cultural variation in symptoms. Marie Haug and her colleagues (1991) also found a low incidence of symptoms in Japan. Marcha Flint and R. S. Samil (1990) found low reporting of hot flashes in Indonesia.

TABLE 14.3 Rates of Reporting Symptoms in Previous Two Weeks, by Country
Margaret Lock (1993) found that women between the ages of forty-five and fifty-five in Japan reported far fewer menopausal symptoms than did those in Canada and the United States.

Symptom	Japan	Canada	United States
Headache	27.5%	33.8%	37.2%
Aches or stiffness in the joints	14.5	31.4	38.6
Fatigue	6.0	39.8	38.1
Feeling blue or depressed	10.3	23.4	35.9
Insomnia	11.7	30.4	30.6
Hot flashes or sudden perspiration	12.3	31.0	34.8

Source: Adapted from Lock (1993).

Women with a history of breast cancer in the family are usually discouraged from taking replacement hormones, either ERT or HRT, whereas women with heart disease or osteoporosis in their backgrounds are usually encouraged to do so.

The Male Climacteric

The male climacteric is a gradual process that produces changes in the reproductive system and reduces fertility but, unlike menopause, does not lead to sterility. Men have been known to father children in their seventies and eighties. The male climacteric starts in the forties or fifties and continues over a longer period of time and at a much slower rate than the female climacteric does.

Physical Changes Decreased testicular functioning characterizes the male climacteric. The testes decrease in size and firmness with age. Age-related changes cause the somniferous tubules in the testes to produce fewer viable sperm. The pituitary

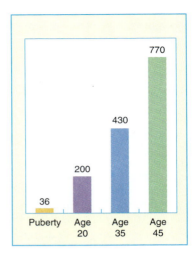

FIGURE 14.5
Number of Divisions a Man's Sex Cells Undergo at Various Ages
Although men often continue to be fertile into late adulthood, older males' sperm are more likely to carry genetic defects because the older the man, the more cell divisions the sperm have made.
Source: Angier (1994, p. C12).

gland responds to the reduction in sperm production by increasing the secretion of FSH. Corresponding to the female case, the testes are not able to respond by producing more sperm. As a result, the number and vitality of sperm go down. Unlike women's eggs, which are fully formed during fetal development, the progenitor sex cells, which create men's sperm, continue to divide throughout a man's life. Older males' sperm are more likely to carry genetic defects because, as Figure 14.5 shows, the older the man, the more cell divisions the sperm have made. Testosterone production very gradually decreases between ages of twenty and ninety, but most men see no noticeable functional change until age sixty (Doering, 1980). Considerable individual differences exist, however: some older men continue to have testosterone levels as high as those of younger men.

The most notable physical changes affect the prostate gland. The prostate gland contributes secretions that make up the largest volume of the semen during ejaculation. Glandular cells in the prostate begin to atrophy after age forty-five, leading to a gradual decrease in the volume of ejaculated fluid. By age sixty-five the prostate gland may show other signs of deterioration, including development of benign hard masses, replacement of muscle fibers with connective tissue, and abnormal overgrowth of tissue. This overgrowth of tissue, or **hypertrophy**, produces pressure on the urethra that may restrict and eventually block urine flow. Whereas only 10 percent of men require surgery to improve urine flow, many others experience frequency of urination, waking at night to urinate, and some difficulty with bladder control (Christiansen & Grzybowski, 1993).

Physical Signs   Many signs attributed to the male climacteric are similar to those attributed to menopause, including mood swings, irritability, alterations in concentration span, and memory lapses (Pesmen, 1984). As with women, these symptoms may be part myth and at least partly due to changes in life circumstances that occur in midlife. Some men report decreased interest in sex. Some even have hot flashes (Jovanovic & Subak-Sharpe, 1987). The prevalence of male symptoms is not known, in part because men are not willing to openly discuss them.

What Do You Think?

Discuss with a few of your classmates the benefits and costs to the reproductive changes that occur during middle adulthood. How do you think life circumstances would affect their impact? How might midlife parents of three adolescents feel? How might midlife newlyweds feel?

SEXUALITY IN MIDDLE ADULTHOOD

The changes in the reproductive systems of men and women have implications for sexual functioning in middle adulthood. Both men and women tend to become aroused more slowly, have less intense orgasms, and return to prearoused levels more quickly (Masters et al., 1994). Men have longer refractory periods. These changes occur over many years and sometimes go unnoticed until late adulthood. This is especially true if a person continues to be sexually active. External factors, such as side effects of medications for hypertension, may also negatively affect sexual response, particularly in older adults.

Female Sexuality

Most women find that the hormonal changes of menopause affect their sexual responsiveness. All phases of the sexual response cycle (see Chapter 12) continue in middle adulthood, but with diminished speed and intensity. The most annoying

Menopause does not significantly affect sexual drive, which depends on androgens, not estrogen. Some women report more enjoyment from sex after menopause when they no longer have to worry about becoming pregnant and when sex is likely to proceed at a slower pace.

change is the slower rate and reduced amounts of vaginal lubrication compared to those at younger ages, which can cause irritation or pain during intercourse. This can also be a problem if the woman feels out of touch with her level of arousal because her degree of vaginal lubrication has always served as an indicator of her sexual readiness. Vaginal dryness can usually be overcome by the use of saliva or water-based lubricants during lovemaking. Estrogen cream or other medications can be prescribed if surface lubricants do not help.

In lesbian couples, both women may be going through menopausal changes at the same time, so each partner's physical and psychological complaints may affect sexual interest and performance. In a study of forty-one middle-aged lesbians, Ellen Cole and Esther Rothblum (1991) found that 76 percent reported no sexual problems. The remaining women reported changes involving vaginal dryness, difficulty finding a partner, less interest in initiating sex, and taking longer to reach orgasm, changes no different than those heterosexual women report.

There is no evidence of decline in postmenopausal women's physical capacity for sex. Aging does not seem to affect the clitoris, which continues to enlarge with sexual arousal. The capacity for orgasm is unimpaired. Female sexual interest typically does not diminish, though hot flashes and disrupted sleep may reduce it temporarily. Menopause does not significantly affect sexual drive, which depends on androgens, not estrogen. In fact, some women report more enjoyment from sex after menopause, when they no longer have to worry about becoming pregnant.

Male Sexuality

The most noticeable change in sexuality for men is the fact that erections take longer to obtain—minutes rather than seconds—and are not as hard as they were in younger years. This is due to changes in the vascular supply and spongy tissue beds running along the length of the penis. Men in their middle adult years often need more direct genital stimulation to become fully erect. These changes often upset even men in their thirties because they are used to the instantaneous erections of their youth and fear they are becoming impotent. Heterosexual women too are sometimes upset by these changes because they fear their partners are less interested in them or less interested in sex. Just as men have mistakenly taken speed of erection as a measure of their potency, women have taken it as a measure of their desirability. On the other hand, many women enjoy the slower pace of sex that middle age brings because it allows more time for their own arousal and enjoyment.

Aging men also experience changes in orgasm. Reduced semen production makes the need to ejaculate feel less intense. This, combined with reduced pumping action on the part of the prostate, leads to a reduction in the intensity of orgasm. In addition, the refractory period, the time between orgasm and the possibility of another erection, lengthens with age. These changes occur gradually and at different rates for different men. While things typically just take longer in the forties and fifties, by the sixties the frequency of ejaculation may be down to twice a week and by age seventy-five to once a week (Masters et al., 1994). Older men feel less of a need to ejaculate at the end of every sexual experience.

Although the physical changes of aging do affect sexuality, there are no physical reasons based on age alone that sex cannot be enjoyed throughout life. In fact, the age-related changes can actually bring some benefits. Slower can be better when it comes to sex. A man in his forties is likely to have more control over ejaculation than he did when he was younger. This gives both him and his partner more time to enjoy sex and reach orgasm. With continuing sexual activity, whether self-pleasuring or with a partner, the capacity for satisfying sexual relations can be preserved well beyond middle age.

What Do You Think?

How do you think young adults can best prepare for the changes in sexuality that occur during the middle years?

GRADUAL DECLINE

Middle adulthood is a time of physical well-being during which the signs of decline become apparent. Most of the decline of primary aging is so slight that it has only a minor impact on daily life. The speed of decline and the risks of morbidity and mortality associated with secondary aging are linked to genetic make-up, health behaviors, and health-compromising behaviors. Thus, it is important to make life-promoting changes where necessary to maintain optimal health and well-being into the older years.

Physical changes are only one aspect of the middle years. Intellectual growth and expanded social roles bring many pleasures to this time of life. We now turn to the issues of cognitive development during middle adulthood. How does it change? What are the gains and what are the losses?

COGNITIVE DEVELOPMENT

James will turn fifty on his next birthday. During his early adulthood he started graduate school and stopped, married, started a family, held several jobs, returned to graduate school, divorced, and remarried. He earned his doctorate at age thirty-two and began the slow climb to a secure position in the academic world. At age forty-eight, he accepted an offer for a full professorship with an endowed chair at an elite university. More than ever before, his work now calls on him to view his field broadly, to comment on it for the academic and general public, and to train graduate students. James is an example of a successful man in his middle years. He has power in his field and is called on to exercise it nearly every day. He is at the height of what John Horn and Scott Hofer (1992) refer to as "the vital period of life," the time when adults are responsible for maintaining and enhancing the culture.

The reality of power and influence during middle adulthood is often overlooked because youth and youthfulness are so much admired in contemporary America. Conflicting ideas from cognitive psychologists about when intellectual capacities peak and the speed of their decline contribute to contradictory popular images of the middle years as "the intellectual peak" or being "over the hill." For this reason, we start our discussion of cognitive development in middle adulthood with an examination of that controversy.

DOES INTELLIGENCE DECLINE WITH AGE?

Several problems confront us when we try to determine the course of cognitive competence or intelligence over the adult years. Intelligence, as we saw in Chapter 8's discussion of cognitive development in middle childhood, refers to the general ability to learn from experience. This ability is not directly observable; it is a quality of a person that we infer from competent behaviors we consider characteristic of intelligent people, such as learning a new task quickly, solving a difficult problem, or performing well on a test. Competent behaviors, however, depend on more than intelligence alone. A person may do poorly on a test for reasons other than lack of ability to learn. Immediate factors such as illness or anxiety may negatively affect performance on a math test, for example, even though the individual knows the relevant concepts. Longer-range factors such as lack of training in math or inexperience with tests may also negatively affect performance, particularly when we test adults of different ages. Young adults who are still in school are likely to be more comfortable taking tests than older adults who have not been to school for decades or perhaps ever. Likewise, visual loss or arthritis may make filling in an answer sheet problematic for an older test taker. Timed tests may also cause lower performance by elderly individuals due to slower response rather than lower intelligence. If we add to these problems the lack of agreement as to which and how many abilities the term *intelligence* refers to (see Chapter 8 for a full discussion of this issue), it is little wonder that different investigators have arrived at different answers to the question of how intelligence fares during the adult years.

Early Negative Studies

Before the mid-1950s, developmental psychologists believed intellectual decline begins in the teenage years (Botwinick, 1977). This idea, you may remember from Chapter 12, is in keeping with the Piagetian notion that cognitive development reaches its highest level during adolescence. A study by Nancy Bayley (1955) demonstrated that this is not the case. Bayley found that intellectual growth continued until at least age thirty-six. It then seemed that early adulthood, not adolescence, is the peak of intellectual functioning. Research during the 1960s commonly found that young adults perform at a somewhat higher level than adults in their middle years, who in turn perform at a somewhat higher level than older adults (Willis, 1989). These differences were interpreted as reflecting age-related declines. "Early investigators had little doubt that increasing adult age brought about intellectual decline" (Botwinick, 1977, p. 583). Do these differences in performance actually reflect age-related decline, or can they be explained in other ways? To answer that question, we must examine the method used to conduct these early studies.

Cross-sectional Versus Longitudinal Studies

A typical early study would compare the performance of separate groups of adults aged 20, 30, 40, 50, 60, 70, 80, and 90 on a test of one or more abilities. This is called a *cross-sectional study* (see Chapter 1) because it compares groups of people of different ages at the same point in time. A cross-sectional study assumes the older groups all performed at the same level the twenty-year-olds did when they were twenty. If at their current ages they perform lower than the young adults, they are assumed to have declined because of their increased age. But when cross-sectional studies compare individuals of different ages, they also compare individuals of different cohorts. Cohort, or generational, differences include differences in educational level, medical care, nutritional resources, and experience with historical events such as war or economic depression.

Consider educational level. If, as in many families, you and your brothers and sisters attend college while your parents' generation went only to high school and your grandparents' generation went only to grade school, your respective opportunities for learning have been very different. Researchers have found higher correlations between intelligence test scores and educational level than between these scores and age (Botwinick, 1977). Cohort differences in educational level and other life experiences challenge the assumption that an older cohort performed as well as earlier cohorts even when they were the same age. Comparisons of different cohorts at the same ages indicate that this is rarely the case. Cohort differences in performance level exist and vary with the ability studied (Willis, 1989). The cross-sectional method may "create" age decline because it confounds cohort differences with age.

Using the longitudinal method to study changes in intelligence across adulthood minimizes negative age patterns. A longitudinal study (see Chapter 1) tests the same subjects periodically over an extended time period. Testing the same individuals at different ages controls the cohort differences. Figure 14.6 compares age gradients for the Verbal Meanings Test derived from cross-sectional and longitudi-

FIGURE 14.6
Comparable Cross-Sectional and Longitudinal Age Gradients for the Verbal Meanings Test
Cross-sectional studies show earlier and steeper declines than do longitudinal studies. Cohort differences contribute to the decline in cross-sectional studies.
Source: Schaie (1968).

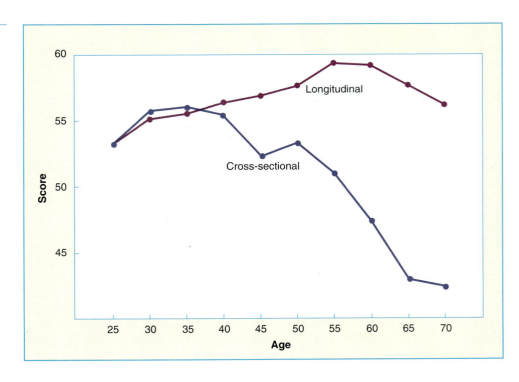

nal studies. While the cross-sectional curve shows decline beginning around age forty, the longitudinal curve shows gain until around age sixty. The difference between these two curves is in part due to the control of cohort differences. A methodological problem may also contribute to the difference: longitudinal data may be biased in a positive direction because people who perform poorly are less likely to be available for retesting. Individuals who are less advantaged in terms of education, health, and SES are more likely to drop out of the study than are more advantaged individuals. If the older groups contain only the scores of the more able participants, the curve is biased in a positive direction. This bias in the experimental design is usually corrected for statistically (Schaie, 1994).

In contrast to findings from cross-sectional studies, findings from longitudinal research present a positive view of intellectual competence in middle adulthood. For many mental abilities, middle adulthood is a period of stability in intellectual functioning. Some abilities, such as verbal ability, peak in the middle years. "Continued development in midlife is most evident for abilities that are extensively employed in tasks and responsibilities of daily living" (Willis, 1989).

Schaie's Sequential Studies

Confronted early in his career with the discrepancies between cross-sectional and longitudinal findings in the study of adult intellectual development, K. Warner Schaie began a longitudinal study of a cross-sectional sample that he had collected for his dissertation in 1956. (Early data from this study formed the basis for Schaie's stages of adult development, discussed in Chapter 12.) In 1963 he tracked down and retested as many of the sample of 500 twenty-two-to-seventy-year-olds he had tested in 1956 as he could find and added a new cross-sectional sample of 997 twenty-two-to-seventy-year-olds. He retested and added new samples again in 1970, 1977, 1984, and 1991. This combination of cross-sectional and longitudinal characteristics produced a sequential study of adult intellectual development. Recall from Chapter 1 that a sequential study allows comparisons among cohorts at any one time and traces individuals' actual development over time.

In what is known as the ongoing Seattle Longitudinal Study (SLS), Schaie and his associates have assessed mental abilities of more than five thousand adults, some of whom have participated for as long as thirty-five years (Schaie, 1994).

Environmental and personality factors in early and middle adulthood account for the large differences in how long individuals maintain their mental abilities. Learning new things and traveling, as this couple is doing in France, are activities associated with less mental decline.

Schaie has recruited all participants from a health maintenance organization (HMO) in Seattle that serves a wide range of professionals, craftspeople, white-collar and blue-collar employees, and their families. While HMO membership underrepresents the lowest socioeconomic segment of the population, who likely have no health insurance, it adequately represents at least the upper 75 percent of the socioeconomic spectrum (Schaie, 1994).

The SLS used the same test battery throughout the study. The Primary Mental Abilities (PMA) battery includes subtests for verbal meaning (understanding what a word or a sentence means), spatial orientation (being able to use a map), inductive reasoning (finding the guiding rule to make a decision, such as reading a bus timetable), number skill (using numbers in simple arithmetic), and word fluency (being able to readily think of a word). Participants also periodically take a test of mental rigidity-flexibility; they have taken additional tests of mental abilities at later intervals. The test administrators also collected demographic data at each testing. During the first three intervals limited information was collected, but in subsequent intervals a more complete inventory asked about major work circumstances (with homemaking defined as a job), friends and social interactions, daily activities, travel experiences, physical environment, and lifelong educational pursuits. The researchers have obtained health history records for participants encompassing at least fourteen years.

Different Patterns for Different Abilities   The SLS data show no uniform pattern of age-related changes in adulthood across all intellectual abilities. Schaie and his colleagues combined their cross-sectional and longitudinal data to see the overall picture for each of the primary mental abilities. They combined data such that each age segment involves a longitudinal follow-up but successive segments are on different individuals. The resulting longitudinal curves show at least a modest gain for all abilities from early adulthood to early middle age. As Figure 14.7 shows, the abilities peak at different ages, change at different rates, and differ systematically for women and men. Women maintain stronger verbal meaning and inductive reasoning skills, whereas men do better in tests of spatial orientation and number skill.

Age-Related Changes   Schaie (1994) found that word fluency, which significantly declined by the early fifties, was the only primary ability that clearly decreased in middle adulthood. All abilities showed some decline by age sixty-seven, but these declines were modest until the eighties and even then were slow for more than half the participants. Remember, performance is not the same as cognitive ability; other factors may interfere with performance. According to Schaie (1994), "Much of the late life decline . . . must be attributed to slowing of processing and response speed" (p. 308).

Cohort Differences   The SLS assessed cohort trends by comparing successive cohorts observed at the same age. In tests of inductive reasoning, verbal meaning, and spatial orientation, cohorts born later performed better than those born earlier. Performance on number skills peaked with the 1924 cohort and declined progressively in later cohorts. More recently born cohorts also scored lower on word fluency. These findings provide evidence that cross-sectional studies may overestimate or underestimate the age-related decline depending on the ability being measured. Increasing educational opportunities probably explain the rising abilities of successive cohorts, and changes in teaching methods and life experiences may account for the decrements in abilities. With the availability of, for example, automatic cash registers, pocket calculators, and, most recently, computers, younger cohorts do less arithmetic and so are less practiced in number skills.

Individual Differences in Age-Related Change   Individual performance on the PMA varied widely among SLS participants. Some individuals' intellectual performance changed significantly in midlife, while a few declined little even into the eighties. In addition to mapping the general pattern of age-related changes, the SLS looked at individual differences in life experiences that led to early loss for some in-

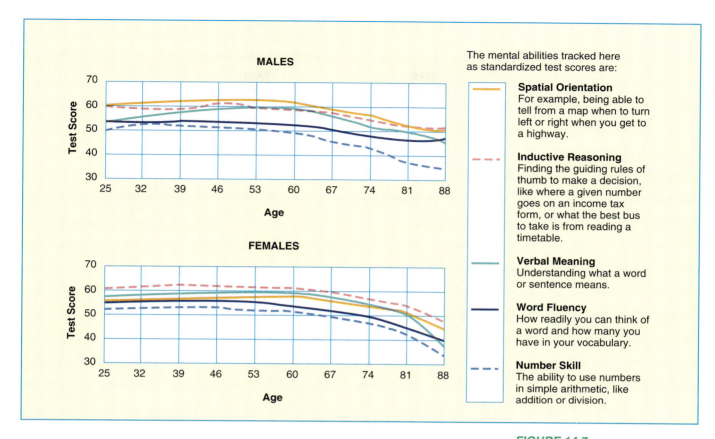

MALES

Test Score

FEMALES

Test Score

The mental abilities tracked here as standardized test scores are:

Spatial Orientation
For example, being able to tell from a map when to turn left or right when you get to a highway.

Inductive Reasoning
Finding the guiding rules of thumb to make a decision, like where a given number goes on an income tax form, or what the best bus to take is from reading a timetable.

Verbal Meaning
Understanding what a word or sentence means.

Word Fluency
How readily you can think of a word and how many you have in your vocabulary.

Number Skill
The ability to use numbers in simple arithmetic, like addition or division.

FIGURE 14.7
Changes in Cognitive Abilities with Age
Findings from the thirty-five-year Seattle Longitudinal Study (SLS) indicate that cognitive abilities peak at different ages, change at different rates, and differ systematically for women and men.
Source: Goleman (1994).

dividuals and maintenance of high levels for others. Schaie (1994) identified seven factors that reduce the risk of cognitive decline in old age, which are presented in Table 14.4. As you can see, advantageous genetic, personality, and environmental circumstances all contribute to the maintenance of cognitive abilities.

The SLS data provide a picture of age-related decline in intellectual abilities that is multifaceted and multidirectional. On average, decline begins gradually in the mid-sixties and accelerates in the late seventies. The onset and rate of decline differ for the various abilities and with gender. Number skills show the sharpest decline overall, although word fluency begins to decline the soonest. For men, the slowest decline is

TABLE 14.4 *Factors That Maintain Good Cognitive Functioning in Later Life*
The seven factors that reduce the risk of cognitive decline in old age reflect advantageous genetic, personality, and environmental circumstances.

1. *The absence of cardiovascular disease and other chronic diseases.* Behaviors that lead to early onset of disease probably reflect lifestyles that are unfavorable to maintaining cognitive functioning as well.

2. *Living in favorable circumstances.* Favorable circumstances, as would be likely for people with high SES, include above-average education, occupational pursuits high in complexity and low in routine, above-average income, and intact families.

3. *Substantial involvement in complex and intellectually stimulating activities.* Reading extensively, traveling, attending cultural events, belonging to clubs and professional associations, and pursuing continuing education are all activities of this type.

4. *Flexible personality style at midlife.* Being able to change plans, adjust to new circumstances, and cope with life's surprises demonstrate a flexible personality style.

5. *Being married to a spouse with high cognitive functioning.* When people of different cognitive levels marry, the lower-functioning spouse has been found to maintain or improve his or her level.

6. *High levels of performance speed.* Since the measurement of cognitive abilities depends somewhat upon perceptual and response speed, those who maintain high levels of perceptual processing speed because of genetics and/or health-promoting behavior have an advantage.

7. *Personal satisfaction with one's life's accomplishments in midlife or early old age.*

Source: Adapted from Schaie (1994).

in spatial orientation; for women, it is in inductive reasoning. Environmental and personality factors in early and middle adulthood account for the large differences in how long individuals maintain their mental abilities. People who like learning new things and going new places and who adapt easily to change show less mental decline. We will see in Chapter 16's discussion of cognitive development in late adulthood that some of the decline is reversible. Schaie and his associates are generally optimistic about maintenance of cognitive abilities into late adulthood. Other investigators, however, view this multifaceted and multidirectional picture negatively.

What Do You Think?

Do you think the biases imposed by cross-sectional and longitudinal methods create more distortion of age-related differences in adult intelligence than in child and adolescent intelligence? Why or why not?

FLUID AND CRYSTALLIZED INTELLIGENCE

John Horn (1970) developed the theory of fluid and crystallized intelligence first proposed by Raymond Cattell (1963). Fluid and crystallized intelligence are two general types of abilities, both of which are influenced by hereditary and environmental factors. Both rely on memory, but on different types of memory. They show different patterns of age-related decline, which led Horn and his associates (Horn & Donaldson, 1976, 1977; Horn & Hofer, 1992) to take a much dimmer view of age-related changes in intellectual functioning than Schaie and his colleagues do.

Two Types of Intelligence

Crystallized intelligence refers to learned cognitive processes and primary abilities, such as vocabulary, general information, and word fluency, that remain relatively stable with increasing age. Institutional aspects of culture, such as formal education, shape crystallized intelligence. Researchers use vocabulary tests, simple analogies, remote associations, and social judgment tests to measure it. An example of a remote association test item used to measure crystallized intelligence is:

> What one word is well associated with the
> words *bathtub, prizefighting,* and *wedding*?

Here is an example of a judgment item that is used to test crystallized intelligence:

> You notice that a fire has just started in a crowded café.
> What should one do to prevent death and injury?

Fluid intelligence is the ability to process new information in novel situations. Fluid intelligence includes reasoning, which is central to almost any definition of intelligence. It concerns the processing of information that is less tied to education and depends more on neurological development than on transmission of formal knowledge about one's culture. Horn and Hofer (1992) report that high scores on measures of fluid intelligence can be obtained by people of relatively low education and SES, reflecting that it is acquired by personal experience that is not tied to formal education or acculturation and thus is relatively culture free. Tasks such as letter series, matrices, concept formation, common word analogies, and analysis synthesis are measures of fluid intelligence. An example of a letter series test item used to measure fluid intelligence presents the following letter series and asks which letter comes next:

ADGJMP

Another test item would entail flashing on a screen for a fraction of a second the following matrix:

YOUA
REAC
UTIE

The viewer is asked to remember as many letters as possible. If he or she can see the embedded words in the fraction of a second, remembering all twelve letters is easy.

These two types of memory change differently with age, as Figure 14.8 shows. Crystallized intelligence, or stored memory, improves or stabilizes with age; as you have probably noticed, older adults are frequently better informed than younger adults. In contrast, fluid intelligence peaks in late adolescence and declines rapidly as individuals go from early adulthood to old age. While a great deal of variability exists in performance on measures of crystallized intelligence, with some elderly people showing loss while most are showing gain, there is little variability in the decline in fluid intelligence (Wang & Kaufman, 1993). Early in life, fluid intelligence and crystallized intelligence are indistinguishable because neurological growth during childhood and adolescence masks any damage to the central nervous system. In adulthood, however, the different patterns of these two kinds of intelligence become more noticeable as growth tapers off and damage accumulates (Horn, 1970).

Negative Assessment

In their negative assessment of age-related changes in intellectual functioning, Horn and his colleagues (Horn & Donaldson, 1976; Horn & Hofer, 1992) focused on the vulnerability of fluid intelligence. They saw fluid intelligence as being the

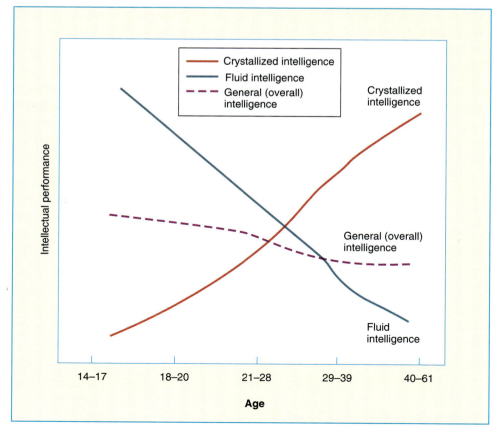

FIGURE 14.8
Age-Related Changes in Crystallized Intelligence and Fluid Intelligence from Adolescence through Adulthood
Crystallized intelligence improves with age, whereas fluid intelligence peaks during adolescence and decreases with age.
Source: Horn (1970, p. 963).

most salient indicator of intellectual capacities because it enables an individual to understand relations, comprehend implications, and draw inferences using inductive and deductive reasoning and is relatively independent of cultural and experiential influences. Earl Hunt (1993) agrees in the context of a changing work world. Whereas machines can handle routine problems, only people can deal with the "novel" problems that arise in any occupation. Hunt, like Horn, believes this ability depends on fluid intelligence. Horn and Hofer posit that age-related declines in fluid intelligence result from accumulations of small losses of brain function. These losses are related to lifestyle factors that have harmful effects on the nervous system, such as drug or alcohol abuse, poor diet, or inactivity, health-compromising behaviors we discussed in Chapter 12.

Conflicting Views

Horn's theory has been criticized on several grounds. First, because it is based on cross-sectional research, it confounds cohort differences with age differences (Labouvie-Vief, 1985). Gisela Labouvie-Vief points out that in times of rapid cultural and technological change, aged individuals seem deficient in comparison to younger adults rather than in comparison to their younger selves and that "these changes may not impact only on such 'crystallized' functions as information-related tests . . . but also on ones much closer to fluid functions (Reasoning, and, to a less extent, Space)" (Labouvie-Vief, 1985, p. 505). In other words, fluid intelligence is not totally unaffected by cultural and experiential influences. Also on methodological grounds, Jing-Jen Wang and Alan Kaufman (1993) point out that researchers disagree as to which scales are unequivocally crystallized or fluid.

As we discussed earlier, Schaie's sequential studies show gains in all but one of the primary mental abilities until the sixties. In response, Horn and Hofer (1992) criticize longitudinal research for painting a falsely positive picture, which they refer to as the "class reunion" effect: "If one were to estimate age changes in income from longitudinal samples of people returning for class reunions, one would be drawn to the conclusion that income increases with age. But this could mainly represent the fact that people who return for reunions have made money and want others to know this, but those who have not made money do not return for reunions" (p. 76).

Jack Botwinick (1977) sees the different patterns of age-related decline as being due to speed rather than to fluid-crystallized differences. Primarily because of changes in motor coordination, ability in tasks that involve speed, performance tests such as Digit Symbol and Picture Arrangement decline while ability in non-speeded tasks does not. James Birren (Birren et al., 1980) suggests that primary aging of the central nervous system and secondary aging due to disease and lack of physical fitness both affect processing speed. Other critics argue that fluid abilities are not a good measure of intelligence for older adults because in later life much of everyday cognitive performance depends less on fluid abilities than on contextual factors (Rybash et al., 1986). The conflict over whether intelligence declines during adulthood has not been resolved, nor have the methodological issues.

Thus far, we have been evaluating quantitative measures of adult intellectual functioning, using what we referred to in Chapter 8 as the psychometric approach to measuring intelligence. Do problem-solving measures of cognitive abilities show age-related changes? Do the kinds of problems to be solved matter? We explore these questions next.

What Do You Think?

Does intelligence decline with age? Set up a mock debate between Schaie and Horn/Hofer to examine this question.

COMPETENCE

Performance on traditional laboratory problem-solving tasks decreases during the adult years, while performance in the real world increases at least through middle age (Denney, 1989). In real life, many of us prefer to hire heart surgeons, attorneys, or investment advisers who are middle aged or older because we want experienced specialists to address our problems. As with James, whose work is in great demand in his middle years, we assume experience matters in real-world performance. How can we explain this multidirectional picture of adult performance?

Laboratory measures of problem solving were developed to measure intellectual development in children and young adults. Schaie (1977/1978) pointed out that these measures have limited value testing intellectual functioning in middle and late adulthood (see Chapter 12) because adults' abilities may qualitatively differ from children's. For this reason, investigators have turned to the study of real-world problem solving to better measure adult problem-solving abilities. Among studies that focus on real-world problem solving, Schaie (1990) distinguishes among practical intelligence, expertise, and wisdom. **Practical intelligence** involves the application of intellectual skills to everyday activities, whereas **expertise** and *wisdom* refer to behaviors that require intelligence as well as specialized experience in specific domains, as you may recall from Chapter 10's discussion of cognitive development in adolescence. We will look at practical intelligence and expertise in this section; wisdom is discussed in Chapter 16.

Practical Intelligence

If we view intelligence as the mental abilities that enable individuals to adapt successfully to their environment, looking at practical problem solving may be a better assessment tool than performance on traditional abstract problem solving. Studies of practical problem solving use realistic stimuli, sometimes in a novel situation and sometimes in a realistic situation. For example, David Arenberg (1968), in a traditional concept-learning problem, used food stimuli instead of abstract geometric figures so that the stimuli were familiar while the situation was novel. He told the subjects that one of the foods was poisoned and they were to figure out which one. Subjects were told whether they "lived" or "died" after each "meal" of three foods was presented. If they "lived," the poisoned food was not included in the three foods they had just "eaten"; if they "died," it was. From this information they had to solve the problem. Studies of this type have found that both older and younger subjects perform better with the use of realistic stimuli, but, if anything, the younger adults outperform the older by even more (Denney, 1989).

Nancy Denney (1989) and her colleagues conducted a series of practical problem-solving experiments using realistic stimuli in realistic situations. They gave the subjects real-life problems dealing with issues such as cooking, consumer issues, weather, crime, housing, and work and judged responses based on how many solutions were both safe and effective. Participants in these cross-sectional studies were men and women twenty to eighty years of age recruited from the community by calling individuals randomly selected from the census lists for Lawrence, Kansas. In the first study, Denney used problems such as the following:

> Let's say that one evening you go to the refrigerator to get something cold to drink. When you open the refrigerator, you notice that it is not cold inside, but rather is warm. What do you do?

Performance on the problems increased from age twenty to age fifty and then declined after that. Because the investigators were concerned that the initial set of problems may have been biased toward middle-aged individuals, they constructed

This woman is applying her intelligence to a practical problem. Studies show that practical abilities increase through middle age.

problem sets that focused on issues young, middle-aged, and elderly adults would typically face.

In the two subsequent studies, Denney gave individuals between ages twenty and eighty three sets of problems, one geared to each adult stage. Here is an example of a young adult problem:

> Let's say that a young man who is living in an apartment building finds that the heater in his apartment is not working. He asks his landlord to send someone out to fix it and the landlord agrees. But, after a week of cold weather and several calls to the landlord, the heater is not fixed. What should the young man do?

An example of a middle-aged adult problem is the following:

> Let's say that a middle-aged woman is frying chicken in her home when, all of a sudden, a grease fire breaks out on top of the stove. Flames begin to shoot up. What should she do?

Here is an example of an elderly problem:

> Let's say that a 60-year-old man who lives alone in a large city needs to go across town for a doctor's appointment. He cannot drive because he does not have a car and doesn't have relatives who live nearby who could drive him. What should he do?

In the first of these studies, performance on the young adult problems decreased with increasing age, while performance on the middle and late adult problems increased up to middle age and decreased after that. In the next study, the young and middle-aged groups performed best on the problems designed for them, but the elderly subjects did not perform best on their problems. Even when elderly adults were recruited to help design problems that would give them an advantage, their performance peaked at fifty and declined after that.

Studies of practical intelligence do show that practical abilities increase with age, and most show an improvement in performance through middle age (Cornelius, 1990). It is easy to construct problems that give either the young adult or the middle-aged adult an advantage. Although they have tried, researchers have been unable to develop a set of problems on which older individuals perform better than middle-aged or younger individuals (Denney, 1989). These findings are consistent with real-life experience, in which middle-aged adults typically are more knowledgeable than young adults. Many older adults are too, but that is harder to demonstrate in problem-solving studies.

Expertise

Adults in their sixties and seventies hold many of the most responsible and challenging leadership positions in society and are seldom perceived as being less cognitively competent than adults in the twenties, thirties, forties, and fifties. Yet, as we have seen, their performance on conventional psychometric and abstract problem-solving measures are lower than those of young adults and their performance on practical problem-solving measures are lower than those of both young and middle-aged adults. How can we resolve this paradox between competence in the real world and ability as measured in the laboratory?

Experience may be the answer. Experience is highly relevant to competence and much less relevant to abstract assessment of cognitive abilities. An expert has a lot of experience in a particular task or domain of knowledge, as we saw in Chapter 10. Years of cooking, playing chess, gardening, or any of the many activities adults do make them expert. Compared to novices, experts can accomplish their tasks with fewer steps and better results. Consider baking a pie. An expert combines the ingredients with less measuring than a novice would use because knowing what the pastry should look and feel like at each stage enables taking shortcuts. Similarly, expert physicians diagnose illnesses more efficiently than novices do because they recognize and interpret signs without having to go through the formal steps of asking and answering questions (Rybash et al., 1986). Well-rehearsed activities, such as tying your shoes, can be done automatically, although mastering those activities takes a lot of time.

Adults continue to accumulate knowledge, refining it with age and experience. Despite declining fluid abilities, they continue to function efficiently when given tasks that allow them to call on their expert knowledge (Hoyer & Rybash, 1994). Timothy Salthouse (1990) has suggested several ways in which experience might operate. First, experience may maintain or preserve abilities that would decline in the absence of experience. Continuing to play the piano, for example, keeps fingers limber and the connections among written notes, sounds, and keys sharp. Second, development of competence may depend on a certain level of fluid intelligence, whereas maintenance of competence no longer requires the same level. Skill in diagnosing mechanical problems, for example, would be difficult to learn in later years, when fluid abilities have declined, but maintaining a well-developed skill would be no problem. Third, increased experience may somehow lead to compensation for declining abilities. Considerable evidence supports this last explanation; domain-specific advantage has been demonstrated in experts in several different fields.

Salthouse (1984) compared typists who differed in age (young versus older adults) and skill level (novices versus experts). He tested them on three traditional laboratory tasks: simple reaction time, the fastest speed at which they could tap their fingers, and digit symbol substitution, then tested their actual typing speed. As you might predict from our discussion so far, the older typists performed less well than the younger typists on the three laboratory tasks, whereas the expert typists, both young and old, performed faster on the typing test than the novices. Salthouse determined that the older expert typists compensated for age-related declines in speed by looking farther ahead in the printed text, which gave them more time to plan their next keystrokes. They did not use the same strategy in the other tasks, though it could have helped to improve their performance. Salthouse concludes that the compensatory mechanism is domain specific.

Neil Charness (Charness & Bosman, 1990) studied chess players of varying ages but equal in skill level. He found that older players were no better or worse than equally skilled younger ones in choosing the best move from four chess positions, but the older skilled players were faster. They thought through their moves just as far ahead as the younger players did, but did it much more efficiently. Charness suggests that over their years of practice, older chess experts develop elaborate retrieval structures that enable them to search for appropriate moves quickly.

Stephanie Clancy and William Hoyer (1988, 1993) studied medical technologists who differed in age (young versus older adults) and skill level (novices versus experts). First, they tested their ability to identify abstract geometric figures flashing on a video screen. As you might expect, younger subjects performed better than older subjects at this task. Then Clancy and Hoyer showed subjects pictures of complex microscopic slides of actual laboratory specimens. Each slide had some elements of clinically significant information and some of clinically insignificant information. The subjects were shown a single piece of information and asked whether or not it had been on the slide. Experts in both age groups were equally fast and accurate at identifying whether clinically significant information had been on the slide and could do this even while performing another task simultaneously. Novices performed poorly at the microscopic identification task, especially when doing another task at the same time. Again, skill mattered more than age in the domain-specific task, whereas age was important in the general, abstract task.

Aging, then, appears to lead to poorer performance in nonpracticed tasks and slower acquisition of new skills, particularly those that depend on new types of knowledge. However, practice speeds up performance for both young and old. Evidence suggests that skilled older individuals (age sixty-five and older) who perform at levels similar to those of younger adults do so via some compensatory mechanism (Charness & Bosman, 1990). They look farther ahead, as the expert typists did, or identify critical elements more quickly as the lab technicians did. This explains how older skilled performers, doctors, attorneys, and so on, continue to perform expertly and how older adults can perform competently in most real-world tasks.

The overall picture of intellectual functioning among individuals in middle adulthood is very positive. Most functions do not decline before the mid-sixties, and frequently used skills typically are maintained well beyond that. Middle-aged adults continue to be competent in the areas in which they have developed skills and expert in the areas in which they have well-developed skills. But what about new learning? In the middle years adults often want to change jobs, take on new hobbies, and expand their horizons. Where do adults go to learn new things, and what kind of students do they make? In the next section, we look at the adult learner.

What Do You Think?

What evidence do you see of increased performance through the middle adult years in people you know? Share your evidence with other members of the class. Do you see any patterns?

THE ADULT LEARNER

For most adults, learning projects are motivated by some fairly immediate problem, task, or decision that requires new skills or information. Adults have a variety of motivations for adult learning. Allen Tough (1981) found that most of the reasons people gave for efforts to learn fell into four broad categories: job or occupation, managing the home and family, hobby or leisure time activity, or puzzlement or curiosity. They turn to adult education programs, self-study, and colleges and universities for lifelong learning.

Adult Education

The last two decades have brought an explosion of adult education. *Adult education* refers to all non-full-time educational activities, such as part-time college attendance, classes or seminars given by employers, and classes taken for adult literacy purposes or for recreation and enjoyment. In 1991, 51 percent of adults ages thirty-four to forty-four, 37 percent ages forty-five to fifty-four, 26 percent ages fifty-five to sixty-four, and 13 percent ages sixty-five and over had participated in adult education in the past three years (U.S. Department of Education, 1992). Women outnumbered men in all age groups, predominantly in the older groups. Adult education participants tend to be well educated, have high incomes, live in the suburbs rather than in cities or rural areas, and hold primary-sector jobs; blue-collar and farm workers, unemployed individuals, African Americans, and Hispanics are underrepresented (Schlossberg, 1984). In a study of nearly eight hundred adults age fifty-five and older, awareness of where educational activities were available was the best predictor of participation (Fisher, 1986). These figures describe participants in instructor- or institution-planned adult learning; many adults are involved in less formal lifelong learning.

To understand the entire range of learning efforts that are made by adult learners, Tough (1981) undertook a series of studies that interviewed a wide range of adults in depth about their learning projects during the prior year. Twenty-seven surveys were done in the United States and four other countries; many types of respondent populations were surveyed, including older adults and unemployed persons, as well as groups from specified geographical areas and occupational categories. Tough reported "Only major, highly deliberate efforts to gain and retain some definite knowledge or skill were recorded by the interviewers" (p. 297). Learning projects included job-related learning, such as electronics, law, and typing; home-related learning, such as investing and childrearing; and leisure-related learning, such as scuba diving and drawing. Tough found the typical learning effort involved one hundred hours of sessions or episodes in which the primary purpose was to learn. (To be counted, an effort had to involve at least seven hours within a period of six months.) Tough reported that 90 percent of all adults conducted at least one major learning effort each year and that the average adult conducted five learning projects in one year. He also found that most of the learning was self-planned. Only 20 percent of learning projects were planned by professionals, while 80 percent were planned by the learners themselves or occasionally by friends (3 percent) or a group of peers (4 percent). Respondents indicated that these learning programs were extremely important to them, but they did not generally discuss their efforts at self-improvement.

In another broad study of adult learning that encompassed independent learning activities as well as organized instruction, Carol Aslanian and H. M. Brickell (1980) found that life changes, or transitions, often provide the impetus for adult learning. They define a *transition* as a "change in status . . . that makes learning necessary. The adult needs to become competent at something that he or she could not do before in order to succeed in the new status" (pp. 38–39). Often the transition is precipitated by what Aslanian and Brickell call a *trigger,* a specific life event that generates the decision to learn at that time, such as becoming widowed, losing a job, or having a health crisis. They identify seven life areas into which both transitions and triggers may be classified: career, family, health, religion, citizenship, art, and leisure. From their telephone interviews with about fifteen hundred adults over age twenty-five, they found that about half had engaged in some kind of adult learning in the previous year. Of the learners, 83 percent reported being motivated by a transition, 56 percent cited career transitions, 16 percent cited family transitions, and 13 percent cited leisure transitions.

Women showed greater variation in their reasons for adult learning than men did. While career transitions were the most frequent triggers for both men and women, family was more often the trigger for women (52 percent) than for men (20 percent). The desire to cook, can, or sew, pregnancy, and changes in the health of a

While most adult education occurs outside of educational institutions, in recent years adults have been attending adult education programs and returning to college in record numbers.

family member were all examples of family motivations for education. Just as family may trigger learning, it may also serve as a barrier to women pursuing adult education. Middle-aged women are often subject to the multiple pressures of employment, children, homemaking, and care of older relatives. This is why women in the thirty-five-to-fifty-four age group participate in adult learning at lower rates than women in the older age groups (Schlossberg, 1984).

Returning to College

While most adult education occurs outside of educational institutions, "when learning is measured in terms of effort or time invested, college easily emerges as the largest source for adult learning" (Peterson, 1981, p. 320). In recent years, adults have been returning to college in record numbers; the growth in the number of older students has been greater than that for younger students. Between 1980 and 1990, enrollment of students under age twenty-five increased by 2 percent at the same time enrollment of persons twenty-five and over rose by 32 percent (U.S. Department of Education, 1992).

Typically adults return to college because they are dissatisfied with their lives and regard finishing their education as a way to improve themselves (Campbell et al., 1980). Rose is an example. After high school, she attended college for a year and earned twenty-five credits before dropping out and enrolling in secretarial school. Thirteen years later, Rose returned to college. She was now a married mother of three and wanted to become a lawyer. She took one course per semester until her youngest child was in nursery school, then increased to two and sometimes three courses. Friends helped her out with child care. It took her nine years to complete her bachelor's degree as a continuing education student, at which point she entered law school as a full-time student. She will graduate from law school twelve years after returning to college, at age forty-two. Like Rose, most adults return with specific career goals in mind; see the Working With interview with Caroline Singer, dean of continuing education, on page 531.

Besides dissatisfaction with their lives, what other characteristics do returning college students share? Nontraditional-age students tend to already be relatively well educated and earn high incomes; like Rose, they have often had some college or post–high school education (Peterson, 1981). Costs for continuing education in colleges and universities tend to be high, which limits its availability to those with high incomes or with employers who will reimburse all or part of tuition costs. Indirect costs, such as forgone income, child care, and transportation, must be borne as well. Between 1970 and 1990, the number of men thirty-five years old and over returning to higher education more than doubled and the number of women in that age group more than quadrupled (US Department of Education, 1992). The vast majority of both women and men (more than 80 percent) were part-time students.

The cognitive gains in critical thinking that occur during college (discussed in Chapter 12) also benefit nontraditional/older students. Karen Kitchener and Patricia King (1990) compared senior college students with two groups of students entering college for the first time, traditional first-year students and nontraditional first-year students. They found that the two groups of first-year students had similar critical thinking scores, while the scores of seniors were substantially higher. Growth in critical thinking seemed to be more closely related to the amount of postsecondary education than to increasing age. In a longitudinal study of returning students who completed a multicourse weekend program in the social sciences, the sixty-seven adults showed a statistically significant increase in critical thinking as measured before and after the program (Klassen, 1983/1984).

Career development is the most frequent reason for returning to college in the middle years. In the long term, a college degree leads to higher job status and in-

Working with Caroline Singer, ASSOCIATE DEAN OF CONTINUING EDUCATION

Counseling Students Returning to College

Caroline Singer, associate dean of continuing education at a small, private New England college, began her career as a high school teacher. After earning her master's degree, she began teaching at a junior college. She continued graduate work, earned her Ph.D. in higher education, and became a professor at a four-year college. Now in her fifties, Caroline also advises continuing education students. Her own career is a good example of the many job changes that are often part of contemporary adult life.

Michele: How did you get started working in continuing education?

Caroline: I evolved into it. The program I taught in was being phased out of the college. When that happened, I gradually started to advise continuing education students. I saw a need, and I filled it. I found I was happiest working with nontraditional-age students.

Michele: What are your continuing education students like?

Caroline: Most start in their early to mid-thirties, others in their late twenties. Three out of four are women. Many are single parents. I am continually impressed by their extraordinary accomplishments. The single parents have support groups of friends or parents. If they don't, they stop coming. Most are working full time. A degree requires forty courses. If you take five per year, that takes eight years. Most of our students take five or six years for their bachelor's degree because they start out with some credits. They have so much else besides college going on in their lives that they rarely go straight through. Things intervene: they have a baby, their mother has an operation, they get sick. They are older, so they have different kinds of commitments; yet many excel in their academic work.

Michele: You say your students work full time. What kinds of jobs do they have?

Caroline: Secretaries, computer programmers, assistant managers, supervisors. Some have very high salaries, $45,000, but no college credentials. They often have unusually good jobs with less education than others around them. I hear, "I'm talking to Ph.D.'s and M.B.A.'s. I need to get my degree." Their companies often help pay their tuition. Now that women are able to take jobs where credentials count, they are returning to college.

Michele: What motivates your continuing education students?

Caroline: The students I see here are very focused. They want to improve their skills or get their degree so they can move up in their organization or into another company. Personal satisfaction motivates them too. They want to complete something they started. A high percentage, 85 to 90 percent, started college before and are returning. Very few come back just to expand their horizons.

Michele: Are your male and female students motivated by different things?

Caroline: I don't think so. I'm surprised by how few men there are, though. When they were nineteen, they didn't know what they wanted to do. Now they feel pressure to have a degree. Usually they are married or divorced. They say, "I never got this done; I need to get closure." Men in their mid-twenties don't stay in continuing education for very long. They get someone to finance them, or they get financial aid and they go full time.

Michele: Do you find your work satisfying?

Caroline: It's extraordinary work! I see these nontraditional students grow and change. One thing I've realized is that there is no typical continuing education student. They are a diverse group. They have some commonalties, but it's dangerous to generalize about nontraditional-age students. I often hear the same story: "I don't know how to get started." "I'm too old." "My brain cells are going." One totally competent-looking student, a personnel director for a nursing home, told me that the first day of class she sat in the parking lot for twenty minutes, afraid to come in. I've heard that again and again. They go from terrified to articulate; they become totally different people.

What Do You Think?

1. How do Caroline Singer's advisees reflect the profile of the adult learner discussed in the chapter?

2. What kinds of challenges might a nontraditional-age student face on campus?

come. It also influences how employees are regarded by their employers and by themselves (Pascarella & Terenzini, 1991). Because of the nature of work in middle adulthood, these aspects of returning to college often appeal to nontraditional-age individuals who did not finish college as young adults.

What Do You Think?

Interview several men and women that you know about their learning projects. Combine your results with those of several classmates and see how they compare to Tough's findings.

WORK IN MIDDLE ADULTHOOD

As we discussed in Chapter 12, careers progress through a series of stages. Though young adults often believe the difficult parts of career development are figuring out the kinds of jobs for which they are suited, getting training, and finding employment, by the middle years other work concerns are often apparent. As Table 12.5 (page 450) indicates, mid-career, ages forty to fifty-five, is the time to reappraise early career decisions, reaffirm or modify goals, and make choices that enable continuing challenge and productivity. Late career, age fifty-five to retirement, entails remaining productive, maintaining self-esteem, and preparing for retirement by balancing nonwork and work involvements. During mid- and late-career stages, problems can arise from both success and lack of success.

Because of changes in the work world, "today's employee often experiences a dead-end job in a turbulent, financially constrained organization, which has just been restructured (or acquired or divested) and which cannot even promise that the present job will be there next year" (Hall & Rabinowitz, 1988, p. 67). Fear of job loss and **plateauing**, or reaching a point of constricted occupational opportunity, are serious concerns for midlife workers. Plateauing generally occurs in mid-career, when boredom may replace the feelings of activity, growth, and change that accompany earlier career stages. Pay raises may level off, assignments may all feel the same, and a sense of stagnation may set in.

Even for successful people at the executive/responsible stages of their careers, negative emotions and feelings of personal failure sometimes accompany the mid-to-late-career stages. From a review of research studies and anecdotal reports of successful managers, executives, and entrepreneurs, Abraham Korman (1988) concluded that no relationship exists between career success and personal life satisfaction among mid-to-late-career individuals. Successful individuals frequently complain that the stresses of their careers have damaged their relationships with their spouses and children. Korman attributes this age-related problem to emotions resulting from midlife crisis, a topic we focus on in the next chapter. Whether as a result of crisis or not, changes in the midlife adult's perspective on life may result in a greater orientation toward the inner self and personal needs and a decreased interest in the incentives and promises offered by others, especially if earnings are already high. This may be accompanied by decreased interest in achievement, in looking toward future possibilities, and in having an impact on others through work activities.

Mid-career issues are not the same for all working adults, however. **Burnout**, or disillusionment and exhaustion on the job, may result from a variety of causes. Discrimination based on race/ethnicity and gender, as well as different role expectations based on gender, often lead to different midlife work issues for white men, women, and minorities. Men are more likely than women in our society to have given up time with their families to pursue success in their occupations. Successful women are more likely to have maintained relationships during the course of their careers by juggling the roles of wife, mother, and extended family member (Crosby, 1991). Some successful women have delayed childbearing so that at midlife they are balancing careers and babies. These women may experience role strain as a result of their many commitments. On the other hand, women whose attention was divided between family and occupation while their children were young may feel free at midlife to devote more time and energy to their careers, whereas their husbands may feel regret for not having spent more time with their children when the children were still at home.

Age and Job Satisfaction

Research on work satisfaction has consistently shown that older people are more satisfied with their jobs than younger people are. There are several possible explanations for this. First, older workers belong to a different cohort than younger workers, and that cohort may have learned to value work more highly. When your grandfather tells you he never missed a day of work from the day he turned sixteen, he is bragging about his work ethic. Second, as workers spend time on their jobs, they may accommodate so that they become happier with less. An older worker who encourages a younger worker to slow down and relax may be expressing this kind of accommodation. Third, older workers have better jobs than younger workers and therefore find them more satisfying. In most fields, middle-aged workers hold the upper-level positions. In a study of 1,102 economically active, salaried white males between ages sixteen and sixty-four, James Wright and Richard Hamilton (1978) found that a decisive choice among these hypotheses could not be made, but the bulk of the evidence favored the hypothesis older workers have better jobs. Clifford Mottaz (1987) studied the relationship between age and overall work satisfaction using data from 1,385 full-time workers in professional, managerial, clerical, and service occupational groups. He found some support for the second explanation, that age has an indirect positive effect on work satisfaction through its relationship to work rewards and values. Data suggested that in situations in which intrinsic rewards were not generally available, extrinsic rewards tended over time to become increasingly important sources of work satisfaction. Gerald Zeitz (1990) found distinctly different age satisfaction curves among three employee groups: nonprofessionals, elite professionals, and ordinary professionals. He suggests a situational explanation of work satisfaction like the third explanation.

Racial and Ethnic Minorities

Because racial and ethnic minorities face discrimination in corporate America, they are more likely to plateau long before they reach their corporate dream. In a 1984 to 1986 survey of more than twelve thousand people in thirteen companies, John Fernandez (1988) found that 92 percent of African Americans, 77 percent of other minorities, and 63 percent of whites reported that racism existed in their companies. Minorities and women at the higher levels of management were substantially more likely to perceive racism than those at lower levels. The Glass Ceiling Commission report (1995) found that while white men make up only 43 percent of the work force, they hold 95 percent of the senior management positions, defined as vice president or higher. White women (36 percent of the work force) progress as far as middle management, holding 40 percent of assistant vice president and office manager positions. African American women (10 percent of the work force) hold only 5 percent of the middle management positions, and African American men (11 percent of the work force) hold only 4 percent of those positions. This helps to explain why while white men develop a more optimistic view of their careers and work situations as they move up the corporate ladder, minorities and women do not. As the latter go up, they find themselves more isolated from same-sex or same-race superiors or peers, their status becomes more obviously "token," and they are more likely to feel alienated.

Fernandez (1988) found that minorities and women face problems that do not affect white males. First, he found evidence of racial and gender stereotypes. The same assertive, self-confident, and ambitious behavior that would lead a white male to be considered a "go getter" is interpreted differently when exhibited by an African American male or a woman, who would likely be considered too aggressive, arrogant, and wanting too much too fast. Second, he found that women and minorities held less power and authority. Third, he found they were systematically excluded from "powerful, political, informal groups" (Fernandez, 1988, p. 234). As the Glass Ceiling Commission report (1995) describes it, "Many middle- and upper-level white male managers view the inclusion of minorities and women in management as a direct threat to their own chances for advancement." As a result of these problems, minorities and women must meet higher performance standards than white men while they have fewer resources at their disposal, and white men create barriers to their progress.

Gender

Men constitute the majority of full-time workers age fifty and older, and women comprise the majority of part-time workers. While four out of nine workers age forty-five or over are female, more male workers in this age group (38 percent) hold managerial and professional jobs than do female workers (30 percent) (American Association of Retired Persons, 1993). As women get older, the earnings gap between men and women that we discussed in Chapter 12 widens. Women reach their peak earnings when at ages thirty-five to forty-five, ten years before men do. This is a result of the cumulative discriminatory forces we have discussed in relation to women's employment.

New family issues may put pressure on midlife women's employment as well. With more women in the labor force and increasing life expectancies, the number of working women who provide unpaid, informal caregiving for aging parents and other relatives has grown dramatically and will continue to grow (Stoller & Pugliesi, 1989). While some progress has been made in developing parental leaves and childcare programs to help parents balance the demands of family and employment, almost no attention has been given to the demands of family caregiving of aging and ailing relatives and how they affect women's employment in the middle and later years (Seccombe, 1992).

What are the effects of women's caregiving on employment? Caregivers are more likely than other employees to report conflicts between work and family responsibilities and more likely to miss work (Scharlach & Boyd, 1989). Unlike the research on multiple roles of spouse, parent, and worker that has shown benefits to health and well-being (see the Perspectives box on stress and women's employment in Chapter 12), research on caregiving documents, stress, strain, and burden on caregivers, especially those who are employed (Seccombe, 1992). Employed caregivers report more missed meetings, losses in overtime pay, forgone promotions, and reduced job offers as a result of their conflicts between caregiving and work (Gibeau & Anastas, 1989). They also report that they have considered quitting. In one national representative sample, 9 percent of nonemployed respondents said they had left their jobs to care for aging relatives (Stone et al., 1987). Dropping out of the labor force, switching to part-time employment, and missing out on raises and promotions all contribute to poverty among older women. Because family caregiving relies on the informal work of families, and because women perform 80 percent of family caregiving, women become further disadvantaged in the labor force and suffer financial, emotional, and physical costs (Hooyman, 1992).

Unemployment

Susan began working for a publishing company in her mid-twenties. She worked her way up the editorial ladder and by her late forties had considerable decision- making power and income. Then a takeover of her company led to a new boss and, soon thereafter, to Susan's firing. Shock and disbelief hit her and all who had worked with her. In an instant she went from "in charge" to unemployed. After the shock wore off, Susan took some time to relax and consider her next career move. With a family that included one daughter in college, finances were very important; so was continuing her career. After an initial period of coming to terms with her situation, Susan began looking for new employment. About six months later she found a similar position in a much smaller company, though at a substantially lower salary.

George was not so lucky. He started working for a moving company after high school, and by age fifty he had achieved seniority and a comfortable salary. But also at age fifty, he had a heart attack and underwent bypass surgery, which limited his ability to lift heavy things and drive long distances. He continued to work, but his company increased the pressure on him instead of reducing it. They began to assign

Career change during middle adulthood may be more difficult than during early adulthood because of more limited reemployment opportunities.

him cross-country moves instead of local ones. At age fifty-two, George had another heart attack and additional bypass surgery. When he went back to work, he told his company he had to take it easier; they demoted him from driver to passenger, decreased his salary, and continued to give him long-distance assignments. When he tried to negotiate with them, they fired him. One of the companies he had moved offered him a position. Now, at age fifty-seven, he is doing entry-level work and earning a third less than he did before. This situation, coupled with the fear of a third heart attack, has left him very depressed.

Unemployed individuals such as Susan and George lose much more than a regular paycheck when they lose their jobs. "They lose social contacts, a regular structure for the day, and a connection with goals and a sense of larger purpose" (Latack & Kaufman, 1988). Work is an important aspect of a person's identity, especially for managers and professionals (Kaufman, 1982). Being without their jobs leaves adults without part of themselves. Responses to job loss have been found to follow several stages (Latack & Kaufman, 1988). The initial reaction is likely to be shock, disbelief, and anger as the person copes with the news of being fired. After the initial shock, the first stage is likely to be relief and relaxation, as we saw in Susan's case. The second stage includes efforts to become reemployed. If these efforts are not successful in a few months, the third stage, frustration at not finding work, sets in. The fourth stage is resignation to being out of work. Because Susan found reemployment during the second stage, she is among the group of unemployed who will suffer the least.

Unemployment has been shown to have a negative impact on physical, mental, and social well-being. Job loss has been linked to increases in rates of suicide, diagnosed cases of mental illness, use of mental health services, alcohol abuse, lowered self-esteem, and severe depression (Mallinckrodt & Fretz, 1988). It may have particularly severe effects on older workers because workers age forty-five and over who are laid off remain unemployed longer than their younger counterparts (American Association of Retired Persons, 1993). For those in mid-to-late-career phases, job loss may result in permanent career damage because some will never be reemployed in satisfactory positions. Susan, for example, is unlikely to ever regain the status or salary of her old position, although she is fortunate to have a good new job. George's new job is not a good one, and he can never expect to regain his former pay or seniority.

The psychological impact of unemployment may be greater for male workers than for female workers. In a study of members of a self-help organization for unemployed professionals over forty, Brent Mallinckrodt and Bruce Fretz (1988) measured stressors, stress symptoms, and job-seeking behaviors in twenty-seven men and eight women. They found no gender differences in job-seeking efforts, stress symptoms, or stressors except for social support. Women reported more available social support than men did. Perceived availability of social support was associated with positive self-esteem and lower levels of stress symptoms. Absence of social support was related to higher levels of a variety of stress symptoms, including physical health complaints, lower self-esteem, and depression. Social support was most beneficial when it provided reassurance of worth and shared values and interests. Under the stressful conditions of unemployment, the fact that women have more social connections with relatives and friends outside of the work setting may buffer them from some of its negative effects. Heimo Viinamaki and his colleagues (1993) studied Finnish workers laid off from a wood-processing factory (study group) and workers in a similar wood-processing factory (controls) that stayed in operation. They found that women in the study group were no more depressed or in need of psychological help than women in the control group, but the men in the study group were more depressed than the male controls.

This serves as another example of how multiple roles often benefit women, as we saw in Perspectives box on "How Does Stress Relate to Women's Employment?" in Chapter 12. Because they generally assume kinkeeping functions in the family, women are more likely than men to develop social supports outside of workplace that can help buffer the psychological distress associated with unemployment. While multiple roles create stressors, as when aging parents need caregiving at the same time that work is demanding, they also provide multiple avenues for support and self-esteem.

What Do You Think?

Given your own race, ethnicity, and gender, what work-related issues might you expect to face in the years to come?

CHANGE AND GROWTH

As we have seen in this chapter, midlife is a time of new challenges, readjusting goals, learning new things, and adjusting to occupational changes. Looking at cognitive development, we see continued growth in many areas, particularly in practical intelligence and expertise. Looking at the issues of work and unemployment, we see that social forces have a great impact on the work experiences of adults in their middle years, as do earlier choices and opportunities. The economy determines whether people will face layoffs or job openings. As we saw in Chapter 12, socioeconomic factors affect the educational and career opportunities an individual had in the early adult years. As a result, adults encounter no single midlife experience but a wide range of experiences. They also encounter changes in family and other social relationships, which take different forms in the lives of different individuals. In the next chapter, we examine these and other aspects of psychosocial development in the middle adult years.

SUMMARY OF MAJOR IDEAS

PHYSICAL DEVELOPMENT

The Biology of Aging

1. Middle adulthood, roughly the period from ages forty to sixty, is characterized by changes in appearance and physical functioning.

2. Primary aging refers to normal age-related changes that everyone experiences, such as the climacteric; secondary aging refers to pathological aging. Because of differences in genetic make-up, health-compromising behaviors, and environmental exposure that lead to secondary aging, people age at different rates.

Physical Functioning in Middle Adulthood

3. Though strength peaks during early adulthood and then slowly and steadily declines, during middle adulthood the loss is so minimal that increased skill and experience can often compensate.

4. Age-related changes in appearance become apparent during the middle years as skin loses its elasticity, hair thins and grays, and weight tends to increase.

5. The cardiovascular system loses efficiency during middle adulthood because of changes in the left ventricle and the arterial walls. Regular exercise can considerably reduce, but not eliminate, these changes.

6. The respiratory system continues to decrease in its ability to oxygenate the blood, a change that begins in early adulthood. Avoiding smoking and environmental pollutants and engaging in regular aerobic exercise can slow, but not stop, aging of the respiratory system.

7. Changes in vision and hearing become noticeable during the forties and fifties.

Health in Middle Adulthood

8. Health is more of a concern during middle adulthood than in early adulthood as men, more often than women, become victims of premature death and chronic diseases.

9. Health behaviors in early adulthood, such as regular aerobic exercise, a low-fat diet, weight control, and avoidance of tobacco smoke and abuse of alcohol can lead to healthy middle and later years.

10. Rates of breast and prostate cancer increase during the middle years. Ethnic differences reflect differences in stage of diagnosis as well as in genetic and cultural factors.

Reproductive Changes

11. The climacteric is the gradual process of decline in reproductive capacity. In women it is called menopause and ends with the cessation of the menstrual cycle and the ability to have children. For men, the climacteric reduces fertility but does not lead to sterility.

Sexuality in Middle Adulthood

12. The changes in the reproductive systems of men and women affect sexual functioning. All phases of the sexual response cycle continue, but with diminished speed and intensity. The capacity for satisfying sexual relations can continue well beyond middle age for healthy individuals.

COGNITIVE DEVELOPMENT

Does Intelligence Decline with Age?

13. How intelligence changes with age depends on the methods used to study the question. Cross-sectional studies show decline beginning around age forty, whereas longitudinal studies show gain until around age sixty.

14. Schaie's sequential studies show at least modest gain for all abilities from early adulthood to early middle age. Abilities peak at different ages, change at different rates, and differ systematically for women and men.

15. Schaie's studies show large differences in how long individuals maintain their mental abilities. People who like learning new things and going new places and who adapt easily to change show less mental decline.

Fluid and Crystallized Intelligence

16. Fluid and crystallized intelligence show differential age-related decline. Crystallized intelligence improves with age, whereas fluid intelligence declines. Developmental psychologists disagree about how to interpret these changes.

Competence

17. Real-world performance increases at least through middle age. Measures of practical intelligence show increased performance, although laboratory measures do not. Experience seems to explain the discrepancy. Experts rely on frequently used skills that are well maintained with age.

The Adult Learner

18. Studies indicate that 90 percent of all adults conduct at least one major learning effort each year. While most of these projects are self-planned, well-educated, high-income, suburban adults are likely to participate in formal adult education.

19. Since 1980, record numbers of nontraditional-age students have been returning to college to improve themselves and to complete what they started but did not finish as young adults. They receive cognitive and career advantages similar to those of traditional-age students.

Work in Middle Adulthood

20. Mid- and late-career stages call for reappraisal of early career decisions and new choices that provide continuing challenge. Many factors, however, can lead to plateauing. Women and racial and ethnic minorities are more likely to plateau before reaching the top because of stereotyping and unequal treatment.

21. Family caregiving for aging parents and relatives puts pressure on midlife women's employment as life expectancies increase but care for the elderly is left to informal networks.

22. Unemployment has particularly severe effects on older workers, who typically remain unemployed longer than their younger counterparts. Men may be more negatively affected than women because they have less social support.

KEY TERMS

life expectancy (497)
primary aging (498)
secondary aging (498)
vital capacity (501)
morbidity (503)
mortality (503)
climacteric (509)
menopause (509)
hysterectomy (511)
oophorectomy (511)
estrogen replacement therapy (ERT) (511)

hormone replacement therapy (HRT) (511)
osteoporosis (512)
hypertrophy (514)
crystallized intelligence (522)
fluid intelligence (522)
practical intelligence (525)
expertise (525)
plateauing (532)
burnout (532)

15

MIDDLE ADULTHOOD

Psychosocial Development

Focusing Questions

- How typical is "midlife crisis"?

- How are marriage and divorce different in middle age than in earlier years?

- What are the important family relationships at midlife, and what changes can be expected in them?

- Why is the loss of a parent a significant event during middle age?

- Is there continuity or change in leisure activities during this stage of life?

- How do wills and retirement planning help individuals prepare for late adulthood?

Marcia is forty-eight. She has been a teacher for twenty-five years, married to Ed for twenty years, and a mother for seventeen years. These facts about her life make her sound very middle-aged and established, which she is. She is also currently going through some very big life changes. Her older child, Adam, is now a difficult teenager. He is a new driver, which worries his parents. He does not do what Marcia and Ed expect of him, especially in terms of school. He demands "the right to be a C student," while his well-educated parents want him to get into college and have choices about his future. Marcia's younger child, Shelly, is now thirteen and needs less supervision than she used to. These family changes have left Marcia with both more worries and more time to devote to her own career. She has recently taken on a contract to write a textbook. She finds this new commitment both exciting and challenging. She knows she must separate from her growing children while continuing to be a good parent to them. How to do that is not always clear.

Marcia is also confronting the aging of her parents. She sees them becoming frail and feels the need to cherish what time she has left with them. Their aging adds to her own sense of growing older. Her periods have become less regular, and she knows she will soon have to face the choice of whether or not to take hormone replacement therapy (HRT). In her desire to avoid HRT, Marcia has become health conscious. She is more careful than she used to be about what she eats. She exercises more regularly than ever before, walking at least three miles each day and going to a gym three days a week to lift weights. She also meditates.

As you can see, Marcia is involved in the tasks of middle adulthood. She is shifting her commitment to work as she adjusts to changes in her family relationships. She recently helped Ed bury and mourn for his mother. She has begun to anticipate an empty nest in the not so distant future. As Adam has become harder to live with, the idea of having him away at college has become something she looks forward to. She knows her marriage will change when the kids leave home. Middle adulthood is a period of many changes and challenges.

A MULTIPLICITY OF IMAGES
OF MIDDLE AGE

To many people, changes and challenges are not terms associated with middle age. The stereotype of midlife as a boring plateau is one shared by many young adults and some researchers (Chiriboga, 1989). Other researchers and many popular books present the opposite stereotype of midlife as a time of inevitable crisis. We have all heard stories of the seemingly stable husband/father hitting fifty, buying a sports car, and driving off with a woman young enough to be his daughter. How can two such contrasting views continue to coexist? One answer is that middle-aged

No single experience represents middle adulthood. Blue-collar individuals are more likely to describe it as a period of slowing down and physical weakening, whereas upper-middle class individuals usually describe it as the period of greatest productivity.

people are at least as different from one another as younger adults are. Some have boring lives, and some do not. Some have crises, and some do not. We have a multiplicity of images of the middle years because no single experience represents this stage of life. Another answer is that midlife looks different depending on whether we consider social roles—which are very likely to change, as we saw in the case of Marcia—or personality traits, which research indicates are fairly stable after age thirty (Costa & McCrae, 1989; Costa et al., 1994).

What are people's conceptions about stability and change of personality in the adult years? Joachim Krueger and Jutta Heckhausen (1993) asked thirty young, thirty middle-aged, and thirty old adults in Germany to rate one hundred trait-descriptive adjectives along several dimensions, including desirability ("How desirable is it to have this trait?") and self-descriptiveness ("How well does the trait describe you?"). The subjects also rated whether each trait changed and, if so, how much and in which direction, for each of seven decades of the adult lifespan. All age groups judged desirable traits (such as energetic, good-natured, purposeful, realistic, intelligent) to increase in early adulthood (growth), followed by moderate decreases in old age (decline), and undesirable traits (such as discourageable, quarrelsome, irresponsible, nervous, blunt-witted) to moderately decrease in early adulthood (growth), then slightly increase in old age (decline). Based on self-descriptions, the overall personality was seen to be at its best during the decade of the sixties, when subjects judged they had the most positive traits and the fewest negative traits. Respondents of all ages were optimistic about development. They judged that more growth than decline occurs during the decades of adulthood. Older subjects considered personality to be quite stable and were more optimistic than their younger counterparts with regard to late-life development. As Figure 15.1 shows, views of development were related to age of the respondents. There were no differences for the young and the middle-aged groups, but for the sixties the older group gave higher ratings for growth than did young or middle-aged subjects. Also, whereas the two younger groups expected decline in the seventies, the older subjects had balanced conceptions of growth and decline.

Perceptions of life periods vary by social class and by gender as well as by age. Upper-middle-class individuals usually describe middle age as the period of greatest productivity, the "prime of life," whereas blue-collar individuals are more likely to describe it as a period of slowing down, physical weakening, or becoming a "has-been" (Neugarten, 1977). By age forty, blue-collar workers are likely to consider

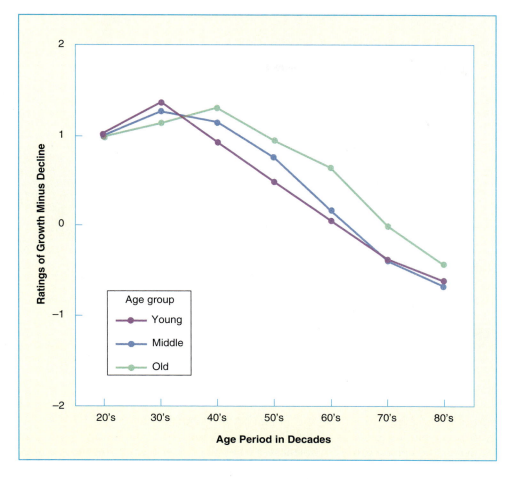

FIGURE 15.1
Optimism About Personality Change by Age
When adults of different ages rated growth and decline at each decade, there were no differences for the young and the middle-aged groups. For the sixties, the older group gave higher ratings for growth than did young or middle-aged subjects and saw less decline in the later years.
Source: Krueger & Heckhausen (1993).

themselves middle-aged, whereas upper-middle-class men often do not consider themselves middle-aged until the early fifties (Tamir, 1989). Lower-middle-class men fall somewhere between these two extremes. Women are more likely than men to perceive themselves as younger than their chronological ages, and this judgment becomes more pronounced as they get older (Rodeheaver & Stohs, 1991).

CRISIS OR NO CRISIS?

What do psychologists have to tell us about the experience of midlife? Again we find a multiplicity of images. As we discussed in Chapter 2, Freud saw development as complete by the end of childhood, while Erikson extended Freud's stages beyond adolescence and throughout adulthood. Carl Jung (1933), one of the earliest theorists to suggest that psychological development is lifelong, found middle age more interesting than any other stage of life because once one achieves an acceptable level of status according to societal expectations, one diverts "serious attention" from the demands of society to one's inner self.

Jung defined the personality, or *psyche*, as a collection of conflicting forces. The unconscious, for example, consists of the *collective unconscious*, thought-forms or memory traces from our ancestral past, and the *personal unconscious*, personal experiences that have been suppressed or forgotten. Jung believed the collective unconscious and the personal unconscious are often in conflict, just as the personal unconscious is often in conflict with conscious desires and goals. The psyche in both men and women also includes the *anima*, or primitive female force, as well as the *animus*, or primitive male force, which are often in conflict. The *shadow* is the

THE TERRIBLE FORTY-TWOS

Although inevitable crisis has become a stereotype of middle age, studies have not found universal midlife crisis.

part of the psyche that reflects the animal instincts humans have inherited in their evolution from lower forms of life. The *self* is the unifying force in the psyche that motivates the person toward wholeness. Although present from birth, the self does not develop until middle age, when the individual has amassed enough discipline, effort, and wisdom to appraise and evaluate the conflicting aspects of the psyche and work toward integration. The integrating process is *individuation*, through which the useful and creative aspects of the unconscious are made conscious and channeled into productive activity. As the self develops, it takes over the central role that the ego, which organizes the conscious mind, has been playing. Because of this, during middle age significant changes in personality occur as the self establishes a new balance between the conscious and the unconscious elements in the psyche. Men, for example, recognize their nurturant (anima) impulses, while women recognize assertive and independent (animus) impulses, leading both to be more balanced in their middle years (Helson, 1993).

Robert Havighurst (1953) identified seven developmental tasks of middle age: achieving civic and social responsibility, establishing and maintaining economic stability, assisting teenage children to become responsible adults, developing adult leisure time activities, relating to one's spouse and to oneself as individuals, accepting physiological changes in oneself, and adjusting to the aging and even the death of parents. Havighurst's focus on the timing of these developmental tasks makes it a timing of events model, as discussed in Chapter 13. The developmental tasks are associated with normative and nonnormative transitions that are likely to occur during the middle years. A **normative life event** is a life transition that occurs within a restricted time period, such as marriage, children leaving home, or retirement. A **nonnormative life event** is one that occurs at any point in life. A normative event may be experienced as nonnormative if it occurs "off time," for example, being widowed as a young adult or returning to college in middle age.

Erikson's theory predicts a normative crisis as the midlife individual faces the task of **generativity versus stagnation**. Generativity requires expanding ego interests and developing a deep concern for the establishment and nurturance of the next generation. It involves creating a *personal legacy* that can serve as an enduring symbol of one's own existence. Stagnation results in life no longer feeling purposeful or having long-term meaning. According to Erikson, generativity appears to increase in importance and strength up through the middle adult years and then taper off somewhat in old age. It may be expressed through nurturing, teaching, mentoring, leading, and promoting the next generation. In the process of dealing with the crisis of generativity versus stagnation, an earlier conflict, such as intimacy versus isolation, may be reawakened and an earlier resolution reworked. Later in the chapter we will see that middle-aged men, feeling they have missed some of the intimacy of family life, sometimes readjust their priorities from an emphasis on career toward an emphasis on family. Ellen, for example, has been surprised by her father's caregiving devotion to his grandchildren, since he was always working when she and her brothers were children.

Dan McAdams, Ed de St. Aubin, and Regina Logan (1993) measured differences in generativity among young (ages twenty-two to twenty-seven), midlife (ages thirty-seven to forty-two), and older (ages sixty-seven to seventy-two) adults. They found that midlife adults scored higher than young adults on generativity, but not higher than older adults. Both middle and older adults expressed high generative commitments compared to young adults, as shown in Table 15.1, which presents examples of their answers to the open-ended question "I typically try to . . . ." This study supports Erikson's contention that generativity increases in middle adulthood, but not that it decreases during late adulthood. Notice, however, that the older adults in the McAdams et al. study represented a narrow, young range of older adult ages. It is possible that generativity declines later in older adulthood.

Erikson's theory does not apply as well to women as to men, as we saw in Chapter 13 in our discussion of intimacy versus isolation. Suzanne Slater (1995) points out obstacles to applying generativity theory to women in general and to lesbian women in particular. First, men often give priority to individual pursuits and underestimate the role of relationships in their personal identities, but women do not. Recall from our earlier discussion of Daniel Levinson's work that women more often have a split Dream, one of achievement and relationships, whereas men dream of achievement. While this may create stress during early adulthood, it may

TABLE 15.1 *Strivings of Young, Midlife, and Older Adults*
When asked about their strivings, middle-aged and older adults expressed high generative commitments compared to young adults.

Age of Respondent	Completion of the Statement "I typically try to . . ."
26-year-old woman	"make my job more interesting than it really is" "be more open to others" "figure out what I want to do with my life" "be a good person" "enjoy life" "avoid uncomfortable situations" "keep up with current events" "be well liked" "make life more interesting and exciting" "make others believe I am completely confident and secure"
40-year-old woman	"be a positive role model for young people" "explain teenage experiences to my son and help him work through difficult situations" "provide for my mother to the best of my ability" "be helpful to those who are in need of help"
68-year-old woman	"counsel a daughter who has recently been let go from a job due to cutbacks" "help another daughter with her sick child" "help as a volunteer in a nonprofit organization" "assist a candidate running for election" "offer financial aid to someone close (friend or relative) if needed"

Source: Adapted from McAdams et al. (1993).

spare women from experiencing crisis at midlife that leads to reordering their priorities. Second, women who have children in their twenties and thirties broaden their focus beyond themselves to include essential relational ties to their children. The family life cycle presents them with issues of generativity before midlife. Third, generativity theory assumes that fears of becoming invisible and obsolete are new stresses that occur during middle age in our youth-oriented culture. Lesbians frequently lack social recognition and family support and therefore experience this kind of social exclusion before midlife. Because they face this exclusion earlier, Slater argues, they confront the need in themselves for generativity sooner. Denied access to social relationships, lesbians frequently join efforts for progressive social change and take up the helping professions to establish a personal legacy without ever experiencing the normative crisis of generativity versus stagnation.

Building on the theoretical conceptions of Erikson and Jung, some psychologists have developed stage theories of adult development that focus on crisis as a normal component of midlife. The term **midlife crisis** refers to radical changes within the personality associated with the adult's reexamination of goals, priorities, and life accomplishments as the midpoint of life is passed. Other researchers see no evidence that midlife crisis is characteristic of the adult experience. Still others see midlife as a time of transition, though not necessarily of crisis. In the following sections, we review some of the evidence for each of these positions.

Normative Crisis Models: Midlife Crisis

Three studies support the crisis position: Robert Gould's (1978) study of five hundred adults, known as the UCLA study; George Vaillant's (1977) study of ninety-five men, known as the Harvard Grant study (see Chapter 13); and Daniel Levinson's (1978) study of forty men, done at Yale (see Chapter 13). Each of these studies provides evidence for regular stages of adult development that include a midlife crisis.

The UCLA Study   Roger Gould, a psychiatrist, noticed that many of his patients at the psychiatric clinic were seeking help with problems that appeared to be age related. To investigate this idea, Gould established a sample of five hundred individuals ages sixteen to fifty who were not patients. Gould used interview and questionnaire data gathered from these women and men to describe the major periods of adulthood. His methodology, it must be noted, was that of a clinician. His data are qualitative rather than quantitative, and his book is based on case material drawn from the study without any statistical analysis. This means the interpretation is distinctly subjective.

Gould found the transformation of middle adulthood to be the most significant one in adulthood. As parents become ill and die, children leave home and become independent, one's position at work changes, and one's body shows signs of physical aging, the individual in middle adulthood confronts the long-held, false assumption of immortality. As when adolescents begin to realize they are not invincible, recognizing one's own mortality engenders strong negative feelings of "passivity, rage, depression and despair" (p. 218). Faced with these feelings, middle adults may question how to spend their time and reassess their priorities. The outcome of the midlife crisis—for example, taking courses, meeting new friends, or reestablishing old relationships—can lead to increased vitality and "deep self-renewal" (p. 307). According to Gould, how an individual negotiates the midlife crisis determines the individual's adaptation to old age.

The Harvard Grant Study   George Vaillant's study of midlife is part of the ongoing longitudinal study of Harvard men we described in Chapter 13. The men were all selected as young adults at Harvard because they were considered healthy and well adjusted. At midlife, these privileged men expressed feelings of turmoil and a heightened awareness of aging (Vaillant & McArthur, 1972). The fifth decade, Vaillant and McArthur found, brings "once again the *sturm und drang* [storm and stress] of adolescence. As adolescence is a period for acknowledging parental flaws and discovering the truth about childhood, so the forties are a time for reassessing and reordering the truth about adolescence and young adulthood" (Vaillant, 1977, pp. 219–220). The personal fable of invincibility gives way to a sense of life's limits and a need to use time wisely. Vaillant saw the pain of the forties as preparation for entering a new stage in which the values and career goals of the thirties are found to be too constraining and the interactions with adolescent children reawaken parts of the forgotten inner self. This heightened self-awareness leads to further growth and opens the way for achieving a sense of generativity. Vaillant's theory assumes everyone has kids "on time." As we will soon see, the stage of the family has an impact on the issues parents face.

The Era of Middle Adulthood   Levinson (1978) studied forty men between ages thirty-five and forty-five, a very narrow portion of midlife. He interviewed them intensively over several months and reinterviewed them two years later. From this biographical information, he discovered that *"the life structure evolves through a relatively orderly sequence during the adult years.* The essential character of the sequence is the same for *all* the men in our study and for the other men whose biographies we examined" (p. 49). Figure 13.1 on page 461 shows Levinson's stages of adult life. (See Chapter 13 for a discussion of the era of early adulthood.) The mid-life transition, which begins between ages thirty-eight and forty-three, bridges early adulthood and middle adulthood. During this transition, the emphasis shifts from past to future. A man comes to terms with his Dream not having come to fruition; he revises his Dream for the future and makes changes in his lifestyle around the themes of a new life structure. The Dream, remember, is idealized and never fully attainable. For some men this means drastic changes such as divorce, remarriage, or major shifts in occupation. For others it means less obvious but still important changes. For 80 percent of the men in his sample, Levinson found tumultuous struggles within the self and with the external world. For those who were not struggling with the "difficult questions regarding the meaning, value and direction of their lives" (p. 198), he predicted a later developmental crisis or a withering of the self. During the midlife transition the man confronts his own mortality, integrates aging in a way appropriate for middle adulthood rather than revisiting adolescent behavior, and establishes the conditions for mentoring and creating a legacy. (Levinson's theory leaves women out, as we discussed in Chapter 13.)

Women and Crisis   Research with women shows relatively little evidence for normative midlife crisis. As men reappraise their own values, women's tendency toward nurturance and investment in relationships appears more admirable and desirable than it did in younger years. Midlife women whose children have left home have a greater sense of well-being, a lower rate of depression, and improved marriages compared to younger women with children at home (Todd et al., 1990). Grace Baruch and Rosalind Barnett (1986) found that the combination of paid worker, wife, and mother roles promotes psychological well-being in midlife women. In both the United States and Kenya, higher-status (based on SES) women over age forty-four shifted toward greater interpersonal power compared to women under age thirty-six (Todd et al., 1990). Whereas women with little basis for power did not increase interpersonal power with age, those with some type of resources did.

No Crisis

David Chiriboga (1989) points out that the evidence for midlife crisis is derived from clinical impressions from people seeking help dealing with issues related to their stage of life or from nonrandomly selected samples of research participants studied by clinicians. He suggests that helping professionals are likely to overestimate the frequency of midlife crisis because they come into contact primarily with people seeking help. They may interpret evidence of "change" as evidence of "crisis." In contrast, when social and developmental psychologists randomly select middle-aged respondents drawn from the community, estimates of midlife crisis are only 2 to 5 percent. These researchers generally use checklists and rating scales rather than interviews. When people tell stories in interviews, they are more likely to dramatize their lives; in contrast, when they fill in scales, they rarely report a crisis (Haan, 1989). As further evidence of no crisis, Chiriboga (1989) reports that depression and other signs of stress and crisis do not increase during the middle years and that rates of suicide go down.

Personality Traits Paul Costa and Robert McCrae (1989) argue that "adult development should be viewed as the development not of social roles, or life structures, but of personality" (p. 49). While life events cause changes in social roles, they do not necessarily cause changes in the psychology of the individual. Costa and McCrae criticize normative crisis models of adulthood because those models show little agreement as to which phenomena constitute the core of adult development. Instead of looking for stages or structures, Costa and McCrae (1989; Costa et al., 1994) focus on the trait as a dimension of psychological functioning. A **trait** is a relatively enduring disposition of an individual, a characteristic way of thinking, feeling, and acting. While thousands of different traits are used in natural language and in personality assessment, most traits can be categorized within five broad dimensions, as Table 15.2 shows.

Personality traits, according to Costa, Metter, and McCrae (1994), contribute to the person's basic tendencies. Other factors, such as gender, intelligence, and left-handedness, also contribute, but they are not part of the personality. Basic tendencies must be distinguished from specific behaviors. A ninety-year-old who was the life of the party and danced on the tables in the Roaring Twenties is unlikely to do that today, but she is still likely to enjoy social gatherings and spirited conversation. Her specific behaviors have changed, but the basic tendency is still the same.

The Stability of Traits Hundreds of studies have been done to find out if personality traits change as people age. Most of these studies have been cross-sectional and show very little consistency (Neugarten, 1977). Because cross-sectional studies confound cohort effects with age changes, as we discussed in Chapter 14's discussion of cognitive development in middle adulthood, they are not able to provide answers to the question of stability or change in personality traits. Longitudinal studies show that personality is quite stable after about age thirty (Costa et al., 1994). In a characteristic longitudinal study, Costa and his associates (Costa et al., 1986) gave brief scales to measure neuroticism, extraversion, and openness to experience to a national sample of ten thousand individuals ages thirty-five to eighty-four. Ten years later, they relocated and retested two-thirds of the initial sample. They found little effect of age on any of the three personality dimensions for men or women, African Americans or whites.

TABLE 15.2 *The "Big Five" Dimensions of Personality*
Personality traits, which can be categorized within these five broad dimensions, show considerable stability after age thirty.

- **Neuroticism:** the tendency to experience negative emotions such as fear, anger, and sadness
- **Extraversion:** sociability, but closely associated with the tendency to experience excitement, joy, and good spirits
- **Openness to experience:** welcoming new experiences; imaginative and curious
- **Agreeableness:** sympathy, trust, cooperativeness, and altruism
- **Conscientiousness:** organization, scrupulousness, persistence, and achievement motivation

Source: Adapted from McCrae and John (1992).

In an extensive longitudinal study of men at midlife, McCrae and Costa (1984) used a Midlife Crisis Scale based on the work of Roger Gould, intensive interviews, and several personality inventories and found no evidence of universal midlife crisis. Although some people do experience crisis, these researchers see little evidence that most people do. They argue, rather, that "personality is highly predictable over long periods of time" (Costa et al., 1994, p. 48), which enables us to prepare for successful aging. "We know that aging men and women face many adaptational challenges, from declining health to death of loved ones to, in many cases, economic hardships. . . . How much more complicated life would be if, in addition to these external conditions, one had to adapt to new personality traits. Instead, enduring personality dispositions provide a dependable basis for adaptation to a changing world" (p. 56).

Midlife Transition

Lois Tamir (1989) takes a third position, which represents a timing of events approach. She believes men in their forties experience a transition to middle age in which their perspective on life changes, but the transition may or may not reach crisis proportions. Why men? For one thing, they face more rigid expectations for occupational success than women do. Women who are now middle-aged or older, even career women, have organized their lives around the life cycle of the family, whereas men have organized their lives around work. Family life cycle changes vary far more for women than do expectations of work for men. A woman may send her youngest child to college when she is thirty-eight, fifty-eight, or anywhere in between. While women are evaluated by themselves and others on a combination of family and work dimensions, men at age forty-five are evaluated according to career expectations (Tamir, 1989). In addition, because women are typically more interpersonally expressive, men find it more psychologically stressful to undergo the self-assessment that is a task of middle age.

Michael Farrell and Stanley Rosenberg (1981) found that not all men are willing to undergo self-examination, to openly recognize and confront the disturbing issues in their lives. They studied two hundred men ages twenty-five to thirty and three hundred men ages thirty-eight to forty-eight using intensive interviews, questionnaires, and several other measures. As Table 15.3 shows, Farrell and Rosenberg categorized these men into four major personality types based on two factors: their degree of life satisfaction and their ability to confront stress.

Anti-heroes and *transcendent-generative* men openly confronted stress. About 12 percent of the sample were categorized as anti-heroes. They were notably in crisis: dissatisfied, stressed, and alienated. They expressed regrets over the past, dissatisfaction with their occupations, and a wish to start anew, especially in the area of work. They expressed a strong personal sense of midlife crisis and did not deny or project these feelings onto others. Transcendent-generative men made up the largest group, 32 percent of the sample. While not denying there were stresses in their lives, they had no sense of crisis or turmoil and were the most satisfied. They seemed to have everything: satisfaction from work and family, freedom from anxiety and stress-related symptoms, open-mindedness, self-assurance, and a history of successful coping with adversity. They were primarily from the affluent upper middle class.

Pseudo-developed and *punitive-disenchanted* men denied stress. About 26 percent of the sample was categorized as pseudo-developed. The pseudo-developed men attempted to appear perfect. They denied problems in work and family and reported high levels of mental health, but psychological tests and interviews revealed self-deception, rigid personalities, and bigotry toward others. The punitive-disenchanted respondents, 30 percent of the sample, also denied stress but were clearly dissatisfied with their lives. They were truly in crisis: depressed, alienated, and likely to experience problems at work and at home. These men blamed their

TABLE 15.3 *Typology of Men's Responses to Middle Age Stresses*
Farrell & Rosenberg (1981) categorized the midlife men they studied into four major personality types based on their degree of life satisfaction and their ability to confront stress.

	Denial of Stress	Open Confrontation with Stress
Dissatisfied	**IV Punitive-Disenchanted** 1. Highest in authoritarianism 2. Dissatisfaction associated with environmental factors 3. Conflict with children	**I Anti-Hero** 1. High alienation 2. Active identity struggle 3. Ego-oriented 4. Uninvolved interpersonally 5. Low authoritarianism
Satisfied	**III Pseudo-Developed** 1. Overtly satisfied 2. Attitudinally rigid 3. Denies feelings 4. High authoritarianism 5. High on covert depression and anxiety 6. High in symptom formation	**II Transcendent-Generative** 1. Assesses past and present with conscious sense of satisfaction 2. Few symptoms of distress 3. Open to feelings 4. Accepts out-groups 5. Feels in control of fate

Source: Farrell & Rosenberg (1981).

families and social circumstances for their misery, were the most bigoted, and were largely from lower-SES groups.

This study highlights the lack of uniformity of the midlife male experience. Some men experienced midlife crisis, others did not. Farrell and Rosenberg found that "a variety of reactions appear, ranging from heightened awareness of self to increased rigidity and defensiveness. The resurgence of old memories, conflicts, and aspirations is generally not a welcomed experience, but one that intrudes itself in situations of personal disruption and vulnerability. The only exception, and a relatively rare one, is among upper-class or well-educated middle-class men. These men may, in the context of positive self-esteem, utilize the midlife transition as an opportunity to reexamine and change earlier choices and solutions" (p. 206). The social and psychological resources of the upper class seem to facilitate more optimal development. The class-based nature of midlife crisis may explain why the Harvard Grant and Levinson studies found evidence of midlife crisis, since their samples were nonrandom and heavily tilted toward the privileged. Tamir (1989), on the other hand, has criticized the Farrell and Rosenberg study for having too narrow an age range to encompass working-class and upper-middle-class experiences of midlife crisis. Working-class men at forty-five might already have been over their crisis, while middle-class men might not yet have begun it.

We see no universal midlife crisis here. Men appear to be more prone to crisis than women are. Privileged men seem more likely to engage in the self-exploration associated with midlife crisis than men with few material and social resources. At the same time, we know there are life changes associated with midlife. We saw in Chapter 14 that middle age is the time when men and women reach the peak of their influence on society. It is also the time when society makes its maximum demands on them for social and civic responsibility. At the same time expectations of one's partner, friends, and family may also be changing. We turn now to a look at home and family life in normative and nonnormative transitions in the middle years.

What Do You Think?

Consider a middle-aged adult you know well. Has that person experienced a midlife crisis or not? What is your evidence? What characteristics does that person have that may have contributed to the crisis or no-crisis experience?

MARRIAGE AND DIVORCE

During the middle years marriages may just be starting, may be ending, or may be continuing. Although divorce rates are relatively high, one-fifth of first marriages will last for fifty years or more (Condie, 1989). Because people typically marry for the first time and most often remarry as young adults, our focus in Chapter 13 was on the formation of new marriages. Middle-aged adults who newly marry or remarry face similar issues of marriage formation. In this section we focus on continuing marriages, within which many couples in middle adulthood face the normative changes of their lives.

Long-Term Marriage

When Francis and Tom were in their fifties, they appeared to have little in common. She was a full-time homemaker; her youngest two children were still at home, going through difficult adolescent years. Tom managed a small construction business. They both worked very hard; money was tight, and family time was stressful. Now in their seventies, Francis and Tom have only a dog and two cats living with them. Tom has retired and they spend most of each day together, taking a long morning walk, doing the marketing, or caring for assorted grandchildren. As older adults married for more than fifty years, they seem to enjoy each other's company in a way that was not apparent in their middle years. Each rarely complains about the other, and both are warm and supportive in their interactions with each other.

Laura Carstensen and her associates (1995) compared the emotional behavior of middle-aged and old adults in long-term marriage. They recruited participants on

Husbands and wives in long-term marriages agree that being friends, liking one's spouse as a person, and laughing frequently together leads to long, stable, and satisfying marriage. This couple's relationship appears to have all of these qualities.

the basis of marriage (middle-aged couples had to be married for fifteen years, older couples for thirty-five years), age (the older spouse in middle-aged couples had to be forty to fifty years old, in older couples sixty to seventy years old), and marital satisfaction (both spouses relatively happy or both spouses relatively unhappy). Their sample included 156 couples: 86 percent white, 6 percent African American, 3 percent Hispanic, 3 percent Asian, and 2 percent with spouses of different races. Couples came to the laboratory and were recorded while they engaged in three conversational interactions: discussing events of the day, discussing an area of continuing disagreement in their marriage, and discussing a mutually agreed-on pleasant topic. A team of coders used a carefully constructed coding system to rate the interactions. Elderly couples were coded as being more affectionate than middle-aged couples, while middle-aged couples were coded as displaying more interest, humor, anger, and disgust. Even when discussing conflict in their relationship, older couples managed to express higher levels of affection and lower levels of negative feelings toward their partners. In addition to these differences, there were similarities between older couples and findings from studies of younger couples. Regardless of age, positive emotions of humor, affection, and validation were more likely to emerge in happy marriages than in unhappy marriages even when discussing marital conflict. Also, wives showed more emotion and a greater range of emotions than husbands, while husbands showed more defensiveness. Other researchers have asked couples in long-term marriages to what factors they attribute their success (Lauer et al., 1995). Husbands and wives mention very similar qualities; Table 15.4 shows they agree on eight of the top ten factors.

The Family Life Cycle

To analyze the similar activities, joys, and problems people experience at different points in their married lives, some scholars have developed the concept of the **family life cycle**, a series of predictable stages through which families pass. You may recognize this as a timing of events model from our discussion in Chapter 13. Families are placed into stages based on the ages of the children and the age of the wife. Young families (stage I) have young children; the wife is less than forty-five years old, and at least one child is under six. Maturing families (stage II) have school-age children; at least one child is between six and eighteen years old. Middle-aged

TABLE 15.4 *Perceived Reasons for Successful Long-Term Marriages (Top Ten, Listed in Order of Frequency of Naming)*
When Lauer et al. (1995) asked one hundred couples who had been married for forty-five to sixty-four years the reasons for the success of their marriage, husbands and wives mentioned very similar factors as leading to a long, stable, and satisfying marriage.

Husbands	Wives
Mate is best friend	Marriage a long-term commitment
Like mate as person	Like mate as person
Marriage a long-term commitment	Mate is best friend
Marriage a sacred institution	Laugh together frequently
Agree on aims and goals	Agree on aims and goals
Laugh together frequently	Marriage a sacred institution
Proud of mate's achievements	Agree on expression of affection
Mate more interesting now than when first married	Agree on philosophy of life
Engage in outside interests	Proud of mate's achievements
Agree on major decisions	Mate more interesting now than when first married

Source: Lauer et al. (1995).

empty-nest families (stage III) have no children at home; the wife is age forty-five or older. Older families (stage IV) have no children at home; the wife is sixty years or older. Figure 15.2 shows that different stages of the family life cycle are associated with different levels of marital satisfaction. Stage analysis deemphasizes the irregularities in family life. It excludes families that are exceptions to the stages, for example, those without children, those in which all of the children are over eighteen but some are still living at home, or those in which adult children have special problems, which are discussed in the accompanying Perspectives box.

Marital Satisfaction and Family Stage   Pat Keith and Robert Schafer (1991) investigated well-being in households with different lifestyles (one- and two-job families, modern and traditional spouses) and in each of the four family stages just described, as well as in single-parent households containing at least one child less than nineteen years old. They interviewed 750 individuals: 85 husbands and wives at stage I, 88 husbands and wives at stage II, 81 husbands and wives at stage III, 82 husbands and wives at stage IV, and 78 single-parent women. Married couples were interviewed separately. Interview questions asked about work-family roles, dissatisfaction, disagreement, role performance, equity and inequity, depressive symptoms, role strain, attitudes toward gender roles, work commitment, comparisons of family type, and involvement in "masculine" and "feminine" tasks. Their study is outstanding because it allows for comparisons between (1) one- and two-job families, (2) single-parent women and their married counterparts, (3) older and younger couples, (4) modern and traditional spouses, and (5) the experiences of husbands and wives.

Keith and Schafer found that gender role attitudes correlated with many of the other factors measured: "Whether gender-role attitudes were modern or more traditional was linked to the household involvement of husbands and wives in most of the life stages. Thoughts about gender roles were especially salient in predicting the division of labor in younger families . . . traditional wives spent more time on feminine tasks and, correspondingly, nontraditional husbands did more housework" (p. 152). The oldest families were an exception to this trend: "Older men were more involved than younger men in housekeeping, but their behavior was not directly affected by their gender-role attitudes, their own employment status, or that of their wives" (p. 152). More stage I and II families aspired to equal partnerships (modern),

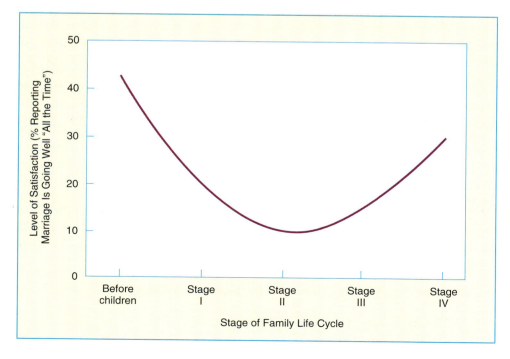

FIGURE 15.2
Level of Satisfaction at Stages of the Family Life Cycle
Marital satisfaction appears to follow a curvilinear path over the family life cycle, starting high, dropping sharply after the birth of the first child, reaching an all-time low when the children are adolescents, and increasing when the children leave home and the couple retires.

The Effects of Middle-Aged Adult Children's Problems on Older Parents

The family life cycle emphasizes predictable parental responsibilities when children are young and subsequent freedom from these responsibilities when children reach adulthood. By the time one's children are middle aged, they are expected to begin caring for their parents. But what if adult offspring have problems? Studies of young children and young adult children have shown that their physical and mental disorders often lead to parental distress (Cook, 1988; Noh et al., 1989). Does this relationship between children's problems and parental distress continue into later life, when the children are middle-aged adults and the parents are elderly?

Karl Pillemer and Jill Suitor (1991) set out to investigate this question. They believed that because parents identify with their children and view their children's accomplishments and difficulties as indicators of their own success and failure, elderly parents would be affected by the problems of their adult offspring. Also, because mothers typically invest more of their time and energy in childrearing, elderly mothers were expected to be more distressed by their children's problems than would elderly fathers.

Pillemer and Suitor conducted a telephone survey of 1,421 noninstitutionalized elderly (ages sixty-five to one hundred) women (67 percent) and men (33 percent) in Canada, asking them about their relationships with their children. People with no living children were excluded. Up to two children were selected in each case: one child who lived with the respondent (if any did) and one child who lived independently. If there was more than one child in either category, the respondents were asked to select "the child with whom they had the hardest time getting along" (p. 588).

The interviews measured psychological distress and children's problems, along with several other variables. The psychological distress scale asked questions about how frequently in the preceding week the respondent felt a certain way (e.g., "You felt downhearted or blue"). The respondent could answer "very often," "fairly often," "once in a while," or "never." Children's problems were measured by asking the respondent whether the target child (or, if two, either child) had any of four problems: mental or emotional problems (3.5 percent of respondents reported these), serious problems with his or her

while in stage III and IV families the wife was likely to be modern and the husband traditional. This may well be due to cohort differences, since age and stage are not possible to separate in this cross-sectional study. Gender role attitude correlated with employment of stage I and II wives; when husbands and wives were both traditional, the young wife was unlikely to be employed. By middle age, wives were employed regardless of gender role attitudes because child care needs no longer conflicted with employment.

Dual-Earner Families   Keith and Schafer found that wives and husbands in dual-earner families responded differently to the strain of balancing the demands of home and work. Wives reported distress when their husbands experienced competing demands, while husbands reported distress when their wives spent large amounts of time at work. Younger dual-earner husbands experienced more strain than older ones, especially if they felt negative about their family incomes or about themselves as providers. Age was not related to role strain among dual-earner women or single-earner men who were troubled when their at-home wives felt overloaded.

Family life stage was highly correlated with strain for dual-earner families. More than one-third of the young families reflected high role strain between occupational and family demands for both partners, compared to fewer than 10 percent of the middle-aged and older couples. This is probably due to the intensity of the demands of establishing new careers and parenting young children that we considered in our discussion of early adulthood. Wives had the most intense role strain, but it was the level of the husbands' role strain that differentiated the harried families from the calmer ones. Since wives are generally strained, perhaps having a highly stressed husband as well pushes the family over the edge.

Which Family Stages Are Happier?   Some studies indicate that middle-aged (stage III) and older (stage IV) marriages are happier than those in the earlier

physical health (14.2 percent), a drinking or alcohol problem (2.2 percent), or serious stress during the past year (21.3 percent). Twenty-six percent of the respondents reported that their child had at least one of these problems. One question assessed parent-child conflict: "How often does your child create tensions or arguments with you?" Another measured the amount of support received from the child: "How often does your child make you feel loved or cared for?" Another asked the extent to which the child depended on the parent for financial support. Respondents also answered questions about their own health, marital status, education, and whether they had a confidant.

Parents who reported that their child had at least one of the four problems received higher depression scores than parents who did not report a child with a problem. The strength of the relationship between children's problems and parents' psychological distress was the same for mothers and fathers and for parents living with their children and those living independently. Pillemer and Suitor thought the direct practical impact of the children's problems on the parents might explain the parents' depres-

sion: perhaps the problem children were more financially dependent, or they did not provide their parents with emotional support. However, they found no such relation existed. Conflict with children, on the other hand, was positively related to depression.

This study clearly shows that even when the children are themselves adults in their middle years, their problems affect the well-being of their parents. This is not because they coreside, need financial help, or fail to provide emotional support but because elderly parents continue to identify with their children and to conclude that if the child does not "turn out right," they are at fault (Strom & Strom, 1995). Earlier studies have shown this to be true at earlier stages of the parent-child relationship (Goldsteen & Ross, 1989; Umberson, 1989). As with any timing of events theory, the family life cycle cannot account for the unpredictable problems that occur in families.

stages. Marital satisfaction appears to follow a curvilinear path over the family life cycle, starting high during the honeymoon, dropping sharply after the birth of the first child, reaching an all-time low when the children are adolescents, and increasing when the children leave home and the couple retires, as Figure 15.2 shows (Anderson et al., 1983; Levenson et al., 1993). The presence of younger children at home creates demands that lower both marital interaction and marital happiness for husbands and wives (Zuo, 1992). Women and men in long-term happy marriages report increasing satisfaction over time, with a dip during the childrearing years (Lauer et al., 1995). On the other hand, Caroline Vaillant and George Vaillant (1993) analyzed data from men in the Harvard Grant study and their wives and found little support for the family life cycle curve. They suggest that the curve may be an artifact of cross-sectional methodology, but their sample was so small and so select that it alone is not a good test of the U-shaped curve of marital satisfaction. (See Chapter 13 for a description of the sample.) Financial stress is one important factor that brings on decline in marital satisfaction, and that is missing in the privileged Harvard Grant sample (Norris & Tindale, 1994).

Middle-aged people are often in stage II and stage III families, depending on how young they were when they had children. Marcia and Ed, the couple in our opening example, are living through the parental side of the difficulties of adolescent children (stage II) that we discussed from the children's perspective in Chapter 11, but in five years, when Shelly enters college, their nest will be empty (stage III). Marital quality is then likely to improve when Marcia and Ed have more time for each other without the stresses of adolescent demands, temperaments, and misbehaviors orchestrating family life. In addition to having children successfully launched, Marcia and Ed will each have achieved a career plateau and be looking forward to retirement. In a study comparing long-term first marriages of middle-aged and old couples, Robert Levenson, Laura Carstensen, and John Gottman (1993) found that children were rated as the largest source of marital conflict for middle-aged couples and only the fourth in importance for old couples. Other sources of conflict middle-aged couples rated significantly higher than old couples did include money, religion, and recreation. No sources of conflict were significantly greater for old couples than for middle-aged ones, but old couples rated four areas as significantly higher sources of pleasure: children or grandchildren, things done together recently, dreams, and vacations taken. These sources of pleasure reflect more time to spend together in the later stages of marriage. Jiping Zuo (1992) found a positive relationship between marital interaction and marital happiness; each factor had a positive impact on the other.

Divorce

Although marital satisfaction tends to increase among long-term married couples, divorce does occur. The divorce rate for couples married more than fifteen years is over 20 percent, considerably lower than that for shorter-term marriages but increasing (Cooney, 1994). Still, most divorces occur before the middle years: only 15 percent of recent separations and divorces occurred among women over age forty (Bumpass et al., 1990). The rate of separation and divorce for African Americans is higher than for whites. Divorce during middle adulthood has a significant impact on women, men, and their children.

For those who do not remarry, divorce represents entry into a lifetime single status. As Table 15.5 shows, the younger a woman is when she divorces and the fewer children she has, the more likely she is to remarry. This reflects in part the decrease in the number of potential marriage partners. Remarriage is less common among African Americans and Hispanics than among whites. Men are more likely to remarry than women.

For women, separation and divorce usually lower the standard of living significantly. This is especially true while there are still children in the home. Since 45 percent of mother-only families live in poverty, divorce has a substantial impact on the quality of life for children (Edmondson et al., 1993). Even when women remarry, the majority of children living in single-parent families because of divorce will live out their childhood without ever entering a second family (Bumpass & Sweet, 1989). "It is 7 years before half of the mothers with one or two children at separation have remarried, and it is almost 14 years for those with three or more children" (Bumpass et al., 1990, p. 753).

For men, divorce or separation usually means they see their children far less often. Because custody of young children is most frequently awarded to mothers, fathers' interactions with their children are often disrupted due to physical separation. Teresa Cooney (1994) estimates that 13 to 51 percent of children of divorce have infrequent, if any, contact with their noncustodial parent. Alan Booth and Paul Amato (1994) found that divorce was most disruptive to father-child relations when it occurred early in the children's life. This has implications for the well-being of men after age fifty, when divorce has a pronounced negative effect on the frequency of fathers' contacts with their adult offspring and sharply reduces the probability that fathers consider their adult children as potential sources of support in times of need (Cooney & Uhlenberg, 1990).

What happens if divorce does not occur until the parents are in their middle years and the children are already out of the house? Cooney (1994) studied the influence of recent parental divorce on contact and feelings between 485 young white adults (ages eighteen to twenty-three) and their parents, half of whom had experienced divorce in the past fifteen months. Because these children were already adults, Cooney could assess the changes in the relationship with each parent in the absence of court-imposed custody. Recent parental divorce was associated with reduced intimacy and contact between fathers and their children, but not mothers. Approximately 15 percent of nonresident adult children of recent divorce saw their fathers less than once a month, which was virtually unheard of in intact families.

TABLE 15.5 Expected Proportion of Women Ever Remarrying after Separation (Experience Centering on 1982)
The younger a woman is and the fewer children she has when she divorces, the more likely she is to remarry.

Variable	Percentage Remarrying
Age at separation	
Under 25	89
25–29	79
30–39	59
40+	31
Duration of first marriage	
0–1 years	89
2–4 years	82
5–9 years	76
10+ years	52
Age at first marriage	
14–17	84
18–19	79
20–22	67
23+	51
Children at separation	
0	81
1–2	73
3+	57
Race	
White non-Hispanic	76
African American	46
Education	
0–11 years	67
12 years	75
13 + years	72
Region	
Northeast	60
North Central	70
South	77
West	78
Total	72

Source: Adapted from Bumpass et al. (1990).

"Less than 60% of children of divorce had weekly contacts with their absent fathers, compared to 80% of those in intact families" (p. 53).

Speculations as to the reasons for this lack of contact include lack of interest on the part of the father (Furstenberg & Cherlin, 1991), ongoing conflict with the ex-partner that could force the children to take sides, personal problems such as alcoholism, and geographic distance (Dudley, 1991), but it is hard to understand why some of these reasons would not affect mothers' contact as well. It seems likely that these fathers lack the kinkeeping skills that are necessary for continuing contact. *Kinkeeping skills* are those skills that keep the individual in touch with other family members, such as phoning, sending birthday cards, or visiting. These are skills that men can learn but have traditionally been the province of women. "Perhaps as the scope of men's responsibilities in the home widens, more fathers will have the opportunity to develop their relationship skills and form stronger, independent relations with their children and other kin" (Cooney, 1994, p. 54).

What Do You Think?

Suppose you have a friend who has two teenagers and is having some problems in her marriage. If she obtained the help of a marriage counselor, what advice do you think this professional would be likely to give to your friend based on what you have learned about the family life cycle?

FAMILY RELATIONSHIPS

The concept of the family life cycle clearly indicates how closely intertwined marriage is with other family relationships. As we have seen, the ages of the children affect the marital relationship, and marital disruption affects parental relationships with children. Yet, married or not, adults in their middle years tend to have a rich array of family relationships. For adults, attachment is an emotional closeness that does not depend on physical immediacy. (See the Chapter 5 discussion of attachment formation in early life.) Adults who feel secure in their attachments approach work with confidence and report greater well-being than those who do not (Hazen & Shaver, 1990). Without necessarily being in constant contact, middle-aged adults maintain relationships with the younger generations of children and grandchildren, with the older generations of parents and grandparents, and with their own generation of siblings. Because their loved ones call on them when they are in crises, middle-aged adults have been called the **sandwich generation**, caught between the needs of the adjacent generations. As we discuss the various relationships, it is necessary to keep in mind the diversity among middle-aged adults in terms of race/ethnicity, educational level, occupational attainment, gender, and health status to understand that each midlife adult will not have all of the relationships we consider and each relationship will not be experienced in the same way by different individuals. Disjunction and disruption sometimes occur in family relationships as well, as Joan Stone, a victim advocate, mentions in the Working With interview on page 558.

Adolescent Children

Although the transition to parenthood puts a lot of strain on the marital relationship, as we discussed in Chapter 13, adolescent children have the most detrimental impact on marital satisfaction (Gecas & Seff, 1990). As children grow into adolescence, parents need to become less hierarchical and more flexible in their parenting style (Norris & Tindale, 1994). Adolescents need the opportunity to make their own decisions and make their own mistakes within the safe confines of parental supervision. As you may remember from Chapter 11, an authoritative style that combines high acceptance, supervision, and respect for adolescent autonomy promotes adolescent development. Adolescent adjustment in both biological families and stepfamilies is positively related to parental supervision, warmth, and interest and negatively related to conflict (Fine & Kurdek, 1992; Reuter & Conger, 1995). Parents of adolescents face continual challenges to their judgment, which often results in discomfort and conflict between the parents. Parents may revisit their own adolescent conflicts and want to prevent their children from making the same mistakes. Realizing their offspring are close to independence may spur midlife reassessment of self and goals that in itself is often disconcerting and may cause crises. Parents who have not lived alone with each other for years may worry about how they will get along without children. In addition, adolescents take up a lot of space and time. Unlike younger children, they do not have a bedtime that allows parents private

The woman pushing the wheelchair provides care for both her mother and her son. This makes her a member of the sandwich generation, caught between the needs of the adjacent generations.

time. Few parents can even stay up as late as their teenagers do, because parents generally must wake early to days filled with work and family responsibilities.

While adolescence is characterized by reduced interaction and closeness with parents, especially for sons (Youniss & Smollar, 1985), this is not uniformly true when family diversity is taken into account. As visible minorities within an often hostile majority environment, African American adolescents may see their families as a "safe haven" or anchor. They report significantly higher levels of parental control and family intimacy than do white adolescents (Giordano et al., 1993). This may reduce adolescent-parent conflict within African American families. The adolescent years are a time when children do not like to be different in any way. Matile Rothschild (1991) found that most teenagers, especially in the years between twelve and fifteen, react negatively to having a lesbian mother or a gay father. This may increase adolescent difficulties in families with gay or lesbian parents. While the level of conflict between adolescents and parents varies, Alice Schlegel and Barry Herbert (1991) found some amount of conflict over control in every culture and every historical period.

Young Adult Children

Relationships change as children move out to attend college or to begin their own adult lives, but this does not mean they have become fully independent. As you may remember from Chapter 11, entry into adulthood increases interaction and closeness between child and parents compared to adolescent levels (Rossi & Rossi, 1990). Parents are often pleasantly surprised to discover that the same child who, while living at home during high school, answered questions with monosyllables calls from college with lots to talk about. Parents continue to provide financial and emotional support for children in college and reside in what have been called "semi-autonomous households" because the children return for holidays, summer vacations, and whenever they feel the need (Goldscheider & DaVanzo, 1986). Even when the young adult offspring have established households of their own, like Bill and Karen in Chapter 13, parents are likely to continue to give emotional and material support.

Working with | Joan Stone, VICTIM ADVOCATE

Helping Victims of Abusive Family Relationships

Joan Stone graduated from college a year ago with a major in psychology and a minor in women's studies. Since then she has been working as a victim advocate for victims of domestic violence. She provides legal assistance and referrals for services and counseling.

Michele: What is a victim advocate?

Joan: Connecticut mandated the victim advocate position in response to a case in which a woman who had no adequate protection from domestic violence was disabled by her husband. The Domestic Violence Project, where I work, places victim advocates in the courts so we are readily available for those who need us. The Project provides victims with a safe place to live for up to ninety days, counseling, legal assistance, referrals for services, and other social supports. To qualify you have to be a victim of abuse by someone you are intimate with or are related to, such as a husband, a father of your children, or a child.

Michele: What training did you have?

Joan: I did a year-long internship my senior year. I also earned a twenty-hour certificate of training before the internship.

Michele: What exactly do you do?

Joan: I help victims in both civil and criminal court. If a person is in an abusive relationship but can't get the abuser arrested, I help get a restraining order through civil action. The victim calls the twenty-four-hour hot line for our help, which takes an enormous amount of self-confidence to do. In contrast, when the abuser has been arrested, the case goes to criminal court. In criminal court, the victim can receive a protective order through the state-mandated law. In criminal cases, the victim advocate sees the victim in person or makes contact by phone or letter. Most victims cooperate, but some are unwilling.

Michele: How are cases assigned to you?

Joan: An arrest takes place. The defendant is arraigned the next day. Speedy results are mandated due to the severity of domestic violence. The only way the victim advocates can initiate contact with victims is if they go through the court process. On the first offense the defendant is often referred to the family violence course, and if the defendant finishes the course, the charges are dropped. The victim can be referred to the domestic violence program and to counseling.

Michele: Can you give me some examples of your cases?

Joan: Some victims in criminal cases will say, "Yes, I want him out of the house," but a lot will drop charges. They will say, "It was a one-time thing," although if you look at the records, you see they have been to court before. Experienced victim advocates say it takes eight or nine arrests before the victims leave their relationships.

I once worked with a woman in her late eighties whose son, in his mid-forties, was abusing her. She was rushed to the emergency room, she was beaten so badly. We called elderly services to help her. She needed her son to care for her but wanted him out. I worked with another elderly woman who lived with her three middle-aged unmarried children. They all abused each other. There was a cycle of violence in the family.

While emotional support is a two-way interaction between adult children and their parents, material support tends to be parent to child until parents are well into their seventies and the children are in their forties (Spitze & Logan, 1992). There is some evidence, however, that ethnicity and family income strongly influence the flow of money between generations. In a comparison of student and nonstudent young adults after high school graduation, Frances Goldscheider and Calvin Goldscheider (1991) found that white parents contributed more to their young adult children who were students than did African American parents, not because of race but due to several family structure variables associated with race, including a lower likelihood of living in a mother-headed family, higher family income, and parents' later entry into parenthood.

The Empty Nest   Children moving out appears to be conducive to well-being in parents, especially mothers, and to improved marital satisfaction for the couple (Norris & Tindale, 1994). Having an "empty nest" typically results in time to spare and, when the children are out of college, money to spare as well. This provides midlife parents with opportunities for self-development and autonomy. When the children leave home, mothers have the freedom to develop occupations or careers

Michele: So far you have spoken of women victims. What are they like?

Joan: Well, it depends. Those who come to the office are seeking counseling and support voluntarily, but when we meet clients in court, they are there because police officers directed them. That puts me in the position of working with people who don't want help. I have to let them make decisions themselves. For example, a woman in her late thirties was in court because her boyfriend, who had a drinking problem, had been beating her sixteen-year-old daughter. She was very upset and wanted him to stop. Even though the woman didn't ask for one, the court assigned a protective order. She was trying to protect her daughter and the defendant at the same time, although she certainly understood the problem. I talked to her for a long time and got her to let me talk to the daughter. The daughter said, "I really like this man, but when he drinks they get into a fight." The mother and daughter were hesitant, but with help and support they made a decision to restrict him to visits, which was positive and productive for them.

Michele: What segment of the population do victims come from?

Joan: All types of people are victims of domestic violence: minority, lower-class white, and upper-class white. In fact, the person sitting next to you may be a victim of domestic violence. The other day I called a prominent woman in town because her husband was arrested for harassment. She was in her fifties; they were married over thirty years. It turns out he was a problem drinker, and she wanted him to get help. He was arraigned in court and assigned counseling. She got a partial protective order, which means he can continue to live at home but not harass her. This solution fit her needs, but it wouldn't work for everyone. Part of what I do as a victim advocate is help victims come up with the best solution given the specifics of their situation.

Michele: Do you deal only with spousal abuse cases?

Joan: No, we see a lot of victims abused by their children. I have seen middle-aged fathers abused by sons in high school or college. The child often has a drug or alcohol problem. The father may not like the friends his son is hanging out with or that the son's grades are going down. The father and son get into a fight that turns physical. The child may threaten, "I'm going to kill you." It's hard for parents to call the police. It is sad to see people abused like this.

Michele: What do you like about your work?

Joan: It's exciting. I learn how different people think. It's also frustrating. You can't tell people what to do. You don't want to be judgmental, but I have a hard time accepting what they want. If a victim wants her abuser back, she has a right even if she is in danger. The best thing is the gratification I get when the victim has a positive outcome and is *safe*!

What Do You Think?

1. What strains in family relationships are reflected in the types of domestic violence Joan describes?

2. Why might women with children be reluctant to leave their marriages or cohabiting relationships even though those relationships are abusive?

or increase their commitment to those they have, and couples have the opportunity to do more things together, especially travel. One result is that, regardless of marriage type or gender role attitudes, middle-aged wives tend to be employed (Keith & Schafer, 1991). Studies have focused on mothers rather than on fathers because mothers have traditionally been the more involved parents.

Mothers tend to benefit more than fathers, either because they have put off or limited independent activities to tend to family needs or have been doing a "second shift" (first shift at work, second shift at home), as we saw in Chapter 13's discussion of parenting issues in early adulthood. Mothers in young dual-earner families experience the most intense role strain (Keith & Schafer, 1991). The empty nest is a source of freedom for women; they become more assertive, less depressed, and less strained (Cooper & Gutman, 1987; Norris & Tindale, 1994). This appears to be true regardless of ethnicity. In a study of 243 middle-aged, empty-nest Mexican American mothers, Linda Rogers and Kyriakos Markides (1989) found that the women enjoyed levels of well-being equal to those of other ethnic groups. In their study, the women who were employed were, on average, five years younger and less likely to report depressive or physical symptoms than were the nonemployed mothers. This is consistent with findings from research with white middle-aged mothers (Barnett & Baruch, 1985).

Many contemporary, unmarried, young adults never leave home or return one or more times to the parental household. Middle-aged parents tend to fare best emotionally when adult children physically move out but remain in close contact.

Multigenerational Households   Parents tend to fare best emotionally when children physically move out but remain in close contact (White & Edwards, 1990). The parents can reorganize their time and interests but still maintain their parenting relationship. However, many young adults never leave home or return one or more times to the parental household (Thornton et al., 1993). The individuals who reached early adulthood in the 1980s were more likely to reside with their parents than were those who came of age in the 1960s or 1970s, probably because they remained single much longer (Glick & Lin, 1986). William Aquilino (1990) used an extensive collection of family life interviews to study African American, white, and Mexican American parents who had at least one child or stepchild over nineteen years of age. He found that middle-aged parents (age fifty-four or younger) were more likely to have an adult child living with them than were older parents (fifty-five or older); 28 percent reported adult coresident children. Children's marital status was the best predictor of coresidence: only parents with *unmarried* adult children were likely to have children coresiding. Parents whose youngest adult child was age nineteen to twenty-one were more likely to have children at home than parents with older children. Sons were more likely to live with their middle-aged parents than daughters. Married parents, particularly those still married to each other, were most likely to have adult children coresiding. There was little evidence for stronger preference for coresidency among minorities than among whites. While more African American and Mexican American adult children lived with their parents, the racial differences were entirely accounted for by the children's marital status. Minority parents were more likely to have adult children living with them because they were more likely to have unmarried adult children. James Jackson, Toni Antonucci, and Rose Gibson (1990) report that all racial and ethnic minorities, especially Native Americans, are more likely than whites to live in multigenerational households. They suggest socioeconomic differences, cultural preferences, values, and feelings of filial devotion as reasons for maintenance of these multigenerational households.

For good or ill, coresident parents and adult children keep tabs on one another. Parents evaluate and monitor their child's dating, eating, and exercising behaviors, and children evaluate and monitor their parents' behaviors. As a result, each influences the other (Boyd & Pryor, 1989). Differences in attitudes about these daily issues can lead to conflict. How well coresidence works out is best predicted by the presence or absence of conflict between the parents and the child (Aquilino & Supple, 1991). Conflict increased and parental satisfaction declined if the children were financially dependent or unemployed and separated or divorced with accompanying grandchildren. When children return to the parental home under such conditions, parents have to resume responsibility for their children's welfare, and this is likely to interfere with meeting their own independent needs and ambitions (Clemens & Axelson, 1985).

Grandparenting

Couples today typically become grandparents in their late forties and early fifties, which is young compared to couples in the early 1900s (Gee, 1991). This is likely to change in the future as more young adults delay starting families. Because contemporary grandparenting begins early and life expectancies are long, the role of grandparent is likely to last for three or four decades. As the accompanying Multicultural View box indicates, contact between the generations shows considerable diversity. Women, who tend both to be younger than men when their children are born and to live longer, have a particularly long period of grandparenthood. Frances was forty-six and Tom was fifty-one when their first grandchild was born. Still healthy and vigorous, they have already been grandparents for more than twenty-five years and step-great-grandparents for five years.

Timing affects how people experience the transition to grandparenting. Most Canadian women state that late middle age is the "right time" (Gee, 1991). Very early "off-time" grandparenthood can be very distressing. It is likely to be caused by a teenage pregnancy (which may in itself be upsetting) and provides less time for the grandparent-to-be to prepare for the new role (Norris & Tindale, 1994). It also pushes a person to feel older, a negative feeling in our youth-oriented culture. Social class has a significant impact on timing of grandparenthood. Teenage childbearing is more common among working-class women and, after several generations, can produce a grandmother in her late twenties and a great-grandmother in her forties. Linda Burton (Burton & Bengtson, 1985) found that many very young African American grandmothers rejected the role of grandmother and shifted the responsibilities to the great-grandmother. These young great-grandmothers assumed responsibility for their great-grandchild and their adolescent granddaughter (the child's mother), as well as for their own aging parents. When grandparenting is on time, the transition is typically a positive experience for the older couple and one that is likely to reinforce the connections between the two older generations as they both form attachments to the new generation.

Grandparents as a Family Resource   Families generally view grandparents as a valuable resource, although the ways that resource is called on depends on the family's circumstances (Bengtson et al., 1990). Grandparents help by just being there, providing a sense of family continuity and family history. In times of crises in the lives of children, such as divorce, widowhood, teenage pregnancy, or prolonged unemployment, grandparents frequently provide substantial assistance to their adult children and become more involved in the daily lives of their grandchildren. When the crises pass, the adult children are likely to resume fuller responsibility. For example, when Frances and Tom's younger daughter's marriage broke up, their granddaughter was only two months old. Lauren moved back into the parental home with baby Rachel. Frances became Rachel's caregiver while Lauren worked and found her emotional balance. Rachel was already in first grade by the time Lauren remarried and moved in with her new husband. By then the bonds between grandparents and grandchild were very strong. Frances and Tom have also provided financial assistance to a married adult son out of work, after-school and vacation care for grandchildren, and care for grandchildren too sick to attend school.

In most respects, grandmothers and grandfathers view their relationships with their grandchildren similarly, but some gender differences exist (Thomas, 1995). Both expressed a similar sense of responsibility toward the grandchild, similar feelings of centrality of the relationship in their own lives, similar feelings that the relationship permitted reinvolvement with their past, and placed similar value on sharing wisdom with the grandchild. Grandmothers reported greater satisfaction from these relationships than did grandfathers; grandfathers placed greater stress on generational extension of the family and indulging grandchildren than did grandmothers. Jeanne Thomas (1995) interprets her results as being in keeping with the

A Multicultural View

Diversity in Intergenerational Families

Contemporary Americans have fewer children and live longer and thus spend more years in intergenerational families than did earlier generations (Bengtson et al., 1990). Families have changed structurally, too. As couples have fewer children, young people have fewer aunts, uncles, and cousins. As family members live longer, young people are more likely to know their grandparents, great-grandparents, and even great-great-grandparents. "Individuals are now more likely to grow older in four- or even five-generation families, spend an unprecedented number of years in family roles such as grandparenthood, and be part of a more complex and varied web of intergenerational family ties" (Burton, 1992b). These changes have produced the **beanpole family structure**, which has more generations but fewer people in each generation. Authors Robert and Michele Hoffnung, for example, grew up with twenty-two aunts and uncles and twenty-three first cousins. They have one brother. The three Hoffnung siblings have, respectively, one, three, and two children. Their children have many relatives in the two generations ahead of them, but few in their own generation. Robert and Michele were born into a three-generational family; their grandchildren are likely to be born into four generational families on the Hoffnung side and perhaps five on the other side.

Declining birth rates have produced similar changes in family structure around the world, with the exception of sub-Saharan Africa (Caldwell & Caldwell, 1990). In

India, for example, conditions that tend to discourage couples from having large families include the general scarcity of goods and services, limited opportunities for a good education and subsequent employment, and the dowry-dominated marriage market (Ramu, 1991). Social policy, such as the one-child policy in China, has also contributed to a decline in births and an increase in the beanpole family structure in Asia.

Intergenerational bonds show considerable diversity among contemporary families, reflecting gender, ethnic, and social class differences. Four social characteristics above and beyond individual circumstances and choices predict interaction among American family members (Bengtson et al., 1990). First, gender matters. Daughters tend to interact more frequently with their parents than do sons, and middle-aged daughters assume the responsibilities of kinkeepers (Rossi & Rossi, 1990). Second, marital status of both generations predicts contact. Widowhood brings more frequent contact with children, and unmarried children have more contact with parents (Lopata, 1973). Third, social class seems to have an impact. Working-class children have more contact with parents than do white-collar children, in part because they live closer to home. Fourth, ethnic or racial differences affect contact. Hispanics show the highest levels of interaction, while African Americans and whites are quite similar (Mitchell & Register, 1984). In a comparison of African American, white, and Mexican American grand-

earlier experiences of men and women. Grandmothers enjoy the continuity of family experiences, while grandfathers are concerned with continuing the family line. Grandfathers' indulgence of their grandchildren "may reflect male nurturance and expressivity of middle and later adulthood" (p. 191).

Grandparents as Surrogate Parents   When their children are unable to act as parents, grandparents are called on to become surrogate parents. In 1990, 5 percent of children in the United States lived with grandparents without their parents present in the household (Atchley, 1994). This is more frequent among African American families (13 percent of children) and Hispanics (6 percent) than among whites (3 percent) (Strom et al., 1995). Margaret Jendrek (1992) found that in a largely white sample of thirty-six grandparents (average age fifty-six) with formal custody of their grandchildren, emotional problems, drug addiction, mental problems, and alcohol abuse were the factors that prevented their children from doing the parenting. Linda Burton (1992a) studied African American grandparents who were parenting their grandchildren and found that drug addiction was a leading cause. In addition to substance abuse, violence, incarceration, and AIDS are major factors that have brought grandchildren into their grandparents' care.

The pain endured by middle-aged parents whose adult children have these problems is one of the difficulties of surrogate parenting (discussed in the Perspectives box on page 552). In ethnographic studies of African American grandparents who were surrogate parents, Linda Burton and Cynthia DeVries (1992) found that the role was associated with both challenges and rewards. The grandparents had

parents, Vern Bengtson (1985) found that Mexican American grandparents had many more grandchildren and reported higher levels of contact and more satisfaction from that contact.

We see, then, that although family structures are changing as fertility and mortality rates change, a great deal of diversity remains in family relationships.

Beanpole families, with many generations but few people in each generation, have become prevalent as people around the world have fewer children and live longer. The Chinese one child policy contributes to this trend.

many other responsibilities: they were often caring for adults who were drug addicted and/or elderly relatives as well as the grandchildren. This left them no time for their personal needs. On the other hand, they reported enjoying the opportunity to parent again, the companionship, and love, and saw being needed by their grandchildren as the reason for living. Burton (1992a) found that all of the African American grandparents who were surrogate parents reported one or more stressful outcomes, such as feeling "depressed and anxious" most of the time, smoking more than ever before, drinking heavily, or having heightened medical problems. "The rewards of caregiving did not entirely offset these negative outcomes" (p. 750).

Effectiveness of Grandparents   In a study designed to assess the performance and effectiveness of African American and white grandparents, Robert Strom and his colleagues (1995) selected 204 white and 204 African American grandparents from churches and senior centers. White grandmothers (74 percent) and grandfathers (26 percent) were mostly from middle-class backgrounds, while African American grandmothers (79 percent) and grandfathers (21 percent) reported substantially lower annual incomes. Strom and associates also selected 470 grandchildren, 175 white and 295 African American. The seven-to-eighteen-year-olds were not relatives of the grandparents in the sample but came from families of similar income levels. Grandparents were asked to choose one grandchild to think about while completing the questionnaire. Grandchildren were asked to choose a particular grandparent and describe how that grandparent performed his or her role. Each participant was asked to complete the Grandparent Strengths and Needs Inventory, which had questions about six areas: satisfaction, success, teaching, difficulty, frustration, and information needs. There were separate forms of the inventory for the adults and the children.

Both groups of grandparents had self-perceptions that were favorable overall, but the African Americans scored higher than the whites in each of the six areas. African Americans grandparents saw teaching as their greatest strength, and African American grandchildren agreed. African American grandchildren saw their grandparents as needing improvement in the way they handled difficulties, coped with frustrations, and understood what it is like to be growing up today. White grandchildren scored their grandparents higher in each of these areas than did African American grandchildren. Regardless of ethnicity, grandparents who spent the most time with their grandchildren scored themselves as being more effective, and so did the grandchildren. Both age groups indicated that more African American grandparents (72 percent) spent five or more hours a month with their grandchildren than did white grandparents (30 percent). Older African American grandparents (age sixty and over) and younger white grandparents (under age sixty) regarded themselves as more effective in their role. African American grandchildren considered their older grandparents to be more successful and more influential, while white grandchildren considered their younger grandparents to be more effective. Grandchildren of both races considered their grandmothers to be more effective in teaching and their grandfathers to be better at coping with frustration.

The Strom et al. study is a good example of why we must be cautious in interpreting racial differences. Race/ethnicity and social class are confounded in the study (African American grandparents and grandchildren were from families with lower incomes than their white counterparts), as they often are in real life. Social class has an impact on family structure in several ways. First, it is related to patterns of childbearing; working-class families are more likely to have teenage childbearing, whereas upper-middle-class families are more likely to have delayed childbearing. This means working-class grandparents more likely to be called on to help raise their grandchildren and, as a result, to have more contact with them. Second, working-class families are more likely to have children who need help because of unemployment or underemployment, so grandparents are more likely to be involved. Third, middle-class children are more likely to move away from their parents' home, so contact between the generations is more limited. Another confound in the study is that significantly more white grandchildren lived in two-parent families than did African American grandchildren. Since marital status is an important factor in contact between the generations, the fact that more African American custodial parents were single may be the reason for more contact between the grandparents and grandchildren. Race/ethnicity may be an additional factor, but it is not possible to verify this from the Strom et al. study, and other studies have failed to show this relationship (Mitchell & Register, 1984; Bengtson, 1985).

Aging Parents

As middle-aged adults become grandparents, their own parents are likely to be reaching late adulthood. Middle-aged adults and their aging parents report high levels of regard, closeness, warmth, and satisfaction with their interactions (Atchley, 1994; Rossi & Rossi, 1990). This seems to be especially true of African American and Hispanic families (Bengtson et al., 1990). Mothers and daughters are more likely to be close than any other family combination. In a study of the patterns of intergenerational contact among parents over sixty-five years old who were not in any particular need of help, Glenna Spitze and John Logan (1990) analyzed 8,516 sets of responses to a national health survey. They found that daughters telephoned and visited their parents more often than sons did. More highly educated aging par-

The relationship of this middle-aged daughter and her mother reflects the closeness, warmth, and satisfaction characteristic of connections between middle-aged adults and their aging parents.

ents had less contact with their children. Older and less healthy unmarried parents and married parents with more needs experienced more contact. Those who lived farthest from a child had less contact and fewer visits and telephone calls. Unmarried mothers were visited somewhat more often and called significantly more than married parents.

Still-healthy aging parents tend to provide the most financial and emotional support to their children (Bengtson et al., 1990). Parents seem to give to their children in one way or another as long as they are able. When adult children have stressful problems, older parents often assume responsibility by providing, for example, care for developmentally disabled adults, housing and financial assistance for divorcing adult children, and emotional support for middle-aged widowed children (Atchley, 1994). Donna Hoyert (1991) examined intergenerational household and financial aid flows between adult children and older parents and found that young-old parents (under age eighty) tended to give more aid, while old-old parents (over age eighty) tended to receive more aid. The aging parents who gave aid tended to be middle to upper income, white, and married. The adult children they aided tended to be young adults, particularly previously married daughters and sons and never-married daughters. Adult children tended to aid aging mothers who were older, low income, widowed, or divorced. African American adult children were more likely to provide both household aid and financial aid to their parents. Mexican American older parents expected more aid from their adult children than did white parents and were more likely to be disappointed with the aid they received (Markides & Krause, 1986).

When aging parents become frail, middle-aged adult children are second only to spouses in providing care. Gender plays an important role in family caregiving; parental care falls primarily on a particular daughter as principal caregiver, if there is a daughter (Brody, 1990; Cicirelli, 1992). Daughters not only are more likely than sons to provide assistance but are also likely to provide a different type of assistance. Daughters are more likely than sons to help with household chores, such as food preparation and laundry, and personal care tasks that require daily "hands-on" assistance (Montgomery, 1992). Sons are more likely to perform home repair and maintenance tasks. When sons are primary caregivers, they are more likely to be managers of care rather than direct providers. Never-married and widowed daughters, who are likely to have the fewest competing family roles, provide the largest proportions of care themselves, while married, remarried, and divorced or separated daughters have informal and paid helpers (Brody et al., 1994). Employed daughters provide as much shopping, transportation, household maintenance, emotional support, and service management as do nonworking daughters but provide somewhat less personal care and help with cooking, with the reduction being offset by purchased services (Brody et al., 1987).

Joyce Warshow (1991) sees special problems for midlife lesbians with aging mothers. As she points out, the "unmarried" daughter has historically been considered the best candidate for caregiving. While this may be an enormous burden for any single woman to integrate with her career and friendship network or intimate relationships, a lesbian daughter faces the additional issue of whether the parent accepts her lifestyle and her partner and whether the partner accepts the need for caregiving.

Raymond Coward and Jeffrey Dwyer (1990) interviewed 683 caregiving sons and daughters who were part of a large national survey. Participants were grouped according to the nature of their sibling group—single-gender, mixed-gender, and only children—to determine the effects of gender composition of sibling group on parental caregiving. Sons from all three sibling groups were less likely to provide parent care or to be the primary caregiver than daughters were. Sons from families with no available sisters who provided care, however, provided as many hours of care as did daughters from families where no brothers were available. Only in mixed-gender sibling groups did daughters provide significantly more hours of care than did sons. Since mixed-gender sibling groups are the most frequent, daughters were providing the majority of care.

Siblings

Sibling relationships are special because they are among age peers, meaning they are longer lasting, more egalitarian, more sociable, and more like friendships than other family relationships (Connidis, 1992). As children, siblings are in daily contact and share a sense of family belonging. As young adults, they tend to go their separate ways and contact is likely to be the most limited. During the period when young adults are establishing their own homes siblings may not see one another very much, but they find communication easy when they do get together. Two-thirds report feeling close or very close to the sibling with whom they have the most contact (Cicirelli, 1980). During middle adulthood, when children are leaving home, siblings often increase contact and get closer as they face family crises of divorce, illness, or decline of a parent.

Ingrid Connidis (1992) studied how various life transitions changed ties among adult siblings. Sixty sibling pairs (120 respondents) were interviewed separately about marriage, children, divorce, widowhood, and other life events of both the respondent and any of his or her siblings. Respondents ranged in age from twenty years to over eighty. About 40 percent of the respondents reported that marriage, childbearing, maturing children, or their own widowhood had affected their relationships with their siblings. Greater emotional closeness was the most commonly noted effect reported for all transitions except the marriage of the respondent. Marriage led to improved relations but a decline in contact and a reduction in emotional closeness.

Why is marriage different? Often marriage is the reason for moving out of the parental home, in which case it separates siblings and reduces contact. In addition, marriage requires integrating roles and habits from two different families in a way that is mutually acceptable to the couple, which may require some emotional distancing from the spouses' respective siblings. On the other hand, equal numbers of respondents reported that the arrival of children increased or decreased the amount of sibling contact they had. "Understandable factors such as moving farther away,

During middle adulthood, siblings often increase contact and get closer as they face the aging, illness, or decline of a parent.

having new commitments, and having less time accounted for less contact" (Conni-dis, 1992, p. 977). Shifts in contact between siblings did not seem to reflect shifts in emotions. Divorce and widowhood led to closer, more supportive, and more active sibling ties. Siblings often have dormant emotional ties, such as protective-ness and loyalty, that are mobilized by crises. Death or poor health of parents or other family members typically drew siblings closer together and strengthened their ties with one another.

Helping aging parents is a new developmental task for middle-age siblings. Based on clinical work with adult children, Tonti (1988) outlined a series of stages they go through as they face this challenge, as shown in Table 15.6. Most adult chil-dren deny the parent's aging until some critical event, often a health crisis, forces a reappraisal. Increased communication about the parent's situation initially moves the siblings emotionally closer together. As the parent's needs increase to the point where the children need to provide more care, one sibling assumes the role of pri-mary caregiver. As the parent becomes more frail, he or she may move in with the primary caregiver. Finally, when the parent's needs become more intense, the parent may be transferred to a long-term care facility.

Parental caregiving arrangements can be a source of conflict for middle-aged siblings. Sarah Matthews and Tena Rosner (1988) found that about half of the fam-ilies they studied experienced such conflict, although much of this conflict stemmed from events of the past and had longer histories than did the caregiving responsibil-ities. Brothers and sisters often have a backlog of tensions that current issues can reawaken. The current source of conflict tended to center on the issue of whether or not a sibling had met her or his filial responsibilities. Elaine Brody (1990) found that 30 percent of principal caregivers, 40 percent of their sisters, and 6 percent of their brothers reported strain with siblings regarding parent care. Principal caregivers had difficulty with their siblings not doing their fair share, while other

TABLE 15.6 *Stages in Sibling Response to Parent's Aging*
Based on clinical work with adult children, Tonti (1988) outlined a series of stages they go through as they face the challenge of helping their aging parents.

1. Denial	Adult children deny the age-related changes in their parent and continue to count on the parent's assistance as they have all their lives.

Health or Other Crisis Forces Reappraisal

2. Increased sibling communication	Siblings agree to monitor and/or provide assistance for parent.
3. Primary caregiver emerges	One sibling assumes the role of primary caregiver.
4. Coresidence with primary caregiver	The parent moves in with the primary caregiver.
5. Long-term care	The parent needs such comprehensive care that a long-term facility is chosen and the parent is moved.

Source: Based on Tonti (1988).

siblings were critical of the caregiver's performance. When the parent dies, siblings can be both a comfort and a source of unresolved old conflicts (Dane, 1989).

What Do You Think?

Given your gender, what benefits and costs might you expect (or have you experienced) in your relationships with your family during middle adulthood? How would those benefits and costs differ for a sibling of the other gender?

BEREAVEMENT

Parental death has become a normative feature of midlife; more than half of American women between ages forty and sixty will experience the death of one or both parents (Scharlach & Fuller-Thomson, 1994). No matter what our age, a parent's death involves many emotions because of the intensity and uniqueness of the parent-child relationship. The child in each of us may feel abandoned in losing a parent, our first deep attachment. **Bereavement**, the process of getting over another person's death, elicits feelings of being alone or unattached, memories of earlier losses, guilt over unresolved conflicts or imagined wrongs, and questions concerning our purpose in life. Roslyn was forty-three years old when her mother died. She was divorced and had two young children. Her mother had always been healthy and seemed very young at age sixty-nine, when she became ill and died within six months. This six months of warning enabled the mother to make provisions for her husband, children, and grandchildren and allowed Roslyn to spend time with her mother sharing feelings and providing mutual support. Nonetheless, when her mother died Roslyn felt orphaned. In her grief, she felt as sorry for herself being left without her mother as she did for her mother who had died.

Mourning for One's Parents

According to Barbara Dane (1989), the mourning middle-aged sons and daughters undergo entails three tasks: stocktaking, reminiscence of harsh and meaningful memories, and internalization and passage. Each of these tasks focuses on a different aspect of the child's relationship to the deceased parent. Stocktaking involves exploration of changes caused by the parent's death. For Roslyn that included the loss of her mother's kinkeeper function, which kept her in touch with the extended family. It included the loss of her mother's grandparenting role with her children. It

Parental death has become a normative feature of midlife. Getting over a parent's death often provides an impetus to resolve midlife developmental tasks and promotes maturity, responsibility, and generativity.

also included an increased sense of responsibility for her aging father and a better financial situation due to a small inheritance from her mother.

The second task, reminiscence of harsh and meaningful memories, involves reviewing memories that were wonderful and positive as well as those that were harsh and unfulfilling. Roslyn's initial memories were all positive; she would dream of earlier times when she felt totally cared for and loved by her mother. Part of the grieving process is to explore the ambivalent feelings about the deceased parent, which provides comfort and encourages growth. When a person clings only to the good memories, there is denial that every relationship involves some conflict (Weizman & Kamm, 1985). For adult children who have experienced a difficult relationship with their parent, angry, hostile, or resentful memories are the first ones they experience. Mourning occurs for the disappointments in the relationship as well as for the death. It is still necessary to find the good memories to be able to deal with the total relationship.

The third task of bereavement, internalization and passage, involves discussion about the present without denying the past. In this task, the adult child attains satisfaction with having known the deceased parent and sees herself or himself as conveying the internalized values of that parent in her or his own middle-aged life. Holding onto the values and ideals by which your parent lived provides nurturance. Remembering your parent's wisdom and errors in parenting can bring both laughter and tears and keep your parent nurturing you after he or she has died. Roslyn found herself seeing similarities with her mother in her appearance, her parenting style, her political commitments, and her devotion to her brothers and extended family. Acknowledging these similarities to herself and to her children made her feel that her mother was still with her symbolically.

Bereavement and Growth

Bereavement for a parent during middle age may promote personal growth. Parental death often provides an impetus to resolve midlife developmental tasks and promotes age-appropriate levels of maturity, responsibility, and generativity (Douglas, 1990/1991; Scharlach & Fredriksen, 1993). Based on interviews with eighty-three middle-aged adult children (ages thirty-five to sixty) who had lost a parent in the previous five years, Andrew Scharlach and Karen Fredriksen (1993) found that most respondents reported a greater sense of personal maturity. They spoke of "feeling more autonomous, more self-reliant, and more responsible for themselves and others. Respondents also reported increased awareness of the eventuality of their own deaths, often leading to a reevaluation of personal priorities, significant changes in career plans and personal relationships, and modifications in religious practices" (pp. 314–315). These changes are consistent with the midlife developmental theories of Gould, Grant, and Levinson that we examined earlier.

Joan Douglas (1991) interviewed forty midlife adult children (ages thirty-five to fifty-five) who had lost a parent as an adult. She also found that the parent's death was followed by a time of upheaval and, for most of the sample, a change in outlook on life. Issues of mortality, moving to the head of the line, loss and finality, and feeling alone and orphaned were common. "Some said they grew up, that the deaths had liberated them to become more independent and more themselves," and two-thirds "spoke of positive changes in other relationships" (p. 134). While there was loss, from the loss had come "new beginnings" (p. 134). The initial reactions to grief that precede these new beginnings can be emotionally and physically challenging.

Reactions to Grief

Initial grief reactions to parental death include a substantial increase in psychological distress (for example, difficulty sleeping) and a reduced sense of personal mastery (for example, finding it hard to keep up with normal activities). Unresolved grief reactions include depression, thoughts of suicide, and other psychiatric symptoms (Scharlach & Fuller-Thomson, 1994). In a study of initial and residual grief reactions in 220 adult children ages thirty-five to sixty, Scharlach (1991) found that primary factors contributing to both kinds of grief were the expectedness of the parent's death and the extent of filial autonomy. Expected deaths allow for preparatory grief and reduce the impact of the immediate loss. Adult children who have achieved mature relationships with their parents are less vulnerable when the parent dies than adult children who still look primarily to the parent for validation and support. Other factors that contributed to grief reactions were the respondent's age for initial reaction to the mother's death, with younger adults having more grief reaction, and gender for initial reaction to the father's death, with daughters having more grief reaction. Table 15.7 shows the resources middle-aged children considered helpful in coping with their parent's death.

Because society does not support adults' overreacting to the loss of a loved one, many adults deny the impact of the loss and express their feelings of pain through

TABLE 15.7 *Resources Considered Helpful in Coping with Parent's Death*
Scharlach and Fuller-Thomson (1994) found that having these resources was considered helpful in relieving the psychological distress that accompanies the initial grief reaction to a parent's death.

	Mother's Death (n = 72)	Father's Death (n = 66)
Friends	79%	75%
Peer whose parent had died	77	78
Family	76	66
Spouse or partner	73	69
Work	71	75
Religion	61	55

Source: Adapted from Schanlach & Fuller-Thomson (1994).

physical symptoms. Andrew Scharlach and Esme Fuller-Thomson (1994) found that 40 percent of their middle-aged respondents who had lost a parent one to two years earlier reported experiencing physical reactions, including poorer overall health, physical illness, and fatigue. Using survey data from a large national sample, Wesley Perkins and Lynne Harris (1990) compared personal health status reports for young, middle-aged, and older adults who had and had not experienced familial deaths within the last five years. Personal health status of the respondents was assessed on the basis of three questions: subjective assessment of health, relative satisfaction with health, and whether they had been hospitalized or disabled in the past year. Figure 15.3 shows Perkins and Harris's comparisons of each age group for each of the three personal health measures. As you can see, neither young adults nor older adults exhibited much evidence of a relationship between bereavement in the last five years and current health. Among the middle-aged adults, however, Perkins and Harris found significant differences in reported health. All three health measures indicated poorer health among the bereaved (loss) and the nonbereaved (no loss) respondents in their middle years. When the middle-aged respondents' bereavement status and health reports were broken down by the four types of familial deaths, Perkins and Harris found that the negative effect came primarily from the loss of a sibling or a sibling-in-law and the loss of a spouse.

Why would the death of a family member, particularly a sibling and a spouse, have more of an impact on the health of a middle-aged adult than on younger or older adults? Perkins and Harris suggest that younger adults may be protected by their greater physical capacities, which buffer them against the strain of readjustment. This is consistent with our discussion in Chapter 12 of how stress and health-compromising behaviors may exhibit little effect on health in early adulthood because the damage does not reach a critical threshold. Young adults may also feel invulnerable to death because of their youth. Older adults, on the other hand, are likely to be better prepared for the death of other family members as they prepare for their own deaths and as their friends experience similar losses. Death is "on time" in late adulthood. Middle-aged adults may have a similar buffer concerning the death of a parent that is "on time," but they have neither of these protective mechanisms in the case of death of siblings and spouses, who are more likely to be members of their own generation. The deaths of spouses and siblings are most likely to affect their

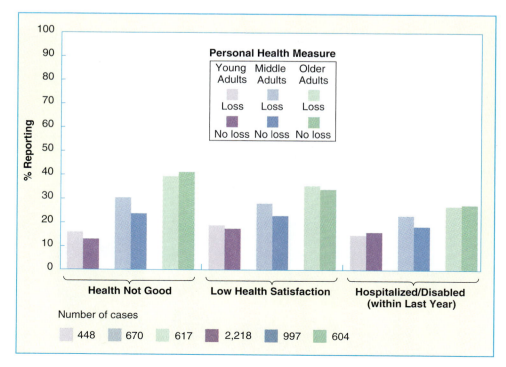

FIGURE 15.3
Percentage of Young (20 to 39), Middle-Aged (40 to 59), and Older (60 to 79) Adults Indicating Poor Personal Health, by Bereavement Status (Familial Loss or No Loss Experience in Last Five Years)
Perkins and Harris (1990) assessed personal health status of respondents on the basis of three questions: subjective assessment of health, relative satisfaction with health, and whether they had been hospitalized or disabled in the past year. Only among the middle-aged subjects did they find differences between the loss and no-loss groups on all three health measures.
Source: Adapted from Perkins & Harrris (1990).

daily lives on the one hand and remind them of their own mortality on the other. We return to the topic of bereavement when we discuss death and dying in Chapter 18.

What Do You Think?

In addition to loss, bereavement brings impetus for growth. What developmental experiences have you had that combined loss with positive growth?

LEISURE

We have seen that middle age is a time of many changes: physical changes, cognitive changes, occupational changes, changes in family relationships, changes in priorities, and changes in perspective on mortality. As a result of many of these changes, midlife adults often feel less constrained than they did in their early adulthood. Like Marcia, they find their children need them less, their parents are still relatively healthy, their work has plateaued, and they can make choices about what to do with their time. **Leisure,** according to John Neulinger (1981), is choosing whatever activities one enjoys and participating in them at one's own pace. Marcia, for example, took on a new writing project and increased her exercise activities. To many other individuals these new activities sound like work rather than leisure, which illustrates a difficulty in defining leisure.

The same activities have different meanings for different individuals. Michael Jordan plays basketball for a living, while Bill, whom you met in Chapter 13, plays basketball for recreation. Bill writes and edits for a living, while many individuals write prose or poetry for recreation. Although both Michael Jordan and Bill enjoy many aspects of their work, they are constrained to doing it on a schedule that others determine and to get a paycheck. Leisure, then, is freedom from constraint. It includes activities chosen freely and done for intrinsic reward (enjoyment). In contrast, *job* is activity that is highly constrained and done for extrinsic reward (pay). Obviously, some activities people do as work also give them pleasure. Ballplayers such as Michael Jordan usually love to play ball. Their work is not pure leisure

Choice of leisure activities during middle adulthood often result from preferences that have been learned during childhood and early adulthood. When leisure activities are shared, as in this family, patterns of leisure pass from one generation to the next.

(because of the constraints), but it is not pure job either (because of the enjoyment). People are most satisfied with their jobs when the jobs include larger aspects of leisure, namely discretion over time and intrinsically rewarding activities. People are least satisfied when the job is pure job (no discretion over time and all extrinsic reward) (Neulinger, 1981). Notice that none of these definitions are based on the amount of physical energy expended. Playing tennis works up a sweat and answering the phone is physically easy, but playing tennis is leisure if you choose to do it in your free time and answering the phone is job if you earn a living as a receptionist.

Do leisure activities change in middle adulthood? Cross-sectional studies provide some evidence that as people enter middle age, their view of leisure shifts (Kelly et al., 1987). They seek out new avenues for gratification and affirmation as their roles change. By shifting some of her focus from her family to her new writing project, for example, Marcia expects validation to come from this new activity. As people age, they tend to shift from activities requiring physical exertion and high-intensity involvement to more sedentary, moderate-intensity activities (Cutler & Hendricks, 1990; Iso et al., 1994). Young adults play more sports and do more running with friends, for example, whereas older adults play more golf and more cards. But Marcia has started to lift weights at age forty-seven, and Tom began running every morning only after retiring at age seventy. Perhaps today's health-conscious midlife and older adults will establish new trends for leisure, at least while they remain healthy. Once again, remember the key limitation to cross-sectional studies: because they have different individuals in each age group, they cannot separate cohort effects from age-related changes.

Longitudinal studies, on the other hand, provide some evidence of continuity in level and types of leisure activities over the life course. A pattern of frequent childhood leisure participation is associated with higher levels as an adult (Cutler & Hendricks, 1990). Adult leisure activities have been found to be evenly divided between those begun during childhood and those begun during adulthood. The longitudinal studies have most often been retrospective or of limited duration, which may account for the high rate of continuity they have found.

How do socioeconomic status (SES), race/ethnicity, and gender affect leisure activities? Higher SES is associated with greater leisure involvement (Lawton, 1985). Individuals in professional occupations engage in a greater variety of activities and participate more frequently in activities that require a certain expense of energy (Burrus-Bammel & Bammel, 1985). Higher income, higher educational level, and higher occupational attainment all provide more options for leisure. Racial and ethnic minorities have been relatively worse off than the general population on all of these dimensions of SES and therefore have had more limited leisure options. In an examination of the relationship among race, leisure preferences, and class, Myron Floyd and his colleagues (1994) found similarities in leisure preferences between African Americans and whites who defined themselves as middle class, but leisure preferences diverged among those who defined themselves as poor or working class, especially women. Whites expended more energy in leisure-time physical activity than African Americans, but once again SES played a role (Folsom et al., 1991). Leisure time physical activity increased with level of formal education; the largest racial differences were found between those who had a high school diploma or less. These differences in leisure activities were likely the result of both differences in what people are taught to prefer and differences in financial resources. Little difference has been found in membership in voluntary organizations between whites and ethnic/racial minorities (Jackson et al., 1990).

Gender also affects the leisure activities people choose. Women are more likely than men to engage in social and home-based activities and in cultural activities such as attending plays, concerts, or art exhibitions. Men, in contrast, are more likely to be involved in exercise and outdoor recreation, which is a continuation of the childhood patterns discussed in Chapter 8. Men also attend spectator sports and travel more than women do (Atchley, 1994). In a study of nearly thirty-three thousand adult women, Kimberly Yeager and her associates (1993) found that 30 percent of white women and 45 percent of African American women had no leisure time physical activity. While these percentages decreased for both groups as their SES increased, controlling for SES did not eliminate the ethnic difference in sedentary behavior. Girls and young women are now being encouraged to engage in sports, exercise, and outdoor recreation. Since choices of activities result from preferences that have been learned by trying the alternatives available in childhood and early adulthood, these changes may very well alter the pattern of leisure activities for future cohorts of middle-aged and older adults.

Involvement in leisure activities seems to promote psychological well-being. The number and types of activities appear to be less important than the degree of satisfaction derived from them. People who spend time doing what they wish have higher life satisfaction than those who desire to change their allocation and use of time (Seleen, 1982). Once adults establish an activity pattern, it tends to persist. Middle adulthood, when family and work are less demanding than in early adulthood, affords an opportunity to expand leisure pursuits. Positive attitudes toward leisure are associated with more positive attitudes toward retirement, consideration of early retirement, and more thought given to retirement (Cutler & Hendricks, 1990). Pursuing leisure activities that give satisfaction, then, is good preparation for some of the life changes associated with late adulthood.

What Do You Think?

Consider with several of your classmates the leisure activities you engage in. What are they? When did you begin them? Are you likely to pursue them as you get older? In what ways do you think they will change? Why?

PREPARING FOR LATE ADULTHOOD

While many aspects of adulthood are continuous, aging changes activities and perspectives in several predictable ways. We have seen how the demands of childrearing decrease as parents launch their children into adulthood. We have seen how more leisure time results from that change in the family life cycle and from occupational changes in mid- and late-career stages (see Chapter 14). We have seen how the death of a parent enhances awareness of one's own mortality. With late adulthood comes the additional changes of retirement and even less need on the part of adult children for assistance. Physical changes occur as well (a focus of the next chapter), and death approaches. Beginning preparation for these new challenges in middle adulthood is a good way to face them. Richard Schulz (1978) found that the more opportunities and time people have to prepare for stressful events such as death, the more they will feel in control and the less they will feel helpless and anxious. Taking more responsibility for one's own life increases the middle-aged adult's sense of mortality, which leads to specific concrete behaviors such as drafting a will or making funeral arrangements (Scharlach & Fredriksen, 1993).

Wills and Advance Directives

A *will* is a legal document that can distribute property, appoint a guardian for children, provide for pets, provide for funeral and burial, and appoint an executor to oversee distribution of property. Although many people think one needs a will only if one has property, that is not necessarily so. Adults with personal wishes that run contrary to those of their blood families or with lifestyles that are unconventional can arrange for after-death choices, such as cremation rather than burial, and provide for nonkin loved ones. If you are not married but cohabit, you will need a will to ensure that your property goes to your partner rather than your blood kin, if that is what you desire. This is a special problem for lesbians and gay men who do not have the legal right to marry and may have families that do not accept their partners' legitimacy (Ettelbrick, 1991). Because wills serve many functions, people write wills at all stages of adulthood and revise them as life circumstances change.

An **advance directive** is a legal document specifying what medical care can be given in the event the person becomes unable to make or communicate his or her decisions. They allow an individual to arrange to die with dignity and to avoid expensive, invasive, and fruitless procedures. Most states have two types of advance directives. The **living will** notifies your physician of your wishes regarding the withdrawal of life-sustaining equipment even if the result is your death (see Figure 15.4 for an example). A living will goes into effect only when you are unable to make or communicate your decision about your medical care *and* when you are in a terminal condition or permanently unconscious. A **durable power of attorney for health care** designates a person to make medical decisions on your behalf other than the withdrawal of life support systems. The designee could decide, for example, whether to change physicians, obtain a second opinion, reject surgery, or provide physical therapy. Once again, designating a person to make health care decisions may be especially important if your choices would differ from those of your blood family or if your closest relationship is one that is not legally recognized.

FLORIDA LIVING WILL

Declaration made this _____ day of _____ ,19 ___ .
I,_____ , willfully and voluntarily make known my desire that my dying not be artificially prolonged under the circumstances set forth below, and I do hereby declare:

If at any time I have a terminal condition and if my attending or treating physician and another consulting physician have determined that there is no medical probability of my recovery from such condition, I direct that life-prolonging procedures be withheld or withdrawn when the application of such procedures would serve only to prolong artificially the process of dying and that I be permitted to die naturally with only the administration of medication or the performance of any medical procedure deemed necessary to provide me with comfort care or to alleviate pain.

It is my intention that this declaration be honored by my family and physician as the final expression of my legal right to refuse medical or surgical treatment and to accept the consequences for such refusal.

In the event that I have been determined to be unable to provide express and informed consent regarding the withholding, withdrawal, or continuation of life-prolonging procedures, I
wish to designate, as my surrogate to carry out the provisions of this declaration:
Name:_____
Address:_____
_____ Zip code: _____
Phone: _____

I wish to designate the following person as my alternate surrogate, to carry out the provisions of this declaration should my surrogate be unwilling or unable to act on my behalf:
Name:_____
Address:_____
_____ Zip code: _____
Phone: _____

Additional instructions (optional):

I understand the full import of this declaration, and I am emotionally and mentally competent to make this declaration.
Signed:_____
Witness 1:_____
Signed:_____
Address:_____
Witness 2:_____
Signed:_____
Address:_____

FIGURE 15.4
The Living Will
Note: This is an example of a living will for the state of Florida. Please contact Choice in Dying at 200 Varick Street, New York, NY 10014, (212) 366-5540, to receive a copy of appropriate advance directives for your state.
Reprinted courtesy of Choice in Dying

Middle age is the optimal time to make decisions about long-term care because, on the one hand, you are not facing the immediate crisis of an illness and, on the other hand, you are thinking about these issues as you and your friends assume responsibility for your aging parents. As Figure 15.4 shows, the living will requires that you understand the full impact of your decision. Middle adults have the emotional and mental competence to consider and decide on these issues. Public opinion polls show that almost 90 percent of American adults would not want life support systems in place if there were no prospect of recovery, yet fewer than one in five have actually prepared any written advance directive (Moody, 1994). Eric Diamond and his associates (1989) found that supportive counseling regarding planning for terminal illness and death was very helpful in enabling people to specify their wishes.

Retirement Planning

Another developmental task of midlife is planning both financially and psychologically for retirement, one of the normative life events of late adulthood. Midlife is traditionally a time of peak earning years and thus is a time to save a portion of income for the future. As we saw in our discussion of leisure, midlife is also a time for developing interests and activities that can continue after retirement. Individuals who prepare for retirement have a better idea of their retirement needs, more favorable attitudes toward retirement, higher morale, and fewer longings for their jobs once they retire (Teaff & Johnson, 1983). Research indicates that a highly work-committed professional may avoid retirement planning and have difficulties just before and just after retirement (Kilty & Behling, 1985; Richardson & Kilty, 1992).

What Do You Think?

Will your generation be better prepared for late adulthood than your parents' and grandparents' generations? If so, in what ways? If not, why not?

LOOKING BACK/LOOKING FORWARD

In Part Seven, we have focused on the developmental issues of middle adulthood: reassessing goals and priorities, launching children, caring for aging relatives, and preparing for late adulthood. Though these tasks are stage related, they do not occur in each person's life at the same time or in the same way. While some middle-aged adults are celebrating silver anniversaries, others are newly marrying or discovering their gay or lesbian identities, and still others are adjusting to widowhood. While some are launching children and becoming grandparents, others are parenting young children, and still others have no children. More than anything, variety characterizes middle adulthood. Differences in genetic heritage, social and economic resources, and life circumstances mean that age fifty finds some individuals healthy, happily employed, and rich in family relationships; others chronically ill, disappointed in work, and isolated from others; and still others in between these extremes. Many contemporary midlife adults are more physically fit than typical young adults; others face chronic illnesses that push them prematurely into life changes more typical of late adulthood. Middle adulthood is a time of changes, but for some it is just a change in perspective and for others it is a change in daily life due to illness, unemployment, or bereavement. As we turn our focus to the issues of late adulthood in Part Eight, remember that many individuals face some of those issues at younger life stages. As we have said before, there are many different patterns to adult life; when we discuss stages of adulthood, the boundaries are unclear.

SUMMARY OF MAJOR IDEAS

A Multiplicity of Images of Middle Age

1. Contrasting stereotypes of middle age present it as a boring plateau and as a time of inevitable crisis. Perceptions of this stage of life vary by social class, gender, and age.

Crisis or No Crisis?

2. Psychologists also have differing views of midlife. Theorists such as Gould, Vaillant, and Levinson build on Erikson's model of midlife crisis; other researchers find little evidence of crisis; and still others see transition rather than crisis as the normative midlife experience.

3. Personality traits show stability after about age thirty.

4. Gender and class are factors determining whether the transition of midlife will result in crisis. Men are more likely than women to experience a midlife crisis, especially upper-class and well-educated, middle-class men.

Marriage and Divorce

5. There is evidence that middle-aged and older marriages are happier than those in earlier stages of the family life cycle.

6. Although divorce is less frequent in middle adulthood than in early adulthood, it has a significant impact on women, men, and children. For women, especially those with children at home, marital separation is associated with markedly lower economic well-being. For men, it is associated with less contact with their children, even if the children are adults.

Family Relationships

7. Middle age is a time of many family relationships with older and younger generations, which has led to the label the sandwich generation. Gender, race/ethnicity, and SES have an impact on the various relationships.

8. Parenting adolescent children has a large negative impact on the marital relationship.

9. Parents and young adult children have increased interaction and closeness compared to parent-adolescent relationships. Emotional support is a two-way interaction, while material support is generally parent to child, depending on ethnicity and family income.

10. Many young adults remain at home or return home; parental well-being is optimized when children physically move out but remain in close contact.

11. Grandparents are called on to assist in many different ways depending on the SES, race/ethnicity, and circumstances of the family. Grandparents help by just being there, providing regular caregiving, assisting in times of crisis, and becoming surrogate parents.

12. Middle-aged adults generally have warm and satisfying relations with their aging parents, especially in African American and Hispanic families. Daughters have more contact with their parents than sons do. Older, unmarried, and needy parents are visited and called more often.

13. While aging parents are still healthy, they continue to give financial and emotional support if they are able. When they become frail, they tend to receive more support than they give.

14. Daughters typically provide more care for aging parents than do sons.

15. Siblings often increase their adult contact during the middle years in response to children leaving or family crisis, such as illness of a parent.

Bereavement

16. Parental death is a normative feature of midlife and involves many emotions because of the importance of this first deep attachment.

17. In addition to grief, parental death often leads to growth-producing changes in levels of maturity, responsibility, and generativity.

Leisure

18. There is evidence of both continuity and change in leisure activities during midlife, depending on whether the studies are cross-sectional or longitudinal.

19. Higher SES provides more options for leisure; race/ethnicity, and gender are associated with different patterns of leisure activities.

Preparing for Late Adulthood

20. Wills and advance directives enable individuals to take control of after-death choices as well as choices about medical care and life-sustaining equipment in the event of terminal illness or permanent unconsciousness.

21. Midlife is a time to prepare for retirement. Professionals who have high commitment to work tend to avoid retirement planning and adjust less well to retirement.

KEY TERMS

normative life event *(542)*
nonnormative life event *(542)*
generativity versus stagnation *(542)*
midlife crisis *(544)*
trait *(546)*
family life cycle *(550)*
sandwich generation *(556)*
beanpole family structure *(562)*
bereavement *(568)*
leisure *(572)*
advance directive *(575)*
living will *(575)*
durable power of attorney for health care *(575)*

PART EIGHT

Late Adulthood

Late adulthood refers to the years after age sixty. Because of the increasing longevity of our population, which we discuss in Chapter 16, this designation has become too broad to meaningfully describe the wide variety of individuals it encompasses. K. Warner Schaie (1988) likens grouping all individuals "over sixty" to grouping all individuals "under twelve." As we know from the first nine chapters in this book, too much development occurs within the first eleven years of life to meaningfully lump all individuals into one age category. For the same reason, Schaie encourages making a distinction between the young-old (those in their sixties and early seventies), the old-old (those in their late seventies and early eighties), and the very old (those in their late eighties and beyond). It is important to keep in mind the great diversity among elderly individuals.

Although we tend to think of all old people as frail, that stereotype fits only the very-old, and not even all individuals in that category. The young-old are often more like individuals in middle adulthood, except they are more likely to be retired. As we will see in Part Eight, the elderly are a diverse population that can be understood only within the context of their ethnicity, gender, level of education, income, occupational status, family status, and health status. "Many age differences that are reported in the literature, instead of being 'caused' by aging, are more likely to be attributable to differences in demographic characteristics and cohort-specific experiences than to adverse maturational changes" (Schaie, 1988).

16

LATE ADULTHOOD

Physical and Cognitive Development

AGING AND AGEISM

When Mariko came to the United States to visit her first grand-child, she was shocked at how disrespectfully she was treated. Her friends in Tokyo enjoyed caring for their grandchildren and the honor grandparenthood brought them. But during her stay in New York, Mariko felt ignored at best and rudely treated at worst. Age appeared to be seen in a very different light.

Societies differ in their treatment of the elderly. In Japan, old age is revered and chronological age is used as a literal measure of social status (Kimmel, 1988). Sixty-first birthdays are celebrated as a coming of age, much as twenty-first birthdays are celebrated in the United States. In contrast, in the United States elderly people are viewed negatively. This has not always been true, however; the people of early America exalted old age. According to David Hackett Fischer (1977), age bias has changed dramatically in the United States over the past three centuries. As evidence of changing attitudes, he reports that people in the seventeenth and eighteenth centuries tended to represent themselves as older than they really were, whereas in the nineteenth and twentieth centuries people typically represented themselves as younger than their true age. The years between 1770 and 1830 brought a revolution in age relations as the population grew older, most notably because birth rates were decreasing. By the twentieth century, old age was being viewed as a social problem. Fernando Torres-Gil (1992) has called the years from 1930 to 1990 the period of Modern Aging. The Modern Aging period, according to Torres-Gil, brought about the age segregation of the elderly and the delegation of their care to the government, which further contributed to negative attitudes toward elderly people.

On his eighty-fifth birthday, John Kenneth Galbraith, renowned economist, retired economics professor, former economic adviser to government agencies, and U.S. ambassador, reflected on modern attitudes toward old people that he had experienced:

[I]n my youth the sensitivity of the old was greatly respected. One did not emphasize physical and mental decline, inevitable and apparent though these are. Now, I find, they receive daily, even hourly, mention. "*Still* getting that exercise," I hear when I go out for a walk. "*Still* lecturing," I hear when I give a talk. "*Still* writing," many say when I pub-lish a book or even a review. "*Still* interested in politics," I'm told when I show up at a

Focusing Questions

- What historical changes have occurred in the lifespan and in life expectancy, and what further changes can we anticipate?

- What factors affect changes in physical functioning during late adulthood?

- Do health-promoting behaviors change in importance once a person is old?

- What chronic illnesses become common, and how do they affect daily life?

- What are the age-related losses and gains in cognitive functioning?

- In what ways is the aging brain a good example of both the loss and the compensation that are evident during late adulthood?

- What factors influence how retirees adjust to their new life circumstances?

meeting. "*Still* imbibing," when I have a drink. "*Still* that way," someone observes when my eyes are seen to light up on encountering a beautiful woman . . . ." (*Harvard Magazine*, 1994, 96[3], p. 108).

Robert Butler (1993) coined the term *ageism* in 1968 when middle-aged citizens protested the building of a high-rise "luxury" apartment building for the use of elderly poor. **Ageism**, according to Butler, "can be seen as systematic stereotyping of and discrimination against people because they are old, just as racism and sexism accomplish this with skin color and gender." From the very beginning, ageism has been linked to social policy that is seen as potentially discriminatory and unfair in an egalitarian society (Kimmel, 1988). Distributing social services on the basis of age rather than need denies the diversity among people of the same age and promotes discrimination and prejudice. Ageism reflects tension about the growing number of older Americans in the population and the cost of entitlement programs that benefit them, such as social security, Medicare, and Medicaid.

In our society, prejudicial attitudes toward elderly persons abound; more stereotypes exist about old age than about any other period of life. Stereotyped images of the aging and elderly can be positive or negative, but because they are based on general characterizations of "old people" rather than on actual appraisals of individuals, they reflect preconceived notions or prejudices. Anxieties about our own aging contribute to negative attitudes, as do the messages of the media that feed on these anxieties in an attempt to sell creams, pills, cosmetics, and hair colors that promise to make us look and feel younger. Negative stereotypes of elderly people include physical traits such as *slow, feeble*, and *gray-haired*, as well as personality traits such as *cranky* and *repetitive;* positive stereotypes include *sweet, caring, pleasant* and *storytellers* (Shenk & Achenbaum, 1993). Stereotypes such as *wealthy, greedy, dependent, burdensome,* and *idle freeloaders* ignore the diversity of the elderly population (Adamchak, 1993). When college students are asked to describe a particular elderly person, stereotypes break down and the descriptions are often of healthy, active individuals who happen to be older. Unfortunately, it is easy to consider elderly individuals who defy the stereotypes as exceptions while continuing to hold the stereotypes (Shenk & Achenbaum, 1993).

Ageism abounds among professionals as well as in the general population. Nicknames such as "vegetable" or "Gork" ("God only really knows" the basis of the person's symptoms) are part of medical students' everyday vocabulary. Few medical students choose geriatrics as a specialty, and few doctors devote as much energy to their elderly patients as they do to their young patients (Butler, 1993). Clinicians prescribe drug treatments to elderly depressed patients more often than they refer them to psychotherapists because they assume elderly people are too "stuck in their ways" to be introspective (Pasupathi et al., 1995). K. Warner Schaie (1988) describes similar problems of ageism among psychological researchers who assume lowered competence in elderly people and fail to use proper comparison groups in their research. Because the elderly are a heterogeneous group, health status, education, occupational status, gender, and race must be specified and generalizations to other populations made cautiously. Lars Tornstam (1992) criticizes gerontological researchers for their tendency to approach their work from a "misery perspective" (older people as a problem) rather than from a "resource perspective" (older people as a resource). Tornstam points out that the common assumption is that the processes of industrialization and urbanization distanced older people and their children from each other; however, as we saw in Chapter 15, elderly people have close contact with their children.

What Do You Think?

Discuss with your classmates the stereotypes you hold about aging and old people. Where did these attitudes come from? In what ways could negative stereotypes be overcome?

PHYSICAL DEVELOPMENT

Grace, now in her early sixties, has had high blood pressure for twelve years. She walks vigorously at least three times a week, takes medication to control her blood pressure, and tries to limit her intake of salt and fat. She likes to eat and drink, however, so she struggles with the dietary changes. Her career in publishing keeps her happily busy most of the time, although she sometimes feels so stressed that she wonders if she should continue at her current pace. Her husband, Larry, recently retired at age sixty-five. Grace enjoys the intellectual challenge and sociability of her work and fears retirement may lead to mental stagnation and isolation. While Larry has many house and yard projects that occupy him, Grace has always been more outgoing than he. Continuing her current activities seems best for now, although she has begun to think about ways to be active after retirement.

Most elderly individuals continue to be productive contributors to their families and their communities long after retirement, and others never really retire. Vladimir Horowitz performed as a concert pianist in his eighties. In his nineties, George Burns continued to delight audiences and make them laugh. Lena Horne and Katherine Hepburn are examples of elderly women who continued to be attractive and productive well into late adulthood. Pablo Picasso, Charlie Chaplin, and many other public (and private) figures have continued to actively contribute to society in their late adulthood.

LONGEVITY

As we saw in our discussion of physical development in middle adulthood in Chapter 14, the average life expectancy in the United States has gone from forty-seven years in 1900 to seventy-five years today. During the nineteenth and twentieth centuries improvements in diet, sanitation, and medicine contributed to the increase in average life expectancy. Most of the increase has come from the eradication of diseases that caused high infant and child mortality; since World War II, some has come from the control of fatal diseases of adult life, such as influenza and pneumonia. As a result, the young-old group (ages sixty to seventy-four) is eight times larger than in 1900; the old-old (ages seventy-five to eighty-four) group is twelve times larger; and the very-old group (over eighty-five) is twenty-two times larger (American Association of Retired Persons [AARP], 1990).

In addition to getting older, as Figure 16.1 shows, the population of the United States has been getting more diverse during this century. Although never homogeneous, recent immigrants have added Latin American and Asian influences. In 1990, the elderly population was 14 percent nonwhite. Minorities make up a smaller proportion of the elderly population and a larger proportion of the early adult population than do whites because of higher fertility and mortality rates (Hooyman & Kiyak, 1993). Beginning in the early part of the next century, the proportion of minority older adults is expected to increase at a faster rate than whites because so many children will be growing older and mortality rates are decreasing. The faulty stereotype of elderly people as white, middle-class, and part of traditional families will become even harder to maintain.

The growing number of older adults from a wider diversity of backgrounds has resulted in a wide range of economic and social conditions among the elderly. The elderly as a group has made social and economic progress. Poverty levels have

The growing number of older adults from a wider diversity of backgrounds has resulted in a wide range of economic and social conditions among the elderly. White, married, young-old men tend to be the most advantaged, whereas women, minority older people, people living alone and in rural areas, and the very old are the least advantaged.

declined, and median income for people sixty-five and over has increased. But poverty and near-poverty still characterize subgroups of the elderly population, namely women, minority older people, people living alone and in rural areas, and the very old (Torres-Gil, 1992). Married individuals as a group are less likely to be below the poverty level than any of the other marital statuses. The most advantaged segment of the late adult population is employed, married men in their early sixties. The least advantaged is widowed women over seventy-five years old who rely on social security for their incomes. Not surprisingly, SES, which we saw in our discussion of physical development in early adulthood in Chapter 12 as being strongly related to health, affects mortality and morbidity among the elderly.

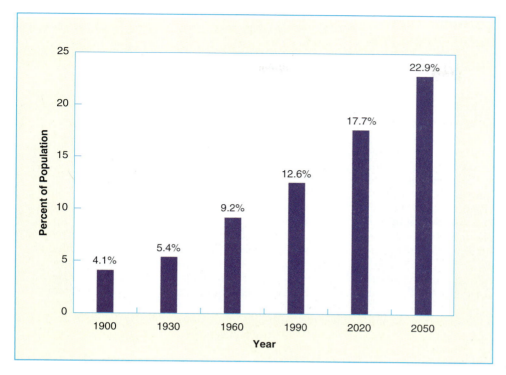

FIGURE 16.1
Growth of Population
Sixty-five Years Old and Over
During the twentieth century, the population of the United States has been getting older. This trend is projected to continue.
Source: U.S. Bureau of the Census (1993).

Mortality

In the late 1960s, after two decades of stability, mortality rates began to fall steadily. Experts attribute these declines to improvements in medical care and drugs for cardiovascular disease and hypertension; wider access to medical care; and improved health behaviors, especially reduced smoking and alcohol consumption, and improved diet and physical fitness. Men, who started out with higher mortality rates, have made larger gains than women, except at advanced ages of seventy-five and above and except for African American and other nonwhite men. Nevertheless, women continue to have longer life expectancies. All age groups have made improvements except the very oldest group (age eighty-five and above) (Verbrugge, 1989a). These data reflect several important dimensions of health in late adulthood: gender, race, and lifestyle improvements.

Gender and Mortality   Table 16.1 shows that though their rates differ, women and men die from the same causes. Men have higher mortality from all the leading causes of death except diabetes mellitus. As we saw in the Chapter 14 discussion of physical development in middle adulthood, many more males die during middle adulthood as a result of cardiovascular and respiratory diseases. Males also die more frequently of chronic liver disease, accidents, suicide, and homicide, all of which are lifestyle related. In late adulthood, the gap between men's and women's mortality rates narrows as the pace of death and disease for older women increases relative to middle-aged women. But the gender gap continues to widen with age for cancer, heart disease, kidney disease, and suicide. As both genders get older and frailer, the body becomes more vulnerable to *septicemia* (infection that has entered the blood stream), pneumonia/influenza, and atherosclerosis, and these rise as causes of death, whereas deaths that are closely related to lifestyle behaviors, such as smoking and drinking, go down because these conditions have already taken their toll at earlier ages.

Race and Mortality   Mortality rates differ between whites and African Americans. In 1990, the life expectancy of a white newborn male was 72.7 years, for an African

A Multicultural View

The Mortality Crossover

While over most of the lifespan African American and Native American populations are at higher risk for mortality and morbidity than whites, at advanced ages these minority populations are more robust. In contrast to any earlier age, if African Americans or Native Americans live to reach eighty, they can expect to outlive their white counterparts. The point at which the death rates and probabilities are reversed and the previously lower white rates become and remain higher than those of African Americans is called the *mortality crossover*. Not all minority populations are similarly affected. Hispanic mortality rates, which are closer to white than African American rates all along, do not reverse themselves in old age. Asian Americans have age-adjusted mortality rates that are consistently lower than those for the general population (Jackson et al., 1990).

Although a couple of explanations for mortality crossover have been proposed, considerable evidence has accumulated for the selective survival thesis (Jackson et al., 1990; Markides, 1989). According to this theory, high-mortality populations experience the deaths of a greater number of the least robust members before they reach old age. This leaves only very hardy individuals at very old ages. In comparison, low-mortality populations have more weak individuals reaching very old ages, and they are more vulnerable.

This leads to the question of why some populations have mortality crossovers and others do not. We know, for example, that males have higher mortality rates than females in middle and early old age (see the Perspectives box on the gender gap in life expectancy in Chapter 14). Why is there no gender mortality crossover? The answer

seems to be that mortality crossover is a result of extreme environmental situations. Different environmental factors affect men and women, as do differences in biology. Women have increased their rate of smoking and their participation in hazardous occupations, narrowing the gender gap in life expectancy. But there is no crossover because women and men are not similarly genetically endowed. Although environmental factors have become more similar, the biological advantage of being female remains.

The mortality crossover shows up among poor populations that experience high mortality in the childhood, adolescent, early adult, and middle adult years. Causes of death among these populations differ from those for more affluent ones. Poor populations tend to die from infectious diseases and accidents, or exogenous causes, whereas affluent populations typically die from cardiovascular disease and cancers, or endogenous causes (Kunitz & Levy, 1989).

The Navajo Indians can serve as an example. Stephen Kunitz and Jerrold Levy (1989) found that heart disease, cancer, and hypertension were all much lower among Navajo than among non-Navajo elderly, yet many external factors have contributed to Navajo high mortality rates. During 1988–1991, the age-adjusted motor vehicle–related death rates for Navajos were fivefold greater than for the total U.S. population (97.9 per 100,000 versus 19.5 per 100,000) and almost three times the rate for all New Mexico residents (35.2 per 100,000). Like other Native Americans and Alaskan Natives, Navajos are at increased risk for motor vehicle–related deaths and injuries, for at least three reasons. First, because many live in rural

TABLE 16.1   *Rank Orders of Causes of Death by Sex*
Although men have higher rates of mortality from most of the leading causes of death, women and men die from the same causes.

	Men 65–74	Men 75 and Over	Women 65–74	Women 75 and Over
Heart disease	1	1	2	1
Cancer	2	2	1	2
Accidents	7	6	7	7
Cerebrovascular disease	4	3	3	3
Chronic obstructive pulmonary diseases	3	4	4	5
Pneumonia, influenza	6	5	6	4
Suicide	9	8	9	9
Chronic liver disease	8	9	8	8
Diabetes mellitus	5	5	5	6

Source: National Center for Health Statistics (1993).

Because Navajo Indians have high mortality rates from external factors such as accidents and infectious disease, the hardy elderly who survive, like this couple in their eighties, are likely to outlive their white counterparts.

as drinking and driving and not wearing safety belts. In addition, because alcohol is not legally available in the Navajo Nation, those residents who drink may drive long distances while impaired (Safety-Belt Use, 1993).

The recent news about the hantavirus, or "Navajo flu," is an example of an infectious disease causing disproportionate premature death among the Navajo. Mortality from this respiratory ailment in confirmed patients has exceeded 75 percent, frequently in previously healthy adults between twenty and forty years of age (Nichol et al., 1993). Non-Navajo populations are not genetically immune to the virus, but their life circumstances are less likely to bring them into contact with it. The Navajo live in rural Arizona and New Mexico (the Four Corners area), where there is a high deer mouse population. The hantavirus is an airborne virus spread in deer mouse droppings and saliva.

According to the selective survival thesis, exogenous factors such as these contribute to the high mortality rates of poor minority populations. Poverty and powerlessness create life circumstances that predispose people to the highest rates of social dysfunction, the highest rates of morbidity and mortality, the lowest access to primary care, and little or no access to primary preventive programs (Braithwaite & Lythcott, 1989). Only the hardiest survive to be very old. Since these populations are initially similar to the general population with regard to genetic endowment for longevity, these hardy elderly are likely to live longer than the mix of survivors in the general population (Clark et al., 1993; Markides, 1989).

areas, their access to advanced emergency medical care may be limited when a crash occurs, and as a consequence, treatment for injuries may be delayed. Second, they may travel more on isolated two-lane highways and ride unprotected in the backs of open pickup trucks, placing them at higher risk for injury if a crash occurs. Third, this population is younger than the total U.S. population (median age twenty-three years versus thirty years); young people are at higher risk for injury because of risk-taking behaviors such

American male 64.5 years, for a white female 79.4 years, and for an African American female 73.6 years. By age sixty-five the gap narrows, so that white men can expect only 2.0 more years than African American men and white women only 1.9 more years than African American women (National Center for Health Statistics, 1993). The gap shrinks because the less hardy have already died. The accompanying Multicultural View box explores the *mortality crossover*, the age at which African Americans can expect to live longer than whites.

Hispanics are the second largest ethnic minority population in the United States and the fastest growing. They are expected to exceed African Americans in numbers by the end of this century. Most Hispanics are Mexican Americans living in the five southwestern states. Hispanic mortality is closer to whites' than to African Americans'. In some age groupings and by some definitions (for example, Spanish origin rather than Spanish surname), Hispanic life expectancies are higher than those for whites and are always higher than those for African Americans. Hispanics also have higher mortality rates from infectious and parasitic diseases, influenza and pneumonia, and accidents and all violent deaths than whites (Markides et al., 1989).

Life Expectancy

While life expectancy has increased, the human lifespan has not changed. *Lifespan* refers to the maximum possible period of time a species could be expected to live if environmental hazards were eliminated. For humans, the maximum lifespan is 115 years. This lifespan is based on the laboratory work of Leonard Hayflick (1994), which demonstrated that normal human cells can reproduce by doubling a maximum of fifty times and that as they approach that limit they undergo changes that affect every aspect of their functioning. As of 1995, the oldest verified age to which an individual has lived is just over 120½ years. Jeanne Calment, a French woman who celebrated her 120th birthday February 21, 1995, was living in a nursing home in October of that year when she broke the previous verified world longevity record of 120 years and 237 days. At 120 years of age, Jeanne was described in the French press as frail, blind, and almost totally deaf, all age-related changes that we will soon see are associated with very old late adulthood, but still having her mental faculties.

Increased life expectancy means more individuals' lives are approaching the maximum lifespan in length. As this happens, it is expected that more cases of extreme longevity will occur as, with larger numbers of elderly, the statistical probability of living past the average lifespan increases. Nonetheless, without some unanticipated and extraordinary biological discoveries, the average lifespan is not expected to go beyond eighty-five years (Olshansky et al., 1990). An extension of the lifespan would require a change in the rate of primary aging, which depends on biological factors that scientists do not know how to control.

What Do You Think?

Why do you think different races have different mortality rates? What information would you need to be sure your reason was correct? What other possible reasons can you think of?

THEORIES OF AGING

Throughout life the cells of most of the body's tissue die and are replaced. Exceptions are muscle and nerve cells, which are formed at birth and may live as long as the body does. In day-to-day life, body tissue is damaged and repaired and cancers begin to grow and are destroyed by the immune system. This maintenance function breaks down in humans sometime between ages fifty and one hundred. The breakdown of the surveillance, repair, and replacement process of the body is known as *senescence*. **Senescence,** the degenerative phase of the aging process, causes an individual to become more vulnerable to disease and mortality as the years go by.

Many theories attempt to explain senescence. To do this they must account for why aging is universal in a given species, why it progresses with time, and why it leads to the failure of the organism. No one theory does this perfectly, which is perhaps why so many theories currently exist. Theories of senescence fall into two distinct types: cellular theories and programming theories.

Cellular theories focus on the processes that take place within and between the cells and lead to the breakdown of cells, tissue, and organs. They are sometimes referred to as "wear and tear" theories because they explain the loss of function by repeated errors of transmission of genetic material resulting from toxins, pollutants, free radicals (highly reactive molecular fragments released by chemical reactions in the body), and other factors that affect cell reproduction. These stressors result from continuous use. As cells are replicated, some number of the new cells will contain genetic errors. The older the individual, the greater the number of the cells that will have errors and the greater the number of the cells that will have multiple errors. The increase in genetic errors causes inefficiency in the cell, leading to cell death and eventually to organism death.

Programming theories consider the maximum lifespan to be predetermined by the genes in each species. Leonard Hayflick (1994) demonstrated that human cells in the laboratory will replicate only to a certain point, about fifty replications, which constitutes the Hayflick Limit. After that the genetic material runs out. Hayflick believes death is programmed into complex organisms. Each species has its own characteristic lifespan that is preset by the number of possible cell replications. Other variations of programming theories posit other preprogrammed mechanisms. Daniel Rudman and his colleagues (1990) administered human growth hormone to adult men ages sixty-one to eighty-one and reversed some of the effects of aging. The decline in the growth hormone with age may lead to the changes of primary aging, such as atrophy of muscles and organs. The point of programming theories is that at birth our eventual deaths are already built in; anything less than *ideal* environmental conditions may shorten it, but nothing can lengthen it.

It is very likely that both cellular wear and tear and genetic preprogramming operate to produce senescence. Breakdown occurs in many different forms: the generating of free radicals, the instability of molecules, finite cell life, accumulated genetic and metabolic errors, and cross-linkage of collagen, the main supportive and connective tissue in the body. Wear and tear theories encourage consideration of how to reduce stressors to inhibit secondary aging and prolong life. Programming theories remind us that the gradual declines of primary aging are beyond our control.

What Do You Think?

Compare the implications of cellular theories and programming theories for health behaviors. According to each theory, what can people do to affect their longevity?

PHYSICAL FUNCTIONING IN LATE ADULTHOOD

Late adulthood is a time of loss in efficiency of body systems, but it is also a time of compensation. The most significant age-related changes are diminished pumping capacity of the heart, which we discussed in Chapter 14 because it begins early and continues throughout adulthood, and loss of neurons from the central nervous system. These changes have a negative impact on other body systems as well. But the aging process is not one of unmitigating and increasing loss. The body is an organism that repairs and restores itself as damage occurs. In some cases there is regeneration, in others compensation, and in still others growth due to the plasticity of the system. While it is not possible for the body to prevent eventual death; it is possible for it to work to enhance life. In this section, we consider the age-related changes that constitute primary aging in late adulthood.

Slowing with Age

Research examining motor responses, sensory processes, and intellectual functioning consistently shows that behavior slows with age (Spirduso, 1995). Older individuals can do what younger ones can, but it takes more time. The cause of the slowing is not fully understood, although animals of all species become slower as they age. It may be due to aging in the peripheral nervous system, the sensory receptors and nerves that transmit sensations from the outside world to the central

Although it is generally true that behavior slows with age, physical fitness serves to minimize age differences in speed. This man doing the long jump in the senior olympics is fitter and faster than most younger men who are not athletes.

nervous system and motor commands back to the muscles (Salthouse, 1989). It may be due to slowing throughout the central nervous system as well as in the peripheral nervous system (Cerella, 1990). Health and physical fitness, however, are more closely related to performance than is age. Waneen Spirduso and Priscilla MacRae (1990) found that levels of physical fitness and effects of exercise were among factors that minimized age differences in speed. Unfortunately, many of the studies that compare speed among adults of different ages have used as the older adults in their samples, nursing home residents, who are rarely physically fit and free of disease.

Skin, Bone, and Muscle Changes

The most noticeable changes of late adulthood occur to the skin. Aging skin becomes more wrinkled, dry, sagging, and less regular in pigmentation, especially on the face, hands, and neck, which are exposed to the sun and wind. Very old skin is likely to bruise more easily, heal more slowly, and grow lesions. Several age-related changes cause wrinkling: thinning of the skin, changes in blood vessels that impede circulation to the skin's surface, loss of skeletal and muscle mass, and the loss of subcutaneous fat (Christiansen & Grzybowski, 1993). Age-related decrease of melanocytes, which give the skin its color, cause pigmentation changes. After age thirty active melanocytes decrease 8 to 20 percent in each decade, causing the skin to become paler (Kligman et al., 1985). The remaining melanocytes may be irregularly distributed, leading to irregular pigment deposits—so called "age spots." Light-skinned people are more affected by ultraviolet light than darker-skinned people and are likely to develop more pigmentation irregularities. As we saw in Chapter 14's discussion of physical development in middle adulthood, aging of the skin can best be prevented by avoiding sun exposure, especially during childhood.

Another aspect of primary aging, demineralization, results in a lighter bone mass in older adults. The bone becomes more porous and brittle as the supporting bone matrix breaks down. This bone degeneration is called *osteoporosis,* which you may remember from Chapter 14. Osteoporosis has a two-phase pattern

"Is that man's skin wrinkled 'cause he stayed in the bathtub too long?"

The most noticeable changes of late adulthood are to the skin. Aging skin becomes more wrinkled, dry, sagging, and less regular in its pigmentation, especially where it has been exposed to the sun and wind.

of bone loss. The first phase is gradual and occurs in both sexes throughout adulthood. Maintaining a calcium-rich diet and regularly engaging in weight-bearing exercise can prevent this phase of osteoporosis. The second is rapid and occurs in postmenopausal women (Riggs & Melton, 1986). Women experience far greater bone loss than men do; women lose about 30 percent of their bone mass, whereas men lose about 17 percent (Hayflick, 1994). Table 16.2 shows risk factors for osteoporosis. Clinical osteoporosis is not a separate disease of old age but an extreme form of primary aging (Whitbourne & Weinstock, 1986). It puts elderly women at risk for hip fractures. Regular weight-bearing exercise, estrogen replacement therapy, and calcium supplements, separately or together, have been shown to slow bone loss and reverse osteoporosis in postmenopausal women (Hayflick, 1994).

TABLE 16.2   *What Puts You at Risk for Osteoporosis: A Checklist*
While some of the risk factors for osteoporosis, such as gender, body build, and family history, are beyond an individual's control, many are linked to health-compromising behaviors.

- **Increasing age.**
- **Being female.** By age 65, the average man still has 91% of his bone mass, but the average woman has only about 74%.
- **Being chronically underweight** or having a slight frame.
- **Being Caucasian or Asian** (usually small-boned).
- **Having osteoporosis in the family.**
- **A poor diet,** low in vitamins and minerals, especially calcium.
- **Being sedentary** and lack of weight-bearing exercise.
- **Smoking.** In women this lowers the estrogen content of the blood, thus weakening the bones. Smoking is particularly dangerous for women who have other risk factors for osteoporosis.
- **Heavy drinking.** It's not known why heavy drinking weakens the bones—perhaps because heavy drinkers often eat a poor diet.
- **Long-term use of certain medications.** Some people with asthma and rheumatoid arthritis take cortisone for long periods, which can diminish bone strength. So can long-term use of thyroid hormones, which are sometimes used to treat obesity, although most physicians do not recommend them for this purpose.

With aging comes a progressive loss of muscle strength and speed. As we saw in Chapter 14, muscle mass starts its gradual decline in middle adulthood. By age sixty or seventy, the rate of loss doubles to 10 to 20 percent per decade (Grimby & Saltin, 1983). Loss of muscle mass varies with the muscle and how much it is used; muscles used in daily activities are maintained, whereas those used infrequently decline. For instance, muscles in the arms and shoulders used to pull weights maintain their strength to age eighty, whereas hand grip strength begins to decrease by age fifty or sixty (Whitbourne & Weinstock, 1986). Loss of muscle fibers results from atrophy due to disuse or to damage and atrophy of the nerve fibers that carry impulses to the muscle. Older adults maintain strength if they have engaged in life-long patterns of physical exercise and can overcome losses by taking up regular exercise training. While atrophied muscles do not regenerate, exercise helps muscle fibers that have not yet atrophied to function more efficiently (Grimby, 1988).

Cardiovascular System Changes

The heart is a muscle too, and like all muscles it changes with age. Cardiovascular changes begin in early adulthood and continue throughout middle and later adulthood. With increasing age, the muscle cells of the heart contract at a slower rate and respond less well to the pacemaker cells that synchronize the contractions. Older hearts have fewer muscle fibers and more fat and connective tissue. They eject a lower volume of blood as the left ventricle becomes weaker and less expandable. The atherosclerotic changes we discuss in Chapters 12 and 14 also contribute to the reduction of blood flow. As physician Sherwin Nuland (1994) describes it, "each cigarette, each pat of butter, each slice of meat, and each increment of hypertension make the coronary arteries stiffen their resistance to the flow of blood." Even a heart that is free of cardiovascular disease has reduced *maximum cardiac output*, the volume of blood pumped by the heart every minute under conditions of peak exertion, and *aerobic power*, the amount of oxygen carried by the blood every minute under conditions of peak exertion, although resting cardiac output does not decline (Lakatta, 1990). These changes can be kept to a minimum by regular aerobic exercise and good nutrition, as we discuss in Chapter 14. Even among sedentary elderly people, physical training has been shown to increase aerobic capacity and reduce fat composition (O'Brien & Vertinsky, 1991). And in many conditioned elderly individuals, maximum oxygen consumption rate is equal to or better than those of younger sedentary individuals (Spirduso, 1995). Exercise also keeps the respiratory system healthier.

Respiratory System Changes

The lungs in even healthy older adults become smaller and less elastic; their weight decreases by about 20 percent (Krumpe et al., 1985). The respiratory system becomes less efficient in gas exchange as a function of age, as we noted in our discussion of age-related changes in physical functioning during early and middle adulthood. Weakening of the muscles in the chest wall and reduction in lung elastic recoil lead to a decrease in oxygenation of the arterial blood. The decease is gradual, but by late adulthood the loss is considerable (Sparrow & Weiss, 1988). Because brain cell functioning relies on oxygen and nutrients, decreased efficiency of the heart and lungs increases risk of stroke or loss of brain functions. Older adults compensate by using accessory muscles, particularly the diaphragm, to facilitate respiration (Miller, 1992). Normal daily functioning is unlikely to be impaired, but under conditions of stress an older adult may have difficulty breathing or become fatigued. Cilia, the hairlike structures in the air passages, become fewer in number and less effective in removing foreign particles. Declining muscle strength makes coughing less efficient. These changes make older people more susceptible to chronic bronchitis, emphysema, and pneumonia. The rate of aging of the respiratory system varies from individual to individual and is strongly influenced by lifestyle factors such as regular aerobic exercise, smoking, and exposure to air pollutants.

Sensory System Changes

Visual loss is part of the primary aging process. As Figure 16.2 shows, the percentage of elderly people with significant visual loss increases with age.

Loss of accommodation, the ability to change the focus of the eye, is a nearly universal aspect of senescence. By age fifty people need reading glasses to see things close up. Sensitivity to dim light also decreases steadily with advancing age. In addition to these age-related developments, two visual diseases affect older adults. *Cataract,* a clouding of the lens, is the most common correctable cause of blindness. Cataracts usually develop first around the periphery and impair vision when they spread to the central portion of the lens. *Glaucoma,* increased pressure in the eyeball, can also cause blindness. Glaucoma is caused by blockage of the Canal of Schlemm, which drains aqueous humor from the eye and returns it to the bloodstream. The aqueous humor continues to be produced, which builds up pressure in the eye. Topical drugs usually control glaucoma. It is the leading cause of blindness among African Americans. Even when socioeconomic differences and access to health care are controlled, glaucoma is more prevalent and more difficult to treat in African Americans than in whites (Wilson, 1989).

Hearing loss is also a part of the primary aging process. *Presbycusis* is age-related hearing loss caused by changes in the conductive system in the outer and middle ear and loss of hair cells and nerves in the inner ear. It interferes with the ability to hear high-pitched sounds and consonants in normal speech. It is difficult to separate deafness due to presbycusis from deafness due to loud noise, damage from past infections, or other causes. The percentage of elderly Americans with significant hearing loss increases with age, as is shown in Figure 16.3. Men have greater hearing loss than women, probably due to greater exposure to occupational and recreational noise. Noise is the largest contributor to hearing loss. Adolescents who attend rock concerts or listen to their stereos at high volume put themselves at risk for hearing impairment later in life. Figure 16.4 shows speech intelligibility as a function of age. Hearing aids can compensate for hearing loss to some extent, but because they magnify background noise as well as speech, they are not helpful in all

Hearing loss is part of the primary aging process. While the man on the left uses a hearing aid to compensate for his loss, the other also seems to have a problem hearing. Because there is less acceptance of hearing aids than of glasses, individuals are more likely to resist their use.

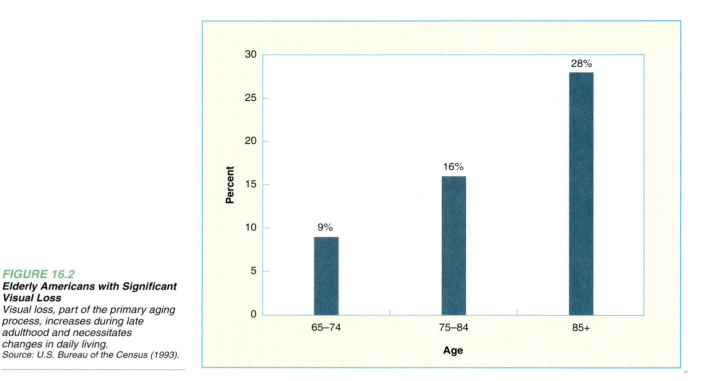

FIGURE 16.2
Elderly Americans with Significant Visual Loss
Visual loss, part of the primary aging process, increases during late adulthood and necessitates changes in daily living.
Source: U.S. Bureau of the Census (1993).

settings. There is also much less acceptance of hearing aids than of glasses, so a person may feel self-conscious or "old" wearing them.

Primary aging affects both taste and smell, with age-related declines in smell being greater than those in taste (Bartoshuk & Weiffenbach, 1990). Taste buds continually regenerate and do not show reduction in numbers with age (Miller, 1988).

FIGURE 16.3
Elderly Americans with Significant Hearing Loss
Hearing loss increases during late adulthood due to both primary and pathological aging.
Source: U.S. Bureau of the Census (1993).

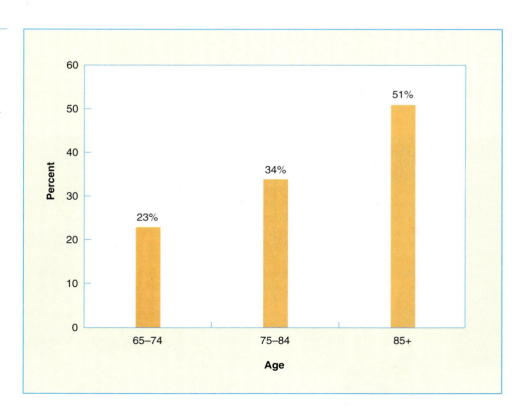

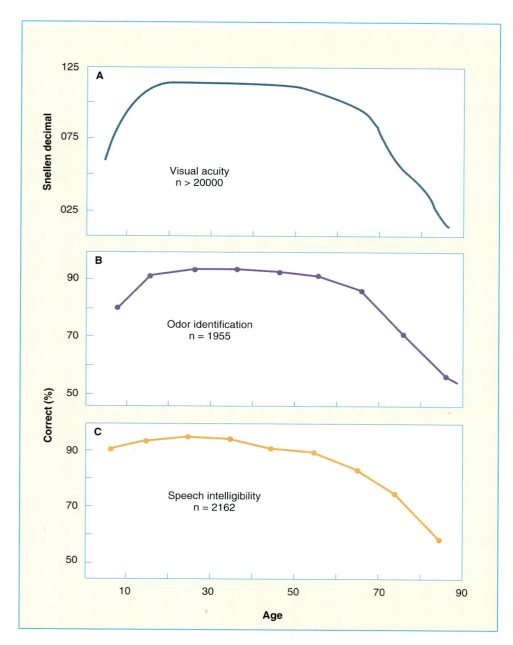

FIGURE 16.4
Suprathreshold Measures Across Age for Three Major Sensory Systems
Visual acuity, odor identification, and speech intelligibility all show similar age-related changes
Source: Doty et al. (1984).

While cross-sectional studies have shown that sensitivity to the four basic tastes (sweet, salty, sour, and bitter) decreases over the adult years, longitudinal studies have found much smaller age-related declines, rarely involving more than one of the four basic tastes (Hooyman & Kiyak, 1993). Ability to recognize a large number of foods goes down with age. These findings are based on cross-sectional studies, however, and may be affected by tobacco smoking, use of dentures, and presence of dental diseases in the older cohorts (Whitbourne & Weinstock, 1986). Because taste and smell work together in helping to identify foods, losses in smell may be responsible. Using a longitudinal design, Carolyn Tylanda and Bruce Baum (1988) found perception of taste intensity to be remarkably robust with age. The sweetness of sugar appears to be the most robust of all tastes (Bartoshuk & Weiffenbach, 1990).

Olfactory (smell) receptors regenerate continually too, but their numbers begin to decrease at about thirty years of age. As Figure 16.4 shows, ability to

Older Adults Have Healthier Lifestyles Than Young and Middle-Aged Adults

Adopting a healthy lifestyle is the best strategy for decreasing illness and enhancing health throughout life. All adults are encouraged to avoid health-compromising behaviors and adopt health-promoting behaviors, but who actually follows that advice? Susan Walker, Kevin Volkan, Karen Sechrist, and Nola Pender (1988) set out to compare young, middle-aged, and older adults in their patterns of health-promoting behaviors. They recruited 452 volunteers between ages eighteen and eighty-eight to fill out their Health-Promoting Lifestyle Profile. Their sample included 167 young adults (ages eighteen to thirty-four), 188 middle-aged adults (ages thirty-five to fifty-four), and 97 older adults (ages fifty-five to eighty-eight). Participants rated forty-eight items on a 1 to 4 scale (1 = never, 2 = sometimes, 3 = often, 4 = routinely). Table 16.3 shows representative items for each of the six subscales of the profile.

Older adults had significantly higher total heath-promoting scores and higher scores for the subscales health responsibility, nutrition, and stress management than young or middle-aged adults. There were no significant differences among age groups for self-actualization, exercise, and interpersonal support. For every age group, average scores for exercise were the lowest of all the subscales.

In addition to age, the researchers looked at educational level, gender, and income to see if these demographic factors were related to healthy lifestyles. Gender was found to be related to an overall health-promoting lifestyle and to the dimensions of health responsibility, exercise, nutrition, and interpersonal support. In all cases, women had significantly higher scores than men.

Higher income was associated with health responsibility and exercise, and more education was associated with nutrition, interpersonal support, and stress management. Marital status and employment status were both related to nutrition. Being married and not being employed were associated with higher health-promoting nutrition scores. In this sample, not being employed meant being a homemaker or being retired (only 2 percent of each age group was unemployed).

What do these findings tell us? In this sample the older adults had healthier lifestyles, but why? Perhaps with maturity people become more health conscious and adopt healthier habits. Perhaps older adults have more time and resources to devote to health promotion than do younger adults. Other studies have also shown that desirable health practices increase with age (Bausell, 1986; Prohaska et al., 1985). Thomas Prohaska, Elaine Leventhal, Howard Leventhal, and Mary Keller (1985) found that elderly people considered themselves more vulnerable to disease and saw it as more serious for them. On the other hand, it may be that the older adults with less healthy habits had already died or become too sick to be part of this sample. Because the Walker et al. findings came from a cross-sectional study (a separate sample at each age group), it is impossible to knowledgeably choose between these explanations. A longitudinal study that followed the same adults from early to late adulthood and periodically measured their health practices would provide a clearer answer to who has the healthiest lifestyles. These data do, however, contradict the negative stereotype of elderly people as unable or unlikely to care for themselves.

detect various types of odors peaks between ages twenty and fifty, decreases slightly over the fifties and sixties, and decreases markedly after seventy (Doty et al., 1984). In a study of 1,955 individuals ages five to ninety-nine years, Richard Doty and his colleagues (1984) found that 50 percent of adults sixty-five to eighty years old and more than 75 percent of those over eighty years old showed major olfactory impairment. They also found that at every age females were better at identifying odors than males, and nonsmokers were better than smokers. Using a large, nationwide sample, Avery Gilbert and Charles Wysocki (1987) found that the ability to smell odors did not decline with age until respondents were in their seventies. However, the perceived intensity of an odor and the ability to identify it began to decline much earlier. Mercaptans, the odors added to natural gas, became harder to detect at about age fifty, whereas rose odor did not begin to decline until age seventy.

Thus far we have been discussing aspects of primary aging, age-related changes that all people in late adulthood experience to some degree. Older adults vary greatly in their levels of physical functioning. Many experience secondary aging caused by health-compromising behaviors, such as smoking, or environmental factors, such as pollution. Others continue to function as they did in middle age because of favorable genetic make-up and health behaviors.

The findings that gender, SES, and marital status are positively associated with health promotion are consistent with the positive relationship each of these demographic variables has with health status. The most distressing finding is that the lowest scores in all age groups were for the exercise dimension of health promotion, since regular exercise throughout life has repeatedly been demonstrated to enhance health and longevity.

TABLE 16.3 *Sample Items for Each Subscale of the Health-Promoting Lifestyle Profile*
Susan Walker and her colleagues (1988) found that older adults had significantly higher total health-promoting scores than young or middle-aged adults.

Self-actualization
  Like myself
  Look forward to future
  Know what is important

Health Responsibility
  Check cholesterol level
  Report symptoms to M.D.
  Observe body for changes

Exercise
  Exercise three times/week
  Recreational activities
  Check pulse rate

Nutrition
  Eat three meals daily
  Eat roughage/fiber
  No preservatives

Interpersonal Support
  Discuss concerns/problems
  Enjoy touching and being touched
  Time with close friends

Stress Management
  Meditation/relaxation
  Express feelings
  Aware of stress sources

Source: Adapted from Walker et al. (1987).

What Do You Think?

Imagine that your eyesight is failing and you find it difficult to drive. How would you go shopping and get to the other places you usually go? What changes would you need to make in your lifesyle?

HEALTH BEHAVIORS IN LATE ADULTHOOD

Health and fitness are no less important in the later years than in early or middle adulthood; if anything, increased physical vulnerability may make them more important. Older adults seem to be aware of this and engage in more health-promoting behaviors than their younger counterparts, as the accompanying Perspectives box suggests. Table 16.4 presents seven health habits that are considered effective in improving health and prolonging life. Beginning these habits early in adulthood can provide cumulative benefits in later adult years, but they need to be

TABLE 16.4   Behaviors That Improve Adult Health and Longevity
Beginning health behaviors in early adulthood can provide cumulative benefits in later adult years, but they need to be continued. Health behaviors can improve health even if started during late adulthood.

- Sleeping an average of 7 to 8 hours nightly
- Eating breakfast almost every day
- Seldom, if ever, eating snacks
- Controlling weight
- Exercising regularly
- Limiting alcohol consumption
- Never having smoked cigarettes

Source: Adapted from Shoenborn & Danchik (1980).

continued. Of special concern during the later years are diet, exercise, and alcohol consumption.

Diet

Nutritional concerns increase during late adulthood because at the same time caloric needs decline, the need for many nutrients rises. Problems arise when older adults consume too few vitamins and minerals or take medications that prevent them from getting the full benefits of the nutrients in the foods they eat. Undernutrition can increase the risk of developing heart disease, cancer, osteoporosis, infectious illnesses, and acute brain syndromes. Obesity can contribute to a variety of health problems, such as troubled breathing, diabetes mellitus, gallstones, hypertension, atherosclerosis, and heart disease. The elderly have more varied caloric requirements than any other age group, but any given elderly individual needs fewer calories than in earlier years. Activity levels, gender, weight, height, genetic makeup, social environment, and SES all affect dietary needs. To control weight and meet nutritional requirements, it becomes more important in late adulthood to avoid eating empty calories and choose foods that are high in nutrients and fiber and low in fats and cholesterol.

A variety of physical, social, and emotional factors can contribute to nutritional deficits among the elderly. Declining health or medications may make food uninviting. Dental problems, such as missing teeth or poorly fitting dentures, may make chewing difficult. Changes in taste and smell may make food less enjoyable. Reduced income from retirement or widowhood may make food less affordable. Loss of mobility because driving is no longer safe or walking is too difficult may make regular grocery shopping impossible. Social changes, such as the loss of a partner, may make meal preparation more problematic. Cooking for one can challenge a person's dedication to variety and nutrition. Widowed men may find themselves alone and responsible for their own food preparation for the first time. These kinds of difficulties often lead to skipping meals or eating snack foods and TV dinners rather than properly balanced meals.

Exercise

Judging from the average daily expenditure of calories, as people get older routine physical activity decreases (Lakatta, 1990). In Chapter 12, we discussed the challenge to young adults to lower their caloric intake as they experience a decrease in activity level from adolescence to adulthood. In late adulthood retirement brings further decreases in physical activity, especially for men. Women have a greater variation of lifestyles. Elderly homemakers may continue to care for large homes, entertain extended family, and tend their grandchildren, which may require working as actively as they ever did. Although physical activity is less a part of the daily

Reduced income from retirement or widowhood may make food less affordable during late adulthood. This couple supplements their diet by searching for discarded food at the Boston Haymarket.

routine, exercise, along with good nutrition and adequate sleep, is considered a significant health need for today's elderly (Evans & Meredith, 1989). About half of what has generally been accepted as part of aging is now understood to be **hypokinesia,** a disease of disuse that causes degeneration and functional loss of muscle and bone tissue (Drinkwater, 1988). In addition to preventing hypokinesia, regular exercise makes people feel better, reduces stress, facilitates weight loss, lowers blood pressure, controls depression, heightens resistance to disease, and improves the quality of life for elderly people (McNeil et al., 1991; O'Brien & Vertinsky, 1991; Solomon, 1991). It also increases longevity (Blair, Brill & Kohl, 1989).

Few adults get regular, vigorous, physical exercise, and older women appear to get even less. While the Perspectives box on p. 596 indicates older adults engage in more health-promoting behaviors than their younger counterparts, this isn't true of exercise. Rod Dishman (1990) found that only 10 percent of Americans were regularly and vigorously active. Carl Caspersen and his colleagues (1986) found that only 5.0 to 7.5 percent of those over sixty-five had "appropriate levels of physical activity," while 42 percent said they were sedentary. Although older women may be active, of those who were exercising, most were men. Other studies have found somewhat higher percentages of older adults who exercise, but the gender difference persists (Blair, Brill & Kohl, 1989). Lois Verbrugge (1989a) sees the gender difference in late adulthood as a continuation of a pattern, established during adolescence, in which boys are more physically active than girls. Poor exercise habits learned early in life and continued through middle-age do not help women when they become older. For healthy adults, the recommendation on exercise by the American College of Sports Medicine is moderate training three to five times a week at 65 to 75 percent of maximal heart rate. Health professionals have tended to be overcautious in prescribing exercises for the elderly that are sufficiently challenging to yield the full benefits of an exercise program (Frontera & Meredith, 1989).

Alcohol Consumption

Alcohol poses serious problems for older people. During late adulthood, sensitivity to alcohol increases. For any given amount consumed, blood alcohol concentration is higher in an older individual than in a younger one, probably due to less dilution by body water volume, which decreases with age (Christiansen & Grzybowski. 1993). Alcohol can block reaction time, impair coordination, and cloud mental abilities, especially memory. It may accelerate some of the cognitive changes associated with aging, as well as lead to damage in the gastrointestinal, cardiovascular, and central nervous systems.

Levels of alcohol consumption and the number of problem drinkers are lower in older age groups, as Figure 16.5 shows. In a seven-year longitudinal study, Wendy Adams and her colleagues (1990) found that the number of elderly people who abstained from alcohol increased by 2 percent each year. In a detailed examination of drinking patterns of 1,070 community-living English elderly people and a three-year follow-up, Paul Saunders and his associates (1989) found a decline in the number of people drinking regularly and a trend toward reduction in alcohol consumption with age. Similar reductions were found in a twenty-five-year study of three Navajo populations (Kunitz & Levy, 1994).

Although alcohol consumption decreases in late adulthood, it remains a problem for some groups. Elderly alcoholics may be continuing a pattern established in early life or may be responding to stressful social changes in their lives, such as loneliness, bereavement, or retirement. Elderly males are at greater risk for alcoholism than females. Scot Adams and Shirley Waskel (1993) found that among elderly alcoholic men, the onset of problem drinking was due less to stress than to the loss of a spouse, who may serve to regulate the man's drinking. Other risk factors are low income, low level of education, and a history of depression. Regular drinking is more common in retirement communities, where it is associated with social

FIGURE 16.5

Alcohol Dependence by Age
Although abuse of alcohol is a problem for some groups of elderly, levels of consumption and numbers of problem drinkers decrease with age.
Source: Adapted from Christiansen & Grzybowski (1993).

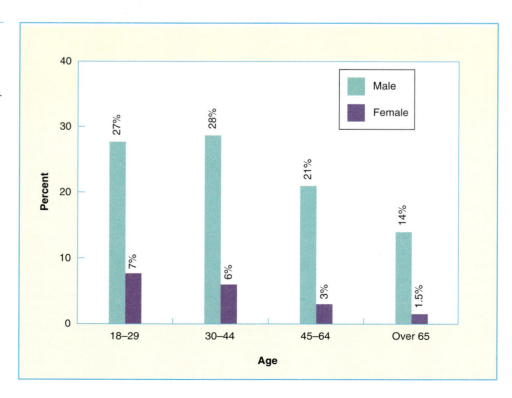

activity, than in the general population of senior citizens (Alexander & Duff, 1988). Although stress has been associated with alcohol use, Neal Krause (1991) found that not all stressors led to an increase in alcohol use among the elderly. Health problems were associated with a greater probability of elderly individuals abstaining from alcohol, while financial difficulties were associated with a lower probability of abstaining. Gender and race were also found to be significant factors; being a woman or being an African American increased the probability of abstaining. Being religious was also associated with a higher probability of abstinence.

Prescription Drugs

Increased sensitivity to drugs puts elderly individuals at high risk for adverse drug effects, especially if they take multiple drugs. In part because of the chronic illnesses discussed in the next section, older adults take one-third of the prescription drugs used. Sharon Willcox and her associates (1994) found that 23.5 percent of community-living adults age sixty-five and over had been prescribed one or more of twenty drugs that elderly people should avoid because of adverse side effects. Individuals most likely to receive hazardous prescriptions were women, people living in the South, those who rated their health as poor, and those on Medicaid. Improper medications may cause physical, cognitive, and social dysfunction, which sometimes leads to a misdiagnosis of dementia, as we will see later in this chapter.

The later years are characterized in far more negative terms than many individuals experience them. While losses in physical functioning occur during late adulthood, normal aging is not synonymous with a loss. There are large differences in how different body system age and in how different individuals age. Severe losses are the function of disease and disuse, not of normal aging, and do not affect everybody.

What Do You Think?

Assess your health-promoting behaviors. What improvements can you make?

CHRONIC ILLNESSES

Chronic illness, a medical condition that cannot be cured but can only be managed, is a common feature of late adulthood. Most of us will eventually develop at least one chronic disease or disability that may ultimately cause our death. Chronic diseases are incremental, universal, and characterized by progressive loss of organ reserve (the extra capacity to respond to stress). All chronic conditions have a clinical threshold, the point when the symptoms appear. The key to preventing chronic illness is to delay reaching the clinical threshold (Fries & Crapo, 1981).

While chronic illness is associated with age, it is not special to late adulthood. Many children suffer from asthma, for example, which is a chronic illness. At any given time, half of the population has some chronic condition that requires medical management (Taylor, 1995). Even if we focus only on chronic illnesses in adults, the lines between middle and late adulthood are blurring as increasing numbers of Americans continue to be healthy and vigorous well into their later years. While some middle-aged adults already suffer from chronic diseases, many young-old adults do not.

Because people may live with chronic diseases for many years, they often find all aspects of their lives affected (Taylor & Aspinwall, 1990). At its most acute—for example, a person has a heart attack—a chronic disease disrupts all life activities, throwing the person into a state of physical, social, and psychological crisis. Once the crisis phase passes, people begin to develop a sense of how the chronic illness will alter their lives. They may need to make permanent changes in physical, vocational, and social activities and often need to learn to accept the role of patient. Denial, anxiety, and depression are common emotional reactions (Taylor & Aspinwall, 1990). We will see the implications of these psychological aspects of chronic disease when we discuss psychosocial development in the next chapter. Here we discuss the chronic diseases that become frequent in middle and late adulthood.

Cardiovascular Disease

Cardiovascular disease, any disease of the heart and blood vessels, is the major chronic illness in the United States. It is responsible for most illness and death among men during middle adulthood, usually after age forty-five (Wegner et al., 1986). Coronary heart disease (CHD) refers to illnesses caused by atherosclerosis, the narrowing of the arteries that supply the heart. Atherosclerosis is the most common heart disorder in the United States (Ashburn, 1992). Wastes in the form of fatty deposits (plaques) build up over the years, impeding blood flow. Narrowed or closed arteries wholly or partially block the flow of oxygen and nutrients to the heart. Figure 16.6 shows how atherosclerosis may progress evenly or may result in a sudden, catastrophic event. Temporary blockage may cause pain or tightness in the chest and radiating down the arms, called *angina pectoris*. The pain is due to insufficient oxygen and nutrients getting to the heart cells and is likely to occur when the body is under stress and the heart rate is elevated. Severe blockage may result in *myocardial infarction*, or heart attack. Heart attacks damage heart cells beyond repair.

Risk Factors   CHD, the leading cause of death in the United States, is common among males and elderly people in general. Men are three times more likely than women to experience a major cardiovascular event before age sixty. At any level of risk factors, women have half the risk men of the same age do and tend to show signs of it ten years later than men. This biological advantage is heavily influenced by environmental factors, as indicated by the finding that wives of men with CHD have twice the risks that wives of men who do not have it do (Strickland, 1988b). The biological advantage does not protect women from CHD indefinitely either.

FIGURE 16.6
The Clinical Course of Atherosclerosis
Atherosclerosis may progress relatively evenly, or it may result in a sudden, catastrophic event such as heart attack or stroke. The other major chronic illnesses show similar progressions.
Source: Fries & Crapo (1981).

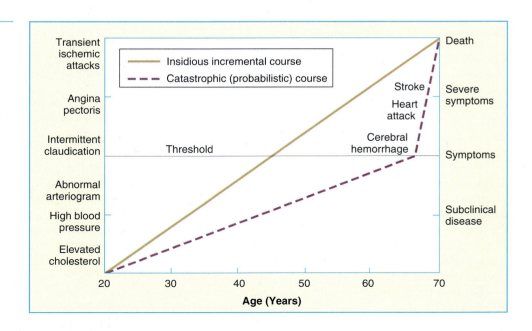

While among women twenty-five to sixty-four years old only 10 percent suffer from CHD, about 90 percent of women above age sixty-five die from it (Nachtigall, 1987).

Risk factors for heart disease include family history, health-compromising behaviors, personality type, and stress. Offspring of parents who have had CHD are at greater risk. A diet high in fats and cholesterol, obesity, tobacco smoking, and low levels of physical activity are all risk factors a person can control, as we discussed in Chapter 12. A CHD-prone personality is characterized by strong feelings of hostility (Eysenck, 1990). Other risk factors include diabetes and high blood pressure.

Hypertension   Blood pressure, the pressure exerted when the left ventricle of the heart contracts, maintains equilibrium throughout the vascular system as it responds to the needs of the cells for oxygen during varying levels of physical exertion. Blood pressure varies greatly from individual to individual and according to activity. Hypertension, or high blood pressure, is determined by the systolic and diastolic blood pressure. *Systolic pressure* is the greatest amount of force developed during the contraction of the ventricles; *diastolic pressure* is the lowest pressure in the arteries when the heart is relaxed. Systolic pressure consistently over 140 and diastolic pressure consistently 90 or above constitute hypertension. Continuing high blood pressure can cause deterioration of the arterial walls and of the cell tissue. The arterioles, or small arteries, become thicker and less elastic, causing arteriosclerosis. Arteriosclerosis puts a person at risk for heart attack, kidney damage, and *stroke*, which is a rupture or leak of an arteriole in the brain. Men are more at risk for heart attack. Women are more at risk for stroke; they experience 60 percent of all stroke deaths (U.S. Department of Health and Human Services, 1991). As Figure 16.7 shows, the risk for African American women is higher than that for white women.

Risk factors for hypertension include genetic predisposition, obesity, poor diet, and, perhaps, personality characteristics (Taylor, 1995). Males are at greater risk than females; African Americans are more at risk than whites; and older people are more at risk than younger people. Low-income African Americans are at highest risk. They are more likely to have parents with a history of hypertension and to live

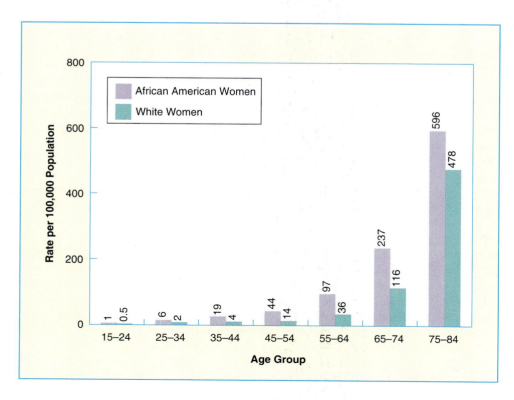

FIGURE 16.7
Death Rates for Stroke Victims Among Women, Ages Fifteen to Eighty-four
African American women are at greater risk for stroke than are white women, and this risk increases with age.
Source: U.S. Department of Health and Human Services (1993).

in neighborhoods and work in jobs that cause chronic stress. Racism may also contribute to hypertension. Cheryl Armstead and her associates (1989) found that exposure to racist stimuli was associated with blood pressure increases among African American college students. Stress also seems to be a contributing factor. Treatment of hypertension often includes medication and adopting healthier behaviors.

Cancer

Cancer is actually a set of more than one hundred diseases characterized by uncontrolled cellular growth and reproduction due to a dysfunction of the DNA, the part of the cell that regulates these processes. Cancerous growths, called *malignant tumors,* can spread by invading other tissues and organs. This process of spreading is called *metastasis*. Once cancer has metastasized, local surgical removal usually becomes impossible.

Cancer is the second most frequent cause of death in the United States and the leading cause of morbidity and mortality for women ages forty-five to seventy-four (American Cancer Society, 1993). The leading cause of cancer deaths for both men and women is lung cancer, usually *bronchial carcinoma*, most likely caused by smoking. For men over fifty, prostate cancer is the most common cancer (Christiansen & Grzybowski, 1993). For women between ages thirty-five and fifty-five, breast cancer is second (Strickland, 1988b). As discussed in Chapter 14, these cancers are common enough in middle adulthood that regular breast self-examination (BSE) and professional breast and prostate examination are considered important health behaviors. BSE entails systematic palpation of each breast to detect alterations or lumps in the underlying tissue. Although regular mammograms and annual professional breast exams are recommended for women forty and older, 85 percent of lumps are still detected by women themselves. Professional digital rectal examination of the prostate is recommended as part of an annual physical for men starting at age fifty. Because both are curable in their early stages, early detection of breast and prostate cancers saves lives.

Risk Factors   The causes of cancer are not fully understood, but some risk factors are known. Some cancers run in families; some are linked to gender, ethnicity, lifestyle, or marital status; and most are linked to diet. Cancer rates among African Americans average 10 to 20 percent higher than among whites (Garfinkel, 1991). Cancer-related mortality rates for African Americans are higher than for nonminorities and are increasing faster. And in areas where mortality rates are decreasing for whites, they are still increasing for African Americans or not decreasing as rapidly (National Cancer Institute, 1990). Hispanics appear to have lower rates of major cancers, especially cancers of the lung, breast, colon/rectum, prostate, and pancreas. They have higher rates for cancers of the cervix, stomach, liver, and gall bladder. Overall, Hispanic women have slightly higher cancer rates than white women and substantially lower ones than African American women. Hispanic men have lower cancer rates than white and African American men (Markides et al., 1989).

Charles Longino and his colleagues (1989) found that incidence of cancer was directly related to SES (the higher the SES, the higher the incidence of cancer). Yet lower-SES people with cancer have lower survival rates than wealthier people. Whereas 78 percent of white women earning more than $30,000 survived breast cancer over five years, only 63 percent of women earning under $15,000 did (Hardisty & Leopold, 1992). SES is directly related to health status, as discussed in Chapter 12. Lack of health insurance makes early detection of cancers less likely, but it is only one of many factors that put low-SES groups at higher risk for cancer and other chronic diseases. Low SES typically means greater exposure to *carcinogens* (cancer-causing substances) in workplaces and neighborhoods, higher rates of smoking, and greater exposure to chronic stress.

Stress   Research suggests that the onset of cancer is related to the experience of uncontrollable stressful life events, such as divorce or death of a spouse. Stressful events may suppress the immune system (Eysenck, in press). Stress may also interfere with DNA repair (Glaser et al., 1985), as well as with the ability of the immune system to survey and destroy tumor cells (Glaser et al., 1986). Personality also has an influence on a person's likelihood of developing cancer. The cancer-prone personality is characterized as "overly cooperative, pleasing, unassertive, over-patient, conflict avoiding, harmony seeking, compliant, defensive, emotion suppressing, and unable to deal with interpersonal stress, which leads to feelings of hopelessness/helplessness, and finally to depression" (Grossarth-Maticek et al., 1990, p. 199).

Arthritis

Arthritis, a set of more than eighty autoimmune diseases in which the body incorrectly identifies its own tissue as foreign matter and attacks it, is the second leading chronic disease in the United States. Arthritis attacks the joints and connective tissue and causes inflammation, pain, stiffness, and sometimes swelling of the joints. Although arthritis rarely leads to death, it can be crippling. *Osteoarthritis* is the most common type of arthritis, affecting mostly elderly people and some athletes. This degenerative joint disease wears down the cartilage through overuse, injury, or other causes. It most often affects weight-bearing joints: the hips, knees, and spine. *Rheumatoid arthritis* affects the whole body rather than specific, localized joints. The lining of the joint capsule becomes inflamed, producing enzymes that attack the cartilage, bone, and soft tissue. In severe cases, the joint is destroyed. The exact cause of rheumatoid arthritis is unknown, but it is brought on by autoimmune processes. It is the most crippling form of arthritis and is most prevalent among people ages forty to sixty.

Rheumatoid arthritis afflicts three times more women than men. The onset usually occurs between ages twenty-five and forty-five; half of women over fifty suffer from it. Incidence is particularly high among women who have had an oophorectomy (surgical removal of the ovaries). Early diagnosis and treatment can prevent the disabling aspects of the disease. While it is not clear whether stress causes rheumatoid arthritis, it is known to exacerbate the disease.

Half of women over 50 suffer from rheumatoid arthritis. Regular, gentle stretching can prevent or reduce its disabling effects.

Common Symptoms in Later Years

Based on two community-based studies in which participants kept daily diaries of symptoms, Lois Verbrugge (1989a) provides a view of what symptoms pervade daily life in middle and late adulthood and how frequent they occur. As Table 16.5 indicates, both older men and women most frequently report musculoskeletal symptoms, about half from disease (usually arthritis) and half from overexertion, strains, and sprains. Headaches and respiratory symptoms rank high for middle-aged (forty-five to sixty-five) men and women. Cardiovascular symptoms are rare in daily life, even though they are the leading cause of death. Lower-SES people report they are less healthy and suffer from more chronic diseases (Longino et al., 1989; Rakowski et al., 1993).

Gender   Lois Verbrugge's data indicate that the kinds of symptoms that bother men and women are very similar but are much more frequent in women. Women's chronic conditions tend to be nonfatal, such as arthritis, and men's tend to be fatal or precursors to fatal conditions, such as heart disease. As a result, men die at a faster rate and women experience more frequent symptoms and health care. Women can look forward to longer lives, but lives filled with more sickness and disability, whereas men can look forward to shorter lives with fewer years of health trouble while alive.

Race/Ethnicity   Incidence of chronic diseases varies among racial/ethnic groups. Among African Americans, the three most prevalent chronic conditions for middle-aged adults (forty-five to sixty-four years) are hypertension, arthritis, and sinusitis; for older adults (sixty-five–seventy-five years) arthritis, hypertension, and heart disease; and for the very old (seventy-five or older) arthritis, hypertension, and hearing impairment. If you compare these to the chronic conditions in Table 16.5, you will notice that although there are variations in rank ordering among African Americans, the most prevalent conditions are similar to those of the total adult population. The frequency of these conditions, however, is higher for African Americans (Jackson & Perry, 1989). Hispanics living in the five southwestern states have a lower prevalence of cardiovascular disease than do whites or African Americans; Hispanic men have lower rates than non-Hispanic men, and Hispanic women have slightly higher rates than non-Hispanic women.

While chronic diseases become more frequent in late adulthood, they generally have their beginning in earlier life stages and often have their onset earlier as well. In part, the great frequency of these illnesses is a result of people living longer. For many older adults, chronic diseases do not interfere with everyday activities. Faced with physical limitations, people have ingenious ways of adapting and compensating for losses. Nonetheless, late adulthood is a time when body decline is a part of

TABLE 16.5   *Rank Order of Chronic Conditions by Sex*
Men and women suffer from similar chronic conditions, but because men die sooner, women tend to experience more sickness and disability.

	Men 65–74	Men 75 and Over	Women 65–74	Women 75 and Over
Arthritis	1	2	1	1
High blood pressure	2	3	2	2
Hearing impairment	3	1	3	3
Heart disease	4	5	—	—
Cataracts	—	4	5	4
Chronic sinusitis	5	—	4	5

Sources: Verbrugge (1989a); National Center for Health Statistics (1993).

life. While physical fitness accomplished by lifelong heath behaviors can maintain most body systems at high levels of functioning, the levels are not as high as they were before because primary aging cannot be stopped. Losses in vision, hearing, smell, and, to a lesser extent, taste all affect the way elderly people perceive and interact with the world. What are the views on cognitive changes in late adulthood, and what changes are likely to be encountered?

What Do You Think?

Imagine what your life would be like if you had severe arthritis or some other debilitating chronic disease. How would such a condition change your current lifestyle?

COGNITIVE DEVELOPMENT

At age seventy-three, Sally occasionally can't find her keys or think of a name and worries that she is losing her memory. Yet, she manages the household she shares with her husband and keeps track of her large extended family's many birthdays and anniversaries without mishap. She cooks and bakes from her vast mental store of recipes and shares news of everyone during calls and visits with her adult children and grandchildren.

As we saw in Chapter 14's discussion of cognitive development in middle adulthood, patterns of age-related changes in cognitive abilities in adulthood differ widely. Both objective performance on memory tests and subjective appraisals of memory functioning are negatively associated with age (Ryan, 1992; West et al., 1992). Performance on unfamiliar laboratory tasks show greater age-related differences than performance on familiar real-life tasks (Hultsch & Dixon, 1990). Older adults maintain domain-specific knowledge in areas of expertise. Schaie and his colleagues (1994) found that some individuals showed significant changes in intellectual performance in midlife, while a few showed little decline even into their eighties. Absence of chronic diseases, high SES, involvement in intellectually stimulating activities, a flexible personality style, marriage to a spouse with high cognitive functioning, and satisfaction with one's life accomplishments were all factors that reduced the risk of cognitive loss. But are there age-related gains? Do we become wiser with experience? This is the question to which we now turn.

WISDOM

Wisdom, expert knowledge and good judgment about important but uncertain matters of life, is a positive change associated with late life. Jutta Heckhausen et al. (1989) asked groups of young, middle-aged, and old respondents about their views on the nature of adult development and aging. Respondents were given more than three hundred psychological attributes (such as aggressive, curious, excitable, intelligent, materialistic, proud) and asked which of these attributes they expected to change with age ("become more apparent, stronger and/or more frequent") during the decades of adult life. They also were asked to indicate the degree of desirability of the expected change. Overall, subjects believed the attributes likely to change in early adulthood were more desirable than those expected to change in later adulthood. The two desirable attributes they expected to be more frequent and stronger in late adulthood were wisdom and dignity.

During recent years, wisdom has become an area in which psychologists have made efforts to measure cognitive growth or potential for growth in late adulthood. Paul Baltes and Ursula Staudinger (1993) and their associates at the Berlin Max Planck Institute for Human Development and Education have been studying the losses and gains of the aging mind. They distinguish between *cognitive mechanics* (content free) and *cognitive pragmatics* (knowledge rich) as two major intellectual categories, extending the distinction between fluid and crystallized intelligence presented in Chapter 14. They believe that in the fluid mechanics of the mind, biological conditions are most significant, and, therefore, decline with aging is likely. In the crystallized pragmatics of the mind, culture is most significant, and, therefore, progress may be possible in old age.

Cognitive Mechanics

Cognitive mechanics refers to basic memory processes, which, as we saw in Chapter 14, are likely to decline in late adulthood. Baltes and Staudinger (1993) developed a memory technique that requires creative, quick, and accurate use of all of the cognitive mechanical operations (processes of sensory information input; visual and motor memory; the processes of discrimination, categorization, and coordination) to measure age-related changes in cognitive mechanics. They asked subjects to remember a long list of words, such as thirty nouns (*car, plane, house, chair,* etc.) in the order of presentation. Most people can remember five to seven words if they do not use a memory technique, but can remember much longer strings of words when taught to create mental images that link the words to be remembered to a set series of mental locations. At recall, subjects recreate the images, location by location, and decode the images into the original memory words. Table 16.6 shows this and other memory techniques. Baltes and Staudinger have found that when seventy-year-olds learn and practice memory techniques they do reasonably well, but they do not approach the performance of thirty-year-olds. "Even after about 35 sessions of training and assessment, most older adults do not reach the level that young adults display after a few training sessions. . . . this age-related decrement is robust and appears irreversible" (p. 76).

Cognitive Pragmatics

Cognitive pragmatics refers to intellectual problems in which culture-based knowledge and skills are primary, such as reading and writing skills, language comprehension, professional skills, and knowledge about strategies to manage the peaks and valleys of life. Baltes and Staudinger (1993) consider wisdom to be one of the prototypes for growth in the pragmatics of intelligence in adulthood. To measure age-related

---

TABLE 16.6   *Techniques for Maintaining or Improving Memory*
People as old as seventy have been shown to benefit from memory techniques.

Use places. Link a string of facts you must remember to familiar places. "Place" one fact at each location and "pick them up" when you need them by revisiting the locations in your mind.

Use rhymes. Create your own rhymes, such as "*I* before *E*, except after *C*," to string together what you need to remember.

Rehearse new facts. Repeat the name of the person who has just been introduced to you, and make a point of using the name several times as you speak to that person.

Chunk or regroup. Turn directions to a new place into fewer items to remember by making up a sentence or story that includes each street you must turn on.

Make notes. A shopping list or list of errands will be fixed in your mind if you write them down. If they are not, you have the list to consult.

Structure your life. Put your keys on their special hook, your glasses on a particular shelf, and your checkbook in a particular drawer. You will then remember where they are.

Leading museum tours calls on this woman's store of knowledge, as well as her language and interpersonal skills, all of which are aspects of cognitive pragmatics that may increase in old age.

changes in wisdom, they use verbal responses to various types of life dilemmas. An example of a dilemma they use is "A 15-year-old girl wants to get married right away. What should one/she do and consider?" Another example is "Imagine a good friend of yours calls you up and tells you that she can't go on anymore and has decided to commit suicide. What would one/you be thinking about? How would you deal with this situation?" Participants are asked to "think aloud" about the dilemmas. Table 16.7 shows the five wisdom-related criteria researchers use to evaluate the responses and how they are applied to the dilemma about the fifteen-year-old. In a comparison of young (average age thirty-two years) and older (average age seventy-one years) adults on wisdom-related dilemmas, the researchers found no differences in overall performance. Older adults showed higher levels of wisdom-related knowledge on tasks specific to their own age group than young adults. A fairly large number of old adults were among the top scorers. Few responses among a well-educated group of participants were considered wise, however, so wisdom is not inevitable (Smith & Baltes, 1990). Ursula Staudinger and her colleagues (1992) compared clinical psychologists, a professional specialty that involves a higher than average level of exposure to giving advice about the uncertain matters of life, and matched controls of various ages. The clinical psychologists did better than the controls, and at least as many old clinical psychologists as young ones were among the top scorers. Clearly the research on wisdom, in which older participants are among those who do well, shows a very different age-related pattern than that of mechanics, where none of the older participants are among the top scorers.

Critics of the Berlin institute researchers' optimism about gains in wisdom in late life point out that as yet no empirical evidence suggests that older adults *on the average* perform better on wisdom-related tasks than younger adults and that creativity is "the privilege of youth" (Simonton, 1990, p. 321). Baltes and Staudinger (1993) respond that old age is very young (only recently have many people lived to reach it), so we do not yet know what is possible. The prevailing negative images still influence everyday life; measures and criteria used to evaluate performance are still youth oriented. The fact that any older adults perform at peak or near-peak levels demonstrates that high levels of functioning are possible and, with cultural change, may become normative. These researchers are not the only ones who are optimistic about the possible cognitive gains of later life.

TABLE 16.7   *Use of the Wisdom-Related Criteria to Evaluate Discourse About Life Matters*

This table illustrates how Baltes and Staudinger (1993) evaluated the wisdom of responses to the dilemma "A 15-year-old girl wants to get married right away. What should one/she do and consider?"

Criterion	Evidence
Factual knowledge	Who, when, where? Examples of possible different situations Multiple options (forms of love and marriage)
Procedural knowledge	Strategies of information search, decision making, and advice giving Timing of advice Monitoring of emotional reactions Cost-benefit analysis; scenarios Means-ends analysis
Lifespan contextualism	Age-graded contexts (e.g., issues of adolescence) Culturally graded contexts (e.g., change in norms) Idiosyncratic contexts across time and life domains (e.g., terminal illness) Interrelations, tensions, priorities of life domains
Relativism	Religious and personal preferences Current versus future values Historical period Cultural relativism
Uncertainty	No perfect solution Optimization of gain versus loss Future not fully predictable Backup solutions
	Examples of responses (abbreviated)
Low score	A 15-year old girl wants to get married? No, no way. Marrying at age 15 would be utterly wrong. One has to tell the girl that marriage is not possible. [After further probing] it would be irresponsible to support such an idea. No, this is just a crazy idea.
High score	Well, on the surface, this seems like an easy problem. On average, marriage for 15-year-old girls is not a good thing. I guess many girls might think about it when they fall in love for the first time. And, then, there are situations where the average case does not fit. Perhaps in this instance, special life circumstances are involved, such that the girl has a terminal illness. Or this girl may not be from this country. Perhaps she lives in another culture and historical period. Before I offer a final evaluation I would need more information.

Source: Baltes & Staudinger (1993).

What Do You Think?

When you need help with a life problem, to whom do you turn? Does your answer reflect that you expect to find older people have more wisdom? Does your answer depend on the type of problem?

COGNITIVE PLASTICITY AND TRAINING

Research showing that the environment has a significant impact on the structure and functioning of the brain has also led to optimism about cognitive functioning in late adulthood. Studies with animals have demonstrated plasticity of the neurons in the cerebral cortex. **Plasticity** refers to the ability of other neurons to take over the functions of neurons that have been damaged or lost. We will discuss changes in the

This man in late adulthood demonstrates cognitive plasticity with his use of computer technology that was not yet invented when he was a young adult. Environmental factors, such as exposure to new experiences, influence the course of cognitive functioning in adulthood.

brain more specifically in the next section. Here we look at research, first with animals and then with humans, demonstrating that aging brains can respond positively to enrichment in the environment and cognitive training.

Animal Research

Marian Cleeves Diamond (1993) and her colleagues at the University of California at Berkeley have spent thirty years doing a series of experiments with rats that have given a new perspective on the brain, its functioning, and its aging. Their investigations have led to the understanding that environmental living conditions have an impact on the state of the cerebral cortex. In the enrichment condition, twelve rats live together in a large cage in which they have access to objects to explore. In the standard condition, three rats live together in a small cage with no objects to explore. In the impoverished condition, one rat lives alone in a small cage with no objects to explore. Diamond and her colleagues have shown that enrichment of the environment causes an increase in the growth of dendrites (the part of the nerve cell that connects with other nerve cells) and thickening of the cerebral cortex in the brains of rats, while impoverishment of the environment causes decreases in thickness of the cerebral cortex. Greater thickness of the cortex reflects more connections among nerve cells. First, the researchers found evidence of these cortical changes in young animals placed in enriched environments. Then they found measurable changes with prenatal enrichment. Later they looked at young, middle-aged, and old adult rats and found that at all ages environmental enrichment produced significantly thicker cortices, while environmental impoverishment produced diminished cortices (Diamond, 1988).

Let us look at an experiment done with very old rats. A particular breed of rat can live 904 days in the laboratory. (On average, rats have a life expectancy of two to three years.) At 766 days, after spending most of their lives in standard colony living conditions, Diamond (1988) and her research team separated these old rats into enriched or standard conditions, with new living partners. After 138 days in these new living conditions (at 904 days old), the experiment was ended and the cerebral cortices were examined. The enriched rats had 10 percent thicker cortices than those in the standard condition, a difference as great as that seen among young rats. These old rats were in the enriched condition for 138 days rather than the 30 days typically used with the young rats. We do not know if the old rats would have responded in only thirty days, but we do know that the cortices of very old animals did respond positively to enriched conditions.

Obviously it would be unethical to do similar studies with humans, but "the results from enriched animals provide a degree of optimism about the potential of the brain in elderly human beings, just as the effects of impoverishment warn us of the deleterious consequences of inactivity" (Diamond, 1988, p. 157). Human studies have focused on whether older adults' cognitive performance can be improved through training, the nature of the training, and the training conditions under which improvement occurs. They demonstrate the ability of social and behavioral science to improve cognitive functioning in the later years (Lerner, 1990).

Human Research

As we saw in Chapter 14, normative patterns of age-related changes in cognitive functioning begin in the early sixties, but great individual differences exist, with some individuals showing large changes in midlife and others showing only small changes in their eighties. K. Warner Schaie's (1994) sequential studies, you may remember, also indicate cohort differences in the course of cognitive functioning. Individual and cohort differences suggest that environmental factors influence the course of cognitive functioning in adulthood. Researchers have designed studies to test whether declines among elderly people can be remedied by training. They have focused on those abilities and processes that longitudinal studies have shown to exhibit earlier patterns of decline, such as abstract problem solving, fluid intelligence, formal operations, perceptual speed, and associative memory and memory span, to test the effects of cognitive interventions in late adulthood (Willis, 1990).

How do researchers train older adults and test for improvement? Willis and Schaie (Schaie, 1994) did a longitudinal training study using the participants in the Seattle Longitudinal Study (SLS) (see Chapter 14). Sherry Willis developed training materials to provide five one-hour sessions of individual strategy training in inductive reasoning and spatial orientation, two fluid abilities that tend to decline early and to be considered resistant to training. Schaie and Willis used the longitudinal information from the SLS to identify individuals who had declined in one or both of these abilities in the previous fourteen years. They selected individuals who were sixty-five in 1983 and later those who were sixty-five in 1990. Each subject received training in one ability. Subjects who had declined in only one ability got training for that ability; those who had declined in both abilities or neither ability were assigned to the training groups randomly. All subjects received a pretest, then training, then a posttest. The inductive reasoning group served as a control for the spatial orientation group, and vice versa, since each person was in only one training group.

In the initial training study (1983–1984) about two-thirds of the experimental subjects showed significant improvement and about 40 percent who had declined in the previous fourteen years returned to their predecline level. The 1990–1991 sample produced similar findings. Training was more effective for inductive reasoning than for spatial orientation. Men tended to benefit more from inductive reasoning training, while women benefited more from spatial orientation training. Training was somewhat more effective for those who had declined than those who had not. Subjects who had been trained in the initial study still maintained a significant advantage over the controls seven years later. The improvements were not limited to laboratory tasks. Willis and her associates (1992) showed substantial correlations between the abilities that were trained and objective measures of performance on tasks of daily living.

These and similar studies show that intellectual decline is not necessarily irreversible and that intervention strategies may allow for longer maintenance of high levels of intellectual functioning in community-dwelling older persons (Schaie, 1990). These findings highlight the considerable plasticity in older adults' cognitive performance. Such evidence of plasticity provides a very optimistic counterpoint to the irreversible cognitive decrements from which some elderly people suffer, which we will consider in the next section.

What Do You Think?

Given the evidence that older people can benefit from plasticity and training, in what ways do you think ageism might contribute to decline in older adults? What life circumstances might help older adults maintain cognitive abilities?

THE AGING BRAIN

As with other bodily systems, age-related changes occur in the central nervous system. Brain weight and brain mass start to decrease gradually at age twenty, although in both cases the loss is moderated by health status. The decreases are very small by age fifty and accelerate after age sixty (Christiansen & Grzybowski, 1993). These cross-sectional differences in brain size may not be simply a function of age but may in part be due to the secular trend that has produced increased height and weight in succeeding generations (Whitbourne, 1985). Without knowing for sure what the brain weight and mass of older adults were when they were young, we cannot be certain how much of their smaller brain size is due to age-related loss and how much is due to their being smaller as young adults than the young adults to whom they are being compared.

Brain Changes

Cross-sectional studies show loss of nerve cells in some areas of the brain over the adult years, but most brain changes are not apparent until after age sixty. In the cerebral cortex, the neuronal loss seems to be greatest in the sensory and motor areas and smallest in the association areas. This may explain why we see a steady decrease in fluid intelligence, which is more closely tied to sensory input, over middle adulthood but an increase in crystallized intelligence, which, as discussed in Chapter 14, is the knowledge of specific information and the use of judgment.

Neuronal Loss and Growth   Brain cells do not regenerate. Many more are produced than are needed. During fetal development, nerve cells form at the rate of fifty thousand per second (Diamond, 1993). A newborn has approximately 100 billion brain cells. A small loss in brain cells is apparent by age fifty, and accelerates after age sixty. By age 80, brain mass has decreased by about 10 percent.

Neuronal loss is not the only age-related change that we see in the brain. Plasticity enables other neurons to take over the functions of neurons that have been lost. Some neurons have the inherent capacities to grow and repair their circuitries. They do this through axon sprouting and synaptogenesis. *Axon sprouting* means that when part of the input to a neuron or group of neurons is lost, the nerve fibers from undamaged neurons sprout and form new connections to replace those lost. *Synaptogenesis* refers to the creation of new synapses to replace old ones that have been lost (Cotman, 1990). While many studies have demonstrated the loss in number of neurons in the brain as it ages, others have shown that the density of synapses increases with age (Labouvie-Vief, 1985; Whitbourne & Weinstock, 1986). Sherwin Nuland (1994) has suggested that this may be the neurological source of wisdom that people are believed to accumulate with advancing age.

Other Changes   Besides the decrease in neurons, other significant changes occur in the aging nervous system. As the aging cardiovascular system functions less efficiently, the blood flow to the brain is reduced. This contributes to the death of neurons, which cannot store oxygen and depend on the blood flow to keep them supplied. The neurons themselves develop *neurofibrillary tangles* within the cell body and dendrites. The brain develops *granulovascuolar degeneration*, empty spaces called *vacuoles* surrounding densely stained granules, and *senile plaques,* clusters of degenerating neurons. The brains of elderly individuals with senile dementia show these structural changes. It is not clear whether they occur in normal aging brains. Chemicals called *neurotransmitters* that regulate the nervous system also change, altering the patterns of communication among neurons.

Changes in the brain are the aspect of aging that people generally fear most. The word *senility,* which, like *senescence,* used to be a neutral term referring to old age, has become a negative term referring to mental and physical infirmity of old age (Covey, 1988). This usage implies that cognitive impairment is a normal consequence of aging and is another example of the historical changes in ageism we discussed earlier in this chapter. In fact, most declines in mental functioning are related to changes in health and are not a function of age. Better cognitive functioning in old age is also associated with social factors such as more education, professional occupations, and being active during retirement. There are, however, several brain disorders of age.

Organic brain syndromes are pathological states of the brain caused by physical damage of brain tissue. Physicians diagnose organic brain syndrome based on behaviors and not by examining the brain. Behaviors associated with organic brain syndrome include mood changes, irritability, fatigue, agitation, disorientation, and deficits of memory, learning, and judgment. Since any number of factors may cause these behaviors, there is ample room for misdiagnoses, which can be tragic since some syndromes are treatable whereas others are not. Metabolic malfunctions such as diabetes, liver failure, or anemia and those due to medication effects, benign brain tumors, vitamin deficiencies, or alcoholism cause **acute brain syndromes**. Although the symptoms often appear to be the same as those linked to irreversible brain damage, people with acute brain syndrome are likely to have fluctuating periods of awareness when they are lucid. While these periods may be brief, they suggest that the damage is treatable and reversible. Physicians must attempt to rule out these potentially curable causes of dementia before diagnosing chronic brain syndrome (Prayson & Estes, 1994). Irreversible changes in the brain cause **chronic brain syndromes**, including multiinfarct dementia, Alzheimer's disease, and senile dementia.

Multiinfarct Dementia

Vascular disease causes **multiinfarct dementia**, which accounts for 10 to 20 percent of organic brain syndrome in adults (Christiansen & Grzybowski, 1993). Risk factors include hypertension, diabetes mellitus, advanced age, being male, and smoking (Skoog, 1994). Blockages in the blood vessels reduce or prevent blood flow to the brain, depriving it of oxygen and nutrients. This results in a series of tiny strokes, which may be so small that they go unnoticed at the time or may be accompanied by headaches or dizziness. An attack of confusion or spotty memory may be the first sign of multiinfarct dementia. It is important to diagnose multiinfarct dementia, because treating the hypertension and underlying vascular disease can slow the progress of the brain disease. Multiinfarct dementia is distinguished from other dementias by sudden rather than gradual onset and a steplike progression (Elias et al., 1990). Unlike with other chronic brain syndromes, individuals with multiinfarct dementia have periods when they are lucid and memories return.

This wife shows a leaf to her husband with Alzheimer's disease. Caring for a husband with Alzheimer's disease is a tremendous burden because as it progresses he may no longer recognize his wife or other loved ones.

Alzheimer's Disease

When a popular president of the United States begins to forget things, he has many people around him who provide him with notes, whisper cues from the sidelines, or fill in for him. All of these memory aids were in use at the end of Ronald Reagan's presidency. Only after he was out of office did the family announce that President Reagan was suffering from Alzheimer's disease.

Senile dementia of the Alzheimer's type, or **Alzheimer's disease**, affects more than 11 percent of individuals over sixty-five years of age and, including those patients under sixty-five, around 4 million Americans. It accounts for 50 to 60 percent of organic brain syndrome patients over sixty-five, as well as many in their middle years (Nuland, 1994). Alzheimer's disease is caused by degeneration of the brain cells in those portions of the cerebral cortex that are associated with memory, learning, and judgment. The progressive deterioration worsens the patient's dementia as it affects an increasing proportion of these cells. In addition to the loss of brain cells, the chemical neurotransmitter decreases, and lipofuscin granules (yellow-brown pigments that may interfere with cell activities), neurofibrillary tangles, and senile plaques increase. The hippocampus, a part of the temporal lobe associated with the storage of memories, degenerates. The presence of senile plaques and neurofibrillary tangles in the brain are the bases for the microscopic diagnosis of Alzheimer's disease. While these sometimes appear in the normal aging brain, they show up in large quantity in Alzheimer's patients.

Forgetfulness or confusion are typically the first symptoms of Alzheimer's. At this early stage of the disease, a person may get lost on the way home from work or forget what happened the previous evening. As the disease progresses the confusion becomes intense and often includes belligerence. A husband, for example, may become violent with his wife for the first time after thirty-five years of marriage.

Working with Mark John Isola, THERAPEUTIC RECREATION DIRECTOR

Helping Alzheimer's Patients and Their Families

After first attending community college, Mark John Isola earned his bachelor's degree in gerontology. He was then hired as a therapeutic recreation director by the Alzheimer's Resource Center of Connecticut.

Michele: What is the Alzheimer's Resource Center?

Mark John: It's a long-term care facility for clients with dementias, primarily Alzheimer's. It provides care while preserving the dignity of the clients as much as possible. It's designed to be light, airy, and safe. The resident living areas are on an atrium, so there are no long halls. Clients can walk without interruption and not feel lost or frustrated by walls.

Michele: What does a therapeutic recreational director do?

Mark John: All long-term care facilities are required by state mandate to have therapeutic recreation directors or TRDs. The Resource Center has two full-time TRDs for 120 residents. Institutional life, no matter how good the institution, is very upsetting, so we try to alleviate that by developing therapeutic activities for the clients.

Michele: What kinds of activities?

Mark John: I run eight activities a day to help maintain and stimulate abilities. I gear them to three different levels: high-, moderate-, and low-functioning clients. I also design activities to provide social, task-oriented, and cognitive stimulation. Although word games and ballplaying activities are basic to therapeutic recreation programs, the real substance of the program includes art therapy, music therapy, sensory programs, arts and crafts activities, and live entertainment.

We are very concerned with maintaining the dignity of our clients. We make sure our activities are age appropriate. If we want to hold a large-motor activity, for example, we don't blow bubbles and have the clients break them by waving their arms. Instead of stuffed animals, the Humane Society brings in real pets once a month.

Michele: How do your clients respond?

Mark John: It varies with the client. The activities keep clients involved. In most long-term care facilities, the TRDs try to cultivate a peer support group for each client. A support group of other clients and a TRD helps prevent disengagement and depression.

Michele: So do you mainly work with groups?

Mark John: No, I do a lot of one-on-one work, too. With dementia clients, the TRD becomes a caregiver working to balance out mood states and anticipate needs of the clients. I'm responsible for the thirty residents in one of our four units. I'm with them eight hours a day. I constantly help them make decisions or intervene in the things they're doing. Sometimes I help them to the bathroom or stop them from playing with dirty clothes in the hamper. Many have lost the ability to communicate, so I try to interpret from their behavior whether they are thirsty or hungry, or need personal attention.

Michele: What do you try to accomplish?

Mark John: With Alzheimer's, there is no rehabilitation. There is no time limit. I'm content when the client is

Patients may no longer recognize their loved ones or may forget to dress before going outside. As the Alzheimer's progresses, symptoms include greater confusion and hyperactivity, often in the form of aimless but continual walking. In the final stages sleep increases, then come coma and death. The course of the disease is usually seven to ten years, but death can come as quickly as three or as slowly as fifteen years after its onset. As Alzheimer's progresses, patients become less able to care for themselves and require more care and controlled environments to enable them to wander in safety.

Neither the causes of nor the cure for Alzheimer's disease are understood. Although some evidence suggests that genetic defects are involved, in many cases genetic involvement has not been found (Marx, 1991). Rare early-onset forms of Alzheimer's tend to pass from generation to generation and have been most clearly linked with abnormalities in two of the three genes associated with Alzheimer's (Hardy, 1994; Nuland, 1994). More common variations have been found in APOE, a gene on chromosome 19 that produces a blood lipoprotein. Testing for APOE cannot predict if or when a person will get Alzheimer's, because not everyone who suffers from Alzheimer's carries APOE and some who have the gene show no signs of Alzheimer's even in very old age (Sachs, 1995). Researchers can use APOE to identify people who are at greater biological risk for the disease to study progression of

content or in the best mood state he or she can be in. I ask myself: Why are people crying? Why are people tearing things off the wall? Why are they undressing themselves? It's not that I care if their briefs are off, but then they find themselves naked and feel embarrassed. I manage mood states to the best of my ability. If I see someone sobbing uncontrollably, I try music, I try touch, I try everything I know to help. Sometimes it works and sometimes I just have to walk away, but I go back two minutes later and try again.

Keep her safe. Keep him safe. It's hard. The burnout rate is high, much higher than with other long-term care facilities. Working exclusively with this population is brutal. At the end of the day, you must let go of it and walk away. A blessing of the disease is that most of the clients achieve some level of contentment. It's harder on the families. I worry that many families keep Alzheimer's patients at home too long. It's often not functional in this day and age. If the adult child does not have the coping skills, it isn't nec-

essarily better for the patient just to keep him in familiar surroundings. It's also a terrible burden on women.

Michele: Do you work with the families too?

Mark John: Often dealing with the family is more difficult than dealing with the actual client. A caregiver wife of that generation, who was a dependent spouse, is likely to be stressed and fearful. At age sixty, sixty-five, or seventy, she may be dealing for the first time with transportation, finances, and care-plan meetings. She misses her spouse and is going through anticipatory widowhood. She wants to be a caregiver, but can't any longer. Her husband may not even recognize her anymore, although there is often a sense of familiarity.

Michele: How do the clients' children take it?

Mark John: Adult children and spouses both find Alzheimer's frightening. Children can be more confused by seeing their parent change, but they see the light beyond. They have more life flexibility. Children are more likely to say, "We will do what is needed."

Many wives see it as the end of the road. On the other hand, some spouses are as supportive of you and the staff as you are of them. You wonder in those cases who is helping whom.

Michele: Do you find your work gratifying?

Mark John: I like it. It's an opportunity to view the disease right up front. I feel I am helping people. I always knew I wanted a helping profession— I just wasn't sure what population. I think I have a talent for this. My coping skills are good; it doesn't drain me. I bring life and I bring balance to it. You need to have balance within yourself.

What Do You Think?

1. Why is there no rehabilitation among Mark John's clients? How is this outcome for Alzheimer's similar to that for other ailments discussed in this chapter? How is it different?

2. How might a facility designed for Alzheimer's patients be better for the patient than at-home care provided by the family? How might it be better for the family?

and treatments for the disease. Preliminary tests indicate that special eye drops may identify Alzheimer's patients, but since there is no preventive treatment or cure it is unclear whether early diagnosis would be beneficial.

As people have learned more about Alzheimer's, fear of the disease has grown. Older adults often experience *anticipatory dementia,* the concern that normal age-associated memory changes are signs of the onset of Alzheimer's disease. Stephen Cutler and Lynne Hodgson (in press) examined the link between memory appraisal and personal concerns about developing Alzheimer's among fifty adults ages forty to sixty, half with a living parent diagnosed with Alzheimer's and half a matched group with no family history of Alzheimer's. They found that changes in memory functioning created concern about developing Alzheimer's regardless of whether one had a family member with dementia; those with more memory loss had more anxiety. Among the adult children of Alzheimer's patients, concern about developing the disease was greater among women, among unmarried people, and among those who believed Alzheimer's is inheritable. Perhaps women have greater concern because as female adult children they are more likely to be caregivers, as we saw in Chapter 15. Cutler and Hodgson express concern that since anticipatory dementia may discourage people with remediable memory complaints from seeking help, it may represent a potential threat to well-being.

Alzheimer's patients are sometimes given drugs to lessen their agitation. Memory aids, such as making lists of things to do before leaving the house, can sometimes help patients in the early stages of Alzheimer's maintain their functioning. But at this time, the best we can do is provide loving care for the patients and support the families and friends who suffer the loss of their loved one while carrying the enormous burden of providing care. The Working With interview on page 616 describes a caregiver in a long-term care facility.

Senile Dementia

Like Alzheimer's, the loss of brain cells causes **senile dementia**, which impairs orientation, intellect, judgment, and memory. Senile dementia is more frequent among females, whereas Alzheimer's is more common among males. Senile dementia typically starts at about age seventy-five, which is later than the average onset of Alzheimer's. Senile dementia is terminal; there is no cure.

While people often exaggerate how frequently the dementias occur, the heartbreak for afflicted individuals and their families cannot be overstated. Slightly fewer than 5 percent of all persons over sixty-five suffer so severely from dementia (including all types of dementia) that they require institutional care or a full-time custodian, and another 10 percent have mild to moderate dementia (Horvath & Davis, 1990). But these statistics do not lessen the burden of those families with a member who has dementia. Mild to moderate dementia requires special attention to care and safety on the part of the family or caregivers. It also requires a sense of humor to deal with the pain of seeing once competent and capable partners, parents, and siblings act in forgetful and foolish ways. Severe dementia causes agony because in addition to exhibiting totally new patterns of behavior that require constant supervision, patients cease to recognize loved ones who provide care or make arrangements for care. The personal anguish of having your spouse or parent not recognize you or remember your shared history compounds the pain of watching the disease take its toll and the pressure of providing care. In addition, adult children worry about their chances of suffering the same fate.

Although we have come to associate dementia with being old, it is not inevitable. Most older adults are in good cognitive health. Changes in functioning should not simply be accepted as the inescapable effects of age. Some organic brain syndromes are treatable, as are many physical symptoms. Likewise, good health and good health behaviors can contribute to maintaining brain functioning well into the later years, as we saw in our earlier discussion. In addition, because the physical, cognitive, and psychosocial domains interact, treatable psychological problems such as depression may contribute to the misdiagnosis of dementia. We turn to the mental health issues of aging next.

What Do You Think?

Imagine that one of the tests designed to identify risk for Alzheimer's indicates that a person is likely to develop the disease. Should the person be told? Debate this issue with one or more classmates.

MENTAL HEALTH AND AGING

Depression is the most common psychiatric complaint of elderly adults (Cohen, 1990). Although its incidence is higher among older adults, the experience of depression and its responsiveness to treatment are the same as for younger adults

(LaRue et al., 1985). Symptoms associated with depression include appetite or weight loss; sleep disturbance; lethargy or agitation; loss of interest or pleasure in activities; feelings of worthlessness, guilt, or self-reproach; cognitive complaints; and suicidal ideation or behavior. Because many of the symptoms of depression, such as sleep problems or memory complaints, are thought to be normal changes associated with aging or illness, they may go undiagnosed. Elderly patients tend to report physical symptoms such as appetite loss but deny affective symptoms such as feeling worthless, which can mask the depression (Rabins, 1992). In addition, the symptoms of depression in elderly people often mimic dementia, leading to misdiagnosis. As a result of underdiagnosing or misdiagnosing of depression among the elderly, curable problems are often left untreated (LaRue et al., 1985).

Although we do not know how many older adults suffer from depression, clinicians generally agree that between 4 to 7 percent experience depression severe enough to require intervention (Anthony & Aboraya, 1992). Rates as high as 20 to 25 percent have been reported among nursing home residents (Adler, 1992). Depression is more common in very old adults. In a cross-sectional comparison of eighteen-to-ninety-year-olds, John Mirowsky and Catherine Ross (1992) found that depression was least frequent during middle age and most frequent in people over eighty. Chronic diseases and reactions to medications have been cited as factors leading to depression during late adulthood (Husaini et al., 1991; Taylor & Aspinwall, 1990). The role of social factors, such as lower social support or stressful life events, is less clear (Husaini et al., 1991; Mirowsky & Ross, 1992). Among elderly people in institutions, deteriorating health and associated increases in depression have been found to be predictive of death (Parmelee et al., 1992).

Gender, race/ethnicity, and SES are associated with depression among the elderly. Women are at somewhat more risk for depression, whereas men are more likely to be diagnosed with substance abuse or antisocial personality. For both men and women over age sixty-five, rates of these disorders are lower than for younger adults (Wykle & Musil, 1993). Marjorie Feinson (1987) found that gender was associated with depression only among the bereaved. Since women more often outlive their partners, they are at particular risk for bereavement depression.

Economic strain is associated with poor mental health, lower life satisfaction, and depressive symptoms (Wykle & Musil, 1993). Rates of depression among elderly African Americans are comparable to those of whites (Stanford & DuBois, 1992). Older Hispanics who have high illiteracy and poverty rates also have poor mental health. For instance, older Hispanic women who are widowed, have little education and low income, and are not English speaking are particularly vulnerable to depression (Stanford & DuBois, 1992). The interrelatedness of race and/or gender and SES, physical health, and negative life events may help explain the apparent associations between gender and race/ethnicity and mental health. Elderly women and minorities are often disadvantaged in terms of economic resources and, as we have seen, are more prone to depression.

Untreated depression increases the incidence of suicide among all age groups, especially elderly, white males. Older persons commit 17 percent of all suicides (Koenig & Blazer, 1992). Men age sixty-five and older are more likely to commit suicide than any other age group; white men in this age group are more likely to do so than African American men (Kaplan et al., 1994). Kevin Early and Ronald Akers (1993) suggest that African Americans are protected by a belief that suicide is a "white thing" alien to African American culture. Suicide rates for females are much lower than for males and lower for African Americans than whites.

Effective treatments for elderly depression include pharmacotherapy (antidepressants) and psychotherapy. Few comparisons between treatments based on drugs versus psychotherapy have been conducted with populations over age sixty-five, so the relative merits of the two are undocumented (Adler, 1992). Exercise may reduce depression. While most studies of physical activity and depression have excluded

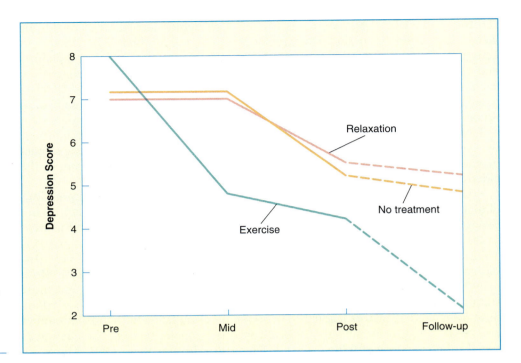

FIGURE 16.8
Beck Depression Inventory Scores from Subjects in the Aerobic Exercise Training, Progressive Relaxation Training, and No-Treatment Control Conditions
Shorter-term exercise programs have been shown to have a therapeutic effect on mild to moderate forms of depression.
Source: Roth & Holmes (1987), p. 362.

older adults, Terry Camacho et al. (1991) used data from a longitudinal study of 8,023 adults, half of whom were over age forty. They took baseline measures of physical activity and depression in 1965, then again in 1974 and 1983. They wanted to know whether people who participated in physical activity were at a lower or higher risk for developing depression and whether a change in exercise pattern could predict depression.

They found that men and women who reported low physical activity at the beginning of the study were at a much higher risk for developing depression ten or twenty years later than were those who reported high physical activity when the study began. Even when the researchers statistically controlled for physical health, SES, social supports, life events, and other health habits, this relationship between physical activity and depression persisted. Adults who began the study "inactive" and changed their pattern to "active" by 1974 had no greater risk of depression in 1983 than those who had been active continuously. On the other hand, those who had been active in 1965 and became inactive in 1974 had a 1½ times greater risk of being depressed in 1983. For those who had been inactive continuously, risk of depression was highest. Statistical analysis revealed that the direct relationship was between physical health and depression. As Figure 16.8 shows, shorter-term exercise programs have been shown to have a therapeutic effect on mild to moderate forms of depression (Martinsen, 1990). Once again we see how health-promoting behaviors adopted early in life can have long-term benefits.

What Do You Think?

What do you do when you are depressed? Do you think these same strategies would be effective if you were elderly? Why or why not?

WORK AND RETIREMENT

While establishing a career or an occupation and achieving within it are the focus of early and middle adulthood, most Americans look forward to retirement in their

Race, ethnicity, gender, and occupational level all effect retirement possibilities and choices. His noncareer job at a dry cleaners does not provide this older man with pension benefits, which makes his retirement difficult.

later years. Although stereotypes often depict retirement as a time of depression and low life satisfaction, the reality turns out to be quite different. As with many areas of life, people who can control whether and when they retire can plan for and anticipate the change. This enables retirees to make a positive adjustment to retirement and contrasts sharply with the experience of involuntary retirement or losing a job that we discussed when we addressed cognitive development in middle adulthood in Chapter 14. The statistics on when people retire, however, are contradictory. The U.S. Bureau of the Census (1993) indicates that most adults retire by age sixty-five, and almost all by age seventy. Yet an AARP survey (1993) indicates that fewer than one-fourth of Americans ages sixty-five to seventy-four and fewer than one-third seventy-five and older describe themselves as retired. To understand this contradiction, let's consider how retirement is defined.

What Is Retirement?

When Neal retired after twenty-five years on the police force, he didn't stop working. He began driving people to various places in their own cars and delivering packages. Because he knew so many people from his work on the force, his new business developed by word of mouth. He drives his regular customers to doctors' appointments, to the theater, and to and from airports. Often he makes several trips in a day.

Continuous Work   Retirement often means departure from a *career job*, a job at which the individual has been employed at least thirty-five hours per week for ten or more years. Leaving a career job is a significant life event, but it does not necessarily mean leaving the labor force. In a study of more than eleven thousand respondents, Joseph Quinn and associates (1990) found that over one-quarter of the wage and salary employees did not stop working when they left their full-time career jobs. Like Neal, most of these people started a new full- or part-time job, and only a few moved to part-time status on their current jobs. Table 16.8 shows exit patterns from career jobs for women and men. There is no column for self-employed women, because only 50 of the 3,021 women in the sample fit this category of self-employed

TABLE 16.8 **Exit Patterns from Career Jobs for Individuals with Four Years of Subsequent Data**
Joseph Quinn and his associates (1990) found that more than one-quarter of the wage and salary employees in their retirement history study did not stop work when they left their full-time career jobs.

Type of Transition	Wage and Salary Men	Self-employed Men	Wage and Salary Women
Part time on career job	5%	25%	10%
Part time on new job	10	13	10
Full time on new job	12	13	7
Out of labor force	73	49	74
(Sample size)	(1,446)	(241)	(368)

Source: Quinn et al. (1990).

career job. This seems likely to change as younger cohorts of women, who have entered professions and started businesses in greater numbers, reach retirement age. Most of the men and women left their career jobs between ages sixty-two and sixty-four. Those who left earlier, between fifty-eight and sixty-one, were the most likely to take another full-time job. Those who stayed on career jobs after age sixty-five (6 percent of the men and 11 percent of the women) were least likely to leave the labor force for good. Retirement, then, may mean changed or reduced employment, not simply stopping work.

Discontinuous Work   Many adults, especially racial/ethnic minorities, never have held career jobs and thus never consider themselves to be retired. Only 5 percent of those who described themselves as retired in the AARP survey were African Americans. Rose Gibson (1991) found that many older African Americans did not define themselves as retired because they had discontinuous lifetime work patterns, thought of themselves as disabled, and felt economic need that pressed them to work from time to time. Perceptions of a discontinuous work life made the line between work and nonwork indistinct and created ambiguity of retirement status. Similar difficulties have been identified in defining retirement among Mexican Americans who often work, voluntarily or not, in part-time and seasonal jobs for much of their working lives. Because their lifetime work patterns have no clear line between work and nonwork and they lack access to private pensions, they do not define themselves as retired (Zsembik & Singer, 1990).

In terms of retirement, women face problems similar to those of racial/ethnic minorities. Although women's labor force participation has increased dramatically, many older women have been homemakers for most, if not all, of their adult lives. Consider Tom and Frances, whom you met in the last chapter. When Tom retired at age seventy, Frances continued her homemaking tasks. Although she had held a small number of jobs over the years, they had always been part time, short term, and secondary to homemaking for her family of ten. As Tom naps in his recliner during the afternoon, she often asks herself when *she* will get to retire. Even women who have had more labor force commitment than Frances are less likely than men to be covered by pension plans because they are more likely to have held part-time jobs or taken leaves to raise children or care for aging parents (AARP, 1993; Hatch, 1995). Mexican American women are almost five times more likely than Mexican American men to describe themselves as retired, but they are one-third as likely to be considered retired when in terms of receiving retirement income (Zsembik & Singer, 1990). This gender disadvantage is likely to change as younger cohorts of women establish steady patterns of labor force participation in jobs that provide retirement benefits.

Retirement Patterns   We see, then, that retirement is not simply a *yes* or *no* status; nontraditional retirement patterns are common among older Americans. Even those who retire experience different phases as they adjust to their new status, as Table 16.9 shows. Retirement is best defined by both substantial withdrawal from the labor force and receipt of retirement benefits (Atchley, 1994). White men are most likely to meet both criteria. Race, ethnicity, gender, and occupational level all affect retirement possibilities and choices. Health and pension status are both important (Quinn et al., 1990). Physical and mental capabilities interact with the demands of the job to influence retirement decisions. Sam, for example, was a pipe fitter who counted the days until he reached retirement age and would no longer have to bend and lift. His brother, a pharmacist, had less physically demanding work, but his health was poor, so he reluctantly retired. The third brother, a teacher, suffered small strokes that gave him episodes of incoherence that made continuing his work impossible. If there had been a fourth brother with an intellectually but not physically demanding job and no physical or mental health problem, he likely would have delayed retirement. People with poor health or physically demanding work are more likely to leave the labor force, as are those with pension benefits. Those who are healthy and those without benefits are more likely to continue working. Self-employed individuals are more likely to simply reduce hours on their current jobs. Other individuals will likely have to change jobs and take lower-status jobs to reduce work hours.

How much individuals enjoy their work also influences retirement decisions. Workers with boring, repetitive jobs, such as assembly line and office work, are likely to choose retirement as early as they can afford it. In contrast, workers with interesting jobs that give them high satisfaction are less likely to retire early and more likely to continue to work. Well-educated employees are less likely to retire early than those with high school education or less (Hooyman & Kiyak, 1993). Perhaps for these reasons, early retirement is more prevalent among African Americans and Mexican Americans with career jobs than among whites (Gibson & Burns, 1991). Three-quarters of employees would choose to retire gradually, but few jobs make this option possible (Jondrow et al., 1987).

TABLE 16.9   *Atchley's Phases of Retirement*
Based on studies of people facing retirement, Robert Atchley and his colleagues identified phases through which the retirement role is approached, taken on, and relinquished. Phases are not tied to particular chronological ages, and individuals do not go through all of the phases.

Preretirement: People gear themselves up for separation from their jobs.

Honeymoon: New retirees experience a euphoric period of doing the things they "never had time for" before.

Immediate retirement routine: People settle into new routines. Those whose off-the-job-lives were full prior to retirement often find new routines more easily than those who have focused exclusively on work.

Rest and relaxation: Instead of a honeymoon phase, many people go through an initial period of inactivity or "taking it easy" after working for a long period of time. After about three years, activity levels return to normal.

Disenchantment: After the honeymoon is over and a routine is established, a small number of people feel let down or even depressed. They may have had an unrealistic fantasy of retirement or may have encountered a disruption in their retirement plans due to the death of a spouse.

Reorientation: Those who are disenchanted usually go through a process of exploring realistic choices and choosing a retirement routine that is satisfying. Friends, family, and community groups often help people to reorient.

Retirement routine: Whether they first go through the honeymoon, rest and relaxation, disenchantment, or directly from employment, most people master the retirement role and settle into a satisfying routine.

Termination of retirement: While some people return to a job, for many retirement is overshadowed by illness and disability, which gradually leads to the loss of independence.

Source: Adapted from Atchley (1994).

Well-Being in Retirement

Although retirement is a major life transition, 60 percent of retirees are relatively satisfied and adjust well to their new life circumstances (U.S. Senate Special Committee on Aging, 1990). Health and financial security seem to be the major determinants of life satisfaction after retirement. Poor health, low income, negative attitudes toward retirement, difficulty making transitions, and inability to confront job loss have been found to make retirement adjustment difficult; early retirement has more negative effects than later retirement (Atchley, 1994). Retiring early often results from ill heath, dissatisfaction at work, or involuntary job loss, which probably accounts for its negative impact. Occupational status also predicts retirement satisfaction, with lower-status workers having more health and financial difficulties, and therefore less satisfaction, than higher-level, white-collar workers. Higher-status occupations are likely to provide options for nonwork pursuits throughout life, including retirement. Harold, for example, recently retired at age seventy from his career as a college professor. He enjoyed his work and retired with a good pension. Because of his expertise, he is still sought after to lecture on trips and at special events, which provides opportunities for him and his wife to travel and enables him to continue to teach about the issues about which he has developed wisdom. In addition, Harold has research and writing projects that he never had enough time for when he was teaching. For those who, like Harold, have lifelong activities they can expanded on during retirement, the transition is easier.

Retirement is just one of the role changes in the later years. Loved ones die and become ill; living situations must be adjusted to new physical, social, and economic circumstances. Physical and cognitive changes are a significant part of the later years as people adjust to and care for their aging bodies, but social changes are dramatic as well. Whether a person reduces his or her work force participation gradually or abruptly, early or late, retirement leads to new options: leisure pursuits, community involvement, and adult education, to name a few. How people cope, grow, and change with these circumstances during late adulthood is the focus of the next chapter.

What Do You Think?

Discuss with your classmates the retirement patterns of your elderly relatives and friends. In what ways have finances and health affected their retirement decisions? What other factors have influenced their choices?

SUMMARY OF MAJOR IDEAS

Aging and Ageism

1. Ageism, or the stereotyping of and discrimination against people because they are aging or old, is a part of contemporary American culture.

PHYSICAL DEVELOPMENT

Longevity

2. Life expectancy in the United States has gone from 47 years in 1900 to 75 years today, but the maximum lifespan for humans remains 115 years and is not expected to change.

3. During the twentieth century, the U.S. population has been getting older and the elderly population has been growing in diversity. Gender, race/ethnicity, and SES affect mortality rates.

Theories of Aging

4. Cellular theories of aging attribute the breakdown of cells, organs, and the organism to "wear and tear" on the cells caused by stressors such as toxins, pollutants, and free radicals.

5. Programming theories consider the maximum lifespan to be built into the genes of each species and beyond human control.

Physical Functioning in Late Adulthood

6. Late adulthood is a time of loss in efficiency of bodily systems, but it is also a time of compensation. As loss occurs, some systems experience regeneration and growth due to their plasticity.

7. Slowing of behavior with age is a consistent finding in research examining motor responses, sensory processes, and intellectual functioning. Health and fitness, however, are more closely related to performance than is age.

8. Skin, bone, and muscle all show age-related changes. Protection from sun and other elements in early life can prevent some of the skin changes just as regular exercise can prevent some of the bone and muscle mass loss.

9. Cardiovascular and respiratory system changes that begin in early adulthood continue into the later years. The rate of aging of these systems is strongly influenced by lifestyle factors such as diet, regular aerobic exercise, smoking, and exposure to air pollutants.

10. Age-related loss occurs in all of the senses. Visual and hearing loss begin by age fifty; loss of smell shows a similar pattern; taste seems to undergo smaller and later decline.

Health Behaviors in Late Adulthood

11. Health and fitness continue to be important in the later years. Nutritional concerns increase as caloric needs decline while the need for many nutrients rises. Regular aerobic exercise is needed to prevent hypokinesia and to maintain cardiovascular and respiratory fitness. Alcohol and drug sensitivity increase.

Chronic Illnesses

12. Chronic illness, a common feature of late adulthood, often begins during middle adulthood or earlier.

13. Cardiovascular disease, the major chronic disease in the United States, is responsible for most illness and death of men during the middle years. Risk factors include family history, health-compromising behaviors, personality type, and stress.

14. Hypertension can cause arteriosclerosis, which puts a person at risk for heart attack, kidney damage, and stroke. Risk factors include genetic predisposition, obesity, poor diet, personality characteristics, and stress.

15. Cancer, the second most frequent cause of death in the United States, is a set of more than one hundred diseases characterized by uncontrolled cellular growth. Different cancers have different risk factors; all are linked to race, SES, and stress.

16. Arthritis, the second leading chronic disease in the United States, consists of more than eighty diseases that attack the joints and connective tissue. It afflicts three times more women than men and is exacerbated by stress.

COGNITIVE DEVELOPMENT

Wisdom

17. Wisdom is a positive cognitive change associated with later life. Research has shown that some older adults perform at near-peak levels on wisdom-related tasks.

Cognitive Plasticity and Training

18. Research with both animals and humans shows that enrichment and training can lead to positive changes in elderly brains and in cognitive performance

The Aging Brain

19. Normal aging of the brain is associated with neuronal loss as well as increased density of synapses.

20. Organic brain syndromes can be acute or chronic. Though the symptoms are similar, acute syndromes are treatable and reversible, whereas chronic syndromes are not reversible and are often fatal. Alzheimer's disease is the most frequent chronic organic brain syndrome.

Mental Health and Aging

21 Depression is more common among the elderly than among younger adults and, if untreated, can put them (especially white men) at risk for suicide. Low SES is associated with depression, which puts women and racial/ethnic minorities at greater risk because they are economically disadvantaged.

Work and Retirement

22. Retirement is not simply a work/stop work decision; many individuals follow nontraditional retirement patterns. Health status and financial security affect satisfaction with retirement.

KEY TERMS

ageism *(582)*
senescence *(588)*
cellular theories *(588)*
programming theories *(589)*
hypokinesia *(599)*
wisdom *(607)*
cognitive mechanics *(608)*
cognitive pragmatics *(608)*

plasticity *(610)*
acute brain
   syndromes *(614)*
chronic brain
   syndromes *(614)*
multiinfarct dementia *(614)*
Alzheimer's disease *(615)*
senile dementia *(615)*

17

LATE ADULTHOOD

Psychosocial Development

Focusing Questions

- What is successful aging, and what contributes to it?

- Which relationships are significant in late life, and in what ways?

- Why is choice in housing critical in old age?

- How do the interests and activities of late life show both continuity and change?

Marcellus was born and raised in southern Illinois. It is there that he and his wife married and had their five children. He worked as a butcher and as a blacksmith. When Marcellus was forty-two, the butcher he worked for was diagnosed with tuberculosis. To protect himself and his family from the disease, Marcellus moved them to Colorado, where he had siblings. There he became a farmer. At age fifty-eight he and his wife moved again, this time to southern California to help their youngest daughter and her two young children. At age twenty-two, she was getting a divorce. They lived with her in Los Angeles, except in the summer, when they would go north to pick oranges with the other seasonal workers. Marcellus transformed his skills as a blacksmith by learning to be a mechanic. At age sixty-eight, when his wife died, he lived by himself and worked as the mechanic at a gas station. His flexible attitude and his thoughtful approach to figuring things out served him in good stead as he faced the transition of two major relocations during middle adulthood. He continued employment well into late adulthood. When he became old-old, he turned his attention to his daughter's yard, planting, weeding, and pruning as attentively as he had cared for his farm. He was always busy. As his physical mobility decreased in his very-old years, he found new ways to tend the yard. When, in his nineties, he needed to use a walker to get around, he tied a box to it and would rake the leaves and put them in the box. When an olive tree needed to come down, he sat in the yard and sawed branches one at a time, methodically cutting each one into pieces before tackling the next one. Marcellus lived almost to his 102nd birthday. He is an example of successful aging.

PERSONALITY DEVELOPMENT
IN LATE ADULTHOOD

Successful aging, from a psychological perspective, refers to the maintenance of psychological adjustment and well-being across the full lifespan. Recent research indicates that, like Marcellus, the vast majority of older men and women who are not cognitively impaired show considerable psychological resilience in the face of stress (McCrae & Costa, 1988). Although older individuals are less satisfied than younger adults with their health, they are more satisfied with most other aspects of their lives. Happiness is not correlated with age but appears to be a stable outcome of personality traits (Costa et al., 1994). Personality traits are remarkably stable in adulthood, as we saw in Chapter 15's discussion of psychosocial development in middle adulthood. Old age brings many adaptational challenges, including death of loved ones, declining health, and often economic hardship. Old people call on the skills and styles they have honed over a lifetime to adapt to these new situations. Marcellus is a good example of this. He continued his interests in making things work and helping things grow as his environment changed. As his physical mobility decreased in very old age, he resourcefully applied his interests and abilities to the narrowing tract of land he could navigate.

Continuity and Change in Late Life

George Vaillant and Caroline Vaillant (1990) reexamined the lives of the men in the Harvard Grant study (see Chapter 13) to determine predictors of physical health, mental health, and life satisfaction at age sixty-five. In 1990 the 173 remaining participants were examined by an internist to assess physical health, given a psychosocial adjustment scale to assess mental health, rated on life satisfaction, and asked to rate themselves on life satisfaction. Since this was a longitudinal study begun in 1940, the investigators already had many measures of adjustment and experiences from earlier stages of life.

What did they find? The authors identify five variables that contributed to late life adjustment: First, long-lived ancestors predicted physical health only. Second, sustained family relationships predicted physical and mental health. Closeness to siblings was a powerful predictor of late life adjustment. More than half of the men with a lifetime diagnosis of depression were only children or estranged from siblings, while only 7 percent of the men with the best psychosocial outcome had such a family history. Third, maturity of ego defenses assessed before age fifty contributed to psychosocial adjustment at age sixty-five (see Chapter 13). Fourth, absence of alcoholism and, fifth, absence of depressive disorder promoted health. The use of tranquilizers before age 50 (indicative of both depression and alcoholism) was the most significant predictor of both physical and mental ill health at age sixty-five. While childhood strengths were positively associated with health in late life and difficulty coping in early life negatively affected both mental and physical health in late life, many variables often thought to be associated with adjustment in early adulthood were not linked to late life adjustment. These included childhood SES, orphanhood, and college scholastic aptitude.

The Grant study found that closeness to siblings is a powerful predictor of late life adjustment for men. Although women were not part of the study, sisters often are close friends and companions during later life.

Limitations of the Grant Study   While the Harvard Grant study provides longitudinal data into late adulthood, it has several important limitations. First, it includes only men. Second, the sample, selected as successful young adults at Harvard, was very privileged. Consider, for example, Vaillant and Vaillant's finding that SES during childhood was not associated with late life outcome. These men represented a narrow range of SES; all were from families that had enough food, shelter, and medical attention. We cannot tell from this study how other levels of SES would affect late life outcomes. The same criticism applies to the restricted range of college scholastic aptitude; all of these men were successful enough to be admitted to Harvard. Third, sixty-five is only young-old age. What happens in the next twenty or more years? In summary, while the Harvard Grant study tells us a good deal about the aging of privileged men into young-old age, it does not answer questions about women, less privileged men, or people in old-old and very-old late adulthood.

The Berkeley Older Generation Study is a longitudinal study that includes women as well as men, has been going on for more than fifty-five years, and started out with a more representative sample than the Harvard Grant study. In 1928 about 420 young adult residents of Berkeley, California, were first interviewed. Every third child born in that city was selected for a child study, and these adults were their parents. Dorothy Field and Roger Millsap (1991) report on interview data collected from seventy-two survivors in 1969 (average age 69.0), when the respondents were young-old, and 1983 (average age 82.7 years), when forty-seven were old-old (74 to 84 years) and twenty-seven were very old (85 to 93 years). The survivors, fifty-one women and twenty-one men, were educationally, intellectually, and financially advantaged (as survivors in longitudinal studies usually are, because the less advantaged stop participating or die) and community dwelling. All had been married at one time and had living children.

Stable Traits in Late Life   What does the Berkeley study tell us about stability and change in later life? Using statistical procedures to analyze ratings on twenty-one personality characteristics at each of the two interviews, Field and Millsap (1991) found five personality components that were stationary across the two time periods: intellect, agreeableness, satisfaction, energetic, and extraversion. If you look back at Table 15.2, you will see that four of these five components are similar to those identified by Robert McCrae and Paul Costa (McCrae, 1992), which we discussed in Chapter 15. *Intellect* represents cognitive functioning and openmindedness. *Agreeableness* describes a person who is openminded, cheerful, and accepting of his or her offspring and "things in general." *Satisfaction* describes a person with high self-esteem and life satisfaction. *Energetic* reflects activity and health and correlates highly with self-reports of health in the later years. *Extraversion* includes talkativeness, frankness, and emotionality. Field and Millsap found that four components—intellect, agreeableness, satisfaction, and extraversion—reflected enduring traits during the fourteen years between their two interviews. Notice that these are four of the traits that Costa and associates (1994) indicate are stable after age thirty. The trait that Field and Millsap add, *energetic*, showed low stability in their study, probably because it is linked to health and health declines for most individuals in old-old age.

When they compared old-old and very old adults, Field and Millsap found that the very-old were less energetic than the old-old and were declining on this trait more rapidly. The very-old showed some decline in intellect, but this was unchanged for the old-old. The most stable trait they found was satisfaction. While most of the respondents showed no change on this trait, 20 percent went up in satisfaction. More than a third of the respondents increased in agreeableness. The investigators saw evidence of Eriksonian generativity (see Chapter 15) in the respondents' interest, concern, and care for their offspring. Extraversion showed a decline for both genders. The Berkeley data indicate that longitudinal change was more likely to be age related than gender related. Only one trait, satisfaction, showed a gender difference at both points of measurement, with men having higher ratings than women. The data show relative stability in satisfaction and intellect well into very old age, an increase in agreeableness, and a decline in extraversion. Certainly this is a far cry from the stereotype of cranky, conservative old people. In fact, Field and Millsap saw considerable evidence for the development of integrity.

Integrity Versus Despair

Eric Erikson's eighth stage of life, **integrity versus despair,** describes the developmental task of late adulthood (see Chapter 2). In the face of the loss of loved ones, declining health, and loss of meaningful work that can lead to *despair*, can the individual find *integrity*, or "acceptance of one's one and only life cycle and of the people who have become significant to it, as something that had to be" (Erikson, 1968, p. 139). Successful resolution of the previous stage, *generativity versus isolation*, shifts the aging adult's focus from personal concern for self and family to altruistic concern for guiding the next generation. This paves the way for finding enduring meaning for one's life, or integrity, in late adulthood. Only in late adulthood can "the fruit of the seven stages gradually ripen" (Erikson, 1968, p. 139). The progression of Erikson's adult stages moves the individual beyond adolescent identity to include a significant other in early adulthood (intimacy versus isolation), expands to the next generation during middle adulthood (generativity versus stagnation), and expands further to the sequence of the generations (integrity versus despair) so that the person becomes what survives after death, faith, love, care, and wisdom (Erikson, 1968).

According to Erikson, wisdom, which we discussed in the previous chapter as a late life cognitive development, is born of the conflict between integrity and despair. Dorothy Field and Roger Millsap (1991) found a normative, developmental increase in agreeableness that they interpret as evidence for ego integrity. While not representing "the breadth and subtlety of Erikson's life stage," agreeableness described "a person who is coming to terms with life and accepting what it has been" (p. 306). They also note that the old-old increased in agreeableness, which Erikson would expect, while the very old, who he would expect to have attained this stage already, held steady. Erik Erikson, Joan Erikson, and Helen Kivnick (1986) interviewed participants in the Berkeley Older Generation Study and found convincing evidence for the stage of integrity versus despair. Eugene Thomas (1991) also found clear evidence for ego integrity in a study of Hindu religious renunciates in India. The elderly men he interviewed accepted their past as "something that had to be." Thomas, however, points out the culture-bound nature of Erikson's formulation. These Hindus did not accept their lives as their "one and only life cycle" because of their belief in previous and future reincarnations as well.

Theories of Successful Aging

What makes for successful aging? Psychologists and sociologists have been interested in what elderly people can do and what society can do with regard to the elderly to promote successful aging. Since the 1950s and 1960s, several theories have been advanced that try to describe or explain how people adapt to the changes characteristically associated with aging. As Table 17.1 indicates, *activity theory* and *disengagement theory* take opposing perspectives on the problem of adapting to the loss of roles or activities that occurs in late adulthood.

Activity Theory   According to **activity theory,** the maintenance of social, physical, and intellectual activity contributes to successful aging. This theory assumes older people who are active will be more satisfied and better adjusted than those who are

TABLE 17.1 *Activity and Disengagement Theories Compared*
Activity theory and disengagement theory take opposing perspectives on adapting to the loss of roles or activities that occurs in late adulthood.

Activity Theory	Disengagement Theory
Older people have the same psychosocial needs middle-aged people do.	Older people have increased preoccupation with the self and decreased investment in society.
Decreased social interaction in old age comes from withdrawal by society from the aging person.	Decreased social interaction in old age comes from mutual withdrawal of both the individual and society.
Optimal aging occurs when the person stays active.	Optimal aging occurs when the aging person establishes greater psychological distance from those around him or her.
Substitute activities should be found for those that are lost (e.g., for work at retirement).	Decreased social interaction should be expected.

less active. When they articulated activity theory, Robert Havighurst, Bernice Neugarten, and Sheldon Tobin (1968) were presenting what has become both a dominant gerontological and commonsense perspective on aging. They proposed that unless constrained by poor health or disability, older people have the same psychological and social needs middle-aged people do. Older people who are aging optimally stay active and resist shrinkage of their social world by maintaining activities or finding substitutes for the ones they must give up. When disengagement occurs, it is because society withdraws from the elderly, giving them gold watches and sending them home, rather than because older people seek this withdrawal.

Activity theory and common sense share the view that older people who are active will be more satisfied end better adjusted than those who are less active. Older adults can remain active without having the same activity levels they did when younger. Golf, for example, may replace basketball or racquetball in the later years when men have more time and less energy.

While research supports the idea that healthy, active people have higher life satisfaction than those who are inactive or in poor health, one can be active without maintaining levels of activity typical of middle age (Atchley, 1994). Many people feel too busy in their middle years and enjoy reducing their activity levels at retirement, though they remain active. When Tom, whom we met in Chapter 15, retired, for example, he added some new activities (such as his long walk with Frances each morning), expanded some activities (time caring for grandchildren, home maintenance and yard work), and left himself more unassigned time than his life had ever before allowed. He keeps time in the afternoon to nap, read, or socialize. While still vital and active, Tom has not kept up his middle-years level of activity.

As a test of activity theory, David Lee and Kyriakos Markides (1990) studied 508 older (age sixty or over) Mexican Americans and Anglos (whites) over an eight-year period to see if activity level would predict mortality. Participants were interviewed in 1976 and reinterviewed in 1980 and 1984. Activity level was assessed at each interview by means of a scale that asked questions such as "During the last two weeks, what was the farthest distance you traveled from your home (other than going to work)?"; "How often do you get together with friends or neighbors to play such things as bingo, cards, dominoes, etc.?"; "How often do you go sightseeing in the city or countryside?" By the end of the study, 119 participants were confirmed to have died. The researchers found that activity level did not predict mortality or life satisfaction. Poorer self-rated health and advanced age did predict mortality. The researchers found no differences based on race/ethnicity.

Disengagement Theory   In contrast to activity theory, **disengagement theory** views the reduction in elderly adults' social involvement as the consequence of a mutual process between the elderly and society. Proposed by Elaine Cumming and William Henry (1961), disengagement theory assumes aging individuals experience inevitable decline in abilities and, as a result, want to be released from societal expectations. As the older person retires and children leave home, his or her social circle begins to shrink. The individual anticipates, adjusts to, and participates in this shrinking. As people have fewer roles, their style of interaction changes from active to passive. Because they have become passive, they are less likely to be sought out for new roles.

While disengagement occurs for some people, there is little evidence that it is normative. Reed Larson, Jiri Zuzanek, and Roger Mannell (1985) studied ninety-two retired adults who carried electronic pagers for one week. At randomly selected times throughout the week, a researcher would page the respondents and they would fill out a questionnaire about their companionship and internal states. From the 3,412 self-reports generated, the researchers found that half of the respondents' waking hours were spent alone. Alone, however, was not a negative or disengaged experience for most of them. When alone, they tended to do things that challenged them and demanded concentration. They reported feeling highly engaged, but in activities that were not interpersonal.

Critics of both activity and disengagement theory point out that the theories place the burden of adjustment on aging individuals, independently of the circumstances in the world around them (Cutler & Hendricks, 1990). One of the major reasons the activities of older people change is that they have reduced financial circumstances. Economizing to live within one's reduced retirement income often includes, for example, entertaining less often. As we saw in our discussion of leisure in Chapter 15, higher income, higher educational level, and higher occupational attainment all provide greater financial security and more options for leisure activities. In activity theory, we have the socially sanctioned value of productivity and keeping busy prodding elderly people to "act middle aged." In disengagement theory, we have the acceptance of the stereotypes of passive, disengaged, decaying old people. Neither theory can account for the range of activity levels of successfully aging individuals; people have different levels of activity and life satisfaction based on their personalities and life experiences. Nor do these theories consider the role of social support in successful aging, to which we turn next.

What Do You Think?

Do you know any older adults who are very active? Do you know any who are disengaged? What personality and social factors can you identify that may have contributed to these individuals' ways of aging?

MARRIAGE AND SINGLEHOOD

Older married people appear to be happier, be healthier, and live longer than widowed and divorced people of the same age (Brubaker, 1985). Most older marriages have existed since early adulthood and, as we saw in Chapter 15, marital satisfaction generally increases among long-term married couples. Compared to middle-aged long-term marriages, old long-term marriages have reduced potential for conflict and greater potential for pleasure (Levenson et al., 1993; Ward, 1993). As older couples face retirement, relocation, and declining health, the marital relationship plays important support functions, especially for men. Marriage provides emotional intimacy, sexual intimacy, interdependence, and belonging. Although all stages of the sexual response take longer with increasing age, as our discussion of physical development in middle adulthood in Chapter 14 indicates, sex can be enjoyed throughout life. Men seem to depend emotionally on their spouses more exclusively than do women. While men and women are just as likely to consider their spouses to be companions, men are more likely to name their wives as confidants (Chappell, 1990). Married women are more likely to name a daughter or a friend as their confidants, either instead of or in addition to their spouses. Perhaps that is why while most older married people report satisfaction with marriage, men tend to report more satisfaction than women (Quirouette & Gold, 1995).

Both gender and race/ethnicity are related to marital status in later life. As Figure 17.1 shows, women over age sixty-five are much more likely to be widowed than men, especially in the oldest cohorts. African American women age eighty-five

Older married people appear to be happier, healthier, and live longer than widowed and divorced people of the same age. Marriage provides intimacy, sexual intimacy, interdependence, and belonging as older couples face retirement, relocation, and declining health.

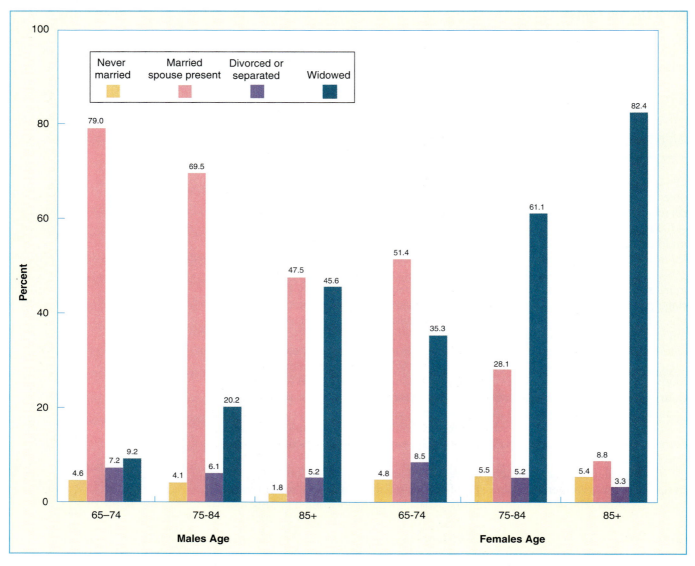

FIGURE 17.1

Marital Status of Elders by Age and Sex, United States, 1991
Women over age sixty-five are much more likely to be widowed than men, especially in the oldest cohorts.
Source: U.S. Bureau of the Census (1992).

and over make up the highest proportion of widows (83.3 percent in 1991). Hispanic and African American women are more likely than white women to be divorced. White men are more likely to be married than Hispanic and African American men. Older widowed men are seven times more likely to remarry than widowed women (Longino, et al., 1990). Divorced individuals are more likely to remarry than widowed people. Older women have fewer options for remarriage because they outlive men in their cohort and because older men tend to marry younger women. Widowed women may also find satisfaction in being single, especially if they have adequate financial resources, and may be reluctant to become caregivers to another aging husband.

Spouses as Caregivers

Declining health presents new challenges for older couples and brings changes to the couple relationship. Spouses serve as the first line of defense in coping with disease and disability. Spouses provide more hours of care and more personal care, and tolerate greater disability in their spouses for a longer period of time than other caregivers (Stoller, 1992). Since caring for each other is a normative expectation of

Though spouses serve as the first line of defense in coping with disease and disability, having help from a grand-daughter or other relatives can relieve some of the caregiving spouse's strain.

marriage, it is unlikely to stop until deterioration of health of the caregiving spouse prevents it. The rate of married elderly adults entering institutions such as nursing homes is about half that of never-married or previously married adults, even when the disability is extreme and the age very old (Stoller, 1992). Coping with disease and disability can increase closeness as the elderly partners express their love and gratitude by caring for each other (Ade-Ridder & Kaplan, 1993). The caregiving role is not limited to elderly spouses. Chronic illness and disability may strike in middle or even early adulthood, but it is more common in late life. Caregivers may receive satisfaction from working to maintain a high quality of life for their spouses, but they face burdens as well.

Psychosocial Aspects of Chronic Illness   As we discussed in Chapter 16, chronic illness generally begins with a crisis, such as a heart attack or a cancer diagnosis, and from that moment on the patient and his or her family face a changed future. Plans for daily living must be altered to include medical treatment and revise exercise patterns, dietary practices, travel plans, and, perhaps, work and household chores. To adjust to chronic illness, patients must somehow integrate their illness into their lives. For example, a heart disease patient who continues to smoke or fails to exercise is a poor patient. Most patients cope with chronic illness in ways similar to how they cope with other stressful life events. Although most experience denial, anxiety, and depression as they adjust to the demands of the illness, many ultimately adopt active coping strategies, such as modifying health and lifestyle habits to reduce subsequent risk. In contrast to avoidant strategies, such as denial, active coping has generally been found to accompany good adjustment (Taylor, 1995).

Chronic illness can lead to interpersonal strains for patients and their families. Pity or social rejection may follow diagnosis, especially if negative stereotypes are associated with the illness, such as in the case of cancer (Rounds & Zevon, 1993). Cancer, AIDS, and other chronic illnesses may cause fear and aversion in family and friends at the same time they call forth desire to provide social support. This ambivalence can lead to tense relationships and ineffective social support (Varni et al., 1992). Spouses, lovers, and other intimates may themselves be depressed by their loved one's condition (Stein et al., 1992).

Chronic illness also leads to positive outcomes. Patients report a greater ability to appreciate each day, to do things now rather than put them off, to put more effort into their relationships, to be more sensitive to others' feelings, and to be more compassionate (Taylor, 1995). They also report feeling stronger and more self-assured. People offset the negative impact of their chronic diseases by rearranging their priorities and extracting meaning and benefit from their experiences (Schaefer & Moos, 1992).

Problems of Caregiving Spouses   Spousal caregivers are subject to emotional, social, economic, and physical strain. Emotional stress results from concern for the spouse's physical and mental well-being, as well as from the need to establish new patterns of roles and responsibilities within the relationship. Not only is the caregiver likely to need to do more, but he or she is likely to get less. One of the most frequent problems of spousal caregivers is missing the way the spouse "used to be" (Chappell, 1990). Psychological reactions to many chronic illnesses, such as heart disease, stroke, and cancer, lead to decreased sexual activity (Taylor, 1995). The disability of a spouse, especially if it entails cognitive impairment, removes emotional and social support and limits the personal freedom of the caregiver. Healthy spouses may restrict social activities to provide care and companionship or because they feel guilty enjoying themselves while their partners cannot. When Benny became disabled, Bertha needed to assume all household and financial management. She also felt bound to the house to tend to his physical needs. When Bertha finally hired a nurse's aide to bathe him and watch him while she went for a walk or to the market, Benny became upset and scared the helper away. As a result Bertha left the house infrequently, only when responsibilities demanded it, and felt embarrassed to invite people in. Although financial strain was only a small part of Bertha's troubles, it often contributes to the caregiver's burden as the medical expenditures shrink the shared economic resources. The cost of nursing home care, which can cause impoverishment, adds to the caregiver's desire to keep the spouse at home. These stresses may be greater on recently married older couples who do not have a lifetime of shared experiences to draw on. Among younger married persons, declining health of a spouse has been shown to have an adverse influence on marital quality (Booth & Johnson, 1994).

Gender and Caregiving   Gender has a significant impact on the caregiving role. Because wives generally outlive husbands, more women than men provide spousal care. Husbands also appear to be less tolerant of caregiving burdens, since a higher percentage of married women are institutionalized compared to married men and married women spend more days in nursing homes than married men do (Freedman, 1993; Stoller, 1992). Eleanor Stoller and Stephen Cutler (1992) found gender differences in husbands' and wives' responses to their spouses' need for help among the frail elderly. Still, more than one-third of spousal caregivers in the United States are men (Miller, 1990). This contrasts with fewer than 10 percent male caregivers in Japan, where wives typically take care of older men and daughters-in-law take care of older women (Kiefer, 1987). There is evidence that men and women experience spousal caregiving differently, which may reflect the traditional division of labor within marriages among the now old. The way a relationship is organized before the disease or disability strikes influences how the couple copes with it (Grand et al., 1995). A lifetime of traditional gender roles leads wives more than husbands to be responsive to the physical and emotional needs of their spouses. Baila Miller (1987) found that caregiving wives paid closer attention to interpersonal situations and focused on the changes in the marital relationship, while caregiving husbands emphasized structural activities. Wives, for example, would devise explanations for hiring a helper when they went out so that their impaired spouses would not feel demeaned by having a "baby sitter."

Susan Allen (1994) found that wives provided about twice the hours of care husbands provided. Compared to caregiving wives, caregiving husbands had more outside help, and their spouses were left with more unmet needs. In terms of roles, the incapacity of a husband means a wife must assume his responsibilities, and vice versa. Since wives already do most of the household tasks, the change is greater for caregiving husbands than for caregiving wives. Illness is the factor that causes the traditional division of labor to change in elderly households (Brubaker & Kinsel, 1988). Caregiving husbands are more likely to experience decline in social contacts because wives are generally the kinkeepers. On the other hand, men are acknowledged more for their caregiving because it is less expected of them. Although some studies show that men experience less caregiving stress, more studies report no difference between the genders (Miller, 1990; Stoller, 1992).

The impact of race/ethnicity is hard to determine because most of the available research has focused on white couples. Rose Gibson (1986) found that older African American couples were less likely to face caregiving responsibilities alone than were white couples; extended families shared in the care of elderly relatives. In a study of older inner-city African Americans and whites, Colleen Johnson and Barbara Barer (1990) found that African Americans had more active support networks than did whites despite the low incidence of support from spouses and children for both groups. Shirley Lockery (1991) points out that strong family ties among racial and ethnic minorities have been assumed to provide social support for their elders, but the little research that has been done has ignored the diversity among and within minority groups. She suggests that SES, extent of acculturation, length of time in this country, and circumstances in which the group or individuals arrived in this country are all factors that affect caregiving for the elderly.

Widowhood

While illness of a spouse requires significant adjustment, the death of a spouse causes disruption to self-identity and relationships with others. The impact of widowhood depends on the age and social class of the widow. Older widows adjust better than younger widows. Becoming a widow late in life is "on time," whereas at younger ages it puts a woman into minority status. Young widows are stigmatized and allowed to play the widow role for only a short time before they are considered single again (Lopata, 1973). For most lower-SES women, widowhood means poverty, which results in lower social participation outside the home (Atchley, 1994). The disruption of social roles depends on the number of role relationships affected by the spouse's death. Helen Lopata (1973) found that widows who did not have their own friends or who had only couple-based friendships before their spouses' death generally had more difficulty. Middle-class widows who viewed themselves as part of a team in a couple-operated family farm or business, for example, have their roles impaired by widowhood. Family relationships are affected as well. Older widows usually lose their contact with in-laws, though interaction with their own families increases (Morgan, 1984).

Although far more women are widowed than men, in 1988 about 25 percent of males over age seventy-five were widowers. What impact does gender have on the experience of widowhood? This is one of the few research areas in which much less is known about men than about women. If the role of wife has been central to a woman's identity, the loss of the role may leave her wondering who she is. Men typically have other roles besides husband that are important to them, which may make widowhood a less severe identity crisis for them. On the other hand, men often see their wives as part of themselves and rely more exclusively on them as confidants. Thus, both widows and widowers face problems. Because there are so many more older widows, women are likely to have friends with whom they can share activities. A less established widowers' community is available for men to take part in. Widowers tend to be more cut off from families than widows, although no apparent difference exists in the extent of older widows' and widowers' loneliness. Widows seem to expect more, get more, and want even more social interactions,

The Double Standard of Sexuality in Late Adulthood

Ageism makes being "older" difficult. We live in a youth-oriented culture. Youth is used as a metaphor for energy, mobility, appetite, and well-being. This makes us all aware of our age long before we approach old age. Men and women alike are made defensive about gaining years and losing the prestige of youth, but the glorifying of youth affects women much more harshly than it does men.

Women in our society are judged primarily on their physical attractiveness, whereas men are judged mainly on their accomplishments (Gergen, 1990). Since the contemporary standard of female beauty is a slender and youthful one, as women age they naturally move away from it; youthful appearance is something one outgrows rather than develops over the adult years. Accomplishments, in contrast, are achieved over time. As a man ages he is more likely to be successful at work and gain money, power, and status. All of these things make him more attractive than he was before despite his graying hair, wrinkles, and other signs of physical aging. The result is the *double standard of aging,* whereby getting older enhances a man's value but diminishes a woman's. There are, of course, men who are not successful and distinguished, and many of them suffer profoundly in their middle and later years. All women, however, learn that they should hide their age by staying "thirty-nine" indefinitely and doing all they can to remain young looking. This is not a growth-producing or affirming process and puts women at a distinct disadvantage when looking for new sexual partners in their later years.

Women are judged to be older than men of the same age. When asked to categorize photographs of men and women into adolescent, young, middle-aged, elderly, and aged adult, both men and women assigned the women to older age groups (Kogan, 1989). Wrinkles and gray hair, early signs of aging, are considered ugly on a woman. "Why doesn't she do something with herself?" people ask, meaning dye her hair, use cosmetics, or get a facelift. On men, however, wrinkles are considered "character" lines, and gray hair is considered distinguished.

Women are considered sexually unattractive at a much earlier age than men are. African American women are an exception. While young women can expect to attract men about their own age, middle-aged women have to settle for men who are considerably older. Older men, on the other hand, can date and marry women much younger than themselves. Films abound in which a young actress plays the romantic partner of an aging actor, and moviegoers find the pair quite believable. Imagine the age difference was reversed and the woman was twenty or so years older than the leading man. How would audiences react? In real life, older men often choose partners who are or look younger than themselves. In 1995, the seventy-five-year-old actor Tony Randall married a woman fifty years his junior. We are used to this arrangement. We are not used to couples in which the woman is

whereas widowers expect little and get what they expect and are satisfied (Atchley, 1994). Widowers generally have better financial resources than widows and greater opportunities for remarriage because there are more older women and because society is more accepting of marriages between older men and younger women than the reverse for reasons presented in the accompanying Perspectives box.

What effect does widowhood have on quality of life? Robert McCrae and Paul Costa (1988) conducted a ten-year longitudinal study to assess the effects of widowhood on health, ability to function, and well-being. Using data from a national survey, they compared those who were married at the start of the study with those who were widowed at the start of the study ten years later. They ended up with three groups: those still married; those still widowed; and those widowed during the interval. They found that being widowed did not increase the risk of earlier mortality. It did, however, have significant impact on lifestyle. Respondents who were married had a substantially lower rate of being institutionalized (as we discussed in regard to spouse caregiving). Widowhood was also associated with a reduction in family income for both genders. The investigators found no differences among their seven variables used to assess personality, level of psychosocial functioning, or well-being. They found such strong signs of psychological resilience from bereavement and the burdens of widowhood that they conclude, "the great majority of individuals show considerable ability to adapt to a major life stress and continuing life strains—an ability we would call remarkable if it were not so nearly universal a process" (p. 138).

much older than the man, and research shows that people judge such marriages to be less likely to survive (Cowan, 1984). Older men marrying younger women leaves older women (and older-looking women) with few available partners.

Not only are older women seen as sexually unattractive; they are often thought of as not being sexual. Ageism includes the stereotype that old people are not interested in sex, that they are not sexual beings, and that sex is the province of the young. Since women are considered "old" sooner, they often fall subject to this prejudice when they are still in their middle years. While people are likely to admire an old man's interest in sex, they see an old woman's sexual interest as being in bad taste. This is an extension of the sexual double standard, in operation during adolescence and early adulthood, that condones promiscuity in men but condemns it in women. Stereotypes and social expectations can affect how we think about our sexual feelings and make us feel guilty, ashamed, or inappropriate. Women more than men are subject to negative sanctions against sexual expression, and this situation worsens as they get older.

In fact, sexual activity has been shown to predict health, happiness, and longevity among older men and women (Busse & Maddox, 1985). There is no evidence that either men or women lose interest in or the ability to enjoy sex as they age. The best predictor of sexual interest in middle and late adulthood is frequency and enjoyment of sex at younger ages. The best predictor of sexual activity is having a partner. The vast majority of older adults consider sexual satisfaction to be an important component of their quality of life. In one survey of sixty-to-ninety-one-year-olds, 91 percent enjoyed sex for a variety of reasons: it reduced tension, made women feel more feminine, helped people sleep, and provided a physical outlet for emotions (Starr & Weiner, 1981). Among married women and men age sixty and over, a person's sense of self-worth/competence and his or her partner's health status are positively related to the frequency of sex (Marsiglio & Donnelly, 1991).

While the double standard of sexuality is apparent in late adulthood, gender stereotypes are changing, and hopefully these changes will diminish it. As women have moved into the public arena in full force, their accomplishments have been mounting and receiving more recognition. As women devote their time and energies to being competent, strong, and accomplished instead of just nice, pretty, and graceful, we can hope that female desirability and self-confidence will be based on more than physical attributes, just as men's are. And as women allow their bodies to age more naturally, without hair dyes and facelifts, they will gain self-respect, and perhaps that will lead to new standards of attractiveness for older women. Many older women are indeed quite beautiful, but not in eighteen- or twenty-five-year-old ways.

Dating and Remarriage

One type of resiliency is to form new intimate relationships in later life. Socially active older adults are more likely to meet people who are potential dating partners. Health, driving ability, organizational memberships, and contact with siblings are all positively associated with dating (Bulcroft & Bulcroft, 1991). Compared to younger daters, older ones are not experimenting with marital roles (because they have been married before) and place more emphasis on companionship. They date to select a marriage partner and to maintain social activity. Older women report that dating increases their self-esteem because it makes them feel desirable. Older men report that dating gives them an avenue for self-disclosure. Both men and women expect the functions of dating relationships to include friend, confidant, lover, and, to a lesser extent, caregiver (McElhaney, 1992). The Perspectives box on page 638, examines some of the issues surrounding sexuality in late adulthood.

Marriage in later life is not uncommon, but it is likely to be remarriage. Of the fifty thousand people over age sixty-five who got married in 1987, only 4 percent were marrying for the first time (Vera et al., 1990). Previous experience with marriage predisposes people to remarry. The major reasons for remarriage are companionship and economic resources. Older mate selection follows the same principle of similarity that we noted among younger adults (see the discussion of mate selection in Chapter 13). Older adults choose mates who have similar backgrounds and interests; often they choose partners whom they have known for a long time. While elderly adults meet dating partners in public places or through friends, new spouses are more often known from the past (McElhaney, 1992). Successful late life remarriage is more likely when there has been a long prior friendship, when family and friends approve, when the pooled financial resources of the new couple are adequate, and when the marriage partners are personally adaptable (Brubaker, 1985). Some older couples choose to live together without remarriage. Charlie, for example, became a widower shortly after he retired at age sixty-five. Just as he and his wife were preparing to travel and enjoy their leisure years, she discovered she had cancer and died in less than a year. Ruth had lost her husband a few years earlier. The two couples had been close friends for many years. Now Charlie and Ruth are together, although they have chosen not to remarry. They travel together and are accepted by each other's children, but they like things the way they are.

Older Lesbians and Gay Men

While most older adults are married and living with a spouse, an estimated 10 percent are lesbian women and gay men (Quam & Whitford, 1992). Long-term relationships are much more frequent among gay men and lesbians than is commonly assumed, as we discussed in Chapter 13. While currently it is not legal for these couples to marry, many have ceremonies to celebrate their partnerships and, in several municipalities, receive "marriage" benefits such as health insurance and bereavement leave (Kimmel, 1992). Based on his own research as well as a review of the literature, Douglass Kimmel (1992) found that "when matched on age and background, lesbian, gay, and heterosexual couples do not differ on standard measures of relationship quality or satisfaction" (p. 38). Older lesbian and gay couples, like older heterosexual couples, tend to be more content in their relationships than their middle-aged counterparts (Berger, 1982).

In a survey of eighty gay men and lesbians ages fifty to seventy-three, Jean Quam and Gary Whitford (1992) found a minority were currently in a same-sex relationship, as Figure 17.2 shows. Respondents' areas of concerns were primarily the same as those for most aging adults: loneliness, health, and income. They had additional concerns about being rejected by adult children (58.7 percent reported having children) and grandchildren when they "came out" to their families and about discrimination in health care, employment, housing, and long-term care, which

Long-term relationships are much more frequent among gay men and lesbians than is commonly assumed. Older lesbian and gay couples, like heterosexual couples, tend to be more content in their relationships than middle-aged couples.

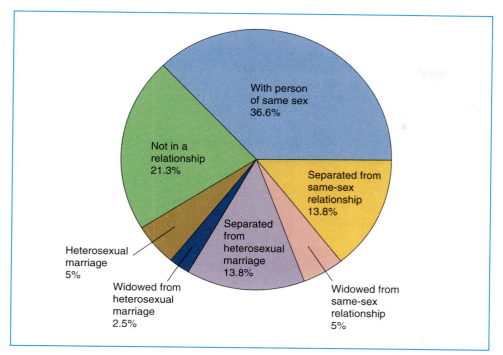

FIGURE 17.2
Relationship Status of Self-Identified Lesbians and Gay Men over Fifty Years Old
Only a minority of older lesbians and gay men are currently in a same-sex relationship.
Source: Adapted from Quam & Whitford (1992).

compounded their anxieties about aging. Older gay men and lesbians have lived most of their lives in a society that has been actively hostile and oppressive toward homosexuality. Discrimination and stigma have profoundly affected their aging experience, life satisfaction, and quality of life (Friend, 1990).

Never-Married Older Adults

In 1991 only 5 percent of older adults in the United States had never married, as Figure 17.1 shows. Because never-married adults have been on their own their entire lives, they have learned to cope with aloneness and to be autonomous and self-reliant, qualities that facilitate successful aging (Essex & Nam, 1987). Jaber Gubrium (1975) found that elderly never-marrieds tended to be lifelong isolates, although they were not especially lonely in old age. Robert Rubinstein (1987) challenged this image of never-married people as isolates. He found that many had not lived alone most of their adult lives, and almost all had family with whom they were close. Olga, for example, chose not to marry because she was blind, which she believed would prevent the marriage that was proposed from having enough privacy. She lived with her never-married sister and mother for almost all of her adult life. By the time her mother died, two other sisters had become widows and moved back "home." She survived all three sisters and, in her seventies, moved in with a fourth sister and her husband. Although never married, she was never isolated and had many close family relationships.

In a comparison of loneliness among older married, never-married, and formerly married women, Marilyn Essex and Sunghee Nam (1987) found that married and never-married people reported less loneliness than those formerly married. Robert Atchley (1994) found that social contact of never-married women depended on SES. Middle-class never-married older teachers had about the same level of social interaction married older teachers did, but never-married older telephone operators had much lower social interaction than married telephone operators.

Using intensive interviews with thirty-one never-married, childless women over sixty years of age, Robert Rubinstein and his colleagues (1991) examined the key interpersonal relationships in their lives. They found three types of key relationships:

blood relationships, such as daughter, sibling, aunt, or niece; *constructed relation-ships,* such as "like a son," "like a sister," or same-generation companionate relation-ships; and *friendships.* Coresident daughter was a frequent blood relationship; like Olga, 71 percent of these women had lived with their parents until the parents' death. Nearly 60 percent had key relationships with siblings, nieces, and nephews. Many had constructed relationships as well. More than a third had been "adopted into" a family to which they were not biologically related, such as a friend's or a min-ister's family. About 20 percent had key relationships with younger nonrelatives to whom they acted as parents. One-quarter of these women had same-generation, same-gender companionate relationships that were key in their lives. These relation-ships typically had characteristics that included enduringness, subjective closeness, periods of coresidence, extensive traveling together (such as on vacations and holi-days), and involvement with the other's extended family. All but two of the never-married women in Rubinstein's study had close friends. Some had remained close to key friends from youth into late life. Almost all of the key friends these women named were women. When asked to compare their relationships to relationships others had, some of the respondents considered their relationships as equally or more successful than key relationships others had with spouses and children, and some viewed them as problematic in terms of the potential need for caregiving. While companionate relationships clearly included a sense of obligation with regard to caring for each other, the other key relationships were far less certain. The never married do not represent all elderly people, but their experiences point out the rich variety of important relationships older adults form with family and friends.

What Do You Think?

How would you advise a young-old person to prepare for later stages of adulthood? Would your advice differ for a person in a couple or for a single person? Would it differ for a man and a woman?

RELATIONSHIPS WITH FAMILY AND FRIENDS

Relationships with family and friends are important at all stages of life. Social sup-port has been shown to affect mental health, ability to cope with stressful events, health, and mortality from infancy to late life (Antonucci, 1991). It is a direct par-allel to attachment, a concept we introduced in our discussion of infancy in Chapter 5. Secure relationships have lifelong importance; family and friend relationships among elderly adults emerge from the early social relationships between mothers and infants (Hazen & Shaver, 1987, 1990). The term **social convoy** is used to de-scribe the dynamic concept of lifelong social networks. Figure 17.3 shows two ex-amples of social convoys. The convoy model of social relations emphasizes, first, that some relations are more important than others; spouses, parents, and children are more important than other relatives, friends, and coworkers. Second, relation-ships develop over time. The mother-infant relationship grows and develops as both child and mother grow and change, but stability and continuity exist in the relation-ship as well. Third, social relations are influenced by characteristics of the individ-ual such as age, gender, ethnicity, marital status, and situational characteristics (for example, employment status). Toni Antonucci (1991) used data from a study of re-lationships among mature adults (age fifty or older) to provide evidence for the life course continuity of attachment and social support. Her data were both cross-sectional (ages fifty to ninety-eight) and longitudinal because she recontacted as many respondents as she could (404) four years later. She found that respondents had an easy time categorizing their social relations into three levels of closeness and

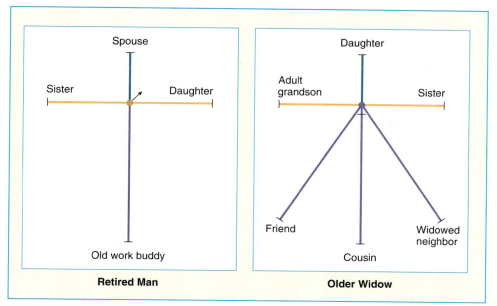

FIGURE 17.3
Examples of Social Convoys
As these two social convoys of an older adult man and woman show, members of convoys fall into three levels of closeness.

that these categories stayed stable over the four-year interval. She found no gender differences in network composition—both men and women had more women in their network—and no age differences in the number of people who provided support. Older people were more likely to have network members who were older and had been in their network longer. They were less likely to live within an hour of the members of their network or to see them as often as younger people saw their network members. While no difference was found in how many people they received support from, they provided support for fewer network members than younger adults did. Antonucci also found that early social support had a positive influence on well-being, even in the presence of negative life events.

The most important relationships are with spouses, parents, and children. We discussed all of these relationships either earlier in this chapter or in Chapter 15 in our consideration of relationships during middle adulthood. For the young-old, the issues of aging parents and young adult children are the same as those for middle-aged adults facing the same family stage issues. Remember that the boundary between middle and late adulthood in not clear; family stage is usually more relevant than age. For the old-old and very old, the issues surrounding being cared for by middle-aged children become relevant. We looked at this from the perspective of middle-aged children in Chapter 15 and will address it again from the elderly parent's perspective when we consider the "problems of living" later in the chapter. Here we focus on later life relationships with siblings, adult grandchildren, friends, and fictive kin.

Siblings

When relatives outside of the inner circle of spouse, parents, and children are considered, the sibling relationship appears to be the strongest bond for those who have a surviving sibling (Johnson & Barer, 1990). After being very important in the child and adolescent years, relationships with siblings often go underground during early adulthood, when energy is devoted to establishing independent lives and new families. As we discussed in Chapter 15, middle-aged siblings often focus on one another again for the first time when their aging parents need care. Siblings who may have had little involvement with one another find themselves in more frequent contact as they cooperate around arrangements for their parents' care. While tensions from earlier years are likely to affect families that come together in this way, most siblings work to keep their mutual rivalries and grudges from interfering with parental care, and many are able to get to know one another better and defuse petty issues from childhood (Moyer, 1992). This often enables the siblings to overcome residual family problems so the later years can be a time of increased closeness and sharing (Bedford, 1989; Gold 1990).

Older adult siblings often form one of the strongest social support systems for the older adult, during good times and bad. The tie between siblings is particularly enduring, at least on the emotional level; siblings can act as confidants, caregivers, and cherished friends. Paula Avioli (1989) found that 74 percent of older adults considered at least one of their siblings to be a close friend. Colleen Johnson and Barbara Barer (1990) found that three-quarters of older adults with siblings reported that the relationship was emotionally rewarding. In a study of immigrant Italian American siblings, Johnson (1985) also found a positive impact of ethnicity on late life sibling interactions. Siblings travel together, provide emotional support, and share family memories. They knew us when we were young and energetic and provide a generational solidarity as we get old. The death of older adult siblings has a profound effect on each sibling, because it changes the family constellation: a younger sister may become the oldest, one of many may become the only one remaining. As each sibling dies, those who remain feel less buffered from their own mortality (Moyer, 1992).

While many studies have suggested that African American families have greater solidarity than white families, only a few studies have focused on sibling ties (Johnson & Barer, 1990). In a comparison between suburban African American and white late life sibling pairs, Deborah Gold (1990) found that African Americans tended to report more positive attitudes toward their siblings and to show greater interest in providing support for them than did whites. In analyzing the descriptions of eighty-nine white and sixty-four African American sibling pairs, Gold coded for mention of closeness, envy, resentment, instrumental support, emotional support, acceptance/approval, psychological involvement, and contact. Figure 17.4 shows that although an overwhelming majority of the sibling relationships were categorized as intimate, congenial, or loyal (95 percent African American and 78 percent white), a substantially greater percentage of the white relationships were categorized as apathetic or hostile (22 versus 4.5 percent). The concepts of envy and re-

FIGURE 17.4

A Comparison of White and African American Sibling Relationships
Deborah Gold (1990) found that although an overwhelming majority of sibling relationships were categorized as intimate, congenial, or loyal, a substantially greater percentage of the white relationships were categorized as apathetic or hostile.
Source: Adapted from Gold (1990).

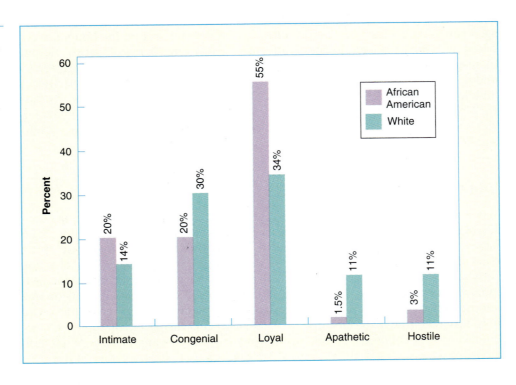

sentment were used far less frequently by African Americans than by whites to describe their sibling relations, but only among gender combinations that included men (male-male and male-female pairs).

In a large, national survey of adults with at least one full sibling who had left the parental home, Lynn White and Agnes Riedmann (1992) also found that gender was important to sibling relationships. This may well be because of the gender differences in kinkeeping skills we discussed in Chapter 15. The presence of any living sister was associated with large increases in sibling contact, and this effect doubled for female respondents. Sister-sister ties were the strongest and brother-brother ties the weakest. White and Riedmann found that African Americans, Mexican Americans, and whites were no different in the degree to which they viewed their siblings as a source of support, while Asian Americans had more faith in their sibling networks. In contrast to similarities in perceived availability, African Americans were less involved in actual exchange with their siblings, which may be related to the finding that respondents' educations and family incomes were positively associated with actual exchange and contact among siblings. Robert Taylor (1990) also found that among African Americans, those with higher educations and incomes have the most social support.

The importance of siblings in later life shows that the extended family rather than the nuclear family can serve as a source of social support. Siblings have a life-long bond that can be rekindled or refined in late adulthood. Among inner-city African Americans, Johnson and Barer (1990) found that relationships with nieces and nephews often persisted after the deaths of their siblings. More distant relatives, such as cousins, may also become close friends. Only children, siblings who cannot reconcile their resentment or estrangement, and those whose siblings live very far away must look to other family members or friends as family.

Adult Grandchildren

Given the changing patterns of mortality we saw in Chapter 16, more grandchildren know their grandparents not only as children but as adults, and more older people function as grandparents. Since grandparenthood usually begins in the middle years, we began our discussion in Chapter 15. Once again, the problems and pleasures of being a grandparent to young grandchildren do not differ for people who

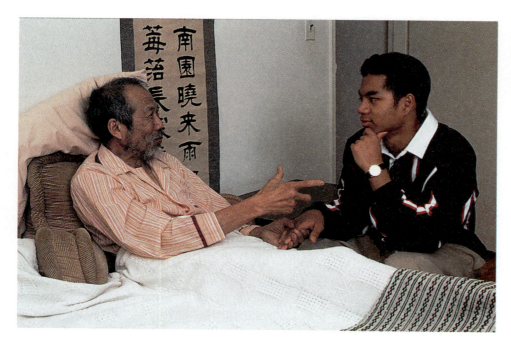

Although relationships between adult grandchildren and their aging grandmothers tend to be stronger than those with their grandfathers, this grandson and grandfather have a close relationship.

are already in late adulthood when they become grandparents. Stage of life is more important than age. In this section, we focus on the relationships of older grandparents and their adult grandchildren. Do grandchildren grow away from their grandparents as they grow up, or do they form more voluntary relationships with them? What characteristics of the grandparent and the grandchild lead to continuing association?

Continuing Connection   Research points to a continuation of the bond between grandparents and grandchildren that, as we saw in Chapter 15, begins early in the grandchildren's lives. Karen Roberto and Johanna Stroes (1995) distributed questionnaires to 142 college students. Eighty-nine percent had living grandparents; 25 percent had both sets of grandparents still living. On average, the grandchildren interacted with their grandparents once a month or less. The researchers found that adult grandchildren, both grandsons and granddaughters, did more activities with their grandmothers than with their grandfathers, particularly participating in brief visits, attending family gatherings, talking over important issues, and helping with chores. Grandchildren reported being more influenced by their grandmothers than their grandfathers in religious beliefs, sexual beliefs, family ideals, educational beliefs, moral beliefs, and personal identity issues. There was no difference in the degree to which their grandmothers and grandfathers influenced their political beliefs and work ethics. Grandchildren rated their relationships with their grandmothers to be stronger than their relationships with their grandfathers. They believed their grandmothers understood them better, and vice versa, communication was better with their grandmothers, and they shared more similar life views with their grandmothers. No differences were found in grandchildren's appraisals of their relationships with maternal and paternal grandparents. The college students reported that enjoyment in being with their grandparents was a strong motivation for maintaining a relationship with them.

Using a national telephone survey, Lynne Hodgson (1995) located 208 respondents who were age eighteen or older and had at least one living grandparent. Respondents were interviewed about the level of contact, the type of contact, and perceived closeness in their relationships with their grandparents. The mean age of the sample was 27.4 years and included eighteen-to-fifty-one-year-olds. When respondents were asked to identify the grandparent with whom they were emotionally closest, 75 percent mentioned a grandmother. This reflects the fact that many had only a grandmother living, in addition to a preference for the grandmother when the grandfather was also alive. Although the degree of association between these adult children and their grandparents varied, overall it was "remarkably high." Contact was more frequent for younger than older grandchildren, for those living within an hour's drive than those living farther away, for those who felt emotionally close to their grandparent than those who did not, and for those who had frequent contact with their parents than those who had infrequent contact. Seventy percent of the grandchildren rated their relationship with their closer grandparent as "close" or "quite close." In addition to grandmothers being chosen as closer more frequently than grandfathers, maternal grandparents were chosen more frequently than paternal ones. When respondents were asked why they were emotionally closer to the grandparent they chose, "living close by" and "seeing often" were the most frequently given reasons. Another important element was whether the grandchild had lived with the grandparent at some point in his or her life. If the grandparent had acted as a surrogate parent for the grandchild, the attachment was strong and permanent. While closeness often began early in life, many in the sample reported their relationships had become closer over time. As adults, the grandchildren appreciated their grandparents more and wanted their own children to know the grandparents, as their great-grandparents. In addition, a personal crisis or increasing need on the part of the aging grandparent had brought them together.

Cultural Variation   Culture provides different attitudes toward behaviors in different ethnic groups. Nieli Langer (1995) found that middle-class Jewish elderly adults had few expectations of material support from grandchildren. Their relationships with their adult grandchildren were based on reciprocity of meaningful emotional support. In contrast, the active role of grandparent in African American life is thought to be critical (Yee, 1992). As we saw in Chapter 15, African American grandmothers take in grandchildren at a much higher rate than do white grandmothers and thus develop strong emotional bonds with at least some of their grandchildren that continue when the grandchildren are adults. Among older inner-city African Americans, Johnson and Barer (1990) found that some had so many grandchildren that they could not keep track of them all; only grandchildren who were bound by ties of affection were counted. More than half of the respondents reported they had at least one grandchild who provided them with emotional support. While African American families often have a great many grandchildren, they are not the only families that do. Authors Robert and Michele Hoffnung were, respectively, the twelfth and fourteenth of their maternal grandmother's twenty grandchildren. While we saw this grandmother fairly often, it was usually in the company of many other aunts, uncles, and cousins. Although warm, there was nothing distinctive about our bond with her. We were part of an undifferentiated group of grandchildren.

Friends

While interactions with family are crucial at times of crisis, studies show that interaction with friends is more important to everyday well-being in later life (Hatch & Bulcroft, 1992). Having friends is prevalent in middle age and later life; 85 to 93 percent of middle-aged and older people report they have close friends (Atchley, 1994). Individuals without close friends are more likely to be men, older, and working class. Of all types of support, friends most often provide emotional intimacy and companionship (Connidis & Davies, 1990). Larry Mullins and Mary Mushel (1992) found that among older persons having friends was associated with not being lonely, while the presence or absence of spouse or children did not affect level of loneliness. Unlike family ties, which remain fairly consistent through old age, contact with friends can be subject to more variation. Health or economic problems, geographic distance, retirement, or neighborhood change may make interaction difficult. Bertha, for example, had many good friends in her neighborhood. When Benny became ill, Bertha and Benny sold their home and relocated to an apartment near a middle-aged niece and nephew. Bertha found it difficult to make new friends in her new neighborhood because she could not get out and would not invite people in due to Benny's invalid behavior. She remained in phone contact with her old friends, but missed their companionship very much.

Does gender affect friendship in later life? The findings are generally inconsistent, with some studies showing no differences and others showing some. When differences are found, they indicate that men tend to have larger friendship networks and engage in more frequent interaction with their friends, whereas women place greater importance on friendship and engage in more intimate relationships. Believing that some of the inconsistency in previous findings was related to the importance of life circumstances, such as marital status and retirement status, Laurie Hatch and Kris Bulcroft (1992) used a longitudinal design to investigate gender differences in friendship contacts in never-married, widowed, and divorced African American and white women and men. They found that widowed women had more frequent contacts with friends than all other gender and marital groups. They also found declines in the frequency of contact with friends over time, with the declines greatest among formerly married men.

The emotional intimacy and companionship these older friends provide each other are important to their everyday well-being. Men tend to have larger friendship networks with whom they engage in more frequent interaction, whereas women place greater importance on friendship and engage in more intimate relationships.

Fictive Kin

Often members of the social convoy become so important that the relationship between kin and friends becomes blurred. Parents' best friends often are treated like aunts and uncles while children are young and assume some of the attendant responsibilities. This family closeness can persist into adulthood. One mechanism for formalizing such relationships is through godparentage. Likewise, some relatives are so close in affection and interests that they become best friends. The merging of voluntary and obligatory relations sometimes produces **fictive kin,** or, as we referred to these relationships when discussing never-married adults, *constructed relationships*. Among the Herero of Botswana, fictive kin relationships are common and provide flexibility in "family" caregiving for elderly adults (Keith et al, 1994). Fictive kin are particularly prevalent in the African American kinship system, in which foster parents or foster children, for example, are often considered equivalent to relatives by blood or marriage (Johnson & Barer, 1990). Sometimes fictive kin result from formal relationships; for example, a nanny may always hold the kinship title of granny in a child's life. Among older adults a homemaking/companion may visit several times a week, share the same cultural background, and become an intimate companion thought of as a "daughter," "granddaughter," or "pal." (See the Working With interview on page 653.) Although fictive kin are sometimes accepted as though they were family members, they are not expected to fulfill the responsibilities of kin (Cicirelli, 1994). This is particularly significant to older adults as they consider their prospects for caregiving, as we saw in our discussion of never-married adults.

Childlessness

Perhaps because of the ability of people to create fictive kin, as well as the importance of friends in late life, studies indicate that being without children does not have a negative impact on well-being in later life. Since none of the studies separate child free by choice, childless by circumstance, and childless due to death, *childless* refers here to all of these situations. In a study of confidant and companion networks, Ingrid Connidis and Lorraine Davies (1990) found that childless women tend to develop ties with friends as both companions and confidants to a greater extent than older adults who are parents. Siblings are a more primary component of their confidant network than for older parents, especially for a childless woman who is single or widowed. Childless men place greater emphasis on friends as companions as well, but turn to relatives for confidants. Among childless women, friends and siblings are especially important as confidants, while among childless men, siblings are less important in this role than other relatives. Larry Mullins and Mary Mushel (1992) compared elderly men and women who had children with whom they were emotionally close, those who had children with whom they were not close, and those without children. They found no difference in the degree of loneliness experienced by any of the three groups. Sibling ties are more important and contact with family more frequent for childless adults than for those with children. Living parents or children occupy the center stage in most adults' lives; when that inner circle is reduced, siblings become a more important part of adults' social support networks (White & Riedmann, 1992).

What Do You Think?

Based on what you have read about relationships in late adulthood in this chapter, what family relationships do you imagine will be important to you in your old age? Why? In what ways does thinking about this issue make you want to change the way you relate to your kin?

PROBLEMS OF LIVING: THE HOUSING CONTINUUM

Aging in place—not moving to a nursing home—has become the ideal for both gerontologists and elderly people themselves. From the perspective of gerontologists, too many older people enter nursing homes when they could and should have remained in their own households (Callahan, 1992). From the perspective of older adults, they prefer to grow older where they have been younger; 86 percent wish to continue to live in their own homes and never move (American Association of Retired Persons (AARP), 1990). They feel comfortable and familiar with their surroundings and have developed informal support networks nearby. Elderly adults are likely to relinquish their own households only when they have limited economic resources and become frail or widowed. This is true for apartment dwellers as well as homeowners. Fully 95 percent of older people live in the community (outside of institutions), and only 10 to 20 percent live in households headed by adult children or others besides their spouses (Kendig, 1990).

Economics plays a large part in the housing decisions of late adulthood, just as it does earlier in life. Seventy-five percent of all older persons live in their owner-occupied dwellings, 83 percent of which no longer have a mortgage (Mutschler, 1992). Older adults who own their homes can cash them in and buy entry into a home for the aged, provide housing for adult children, or continue to live on their own as independent couples or widows. Not surprisingly, large differences exist in the distribution of housing assets among older Americans. Women and racial/ethnic minorities have fewer assets. Only 48 percent of widows own their own homes, whereas 84 percent of couples do (Kendig, 1990). Homeownership rates are low among never-married, separated, or divorced adults, among nonwhites and Hispanics, and among urban dwellers. African Americans, more than any other group, have been systematically limited as to choice of housing because of residential segregation. As older adults, they suffer from the multiple effects of low income, racial segregation, and ageism, which leave them with fewer housing choices (Skinner, 1992).

While most adults prefer to continue living on their own, frailty brings the needs for housing modifications and special services. Stairs are likely to cause difficulty, for example, and shopping may become problematic. Limited finances may also push older adults to consider other housing alternatives. The elderly need a range of options, including independent living, semi-independent living, and group housing that provides long-term care. Table 17.2 lists housing types by the degree of independence they offer. As we discuss the various options, you will see that some facilities provide more than one level of independence and that similar housing types may provide elderly residents with different levels of control over their living conditions.

Independent Living

Homeownership is frequent among today's elderly. Because elderly people's homes are often debt free (83 percent), housing costs are generally low. Nonetheless, taxes and home maintenance costs can be a financial burden for older adults who are property rich but income poor. While all homeowners face the time-consuming and costly demands of home maintenance, older people tend to live in older homes, which are often particularly difficult to maintain. In addition, maintenance of a house is likely to become too much to handle when health problems and functional impairments accumulate. Tom and Frances, for example, always did their own home maintenance. Tom, a jack of all trades, did carpentry, electrical work, plumbing, and

TABLE 17.2 Levels of Housing by Degree of Independence
Notice that some types of housing, such as an independent household, provide the possibility of more than one degree of independence.

Type of Housing	Description	Examples
Independent household:		
Fully independent	Household is self-contained and self-sufficient; residents do almost all of the cooking and household chores	Private home, apartment, shared housing
Semi-independent	Household is self-contained but not self-sufficient; requires help with household chores	Utilizes homemaker/companion, Meals on Wheels, adult foster care, or family caregiving
Group housing:		
Congregate housing	Household may be self-contained but receives some communal services, typically meals	Retirement community, assisted-living facility
Personal care home	Resident unit is neither self-contained nor self-sufficient	Group home or adult care facility
Nursing home	Resident unit is neither self-contained nor self-sufficient; total care is provided, including personal and health care	Skilled nursing facility

painting as needed. Frances cleaned their large Victorian home and devised creative ways to cover up some of the problems that were not adequately repaired. By the time Tom retired, the house was very old and needed either a costly major overhaul or endless daily attention. After several years of balancing on ladders and even hiring some help, Tom decided it was too much for him and bought a very new, very clean, smaller house with a single-floor layout that would be easier for him and Frances to maintain and to grow frail in. Having the resources of their old home made purchase of the new one possible. When older people become frail, the home environment needs to be more supportive to compensate for their limitations or disabilities. Homeowners have discretion over modifications and repairs that can ac-

Most adults prefer to continue living independently for as long as they are able. Health and economics play a large part in the housing decisions of late adulthood.

commodate their late life needs and have the potential to trade in their assets for more age-appropriate housing, as Tom and Frances did. Homeowners live mostly in single-family homes. Because of the dispersion of single-family homes, elderly homeowners are more likely to become isolated or receive less adequate care than apartment dwellers. Tom and Frances's decision to buy a new house enabled them to move closer to their daughter and her family, which will provide them with social support as well as assistance with transportation. When it becomes necessary, their daughter will be there for other levels of caregiving.

Elderly renters tend to be older than elderly homeowners, are more likely to be women, and are disproportionately African Americans. Renters are significantly more likely than homeowners to pay excessive housing costs, defined as more than 30 percent of their before-tax income (Mutschler, 1992). Sixty-nine percent of elderly women renters compared to 25 percent of elderly women owners paid excessive housing costs in 1987; for elderly men the figures were 59 percent and 17 percent, respectively (U.S. Senate Special Committee on Aging, 1992). Most renters live in apartments in buildings with more than five units. This provides them with the advantage of neighbors close by, affording some security and some social support. Another advantage of renting is not being responsible for yard and building maintenance; the management may also provide some routine inside maintenance, such as installing storm windows. On the other hand, renters may not be allowed to modify their homes to facilitate their functioning as they face increasing physical limitations.

Naturally occurring retirement communities (NORCs) are housing developments that are not planned or designed for older people but attract a majority of residents age sixty or more. They provide a supportive social environment and access to services and facilities that can prolong independent living among elderly residents. They are unlike planned elderly housing in that they are not specifically designed for the elderly, are age integrated, are often single buildings or small complexes of buildings, and go unnoticed as retirement communities (Hunt & Ross, 1990). NORCs are the most common form of alternative housing for older people in the United States; only 5 percent live in planned retirement communities, and 27 percent live in NORCs (AARP, 1990). NORCs develop both by aging in place and by in-migration. These apartments are attractive to both younger and older people because of their location. Younger residents like being close to public transportation, work, and leisure activities, while older residents like being close to grocery stores, drugstores, banks, variety stores, department stores, post offices, doctors' offices, cleaners, libraries, churches and synagogues, and restaurants (Hunt & Ross, 1990). Safety of the neighborhood is of primary importance to both age groups. Older residents also value the proximity of friends and age peers. John Skinner (1992) points out that many older African American and other minority elders end up in inner-city neighborhoods that, although the buildings take on the identity of NORCs because of the density of the aging population, lack the services necessary to support the aging residents. Inner-city aging housing is likely to lack security and protection, convenience shopping, and transportation. This leaves the elderly residents confined to their homes out of fear and frailty. These elders "are not only aging in place, they are stuck in place, prisoners in their own homes, without the ability to move to more appropriate housing" (p. 51). Safe neighborhoods, household modifications, and services and age peers available within walking distance facilitate independent living, but frailty or disability may render them insufficient.

The formal support of home health care enables this elderly woman to live semi-independently. Assisted living often includes informal help from family and friends as well as formal services.

Assisted Living

Assisted living, or *semi-independent living,* refers to some degree of help with daily living that enables older adults to age in place. Assisted living can include informal and formal supports. Over the past twenty-five years, informal supports have been predominant at the same time formal service supports have expanded (Morris & Morris, 1992). Informal supports are provided by relatives and friends; formal services include elderly housing, retirement communities, and community services. Informal supports, "the good efforts of their relatives and friends," enable at least three out of five marginally functioning elders to continue to reside in the community (Morris & Morris, 1992, p. 41). Retirement communities provide a range of options from independent living to twenty-four-hour skilled nursing as the aging individual's needs change. Community services include senior centers, special transportation, Meals-on-Wheels, visiting nurses or health aides, homemaking companions, telephone reassurance, and adult day care. The accompanying Working With interview describes one such provider of help to community living elderly.

An elderly person needs assistance when she or he is unable to perform at least one daily activity. The largest source of help is relatives. Spouses provide care if they are present; those who live alone often must rely on their children. As Figure 17.5 shows, more than half of elderly people who live alone have a child living nearby. Older African Americans who live alone are less likely than whites or Hispanics to have a child who lives nearby. With advancing age, more people have no living child or sibling and more people rely on formal support, especially community services (U.S. Senate Special Committee on Aging, 1992).

Elderly or senior housing is federally subsidized and specially designed to meet the needs of old and disabled adults who are poor and have few other alternatives. Construction is barrier free so that walkers and wheelchairs can navigate easily and provides emergency alarm buttons and architectural features that can enhance functioning. There are common social areas, and residents usually have the opportunity to receive some supportive services, such as meals, transportation, homemaking, and nursing, depending on the facility. Despite the high visibility of elderly housing, however, only 3 to 5 percent of older Americans live in these projects (Kendig, 1990).

Retirement communities are private, age-specific housing alternatives. Older people of means buy into nonprofit continuing care retirement communities before they are in need of care. The cost often amounts to a person or couple's life savings. The benefit is availability of a range of care options from congregate housing to

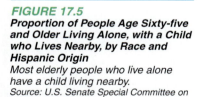

FIGURE 17.5
Proportion of People Age Sixty-five and Older Living Alone, with a Child who Lives Nearby, by Race and Hispanic Origin
Most elderly people who live alone have a child living nearby.
Source: U.S. Senate Special Committee on Aging (1991).

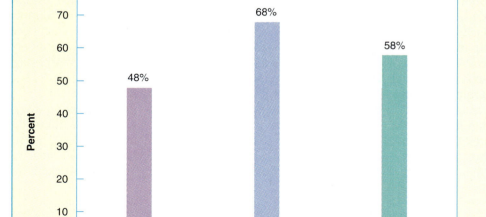

Working with   Debbie Holt, HOMEMAKING/COMPANION

Helping Community-Living Elderly Adults

Debbie Holt works for a private for-profit agency doing light housekeeping, errands, marketing, and some meal preparation and providing transportation to doctors' appointments and companionship for homebound elderly Medicaid and Medicare clients. Although most homemaking/companions are mothers of school-age children who have high school educations and are attracted by the flexible hours, Debbie is in her twenties and college educated.

Michele: Do you take your clients with you to do their errands and marketing?

Debbie: It varies. I have two clients who are consistently homebound, in wheelchairs. One was hit by a drunk driver when she was twenty-two, and now she is eighty-seven. She has six kids. She has been in a wheelchair since she was about forty. I have two clients who can do minimal walking. I take them walking a certain amount, and then we use a wheelchair. I see a ninety-one-year-old women who jumps at the chance to get out of what she calls "her corner."

Michele: Where do you take her?

Debbie: I take her to the doctor and to the grocery store. She doesn't get out of the car, but even that is good for her. Sometimes we just go toodling around town. We are supposed to have a practical reason to go out, but I fudge. We had an extra hour the other day, so I said, "It will be on my mileage, let me take you to see the north part of town where they are building." It was worth it just to see her smile and her eyes light up.

Michele: You obviously like her. Does she have other social supports?

Debbie: She has a daughter in her late fifties who lives with her family in New York and a son who lives nearby, but he's very sick with lung cancer. The daughter has it tough: she comes from New York every Sunday, spends time with her mother, then with her brother, then goes back

to New York on Monday. She also has other "girls," which is what she calls us. She gets a lot of help from the agency, mostly meal preparation. I'm with her three hours every Tuesday and Friday morning. She also has one hour of help every other morning and afternoon. She likes to cook. Half the time she'll get herself downstairs and into the kitchen with her walker and put a pot roast or pork ribs on to cook. The kitchen is a disaster because she knocks things over with the walker, but she manages. I'm not supposed to eat with my clients, but often I bring my own lunch. Many clients have Meals on Wheels or Catered with Care bring their meals, so prep is just microwaving the meal. It's a lot more fun to prepare the food.

Michele: What do you see as your major function in your clients' lives?

Debbie: Companionship. I think a lot of my clients would argue—they wouldn't want to admit it. While I vacuum and dust, most of my clients talk with me the whole time.

Michele: Have you formed emotional bonds with any of them?

Debbie: Three, so far. When I leave this job, I'll stay in touch with them. When I was still a student, I used to take my papers to one client, and while I cleaned she would give me critiques. She is elderly and homebound, and it's good for her to be involved. She was a homemaker and raised six kids. She gets help from me twice a week. One of her daughters comes once a month. She gets a lot. Her family is very supportive, very caring. She still reads the paper every day. She hates television and loves the radio.

Then there are the other two. One is the ninety-one-year-old I already mentioned. The other is an eighty-six-year-old who is virtually blind from cataracts. She remains very independent and stubborn; she makes rosaries for people in jail, eight a day.

She also has a great sense of humor. When I took her to the doctor, I chose to valet park for five dollars. I told her it was my treat, but when we went home she insisted on paying me for it. As she pulled out bills and asked me what they were (because she can't see), she said, "When I was in my twenties and lit off my brain, I knew better how much money I had than I do now." A lot of clients don't laugh. When you get ones who do, it's a real joy.

Michele: How do your clients treat you?

Debbie: The majority treat me like a granddaughter. Only one client treats me like a worker. She makes less conversation. Instead of greeting me with "How are you?" she is likely to say, "We are going to do the drapes today." But she has speech difficulties.

Michele: What do you see as the benefits of the job?

Debbie: I learn about cooking. I listen to stories about what life was like in the twenties and thirties. Old people can offer a lot of wisdom; that's why I've chosen to go into this field.

Michele: What are your long-term plans?

Debbie: There is an organization that was started in France by a bunch of monks called Little Brother. There are now branches in Chicago, San Francisco, and several other cities. I hope to organize one here. They match volunteers with elderly to provide "flowers before bread."

What Do You Think?

1. All of the clients Debbie talks about have help from children, as well as paid help from a homemaking/companion. Why do they need both types of help? How does combining formal and informal caregiving benefit the client and the client's adult children?

2. Where would you place Debbie's clients on the housing continuum? If Debbie's clients did not have paid homemaking/companion assistance, what other housing options would be possible for them?

long-term care for life as the individual's needs change. **Congregate housing** provides some communal services, at least a central kitchen and dining room. Amos and Barbara bought membership in a retirement community when both were seventy and in good health. Since they still needed to help their only daughter to manage her own life, they felt it was imperative to plan for their own caregiving. They sold their two homes and moved into an attractive, self-contained apartment in the retirement community. They made the choice to eat breakfasts and lunches in their own kitchen and dinners in the main dining room. If and when either needs more care, the community will provide increasing levels of assistance to long-term care. And if one of them needs institutionalization, this choice will enable them to continue to live together. Private retirement communities serve only a small percentage of older people, but recently have become more popular (Kendig, 1990). Lower-SES elderly adults are more likely to rely on the community services discussed earlier as they age in place. Figure 17.6 shows that with increasing age, a greater proportion of elderly people who live alone use community services, and that use is more prevalent among the poor.

Long-Term Care

The term *long-term care* generally brings to mind nursing homes, which are stereotyped as the final destination of the very old. But **long-term care** is a much broader concept that refers to ongoing assistance to people with chronic illnesses and disabilities in a wide variety of settings. While some long-term care is *health care*, most of it is *personal care* and consists of help with everyday activities such as bathing, getting in and out of bed, using the toilet, grocery shopping, doing laundry and housework, and preparing meals. Most long-term care is provided by relatives and friends in the person's independent household. Only about 6 percent of older people live in institutions, including nursing homes, boarding homes, and psychiatric hospitals, although somewhere between 30 and 50 percent will spend a short time in a nursing home after an early discharge from the hospital (Atchley, 1994).

FIGURE 17.6
Proportion of People Age 65 and Older Who Live Alone and Use Community Services, by Age Group and Poverty Status, 1990
Elderly people who cannot afford private services are more likely to use community services.
Source: U.S. Senate Special Committee on Aging (1991).

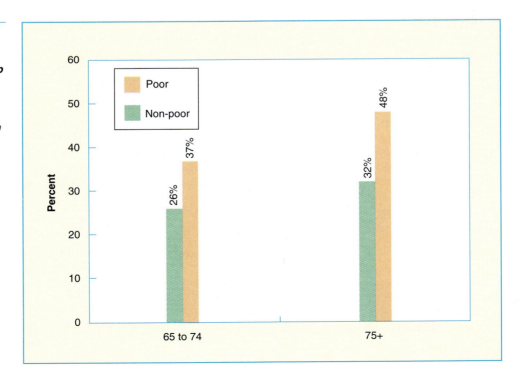

Spouses, adult children, and other relatives are the major providers of personal care, as we have discussed, but paid help is also important. Robyn Stone, Gail Cafferata, and Judith Sangl (1987) found that the average caregiver spent four hours a day, seven days a week providing care for an aging relative. Many families combine informal caregiving with some formal services to enable the family to meet the heavy burden of providing personal care. Paid help seems to work best when it is supervised by family, since the people who need the care are vulnerable to abuse and exploitation by strangers. African American elderly who experience functional declines are less likely to be institutionalized and more likely to rely on coresidence and informal caregiving than are whites (Skinner, 1992). This is a joint result of the availability of social support systems in the African American community as well as poverty. Nursing homes are expensive, and those that participate in Medicaid often have long waiting lists. Adult day care, another formal service that can supplement family caregiving, can be especially helpful for people with Alzheimer's disease or other dementias. It is a community-based group program designed to meet the needs of adults with functional impairments. Within a safe, supervised environment, staff provide a comprehensive program of physical, social, cognitive, and functional activities to maximize remaining strengths and minimize deficits. Individuals participate on a planned basis, during specified hours, two to five days a week. This provides some relief and support to caregivers and enables them to continue caring for the impaired family member at home. Staff members also acquaint the caregivers with other community resources and provide them with emotional support (Engstrom et al., 1993).

Control over Living Conditions

It is not always possible for people to age in place. Their losses of function may be too great, or the place may become inappropriate to their needs for safety and maneuverability. When they move, whether to the home of a family member or to group housing, the strong preference is for some space that they personally control. In a study of life satisfaction in a variety of elderly housing situations, Robert Vallerand, Brian O'Connor, and Marc Blais (1989) found that French-speaking Canadian residents of "high self-determination" nursing homes had levels of satisfaction comparable to those of community-dwelling elderly and significantly higher than those of residents of "low self-determination" nursing homes. Table 17.3 presents the five criteria they used for self-determination.

In a review of the literature, Judith Rodin (1986) found negative effects on the health of older people when personal control of their activities is restricted. For example, being forced to move has been associated with adverse health outcomes among elderly adults, such as more hospitalizations and nursing home admissions, greater incidence of stroke and angina pectoris, and poorer self-health assessment. When the older people were exposed to any control-enhancing experimental manipulation, such as choice of when or where to move or about aspects of their

---

TABLE 17.3 *Criteria for Self-Determination in Nursing Homes*
Residents of "high self-determination" nursing homes had levels of satisfaction comparable to those of community-dwelling elderly and significantly higher than those of residents of "low self-determination" nursing homes.

1. How much choice do residents have regarding mealtimes?
2. To what extent are nursing home staff responsible for residents' personal care?
3. How free are residents to decorate and arrange the furniture in their rooms?
4. Are the residents allowed to have or care for a pet?
5. To what degree does the staff encourage or discourage personal initiative?

Source: Based on Vallerand, O'Connor, & Blais (1989).

new living arrangements, little decline in health and psychological status was found.

Studies designed to encourage self-reliance among elderly in institutions such as convalescent and nursing homes have shown that increasing responsibility among elderly residents led to increased alertness, more activity, and reports of feeling happier, in contrast to those who were encouraged to believe the staff would tend to their needs (Rodin, 1986). Enhanced control has also led to improvements in memory, satisfaction, and physical health in some studies. Rodin points out, however, that although "the strength of the relation between control and health increases with aging . . . there is more variability in perception and desire for control with advancing age, presumably because of the accumulation of different life experiences" (p. 1271). This means that most elderly people respond positively to the opportunities for control, but others prefer not to be responsible.

Choice, then, becomes one of the most important aspects of the housing continuum. It is wise for older people and their families to consider options and make housing choices in advance of health crises; yet a recent survey revealed that more than half of older people have done little or no planning for their future housing needs (AARP, 1990). Looking into the possibilities for home remodeling or relocation to prolong independent living is best done in advance, as is learning about the opportunities for congregate housing in the geographic region most convenient to family and friends. As we have seen, Tom and Frances and Amos and Barbara made different choices at the same stage of life, but both couples chose before they experienced a crisis. Even when long-term care requires institutionalization, a nursing home should be chosen carefully, with an attempt to match the individual's need for control to the level of control available. While more than half of people over sixty-five will spend some time in a nursing home, it is not the end of meaningful and enjoyable life. This becomes exquisitely clear in Tracy Kidder's (1993) description of the friendship and daily lives of two old men who met and became roommates in a nursing home. The nursing home Kidder studied has two levels of residency providing more or less control based on the resident's level of functioning. Despite increasing frailty, older adults continue to have interests that extend beyond their aging bodies. Even for individuals with dementia, a client-centered approach provides age-appropriate activities rather than treating them like children, promotes use of the cognitive abilities that remain intact, and encourages day-to-day decision making about clothing, food, and activities (Hofland, 1994). (See the Working With interview in Chapter 16 on page 616.)

What Do You Think?

Consider one of your relatives who is in late adulthood. How suitable are his or her housing arrangements for aging in place? Consider the available housing alternatives. Role-play with a classmate how you might discuss the pros and cons of each alternative with your relative.

INTERESTS AND ACTIVITIES

We know from Chapter 16 that many older adults continue to work, although most retire from their career jobs or reduce their hours if they are self-employed, especially after age seventy. How do they spend the hours that are freed from the constraints of employment? The answer to that question depends to a large extent on the socioeconomic standing of the aging person. Those who have enjoyed high levels of education, occupational status, and income are likely to be in good health and to have resources that provide many options for activities, whereas those who have had low levels of education, occupation, and income likely have health limitations

Activities in late adulthood, such as travel, depend on having good health and financial resources that typically result from educational and occupational opportunities in early and middle adulthood.

and fewer resources in their later years. Health acts as a threshold for leisure, and financial security plays a critical role in supporting various activities (Cutler & Hendricks, 1990). Poverty is a barrier to involvement in community activities, especially among people who formerly were middle class (Kelly, 1993). For low-income or ethnic/racial minority older adults who have never had secure regular employment, increased leisure may not be part of late adulthood because they need to continue earning.

Other factors influence the use of leisure time in late adulthood as well. Educational attainment and occupation influence the preference for activities. Although some individuals learn to dance or draw in their later years, there is evidence that developing **activity competence,** the skills and knowledge needed to take advantage of opportunities for activities, is generally established in earlier adult years. Those who are better educated therefore are better prepared to feel competent engaging in a variety of activities. Individuals with spouse, family, or friends tend to be more active in communal activities than those who are alone. Using an eight-year longitudinal method to study older adults (average age seventy-two at the start of the study), Frances Carp (1978/1979) found that type of living arrangement affected leisure activity patterns. People who moved to retirement communities or other congregate housing increased their activity levels, whereas those who remained in the community decreased their activity levels. Obviously self-selection was a factor; those who selected living situations with extensive activity programs must have desired such activities. As we saw in Chapter 15, gender affects choice of leisure activities: women are more likely to choose passive, social, and expressive activities, whereas men tend to choose active and less expressive activities and join more organizations (Cutler & Hendricks, 1990). As a result of these many factors, the leisure pursuits of older people vary greatly.

Past patterns of activity shape the way older adults use their time. When they retire, for example, most people continue to do the same activities they did before retirement, but at a different pace (Kelly, 1993). As we saw in the story of Marcellus at the beginning of this chapter, activity patterns of middle age tend to persist into the later years, but gradually, as people become frail, the activity becomes constricted. In his nineties, Marcellus was tending a yard instead of a farm. Because of his interest in inventing things, he was able to continue tending the yard despite his frailty. Another old man might have eventually restricted his gardening even more, to tending flower boxes, for example. We discussed in Chapter 15 how older adults continue to work. Much of this chapter has indicated how their involvement with family continues. Here we examine older adults' involvement in community organizations, religion and spirituality, and the more solitary activity of contemplation.

Community Involvement

Community organizations include political parties, labor unions, veterans groups, fraternal organizations, community service groups, professional organizations, religious institutions, parent-teacher organizations, neighborhood associations, and many other groups designed to achieve a purpose or pursue some shared interest. People show considerable stability in their general levels of participation in community organizations from middle age until their sixties, when involvement gradually decreases (Cutler & Hendricks, 1990). Poor health, inadequate income, and problems with transportation all contribute to decreases in participation (Atchley, 1994). While membership in community organizations has been associated with well-being, it is impossible to separate the fact that members tend to have higher levels of health, income, and education—all of which are linked to well-being—than do nonmembers.

Volunteerism   Efforts have been made to involve older adults as volunteers to provide services for the community, enable older adults to pass on their knowledge to younger people, and provide the volunteers with meaningful activity (Chambré, 1991). The Foster Grandparent Program, Retired Senior Volunteer Program (RSVP), and Service Corps of Retired Executives (SCORE) are just three organizations formed especially for seniors. Volunteerism provides a continuing link with the community, as well as ways to substitute similar activities for the reduced work and family roles of later life (Chambré, 1991). Nevertheless, despite the many organizations that try to recruit senior volunteers, only about 16 percent of people over sixty-five are volunteers compared to 23 percent of all Americans (U.S. Special Committee on Aging, 1992). This figure greatly underestimates the amount of volunteering older adults actually do because it considers only formal organizations and does not include informal helping within the family and community.

If we broaden the definition of volunteerism to include providing informal service, almost all retired adults do volunteer work. In a study of retired Minnesota workers, Lucy Fischer, Daniel Mueller, and Philip Cooper (1991) found that nearly 60 percent of the older adults provided help for their families, most by caring for grandchildren. More than 40 percent provided help to their neighbors, usually in the form of transportation or visiting. In addition, 53 percent were doing organized volunteer work, mostly through their religious institutions. When all types of volunteer work were considered, only 17 percent of this elderly population were not doing any. On average, these Minnesota adults were spending fourteen hours a month doing voluntary service. If we added caregiving to family members within the home, the percentages would likely be even higher. In a study of help and support older women provide to kin and friends, Sally Gallagher and Naomi Gerstel (1993) found that 96 percent of married women and 92 percent of widows had provided some type of help to at least one relative or friend in the previous month.

Older volunteers face some problems. First, talented older people sometimes find themselves assigned to menial work that is beneath their knowledge, experience, and dignity. This makes them feel undervalued. Second, volunteers are sometimes placed in positions without sufficient training. This puts them in the unfortunate position of feeling tested rather than feeling prepared and welcomed. Third, many older volunteers need additional income and would prefer paid part-time work. This has led the National Council of Senior Citizens to object to any program that recruits older people to do on a volunteer basis work for which younger people are paid. Fourth, people who are retired may be unwilling to commit to a rigid volunteer schedule that would limit their freedom to travel. Organizations need to find ways to encourage short-term contributions, such as to one-time events or recurring events. Fifth, transportation is often a problem for older volunteers. If it were provided, older adults who no longer feel comfortable driving would be able to volunteer their services.

Continuing Education   Another kind of community involvement is through Elder-hostel programs. Begun in 1975, Elderhostel is a nationwide program in continuing higher education that has been extremely successful (Brady, 1984). It offers one-week summer programs that include a campus dorm room, cafeteria meals, college-level courses, and extracurricular activities at low cost. Participants are not expected to have prior knowledge of the subject matter and receive no grades. Elderhostel now has nearly two thousand educational sites in the United States, Canada, and forty-five countries worldwide (Goggin, 1992). Michael Brady (1984) sampled 560 Elderhostel participants in twenty New England programs and found that the typical participant was sixty-eight years old, retired, married, and well educated. Only 12 percent had high school education or below, while 42 percent of the men and 24 percent of the women had graduate or professional degrees. More of the participants were women (67 percent) than men (33 percent), and more of the women (37 percent) than the men (9 percent) were widowed. Brady's participants completed two scales that measured their perceived academic benefit. Those persons with lower levels of education and lower annual incomes reported receiving more benefits from the Elderhostel programs than the more privileged participants. This may be because they were attending college for the first time and therefore derived more benefits from the noncognitive elements of college life, they actually learned more from the courses, or they were more willing to report having benefited.

Religion and Spirituality

Churches or synagogues are the organizations to which older people most frequently belong. Membership in religious organizations is higher at older ages, especially after age seventy-five (Atchley, 1994). Church and synagogue attendance and membership in church-affiliated groups and fraternal organizations, as well as leadership positions in these organizations, all reflect greater involvement of people over age sixty-five than under (Koenig et al., 1988). Attendance at services increases steadily from the teens and peaks in the late fifties to early sixties at about 60 percent; then there is a gradual decline, more gradual than with any other type of organization (Cutler & Hendricks, 1990). While leadership in a congregation enhances the status of older members, participation provides older people with continuity, social identity, and access to meaningful social roles (Payne & McFadden, 1994). Abraham, for example, was raised in an orthodox Jewish family. He was not religious as an adult, but he belonged to a synagogue, sent his children for religious instruction, and attended services on the High Holy Days because he enjoyed them. In his sixties, after his wife died, his involvement with his synagogue increased dramatically. He attended services regularly and spent hours discussing religious and political issues with his rabbi. He felt both comfortable and comforted as a member of the congregation.

Lack of church or synagogue attendance does not necessarily mean lack of religious involvement, just as attending services does not necessarily mean being religious. When attending formal services becomes too difficult as a result of declining health, disability, transportation problems, or relocation, many older adults compensate by increasing religious practices at home, such as reading the Bible, listening to religious broadcasts, praying, or studying religion (Ainlay & Smith, 1984). Older people continue to feel an emotional attachment to the religious institution where they had been involved even when they have relocated and that institution is many miles away or when they are homebound and can no longer participate (Payne & McFadden, 1994). On the other hand, churches and synagogues offer opportunities for contact with people that may be especially attractive to widowed adults such as Abraham, because such contact does not depend on having a spouse.

The Social Support of Religious Institutions   Religious institutions form an important source of social support among racial/ethnic minorities, especially African Americans. Kyriakos Markides (1983) found that church attendance, self-rated religiousness, and private prayer were all positively related to life satisfaction among Mexican Americans. After the family and before formal sources, older African Americans turn to the church for assistance (Walls, 1992). Some African American churches create spiritual families and assign kin terms to their members, fostering the development of fictive kin. "Church mothers" are available as lay therapists and confidants to members of the church who have problems (Johnson & Barer, 1990). To investigate the relationship among church support, religious involvement, and psychological well-being among elderly African Americans, Carla Walls (1992) interviewed ninety-eight African American church members ages 65 to 104 and had them complete a series of scales to measure social support, religiosity, well-being, health status, and functional health status. Walls found that most of the friends and family members of the respondents were members of the same church. Family members were perceived as providing more emotional than instrumental support, while church members provided more instrumental than emotional support. Both church and family networks were important predictors of well-being; support from either source was associated with high levels of well-being, and support from both sources was associated with the highest levels. Walls points out that it was "the perceptions the African American elders had of the church, and not the ideology (spiritual aspects) or involvement in the organizational aspects of the church, that generated feelings of well-being" (p. 35). This is important because it raises the question of how much perceptions of religious institutions are related to age and how much to cohort.

Cohort Effects of Religious Involvement   While religion is clearly very important to older Americans, that does not necessarily mean people become more religious with age. The now old grew up in an era of more widespread religious involvement than the now middle aged and, like Abraham, are likely to have lived in religious households and to have valued religion when young. As the accompanying Multicultural View box shows, some elderly adults postpone death for religious holidays. The few longitudinal studies of religiosity show that cohort differences may be more important than age differences (Hunsberger, 1985). It is also possible that more older people who are religious have survived, since orthodox individuals are less likely to smoke, drink excessively, or engage in other behaviors that put them at risk for premature death. This would make the surviving older population appear more religious than if the entire cohort had survived. Because subsequent cohorts have grown up with different levels of religious involvement, it is important to distinguish between religion and spirituality. Whereas *religion* generally refers to organized religion, **spirituality** refers to the human need to construct a sense of meaning in life. Spirituality can occur within or outside of a specifically religious context.

Spirituality and Faith   Spiritual development appears to be age related but not age determined. Among members of more than five hundred Protestant congregations, individuals judged to have *mature faith* were likely to be older (Benson & Elkin, 1990). Mature faith is the final stage of James Fowler's (1991) faith-knowing system of growth and development of the spiritual domain, as Table 17.4 indicates. The growth of faith, according to Fowler, is a universal process that is not necessarily religious in orientation. Rather, it is an integral aspect of daily life that "serves to

A Multicultural View

Can Individuals Postpone Dying for a Special Event?

Students of American history are impressed when they learn of the nearly simultaneous deaths of John Adams and Thomas Jefferson on July 4, 1826. It can hardly be an accident that these two founders and signers of the Declaration of Independence both died on the fiftieth anniversary of its signing. The odds of this happening by chance are one in twelve hundred million. Jefferson, who was unconscious for much of July 3, woke that night and asked "Is it the Fourth?" (Ellis, 1993). This confirms the impression that he wanted to live until that special day.

Do symbolic events that are anticipated with pleasure serve as a lifeline, keeping people alive so they can celebrate? Can people really time their own deaths around events that are special to them? In the last fifty years, many studies have examined this phenomenon. The death rate of Jews has been shown to dip below normal before the Jewish holiday of Passover and then peak by the same amount right after the holiday (Phillips & King, 1988). A similar finding has shown Chinese mortality to dip before a Chinese holiday and rise right after it (Phillips & Smith, 1990).

The most extensive studies have used the birthday as the special event. Some people perceive the birthday as a positive event: a time to celebrate with friends, to get presents and attention. Others see it as a negative occasion: a time to reflect on whether they have achieved their goals and to focus on the ways they have failed. David Phillips and his colleagues (1992) used birth and death records of nearly 3 million individuals to see if birthdays functioned as a lifeline (a dip in deaths before and a peak after) or a deadline (no dip before but a peak

after). They looked only at records of people who died from natural causes, were at least eighteen years old, and were not born on February 29. They found that for women, the birthday functioned as a lifeline. There was a dip in deaths before women's birthdays, a peak in the week after the birthdays, and then a smaller dip several weeks after the birthdays. This was true for younger and older women and for white and African American women. For men the birthday functioned as a deadline; a peak in deaths occurred right before the birthdays.

To focus on a group that was likely to see the birthday as a positive event, the investigators also analyzed a sample of famous people taken from the *Encyclopedia of American History*. They figured that famous people would evaluate their lives in positive terms because of their accomplishments and receive considerable attention on their birthdays. These two things would make the birthday a positive experience. They indeed found a stronger lifeline effect among famous Americans than they had found among ordinary women.

It is clear from these data that symbolic events can have psychosomatic effects. Women are able to briefly prolong their lives for a positive, symbolically meaningful occasion such as the birthday. Famous Americans (mostly men) can do this as well, but the birthday typically does not function as a positive occasion for ordinary men. This may be because men have more at stake in their workplace achievements and suffer more from their lack of accomplishment, whereas women have a set of expectations that include social relationships as well as workplace achievements.

TABLE 17.4 *Fowler's Faith-Knowing System*
The growth of faith, according to James Fowler, is a universal progression through stages of spiritual development that is not necessarily religious in orientation. Mature or universalizing faith is the final stage of his faith-knowing system.

Stage	Age	Center of Power	Process	Value
0: Undifferentiated Faith	Birth–2 years	Symbiotic relationship with parent	Egocentric perceptions	Own needs
1: Intuitive-Projective Faith	2–6 years	Caregiving adult	Magical thought	Appeasement
2: Mythical-Literal Faith	6–12 years	Cultural and religious rules and traditions	Rituals and rules	Order, rituals, fairness
3: Synthetic-Conventional Faith	12 and beyond	Peers, cultural or religious leader	Symbols provide meaning	Approval
4: Individuative-Reflective Faith	Early adulthood and beyond	Self	Construct own symbols	Own meaning
5: Conjunctive Faith	Midlife and beyond	Truth	Verities expressed through symbols, awe	Openness to others, humility
6: Universalizing Faith	Midlife and beyond	The Ultimate God	Relationship expressed through life lived	Love, others' need

Source: Fowler (1991).

organize the totality of our lives and gives rise to our most comprehensive frames of meaning" (Fowler, 1986). Peter Benson and Carolyn Elkin (1990) conclude that "Maturity of faith is strongly linked to age, increasing with each successive decade, and is most likely to be found among those over 70" (p. 3).

Spiritual Integration   Spirituality has been found to influence one's perception of quality of life and will to live, even in the face of loss and infirmity (Thorson, 1983). It is associated with "the human capacity to experience a transcendental sense of wholeness within the self, with other persons, the world, and with God" (Payne & McFadden, 1994, p. 23). The transcendent sense of connection with other people, even when not in actual physical contact, conveys a sense of life's meaning and purpose. This sense of connectedness can reinforce life's meaning even when the older person is alone. Our discussion of the social convoy and the array of social relationships older people experience indicates that old people generally are not overwhelmed by loneliness. Yet many forces do compel old adults to find a new balance between intimacy and isolation by reworking Erikson's early adult normative crisis discussed in Chapter 13 (Payne & McFadden, 1994). Spouse, siblings, and friends die. Visual impairment may make letter writing impossible. Hearing impairment may interfere with conversation. Motor impairment may reduce social contact. Spirituality can enable old people to remain meaningfully connected with others. Erik Erikson suggested that this may be an aspect of ego integrity. He also proposed that it may be necessary to add a ninth stage to his theory of development that would include "a sense of premonition of immortality . . . as creatively given form in the world religions" (Erikson et al., 1986, pp. 336–337). Spiritual integration among older adults is supported by autobiographical storytelling, journal keeping, and empathic interactions with others (McFadden & Gerl, 1990).

Contemplation   Some of the activities that promote spiritual integration are solitary ones. Robert Butler (1975) has suggested that contemplation is a valuable use

Reminiscence, the recall of past experiences and events that occurs among people of all ages, is thought to serve a special function in late life. Through reminiscence this man reduces his likelihood for depression and increases his ability to cope with a health problem.

of time in the later years. Reminiscence and life review are two contemplative processes that are thought to serve special functions in late life. **Reminiscence** is the recall of past experiences and events and occurs among people of all ages. Reminiscence has been associated with measures of life satisfaction and sense of well-being. Utilizing the Uses of Reminiscence scale shown in Table 17.5, Sharan Merriam (1993) compared African American and white men and women in their sixties, eighties, and one hundreds. She found no age differences in the uses of reminiscence among these three groups of older adults. She did find significant race and gender differences, though. African Americans more than whites used reminiscence to teach others about the past, lift their spirits, understand themselves better, tell of their accomplishments, combat loneliness, help them accept changes in their lives, understand what life is all about, put their lives in order, and deal with knowing that life is finite. Men more than women used reminiscence to teach others about the past, tell of their accomplishments, make future plans, deal with a present problem, put their lives in order, cope with knowing that life is finite, and deal with unpleasant or troublesome memories. Those who reminisced more were less depressed and coped with health problems more effectively.

Life review, according to Robert Butler (1975), is a universal inner experience of older people "characterized by the progressive return to consciousness of past experiences, in particular the resurgence of unresolved conflicts which can now be surveyed and reintegrated" (p. 412). This evaluative process, an aspect of Erikson's developmental stage of integrity versus despair, enables old people to take stock of themselves and decide what they will do with the rest of their lives. It enables them to find new significance and meaning in their lives and to prepare for death. This preparation often includes decisions about the material and emotional legacies they wish to leave to others. Life review can lead to family reconciliation, which, as we saw in Chapter 15, may enable adult children to become friends as they arrange for care of aging parents. Life review may make the experience of social isolation one of solitude rather than loneliness.

TABLE 17.5 Uses of Reminiscence Scale
Reminiscence, the recall of past experiences and events, occurs among people of all ages and has been associated with measures of life satisfaction and sense of well-being.

People think about or talk about their past for many different reasons. Do you think about or talk about your past in order to:				
	Never			Very Often
relive a pleasant experience	1	2	3	4	5
teach others about the past	1	2	3	4	5
lift your spirits	1	2	3	4	5
get relief from boredom	1	2	3	4	5
entertain others	1	2	3	4	5
understand yourself better	1	2	3	4	5
cope with a loss	1	2	3	4	5
tell of your accomplishments	1	2	3	4	5
make future plans	1	2	3	4	5
get over feeling lonesome	1	2	3	4	5
help accept changes in your life	1	2	3	4	5
understand what life is all about	1	2	3	4	5
deal with a present problem	1	2	3	4	5
put your life in order	1	2	3	4	5
deal with knowing your life is finite	1	2	3	4	5
help you to relax	1	2	3	4	5
deal with unpleasant or troublesome memories	1	2	3	4	5

Adapted from Merriam (1993).

What Do You Think?

For a week, keep a list of your daily contacts with people who are in late adulthood. You will probably have only limited contact if you are rarely off campus, but pair up with someone who commutes to broaden the possibilities. Where do you see older adults? What are they doing? What does your list reveal about their activities and interests?

LOOKING BACK/LOOKING FORWARD

Late adulthood depends for its quality on all that has come before. Physical well-being is greatly affected by lifelong health behaviors and health-compromising behaviors. Cognitive well-being is greatly affected by educational, occupational, and leisure activities of earlier years. Psychological well-being is greatly influenced by the social convoy of relationships formed and maintained throughout the adult years. Continuity of abilities, activities, and relationships is the basic pattern. This results in enormous variability in the experiences of later life due to gender, race/ethnicity, and culture as well as socioeconomic factors. Poverty and lack of educational and occupational opportunities often lead to premature aging and death, just as privilege often promotes physical and mental vigor well into the late adult years. In this stage of life more than any other, the variability is so great that age is not a good indicator of what a person can do. Yet there are new elements to being old that eventually everyone will face. Age-related physical changes slow behavior and reduce sensory acuity. If one is lucky enough to live to be very old, increasing frailty is part of the experience. There are social losses as well. Loved ones become sick and die. Housing that was appropriate in earlier stages of life needs to be modified. Assistance becomes necessary as sensory and motor changes occur. For many old people, late adulthood brings new development as well, including the emergence of ego integrity, wisdom, and mature faith. These help old people look ahead and prepare for death, the final stage of life.

SUMMARY OF MAJOR IDEAS

Personality Development in Late Adulthood

1. Successful aging refers to the maintenance of psychological adjustment and well-being across the full lifespan. It requires psychological resilience in the face of age-related stress.

2. Longitudinal studies such as the Harvard Grant and Berkeley Older Generation studies show considerable evidence for continuity of psychological adjustment into late adulthood, as well as increased agreeableness and acceptance of the past as "something that had to be." These findings provide support for Erikson's eighth stage of life, integrity versus despair.

3. Neither activity theory nor disengagement theory can account for successful aging. While remaining active has been associated with high life satisfaction, successfully aging individuals exhibit a range of activity levels based on their life experiences and personalities.

Marriage and Singlehood

4. Older married people appear to be happier, be healthier, and live longer than widowed and divorced people of the same age. They rely on their spouses to provide care when coping with disease or frailty.

5. Wives are spousal caregivers more often than husbands are. They also tend to provide more hours of care, get less outside assistance, and experience considerable stress as a result.

6. Widowhood causes a disruption to self-identity and relationships with others, but does not appear to have negative impacts on subsequent health, ability to function, or well-being.

7. Socially active unmarried older adults are more likely to meet potential dating partners. Successful remarriage is more likely when there has been a long prior friendship and the couple has social and financial resources.

8. Older lesbian and gay couples have satisfactions in their relationships similar to those of heterosexual couples and concerns similar to those of most aging adults. They have additional concerns about sexual preference discrimination in health care, housing, and long-term care.

9. Never-married adults learn to cope with aloneness and to be autonomous and self-reliant, qualities that facilitate successful aging. They develop a rich variety of supportive relationships.

Relationships with Family and Friends

10. Starting in infancy, individuals develop social convoys of stable and continuous relationships that develop and change over time. The most important realtionships are with spouses, parents, and children.

11. Siblings provide the strongest bond outside of spouse, parents, and children. They provide emotional support, share memories, and sometimes provide instrumental support as well.

12. Adult grandchildren sustain their bonds with their grandparents. They tend to be closer to grandmothers than to grandfathers and closer to grandparents they knew well as children.

13. Interaction with friends in later life is more important to well-being and more subject to variation than relationships with kin.

14. Fictive kin are constructed relationships that blur the distinction between friends and family. They appear particularly important in the lives of never-married adults and in the African American community.

15. Childless older adults develop ties with friends and other relatives who provide them with a social network that sustains their well-being.

Problems of Living: The Housing Continuum

16. Older adults generally prefer to age in place. This is generally easier for homeowners than for renters, but in either case disability or frailty may require modification of the old home or change to a new housing alternative.

17. Independent living refers to maintaining a household with little assistance. Older adults often choose naturally occurring retirement communities (NORCs), which provide a supportive social environment that can prolong independent living.

18. Assisted living can occur in one's own home, in a retirement community, or in elderly housing. Informal services of relatives and friends, formal services, or a combination of both can provide assistance with activities of daily living that enable semi-independence.

19. Long-term care can also be found in a variety of settings, such as a relative's home, a retirement community, or a nursing home. The level of self-determination in these settings is related to levels of satisfaction of the residents.

Interests and Activities

20. Though formal volunteering among the elderly is rather low, most older adults do volunteer when informal work is also considered.

21. Membership in religious institutions is higher at older ages and declines more slowly than other community memberships. This is probably due to cohort effects, as well as to an increase in spirituality in late life.

22. Reminiscence and life review are two contemplative activities that are associated with better adjustment among old adults.

KEY TERMS

integrity versus
   despair *(630)*
activity theory *(630)*
disengagement
   theory *(632)*
social convoy *(642)*
fictive kin *(648)*
naturally occurring
   retirement community
   (NORC) *(651)*

assisted living *(651)*
congregate housing *(654)*
long-term care *(654)*
activity competence *(657)*
spirituality *(660)*
reminiscence *(663)*
life review *(663)*

PART NINE

Death, Loss, and Bereavement

The final stage of life is death. For those who are fortunate, death comes at the end of a long life. Though most people die in late adulthood, this is not always the case. Because illness and death occur during all life stages, we have discussed aspects of death, loss, and bereavement while focusing on each stage of lifespan development. When death comes early in life, it is usually sudden and unexpected. During middle adulthood, chronic diseases make death more frequent. During late adulthood, death is expected.

Ways of coping with death of a loved one also change over the lifespan. Children find it hard to grasp the finality of death and are less able to manage the loss of a significant person. Adults learn to cope with the loss of their parents and other loved ones and become increasingly aware of their own mortality. During late adulthood, grief and mourning become normative aspects of life. Concerns about care during terminal illness increase as well.

In Part Nine we explore death, loss, and bereavement with a focus on late adulthood. As you read this final section, keep in mind that life circumstances sometimes make these issues relevant at earlier stages too.

18

Death, Dying, and Bereavement

Focusing Questions

- What are contemporary attitudes toward death, and how do they affect the treatment of the dying?

- Why are elderly adults likely to be more accepting of death than younger people?

- What choices are available for terminal care, and how do they differ?

- How does bereavement affect survivors, and what supports are available to help their recovery?

Betty entered the hospital on November 26, her seventieth birthday. She had been feeling very tired and finally decided to go for tests. The tests revealed widespread cancer; whether it had started in her colon or in her ovaries was unclear. The doctor surgically removed a large portion of her intestines and sent her home to enjoy what he said might be six good months. Betty returned to the home she shared with her husband George. A hospital bed was placed in the sun room that for years had served as her home office. She had been an antique dealer and, although retired from her shop, until her hospitalization had continued to appraise and lecture on American antiques. Her office was filled with beautiful and familiar things. An around-the-clock nurse's aide tended to her personal care, and a licensed nurse visited daily to attend to her medications.

At home Betty was able to continue to be part of the family. From her bed she arranged for Christmas dinner. She and George had three adult children, one living in the same town, one an hour away, and the other a two-day drive away. They also had five grandchildren. At home the children were able to visit often, to help their father and talk to their mother about how much they would miss her. On January 14, George called the children to say that Mom was "really bad." The two children who lived close enough got there in time to spend the day. They left thinking Mom had pulled out, but that night she died in her sleep.

Betty's family arranged a day of viewing at a local funeral parlor. Friends and associates came to see her and then went to the family home to eat and pay condolences to George and the three adult children. After the viewing day, Betty was cremated and her ashes were scattered by plane into the Pacific Ocean. Betty's daughter wrote an obituary and distributed it to all the papers in the towns where Betty had done business.

Since all humans die, Betty's death was in some ways a universal experience, but it was also particular to the contemporary American cultural tradition of which she and her family were a part. Specifically, Betty died in late adulthood of a degenerative disease. She received acute care in the hospital and terminal care in her home. She was prepared for viewing and viewed at a professional funeral home and then cremated. Compared to earlier times in the United States and to contemporary times in less developed countries, death is likely to be a late adult experience. Changing mortality rates mean most Americans will live past age sixty-five and die from **degenerative diseases**, such as cardiovascular disease and cancer, as we discussed in Chapter 16. This is in contrast to earlier times when **communicable diseases**, such as influenza, cholera, scarlet fever, measles, or smallpox, spread from person to person and killed large numbers of old and young people alike. Because degenerative diseases generally cause slower deaths than do communicable diseases, the dying process in twentieth-century America is more likely to be prolonged and painful. Although Betty died less than three months after she was officially diagnosed, her daughter believes Betty knew she was ill for some time but chose to be private about it.

Betty and her family made several choices. After surgery they decided on home care rather than a nursing home. After death they decided on a viewing day rather than a funeral or memorial service. They chose cremation rather than burial. While their choices are consistent with a recent trend toward swift and inexpensive disposal

Perspectives

How Children Understand Death

In modern society, death has become rare in childhood and common in old age. This seemingly natural state of affairs actually is quite unusual; throughout history and around the world, the majority of deaths have occurred among infants and children. Today's reversal of this trend has had benefits, of course, but it may also leave children unprepared to understand and cope with death when they do experience it at close hand. Instead of seeming natural, inevitable, and universal, death may seem a rare and arbitrary event, a catastrophe that befalls only a few people. Such a view may create confusion about the nature and meaning of death.

Studies confirm that children have only a hazy understanding of death, even well into middle childhood. Early in this period, around age six, they describe death with analogies that are often reversible: "Death is when you go to sleep," said one six-year-old, as though death ended in waking up again. Often the analogies refer not to universal events but to special ones; "Death is going on a trip," for example, implying that not everyone will die since not everyone goes on trips (Webb, 1993). Perhaps for these reasons, young children do not seem to fear death as much as older children and adults do. They reveal concern and distress about the general idea of death, but unless they experience the death of a close relative (such as a parent) directly, their concerns tend to be comparatively limited. Not until around age ten do the large majority of children realize that death is irreversible, permanent, and universal. But even then their concern is rather abstract and emphasizes physical inevitability rather than psychological repercussions: "Dying is when your heart stops beating forever."

All of these developments occur more rapidly and vividly, though, if a child has had a life-threatening illness (such as leukemia) or has lost a close relative, especially a parent (Bertoia, 1993). These children face challenges that develop their understanding of death very quickly. First, they must *understand* the death as realistically as possible: it indeed has occurred, cannot be ignored, and will never be undone. Unfortunately, younger children may have trouble understanding this reality because their general cognitive understanding is limited. Second, children must have chances to *grieve* or mourn their loss and work through the feelings they still have about the per-

of the body, many different cultural and religious traditions lead to different choices as contemporary Americans try to find personally meaningful responses to death (De-Spelder & Strickland, 1996). In this chapter we examine the various options available as we look at changing attitudes toward death, preparation for one's own death, caring for the dying, and bereavement.

ATTITUDES TOWARD DEATH

Social and technological changes in developed nations have made death less familiar in the twentieth century than ever before. While in 1900 more than half of reported deaths were among children age fourteen or younger, today fewer than 3 percent of deaths occur among this age group (U.S. Bureau of the Census, 1995). When infants died frequently, children commonly died of childhood diseases, and many women died giving birth, death was witnessed often by young and old alike. Today even an at-risk infant is kept in the hospital, where life-extending technologies increase its chances of survival. If the infant dies, it is in an institution away from siblings, parents, and other family. Eighty percent of contemporary deaths take place in hospitals, nursing homes, and other formal settings. Death therefore has been removed from everyday life. Even when it is not, geographical mobility makes it likely that members of the extended family will not be present when their relatives die. The attitude conveyed by this separation is that death is or should be invisible. The cultural historian Philippe Ariès (1981) refers to this attitude toward death as *death denied*. Historically this is, according to Ariès, a totally new attitude toward death, one that makes death private rather than public, denies mourning, and includes funerary rites that erase signs of death. Coffins become caskets. Morticians beautify dead bodies so they look alive. Grief is expressed only privately, while community life goes on as normal.

son who died. The extent and nature of their grieving will depend on how emotionally attached they were to the deceased person, their overall cognitive maturity, and the support they receive for expressing their sadness. As one nine-year-old girl put it, "What bothered me most about my mother's death was that no one gave me a chance to talk about it; they were too busy with their own problems." Another child said, "My little brother didn't seem to react when my sister died [of meningitis], but I can't tell if it's because he wasn't very close to her emotionally, or because he was only four at the time, or because Mom and Dad kept telling him how 'strong' he was not to cry."

Either despite or because of their cognitive limitations, children react strongly to the deaths of the most important people in their lives, usually their parents. Research shows that the effects can be quite long-lived (Silverman & Worden, 1993). Even ten years after losing a parent, bereaved children tend to be more submissive and introverted and less aggressive than other children, even including children who lose a parent through divorce. As you might expect, though, the extent and nature of a child's reactions depend heavily on the circum-

stances: losing a mother can be harder for a child than losing a father, on average, because the remaining parent—the father—more often has had less practice expressing his own grief and has fewer social relationships to offer emotional support. Furthermore, the reactions of the surviving parent and other relatives affect the child's ability to come to terms with the death. A parent depressed with his or her own grief has reduced ability to comfort a school-age child.

What can professionals do to help children come to terms with death in general and a specific person's death in particular? The answer depends partly on the extent of their own involvement. Social workers and nurses who assist families during particular deaths can encourage children to talk about the death, say what they think and feel, and ask about what perplexes them. Teachers and school counselors also can do this when a classmate has died. In addition, they can explore the issues and feelings about death in more general ways, such as by incorporating the topic into the overall school curriculum (U.S. Department of Health and Human Services, 1993).

What is the impact of this attitude toward death? Most people feel uncomfortable around death. As we see in the accompanying Perspectives box, because of this discomfort we may send confusing messages about death to children, whose understanding of death is already vague. Not only are dying people usually placed in formal settings, but we are unlikely to visit them. We tell ourselves they would rather not be disturbed. We assign their care to specialists for whom contact with death has become routine and impersonal (Marshall & Levy, 1990). As a result, the dying

This man with AIDS is dying the good death surrounded by family and friends with minimal technological interference.

often experience a *social death* before their biological death, isolated in institutions away from family and friends and shunned by their medical caregivers as well (Kastenbaum, 1992b). Even in speaking we avoid death. People refer to it by euphemism; in polite conversation people *pass away*, are *called home,* or *go to heaven* rather than die. Caskets are likely to be closed so that people do not have to view death. If the casket is open, the deceased has been embalmed and made up to look alive. Children are likely to be kept away from funerals and burials. Mourning rites and bereavement leave have become shorter in the United States and are shaped to the time constraints of the business world (Pratt, 1981).

Partially in response to the lack of opportunities to learn about death and dying through direct observation, in the 1970s a movement to forge new meanings and patterns for handling dying and death emerged. The **death awareness movement** responded to the increasing number of very old people in American society, the prolongation of the dying process, the anxieties of the nuclear age, and the 1960s perspective that asserted the rights of the ignored and underprivileged, in this case the dying (DeSpelder & Strickland, 1996). Social issues of our time, such as abortion, AIDS, drug abuse, and alcoholism, also have pushed us to face death and dying (Feifel, 1990). The death awareness movement has led to the analysis of cultural messages about death. It has challenged the isolation of the dying and promoted the idea of *the good death,* in which the dying person is surrounded by family and friends with minimal technological interference. It has also led to the development of death education (Durlak & Riesenberg, 1991). As a result of the death awareness movement, most colleges and universities and a few elementary and high schools now offer courses on death and dying; the topic permeates many books and chapters in textbooks such as the one you are now reading.

What Do You Think?

With several classmates, list as many euphemisms for dying that you can think of. Which ones were used in your families? What did they mean to you as a child when you heard them? What does their use teach children about death?

FACING ONE'S OWN DEATH

Death does not come only to the old, but it does so more frequently. In 1990, 72 percent of deaths in the United States were among people age sixty-five and older (National Center for Health Statistics, 1993). There is evidence that as people age, recognition of their own mortality increases. Most people eighty-five or older expect to die within five years, compared to only 7 percent of those ages sixty-five to seventy-four (Marshall, 1980). Witnessing the death of peers, reaching the age of one's parent's death, and confronting health problems increase the salience of one's own mortality. While these experiences are more typical of middle age, younger people are affected by them as well. When an adolescent or a young adult peer dies, it is most likely a result of accident, homicide, or suicide. Such deaths are typically unexpected, traumatic or violent, shocking, and off time. All of these characteristics make the deaths difficult to accept, especially if schools and parents respond by continuing life as usual rather than taking time out for bereavement (Corr et al., 1994). Adults may give little thought to the effects of the deaths of young cultural icons, such as rock stars Kurt Cobain and Selena, basketball player Reggie Lewis, and teenage AIDS activist Angel Velasquez, on their teenage children, but adolescents respond with grief. Consistent with their developmental stage, teenage grieving tends to come and go and may extend over a long period of time (Hogan & DeSantis, 1992).

Starting in midlife, people begin to estimate the amount of time they have left before they are likely to die. While not everyone makes such estimates, Pat Keith

Millions of school children were watching the live broadcast of the Challenger launching when an explosion killed the astronauts. As a result, teachers had little choice but to help children with their concerns and anxieties about the deaths.

(1982) found that doing so was associated with planning for the future and more favorable attitudes toward death. Perceptions of the amount of time left are affected by the ages at which one's parents died as well as by one's own age.

Death Acceptance

Studies show that people both accept and deny the reality of their dying; while we know that dying is universal, we find it hard to comprehend our own mortality (Wiseman, 1972). Young children see death as reversible or temporary, as we see in Perspectives: How Children Understand Death. Adolescents tend to deny their own mortality, as they cling to the personal fable of invincibility. Young adults are often very angry when faced with their own death because they are just beginning the tasks of building intimate relationships, establishing occupations, and raising children and feel frustrated that their dreams will go unfulfilled. As we saw in Chapter 15, middle-aged adults' awareness of their own mortality increases as they bury and mourn for their parents. Late adulthood is associated with an increasing acceptance of death or "nonbeing" and increasing concern about the process of dying, with wishes to not die in pain, immobile, alone and irreversibly confused (Marshall & Levy, 1990; Tobin et al., 1994). That is one of the reasons, as we saw in our discussion of wills and advance directives in Chapter 15, that planning and leaving instructions for terminal care and death can reduce death anxiety.

Impact of Advance Directives   Public opinion polls show almost 90 percent of American adults would not want life support systems in place if there were no prospect of recovery, yet fewer than one in five have actually prepared any written advance directive (Moody, 1994a). Eric Diamond and his associates (1989) assessed the preferences regarding advance directives among thirty-nine nursing home patients ages fifty-eight to ninety-six. Half of the respondents had given prior thought to life support decisions but only six recalled signing a declaration. While 59 percent said they preferred forgoing life-prolonging measures, 48 percent signed the advance directive declaration, 8 percent chose not to sign, 21 percent deferred their decision, and 23 percent were unable to adequately respond to the form. Most patients preferred hospitalization for nonterminal but potentially life-threatening conditions but preferred to forgo burdensome measures in the event of terminal status. Martha Henderson (1990) studied sixty-three generally well-educated, middle-class retirement community residents with living wills to see if more specific planning for their dying process would decrease their anxiety about death. Residents were randomly assigned to an experimental and a control group. All participants completed a Death Anxiety Scale at the beginning of the study. The experimental group was then given a questionnaire about specific treatment options in the face of terminal illness and the opportunity to discuss any items, feelings, and concerns the questionnaire engendered. A week later, both groups completed the Death Anxiety Scale once again. The mean death anxiety score for the experimental group decreased significantly after the intervention. No change occurred for the control group.

Residents who wanted little or no medical intervention in the event of a terminal illness benefited most from the opportunity to specify what they did not want. Participants said they found the study useful because they would not have done such planning without the supportive counseling the study provided. "Themes of usefulness included the opportunity to clarify treatment options and wishes, and to share these with their children; the chance to make specific plans, such as contacting their minister about their memorial service or making arrangements for the disposition of their body; time for introspection, reminiscing, and affirmation of beliefs . . ." (Henderson, 1990, p. 483). By specifying their wishes regarding treatment and other care issues, the individuals were able to increase their control over their dying process and decrease their anxiety. Unfortunately, there are no studies of the impact of advance directives on a broader spectrum of adults with respect to age, race/ethnicity, and SES.

Differences in Death Anxiety   Older people talk about death more than younger people do and seem to be less fearful of it (Kalish, 1985; Thorson & Powell, 1988). Conflicting evidence exists on gender differences. James Thorson and F. C. Powell (1988) found that women seem to be more accepting of death than are men. While they fear their own deaths, they see death as peaceful, whereas men view it as antagonistic. Women express more death anxiety than men do (Dattell & Neimeyer, 1990). Fear of death is also related to religiosity. Richard Kalish (1985) found that people who were strongly religious and those who were affirmed atheists showed few death fears. Those with strong inner beliefs, whether in a traditional God or in a personal philosophy, seemed better able to contend with death. Those who were sporadically religious or uncertain about their religious beliefs showed the most death fears (Glass, 1990).

Factors That Reduce Death Anxiety   Why are older people less fearful of death even though they are closer to it? Several explanations have been proposed. First, because our society has negative views of aging and old people, as we discussed in Chapter 16, older people may come to value themselves and their lives less (Stillion, 1985). This may lead them to see their lives as having fewer prospects for the future. Second, older people deal frequently with the deaths of their friends and associates, especially if they live in age-segregated retirement communities or nursing homes. This helps to socialize them into acceptance of their own death. Third, if they have lived past the time they expected to, they may view themselves as living on "borrowed time" (Kalish, 1985). Fourth, a painless death is viewed more favorably than slow mental or physical deterioration and becoming a burden to loved ones (Marshall, 1980). Fifth, as we discussed in Chapter 17, during Erikson's late adult developmental stage of ego integrity versus despair, the process of life review may enable the resolution of conflicts and relieve death anxiety. Robert Kastenbaum (1992a) found evidence of ego integration and life review among hospitalized geriatric patients. In a study of death anxiety among older women, Patrick Quinn and Marvin Reznikoff (1985) found that those women with high death anxiety had less sense of purpose in life, saw time as marching relentlessly on, felt harassed by time pressures, and saw less continuity in their lives than those with low death anxiety.

Impact of Off-Time Responsibilities   Unfinished business can interfere with the normative process of accepting death as one gets old. Young and middle-aged parents of dependent children typically feel concern about the impact of their death on their children. Lillian Rubin (1979) found that midlife women whose children were leaving home expressed relief from this concern. As one of them said, "It would be a tragedy, wouldn't it, to be a mother and to die before you thought your kids were ready?" (p. 29). Sheldon Tobin, Elise Fullmer, and Gregory Smith (1994) interviewed a sample of 235 mothers ages fifty-eight to ninety-six who were caring at home for an adult child with mental retardation. Unlike most older mothers, although they had successfully launched other adult children, they still had a dependent offspring, which made it difficult for them to accept their own death. The mothers were given the Sentence Completion Test (SCT) stem *Death is . . .* and asked to complete the sentence. Responses were scored on a five-point scale. A score of 1 was assigned to completions reflecting fear or denial, such as "not being afraid if she were taken care of." A 2 was assigned to themes of loss, such as "losing everything." A 3 was assigned to themes that were neutral, such as "natural" or "inevitable." A 4 was assigned to themes of relief from pain or suffering, such as "knowing he will let me die in peace." And a score of 5 was given when there was a transcendental quality, such as "going to heaven." The responses to the SCT did not suggest a great fear of dying: 62 percent scored 3 (natural or inevitable); 20 percent scored 1 or 2 (indicating fear or loss); and 18 percent scored 4 or 5 (indicating death was a blessing).

However, when the mothers were further asked, "Has being a parent and caregiver of a mentally retarded son/daughter affected your feelings about your own death?" responses reflected internal conflict regarding death. Those who had said death was "natural" or "inevitable" also said things such as: "I don't want to go before her"; "I hate the thought of leaving her; I wish I could live forever"; "I worry about him. He'll miss me"; and "I can't die." Tobin and his associates (1994) interpret these conflictual responses as indicating that "If they were not perpetual parents, death would be acceptable" (p. 192). Among their sample they found that death acceptance decreased with age and fears and losses increased, which is counter to normative aging. Only the handful of mothers who had made future plans for their dependent offspring with which they were comfortable could talk positively about dying.

Unfinished business can come in forms other than a dependent adult child with a disability. An older person with dependent grandchildren or a disabled spouse may be less accepting of death than one who does not have those social responsibilities. The same may be true of older people still deeply involved in their careers, such as Supreme Court justices or artists still seeking to express the essence of their work (Tobin, 1991). There may also be cohort effects in death acceptance. The now old cohort has less education than the cohorts that follow, and there is evidence that among the better educated more awareness of life's uncertain length exists at all ages (Marshall, 1980). On the other hand, in the absence of mandatory retirement, more elderly individuals may continue active careers that interfere with death acceptance. We do not know how much of the documented differences in death acceptance have to do with age and how much with cohort effects. Although we know differences exist among ethnic and religious groups, little research has systematically measured them. We do know more African American grandparents are raising their grandchildren, as we discussed in Chapter 15, which may have a negative impact on their death acceptance.

Elder Suicide

"The fact that elderly men and women often can accept the inevitability of death with a sense of composure does not mean that they have had enough of life" (Kastenbaum, 1992a, p. 12). It is important not to confuse age-related death acceptance with desire for death. Robert Kastenbaum and his colleagues (1992a) found that among hospitalized geriatric patients, two psychological patterns occurred with about equal frequency: a gradual withdrawal and closing down of operations and a continuation of customary activities. He quotes one woman in the second group as having said, "Death wants me—he'll have to find me at Bingo!" Among a sample of terminally ill late-middle-aged and elderly adults, Kastenbaum found that the desire and opportunity to affirm personal relationships through a process of leave-taking helped to control anxiety and reduce impulses to end one's life through suicide, assisted suicide, or euthanasia (we will discuss these last two topics in the next section).

Nonetheless, an association has been found between age and suicide; cross-sectional studies report that suicide rates are higher in later life (Koenig & Blazer, 1992). Elderly people commit 17 percent of the suicides but make up only 11 or 12 percent of the population. Longitudinal data, however, present a different picture of the age-suicide relationship. Since World War II the suicide rate has been relatively stable despite an increasing elderly population, then it started to rise around 1986, particularly among those ages seventy-five to eighty-four (U.S. Bureau of the Census, 1995). Harold Koenig and Dan Blazer (1992) point out that both period effects and cohort effects must be considered when looking at the impact of age on suicide rates. *Period effects* refer to the impact of a unique stressor on the suicide rates for a particular age group. Legalizing the use of handguns, for example, as the state of Virginia recently did, may increase the suicide rate among the elderly, since older men are more likely than younger men to use firearms. *Cohort effects* on suicide rates refer to stressors that affect members of a particular age group because of the generation into which they were born. Because of social security and Medicare, the current cohort of elderly has had fewer financial pressures and better health than other post–World War II cohorts, and that would predict lower suicide rates.

Not all elderly are equally likely to attempt or commit suicide. Most of us know individuals who in late adulthood are full of zest for life. What factors put individuals at risk for suicide in later life? As Table 18.1 shows, the elderly who are at high risk are those with reduced opportunity or inclination to communicate (Kastenbaum, 1992a). Living alone cuts down opportunities to share feelings, which is why married persons of all ages have the lowest risk of suicide and widowed or divorced people have the highest. Residing in a low-income, transient urban area tends to cut down social contacts, whereas high-SES individuals seem buffered against the risk of suicide. Being depressed, dependent on alcohol, or mentally ill reduces communication and is likely to drive other people away and increase the suicide risk. A very large proportion of elderly men and women who kill themselves do so because they suffer from quite remediable depression, as we discussed in Chapter 16.

As Figure 18.1 shows, being male and white greatly increases the risk of suicide. Elderly white males take their own lives at a rate five times the national average (Nuland, 1994). Men show reluctance to seek help or to accept opportunities to express grief or suffering. Race is also a risk factor, although the reason is not fully understood. Suicide seems to be alien to African American culture, where people consider it to be a "white thing" (Early & Akers, 1993). The rate of suicide for white males age eighty-five or older is about three times that of African American males in this age group (Koenig & Blazer, 1992). Anger, despair, and suicidality are more char-

TABLE 18.1 *Risk Factors for Suicide in Late Adulthood*
Factors that reduce opportunity or inclination to communicate with others during late adulthood increase the risk of suicide.

- Living alone and being social isolated
- Experiencing financial difficulty
- Feeling depressed or useless
- Being alcohol or drug dependent
- Having a mental illness that reduces communication
- Suffering from chronic pain, illness, or incapacity
- Being unable to express grief or suffering
- Losing significant relationships due to the death of loved ones

acteristic of the hospitalized elderly than of the independently living, which indicates that those committing suicide are uncomfortable with life rather than looking forward to death (Kastenbaum, 1992a). Poor health status, a precursor to hospitalization, is also a major risk factor. Because of this relationship between illness and suicide among the elderly, suicide among this group is probably seriously underestimated. Neglecting to take medication, refusing to undergo life-saving surgery or other treatments, or neglecting to seek medical care may lead to intentional deaths that get recorded as due to natural causes (Rodin et al., 1981).

Older suicides may be harder to predict, and therefore, prevent, than younger suicides. In a study designed to assess what risk factors distinguish older from younger suicides, Susanne Carney and her associates (1994) compared early (sixteen to thirty years), middle (thirty-one to fifty-nine years), and older (sixty to eighty-eight years) adult suicides that had occurred during one year in San Diego County. Using extensive data-gathering techniques, they found that mental disorders played a major role in suicide at all ages, with depression the most common disorder. Interpersonal loss was a stressor associated with 43 percent of the older suicides, but it was also very common among the younger (64 percent) and middle-age suicides (59 percent). While older people generally experienced the death of a spouse or long-term partner, young and middle-aged people tended to lose significant relationships because of

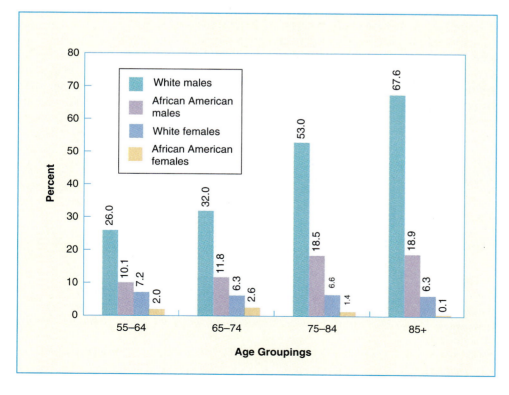

FIGURE 18.1
Older Suicide by Race and Gender, 1992* (Rate per 100,000 Population)
Being white and male increases the risk of suicide.
Source: U.S. Bureau of the Census (1995), Table 136.
*When the 1992 data were unreliable, earlier data from the same table were used.

fights or separations. Financial stressors were less frequent among the older group than the two younger groups. Health problems were more common in the older group of suicides. The older individuals were not more isolated socially, but were less likely to have talked of suicide or to have made a prior suicide attempt. The investigators conclude that the major risk factors of suicide differ little between older and younger people, but older adults seem to communicate warnings less frequently.

Suicide at any age appears sudden and unexpected to the people left behind. It also appears to have been chosen, although more frequently it is an escape or an inability to live with the human condition. These characteristics make suicide deaths hard for survivors to cope with, as they leave a complex combination of anger, sadness, and guilt (Corr et al., 1994). While family and peers may be more accepting of suicide in the face of poor health and deteriorating quality of life among the elderly, suicide is still more difficult to accept than the unchosen, often protracted death that is the normal end to life.

The Dying Process

The understanding of how people come to accept their own deaths has been greatly influenced by the work of Elisabeth Kubler-Ross (1969, 1981).

Working within a psychoanalytic framework, Kubler-Ross (1969) interviewed more than two hundred dying patients and proposed five distinct stages through which individuals pass. Table 18.2 shows these stages. Although the stages are distinct, they are not necessarily progressive and are likely to overlap. Denial, the refusal to believe the terminal diagnosis, is the initial response as the person defends against the news of impending death. Anger is often displaced onto the family or medical staff and is likely to be a hard stage for the caregivers to tolerate. Bargaining with a higher being often takes the form of asking for more time to do something good, such as be more religious or finish a project. Depression is the stage in which the individual begins to acknowledge and mourn the impending loss. It represents the natural grieving process of separation from loved ones and life. Acceptance, the final stage, is reached only if the individual is allowed to express and work out the earlier feelings. Kubler-Ross (1981) emphasizes the importance of informing patients about their condition so that dying can be a time of growth as individuals come to terms with their past and who they really are.

Although Kubler-Ross's stage formulation has been widely accepted by clinicians who work with dying patients, it has also been amply challenged by research and theory (Corr, 1993; Marshall & Levy, 1990). The patients Kubler-Ross studied were young and middle-aged adults dying of cancer, which may account for the anger and bargaining she found. The age range of her sample makes generalizing to older adults problematic. As we have already discussed, older people are generally more accepting of death. Among people who were sixty years old on the average, Avery Wiseman

Elisabeth Kubler-Ross emphasized the importance of informing patients about their condition so that dying can be a time of growth. This became a basic premise of the death awareness movement.

TABLE 18.2 Elisabeth Kubler-Ross's Stages of Coping with Death
Kubler-Ross's stages are not necessarily progressive and are likely to overlap. Since they are based on young and middle-aged adults dying of cancer, they do not represent the variability that exists in the course of dying.

Stage	Associated Feelings
Denial	"Not me."
Anger	"Why me?"
Bargaining	"Yes me, but . . ."
Depression	"Yes me." Begin to mourn.
Acceptance	"My time is very close now, and it's all right."

Source: Kubler-Ross, E. (1969), On death and dying, New York: MacMillan.

THE LAST DAYS OF A HYDRANGEA

DENIAL — OH, ISN'T IT PRETTY? IT'S VERY SUBTLE.

ANGER — STAND UP STRAIGHT! HOW MUCH SUNLIGHT CAN I GIVE YOU?

BARGAINING — O.K. GIVE ME ONE LITTLE BLOSSOM AND I'LL NEVER GOSSIP AGAIN.

DEPRESSION — WHY? WHY?

ACCEPTANCE — FELLAS, SAY HELLO TO YOUR NEW FRIEND.

Kubler-Ross's five-stages of dying have been so widely popularized they are sometimes the subject matter of cartoons. Nevertheless, variations in cultural context and circumstances of death make general application of her formulation too simplistic.

(1972) found that acceptance of death without denial was possible. Kastenbaum (1992b) points out that the course of dying is much more variable than Kubler-Ross's stages imply. For example, cancer may go in and out of remission, which can cause alternation between acceptance and denial rather than a clear first and last stage. Besides variation due to age or type of death, a larger criticism is that Kubler-Ross focuses on the individual rather than the social relationships in which dying is embedded and one's cultural setting. Kathy Charmaz (1980) suggests that "the stages of dying . . . may indeed be a consequence of how illness and dying are socially handled in this society, rather than a psychological process of adjustment to death" (p. 155). In particular, since Kubler-Ross's dying patients were all in the hospital, "Denial may occur when the patients have not yet put together the cues [that they are dying], . . .

anger when they learn that everyone else knew long before, depression when there is not much time and so much left unfinished, and acceptance when they realize that nothing more can be done" (Charmaz, 1980, p. 155). If our society did not deny death and isolate the dying, perhaps the experience of dying would be different. Although Eastern religions include a variety of traditions, they represent views of death and rebirth that place the experience of dying in a different perspective. Hindus seek a state of blissful union with a higher state of being-as-blissful consciousness. Buddhists consider "right livelihood" and the avoidance of nonvirtue as an avenue to correct understanding of the universe. By teaching that a meaningful life can be found by the individual detaching from self and finding unity with all, these beliefs contrast with Western views of dying. Despite the criticism of her work, Kubler-Ross has had a profound effect on making people more sympathetic to death and dying.

The Good Death

The good death is one that is appropriate to the person who is dying. This shows considerable cultural variation (see Table 18.3). For Buddhists and Hindus, who believe the last thought at the moment of death determines the character of the next incarnation, the good death is one in which the individual uses the *bardo*, or interval of suspension between death and rebirth, to awaken a more enlightened incarnation (DeSpelder & Strickland, 1996). In Indian culture, for instance, the final or *sannyasi* stage of Hindu life is initiated with a ritual that symbolizes death of the old self. The individual renunciates his former life and directs his mind to the attainment of liberation. Family and acquaintances respect and admire the individual renouncing former status and power, which gives his life new meaning and purpose. As part of the initiation rite, the individual conducts his own funeral ceremonies. He is not cremated at his actual death because he has already experienced ritual death (Thomas, 1994).

When Robert Kastenbaum and Claude Normand (1990) asked American college students to picture their deathbed scene, they generally described being alert, lucid, and aware of their coming death as they died of old age, at home, with their friends and family gathered around them. Missing from their descriptions are institutional settings, medical interventions, pain, and long-term suffering that are the realities of modern life. A recent large-scale hospital study attempted to improve end-of-life decision making and reduce frequency of the mechanically supported, painful, and prolonged dying process by having a specially trained nurse facilitate understanding and planning through discussions with patient, family, and physician (SUPPORT Principal Investigators, 1995). Having a nurse work to enhance communication did not result in improved care. Patient-physician communication was not increased, do-not-resuscitate orders were not made more quickly, and level of pain during the patient's last days was not reduced. Improving the quality of end-of-life care will require changes in the organization and culture of the hospital and active support from hospital leaders (Improving Care, 1995). Nurses are not powerful enough that their intervention can effect these changes, and doctors receive little training in talking to patients about life-sustaining equipment.

The death awareness movement has promoted conditions that can make the good death possible, such as honesty with the dying person, home and hospice settings that enable friends and family to remain close, and control of pain and tech-

TABLE 18.3 *Ways in Which Culture Influences Death Concerns*
Like all other stages of life, death is influenced by culture.

- It affects the assessment of comfort needs of the dying and the kind of care provided.
- It influences selection, perception, and evaluation of health care givers and their methods.
- It shapes beliefs about causes of death.
- It determines the disposition of the body and funeral and burial rituals.
- It patterns grief responses and bereavement roles.

Source: Adapted from Ross (1994).

nological interventions. The goal is to enable the dying individual to experience personal growth in this final stage of life. Increasing the conditions for the good death can foster hope in the dying person, which can motivate attempts to control the disease and establish continuity between oneself and one's survivors (Kastenbaum, 1992b). As is evident in Chapter 17's Multicultural View box, "Can Individuals Postpone Dying for a Special Event?" individuals can influence the course of their dying to enable them to celebrate a final special holiday or birthday. One aspect of the good death that terminally ill patients emphasize is looking after the needs of survivors in a practical manner; material preparations take precedence over religious concerns in the preterminal phase (Kastenbaum, 1992a).

What Do You Think?

In what ways do you think death acceptance can help set the conditions for the good death? What evidence for this idea do you see in the vignette about Betty at the start of this chapter?

CARING FOR THE DYING

The way the dying are cared for influences the quality of their deaths. Often older adults facing a terminal illness are in need of both acute care and long-term care. Though not curative, surgery or other aggressive treatment may be able to slow the progress of the disease or make the dying person more comfortable. Pain control can also make a person more comfortable even though it does not cure the cause of the pain. Sometimes surgery reveals the terminal nature of the disease, as was the case for Betty in our opening vignette. A person therefore may need hospital or other acute care at some stages of the terminal illness and long-term care at others.

Terminal Care Alternatives

Contradiction is inherent in the fact that so many individuals die in hospitals. Hospitals are designed to prolong life, not to promote the good death. People like Betty go to the hospital to get sophisticated health care, not for personal comfort as they face death. Betty's decision to go home to die is one more families are now making in the wake of the death awareness movement. At home Betty was able to be with her family, eat her favorite foods, and enjoy her own familiar things. What would she have faced in the hospital? Routine care by impersonal caregivers. Medical intervention that would have been painful and costly but not curative. Not only would Betty's death have been more difficult for her; it would have been harder for her family. Being with Betty would have been limited by hospital rules concerning visiting hours and number of visitors, as well as the discomforts of a small, impersonal hospital room and dreary hallways. The family's focus might have been fighting the rules rather than engaging in grief work. **Grief work**, an initial phase of the bereavement process, entails anger, self-recrimination, depression, and taking care of unfinished business. Instead of the joy of having the family together for one last Christmas dinner, there would have been guilt had the rest of the family left Betty alone while they had Christmas dinner, or there may have been no annual family dinner at all as they hung around the hospital.

Home Death   Home used to be where elderly people died in the United States and continues to be where most people die in nonindustrialized countries. Caring for the dying was an integral part of American women's work until early in this century (Abel, 1991). Only when advances in medicine and nursing made it possible to delay death, about fifty years ago, did dying move to hospitals. By the 1980s, most deaths were occurring outside of the home.

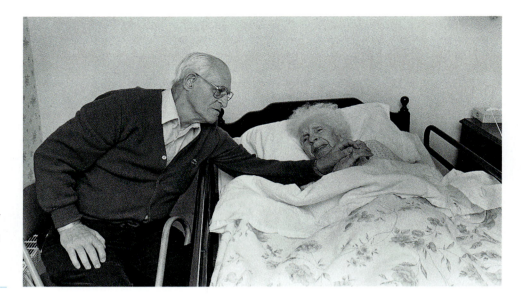

Home care provides familiarity, a sense of normalcy, greater opportunities for sustaining relationships, and allows for mutual sharing of concerns and feelings. Long-term married couples, like this one, often choose to be together for as long as possible.

Several recent developments have led to a reversal of this trend and the reemergence of home death (Sankar, 1993). First, the death awareness movement has encouraged the elderly, the terminally ill, and their families to control the conditions of their own deaths. Second, the hospice movement has promoted the expectation of the good death. **Hospice** takes an holistic approach to death by attending to the physical, emotional, spiritual, and aesthetic needs of patients and their families, predominantly in their own homes. The most important criteria for eligibility for hospice care is that the patient and family be choosing supportive care for a terminal disease with the care delivered primarily in the home setting (Gentile & Fello, 1990). Hospice is now formally recognized by Medicare and private insurance companies, enabling many more people to utilize its services. Third, recognition of the limits of medical care has been growing. Heroic measures may prolong life, but they do not ensure quality of life. Care for pain and symptom relief may be preferable to invasive or aggressive medical treatment. Fourth, improvements in technology and pharmacology have made home-based care possible, particularly in the areas of pain control, oxygen therapy, intravenous treatments, nutritional supplements, and chemotherapy. Fifth, insurance companies have limited the duration of a hospital stay for which they will reimburse unless the patient is receiving active treatment. As a result of these diverse forces, people are increasingly choosing home death over hospital death.

While it is easy to see the benefits of home death, that choice has several difficult aspects for which many families are unprepared. On the positive side, home care provides familiarity, a sense of normalcy, and greater opportunities for sustaining relationships and allows for mutual sharing of concerns and feelings (DeSpelder & Strickland, 1996). On the negative side, today's dying typically are much sicker than they used to be (Sankar, 1991). Medical advances have led to fewer deaths from secondary infections such as pneumonia and more from primary diseases such as cancer. (The exception is people with HIV.) One result is that by the time death comes, the patient is likely to be very weak and debilitated. Except for AIDS patients, dying people are also likely to be older and frailer than they used to be. Home death, then, usually means having not a clear-headed and active patient but a very fragile patient for whom routine activities such as eating, eliminating, and bathing are major undertakings. Often it requires establishing the equivalent of an intensive care unit in the home. Many caregivers are not prepared for the level of care home death requires.

Another important change has occurred in the lives of women, who are most often the caregivers. While fifty and more years ago few women worked outside the home, today most are employed. Since a high percentage of primary caregivers are employed, the risk for potential emotional, physical, and financial stress is considerable (Cantor, 1992). Home care requires that someone be on call around the clock. This is very difficult for many families to arrange. Hospice and other home care programs are designed to provide information and support services, which can be invaluable, but they may not be enough. In real (rather than ideal) families, conflict among family members may make caregiving under such demanding circumstances too difficult. The dying person may be having a difficult time accepting death. The caregiver may have unresolved anger and bitterness toward the dying family member. In addition, cognitive impairment of the dying person may make home care too difficult because the caregiver has to interpret what the patient cannot say and also assess whether what is said is actually meant (Sankar, 1993).

Home care is not always the best way to facilitate the good death. If dying is prolonged and disability is pronounced, moving the patient to a hospice or other acute care facility for palliative care can enable the stressed caregiver to relax and be with the dying relative emotionally. Not every family has the emotional and physical resources to sustain home care, and not every patient is able to appreciate being at home. On the other hand, many caregivers who have provided home care through a home death experience found it a very rewarding moment in their lives, as well as the most difficult and challenging thing they have accomplished (Sankar, 1991).

Home care, then, is one alternative to hospital care. Home care is most appropriate when the patient is alert enough to relate to the caregiver and benefit from the familiar surroundings. Since it is predicated on close caring relationships, it works best when honesty characterizes the terminal diagnosis. Figure 18.2 presents some of the positive ways a person can support someone who is facing a life-threatening illness. Secrecy or denial can make it difficult to continue to be close and prevent the dying and the bereaved from resolving the issues surrounding the death (Kalish, 1985).

Acute Care Facilities   What other options are available for patients besides hospital and home? Nursing homes are the institutions other than hospitals in which Americans most frequently die. Hospitals generally provide only short-term, aggressive care and then release the patient to nursing home or home care. Nursing homes have around-the-clock skilled nursing facilities but provide less sophisticated care than do hospitals. They also tend to be impersonal in style and setting. Other innovative long-term care programs, such as On Lok Senior Health Services of San Francisco, enable elderly persons who are certified for nursing home care to remain in the community as long as possible (Der-McLeod & Hansen, 1992). On Lok combines primary medical, adult day health, and home care services complete with transportation. On Lok works with the patient and the family of culturally diverse elders; its participant population includes Chinese, Italian, Spanish, African American, German, Greek, Irish, Filipino, and Korean. The staff works with the family to supplement their care and relieve some of the caregiving stress, teaches new knowledge and management skills that increase the family's ability to cope with the difficulties of caregiving, and provides crisis intervention. The staff also works with the patients to establish what their health wishes are. This is an ongoing process that has enabled some elderly people—even among the Chinese and Italians, who have an unspoken tradition of not discussing matters of death or dying—to express their wishes concerning resuscitation (Der-McLeod & Hansen, 1992). On Lok in San Francisco has served as a model for similar organizations in other locations.

Hospice Service   In addition to home care services, some hospices have centers that provide acute care. Whether at home or at a facility, hospice care is specifically designed to meet the needs of the dying patient and the bereaved family members. Hospices offer services that enable individuals to die with dignity and maintain a purposeful life to the end. The hospice philosophy is to provide **palliative care**, to manage the pain and other symptoms so that the dying individual can enjoy what remains of life. In addition to medical and nursing staff, trained volunteers and family members serve as caregivers, and there is a bereavement program for survivors. Hospice

Your Caring Presence: Ways of Effectively Providing Support to Others

1. Be honest about your own thoughts, concerns, and feelings
2. When in doubt, ask questions:
   How is that for you?
   How do you feel right now?
   Can you tell me more about that?
   Am I intruding?
   What do you need?
   What are the ways you can take care of yourself?
3. When you are responding to a person facing a crisis situation, be sure to use statements such as:
   I feel __________
   I believe __________
   I would want __________

   Rather than:
   You should
   That's wrong
   Everything will be ok

   which are statements that may not give the person the opportunity to express his/her own unique needs and feelings.
4. Stay in the present as much as possible: How do you feel RIGHT NOW? What do you need RIGHT NOW?
5. Listening is profoundly healing. You don't have to make it better. You don't have to have the answers. You don't have to take away the pain. It's his pain. He needs to experience it in his own time and in his own way.
6. People in crisis need to know they have decision-making power. It may be appropriate to point out alternatives.
7. Offer any practical assistance that you feel comfortable giving.
8. If the situation warrants it, feel free to refer individual to appropriate agency.

FIGURE 18.2
Your Caring Presence: Ways of Effectively Providing Support to Others Who Face Life-Threatening Illness
Source: The Centre for Living with Dying.

facilities are designed more like homes than hospitals. As the Working With interview on page 686 shows, hospice care encourages friends and family to be with their loved ones. The Connecticut Hospice was the first American hospice and is based on the model of St. Christopher's Hospice in Sydenham, England. The building, designed to handle fifty-three patients, provides natural lighting and garden views in every room, allowing even immobile patients to enjoy them. The commons has a glass ceiling so that daily performances and activities happen "outside" rain or shine. Doors are wide enough for beds to be wheeled to where the activities are. Flower beds are at wheelchair level so that patients can tend the flowers. Hospice pets come in regularly to visit. Arts and crafts keep patients involved in meaningful, goal-directed activities.

While there are some freestanding hospice facilities in the United States that offer both inpatient and home care programs, such as the one in Connecticut, many hospices are simply home care programs, and some hospice programs are set within traditional medical facilities. Most hospice care is provided at home. Even those patients who eventually move to an inpatient facility start with home care. Hospice provides social workers, nurses, and aides to assist families care for patients and help them with bereavement. Some hospices have arrangements with inpatient facilities and some do not.

Assisted Suicide

Given that many individuals face long, painful, debilitating terminal illnesses, some choose (or would like to choose) to end their lives while they are still rational rather than suffer and be a burden to their loved ones. As we have seen, the elderly may welcome a timely death with dignity, the good death, over the pain and ravages of an incurable disease. This may be true as well for younger adults who face incurable and debilitating illnesses such as AIDS or cancer. As physician and writer Sherwin Nuland (1994, p. 151) articulates it, "Taking one's own life is almost always the wrong thing to do. There are two circumstances, however, in which that may not be so. Those two are the unendurable infirmities of a crippling old age and the final devastations of terminal disease." He emphasizes *unendurable*, *crippling*, *final*, and *terminal* because he sees them as the critical conditions for euthanasia. *Euthanasia* is the voluntary ending of life when illness makes it intolerable. In the Netherlands, a distinction is made between ordinary suicide and death under the circumstances of euthanasia. Although illegal in the Netherlands, euthanasia is not prosecuted as long as it meets certain guidelines. The guidelines require that there be "severe suffering without the hope of relief; a financially and emotionally uncoerced, informed, and consistent choice by the patient; the absence of treatment options and second opinions from other professionals" (Cassel & Meier, 1990).

Contemporary debate in the United States has focused on the role of doctors in assisting the suicide of their patients and the role of family and friends in assisting the suicide of their loved ones. Euthanasia can be passive or active. **Passive euthanasia** refers to not doing something to prolong life, such as not utilizing life support equipment or not giving antibiotics, as you may remember from our discussion of advance directives in Chapter 15. **Active euthanasia** refers to taking steps to end life, such as giving a fatal dose of painkilling medication. *Assisted suicide* refers to helping with active euthanasia. In 1996, assisting in suicide was illegal in all fifty states. While most people condemn involuntary euthanasia, or killing someone "for his or her own good" but without the person's consent, opinions about voluntary euthanasia differ widely. Some, like the Hemlock Society, advocate legalizing assisted suicide and voluntary euthanasia so that patients have self-determination regarding the termination of their lives. Others fear this would encourage depressed elderly people to end their lives instead of changing the conditions that cause their depression (Moody, 1994b). A request for euthanasia may be a plea for help, a choice made in ignorance of other alternatives to alleviate pain, or a response to rejection from family or friends rather than a rational decision.

Still others fear that loosening the restraints on active euthanasia could lead to abuses by unethical and incompetent doctors (Kass, 1994). Dr. Jack Kevorkian's role in the assisted suicide of Mrs. Janet Adkins in June 1990 is an example of what these critics fear (Cassel & Meier, 1990). Mrs. Adkins, only fifty-four years old, was in the early stages of Alzheimer's disease and was in excellent health and functional status at the time Dr. Kevorkian assisted with her suicide. As we discussed in Chapter 16, the diagnosis of Alzheimer's disease is less than certain. While Mrs. Adkins may have faced the terrible cognitive losses that accompany Alzheimer's, Dr. Kevorkian was not her regular physician and was in no position to confirm the diagnosis. He decided her euthanasia request was rational on the basis of one face-to-face meeting (Worsnop, 1992). She may well have had good years ahead.Frances Moore (1995), a surgeon for fifty years, argues it is the physician's responsibility to help patients have the best chance for good minutes, hours, and days without prolonging their agony. In descriptions of patients he has treated, he points out how clinical judgment and long experience are necessary when deciding whom to treat aggressively and whom to just make as comfortable as possible, whom to keep on life supports and whom to disconnect.

What Do You Think?

What is your position on assisted suicide? Should it be legal? If so, under what conditions? Do you have misgivings about your position? Why or why not?

Helping the Dying and Bereaved

Susan Gardner is a social worker at The Connecticut Hospice, where she has worked for eight years. Before that she worked in medical social work, counseling patients with acute and chronic illnesses.

Michele: What is Hospice?

Susan: Hospice is a licensed acute care facility that provides highly skilled, not aggressive, intervention for advanced stages of life-threatening diseases. We provide home care and short-term care—two weeks, on average, although some patients are here three or four months. We have two groups of patients: those who have pain and symptoms and come for pain management and those who are at the end of the disease and come to die. The key is a need for highly specialized acute care.

Michele: When do patients change from home care to residential care?

Susan: When pain and symptoms get out of control. A patient may be afraid of getting addicted to strong medicine. Or the family may want a patient to stay alert. Or the patient may no longer be able to swallow pills and be scared of injections. Some patients can't let go because of the family's need to have them live.

Others don't know how to read their own bodies. They can't describe what's happening verbally. Nurses and doctors can see changes and read body language. Sometimes home care patients come in for awhile. There was a home care patient who was in twice. He lived alone and didn't eat right. He began to dwindle. When he came here, he felt better. He ate better and got into pain control. Then he went back home.

Michele: I didn't think you would accept a patient who lived alone.

Susan: We try to identify a primary care person. Ideally the primary care person is someone who lives with the patient—usually a spouse, son, or daughter—who can notice if a change occurs. But it doesn't need to be a family member. In this man's case, it was a neighbor. The primary care person has to be a back-up for everything. We have aides and nurses, but sometimes they can't get out.

Michele: Who are your patients?

Susan: About 70 percent are over sixty-five. About two-thirds have children. About half have spouses. Sometimes a grandchild is the primary care person, sometimes a sib-

ling. A patient with a big Italian family, four brothers and four sisters, was recently here. She was single and had two unmarried sisters. The three had lived together all their lives. The youngest was the caregiver. The other sister and the brothers were married. The married sister came every day. The brothers all came with their spouses. But the unmarried sisters were mutually dependent on each other, and the loss of one was devastating.

Michele: I know you encourage family to be here with the patient. How do you facilitate that?

Susan: Each unit has a family room. These include kitchen facilities so families can heat up or prepare the patient's favorite foods. We also have a dining room people can use. We have a couple of rooms with double beds for conjugal visits. Families often stay here when the patient is close to death. We set up cots next to the patient's bed. The rooms are big and have curtains for privacy.

We had a young woman in her early thirties. She had epileptic seizures since childhood and developed a brain tumor. Her parents lived in New York. They slept by her bed for

BEREAVEMENT

Dying affects not only the person who dies but those with whom the person has close relationships. **Bereavement** is the experience of loss of a loved one through death. Nearly everyone experiences bereavement at some time in their lives, most of us long before reaching late adulthood. College students asked to recall their first experience with death indicated it was the death of a grandparent (42 percent), a pet (28 percent), another relative (15 percent), or an unrelated person (15 percent) and occurred at an average age of eight years old (Dickinson, 1992). The death of a significant person creates more difficulty for children than for adults because children are cognitively immature and have less ability to manipulate their environment to find new sources of love and nurturance. Adolescents tend to live in the present and deny death. This denial of death often leads them to act out their grief in acts against society rather than mourning openly. As we saw in Chapter 15, the death of a sibling, spouse, or partner in middle adulthood is not uncommon, and the death of a parent is normative. During late adulthood, however, deaths of loved ones become more frequent. Bereavement has two important components: grief and

2½ months. It worked very well. For awhile I feared they weren't dealing with her death, but they really needed to be with her. At the end, they were ready to give her up.

Michele: What do you do here as a social worker?

Susan: There are seven social workers. We start with home care and follow the family through. Each of us generally has fifteen to twenty families at different stages. We spend about two-thirds of our time with the family and a third with the patient. Bereavement is a monumental event in people's lives. Some do well and go on to have healthy lives; others suffer for long periods of time, especially older people. That's why Hospice got started. Bereavement has a big effect on emotional and physical wellness.

Michele: What factors make anticipatory grief more difficult?

Susan: Communication problems. It might be a close family, but if the members aren't honest and use euphemisms and denial, then it's difficult. Unclear communication tends to create conflict. People with a lot of unfinished business have a tough time. They are usually younger. Previous losses in life, such as the death of

a parent when a person was very young, can cause problems now with one's own or spouse's death. Also, those who are unsure about seeking treatment have difficulty. For example, if the diagnosis is recent and the patient and family haven't accepted it, they may be actively seeking more treatment while the doctor is telling them there is no more treatment.

Michele: What is your commitment to the bereaved after the death?

Susan: They are followed by the bereavement department for thirteen months after the death. An assessment is made on every patient to identify the people at high risk. Normal follow-up includes support groups, letters four times a year, and an annual healing/grief day early in November. There are talks about how to cope, physical and emotional health, what to do if you are worried about yourself, and how to handle the holidays. Also, people make friends and follow up with each other. People at greater risk receive counseling by trained volunteers, counseling by social workers, and referrals for professional counseling.

Michele: How expensive is Hospice care?

Susan: Anybody can come regardless of ability to pay or insurance. We have had people without a penny. We get funds from Medicare, private insurance, and firm donations. We even have a small facility for people who don't have a home. Often those are AIDS patients.

Michele: You obviously like your work. Why?

Susan: I like being a little bit helpful at a difficult time. Any social worker wants to be helpful—that's why we become social workers. Patients are very courageous. I find it very rewarding to work with families and help them grow to survive death and deal with grief. Also, there is a big spiritual component to Hospice care. The building has a nondenominational chapel at its center. Most people here are spiritual, not necessarily religious, and I like that. The older people feel they've had a good or meaningful life and are more ready to die.

What Do You Think?

1. In what ways is Hospice care consistent with the concept of the good death?

2. How does Hospice address the special problems of bereavement presented in the chapter?

mourning. **Grief** is the emotional response to one's loss. **Mourning** refers to the actions and manner of expressing grief, which reflect social and cultural prescriptions.

Grief

Grief results when people lose certain primary relationships, but not when they lose others. *Primary relationships* are close, face-to-face, emotionally important, and special to the particular relational partner. Robert Weiss (1993) distinguishes what he calls *relationships of attachment* from *relationships of community*. Relationships of attachment include spouses or partners, parents, and children. Grief, often in the form of severe and persisting distress, follows the death of any single relationship of attachment. Relationships of community include friends, work colleagues, and other family relationships. The death of one relationship of community, such as an adult sibling living in a different household, is followed by distress and sadness but not persisting grief. Only the loss of an entire group or network of relationships of community produces grief (Weiss, 1993). Bertha, for example, expressed deep sadness after the death of each of her seven adult siblings, but her grief after the last

Anticipatory grief during the caregiving period is common in cases of Alzheimer's disease, especially when the patient no longer recognizes the caregiving loved one.

died was immense. When the last sister died, she was likely grieving for them all. Loss of relationships of attachment trigger grief because we count on these relationships for security, as we discussed in Chapter 5. In relationships of attachment, another, similar relationship, such as a new spouse or another child, cannot substitute for the person who is lost, in contrast to relationships of community, which allow a new friend or colleague at work to be substituted.

Grief is a natural process that occurs after the loss of a loved one. Yet grief is a highly individualized process. "There are many and varied ways people grieve, . . . even one individual's grief varies from moment to moment" (M. S. Stroebe et al., 1993). All losses are not equivalent. The loss of a child, for example, will be experienced differently at different stages of the family life cycle (DeVries et al., 1994). As Table 18.4 shows, the quality of the parent-child relationship changes as the child grows, and thus parents feel different types of loss. The loss of an infant is felt more strongly by the mother than the father, perhaps because the connection for the mother begins during pregnancy. Brian DeVries and associates (1994) found that while child's age did not affect how much grief mothers experienced, fathers showed increasing intensity of grief with increasing age of the child at death. While the loss of an adult child typically causes the most pain because of the degree of relationship and interconnection, the parent who loses an adult child receives little social recognition; the child's spouse and children are the recipients of the condolences and comfort. As we see in the accompanying Multicultural View box on page 690, people grieve in different ways. Although the grief process has three recognizable phases—(1) an initial period of shock, disbelief, and denial; (2) an intermediate intense mourning period of acute physical and emotional discomfort and social withdrawal; and (3) a culminating period of restitution (Shuchter & Zisook, 1993)—these phases at least partially overlap and do not reflect a unified experience.

TABLE 18.4 *The Perception of Loss for Bereaved Parents at Different Family Stages*
As the child grows, the quality of the parent-child relationship changes, and thus parents feel different types of loss if the child dies.

	Infant	Young Child	Adult
Time	Dissynchrony (infant is antithesis of death) Loss of potential	Futility (child on verge of productivity) Loss as deprivation	Dissynchrony (old die before the young) Loss of long lasting relationship (survival guilt)
Nature/quality	Loss as incompetence, failure, violation (guilt)	Loss as incompetence exacerbated by ambivalence (future expressions)	Loss of social heirs and continuity
Role deceased played	Loss of defining family feature (basis of parent role and adult identity)	Loss of family system/organization	Loss as inability to procreate Loss of control and meaning Loss of beneficiary
Characteristics of the death	Loss as failure to protect (guilt) (congenital birth defects, SIDS)	Loss as failure to protect (guilt and stigma) (accidents, homicide, suicide)	Loss exacerbated by reduced involvement (disease: cancer, AIDS)
Social support system	Loss of young infant discounted or minimized (not yet a relationship)	Loss of social world (social withdrawal)	Loss discounted or minimized (forgotten grievers) Loss of confidant Loss as threatened health and independence

Source: DeVries et al. (1994).

In an attempt to understand people's conceptualizations of the normal bereavement reaction, Paul Burnett and his colleagues (1994) had seventy-seven workers in the field of bereavement fill out a scale designed to measure perceptions of bereavement phenomena. The scale was filled out twice, once for the first six weeks of acute bereavement and once for the longer bereavement extending beyond the first anniversary of loss. Although crying and distressing thoughts concerning the loss were perceived as common to acute bereavement and nostalgia was perceived as typical of longer-term bereavement, most common phenomena were seen as applying to both phases. These included sadness, yearning or pining for the lost person, a need to talk about the lost person, intrusive thoughts about the lost person, preoccupation with images/thoughts of the lost person, and distress at reminders of the lost person.

In many situations, there is a warning that a loved one is in the process of dying, such as when a terminal illness is diagnosed. Caregivers of dementia victims, for example, often experience a prolonged period during which they see their relative steadily lose dignity and quality of life as death approaches. In a study of caregivers of family members with Alzheimer's disease, Patricia Jones and Ida Martinson (1992) found that intense sadness and grief during the caregiving period were common, especially when the family member no longer recognized the caregiver. The grief one feels before the death occurs is referred to as **anticipatory grief**. Jennifer Klapper, Sidney Moss, Miriam Moss, and Robert Rubinstein (1994) found that 70 percent of their sample of adult married daughters who had lost their elderly mothers in the prior three to six months reported they had actually grieved for their mothers before the deaths. Anticipatory grief was more likely if the elderly parent had been ill for a long time and was not cognitively intact. Providing care to a family member during a prolonged and debilitating illness can result in grief before the death and relief after the death. Jones and Martinson (1992) found that clear relief was more characteristic of the bereavement experiences of caregivers who felt comfortable with decisions made and care given during the illness, whereas relief mixed with guilt was more characteristic of caregivers who had ambivalent feelings about the care given and the feelings expressed. If, for example, they had expressed anger and frustration during the caregiving, they might have felt guilt later.

While anticipatory grieving sometimes begins the grief process, grief is a powerful emotion that is stimulated by the actual death. Funerals serve to support the

A Multicultural View

Men and Grief

Grief is a natural and universal reaction to loss, but in the United States males and females express it differently. Although ethnicity and social class contribute to norms regarding the expression of grief, in our society gender has a large impact as well (Lister, 1991). In their study of 434 adult African Americans, Japanese Americans, Mexican Americans, and white Americans, Richard Kalish and David Reynolds (1981) found that men more often than women reported that they "never" thought of their own deaths, that would fight rather than accept their own deaths, they would try very hard to control their grief-related emotions in public, and grief should last three months or less. Men, especially Japanese American men, had attended more funerals than women in the prior year. Mexican American men were more accepting of crying than were other men.

Men fare less well than women when their spouses die. In a study of 350 widowed adults, Stephen Shuchter and Sidney Zisook (1993) found that compared to women, men showed less acceptance of the deaths of their spouses, became involved in romantic relationships sooner, expressed themselves less, and drank more. Women felt a greater degree of helplessness and tended more to experience their dead spouses in a protective role. A greater proportion of women had an overall "good" or "excellent" adjustment to widowhood. While

widows are at a somewhat higher risk for mortality than married women, widowers have an excessive mortality rate compared to married men and a rate typically higher than that of widows (M. S. Stroebe & Stroebe, 1993). In a study of older newly widowed men and women, Delores Gallagher-Thompson and her colleagues (1993) found that bereaved males faced a substantially higher risk of death, particularly within the first year of bereavement. Widowers also suffer greater health impairment compared to married men than widows compared to married women (W. Stroebe & Stroebe, 1993).

Why do men adjust so relatively poorly after losing their spouses? Two explanations have been advanced. First, gender differences in adjustment, health, and mortality after widowhood have been attributed to the greater availability of social support to women than to men. Men are more likely to depend on their spouses for emotional support, nurturance, and connections to other social relationships with family and friends so that the loss of a partner results in a decrease of social supports for widowers but not for widows. Men have a difficult time assuming the kinkeeping and other social roles their wives have handled. Camille Wortman and her colleagues (1993) found that widowhood was associated with significantly more strained relationships, particularly with children, for men but not for women. Loneli-

reality and finality of death, an important step in the resolution of grief (Leming & Dickinson, 1994). Funerals also provide social support and human interaction for mourners, which facilitates sharing and diminishing of grief.

Funeral and Ritual Practices

Funerals are ritual practices associated with death. Death constitutes a major rite of passage in the human experience for the deceased and for the mourners, one with which all societies have to cope. While anthropology suggests that funeral rituals were born of fear and designed to appease the dead, modern rituals focus on the expression of both grief and hope (Irion, 1990/1991). Anthropologists and sociologists have found that funeral rituals have three functions (Corr et al., 1994). First, they organize for the appropriate disposal of the body. In contemporary American society, the choices for disposal of the body are burial, cremation, and donating the body for science (which requires prior arrangements).

Second, funerals contribute to the realization of the implications of the death. During a wake or a funeral survivors can view, touch, or kiss the dead body and make the death more real. When each of her parents died, looking at and touching their dead bodies felt necessary to author Michele Hoffnung, because it was so hard to comprehend their not being alive. The mental image of each parent in the coffin remains an important memory for her. In contrast, Ben remembers how difficult it was for him at age fourteen when, after his brother's death, the corpse was removed and cremated without an opportunity to see and say goodbye to it. After spending more than a week at the hospital bedside, Ben missed having a sense of closure. Funeral rit-

ness and lack of social support are major problems in adaptation to loss (Lopata, 1993). Widowed men who were active in church or synagogue were less depressed than those without this social connection (Siegel & Kuykendall, 1990).

Second, although men experience loss and grief, in American society their expression of grief is not always apparent. Bereaved individuals who are communicative with others about their thoughts and feelings are more likely to have a positive adjustment (Lund et al., 1993). When controlled and not dealt with, a man's grief may lead to dysfunctional behaviors and self-destructive activities. Men are likely to report fewer symptoms and less affective distress than are women when their spouses die. Perhaps because of this, though widows have higher depression scores one year after the death of their spouses, widowers have higher depression scores two to four years later (Sanders, 1993). Women often respond more dramatically than men to the death of a child as well (Rubin, 1993).

Although grief is expected of men following the death of a spouse or child, this is mediated by the cultural message that men should be stoic and controlled. Male socialization includes a sanction against the expression of feelings as well as an ideal of independent action (Lister, 1991). Taken together, these proscriptions on male be-

havior prepare men poorly for expressing grief. As a result, men tend to be instrumental, to "do something" after a death, rather than allow themselves to feel. Men tend to return to their usual activities sooner than women. Women are more likely to turn their feelings into social actions that do not deny the feelings, such as Mothers Against Drunk Driving and the movement to develop resources for AIDS babies and children. Men are also less likely to seek assistance, whereas women more often will turn to relatives, friends, or professionals for help with their grief. Men are much less interactional about their feelings and more likely to deny them or drown them in drink or drugs.

While individual men do express their grief and it is possible to imagine a culture in which men would be encouraged to do so, we have not found such a culture to describe. Perhaps some cultures exist and have not been studied, but the literature overwhelmingly indicates that men are encouraged to act and discouraged to express feelings. In anthropological studies of death rituals in diverse societies, "men say it is the women who feel the death most and it is they who do most of the crying and wailing" (Woodburn, 1982, p. 189), and "it is women who take on mourning for death" (Bloch, 1982, p. 215).

uals serve to free people "to act out feelings of meanings that might not be expressible otherwise" (Irion, 1990/1991, p. 161). Kathryn remembers her Irish Catholic grandfather at the wake of his dead wife pouring whiskey into her mouth to "wake her up."

Third, funerals assist in social reintegration and meaningful ongoing life. Funerals and memorial services pull people together and show mourners they are not alone. People who do not regularly see one another share their memories and feelings and sometimes become closer as a result. Funerals are significant ritual occasions, particularly for the elderly, who are more likely to attend them (Marshall & Levy, 1990).

These ritual functions of funerals take different forms in different cultures. Cuaxomulco is a typical village of the Mexican highlands. When Don Indalecio, a political leader of the village, died in middle age of a burst appendix, his family and community responded with the patterned cultural response of that region (Grunloh, 1978). The early phase of the funeral focused the initial shock and anxiety of the loss of an important community member on the necessary tasks of food preparation. Being able to provide food demonstrates the family's vitality and the culture's ability to survive. Once the casket with Don Indalecio's body arrived, the large gathering of family and community members began wailing, shrieking, praying, and remembering. It was not until the third day of the funeral that a brass band from another village arrived, breakfast was served, and the casket was finally taken to the graveyard. The funeral procession stopped along the way at the schoolyard, where the teacher came out to honor Don Indalecio; the municipal hall, where the president honored him; and the church for a mass. After the burial, the rosary was said every night for eight days and then a cross was erected at the grave. The funeral provided an opportunity for people to come to terms with the death by gathering together and remembering, as well as for social reintegration as Don Indalecio's

Funerals are significant ritual occasions that take different form in different cultures and in different circumstances in the same culture. Though a policeman's funeral in the United States and a Buddhist cremation in South Korea look very different, they serve many of the same functions.

brothers reaffirmed the widow's ties to her husband's clan and assumed his community roles and responsibilities.

Funeral rituals also take different forms in different circumstances in the same culture. Funerals of public figures—especially those killed in the line of duty, such as Israeli Prime Minister Yitzhak Rabin or President John F. Kennedy—include ceremonies that help to ensure the continuity of leadership. Assassinations, like other off-time and sudden deaths, cause shock and grief but also fear. The public viewing of the casket, the gathering of public officials from many countries, the eulogies that exalt the significance of the life of the deceased, and the familiarity of the rituals all reassure the family and community that the culture will continue.

American funerals have been criticized because they have failed to serve these necessary functions and because they have become elaborate due to commercial pressure. The use of embalming, cosmetics, and expensive linings for caskets seem to promote an image of life rather than death (Mitford, 1963). Closed caskets seem to deny death. In an effort not to upset the mourners, the casket often is not lowered or the grave refilled until after survivors have left the cemetery. This removes the mourners from the reality of the death. In addition, at a time when they are least able to resist because of their grief, the mourners are sometimes sold expensive products and services of dubious value, such as airtight caskets or big limousines. Some funeral directors may take advantage of guilt the bereaved feel for what they did not do while the deceased was living to sell expensive funeral amenities.

In response to these criticisms, there has been a countermovement toward simpler funerals and cremation rather than burial (Marshall & Levy, 1990). Mortuary science colleges have added psychology, sociology, and ethics to their course requirements to better prepare their graduates to be sensitive practitioners (Gose, 1995). Paul Irion (1990/1991) reports developments within most religious denominations of new rituals that take into account growing psychological knowledge of the grieving process and are more sensitive to the fact that those attending a funeral are likely to include members of several faiths and ethnic communities. Even when wakes, funerals, and memorial services do function to pull survivors together and help them face the reality of the death, they do not go far enough in accomplishing these tasks. Mourning is a much longer process.

Mourning

Mourning is the social experience of grief. In all societies there are some things a person cannot do (restrictions) and some that must be done (obligations), although these things vary from one culture to the next. In a study of seventy-eight societies in Europe, America, Japan, Africa, and the Pacific Islands, Paul Rosenblatt, Patricia Walsh, and Douglas Jackson (1976) found striking similarities in grieving as well as wide differences in defining what is an appropriate expression of grief. Table 18.5 shows some ethnic differences in behaviors considered appropriate after the death of a spouse. Because the United States is culturally diverse, what is an "ethnically normal" expression of grief for one individual or family may be deviant for another. In families consisting of people from different cultures or in families that are assimilating and between cultures, the differences may cause discomfort and misunderstanding. For instance, in Japan and China white is the color of mourning, so imagine an immigrant's feelings when other mourners show up in black at their loved one's funeral.

American society, as represented by white, Anglo-Saxon, Protestant behavior, does not approve of mourning except within the rigid confines of the funeral. Grief is something to be mastered, and mourners are expected to return to their normal routines quickly and not burden others with public displays of grief (Rosenblatt, 1993). Also, there are few prescriptions for how to interact with one who is mourning. In a study that asked people how they would respond if they met someone who had lost a loved one through death since their last meeting, only 25 percent of the respondents said they would mention the death (Stephenson, 1985). Most reported they would not know what to say. The lack of rituals of mourning and rituals of interacting with mourners pushes people to deny their need to mourn. The status of the lost loved one is considered to warrant different levels of grief, which reflects a "widespread cultural sense of hierarchy in the permitted severity of grief: loss of a child (at any age) at the nadir, followed by loss of spouse, and finally the on-time loss of an elderly parent" (Klapper et al., 1994, p. 34). This too can push one toward denial of a need to mourn. Despite the grief an adult daughter may feel due to the death of her elderly mother, she may believe she must control the expression of that grief because her mother was old and the death was on time. Off-time losses are expected to produce more expression of grief. The death of a child, a teenager, or a young adult is unexpected and tragic, whereas the death of an older person is expected and sad.

This denial of one's need to mourn and lack of customary mourning behavior contrasts with the customs of Orthodox Jews in this country. Jewish law and custom give mourners a structure that encourages feeling their loss and thus healing. After

TABLE 18.5 *Behaviors Considered Appropriate After the Death of a Spouse*
In the culturally diverse United States, it is important to understand ethnic differences in what are considered appropriate behaviors after the death of a loved one, in this case a spouse.

	African Americans	Japanese Americans	Mexican Americans	White Americans
To remarry				
Unimportant to wait	34%	14%	22%	26%
1 week–6 months	15	3	1	23
1 year	25	30	38	34
2 years or more	11	26	20	11
Other (including never/depends)	16	28	19	7
To stop wearing black				
Unimportant to wait	62	42	52	53
1 week–1 month	24	26	11	31
6 months	11	21	35	6
1 year or more	4	11	3	11
To return to place of employment				
Unimportant to wait	39	22	27	47
1 day–1 week	39	28	37	35
1 month or more	17	35	27	9
Other/depends	6	16	9	10
To start going out with other men/women				
Unimportant to wait	30	17	17	25
1 week–1 month	14	8	4	9
6 months–1 year	24	22	22	29
2 years or more	11	34	40	21
Other/depends	21	19	18	17

Source: Adapted from Kalish & Reynolds (1981).

the funeral, immediate mourners (parents, spouse, children) sit *shiva* for seven days, which is the intense period of formal mourning (Diamant & Cooper, 1991). Together in one home, they grieve, accept visitors, talk of their feelings, and share memories of the deceased. Shiva creates an emotionally protective setting for the mourners in which they are not expected to reciprocate what is done for them (Slochower, 1993). Friends and neighbors bring food, mirrors are covered to discourage vanity, and the mourners wear strips of black fabric as a visible symbol of being inwardly torn by grief, and sit on stools. Prayers continue to get said twice a day until, after eleven to twelve months, the family and friends return to the cemetery and the stone is placed on the grave. Only after the *unveiling* of the stone does the mourning period end. Remembering still continues. A special twenty-four-hour memorial candle is lit every year on the eve of the day of the death as an act of remembrance.

Hispanic Americans also believe it takes time to express one's feelings of grief. Funerals and wakes in the Los Angeles Mexican American community mark the coming together of large numbers of supportive people, family and friends, and the outpouring of emotions with little restraint (Kalish & Reynolds, 1981). Using an inventory of grief, Jo-Anne Grabowski and Thomas Frantz (1993) found significantly greater intensity of grief among Latinos than among Anglos. Latinos who were grieving a sudden death had a significantly greater grief intensity than did Latinos grieving an expected death and Anglos grieving either kind of death. Mexican Americans consider the grieving process to involve the gathering together of a large support group of friends, family, and community members (Salcido, 1990). Among Puerto Ricans in New York City, the wake may continue for several days (Eisenbruch, 1984). This is also true of Dominicans. Puerto Ricans prefer lengthy formal mourning periods and strongly prohibit saying anything ill of the person who has died (Campos, 1990). Cultural traditions that facilitate the expression of grief can help survivors mourn and thus heal.

Many Asian Americans believe death allows for a continued relationship between the deceased and the survivors. In keeping with this belief, funerals and memorial services are considered very important events because showing respect for ancestors ensures that the ancestors will contribute to the well-being of the survivors (Kalish & Reynolds, 1981). Japanese Americans and Chinese Americans tend to hold traditional funerals at which people have formal roles, bring gifts, and take extensive photographs. Because of the ongoing interaction between the living and the deceased, Asian Americans make frequent visits to grave sites, have very conservative mourning traditions, and are unlikely to remarry or even date after becoming widowed (Kalish & Reynolds, 1981).

Support Groups

Given that people have complex and varied feelings of grief and that cultural pressures compel one to get on with life, bereavement programs have developed to encourage survivors to feel normal about their grief reactions and to offer empathy (Schneidman, 1992). Although society rushes on, grief takes time and cannot be rushed. Support groups offer the opportunity for bereaved people to share their concerns and feelings with others going through similar experiences. Bereavement support groups take several forms. Some are self-help groups composed entirely of bereaved peers. Widow-to-Widow, a national program that provides mutual aid and bereavement support, has served as a model for many mutual help groups. Self-help groups are a low-cost, community-based alternative that can meet the social and psychological needs of a large segment of the bereaved population (Lieberman, 1993). Other support groups are organized by hospice and other palliative care programs and led by trained

The AIDS quilt enables people to view the panels and remember those who have died. It also provides the opportunity for people to work together to make a panel as a remembrance for a loved one.

> ### Questions for Assessment of the Vulnerability of the Bereaved
>
> Can you tell me about him/her?
>
> Can you tell me about the death, how he/she died?
>
> Can you tell me about how others have responded to you since—what they said and did, what it meant to you?
>
> Can you tell me about the other things that happened to you, or are happening to you, that are making things harder as well?
>
> Can you tell me about yourself as a person and your life before this happened—how has it been, and what sorts of things have you had to face in the past?
>
> Can you tell me about the family—how this has affected the family as a whole, and what you feel it has meant for each person?

FIGURE 18.3
Questions for Assessment of the Vulnerability of the Bereaved
Therapists use these questions to assess the vulnerability of a person seeking bereavement counseling. Source: Adapted from Raphael et al. (1993).

volunteers who assist bereaved family members. Still other groups are led by trained professional social workers or bereavement counselors. In addition to support groups, individual bereavement counseling has been shown to be effective, both as a preventative measure for people who are high risk and as a therapeutic intervention (Raphael et al., 1993). Figure 18.3 shows key questions that are used for therapeutic assessment of the vulnerability of a person seeking bereavement counseling.

Recovery

Grief involves a process of transition, a change in both the self and the family. "Severe grief, no matter how fully individuals emerge from it, should be expected to produce character change" (Weiss, 1993, p. 277). Survivors take on new roles and see themselves from a new perspective. As we discussed in Chapter 15, as a result of parental death middle-aged adult children are likely to be more conscious of their own mortality, feel more responsible for themselves, and take on new kinkeeping responsibilities in the family. Likewise, as we discussed in Chapter 17, a bereaved spouse is likely to take on new roles and interact with the world in new ways. Grief therefore leads not simply to recovery but to change and transformation (Klapper et al., 1994). Notice, for instance, how Susan Gardner talks about helping the bereaved "to grow to survive death" in the Working With interview on page 686.

What, then, is recovery if it is not a return to one's former self? Recovery is best understood as a return to previous levels of functioning. Indicators of recovery are the ability to find energy in everyday life, freedom from psychological pain and distress, the ability to feel pleasure when desirable events occur, hopefulness regarding

Grief can help survivors mourn and thus heal. Recovery, a return to previous levels of functioning, typically entails taking on new roles and interacting with the world in new ways. Here a widow mows her lawn.

the future, and the ability to function with reasonable adequacy as spouse, parent, and member of the community (Weiss, 1993). Not everyone goes through the same grieving process to reach recovery. In a series of studies of emotional reactions to significant loss, Camille Wortman, Roxane Silver, and Ronald Kessler (1993) found great variability in response. Intense distress or depression was not inevitable following a major loss, and the failure to experience such distress did not predict poor adaptation to loss. Among their sample of widows, for example, those with the best marriages were particularly distressed by the loss of a spouse, whereas those in unhappy marriages showed less depression after the loss. The data suggest that the meaning of the loss to the survivor and the survivor's coping resources have an impact on the grieving and recovery process. As with any other life experience, the social and cultural contexts affect the recovery process.

What Do You Think?

Consider the last wake, funeral, or memorial service you attended. In what ways did it meet the ritual functions that can help the mourners? (If you have not been to any, interview someone who has.)

SUMMARY OF MAJOR IDEAS

Attitudes toward Death

1. Social and technological changes in the twentieth century have led to a separation of death from everyday life and to an attitude that denies death.

2. Recently the death awareness movement has promoted the idea of the good death and raised consciousness about issues of dying and bereavement that have influenced care of the dying and death education.

Facing One's Own Death

3. Aging is associated with increasing acceptance of death and heightened concern about the process of dying. Unfinished business can interfere with normative death acceptance among the elderly.

4. Suicide rates are higher in later life, especially among white males and others who have reduced opportunity or inclination to communicate.

5. Elisabeth Kubler-Ross has outlined five stages of reactions to dying. While these stages have been widely accepted by clinicians who work with dying patients, they have been challenged by theory and research.

6. The good death is one that enables the dying individual to experience growth in this final stage of life. It emphasizes honesty, homelike settings, and control of pain.

Caring for the Dying

7. Nursing homes, hospices, and home care provide terminal care alternatives to hospital death.

8. Home death provides familiarity and greater opportunities for sustaining relationships and allows for mutual sharing of concerns and feelings. There are also many difficult aspects to that choice for which many families are unprepared.

9. Controversy surrounds the issue of whether individuals suffering from a terminal disease should be allowed assistance in ending their lives.

Bereavement

10. Grief is a highly variable experience. Although certain grief reactions are considered common, differences abound based on the nature of the relationship, the on-time or off-time nature of the loss, whether there is time to anticipate the loss, and cultural expectations.

11. Funerals and other ritual practices serve important functions for mourners, but the mourning process takes longer than the duration of these rituals.

12. Although the white, Anglo-Saxon, Protestant expectation is that grief will be mastered and the person will return to normal routines quickly, different ethnic cultural traditions within the United States express mourning differently.

13. Bereavement support groups bring people going through similar experiences together to provide empathy and encourage survivors to feel normal about their grief reactions.

14. Recovery entails growth and change as a survivor returns to previous levels of functioning while adjusting to a new set of life circumstances.

KEY TERMS

degenerative diseases (669)
communicable
   diseases (669)
death awareness
   movement (672)
the good death (680)
grief work (681)
hospice (682)

palliative care (683)
euthanasia, passive (685)
euthanasia, active (685)
bereavement (686)
grief 687)
mourning (687)
anticipatory grief (689)

Glossary

accommodation According to Piaget, the process of modifying existing ideas or action-skills to fit new experiences.

achievement motivation Behavior that enhances competence or enhances judgments of competence.

achievement test A test designed to evaluate a person's current state of knowledge.

achieving stage Schaie's first stage of adult thinking during which young adults direct their intelligence toward specific goals rather than following every inclination as might adolescents who have not yet formulated clear personal choices.

active euthanasia Taking steps to end life, such as giving a fatal dose of painkilling medication, when unendurable illness makes living intolerable.

activity competence The skills and knowledge necessary to take advantage of opportunities for leisure activities. Because it is generally established in earlier adult years, older adults who are better educated are more prepared to feel competent engaging in a variety of activities.

activity theory The theory of aging that assumes older people who maintain social, physical, and intellectual activity levels similar to those during their middle years age more successfully than those who are less active.

acute brain syndromes Pathological states of the brain caused by metabolic malfunctions, such as diabetes, liver failure, or anemia, and those due to medication effects, benign brain tumor, vitamin deficiencies, or alcoholism. The damage is treatable and reversible.

acute illness A disease with a definite time of onset and lasting for a fixed and relatively short period of time.

adaptive mechanisms George Vaillant's term for the coping styles that people use to adapt to life events and that determine their levels of mental health. Vaillant categorized four types: mature mechanisms, immature mechanisms, psychotic mechanisms, and neurotic mechanisms.

adolescence The stage of development between childhood and adulthood, around ages ten to twenty-two.

adolescent egocentrism The tendency of adolescents to perceive the world (and themselves) from their own perspective.

adoption study A research method for studying the relative contributions of heredity and environment in which genetically related children reared apart are compared with genetically unrelated children reared together.

advance directive A legal document specifying what medical care can be given in the event the person becomes unable to make or communicate his or her decisions.

ageism Stereotyping of and discrimination against people because they are old.

aggression A bold, assertive action that is intended to hurt another person or to procure an object.

allele One of several alternative forms of a gene.

Alzheimer's disease A chronic brain syndrome caused by degeneration of the brain cells in those portions of the cerebral cortex that are associated with memory, learning, and judgment. Patients go through a series of stages beginning with loss of memory and ending with coma and death.

American Sign Language (ASL) A system of gestures used in place of oral language by individuals with hearing impairments.

amniotic sac A tough, spongy bag filled with salty fluid that surrounds the embryo, protects it from sudden jolts, and helps to maintain a fairly stable temperature.

androgyny A tendency to integrate both masculine and feminine behaviors into the personality.

anorexia nervosa A physical and psychological disturbance that causes a person to refuse to eat sufficient food and to develop an increasingly unrealistic view of his or her body; most individuals with anorexia are teenage girls.

anticipatory grief The intense sadness and grief that one feels when a loved one is in the process of dying, such as when a terminal illness is diagnosed.

anxious-avoidant attachment An insecure bond between infant and caregiver in which the child rarely cries when separated from the caregiver and tends to avoid or ignore the caregiver when reunited.

anxious-resistant attachment An insecure bond between infant and caregiver in which the child shows signs of anxiety preceding separation, is intensely upset by separation, and seeks close contact when reunited while at the same time resisting the caregiver's efforts to comfort.

Apgar Scale A system of rating newborns' health immediately following birth based on heart rate, strength of breathing, muscle tone, color, and reflex irritability.

aptitude test A measurement of ability that estimates future performance in some realm of behavior.

assimilation According to Piaget, a method by which a person responds to new experiences by using existing concepts to interpret new ideas and experiences.

assisted living Semi-independent living in which some degree of informal and formal help with daily living enables older adults to continue to live in the community.

attachment An intimate and enduring emotional relationship between two people, such as infant and caregiver, characterized by reciprocal affection and a periodic desire to maintain physical closeness.

attention deficit hyperactivity disorder (ADHD) See *hyperactivity*.

authoritarian parenting A style of childrearing characterized by a high degree of control and demands on children's maturity and a low degree of clarity of communication and nurturance.

authoritative parenting A style of childrearing characterized by a high degree of control, clarity of communication, maturity demands, and nurturance.

autonomy In Erikson's theory, an individual's ability to govern and regulate her or his own thoughts, feelings, and actions freely and responsibly while at the same time overcoming feelings of shame and doubt.

autonomy versus shame and doubt According to Erikson, the psychosocial crisis of children ages one to three involving the struggle to control their own thoughts, feelings, and actions; the second of Erikson's developmental stages.

balanced bilingual   A person who is equally fluent in two languages rather than more fluent in one language than in the other.

basic dualism   William Perry's term for a perspective toward intellectual and ethical problems from which students view truth in terms of right or wrong, good or bad, and we or they.

beanpole family structure   The contemporary family structure, which has more generations but fewer people in each generation because of increased longevity and a decreased birth rate.

behaviorism   A learning theory that focuses on changes in specific observable behaviors and their causes.

behavior modification   A body of techniques based on behaviorism for changing or eliminating specific behaviors.

bereavement   The process of getting over the loss of a significant relationship, usually through death.

biographical method   Daniel Levinson's method for reconstructing the life course by interviewing the person and using a variety of other sources, such as visiting the person's workplace and home.

Black English   A dialect or version of English spoken by many African Americans.

blended family   A family created from a combination of stepchildren, stepparents, and stepsiblings.

bulimia   A disorder in which a person, usually a teenage girl, eats huge amounts of food and then vomits it to avoid gaining weight.

burnout   Disillusionment and exhaustion on the job that may result from stress caused by multiple role commitments, discrimination based on race/ethnicity or gender, or other factors.

canalization   The tendency of many developmental processes to unfold in highly predictable ways under a wide range of conditions.

career consolidation   A stage George Vaillant identified as fitting between Erikson's stages of intimacy and generativity and occurring in one's thirties. The men Vaillant studied tended to work hard, devote themselves to career advancement, and sacrifice play.

caregiver-infant synchrony   Patterns of closely coordinated social and emotional interaction between caregiver and infant.

case study   A research study of a single individual or small group of individuals considered as a unit.

cellular theories   Theories of aging that focus on the processes that take place within and between the cells, leading to the breakdown of cells, tissue, and organs. Sometimes referred to as *wear and tear theories.*

central nervous system   The brain and nerve cells of the spinal cord.

cephalocaudal principle   The tendency for organs, reflexes, and skills to develop sooner at the top (or head) of the body and later in areas farther down the body.

chromosome   A threadlike, rod-shaped structure containing genetic information that is transmitted from parents to children; each human sperm or egg cell contains twenty-three chromosomes, and these determine a person's inherited characteristics.

chronic brain syndromes   Pathological states of the brain, including multiinfarct dementia, Alzheimer's disease, and senile dementia, caused by changes in the brain that are irreversible.

chronic illness   A disease lasting a long period of time (such as several months or more) and changing only very slowly.

circular reaction   Piaget's term for an action often repeated, apparently because it is self-reinforcing.

classical conditioning   According to Pavlov, learning in which a neutral stimulus gains the power to bring about a certain response by repeated association with another stimulus that already elicits the same response.

classification   Putting objects in groups or categories according to some set of standards or criteria.

climacteric   The gradual reduction in sex hormone production that is an aspect of primary aging during middle adulthood, leading to menopause in women and to reproductive system changes in men that decrease fertility.

clinical depression   A pattern of depressive symptoms that is severe enough to require treatment by mental health professionals. Symptoms include depressed or irritable mood, decreased interest in pleasurable activities, abnormal weight gain or loss, sleep problems, over- or underactivity, fatigue or loss of energy, excessive feelings of worthlessness and guilt, impaired concentration and decision making, and thoughts about, plans for, or attempts at suicide.

clique   A small, closely knit peer group of two or more members (average of six members) who are intimately involved in a number of shared purposes and activities and exclude those who are not.

cognition   All processes by which humans acquire knowledge; methods for thinking or gaining knowledge about the world.

cognitive development   The area of human development concerned with cognition; involves all psychological processes by which individuals learn and think about their environment.

cognitive mechanics   Basic memory processes, such as sensory information input, visual and motor memory, and the processes of discrimination, categorization, and coordination, that are likely to decline in late adulthood.

cognitive pragmatics   Intellectual problems in which culture-based knowledge and skills are primary, such as reading and writing skills, language comprehension, professional skills, and knowledge about strategies to manage the peaks and valleys of life, that may grow in late adulthood.

cohabitation   Unrelated adults living together in a sexual partnership.

communicable diseases   Diseases that spread from person to person and formerly killed large numbers of old and young people alike, such as influenza, cholera, scarlet fever, measles, and smallpox.

competence   According to Robert White, individuals' increased skill and capability in successfully exploring, mastering, and controlling the world around them.

conception   The moment at which the male's sperm cell penetrates the female's egg cell (ovum), forming a zygote.

concrete operations   Logical thinking about concrete or tangible objects and processes; especially characteristic of middle childhood.

congregate housing   Housing that provides elderly residents with some communal services, at least a central kitchen and dining room.

conservation   A belief that certain properties (such as quantity) remain constant despite changes in perceived features such as dimensions, position, and shape.

constructive play   A type of play that involves manipulation of physical objects to build or construct something.

contextual relativism William Perry's term for a perspective toward intellectual and ethical problems from which students begin to see that truth is relative and that the meaning of an event depends on its context and on the framework of the knower who is trying to understand the event.

control group In an experimental research study, the group of subjects who experience conditions similar or identical to the experimental group, but without experiencing the experimental treatment.

conventional relationship A couple relationship based on gender-stereotyped division of responsibilities; the man is the head of the household and sole economic provider, and the woman is the mother and homemaker.

correlation An association between two variables in which changes in one variable tend to occur with changes in the other. The association does not necessarily imply a causal link between the variables.

critical period Any period during which development is particularly susceptible to an event or influence, either negative or positive.

critical thinking Reflection or thinking about complex issues, usually to make decisions or take actions.

cross-sectional study A study that compares individuals of different ages at the same point in time.

crowd A large, loosely knit peer group of between fifteen and thirty members (average of twenty members) that generally consists of from two to four cliques.

crystallized intelligence The cognitive processes and primary abilities, such as vocabulary, general information, and word fluency, that are strongly shaped by formal education and increase or remain relatively stable with age.

death awareness movement A response to the increasing number of very old people in American society, the prolongation of the dying process, the anxieties of the nuclear age, the 1960s perspective that asserted the rights of the ignored and underprivileged (in this case the dying), and the AIDS epidemic. It has led to the analysis of cultural messages about death, increased sensitivity to the dying, and increased education about death.

degenerative diseases Diseases that cause the slow, prolonged, and painful deaths typical of late adulthood, such as cardiovascular disease and cancer.

dependent variable A factor that is measured in an experiment and that *depends on,* or is controlled by, one or more independent variables.

development Long-term changes in a person's growth, feelings, patterns of thinking, social relationships, and motor skills.

developmentally appropriate practice Methods and goals of teaching considered optimal for young children given current knowledge of child development.

discrimination In terms of the labor market, the valuation of personal characteristics of a worker that are not related to productivity, such as educational background, health, and marital status, or based on prejudice on the part of employers, coworkers, employees, or customers.

disengagement theory The theory of aging that views the reduction of elderly people's social involvement to be a natural and mutual process between the elderly and society.

displaced homemaker A woman who committed herself to the conventional roles of wife and mother, lost these roles due to separation, divorce, or widowhood, and was unprepared for employment and single parenthood.

domain A realm of psychological functioning.

dominant gene In any paired set of genes, the gene with greater influence in determining physical characteristics that are physically visible or manifest.

Down syndrome A congenital condition that causes mental retardation.

durable power of attorney for health care A legal document designating a person to make medical decisions on one's behalf other than the withdrawal of life support systems.

early articulator Jean Veevers' term for someone who knew from childhood that she did not want to have children.

ego According to Freud, the rational, realistic part of the personality; coordinates impulses from the id with demands imposed by the superego and by society.

egocentrism The inability of a person to distinguish between her or his own point of view and that of another person.

ego integrity versus despair According to Erikson, the final psychosocial crisis, reached during late adulthood and old age, in which one looks back on one's life with dignity, optimism, and wisdom while facing the despair resulting from the negative aspects of old age.

embryonic stage The stage in prenatal development that lasts from week 2 through week 8.

empathy A sensitive awareness of the thoughts and feelings of another person.

equal-partner relationship A couple relationship based on the principle of negotiating about shared concerns and responsibilities. Instead of a preset assignment of roles and responsibilities, everything (who works, who cooks, who pays the bills) is open for renegotiation except the principle that everything is negotiable.

estrogen A sex hormone, sometimes called the *female sex hormone* because its high concentration in girls stimulates the growth of the ovaries and vagina during puberty.

estrogen replacement therapy (ERT) The taking of replacement estrogen to alleviate menopausal symptoms; often recommended for women who have surgical menopause.

executive stage Schaie's stage of adult thinking that applies to some middle adults who have powerful positions that bring broader and more complex responsibilities and require a new type of cognition, applying postformal thinking about systems to practical problems, as they work to understand and meet the needs of competing groups in a large organization that affects many people beyond self and family.

experimental group In an experimental research study, the group of subjects who experience the experimental treatment while in other respects experiencing conditions similar or identical to the those of control group.

experimental study A study in which circumstances are arranged so that just one or two factors or influences vary at a time.

expertise Specialized experience in specific domains of knowledge that enables efficient and effective performance and is not hampered by age.

failure to thrive A condition in which an infant seems seriously delayed in physical growth and is noticeably apathetic in behavior.

family life cycle   A series of predictable stages that families experience based on the age of the children.

fetal alcohol syndrome (FAS)   A congenital condition exhibited by babies born to mothers who consumed too much alcohol during pregnancy. They do not arouse easily and tend to behave sluggishly in general; they also have distinctive facial characteristics.

fetal presentation   Refers to the body part of the fetus that is closest to the mother's cervix; may be head first (cephalic), feet and rump first (breech), or shoulders first (transverse).

fetal stage   The stage in prenatal development that lasts from the eighth week of pregnancy until birth.

fictive kin   Constructed relationships, such as foster child or godparent, that by merging voluntary and obligatory relations take on the significance of blood kin.

fifth stage of cognitive development   An adult stage of cognitive development that follows formal operations, the last of Piaget's four stages. Although different theorists use different terms, postformal thought is characterized by relative and nonabsolute thinking that accepts and synthesizes contradiction and helps adults deal with the ambiguities of real-life problems.

fine motor coordination   The ability to carry out smoothly small movements that involve precise timing but not strength.

fluid intelligence   The cognitive processes and primary abilities, such as information processing and reasoning, that depend more on neurological development and less on formal education and peak in late adolescence, followed by rapid decline.

formal curriculum   The traditional academic curriculum that helps students acquire the knowledge and skills thought to be necessary for successful participation in society.

formal operational thought   Thinking based on previously acquired concrete mental operations and involving hypothetical reasoning and attention to the structure or form of ideas.

functional play   A cognitive level of play that involves simple, repeated movements and a focus on one's own body.

games with rules   A cognitive level of play involving relatively formal activities with fixed rules.

gender   The thoughts, feelings, and behaviors associated with being male or female.

gender role stereotypes   The culturally "appropriate" patterns of gender-related behaviors expected by society. Also called sex roles.

gene   A molecular structure, carried on chromosomes, containing genetic information; the basic unit of heredity.

general adaptation syndrome   The pattern of physical response to stress identified by Hans Seyle, which has three stages: alarm, resistance, and exhaustion. Confrontation with a stressor sets the stress response in motion. The syndrome appears to be irreversible and accumulates to constitute the signs of aging.

generativity versus stagnation   The seventh of Erikson's psychosocial crises, reached in middle adulthood, in which one must balance the feeling that one's life is personally satisfying and socially meaningful with feelings of purposelessness.

genotype   The set of genetic traits inherited by an individual. See also *phenotype*.

germinal stage   The stage in prenatal development that occurs during the first two weeks of pregnancy; characterized by rapid cell division. Also called the *period of the ovum*.

grief   The emotional response to the loss of a relationship of attachment, such as a spouse, partner, parent, or child.

grief work   An initial phase of the bereavement process that entails anger, self-recrimination, depression, and taking care of unfinished business.

growth spurt   A rapid change in height and weight that occurs in puberty and is preceded and followed by years of comparatively little increase.

habituation   The tendency to attend to novel stimuli and ignore familiar ones.

health-compromising behaviors   Behaviors that lead to illness, pathological aging, and premature death, such as smoking, drug and alcohol abuse, and unsafe sex.

homophobia   Fear, dread, hostility, or prejudice directed toward gay and lesbian persons and the resulting mistreatment and discrimination.

hormone replacement therapy (HRT)   The taking of replacement estrogen in combination with progestin (artificial progesterone) to alleviate menopausal symptoms that is recommended for women who have not had a hysterectomy because ERT has been shown to increase the rate of endometrial cancer.

hospice   An interdisciplinary team and holistic approach to death by attending to the physical, emotional, spiritual, and aesthetic needs of patients and their families, primarily in their own homes but also at acute care facilities.

hostile aggression   Aggressive behavior in which harm is a primary intent.

hyperactivity   Excessive levels of activity and an inability to concentrate for normal periods of time. See *attention deficit hyperactivity disorder*.

hypertrophy   The overgrowth of tissue in the prostate gland that is one of the physical changes of the male climacteric and sometimes leads to pressure on the urethra, which interferes with urine flow.

hypokinesia   A disease of disuse that causes degeneration and functional loss of muscle and bone tissue and can be prevented by regular exercise.

hypothesis   A precise prediction based on a scientific theory; often capable of being tested in a scientific research study.

hysterectomy   The surgical removal of the uterus.

id   In Freud's theory, the part of an individual's personality that is present at birth, unconscious, impulsive, and unrealistic, and that attempts to satisfy a person's biological and emotional needs and desires by maximizing pleasure and avoiding pain.

identity diffusion   A failure to achieve a relatively coherent, integrated, and stable identity.

identity status   Marcia's four categories of identity development: identity achievement, identity diffusion, moratorium, and foreclosure.

identity versus role confusion   The fifth of Erikson's psychosocial crises, in which one must integrate one's many childhood skills and beliefs and gain recognition for them from society.

imaginary audience   A characteristic of young adolescents in which they act as though they are performing for an audience and believe that others are as concerned with their appearance and behavior as they themselves are.

independent variable   A factor that an experimenter manipulates (varies) to determine its influence on the population being studied.

individuation   The process by which an adolescent develops a unique and separate personal identity. Consists of four subphases: differentiation, practice and experimentation, rapprochement, and consolidation.

industry versus inferiority   Erikson's fourth crisis, during which children concern themselves with their capacity to do good work and thereby develop confident, positive self-concepts or else face feelings of inferiority.

infant-directed speech   The style or register of speech used by adults and older children when talking with a one- or two-year-old infant.

infant mortality rate   The frequency with which infants die compared to the frequency with which they live.

infertility   A couple's inability to conceive a pregnancy after one year of sexual relations without contraception.

informal curriculum   The implicit norms, expectations, and rewards for certain ways of thinking and acting that are conveyed by a school's social and authority relationships; teaches students the social roles and behaviors society expects.

informed consent   An agreement to participate in a research study based on understanding the nature of the research, protection of human rights, and freedom to decline to participate at any time.

initiative versus guilt   Erikson's third crisis, during which a child's increasing ability to initiate verbal and physical activity and expanding imaginative powers lead to fantasies of large and sometimes frightening proportions.

instrumental aggression   Assertive behavior with a goal in mind; the action ends when the goal is achieved and sometimes may unintentionally hurt others.

integrity versus despair   The eighth and final crisis of development in Erikson's theory, in which older adults assess the value of their life's work and fight the tendency to lose hope about life in general.

intelligence   A general ability to learn from experience; also refers to ability to reason abstractly.

interview   A face-to-face, directed conversation used in a research study to gather in-depth information.

intimacy versus isolation   The sixth of Erikson's psychosocial crises, in which young adults must be able to develop intimate relationships with others while dealing with the fear of loss of identity that such intimacy entails.

junior-partner relationship   A couple relationship that has elements of both equal partnership and conventional relationships. The junior partner, typically the wife, brings in some of the income and takes on some decision-making responsibilities while the senior partner, usually the husband, often helps at home but does not share family responsibilities.

juvenile delinquency   A pattern of destructive or antisocial activities and lawbreaking offenses committed by adolescents.

juvenile period   Proposed by Sullivan, a period between ages five and ten when children show increasing interest in developing intense friendships or "chum relationships" with peers of the same gender.

latency   According to Freud, the stage of development between the phallic and genital stages. Sexual feelings and activities are on hold as the child struggles to resolve the oedipal conflict.

learning disability   Difficulty in learning a specific academic skill such as reading or arithmetic.

learning orientation   Achievement motivation that comes from the learner and the task.

leisure   Activities chosen freely and enjoyed at one's own pace.

life expectancy   A statistical estimate of the probable number of years remaining in the life of an individual based on the likelihood that members of a particular birth cohort will die at various ages. It changes for each cohort from year to year as some die and some survive.

life review   According to Robert Butler, a universal inner experience of older people that helps them evaluate their lives, resolve remaining conflicts, and make decisions about material and emotional legacies. Life review promotes the resolution of Erikson's conflict of *integrity versus despair.*

living will   A legal document notifying one's physician of one's wishes regarding the withdrawal of life-sustaining equipment even if the result is death.

longitudinal study   A study of the same subjects over a relatively long period, often months or years.

long-term care   Health care and personal care, such as bathing, shopping, and laundry, usually provided by friends and relatives but sometimes by nursing homes and boarding homes.

low birth weight   A birth weight of less than 2,500 grams (about 5½ pounds).

menarche   The first menstrual period.

menopause   The second stage in the female climacteric during which hormone production is reduced, the ovaries cease to produce eggs, and menstruation ceases.

metalinguistic awareness   The ability to attend to language as an object of thought rather than attending only to the content or ideas of a language.

metaphor   A word or term used to compare one idea or behavior or event with another.

midlife crisis   Radical changes within the personality associated with the adult's reexamination of goals, priorities, and life accomplishments as the midpoint of life is passed.

morality   Sensitivity to and knowledge about what is right and wrong.

morbidity   The measure of health that refers to the number of cases of a disease in a given population.

mortality   The proportion of persons who die at a given age; the rate of death.

motor skills   Physical skills using the body or limbs, such as walking and drawing.

mourning   The actions and manner of expressing grief that reflect social and cultural prescriptions.

multiinfarct dementia   A chronic brain syndrome that results from blockages in the blood vessels that reduce or prevent blood flow to the brain, depriving it of oxygen and nutrients and causing a series of tiny strokes.

multiple intelligences   According to Howard Gardner's theory of intelligence, alternative forms of intelligence or adaptability to the environment.

naturalistic study   A study in which behavior is observed in its natural setting.

naturally occurring retirement community (NORC) A housing development that is not planned or designed for older people but attracts a majority of elderly residents because it provides a supportive social environment and access to services and facilities that can prolong independent living.

nature (1) The essence or basic character of a person or thing. (2) The inborn qualities of a person.

negative identity A form of identity diffusion involving rejection of the roles preferred by one's family or community in favor of socially undesirable roles.

neonate A newborn infant.

neostructuralist theory Theories of cognitive development that are based on the general notion of stagelike development but focus on more precise areas of thinking and mechanisms of development than Piaget's original theory proposed.

neurons Nerve cell bodies and their extensions or fibers.

non-REM sleep A relatively quiet, deep period of sleep. See also *REM sleep*.

nonnormative life event A life transition that occurs in the lives of people but is not associated with a particular stage of life.

normative life event A life transition that occurs within a time period strongly associated with chronological age, such as marriage, children leaving home, or retirement.

norms Behaviors typical at certain ages and of certain groups; standards of normal development.

nurture Environmental influences and experiences that affect a person's development.

obesity The state of being extremely overweight, specifically more than 130 percent of normal weight for height and bone size.

object permanence According to Piaget, the belief that people and things continue to exist even when one cannot experience them directly; emerges around age two.

object relations The child's relationships with the important people (called *objects*) in his or her environment and the process by which their qualities become part of the child's personality and mental life.

observational learning The tendency of a child to imitate or model behavior and attitudes of parents and other nurturant individuals.

occupational segregation The reality that most jobs in the United States are held by females (e.g., typists) or males (e.g., architects) and few are truly integrated.

oophorectomy The surgical removal of the ovaries that triggers surgical menopause.

operant conditioning According to Skinner, a process of learning in which a person or an animal increases the frequency of a behavior in response to repeated reinforcement of that behavior.

organ reserve The extra capacity the lungs, heart, and other organs have to respond to particularly intense or prolonged effort or unusually stressful events. Primary aging affects organ reserve so that most people first notice decline under stressful conditions.

osteoporosis The degeneration of bone; affects about one in three postmenopausal women and can be prevented by ERT or HRT in combination with weight-bearing exercise and a calcium-rich diet.

overgeneralizations Utterances in which a child shifts from using correct but irregular forms to using wrong but more regular forms; represent efforts to try out newly noticed rules of syntax.

ovum The reproductive cell, or gamete, of the female; the egg cell.

palliative care Management of pain and other symptoms of terminally ill patients that allows them to enjoy what remains of life.

passive euthanasia Not doing something to prolong life, such as not utilizing life-support equipment or not giving antibiotics, when unendurable illness makes living intolerable.

pathological aging Losses in functioning people suffer as they age that result from illness, abnormality, genetic factors, or exposure to unhealthy environments rather than from the normal aging process.

peers Individuals who are of approximately the same age and developmental level and share common attitudes and interests.

perception The neural activity of combining sensations into meaningful patterns.

performance orientation Achievement motivation stimulated by other individuals who may see and evaluate the learner rather than by the intrinsic nature of the task itself.

period of acquisition Schaie's term for all four of Piaget's stages, during which the child/adolescent builds basic skills and abilities and that precede Schaie's stages of adult thinking.

permissive-indifferent parenting A style of parenting in which parents' permissiveness reflects an avoidance of childrearing responsibilities, sometimes with detrimental results.

permissive-indulgent parenting A style of parenting in which parents make relatively few demands on their children but clearly communicate their warmth and interest and provide considerable care and nurturance.

personal fable Adolescents' belief that their own lives embody a special story that is heroic and completely unique.

phenotype The set of traits an individual actually displays during development; reflects the evolving product of genotype and experience. See also *genotype*.

phonemes Sounds that combine with other sounds to form words.

physical development The area of human development concerned primarily with physical changes such as growth, motor skill development, and basic aspects of perception.

placenta An organ that delivers oxygen and nutrients from the mother to the fetus and carries away the fetus's waste products, which the mother will excrete.

plasticity The ability of other neurons in the cerebral cortex to take over the functions of neurons that have been damaged or lost.

plateauing Reaching a point of constricted occupational opportunity, usually in mid-career, resulting in boredom and feelings of stagnation.

postconventional moral judgment In Kohlberg's theory, an orientation to moral justice that develops beyond conventional rules and beliefs.

postformal thought A level of thought that may develop after formal operations and is characterized by relative and nonabsolute thinking that accepts and synthesizes contradiction.

postponer Jean Veevers' term for someone who was less definite about whether she would have children and made the decision to remain child-free after first delaying childbearing for a definite time and then for an indefinite time.

posttraumatic stress disorder (PTSD) The physical and psychological symptoms of a person who has been the victim of a highly stressful event, such as violent war, rape, or earthquake, that last long after the event is over. Typical reactions include feeling numb, reliving aspects of the trauma, having sleeping problems, finding it difficult to concentrate, and reacting strongly to other stressful events.

practical intelligence   A form of real-world problem solving that involves applying intellectual skills to problems of everyday life and shows improved performance through middle age.

prepared childbirth   A method of childbirth in which parents have rehearsed or simulated labor and delivery well before the actual delivery date.

pretend play   Play that substitutes imaginary situations for real ones. Also called *fantasy* or *dramatic play*.

primary aging   Normal age-related changes that everyone experiences, such as the climacteric.

primary sex characteristics   Characteristics that make sexual reproduction possible. For females, consist of the vagina, uterus, fallopian tubes, and ovaries; for males, consist of the penis, scrotum, testes, prostate gland, and seminal vesicles.

problem finding   Patricia Arlin's proposed postformal mode of thinking, which entails generating new questions about oneself, one's work, or one's surroundings, in contrast to the problem-solving nature of formal operational thought.

programming theories   Theories of aging that consider the maximum lifespan to be predetermined by the genes in each species.

proximodistal principle   Growth that exhibits a near-to-far pattern of development, from the center of the body outward.

psychometric approach to intelligence   A view of intelligence based on identifying individual differences in ability through standardized test scores.

psychosocial development   The area of human development concerned primarily with personality, social knowledge and skills, and emotions.

psychosocial moratorium   According to Erikson, the latency period that precedes puberty and provides a temporary suspension of psychosexual development.

puberty   The period of early adolescence characterized by the development of full physical and sexual maturity.

pubic hair   Hair that grows around the genital area as a result of puberty.

punishment   According to Skinner, any stimulus that temporarily suppresses the response that it follows.

random sample   In research studies, a group of subjects from a population chosen such that each member of the population has an equal chance of being selected.

range of reaction   The range of possible phenotypes that an individual with a particular genotype might exhibit in response to the particular sequence of environmental influences he or she experiences.

recall memory   Retrieval of information by using relatively few external cues.

recessive gene   In any paired set of genes, the gene that influences or determines physical characteristics only when no dominant gene is present.

recognition memory   Retrieval of information by comparing an external stimulus or cue with preexisting experiences or knowledge.

reflex   An involuntary, automatic response to a stimulus. The very first movements or motions of an infant are reflexes.

reinforcement   According to Skinner, any stimulus that increases the likelihood that a behavior will be repeated in similar circumstances.

reintegrative stage   Schaie's last stage of adult thinking during which late adults focus again on their personal interests and values.

reminiscence   Recall of past experiences and events that occurs among people of all ages and promotes spiritual integration in late adulthood.

REM sleep   A relatively active period of sleep, named after the rapid eye movements that usually accompany it. See also *non-REM sleep*.

responsible stage   Schaie's second stage of adult thinking during which middle adults also consider their responsibility to others—mates, children, aging parents, and community—when making decisions.

reversibility   Piaget's term for the ability to undo a problem mentally and go back to its beginning.

sandwich generation   Middle-aged adults caught between the needs of adjacent generations, their children and their aging parents.

scheme   According to Piaget, a behavior or thought that represents a group of ideas and events in a person's experience.

scientific methods   General procedures of study involving (1) formulating research questions, (2) stating questions as a hypothesis, (3) testing the hypothesis, and (4) interpreting and publicizing the results.

secondary aging   Pathological aging, or the effects of illness and disease on the body due to genetic predisposition, environmental exposure, or health-compromising behaviors.

secondary sex characteristics   Sex characteristics other than the sex organs, such as extra layers of fat and pubic hair.

secure attachment   A healthy bond between infant and caregiver. The child is happy when the caregiver is present, somewhat upset during the caregiver's absence, and easily comforted upon the caregiver's return.

self-constancy   The belief that one's identity remains permanently fixed; established sometime after age six.

self-esteem   An individual's belief that he or she is an important, competent, powerful, and worthwhile person who is valued and appreciated.

semantics   The purposes and meanings of a language.

senescence   The degenerative phase of the aging process that causes an individual to become more vulnerable to disease and mortality as the years go by.

senile dementia   A chronic brain syndrome, caused by the loss of brain cells, that impairs orientation, intellect, judgment, and memory. Although the symptoms are similar to Alzheimer's, it usually has a later onset and is more frequent among women than men.

sense of self   A structured way in which individuals think about themselves that helps them to organize and understand who they are based on the views of others, their own experiences, and cultural categories such as gender and race.

sensorimotor intelligence   According to Piaget, thinking that occurs by way of sensory perceptions and motor actions; characteristic of infants.

sequential study   Research in which at least two cohorts are compared both with each other and at different times.

serial monogamy   A series of committed, intimate, sexually exclusive relationships with one person at a time.

SES   The socioeconomic status of an individual or family that is determined by level of education, income, and type of work, as well as by lifestyle and social values. Also called social class.

sex-linked recessive traits   Recessive traits resulting from genes on the X chromosome.

sexual dysfunction   An inability, often temporary, to function adequately in or enjoy sexual activities.

sickle-cell disease   A genetically transmitted condition in which a person's red blood cells intermittently acquire a curved, sickle shape. The condition sometimes can clog circulation in the small blood vessels.

social clock   Bernice Neugarten's timing of events approach to understanding the consistencies among disparate lives. Cultural groups tend to develop a shared sense of when certain life transitions, such as marriage or retirement, should occur, and people strive to time their major life events to match societal expectations.

social cognition   Knowledge and beliefs about interpersonal and social matters.

social conventions   Arbitrary customs and agreements about behavior that members of a society use.

social convoy   The term used to describe the lifelong social network of family and friend relationships that develop over the life course and provide social support from infancy through old age.

social referencing   The child's sensitive awareness of how parents and other adults are feeling and ability to use these emotional cues as a basis for guiding his or her own emotional responses and actions. Social referencing is important for the development of autonomy.

sociocultural perspective on intelligence   A view of intelligence that emphasizes the social and cultural influences on ability rather than the influence of inherent or learned individual differences.

sperm   Male gametes, or reproductive cells; produced in the testicles.

spirituality   The human need to construct a sense of meaning in life that occurs within or outside of a specifically religious context.

Strange Situation   A widely used method for studying attachment; confronts the infant with a series of controlled separations and reunions with a parent and a stranger.

superego   In Freud's theory, the part of personality that acts as an all-knowing, internalized parent. It has two parts: the conscience, which enforces moral and social conventions by punishing violations with guilt, and the ego-ideal, which provides an idealized, internal set of standards for regulating and evaluating one's thoughts, feelings, and actions.

survey   A research study that samples specific knowledge or opinions of large numbers of individuals.

symbolic thought   Cognition that makes one object or action stand for another.

syntax   The organizational rules of words and phrases in a language; its grammar.

telegraphic speech   Early utterances that leave out most articles, prepositions, and conjunctions.

temperament   Individual differences in quality and intensity of emotional responding and self-regulation that are present at birth, are relatively stable and enduring over time and across situations, and are influenced by the interaction of heredity, maturation, and experience.

teratogen   Any substance ingested by a pregnant woman that can harm the developing embryo or fetus.

testosterone   A sex hormone; sometimes called the *male sex hormone* because its high concentration in boys stimulates the growth of the penis and related male reproductive organs.

the good death   A death that is appropriate to the dying person. In the contemporary United States, it typically refers to a death in which the dying person is surrounded by family and friends with minimal technological interference.

trait   A relatively enduring disposition of an individual; a characteristic way of thinking, feeling, and acting.

triarchic theory of intelligence   A view of intelligence as consisting of three components: (1) adaptability, (2) information-processing skills, and (3) the ability to deal with novelty.

trust versus mistrust   In Erikson's theory, the psychosocial crisis of children from birth to one year involving whether they can rely on their parents to reliably meet their physical and emotional needs.

twin adoption study   Research that compares twins reared apart with unrelated persons reared together.

twin study   A research method for studying the relative contributions of heredity and environment in which the degree of similarity between genetically identical twins (developed from a single egg) is compared with the similarity between fraternal twins (developed from two eggs).

umbilical cord   Three large blood vessels that connect the embryo to the placenta, one to provide nutrients and two to remove waste products.

validity   The degree to which research findings measure or observe what is intended.

visual cliff   The classic laboratory setup of a ledge covered by a sheet of glass; used to test the acquisition of depth perception. Young babies crawling on the glass discriminate between the two sides of the "cliff."

vital capacity   The total volume of air that moves in and out of the lungs during maximal exertion.

wisdom   Expert knowledge and good judgment about important but uncertain matters of life; a positive change associated with late life.

zone of proximal development   According to Vygotsky, the level of difficulty at which problems are too hard for children to solve alone but not too hard when given support from adults or more competent peers.

zygote   The single new cell formed when a sperm cell attaches itself to the surface of an ovum (egg).

References

Abel, E. (1991). *Who cares for the elderly: Public policy and experiences of adult daughters.* Philadelphia: Temple University Press.

Abler, R. M., & Sedlacek, W. E. (1989). Freshman sexual attitudes and behaviors over a 15-year period. *Journal of College Student Development, 30,* 201–209.

Adamchak, D. J. (1993). Demographic aging in the industrialized world: A rising burden? *Generations, 17*(4), 6–9.

Adams, S. L., & Waskel, S. A. (1993). Late onset alcoholism: Stress or structure. *Journal of Psychology, 127*(3), 329–334.

Adams, W., Garry, P., Rhyne, R., Hunt, W., & Goodwin, J. (1990). Alcohol intake in the healthy elderly: Changes with age in a cross-sectional and longitudinal study. *Journal of the American Geriatrics Society, 38,* 211–216.

Ade-Ridder, L., & Kaplan, L. (1993, October). Marriage, spousal caregiving, and a husband's move to a nursing home. *Journal of Gerontological Nursing,* pp. 13–23.

Adler, N. E., Boyce, T., Chesney, M. A., Cohen, S., Folkman, S., Kahn, R. L., & Syme, S. L. (1994). Socioeconomic status and health: The challenge of the gradient. *American Psychologist, 49,* 15–24.

Adler, T. (1992, February). For depressed elderly, drugs advised. *The APA Monitor,* pp. 16–17.

Adlercreutz, H., Hämäläinen, E., Gorbach, G., & Goldin, B. (1992). Dietary phyto-oestrogens and the menopause in Japan. *The Lancet, 339,* 1233.

Agras, W. S., Kraemer, H. C., Berkowitz. R. I., Korner, A. F., & Hammer, L. D. (1987). Does a vigorous feeding style influence early development? *Journal of Pediatrics, 110,* 799–804.

Ainlay, S. C., & Smith, D. R. (1984). Aging and religious participation. *Journal of Gerontology, 39,* 357–564.

Ainsworth, M. (1973). The development of infant mother attachment. In B. M. Caldwell & H. N. Ricciuti (Eds.), *Review of child development research: Vol. 3.* Chicago: University of Chicago Press.

Ainsworth, M. (1979). Infant-mother attachment. *American Psychologist, 34,* 932–937.

Ainsworth, M., Blehar, M., Waters, E., & Wall, S. (1978). *Strange-situation behavior of one-year-olds. Its relation to mother-infant interaction in the first year and to qualitative differences in the infant-mother attachment relationship.* Hillsdale, N.J.: Erlbaum.

Akande, A. (1994). What meaning and effects does fatherhood have in child development? *Early Child Development and Care, 101,* 51–58.

Alexander, F., & Duff, R. W. (1988). Social interaction and alcohol use in retirement communities. *The Gerontologist, 28,* 632–636.

Alexander, G. M., & Hines, M. (1994). Gender labels and play styles: Their relative contribution to children's selection of playmates. *Child Development, 65,* 869–879.

Alexander, K. L., & Entwisle, D. R. (1988). Achievement in the first 2 years of school: Patterns and processes. *Monographs of the Society for Research in Child Development, 53*(2, Serial No. 218).

Alexander, L. L., & LaRosa, J. H. (1994). *New directions in women's health.* Boston: Jones and Bartlett.

Allen, J. P., Hauser, S. T., Bell, K. L., & O'Conner, T. G. (1994). Longitudinal assessment of autonomy and relatedness in adolescent-family interactions as predictors of adolescent ego development and self esteem. *Child Development, 65,* 179–194.

Allen, S. M. (1994). Gender differences in spousal caregiving and unmet need for care. *Journal of Gerontology, 49,* S187–195.

Almada, S. J., Zonderman, A. B., Shekelle, R. B., & Dyer, A. (1991). Neuroticism and cynicism and risk of death in middle-aged men: The Western Electric Study. *Psychosomatic Medicine, 53,* 165–175.

Alpert, D., & Culbertson, A. (1987). Daily hassles and coping strategies of dual-earner and nondual-earner women. *Psychology of Women Quarterly, 11,* 359–366.

Ambry, M. K. (1992). Childless chances. *American Demographics, 14*(4), 55.

American Academy of Pediatrics. (1985). *Pediatric nutrition handbook* (2nd ed.). Elk Grove Village, Ill.: Author.

American Academy of Pediatrics. (1991). *Facts about children with AIDS.* Elk Grove Village, Ill.: Author.

American Academy of Pediatrics. (1993). *Pediatric nutrition handbook.* Elk Grove Village, Ill.: Author.

American Association of Retired Persons. (AARP). (1990). *Understanding senior housing for the 1990s: An American Association of Retired Persons survey of consumer preferences, concerns and needs.* Washington, D.C.: Author.

American Association of Retired Persons (AARP). (1990). *A profile of older Americans: 1990.* Washington, D.C.: Author.

American Association of Retired Persons (AARP). (1993). *America's changing workforce: Statistics in brief.* Washington, D.C.: Author.

American Cancer Society. (1993). *Cancer facts and figures, 1993.* Atlanta: Author.

American College of Obstetricians and Gynecologists (ACOG). (1990). *Planning for pregnancy, birth, and beyond.* New York: Dutton.

American Psychiatric Association. (1994). *Diagnostic and statistical manual of mental disorders* (4th ed.). Washington, D.C.: Author.

American Psychological Association. (1992). Ethical principles of psychologists and code of conduct. *American Psychologist, 47*(12), 1992.

Ames, L. B. (1983). *Your one-year-old.* New York: Dell.

Amott, T. (1995*).* Shortchanged: Restructuring women's work. In M. L. Andersen & P. H. Collins (Eds.), *Race, class, and gender* (2nd ed., pp. 207–217). Belmont, Cal.: Wadsworth.

Amschler, D. H. (1991). The rising incidence of HIV infection and its implications for reproductive health. *Journal of Sex Education and Therapy, 17,* 244–250.

Anastasi, A. (1989). *Psychological testing* (6th ed.). New York: Macmillan.

Anderson, B. (1989). Effects of public day care: A longitudinal study. *Child Development, 60,* 857–866.

Anderson, S. A., Russell, C. S., & Schumm, W. A. (1983). Perceived marital quality and family life-cycle categories: A further analysis. *Journal of Marriage and the Family, 45,* 127–139.

Andrews, E. (1996, February 29). TV executives reach broad accord on rating violent shows. *The New York Times,* p. A15.

Andrien, M. (1994). *Social communication in nutrition: A methodology for intervention.* Rome: Food and Agricultural Organization of the United Nations.

Angier, N. (1994, May 17). Genetic mutations tied to father in most cases. *The New York Times,* p. C12.

Anglin, J. (1993). Vocabulary development: A morphological analysis. *Monographs of the Society for Research on Child Development, 58*(10, Serial No. 238). Chicago: University of Chicago Press.

Anson, O. (1989). Marital status and women's health revisited: The importance of a proximate adult. *Journal of Marriage and the Family, 51,* 185–194.

Anthony, J. C., & Aboraya, A. (1992) The epidemiology of selected mental disorders in later life. In J. E. Birren, R. B. Sloane, & G. D. Cohen (Eds.). *Handbook of mental health and aging* (2nd ed., pp. 27–73). San Diego: Academic Press.

Antonucci, T. C. (1990). Social supports and relationships. In R. H. Binstock & L. K. George (Eds.), *Handbook of aging and the social sciences* (3rd ed., pp. 205–226). San Diego: Academic Press.

Antonucci, T. C. (1991). Attachment, social support, and coping with negative life events in mature adulthood. In E. M. Cummings, A. L. Greene, & K. H. Karraker (Eds.), *Life-span developmental psychology: Vol. 11. Stress and coping across the life-span* (pp. 261–276). Hillsdale, N.J.: Erlbaum.

Antonucci, T. C., Jackson, J. S., & Gibson, R. (1989). Social relations, productive activities and coping with stress in late life. In M. A. P. Stephens, J. H. Crowther, S. E. Hobfoll, & D. L. Tennenbaum (Eds.), *Stress and coping in later life families.* Washington, D.C.: Hemisphere Publishers.

Apgar, V. (1953). A proposal for a new method of evaluation in the newborn infant. *Current Research in Anesthesia and Analgesia, 32,* 260.

Apgar, V., & Beck, J. (1973). *Is my baby all right?* New York: Trident.

Aquilino, W. S. (1990). The likelihood of parent-adult child coresidence: Effects of family structure and parental characteristics. *Journal of Marriage and the Family, 52,* 405–419.

Aquilino, W. S., & Supple, K. R. (1991). Parent-child relations and parent's satisfaction with living arrangements when adult children live at home. *Journal of Marriage and the Family, 53,* 13–27.

Archer, S. L. (1982). The lower age boundaries of identity development. *Child Development, 53,* 1551–1556.

Archer, S. L., & Waterman, A. S. (1988). Psychological individualism: Gender differences or gender identity? *Human Development, 31,* 65–81.

Archibald, J. (Ed.). (1995). *Phonological acquisition and phonological theory.* Hillsdale, N.J.: Erlbaum.

Arditti, J. A. (1992). Differences between fathers with joint custody and noncustodial fathers. *American Journal of Orthopsychiatry, 62,* 186–195.

Arenberg, D. (1968). Concept problem solving in young and old adults. *Journal of Gerontology, 23,* 279–282.

Arend, R., Gove, F., & Sroufe, L. (1979). Continuity of individual adaptation from infancy to kindergarten: A predictive study of ego-resiliency and curiosity in preschoolers. *Child Development, 50,* 950–959.

Ariès, P. (1962). *Centuries of childhood: A social history of family life* (R. Baldick, trans.). New York: Vintage.

Ariès, P. (1981). *The hour of our death.* (J. Lloyd, Trans.). Cambridge, Mass.: Harvard University Press.

Arlin, P. K. (1989). Problem solving and problem finding in young artists and young scientists. In. M. L. Commons, J. D. Sinnott, F. A. Richards, & C. Armon (Eds.), *Adult development: Vol. 1. Comparisons and applications of developmental models* (pp. 197–216). New York: Praeger.

Arliss, L. (1991). *Gender communication.* Englewood Cliffs, N.J.: Prentice-Hall.

Armstead, C. A., Lawler, K. A., Gordon, G., Cross, J., & Gibbons, J. (1989). Relationship of racial stressors to blood pressure responses and anger expression in black college students. *Health Psychology, 8,* 541–557.

Aro, H. M., & Palosaari, U. K. (1992). Parental divorce, adolescence, and transition to young adulthood: A follow-up study. *American Journal of Orthopsychiatry, 62,* 421–429.

Aro, H. M., & Taipale, V. (1987). The impact of timing of puberty on psychosomatic symptoms among fourteen- to sixteen-year-old Finnish girls. *Child Development, 58,* 261–268.

Aronson, E., & Bridgeman, D. (1979). Jigsaw groups and the desegregated classroom: In pursuit of common goals. *Personality and Social Psychology Bulletin, 5,* 438–446.

Ashburn, S. S. (1992). Biophysical development during middlescence. In C. S. Schuster & S. S. Ashburn (Eds.), *The process of human development: A holistic lifespan approach* (3rd ed., pp. 756–778). New York: J. B. Lippincott.

Asher, S., Renshaw, P., & Hymel, S. (1982). Peer relations and the development of social skills. In S. Moore & C.

Cooper (Eds.), *The young child: Reviews of research: Vol. 3.* Washington, D.C.: National Association for the Education of Young Children.

Aslanian, C. B., & Brickell, H. M. (1980). *Americans in transition: Life changes as reasons for adult learning.* New York: College Entrance Examination Board.

Atchley, R. C. (1994). *Social forces and aging* (7th ed.) Belmont, Cal.: Wadsworth.

Atkinson, J., & Feather, N. (Eds.). (1966). *A theory of achievement motivation.* New York: Wiley.

Attie, I., & Brooks-Gunn, J. (1989). Development of eating problems in adolescent girls: Response or cause of stress? In R. Barrett, L. Biener, & G. Baruch (Eds.), *Gender and stress* (pp. 218–254). New York: The Free Press.

Attie, I., Brooks-Gunn, J., & Petersen, A. (1990). A developmental perspective on eating disorders and eating problems. In M. Lewis & S. M. Miller (Eds.), *Handbook of developmental psychopathology* (pp. 409–420). New York: Plenum Press.

Aviezer, O., van Ijzendoorn, M. H., Sagi, A., & Schuengel, C. (1994). "Children of the Dream" revisited: 70 years of collective early child care in Israeli kibbutzim. *Psychological Bulletin, 116,* 99–116.

Avioli, P. S. (1989). The social support functions of siblings in later life. *American Behavioral Scientist, 33*(1), 45–57.

Azmitia, M., & Hesser, J. (1993). Why siblings are important agents of cognitive development: A comparison of siblings and peers. *Child Development, 64,* 430–444.

Bachmann, G. A. (1990). Hysterectomy: A critical review. *Journal of Reproductive Medicine, 35,* 862.

Bailey, J. M., & Zucker, K. J. (1995). Childhood sex-typed behavior and sexual orientation: A conceptual analysis and quantitative review. *Developmental Psychology, 31,* 43–55.

Baillargeon, R. (1993). The object concept revisited: New directions in the investigation of infants' physical knowledge. In C. Granrud (Ed.), *Visual perception and cognition in infants,* pp. 265–316. Hillsdale, N.J.: Erlbaum.

Bain, L. (1993). *Parents' guide to childhood emergencies.* New York: Delta.

Baird, P., & Sadovnick, A. D. (1987). Life expectancy in Down syndrome. *Journal of Pediatrics, 110,* 849–854.

Bakan, D. (1975). Adolescence in America: From idea to social fact. In R. E. Grinder (Ed.), *Studies in adolescence* (3rd ed.). New York: Macmillan.

Baker, C. (1995). *English syntax* (2nd ed.). Cambridge, Mass.: MIT Press.

Baker, J. E., Sedney, M. A., & Gross, E. (1992). Psychological tasks for bereaved children. *American Journal of Orthopsychiatry, 62,* 105–116.

Baltes, P. B., Smith, J., & Staudinger, U. M. (1992). Wisdom and successful aging. In T. B. Sonderegger (Ed.), *Psychology and aging: Nebraska symposium on motivation 1991* (Vol. 39). Lincoln, Neb.: University of Nebraska Press.

Baltes, P. B., & Staudinger, U. M. (1993). The search for a psychology of wisdom. *Current Directions in Psychological Science, 2*(3), 75–80.

Bamford, F., Bannister, R., Benjamin, C., Hillier, V., Ward, B., & Moore, W. (1990). Sleep in the first year of life. *Developmental Medicine and Child Neurology, 32,* 718–724.

Bandura, A. (1989). Social cognitive theory. In R. Vasta (Ed.), *Annals of Child Development. Theories of child development: Revised formulations and current issues.* Greenwich, Conn.: JAI Press.

Bandura, A. (1991). Social cognitive theory of moral thought and action. In W. Kurtines & J. Gewirtz (Eds.), *Handbook of moral behavior and development: Vol. 1* (pp. 45–104). Hillsdale, N.J.: Erlbaum.

Bandura, A., Cioffi, D., Taylor, C. B., & Brouillard, M. E. (1988). Perceived self-efficacy in coping with cognitive stressors and opoid activation. *Journal of Personality and Social Psychology,* 55, 479–488.

Banks, M., & Dannemiller, J. (1987). Infant visual psychophysics. In P. Salapatek & L. Cohen (Eds.), *Handbook of infant perception: Vol. 1.* Orlando, Fla.: Academic Press.

Bardige, B., Ward, J. V., Gilligan, C., Taylor, J. M., & Cohen, G. (1988). Moral concerns and considerations of urban youth. In C. Gilligan, J. V. Ward, & J. M. Taylor (Eds.), *Mapping the moral domain* (pp. 159–173.) Cambridge, Mass.: Harvard University Press.

Barkley, R. (1985). Developmental changes in the mother-child interactions of hyperactive boys: Effects of two dose levels of Ritalin. *Journal of Child Psychology and Psychiatry, 26*(5), 705–715.

Barlow, D. H., & Durand, V. M. (1995). *Abnormal psychology: An integrative approach.* Pacific Grove, Cal.: Brooks/Cole.

Barnes, G. M., Welte, J. W., & Dintcheff, B. (1992). Alcohol misuse among college students and other young adults: Findings from a general population study in New York State. *The International Journal of the Addictions, 27,* 917–934.

Barnett, R. C., & Baruch, G. K. (1985). Women's involvement in multiple roles and psychological distress. *Journal of Personality and Social Psychology, 49,* 135–145.

Barr, H. M., Streissguth, A. P., Darby, B. L., & Sampson, P. D. (1990). Prenatal exposure to alcohol, caffeine, tobacco, and aspirin: Effects on fine and gross motor performance in 4-year-old children. *Developmental Psychology, 26,* 339–348.

Bartoshuk, L. M., & Weiffenbach, J. M. (1990). Chemical senses and aging. In E. L. Schneider & J. W. Rowe (Eds.), *Handbook of the biology of aging* (3rd ed., pp. 429–443*)*. San Diego: Academic Press.

Bartsch, K. (1993). Adolescents' theoretical thinking. In R. Lerner (Ed.), *Early adolescence: Perspectives on research, policy, and intervention,* pp. 143–159. Hillsdale, N.J.: Erlbaum.

Bartsch, K., & Wellman, H. (1995). *Children talk about the mind.* New York: Oxford.

Baruch, G. K., & Barnett, R. (1986). Role quality, multiple role involvement, and psychological well-being in midlife women. *Journal of Personality and Social Psychology, 51,* 578–585.

Baruch, G., Barnett, R., & Rivers, C. (1983). *Lifeprints: New patterns of love and work for today's woman.* New York: McGraw Hill.

Basseches, M. (1984*)*. *Dialectical thinking and adult development.* Norwood, N.J.: Ablex.

Bauman, K. E., & Ennett, S. T. (1994). Peer influence on adolescent drug use. *American Psychologist, 49,* 820–822.

Baumrind, D. (1971). Current patterns of parental authority. *Developmental Psychology, 4,* 1–103.

Baumrind D. (1989). Raising competent children. In W. Damon (Ed.), *Child development today and tomorrow* (pp. 349–378). San Francisco: Jossey-Bass.

Baumrind, D. (1991a). Effective parenting during the early adolescent transition. In P. Cowan & M. Hetherington (Eds.), *Family transitions.* Hillsdale, N.J.: Erlbaum.

Baumrind, D. (1991b). Parenting styles and adolescent development. In R. M.Lerner, A. C. Petersen, & J. Brooks-Gunn (Eds.), *The encyclopedia of adolescence.* New York: Garland.

Bausell, R. B. (1986). Health-seeking behavior among the elderly. *The Gerontologist, 26,* 556–559.

Bayley, N. (1955). On the growth of intelligence. *American Psychologist, 10,* 805–823.

Beck, R. (1978). *Motivation: Theories and principles.* Englewood Cliffs, N.J.: Prentice-Hall.

Becker, A. (1994). Nurturing and negligence: Working on others' bodies in Fiji. In T. Csordas (Ed.), *Embodiment and experience: The existential ground of culture and self* (pp. 100–115). New York: Cambridge University Press.

Bedford, V. (1989). Understanding the value of siblings in old age. *American Behavioral Scientist, 33*(1), 33–44.

Behrman, R. (Ed.). (1993). *The future of children: School-linked services.* Los Altos, Cal.: Center for the Future of Children, The David and Lucille Packard Foundation.

Belenky, M. F., Clinchy, B. M., Goldberger, N. R., & Tarule, J. M. (1986). *Women's ways of knowing: The development of self, voice, and mind.* New York: Basic Books.

Bell, A. P., & Weinberg, M. S. (1978). *Homosexualities: A study of diversity among men and women.* New York: Simon & Schuster.

Bell, A. P., Weinberg, M. S., & Hammersmith, S. K. (1981). *Sexual preference: Its development in men and women.* Bloomington, Ind.: Indiana University Press.

Bellugi, U., Van Hoek, K., Lillo-Martin, D., & O'Grady, L. (1993). The acquisition of syntax and space in young deaf signers. In D. Bishop & K. Mogford (Eds.), *Language development in exceptional circumstances* (pp. 132–149). Hillsdale, N.J.: Erlbaum.

Belsky, J. (1980). Child maltreatment: An ecological integration. *American Psychologist, 35,* 320–335.

Belsky, J. (1988a). The "effects" of infant day care reconsidered. *Early Childhood Research Quarterly, 3,* 235–272.

Belsky, J. (1988b). Child maltreatment and the emergent family system. In K. Browne, C. Davies, & P. Strattan (Eds.), *Early prediction and prevention of child abuse* (pp. 291–302). New York: Wiley.

Belsky, J. (1993). Etiology of child maltreatment: A developmental-ecological analysis. *Psychological Bulletin, 114,* 413–434.

Belsky, J., Crnic, K., & Gable, S. (1995). The determinants of coparenting in families with toddler boys: Spousal differences and daily hassles. *Child Development, 66,* 629–642.

Belsky, J., Gilstrap, B., & Rovine, M. (1984a). Stability and change in mother-infant and father-infant interaction in a family setting: One-to-three-to-nine months. *Child Development, 5,* 706–717.

Belsky, J., Gilstrap, B., & Rovine, M. (1984b). The Pennsylvania Infant and Family Development Project, I: Stability and change in mother-infant and father-infant interaction in a family setting. *Child Development, 59,* 692–705.

Belsky, J., Lerner, R., & Spanier, G. (1984). *The child in the family.* Reading, Mass.: Addison-Wesley.

Belsky, J., & Nezworski, T. (Eds.). (1988). *Clinical implications of attachment.* Hillsdale, N.J.: Erlbaum.

Belsky, J., & Rovine, M. (1988). Nonmaternal care in the first year of life and the security of infant-parent attachment. *Child Development, 59,* 157–176.

Belsky, J., & Rovine, M. (1990). Patterns of marital change across the transition to parenthood: Pregnancy to three years postpartum. *Journal of Marriage and the Family, 52,* 5–19.

Bem, S. L. (1974). The measurement of psychological androgyny. *Journal of Consulting and Clinical Psychology, 42,* 155–162.

Bem, S. L. (1976). Probing the promise of androgyny. In A. Kaplan & J. Bean (Eds.), *Beyond sex-role stereotypes: Readings toward a psychology of androgyny.* Boston: Little, Brown.

Bem, S. L. (1981). Gender schema theory: A cognitive account of sex typing. *Psychological Review, 88,* 354–364.

Bem, S. L. (1983). Gender schema theory and its implications for child development: Raising gender-aschematic children in a gender-schematic society. *Signs, 8,* 598–616.

Bengtson, V. L. (1985). Diversity and symbols in grandparent roles. In V. L. Bengtson & J. F. Robertson (Eds.), *Grandparenthood* (pp. 51–57). Beverly Hills, Cal.: Sage.

Bengtson, V. L., Rosenthal, C., & Burton, L. (1990). Families and aging: Diversity and heterogeneity. In R. H. Binstock & L. K. George (Eds.), *Handbook of aging and the social sciences* (3rd ed., pp. 263–287). San Diego: Academic Press.

Benson, P., & Elkin, C. (1990). *Effective Christian education: A national study of Protestant denominations.* Minneapolis: Search Institute.

Berg, W. K., & Berg, K. (1987). Psychophysiological development in infancy: State, startle, and attention. In J. Osofsky (Ed.), *Handbook of infant development* (2nd ed.). New York: Wiley.

Berger, R. M. (1982). *Gay and gray: The older homosexual man.* Chicago: University of Illinois Press.

Bergmann, M. S. (1988). On the intrapsychic function of falling in love. *Psychoanalytic Quarterly, 69,* 56–78.

Berko, J. (1958). The child's learning of English morphology. *Word, 14,* 150–177.

Berkowitz. R. I., Agras, W. S., Korner, A. F., Kraemer, H. C., & Zeanah, C. H. (1985). Physical activity and adiposity: A longitudinal study from birth to childhood. *Journal of Pediatrics, 106,* 734–738.

Berlin, B., & Kay, P. (1969). *Basic color terms: Their universality and evolution.* Columbus, Ohio: Merrill.

Berndt, T. J. (1988). The nature and significance of children's friendships. In R. Vasta (Ed.), *Annals of child development: Vol. 5* (pp. 155–186). Greenwich, Conn.: JAI Press.

Bernhardt, J. S. (1990). Potential workplace hazards to reproductive health. *Journal of Obstetrical and Gynecological Nursing, 19,* 53–62.

Bertoia, J. (1993). *Drawings from a dying child: Insights into death from a Jungian perspective.* London: Routledge.

Bialystok, E., & Hakuta, K. (1994). *The science and psychology of second language acquisition.* New York: Basic Books.

Bian, Z. (1994). New childless families in China. *Beijing Review, 37*(5), 24–25.

Bibby, R. W., & Posterski, D. C. (1985). The emerging generation: An inside look at Canada's teenagers. Toronto: Irwin.

Bierman, K. L., Smoot, D. L., & Aumiller, K. (1993). Characteristics of aggressive-rejected, aggressive (nonrejected), and rejected (nonaggressive) boys. *Child Development, 64,* 139–151.

Bijstra, J., Jackson, S., & Van Geert, P. (1991). Progress to conservation: Conflict or correct answer? *European Journal of Psychology of Education, 3,* 291–301.

Binder, J., Dobler-Mikola, A., & Angst, J. (1981). An epidemiological study of minor psychiatric disturbances. A field study among 20-year-old females and males in Zurich. *Social Psychiatry, 16,* 31–41.

Birenbaum, L. K., Robinson, M. A., Phillips, D., Stewart, B., et al. (1991). The response of children to the dying and death of a sibling. *Omega: Journal of Death and Dying, 20,* 213–228.

Biringen, Z. (1990). Direct observation of maternal sensitivity and dyadic interaction in the home: Relations to maternal thinking. *Developmental Psychology, 26,* 278–284.

Birren, J. E., Woods, A. M., & Williams, M. V. (1980). Behavioral slowing with age: Causes, organization, and consequences. In L. W. Poon (Ed.), *Aging in the 1980s: Psychological issues* (pp. 293–308). Washington, D.C.: American Psychological Association.

Blackburn, J. A., & Papalia, D. E. (1992). Adult cognition from a Piagetian perspective. In R. J. Sternberg & C. A. Berg (Eds.), *Intellectual development* (pp. 141–160). New York: Cambridge University Press.

Blackman, J. A. (1990). *Medical aspects of developmental disabilities in children birth to three* (2nd ed). Rockville, Md.: Aspen Publishers, Inc.

Blair, S. N., Brill, P. A., & Kohl, H. W. (1989). Physical activity patterns in older individuals. In W. W. Spirduso & H. M. Eckert (Eds.), *The academy papers: Physical activity and aging* (pp. 120–139). Champaign, Ill.: Human Kinetics.

Blair, S. N., Kohl, H. W., III, Paffenberger, R. S., Clark, D. B., Cooper, K. H., & Gibbons, L. W. (1989). Physical fitness and all-cause mortality: A prospective study of healthy men and women. *Journal of the American Medical Association. 262,* 2395–2401.

Blanck, G. (1990). The man and his cause. In L. C. Moll (Ed.), *Vygotsky and education: Instructional implications and applications of sociohistorical psychology.* Cambridge, U.K.: Cambridge University Press.

Blatt, R. J. R. (1988). *Prenatal tests.* New York: Vintage.

Blier, M. J., & Blier-Wilson, L. A. (1989). Gender differences in self-rated emotional expressiveness. *Sex Roles, 21*(3–4), 287–295.

Bloch, M. (1982). Death, women and power. In M. Bloch & J. Parry (Eds.), *Death and the regeneration of life* (pp. 211–230). Cambridge, U.K.: Cambridge University Press.

Block, J. H., Block, J., & Morrison, A. (1981). Parental agreement-disagreement on child-rearing orientations and gender-related personality correlates in children. *Child Development, 52,* 965–974.

Bloom, L. (1993). *The transition from infancy to language: Acquiring the power of expression.* New York: Cambridge University Press.

Blumberg, M. L., & Lester, D. (1991). High school and college students' attitudes toward rape. *Adolescence, 26,* 727–729.

Blumstein, P., & Schwartz, P. (1983). *American couples: Money, work, sex.* New York: William Morrow.

Bock, R. D., & Moore, E. G. J. (1986). *Advantage and disadvantage: A profile of American youth.* Hillsdale, N.J.: Erlbaum.

Bogdon, J. C. (1993). Childbirth practices in American history. In B. K. Rothman (Ed.), *The encyclopedia of childbearing.* New York: Henry Holt, 1993.

Bojko, M. (1995). The multi-cultural program at O'Brien Elementary School. Personal communication.

Bolger, K. E., Patterson, C. J., Thompson, W. W., & Kupersmidt, J. B. (1995). Psychosocial adjustment among children experiencing persistent and intermittent family economic hardship. *Child Development, 66,* 1107–1129.

Bollerud, K., Christopherson, S., & Frank, E. (1990). Girls' sexual choices: Looking for what is right: The intersection of sexual and moral development. In C. Gilligan, N. Lyons, & T. Hanmer (Eds.), *Making connections: The relational worlds of adolescent girls at Emma Willard School* (pp. 274–285). Cambridge, Mass.: Harvard University Press.

Booth, A., & Amato, P. R. (1994). Parental marital quality, parental divorce, and relations with parents. *Journal of Marriage and the Family, 56,* 21–34.

Booth, A., & Johnson, D. R. (1994). Declining health and marital quality. *Journal of Marriage and the Family, 56,* 218–223.

Booth, A., & Johnson, E. (1988). Premarital cohabitation and marital success. *Journal of Family Issues, 9,* 387–394.

Bordo, S. (1993). *Unbearable weight: Feminism, Western culture, and the body.* Berkeley, Cal.: University of California Press.

Bornstein, M. (1989). Information processing (habituation) and stability in cognitive development. *Human Development, 32,* 129–136.

Bornstein, M., & Tamis-Lemonda, C. (1989). Maternal responsiveness and cognitive development in children. In M. Bornstein (Ed.), *Maternal responsiveness: Characteristics and consequences.* San Francisco: Jossey-Bass.

Botvin, G. J., & Tortu, S. (1988). Preventing adolescent substance abuse through life skills training. In R. H. Price, E. L. Cowen, R. P. Lorion, & J. Ramos-McKay (Eds.), *Fourteen ounces of prevention: A casebook for practitioners.* Washington, D.C.: American Psychological Association.

Botwinick, J. (1977). Intellectual abilities. In J. E. Birren & K. W. Schaie (Eds.), *Handbook of the psychology of aging* (pp. 580–605). New York: Van Nostrand Reinhold.

Bouchard, C., & Shephard, R. J. (1993). Physical activity, fitness, and health: The model and key concepts. In C. Bouchard, R. J. Shephard, & T. Stephens (Eds.), *Physical activity, fitness, and health* (pp. 11–23). Champaign, Ill.: Human Kinetics.

Bouchard, C., Shepard, R. J., Stephens, T., Sutton, J. R., & McPherson, B. D. (Eds.). (1990). *Exercise, fitness and health: A consensus of current knowledge.* Champaign, Ill.: Human Kinetics.

Bowers, R. (1995). Early adolescent social and emotional development: A constructivist perspective. In M. Wavering (Ed.), *Educating young adolescents,* pp. 79–110. New York: Garland.

Bowlby, J. (1969). *Attachment and loss: Vol. 1. Attachment.* New York: Basic Books.

Bowlby, J. (1973). *Attachment and loss: Vol. 2. Separation, anxiety, and anger.* New York: Basic Books.

Bowlby, J. (1979). *The making and breaking of affectional bonds.* London: Tavistock Publications.

Bowlby, J. (1980). *Attachment and loss: Vol. 3. Loss, sadness, and depression.* New York: Basic Books.

Bowlby, J. (1988). *A secure base: Clinical applications of attachment theory.* London: Routledge.

Bowman, P. J. (1990). The adolescent-to-adult transition: Discouragement among jobless Black youth. *New Directions for Child Development, 46,* 87–105.

Boyd, M., & Pryor, E. T. (1989). The cluttered nest: The living arrangements of young Canadian adults. *Canadian Journal of Sociology, 14,* 461–477.

Boyd, R. L. (1989). Minority status and childlessness. *Sociological inquiry, 59*(3), 331–342.

Boyer, E. L. (1983). *High school: A report on secondary education.* New York: Harper & Row.

Brady, E. M. (1984). Demographic and educational correlates of self-reported learning among older students. *Educational Gerontology, 10,* 25–38.

Braithwaite, R. L., & Lythcott, N. (1989). Community empowerment as a strategy for health promotion for black and other minority populations. *Journal of the American Medical Association, 261,* 282–283.

Brasel, J., & Gruen, R. (1978). Cellular growth: Brain, liver, muscle and lung. In F. Falkner & J. Tanner (Eds.), *Human growth: Vol. 2.* New York: Plenum Press.

Brazelton, T. B. (1976). Early mother-infant reciprocity. In V. C. Vaughn III & T. B. Brazelton (Eds.), *The family: Can it be saved?* Chicago: Yearbook Medical Publishers.

Brecher, E. (1984). *Love, sex, and aging.* Boston: Little, Brown.

Bredekamp, S. (Ed.). (1987). *Developmentally appropriate practice in early childhood programs serving children from birth through age 8* (expanded ed.). Washington, D.C.: National Association for the Education of Young Children.

Bredkamp, S. (Ed.). (1987). Integrated components of developmentally appropriate practice for infants. In *Developmentally appropriate practice in early childhood programs serving children from birth through age 8* (pp. 34–38). Washington, D.C.: National Association for the Education of Young Children.

Bretherton, I., McNew, S., & Beeghly-Smith, M. (1981). Early person knowledge as expressed in gestural and verbal communications. In M. Lamb & L. Sherrod (Eds.), *Infant social cognition.* Hillsdale, N.J.: Erlbaum.

Bretherton, I., & Waters, E. (1985). Growing points in attachment theory. *Monographs of the Society for Research in Child Development, 50* (12, Serial No. 209).

Brislin, R., & Yoshida, T. (1994). *Intercultural communication training: An introduction.* Thousand Oaks, Cal.: Sage.

Broderick, V. (1991). Young children's comprehension of similarities underlying metaphor. *Journal of Psycholinguistic Research, 20,* 65–81.

Brody, E. M. (1990). *Women in the middle: Their parent-care years.* New York: Springer.

Brody, E. M., Litvin, S. J., Albert, S. M., & Hoffman, C. J. (1994). Marital status of daughters and patterns of parent care. *Journal of Gerontology, 49,* S95–S103.

Brody, E. M., Morton, H. K., Johnsen, P. T., Hoffman, C., & Schoonover, C. B. (1987). Work status and parent care: A comparison of four groups of women. *The Gerontologist, 27,* 201–208.

Brody, G. H., Graziano, W. G., & Musser, L. M. (1983). Familiarity and children's behavior in same-age and mixed-age peer groups. *Developmental Psychology, 19,* 569–576.

Brody, G. H., Stoneman, Z., & Burke, M. (1987). Family system and individual child correlates of sibling behavior. *American Journal of Orthopsychiatry, 57,* 561–569.

Brody, G. H., Stoneman, Z., McCoy, J. K., & Forehand, R. (1992). Contemporary and longitudinal associations of sibling conflict with family relationship assessments and family discussions about sibling problems. *Child Development, 63,* 391–400.

Brody, J. E. (1993, February 10). Adult years bring new afflictions for DES "babies." *The New York Times,* p. C–12.

Bronfenbrenner, U. (1989). Ecological systems theory. In R. Vasta (Ed.), *Annals of child development: Vol. 6. Six theories of child development: Revised formulations and current issues.* Greenwich, Conn.: JAI Press.

Bronstein, P. (1988). Marital and parenting roles in transition. In P. Bronstein & C. Cowan (Eds.), *Fatherhood today: Men's changing role in the family* (pp. 3–12). New York: Wiley.

Brooks-Gunn, J. (1987). Pubertal pressures: Their relevance for developmental research. In V. B. Van Hasselt & M. Hersen (Eds.), *Handbook of adolescent psychology* (pp. 111–130). New York: Pergamen Press.

Brooks-Gunn, J., & Furstenberg, F. (1989). Adolescent sexual behavior. *American Psychologist, 44,* 249–257.

Brooks-Gunn, J., & Warren, M. (1989). Biological and social contributions to negative affect in young adolescent girls. *Child Development, 60,* 40–55.

Brooten, D. (Ed.). (1992). *Low-birth-weight neonates.* Philadelphia: Lippincott.

Brophy, J. (1983). Research on the self-fulfilling prophecy and teacher expectations. *Journal of Educational Psychology, 75,* 631–666.

Brown, B. B. (1990). Peer groups and peer cultures. In S. S. Feldman & G. R. Elliot (Eds.), *At the threshold: The developing adolescent* (pp. 171–196). Cambridge, Mass.: Harvard University Press.

Brown, B. B., Mocents, N., Lamborn, S. D., & Steinberg, L. (1994). Parenting practices and peer group affiliation in adolescence. *Child Development, 64,* 467–482.

Brown, J. L., & Pollitt, E. (1996, February). Malnutrition, poverty and intellectual development. *Scientific American,* 38–43.

Brown, J. R. (Ed.). (1990). *Plant population genetics, breeding, and genetic resources.* Sunderland, Mass.: Sinauer Associates.

Brown, J. R., & Dunn, J. (1992). Talk with your mother or your sibling? Developmental changes in early family conversations about feelings. *Child Development, 63,* 336–349.

Brown, L., & Gilligan, C. (1992). *Meeting at the crossroads: Women's psychology and girls' development.* Cambridge, Mass.: Harvard University Press.

Brown, R. (1973). *A first language: The early stages.* Cambridge, Mass.: Harvard University Press.

Brubaker, T. H. (1985). *Later life families.* Beverly Hills, Cal.: Sage.

Brubaker, T. H., & Kinsel, B. (1988). Who is responsible for household tasks in long-term marriages of the young old elderly? In L. Ade-Ridder & C. Hennon (Eds.), *Lifestyles of the elderly: Diversity in relationships, health, and caregiving.* New York: Human Sciences Press.

Bruch, H. (1979). *The golden cage: The enigma of anorexia nervosa.* New York: Vintage.

Bruch, H. (1988). *Conversations with anorexics.* New York: Basic Books.

Bruner, J. (1983). *Child's talk: Learning to use language.* New York: Norton.

Bryant, B. K. (1985). The neighborhood walk: Sources of support in middle childhood. *Monographs of the Society for Research on Child Development, 50* (3, No. 210).

Bryant, B. K. (1990). The richness of the child-pet relationship: A consideration of both benefits and costs of pets to children. *Anthrozoos, 3,* 253–261.

Buckley, K., & Kulb, N. (Eds.). (1983). *Handbook of maternal-newborn nursing.* New York: Wiley.

Buhrmester, D. (1990). Intimacy of friendship, interpersonal competence, and adjustment during preadolescence and adolescence. *Child Development, 61,* 1101–1111.

Buhrmester, D., & Furman, W. (1987). The development of companionship and intimacy. *Child Development, 58,* 1101–1113.

Buhrmester, D., & Furman, W. (1990). Perceptions of sibling relationships during middle childhood and adolescence. *Child Development, 61,* 1387–1398.

Bulcroft, R., & Bulcroft, K. (1991). The nature of the function of dating in later life. *Research on Aging, 13*(2), 244–260.

Bumpass, L. L., & Sweet, J. A. (1989). Children's experience in single-parent families: Implications of cohabitation and marital transitions. *Family Planning Perspectives, 21,* 256–260.

Bumpass, L. L., Sweet, J. A., & Cherlin, A. (1991). The role of cohabitation in declining rates of marriage. *Journal of Marriage and the Family, 53,* 913–927.

Bumpass, L. L., Sweet, J. A., & Martin, T. C. (1990). Changing patterns of remarriage. *Journal of Marriage and the Family, 52,* 747–756.

Burnett, P., Middleton, W., Raphael, B., Dunne, M., Moylan, A., & Martinek, N. (1994). Concepts of normal bereavement. *Journal of Traumatic Stress, 7,* 123–128.

Burrus-Bammel, L. L., & Bammel, G. (1985). Leisure and recreation. In J. E. Birren & K. W. Schaie (Eds.), *Handbook of the psychology of aging* (2nd ed., pp. 848–863). New York: Van Nostrand Reinhold.

Burton, L. M. (1992a). Black grandparents rearing children of drug-addicted parents: Stressors, outcomes, and social service needs. *The Gerontologist, 32,* 744–751.

Burton, L. M. (1992b). Families and the aged: Issues of complexity and diversity. *Generations, 17*(3), 5–6.

Burton, L. M., & Bengtson, V. L. (1985). Black grandmothers: Issues of timing and continuity of roles. In V. L. Bengtson & J. F. Robertson (Eds.), *Grandparenthood* (pp. 61–77). Beverly Hills, Cal.: Sage.

Burton, L. M., & DeVries, C. (1992). Challenges and rewards: African American grandparents as surrogate parents. *Generations, 17*(3), 51–54.

Buss, A. H., & Plomin, R.(1984). *Temperament: Early developing personality traits.* Hillsdale, N.J.: Erlbaum.

Busse, E. W., & Maddox, G. L. (1985). *The Duke longitudinal studies of normal aging, 1955–1980: Overview of history, design, and findings.* New York: Springer.

Butler, R. N. (1975). *Why survive? Being old in America.* New York: Harper & Row.

Butler, R. N. (1993). Dispelling ageism: The cross-cutting intervention. *Generations, 17*(2), 75–78.

Byard, R., & Cohle, S. (1994). *Sudden death in infants, children, and adolescents.* New York: Cambridge University Press.

Byne, W. (1994, May). The biological evidence challenged. *Scientific American,* pp. 50–55.

Caldwell, J. C., & Caldwell, P. (1990). High fertility in sub-Saharan Africa. *Scientific American, 262*(5), 118–125.

Caliso, J., & Milner, J. (1992). Childhood history of abuse and child abuse screening. *Child Abuse and Neglect, 16,* 647–659.

Call, V., Sprecher, S., & Schwartz, P. (1995). The incidence and frequency of marital sex in a national sample. *Journal of Marriage and the Family, 57,* 639–652.

Callahan, J. J., Jr. (1992). Aging in place. *Generations, 16*(2), 5–6.

Camacho, T. C., Roberts, R. E., Lazarus, N. B., Kaplan, G. A., & Cohen, R. D. (1991). Physical activity and depression: Evidence from the Alameda County study. *American Journal of Epidemiology, 134,* 220–231.

Campbell, M. D., Wilson, L. G., & Hanson, G. R. (1980). *The invisible minority: A study of adult university students.* (Final report submitted to the Hogg Foundation for Mental Health). Austin, Tx.: Office of the Dean of Students, University of Texas.

Campos, A. P. (1990). Social work practice with Puerto Rican terminally ill clients and their families. In J. K. Parry (Ed.), *Social work practice with the terminally ill: A transcultural perspective* (pp. 129–143). Springfield, Ill.: Charles C Thomas.

Campos, J., & Stenberg, C. (1981). Perception, appraisal, and emotion: The onset of social referencing. In M. Lamband & L. Sherrod (Eds.), *Infant social cognition.* Hillsdale, N.J.: Erlbaum.

Campos, R., Raffaelli, M., Ude, W., Greco, M., Ruff, A., Rolf, J., Antunes, C. M., Halsey, N., Greco, D., & Street Youth Study Group. (1994). Social networks and daily activities of street youth in Belo Horizonte, Brazil. *Child Development, 65,* 319–330.

Camras, L. A., Sullivan, J., & Michel, G. (1993). Do infants express discrete emotions? Adult judgments of facial, vocal, and body actions. *Journal of Nonverbal Behavior, 17,* 171–186.

Cancian, F. M. (1986). The feminization of love. *Signs: Journal of Women in Culture and Society, 11,* 692–709.

Cantor, M. H. (1992). Families and caregiving in an aging society. *Generations, 16*(3), 67–70.

Cantos, A. L., Neidig, P. H., & O'Leary, K. D. (1994). Injuries of women and men in a treatment program for domestic violence. *Journal of Family Violence, 9*(2), 113–124.

Card, C. (1995). *Lesbian choice.* New York: Columbia University Press.

Carlson, C. I., Cooper, C. R., & Spradling, V. Y. (1991). Developmental implications of shared versus distinct perceptions of the family in early adolescence. *New Directions for Child Development, 51,* 13–32.

Carlson, E. A., Jacobvitz, D., & Sroufe, A. L. (1995). A developmental investigation of inattentiveness and hyperactivity. *Child Development, 66,* 37–54.

Carnegie Council on Adolescent Development. (1989). *Turning points: Preparing American youth for the 21st century.* Washington, D.C.: Task Force on Education of Young Adolescents.

Carnegie Council on Adolescent Development. (1992). A matter of time: Risk and opportunity in the nonschool hours. Report of the task force on youth development and community programs. New York: Carnegie Corporation of New York.

Carney, S. S., Rich, C. L., Burke, P. A., & Fowler, R. C. (1994). Suicide over 60: The San Diego study. *Journal of the American Geriatric Society, 42,* 174–180.

Carp, F. M. (1978/1979). Effects of the living environment on activity and the use of time. *International Journal of Aging and Human Development, 9,* 74–91.

Carstensen, L. L., Gottman, J. M., & Levenson, R. W. (1995). Emotional behavior in long-term marriage. *Psychology and Aging, 10,* 140–149.

Carter, R. T., & Swanson, J. L. (1990). The validity of the strong inventory with Black Americans. *Journal of Vocational Behavior, 36,* 195–209.

Case, R. (1991a). *The mind's staircase: Exploring the conceptual underpinnings of children's thought and knowledge.* Hillsdale, N.J.: Erlbaum.

Case, R. (1991b). General and specific views of the mind, its structure, and its development. In R. Case (Ed.), *The mind's staircase* (pp. 3–16). Hillsdale, N.J.: Erlbaum.

Case, R. (1991c). A neo-Piagetian approach to the issue of cognitive generality and specificity. In R. Case (Ed.), *The mind's staircase* (pp. 17–36). Hillsdale, N.J.: Erlbaum.

Case, R. (1991d). Advantages and limitations of the neo-Piagetian position. In R. Case (Ed.), *The mind's staircase* (pp. 37–51). Hillsdale, N.J.: Erlbaum.

Case, R. (1992). Neo-Piagetian theories of intellectual development. In H. Beilin & P. Pufall (Eds.), *Piaget's theory: Prospects and possibilities.* Hillsdale, N.J.: Erlbaum.

Case, R., & Edelstein, W. (1993). *The new structuralism in cognitive development: Theory and research on individual pathways.* New York: Karger.

Caspersen, C. J., Christenson, G. M., & Pollard, R. A. (1986). Status of the 1990 physical fitness and exercise objectives—Evidence from NHIS. *Public Health Reports, 101,* 589–592.

Cassel, C. K., & Meier, D. E. (1990). Morals and moralism in the debate over euthanasia and assisted suicide. *New England Journal of Medicine, 323,* pp. 750–752.

Cassell, D. (1994). *Encyclopedia of obesity and eating disorders.* New York: Facts on File Press.

Castañeda, D. M. (1993). The meaning of romantic love among Mexican-Americans. *Journal of Social Behavior and Personality, 8,* 257–272.

Cates, W., Jr., & Rauh, J. L. (1985). Adolescents and sexually transmitted diseases: An expanding problem. *Journal of Adolescent Health Care, 6,* 1–5.

Cattell, R. B. (1963). Theory of fluid and crystallized intelligence: A critical experiment. *Journal of Educational Psychology, 54,* 1–22.

Cazden, C. (1988). *Classroom discourse.* Portsmouth, N.H.: Heinemann.

Cazenave, N. A., & Straus, M. A. (1990). Race, class network embeddedness, and family violence: A search for potent support systems. In M. A. Straus & R. J. Gelles, with C. Smith, (Eds.), *Physical violence in American families: Risk factors and adaptations to violence in 8,145 families* (pp. 321–339). New Brunswick, N.J.: Transaction.

Centers for Disease Control. (1990). Use of mammography, United States, 1990. *Morbidity Mortality Weekly Reports, 39,* 621–627.

Centers for Disease Control. (1991a). *Health objectives for the nation. Tobacco use among high school students—United States, 1990* (Vol. 40, No. 36, pp. 617–619. Washington, D.C.: Author.

Centers for Disease Control. (1991b, October). *HIV/AIDS surveillance report.* Atlanta: Author.

Centers for Disease Control. (1993a). *National overview of sexually transmitted diseases: STD/HIV problem assessment.* Washington, D.C.: Author.

Centers for Disease Control. (1993b, February). *HIV/AIDS surveillance report* (year-end edition). Washington, D.C.: Author.

Cerella, J. (1990). Aging and information processing rate. In J. E. Birren & K. W. Schaie (Eds.), *Handbook of the psychology of aging* (3rd ed., pp. 201–221). San Diego: Academic Press.

Chafel, J. (1993). *Child poverty and public policy.* Washington, D.C.: The Urban Institute.

Chaiklin, S., & Lave, J. (Eds.). (1993). *Understanding practice: Perspectives on activity and context.* New York: Cambridge University Press.

Chambré, S. M. (1991). Volunteerism by elders: Demographic and policy trends, past and future. In *Resourceful aging: Today and tomorrow: Vol. II. Volunteerism* (pp. 33–36). Washington, D.C.: American Association of Retired Persons.

Chan, S. (1991). *Asian Americans: An interpretive history.* Boston: Twayne Publishers.

Chang, H., & Trehub, S. (1977a). Auditory processing of relational information by young infants. *Journal of Experimental Child Psychology, 24,* 324–331.

Chang, H., & Trehub, S. (1977b). Infants' perception of temporal grouping in auditory patterns. *Child Development, 48,* 1666–1670.

Chao, R. K. (1994). Beyond parental control and authoritarian parenting style: Understanding Chinese parenting through the cultural notion of training. *Child Development, 65,* 1111–1119.

Chapman, M., & Skinner, E. A. (1989). Children's agency beliefs, cognitive performance, and conceptions of effort and ability: Individual and developmental differences. *Child Development, 60,* 1229–1238.

Chappell, N. C. (1990). Aging and social care. In R. H. Binstock & L. K. George (Eds.), *Handbook of aging and the social sciences* (3rd ed., pp. 438–454). San Diego: Academic Press.

Charbonneau, C., & Lander, P. S. (1991). Redefining sexuality: Women becoming lesbian in midlife. In B. Sang, J. Warshow, & A. J. Smith (Eds.), *Lesbians at midlife: The creative transition* (pp. 35–43). San Francisco: Spinster Book Company.

Charmaz, K. (1980). *The social reality of death.* Reading, Mass.: Addison-Wesley.

Charness, N., & Bosman, E. A. (1990). Expertise and aging: Life in the lab. In T. M. Hess (Ed.), *Aging and cognition: Knowledge, organization, and utilization* (pp. 343–385). Amsterdam: North-Holland/Elsevier.

Chasnoff, I. J., Griffith, D. R., MacGregor, S., Dirkes, K., & Burns, K. A. (1989). Temporal patterns of cocaine use in pregnancy: Perinatal outcome. *Journal of the American Medical Association, 262,* 1741–1744.

Cheatham, H. E., & Berg-Cross, L. (1992). College student development: African Americans reconsidered. Special issue: College student development. *Journal of College Student Psychotherapy, 6*(3–4), 167–191.

Cheek, D. (1974). Body composition, hormones, nutrition and growth. In M. Grumbach, G. Grave, & F. Mayer (Eds.), *Control of the onset of puberty.* New York: Wiley.

Cherry, F. (1995). *"Stubborn particulars" of social psychology: Essays on the research process.* New York: Routledge.

Chi, M. (1985). Interactive roles of knowledge and strategies in the development of organized sorting and recall. In S. Chipman, J. Segal, & R. Glaser (Eds.), *Thinking and learning skills: Vol. 2. Research and open questions* (pp. 457–483). Hillsdale, N.J.: Erlbaum.

Chi, M., Glaser, R., & Farr, M. (1989). *The nature of expertise.* Hillsdale, N.J.: Erlbaum.

Children's Defense Fund. (1992). *The state of America's children, 1992.* Washington, D.C.: Author.

Children's Defense Fund. (1993). *Progress and peril: Black children in America: A fact book and action primer.* Washington, D.C.: Author.

Children's Defense Fund. (1995). *The state of America's children.* Washington, D.C.: Author.

Chiriboga, D. A. (1989). Mental health at the midpoint: Crisis, challenge, or relief? In S. Hunter & M. Sundel (Eds.), *Midlife myths* (pp. 116–144). Newbury Park, Cal.: Sage.

Chodorow, N. (1978). *The reproduction of mothering.* Berkeley: University of California Press.

Chomsky, N. (1994). *Language and thought.* Wakefield, R.I.: Moyer Bell Publishers.

Christiansen, J. L., & Grzybowski, J. M. (1993). *Biology of aging.* St. Louis: Mosby.

Chumlea, W., Knittle, J., Roche, A., Siervogel, R., & Webb, P. (1983). Size and number of adipocytes and measures of body fat in boys and girls 10 to 18 years of age. *American Journal of Clinical Nutrition, 37.*

Cicchetti, D., & Olson, K. (1990). The developmental psychopathology of child maltreatment. In M. Lewis & S. Miller (Eds.), *Handbook of development psychopathology.* New York: Plenum Press.

Cicirelli, V. G. (1980). Sibling relationships in adulthood: A life span perspective. In L. W. Poon (Ed.), *Aging in the 1980s: Psychological issues.* Washington, D.C.: American Psychological Association.

Cicirelli, V. G. (1992). Siblings as caregivers in middle and old age. In J. W. Dwyer & R. T. Coward (Eds.), *Gender, families, and elder care* (pp. 84–101). Newbury Park, Cal.: Sage.

Cicirelli, V. G. (1994). Sibling relationships in cross-cultural perspective. *Journal of Marriage and the Family, 56,* 7–20.

Clancy, S. M., & Hoyer, W. J. (1988). Effects of age and skill on domain specific search. In V. L. Paterl, & G. J. Groen (Eds.), *Proceedings of the tenth conference of the Cognitive Science Society* (pp. 398–404). Hillsdale, N.J.: Earlbaum.

Clancy, S. M., & Hoyer, W. J. (1993). Skill and hemispheric specialization in detecting featural differences in visual images. *Brain & Cognition, 21,* 192–202.

Clark, C. S. (1993). Child sexual abuse. *CQ Researcher, 3,* 25–48.

Clark, D. O., Maddox, G. L., & Steinhauser, K. (1993). Race, aging, and functional health. *Journal of Aging and Health, 5,* 536–553.

Clarke-Stewart, K. A. (1989). Day care: Maligned or malignant? *American Psychologist, 44,* 266–273.

Clemens, A. W., & Axelson, L. (1985). The not-so-empty nest: The return of the fledgling adult. *Family Relations, 34,* 259–264.

Clopton, N. A., & Sorell, G. T. (1993). Gender differences in moral reasoning: Stable or situational. *Psychology of Women Quarterly, 17,* 85–101.

Coates, J. (1993). *Women, men, and communication* (2nd ed.). New York: Longman.

Cogan, R. (1980). Effects of childbirth preparation. *Clinical Obstetrics and Gynecology, 23,* 1–14.

Cohen, D. (1983). *Piaget: Critique and reassessment.* New York: St. Martin's press.

Cohen, G. D. (1990). Psychopathology and mental health in the mature and elderly adult. In J. E. Birren & K. W. Schaie (Eds.), *Handbook of the psychology of aging* (3rd ed., pp. 359–371). San Diego: Academic Press.

Coie, J. D., Dodge, K. A., & Coppotelli, H. (1982). Dimensions and types of social status: A cross-age perspective. *Developmental Psychology, 18,* 557–570.

Coie, J. D., Dodge, K. A., Terry, R., & Wright, V. (1991). The role of aggression in peer relations: An analysis of aggression episodes in boys' play groups. *Child Development, 62,* 812–826.

Coiro, M. (1994). *Health of our nation's children.* Hyattsville, M.B.: United States Department of Health and Human Services.

Colby, A., & Damon, W. (1992). *Some do care: Contemporary lives of moral commitment.* New York: The Free Press.

Colby, A., & Kohlberg, L. (1987). *The measurement of moral judgment.* New York: Cambridge University Press.

Colditz, G. A., Hankinson, S. E., Hunter, D. J., Willett, W. C., Manson, J. E., Stampfer, M. J., Hennekens, C., Rosner, B., & Speizer, F. E. (1995). The use of estrogens and progestins and the risk of breast cancer in postmenopausal women. *New England Journal of Medicine, 332,* 1589–1593.

Cole, E., & Rothblum, E. (1991). Lesbian sex at menopause: As good or better than ever. In B. Sang, A. Smith, & J. Warshow (Eds.), *Lesbians at midlife: The creative transition* (pp. 184–193). San Francisco: Spinsters Book Company.

Cole, M. (1990). Cultural psychology. In J. Berman (Ed.), *Nebraska symposium on motivation, 1989: Cross-cultural psychology* (pp. 279–336). Lincoln, Neb.: University of Nebraska Press.

Coleman, J. (1988). Social capital in the creation of human capital. *American Journal of Sociology, 94,* 95–120.

Coles, R. (1992). *Their eyes meeting the world: Drawings and paintings of children.* Boston: Houghton Mifflin.

Coles, R., & Stokes, G. (1985). *Sex and the American teenager.* New York: Harper & Row.

Collins, W. A. (1991). Shared views and parent-adolescent relationships. *New Directions for Child Development, 51,* 103–110.

Collins, W. A., Sobol, B., & Westby, S. (1981). Effects of adult commentary on children's comprehension and inferences about a televised aggressive portrayal. *Child Development, 52,* 158–163.

Comer, J. P., & Poussaint, A. F. (1992). *Raising black children.* New York: Plume.

Commons, M. L., & Richards, F. A. (1984a). A general model of stage theory. In M. L. Commons, F. A. Richards, & C. Armon (Eds.), *Beyond formal operations: Late adolescent and adult cognitive development* (pp. 120–140). New York: Praeger.

Commons, M. L., & Richards, F. A. (1984b). Applying the general stage model. In M. L. Commons, F. A. Richards, & C. Armon (Eds.), *Beyond formal operations: Late adolescent and adult cognitive development* (pp. 141–157). New York: Praeger.

Comstock, F. (1991). *Television and the American child.* San Diego: Academic Press.

Condie, S. (1989). Older married couples. In S. Bahr & E. Peterson (Eds.), *Aging and the family.* Lexington, Mass.: Lexington Books.

Connidis, I. A. (1992). Life transitions and the sibling tie: A qualitative study. *Journal of Marriage and the Family, 54,* 972–982.

Connidis, I. A., & Davies, L. (1990). Confidants and companions in later life: The place of family and friends. *Journal of Gerontology: Social Sciences, 45,* S141–149.

Connolly, J., White, D., Stevens, R., & Burstein, S. (1987). Adolescent self-reports of social activity: Assessment of stability and relations to social adjustment. *Journal of Adolescence, 10,* 83–95.

Cook, J. (1988). Who "mothers" the chronically mentally ill? *Family Relations, 37,* 42–49.

Cooney, T. M. (1994). Young adults' relations with parents: The influence of recent parental divorce. *Journal of Marriage and the Family, 56,* 45–56.

Cooney, T. M., & Uhlenberg, P. (1990). The role of divorce in men's relations with their adult children after mid-life. *Journal of Marriage and the Family, 52,* 677–688.

Cooper, K. L., & Gutman, D. L. (1987). Gender identity and ego mastery style in middle-aged, pre- and post-empty nest women. *The Gerontologist, 27,* 347–352.

Cooper, M. H. (1994). Regulating tobacco. *CQ Researcher, 4*(36), 844–858.

Cornelius, S. W. (1990). Aging and everyday cognitive abilities. In T. M. Hess (Ed.), *Aging and cognition: Knowledge, organization, and utilization* (pp. 411–459). Amsterdam: North-Holland/Elsevier.

Corr, C. A. (1993). Coping with dying: Lessons that we should and should not learn from the work of Elisabeth Kubler-Ross. *Death Studies, 17,* 69–83.

Corr, C. A., Nabe, C. M., & Corr, D. M. (1994). *Death and dying: Life and living.* Pacific Grove, Cal.: Brooks/Cole.

Costa, P. T., Jr., & McCrae, R. R. (1989). Personality continuity and changes of adult life. In M. Storandt & G. R. VandenBos (Eds.), *The adult years: Continuity and change* (pp. 45–77). Washington, D.C.: American Psychological Association.

Costa, P. T., Jr., McCrae, R. R., Zonderman, A. B., Barbano, H. E., Lebowitz, B., & Larson, D. M. (1986).Cross-sectional studies of personality in a national sample: 2. Stability in neuroticism, extraversion, and openness. *Psychology and Aging, 1,* 144–149.

Costa, P. T., Jr., Metter, E. J., & McCrae, R. R. (1994). Personality stability and its contribution to successful aging. *Journal of Geriatric Psychiatry, 27*(1), 41–59.

Cotman, C. W. (1990). Synaptic plasticity and transplantation in the brain. In E. L. Schneider & J. W. Rowe (Eds.), *Handbook of the biology of aging* (3rd ed., pp. 255–274). San Diego: Academic Press.

Covey, H. (1988). Historical terminology used to represent older people. *The Gerontologist, 28,* 291–297.

Cowan, C., Cowan, P., Heming, G., & Miller, N. (1991). Becoming a family: Marriage, parenting, and child development. In P. Cowan & M. Hetherington (Eds.), *Family transitions* (pp. 79–110). Hillsdale, N.J.: Erlbaum.

Cowan, G. (1984). The double standard in age discrepant relationships. *Sex Roles, 11,* 17–24.

Cowan, G., Warren, L. W., & Young, J. L. (1985). Medical perceptions of menopausal symptoms. *Psychology of Women Quarterly, 9,* 3–14.

Cowan, N. (1995). *Attention and memory.* New York: Oxford University Press.

Cowan, P. A., & Cowan, C. P. (1988). Changes in marriage during the transition to parenthood: Must we blame the baby? In G. Y. Michaels & W. A. Goldberg (Eds.), *The transition to parenthood: Current theory and research* (pp. 114–154). Cambridge, U.K.: Cambridge University Press.

Coward, R. T., & Dwyer, J. W. (1990). The association of gender, sibling network composition, and patterns of parent care by adult children. *Research on Aging, 12,* 158–181.

Cox, M. J., Owen, M. T., Henderson, V. K., & Margand, N. A. (1992). Prediction of infant-father and infant-mother attachment. *Developmental Psychology, 28,* 474–483.

Crick, N. R., & Grotpeter, J. K. (1995). Relational aggression, gender, and social-psychological adjustment. *Child Development, 66,* 710–722.

Criqui, M. H., & Ringel, B. L. (1994). Does diet or alcohol explain the French paradox? *Lancet (North American Edition), 344* (8939–8940), 1719–1723.

Crockenberg, S. B., & Litman, C. (1990). Autonomy and competence in 1-year-olds: Maternal correlates of child defiance, compliance, and self-assertion. *Developmental Psychology, 26,* 961–971.

Crockenberg, S. B., & McCluskey, K. (1986). Change in maternal behavior during the baby's first year of life. *Child Development, 57,* 746–753.

Crohan, S., & Verhoff, J. (1989). Dimensions of marital well-being among white and black newlyweds. *Journal of Marriage and the Family, 51,* 373–383.

Crosby, F. J. (1991). *Juggling: The unexpected advantages of balancing career and home for women and their families.* New York: The Free Press.

Csikszentmihalyi, M., & Larson, R. (1984). *Being adolescent: Conflict and growth in the teenage years.* New York: Basic Books.

Cuffaro, H. (1991). A view of materials as the texts of the early childhood curriculum. In B. Spodek & O. Saracho (Eds.), *Issues in early childhood curriculum* (pp. 64–85). New York: Teachers College Press.

Cumming, E., & Henry, W. E. (1961). *Grown old: The process of disengagement.* New York: Basic Books.

Cumming, R. G. (1990). Calcium intake and bone mass: A quantitative review of evidence. *Calcified Tissue International, 47,* 194–201.

Curry, G. D. & Spergel, I. (1988). Gang homicide, delinquency, and community. *Criminology, 26,* 381–405.

Cushman, P. (1991). Ideology obscured: Political uses of the self in Daniel Stern's infant. *American Psychologist, 46,* 206–219.

Cutler, S. J., & Hendricks, J. (1990). Leisure and time use across the life course. In R. H. Binstock & L. K. George (Eds.), *Handbook of aging and the social sciences* (3rd ed., pp. 169–185). San Diego: Academic Press.

Cutler, S. J., & Hodgson, L. G. (In press). Anticipatory dementia: A link between memory appraisals and concerns about developing Alzheimer's disease. *The Gerontologist.*

D'Alton, M. E., & DeCherney, A. H. (1993). Prenatal diagnosis. *New England Journal of Medicine, 32,* 114–120.

Dalton, S. T. (1992). Lived experience of never-married women. *Issues in Mental Health Nursing, 13*(2), 69–80.

Damon, W. (1983). *Social and personality development: Infancy through adolescence.* New York: Norton.

Damon, W. (1988). *The moral child.* New York: Cambridge University Press.

Damon, W., & Hart, D. (1988). *Self-understanding in childhood and adolescence.* New York: Cambridge University Press.

Dane, B. O. (1989). Middle-aged adults mourning the death of a parent. *Journal of Gerontological Social Work, 14*(3/4), 75–89.

Daniels, P., & Weingarten, K. (1982). *Sooner or later: The timing of parenthood in adult lives.* New York: Norton.

Darling, C. A., Davidson, J. K., & Passarello, L. C. (1992). The mystique of first intercourse among college youth: The role of partners, contraceptive practices, and psychological reactions. *Journal of Youth and Adolescence, 21,* 97–117.

Darling, N., & Steinberg, L. (1993). Parenting style as context: An integrative model. *Psychological Bulletin, 113,* 487–496.

Darwin, C. (1877). A biographical sketch of an infant. *Mind, 2,* 286–294.

Dattell, A. R., & Neimeyer, R. A. (1990). Sex differences in death anxiety: Testing the emotional expressiveness hypothesis. *Death Studies, 14,* 1–11.

Davajan, V., & Israel, R. (1991). Diagnosis and medical treatment of infertility. In A. L. Stanton & C. Dunkel-Schetter (Eds.), *Infertility* (pp. 17–28). New York: Plenum.

Davies, B. (1991). Accomplishment of genderedness in preschool children. In L. Weis, P. Altbach, G. Kelly, & H. Petrie (Eds.), *Critical perspectives in early childhood education.* Albany, N.Y.: State University of New York Press.

Davies, B. (1995). Sibling bereavement research: State of the art. In I. B. Corless, B. B. Germino, & M. A. Pittman (Eds.), *A challenge for living: Dying, death, and bereavement.* Boston: Jones and Bartlett Publishers.

Davis, E. (1993). Common complaints of pregnancy. In B. K. Rothman (Ed.), *The encyclopedia of childbearing.* New York: Henry Holt.

Davis-Floyd, R. E. (1986). Birth as an American rite of passage. In K. L. Michaelson (Ed.), *Childbirth in America: Anthropological perspectives.* South Hadley, Mass.: Bergin & Garvey.

DeAngelis, T. (1991, January). Living with violence: Children suffer, cope. *APA Monitor, 22,* 26–27.

DeCasper, A. J., Lecanuet, J. P., Busnel, M. C., & Granier-Deferre, C. (1994). Fetal reactions to recurrent maternal speech. *Infant Behavior and Development, 17,* 159–164.

DeCasper, A. J., & Spence, M. J. (1986). Prenatal maternal speech influences newborns' perception of speech sounds. *Infant Behavior and Development, 9,* 133–150.

Deci, E. L., & Ryan, R. M. (1987). The support of autonomy and the control of behavior. *Journal of Personality and Social Psychology, 56,* 1024–1037.

de Cubas, M. M., & Field, T. (1995). Children of methadone-dependent women: Developmental outcomes. *American Journal of Orthopsychiatry, 63,* 266–276.

DeJong, W. (1993). Obesity as a characterological stigma: The issue of responsibility and judgments of task performance. *Psychological Reports, 73,* 963–970.

DeMaris, A., & McDonald, W. (1993). Premarital cohabitation and marital instability: A test of the unconventionality hypothesis. *Journal of Marriage and the Family, 55,* 399–407.

DeMaris, A., & Rao, K. V. (1992). Premarital cohabitation and subsequent marital stability in the United States: A reassessment. *Journal of Marriage and the Family, 54,* 178–190.

Demetriou, A., & Shayer, M. (1992). Neo-Piagetian theories of cognitive development: Implications and applications for education. New York: Routledge.

Dempster, F. (1981). Memory span: Sources of individual and developmental differences. *Psychological Bulletin, 89,* 63–100.

Denney, N. W. (1989). Everyday problem solving: Methodological issues, research findings, and a model. In L. W. Poon, D. C. Rubin, & B. A. Wilson (Eds.), *Everyday cognition in adulthood and late life* (pp. 330–351). Cambridge, U.K.: Cambridge University Press.

Dennis, S. (1992). Stage and structure in the development of children's spatial reasoning. In R. Case (Ed.), *The mind's staircase* (pp. 229–245). Hillsdale, N.J.: Erlbaum.

Der-McLeod, D., & Hansen, J. C. (1992). On Lok: The family continuum. *Generations, 16*(3), 71–72.

DeRosier, M. E., Cillessen, A. H. N., Coie, J. D., & Dodge, K. A. (1994). Group social context and children's aggressive behavior. *Child Development, 65,* 1068–1079.

Desiderato, L. L., & Crawford, H. J. (1995). Risky sexual behavior in college students: Relationships between number of sexual partners, disclosure of previous risky behavior, and alcohol use. *Journal of Youth & Adolescence, 24,* 55–68.

DeSpelder, L. A., & Strickland, A. L. (1996). *The last dance: Encountering death and dying.* Mountain View, Cal.: Mayfield.

DeStefano, L., & Colasanto, D. (1990).The gender gap in America: Unlike 1975, today most Americans think men have it better. *Gallup Poll News Service, 54*(37), 1–7.

DeVries, B., Lana, R. D., & Falck, V. T. (1994). Parental bereavement over the life course: A theoretical intersection and empirical review. *Omega, 29*(1), 47–69.

Diamant, A., & Cooper, H. (1991). *Living a Jewish life.* New York: HarperPerennial.

Diamond, E. L., Jernigan, J. A., Moseley, R. A., Messina, V., & McKeown, R. A. (1989). Decision-making ability and advance directive preferences in nursing home patients and proxies. *The Gerontologist, 29,* 622–626.

Diamond, J. (1989, February). Blood, genes, and malaria. *Natural History,* 8–18.

Diamond, M. C. (1988). *Enriching heredity: The impact of the environment on the anatomy of the brain.* New York: The Free Press.

Diamond, M. C. (1993). An optimistic view of the aging brain. *Generations, 16*(1), 31–33.

Dickinson, G. E. (1992). First childhood death experiences. *Omega, 25,* 169–182.

Dishion, T. J., Andrews, D. W., & Crosby, L. (1995). Antisocial boys and their friends in early adolescence: Relationship characteristics, quality, and interactional process. *Child Development, 66,* 139–151.

Dishion, T. J., Reid, J. B., & Patterson, G. R. (1988). Empirical guidelines for a family intervention for adolescent drug use. *Journal of Chemical Dependency Treatment, 1,* 181–216.

Dishman, R. K. (1990). Determinants of participation in physical activity. In C. Bouchard, R. J. Stephens, T. Stephens, J. R. Sutton, & B. D. McPherson (Eds.), *Exercise, fitness, and health* (pp. 75–102). Champaign, Ill.: Human Kinetics.

Dodge, K. A. (1986). A social information processing model of social competence in children. In M. Perlmutter (Ed.), *Minnesota symposia on child psychology: Vol. 18.* Hillsdale, N.J.: Erlbaum.

Dodge, K. A., & Coie, J. D. (1987). Social-information-processing factors in reactive and proactive aggression in children's peer groups. *Journal of Personality and Social Psychology, 53,* 1146–1158.

Dodge, K. A., Coie, J. D., Pettit, G. S., & Price, J. M. (1990). Peer status and aggression in boys' groups: Developmental and contextual analysis. *Child Development, 61,* 1289–1309.

Dodge, K. A., Pettit, G. S., McClaskey, C. L., & Brown, M. M. (1986). Social competence in children. *Monographs of the Society for Research in Child Development, 51*(2, Serial No. 213).

Doering, C. (1980). The endocrine system. In O. G. Brim, Jr., & J. Kagan (Eds.), *Constancy and change in human development* (pp. 229–271). Cambridge, Mass.: Wiley.

Donati, T. (1995). Single parents and wider families in the new context of legitimacy. *Marriage & Family Review, 20*(1–2), 27–42.

Doren, M., & Schneider, H. P. G. (1989). Overall rationale for Hormonal Substitution Therapy after the menopause. In M. L'Hermite (Ed.), *Update on hormonal treatment in the menopause.* New York: Basel Karger.

Doty, R. L., Shaman, P., Applebaum, S. L., Giberson, R., Sikosorski, L., & Rosenberg, L. (1984). Smell identification ability: Changes with age. *Science, 226,* 1441–1443.

Dougherty, D. M. (1993). Adolescent health: Reflections on a report to the U.S. Congress. *American Psychologist, 48,* 193–201.

Douglas, J. D. (1990/1991). Patterns of change following parent death in midlife adults. *Omega, 22*(2), 123–137.

Dreyer, P. H. (1982). Sexuality during adolescence. In B. B. Wolman (Ed.), *Handbook of developmental psychology.* Englewood Cliffs, N.J.: Prentice-Hall.

Drinkwater, B. (1988). Exercise and aging: The female masters athlete. In J. L. Puhl & R. O. Voy (Eds.), *Sport science perspectives for women.* Champaign, Ill.: Human Kinetics.

Dubois, D. L., & Hirsch, B. J. (1990). School and neighborhood friendship patterns of blacks and whites in early adolescence. *Child Development, 61,* 524–536.

Dudley, J. R. (1991). Increasing our understanding of divorced fathers who have infrequent contact with their children. *Family Relations, 40,* 279–285.

Duffy, K. G. (1996). *Community psychology.* Boston: Allyn & Bacon.

Dunkel-Schetter, C., & Lobel, M. (1991). Psychological reactions to infertility. In A. L. Stanton & C. Dunkel-Schetter (Eds.), *Infertility* (pp. 29–57). New York: Plenum.

Dunn, J. (1985). *Sisters and brothers.* Cambridge, Mass.: Harvard University Press.

Dunn, J. (1988). Connections between relationships: Implications of research on mothers and siblings. In R. A. Hinde & J. Stevenson-Hinde (Eds.), *Relationships within families: Mutual influences.* Oxford: Clarendon Press.

Dunn, J., & Plomin, R. (1990). *Separate lives: Why siblings are so different.* New York: Basic Books.

Dunn, J., & Shatz, M. (1989). Becoming a conversationalist despite (or because of) having an older sibling. *Child Development, 60,* 399–410.

Dunn, J., Slomkowski, C., & Beardsall, L. (1994). Sibling relationships from the preschool period through middle childhood and early adolescence. *Developmental Psychology, 30,* 315–324.

Dunphy, D. C. (1963). The social structure of urban adolescent peer groups. *Sociometry, 26,* 230–246.

Dupont, R. L. (1988). The counselor's dilemma: Treating chemical dependence at college. In T. M. Rivinus (Ed.), *Alcoholism/chemical dependency and the college student* (pp. 41–61). New York: Haworth Press.

Durbin, D. L., Darling, N., Steinberg, L., & Brown, B. B. (1993). Parenting style and peer group membership among European-American adolescents. *Journal of Research on Adolescence, 3,* 87–100.

Durlak, J. A., & Riesenberg, L. A. (1991). The impact of death education. *Death Studies, 15,* 39–58.

Dusek, J. B. (Ed.). (1985). *Teacher expectancies.* Hillsdale, N.J.: Erlbaum.

Dusek, J. B. (1991). *Adolescent development and behavior* (2nd ed.). Englewood Cliffs, N.J.: Prentice-Hall.

Dweck, C. S., & Leggett, E. L. (1988). A social-cognitive approach to motivation and personality. *Psychological Review, 95,* 256–273.

Dyson, A. (1990). Symbol makers, symbol weavers: How children link play, pictures and print. *Young Children, 45*(2), 50–57.

Eagle, M. (1984). *Recent developments in psychoanalysis: A critical evaluation.* New York: McGraw-Hill.

Eakins, P. S. (1993, September). Obstetric outcomes at the birth place in Menlo Park: The first seven years. *Birth, 16,* 123–129.

Earle, J. (1990). *Keeping pregnant and parenting teens in school.* Alexandria, Va.: National Association of State Boards of Education.

Early, K. E., & Akers, R. L. (1993). "It's a white thing": An exploration of beliefs about suicide in the African-American community. *Deviant Behavior, 14*(4), 277–296.

East, M. C., & Steele, P. R. M. (1987). Inhaling heroin during pregnancy: Effects on the baby. *British Medical Journal, 296,* 754.

Eccles, J. S. (1993). Development during adolescence: The impact of stage-environment fit on young adolescents' experiences in schools and families. *American Psychologist, 48,* 90–101.

Eccles, J. S., & Harold, R. D. (1993). Parent-school involvement during the early adolescent years. *Teachers College Record, 94,* 568–587.

Eccles, J. S., Midgley, C., Wigfeld, A., Buchanan, C. M., Reuman, D., Flanagan, C., & MacIver, D. (1993). Development during adolescence: The impact of stage-environment fit on young adolescents' experiences in schools and families. *American Psychologist, 48,* 90–101.

Eckerman, C. O., Davis, C. C., & Didow, S. M. (1989). Toddlers' emerging ways of achieving social coordinations with a peer. *Child Development, 60,* 440–453.

Eder, D., & Hallinan, M. (1978). Sex differences in children's friendships. *American Sociological Review, 43,* 237–250.

Editors of the University of California at Berkeley Wellness Letter. (1995). *The new wellness encyclopedia.* Boston: Houghton Mifflin.

Edmondson, B., Waldrop, J., Crispell, D., & Jacobsen, L. (1993). Single parents. *American Demographics, 15*(12), 36–37.

Edwards, C., Gandini, L., & Furman, G. (Eds.). (1993). *The hundred languages of children.* Norwood, N.J.: Ablex.

Egeland, B. (1988). The consequences of physical and emotional neglect on the development of young children. In A. Cowan (Ed.), *Child neglect.* Washington, D.C.: National Center on Child Abuse and Neglect.

Eifermann, R. (1971). Social play in childhood. In R. Heffon & B. Sutton-Smith (Eds.), *Child's play.* New York: Wiley.

Eisenberg, N., & Fabes, R. A. (1992). Emotion, self-regulation, and social competence. In M. Clark (Ed.), *Review of personality and social psychology. Vol. 14: Emotion and social behavior* (pp. 119–150). Newbury Park, Cal.: Sage.

Eisenberg, N., Fabes, R. A., Nyman, M., Bernzweig, J., & Pinuelas, A. (1994). The relations of emotionality and regulation to children's anger-related reactions. *Child Development, 65,* 109–128.

Eisenberg, N., Fabes, R. A., Schaller, M., & Miller, P. (1989). Sympathy and personal distress: Development, gender differences, and interrelations of indices. In N. Eisenberg (Ed.), *Empathy and related emotional responses: New directions for child development* (pp. 107–126). San Francisco: Jossey-Bass.

Eisenberg, N., Hertz-Lazarowitz, R., & Fuchs, I. (1990). Prosocial moral judgment in Israeli kibbutz and city children: A longitudinal study. *Merrill Palmer Quarterly, 36,* 273–285.

Eisenbruch, M. (1984). Cross-cultural aspects of bereavement. II: Ethnic and cultural variations in the development of bereavement practices. *Culture, Medicine & Psychiatry, 8,* 315–347.

Ekelund, L-G., Haskell, W. L., Johnson, J., Whaley, F. S., Criqui, M. H., & Sheps, D. S. (1988). Physical fitness as a predictor of cardiovascular mortality in asymptomatic American men. *New England Journal of Medicine, 319,* 1379–1384.

Elbers, E., Wiegersma, S., Brand, N., & Vroon, P. (1991). Response alternation as an artifact in conservation research. *Journal of Genetic Psychology, 152,* 47–56.

Elias, M. F., Elias, J. W., & Elias, P. K. (1990). Biological and health influences on behavior. In J. E. Birren & K. W. Schaie (Eds.), *Handbook of the psychology of aging* (3rd ed., pp. 79–102). San Diego: Academic Press.

Elkind, D. (1985). Egocentrism redux. *Developmental Review, 5,* 218–226.

Elkind, D. (1994a). *A sympathetic understanding of the child* (3rd ed.). Boston: Allyn & Bacon.

Elkind, D. (1994b). *Ties that stress: The new family imbalance.* Cambridge, Mass.: Harvard University Press.

Ellis, J. (1993). *The passionate sage: The character and legacy of John Adams.* New York: Norton.

Ellis, S., Rogoff, B., & Cromer, C. (1981). Age segregation in children's social interactions. *Developmental Psychology, 17,* 399–407.

Emery, R. E. (1989). Family violence. *American Psychologist, 44,* 321–328.

Emmerich, W., & Sheppard, K. (1982). Development of sex-differentiated preferences during late childhood and adolescence. *Developmental Psychology, 18,* 407–417.

Endres, J., & Rockwell, R. (1993). *Food, nutrition, and the young child* (4th ed.). Columbus, Ohio: Merrill.

Engels, J. (1993). *Pocket guide to pediatric assessment* (2nd ed.). St. Louis: Mosby.

Engstrom, M., Greene, R., & O'Connor, M. C. (1993). Adult daycare for persons with dementia: A viable community option. *Generations, 17*(1), 75–76.

Epstein, L. H., & Wing, R. R. (1987). Behavioral treatment of childhood obesity. *Psychological Bulletin, 101,* 331–342.

Erikson, E. H. (1963). *Childhood and society* (2nd ed.). New York: Norton.

Erikson, E. H. (1968). *Identity, youth and crisis.* New York: Norton.

Erikson, E. H. (1975). "Identity Crisis" in autobiographical perspective. In E. Erikson, *Life history and the historical moment.* New York: Norton.

Erikson, E. H., & Erikson, J. M. (1981). Generativity and identity. *Harvard Educational Review, 51,* 249–269.

Erikson, E. H., Erikson, J. M., & Kivnick, H. Q. (1986). *Vital involvement in old age.* New York: Norton.

Eron, L. D. (1987). The development of aggressive behavior from the perspective of a developing behaviorism. *American Psychologist, 42,* 435–442.

Ervin-Tripp, S. (1989). Sisters and brothers. In P. Zurkow (Ed.), *Sibling interaction across cultures: Theoretical and methodological issues* (pp. 184–196). New York: Springer-Verlag.

Essex, M. J., & Nam, S. (1987). Marital status and loneliness among older women: The differential importance of close family and friends. *Journal of Marriage and the Family, 49,* 93–106.

Ettelbrick, P. (1991). Legal protections for lesbians. In B. Sang, J. Warshow, & A. J. Smith (Eds.), *Lesbians at midlife: A creative transition* (pp. 258–264). San Francisco: Spinsters Book Company.

Evans, W. J., & Meredith, C. N. (1989). Exercise and nutrition in the elderly. In H. N. Munro & D. E. Danford (Eds.), *Nutrition, aging and the elderly.* New York: Plenum.

Eveleth, P., & Tanner, J. (1990). *Worldwide variation in human growth* (2nd ed.). New York: Cambridge University Press.

Eysenck, H. J. (1990). Type A behavior and coronary heart disease: The third stage. *Journal of Social Behavior and Personality, 5,* 25–44.

Eysenck, H. J. (in press). Smoking, personality and stress as risk factors for cancer and coronary heart disease.

Faber, N. B. (1991). The process of pregnancy resolution among adolescent mothers. *Adolescence, 26,* 697–716.

Fabes, R. A., & Eisenberg, N. (1992). Young children's coping with interpersonal anger. *Child Development, 63,* 116–128.

Fabes, R. A., Eisenberg, N., McCormick, S. E., & Wilson, M. S. (1988). Preschoolers' attributions of the situational determinants of others' naturally occurring emotions. *Developmental Psychology, 24,* 376–385.

Fabrikant, G. (1996). The young and restless audience: Computers, cable and videos cut into children's TV-watching time. In press.

Fagot, B. I. (1982). Adults as socializing agents. In T. Field, A. Huston, H. Quay, L. Troll, & G. Finley (Eds.), *Review of human development*. New York: Wiley.

Fagot, B. I. (1994). Peer relations and the development of competence in boys and girls. In C. Leaper (Ed.), *Childhood gender segregation: Causes and consequences: New directions for child development* (pp. 53–66). San Francisco: Jossey-Bass.

Fagot, B. I., & Hagan, R. (1991). Observations of parent reactions to sex-stereotyped behaviors: Age and sex effects. *Child Development, 62,* 617–628.

Fagot, B. I., & Leinbach, M. D. (1989). The young child's gender schema: Environmental input, internal organization. *Child Development, 60,* 663–672.

Fagot, B. I., Leinbach, M. D., & O'Boyle, C. (1992). Gender labeling, gender stereotyping, and parenting behaviors. *Developmental Psychology, 28,* 225–230.

Falkner, F., & Tanner, J. (Eds.). (1986). *Human growth: Vol. 3. Methodological, ecological, genetic and nutritional effects on growth.* New York: Plenum Press.

Fangos, J. H., & Nickerson, B. G. (1991). Long-term effects of sibling death during adolescence. *Journal of Adolescent Research, 6,* 70–82.

Fantz, R. (1963). Pattern vision in newborn infants. *Science, 140,* 296–297.

Farrangy, P., Steele, H., & Steele, M. (1991). Maternal representations of attachment during pregnancy predict the organization of infant-mother attachment at one year of age. *Child Development, 62,* 891–905.

Farrell, M. P., & Rosenberg, S. D. (1981). *Men at midlife.* Boston: Auburn House.

Farver, J. M., & Branstetter, W. H. (1994). Preschoolers' prosocial responses to their peers' distress. *Developmental Psychology, 30,* 334–341.

Faust, M. S. (1977). Somatic development in adolescent girls. *Monographs of the Society for Research on Child Development,* No. 169.

Fedele, N. M., Golding, E. R., Grossman, F. K., & Pollack, W. S. (1988). Psychological issues in adjustment to first parenthood. In G. Y. Michaels & W. A. Goldberg (Eds.), *The transition to parenthood: Current theory and research* (pp. 85–113). Cambridge, U.K.: Cambridge University Press.

Federal Bureau of Investigation. (1991, August). *Uniform crime reports for the United States.* Washington, D.C.: U.S. Department of Justice.

Feifel, H. (1990). Psychology and death: Meaningful rediscovery. *American Psychologist, 45,* 537–543.

Feinbloom, R. I., & Forman, B. Y. (1987). *Pregnancy, birth and the early months: A complete guide.* Reading, Mass.: Addison-Wesley.

Feinson, M. (1987). Mental health and aging: Are there gender differences? *The Gerontologist, 27,* 703–711.

Feld, S., Ruhland, D., & Gold, M. (1979). Developmental changes in achievement motivation. *Merrill-Palmer Quarterly, 25,* 43–60.

Ferholt, J. B. (1991). Psychodynamic parent psychotherapy: Treating the parent-child relationship. In M. Lewis (Ed.), *Comprehensive textbook of child psychiatry.* New York: Saunders.

Ferketich, S. L., & Mercer, R. T. (1995). Paternal-infant attachment of experienced and inexperienced fathers during infancy. *Nursing Research, 44,* 31–37.

Fernandez, J. P. (1988). Human resources and the extraordinary problems minorities face. In M. London & E. M. Mone (Eds.), *Career growth and human resource strategy* (pp. 227–239). New York: Quorum.

Field, D. (1987). A review of preschool conservation training. *Developmental Review, 7,* 210–251.

Field, D., & Millsap, R. E. (1991). Personality in advanced old age: Continuity or change? *Journal of Gerontology: Psychological Sciences, 46,* P299–308.

Field, J. (1987). Development of auditory-visual localization in infants. In B. McKenzie & R. Day (Eds.), *Perceptual development in early infancy* (pp. 175–198). Hillsdale, N.J.: Erlbaum.

Field, T., & Roopnarine, J. (1982) Infant-peer interactions. In T. Field (Ed.), *Review of human development.* New York: Wiley.

Fine, G. A. (1982). Friends, impression management, and preadolescent behavior. In S. Asher & J. Gottman (Eds.), *The development of children's friendships.* New York: Cambridge University Press.

Fine, G. A., Mortimer, J. T., & Roberts, D. F. (1990). Leisure, work, and the mass media. In S. Feldman & G. Elliott (Eds.), *At the threshold: The developing adolescent* (pp. 225–252). Cambridge, Mass.: Harvard University Press.

Fine, M. (1986).Why urban adolescents drop into and out of high school: The ideology of school and work. *Teachers College Record, 87,* 393–409.

Fine, M. (1991). *Framing dropouts: Notes on the politics of 84 urban public high schools.* New York: State University of New York Press.

Fine, M., & Kurdek, L. A. (1992). The adjustment of adolescents in stepfather and stepmother families. *Journal of Marriage and the Family, 54,* 725–736.

Finkelhor, D. (1995). The victimization of children: A developmental perspective. *American Journal of Orthopsychiatry, 65,* 177–193.

Fischer, D. H. (1977). *Growing old in America.* New York: Oxford University Press.

Fischer, K. (1980). A theory of cognitive development: The control and construction of hierarchies of skills. *Psychological Review, 87,* 477–531.

Fischer, K., & Pipp, S. L. (1984a). The process of stage transition: A neo-Piagetian view. In R. Sternberg (Ed.), *Mechanisms of cognitive development.* San Francisco: Freeman.

Fischer, K., & Pipp, S. L. (1984b). Processes of cognitive development: Optimal level and skill acquisition. In R. J. Sternberg (Ed.), *Mechanisms of cognitive development* (pp. 45–90). New York: Freeman.

Fischer, K., Shaver, P., & Carnochan, P. (1990). How emotions develop and how they organize development. *Cognition and Emotion, 4,* 81–127.

Fischer, L. R., Mueller, D. P., & Cooper, P. W. (1991). Older volunteers: A discussion of the Minnesota Senior Study. *The Gerontologist, 31,* 183–194.

Fish, M., Stifter, C. A., & Belsky, J. (1993). Early patterns of mother-infant dyadic integrations: Infant, mother, and family demographic antecedents. *Infant Behavior and Development, 16,* 1–18.

Fisher, J. C. (1986). Participation in educational activities by active older adults. *Adult Education Quarterly, 36*(4), 202–210.

Fitzgerald, H., Lester, B., & Zuckerman, B. (1994). *Children of poverty: Research, health, and policy issues.* New York: Garland.

Flanagan, C. A. (1990). Change in family work status: Effects on parent-adolescent decision making. *Child Development, 61,* 163–177.

Flavell, J., Green, F., & Flavell, E. (1986). Development of knowledge about the appearance-reality distinction. With commentaries by M. Watson & J. Campione. *Monographs of the Society for Research on Child Development, 51*(1, Serial No. 212).

Flavell, J., Green, F., & Flavell, E. (1995). Young children's knowledge about thinking. *Monographs of the Society for Research on Child Development* 60 (1, Serial No. 243).

Fleming, R., Leventhal, H., Glynn, K., & Ershler, J. (1989). The role of cigarettes in the initiation and progression of early substance use. *Addictive Behaviors, 14,* 261–272.

Fletcher, A. C., Darling, N. E., Steinberg, L., & Dornbusch, S. M. (1995). The company they keep: Relation of adolescents' adjustment and behavior to their friends' perceptions of authoritative parenting in the social network. *Developmental Psychology, 31,* 300–310.

Flint, M., & Samil, R. S. (1990). Cultural and subcultural meanings of the menopause. In M. Flint, F. Kronenberg, & W. Utian (Eds.), *Annals of the New York Academy of Sciences, 592* (pp. 134–148). New York: New York Academy of Sciences.

Floyd, M. F., Shinew, K. J., McGuire, F. A., & Noe, F. P. (1994). Race, class, and leisure activity preferences: Marginality and ethnicity revisited. *Journal of Leisure Research, 26,* 158–173.

Folsom, A. R., Cook, T. C., Sprafka, J. M., & Burke, G. L. (1991). Differences in leisure-time physical activity levels between Blacks and Whites in population-based samples: The Minnesota Heart Survey. *Journal of Behavioral Medicine, 14,* 1–9.

Forrest-Pressley, D., Mackinnon, G., and Waller, T. (1985). *Metacognition, cognition and human performance.* Orlando: Academic Press.

Foster, S. (1990). *The communicative competence of young children: A modular approach.* New York: Longman.

Fowler, J. W. (1986). Faith and the structuring of meaning. In C. Dykstra & S. Parks (Eds.), *Faith development and Fowler* (pp. 15–42). Birmingham, Ala.: Religious Education Press.

Fowler, J. W. (1991). *Stages of faith and religious development.* New York: Crossroads Press.

Fox, N. A., Kimmerly, N. L., & Schafer, W. D. (1991). Attachment to mother/attachment to father: A meta-analysis. *Child Development, 62,* 210–225.

Frank, E. S. (1991). Shame and guilt in eating disorders. *American Journal of Orthopsychiatry, 61,* 303–306.

Frank, E., Anderson, A., & Rubenstein, D. (1978). Frequency of sexual dysfunction in "normal" couples. *New England Journal of Medicine, 299,* 111–115.

Franz, C. E., McClelland, D. C., & Weinberger, J. (1991). Childhood antecedents of conventional social accomplishment in midlife adults: A 36-year prospective study. *Journal of Personality and Social Psychology, 60,* 586–595.

Franz, W., & Reardon, D. (1992). Differential impact of abortion on adolescents and adults. *Adolescence, 27,* 161–172.

Fraser, A. M., Brochert, J. E., & Ward, R. H. (1995). Association of young maternal age with adverse reproductive outcomes. *New England Journal of Medicine, 332,* 113.

Freedman, D. (1976). Infancy, biology, and culture. In L. P. Lipsitt (Ed.), *Developmental psychobiology: The significance of infancy.* New York: Wiley.

Freedman, V. A. (1993). Kin and nursing home lengths of stay: A backward recurrence time approach. *Journal of Health and Social Behavior, 34,* 138–152.

French, D. C. (1984). Children's knowledge of the social functions of younger, older, and same-aged peers. *Child Development, 55,* 1429–1433.

French, J., & Rhodes, C. (1992). *Teaching thinking skills: Theory and practice* (2nd ed.). New York: Garland.

Freud, S. (1983). *A general introduction to psychoanalysis* (rev. ed.). New York: Washington Square Press.

Frezza, M., DiPadova, C., Pozzato, G., Terpin, M., Baraona, E, & Lieber, C. S. (1990). High blood alcohol levels in women. *New England Journal of Medicine, 322*(2), 95–99.

Friedman, G. D., Tekawa, I., Klatsky, A. L., Sidney, S., & Armstrong, M. A. (1991). Alcohol drinking and cigarette smoking: An exploration of the association in middle-aged men and women. *Drug and Alcohol Dependence, 27,* 283–290.

Friedman, H. S., Tucker, J. S., Schwartz, J. E., Tomlinson-Keasy, C., Martin, L. R., Wingard, D. L., & Criqui, M. H. (1995). Psychosocial and behavioral predictors of longevity: The aging and death of the "Termites." *American Psychologist, 50,* 69–78.

Friend, R. A. (1990). Older lesbian and gay people: A theory of successful aging. *Journal of Homosexuality, 20,* 99–118.

Fries, J. F., & Crapo, L. M. (1981). *Vitality and aging.* San Francisco: Freeman.

Frieze, I., Francis, W., & Hanusa, B. (1981). Defining success in classroom settings. In J. Levine & M. Wang (Eds.), *Teacher and student perceptions.* Hillsdale, N.J.: Erlbaum.

Frisch, R. (1983). Fatness, puberty, and fertility: The effects of nutrition and athletic training on menarche and ovulation. In J. Brooks-Gunn & A. Peterson (Eds.), *Puberty in girls: Biological and psychological perspectives.* New York: Plenum Press.

Frontera, W. R., & Meredith, C. N. (1989). Strength training in the elderly. In R. Harris & S. Harris (Eds.), *Physical activity, aging and sports* (pp. 319–331). Albany, N.Y.: Center for the Study of Aging.

Frost, A. K., & Pakiz, B. (1990). The effects of marital disruption on adolescents: Time as a dynamic. *American Journal of Orthopsychiatry, 60,* 544–555.

Fry, J. (1974). *Common diseases: Their nature, incidence, and care.* Philadelphia: Lippincott.

Fuhrman, T., & Holmbeck, G. N. (1995). A contextual-moderator analysis of emotional autonomy and adjustment in adolescence. *Child Development, 66,* 793–811.

Fuligni, A. J. & Eccles, J. S. (1993). Perceived parent-child relationships and early adolescent's orientation toward peers. *Developmental Psychology, 29,* 622–632.

Furman, W. (1982). Children's friendships. In T. Field (Ed.), *Review of human development.* New York: Wiley.

Furman, W. (1989). The development of children's social networks. In D. Belle (Ed.), *Children's social networks and social supports.* New York: Wiley.

Furman, W., & Bierman, K. L. (1983). Developmental changes in young children's conceptions of friendship. *Child Development, 54,* 549–556.

Furman, W., & Bierman, K. L. (1984). Children's conceptions of friendship: A multidimensional study of developmental changes. *Developmental Psychology, 20,* 925–931.

Furman, W., & Buhrmester, D. (1992). Age and sex differences in perceptions of networks of personal friendships. *Child Development, 63,* 103–115.

Furman, W., Jones, L., Buhrmester, D., & Adler, T. (1989). Children's, parents', and observers' perspectives on sibling relationships. In P. G. Zukow (Ed.), *Sibling interaction across cultures* (pp. 165–183). New York: Springer-Verlag.

Furstenberg, F. F., Jr., Brooks-Gunn, J., & Chase-Lansdale, L. (1989). Teenaged pregnancy and childbearing. *American Psychologist, 44,* 313–320.

Furstenberg, F. F., Jr., & Cherlin, A. J. (1991). *Divided families: What happens to children when parents part?* Cambridge, Mass.: Harvard University Press.

Furstenberg, F. F., Jr., Spanier, G., & Rothschild, N. (1982). Patterns of parenting in the transition from divorce to remarriage. In P. Berman & E. Ramey (Eds.), *Women: A developmental perspective.* Washington, D.C.: National Institutes of Health.

Gagnon, J. H., Laumann, E. O., & Michael, R. T. (1994). *The social organization of sexuality.* Chicago: University of Chicago Press.

Galambos, N. L., & Maggs, J. L. (1991). Out-of-school care of young adolescents and self-reported behavior. *Developmental Psychology, 27,* 644–655.

Galinsky, E. (1987). *The six stages of parenthood.* Reading, Mass.: Addison-Wesley.

Gallagher, J. (1993). Comments on McDaniel's "Education of the Gifted and the Excellence-Equity Debate." In J. Maker (Ed.), *Programs for the gifted in regular classrooms* (pp. 19–22). Austin, Tex.: Pro-Ed Publishers.

Gallagher, J., & Gallagher, S. (1994). *Teaching the gifted child* (4th ed). Boston: Allyn & Bacon.

Gallagher, S. K., & Gerstel, N. (1993). Kinkeeping and friend keeping among older women: The effect of marriage. *The Gerontologist, 33,* 675–681.

Gallagher-Thompson, D., Futterman, A., Farberow, N., Thompson, L. W., & Peterson, J. (1993). The impact of spousal bereavement on older widows and widowers. In M. S. Stroebe, W. Stroebe, & R. O. Hansson (Eds.), *Handbook of bereavement: Theory, research, and intervention* (pp. 227–254). Cambridge, U.K.: Cambridge University Press.

Gallaway, C., & Richards, B. (1994). *Input and interaction in language acquisition.* New York: Cambridge University Press.

Gallos, J. V. (1993). Women's experiences and ways of knowing: Implications for teaching and learning in the organizational behavior classroom. *Journal of Management Education, 17,* 7–26.

Galotti, K. M. (1989). Gender differences in self-reported moral reasoning: A review and new evidence. *Journal of Youth and Adolescence, 18,* 475–488.

Gannon, L. R. (1985). *Menstrual disorders and menopause.* New York: Praeger.

Ganong, L. H., & Coleman, M. (1987). Effects of parental remarriage on children: An updated comparison of theories, methods, and findings from clinical and empirical research. In K. Pasley & M. Ihinger-Tallman (Eds.), *Remarriage and stepparenting: Current research and theory* (pp. 94–140). New York: Guilford Press.

Ganong, L. H., & Coleman, M. (1993a). A meta-analytic comparison of the self-esteem and behavior problems of stepchildren to children in other family structures. *Journal of Divorce & Remarriage, 19*(3–4), 143–163.

Ganong, L. H., & Coleman, M. (1993b). An exploratory study of stepsibling subsystems. *Journal of Divorce & Remarriage, 19*(3–4), 125–141.

Ganong, L. H., Coleman, M., & Maples, D. (1990). A meta-analytic review of family structure stereotypes. *Journal of Marriage and the Family, 52,* 287–297.

Garbarino, J. (1982). Sociocultural risk: Dangers to competence. In C. Kopp & J. Krakow (Eds.), *Child development in a social context.* Reading, Mass.: Addison-Wesley.

Garbarino, J. (1992a). *Children and families in the social environment* (2nd ed.). New York: Aldine de Gruyter.

Garbarino, J. (1992b). *Children in danger.* New York: Jossey-Bass.

Garbarino, J. (1993). Reinventing fatherhood. *Families in Society, 74,* 52–54.

Garbarino, J., & Kostelny, K. (1996). The effects of political violence on Palestinian children's behavior problems: A risk accumulation model. *Child Development, 67,* 33–45.

Garbarino, J., Kostelny, K., & Dubrow, N. (1991). What children can tell us about living in danger. *American Psychologist, 46,* 376–383.

Gardner, H. (1990). *Frames of mind: The theory of multiple intelligences.* New York: Basic Books.

Gardner, H. (1993a). *Frames of mind: The theory of multiple intelligences* (2nd rev. ed.). New York: Basic Books.

Gardner, H. (1993b). *Multiple intelligences: Theory in practice.* New York: Basic Books.

Garfinkel, L. (1991). The epidemiology of cancer in black Americans. *Statistical Bulletin, 72*(2), 11–17.

Garland, A. F., & Zigler, E. (1993). Adolescent suicide prevention: Current research and social policy. *American Psychologist, 48,* 169–182.

Garner, P. W., Jones, D. C., & Palmer, D. J. (1994). Social cognitive correlates of preschool children's sibling caregiving behavior. *Developmental Psychology, 30,* 906–911.

Gavin, L., & Furman, W. (1989). Age differences in adolescents' perceptions of their peer groups. *Developmental Psychology, 25,* 827–834.

Gecas, V., & Seff, M. A. (1990). Families and adolescents: A review of the 1980s. *Journal of Marriage and the Family, 52,* 941–958.

Gee, E. M. (1991). The transition to grandmotherhood: A quantitative study. *Canadian Journal on Aging, 10,* 254–270.

Gelles, R. J., & Cornell, C. P. (1983). *International perspectives on family violence.* Lexington, Mass.: D. C. Heath.

Gelman, R., & Greeno, J. (1988). On the nature of competence: Principles for understanding in a domain. In L. Resnick (Ed.), *Knowing and learning: Issues for a cognitive science of instruction* (pp. 125–186). Hillsdale, N.J.: Erlbaum.

Gentile, M., & Fello, M. (1990). Hospice care for the 1990s: A concept coming of age. *Journal of Home Health Care Practice, 3,* 1–15.

Gerbner, G., Gross, L., Signorielli, N., & Morgan, M. (1986). *Television's world: Violence profile No. 14–15.* University of Pennsylvania, Annenberg School of Communications, Philadelphia.

Gergen, M. M. (1990). Finished at 40. *Psychology of Women Quarterly, 14,* 471–493.

Gerson, K. (1985). *Hard choices: How women decide about work, career, and motherhood.* Berkeley, Cal.: University of California Press.

Gerson, M., Berman, L. S., & Morris, A. M. (1991). The value of having children as an aspect of adult development. *Journal of Genetic Psychology, 152*(3), 327–339.

Gesell, A. (1926). *The mental growth of the preschool child* (2nd ed.). New York: Macmillan.

Gianino, A., & Tronick, E. Z. (1988). The mutual regulation model: The infant's self and interactive regulation coping and defense. In T. Field, P. McCabe, & N. Schneiderman (Eds.), *Stress and coping* (pp. 47–68). Hillsdale, N.J.: Erlbaum.

Gibeau, J. L., & Anastas, J. (1989). Breadwinners and caregivers: Interviews with working women. *Journal of Gerontological Social Work, 14,* 19–40.

Gibson, R. C. (1986). Blacks in an aging society. *Daedalus, 115*(1), 349–371.

Gibson, R. C. (1991). The subjective retirement of black Americans. *Journal of Gerontology: Social Sciences, 46,* S204–209.

Gibson, R. C., & Burns, C. J. (1991). The health, labor force, and retirement experiences of aging minorities. *Generations, 15*(4), 31–35.

Gibson, E., & Walk, R. (1960). The visual cliff. *Scientific American, 202,* 64–71.

Gilbert, A. N., & Wysocki, C. J. (1987). The results: Smell survey. *National Geographic, 172,* 514–525.

Giles, H., & Coupland, N. (1991). Language attitudes: Discursive, contextual, and gerontological considerations. In A. Reynolds (Ed.), *Bilingualism, multiculturalism, and second language learning* (pp. 21–42). Hillsdale, N.J.: Erlbaum.

Giles-Sims, J., & Crosbie-Burnett, M. (1989). Adolescent power in stepfather families. *Journal of Marriage and the Family, 51,* 1065–1078.

Gillialand, F. D., Becker, T. M., Key, C. R., & Samet, J. M. (1994, May 30). Contrasting trends of prostate cancer incidence and mortality in New Mexico's Hispanics, non-Hispanic whites, American Indians, and blacks. *Cancer Researcher Weekly,* p. 24.

Gilligan, C. (1982). *In a different voice: Psychological theory and women's development.* Cambridge, Mass.: Harvard University Press.

Gilligan, C. (1987). Adolescent development reconsidered. In C. Irwin (Ed.), *Adolescent social behavior and health.* San Francisco: Jossey-Bass.

Gilligan, C. (1990). Teaching Shakespeare's sister: Notes from the underground of female adolescence. In C. Gilligan, N. Lyons, & T. Hanmer (Eds.), *The relational worlds of adolescent girls at Emma Willard School* (pp. 6–29). Cambridge, Mass.: Harvard University Press.

Gilligan, C., & Attanucci, J. (1988). Two moral orientations: Gender differences and similarities. *Merrill-Palmer Quarterly, 34,* 223–237.

Gilligan, C., & Wiggins, G. (1987). The origins of morality in early childhood relationships. In J. Kagan & S. Lamb (Eds.), *The emergence of morality in young children* (pp. 277–305). Chicago: University of Chicago Press.

Ginsburg, G. S., & Bronstein, P. (1993). Family factors related to children's intrinsic/extrinsic motivational orientation in academic performance. *Child Development, 64,* 1461–1474.

Giordano, P. C., Cernkovich, S. A., & Demaris, A. (1993). The family and peer relations of black adolescents. *Journal of Marriage and the Family, 55,* 277–287.

Gitlin, M. J., & Pasnau, R. O. (1989). Psychiatric syndromes linked to reproductive function in women : A review of current knowledge. *American Journal of Psychiatry, 146,* 1413–1422.

Glaser, R., Rice, J., Speicher, C. E., Stout, J. C., & Kiecolt-Glaser, J. K. (1986). Stress depresses interferon production by leukocytes concomitant with a decrease in natural killer cell activity. *Behavioral Neuroscience, 100,* 675–678.

Glaser, R., Thorn, B. E., Tarr, K. L., Kiecolt-Glaser, J. K., & D'Ambrosio, S. M. (1985). Effects of stress on methyltranferase synthesis: An important DNA enzyme. *Health Psychology, 4,* 403–412.

Glass, J. C., Jr. (1990). Changing death anxiety through education in the public schools. *Death Studies, 14,* 31–52.

Glass, J. C., Jr. (1991). Death, loss, and grief among middle school children: Implications for the school counselor. *Elementary School Guidance and Counseling, 26,* 139–148.

Glasser, W. (1967) *Reality therapy.* New York: Harper & Row.

Glenn, N. D. (1991). The recent trend in marital success in the United States. *Journal of Marriage and the Family, 53,* 261–270.

Glick, P. C., & Lin, S. L. (1986). More young adults are living with their parents: Who are they? *Journal of Marriage and the Family, 48,* 107–112.

Glick, P. C., & Lin, S. L. (1987). Remarriage after divorce: Recent changes and demographic variations. *Sociological Perspectives, 30,* 162–179.

Goggin, J. M. (1992). Elderhostel: The next generation. *Aging Today, 13*(2), 8.

Gold, D. T. (1990). Late-life sibling relationships: Does race affect typological distribution? *The Gerontologist, 30,* 741–748.

Gold, J. M., Bubenzer, D. L., & West, J. D. (1993). Differentiation from ex-spouses and stepfamily marital intimacy. *Journal of Divorce & Remarriage, 19*(3–4), 83–95.

Golden, C. (1994). Our politics and choices: The feminist movement and sexual orientation. In B. Greene & G. M. Herek (Eds.), *Lesbian and gay psychology: Theory, research, and clinical applications* (pp. 54–70). Thousand Oaks, Cal.: Sage.

Goldscheider, C., & Goldscheider, F. (1987). Moving out and marriage: What do adults expect? *American Sociological Review, 52,* 278–285.

Goldscheider, C., & Goldscheider, F. (1989). Family structure and conflict: Nest leaving expectations of young adults and their parents. *Journal of Marriage and the Family, 51,* 87–97.

Goldscheider, F. K., & DaVanzo, J. (1986). Semiautonomy and transition to adulthood. *Social Forces, 65,* 187–201.

Goldscheider, F. K., & Goldscheider, C. (1991). The intergenerational flow of income: Family structure and the status of black Americans. *Journal of Marriage and the Family, 53,* 499–508.

Goldson, E. (1992). The longitudinal study of very low birthweight infants and its implications for interdisciplinary research and public policy. In C. Greenbaum & J. Auerbach (Eds.), *Longitudinal studies of children at psychological risk: Cross- national perspectives* (pp. 43–64). Norwood, N.J.: Ablex.

Goldsteen, K., & Ross, C. E. (1989). The perceived burden of children. *Journal of Family Issues, 10,* 504–526.

Goldstein, A. P., & Soriano, F. I. (1994). Delinquent gangs. In L. Eron & J. Gentry (Eds.), *Violence and youth: Psychology's response: Vol. II. Papers of the American Psychological Association on Violence and Youth.* Washington, DC: American Psychological Association.

Goldstein, S., Field, T., & Healy, B. T. (1989). Concordance of play behavior and physiology in preschool friends. *Journal of Applied Developmental Psychology, 10,* 3337–3351.

Goleman, D. (1994, April 26). Mental decline in aging need not be inevitable. *New York Times,* pp. C1, C10.

Golombok, S., Cook, R., Bish, A., & Clare, M. (1995). Families created by the new reproductive technologies: Quality of parenting and social and emotional development of the children. *Child Development, 66,* 285–298.

Golombok, S., & Tasker, F. (1996). Do parents influence the sexual orientation of their children? Findings from a longitudinal study of lesbian females. *Developmental Psychology, 32,* 3–11.

Gonzalez, G. M. (1989). Early onset of drinking as a predictor of alcohol consumption and alcohol-related problems in college. *Journal of Drug Education, 19,* 225–230.

Good for business: Making full use of the nation's human capital. (1995). A fact-finding report of the Federal Glass Ceiling Commission, Washington, D.C.

Goodnow, J. J. (1976). The nature of intelligent behavior: Questions raised by cross-cultural studies. In L. B. Resnick (Ed.), *The nature of intelligence.* Hillsdale, N.J.: Erlbaum.

Goodnow, J. J. (1996). From household practices to parents' ideas about work and interpersonal relationships. In S. Harkness & C. Super (Eds.), *Parents' cultural belief systems: Their origins, expressions, and consequences.* New York: Guildford Press.

Goodnow, J. J., Miller, P., & Kessel, F. (Eds.). (1995). *Cultural practices as contexts for development.* San Francisco: Jossey- Bass.

Goosens, F. A., & van Ijzendoorn, M. H. (1990). Quality of infants' attachments to professional caregivers: Relation to infant-parent attachment and day-care characteristics. *Child Development, 61,* 832–837.

Gorman, C. (1993, June 13). Thalidomide's return. *Time,* June 13, p. 67.

Gortmaker, S. L., Must, A., Perrin, J. M., Sobol, A. M., & Dietz, W. H. (1993). Social and economic consequences of overweight in adolescence and young adulthood. *New England Journal of Medicine, 329,* 1008–1012.

Gose, B. (1995, November 10). A new approach to mortuary science. *The Chronicle of Higher Education,* p. A7.

Gosman, E. J., Dandridge, B. A., Nettles, M. T., & Thoeny, A. R. (1983). Predicting student progression: The influence of race and other student and institutional characteristics on college student performance. *Research in Higher Education, 18*(2), 209–236.

Gottesman, I. I. (1963). Heritability of personality: A demonstration. *Psychological Monographs, 77* (Whole No. 572).

Gottman, J., & Parkhurst, J. (1980). A developmental theory of friendship and acquaintanceship. In A. Collins (Ed.), *Minnesota symposia on child psychology: Vol. 13.* Hillsdale, N.J.: Erlbaum.

Gould, R. L. (1978). *Transformations: Growth and change in adult life.* New York: Simon & Schuster.

Gove, W. R., Style, C. B., & Hughes, M. (1990). The effect of marriage on the well-being of adults: A theoretical analysis. *Journal of Family Issues, 11,* 4–35.

Graber, J. A., Brooks-Gunn, J., Paikoff, R. L., & Warren, M. P. (1994). Prediction of eating problems: An 8-year study of adolescent girls. *Developmental Psychology, 30,* 823–834.

Grabowski, J., & Frantz, T. T. (1993). Latinos and Anglos: Cultural experiences of grief intensity. *Omega, 26*(4), 273–285.

Gralinski, J. H., & Kopp, C. (1993). Everyday rules for behavior: Mothers' requests to young children. *Developmental Psychology, 29,* 573–584.

Grand, A., Grand-Filaire, A., & Pous, J. (1995). Aging couples and disability management. In J. Hendricks (Ed.), *The ties of later life* (pp. 55–72). Amityville, N.Y.: Baywood.

Green, D. L. (1990). High school student employment in social context: Adolescents' perceptions of the role of part-time work. *Adolescence, 25,* 425–434.

Green, M. (1994). *Sigh of relief: A first-aid handbook for childhood emergencies.* New York: Bantam Books.

Green, R. (1987). *The "sissy boy" syndrome and the development of homosexuality.* New Haven, Conn.: Yale University Press.

Greenberg, B. S. (1986). Minorities and the mass media. In J. Bryant & D. Zillman (Eds.), *Perspectives on mass media effects.* Hillsdale, N.J.: Erlbaum.

Greenberg, R. A., Haley, N. J., Etzel, R. A., & Loda, F. A. (1984). Measuring the exposure of infants to tobacco smoke. *New England Journal of Medicine, 310,* 1075–1078.

Greenberger, E., O'Neill, R., & Nagel, S. K. (1994). Linking workplace and homeplace: Relations between the nature of adults' work and their parenting behaviors. *Developmental Psychology, 30,* 990–1002.

Greene, B. (1994). Lesbian and gay sexual orientations: Implications for clinical training, practice, and research. In B. Greene & G. M. Herek (Eds.), *Lesbian and gay psychology: Theory, research, and clinical applications* (pp. 1–24). Thousand Oaks, Cal.: Sage.

Greenfield, P. (1994). Independence and interdependence as developmental scripts: Implications for theory, research, and practice. In P. Greenfield & R. Cocking (Eds.), *Cross-cultural roots of minority child development* (pp. 1–40). Hillsdale, N.J.: Erlbaum.

Greenfield, P. (1995, March 30). *Independence and interdependence in school conferences between Anglo teachers and Hispanic parents.* Paper presented at the biennial meeting of the Society for Research on Child Development, Indianapolis.

Greenhaus, J. H. (1987). *Career management.* Hinsdale, Ill.: Dryden Press.

Greenhaus, J. H. (1988). Career exploration. In M. London & E. M. Mone (Eds.), *Career growth and human resource strategy* (pp. 17–30). New York: Quorum.

Greenwood-Audant, L. M. (1989). The internalization of powerlessness: A case study of the displaced homemaker. In J. Freeman (Ed.), *Women: A feminist perspective* (4th ed., pp. 245–262). Mountain View, Cal.: Mayfield.

Gregg, M., & Leinhardt, C. (1995). Mapping out geography: An example of epistemology and education. In *Review of Educational Research, 64*(2), 311–361.

Greil, A. L. (1993). Infertility: Overview. In B. K. Rothman (Ed.), *The encyclopedia of childbearing.* New York: Henry Holt .

Grimby, G. (1988). Physical activity and effects of muscle training in the elderly. *Annals of Clinical Research, 20,* 62–66.

Grimby, G., & Saltin, B. (1983). The aging muscle. *Clinical Physiology, 3,* 209–218.

Grimes, D., & Gross, G. (1981). Pregnancy outcomes in black women aged 35 and older. *Obstetrics and Gynecology, 58,* 614–620.

Grossarth-Maticek, R., & Eysenck, H. J. (1991). Determinants for risk for cancer and coronary heart disease. *Psychological Reports, 61,* 1027–1043.

Grossarth-Maticek, R., Eysenck, H. J., Uhlenbruck, G., Rieder, H., Vetter, H., Freesemann, C., Rakic, L., Gallasch, G., Kanazir, D. T., & Liesen, H. (1990). Sport activity and personality as elements in preventing cancer and coronary disease. *Perceptual and Motor Skills, 71,* 199–209.

Grossmann, K. E., & Grossmann, K. (1990). The wider concept of attachment in cross-cultural research. *Human Development, 33,* 31–47.

Grossmann, K., Grossmann, K., Spangler, G., Suess, G., & Unzner, L. (1985). Maternal sensitivity and newborns' orientation responses as related to quality of attachment in northern Germany. In I. Bretherton & E. Waters (Eds.), Growing points of attachment theory and research. *Monographs of the Society for Research on Child Development, 50,* 233–256.

Grunloh, R. L. (1978, January). To die in Cuaxomulco. *America: Magazine of the Organization of American States.*

Grusec, J. E. (1991). Socializing concern for others in the home. *Developmental Psychology, 27,* 338–342.

Guardo, C., & Bohan, J. (1971). Development of a sense of self-identity in children. *Child Development, 42,* 1909–1921.

Guarnaccia, P. J., Angel, R., & Worobey, J. L. (1991). The impact of marital status and employment status on depressive affect for Hispanic Americans. *Journal of Community Psychology, 19,* 136–149.

Gubrium, J. F. (1975). Being single in old age. *International Journal of Aging and Human Development, 6,* 29–41.

Gunnar, M. R., Proter, F. L., Wolf, C. M., Rigatuso, J., & Larson, M. C. (1995). Neonatal stress reactivity: Predictions of later emotional temperament. *Child Development, 66,* 1–13.

Gurin, P. (1981). Labor market experiences and expectancies. *Sex Roles, 7*(11), 1079–1092.

Guttmacher, A., & Kaiser, I. (1984). *Pregnancy, birth, and family planning.* New York: Signet.

Haan, N. (1989). Personality in midlife. In S. Hunter & M. Sundel (Eds.), *Midlife myths* (pp. 145–156). Newbury Park, Cal.: Sage.

Hall, C. S., & Lindzey, G. (1978). *Theories of personality* (3rd ed.) New York: Wiley.

Hall, D. T., & Rabinowitz, S. (1988). Maintaining employee involvement in a plateaued career. In M. London & E. M. Mone (Eds.), *Career growth and human resource strategy* (pp. 67–80). New York: Quorum.

Hallinan, M. T. (1981). Recent advances in sociometry. In S. Asher & J. Gottman (Eds.), *The development of children's friendships.* New York: Cambridge University Press.

Hallinan, M. T., & Williams, R. A. (1989). Interracial friendship choices in secondary schools. *American Sociological Review, 54,* 67–78.

Hallowell, E., & Ratey, J. (1994). *Driven to distraction: ADHD children as adults.* New York: Pantheon Books.

Hamburg, D. A. (1994). *Today's children: Creating a future for a generation of crisis.* New York: Times Books.

Hamilton, N. G. (1989). *Self and others: Object relations in theory and practice.* Northvale, N.J.: Jason Aronson.

Hamilton, P. M. (1984). *Basic maternity nursing* (5th ed.). St. Louis: Mosby.

Hammond, W. R., & Jung, B. (1993). Psychology's role in the public health response to assaultive violence among African-American men. *American Psychologist, 48,* 142–154.

Hardisty, J., & Leopold, E. (1992, December). Cancer and poverty: Double jeopardy for women. *Sojourner: The Women's Forum,* pp. 16–17.

Hardy, J. B. (1991). Pregnancy and its outcome. In W. R. Hendee (Ed.), *The health of adolescents: Understanding and facilitating biological, behavioral, and social development* (pp. 250–281). San Francisco: Jossey-Bass.

Hardy, J. (1994). Alzheimer's disease: Clinical molecular genetics. *Clinical Geriatric Medicine, 10*(2), 239–247.

Hare-Mustin, R. T., & Marecek, J. (1988). The meaning of difference: Gender theory, postmodernism, and psychology. *American Psychologist, 43,* 455–464.

Hare-Mustin, R. T., & Marecek, J. (1990). Gender and the meaning of difference: Postmodernism and psychology. In R. T. Hare-Mustin & J. Marecek (Eds.), *Making a difference: Psychology and the construction of gender* (pp. 22–64). New Haven, Conn.: Yale University Press.

Hareven, T. (1986). Historical changes in the family and the life course: Implications for child development. In A. Smuts & H. Hagen (Eds.), *History and research in child development. Monographs of the Society for Research on Child Development, 50* (4–5, Serial No. 211).

Harkness, S., & Keefer, C. (1995, February). *Cultural influences on sleep patterns in infancy and early childhood.* Paper presented at the annual meeting of the American Association for the Advancement of Science, Atlanta.

Harkness, S., & Super, C. (1992). Parental ethnotheories in action. In I. Sigel, A. McGillicuddy-DeLisi, & J. Goodnow (Eds.), *Parent belief systems: The psychological consequences for children* (2nd ed., pp. 373–392). Hillsdale, N.J.: Erlbaum.

Harkness, S., Super, C., & Keefer, C. (1992). Learning to be an American parent: How cultural models gain directive force. In R. D'Andrade & C. Strauss (Eds.), *Human motives and cultural models* (pp. 163–178). New York: Cambridge University Press.

Harlan, L., Brawley, O., Pommerenke, F., Wali, P., & Kramer, B. (1995). Geographic, age, and racial variation in the treatment of local/regional carcinoma of the prostate. *Journal of Clinical Oncology, 13,* 93–100.

Harlow, H. (1959). Love in infant monkeys. *Scientific American, 200,* 68–74.

Harlow, H., & Harlow, M. (1962). Social deprivation in monkeys. *Scientific American, 207,* 136–144.

Harris, J. R., Lippman, M. E., Veronesi, U., & Willett, W. (1992). Breast cancer (three parts). *New England Journal of Medicine, 327,* 319–328, 390–398, 473–480.

Harris, M., & Rosenthal, R. (1985). Mediation of interpersonal expectancy effects: 31 meta-analyses. *Psychological Bulletin, 97,* 363–386.

Harris, P. (1983). Infant cognition. In Paul Mussen (Ed.), *Handbook of child psychology: Vol. 4.* New York: Wiley.

Harrison, A. O., Wilson, M. N., Pine, C. J., Chan, S. Q., & Buriel, R. (1990). Family ecologies of ethnic minority children. *Child Development, 61,* 347–362.

Hart, B. (1991). Input frequency and children's first words. *First Language, 11,* 289–300.

Hart, C. H., DeWolf, D. M., Wozniak, P., & Burts, D. C. (1992). Maternal and paternal disciplinary styles: Relations with preschoolers' playground behavioral orientations and peer status. *Child Development, 63,* 879–892.

Hart, C. H., Ladd, G. W., & Burleson, B. R. (1990). Children's expectations of the outcomes of social strategies: Relations with socioeconomic status and maternal disciplinary styles. *Child Development, 61,* 127–137.

Harter, S. (1977). A cognitive-developmental approach to children's expression of conflicting feelings and a technique to facilitate such expression in play therapy. *Journal of Consulting and Clinical Psychology, 45,* 417–432.

Harter, S. (1983). Developmental perspectives on self-system. In E. M. Hetherington (Ed.), *Handbook of child psychology: Vol. 4. Socialization, personality, and social development* (4th ed., pp. 275–285). New York: Wiley.

Harter, S. (1989). Processes underlying adolescent self-concept formation. In R. Montemayor (Ed.), *Advances in adolescent development: Vol 2. Transition from childhood to adolescence.* New York: Russell Sage Foundation.

Harter, S. (1990a). Self and identity development. In S. Feldman & G. Elliot (Eds.), *At the threshold: The developing adolescent.* Cambridge, Mass.: Harvard University Press.

Harter, S. (1990b). Processes underlying adolescent self-concept formation. In R. Montemayor, G. R. Adams, & T. P. Gullotta (Eds.), *From childhood to adolescence: A transitional period?* Newbury Park, Cal.: Sage.

Harter, S., & Barnes, R. (1983). *Children's understanding of parental emotions: A developmental study.* Unpublished paper, 1981. Cited in S. Harter, *Developmental perspectives on the self-system.* In P. Mussen (Ed.), *Handbook of child psychology: Vol. 4.* New York: Wiley.

Harter, S., & Monsour, A. (1992). Developmental analysis of conflict caused by opposing attributes in the adolescent self-portrait. *Developmental Psychology, 28,* 251–260.

Hartup, W. (1983). Peer relations. In P. Mussen (Ed.), *Handbook of child psychology: Vol. 4.* New York: Wiley.

Hartup, W. (1989). Social relationships and their developmental significance. *American Psychologist, 44,* 120–126.

Hartup, W. (1996). The company they keep: Friendships and their developmental significance. *Child Development, 67,* 1–13.

Hatch, L. R. (1995). Gray clouds and silver linings: Women's resources in later life. In J. Freeman (Ed.), *Women: A feminist perspective* (5th ed., pp. 182–196). Mountain View, Cal.: Mayfield.

Hatch, L. R., & Bulcroft, C. (1992). Contact with friends in later life: Disentangling the effects of gender and marital stability. *Journal of Marriage and the Family, 54,* 222–232.

Hatfield, E. (1988). Passionate and companionate love. In R. J. Sternberg & M. L. Brown (Eds.), *The psychology of love.* New Haven, Conn.: Yale University Press.

Haug, M. R., Akiyama, H., Tryban, G., Sonoda, K., & Wykle, M. (1991). Self-care: Japan and U.S. compared. *Social Science and Medicine, 33,* 1011–1022.

Havighurst, R. J. (1953). *Human development and education.* New York: Longmans, Green.

Havighurst, R. J., Neugarten, B. L., & Tobin, S. S. (1968). Disengagement and patterns of aging. In B. L. Neugarten (Ed.), *Middle age and aging* (pp. 161–173). Chicago: University of Chicago Press.

Hayes, C. (1987). *Risking the future: Adolescent sexuality, pregnancy and childbearing.* Washington, D.C.: National Academy Press.

Hayflick, L. (1994). *How and why we age.* New York: Ballantine.

Hayne, H., Rovee-Collier, C., & Borza, M. (1991). Infant memory for place information. *Memory and Cognition, 19,* 378–386.

Haynes, M. A. (1991). Making cancer prevention effective for African-Americans. *Statistical Bulletin, 72,* 18–22.

Hazen, C., & Shaver, P. (1987). Romantic love conceptualized as an attachment process. *Journal of Personality and Social Psychology, 53,* 511–524.

Hazen, C., & Shaver, P. (1990). Love and work: An attachment-theoretical perspective. *Journal of Personality and Social Psychology, 59,* 270–290.

Heath, S. (1993). *Identity and inner-city youth: Beyond ethnicity and gender.* New York: Teachers' College Press.

Heath, S., Mangolia, L., Schlecter, S., & Hull, G. (Eds.). (1991). *Children of promise: Literate activity in linguistically and culturally diverse classrooms.* Washington, D.C.: National Education Association.

Heckhausen, J., Dixon, R. A., & Baltes, P. B. (1989). Gains and losses in development throughout adulthood as perceived by different adult age groups. *Developmental Psychology, 25,* 109–121.

Heidrich, S. M., & Denney, N. W. (1994). Does social problem solving differ from other types of problem solving during the adult years? *Experimental Aging Research, 20*(2), 105–126.

Heilbrun, A., & Friedberg, L. (1990). Distorted body image in normal college women: Possible implications for anorexia nervosa. *Journal of Clinical Psychology, 46,* 398–401.

Hein, K. D., & DiGeronimo, T. F. (1989). *AIDS: Trading fears for facts. A guide for teens.* Mount Vernon, N.Y.: Consumers Union.

Helfer, R. E., & Kempe, R. S. (Eds.) (1987). *The battered child* (4th ed.). Chicago: University of Chicago Press.

Helgeson, V. S., Shaver, P., & Dyer, M. (1987). Prototypes of intimacy and distance in same sex and opposite sex relationships. *Journal of Social and Personal Relationships, 4,* 195–233.

Hellige, J. (1993). *Hemispheric asymmetry: What's right and what's left.* Cambridge, Mass.: Harvard University Press.

Helson, R. (1993). Comparing longitudinal studies of adult development: Toward a paradigm of tension between stability and change. In D. C. Funder, R. D. Parke, C. Tomlinson-Keasey, & K. Widaman (Eds.), *Studying lives through time: Personality and development* (pp. 93–120). Washington, D.C.: American Psychological Association.

Helton, A., McFarlane, J., & Anderson, E. T. (1987). Battered and pregnant: A prevalence study. *American Journal of Public Health, 77,* 1337–1339.

Henderson, M. (1990). Beyond the living will. *The Gerontologist, 30,* 480–485.

Hendler, M., & Weisberg, P. (1992). Conservation acquisition, maintenance, and generalization by mentally retarded children using equality-rule training. *Journal of Experimental Child Psychology, 53,* 258–276.

Hergenrather, J. R., & Rabinowitz, M. (1991). Age-related differences in the organization of children's knowledge of illness. *Developmental Psychology, 27,* 952–959.

Herman, J. (1992). *Trauma and recovery: The aftermath of violence: From domestic abuse to political terror.* New York: Basic Books.

Hershberger, S. L., & D'Augelli, A. R. (1995). The impact of victimization on the mental health and suicidality of lesbian, gay, and bisexual youths. *Developmental Psychology, 31,* 65–74.

Hetherington, E. M. (1988). Family relations six years after divorce. In K. Pasley & M. Ihinger-Tallman (Eds.), *Remarriage and stepparenting: Current research and theory* (pp. 185–205). New York: Guilford Press.

Hetherington, E. M. (1989a). Coping with family transitions: Winners, losers, and survivors. *Child Development, 60,* 1–18.

Hetherington, E. M. (1989b). Divorce: A child's perspective. *American Psychologist, 44,* 303–312.

Hetherington, E. M. (1991). The role of individual differences and family relationships in children's coping with divorce and remarriage. In P. A. Cowan & M. Hetherington (Eds.), *Family transitions* (pp. 165–194). Hillsdale, N.J.: Erlbaum.

Hetherington, E. M. (1995, March 30). *The changing American family and the well-being of children.* Paper presented at the biennial meeting of the Society for Research on Child Development, Indianapolis.

Hetherington, E. M., & Clingempeel, W. (1992). Coping with marital transitions: A family systems perspective. *Monographs of the Society for Research in Child Development, 57* (2–3, Serial No. 227).

Hetherington, E. M., Cox, M., & Cox, R. (1979). Play and social interaction in children following divorce. *Journal of Social Issues, 35,* 26–49.

Hetherington, E. M., Cox, M., & Cox, R. (1982). Effects of divorce on parents and children. In M. Lamb (Ed.), *Nontraditional families: Parenting and child development*. Hillsdale, N.J.: Erlbaum.

Hetherington, E. M., & Furstenberg, F. (1989). Follow-up. Letter to the editor. *Readings: A Journal of Reviews and Commentary in Mental Health*, 22–23.

Hetherington, E. M., Stanley-Hagen, M., & Anderson, E. (1989). Marital transitions: A child's perspective. *American Psychologist, 44*, 303–312.

Hills, T. (1992). Reach potentials through appropriate assessment. In S. Bredekamp & T. Rosegrant (Eds.), *Reaching potentials: Appropriate curriculum and assessment and for young children: Vol. 1* (pp. 43–65). Washington, D.C.: National Association for the Education of Young Children.

Hilton, M. E. (1988). The demographic distribution of drinking problems in 1984. *Drug and Alcohol Dependency, 22*, 37–47.

Hinde, R. A. (1989). Ethological relationships and approaches. In R. Vasta (Ed.), *Annals of Child Development: Six theories of child development—Revised formulations and current issues*. Greenwich, Conn.: JAI Press.

Hirayama, T. (1981). Non-smoking wives of heavy smokers have a higher risk of lung cancer: A study from Japan. *Journal of Behavioral Medicine, 12*, 39–54.

Ho, D. (1994). Cognitive socialization in confucian heritage cultures. In P. Greenfield & R. Cocking (Eds.), *Cross-cultural roots of minority child development* (pp. 285–314). Hillsdale, N.J.: Erlbaum.

Hoare, C. H. (1994). Psychosocial identity development in United States society: Its role in fostering exclusion of cultural others. In E. P. Salett & D. R. Koslow (Eds.), *Race, ethnicity and self: Identity in multicultural perspective*. Washington, D.C.: National Multicultural Institute, 1994.

Hochschild, A. (1989). *The second shift: Working parents and the revolution at home*. New York: Viking.

Hodapp, R., & Mueller, E. (1982). Early social development. In B. Wolman (Ed.), *Handbook of developmental psychology*. New York: Wiley.

Hodgkinson, H. L. (1985). *All one system: Demographics of education, kindergarten through graduate school*. Washington, D.C.: Institute of Educational Leadership.

Hodgson, L. G. (1995). Adult grandchildren and their grandparents: The enduring bond. In J. Hendricks (Ed.), *The ties of later life* (pp. 155–170). Amityville, N.Y.: Baywood.

Hoff-Ginsberg, E., & Krueger, W. (1991). Older siblings as conversational partners. *Merrill-Palmer Quarterly, 37*, 465–482.

Hoffman, K. L., Demo, D. H., & Edwards, J. N. (1994). Physical wife abuse in a non-western society: An integrated theoretical approach. *Journal of Marriage and the Family, 56*, 131–146.

Hoffman, L. W. (1980). The effects of maternal employment on the academic attitudes and performance of school-aged children. *School Psychology Review, 9*, 319–336.

Hoffman, L. W. (1983). Increased fathering: Effects on the mother. In M. Lamb & A. Sagi (Eds.), *Fatherhood and family policy*. Hillsdale, N.J.: Erlbaum.

Hoffman, L. W. (1984a). Maternal employment and the young child. In M. Perlmutter (Ed.), *The Minnesota symposium on child psychology: Vol. 17*. Hillsdale, N.J.: Erlbaum.

Hoffman, L. W. (1984b). Work, family, and the socialization of the child. In R. Parke (Ed.), *Review of child development research: Vol. 7*. Chicago: University of Chicago Press.

Hoffman, L. W. (1989). Effects of maternal employment in the two-parent family. *American Psychologist, 44*, 283–292.

Hoffnung, A. (1992). *Shoeshine boys of Cuenca, Ecuador*. Unpublished paper, Reed College, Portland.

Hoffnung, M. (1992). *What is a mother to do? Conversations on work and family*. Pasadena, Cal.: Trilogy Books.

Hoffnung, M. (1995). Motherhood: Contemporary conflict for women. In J. Freeman (Ed.), *Women: A feminist perspective* (5th ed., pp. 162–181). Palo Alto, Cal.: Mayfield.

Hofland, B. F. (1994). When capacity fades and autonomy is constricted: A client-centered approach to residential care. *Generations, 18*(4), 31–35.

Hogan, N. S., & DeSantis, L. (1992). Adolescent sibling bereavement: An ongoing attachment. *Qualitative Health Research, 2*, 159–177.

Holden, C. (1986). Youth suicide: New research focuses on growing social problem. *Science, 233*, 839–841.

Hollis, J. F., Carmody, T. P., Connor, S. L., Fey, S. G., & Matarazzo, J. D. (1986). The nutrition attitude survey: Associations with dietary habits, psychological and physical well-being, and coronary risk factors. *Health Psychology, 5*, 359–374.

Holloway, J., & Vass, W. (1993). *African heritage of American English*. Bloomington, Ind.: Indiana University Press.

Holmbeck, G., & O'Donnell, K. (1991). Discrepancies between perceptions of decision making and behavioral autonomy. In R. Paikoff (Ed.), *Shared views of the family during adolescence* (pp. 51–70). San Francisco: Jossey-Bass.

Hooyman, N. R. (1992). Social policy and gender inequalities in caregiving. In J. W. Dwyer & R. T. Coward (Eds.), *Gender, families, and elder care* (pp. 181–201). Newbury Park, Cal.: Sage.

Hooyman, N. R., & Kiyak, H. A. (1993). *Social gerontology*. Boston: Allyn & Bacon.

Horgan, J. (1993, June). Eugenics revisited. *Scientific American*, 120–128.

Horn, J. L. (1970). Organization of data on life-span development of human abilities. In L. R. Goulet & P. B. Baltes (Eds.), *Life-span developmental psychology: Research and theory* (pp. 424–466). New York: Academic Press.

Horn, J. L., & Donaldson, G. (1976). On the myth of intellectual decline in adulthood. *American Psychologist, 31*, 701–719.

Horn, J. L., & Donaldson, G. (1977). Faith is not enough: A response to the Baltes-Schaie claim that intelligence does not wane. *American Psychologist, 32*, 369–373.

Horn, J. L., & Hofer, S. M. (1992). Major abilities and development in the adult period. In R. J. Sternberg & C. A. Berg (Eds.), *Intellectual development* (pp. 44–99). New York: Cambridge University Press.

Horvath, T. B., & Davis, K. L. (1990). Central system disorders in aging. In E. L. Schneider & J. W. Rowe (Eds.), *Handbook of the biology of aging* (3rd ed., pp. 306–329). San Diego: Academic Press.

Horwitz, R. A. (1979). Psychological effects of the "open classroom." *Review of Educational Research, 49*, 71–86.

House, S. J., Landis, K. R., & Umberson, D. (1988). Social relationships and health. *Science, 241*, 540–544.

Howes, C. (1988). Peer interaction of young children. *Monographs of the Society for Research in Child Development, 53*(Serial No. 2170), 1–78.

Howes, C., & Farver, J. M. (1987). Toddlers' responses to the distress of their peers. *Journal of Applied Developmental Psychology, 8*, 441–452.

Howes, C., & Matheson, C. C. (1992). Sequences in the development of competent play with peers: Social and social pretend play. *Developmental Psychology, 28*, 961–972.

Howes, C., & Wu, F. (1990). Peer interactions and friendships in an ethnically diverse school setting. *Child Development, 61*, 537–541.

Hoyer, W. J., & Rybash, J. M. (1994). Characterizing adult cognitive development. *Adult Development, 1*, 7–12.

Hoyert, D. L. (1991). Financial and household exchange between generations. *Research in Aging, 13*, 205–225.

Huang, L., & Ying, Y. (1989). Chinese-American children and adolescents. In J. Gibbs & L. Huang (Eds.), *Children of color* (pp. 30–66). San Francisco: Jossey-Bass.

Hudley, C., & Graham, S. (1993). An attributional intervention to reduce peer-directed aggression among African-American boys. *Child Development, 64*, 124–138.

Huesmann, L. R., Eron, L. D., Lefkowitz, M. M., & Walder, L. O. (1984). Stability of aggression over time and generations. *Developmental Psychology, 20*, 1120–1134.

Hughes, M. S. (1987). Black students' participation in higher education. Special issue: Blacks in U.S. higher education. *Journal of College Student Personnel, 28*(6), 532–545.

Hultsch, D. F., & Dixon, R. A. (1990). Learning and memory in aging. In J. E. Birren & K. W. Schaie (Eds.), *Handbook of the psychology of aging* (3rd ed., pp. 258–274). San Diego: Academic Press.

Hunsberger, B. (1985). Religion, age, life satisfaction and perceived sources of religiousness: A study of older persons. *Journal of Gerontology, 40*, 615–620.

Hunt, C. (Ed.). (1992). *Apnea and SIDS*. Philadelphia: Saunders.

Hunt, E. (1993). What we need to know about aging. In J. Cerella, J. Rybash, W. Hoyer, & M. L. Commons (Eds.), *Adult information processing: Limits on loss* (pp. 587–589). San Diego: Academic Press.

Hunt, M. E., & Ross, L. (1990). Naturally-occurring retirement communities: A multiattribute examination of desirability factors. *The Gerontologist, 30*, 667–674.

Hunter-Griffin, L. (1990). The young female athlete. In J. Sullivan & W. Grana (Eds.), *The pediatric athlete* (pp. 69–78). Park Ridge, Ill.: American Academy of Orthopedic Surgeons.

Husaini, B. A., Moore, S. T., Castor, R. S., Neser, W., Whitten-Stovall, R., Linn, J. G., & Griffin, D. (1991). Social density, stressors, and depression: Gender differences among the black elderly. *Journal of Gerontology, 46*, P236–242.

Huston, A. C. (1983). Sex-typing. In P. Mussen (Ed.), *Handbook of child psychology: Vol. 4*. New York: Wiley.

Huston, A. C. (1994). *Children in poverty: Designing research to affect policy*. Social policy report, vol. 8(2). Ann Arbor, Mich.: Society for Research on Child Development.

Huston, A. C., & Alvarez, M. M. (1990). The socialization context of gender role development in early adolescence. In R. Montemayor, G. R. Adams, & T. P. Gullota (Eds.), *From childhood to adolescence: A transitional period?* Newbury Park, Cal.: Sage.

Huston, A. C., Watkins, B., & Kunkel, D. (1989). Public policy and children's television. *American Psychologist, 44*, 424–433.

Huston, A. C., Wright, J. C., Rice, M. L., Kerkman, D., & St. Peters, M. (1990). Development of television viewing patterns in early childhood: A longitudinal investigation. *Developmental Psychology, 26*, 409–420.

Hwang, C. P. (1986). Behavior of Swedish primary and secondary caretaking fathers in relation to mother's presence. *Developmental Psychology, 22*, 749–751.

Ickovics, J. R., & Rodin, J. (1992). Women and AIDS in the United States: Epidemiology, natural history, and mediating mechanisms. *Health Psychology, 11*, 1–16.

Improving care near the end of life: Why is it so hard? (1995). *Journal of the American Medical Association, 274*, 1634–1636.

Ingersoll, B., & Goldstein, S. (1993). *Attention deficit disorder and learning disabilities: Realities, myths and controversial treatments*. New York: Doubleday.

Inglis, A., & Greenglass, E. R. (1989). Motivation for marriage among women and men. *Psychological Reports, 65*, 1035–1042.

Inhelder, B., & Piaget, J. (1958). *The growth of logical thinking from birth to adolescence*. New York: Basic Books.

Irion, P. E. (1990/1991). Changing patterns of ritual response to death. *Omega, 22*(3), 159–172.

Isabella, R. A. (1993). Origins of attachment: Maternal interactive behavior across the first year. *Child Development, 64*, 605–621.

Isabella, R. A., & Belsky, J. (1991). Interactional synchrony and the origins of infant-mother attachment: A replication study. *Child Development, 62*, 373–384.

Iso, A., Seppo, E., Jackson, E., & Dunn, E. (1994). Starting, ceasing, and replacing leisure activities over the life-span. *Journal of Leisure Research, 26*(3), 227–249.

It's not working. (1986). *American Demographics, 8*(12), 13.

Izard, C. E. (1982). *Measuring emotions in infants and children*. New York: Cambridge University Press.

Izard, C. E. (1994). Innate and universal facial expressions: Evidence from developmental and cross-cultural research. *Psychological Bulletin, 115*, 288–299.

Izard, C. E., & Malatesta, C. (1987). Perspectives on emotional development: I. Differential emotions theory of early emotional development. In J. Osofsky (Ed.), *Handbook of infant development* (2nd ed., pp. 494–554). New York: Wiley.

Jackson, J. J., & Perry, C. (1989). Gender, aging and health. In K. S. Markides (Ed.), *Aging and health: Perspectives on gender, race, ethnicity and class* (pp. 111–176). Newbury Park, Cal.: Sage.

Jackson, J. S., Antonucci, T. C., & Gibson, R. C. (1990). Cultural, racial, and ethnic minority influences on aging. In J. E. Birren & K. W. Schaie (Eds.), *Handbook of the psychology of aging* (3rd ed., pp. 103–123). San Diego: Academic Press.

Jackson, P. (1968). *Life in classrooms.* New York: Holt, 1968.

Jackson, P. (1986). *The practice of teaching.* Chicago: University of Chicago Press.

Jadack, R., Hyde, J., Moore, C., & Keller, M. (1995). Moral reasoning about sexually transmitted diseases. *Child Development, 66*, 167–177.

Jendrek, M. P. (1992). *Grandparents who provide care to grandchildren: Preliminary findings and policy issues.* Paper presented at the annual meeting of Sociologists for Women in Society, Pittsburgh.

Jensen, L. C., McGhie, A. P., & Jensen, J. R. (1991). Do men's and women's world-views differ? *Psychological Reports, 68*, 312–314.

Jessor, R. (1993). Successful adolescent development among high-risk settings. *American Psychologist, 48*, 117–126.

Jimenez, R., Garcia, G., & Pearson, D. (1995). Three children, two languages, and strategic reading: Case studies in bilingual/monolingual reading. *American Educational Research Journal, 32*(1), 67–97.

Johnson, C. L. (1985). *Growing up and growing old in Italian-American families.* New Brunswick, N.J.: Rutgers University Press.

Johnson, C. L., & Barer, B. M. (1990). Families and networks among older inner-city blacks. *The Gerontologist, 30*, 726–733.

Johnson, D. W., Johnson, R. T., & Maruyama, G. (1984). Goal interdependence and interpersonal attraction in heterogeneous classrooms: A meta-analysis. In N. Miller & M. B. Brewer (Eds.), *Groups in contact: The psychology of desegregation.* New York: Academic Press.

Johnson, R. (Ed.). (1995). *African-American voices: African-American health educators speak out.* New York: National League for Nursing.

Johnston, F., Hamill, P., & Lemshow, S. (1974). *Skinfold thickness of youths 12–17 years.* U.S. Public Health Service Publication No. 132. Washington, D.C.: U.S. Government Printing Office.

Johnston, L., O'Malley, P., & Bachman, J. (1992). *Drug use among American high school students, college students and other young adults: National trends through 1991.* Rockville, Md.: National Institute on Drug Abuse.

Johnston, M. W., & Eklund, S. J. (1984). Life-adjustment of the never-married: A review with implications for counseling. *Journal of Counseling & Development, 63*(4), 230–236.

Johnston, R. (1991). *Attention deficits, learning disabilities, and ritalin: A practical guide.* San Diego: Singular Publications.

Jondrow, J., Brechling, F., & Marcu, A. (1987). Older workers in the market for part-time employment. In S. H. Sandell (Ed.), *The problem isn't age: Work and older Americans.* New York: Praeger.

Jones, B. A., Kasl, S. V., Curnen, M. G., Owens, P. H., & Dubrow, R. (1995). Can mammography screening explain the race difference in stage at diagnosis of breast cancer? *Cancer, 75*, 2103–2113.

Jones, P. S., & Martinson, I. M. (1992). The experience of bereavement in caregivers of family members with Alzheimer's disease. *Image: Journal of Nursing Scholarship, 24*(3), 172–176.

Jordan, J. V., Kaplan, A. G., Miller, J. B., Stiver, I. P., & Surrey, J. L. (1991). *Women's growth in connection: Writings from the Stone Center.* New York: Guilford.

Joshi, M., & MacLean, M. (1994). Indian and English children's understanding of the distinction between real and apparent emotion. *Child Development, 65*, 1372–1384.

Josselson, R. (1980). Ego development in adolescence. In J. Adelson (Ed.), *Handbook of adolescent psychology.* New York: Wiley.

Jovanovic, L., & Subak-Sharpe, G. J. (1987). *Hormones: The woman's answer book.* New York: Ballantine Books.

Julian, T. W., & McKenry, P. C. (1993). Mediators of male violence toward female intimates. *Journal of Family Violence, 8*(1), 39–56.

Jung, C. G. (1933). *Modern man in search of a soul* (W. S. Dell & C. F. Baynes, Trans.). New York: Harcourt Brace Jovanovich.

Juvonen, J. (1991). Deviance, perceived responsibility, and negative peer reactions. *Developmental Psychology, 27*, 672–681.

Kagan, J. (1984). *The nature of the child.* New York: Basic Books.

Kagan, J., Arcus, D., Snidman, N., Feng, W. Y., Handler, J., & Greene, S. (1995). Reactivity in infants: A cross-national comparison. *Developmental Psychology, 30*, 342–345.

Kagan, J., & Snidman, N. (1991). Temperamental factors in human development. *American Psychologist, 46*, 856–862.

Kahlbaugh, P., & Haviland, J. (1991). Formal operational thinking and identity. In R. Lerner, A. Petersen, & J. Brooks-Gunn (Eds.), *Encyclopedia of adolescence: Vol. 1* (pp. 369–372). New York: Garland.

Kaitz, M., Meschulach-Sarfaty, O., Auerbach, J., & Eidelman, A. (1988). A re-examination of newborns' ability to imitate facial expressions. *Developmental Psychology, 24*, 3–7.

Kakar, S. (1982). *The inner world: A psychoanalytic study of childhood and society in India.* Delhi: Oxford University Press.

Kalish, R. A. (1985). *Death, grief, and caring relationships* (2nd ed.). Monterey, Cal.: Brooks/Cole.

Kalish, R. A., & Reynolds, D. K. (1981). *Death and ethnicity: A psychocultural study.* Farmingdale, N.Y.: Baywood.

Kallman, D. A., Plato, C. C., & Tobin, J. D. (1990). The role of muscle loss in the age-related decline of grip strength: Cross-sectional and longitudinal perspectives. *Journal of Gerontology: Medical Sciences, 45*, M82–88.

Kalverboer, A., Hopkins, B., & Geuze, R. (1993). *Motor development in early infancy and late childhood.* New York: Cambridge University Press.

Kamerman, S. B. (1991). Child care policies and programs: An international overview. *Journal of Social Issues, 47*, 179–196.

Kantor, G. K., & Straus, M. A. (1990). The "drunken bum" theory of wife beating. In M. A. Straus & R. J. Gelles, with C. Smith (Eds.), *Physical violence in American families: Risk factors and adaptations to violence in 8,145 families* (pp. 203–224). New Brunswick, N.J.: Transaction.

Kao, G. (1995). Asian-Americans as model minorities? A look at their academic performance. *American Journal of Education, 103*, 121–159.

Kaplan, A., & Bean, J. (Eds.). (1976). *Beyond sex-role stereotypes: Readings toward a psychology of androgyny.* Boston: Little, Brown.

Kaplan, H. (1979). *Disorders of sexual desire.* New York: Brunner/Mazel.

Kaplan, K., & Wadden, T. (1986). Childhood obesity and self-esteem. *Journal of Pediatrics, 109*, 367–370.

Kaplan, L. (1995). *No voice is ever wholly lost.* New York: Simon & Schuster.

Kaplan, M. S., Adamek, M. E., & Johnson, S. (1994). Trends in firearm suicide among older American males: 1979–1988. *The Gerontologist, 34*, 59–65.

Kashani, I. A., Langer, R. D., Criqui, M. H., Nader, P. R., Rupp, J., Sallis, J. F., & Houghton, R. (1991). Effects of parental behavior modification on children's cardiovascular risks. *Annals of the New York Academy of Sciences, 623*, 447–449.

Kass, L. (1994). Neither for love nor money: Why doctors must not kill. In H. R. Moody (Ed.), *Aging: Concepts and controversies* (pp. 116–122). Thousand Oaks, Cal.: Pine Forge Press.

Kastenbaum, R. (1985). Dying and death: A life-span approach. In J. E. Birren & K. W. Schaie (Eds.), *Handbook of the psychology of aging* (2nd ed., pp. 619–643). New York: Van Nostrand Reinhold.

Kastenbaum, R. (1992a). Death, suicide and the older adult. *Suicide and Life-Threatening Behavior, 22*, 1–14.

Kastenbaum, R. (1992b). *The psychology of death.* New York: Springer-Verlag.

Kastenbaum, R., & Normand, C. (1990). Deathbed scenes imagined by the young and experienced by the old. *Death Studies, 14*, 201–217.

Kates, E. (1995). Escaping poverty: The promise of higher education. *Social Policy Report 9*(1). Ann Arbor, Mich.: Society for Research on Child Development.

Katz, P., & Zalk, S. (1978). Modification of children's racial attitudes. *Developmental Psychology, 14*, 447–461.

Kaufert, P. A., & McKinlay, S. M. (1985). Estrogen-replacement therapy: The production of medical knowledge and the emergence of policy. In E. Lewis & V. Olesen (Eds.), *Women, health and healing: Toward a new perspective* (pp. 113–138). London: Tavistock.

Kaufman, H. G. (1982). *Professionals in search of work: Coping with the stress of job loss and underemployment.* New York: Wiley-Interscience.

Kavanaugh, T., & Shephard, R. J. (1990). Can regular sports participation slow the aging process? *Physician and Sportsmedicine, 18*, 94–104.

Kazdin, A. E. (1994). *Behavior modification in applied settings* (5th ed.). Pacific Grove, Cal. Brooks/Cole.

Keating, D. (1991). Adolescent cognition. In R. Lerner, A. Peterson, & J. Brooks-Gunn (Eds.), *Encyclopedia of adolescence: Vol. 1* (pp. 119–129). New York: Garland.

Keefe, J., & Walberg, H. (Eds.). (1992). *Teaching for thinking.* Reston, Va.: National Association of Secondary School Principals.

Keith, J., Fry, C. L., Glascock, A. P., Ikels, C., Dickerson-Putman, J., Harpending, H. C., & Draper, P. (1994). *The aging experience: Diversity and commonality across cultures.* Thousand Oaks, Cal.: Sage.

Keith, P. M. (1979). Life changes and perceptions of life and death among older men and women. *Journal of Gerontology, 34*, 870–878.

Keith, P. M. (1982). Perceptions of time remaining and distance from death. *Omega, 12*, 307–318.

Keith, P. M., & Schafer, R. B. (1991). *Relationships and well-being over the life stages.* New York: Praeger.

Keller, J. W. (1985). Career changes: A logical phenomenon. *Journal of College Student Personnel, 26*(3), 249–251.

Keller, M., & Wood, P. (1989). Development of friendship reasoning: A study of interindividual differences and intraindividual change. *Developmental Psychology, 25*, 820–826.

Kelly, J. R. (Ed.). (1993). *Activity and aging.* Newbury Park, Cal.: Sage.

Kelly, J. R., Steinkamp, M. W., & Kelly, J. R. (1987). Later-life satisfaction: Does leisure contribute? *Leisure Sciences, 9*, 189–200.

Kelly, M. P., Strassberg, D. S., & Kircher, J. R. (1990). Attitudinal and experiential correlates of anorgasmia. *Archives of Sexual Behavior, 19*, 165–177.

Kendall-Tackett, K. A., Williams, L. M., & Finkelhor, D. (1993). Impact of sexual abuse on children: A review and synthesis of recent empirical studies. *Psychological Bulletin, 113*, 164–180.

Kendig, H. L. (1990). Comparative perspectives on housing, aging, and social structure. In R. H. Binstock & L. K. George (Eds.), *Handbook of aging and the social sciences* (3rd ed., pp. 288–306). San Diego: Academic Press.

Kenkel, W. F., & Gage, B. A. (1983). The restricted and gender-typed occupational aspirations of young women: Can they be modified? *Family Relations: Journal of Applied Family & Child Studies, 32*(1) 129–138.

Kermoian, R., & Campos, J. (1988). Locomotor experience: A facilitator of spatial cognitive development. *Child Development, 59,* 908–917.

Kerr, M., Lambert, W. W., Stattin, H., & Klackenberg-Larsson, I. (1994). Stability of inhibition in a Swedish longitudinal sample. *Child Development, 65,* 138–146.

Khoo, S. (1987). Living together as married: A profile of de facto couples in Australia. *Journal of Marriage & the Family, 49*(1), 185–191.

Kidder, T. (1993). *Old friends.* Boston: Houghton Mifflin.

Kiefer, C. W. (1987). Care of the aged in Japan. In E. Norbeck, & M. Lock (Eds.), *Health, illness, and medical care: Cultural and social dimensions* (pp. 89–109). Honolulu: University of Hawaii Press.

Kilty, K. M., & Behling, J. H. (1985). Predicting the retirement intentions and attitudes of professional workers. *Journal of Gerontology, 40,* 219–227.

Kimmel, D. C. (1988). Ageism, psychology, and public policy. *American Psychologist, 43,* 175–178.

Kimmel, D. C. (1992). The families of older gay men and lesbians. *Generations, 17*(3), 37–38.

Kindermann, T. (1993). Natural peer groups as contexts for individual development: The case of children's motivation in school. *Developmental Psychology, 29,* 979–977.

King, A. C., Taylor, C. B., & Haskell, W. L. (1993). Effects of differing intensities and formats of 12 months of exercise training on psychological outcomes in older adults. *Health Psychology, 12,* 292–300.

King, P., & Kitchener, K. (1994). *Developing reflective judgment.* San Francisco: Jossey-Bass.

Kinsey, A. C., Pomeroy, W. B., & Martin, C. E. (1948). *Sexual behavior in the human male.* Philadelphia: Saunders.

Kisilevsky, B. S., & Muir, D. W. (1984). Neonatal habituation and dishabituation to tactile stimulation during sleep. *Developmental Psychology, 20,* 367–373.

Kisilevsky, B. S., Muir, D. W., & Low, J. A. (1992). Maturation of human fetal responses to vibroacoustic stimulation. *Child Development, 63,* 1497–1508.

Kitchener, K. S., & King, P. M. (1990). The reflective judgment model: Ten years of research. In M. Common, C. Armon, L. Kohlberg, F. Richards, T. Grotzer, & J. Sinnott (Eds.), *Adult development: Models and methods in the study of adolescent and adult thought.* New York: Praeger.

Klahr, D. (1989). Information processing approaches. In R. Vasta (Ed.), *Annals of child development: Vol. 6. Six theories of child development* (pp. 133–187). Greenwich, Conn.: JAI Press.

Klapper, J., Moss, S., Moss, M., & Rubinstein, R. L. (1994). The social context of grief among adult daughters who have lost a parent. *Journal of Aging Studies, 8*(1), 29–43.

Klassen, P. (1983/1984). Changes in personal orientation and critical thinking among adults returning to school through weekend college: An alternative evaluation. *Innovative Higher Education, 8,* 55–67.

Klatsky, A. L., Armstrong, M. A., & Kipp, H. (1990). Correlates of alcohol beverage preference: Traits of persons who choose wine, liquor, or beer. *British Journal of Addiction, 85,* 1279–1289.

Klein, H. (1995). Urban Appalachian children in northern schools: A study in diversity. *Young Children, 50*(3), 10–16.

Kligman, A. M., Grove, G. L., & Balin, A. K. (1985). Aging of human skin. In C. E. Finch & E. L. Schneider (Eds.), *Handbook of the biology of aging* (pp. 820–841). New York: Van Nostrand Reinhold.

Klimes-Dougan, B., & Kistner, J. (1990). Physically abused preschoolers' responses to peers' distress. *Developmental Psychology, 26,* 599–602.

Kline, M., Tschann, J. M., Johnston, J. R., & Wallerstein, J. S. (1989). Children's adjustment to joint and sole physical custody families. *Developmental Psychology, 25,* 430–438.

Klinnert, M. D., Emde, R. N., Butterfield, P., & Campos, J. J. (1986). Social referencing: The infant's use of emotional signals from a friendly adult with mother present. *Developmental Psychology, 22,* 427–432.

Knox, G. W. (1991). *An introduction to gangs.* Berrien Springs, Mich.: Vande Vere.

Koch, P. B. (1988). The relationship of first intercourse to later sexual functioning concerns of adolescents. *Journal of Adolescent Research, 3,* 345–362.

Kochanska, C., Casey, R. J., & Fukumoto, A. (1995). Toddlers' sensitivity to standard violations. *Child Development, 66,* 643–656.

Kochanska, G. (1992). Children's interpersonal influence with mothers and peers. *Developmental Psychology, 28,* 491–499.

Koenig, H. G., & Blazer, D. G. (1992). Mood disorders and suicide. In J. E. Birren, R. B. Sloane, & G. D. Cohen (Eds.), *Handbook of mental health and aging* (2nd ed., pp. 379–407). San Diego: Academic Press.

Koenig, H. G., George, L. K., & Siegler, I. C. (1988). The use of religion and other emotion-regulating coping strategies among older adults. *The Gerontologist, 28,* 303–310.

Kogan, N. (1979). A study of age categorization. *Journal of Gerontology, 34,* 358–367.

Kogan, N. (1990). Personality and aging. In J. E. Birren & K. W. Schaie (Eds.), *Handbook of the psychology of aging* (pp. 330–346). San Diego: Academic Press.

Kohlberg, L. (1966). A cognitive-developmental view of sex-role development. In E. Maccoby (Ed.), *The development of sex differences.* Stanford, Cal.: Stanford University Press.

Kohlberg, L. (1976). Moral stages and moralization: The cognitive-developmental approach. In T. Lickona (Ed.), *Moral development and behavior.* New York: Holt, Rinehart and Winston.

Kohn, M. L. (1969). *Class and conformity: A study in values.* Homewood, Ill.: Dorsey Press.

Kohn, M. L., Slomczynski, K. M., & Schoenbach, C. (1986). Social stratification and the transmission of values in the family: A cross-national assessment. *Sociological Forum, 1,* 73–102.

Kopp, C. (1982). Antecedents of self-regulation: A developmental perspective. *Developmental Psychology, 18,* 199–214.

Koralek, D., Colker, L., & Dodge, D. (1993). *The what, why, and how of high-quality early childhood education: A guide for on-site supervision.* Washington, D.C.: National Association for the Education of Young Children.

Korbin, J. E. (Ed.). (1981). *Child abuse and neglect: Cross-cultural perspectives.* Berkeley, Cal.: University of California Press.

Korbin, J. E. (1987). Child abuse and neglect: The cultural context. In R. E. Helfer & R. S. Kemp (Eds.), *The battered child* (4th ed.). Chicago: University of Chicago Press.

Korbin, J. E. (1991). Cross-cultural perspectives and research directions for the 21st century. *Child Abuse and Neglect, 15,* 67–77.

Korman, A. K. (1988). Career success and personal failure: Mid- to late-career feelings and events. In M. London & E. M. Mone (Eds.), *Career growth and human resource strategy* (pp. 81–94). New York: Quorum.

Kostelnik, M. (1992). Myths associated with developmentally appropriate practice. *Young Children, 47*(4), 17–25.

Kotelchuck, M. (1976). The infant's relationship to the father: Experimental evidence. In M. E. Lamb (Ed.), *The role of the father in child development.* New York: Wiley.

Kotloff, L. (1993). Fostering cooperative group spirit and individuality: Examples from a Japanese preschool. *Young Children, 48*(3), 17–24.

Kozlowski, L. T., Wilkinson, D. A., Skinner, W., Kent, C., Franklin, T., & Pope, M. (1989). Comparing tobacco cigarette dependence with other drug dependencies: Greater or equal "difficulty quitting" and "urges to use," but less "pleasure" from cigarettes. *Journal of the American Medical Association, 261,* 898–901.

Kozol, J. (1995). *Amazing grace: The lives of children and the conscience of the nation.* New York: Crown Publishers.

Kramer, D. A. (1989). Development of an awareness of contradiction across the life span and the question of postformal operations. In M. L. Commons, J. D. Sinnott, F. A. Richards, & C. Armon (Eds.), *Adult development: Vol. 1. Comparisons and applications of developmental models* (pp. 133–159). New York: Praeger.

Krause, N. (1991). Stress, religiosity, and abstinence from alcohol. *Psychology and Aging, 6,* 134–144.

Krueger, J., & Heckhausen, J. (1993). Personality development across the adult life span: Subjective conceptions vs. cross-sectional contrasts. *Journal of Gerontology, 48,* P100–108.

Krugman, R., & Davidson, H. (1990). *Child abuse and neglect: Critical first steps in response to a national emergency.* Washington, D.C.: Department of Health and Human Services, U.S. Advisory Board on Child Abuse and Neglect.

Krumpe, P. E., Knudson, R. J., Parson, G., & Reiser, K. (1985). The aging respiratory system. In M. C. Geokas (Ed.), *Clinics in geriatric medicine: The aging process* (pp. 143–175). Philadelphia: W. B. Saunders.

Kubler-Ross, E. (1969). *On death and dying.* New York: Macmillan.

Kubler-Ross, E. (1981). *Living with dying.* New York: Macmillan.

Kuczynski, L., & Kochanska, G. (1995). Function and content of maternal demands: Developmental significance of early demands for competent action. *Child Development, 66,* 616–628.

Kunitz, S. J., & Levy, J. E. (1989). Aging and health among Navajo Indians. In K. S. Markides (Ed.), *Aging and health: Perspectives on gender, race, ethnicity and class* (pp. 211–245). Newbury Park, Cal.: Sage.

Kunitz, S. J., & Levy, J. E. (1994). *Drinking careers: A twenty-five year study of three Navajo populations.* New Haven, Conn.: Yale University Press.

Kupersmidt, J. B., Griesler, P. C., DeRosier, M. E., Patterson, C. J., & Davis, P. W. (1995). Childhood aggression and peer relations in the context of family and neighborhood factors. *Child Development, 66,* 360–375.

Kurdek, L. A. (1991). The relations between reported well-being and divorce history, availability of a proximate adult, and gender. *Journal of Marriage and the Family, 53,* 71–78.

Kurdek, L. A. (1994). The nature and correlates of relationship quality in gay, lesbian, and heterosexual cohabiting couples: A test of the individual difference, interdependence, and discrepancy models. In B. Greene & G. M. Herek (Eds.), *Lesbian and gay psychology: Theory, research, and clinical applications* (pp. 133–155). Thousand Oaks, Cal.: Sage.

Kurdek, L. A., Fine, M. A., & Sinclair, R. J. (1995). School adjustment in sixth graders: Parenting transitions, family climate, and peer norm effects. *Child Development, 66,* 430–445.

Kurtz, S. (1992). *All the mothers are one: Hindu India and the cultural reshaping of psychoanalysis.* New York: Columbia University Press.

Kushi, L. H., Lenart, E. B., & Willett, W. C. (1995). Health implications of Mediterranean diets in light of contemporary knowledge: 2. Meat, wine, fats, and oils. *American Journal of Clinical Nutrition, 61*(SUPPL. 6), 1416S–1427S.

Kutner, L. (1989, March 16). Parent and child: Responding to aggressive behavior. *New York Times,* p. C–1.

Labouvie-Vief, G. (1985). Intelligence and cognition. In J. E. Birren & K. W. Schaie (Eds.), *Handbook of the psychology of aging* (2nd ed., pp. 500–539). New York: Van Nostrand Reinhold.

Labouvie-Vief, G. (1992). A neo-Piagetian perspective on adult cognitive development. In R. J. Sternberg & C. A. Berg (Eds.), *Intellectual development.* New York: Cambridge University Press.

Labouvie-Vief, G., & Hakim-Larson, J. (1989). Developmental shifts in adult thought. In S. Hunter & M. Sundel (Eds.), *Midlife myths* (pp. 69–96). Newbury Park, Cal.: Sage.

Lackey, C., & Williams, K. R. (1995). Social bonding and the cessation of partner violence across generations. *Journal of Marriage and the Family, 57,* 295–305.

LaCroix, A. Z., & Haynes, S. G. (1987). Gender differences in health effects of workplace. In R. C. Barnett, L. Biener, & G. K. Baruch (Eds.), *Gender and stress* (pp. 96–121). New York: The Free Press.

Ladd, G. W., & Hart, C. H. (1992). Creating informal play opportunities: Are parents' and preschoolers' initiations related to children's competence with peers? *Developmental Psychology, 28,* 1179–1187.

LaGaipa, J. J. (1990). The negative effects of informal support systems. In S. Duck and R. C. Silver (Eds.), *Personal relationships and social support.* London: Sage.

Lakatta, E. G. (1990). Heart and circulation. In E. L. Schneider & J. W. Rowe (Eds.), *Handbook of the biology of aging* (3rd ed., pp. 181–216). San Diego: Academic Press.

Lakoff, G. (1994). What is a conceptual system? In W. Overton & D. Palermo (Eds.), *The nature and ontogenesis of meaning* (pp. 41–90). Hillsdale, N.J.: Erlbaum.

La Leche League International. (1991). *The womanly art of breastfeeding* (5th ed.). New York: Plume Books.

Lamaze, F. (1970). *Painless childbirth: Psychoprophylactic method.* Chicago: Henry Regnery.

Lamb, M. (1977a). The development of mother-infant and father-infant attachments in the second year of life. *Developmental Psychology, 13,* 637–648.

Lamb, M. (1977b). Father-infant and mother-infant interactions in the first year of life. *Child Development, 48,* 167–181.

Lamb, M., Frodi, A., Hwang, C., & Steinberg, J. (1982). Mother- and father-infant interactions involving play and holding in traditional and nontraditional Swedish families. *Developmental Psychology, 18,* 215–221.

Lamb, M., Pleck, J. H., Charnov, E. L., & Levine, J. A. (1987). A biosocial perspective on paternal behavior and involvement. In J. B. Lancaster, J. Altmann, A. S. Rossi, & L. R. Sherrod (Eds.), *Parenting across the life span: Biosocial dimensions.* New York: Aldine de Gruyter.

Lamb, M., & Roopnarine, J. (1979). Peer influences on sex-role development in preschoolers. *Child Development, 50,* 1219–1222.

Lambert, W., Genesee, F., Holobow, N., & Chartrand, L. (1993). Bilingual education for majority English-speaking children. *European Journal of Psychology of Education, 8,* 3–22.

Lamke, L. K. (1982a) Adjustment and sex-role orientation. *Journal of Youth and Adolescence, 11,* 247–259.

Lamke, L. K. (1982b). The impact of sex-role orientation on self-esteem in early adolescence. *Child Development, 53,* 1530–1535.

Lamport, M. A. (1993). Student-faculty informal interaction and the effect on college student outcomes: A review of the literature. *Adolescence, 28*(112), 971–990.

Lancaster, J., & Hamburg, B. (1986). *School-age pregnancy and parenthood.* New York: DeGruyter.

Langer, N. (1995). Grandparents and adult grandchildren: What do they do for one another? In J. Hendricks (Ed.), *The ties of later life* (pp. 171–179). Amityville, N.Y.: Baywood.

Langlois, J., Roggman, L., Casey, R., & Rieser-Danner, L. (1990). Infants' differential social responses to attractive and unattractive faces. *Developmental Psychology, 26,* 153–159.

Lapsley, D. (1991). Egocentrism theory and the "new look" at the imaginary audience and personal fable. In R. Lerner, A. Petersen, & J. Brooks-Gunn (Eds.), *Encyclopedia of adolescence: Vol. 1* (pp. 281–286). New York: Garland.

LaRossa, R. (1992). Fatherhood and social change. In M. S. Kimmel & M. A. Messner (Eds.), *Men's lives* (2nd ed., pp. 521–535). New York: Macmillan.

Larrabee, M. (1993). *An ethic of care: Feminist and interdisciplinary perspectives.* New York: Routledge.

Larson, R., & Ham, M. (1993). Stress and "storm and stress" in early adolescence: The relationship of negative events with dysphoric affect. *Developmental Psychology, 29,* 130–140.

Larson, R., & Richards, M. H. (1991). Daily companionship in late childhood and early adolescence: Changing developmental contexts. *Child Development,62,* 284–300.

Larson, R., & Richards, M. H. (1994). *Divergent realities: The emotional lives of mothers, fathers and adolescents.* New York: Basic Books.

Larson, R., Zuzanek, J., & Mannell, R. (1985). Being alone versus being with people: Disengagement in the daily experience of older adults. *Journal of Gerontology, 40,* 375–381.

LaRue, A., Dessonville, C., & Jarvik, L. F. (1985). Aging and mental disorders. In J. E. Birren & K. W. Schaie (Eds.), *Handbook of the psychology of aging* (2nd ed., pp. 664–702). New York: Van Nostrand Reinhold.

Larzelere, R. E. (1986). Moderate spanking: Model or deterrent of children's aggression in the family? *Journal of Family Violence, 1,* 27–37.

Lasley, J. R. (1992). Age, social context, and street gang membership. *Youth and Society, 23,* 434–451.

Latack, J. C., & Kaufman, H. G. (1988). Termination and outplacement strategies. In M. London & E. M. Mone (Eds.), *Career growth and human resource strategies* (pp. 289–313). New York: Quorum Books.

Lauer, R. H., Lauer, J. C., & Kerr, S. T. (1995). The long-term marriage: Perceptions of stability and satisfaction. In J. Hendricks (Ed.), *The ties of later life* (pp. 35–41). Amityville, N.Y.: Baywood.

Lawson, A., & Rhode, D. L. (1993). *The Politics of Pregnancy: Adolescent Sexuality and Public Policy.* New Haven, Conn.: Yale University Press.

Lawton, M. P. (1985). Activities and leisure. In M. P. Lawton & G. L. Maddox (Eds.), *Annual Review of Gerontology and Geriatrics,* Volume 5, 127–164. New York: Springer.

Lazarus, R. S. (1993). From psychological stress to the emotions: A history of changing outlooks. *Annual Review of Psychology, 44,* 1–21.

Leadbetter, B. (1991). Relativistic thinking in adolescence. In R. Lerner, A. Petersen, & J. Brooks-Gunn (Eds.), *Encyclopedia of adolescence: Vol. 1* (pp. 921–925). New York: Garland.

Leary, W. E. (1995, January 31). Sickle cell trial called success, halted early. *The New York Times,* p. C–1.

Lee, C. (1992). Gender-related motivational differences in participation in an organized seniors fitness program: Moving beyond sex-role stereotypic motives. *Psychological Reports, 71,* 1085–1086.

Lee, D. J., & Markides, K. S. (1990). Activity and mortality among aged persons over an eight-year period. *Journal of Gerontology, 45,* S39–42.

Lee, F. R. (1995, May 9). For women with AIDS, anguish of having babies. *The New York Times,* pp. A1, B6.

Lee, G. R., Seccombe, K., & Shehan, C. L. (1991). Marital status and personal happiness: An analysis of trend data. *Journal of Marriage and the Family, 53,* 839–844.

Lee, V. E., Mackie-Lewis, C., & Marks, H. M. (1993). Persistence to the baccalaureate degree for students who transfer from community college. *American Journal of Education, 102*(1), 80–114.

Lehman, D. R., & Nisbett, R. E. (1990). A longitudinal study of the effects of undergraduate training on reasoning. *Developmental Psychology, 26,* 952–960.

Leigh, B. C. (1989). Reasons for having sex: Gender, sexual orientation, and relationship to sexual behavior. *Journal of Sex Research, 26,* 199–209.

Leigh, B. C., & Stall, R. (1993). Substance use and risky sexual behavior for exposure to HIV: Issues of methodology, interpretation, and prevention. *American Psychologist, 10,* 1035–1045.

Leming, M. R., & Dickinson, G. E. (1994). *Dying, death, and bereavement* (3rd ed.). New York: Holt, Rinehart & Winston.

Leon, A. S. (1983). Exercise and coronary heart disease. *Hospital Medicine, 19,* 38–59.

Leon, A. S., & Fox, S. M., III. (1981). Physical fitness. In E. L. Wynder (Ed.), *The book of health* (pp. 283–341). New York: Franklin Watts.

Leon, G. R., & Dinklage, D. (1989). Obesity and anorexia nervosa. In T. H. Ollendick & M. Hersen (Eds.), *Handbook of child psychopathology* (2nd ed., pp. 247–263). New York: Plenum Press.

Leor, J., Poole, W. K., & Kloner, R. A. (1996). Sudden cardiac death triggered by an earthquake. *New England Journal of Medicine, 334,* 413–419.

Lerner, J. (1993). *Learning disabilities* (6th ed.). Boston: Houghton Mifflin.

Lerner, R. M. (1990). Plasticity, person-context relations, and cognitive training in the aged years: A developmental contextual perspective. *Developmental Psychology, 26,* 911–915.

LeVay, S., & Hamer, D. H. (1994, May) Evidence for a biological influence in male homosexuality. *Scientific American,* 44–49.

Levenson, R. W., Carstensen, L. L., & Gottman, J. M. (1993). Long-term marriage: Age, gender, and satisfaction. *Psychology and Aging, 8,* 301–313.

Levine, G., & Parkinson, S. (1994). *Experimental methods in psychology.* Hillsdale, N.J.: Erlbaum.

Levinson, D. (1989). *Family violence in cross-cultural perspective.* Newbury Park, Cal.: Sage.

Levinson, D. J. (1978). *The seasons of a man's life.* New York: Knopf.

Levinson, D. J. (1986). A conception of adult development. *American Psychologist, 41,* 1–13.

Levinson, D. J. (1996). *The seasons of a woman's life.* New York: Knopf.

Levitt, M. J., Guacci-Franco, N., & Levitt, J. L. (1993). Convoys of social support in childhood and early adolescence: Structure and function. *Developmental Psychology, 29,* 811–818.

Levitt, M. J., Weber, R. A., & Guacci, N. (1993). Convoys of social support: An intergenerational analysis. *Psychology & Aging, 8*(3), 323–326.

Levy-Shiff, R. (1994). Individual and contextual correlates of marital change across the transition to parenthood. *Developmental Psychology, 30,* 591–601.

Lewis, C. T. (1993). Prenatal care in the United States. In B. K. Rothman (Ed.), *The encyclopedia of childbearing.* New York: Henry Holt.

Lewis, J. M. (1993). Childhood play in normality, pathology and therapy. *American Journal of Orthopsychiatry, 63,* 6–15.

Lewis, M. (1992). *Shame: The exposed self.* New York: The Free Press.

Lewis, M., & Brooks-Gunn, J. (1979a). *Social cognition and the acquisition of self.* New York: Plenum Press.

Lewis, M., & Brooks-Gunn, J. (1979b). Toward a theory of social cognition: The development of the self. In I. Uzgiris (Ed.), *Social interaction and communication during infancy.* San Francisco: Jossey-Bass.

Lewis, M., Brooks-Gunn, J., & Jaskir, J. (1985). Individual differences in visual self-recognition as a function of mother-infant attachment relationship. *Developmental Psychology, 21,* 1181–1187.

Lewis, M., Sullivan, M. W., Stanger, C., & Weiss, M. (1989). Self- development and self-conscious emotions. *Child Development, 60,* 146–156.

Lewkowicz, D., & Lickliter, R. (1994). *The development of intersensory perception.* Hillsdale, N.J.: Erlbaum.

Liebmann-Smith, J. (1993). Infertility: Overview. In B. K. Rothman (Ed.), *The encyclopedia of childbearing.* New York: Henry Holt.

Lickona, T. (1991). Moral development in the elementary school classroom. In W. Kurtines & J. Gewirtz (Eds.), *Handbook of moral behavior and development: Vol. 3* (pp. 143–162). Hillsdale, N.J.: Erlbaum.

Lieberman, M. A. (1993). Bereavement self-help groups: A review of conceptual and methodological issues. In M. S. Stroebe, W. Stroebe, & R. O. Hansson (Eds.), *Handbook of bereavement: Theory, research, and intervention* (pp. 411–426). Cambridge, U.K.: Cambridge University Press.

Liebert, R. M., & Sprafkin, J. (1988). *The early window: Effects of television on children and youth* (3rd ed.).New York: Pergamon Press.

Liem, R., & Liem, J. H. (1988). Psychological effects of unemployment on workers and their families. *Journal of Social Issues,44,* 87–105.

Light, R. (1990). *Explorations with students and faculty about teaching, learning, and student life: The first report.* Cambridge, Mass.: Harvard University Assessment Seminars.

Lightfoot, S. L. (1983). *The good high school: Portraits of character and culture.* New York: Basic Books.

Lindblad-Goldberg, M. (1989). Successful minority single-parent families. In L. Combrinck-Graham (Ed.), *Children in family contexts* (pp. 116–134). New York: Guilford.

Lindell, S. G. (1988). Education for childbirth: A time for change. *Journal of Obstetrics, Gynecology, and Neonatal Nursing, 17,* 108–112.

Linn, S., Lieverman, E., Schoenbaum, S. C., Monson, R. R., Stubblefield, P. G., & Ryan, K. (1988). Adverse outcomes of pregnancy in women exposed to diethylstilbestrol in utero. *Journal of Reproductive Medicine, 33,* 3–7.

Linney, J. A., & Seidman, E. (1989). The future of schooling. *American Psychologist, 44,* 336–340.

Lips, H. M. (1993). *Sex & gender* (2nd ed.). Mountain View, Cal.: Mayfield.

Lipsitt, L. (1990). Learning and memory in infants. *Merrill-Palmer Quarterly, 35,* 53–66.

Lipsitt, L., & Kaye, H. (1964). Conditioned sucking in the newborn. *Psychonomic Science, 1,* 29–30.

Lister, L. (1991). Men and grief: A review of research. *Smith College Studies in Social Work, 61*(3), 220–235.

Livson, N., & Peskin, H. (1981a). Perspectives on adolescence from longitudinal research. In J. Adelson (Ed.), *Handbook of adolescent psychology.* New York: Wiley.

Livson, N., & Peskin, H. (1981b). Psychological health at 40: Predictions from adolescent personality. In D. Eichorn, J. Clausen, N. Haan, M. Honzik, & P. Mussen (Eds.), *Present and past in middle life.* New York: Academic Press.

Lock, M. (1993). *Encounters with aging: Mythologies of menopause in Japan and North America.* Berkeley, Cal.: University of California Press.

Lockery, S. A. (1991). Family and social supports: Caregiving among racial and ethnic minority elders. *Generations, 15*(4), 58–62.

Loeb, R. C., Horst, L., & Horton, P. J. (1980). Family interaction patterns associated with self-esteem in preadolescent girls and boys. *Merrill-Palmer Quarterly, 26,* 203–217.

Logan, D. D. (1980). The menarche experience in twenty-three foreign countries. *Adolescence, 58,* 247–257.

Lohnes, K. L., & Kalter, N. (1994). Preventative intervention groups for parentally bereaved children. *American Journal of Orthopsychiatry, 64,* 594–603.

Londerville, S., & Main, M. (1981). Security of attachment, compliance, and maternal training methods. *Developmental Psychology, 17,* 289–299.

Longino, C. F., Jr., Warheit, G. J., & Green, J. A. (1989). Class, aging, and health. In K. S. Markides (Ed.), *Aging and health: Perspectives on gender, race, ethnicity and class* (pp. 79–109). Newbury Park, Cal.: Sage.

Longino, C. F., Soldo, B. J., & Manton, K. G. (1990). Demography of aging in the United States. In K. Ferraro (Ed.), *Gerontology issues and perspectives.* New York: Springer.

Lopata, H. Z. (1973). *Widowhood in an American city.* Cambridge, Mass: Schenkman.

Lopata, H. Z. (1993). The role of social support in bereavement. In M. S. Stroebe, W. Stroebe, & R. O. Hansson (Eds.), *Handbook of bereavement: Theory, research, and intervention* (pp. 381–396). Cambridge, U.K.: Cambridge University Press.

Lorenz, K. (Ed.). (1970). *Studies in animal and human behavior: Vol. 1.* Cambridge, Mass.: Harvard University Press.

Lozoff, B. (1989). Nutrition and behavior. *American Psychologist, 44,* 231–236.

Lund, D. A., Caserta, M. S., & Dimond, M. F. (1993). The course of spousal bereavement in later life. In M. S. Stroebe, W. Stroebe, & R. O. Hansson (Eds.), *Handbook of bereavement: Theory, research, and intervention* (pp. 240–254). Cambridge, U.K.: Cambridge University Press.

Luria, A. R. (1976). *Cognitive development: Its cultural and social foundations.* Cambridge, Mass.: Harvard University Press.

Luster, T., & McAdoo, H. (1996). Family and child influences on educational attachment: A secondary analysis of the High/Scope Perry Preschool data. *Developmental Psychology, 32,* 26–35.

Lustig, M., & Koester, J. (1993). *Intercultural competence: Interpersonal communication across cultures.* New York: HarperCollins.

Lutz, P. (1983). The stepfamily: An adolescent perspective. *Family Relations, 32,* 367–376.

Lu-Yao, G. L., & Greenberg, E. R. (1994). Changes in prostate cancer incidence and treatment in USA. *Lancet, 343,* 251–254.

Lyon, G. (1993). *Better understanding learning disabilities: New views on research and their implications for education and public policy.* Baltimore: Paul Brookes.

Lytinen, P. (1991). Developmental trends in children's pretend play. *Child Care, Health and Development, 17,* 9–25.

Lytton, H., & Romney, D. M. (1991). Parents' sex-related differential socialization of boys and girls: A meta-analysis. *Psychological Bulletin, 109,* 267–296.

Maccoby, E. E. (1980). *Social development, psychological growth, and parent-child relations.* New York: Harcourt Brace Jovanovich.

Maccoby, E. E. (1984). Socialization and developmental change. *Child Development, 55,* 317–328.

Maccoby, E. E. (1990). Gender and relationships: A developmental account. *American Psychologist, 45,* 513–520.

Maccoby, E. E., & Jacklin, C. (1980). Sex differences in aggression: A rejoinder and reprise. *Child Development, 48,* 964–980.

Maccoby, E. E., & Jacklin, C. (1987). Gender segregation in childhood. In H. Reese (Ed.), *Advances in child development and behavior: Vol. 20.* New York: Academic Press.

Maccoby, E. E., & Martin, J. A. (1983). Socialization in the context of the family: Parent-child interaction. In E. M. Hetherington (Ed.), *Handbook of child psychology: Vol. 4. Socialization, personality, and social development* (4th ed., pp. 1–101). New York: Wiley.

MacGregor, S. N., Keith, L. G., Chasnoff, I. J., Rosner, M. A., Chisum, G. M., Shaw, P., & Minogue, J. P. (1987). Cocaine use during pregnancy: Adverse perinatal outcome. *American Journal of Obstetrics and Gynecology, 1,* 66–90.

Magolda, M. B. (1989). Gender differences in cognitive development: An analysis of cognitive complexity and learning styles. *Journal of College Student Development, 30*(3) 213–220.

Maher, F. A., & Tetreault, M. K. T. (1994). *The feminist classroom.* New York: Basic Books.

Mahler, M., Pine, F., & Bergman, A. (1975). *The psychological birth of the human infant: Symbiosis and individuation.* New York: Basic Books.

Main, M., & George, C. (1985). Responses of abused and disadvantaged toddlers to distress in agemates: A study in the day care setting. *Developmental Psychology, 21,* 407–412.

Main, M., & Goldwyn, R. (1989). Predicting rejection of her infant from mother's representation of her own experience: Implications for the abused-abusing intergenerational cycle. *Child Abuse and Neglect, 8,* 203–217.

Maker, J. (Ed.). (1993). *Programs for the gifted in regular classrooms.* Austin, Tex.: Pro-Ed Publishers.

Malina, R. M. (1990). Physical growth and performance during the transition years (9–16). In R. Montemayor, G. R. Adams, & T. P. Gullotta (Eds.), *From childhood to adolescence: A transitional period?* (pp. 41–62). Newbury Park, Cal.: Sage.

Malina, R. M., & Bouchard, C. (1991). *Growth, maturation, and physical activity.* Champaign, Ill.: Human Kinetics Books.

Malincsky-Rummell, R., & Hansen, D. J. (1993). Long-term consequences of childhood physical abuse. *Psychological Bulletin, 114,* 68–79.

Mallinckrodt, B., & Fretz, B. R. (1988). Social support and the impact of job loss on older professionals. *Journal of Counseling Psychology, 35*(3), 281–286.

Mallory, G., & New, R. (Eds.). (1994). *Diversity and developmentally appropriate practice: Challenges for early childhood education.* New York: Teachers' College Press.

Maloney, M. J., & Klykylo, W. M. (1983). An overview of anorexia nervosa, bulimia and obesity in children and adolescents. *Journal of the American Academy of Child Psychiatry, 22,* 99–107.

Marcia, J. (1967). Ego identity status: Relationship to change in self-esteem, "general maladjustment," and authoritarianism. *Journal of Personality, 35,* 119–133.

Marcia, J. (1980). Identity in adolescence. In J. Adelson (Ed.), *Handbook of adolescent psychology.* New York: Wiley.

Marcus, D., & Overton, W. (1978). The development of cognitive gender constancy and sex role preferences. *Child Development, 49,* 434–444.

Marcus, G., Pinker, S., Ullman, M., Hollander, M., Rosen, T., & Xu, F. (1992). Overregularization in language acquisition. *Monographs of the Society for Research on Child Development, 57*(4, Serial No. 228).

Margolin, L. (1994). *Goodness personified: The emergence of gifted children.* New York: Aldine de Gruyter.

Markides, K. S. (1983). Aging, religiosity and adjustment: A longitudinal analysis. *Journal of Gerontology, 38,* 621–626.

Markides, K. S. (1989). Aging, gender, race/ethnicity, class, and health: A conceptual overview. In K. S. Markides (Ed.), *Aging and health: Perspectives on gender, race, ethnicity and class* (pp. 9–21). Newbury Park, Cal.: Sage.

Markides, K. S. (1990). Risk factors, gender, and health. *Generations, 14*(3), 17–21.

Markides, K. S., Coreil, J., & Rogers, L. P. (1989). Aging and health among southwestern Hispanics. In K. S. Markides (Ed.), *Aging and health: Perspectives on gender, race, ethnicity and class* (pp. 177–210). Newbury Park, Cal.: Sage.

Markides, K. S., & Krause, N. (1986). Older Mexican Americans (family relationships). *Generations, 10*(4), 32–35.

Markman, H. J., & Kadushin, F. S. (1986). Preventive effects of Lamaze training for first-time parents: A short-term longitudinal study. *Journal of Consulting and Clinical Psychology, 54,* 872–874.

Marks, L., Hammeal, R., & Bornstein, M. (1987). Similarity and comprehending metaphor. *Monographs of the Society for Research in Child Development, 52*(1, Serial No. 215).

Marschark, M. (1993). *Psychological development of deaf children.* New York: Oxford.

Marsh, C. E. (1993). Sexual assault and domestic violence in the African American community. *Western Journal of Black Studies, 17*(3), 149–155.

Marshall, V. W. (1980). *Last chapters: A sociology of aging and dying.* Monterey, Cal.: Brooks/Cole.

Marshall, V. W., & Levy, J. (1990). Aging and dying. In R. H. Binstock & L. K. George (Eds.), *Handbook of aging and the social sciences* (3rd ed., pp. 245–260). San Diego: Academic Press.

Marshall, W. (1978). Puberty. In F. Falkner & J. Tanner (Eds.), *Human growth: Vol. 2.* New York: Plenum Press.

Marshall, W., & Tanner, J. (1974). Puberty. In J. Davis & J. Dobbing (Eds.), *Scientific foundations of pediatrics.* London: Heinemann Publishers.

Marsiglio, W., & Donnelly, D. (1991). Sexual relations in later life: A national study of married persons. *Journal of Gerontology, 46,* S338–344.

Martin, B. (1975). Parent-child relations. In F. Horowitz (Ed.), *Review of child development research: Vol. 4.* Chicago: University of Chicago Press.

Martin, C. L., Wood, C. H., & Little, J. K. (1990). The development of gender stereotype components. *Child Development, 61,* 1891–1904.

Martinsen, E. W. (1990). Benefits of exercise for the treatment of depression. *Sports Medicine, 9,* 380–389.

Marx, K. H. (1991). Mutation identified as a possible cause of Alzheimer's disease. *Science, 251,* 867–877.

Masters, W. H., & Johnson, V. E. (1966). *Human sexual response.* Boston: Little, Brown.

Masters, W. H., Johnson, V. E., & Kolodny, R. C. (1992). *Human sexuality* (4th ed.). Boston: Little, Brown.

Masters, W. H., Johnson, V. E., & Kolodny, R. C. (1994). *Heterosexuality*. New York: HarperCollins.

Matas, L., Arend, R. A., & Sroufe, L. A. (1978). Continuity of adaptation in the second year: The relationship between quality of attachment and later competence. *Child Development, 49,* 547–555.

Matthews, K. A., Wing, R. R., Kuller, L. H., Meilah, E. N., & Kelsey, S. F. (1990). Influences of natural menopause on psychological characteristics and symptoms of middle-aged healthy women. *Journal of Consulting and Clinical Psychology, 58,* 345–351.

Matthews, S. H., & Rosner, T. T. (1988). Shared filial responsibility: The family as the primary caregiver. *Journal of Marriage and the Family, 50,* 185–195.

McAdams, D. P., de St. Aubin, E., & Logan, R. L. (1993). Generativity among young, midlife, and older adults. *Psychology and Aging, 8,* 221–230.

McCabe, A., & Lipscomb, T. J. (1988). Sex differences in children's verbal aggression. *Merrill-Palmer Quarterly, 34,* 389–401.

McCall, R. (1981). Nature-nurture and the two realms of development: A proposed integration with respect to mental development. *Child Development, 52,* 1–12.

McCall, R., & Kagan, J. (1967). Stimulus schema discrepancy and attention in the infant. *Journal of Experimental Child Psychology, 5,* 381–390.

McCrae, R. R. (Ed.). (1992). The five-factor model: Issues and applications [Special issue]. *Journal of Personality, 60*(2).

McCrae, R. R., & Costa, P. T., Jr. (1984). *Emerging lives, enduring dispositions.* Boston: Little, Brown.

McCrae, R. R., & Costa, P. T., Jr. (1993). Psychological resilience among widowed men and women: A 10-year follow-up of a national survey. In M. S. Stroebe, W. Stroebe, & R. O. Hansson (Eds.), *Handbook of bereavement: Theory, research, and intervention* (pp. 196–207). Cambridge, U.K.: Cambridge University Press.

McCrea, R. R., & John, O. P. (1992). An introduction to the five-factor model and its applications. *Journal of Personality, 60,* 175–216.

McCullough, M., & Scherman, A. (1991). Adolescent pregnancy: Contributing factors and strategies for prevention. *Adolescence, 26,* 809–816.

McDaniel, K. D. (1986). Pharmacological treatment of psychiatric and neuro-developmental disorders in children and adolescents (Parts 1, 2, & 3). *Clinical Pediatrics, 25,* 65–71, 198–224.

McDonald, M., Sigman, M., Espinosa, M., & Neumann, C. (1994). Impact of a temporary food shortage on children and their mothers. *Child Development, 65,* 404–415.

McElhaney, L. J. (1992). Dating and courtship in the later years: A neglected topic of research. *Generations, 17*(3), 21–23.

McFadden, S. H., & Gerl, R. (1990). Approaches to understanding spirituality in the second half of life. *Generations, 14*(3), 35–38.

McGinnis, J. M., & Foege, W. H. (1993). Actual causes of death in the United States. *Journal of the American Medical Association 270,* 2207–2212.

McGinnis, M., Richmond, J. B., Brandt, E. N., Windom, R. E., & Mason, J. O. (1992). Health progress in the United States: Results of the 1990 objectives for the nation. *Journal of the American Medical Association, 268,* 2545–2552.

McGoldrick, M., Pearce, J. K., & Giordano, J. (Eds.). (1982). *Ethnicity and family therapy.* New York: Guilford.

McKay, M. M. (1994). The link between domestic violence and child abuse: Assessment and treatment considerations. *Child Welfare, 73,* 29–39.

McKay, S. (1993). Labor: Overview. In B. K. Rothman, (Ed.), *The encyclopedia of childbearing.* New York: Henry Holt.

McKinlay, J. B., McKinlay, S. M., & Brambilla, D. (1987). The relative contributions of endocrine changes and social circumstances to depression in mid-aged women. *Journal of Health and Social Behavior, 28,* 345–363.

McKinlay, S. M., Brambilla, D. J., & McKinlay, J. B. (1991). Women's experience of the menopause. *Current Obstetrics and Gynecology, 1,* 3–7.

McKussick, V. A. (1988). *Mendelian inheritance in man: Catalogues of autosomal dominant, autosomal recessive, and X-linked phenotypes* (7th ed.). Baltimore: Johns Hopkins University Press.

McLoyd, V. C. (1989). Socialization and development in a changing economy: The effects of paternal job and income loss on children. *American Psychologist, 44,* 243–252.

McNamara, T., Miller, D., & Bransford, J. (1991). Mental models and the construction of meaning. In P. Pearson (Ed.), *Handbook of reading research: Vol. 2* (pp. 490–511). New York: Longman.

McNeil, K. J., LeBlanc, E. M., & Joyner, M. (1991). The effect of exercise on depressive symptoms in the moderately depressed elderly. *Psychology and Aging, 6,* 487–491.

Meehan, P. J., Lamb, J. A., Saltzman, L. E., & O'Carroll, P. W. (1992). Attempted suicide among young adults: Progress toward a meaningful estimate of prevalence. *American Journal of Psychiatry, 149,* 41–44.

Meilman, P. (1979). Cross-sectional age changes in ego identity status during adolescence. *Developmental Psychology, 15,* 230–231.

Meltzoff, A., Kuhl, P., & Moore, M. K. (1991). Perception, representation, and control of action in newborns and young infants. In M. Weiss & P. Zelazo (Eds.), *Newborn attention: Biological constraints and the influence of experience* (pp. 377–411). Norwood, N.J.: Ablex.

Meltzoff, A., & Kuhl, P. (1994). Faces and speech: Intermodel processing of biologically relevant signals in infants and adults. In D. Lewkowicz & R. Lickliter (Eds.), *The development of intersensory perception* (pp. 335–370). Hillsdale, N.J.: Erlbaum.

Melville, K. (1988). *Marriage and family today* (4th ed.). New York: Random House.

Mendelson, B., & White, D. (1995). Children's global self-esteem predicted by body-esteem but not by weight. *Perceptual & Motor Skills, 80,* 97–98.

Menkes, J. (1994). *Textbook of child neurology* (5th ed.). Philadelphia: Williams and Wilkins.

Mennuti, R. B., & Creamer, D. G. (1991). Role of orientation, gender, and dilemma content in moral reasoning. *Journal of College Student Development, 32,* 241–248.

Meredith, H. (1967). A synopsis of pubertal changes in youth. *Journal of School Health, 37,* 171–176.

Merriam, S. B. (1993). Race, sex, and age-group differences in the occurrence and uses of reminiscence. *Activities, Adaptation and Aging, 18*(1), 1–18.

Messer, D. (1994). *The development of communication: From social interaction to language.* New York: Wiley.

Michael, R. T., Gagnon, J. H., Laumann, E. O., & Kolata, G. (1994). *Sex in America: A definitive survey.* Boston: Little, Brown.

Michelsson, K., Rinne, A., & Paajanen, S. (1990). Crying, feeding and sleeping patterns in 1 to 12-month-old infants. *Child: Care, health and development, 116,* 99–111.

Mikaye, K., Chen, S., & Campos, J. (1985). Infant temperament, mother's mode of interaction, and attachment in Japan. In I. Bretherton & E. Waters (Eds.), *Growing points of attachment theory and research. Monographs of the Society for Research on Child Development, 50*(209).

Miller, A. (1990). *For your own good: Hidden cruelty in child-rearing and the roots of violence.* New York: Noonday Press.

Miller, B. (1987). Gender and control among spouses of the cognitively impaired: A research note. *The Gerontologist, 27,* 447–453.

Miller, B. (1990). Gender differences in spouse caregiver strain: Socialization and role explanations. *Journal of Marriage and the Family, 52,* 311–321.

Miller, B. C., & Moore, K. A. (1990). Adolescent sexual behavior, pregnancy, and parenting: Research through the 1980's. *Journal of Marriage and the Family, 52,* 1025–1044.

Miller, C. A. (1992). Biophysical development during late adulthood. In C. S. Schuster & S. S. Ashburn (Eds.), *The process of human development: A holistic lifespan approach* (3rd ed., pp. 804–830). New York: J. B. Lippincott.

Miller, I. J. (1988). Human taste bud density across adult age groups. *Journal of Gerontology, 43,* B26–30.

Miller, M. A. (1993). Smoking in pregnancy. In B. K. Rothman (Ed.), *The encyclopedia of childbearing.* New York: Henry Holt.

Miller, P. (1989). *Theories of developmental psychology* (2nd ed.). New York: Freeman.

Miller, P. (1993). *Theories of developmental psychology* (3rd ed.). New York: W. H. Freeman.

Miller, P., & Simon, W. (1980). The development of sexuality in adolescence. In J. Adelson (Ed.), *Handbook of adolescent psychology.* New York: Wiley.

Miller, T., & Winston, R. (1990). Assessing development from a psychosocial perspective. In D. Creamer & associates (Eds.), *College student development: Theory and practice for the 1990s* (Media Publication No. 49). Alexandria, Va.: American College Personnel Association.

Mills, R. S. L., & Rubin, K. H. (1990). Parental beliefs about problematic behavior in early childhood. *Child Development, 61,* 138–151.

Millstein, S. G. (1989). Adolescent health: Challenges for behavioral scientists. *American Psychologist, 44,* 837–842.

Minuchin, P., & Shapiro, E. (1983). The school as a context for social development. In E. M. Hetherington (Ed.), *Handbook of child psychology: Vol. 4. Socialization, personality and social development* (4th ed.). New York: Wiley.

Mireault, G. C., & Bond, L. A. (1992). Parental death in childhood: Perceived vulnerability and adult depression and anxiety. *American Journal of Orthopsychiatry, 62,* 517–524.

Mirowsky, J., & Ross, C. E. (1992). Age and depression. *Journal of Health and Social Behavior, 33,* 187–205.

Mishell, D. R., & Brenner, P. F. (1986). Menopause. In D. R. Mishell, Jr., & V. Davajan (Eds.), *Infertility, contraception, and reproductive endocrinology* (2nd ed., pp. 179–202). Oradell, N.J.: Medical Economics Books.

Mitchell, J., & Register, J. (1984). An exploration of family interaction with the elderly by race, socioeconomic status, and residence. *The Gerontologist, 11,* 88–93.

Mitford, J. (1963). *The American way of death.* New York: Simon & Schuster.

Moen, P., Dempster-McClain, D., & Williams R. M. (1989). Social integration and longevity: An event history analysis of women's roles and resilience. *American Sociological Review, 54,* 635–647.

Mogford, K. (1993). Language development in twins. In D. Bishop & K. Mogford (Eds.), *Language development in exceptional circumstances* (pp. 80–95). Hillsdale, N.J.: Erlbaum.

Money, J. (1992). *The Kasper Hauser syndrome of "psychosocial dwarfism": Deficient statural, intellectual and social growth induced by child abuse.* Buffalo, N.Y.: Prometheus Books.

Montessori, M. (1964). *The Montessori method.* New York: Schocken Books.

Montgomery, R. J. (1992). Gender differences in patterns of child-parent caregiving relationships. In J. W. Dwyer & R. T. Coward (Eds.), *Gender, families, and elder care* (pp. 65–83). Newbury Park, Cal.: Sage.

Moody, H. R. (1994a). *Aging: Concepts and controversies.* Thousand Oaks, Cal.: Pine Forge Press.

Moody, H. R. (1994b). Should people have the choice to end their lives? In H. R. Moody (Ed.), *Aging: Concepts and controversies* (pp. 99–107). Thousand Oaks, Cal.: Pine Forge Press.

Moore, D. (1984). Parent-adolescent separation: Intrafamilial perceptions and difficulty separating from parents. *Personality and Social Psychology Bulletin, 10,* 611–619.

Moore, D. (1987). Parent-adolescent separation: The construction of adulthood by late adolescents. *Developmental Psychology, 23,* 298–307.

Moore, F. D. (1995). *A miracle and a privilege: Recounting a half century of surgical advance.* Washington, D.C.: Joseph Henry Press.

Moorehouse, M. J. (1991). Linking maternal employment patterns to mother-child activities and children's school competence. *Developmental Psychology, 27,* 295–303.

Moran, E. G. (1993). Domestic violence and pregnancy. In B. K. Rothman (Ed.), *The encyclopedia of childbearing.* New York: Henry Holt.

Morgan, L. A. (1984). Changes in family interaction following widowhood. *Journal of Marriage and the Family, 46,* 323–331.

Morris, J. N., & Morris, S. A. (1992). Aging in place: The role of formal services. *Generations, 16*(2), 41–48.

Morrongiello, B. (1994). Effects of colocation on auditory-visual interactions and cross-modality perception in infants. In D. Lewkowicz & R. Lickliter (Eds.), *The development of intersensory perception* (pp. 235–264). Hillsdale, N.J.: Erlbaum.

Mortimer, J. T., Finch, M., Shanahan, M., & Ryu, S. (1992a). Work experience, mental health, and behavioral adjustment in adolescence. *Journal of Research in Adolescence, 2,* 25–57.

Mortimer, J. T., Finch, M., Shanahan, M., & Ryu, S. (1992b). Adolescent work history and behavioral adjustment. *Journal of Research in Adolescence, 2,* 59–80.

Morton, R. A., Jr. (1994). Racial differences in adenocarcinoma of the prostate in North American men. *Urology, 44,* 637–645.

Mosher, W. D., & Pratt, W. F. (1991). Fecundity and infertility in the United States: Incidents and trends. *Fertility and Sterility, 56,* 192–193.

Mottaz, C. J. (1987). Age and work satisfaction. *Work & Occupations, 14*(3) 387–409.

Moyer, M. S. (1992). Sibling relationships among older adults. *Generations, 17*(3), 55–58.

Muehlenhard, C., & Linton, M. (1987). Date rape. *Journal of Counseling Psychology, 34,* 186–196.

Mullan, J. T., Pearlin, L. I., & Skaff, M. M. (1995). The bereavement process: Loss, grief, recovery. In I. B. Corless, B. B. Germino, & M. A. Pittman (Eds.). *A challenge for living: Dying, death, and bereavement.* Boston: Jones and Bartlett Publishers.

Mullins, L. C., & Mushel, M. (1992). The existence and emotional closeness of relationships with children, friends, and spouses: The effect on loneliness among older persons. *Research on Aging, 14*(4), 448–470.

Munroe, R., Munroe, R., & Whiting, J. (1981). Male sex-role resolutions. In *Handbook of cross-cultural human development.* New York: Garland.

Murphy, J. M., & Gilligan, C. (1980). Moral development in late adolescence and adulthood: A critique and reconstruction of Kohlberg's theory. *Human Development, 23,* 77–104.

Murphy, L. (1937). *Social behavior and child personality.* New York: Columbia University Press.

Murstein, B. I. (1988). A taxonomy of love. In R. J. Sternberg & M. L. Brown (Eds.), *The psychology of love.* New Haven, Conn.: Yale University Press.

Murstein, B. I., Chalpin, M. J., Heard, K. V., & Vyse, S. A. (1989). Sexual behavior, drug, and relationship patterns on a college campus over thirteen years. *Adolescence, 24,* 125–139.

Mutschler, P. H. (1992). Where elders live. *Generations, 16*(2), 7–14.

Myers, J. (1993). Curricular designs that resonate with adolescents' ways of knowing. In R. Lerner (Ed.), *Early adolescence: Perspectives on research, policy, and intervention* (pp. 191–206). Hillsdale, N.J.: Erlbaum.

Nachtigall, L. E. (1987). Cardiovascular disease and hypertension in older women. *Obstetrics and Gynecology Clinics of North America, 14,* 89–105.

Nagata, D. (1989). Japanese-American children and adolescents. In J. Gibbs & L. Huang (Eds.), *Children of color* (pp. 67–113). San Francisco: Jossey-Bass.

National Cancer Institute. (1990). *Cancer statistics review, 1973–87.* (NCI, NIH Pub. No. 90–2789.) Bethesda, Md.: U.S. Government Printing Office.

National Center for Health Statistics. (1993). Advance report of final mortality statistics, 1990. *Monthly Vital Statistics Report, 41*(7) (Supp.). Hyattsville, Md.: U.S. Department of Health and Human Services, Public Health Service, Centers for Disease Control and Prevention.

National Center for Health Statistics. (1993). *Health, United States, 1992.* Hyattsville, Md.: Public Health Service.

National Lesbian and Gay Survey. (1992). *What a lesbian looks like.* London: Routledge.

Neale, A. V. (1994). Racial and marital status influences on 10- year survival from breast cancer. *Journal of Clinical Epidemiology, 47,* 475–483.

Neugarten, B. L. (1967). The awareness of middle age. In R. Owen (Ed.), *Middle age.* London: British Broadcasting Company.

Neugarten, B. L. (1968). Adult personality: Toward a psychology of the life cycle. In B. L. Neugarten (Ed.), *Middle age and aging: A reader in social psychology* (pp. 137–147). Chicago: University of Chicago Press.

Neugarten, B. L. (1968). The awareness of middle age. In B. L. Neugarten (Ed.), *Middle age and aging: A reader in social psychology* (pp. 93–98). Chicago: University of Chicago Press.

Neugarten, B. L. (1977). Personality and aging. In J. E. Birren & K. W. Schaie (Eds.), *Handbook of the psychology of aging* (pp. 626–649). New York: Van Nostrand Reinhold.

Neugarten, B. L., & Neugarten, D. A. (1986, Winter). Age in the aging society. *Daedalus,* 31–49.

Neugarten, B. L., & Neugarten, D. A. (1987). The changing meanings of age. *Psychology Today, 21*(5), 29–33.

Neulinger, J. (1981). *The psychology of leisure.* Springfield, Ill.: Charles C Thomas.

Newcomb, M., & Bentler, P. (1989). Substance use and abuse among children and teenagers. *American Psychologist, 44,* 242–248.

Newman, F., & Holzman, L. (1993). *Lev Vygotsky: Revolutionary scientist.* New York: Routledge.

Nichol, S. T., Spiropoulou, C. F., Morzunov, S., Rollin, P. E., Ksiazek, T. G., Feldmann, H., Sanchez, A., Childs, J., Zaki, S., & Peters, C. J. (1993). Genetic identification of a hantavirus associated with an outbreak of acute respiratory illness. *Science, 262,* 914–917.

Nichols, J., Nelson, J., & Gleaves, K. (1995). Learning "facts" versus learning that most questions have many answers: Student evaluations of contrasting curricula. *Journal of Educational Psychology, 87*(2), 253–260.

Noam, G., & Wren, T. (1993). *The moral self.* Cambridge, Mass.: MIT Press.

Noble, K. D., & Drummond, J. E. (1992). But what about the prom? Students' perceptions of early college entrance. Special issue: Challenging the gifted: Grouping and acceleration. *Gifted Child Quarterly, 36*(2), 106–111.

Noh, S., Dumas, J. E., Wolf, L. C., & Fisman, S. (1989). Delineating sources of stress in parents of exceptional children. *Family Relations, 38,* 456–461.

Nolen-Hoeksema, S., Wolfson, A., Mumme, D., & Guskin, K. (1995). Helplessness in children of depressed and nondepressed mothers. *Developmental Psychology, 31,* 377–387.

Noppe, I. C., Noppe, L. D., & Hughes, F. P. (1991). Stress as a predictor of the quality of parent-infant interactions. *Journal of Genetic Psychology, 152,* 17–28.

Norbeck, J. S., & Tilden, V. P. (1983). Life stress, social support, and emotional disequilibrium in complications of pregnancy: A prospective, multivariate study. *Journal of Health and Social Behavior, 24,* 30–46.

Norman, C. (1988). Math education: A mixed picture. *Science, 241,* 408–409.

Norris, J. E., & Tindale, J. A. (1994). *Among generations: The cycle of adult relationships.* New York: Freeman.

Notman, M. T. (1990). Varieties of menopausal experience. In R. Formanek (Ed.), *The meanings of menopause* (pp. 239–254). Hillsdale, N.J.: Analytic Press.

Nucci, L., & Turiel, E. (1993). God's word, religious rules, and their relation to Christian and Jewish children's concepts of morality. *Child Development, 64,* 1475–1491.

Nuland, S. B. (1994). *How we die? Reflections on life's final chapter.* New York: Knopf.

O'Brien, R. W., Smith, S. A., Bush, P. J., & Peleg, E. (1990). Obesity, self-esteem, and health locus of control in black youths during transition to adolescence. *American Journal of Health Promotion, 5*(2), 133–139.

O'Brien, S. F., & Bierman, K. L. (1988). Conceptions and perceived influence of peer groups: Interviews with preadolescents and adolescents. *Child Development, 59,* 1360–1365.

O'Brien, S. J., & Vertinsky, P. A. (1991). Unfit survivors: Exercise as a resource for aging women. *The Gerontologist, 31,* 347–357.

O'Connor, D. M. (1987). Elders and higher education: Instrumental or expressive goals? *Educational Gerontology, 13*(6) 511–519.

O'Connor, P. (1992). *Friendships between women.* New York: Harvester Wheatshaft.

O'Donnell, J., Hawkins, J. D., Catalano, R. F., Abbott, R. D., & Day, L. E. (1995). Preventing school failure, drug use and delinquency among low-income children: Long-term intervention in elementary schools. *American Journal of Orthopsychiatry, 65,* 87–100.

Offer, D., Ostrov, E., Howard, K. I., & Atkinson, R. (1988). *The teenage world: Adolescent's self-image in ten countries.* New York: Plenum Press.

Offer, D., & Schonert-Reichl, K. A. (1992). Debunking the myths of adolescence: Findings from recent research. *Journal of the American Academy of Child and Adolescent Psychiatry, 31,* 1003–1014.

O'Hara-Devereaux, M., & Johansen, R. (1994). *Globalwork: Bridging distance, culture, and time.* San Francisco: Jossey-Bass.

Olds, D. (1988). The prenatal/early infancy project. In R. H. Price, E. L. Cowen, R. P. Lorion, & J. Ramos-McKay (Eds.), *14 Ounces of Prevention.* Washington, D.C.: American Psychological Association.

Olshansky, S. J., Carnes, B. A., & Cassel, C. (1990). In search of Methuselah: Estimating the upper limits to human longevity. *Science, 250,* 634–640.

Olson, M. R., & Haynes, J. A. (1993). Successful single parents. *Families in Society: The Journal of Contemporary Human Services, 74*(5), 259–267.

Olvera-Ezzell, N., Power, T., Cousins, J., Guerra, A., & Trujillo, M. (1994). The development of health knowledge in low-income Mexican-American children. *Child Development, 65,* 416–427.

Ontario Ministry of Culture, Tourism, and Recreation. (1994). *Policy on full and fair access for women and girls in sport and physical activity.* Toronto: Author.

Opie, I., & Opie, P. (1969). *Children's games in streets and playgrounds.* London: Clarendon Press.

Opinion Roundup. (1980, December/January). Work in the 70's. *Public Opinion, 3,* p. 36.

Oster, H., Hegley, D., & Nagel, L. (1992). Adult judgments and fine-grained analysis of infant facial expressions: Testing the validity of a priori coding formulas. *Developmental Psychology, 28,* 1115–1131.

Page, D. C., Mosher, R., Simpson, E. M., Fisher, E. M., Mardon, G., Pillack, J., McGillivray, B., de la Chapelle, A., & Brown, L. G. (1987). The sex-determining region of the human Y chromosome encodes a finer protein. *Cell, 51,* 1091–1104.

Page, H. (1989). Estimation of the prevalence and incidence of infertility in a population: A pilot study. *Fertility and Sterility, 51,* 571–577.

Parish, W. L., Hao, L., & Hogan, D. P. (1991). Family support networks, welfare, and work among young mothers. *Journal of Marriage and the Family, 53,* 203–215.

Parke, R. D., MacDonald, K. B., Beitel, A., & Bhavnagri, N. (1988). The role of the family in the development of peer relationships. In R. DeV. Peters & R. J. McMahan (Eds.), *Marriages and families: Behavioral treatment and processes.* New York: Brunner/Mazel.

Parkins, E. (1990). *Equilibration, mind and brain: Toward an integrated psychology.* New York: Praeger.

Parmelee, P. A., Katz, I. R., & Lawton, M. P. (1992). Depression and mortality among institutionalized aged. *Journal of Gerontology, 47,* P3–10.

Parten, M. (1932). Social play among preschool children. *Journal of Abnormal and Social Psychology, 27*, 243–269.

Pascarella, E. T., Bohr, L., Zusman, B., et al. (1993). Cognitive impacts of living on campus versus commuting to college. *Journal of College Student Development, 34*(3) 216–220.

Pascarella, E. T., & Terenzini, P. T. (1991). *How college affects students: Findings and insights from twenty years of research.* San Francisco: Jossey-Bass.

Pasupathi, M., Carstensen, L. L., & Tsai, J. L. (1995). Ageism in interpersonal settings. In B. Lott & D. Maluso, *The social psychology of interpersonal discrimination.* New York: Guilford Press.

Patterson, C. J. (1995). Sexual orientation and human development: An overview. *Developmental Psychology, 31*, 3–11.

Patterson, G. R. (1982). *Coercive family processes.* Eugene, Ore.: Castilia Press.

Patterson, G. R. (1985). *A social learning approach to family intervention: Vol. 1. Families with aggressive children.* Eugene, Ore.: Castilia Press.

Patterson, G. R., DeBaryshe, B. D., & Ramsey, E. (1989). A developmental perspective on antisocial behavior. *American Psychologist, 44*, 329–340.

Patterson, G. R., & Dishion, T. J. (1985). Contributions of families and peers to delinquency. *Criminology, 23*, 63–79.

Paulston, C. (1992). *Linguistic and communicative competence: Topics in ESL.* Philadelphia: Multilingual Matters Ltd.

Paulston, C. (Ed.). (1988). *International handbook of bilingualism and bilingual education.* New York: Greenwood Press.

Payer, L. (1992). *Disease-mongers: How doctors, drug companies, and insurers are making you feel sick.* New York: John Wiley.

Payne, B. P., & McFadden, S. H. (1994). From loneliness to solitude: Religious and spiritual journeys in late life. In L. E. Thomas & S. A. Eisenhandler (Eds.), *Aging and the religious dimension* (pp. 13–27). Westport, Conn.: Auburn House.

Pease-Alvarez, L. (1993). *Moving in and out of bilingualism: Investigating native language maintenance and shift in Mexican-descent children.* Santa Cruz, Cal.: National Center for Research on Cultural Diversity, University of California.

Penner, S. (1987). Parental responses to grammatical and ungrammatical child utterances. *Child Development, 58*, 376–384.

Peplau, L. A., & Cochran, S. D. (1990). A relationship perspective on homosexuality. In D. P. McWhirter, S. A. Sanders, & J. M. Reinisch (Eds.), *Homosexuality/heterosexuality: Concepts of sexual orientation* (pp. 321–349). New York: Oxford University Press.

Perez, B., & Torres-Guzman, M. (1992). *Learning in two worlds: An integrated Spanish/English biliteracy approach.* New York: Longman.

Perkins, H. W., & Harris, L. B. (1990). Familial bereavement and health in adult life course perspective. *Journal of Marriage and the Family, 52*, 233–241.

Perry, W. G. (1970). *Forms of intellectual and ethical development in the college years.* New York: Holt.

Peskin, H. (1973). Influence of the developmental schedule of puberty on learning and ego functioning. *Journal of Youth and Adolescence, 2*, 273–290.

Pesmen, C. (1984). *How a man ages?* New York: Ballantine Books.

Petersen, A. C., Compas, B. E., Brooks-Gunn, J., Stemmler, M. E., & Grant, K. E. (1993). Depression in adolescence. *American Psychologist, 48*, 155–168.

Peterson, A. C. (1987). The nature of biological-psychosocial interactions: The sample case of early adolescence. In R. M. Lerner & T. T. Foch (Eds.), *Biological-psychosocial interactions in early adolescence* (pp. 35–61). Hillsdale, N.J.: Erlbaum.

Peterson, R. E. (1981). Opportunities for adult learners. In A. W. Chickering (Ed.), *The modern American college: Responding to the new realities of diverse students and a changing society* (pp. 306–327). San Francisco: Jossey-Bass.

Pettit, G., Dodge, K., & Brown, N. (1988). Early family experience, social problem solving patterns, and children's social competence. *Child Development, 59*, 107–120.

Pettito, L., & Marentette, P. (1991). Babbling in the manual code: Evidence for the ontogeny of language. *Science, 251*, 1493–1496.

Pfeffer, C. R. (1991). Preoccupations with death in "normal" children: The relationship to suicidal behavior. *Omega: Journal of Death and Dying, 20*, 205–212.

Philadelphia Child Guidance Center. (1994). *Your child's emotional health: The middle years.* New York: Macmillan.

Phillips, D. A. (Ed.). (1987). *Quality child care: What does research tell us?* Washington, D.C.: National Association for the Education of Young Children.

Phillips, D. P., & King, E. W. (1988). Death takes a holiday: Mortality surrounding major social occasions. *Lancet, 2*, 728–732.

Phillips, D. P., & Smith, D. G. (1990). Postponement of death until symbolically meaningful occasions. *Journal of the American Medical Association, 263*, 1947–1951.

Phillips, D. P., Van Voorhees, C. A., & Ruth, T. E. (1992). The birthday: Lifeline or deadline? *Psychosomatic Medicine, 54*, 532–542.

Phinney, J. S., Feshbach, N. D., & Farer, J. (1986). Preschool children's response to peer crying. *Early Childhood Research Quarterly, 1*, 207–219.

Piaget, J. (1952). *The child's conception of number.* New York: Norton.

Piaget, J. (1962). *Play, dreams, and imitation in childhood.* New York: Norton.

Piaget, J. (1963). *The origins of intelligence in children.* New York: Norton.

Piaget, J. (1964). *The moral development of the child.* New York: Free Press.

Piaget, J. (1965). *The child's conception of the world.* Totowa, N.J.: Littlefield, Adams.

Piaget, J. (1970). Piaget's theory. In P. Mussen (Ed.), *Carmichael's manual of child psychology* (3rd ed., Vol. 1). New York: Wiley.

Piaget, J. (1983). Piaget's theory. In P. Mussen (Ed.), *Handbook of child psychology: Vol. 1.* New York: Wiley.

Piaget, J., & Inhelder, B. (1967). *The child's conception of space.* New York: Norton.

Pianta, R., Egeland, B., & Erikson, M. (1989). The effects of maltreatment on the development of young children. In D. Cicchetti & V. Carlson (Eds.), *Child Maltreatment.* New York: Cambridge University Press.

Pillemer, K., & Suitor, J. J. (1991). "Will I ever escape my child's problems?" Effects of adult children's problems on elderly parents. *Journal of Marriage and the Family, 53*, 585–594.

Pinon, M. F., Huston, A. C., & Wright, J. C. (1989). Family ecology and child characteristics that predict young children's educational television viewing. *Child Development, 60*, 846–856.

Pirie, P., Murray, D., & Luepker, R. (1991). Gender differences in cigarette smoking and quitting in a cohort of young adults. *American Journal of Public Health, 81*, 324–327.

Pittman, T., & Kaufman, M. (1994). *All shapes and sizes: Promoting fitness and self-esteem in your overweight child.* Toronto: Harper Perennial Books.

Pitts, D. G. (1982). Visual acuity as a function of age. *Journal of the American Optometric Association, 53*, 117–124.

Plante, T. G., & Rodin, J. (1990). Physical fitness and enhanced psychological health. *Current Psychology: Research and Reviews, 9*, 3–24.

Plomin, R. (1989). Environment and genes: Determinants of behavior. *American Psychologist, 44*, 105–111.

Plomin, R. (1990). *Nature and nurture: An introduction to human behavioral genetics.* Pacific Grove, Cal.: Brooks/Cole.

Plomin, R., Emde, R., Braungart, J., Campos, J., Corley, R., Fulker, D., Kagan, J., Resnick, J., Robinson, J., Zahn-Waxler, C., & DeFries, J. (1993). Genetic change and continuity from 14 to 20 months. *Child Development, 64*, 1354–1376.

Plomin, R., & Rowe, D. (1979). Genetic and environmental etiology of social behavior in infancy. *Developmental Psychology, 15*, 62–72.

Pollitt, E. (1987). Effects of iron deficiency on mental development. In F. Johnston (Ed.), *Nutritional anthropology.* New York: Alan R. Liss.

Pollitt, E., Garza, C., & Leibel, R. (1984). Nutrition and public policy. In H. Stevenson & A. Siegel (Eds.), *Child development research and social policy.* Chicago: University of Chicago Press.

Pollock, M. L., Foster, C., Knapp, D., Rod, J. L., & Schmidt, D. H. (1987). Effect of age and training on aerobic capacity and body composition of master athletes. *Journal of Applied Physiology, 62*, 725–731.

Pomerantz, E. M., Ruble, D. N., Frey, K. S., & Greulich, F. (1995). Meeting goals and confronting conflict: Children's changing perceptions of social comparison. *Child Development, 66*, 723–738.

Pomerantz, S. (1979). Sex differences in the relative importance of self-esteem, physical self-satisfaction, and identity in predicting adolescent satisfaction. *Journal of Youth and Adolescence, 8*, 51–61.

Ponterotto, J. G. (1990). Racial/ethnic minority and women students in higher education: A status report. *New Directions for Student Services, 52*, 45–59.

Pope, A. W., Bierman, K. L., & Mumma, G. H. (1991). Aggression, hyperactivity, and inattention-immaturity: Behavior dimensions associated with peer rejection in elementary school boys. *Developmental Psychology, 27*, 663–671.

Portes, P. R., Howell, S. C., Brown, J. H., Eichenberger, S., & Mas, C. A. (1992). Family functions and children's postdivorce adjustment. *American Journal of Orthopsychiatry, 62*, 613–617.

Posner, J. K., & Vandell, D. L. (1994). Low-income children's after-school care: Are there beneficial effects of after-school programs? *Child Development, 65*, 440–456.

Powell, I. J. (1994). Early detection issues of prostate cancer in African American men. *In-Vivo, 8*, 451–452.

Powell, M. (1991). The psychosocial impact of sudden infant death syndrome on siblings. *Irish Journal of Psychology, 12*, 235–247.

Pownall, T., & Kingerlee, S. (1993). *Seeing, reaching, and touching: Relationships between vision and touching in infants.* New York: Harvester and Wheatsheaf.

Pratt, L. V. (1981). Business temporal norms and bereavement behavior. *American Sociological Review, 46*, 317–333.

Prayson, R. A., & Estes, M. L. (1994). The search for diagnostic criteria in Alzheimer's disease: An update. *Cleveland Clinical Journal of Medicine, 61*(2), 115–122.

Price, R. (1992). *Clockers.* Boston: Houghton Mifflin.

Price, R. H. (1992). Psychosocial impact of joblessness on individuals and families. *Current Directions in Psychological Science, 1*, 9–11.

Primeau, M. R. (1993). Fetal movement. In B. K. Rothman (Ed.), *The encyclopedia of childbearing.* New York: Henry Holt.

Prinz, P., & Prinz, E. (1979). Simultaneous acquisition of ASL and spoken English. *Sign Language Studies, 25*, 283–296.

Prior, M., Kyrios, M., & Oberklaid, F. (1987). Temperament in Australian, American, Chinese, and Greek infants: Some issues and directions for future research. *Journal of Cross-Cultural Psychology, 17*, 455–474.

Pritchett, L. (1993). *Wealthier is healthier.* Washington, D.C.: The World Bank.

Prohaska, T. R., Leventhal, E. A., Leventhal, H., & Keller, M. L. (1985). Health practices and illness cognition in young, middle aged, and elderly adults. *Journal of Gerontology, 40*, 569–578.

Pryor, D. W., & McGarell, E. F. (1993). Public perceptions of youth gang crime: An exploratory analysis. *Youth and Society, 24*, 399–418.

Pulakos, J. (1989). Young adult relationships: Siblings and friends. *Journal of Psychology, 123*(3), 237–244.

Putallaz, M. (1987). Maternal behavior and children's sociometric status. *Child Development, 58,* 324–340.

Quadrel, M. J., Fischoff, B., & Davis, W. (1993). Adolescent (in)vulnerability. *American Psychologist, 48,* 102–116.

Quam, J. K., & Whitford, G. S. (1992). Adaptation and age-related expectations of older gay and lesbian adults. *The Gerontologist, 32,* 367–374.

Queen, P., & Lang, C. (1993). *Handbook of pediatric nutrition.* Gaithersburg, Md.: Aspen Publishers.

Quinn, J. F., Burkhauser, R. V., & Myers, D. A. (1990). *Passing the torch: The influence of economic incentives on work and retirement.* Kalamazoo, Mich.: W. E. Upjohn Institute for Employment Research.

Quinn, P. K., & Reznikoff, M. (1985). The relationship between death anxiety and the subjective experience of time in the elderly. *The International Journal of Aging and Human Development, 21,* 197–210.

Quirouette, C., & Gold, D. P. (1995). Spousal characteristics as predictors of well-being in older couples. In J. Hendricks (Ed.), *The ties of later life* (pp. 21–33). Amityville, N.Y.: Baywood.

Rabins, P. (1992). Prevention of mental disorder in the elderly: Current perspectives and future prospects. *Journal of the American Geriatrics Society, 40,* 727–733.

Radke-Yarrow, M., Nottelmann, E., Belmont, B., & Welsh, J. D. (1993). *Journal of Abnormal Child Psychology, 21,* 683–695.

Radke-Yarrow, M., & Zahn-Waxler, C. (1987). Roots, motives, and patterns in children's prosocial behavior. In J. Reykowski, J. Karylowski, D. Bar-Tal, & E. Staub (Eds.), *Origins and maintenance of prosocial behaviors.* New York: Plenum Press.

Raines, S. (1990). Representational competence: (Re)presenting experiences through words, actions, and images. *Childhood Education, 66*(3), 133–139.

Rakowski, W., Fleishman, J. A., Mor, V., & Bryant, S. A. (1993). Self-assessment of health and mortality among older persons. *Research on Aging, 15,* 92–116.

Rakowski, W., Julius, M., Hickey, T., Verbrugge, L. M., & Halter, J. B. (1988). Daily symptoms and behavioral responses results of a health diary with older adults. *Medical Care, 26*(3), 278–297.

Ramey, C. T., Bryant, D. M., Campbell, F. A., Sprling, J. J., & Wasik, B. H. (1988). Early intervention for high-risk children: The Carolina early intervention program. In R. H. Price, E. L. Cowen, R. P. Lorion, & J. Ramos-McKay (Eds.), *Fourteen ounces of prevention* (pp. 32–43). Washington, D.C.: American Psychological Association.

Ramirez, O. (1989). Mexican-American children and adolescents. In J. Gibbs & L. Huang (Eds.), *Children of color* (pp. 224–250). San Francisco: Jossey-Bass.

Ramsey, P. (1995). Changing social dynamics in early childhood classrooms. *Child Development, 66,* 764–773.

Ramu, G. N. (1991). Changing family structure and fertility patterns: An Indian case. *Journal of Asian and African Studies, 26*(3–4), 189–206.

Raphael, B., Middleton, W., Martinek, N., & Misso, V. (1993). Counseling and therapy of the bereaved. In M. S. Stroebe, W. Stroebe & R. O. Hansson (Eds.), *Handbook of bereavement: Theory, research, and intervention* (pp. 427–453). Cambridge, U.K.: Cambridge University Press.

Ratcliff, K. S., & Bogdan, J. (1988). Unemployed women: When social support is not supportive. *Social Problems, 35,* 54–63.

Rawlins, W. K. (1992). *Friendship matters: Communication, dialectics, and the life course.* New York: Aldine De-Gruyter.

Reaves, J., & Roberts, A. (1983). The effect of type of information on children's attraction to peers. *Child Development, 54,* 1024–1031.

Recker, R. R., Davies, K. M., Hinders, S. M., Heaney, R. P., Stegman, M. R., & Kimmel, D. B. (1992). Bone gain in young adult women. *Journal of the American Medical Association, 268,* 2403–2408.

Redl, F., & Wineman, D. (1951) *Children who hate.* New York: The Free Press.

Reed, R. J. (1988). Education and achievement of young black males. In J. T. Gibbs (Ed.), *Young, black and male in America: An endangered species* (pp. 37–93). Dover, Mass.: Auburn House.

Reese, H. W., & Rodeheaver, D. (1985). Problem solving and complex decision making. In J. E. Birren & K. W. Schaie (Eds.), *Handbook of the psychology of aging* (2nd ed., pp. 474–499). New York: Van Nostrand Reinhold.

Reid, M., Landesman, S., Treider, R., & Jaccard, J. (1989). "My family and friends": Six- to twelve-year-old perceptions of social support. *Child Development, 60,* 896–910.

Reif, J. S., Dunn, K., Ogilvie, G. K., & Harris, C. K. (1992). Passive smoking and canine lung cancer risk. *American Journal of Epidemiology, 135,* 234–239.

Reilly, R. R., Brown, B., Blood, M. R., & Malatesta, C. Z. (1981). The effects of realistic previews: A study and discussion of the literature. *Personnel Psychology, 34,* 832–834.

Remafedi, G., Resnick, M., Blum, R., & Harris, L. (1992). Demography of sexual orientation in adolescents. *Pediatrics, 89,* 714–721.

Rennie, J. (1994, June). Grading the gene tests. *Scientific American,* 89–97.

Renzulli, J. (1986). The three-ring conception of giftedness: A developmental model for creative productivity. In R. Sternberg & J. Davidson (Eds.), *Conceptions of giftedness* (pp. 53–92). New York: Cambridge University Press.

Reuter, M. A., & Conger, R. D. (1995). Antecedents of parent-adolescent disagreements. *Journal of Marriage and the Family, 57,* 435–448.

Richardson, J. T., & King, E. (1991). Gender differences in the experience of higher education: Quantitative and qualitative approaches. *Educational Psychology, 11*(3–4), 363–382.

Richardson, V., & Kilty, K. M. (1992). Retirement intentions among black professionals: Implications for practice with older black adults. *The Gerontologist, 32,* 7–16.

Richter, P. (1993). HIV and pregnancy. In B. K. Rothman (Ed.), *The encyclopedia of childbearing.* New York: Henry Holt.

Rickman, M. D., & Davidson, R. J. (1995). Personality and behavior in parents of temperamentally inhibited and uninhibited children. *Developmental Psychology, 30,* 346–354.

Riegel, K. F. (1973). Dialectical operations: The final period of cognitive development. *Human Development, 16,* 346–370.

Riegel, K. F. (1976). The dialectics of human development. *American Psychologist, 31,* 689–700.

Riggs, L. B., & Melton, L. J. (1986). Involutional osteoporosis. *New England Journal of Medicine, 314,* 1676–1685.

Rist, R. (1973). *The urban school: A factory for failure.* Cambridge, Mass.: MIT Press.

Roberto, K. A., & Stroes, J. (1995). Grandchildren and grandparents: Roles, influences, and relationships. In J. Hendricks (Ed.), *The ties of later life* (pp. 142–153). Amityville, N.Y.: Baywood.

Roberts, P., & Newton, P. M. (1987). Levinsonian studies of women's adult development. *Psychology and Aging, 2,* 154–163.

Robinson, I. E., & Jedlicka, D. (1982). Change in sexual attitudes and behavior of college students from 1965 to 1980: A research note. *Journal of Marriage and the Family, 44,* 237–240.

Rodeheaver, D., & Stohs, J. (1991). The adaptive misperception of age in older women: Sociocultural images and psychological mechanisms of control. *Educational Gerontology, 17,* 141–156.

Rodgers, J. L., & Rowe, D. C. (1993). Social contagion and adolescent sexual behavior: A developmental EMOSA model. *Psychological Review, 100,* 479–510.

Rodin, G. M., Chmara, J., Ennis, J., Fenton, S., Locking, H., & Steinhouse, K. (1981). Stopping life-sustaining medical treatment: Psychiatric considerations in the termination of renal dialysis. *Canadian Journal of Psychiatry, 26,* 540–544.

Rodin, J. (1986). Aging and health: The effects of the sense of control. *Science, 233,* 1271–1276.

Rogers, L. P., & Markides, K. S. (1989). Well-being in the postparental stage in Mexican-American women. *Research on Aging, 11,* 508–516.

Rogers, L., & Walsh, J. (1982). Shortcomings of the psychomedical research of John Money and co-workers into sex differences in behavior. *Sex Roles, 8,* 269–281.

Roggman, L. A., Langlois, J. H., Hubbs-Tait, L., & Rieser-Danner, L. A. (1994). Infant day-care, attachment, and the "file drawer problem." *Child Development, 65,* 1429–1443.

Rogoff, B. (1990). *Apprenticeship in thinking.* New York: Oxford University Press.

Rogoff, B., & Chavajay, P. (1995). What's become of research on the cultural basis of cognitive development? *American Psychologist, 50,* 859–877.

Rogoff, B., Mistry, J., Goncu, A., & Mosler, C. (1993). Guided participation in cultural activity by toddlers and caregivers. *Monographs of the Society for Research in Child Development, 58*(8, Serial No. 236).

Roland, A. (1988). *In search of self in India and Japan: Toward a cross-cultural psychology.* Princeton, N.J.: Princeton University Press.

Romeo, F. F. (1984). Adolescence, sexual conflict, and anorexia. *Adolescence, 19,* 551–555.

Romig, D. A., Cleland, C., & Romig, J. (1989). *Juvenile delinquency: Visionary approaches.* Columbus, Ohio: Merrill.

Rook, K. S., Catalano, R., & Dooley, D. (1989). The timing of major life events: Effects of departing from the social clock. *American Journal of Community Psychology, 17,* 233–258.

Rooks, J. P., et al. (1989, December). Outcomes of care in birth centers. *New England Journal of Medicine, 321,* 1801–1822.

Rose, J., & Gamble, J. (1993). *Human walking* (2nd ed.). Baltimore: Williams and Williams.

Rosen, K. S., & Rothbaum, F. (1993). Quality of parental caregiving and security of attachment. *Developmental Psychology, 29,* 358–367.

Rosenberg, M. S. (1979). *Conceiving the self.* New York: Basic Books.

Rosenberg, M. S., & Repucci, N. D. (1985). Primary prevention of child abuse. *Journal of Consulting and Clinical Psychology, 53,* 576–585.

Rosenblatt, P. C. (1993). Grief: The social context of private feelings. In M. S. Stroebe, W. Stroebe, & R. O. Hansson (Eds.), *Handbook of bereavement: Theory, research, and intervention* (pp. 102–111). Cambridge, U.K.: Cambridge University Press.

Rosenblatt, P. C., Walsh, R. P., & Jackson, D. A. (1976). *Grief and mourning in cross-cultural perspective.* New Haven, Conn.: Human Relations Area Files Press.

Rosenthal, R., & Jacobson, L. (1968). *Pygmalion in the classroom: Teacher expectations and pupils' intellectual development.* New York: Holt, Rinehart and Winston.

Ross, C. E., Mirowsky, J., & Goldsteen, K. (1990). The impact of the family on health: A decade in review. *Journal of Marriage and the Family, 52,* 1059–1078.

Ross, H. M. (1994). Societal/cultural views regarding death and dying. In G. E. Dickinson, M. R. Leming, & A. C. Mermann (Eds.), *Dying, death, and bereavement* (2nd ed., pp. 83–90). Guilford, Conn.: Dushkin Publishing Group.

Ross, H., Tesla, C., Kenyon, B., & Lollis, S. (1990). Maternal intervention in toddler peer conflict: The socialization of principles of justice. *Development Psychology, 26,* 994–1003.

Ross, J., & Kahan, J. P. (1983). Children by choice or by chance: The perceived effects of parity. *Sex Roles, 9,* 69–77.

Ross, P. (1993). *National excellence: The case for developing America's talent.* Washington, D.C.: United States Department of Education.

Rossell, C. H. (1988). How effective are voluntary plans with magnet schools? *Educational Evaluation and Policy Analysis, 10,* 325–342.

Rossi, A. S. (1982). Transition to parenthood. In L. R. All-man & D. T. Jaffe (Eds.), *Readings in adult psychology: Contemporary perspectives* (2nd ed., pp. 263–275). New York: Harper & Row.

Rossi, A. S., & Rossi, P. H. (1990). *Of human bonding: Parent child relations across the life course.* New York: Aldine de Gruyter.

Rotatori, A., & Fox, R. (1989). *Obesity in children and youth.* Springfield, Ill.: Thomas.

Roth, D. L., & Holmes, D. S. (1987). Influence of aerobic exercise training and relaxation training on physical and psychological health following stressful life events. *Psychomatic Medicine, 49,* 355–365.

Roth, P. (1987). Temporal characteristics of maternal verbal styles. In K. Nelson & A. van Kleek (Eds.), *Children's language: Vol. 6.* Hillsdale, N.J.: Erlbaum.

Rothbart, M. (1989). Temperament in childhood: A framework. In G. Kohnstamm, J. Bates, & M. Rothbart (Eds.), *Temperament in childhood* (pp. 59–73). New York: Wiley.

Rothbart, M. K., Hanley, D., & Albert, M. (1986). Gender differences in moral reasoning. *Sex Roles, 15,* 645–653.

Rotheram-Borus, M. J., Koopman, C., & Ehrhardt, A. A. (1991). Homeless youths and HIV infection. *American Psychologist, 46,* 1188–1197.

Rothschild, M. (1991). Life as improvisation. In B. Sang, J. Warshow, & A. J. Smith (Eds.), *Lesbians at midlife: The creative transition* (pp. 91–98). San Francisco: Spinster Book Company.

Rounds, J. B., & Zevon, M. A. (1993). Cancer stereotypes: A multidimensional scaling analysis. *Journal of Behavioral Medicine, 16,* 485–496.

Rourke, B., & Del Dotto, J. (1994). *Learning disabilities: Neuropsychological perspectives.* Thousand Oaks, Cal.: Sage.

Royce, J. M., Hymowitz, N., Corbett, K., Hartwell, T. D., & Orlandi, M. A. (1993). Smoking cessation factors among African Americans and whites. *American Journal of Public Health, 83*(2), 220–226.

Rubenstein, J. L., Heeren, T., Housman, D., Rubin, C., & Stechler, G. (1989). Suicidal behavior in "normal" adolescents: Risk and protective factors. *American Journal of Orthopsychiatry, 59,* 59–71.

Rubenstein, J. L., & Howes, C. (1976). The effects of peers on toddler interaction with mother and toys. *Child Development, 47,* 597–605.

Rubenstein, J. L., & Howes, C. (1983). Social-emotional development of toddlers in day care: The role of peers and of individual differences. *Advances in Early Education and Day Care, 3,* 13–45.

Rubin, K. H., Fein, G. G., & Vandenberg, B. (1983). Play. In E. M. Hetherington (Ed.), *Handbook of child psychology: Vol. 4. Socialization, personality and social development* (4th ed.). New York: Wiley.

Rubin, K. H., & Krasnor, L. (1980). Changes in the play behaviors of preschoolers: A short-term longitudinal investigation. *Canadian Journal of Behavioral Science, 12,* 278–282.

Rubin, L. B. (1979). *Women of a certain age: The midlife search for self.* New York: Harper & Row.

Rubin, S. S. (1993). The death of a child is forever: The life course impact of a child loss. In M. S. Stroebe, W. Stroebe, & R. O. Hansson (Eds.), *Handbook of bereavement: Theory, research, and intervention* (pp. 285–299). Cambridge, U.K.: Cambridge University Press.

Rubinstein, R. L. (1987). Never married elderly as a social type: Re-evaluating some images. *The Gerontologist, 27,* 108–113.

Rubinstein, R. L., Alexander, B. B., Goodman, M., & Luborsky, M. (1991). Key relationships of never married, childless older women: A cultural analysis. *Journal of Gerontology, 46,* S270–277.

Ruble, D. N. (1983). The development of social comparison processes and their role in achievement-related self-socialization. In T. Higins, D. Ruble, and W. Hartup (Eds.), *Social cognitive development.* Cambridge, U.K.: Cambridge University Press.

Ruble, D. N. (1988). Sex-role development. In M. H. Bornstein & M. E. Lamb (Eds.), *Developmental psychology: An

advanced textbook (2nd ed., pp. 411–460). Hillsdale, N.J.: Erlbaum.

Rudman, D., Feller, A. G., Nagraj, H. S., Gergans, G. A., Lalitha, P. Y., Goldberg, A. F., Schlenker, R. A., Cohn, L., Rudman, I. W., & Mattson, D. E. (1990). Effects of human growth hormone in men over 60 years old. *New England Journal of Medicine, 323,* 1–6.

Rueter, M. A., & Conger, R. D. (1995). Interaction style, problem-solving behavior, and family problem-solving effectiveness. *Child Development, 66,* 98–115.

Russell, R. M. (1992). Nutrient requirements. In J. B. Wyngaarden, L. H. Smith, & J. C. Bennett (Eds.), *Cecil textbook of medicine, Vol. 2* (19th ed., pp. 1147–1151). Philadelphia: Saunders.

Ruth, S. (1995). *Issues in feminism.* Mountain View, Cal.: Mayfield.

Rutter, M. (1995). *Psychosocial disturbances in young people.* New York: Cambridge University Press.

Ryan, E. B. (1992). Beliefs about memory changes across the adult life span. *Journal of Gerontology, 47,* P41–46.

Rybash, J. M., Hoyer, W. J., & Roodin, P. A. (1986). *Adult cognition and aging: Developmental changes in processing, knowing and thinking.* Elmsford, N.Y.: Pergamon Press.

Rybash, J.M., Roodin, P.A., Hoyer, W.J. (1995). *Adult development and aging* (3rd ed.). Madison: Brown & Benchmark.

Ryckman, R. M. (1993). *Theories of personality* (5th ed.). Pacific Grove, Cal.: Brooks/Cole.

Sachs, J. S. (1995, October). Worrying yourself sick: Alzheimer's anxiety can hit anyone. *Longevity,* pp. 68, 76.

Safety-belt use and motor-vehicle-related injuries—Navajo Nation, 1988–1991. (1992, September 25). *Morbidity and Mortality Weekly Report, 41*(38), 705.

Sagi, A., van Ijzendoorn, M. H., Aviezer, O., Donnell, F., & Mayseless, O. (1994). Sleeping out of home in a kibbutz communal arrangement: It makes a difference for infant-mother attachment. *Child Development, 65,* 992–1004.

Salcido, R. M. (1990). Mexican-Americans: Illness, death and bereavement. In J. K. Parry (Ed.), *Social work practice with the terminally ill: A transcultural perspective* (pp. 99–112). Springfield, Ill.: Charles C Thomas.

Saler, L., & Skolnick, N. (1992). Childhood parental death and depression in adulthood: Roles of surviving parent and family environment. *American Journal of Orthopsychiatry, 62,* 504–516.

Salett, E., & Koslow, D. (1994). Race, ethnicity and self in multicultural perspective. In C. Hoare (Ed.) *Psychosocial identity development in U.S. society: Fostering exclusion of cultural others.* Chicago: University of Chicago Press.

Salthouse, T. A. (1984). Effects of age and skill in typing. *Journal of Experimental Psychology: General, 113,* 345–371.

Salthouse, T. A. (1989). Age-related changes in basic cognitive processes. In APA Master Lectures, *The adult years: Continuity and change.* Washington, D.C.: American Psychological Association.

Salthouse, T. A. (1990). Cognitive competence and expertise in aging. In J. E. Birren & K. W. Schaie (Eds.), *Handbook of the psychology of aging* (3rd ed., pp. 310–319). San Diego: Academic Press.

Sanders, C. M. (1993). Risk factors in bereavement outcome. In M. S. Stroebe, W. Stroebe, & R. O. Hansson (Eds.), *Handbook of bereavement: Theory, research, and intervention* (pp. 255–267). Cambridge, U.K.: Cambridge University Press.

Sanfilippo, J., Finkelstein, J., & Styne, D. (Eds.). (1994). *Medical and gynecological endocrinology.* Philadelphia: Hanley and Belfus.

Sanjur, D. (1995). *Hispanic foodways, nutrition, and health.* Boston: Allyn & Bacon.

Sankar, A. (1991). *Dying at home: A guide for family caregivers.* Baltimore: Johns Hopkins University Press.

Sankar, A. (1993). Images of home death and the elderly patient: Romantic versus real. *Generations, 16*(2), 59–63.

Santrock, J., & Sitterle, K. (1987). Parent-child relationships in stepmother families. In K. Pasley & M.

Ihinger-Tallman (Eds.), *Remarriage and stepparenting: Current research and theory.* New York: Guilford Press.

Santrock, J., & Warshak, R. (1979). Father custody and social development in boys and girls. *Journal of Social Issues, 35,* 112–125.

Sarafino, E., & Armstrong, J. (1986). *Child and adolescent development.* New York: West.

Sato, D. (1993). DES: Diethylstilbestrol. In B. K. Rothman (Ed.), *The encyclopedia of childbearing.* New York: Henry Holt.

Sault, N. (Ed.). (1994). *Many mirrors: Body image and social relations.* New Brunswick, N.J.: Rutgers University Press.

Saunders, P. A., Copeland, J. R. M., Dewey, M. E., Davidson, I. A., McWilliam, C., Sharma, V. K., Sullivan, C., & Voruganti, L. N. P. (1989). Alcohol use and abuse in the elderly: Findings from the Liverpool longitudinal study of continuing health in the community. *International Journal of Geriatric Psychiatry, 4,* 103–108.

Savelsbergh, G. (1993). *Development of coordination in infancy.* New York: North-Holland.

Savin-Williams, R. C. (1995). An exploratory study of pubertal maturation timing and self-esteem among gay and bisexual male youths. *Developmental Psychology, 31,* 56–64.

Savin-Williams, R. C., & Berndt, T. (1990). Peer relations during adolescence. In S. Feldman & G. Elliot (Eds.), *At the threshold: The developing adolescent.* Cambridge, Mass.: Harvard University Press.

Sawin, D. (1979). Assessing empathy in children: A search for an elusive construct. Paper presented at the meeting of the Society for Research on Child Development, San Francisco.

Scanzoni, J., Polonko, K., Teachman, J., & Thompson, L. (1989). *The sexual bond: Rethinking families and close relationships.* Newbury Park, Cal.: Sage.

Scarr, S. (1984). *Mother care, other care.* New York: Basic Books.

Scarr, S. (1991). Protecting general intelligence: Constructs and consequences for intervention. In R. Linn (Ed.), *Intelligence* (pp. 74–118). Urbana, Ill.: University of Illinois Press.

Scarr, S., Phillips, D., & McCartney, K. (1989). Working mothers and their families. *American Psychologist, 44,* 1402–1409.

Schaefer, J. A., & Moos, R. H. (1992). Life crisis and personal growth. In B. N. Carpenter (Ed.), *Personal coping, theory, research, and application* (pp. 149–170). Westport, Conn.: Praeger.

Schafer, W. (1987). *Stress management for wellness.* New York: Holt, Rinehart and Winston.

Schaie, K. W. (1977/1978). Toward a stage theory of adult cognitive development. *Journal of Aging and Human Development, 8*(2), 129–138.

Schaie, K. W. (1988). Ageism in psychological research. *American Psychologist, 43,* 179–183.

Schaie, K. W. (1990). Intellectual development in adulthood. In J. E. Birren & K. W. Schaie (Eds.), *Handbook of the psychology of aging* (3rd ed., pp. 291–309). San Diego: Academic Press.

Schaie, K. W. (1994). The course of adult intellectual development. *American Psychologist, 49,* 304–313.

Schaie, K. W., & Strother, C. R. (1968). A cross-sequential study of age changes in cognitive behavior. *Psychological Bulletin, 70,* 671–680.

Scharlach, A. E. (1991). Factors associated with filial grief following the death of an elderly parent. *Journal of Orthopsychiatry, 61*(2), 307–313.

Scharlach, A. E., & Boyd, S. (1989). Caregiving and employment: Results of an employee survey. *The Gerontologist, 29,* 382–387.

Scharlach, A. E., & Fredriksen, K. I. (1993). Reactions to the death of a parent during midlife. *Omega, 27*(4), 307–319.

Scharlach, A. E., & Fuller-Thomson, E. (1994). Coping strategies following the death of an elderly parent. *Journal of Gerontological Social Work, 21*(3/4), 85–100.

Schlegel, A., & Herbert, B. (1991). *Adolescence: An anthropological inquiry.* New York: The Free Press.

Schlossberg, N. K. (1984). The midlife woman as student. In G. Baruch & J. Brooks-Gunn (Eds.), *Women in midlife* (pp. 315–339). New York: Plenum.

Schneidman, E. (1992). *Death: Current perspectives* (3rd ed.). Mountain View, Cal.: Mayfield.

Schoen, R. (1992). First unions and the stability of first marriages. *Journal of Marriage and the Family, 54,* 281–284.

Schoenborn, C. A., & Danchik, K. M. (1980, November). Health practices among adults. *Advance data, vital health statistics,* No. 64, November 4.

Schrader, D. (Ed.). (1990). *The legacy of Lawrence Kohlberg (New Directions in Child Development,* No. 47). San Francisco: Jossey-Bass.

Schulz, R. (1978). *The psychology of death, dying, and bereavement.* Reading, Mass.: Addison-Wesley.

Schwarzenegger, A., & Gaines, C. (1994). *Arnold's fitness for kids, age 6–10: A guide to health, exercise, and nutrition.* New York: Doubleday.

Schweinhart, L., Barnes, H., & Weikart, D. (1993). Significant benefits: The High/Scope Perry Preschool Study through age 27. (*Monographs of the High/Scope Educational Research Foundation,* No. 10). Ypsilanti, Mich.: High/Scope Press.

Schweinhart, L., & Weikart, D. (1992). The High/Scope Perry Preschool Study, similar studies, and their implications for public policy in the United States. In D. Stegelin (Ed.), *Early childhood education: Policy issues for the 1990's* (pp. 67–88). Norwood, N.J.: Ablex.

Scollon, R., & Scollon, S. (1994). *Intercultural communication: A discourse approach.* Oxford, U.K.: Blackwell.

Scraton, S. (1992). *Shaping up to womanhood: Gender and girls' physical education.* Philadelphia: Open University Press.

Seccombe, K. (1991). Assessing the costs and benefits of children: Gender comparisons among childfree husbands and wives. *Journal of Marriage and the Family, 53,* 191–202.

Seccombe, K. (1992). Employment, the family, and employer-based policies. In J. W. Dwyer & R. T. Coward (Eds.), *Gender, families, and elder care* (pp. 165–180). Newbury Park, Cal.: Sage.

Seidman, E., Allen, L., Aber, J. L., Mitchell, C., & Feinman, J. (1994). The impact of school transitions in early adolescence on the self-esteem and perceived social context of poor urban youth. *Child Development, 65,* 507–522.

Seidman, S. N., & Rieder, R. O. (1994). A review of sexual behavior in the United States. *American Journal of Psychiatry, 151,* 330–341.

Seidner, L. B., Stipek, D. J., & Feshbach, N. D. (1988). A developmental analysis of elementary school-aged children's concepts of pride and embarrassment. *Child Development, 59,* 367–377.

Seifer, R., Sameroff, A. J., Barrett, L. C., & Krafechuk, E. (1994). Infant temperament measured by multiple observations and mother reports. *Child Development, 65,* 1478–1490.

Seifert, K. (1993). Cognitive development in early childhood. In B. Spodek (Ed.), *Handbook of research on the education of young children* (3rd ed., pp. 7–40). New York: Macmillan.

Seitz, V., & Apfel, N. (1994). Parent-focused intervention: Diffusion effects on siblings. *Child Development, 65*(2), 677–683.

Seleen, D. R. (1982). The congruence between actual and desired use of time by older adults: A predictor of life satisfaction. *The Gerontologist, 22,* 995–99.

Selekman, J. (1993). Update: New guidelines for the treatment of infants with sickle cell disease. *Pediatric Nursing, 19,* 800–809.

Selman, R. (1980). *The growth of interpersonal understanding.* New York: Academic Press.

Selman, R. (1981). The child as friendship philosopher. In S. Asher & J. Gottman (Eds.), *The development of children's friendships.* New York: Cambridge University Press.

Selye, H. (1985). History and present status of the stress concept. In A. Monat and R. Lazarus (Eds.), *Stress and coping.* New York: Columbia University Press.

Shafer, M. B., & Moscicki, A. (1991). Sexually transmitted diseases. In W. R. Hendee (Ed.), *The health of adolescents: Understanding and facilitating biological, behavioral, and social development* (pp. 211–249). San Francisco: Jossey-Bass.

Shantz, C. U. (1987). Conflicts between children. *Child Development, 58,* 283–305.

Shapiro, E. G., & Rosenfeld, A. (1987). *The somatizing child: Diagnosis and treatment of conversion and somatization disorders.* New York: Springer-Verlag.

Sharabany, R., Gershoni, R., & Hoffman, J. (1981). Girlfriend, boyfriend: Age and sex differences in intimate friendship. *Developmental Psychology, 17,* 800–809.

Sheldon, S., Spire, J., & Levy, H. (1992). *Pediatric sleep medicine.* Philadelphia: Saunders.

Shenk, D., & Achenbaum, A. (1993). Introduction: Changing perceptions of the aging and the aged. *Generations, 17*(2), 5–8.

Shephard, R. J. (1987). *Physical activity and aging.* Rockville, Md.: Aspen Publishers.

Shepherd-Look, D. (1982). Sex differentiation and the development of sex roles. In B. Wolman (Ed.), *Handbook of developmental psychology.* Englewood Cliffs, N.J.: Prentice-Hall.

Shiao, R., Tao, X., McLeskey, S., Bano, M., Khera, S., Kern, F., Freter, C., & Vincent, T. (1995). Over-expression of IL-6 in MCF-7 breast cancer cells results in increased tumorigenicity in nude mice. *Proceedings of the American Association for Cancer Research Annual Meeting, 36,* 255.

Shrum, W., Cheek, N. H., & Hunter, S. M. (1988). Friendship in school: Gender and racial homophily. *Sociology of Education, 61,* 227–239.

Shuchter, S. T., & Zisook, S. (1993). The course of normal grief. In M. S. Stroebe, W. Stroebe, & R. O. Hansson (Eds.), *Handbook of bereavement: Theory, research, and intervention* (pp. 23–43). Cambridge, U.K.: Cambridge University Press.

Shure, M. B., & Spivak, G. (1988). Interpersonal cognitive problem solving. In R. H. Price, W. L. Cowen, R. P. Lorion, & J. Ramos-McKay (Eds.), *14 ounces of prevention: A casebook for practitioners* (pp. 69–82). Washington, D.C.: American Psychological Association.

Siegel, J. M., & Kuykendall, D. H. (1990). Loss, widowhood, and psychological distress among the elderly. *Journal of Consulting and Clinical Psychology, 58,* 519–524.

Sigelman, C., Maddox, A., Epstein, J., & Carpenter, W. (1993). Age differences in understandings of disease causality: AIDS, colds and cancer. *Child Development, 64,* 272–284.

Silber, S. J. (1991). *How to get pregnant with the new technology.* New York: Warner Books.

Silverman, P. R., Nickman, S., & Worden, J. W. (1992). Detachment revisited: The child's reconstruction of a dead parent. *American Journal of Orthopsychiatry, 62,* 494–505.

Silverman, P., & Worden, J. (1993). Children's reactions to the death of a parent. In M. Stroebe, W. Stroebe, & R. Hansson (Eds.), *Handbook of bereavement: Theory, research, and intervention* (pp. 300–315). Cambridge: Cambridge University Press.

Silverstein, L. B. (1991). Transforming the debate about child care and maternal employment. *American Psychologist, 46,* 1025–1032.

Simenauer, J., & Carroll, D. (1982). *Singles: The new Americans.* New York: Simon and Schuster.

Simmons, R. G. (1987). Social transition and adolescent development. In C. E. Irwin, Jr. (Ed.), *Adolescent social behavior and health* (pp. 33–53). San Francisco: Jossey Bass.

Simmons, R. G., & Blyth, D. (1987). *Moving into adolescence: The impact of pubertal change and school context.* New York: Aldine de Gruyter.

Simmons, R. G., Carlton-Ford, S. L., & Blyth, D. A. (1987). Predicting how a child will cope with the transition to junior high school. In R. M. Lerner & T. T. Foch (Eds.), *Biological-psychosocial interactions in early adolescence* (pp. 325–375). Hillsdale, N.J.: Erlbaum.

Simonton, D. K. (1990). Creativity and wisdom in aging. In J. E. Birren & K. W. Schaie (Eds.), *Handbook of the psychology of aging* (3rd ed., pp. 320–329). San Diego: Academic Press.

Sinclair, D. (1990). *Human growth after birth* (5th ed.). New York: Oxford University Press.

Single parents. (1992). *American Demographics, 14*(7), A14–17.

Singleton, L., & Asher, S. (1979). Racial integration and children's peer preferences: An investigation of developmental and cohort differences. *Child Development, 50,* 936–941.

Sinnott, J. D. (1989). Life-span relativistic postformal thought: Methodology and data from everyday problem-solving studies. In M. L. Commons, J. D. Sinnott, F. A. Richards, & C. Armon (Eds.), *Adult development: Vol. 1. Comparisons and applications of developmental models* (pp. 239–265). New York: Praeger.

Sizer, T. R. (1992). *Horace's compromise: Redesigning the American high school.* Boston: Houghton Mifflin.

Skinner, B. F. (1957). *Verbal behavior.* New York: Appleton-Century-Crofts.

Skinner, J. H. (1992). Aging in place: The experience of African American and other minority elders. *Generations, 16*(2), 49–51.

Skolnick, A., & Skolnick, J. (1989). *Families in transition: Rethinking marriage, sexuality, child-rearing and family organization* (6th ed.). New York: Scott Foresman.

Skoog, I. (1994). Risk factors for vascular dementia: A review. *Dementia, 5*(3–4), 137–144.

Slade, A. (1987). Quality of attachment and early symbolic play. *Developmental Psychology, 23,* 78–85.

Slater, A., & Morrison, V. (1991). Visual attention and memory at birth. In M. Weiss & P. Zelazo (Eds.), *Newborn attention: Biological constraints and the influence of experience* (pp. 256–277). Norwood, N.J.: Ablex.

Slater, S. (1995). Lesbians and generativity: Not everyone waits for midlife. *Work in Progress, No. 72.* Wellesley, Mass.: The Stone Center Working Paper Series.

Slavin, R. E. (1986). Cooperative learning: Engineering social psychology in the classroom. In R. S. Feldman (Ed.), *The social psychology of education: Current research and theory.* Cambridge, U.K.: Cambridge University Press.

Slavin, R. E. (1990a). Achievement effects of ability grouping in secondary schools: A best evidence synthesis. *Review of Educational Research, 60,* 471–499.

Slavin, R. E. (1990b). *Cooperative learning: Theory, research, and practice.* Englewood Cliffs, N.J.: Prentice-Hall.

Slavin, R. E. (1995). *Cooperative learning* (2nd ed.) Boston: Allyn & Bacon.

Slochower, J. A. (1993). Mourning and the holding function of shiva. *Contemporary Psychoanalysis, 29,* 352–367.

Slomin, M. (1991). *Children, culture, and ethnicity: Evaluating and understanding the impact.* New York: Garland.

Sloper, P., Turner, S., Knussen, C., & Cunningham, C. C. (1990). Social life of school children with Down's syndrome. *Child Care, Health, and Development, 16,* 235–251.

Smetana, J. G. (1995). Parenting styles and conceptions of parental authority during adolescence. *Child Development, 66,* 299–316.

Smetana, J. G., Killen, M., & Turiel, E. (1991). Children's reasoning about interpersonal and moral conflicts. *Child Development, 62,* 629–644.

Smilansky, S. (1968). *The effects of sociodramatic play on disadvantaged preschool children.* New York: Wiley.

Smith, J., & Baltes, P. B. (1990). Wisdom-related knowledge: Age/cohort differences in response to life-planning problems. *Developmental Psychology, 26,* 494–505.

Smitherman-Donaldson, G. (1994). *Black talk: Words and phrases from the hood to the amen corner.* Boston: Houghton Mifflin.

Snarey, J. R. (1985). Cross-cultural universality of social-moral development: A critical review of Kohlbergian research. *Psychological Bulletin, 97,* 202–232.

Soldier, L. (1993). Working with Native-American children. *Young Children, 47*(6), 15–21.

Solnit, A. J., Cohen, D. J., & Schowalter, J. E. (1986). *Child psychiatry: Vol. 6.* New York: Basic Books.

Solomon, G. F. (1991). Psychosocial factors, exercise, and immunity: Athletes, elderly persons, and AIDS patients. *International Journal of Sports Medicine, 12,* 250–255.

Somers, M. D. (1993). A comparison of voluntarily child-free adults and parents. *Journal of Marriage and the Family, 55,* 643–650.

Sommerville, J. (1990). *The rise and fall of childhood* (2nd ed.). New York: Vintage Books.

Sonenstein, F. L., Pleck, J. H., & Ku, L. C. (1991). Levels of sexual activity among adolescent males in the United States. *Family Planning Perspectives, 23,* 162–167.

Sorenson, S., & Bowie, P. (1994). Vulnerable populations: Girls and young women. In L. Eron & J. Gentry (Eds.), *Violence and youth: Psychology's response: Vol. II. Papers of the American Psychological Association on Violence and Youth.* Washington, D.C.: American Psychological Association.

Sorsby, A., & Martlew, M. (1991). Representational demands in mothers' talk to preschool children in two contexts: Picture book reading and a modeling task. *Journal of Child Language, 18,* 373–395.

Spaccarelli, S. (1994). Stress, appraisal, and coping in child sexual abuse: A theoretical and empirical review. *Psychological Bulletin, 116,* 340–362.

Sparrow, D., & Weiss, S. T. (1988). Pulmonary system. In J. W. Rowe & R. W. Besdine (Eds.), *Geriatric medicine* (pp. 266–275). Boston: Little, Brown.

Spassov, L., Curzi-Dscalovi, L., Clairambualt, J., Kauffman, F., Eiselt, M., Medigue, C., & Peirano, P. (1994). Heart rate and heart-rate variability during sleep in small-for-gestational-age newborns. *Pediatric Research, 35,* 500–505.

Speece, M. W., & Brent, S. B. (1984). Children's understanding of death: A review of three components of the death concept. *Child Development, 55,* 1671–1686.

Speroff, L., Glass, R. H., & Kase, N. G. (1983). *Clinical gynecologic endocrinology and infertility.* Baltimore: Williams & Wilkins.

Spetner, N., & Olsho, L. (1990). Auditory frequency resolution in human infants. *Child Development, 61,* 632–652.

Spirduso, W. W. (1995). *Physical dimensions of aging.* Champaign, Ill.: Human Kinetics.

Spirduso, W. W., & MacRae, P. G. (1990). Motor performance and aging. In J. E. Birren & K. W. Schaie (Eds.), *Handbook of the psychology of aging* (3rd ed., pp. 183–200). San Diego: Academic Press.

Spirito, A., Stark, L., Fristad, M., Hart, K., & Owens-Stively, J. (1989). Adolescent suicide attempters hospitalized on a pediatric unit. In S. Chess, A. Thomas, A., & M. E. Hertzig (Eds.), *Annual progress in child psychiatry and child development.* New York: Brunner/Mazel.

Spitz, R. A. (1945). Hospitalism: An inquiry in the genesis of psychiatric conditioning in early childhood. In D. Feneschel et al. (Eds.), *Psychoanalytic Studies of the Child: Vol. 1* (pp. 53–74). New York: International Universities Press.

Spitz, R. A. (1946). Hospitalism: A follow-up report. In D. Feneschel et al. (Eds.), *Psychoanalytic Studies of the Child: Vol. 1* (pp. 113–117). New York: International Universities Press.

Spitze, G., & Logan, J. R. (1990). Sons, daughters, and intergenerational support. *Journal of Marriage and the Family, 52,* 420–430.

Spitze, G., & Logan, J. R. (1992). Helping as a component of parent-adult child relations. *Research on Aging, 14,* 291–312.

Spodek, B., & Saracho, O. (Eds.). (1993). *Language and literacy in early childhood education.* New York: Teachers' College Press.

Sponseller, D., & Jaworski, A. (1979). *Social and cognitive complexity in young children's play.* Paper presented at the annual meeting of the American Educational Research Association, San Francisco.

Sroufe, L. A. (1979). The coherence of individual development: Early care, attachment, and subsequent developmental issues. *American Psychologist, 34,* 834–841.

Sroufe, L. A., Fox, N., & Pancake, V. (1983). Attachment and dependency in developmental perspective. *Child Development, 54,* 1615–1627.

St. James-Roberts, I., & Halil, T. (1991). Infant crying patterns in the first year: Normal community and clinical findings. *Journal of Child Psychology and Psychiatry, 32,* 951–968.

St. James-Roberts, I., Harris, G., & Messer, D. (Eds.). (1993). *Infant crying, feeding, and sleeping: Development, problems, and treatments.* New York: Harvester Wheatsheaf.

St. Peters, M., Fitch, M., Huston, A. C., Wright, J .C., & Eakins, D. J. (1991). Television and families: What do young children watch with their parents? *Child Development, 62,* 1409–1423.

Stack, C. B. (1974). *All our kin: Strategies for survival in a black community.* New York: Harper & Row.

Stack, C. B. (1981). Sex roles and survival strategies in an urban black community. In F. C. Steady (Ed.), *The black woman cross-culturally* (pp. 349–367). Cambridge, Mass.: Shinkman.

Stack, C. B. (1993). The culture of gender: Women and men of color. In M. J. Larrabee (Ed.), *An ethic of care: Feminist and interdisciplinary perspectives* (pp. 108–111). New York: Routledge.

Stander, V., & Jensen, L. (1993). The relationship of value orientation to moral cognition: Gender and cultural differences in the United States and China explored. *Journal of Cross-Cultural Psychology, 24,* 42–52.

Stanford, E. P., & DuBois, B. (1992). Gender and ethnicity patterns. In J. E. Birren, R. B. Sloane, & G. D. Cohen (Eds.), *Handbook of mental health and aging* (2nd ed., pp. 99–115). San Diego: Academic Press.

Stanton, A. L., & Dunkel-Schetter, C. (1991). Psychological adjustment to infertility. In A. L. Stanton & C. Dunkel-Schetter (Eds.), *Infertility* (pp. 3–16). New York: Plenum.

Starfield, B., & Pless, I. (1980). Physical health. In O. Brim & J. Kagan (Eds.), *Constancy and change in human development.* New York: Erlbaum.

Starr, B., & Weiner, M. (1981). *Starr-Weiner report.* New York: Stein & Day.

Statton, H., & Magnusson, D. (1990). *Pubertal maturation in female development.* Hillsdale, N.J.: Erlbaum.

Staudinger, U. M., Smith, J., & Baltes, P. B. (1992). Wisdom- related knowledge in a life review task: Age differences and the role of professional specialization. *Psychology and Aging, 2,* 271–281.

Steiger, C. (1993). Midwifery: Overview. In B. K. Rothman (Ed.), *The encyclopedia of childbearing.* New York: Henry Holt.

Steil, J. M. (1989). Marital relationships and mental health: The psychic costs of inequality. In J. Freeman (Ed.), *Women: A feminist perspective* (4th ed., pp. 138–148). Mountain View, Cal.: Mayfield.

Steil, J. M. (1995). Supermoms and second shifts: Marital inequality in the 1990s. In J. Freeman (Ed.), *Women: A feminist perspective* (5th ed., pp. 149–161). Mountain View, Cal.: Mayfield.

Stein, A. (1983). Pregnancy in gravidas over age 35 years. *Journal of Nurse-Midwifery, 28,* 17–20.

Stein, P. N., Gordon, W. A., Hibbard, M. R., & Sliwinski, M. J. (1992). An examination of depression in the spouses of stroke patients. *Rehabilitation Psychology, 37,* 121–130.

Steinberg, L. D. (1986). Latchkey children and susceptibility to peer pressure: An ecological analysis. *Developmental Psychology, 22,* 433–439.

Steinberg, L. D., & Dornbusch, S. M. (1991). Negative correlates of part-time employment during adolescence: Replication and elaboration. *Developmental Psychology, 27,* 304–313.

Steinberg, L. D., Fegley, S., & Dornbusch, S. M. (1993). Negative impact of part-time work on adolescent adjustment: Evidence from longitudinal study. *Developmental Psychology, 29,* 171–180.

Steinberg, L. D., Lamborn, S. D., Dornbusch, S. M., & Darling, N. (1992). Impact of parenting practices on adolescent achievement: Authoritative parenting, school involvement, and encouragement to succeed. *Child Development, 63,* 1266–1281.

Steinberg, L. D., & Levine, A. D. (1990). *You and your adolescent: A parent's guide to development from 10 to 20.* New York: Harper & Row.

Steinberg, L. D., Mounts, N. S., Lamborn, S. D., & Dornbusch, S. M. (1991). Authoritative parenting and adolescent adjustment across varied ecological niches. *Journal of Research in Adolescence, 1,* 19–36.

Steiner, G. (1987). Spatial reasoning in small-size and large-size environments: In search of early prefigurations of spatial cognition in small-size environments. In B. Inhelder, D. de Caprona, & A. Cornu-Wells (Eds.), *Piaget today.* Hillsdale, N.J.: Erlbaum.

Steinglass, P., & Gerrity, E. (1990). Natural disasters and post-traumatic stress disorder: Short-term versus long-term recovery in two disaster-affected communities. *Journal of Applied Social Psychology, 20,* 1746–1765.

Stephenson, J. S. (1985). *Death, grief, and mourning: Individual and social realities.* New York: The Free Press.

Stern, D. N. (1985a). *The first relationship: Infant and mother.* (4th ed.). Cambridge, Mass.: Harvard University Press.

Stern, D. N. (1985b). *The interpersonal world of the infant: A view from psychoanalysis and developmental psychology.* New York: Basic Books.

Stern, D. N. (1992). *Diary of a baby.* New York: Basic Books.

Stern, D. N. (1995). *The motherhood constellation: A unified view of parent-infant psychotherapy.* New York: Basic Books.

Sternberg, R. J. (1987). *The triangle of love: Intimacy, passion, commitment.* New York: Basic Books.

Sternberg, R. J. (1988). *The triarchic mind: A new theory of human intelligence.* New York: Penguin Books.

Sternberg, R. J. (1992). Intellectual development: A satiric fairy tale. In R. J. Sternberg & C. A. Berg (Eds.), *Intellectual development* (pp. 381–394). Cambridge: Cambridge University Press.

Sternberg, R. J. (1994). *Thinking and problem solving.* San Diego: Academic Press.

Sternberg, R. J., & Wagner, R. (Eds.). (1994). *Mind in context: Interactionist perspectives on human intelligence.* New York: Cambridge University Press.

Stets, J. E. (1990). Verbal and physical aggression in marriage. *Journal of Marriage and the Family, 52,* 501–514.

Stevenson, H. W., Chen, C., & Uttal, D. H. (1990). Beliefs and achievement: A study of black, white and Hispanic children. *Child Development, 61,* 508–523.

Stevenson, H. W., & Lee, S. Y. (1990). Contexts of achievement: A study of American, Chinese, and Japanese children. *Monographs of the Society for Research in Child Development, 55.*

Stewart, R. B., Mobley, L. A., Van Tuyl, S. S., & Salvador, M. A. (1987). The firstborn's adjustment to the birth of a sibling: A longitudinal assessment. *Child Development, 58,* 341–355.

Stifter, C. A., Coulehan, C. M., & Fish, M. (1993). Linking employment to attachment: The mediating effects of maternal separation anxiety and interactive behavior. *Child Development, 64,* 1451–1460.

Stiller, N. J., & Forrest, L. (1990). An extension of Gilligan and Lyon's investigation of morality: Gender differences in college students. *Journal of College Student Development, 31,* 54–63.

Stillion, J. M. (1985). *Death and the sexes: An examination of differential longevity, attitudes, behaviors, and coping skills.* Washington, D.C.: Hemisphere.

Stipek, D., & Hoffman, J. (1980). Children's achievement related expectancies as a function of academic performance histories and sex. *Journal of Educational Psychology, 72,* 861–865.

Stokes, G. (1985). The social profile. In R. Coles & G. Stokes (Eds.), *Sex and the American teenager* (pp. 31–144). New York: Harper & Row.

Stolberg, A. L., & Walsh, P. (1988). A review of treatment methods for children of divorce. In S. A. Wolchik & P. Karoly (Eds.), *Children of divorce* (pp. 299–321). New York: Gardner Press.

Stoller, E. P. (1992). Gender differences in the experiences of caregiving spouses. In J. W. Dwyer & R. T.

Coward (Eds.), *Gender, families, and elder care* (pp. 49–64). Newbury Park, Cal.: Sage.

Stoller, E. P., & Cutler, S. J. (1992). The impact of gender on configurations of care among married elderly couples. *Research on Aging, 14,* 313–330.

Stoller, E. P., & Pugliesi, K. L. (1989). Other roles of caregivers: Competing responsibilities or supportive resources. *Journal of Gerontology: Social Sciences, 44,* 231–238.

Stone, R., Cafferata, G. L., & Sangl, J. (1987). Caregivers of the frail elderly: A national profile. *The Gerontologist, 27,* 616–626.

Stout, B. C. (1993). Thalidomide. In B. K. Rothman (Ed.), *The encyclopedia of childbearing.* New York: Henry Holt.

Stratford, B. (1994). Down syndrome is for life. *International Journal of Disability, Development and Education, 41,* 3–13.

Straus, M. A., & Gelles, R. J. (1990). *Physical violence in American families: Risk factors and adaptations to violence in 8,145 families.* New Brunswick, N.J.: Transaction.

Straus, M. A., Gelles, R. J., & Steinmetz, S. (1980). *Behind closed doors: Violence in the American family.* Garden City, N.Y.: Anchor.

Straus, M. A., & Smith, C. (1990). Violence in Hispanic families in the United States: Incidence rates and structural interpretations. In M. A. Straus & R. J. Gelles, with C. Smith (Eds.), *Physical violence in American families: Risk factors and adaptations to violence in 8,145 families* (pp. 341–367). New Brunswick, N.J.: Transaction.

Streissguth, A. P., Barr, H. M., Sampson, P. D., Darby, B. L., & Martin, D. C. (1989). IQ at age 4 in relation to maternal alcohol use and smoking during pregnancy. *Developmental Psychology, 25,* 3–11.

Strickland, B. R. (1988a). Menopause. In E. A. Blechman & K. D. Brownell (Eds.), *Handbook of behavioral medicine for women* (pp. 41–48). New York: Pergamon.

Strickland, B. R. (1988b). Sex-related differences in health and illness. *Psychology of Women Quarterly, 12,* 381–399.

Striegel-Moore, R. H., Silberstein, L. R. & Rodin, J. (1986). Toward an understanding of risk factors for bulimia. *American Psychologist, 41,* 246–263.

Stroebe, M. S., & Stroebe, W. (1993). The mortality of bereavement: A review. In M. S. Stroebe, W. Stroebe, & R. O. Hansson (Eds.), *Handbook of bereavement: Theory, research, and intervention* (pp. 175–195). Cambridge, U.K.: Cambridge University Press.

Stroebe, M. S., Stroebe, W., & Hansson, R. O. (1993). Bereavement theory and research: An introduction to the handbook. In M. S. Stroebe, W. Stroebe, & R. O. Hansson (Eds.), *Handbook of bereavement: Theory, research, and intervention* (pp. 3–19). Cambridge,, U.K.: Cambridge University Press.

Stroebe, W., & Stroebe, M. S. (1993). Determinants of adjustment to bereavement in younger widows and widowers. In M. S. Stroebe, W. Stroebe, & R. O. Hansson (Eds.), *Handbook of bereavement: Theory, research, and intervention* (pp. 208–226). Cambridge, U.K.: Cambridge University Press.

Strom, R., Collinsworth, P., Strom, S., & Griswold, D. (1995). Strengths and needs of black grandparents. In J. Hendricks (Ed.), *The ties of later life* (pp. 195–207). Amityville, N.Y.: Baywood.

Strom, R., & Strom, S. (1995). Raising expectations for grandparents: A three generational study. In J. Hendricks (Ed.), *The ties of later life* (pp. 133–139). Amityville, N.Y.: Baywood.

Sue, S., & Zane, N. (1987). The role of culture and cultural techniques in psychotherapy: A critique and reformulation. *American Psychologist, 42,* 37–45.

Suitor, J. J. (1991). Marital quality and satisfaction with the division of household labor across the family life cycle. *Journal of Marriage and the Family, 53,* 221–230.

Sullivan, H. (1953). *The interpersonal theory of psychiatry.* New York: Norton.

Sullivan, K., & Sullivan, A. (1980). Adolescent-parent separation. *Developmental Psychology, 16,* 93–99.

SUPPORT Principal Investigators. (1995). A controlled trial to improve care for seriously ill hospitalized patients: The study to understand prognoses and preferences for outcomes and risks of treatments (SUPPORT). *Journal of the American Medical Association, 274,* 1591–1598.

Susa, A. M., & Benedict, J. O. (1994). The effects of playground design on pretend play and divergent thinking. *Environment and Behavior, 26,* 560–579.

Sutcliffe, D. (1992). *System in Black language.* Philadelphia: Multilingual Matters.

Swanson, H., Cooney, J., & Brock, S. (1993). The influence of working memory and classification ability on children's word problem solution. *Journal of Experimental Child Psychology, 55,* 374–395.

Taffel, S. M. (1989). Cesarean sections in America: Dramatic trends, 1970 to 1987. *Statistical Bulletin, 70,* 2–11.

Taffel, S. M. (1993). Cesarean birth: Social and political aspects. In B. K. Rothman (Ed.), *The encyclopedia of childbearing.* New York: Henry Holt.

Takahashi, K. (1990). Are the key assumptions of the "Strange Situation" procedure universal? A view from Japanese research. *Human Development, 33,* 23–30.

Takanishi, R. (1993). The opportunities of adolescence—Research, interventions, and policy: Introduction to the special issue. *American Psychologist, 48,* 85–88.

Takata, S., & Zevitz, R. (1990). Divergent perceptions of group delinquency in a midwestern community: Racine's gang problem. *Youth and Society, 21,* 282–305.

Tamir, L. M. (1989). Modern myths about men at midlife: An assessment. In S. Hunter & M. Sundel (Eds.), *Midlife myths* (pp. 157–179). Newbury Park, Cal.: Sage.

Tanfer, K. (1987). Patterns of premarital cohabitation among never-married women in the United States. *Journal of Marriage and the Family, 49*(3), 483–497.

Tannen, D. (1990). *You just don't understand.* New York: Morrow.

Tanner, J. M. (1981). Growth and maturation during adolescence. *Nutrition Review, 39,* 43–55.

Tanner, J. M. (1990). *Fetus into man. Physical growth from conception to maturity* (rev. ed.). Cambridge, Mass.: Harvard University Press.

Tasker, F. L., & Richards, M. P. M. (1994). Adolescents' attitudes toward marriage and marital prospects after parental divorce: A review. *Journal of Adolescent Research, 9*(3), 340–362.

Task Force on Pediatric AIDS. (1989). Pediatric AIDS and human immunodeficiency virus infection: Psychological issues. *American Psychologist, 44,* 258–264.

Taylor, D. K., Miller, S. S., & Moltz, K. A. (1991). Adolescent health: An assessment of referral activities. *Adolescence, 26,* 717–725.

Taylor, R. J. (1990). Need for support and family involvement among Black Americans. *Journal of Marriage and the Family, 52,* 584–590.

Taylor, S. E. (1995). *Health psychology.* New York: McGraw-Hill.

Taylor, S. E., & Aspinwall, L. G. (1990). Psychological aspects of chronic illness. In G. R. VandenBos & P. T. Costa, Jr. (Eds.), *Psychological aspects of serious illness.* Washington, D.C.: American Psychological Association.

Teaff, J., & Johnson, D. (1983). Pre-retirement education. A proposed bill for tuition credit. *Educational Gerontology, 9,* 31–36.

Terre, L., Ghiselli, W., Taloney, L., & DeSouza, E. (1992). Demographics, affect, and adolescents' health behaviors. *Adolescence, 27,* 13–24.

Tesman, J., & Hills, A. (1994). Developmental effects of lead exposure in children. *Social Policy Report: Society for Research on Child Development, 8*(3).

Teti, D., & Ablard, K. (1989). Security of attachment and infant-sibling relationships. *Child Development, 60,* 1519–1528.

The New York Times. (1993, February 5). House and Senate votes on family leave plan, p. A8.

Thissen, D., Bock, R., Wainer, H., & Roche, A. (1976). Individual growth in stature: A comparison of four growth studies in the USA. *Annals of Human Biology, 3,* 529–542.

Thomas, A., & Chess, S. (1977). *Temperament and development.* New York: Bruner/Mazel.

Thomas, A., & Chess, S. (1981). The role of temperament in the contributions of individuals to their development. In R. Lerner & N. Busch-Rossnagle (Eds.), *Individuals as producers of their development: A life-span perspective.* New York: Academic Press.

Thomas, J. L. (1995). Gender and perceptions of grandparenthood. In J. Hendricks (Ed.), *The ties of later life* (pp. 181–193). Amityville, N.Y.: Baywood.

Thomas, L. E. (1991). Dialogues with three religious renunciates and reflections on wisdom and maturity. *International Journal of Aging and Human Development, 32*(3), 211–227.

Thomas, L. E. (1994). The way of the religious renouncer. In L. E. Thomas & S. A. Eisenhandler (Eds.), *Aging and the religious dimension* (pp. 51–64). Westport, Conn.: Auburn House.

Thompson, R. A. (1990). On emotion and self-regulation. In R. A. Thompson (Ed.), *Nebraska symposium on motivation: Vol. 36* (pp. 383–483). Lincoln, Neb.: University of Nebraska Press.

Thompson, S. (1975). Gender labels and early sex role development. *Child Development, 46,* 339–347.

Thomson, E., & Colella, U. (1992). Cohabitation and marital stability: Quality or commitment? *Journal of Marriage and the Family, 54,* 259–267.

Thornborrow, N. M., & Sheldon, M. B. (1995). Women in the labor force. In J. Freeman (Ed.), *Women: A feminist perspective* (5th ed., pp. 197–219). Mountain View, Cal.: Mayfield.

Thorne, B. (1986). Girls and boys together . . . but mostly apart: Gender arrangements in elementary schools. In W. Hartup & Z. Rubin (Eds.), *Relationships and development.* Hillsdale, N.J.: Erlbaum.

Thornton, A., Young-DeMarco, L., & Goldscheider, F. (1993). Leaving the parental nest: The experience of a young white cohort in the 1980s. *Journal of Marriage and the Family, 55,* 216–229.

Thorson, J. (1983). Spiritual well-being in the secular society. *Generations, 8*(3), 10–11.

Thorson, J. A., & Powell, F. C. (1988). Elements of death anxiety and meanings of death. *Journal of Clinical Psychology, 44,* 691–701.

Tobin, S. S. (1991). *Personhood in advanced old age: Implications for practice.* New York: Springer.

Tobin, S. S., Fullmer, E. M., & Smith, G. C. (1994). Religiosity and fear of death in non-normative aging. In L. E. Thomas & S. A. Eisenhandler (Eds.), *Aging and the religious dimension* (pp. 183–202). Westport, Conn.: Auburn House.

Tobin-Richards, M. H., Boxer, A. M., & Petersen, A. C. (1983). The psychological significance of pubertal change: Sex differences in perceptions of self during early adolescence. In J. Brooks-Gunn & A. C. Petersen (Eds.), *Girls at puberty: Biological and psychological perspectives* (pp. 127–154). New York: Plenum.

Todd, J., Friedman, A., & Kariuki, T. W. (1990). Women growing stronger with age: The effect of status in the United States and Kenya. *Psychology of Women Quarterly, 14,* 567–577.

Tolson, T., & Wilson, M. (1990). The impact of two- and three-generational black family structure on perceived family climate. *Child Development, 61,* 416–428.

Tonti, M. (1988). Relationships among adult siblings who care for their aged parents. In M. D. Kahn & K. G. Lewis (Eds.), *Siblings in therapy: Life span and clinical issues* (pp. 417–434). New York: Norton.

Tornstam, L. (1992). The quo vadis of gerontology: On the scientific paradigm of gerontology. *The Gerontologist, 32,* 318–326.

Torres-Gil, F. M. (1992). *The new aging: Politics and change in America.* New York: Auburn House.

Tough, A. (1981). Interests of adult learners. In A. W. Chickering (Ed.), *The modern American college: Responding to the new realities of diverse students and a changing society* (pp. 296–305). San Francisco: Jossey-Bass.

Trautman, P. D., & Shaffer, D. (1989). Pediatric management of suicidal behavior. *Pediatric Annals, 18,* 134–143.

Trends in prostate cancer—United States. (1992, June 12). *Morbidity and Mortality Weekly Report,* pp. 41, 401–404.

Trickett, E. (1991). *Living an idea: Empowerment and the evolution of an alternative high school.* Brookline, Mass.: Brookline Books.

Tronick, E. Z. (1989). Emotions and emotional communication in infants. *American Psychologist, 44,* 112–119.

Tronick, E. Z., Morelli, G. A., & Ivey, P. K. (1992). The Efe forager infant and toddler's pattern of social relationships: Multiple and simultaneous. *Developmental Psychology, 28,* 568–577.

Tronick, E. Z., Ricks, M., & Cohn, J. F. (1982). Maternal and infant affective exchange: Patterns of adaptation. In T. Field & A. Fogel (Eds.), *Emotion and early interaction.* Hillsdale, N.J.: Erlbaum.

Turkheimer, E., & Gottesman, I. I. (1991). Individual differences and the canalization of human behavior. *Developmental Psychology, 27,* 18–22.

Tylanda, C. A., & Baum, B. J. (1988). Oral physiology and the Baltimore Longitudinal Study of Aging. *Gerontology, 7,* 5–9.

United Nations International Children's Emergency Fund (UNICEF). (1993). *The state of the world's children, 1992.* New York: Oxford University Press.

United Nations International Children's Emergency Fund (UNICEF). (1995). *The state of the world's children: 1995.* New York: Oxford University Press.

U.S. Bureau of the Census. (1990a). *Statistical abstract of the United States* (110th ed.). Washington, D.C.: U.S. Government Printing Office.

U.S. Bureau of the Census (1990b). *Who's minding the kids? Current population reports* (Series P-70, No. 20.). Washington, D.C.: U.S Government Printing Office.

U.S. Bureau of the Census. (1991). *Statistical abstract of the United States* (111th ed.). Washington, D.C.: U.S. Government Printing Office.

U.S. Bureau of the Census. (1992a). *Statistical abstract of the United States, 1992* (112th ed.). Washington, D.C.: U.S. Government Printing Office.

U.S. Bureau of the Census. (1992b). *Poverty in the United States, 1991.* Washington, D.C.: U.S. Government Printing Office.

U.S. Bureau of the Census. (1992). Marital status and living arrangements: March 1991. *Current Population Reports,* Series P-20, No. 461. Washington, D.C.: U.S. Government Printing Office.

U.S. Bureau of the Census. (1993). *Statistical abstract of the United States: 1993* (113th ed.). Washington, D.C.: U.S. Government Printing Office.

U.S. Bureau of the Census. (1994). *Statistical abstract of the United States: 1994* (114th ed.) Washington, D.C.: U.S. Government Printing Office.

U.S. Bureau of the Census. (1995). *Statistical abstract of the United States: 1995* (115th ed.). Washington, D.C.: U.S. Government Printing Office.

U.S. Bureau of the Census. (1995a). Live births, deaths, marriages, and divorces: 1900–1994. *Statistical abstract of the United States* (115th ed.). Washington, D.C.: U.S. Government Printing Office.

U.S. Bureau of the Census. (1995b). Marital status and living arrangements: March, 1995 (Series P-20, No. 445). Washington, DC: U.S. Government Printing Office.

U.S. Bureau of the Census. (1995c). Employment status of and presence and age of children: 1960–1994. *Statistical abstract of the United States* (115th ed.). Washington, D.C.: U.S. Government Printing Office.

U.S. Bureau of Labor Statistics. (1995). Bulletin 2307.

U.S. Congress, Office of Technology Assessment. (1988). *Infertility: Medical and social choices* (OTA-BA-358). Washington, D.C.: U.S. Government Printing Office.

U.S. Congressional Budget Office. (1993). *Trends in health spending.* Washington, D.C: Author:

U.S. Department of Commerce. (1995). *Statistical abstract of the United States, 1994.* Washington, D.C.: U.S. Government Printing Office.

U.S. Department of Education. (1992). *Digest of education statistics, 1992.* Washington, D.C.: National Center for Education Statistics.

U.S. Department of Education. (1993). *The condition of education, 1993.* Washington, D.C.: National Center for Education Statistics.

U.S. Department of Education. (1992). *Digest of education statistics, 1992.* Washington, D.C.: National Center for Education Statistics.

U.S. Department of Health and Human Services. (1990a). *Healthy people 2000: National health promotion and disease prevention objectives.* USDHHS HHS/PHS/CDC 91-50212. Washington, D.C.: U.S. Government Printing Office.

U.S. Department of Health and Human Services. (1990b). *The health benefits of smoking cessation: A report of the Surgeon General.* Public Health Service, Centers for Disease Control, Center for Chronic Disease Prevention and Health Promotion, Office on Smoking and Health. DHHS Publication No. (CDC) 90-8416.

U.S. Department of Health and Human Services. (1991). *Health United States, 1990.* (DHHS Pub. No. (PHS) 91-1232.) Washington, D.C.: U.S. Government Printing Office.

U.S. Department of Health and Human Services. (1993). *Health United States, 1992.* (DHHS Pub. No. (PHS) 93-1232.) Washington, D.C.: U.S. Government Printing Office.

U.S. Department of Health and Human Services. (1993). *Talking to children about death.* Washington, D.C.: U.S. Government Printing Office.

U.S. Department of Health and Human Services. (1994a). *Creating a 21st century Head Start: Final report of the advisory committee on Head Start quality and expansion.* Washington, D.C.: U.S. Government Printing Office.

U.S. Department of Health and Human Services. (1994b). *Back to sleep: Reducing the risk of SIDS: What you can do.* Bethesda, Md.: Author.

U.S. Department of Labor. (1994, November). *Monthly labor review.* Washington, D.C.: Bureau of Labor Statistics.

U.S. General Accounting Office. (1993). *Preventive home care for children: Experience from select foreign countries.* Washington, D.C.: Author.

U.S. National Center for Health Statistics. (1991). *Vital statistics of the United States.* Washington, D.C.: U.S. Government Printing Office.

U.S. Select Committee on Children, Youth, and Families. (1992). *Health care reform: How do women, children, and teens fare?* Washington, D.C.: U.S. Government Printing Office.

U.S. Senate Special Committee on Aging. (1990). *Developments in aging: 1989* (Vol. 1.) Washington, D.C.: U.S. Government Printing Office.

U.S. Senate Special Committee on Aging. (1991). *Aging America: Trends and projections.* Washington, D.C.: U.S. Department of Health and Human Services.

U.S. Senate Special Committee on Aging. (1992). *Aging America: Trends and projections.* Washington, D.C.: U.S. Department of Health and Human Services.

Umberson, D. (1987). Family status and health behaviors: Social control as a dimension of social integration. *Journal of Health and Social Behavior, 38,* 306–319.

Umberson, D. (1989). Relationships with children: Explaining parents' psychological well-being. *Journal of Marriage and the Family, 51,* 999–1012.

Vaillant, C. O., & Vaillant, G. E. (1993). Is the U-curve of marital satisfaction an illusion? A 40-year study of marriage. *Journal of Marriage and the Family, 55,* 230–239.

Vaillant, G. E. (1977). *Adaptation to life.* Boston: Little, Brown.

Vaillant, G. E., & McArthur, C. C. (1972). Natural history of male psychologic health: I. The adult life cycle from 18–50. *Seminars in Psychiatry, 4*(4), 415–427.

Vaillant, G. E., & Vaillant, C. O. (1990). Natural history of male psychological health, XII: A 45-year study of predictors of successful aging at age 65. *American Journal of Psychiatry, 147*(1), 31–37.

Vallerand, R. J., O'Connor, B. P., & Blais, M. R. (1989). Life satisfaction of elderly individuals in regular community housing, in low-cost community housing, and high and low self-determination nursing homes. *International Journal of Aging and Human Development, 28*(4), 277–283.

van den Boom, D. C. (1994). The influence of temperament and mothering on attachment and exploration: An experimental manipulation of sensitive responsiveness among lower-class mothers with irritable infants. *Child Development, 65,* 1457–1477.

van den Boom, D. C., & Hoeksma, J. B. (1994). The effect of infant irritabiity on mother-infant interaction: A growth-curve analysis. *Developmental Psychology, 30,* 581–590.

van Ijzendoorn, M. H. (1992) Review. Intergenerational transmission of parenting: A review of studies in nonclinical populations. *Developmental Review, 12,* 76–99.

van Ijzendoorn, M. H., & Kroonenberg, P. M. (1988). Cross-cultural patterns of attachment: A meta-analysis of the Strange Situation. *Child Development, 59,* 147–156.

van-der-Voort, T. H. A., & Valkenburg, P. M. (1994). Television's impact on fantasy play: A review of research. *Developmental Review, 14,* 227–251.

Vandell, D. L. (1980). Sociability with peers and mothers in the first year. *Developmental Psychology, 16,* 355–361.

Vandell, D. L., & Ramanan, J. (1991). Children of the national longitudinal survey of youth: Choices in after-school care and child development. *Developmental Psychology, 27,* 637–643.

Varni, J. W., Setoguchi, Y., Rappaport, L. R., & Talbot, D. (1992). Psychological adjustment and perceived social support in children with congenital/acquired limb deficiencies. *Journal of Behavioral Medicine, 15,* 31–44.

Veevers, J. E. (1980). *Childless by choice.* Toronto: Butterworth.

Vellutino, F. (1991). Dyslexia. In S. William (Ed.), *Emergence of language.* New York: Freeman.

Vera, H., Berardo, F. M., & Vandiver, J. S. (1990). Age irrelevancy in society: The test of mate selection. *Journal of Aging Studies, 4*(1), 81–95.

Verbrugge, L. M. (1982). Women's social roles and health. In P. W. Berman & E. R. Ramey (Eds.), *Women: A developmental perspective* (pp. 49–78). Bethesda, Md.: U.S. Department of Health and Human Services.

Verbrugge, L. M. (1987). Role responsibilities, role burdens, and physical health. In F. J. Crosby (Ed.), *Spouse, parent, worker: On gender and multiple roles* (pp. 154–166). New Haven,, Conn.: Yale University Press.

Verbrugge, L. M. (1989a). Gender, aging and health. In K. S. Markides (Ed.), *Aging and health: Perspectives on gender, race, ethnicity and class* (pp. 23–78). Newbury Park, Cal.: Sage.

Verbrugge, L. M. (1989b). The twain meet: Empirical explanations of sex differences in health and mortality. *Journal of Health and Social Behavior, 30,* 282–304.

Viinamaki, H., Koskela, K., Niskanen, L., Arnkill, R., & Tikkanen, J. (1993). Unemployment and mental well-being: A factory closure study in Finland. *Acta Psychiatrica Scandinavia, 88,* 429–433.

Volling, B. L., & Belsky, J. (1992). Infant, father, and marital antecedents of infant-father attachment security in dual-earner and single earner families. *Journal of Behavioral Development, 15,* 83–100.

Vosler, N. R., & Proctor, E. K. (1991). Family structure and stressors in a child guidance clinic population. *Families in Society: The Journal of Contemporary Human Services, 72*(3), 164–174.

Vuchinich, S., Hetherington, E. M., Vuchinich, R. A., & Clingempeel, W. G. (1991). Parent-child interaction and gender differences in early adolescents' adaptation to stepfamilies. *Developmental Psychology, 27,* 618–626.

Vygotsky, L. S. (1967). Play and its role in the mental development of the child. *Soviet Psychology, 12,* 62–76.

Vygotsky, L. S. (1978). *Mind in society: The development of higher psychological processes.* Cambridge, Mass.: Harvard University Press.

Wadden, T. A., Brown, G., Foster, G. D., & Linowitz, J. R. (1991). Salience of weight-related worries in adolescent males and females. *International Journal of Eating Disorders, 10,* 407–414.

Wadden, T. A., & Stunkard, A. J. (1985). Social and psychological consequences of obesity. *Annals of Internal Medicine, 106,* 1062–1067.

Wadsworth, M. (1986). Serious illness in childhood and its association with later-life achievement. In R. Wilkinson

(Ed.), *Class and health: Research and longitudinal data.* London: Tavistock.

Wadsworth, M., Maclean, M., Kuh, D., & Rodgers, B. (1990). Children of divorced and separated parents: Summary and review of findings from a long-term follow-up study in the UK. *Family Practice, 7,* 104–109.

Wagner, R. M. (1993). Psychosocial adjustments during the first year of single parenthood: A comparison of Mexican-American and Anglo women. *Journal of Divorce and Remarriage, 19*(1–2), 12–33.

Walker, S. N., Sechrist, K. R., & Pender, N. J. (1987). The health-promoting lifestyle profile: Development and psychometric characteristics. *Nursing Journal, 36,* 76–81.

Walker, S. N., Volkan, K., Sechrist, K. R., & Pender, N. (1988). Health-promoting life styles of older adults: Comparisons with young and middle-aged adults, correlates and patterns. *Advanced Nursing Science, 11,* 76–90.

Wallerstein, J. S. (1983). Children of divorce: The psychological tasks of the child. *American Journal of Orthopsychiatry, 53,* 230–243.

Wallerstein, J. S. (1987). Children of divorce: A ten-year follow-up study of early latency-age children. *American Journal of Orthopsychiatry, 57,* 199–211.

Wallerstein, J. S. (1989). Follow-up. Letter to the editor. *Readings: A Journal of Reviews and Commentary in Mental Health, 4,* 21–22.

Wallerstein, J. S., & Blakeslee, S. (1989). *Second chances: Men, women and children a decade after divorce.* New York: Ticknor & Fields.

Wallerstein, J. S., & Corbin, S. B. (1989). Daughters of divorce: Report from a ten-year follow-up. *American Journal of Orthopsychiatry,* 593–604.

Walls, C. T. (1992). The role of church and family support in the lives of older African Americans. *Generations, 17*(3), 33–36.

Wang, J.-J., & Kaufman, A. S. (1993). Changes in fluid and crystallized intelligence across the 20- to 90-year age range on the K-BIT. *Journal of Psychoeducational Assessment, 11,* 29–37.

Wang, V., & Marsh, F. H. (1992). Ethical principles and cultural integrity in health care delivery: Asian ethnocultural perspectives. *Journal of Genetic Counseling, 1,* 81–92.

Ward, J. V. (1988). Urban adolescents' conceptions of violence. In C. Gilligan, J. V. Ward, & J. M. Taylor (Eds.), *Mapping the moral domain* (pp. 175–200.) Cambridge, Mass.: Harvard University Press.

Ward, R. A. (1993). Marital happiness and household equity in later life. *Journal of Marriage and the Family, 55,* 427–438.

Wardle, F. (1995). Alternatives . . . Bruderhof education: Outdoor school. *Young Children, 50*(3), 68–74.

Warren, R., Gartstein, V., Kligman, A. M., Montagna, W., Allendorf, R. A., & Ridder, G. M. (1991). Age, sunlight, and facial skin: A histologic and quantitative study. *Journal of the American Academy of Dermatology, 25,* 751–760.

Warshow, J. (1991). Eldercare as a feminist issue. In B. Sang, J. Warshow, & A. J. Smith (Eds.), *Lesbians at midlife: A creative transition* (pp. 65–72). San Francisco: Spinsters Book Company.

Waterman, A. S. (1982). Identity development from adolescence to adulthood: An extension of theory and a review of research. *Developmental Psychology, 18,* 341–358.

Waterman, A. S. (1985). Identity in the context of adolescent psychology. *New Directions for Child Development, 39,* 5–24.

Webb, N. (Ed.).(1993). *Helping bereaved children: A handbook for practitioners.* New York: Guilford Press.

Wechsler, H., Davenport, A., Dowdall, G., Moeykens, B., & Castillo, S. (1994). Health and behavioral consequences of binge drinking in college: A national survey of students on 140 campuses. *Journal of the American Medical Association, 272,* 1672–1677.

Wegner, N. K., Goodwin, J. F., & Roberts, W. C. (1986). Cardiomyopathy. In J. W. Hurst & R. B. Loque (Eds.), *The heart arteries and veins* (6th ed.). New York: McGraw Hill.

Weinberg, M. K., & Tronick, E. Z. (1994). Beyond the face: The empirical study of infant affective configurations of facial, vocal, gestural, and regulatory behaviors. *Child Development, 65,* 1503–1515.

Weiser, T. (1989). Comparing sibling relationships across cultures. In P. Zukow (Ed.), *Sibling interaction across cultures: Theoretical and methodologial issues.*(pp. 11–25). New York: Springer-Verlag.

Weisner, T. S., & Gallimore, R. (1977). My brother's keeper: Child and sibling caretaking. *Current Anthropology, 18,* 169–190.

Weisner, T. S., & Wilson-Mitchell, J. E. (1990). Nonconventional family life-styles and sex typing in six-year-olds. *Child Development, 61,* 1915–1933.

Weiss, G., & Hechtman, L. (1993). *Hyperactive children grown up* (2nd ed.). New York: Guilford Press.

Weiss, R. (1989). Follow-up. Letter to the editor. *Readings: A Journal of Commentary in Mental Health, 4,* 19–20.

Weiss, R. W. (1993). Loss and recovery. In M. S. Stroebe, W. Stroebe, & R. O. Hansson (Eds.), *Handbook of bereavement: Theory, research, and intervention* (pp. 271–284). Cambridge, U.K.: Cambridge University Press.

Weizman, S. G., & Kamm, P. (1985). *About mourning.* New York: Human Sciences Press.

Wellman, B. (1990). The place of kinfolk in personal community networks. *Marriage and Family Review, 15,* 195–221.

Wellman, H., & Hickling, A. (1994). The mind's "I": Children's conception of the mind as an active agent. *Child Development, 65*(6), 1564–1581.

Wertsch, J. V. (1985). *Vygotsky and the social formation of mind.* Cambridge, Mass.: Harvard University Press.

Wertsch, J. V. (1989). A socio-cultural approach to mind. In W. Damon (Ed.), *Child development today and tomorrow* (pp. 14–33). San Francisco: Jossey-Bass.

Wertsch, J. V., del Rio, P., & Alvarey, A. (1995). *Sociocultural studies of mind.* New York: Cambridge University Press.

West, R. L., Crook, T. H., & Barron, K. L. (1992). Everyday memory performance across the life span. *Psychology and Aging, 7,* 72–82.

Whitbourne, S. K. (1985). *The aging body: Physiological changes and psychological consequences.* New York: Springer-Verlag.

Whitbourne, S. K., & Weinstock, C. S. (1986). *Adult development* (2nd ed.). New York: Praeger.

White, B. (1975). Critical influences in the origins of competence. *Merrill-Palmer Quarterly, 21,* 243–266.

White, B. (1993). *The first three years of life* (Rev. ed.). New York: Simon & Schuster.

White, L. K., & Edwards, J. N. (1990). Emptying the nest and parental well-being: An analysis of national panel data. *American Sociological Review, 55,* 235–242.

White, L. K., & Riedmann, A. (1992). Ties among adult siblings. *Social Forces, 71,* 85–102.

White, S. D., & DeBlassie, R. R. (1992). Adolescent sexual behavior. *Adolescence, 27,* 183–191.

Whitehurst, G., Epstein, J., Angell, A., Payne, A., Crone, D., & Fischel, J. (1994). Outcomes of an emergent literacy intervention in Head Start. *Journal of Educational Psychology, 86*(4), 542–555.

Whiting, B. B., & Edwards, C. P. (1988). *Children of different worlds.* Cambridge, Mass.: Harvard University Press.

Whiting, B. B., & Whiting, J. (1975). *Children of six cultures: A psychocultural analysis.* Cambridge, Mass.: Harvard University Press.

Whiting, J. W. M. (1981). Environmental constraints on infant care practices. In R. Munroe, R. H. Monroe, & B. B. Whiting (Eds.), *Handbook of cross-cultural development.* New York: Garland Press.

Whittemore, A. S. (1994). Prostate cancer. *Cancer Survival, 19–20,* 309–322.

Whittemore, A. S., Wu, A. H., Kolonel, L. N., John, E. M., Gallagher, R. P., Howe, G. R., West, D. W., Teh, C.

Z., & Stamey, T. (1995). Family history and prostate cancer risk in black, white, and Asian men in the United States and Canada. *American Journal of Epidemiology, 141,* 732–740.

Willcox, S. M., Himmelstein, D. U., & Woolhandler, S. (1994). Inappropriate drug perscribing for the community-dwelling elderly. *Journal of the American Medical Association, 272,* 292–296.

Williams, C., & Kimm, S. (1993). *Prevention and treatment of childhood obesity.* New York: New York Academy of Sciences.

Williams, J. D., & Jacoby, A. P. (1989). The effects of premarital heterosexual and homosexual experience on dating and marriage desirability. *Journal of Marriage and the Family, 51,* 489–497.

Willis, D. J., Holden, E. W., & Rosenberg, M. S. (Eds.). (1992). *Prevention of child maltreatment: Developmental and ecological perspectives.* New York: Wiley.

Willis, S. L. (1989). Adult intelligence. In A. Hunter & M. Sundel (Eds.), *Midlife myths: Issues, findings, and practice implications.* Newbury Park, Cal.: Sage.

Willis, S. L. (1990). Introduction to the special section on cognitive training in later adulthood. *Developmental Psychology, 26,* 875–878.

Willis, S. L., Jay, G. M., Diehl, M., & Marsiske, M. (1992). Longitudinal change and prediction of everyday task competence in the elderly. *Research on Aging, 14,* 68–91.

Wilson, M. R. (1989). Glaucoma in Blacks: Where do we go from here? *Journal of the American Medical Association, 261,* 281–282.

Winfree, L. T., Backstrom, T. V., & Mays, G. L. (1994). Social learning theory, self-reported delinquency, and youth gangs. *Youth and Society, 26,* 147–177.

Winner, E. (1988). *The point of words.* Cambridge, Mass.: Harvard University Press.

Wiseman, A. D. (1972). *On dying and denying.* New York: Behavioral Publications.

Wolf, D. (1993). There and then, intangible and internal: Narratives in early childhood. In B. Spodek (Ed.), *Handbook of research on the education of young children* (pp. 42–56). New York: Macmillan.

Wolff, P. (1966). The causes, controls, and organization of behavior in the neonate. *Psychological Issues, 5,* 1–105.

Woodburn, (1982). Social dimensions of death in four African hunting and gathering societies. In M. Bloch & J. Parry (Eds.), *Death and the regeneration of life* (pp. 187–210). Cambridge, U.K.: Cambridge University Press.

Woolston, J. (1993). *Eating and growth disorders.* Philadelphia: Saunders.

World Health Organization. (1995). *World health statistics annual: 1994.* Geneva: Author.

Worsnop, R. L. (1992). Assisted suicide. *CQ Researcher,* 147–163.

Wortman, C. B., Silver, R. C., & Kessler, R. C. (1993). The meaning of loss and adjustment to bereavement. In M. S. Stroebe, W. Stroebe, & R. O. Hansson (Eds.), *Handbook of bereavement: Theory, research, and intervention* (pp. 349–366). Cambridge, U.K.: Cambridge University Press.

Wozniak, R., & Fischer, K. (1993). *Development in context: Acting and thinking in specific environments.* Hillsdale, N.J.: Erlbaum.

Wright, D. J. (1987). Minority students: Developmental beginnings. *New Directions for Student Services, 38,* 5–21.

Wright, J. D., & Hamilton, R. F. (1978). Work satisfaction and age: Some evidence for the job change hypothesis. *Social Forces, 56,* 1140–1158.

Wright, P. H. (1988). Interpreting research on gender differences in friendship: A case for moderation and a plea for caution. *Journal of Social and Personal Relationships, 5,* 367–373.

Wykle, M. L., & Musil, C. M. (1993). Mental health of older persons: Social and cultural factors. *Generations, 17*(1), 7–12.

Wylie, R. (1974/1979). *The self-concept: Vols. 1 & 2*. Lincoln: University of Nebraska Press.

Yacker, N., & Weinberg, S. L. (1990). Care and justice moral orientation: A scale for its assessment. *Journal of Personality Assessment, 56,* 18–27.

Yarrow, M., & Waxler, C. (1978). The emergence and functions of prosocial behavior in young children. In M. Smart & R. Smart (Eds.), *Infants, development and relationships*. New York: Macmillan.

Yeager, K. K., Macera, C. A., & Merritt, R. K. (1993). Socioeconomic influences on leisure-time sedentary behavior among women. *Health Values: The Journal of Health Behavior, Education and Promotion, 17*(6), 50–54.

Yee, B. W. K. (1992). Gender and family issues in minority groups. In L. Glasse & J. Hendricks (Eds.), *Gender and aging* (pp. 69–77). Amityville, N.Y.: Baywood.

Yllo, K., & Bogard, M. (1988). *Feminist perspectives on wife abuse*. Newbury Park, Cal.: Sage.

Yoder, P., & Warren, S. (1993). Can developmentally delayed children's language development be enhanced through prelinguistic intervention? In A. Kaiser & D. Gray (Eds.), *Enhancing children's communication: Vol. 2* (pp. 35–62). Baltimore: Paul Brookes.

Yogman, M., Dixon, S., Tronick, E., Als, H., & Brazelton, T. B. (1977). *The goals and structure of face-to-face interaction between infants and fathers*. Paper presented at the biennial meeting of the Society for Research in Child Development, New Orleans.

Yonas, A. (1988). *Perceptual development in infants. Minnesota Symposium on Child Psychology: Vol. 20*. Minneapolis: University of Minnesota Press.

Youniss, J. (1980). *Parents and peers in social development: A Sullivan-Piaget perspective*. Chicago: University of Chicago Press.

Youniss, J., & Smollar, J. (1985). *Adolescent relations with mothers, fathers, and friends*. Chicago: University of Chicago Press.

Zahn-Waxler, C., Radke-Yarrow, M., & King, R. A. (1979). Child rearing and children's prosocial initiations toward victims of distress. *Child Development, 50,* 319–330.

Zarbatany, L., Hartmann, D. P., & Rankin, D. B. (1990). The psychological functions of preadolescent peer activities. *Child Development, 61,* 1067–1080.

Zeitz, G. (1990). Age and work satisfaction in a government agency: A situational perspective. *Human Relations, 43*(5), 419–438.

Zeskind, P. S., Sale, J., Maio, M. L., Huntington, L., & Weisman, J. R. (1985). Adult perceptions of pain and hunger cries: Asynchrony of arousal. *Child Development, 56,* 549–554.

Zigler, E. F., & Frank, M. (Eds.). (1988). *Infant love and infant care leave*. New Haven, Conn.: Yale University Press.

Zigler, E. F., Taussig, C., & Black, K. (1992). Early childhood intervention: A promising preventative for juvenile delinquency. *American Psychologist, 47,* 997–1006.

Zilbergeld, B., & Ellison, C. R. (1980). Desire discrepancies and arousal problems in sex therapy. In S. R. Leiblum & L. A. Pervin (Eds.), *Principles and practice of sex therapy*. New York: Guilford Press.

Zimmerman, L., & McDonald, L. (1995). Emotional availability in infants' relationships with multiple caregivers. *American Journal of Orthopsychiatry, 65,* 147–152.

Zinn, B. (1989). Family, race, and poverty in the eighties. *Signs: Journal of Women in Culture and Society, 14,* 856–874.

Zsembik, B. A., & Singer, A. (1990). The problem of defining retirement among minorities: The Mexican Americans. *The Gerontologist, 30,* 749–757.

Zuo, J. (1992). The reciprocal relationship between marital interaction and marital happiness: A three-wave study. *Journal of Marriage and the Family, 54,* 870–878.

Acknowledgments

PART AND CHAPTER OPENER PHOTO CREDITS

Part 1: © Bob Daemmrich/The Image Works; **Chapter 1:** © David R. Frazier Photolibrary; **Chapter 2:** © David Harry Stewart/Tony Stone Images; **Chapter 3:** © Donna Day/Tony Stone Images; **Part 2:** © Andrew Cox/Tony Stone Images; **Chapter 4:** © Elizabeth Crews/The Image Works; **Chapter 5:** © Amy C. Etra/PhotoEdit; **Part 3:** Julie Houk/Stock Boston; **Chapter 6:** © Kindra Clineff; **Chapter 7:** © Bob Daemmrich; **Part 4:** © Bob Daemmrich; **Chapter 8:** © David R. Frazier Photolibrary; **Chapter 9:** © Bob Daemmrich; **Part 5:** © D.H. Hessell/Stock Boston; **Chapter 10:** © Lori Adamski Peek/Tony Stone Images; **Chapter 11:** © Richard Hutchings/Photo Researchers; **Part 6:** © Gary W. Nolton/Tony Stone Images; **Chapter 12:** © Elena Rooraid/PhotoEdit; **Chapter 13:** © David Harry Stewart/Tony Stone Images; **Part 7:** © Jim Whitmer; **Chapter 14:** © Bob Daemmrich/Tony Stone Images; **Chapter 15:** © Bob Daemmrich/The Image Works; **Part 8:** © Jim Whitmer; **Chapter 16:** © Christopher Springma/Tony Stone Images; **Chapter 17:** © Frank Siteman/The Picture Cube; **Part 9:** © Michael Newman/PhotoEdit; **Chapter 18:** Skjold/The Image Works.

CHAPTER PHOTO CREDITS

Chapter 1: p. 4: *left,* © Elizabeth Crews; *right,* © Julie O'Neil/The Picture Cube; p. 11: *left,* © *Family Portrait* (1830–1840), Jacob Maentel, Henry Francis du Pont Winterthur Museum; *right, Children Playing on Beach* (1884), Mary Cassatt, National Gallery of Art, Washington, Ailsa Mellon Bruce Collection; p. 1 3: *left,* © Cathlyn Melloan/Tony Stone Images; *right,* © Siteman/Monkmeyer; p. 15: © David R. Frazier/Stock Boston; p. 19: left and right, © Judy Gelles/Stock Boston; p. 21: © Dick Hemingway.

Chapter 2: p. 32: © Kevin Syms/David R. Frazier Photolibrary; p. 34: Mary Evans Picture Library; p. 36: © Paul Merideth/Tony Stone Images; p. 37: Stock Montage; p. 42: © Steven Stone/The Picture Cube; p. 43: © Lawrence Migdale/Stock Boston; p. 44: *left,* © Nita Winter; *right,* © J. Carini/The Image Works; p. 46: © Nita Winter; p. 48: © Bob Daemmrich/Stock Boston; p. 53: Kaluzny/Thatcher/Tony Stone Images.

Chapter 3: p. 64: Custom Medical Stock Photo; p. 64: Lennart Nilsson, *A Child is Born,* Dell Publishing Co.; p. 69: © Dan Bosler/Tony Stone Images; p. 71: © Paul Conklin; p. 77: © Lawrence Migdale/Photo Researchers; p. 78: Drawing by Chas Addams; © 1981 The New Yorker Magazine, Inc.; p. 83: © Lennart Nilsson, *A Child is Born,* Dell Publishing Co.; p. 97: © SIU/Peter Arnold; p. 98: © Spencer Grant/Monkmeyer; p. 102: © Laura Dwight.

Chapter 4: p. 111: © Bill Bachmann/Tony Stone Images; p. 112: © Petit Format/Nestle/Science Source/Photo Researchers; p. 1 18: © Elizabeth Crews/The Image Works; p. 119: © Lionel Delevingne/Stock Boston; p. 122: © Janice Fullman/The Picture Cube; p. 127: © Gale Zucker; p. 129: © Birnbach/Monkmeyer; p. 134: © James Prince/Photo Researchers; p. 140: © Bob Daemmrich; p. 143: © Marianne Gontarz/The Picture Cube; p. 145: Anthro-Photo File no. 6273.

Chapter 5: p. 150: © Lawrence Migdale/Photo Researchers; p. 153: © Susan Woog Wagner/Photo Researchers; p. 156: © Michael Newman/PhotoEdit; p. 157: Deborah Kalas/Stock Boston; p. 161: © Judith Kramer/The Image Works; p. 162: © Elizabeth Crews; *bottom,* © Nancy J. Pierce/Photo Researchers; p. 170: © Elizabeth Crews; p. 173: © Bill Bachman/Photo Researchers; p. 175: © Laura Dwight.

Chapter 6: p. 184: © Lawrence Migdale/Stock Boston; p. 190: © Carol Palmer/The Picture Cube; p. 192: © D. Young-Wolff/PhotoEdit; p. 193: © Bob Daemmrich/The Image Works; p. 195: © Hiller/Monkmeyer; p. 198: © Bob Daemmrich; p. 202: © Bob Daemmrich/Stock Boston; p. 208: © Elizabeth Crews; p. 212: © Bob Daemmrich/Tony Stone Images; p. 216: © Paul Conklin.

Chapter 7: p. 222: © Palmer/Brilliant/The Picture Cube; p. 224: © Elizabeth Crews; p. 225: © Michael Siluk/The Image Works; p. 226: © Barbara Rios/Photo Researchers; p. 229: © Robert Kalman/The Image Works; p. 234: © Andrew Lichtenstein/Impact Visuals; p. 236: © Elizabeth Crews; p. 238: © Elizabeth Crews; p. 249: © Elizabeth Crews; p. 250: © Frank Siteman/Monkmeyer.

Chapter 8: p. 260: © Bob Daemmrich/Stock Boston; p. 264: *top* and *bottom,* © Bob Daemmrich; p. 270: © Elizabeth Crews; p. 272: © Andrew Brilliant; p. 278: © Elizabeth Crews; p. 279: © David Maung/Impact Visuals; p. 287: © Bob Daemmrich; p. 288: © Lawrence Migdale/Stock Boston.

Chapter 9: p. 295: © Jean-Claude LeJeune/Stock Boston; p. 298: © Elizabeth Crews; p. 303: © Robert Brenner/PhotoEdit; p. 307: © Jean-Claude LeJeune/Stock Boston; p. 316: © Bob Daemmrich/Stock Boston; p. 320: © David Young-Wolff/PhotoEdit; p. 322: © Bob Daemmrich/The Image Works; p. 324: © David Young-Wolff/Tony Stone Images; p. 327: © Glen Korengold/Stock Boston.

Chapter 10: p. 334: © Elizabeth Crews; p. 343: © Bob Daemmrich; p. 346: © Dana Schuerholz/Impact Visuals; p. 349: © David R. Frazier Photolibrary; p. 351: © Arlene Collins/Monkmeyer; p. 352: © Bob Daemmrich; p. 356: © Paul Conklin; p. 360: *left,* Laima Druskis/Stock Boston; *right,* Smiley/TexaStock; p. 368: © Mark Tetrault/The Picture Cube.

Chapter 11: p. 372: *top,* © James Holland; *bottom,* © Paul Conklin; p. 378: © Andy Levin/Photo Researchers; p. 383: © Laura Dwight; p. 385: © Spencer Grant/Grantpix/Monkmeyer; p. 388: © Gale Zucker; p. 394: © Spencer Grant/Monkmeyer.

Chapter 12: p. 411: © Willie L. Hill/The Image Works; p. 412: © Michael A. Dwyer/Stock Boston; p. 414: © Dick Hemingway; p. 418: © Spencer Grant/The Picture Cube; p. 423: *Cathy* copyright Cathy Guisewite. Reprinted with permission of *Universal Press Syndicate.* All rights reserved.; p. 426: © Don B. Stevenson/The Picture Cube; p. 433: © Chester Higgins Jr./Photo Researchers; p. 437: © Frank Siteman/The Picture Cube; p. 444: © Mark Richards/PhotoEdit; p. 447: © Joseph Schuyler/Stock Boston; p. 449: © Jim Whitmer.

Chapter 13: p. 457: © Robert Brenner/PhotoEdit; p. 460: © Michael Newman/PhotoEdit; p. 462: © Paula Lerner/The Picture Cube; p. 465: © James Prince/Photo Researchers; p. 472: © Laura Dwight/PhotoEdit; p. 474: Drawing by Cotham; © 1996 The New Yorker Magazine, Inc.; p. 475: © Ursula Markus/Photo Researchers; p. 481: *right,* © David Young-Wolff/PhotoEdit; *left,* © James Wilson/Woodfin Camp; p. 484: © Michael Newman/PhotoEdit; p. 485: © Bob Daemmrich/Stock Boston; p 491: © Jeff Greenberg/PhotoEdit.

Chapter 14: p. 499: © Terry Vine/Tony Stone Images; p. 500: *right* and *left,* © Jim Whitmer; p. 503: © Bob Daemmrich/Image Works; p. 509: © Bob Daemmrich; p. 512: © Michael Newman/PhotoEdit; p. 515: © Mikki Ansin/The Picture Cube; p. 519: © David R. Frazier Photolibrary; p. 526: © D. Wray/The Image Works; p. 529: © Chip Henderson/Tony Stone Images; p. 535: Reprinted with special permission of King Features Syndicate.

Chapter 15: p. 540: © M. Douglas/The Image Works; p. 549: © Gale Zucker; p. 557: © Dick Hemingway; p. 563: Keren Su/Stock Boston; p. 565: © Ursula Markus/Photo Researchers; p. 567: © Elizabeth Crews; p. 569: © Bob Daemmrich/The Image Works; p. 572: © Bachmann/Photo Researchers.

Chapter 16: p. 584: *top,* © Blair Seitz/Photo Researchers; *bottom,* © L. Kolvoord/The Image Works; p. 587: Lionel Delevingne/Stock Boston; p. 590: © Elizabeth Crews; p. 593: © Bob Daemmrich/Stock Boston; p.599: © Michael Dwyer/Stock Boston; p. 605: © Nita Winter 951052N3; p. 609: © Carol Lee/The Picture Cube; p. 6 1 1: © Dick Hemingway; p. 615: © David Young-Wolff/PhotoEdit; p. 621: © Michael Newman/Photo Edit.

Chapter 17: p. 628: © M. K. Denny/PhotoEdit; p. 631: © Lori Adamski Peek/Tony Stone Images; p. 633: © Bill Aron/Tony Stone Images; p. 635: © Lionel Delevingne/Stock Boston; p. 640: © Tom McKitterick/Impact Visuals; p. 645: © Rhode Sidney/PhotoEdit; p. 647: © John Eastcott/YVA Momatiuk/The Image Works; p. 650: © David Woo/Stock Boston; p. 651: © Kindra Clineff/The Picture Cube; p. 657: © Paul Conklin/PhotoEdit; p. 662: © Joseph Nettis/Photo Researchers.

Chapter 18: p. 671: © Bruce Ayres/Tony Stone Images; p. 673: © Sygma; p. 678: © Larry Nelson/Black Star; p. 682: © Frank Siteman/The Picture Cube; p. 688: © Nita Winter; p. 692: *top,* © Greenlar/The Image Works; *bottom,* © Nathan Bena/Stock Boston; p. 695: © Winter/The Image Works; p. 696: © T. Michaels/The Image Works.

TEXT, TABLE, AND LINE ART CREDITS

p. 6: cartoon: For Better or for Worse, copyright 1994 Lynn Johnston Prod., Inc. Reprinted with permission of Universal Press Syndicate. All rights reserved.

p. 7: Figure 1.2 adapted from J. Garbarino (1982), "Sociocultural Risk: Dangers to Competence." From C. Kopp and J. Krakow, *Child development in a social context,* © 1982 by Addison Wesley Publishing Company, Inc. Reprinted by permission of Addison Wesley Publishing Company, Inc.

p. 8: Table 1.1 adapted from J. Garbarino (1982), "Sociocultural Risk: Dangers to Competence." From C. Kopp and J. Krakow, *Child development in a social context,* © 1982 by Addison Wesley Publishing Company, Inc. Reprinted by permission of Addison Wesley Publishing Company, Inc.

p. 20: Cartoon © Bradford Veley.

p. 64: Figure 3.1 from Custom Medical Stock Photo.

p. 65: Figure 3.2 adapted from "Genetic Building Blocks," *Time,* January 17, 1994. © 1994 Time Inc. Reprinted by permission.

p. 66: Figure 3.3 adapted from D. Bukatko, and M. Daehler, *Child Development: A Topical Approach,* 2nd ed., 1995, p. 82. Copyright © 1995 by Houghton Mifflin Company. Used with permission.

p. 66: Figure 3.4 adapted from D. Bukatko, and M. Daehler, *Child Development: A Topical Approach,* 2nd ed., 1995, p. 82. Copyright © by Houghton Mifflin Company. Used with permission.

p. 73: Figure 3.8 adapted from D. Bukatko, and M. Daehler, *Child Development: A Topical Approach,* 2nd ed., 1995. Copyright © 1995 by Houghton Mifflin Company. Used with permission.

p. 78: Drawing by Chas. Addams; © 1981 The New Yorker Magazine, Inc.

p. 80: Figure 3.12 adapted from D. Bukatko, and M. Daehler, *Child Development: A Topical Approach,* 2nd ed., 1995, Copyright © 1995 by Houghton Mifflin Company. Used with permission.

p. 85: Table 3.6 from *Planning for Pregnancy, Birth, and Beyond* by American College of Obstetricians and Gynecologists. Copyright © 1990 by the American College of Obstetricians and Gynecologists. Used by permission of Dutton Signet, a division of Penguin Books USA Inc.

p. 88: Figure 3.14 adapted from *Before We Are Born: Basic Embryology and Birth Defects,* 2nd ed., by K.L. Moore, p. 111, with permission of W.B. Saunders Company, © 1983.

p. 113: Figure 4.1 reprinted by permission from Roftwarg, Muzio & Dement, 1966 (revised 1969), "Ontogenetic Development of the Human Sleep Cycle." *Science,* 152, 604–619. Copyright 1966, 1969 American Association for the Advancement of Science.

p. 137: Figure 4.4 adapted from Renee Baillargeon and Julie DeVos, Object Permanence in Young Children: Further Evidence," *Child Development,* 62 (1991), 1227–1246. Copyright (© 1991 by the Society for Research in Child Development, Inc. Reprinted by permission.

p. 152: Table 5.2 adapted from C. Kopp, (1982), "Antecedents of Self-Regulation: A Developmental Perspective," *Developmental Psychology,* 1982, 18, 199–214, Table 2. Copyright © 1982 by the American Psychological Association. Reprinted by permission.

p. 210: cartoon: Hi and Lois. Reprinted with special permission of King Features Syndicate.

p. 229: Table 7.3 From Hughes, F. P., Children, Play and Development, p. 70. Table 4.1 Copyright © 1991 by Allyn and Bacon. Reprinted by permission.

p. 244: Figure 7.1 adapted from D. Bukatko, and M. Daehler, *Child Development: A Topical Approach,* 2nd ed., 1995, p. 626. Copyright © 1995 by Houghton Mifflin Company. Used with permission.

p. 261: Figure 8.2 adapted from D. Bukatko, and M. Daehler, *Child Development: A Topical Approach,* 2nd ed., 1995, p. 167. Adapted from Meredith, 1978. Copyright © 1995 by Houghton Mifflin Company. Used with permission.

p. 265: Figure 8.3 adapted from D. Bukatko, and M. Daehler, *Child Development: A Topical Approach,* 2nd ed., 1995, p. 188. Adapted from Haubenstriker and Siefeldt, 1986. Copyright © 1995 by Houghton Mifflin Company. Used with permission.

p. 274: Figure 8.5 adapted from D. Bukatko, and M. Daehler, *Child Development: A Topical Approach,* 2nd ed., 1995, p. 335. Original data from Dempster, 1981. Copyright © 1995 by Houghton Mifflin Company. Used with permission.

p. 282: cartoon: Calvin and Hobbes copyright 1989 Watterson. Dist. by Universal Press Syndicate. Reprinted with permission. All rights reserved.

p. 313: cartoon: Drawing by Lorenz; © 1991 The New Yorker Magazine, Inc.

p. 317: Table 9.2 adapted from L.A. Sroufe, C. Bennett, M. Englund, J. Urban, & S. Shulman, (1993), "The Significance of Gender Boundaries in Preadolescence Contemporary Correlates and Antecedents of Boundary Violation and Maintenance." *Child Development,* 64, 455–466. Table 1, p. 456. © The Society for Research in Child Development, Inc. Reprinted by permission.

p. 336: cartoon: Foxtrot. copyright 1996 Bill Amend. Reprinted with permission of Universal Press Syndicate. All rights reserved.

p. 363: cartoon: Drawing by Koren; © 1992 The New Yorker Magazine, Inc.

p. 373: cartoon: © 1996 Jack Ziegler from The Cartoon Bank™ Inc.

p. 387: Figure 11.3 adapted from B. B. Brown, N. Mounts, S. D. Lamborn, & L. Steinberg, "Parenting Practices, and Peer Group Affiliation in Adolescence," *Child Development,* 1993, p. 476, Figure 3, slightly adapted. © The Society for Research in Child Development, Inc.

p. 398: Cartoon reprinted with special permission of North America Syndicate.

p. 417: Table 12.1 from "Overweight in America" from *The New York Times,* July 7, 1994, p. 18. Copyright © 1994 by The New York Times Company. Reprinted by permission.

p. 421: Figure 12.3 from Barnes et al., *The International Journal of the Addictions,* 27, p. 921. Reprinted by permission of Marcel Dekker, Inc.

p. 423: Cartoon Cathy by Cathy Guisewite. Reprinted by permission of Universal Press Syndicate.

p. 429: Table 12.3 from "Selected Sexual Behaviors within Attitudinal Groups," from Michael et al., *Sex in America: A Definitive Survey.*

p. 438: Figure 12.4 from Schaie, *Journal of Aging and Human Development,* 2, 1977–78, p. 129.

p. 461: Figure 13.1 from Levinson, D. J. (1986). "A Conception of Adult Development," *American Psychologist,* 41. Original source: The Seasons of a Man's Life, by D.J. Levinson with C. N. Darrow, E. B. Klein, M. H. Levinson, and B. McKee, 1978, p. 57.

p. 469: Figure 13.2 from "The Kinds of Loving as Different Combinations of the Three Components of Love" from The Triangle of Love, Intimacy, Passion, Commitment by Robert J. Sternberg. Copyright © 1988 by Basic Books, Inc. Reprinted by permission of Basic Books, a division of HarperCollins Publishers, Inc.

p. 470: Table 13.2 from "Top Ten Categories Among Women and Men to Question: What Qualities and Characteristics are Important in a Love Relationship to You Personally?" as adapted from Castañeda, *Journal of Social Behavior and Personality,* 8, 1993.

p. 506: Table 14.2 "Percentage of subjects reporting current cigarette smoking according to race, sex, and alcohol consumption." Reprinted from Friedman et al., *Drug and Alcohol Dependence,* 1991, 27, with kind permission from Elsevier Science Ireland Ltd., Bay 15K, Shannon Industrial Estate, Co. Clare, Ireland.

p. 508: Figure 14.3 from "Older Men's Risk" from *The New York Times,* 5/17/94. Copyright © 1994 by The New York Times Company. Reprinted by permission.

p. 508: Figure 14.4 from "Comparable Cross-Sectional and Longitudinal Age Gradients for the Verbal Meaning Test" from K.W. Schaie and C.R. Strother, *Psychological Bulletin,* 70, 671, 1968. Copyright © 1993 by the American Psychological Association. Reprinted by permission.

p. 518: Figure 14.6 from "Comparable Cross-Sectional and Longitudinal Age Gradients for the Verbal Meaning Test" from K.W. Schaie and C.R. Strother, *Psychological Bulletin,* 70, 671, 1968. Copyright © 1993 by the American Psychological Association. Reprinted with permission.

p. 521: Figure 14.7 from "Changes in Cognitive Abilities with Age" from *The New York Times,* 4/26/94. Copyright © 1994 by The New York Times Company. Reprinted by permission.

p. 535: Cartoon reprinted with special permission of King Features Syndicate.

p. 541: Figure 15.1 from "Optimism Towards Personality Changes by Age," J Journal of Gerontology: Psychological Sciences Vol. 48, No. 3, page 105, May 1993. Copyright © The Gerontological Society of America.

p. 542: Drawing by M. Twohy; © 1990 The New Yorker Magazine, Inc.

p. 543: Table 15.1 "Strivings of Young, Midlife, and Older Adults" from McAdams, de St. Aubin, & Logan, *Psychology and Aging,* 8, p. 221, 1993. Copyright © 1993 by the American Psychological Association. Reprinted with permission.

p. 548: Table 15.3 from "Typology of Responses to Middle Age Stresses" from Farrell and Rosenberg, *Men at Midlife,* 1981.

p. 550: Table 15.4 from *The Ties of Later Life,* edited by Jon Hendricks, copyright 1995. Table 1, page 38, "Perceived Reasons for Successful Long-Term Marriages (Top Ten, Listed in Order of Frequency of Naming)" from Chapter 3 in *The Ties of Later Life.* By Robert Lauer, Jeanette C. Lauer, and Sarah T. Kerr. Published by Baywood Publishing Company, Inc.

p. 560: Cartoon "Passages of Parenthood" Doonsbury Copyright 1991 G.B. Trudeau. Reprinted with permission of Universal Press Syndicate. All rights reserved.

p. 570: Table 15.7 from "Resources Considered Helpful in Respondents' Parent's Death," from Scharlach and Fuller-Thompson (1994), *Journal of Gerontological Social Work,* 21, (3/4).

p. 575: Figure 15.4, The Living Will. Reprinted courtesy of Choice in Dying, 200 Varick St., New York, NY 10014.

p. 591: Cartoon reprinted with special permission of King Features Syndicate.

p. 591: Table 16.2 from "What Puts You at Risk: A Checklist" from *The New Wellness Encyclopedia.* Copyright © 1995 by Health Letter Associates. Reprinted by permission of Houghton Mifflin Company. All rights reserved.

p. 602: Figure 16.6 from Vitality and Aging by Fries and Crapo. Copyright © 1981 by W. H. Freeman and Company. Used with permission.

p. 610: Table 16.7 from *Current Directions in Psychological Science,* Vol. 2, No. 3 (June 1993). "The Search for a Psychology of Wisdom" by Paul B. Baltes and Ursula M. Staudinger. Reprinted by permission of Cambridge University Press.

p. 620: Figure 16.8 from D. L. Roth and D. S. Holmes, "Influence of Aerobic Exercise Training and Relaxation Training on Physical and Psychologic Health Following Stressful Life Events," *Psychosomatic Medicine,* 49, p. 362, 1987.

p. 663: Table 17.5 adapted from Sharan B. Merriam (1993), *Activities, Adaption, and Aging,* 18 (1), 7. Copyright © 1993 by the Haworth Press, Inc., Binghamton, NY. Used by permission.

p. 679: Drawing by Bruce Eric Kaplan; © 1992 The New Yorker Magazine, Inc.

p. 680: Table 18.3 from "Societal/Cultural Views Regarding Death and Dying," *Topics in Clinical Nursing,* Vol. 3, No. 3, October 1981, pp. 1–16.

p. 684: Figure 18.2 from "Your Caring Presence: Ways of Effectively Providing Support to Others," The Centre for Living with Dying.

p. 689: Figure 18.4 from "The perception of loss for bereaved parents of different family stages" from DeVries, et al., "Parental Bereavement Over the Life Course: A Theoretical Intersection and Empirical Review," *Omega,* 29 (1), 1994, 47–69.

p. 694: Table 18.5 from *Death and Ethnicity: A Psychological Study* by Richard A. Kalish and David K. Reynolds. Published by Baywood Publishing Co., Inc.

Author/Name Index

Subject Index